Legal Framework for North Carolina's ELDER PROTECTION SYSTEM

Meredith S. Smith and Aimee N. Wall

The School of Government at the University of North Carolina at Chapel Hill works to improve the lives of North Carolinians by engaging in practical scholarship that helps public officials and citizens understand and improve state and local government. Established in 1931 as the Institute of Government, the School provides educational, advisory, and research services for state and local governments. The School of Government is also home to a nationally ranked Master of Public Administration program, the North Carolina Judicial College, and specialized centers focused on community and economic development, information technology, and environmental finance.

As the largest university-based local government training, advisory, and research organization in the United States, the School of Government offers up to 200 courses, webinars, and specialized conferences for more than 12,000 public officials each year. In addition, faculty members annually publish approximately 50 books, manuals, reports, articles, bulletins, and other print and online content related to state and local government. The School also produces the *Daily Bulletin Online* each day the General Assembly is in session, reporting on activities for members of the legislature and others who need to follow the course of legislation.

Operating support for the School of Government's programs and activities comes from many sources, including state appropriations, local government membership dues, private contributions, publication sales, course fees, and service contracts.

Visit sog.unc.edu or call 919.966.5381 for more information on the School's courses, publications, programs, and services.

Printed in the United States of America

24 23 22 21 20 2 3 4 5

ISBN 978-1-56011-974-6

CONTENTS

CHAPTER 2
ADULT PROTECTIVE SERVICES 29

CHAPTER 3
CRIMINAL INVESTIGATION AND PROSECUTION 61

Introduction

While there are two authors listed on the cover of this publication, this project was truly informed, supported, and improved by many individuals in different ways. The North Carolina Conference of Superior Court Clerks and the Executive Director, Jamie Lassiter, provided not only financial support but also the impetus for creating the manual. The clerks, who are at the center of adult guardianship cases, recognized a need for more information and resources. In response, Jamie Lassiter applied for elder abuse grant funding through the Governor's Crime Commission and contracted with the School of Government (SOG) to assist with the development of resources and training.

At the outset of the project, we recognized that in order to create useful, practical resources we had to start with the professionals who are involved with elder abuse work around the state. Throughout the summer of 2018, we met with individuals and teams in six counties around the state: Alamance, Ashe, Cumberland, Johnston, Mecklenburg, and Pitt. The insight provided by the clerks, social services staff, guardian ad litem attorneys, law enforcement officials, prosecutors, community members, and others was invaluable. Their knowledge and experiences informed every page of this manual.

As the project progressed further, we invited several individuals to join the Elder Abuse Advisory Committee (EAAC). We have called on this group to brainstorm ideas for website design and content, review draft chapters and other resources, and provide quick turn-around feedback about ideas and questions. Committee members include the following individuals.

- Hon. Michelle Ball, Clerk of Superior Court, Johnston County
- Hon. Mandana Vidwan, Assistant Clerk of Superior Court, Mecklenburg County
- Loann Meekins, Attorney, Cleveland County
- Marjorie Brown, Public Guardian, Cabarrus County
- Detective Scott Sluder, Financial Crimes Section, Winston-Salem Police Department
- Kayley Taber, Managing Assistant District Attorney, Chatham County
- Janet Coleman, Assistant District Attorney, New Hanover County
- Karey Perez, Adult Services Section Chief, Division of Aging and Adult Services
- Kim Lassiter-Fisher, Adult Services Supervisor, Orange County
- Felissa Ferrell, Social Services Director, Rockingham County
- Preston Craddock, Protective Services Social Worker, Greene County

We also called on several attorneys, clerks, agency staff, and other professionals outside the EAAC to review chapter drafts and materials throughout the process. We are grateful for their candid feedback and suggestions for improvement.

At about the same time we started working on this project, the North Carolina Conference of District Attorneys also began work on a manual designed specifically for prosecutors. Our work overlapped to a certain degree, and we greatly appreciate the collaboration, resource-sharing, and support from the team involved with that manual. Special thanks to Kim Spahos and the project lead, Nancy Warren.

Within the SOG, this project was supported and improved by many different professionals. Research attorneys Aly Chen and Caitlin Little gathered information, participated in meetings, synthesized content, and did careful citation reviews. Mistyre Bonds made outstanding contributions with her vision, organization, and technical skills related to the website design, roadmap, tools, and other resources. Lindsay Hoyt was the mastermind behind the website, and Stefanie Panke, the overall project lead for the IT team.

A special thanks must go out to the publications and design team, including Melissa Twomey, Robby Poore, Emily Hinkle, Kevin Justice, Jennifer Henderson, and Sonja Matanovic. Work on this manual, in particular, evolved and changed in ways that were not typical for SOG publications. The patience, flexibility, professionalism, and expertise of the publications team have been remarkable and much appreciated.

Finally, we must thank our families for their support as we immersed ourselves in this work for a few years and leaned on their guidance and patience along the way.

Meredith S. Smith
Aimee N. Wall

Preface

When choosing a title for this manual, we recognized that we were taking a bit of a leap of faith. Our research and experiences related to elder abuse suggested that there may not actually be a "system" in place. Rather, we recognized that there are many agencies, organizations, and individuals who are dedicated to this work and are doing everything within their powers to help older adults who may be at risk of or victims of abuse, neglect, or exploitation. In some parts of the state, these groups and individuals work together on a regular basis. But we learned that in most parts of the state, time and resources are so scarce that they are often struggling to connect, collaborate, and create a local elder protection system.

This project, which includes not only this manual but also a website, additional online resources and tools, and workshops, was designed to support connectivity and understanding among the various components of North Carolina's elder protection professionals and organizations.

- **Manual.** The *Legal Framework for North Carolina's Elder Protection System* (*The Legal Framework*) is the foundation for the entire project. One of the key challenges we identified in our preliminary research was that the components of the system understood their own roles within the system, but they did not necessarily understand the roles that others played. Each chapter provides a relatively high-level overview of one component. For example, Chapter 2 describes the work of adult protective services (APS). The first part of each chapter provides an overview of the work of the component and will primarily be helpful for those who work outside the component (e.g., those who are not social workers involved with APS work). The latter part of each chapter includes a "call and response" section that explores challenges faced by the component and possible options for overcoming those challenges.
- **Website.** The project website, protectadults.sog.unc.edu, integrates content from the manual and builds on it to make a more robust and interactive platform to support education and connectivity. The site has several sections.
    - **Resources:** A collection of resources, including the full text of the manual; an interactive roadmap that links out to sections of the manual; and various tools, reference guides, and other materials designed to support local elder protection professionals.
    - **Forum:** A discussion forum for professionals involved with elder protection. The forum is grouped by subjects such as powers of attorney, confidentiality, and adult protective services.

- **Find Your Peers:** A digital map and directory of professionals across the state involved with elder protection. Professionals are added to the map and directory after joining the website.
- **MDT Administrative Space:** This space is designed to support communities as they establish and grow local multidisciplinary teams (MDTs). Each county has one MDT space, which they can use to organize administrative information about their team, such as contact information, meeting calendar, and policies and procedures. For security reasons, the space must not be used to share case-specific or identifiable information.

We plan to revise, update, and expand the site over time as we learn more about and from the elder protection community.

- **Workshops and Training.** In connection with this project, the School of Government (SOG) hosted a two-day workshop for MDTs in Fall 2019. We also expect to host a webinar in Spring 2020 to provide an overview of the project and help clerks and other public officials involved with elder protection offer local training about the law and resources available in their communities. We will continue to look for opportunities to offer training, webinars, and workshops over time that will build on the collaborative learning that is essential to making an elder protection system operate.

We encourage you to use the *Legal Framework* as a reference guide but to also consider consulting additional resources available from the SOG and from others involved in this field when exploring some of the challenging legal and practical questions facing the elder protection community.

Chapter 1
Background and Overview

CONTENTS

I. PURPOSE OF MANUAL

The primary purpose of this manual is to provide a solid base of information to help different public officials work together as part of a coherent whole to address cases involving suspected elder abuse, neglect, or exploitation. It includes overviews of several key governmental functions related to this field, including adult protective services, criminal investigation and prosecution, and guardianship, as well as focused summaries of related areas of law such as powers of attorney, protective orders, and civil actions. Because these areas of the law are so complex and involve different groups of public officials, they are often addressed separately in training and written materials. We integrated them in this manual so that public officials, such as clerks of court, social services staff and attorneys, and law enforcement officials, could develop a more comprehensive understanding of the different components of the elder protection system in North Carolina and identify opportunities for collaboration and cooperation. The manual should also be useful for others, such as private attorneys, advocates, and family members, as they try to identify options for assisting victims of elder abuse and navigate the sometimes-fragmented system.

II. SCOPE OF CHAPTER

This chapter will provide some foundational context for the rest of the manual. It opens by defining two key terms: elder abuse and older adult. It then identifies trends that indicate the likelihood that elder abuse will increase dramatically in the future and highlights the impacts of elder abuse on individuals, families, and society. The chapter also provides some background on why elder abuse has been such a challenging issue for public officials to address. Finally, it includes a brief, high-level overview of the chief elements of the elder protection system in the state—including its three key governmental components, adult protective services, criminal investigation and prosecution, and guardianship—and explores the role that other legal tools and components—such as civil remedies (e.g., powers of attorney), state agencies (e.g., long-term care ombudsman program), health care providers, and financial institutions—play in the system.

III. WHAT IS ELDER ABUSE?

Organizations and government agencies use different terminology in the context of abuse, neglect, and exploitation of older adults. They may use words such as elders, elderly, older adults, seniors, or geriatric to refer to the population affected. They may refer to the actions causing harm as abuse, neglect, exploitation, maltreatment, or mistreatment. Throughout this manual, the terms older adult and elder abuse will be used. Below are brief overviews of how these terms may be understood and applied.

A. ELDER ABUSE

1. TYPES OF ABUSE

When addressing the topic of elder abuse generally, this manual will rely primarily on definitions developed by the U.S. Centers for Disease Control and Prevention (CDC) in 2016. The CDC studied definitions from various organizations in order to develop common uniform definitions of elder abuse that could be adopted across different jurisdictions and fields of study. The CDC defines elder abuse in general as "an intentional act, or failure to act, by a caregiver or another person in a relationship involving an expectation of trust that causes or creates a risk of harm to an older adult."[1] Table 1.1 provides more detailed overviews of the most common types of elder abuse.

Table 1.1. **Types of Elder Abuse (as Defined by the CDC)**

TYPE OF ABUSE	DESCRIPTION	EXAMPLES
Physical abuse	The intentional use of physical force that results in acute or chronic illness, bodily injury, physical pain, functional impairment, distress, or death.	Includes violent acts such as striking (with or without an object or weapon), hitting, beating, scratching, biting, choking, suffocation, pushing, shoving, shaking, slapping, kicking, stomping, pinching, and burning.
Sexual abuse or abusive sexual contact	Forced or unwanted sexual interaction (touching and non-touching acts) of any kind with an older adult.	Includes forced or unwanted • completed or attempted contact between a penis and a vulva or a penis and an anus involving penetration; • contact between a mouth and a penis, vulva, or anus; • penetration of the anal or genital opening of another person by a hand, finger, or other object; and • intentional touching, either directly or through clothing, of a person's genitalia, anus, groin, breast, inner thigh, or buttocks. These acts also qualify as sexual abuse if they are committed against a person who is not competent to give informed approval.

1. U.S. Dep't of Health & Human Servs., Ctrs. for Disease Control & Prevention (CDC), *Violence Prevention*, "Elder Abuse: Definitions," CDC.GOV (last visited May 28, 2019), https://www.cdc.gov/violenceprevention/elderabuse/definitions.html. *See also* Lori Stiegel & Ellen Klem, ABA Comm'n on Law & Aging, Types of Abuse: Comparison Chart of Provisions in Adult Protective Services Laws, by State (2007), https://aemqa.americanbar.org/content/dam/aba/administrative/law_aging/Abuse_Types_by_State_and_Category_Chart.pdf.

Table 1.1, *cont'd*

TYPE OF ABUSE	DESCRIPTION	EXAMPLES
Emotional or psychological abuse	Verbal or nonverbal behavior that results in the infliction of anguish, mental pain, fear, or distress.	Includes behaviors intended to • humiliate (e.g., calling names or insults); • threaten (e.g., expressing an intent to initiate nursing home placement); • isolate (e.g., secluding a person from family or friends); or • control (e.g., prohibiting or limiting access to transportation, telephone, money, or other resources) another person.
Caregiver neglect	A failure by a caregiver or other responsible person to (1) protect an elder from harm or (2) meet an elder's needs for essential medical care, nutrition, hydration, hygiene, clothing, basic activities of daily living or shelter, which results in a serious risk of compromised health and safety.[2]	Includes • not providing adequate nutrition, hygiene, clothing, shelter, or access to necessary health care and • failing to prevent exposure to unsafe activities and environments.
Financial abuse or exploitation[3]	The illegal, unauthorized, or improper use of an older individual's resources by a caregiver or other person in a trusting relationship, for the benefit of someone other than the older individual. This includes depriving an older person of rightful access to, information about, or use of, personal benefits, resources, belongings, or assets.[4]	Includes • forgery, misuse, or theft of money or possessions; • use of coercion or deception to get elder to surrender finances or property; and • improper use of guardianship or power of attorney.

2. *See* Nat'l Adult Protective Servs. Ass'n (NAPSA), *Get Informed*, "What is Neglect?," NAPSA-NOW.ORG, http://www.napsa-now.org/get-informed/what-is-neglect/ (last visited July 5, 2019). Abandonment is considered by some to be a distinct form of abuse. Nat'l Ctr. on Elder Abuse (NCEA), *Types of Abuse*, "Abandonment," NCEANCL.GOV, https://ncea.acl.gov/Suspect-Abuse/Abuse-Types.aspx#abandonment (last visited July 5, 2019).

3. *See* Nat'l Council on Aging (NCOA), *Elder Abuse Facts*, "What Is Elder Abuse?," NCOA.org, https://www.ncoa.org/public-policy-action/elder-justice/elder-abuse-facts/ (last visited July 5, 2019).

4. NAPSA, *Get Informed*, "What Is Financial Exploitation?," NAPSA-NOW.ORG, http://www.napsa-now.org/get-informed/what-is-financial-exploitation/ (last visited July 5, 2019).

Some also consider abandonment to be a distinct form of abuse, but it is often directly connected with caregiver neglect.[5] Examples of abandonment include leaving a cognitively impaired older adult at a hospital emergency room without identification or caregiver contact information or buying an older adult a one-way bus ticket to another town or state.

Self-neglect is also often classified as elder abuse.[6] It involves an adult's lack of self-care, such as failing to seek needed medical care. It can also involve living in conditions that may be unsafe or unsanitary. It is different from other types of elder abuse in a couple of key ways. First, there is not necessarily a "perpetrator." It is possible that the self-neglect could arise as a result of caregiver neglect or abandonment, but that is not always the case. Second, adults may make choices about their food, living conditions, or medical care that differ from those that a social worker, law enforcement official, family member, or friend may make. "It is sometimes difficult to differentiate between an eccentric lifestyle and one that poses an immediate danger to the elder or other people."[7] The goal of protecting adults must be balanced carefully against the importance of preserving an adult's right to self-determination.[8]

Table 1.2. **Some Signs and Symptoms of Abuse**[9]

TYPE OF ABUSE	EXAMPLES OF SIGNS AND SYMPTOMS
Physical abuse	• Bruises, welts, burns, lacerations, and rope marks • Broken bones, sprains, dislocations, and internal injuries • Open wounds, cuts, punctures, and untreated injuries • Broken eyeglasses, physical signs of being subjected to punishment, and signs of being restrained • Overdose or under-use of prescribed drugs • An older adult's report of being hit, slapped, kicked, or mistreated • An older adult's sudden change in behavior • A caregiver's refusal to allow visitors to see an older adult alone • Changes in speaking, breathing, or swallowing that may be the result of strangulation
Sexual abuse or abusive sexual contact	• Difficulty in walking or sitting • Pain or itching in genital area • Unexplained venereal disease or genital infections • Bruises around the breasts, inner thighs, or genital areas • Unexplained vaginal or anal bleeding • Torn, stained, or bloody underclothing

5. BONNIE BRANDL ET AL., ELDER ABUSE DETECTION AND INTERVENTION: A COLLABORATIVE APPROACH 72 (2006); NCEA, *supra* note 2; Stiegel & Klem, *supra* note 1.

6. Jason Burnett et al., *Four Subtypes of Self-Neglect in Older Adults: Results of a Latent Class Analysis*, 62 J. AM. GERIATRICS SOC'Y 1127–32 (2014); NAPSA, *Get Informed*, "Other Safety Concerns and Self-Neglect," NAPSA-NOW.ORG, http://www.napsa-now.org/get-informed/other-safety-concerns-2/ (last visited July 5, 2019).

7. BRANDL ET AL., *supra* note 5, at 72.

8. *Id.*

9. Examples adapted from Lori A. Stiegel, LEGAL ISSUES RELATED TO ELDER ABUSE: A DESK GUIDE FOR LAW ENFORCEMENT, 9-15, American Bar Association Commission on Law and Aging (2015).

Table 1.2, *cont'd*

TYPE OF ABUSE	EXAMPLES OF SIGNS AND SYMPTOMS
Emotional or psychological abuse	• Being emotionally agitated • Being extremely withdrawn and nonresponsive • Depression or suicidal ideation • Signs of self-mutilation • Hypervigilance when in the presence of the abuser • Unusual behavior usually attributed to dementia (e.g., sucking, biting, rocking) • An older adult's report of being verbally or emotionally mistreated
Caregiver neglect	• Dehydration • Malnutrition • Hyperthermia or hypothermia • Hazardous or unsafe living conditions/arrangements • Inadequate or inappropriate clothing • Absence of eyeglasses, hearing aids, dentures, or prostheses • Unexpected or unexplained deterioration of health • Untreated bed sores and other health conditions • Failure to thrive • Lack of routine medical care and/or medications
Financial abuse or exploitation[10]	• Changes in banking practice, including an unexplained withdrawal of large sums of money • Abrupt changes in a will or other financial documents • Unexplained disappearance of funds or property • Substandard care being provided or bills unpaid despite the availability of adequate financial resources • Unexplained sudden transfer of property • Extraordinary interest by family member or "new friend" in older person's assets • Execution of a legal document or transaction that an elder does not understand or was rushed to complete

2. SIGNS AND SYMPTOMS OF ABUSE

Indications that an older adult has been or is being abused may be subtle or they may be glaringly obvious. Individuals who work with older adults should be aware of the different types of abuse and remain alert to potential signs or symptoms.[11] In many cases, the older adult is a victim of more than one type of abuse at the same time.[12] Therefore, if a sign or symptom of one type of abuse is identified, it is essential to search for others. Table 1.2, above, sets out several signs and symptoms that may be associated with the different types of elder abuse. The list should not be viewed as exhaustive but, rather, as a starting point for evaluating individual circumstances.

---

10. *See* NCOA, *supra* note 3.

11. John M. Halphen & Jason Burnett, *Elder Abuse and Neglect: Appearances Can Be Deceptive*, 31 PSYCHIATRIC TIMES 14 (2014).

12. See Valory N. Pavlik et al., *Quantifying the Problem of Abuse and Neglect in Adults—Analysis of a Statewide Database*, 49 J. AM. GERIATRICS SOC'Y 47 (2001) (finding that almost 30 percent of the abuse and neglect reports related to older adults in Texas in a specified period involved more than one type of report).

3. PERPETRATORS OF ABUSE

Perpetrators of elder abuse, other than self-neglect, may be anyone, including family members, friends, informal or formal caregivers, home health workers or in-home aides, guardians, and strangers. Research indicates that perpetrators are "most likely to be adult children or spouses" and have challenges related to behavioral health, substance abuse, social isolation, financial stress, or unemployment.[13] Specifically with respect to financial exploitation, one study found that perpetrators were usually

- family members (in almost 60 percent of cases),
- friends and neighbors (almost 17 percent), and
- home care aides (almost 15 percent).[14]

Potential predictors of elder abuse include poverty, functional and cognitive impairment, worsening cognitive impairment, and living with someone.[15] These risk factors are associated not only with the demographics and abilities of the older adult but also of the perpetrator. Elder abuse is more likely when (1) the perpetrator is suffering from caregiver stress, mental illness or psychological problems, substance abuse, or cognitive impairment and (2) relational issues, such as family disharmony or conflictual relationships, are involved.[16] An abuser's dependency on the older person (often financial) also increases the risk of abuse.[17]

B. OLDER ADULT

Both the CDC and the National Council on Aging (NCOA) consider adults aged 60 and over to be "older adults."[18] In North Carolina, however, some statutes recognize 60 as the age threshold, while others use 65 as a definitional guide.

Two state criminal statutes include the age of an older adult as an element of the particular crime. One law applies to adults aged 60 and older, the other applies to adults 65 and older.

- Domestic abuse, neglect, and exploitation of disabled or elder adults (Chapter 14, Section 32.3 of the North Carolina General Statutes (hereinafter G.S.)): This statute governs abuse of "elder adults," which is defined as persons aged 60 or older who are

---

13. Mark S. Lachs & Karl A. Pillemer, *Elder Abuse*, 373 NEW ENG. J. MED., 1947–56 (2015).

14. Janey C. Peterson et al., *Financial Exploitation of Older Adults: a Population-Based Prevalence Study*, 29 J. GEN. INTERNAL MED. 1615–23, 1620 (Dec. 2014).

15. RON ACIERNO ET AL., NAT'L INST. OF JUST., NATIONAL ELDER MISTREATMENT STUDY 73–74 (Mar. 2009), https://www.ncjrs.gov/pdffiles1/nij/grants/226456.pdf.

16. CDC, *Violence Prevention*, "Risk and Protective Factors," CDC.GOV (last visited May 28, 2019), https://www.cdc.gov/violenceprevention/elderabuse/riskprotectivefactors.html.

17. *Id.*

18. CDC, *supra* note 1; NCOA, *supra* note 3.

"not able to provide for the social, medical, psychiatric, psychological, financial, or legal services necessary to safeguard [their] rights and resources and to maintain [their] physical or mental well-being."

- Exploitation of an older or disabled adult (G.S. 14-112.2): This law defines the term "older adult" to mean a person who is 65 or older.

These two laws represent only a small fraction of the potential crimes that a person abusing an older adult may be committing. The full universe of potential crimes is quite expansive and includes assault, battery, and kidnapping (in cases involving physical abuse or neglect) and forgery, theft, and embezzlement (in financial crimes cases). See Chapter 3 for a list of crimes that may involve elder abuse.

The adult protective services law does not apply exclusively to "older adults" but, rather, it applies to all adults (aged 18 and older) who are disabled.[19] An adult's disability may relate to age, but not necessarily. That body of law is more expansive because it is intended to protect all adults who may be vulnerable due to disability. See Chapter 2 for a discussion of the definition of "disabled" in the context of adult protective services.

Similiarly, incompetency and adult guardianship law does not apply exclusively to "older adults" but instead covers all adults (aged 17.5 and older) who lack the ability to make and communicate decisions or manage their affairs.[20] An adult's lack of competency may relate to age, but not necessarily. That body of law is more expansive because it is intended to protect all adults who may be vulnerable due to incompetency. See Chapter 4 for a discussion of the definition of "incompetency" in the context of guardianship.

IV. WHY IS IT SO IMPORTANT TO ADDRESS ELDER ABUSE?

A. PREVALENCE OF ELDER ABUSE

Many studies and reports related to the prevalence of elder abuse are based on estimates and extrapolations because research and data related to elder abuse lag behind other fields such as child abuse and domestic violence.[21] In addition, experts agree that elder abuse is drastically underreported.[22] One study estimated that only one in fourteen cases of elder abuse is reported to authorities, while another estimated that only one in twenty-four cases is reported. [23]

---

19. Chapter 108A, Section 101(d) of the North Carolina General Statutes (hereinafter G.S.) (defining "disabled adult").

20. G.S. 35A-1101(7) (defining "incompetent adult").

21. NCEA, *Research*, NCEANCL.GOV, https://ncea.acl.gov/About-Us/What-We-Do/Research.aspx (last visited July 5, 2019).

22. UNDER THE RADAR: NEW YORK STATE ELDER ABUSE PREVALENCE STUDY, SELF-REPORTED PREVALENCE AND DOCUMENTED CASE SURVEYS, FINAL REPORT 52 (May 2011), https://ocfs.ny.gov/main/reports/Under%20the%20Radar%20 05%2012%2011%20final%20report.pdf; Ron Acierno, et al., *Prevalence and Correlates of Emotional, Physical, Sexual, and Financial Abuse and Potential Neglect in the United States: The National Elder Mistreatment Study*, 100(2) AM. J. PUB. HEALTH 292, 292–97 (2010).

23. Nat'l Ctr. for Elder Abuse, *Statistics and Data*, "What Is Known about the Incidence and Prevalence of Elder Abuse in the Community Setting?: Prevalence," NCEANCL.GOV, https://ncea.acl.gov/What-We-Do/Research/Statistics-and-Data.aspx (referring to a 2011 New York State Elder Abuse Prevalence Study, which found that only

Despite these limitations, it is still important to examine the data that exists to recognize the scope of the current problem and consider the potential impact of future demographic changes. According to the National Center on Elder Abuse (NCEA), approximately one in ten Americans aged 60 and over have experienced some form of elder abuse.[24] Another study suggests that as many as 5 million older adults are abused each year.[25] The rates are likely higher in institutions such as long-term care facilities.[26]

Like most other states, North Carolina lacks comprehensive state-level data about the prevalence of elder abuse. Some data related to adult protective services is available from the state's Division of Aging and Adult Services (DAAS) within the Department of Health and Human Services. According to DAAS, in state fiscal year 2017–2018, county social services agencies received 30,128 adult protective services reports.[27] Of those reports, 15,563 were screened in and evaluated by social services staff. Of those that were evaluated, 73 percent of the affected adults were 60 years of age or older.[28]

There is some data available regarding criminal charges and convictions under G.S. 14-32.3 and 14-112.2, two state laws that specifically address older adults.[29] See Table 1.3, below, for data from calendar year 2018. There are two important limitations to keep in mind when evaluating this data. First, the statutes also apply to abuse and exploitation of disabled adults who may or may not be older adults. The data does not specify whether the victim was disabled, older, or both. Second, many elder abuse prosecutions in North Carolina and other states rely on other criminal statutes. Therefore, this data is certainly not an accurate representation of the full scope of criminal cases involving elder abuse.

---

one of twenty-four cases of elder abuse gets reported) (last visited July 19, 2019); NCOA, *supra* note 3; NAT'L RESEARCH COUNCIL, ELDER MISTREATMENT: ABUSE, NEGLECT, AND EXPLOITATION IN AN AGING AMERICA (2003), *available through the National Center for Biotechnology Information at* http://www.ncbi.nlm.nih.gov/books/NBK98802/ (estimating that one in fourteen cases of elder abuse is reported).

24. NCOA, *supra* note 3. *See also* NCEA, *Statistics and Data*, "What Is Known about the Incidence and Prevalence of Elder Abuse in the Community Setting?," NCEANCL.GOV, https://ncea.acl.gov/About-Us/What-We-Do/Research/Statistics-and-Data.aspx#prevalence (last visited July 5, 2019).

25. NCOA, *supra* note 3.

26. World Health Org. (WHO), *Elder Abuse*, WHOINT (June 8, 2018), https://www.who.int/news-room/fact-sheets/detail/elder-abuse. *See also* NCEA, *Statistics and Data*, "Abuse in Nursing Homes and Other Long-Term Care Facilities," NCEANCL.GOV, https://ncea.acl.gov/About-Us/What-We-Do/Research/Statistics-and-Data#ltc (last visited Oct. 16, 2019).

27. N.C. DEP'T OF HEALTH & HUMAN SERVS. (NCDHHS), DIV. OF AGING & ADULT SERVS. (DAAS), ANNUAL ADULT PROTECTIVE SERVICES (APS) SURVEY, SFY 2017–2018 (on file at DAAS) (hereinafter APS SURVEY); NCDHHS, DAAS, CLIENT SERVICES DATA WAREHOUSE (CSDW), APS 110 CLIENT DEMOGRAPHICS (on file at DAAS) (hereinafter CSDW APS 110 REPORT). *See also* Thomas Goldsmith, *Mistreated Adults Need Support from State, Not Just Counties and Feds, Advocates Say*, NORTH CAROLINA HEALTH NEWS (Feb. 7, 2019), https://www.northcarolinahealthnews.org/2019/02/07/advocates-want-more-funds-for-adult-protective-services/.

28. APS SURVEY, *supra* note 27; CSDW APS 110 REPORT, *supra* note 27.

29. N.C. ADMIN. OFFICE OF THE CTS., 2018 TALLY OF CRIMINAL CHARGES AND CONVICTIONS (on file with authors).

Table 1.3. **2018 Charges and Convictions for Elder-Specific Crimes**

CRIME	STATUTE (G.S.)	TOTAL # OF CHARGES
Abuse disabled/elderly with injury	14-32.3(a)	27
Abuse disabled/elderly with serious injury	14-32.3(a)	21
Neglect disabled/elderly with injury	14-32.3(b)	16
Neglect disabled/elderly with serious injury	14-32.3(b)	16
Exploit disabled/elderly trust	14-112.2(b)	317
Exploit disabled/elderly capacity	14-112.2(c)	370

Source: N.C. ADMIN. OFFICE OF THE CTS., *supra* note 29.

B. AGING AND DEMOGRAPHICS

Lower fertility rates and increased longevity have led to the rapid growth of the older population across the world and in the United States.[30] In 2015, among the estimated 7.3 billion worldwide population, 617.1 million (9 percent) were aged 65 and older.[31] By 2030, the older population will total roughly 1 billion (12 percent of the projected total world population); by 2050, 1.6 billion (17 percent) of the total world population of 9.4 billion will be 65 and older.[32] The United States will experience further expansion of its older population for many decades to come, fueled by the baby boom cohort that began turning 65 years old in 2011.[33]

Of the more than 10 million people living in North Carolina in 2017, about 16 percent were aged 65 and older.[34] According to the Office of State Management and Budget, this percentage is expected to continue increasing over the next two decades, reaching an estimated 21 percent of the population by 2037.[35] In other words, one in five people will be 65 or older in 2037. The fastest-growing age group will be those 85 and older.[36]

The balance between the older and younger population is also clearly shifting in North Carolina. In 2017, approximately 40 percent of the population was 60 and older.[37] In 2037, it is expected that almost 50 percent of the population will be in that age group.[38] In 2019, it is expected that the state will have more people aged 60 and older than people who are 18 years and younger.[39] (See Figure 1.1, below.)

30. WAN HE ET AL., U.S. CENSUS BUREAU, INTERNATIONAL POPULATION REPORTS, AN AGING WORLD: 2015 1 (2016), https://www.census.gov/content/dam/Census/library/publications/2016/demo/p95-16-1.pdf.

31. *Id.* at 3.

32. *Id.*

33. *Id.* at 9.

34. NCDHHS, DAAS, *North Carolina Is Aging!*, https://files.nc.gov/ncdhhs/documents/files/NC%20State%20Aging%20Profile%202017_0.pdf (last visited July 5, 2019).

35. *Id.*

36. *Id.*

37. *Id.*

38. *Id.*

39. *Id.*

Figure 1.1. **Projected Growth (in Percentages) of Age Groups in N.C. Population from 2017 to 2037**

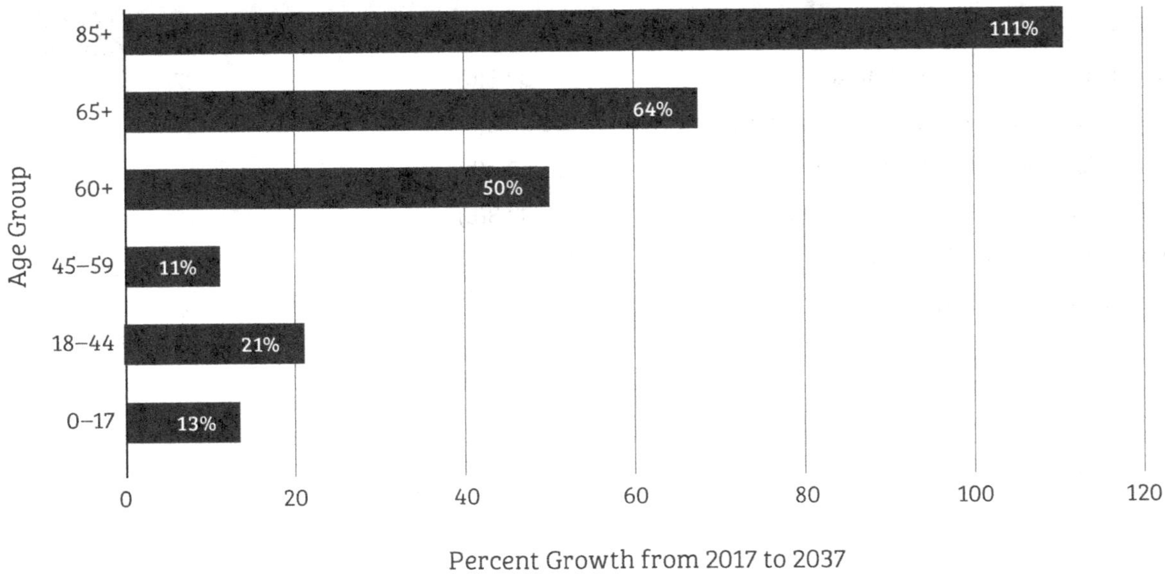

Source: NCDHHS, DAAS, *supra* note 34.

With such a tremendous population expansion on the horizon for older adults in North Carolina, it is reasonable to expect that elder abuse has the potential to increase as well.

C. HEALTH IMPLICATIONS

Elder abuse can lead to physical harm ranging from minor scratches and bruises to broken bones and disabling injuries. It can also lead to serious, sometimes long-lasting, psychological consequences, including depression and anxiety. For older adults, even relatively minor injuries can cause serious and permanent harm or even death. Studies indicate that elder abuse is "predictive of later disability among persons who initially displayed no disability and is associated with increased rates of emergency department utilization, increased risks for hospitalization, and increased risk for mortality."[40] One study found that victims of elder abuse are twice as likely to die prematurely as people who are not victims of elder abuse.[41] Another study found that victims of elder abuse have a 300 percent higher risk of death when compared to those who have not been mistreated.[42]

40. NCEA, *Statistics and Data*, "What Is the Impact of Elder Abuse?," NCEANCL.GOV, https://ncea.acl.gov/About-Us/What-We-Do/Research/Statistics-and-Data#impact (citing Mark S. Lachs et al., *ED Use by Older Victims of Family Violence*, 30 ANNALS EMERGENCY MED. 448–54 (1997); M.W. Baker et al., *Mortality Risk Associated with Physical and Verbal Abuse in Women Aged 50 to 79*, 57 J. AM. GERIATRICS SOC'Y 1799–1809 (2009)) (last visited July 5, 2019).

41. WHO, *supra* note 26.

42. NCOA, *supra* note 3.

D. ECONOMIC IMPACT

It is difficult to estimate the economic impact of elder abuse because such abuse is underreported and there are not consistent definitions and reliable data sources to draw on.[43] When trying to estimate economic impact, one element to consider is direct loss tied to financial exploitation and fraud. These losses are estimated to range anywhere from $2.9 billion to $36.5 billion annually.[44] There are also the financial implications of other types of abuse, which can include medical costs, increased costs related to caregiving for victims, and the decreased financial security of caregivers.[45] Other societal costs may include expenses associated with the prosecution, punishment, and rehabilitation of perpetrators.

V. WHY IS ELDER ABUSE DIFFICULT TO ADDRESS?

Recognizing the need to address elder abuse is relatively easy. Protecting older adults, preserving assets, preventing future abuse, and punishing perpetrators can be much more complicated. Below is a snapshot of some of the potential barriers facing public officials and others trying to address elder abuse, along with at least one suggestion to help make it easier to do.

A. MANY INVOLVED

The various agencies, officials, and organizations involved with elder abuse approach the issue of elder abuse from different perspectives and are governed by different bodies of law. It can be difficult to know who is responsible for what, who has taken which steps, and what the respective roles should be in each situation. Public officials may not fully understand all of the components of the elder protection system in their communities. A concerned family member, neighbor, churchgoer, or professional may not necessarily know where to turn for help.

---

43. Tobie Stanger, *Financial Elder Abuse Costs $3 Billion a Year or Is it $36 Billion?*, CONSUMER REPORTS.ORG (Sept. 29, 2015), https://www.consumerreports.org/cro/consumer-protection/financial-elder-abuse-costs--3-billion-----or-is-it--30-billion-.

44. NCOA, *supra* note 3; True Link Fin., *The True Link Report on Elder Financial Abuse 2015* (Jan. 2015), http://documents.truelinkfinancial.com/True-Link-Report-On-Elder-Financial-Abuse-012815.pdf; NCEA, *Elder Abuse and its Impact: What You Must Know* (last revised Feb. 2015), https://ncea.acl.gov/NCEA/media/Publication/Elder-Abuse-and-Its-Impact-What-You-Must-Know-2013.pdf.

45. NCEA, *Statistics and Data*, NCEANCL.GOV, https://ncea.acl.gov/About-Us/What-We-Do/Research/Statistics-and-Data#impact (last visited July 5, 2019); MetLife Mature Mkt. Inst., *The MetLife Study of Caregiving Costs to Working Caregivers: Double Jeopardy for Baby Boomers Caring for Their Parents* (June 2011), http://www.caregiving.org/wp-content/uploads/2011/06/mmi-caregiving-costs-working-caregivers.pdf.

IDENTIFY PARTNERS AND BUILD STRATEGIC RELATIONSHIPS IN YOUR LOCAL ELDER PROTECTION COMMUNITY. CREATE A COMMON UNDERSTANDING OF THE VARIOUS ROLES OF THE PARTNERS AND THE RESOURCES AVAILABLE IN THE COMMUNITY.

- Identify others in the community who are involved with elder abuse protection. Learn about their missions, the limitations on their roles, and the opportunities presented by their involvement. Build relationships and develop plans for collaboration and coordination. Strive for a no-wrong-door model to ensure that potential victims and reporters are directed to the appropriate resources within the community.
- Consider developing a formalized multidisciplinary team in your community. (See Section VII, below.)
- Develop a public education campaign that simplifies concepts and reporting. (See www.protectadults.sog.unc.edu for more information and resources, including sample training and written materials.)

B. COMPLEX PSYCHOLOGICAL AND EMOTIONAL CONSIDERATIONS

Victims of elder abuse may not be willing to share information or cooperate fully, or they may recant testimony because they are afraid for their own safety or are ashamed to be the subject of an abusive situation or exploitation. They may want to protect a potential abuser who may be a family member or friend. Victims also may be reluctant to seek change because they may be worried about the disruption that would come from reporting abuse, changing living arrangements, or losing a caregiver.

C. DIMINISHED CAPACITY

Older adults may suffer from cognitive impairments, such as dementia, that may prevent them from (1) remaining aware the abuse, (2) providing helpful information to social workers or law enforcement officers, or (3) testifying in proceedings. The presence of cognitive impairments may also present challenges to determining whether an older adult gave consent to a perpetrator's acts.

RESOURCE

What Is Dementia?

Dementia is not a specific disease. It is a general term used to describe conditions that cause losses of memory so severe that they may impact a person's ability to carry out daily activities.[46] It is caused by damage to brain cells.[47] The primary risk factor for dementia is age.[48]

A recent study found that in the United States in 2017, a total of 261,914 reported deaths had dementia as an underlying cause of death.[49] The number of dementia-related deaths has more than doubled in recent years, increasing from 30.5 deaths per 100,000 people in 2000 to 66.7 deaths in 2017.[50] Forty-six percent of these dementia-related deaths were due to Alzheimer's disease,[51] which is the most common form of dementia.[52]

There is no cure and no treatment to stop the progression of Alzheimer's disease.[53] There are drugs and therapies that temporarily improve symptoms.[54]

EARLY SIGNS AND SYMPTOMS OF ALZHEIMER'S DISEASE	TYPICAL AGE-RELATED CHANGES
• Memory loss that disrupts daily life	• Sometimes forgetting names or appointments but remembering them later
• Challenges in planning or solving problems	• Making occasional errors when balancing a checkbook
• Difficulty completing familiar tasks at home, work, or leisure	• Occasionally needing help to use the settings on a microwave
• Confusion with time or place	• Getting confused about the day of the week but figuring it out later
• Trouble understanding visual images and spatial relationships	• Vision changes related to cataracts
• New problems with words in speaking or writing	• Sometimes having trouble finding the right word
• Misplacing things and losing the ability to retrace steps	• Misplacing things from time to time and retracing steps to find them
• Decreased or poor judgment	• Making a bad decision once in a while
• Withdrawal from work or social activities	• Sometimes feeling weary of work, family, and social obligations
• Changes in mood and personality	• Developing very specific ways of doing things and becoming irritable when a routine is disrupted

Note: Adapted from the Alzheimer's Association, *10 Early Signs and Symptoms of Alzheimer's*, "What Is the Difference between Alzheimer's and Typical Age-Related Changes?, ALZ.ORG, https://www.alz.org/alzheimers-dementia/10_signs (last visited July 3, 2019).

---

46. CDC, *Alzheimer's Disease and Related Dementias*, CDC.ORG (last visited Oct. 9, 2018), https://www.cdc.gov/features/alzheimers-disease-dementia/index.html.

47. Alzheimer's Ass'n, *What Is Dementia?*, ALZ.ORG, https://www.alz.org/alzheimers-dementia/what-is-dementia (last visited July 5, 2019).

48. *Id.*

49. CDC, Nat'l Ctr. for Health Statistics, *Dementia Mortality in the United States, 2000–2017*, NAT'L VITAL STATISTICS REPS., vol. 68, no. 2, at 3 (Mar. 14, 2019), https://www.cdc.gov/nchs/data/nvsr/nvsr68/nvsr68_02-508.pdf.

50. *Id.* at 9.

51. *Id.* at 5.

52. *Id.* at 1.

53. Alzheimer's Ass'n, *supra* note 47.

54. *Id.*

INVEST TIME IN DEVELOPING THE EXPERTISE NECESSARY TO COMMUNICATE APPROPRIATELY WITH AND PROVIDE SUPPORT FOR OLDER ADULTS WHO MAY BE VICTIMS OF ABUSE.

Adopt interviewing and information-gathering techniques that are sensitive to potential psychological and emotional barriers, as well as potential limitations related to typical age-related changes in memory or behavior (see Appendix B for more information).

D. LIMITED RESOURCES

All of the public and private agencies involved with the elder protection system have limited financial and human resources. At the same time, they are intensely dedicated to their mission and carrying out their role in protecting older adults.

DEVELOP STRATEGIC PARTNERSHIPS THAT MAXIMIZE THE IMPACT OF EACH PARTNER'S LIMITED RESOURCES.

Each component of a community's elder protection system brings with it opportunities and limitations. They have different missions, expertise, legal authority, and resources. The rest of this manual and the accompanying resources are designed to provide information to help each component understand how the various pieces of the elder protection puzzle fit together. With better understanding, these public and private agencies may be able to find ways to work together to make the most efficient and effective use of the limited resources available.

VI. WHAT ARE THE KEY COMPONENTS OF NORTH CAROLINA'S ELDER PROTECTION SYSTEM?

Elder abuse is a problem that cannot be adequately addressed by over-reliance on one governmental system alone. Rather, it is a societal problem that is cross-cutting in nature. It is therefore useful to take a wider, multidisciplinary view of elder abuse as a topic when trying to ascertain best efforts to combat it. Below is a high-level overview of the chief elements of North Carolina's elder protection system (each is addressed in more detail in the chapters that follow in this manual), including its three key governmental components: adult protective services (APS) (covered in Chapter 2), criminal investigation and prosecution (Chapter 3), and guardianship (Chapter 4). The discussion below also summarizes the roles that other legal tools and components—such as civil remedies (e.g., powers of attorney), state agencies (e.g., long-term care ombudsman program), health care providers, and financial institutions—play in the system (Chapters 4 through 7). Each heading in the subsections immediately below cross-references the manual chapter where readers can find more in-depth information.

A. ADULT PROTECTIVE SERVICES (CHAPTER 2)

Social work is the foundation for adult protective services. According to the National Adult Protective Services Association (NAPSA), the term "adult protective services" (APS) is defined as "a social services program provided by state and/or local governments nationwide serving older adults and adults with disabilities who are in need of assistance" due to abuse, neglect, self-neglect, and/or exploitation.[55] The term "assistance" as used in this definition is vague by necessity because the circumstances in each case are unique and the affected adult's needs will vary tremendously from person to person.

The primary goal of APS is "ensuring that protective services are provided to disabled adults who have been abused, neglected or exploited rather than determining whether a particular abusive incident occurred or punishing the perpetrator."[56] APS social workers are focused on ensuring the well-being of disabled adults. While this goal differs from the one underlying criminal prosecution, it is often essential to involve both APS and law enforcement officials when an older adult has been abused. APS may be able to protect an older adult from abuse, neglect, or exploitation, but law enforcement officials are able to investigate potential crimes, punish a perpetrator, and possibly deter future abuse.

In North Carolina, APS is a governmental function, and front-line APS workers are county government employees. APS workers are often the first people to have contact with a disabled adult, the adult's caregivers, and sometimes with the perpetrators of the alleged abuse. These social workers are not law enforcement officers, they do not carry weapons, and they are limited in their ability to collect evidence, so they may be seen as somewhat less intimidating than sworn officers.

APS involvement begins with a report to a county social services agency. The primary way APS protects and supports older adults is by delivering or arranging for the provision of services that are custom-tailored to address the particular concerns that are putting the older adult at risk. An older adult may consent to the provision of services or a court may order APS to provide them.

B. CRIMINAL INVESTIGATION AND PROSECUTION (CHAPTER 3)

North Carolina law does not establish a specific crime of "elder abuse." Instead, several crimes may be implicated if an older adult is being abused or exploited. Only two crimes focus specifically on older or disabled adults, but many other generally applicable

55. NAPSA, *Get Help*, "What is Adult Protective Services?," NAPSA-NOW.ORG, http://www.napsa-now.org/get-help/how-aps-helps/ (last visited July 5, 2019).

56. NCDHHS, DAAS, DIV. OF AGING & ADULT SERVS. MANUAL I-2 (Apr. 1, 2011), https://files.nc.gov/ncdhhs/documents/files/APS_Manual.pdf.

crimes—such as assault, battery, rape, fraud, forgery, obtaining property by false pretenses, embezzlement, or robbery—may be implicated when a victim is an elder adult. A combination of local, state, and federal officials are involved in both investigating and prosecuting these crimes.

Criminal investigation and prosecution is unique in that it allows for the punishment of perpetrators. The other bodies of law discussed in this manual focus primarily on protecting or providing redress to the affected older person. But punishing a perpetrator can actually prevent further victimization of a particular elder and also potentially deter abuse of other adults in the future.

C. GUARDIANSHIP (CHAPTER 4)

The third governmental component of the elder protection system in North Carolina, guardianship, exists to help individuals who lack capacity to exercise their rights, including the right to remain free from abuse.[57] Guardianship is a "legal relationship under which a person or agency (the guardian) is appointed by a court to make decisions and act on behalf of a minor or an incapacitated adult (the ward) with respect to the ward's personal affairs, financial affairs, or both."[58] A guardian may be appointed for the person, for property, or for both. In North Carolina, clerks of superior court have the exclusive authority to adjudicate incompetency and appoint a guardian. They also have the authority to remove a guardian if the guardian is abusing the older adult.

If an incompetent adult is abused by someone other than a guardian, the appointment of a guardian could help protect the adult in several ways. For example, the guardian could

- move the adult to a different living space or health care facility,
- secure or recover assets that have been stolen or compromised, and
- identify and consent to physical or behavioral health care needed to help the adult recover from the abuse.

A guardian may be appointed relatively quickly in emergency situations or in cases where an imminent risk exists to the older adult or to the older adult's property. A guardian may have broad powers or, if the older adult is determined to have capacity in some areas, the authority of a guardian can be limited. A family member or friend may be appointed to serve as an older adult's guardian or the guardian may be the director of social services or a private guardianship corporation. The court has a continuing role in overseeing the guardianship after the guardian is appointed. Guardianship is seen as a remedy of last resort because of the impact it has on the autonomy of the older adult. Thus, limiting through guardianship the rights of an older adult who lacks capacity should not be undertaken unless it is clear that the guardian will give the older adult a fuller capacity for exercising his or her rights.[59]

57. G.S. 35A-1201(a).
58. JOHN L. SAXON, N.C. GUARDIANSHIP MANUAL § 1.3, at 5 (UNC School of Government, 2008).
59. G.S. 35A-1201(a)(4).

D. POWERS OF ATTORNEY (CHAPTER 5)

A power of attorney (POA) is a legal writing or other record that grants authority to an agent to act in the place of the principal.[60] POAs intersect with all other areas of the elder protection system. A law enforcement officer may be presented with a POA as a defense to a crime. An APS social worker may be presented with a POA as evidence that the older adult does not need protective services. A court may appoint a guardian with the authority to terminate a POA or may enter an order removing an agent.

A POA may grant an agent authority with respect to property and property interests or as to health care. This manual discusses POAs related to property and property interests, sometimes referred to in practice as **durable POAs**. A POA is durable if the incapacity of the principal does not terminate the agent's authority to act. An older adult may execute a POA for any number of reasons, including convenience or as part of planning for future incapacity. Unlike guardianship, which requires a court action, a POA is largely a private arrangement and preserves the self-determination of the older adult. The older adult selects the agent and determines in the POA the extent of the agent's authority to act on his or her behalf.

POAs are regularly used by and often recommended to older adults as a way to avoid guardianship. But POAs may be—and often are—a source of abuse. Because they are private arrangements, unscrupulous individuals may use undue influence or other abusive tactics to get an older adult who lacks capacity to sign a POA. In other cases an older adult with capacity may sign a POA free from undue influence but the agent appointed under the POA may abuse or exceed the authority granted under the POA. Fortunately, there are actions that may be taken by the older adult, by others acting with or on behalf of the older adult, or by the court to protect the older adult from abuse under a POA.

E. CIVIL ACTIONS, DOMESTIC VIOLENCE, AND HOUSING (CHAPTER 6)

In addition to APS, guardianship, and POAs, there are additional civil remedies an older adult or a caregiver may call upon to protect the older adult and provide him or her redress in the event of abuse. Some of these are briefly described below.

- **Private civil actions.** Private civil actions instituted to recover property, seek monetary damages, or rescind a document executed by an older adult include actions alleging breach of fiduciary duty, fraud, conversion, intentional infliction of emotional distress, and civil assault.
- **Domestic violence protective orders.** A victim of domestic violence may be able to obtain an ex parte order of protection in situations involving physical harm or harassment. The terms "domestic violence" and "personal relationship" are defined broadly enough in state law to encompass many of the family relationships that may

60. *See* G.S. 32C-1-102(9) (defining "power of attorney"), (1) (defining "agent"), (11) (defining "principal").

involve elder abuse, such as when abuse is perpetrated by an elder's adult children, grandchildren, or spouses or ex-spouses.[61] The law also applies to situations where people of the opposite sex live together, which may be the case with some in-home aides.[62]

- **Civil no-contact orders.** A victim of unlawful conduct may petition the court for a no-contact order. Under this body of law, "unlawful conduct" is limited to nonconsensual sexual conduct and stalking.[63] These orders apply in situations where an older adult victim has been subjected to unlawful conduct by someone with whom he or she is not in a personal relationship.
- **Housing actions.** Depending on the facts of a particular case, an older adult who is a property owner may bring (1) an action for summary ejectment to remove an abuser or exploiter from his or her home or (2) an action for civil or criminal trespass. An older adult who is a tenant has protections under state and federal law.

If the older adult victim has a low income, Legal Aid of North Carolina may be able to assist the victim in pursuing some of these remedies. Alternatively, private attorneys and elder law clinics may be an option for the older adult to explore.

F. OTHER CRITICAL GOVERNMENTAL COMPONENTS (CHAPTER 7)

While local law enforcement and social services agencies often take the lead in elder abuse cases, it may be possible to collaborate with or transition a case to other government agencies with specific areas of expertise and statutory authority. Several other state agencies are involved in the protection of adults. Some of these organizations are listed below.

- The Division of Health Services Regulation within the Department of Health and Human Services will become involved if an older adult has been abused or neglected in a licensed facility.
- The Department of Justice may become involved if an older adult is the victim of a scam or other consumer fraud.
- The Department of Insurance has law enforcement officers who may become involved if the case involves insurance fraud.
- The Secretary of State's office may become involved if the case involves securities or investment fraud.

61. G.S. 50B-1.
62. G.S. 50B-1(b)(2).
63. G.S. 50C-1(7) (defining "unlawful conduct").

VII. HOW CAN THESE KEY COMPONENTS COLLABORATE TO PROTECT ELDERS?

The term "elder protection system" suggests more connectivity and integration than actually exists in many communities. The various components are often trying to find better ways to collaborate and develop a stronger, more systematic approach to elder protection. One way professionals in various disciplines can collaborate to address elder abuse is through the formation of multidisciplinary teams (MDTs). An MDT is a group of professionals in a geographic region who commit to working together toward a common goal. Elder abuse MDTs have gained traction because the problems they seek to tackle are complex and difficult for any single actor to detect, prevent, and resolve.[64]

For example, APS may intervene in a case to provide protective services to an older adult and to resolve the crisis for that particular adult. However, APS does not have authority to prosecute the perpetrator of the abuse and, therefore, after APS involvement, if no other actor steps in to offer assistance the perpetrator may move on to another victim. Alternatively, an older adult who is the victim of elder abuse may be unable to consent to the protective services offered by APS. In such a case, APS must seek a court-appointed guardian to help implement changes that will protect the older adult from further abuse. APS will then work with that guardian to ensure that protective action is taken on behalf of the older adult.

Some jurisdictions are mandated by law to establish MDTs or protocols for collaboration.[65] Other states expressly authorize public officials to coordinate and provide a collaborative response to elder abuse cases, addressing issues such as information-sharing and confidentiality.[66] The National Adult Protective Services Association's *Recommended Minimum Program Standards* encourage APS systems to form intentional and specific collaborations in order "to provide comprehensive services to alleged victims by building

64. U.S. GOV'T ACCOUNTABILITY OFF., ELDER JUSTICE: STRONGER FEDERAL LEADERSHIP COULD ENHANCE NATIONAL RESPONSE TO ELDER ABUSE (Mar. 2011), https://www.gao.gov/assets/320/316224.pdf; U.S. DEP'T OF JUST., THE ELDER JUSTICE ROADMAP: A STAKEHOLDER INITIATIVE TO RESPOND TO AN EMERGING HEALTH, JUSTICE, FINANCIAL AND SOCIAL CRISIS 5, https://www.justice.gov/file/852856/download (last visited July 5, 2019). ELDER ABUSE: RESEARCH, PRACTICE AND POLICY ch. 19, at 417 (Xin Qui ed., 1st ed. 2017). *See* BUREAU OF CONSUMER FIN. PROT., OFF. OF FIN. PROT. FOR OLDER AMERICANS, REPORT AND RECOMMENDATIONS: FIGHTING ELDER FINANCIAL EXPLOITATION THROUGH COMMUNITY NETWORKS 4 (May 2018), https://files.consumerfinance.gov/f/documents/bcfp_fighting-elder-financial-exploitation_community-networks_report.pdf (recommending the creation of networks to combat financial exploitation of older adults). *See also* Deborah Cox-Roush, *Senior Corps and the Department of Justice: Working Together to Prevent Elder Fraud and Abuse*, DEP'T JUST. J. FED. L. & PRAC., vol. 66, no. 7, at 270 n.22 (Dec. 2018), https://www.justice.gov/usao/page/file/1121446/download (stating that "[m]ultidisciplinary teams are a hallmark of elder abuse prevention programs that reflect the consensus that no single agency has all the resources or expertise needed to effectively resolve all forms of abuse and neglect. Teams may be involved in a variety of collaborative activities, including advocacy, service coordination, professional training, resource development and outreach.").

65. *See* CAL. WELF. & INST. CODE § 15763(A) (requiring adult protective services agencies to lead MDTs in every county).

66. *See, e.g.*, FLA. STAT. §§ 415.1102 (authorizing the state APS agency to establish adult protection teams); 415.106 (requiring the state APS agency to enter into collaborative agreements with others involved with elder protection); 415.107 (specifying when the state APS agency may share confidential information with others involved in elder protection).

on the strengths, and compensating for the weaknesses, of the service delivery system available in the community, and by avoiding working at cross-purposes."[67]

North Carolina does not have specific laws that address elder abuse MDTs. While they are not specifically required or authorized by statute, they are also not prohibited or discouraged.

A. TYPES OF MDTs

There are as many different types of MDTs as there are groups that work together to form them. One of the benefits of an MDT is its flexibility; each group in the MDT is able to decide what approaches and actions will work best for its team or community based on the composition of the community and its resources. That being said, MDTs generally break down in two main types: (1) case-review MDTs and (2) systemic-review MDTs.[68]

1. CASE-REVIEW MDTs

In a case-review MDT, team members recommend specific, complex cases for review by the MDT and collaborate on resolving each selected case. A case-review MDT is typically comprised of the people doing the work out in the field, responding to and resolving reports of abuse on a day-to-day basis. A case-review team may have an information-sharing agreement in place that allows members to share information about specific cases. A case-review MDT may specialize in particular types of cases.[69] Examples of specialized case-review MDTs are set out below.

- **Fiduciary Abuse Specialist Team (FAST).** This type of team specializes in financial exploitation, with an emphasis on early intervention.[70] The team's membership is typically drawn from private sector organizations, such as financial institutions and accountants, and from state and federal regulatory agencies with authority over the investigation and enforcement of financial exploitation.[71]
- **Fatality Review Team.** This kind of team focuses on investigating and sometimes prosecuting elder abuse–related deaths and makes recommendations to improve service systems and professional roles.[72] In addition to traditional MDT members,

67. NAPSA, *Adult Protective Services, Recommended Minimum Program Standards*, at 6 (2013), http://www.napsa-now.org/wp-content/uploads/2014/04/Recommended-Program-Standards.pdf ("The goal of these intentional and specific collaborations is to provide comprehensive services to vulnerable adults in need of protection by building on the strengths, and compensating for the weaknesses, of the service delivery system available in the community, and by avoiding working at cross-purposes. One method to enhance community collaboration is to develop Multidisciplinary Teams as needed or required.").

68. Georgia J. Anetzberger, *The Evolution of a Multidisciplinary Response to Elder Abuse*, MARQUETTE ELDER'S ADVISOR, vol. 13, no. 1, at 119 (2011), https://scholarship.law.marquette.edu/elders/vol13/iss1/1.

69. ELDER ABUSE: RESEARCH, PRACTICE AND POLICY, *supra* note 64, at ch. 19, 419.

70. *Id.* at 420. *See* BUREAU OF CONSUMER FIN. PROT., *supra* note 64 (noting that only 6 percent of known elder abuse networks specialize in financial exploitation).

71. *See* SANTA CLARA CTY. (CAL.), FINANCIAL ABUSE SPECIALIST TEAM PRACTICE GUIDE (v. 2.0, Apr. 2016), https://www.sccgov.org/sites/ssa/daas/aps/Documents/fast_practice_guide.pdf.

72. Lori A. Stiegel, ELDER ABUSE FATALITY REVIEW TEAMS: A REPLICATION MANUAL, AMERICAN BAR ASSOCIATION COMMISSION ON LAW AND AGING (2005), https://www.americanbar.org/content/dam/aba/administrative/law_aging/fatalitymanual.authcheckdam.pdf.

Fatality Review Teams may also include representatives from coroner's offices, funeral homes, state licensing agencies, and hospice agencies.[73]

- **Hoarding Team.** This variety of case-review MDT focuses specifically on older adults who display hoarding behaviors and on the related mental health concerns associated with those behaviors.[74]
- **Elder Abuse Forensic Centers.** These centers/teams focus on conducting investigations and gathering evidence to allow for more efficient prosecution of elder abuse cases by collaborating with health care providers and adult protective services.[75] They may also conduct evidentiary investigations, tape victim interviews, consult on cases, and perform research.[76]

2. SYSTEMIC-REVIEW MDTs

In a systemic-review MDT, team members work together to address systemic problems and service gaps and to develop information networks. A systemic-review MDT is generally staffed by people within organizations who are more senior in rank and who have decisional authority. Examples of actions undertaken by systemic-review MDTs are set out below.

- Disseminating information about new services, legislation, and policy changes to members of the MDT
- Increasing community awareness of elder abuse by offering trainings to the community, including to older adults, caregivers, clergy, financial institutions, and others
- Establishing practical reporting protocols among MDT members
- Forming partnerships and increasing understanding of the various roles, responsibilities, and limitations of each of the professionals on the MDT
- Creating self-help materials for dissemination in the community, such as a community resource guide
- Obtaining and sharing resources

A systemic-review MDT may be organized into separate divisions that carry out each of these actions.

---

73. *Id.*

74. *Id.* For an analysis of hoarding trends in elders, refer to *Hoarding and Elders: Current Trends, Dilemmas, and Solutions*, J. GERIATRIC CARE MGMT. (SPECIAL ISSUE), vol. 20, no. 2 (2010), https://www.aginglifecare.org/ALCA_Web_Docs/memberonly/gcmjournal/GCMJournal-fall10.pdf.

75. See generally the website of the University of California-Irvine Medical Center's Center of Excellence on Elder Abuse & Neglect at http://www.centeronelderabuse.org/EAFC.asp.

76. *Id.*

B. PARTICIPANTS IN MDTs

The question of who should participate on an MDT will depend on the needs and resources of the particular community, as well as on the purpose of the MDT.[77] Some MDTs have members authorized to conduct case reviews and other members that only serve to address systemic issues. Some MDTs engage technical advisors to consult on issues that require specialized knowledge, such as forensic accountants, geriatricians, and neuropsychologists. The composition of an MDT may grow and change over time. It may be preferable, when starting out, for an MDT to have a small group upon which it can build a strong foundation.[78] Figure 1.2 lists possible agencies/organizations/sectors from which MDT members might be drawn.

Figure 1.2. **Possible Members of an MDT**

77. U.S. DEP'T OF JUST., ELDER JUST. INITIATIVE, MDT GUIDE ch. 3, "Selecting Team Members," https://www.justice.gov/elderjustice/selecting-team-members (last visited July 5, 2019).

78. *Id.*

Judges, including clerks of superior court who serve as probate judges in North Carolina, are limited in their ability to serve on MDTs. A judge or clerk could serve on a systemic-review MDT but not on a case-review MDT. This is because judges and clerks must remain impartial and should not be involved in responding to specific cases that come before them outside of a hearing. Judges and clerks may participate, and are important actors, on systemic-review MDTs in order to improve the administration of justice. Judges and clerks can be effective community conveners. Judicial leadership gives a sense of urgency to a matter and emphasizes the importance of an issue.[79] Participation in systemic-review MDTs may help the court to better assess capacity issues, craft more dynamic and responsive court orders, and more effectively oversee cases.[80]

C. POTENTIAL BENEFITS OF MDTs

MDTs provide professionals with an opportunity to step out of their silos and coordinate on the detection, prevention, and resolution of elder abuse in their communities.[81] While research efforts related to the use of MDTs in elder abuse is limited, there have been some studies with positive findings. Below are some examples.

- Staff from agencies involved with the MDT reported believing that they are more efficient and effective when they collaborate with a forensic center.
- Financial exploitation cases that involved collaboration with MDTs or forensic centers were more likely to be referred for prosecution, to result in the filing of charges, and to have an outcome that established the perpetrator's guilt.[82]
- Older adults who received services from an MDT that involved social workers and attorneys were less likely to face future mistreatment.[83]
- Forensic centers were shown to be an effective approach for determining whether a petition for guardianship should be filed in order to protect an older adult.[84]

79. NAT'L CTR. FOR STATE CTS., COURT GUIDE TO EFFECTIVE COLLABORATION ON ELDER ABUSE (2012), http://www.eldersandcourts.org/~/media/microsites/files/cec/court%20collaboration.ashx.

80. *Id.*

81. *See* BUREAU OF CONSUMER FIN. PROT., *supra* note 64; U.S. DEP'T OF HEALTH & HUMAN SERVS., ADMIN. FOR CMTY. LIVING, FINAL VOLUNTARY CONSENSUS GUIDELINES FOR STATE ADULT PROTECTIVE SERVICES SYSTEMS 4–6 (Sept. 2016), https://acl.gov/sites/default/files/programs/2017-03/APS-Guidelines-Document-2017.pdf (guidelines developed in 2016, proposed updates to be incorporated in 2019).

82. Adria Navarro et al., *Holding Abusers Accountable: An Elder Abuse Forensic Center Increases Criminal Prosecution of Financial Exploitation*, GERONTOLOGIST, vol. 53, no. 2, at 303–12 (Apr. 2013), http://gerontologist.oxfordjournals.org/content/early/2012/05/15/geront.gns075; KATHLEEN H. WILBER ET AL., EVALUATING THE ELDER ABUSE FORENSIC CENTER MODEL vii–viii (submitted to U.S. Department of Justice Apr. 3, 2014), https://www.ncjrs.gov/pdffiles1/nij/grants/246428.pdf; Mary S. Twomey et al., *The Successes and Challenges of Seven Multidisciplinary Teams*, J. ELDER ABUSE & NEGLECT, vol. 22, no. 3-4, at 291–305 (2010).

83. Victoria Marie Rizzo et al., *A Systematic Evaluation of a Multidisciplinary Social Work-Lawyer Elder Mistreatment Intervention Model*, J. ELDER ABUSE & NEGLECT, vol. 27, no. 1 (2015).

84. Zachary D. Gassoumis et al., *Protecting Victims of Elder Financial Exploitation: The Role of an Elder Abuse Forensic Center in Referring Victims for Conservatorship*, J. AGING & MENT. HEALTH, vol. 19, no. 9, at 790–98 (2015).

Table 1.4 outlines potential benefits that an MDT may be able to bring to its team members, to victims of elder abuse, and to the community as a whole.

Table 1.4. **Potential Benefits of a Formalized MDT**\[85]

BENEFIT TO THE MDT MEMBERS	BENEFIT TO THE VICTIM	BENEFIT TO THE COMMUNITY
• Increased understanding of the elder protection system in North Carolina • Reduced duplication in the investigation of and response to elder abuse • Strengthened community networks • Better access to information; improved communication among disciplines • Relieved tensions and frustrations	• Improved access to services and supports • Enhanced coordination and efficiency of services • Creation of a "no-wrong-door" system • More complete information about the victim is gathered • Greater expertise is applied to respond to the victim • Increased array of resolutions that are acceptable to the victim	• Increased awareness of the signs of elder abuse • Increased participation in elder abuse prevention • Broadening of the public and private networks that support older adults • Extended reach of limited resources

D. CHALLENGES FOR MDTs

Common challenges faced by MDTs in creating and implementing actions and approaches include[86]

- the establishment of a clear and legal process for information-sharing and confidentiality;
- a lack of participation from key disciplines, such as law enforcement and medical and mental health professionals;
- a failure to get the right people, with necessary authority to make decisions, to the table;
- a lack of legal expertise on teams;
- communication problems across disciplines;
- different goals and expectations among team members;

85. Anetzberger, *supra* note 68, at 126, 143 (noting the importance of a multidisciplinary approach).

86. *Id.* at 127–28. *See also* NCEA, *Multidisciplinary Teams*, NCEANCL.GOV, https://ncea.acl.gov/What-We-Do/Practice/Multidisciplinary-Teams.aspx (last visited July 5, 2019); U.S. DEP'T OF JUST., ELDER JUST. INITIATIVE, Developing an Elder Abuse Case Review Multidisciplinary Team in Your Community (revised Sept. 2016), https://www.justice.gov/elderjustice/file/938921/download.

- mistrust or misperceptions among team members;
- the existence of interpersonal bias or conflicts on teams;
- competition among team members for recognition;
- insufficient administrative support and/or resources;
- competition among team members regarding work demands;
- sustaining interest in the MDT over time;
- unrealistic expectations on the part of team members, the victim, or members of the community; and
- turnover of key team members.

In 2016, the U.S. Department of Justice published a guide called *Developing an Elder Abuse Case Review Multidisciplinary Team in Your Community*. This guide provides a number of solutions for overcoming common obstacles to the creation, effectiveness, and sustainability of MDTs.[87]

RESOURCE

MDT Guide and Toolkit

The U.S. Department of Justice published an MDT guide and toolkit to encourage and facilitate the development and growth of elder abuse MDTs. The toolkit provides general information, checklists, and forms on elder abuse case-review MDTs. The guide and toolkit are accessible at https://www.justice.gov/elderjustice/mdt-toolkit.

87. U.S. DEP'T OF JUST., ELDER JUST. INITIATIVE, *supra* note 77, at ch. 9, "Anticipating Challenges and Troubleshooting," https://www.justice.gov/elderjustice/9-anticipating-challenges-troubleshooting (last visited July 5, 2019).

Chapter 2
Adult Protective Services

CONTENTS

I. SCOPE OF CHAPTER

This chapter describes the role of the county department of social services (DSS) in providing protective services to disabled adults. In addition to protective services, counties provide support to older adults in other ways, such as financial support and in-home assistance to help the adults stay at home rather than move into facilities. This chapter will focus, however, on the agency's statutory mandate related to protective services—which includes receiving reports of abuse, neglect, and exploitation; conducting an evaluation; and, if necessary, providing or arranging for services for the adult.

II. OVERVIEW OF ADULT PROTECTIVE SERVICES

Social work is the foundation for adult protective services (APS). These services, which are provided by government programs and agencies, serve "older persons and adults with disabilities who are in need of assistance due to abuse, neglect, self-neglect and/or exploitation."[1]

In North Carolina, the term "protective services" is defined broadly to encompass evaluating a disabled adult's needs and mobilizing those services necessary to protect the adult from abuse, neglect, or exploitation.[2] This definition is intentionally vague because the circumstances in each APS case are unique and the needs will vary tremendously from person to person.

The primary goal of APS is to ensure "that protective services are provided to disabled adults who have been abused, neglected or exploited rather than determining whether a particular abusive incident occurred or punishing the perpetrator."[3] Because the goals of APS and criminal prosecution are different, it is often essential to involve both APS and law enforcement when an older adult has been abused. APS may be able to protect an older adult from abuse, neglect, or exploitation, while law enforcement officials are able to investigate potential crimes, punish perpetrators, and possibly deter future abuse.

In order to effectively protect and provide services to adults, APS must collaborate with others in the community. For example, they must work with meal delivery services, in-home aide organizations, adult day-care providers, residential placement facilities, and health care providers.

1. NAT'L ADULT PROTECTIVE SERVS. ASS'N (NAPSA), ADULT PROTECTIVE SERVICES RECOMMENDED MINIMUM PROGRAM STANDARDS 5 (2013), http://www.napsa-now.org/wp-content/uploads/2014/04/Recommended-Program-Standards.pdf.

2. Chapter 108A, Section 101(n) of the North Carolina General Statutes (hereinafter G.S.).

3. N.C. DEP'T OF HEALTH & HUMAN SERVS. (DHHS), DIV. OF AGING & ADULT SERVICES (DAAS), DIV. OF AGING & ADULT SERVS. MANUAL I-2 (Apr. 1, 2011) (hereinafter APS MANUAL), https://files.nc.gov/ncdhhs/documents/files/APS_Manual.pdf.

A. WHO IS RESPONSIBLE?

APS is a governmental function. The front-line APS workers are local government employees. Every county is served by an agency that has responsibility for APS. The agency may be a county department of social services (DSS), a regional department of social services, or a consolidated human services agency.[4] To simplify things, this chapter will refer to all three types of agencies as the "local DSS." State law directs these agencies to carry out certain responsibilities involved with APS. In addition, these agencies provide other services for adults, such as helping an adult find a placement in a facility or serving as an adult's representative payee for public benefits.

At the state level, the Division of Aging and Adult Services (DASS), which is part of the N.C. Department of Health and Human Services, is responsible for oversight and supervision of the locally-administered APS programs.

At the local DSS level, APS functions are typically carried out by the individuals listed below.

- **Social services director.** The director has primary responsibility for oversight of the agency and staff. The state APS statutes assign responsibilities to the director, who then delegates authority to staff to carry out the day-to-day APS functions.[5]
- **Adult services supervisor.** This person typically supervises all of the social workers and other staff involved with adult services, including APS.
- **APS social workers.** These staff members are responsible for responding to APS reports; conducting evaluations; and, if a report is substantiated, for offering, providing, or coordinating protective services.
- **Social services attorney.** Every local agency has access to an attorney. The role of the attorney varies from county to county, but he or she typically is available to advise the agency and represent it in judicial proceedings, such as those involving guardianship and protective services. In some counties, the attorney is employed by DSS and reports to the social services director. In others, the attorney is part of the county attorney's office or may be a contractor in private practice.

In North Carolina, most of the APS laws are located in Chapter 108A, Articles 6 and 6A of the North Carolina General Statutes (hereinafter G.S.).[6] These laws require the reporting of suspected elder abuse, outline the scope of DSS's authority to take action, and provide some tools for a county to use when evaluating an abuse report and providing services in response to it. Regulations governing the APS system are found in Title 10A, Chapter 71, Subchapter A of the North Carolina Administrative Code.[7] Important guidance about the program and the scope of DSS's authority can also be found in the state's Division of Aging and Adult Services Manual (*APS Manual*).[8]

4. *See* G.S. 108A-1.
5. G.S. 108A-12 (appointment of director of social services); -14 (duties and responsibilities of director of social services).
6. G.S. Ch. 108A, Arts. 6, 6A.
7. Title 10A, Chapter 71, Subchapter A of the North Carolina Administrative Code (N.C.A.C.).
8. APS MANUAL, *supra* note 3.

B. HOW DOES APS PROTECT OLDER ADULTS?

The primary way APS protects older adults is by delivering tailored services to address the particular concerns that put a certain adult at risk. Specifically, when authorized by law, APS staff is able to mobilize essential services for an older adult who is in need of protective services. The term "essential services" is defined broadly in the law to mean:

> those social, medical, psychiatric, psychological or legal services necessary to safeguard the disabled adult's rights and resources and to maintain the physical or mental well-being of the individual. These services shall include, but not be limited to,
>
> - the provision of medical care for physical and mental health needs,
> - assistance in personal hygiene, food, clothing,
> - adequately heated and ventilated shelter,
> - protection from health and safety hazards,
> - protection from physical mistreatment, and
> - protection from exploitation.[9]

While this definition includes examples of services, it is not an exhaustive list. APS social workers have wide latitude to determine what services are needed for older adults.

Under state APS laws, a "disabled adult" is a person who is

- 18 years of age or older or a lawfully emancipated minor,
- present in the state of North Carolina, and
- physically or mentally incapacitated.[10]

According to G.S. 108A-101, a person may be physically or mentally incapacitated as a result of "an intellectual disability, cerebral palsy, epilepsy or autism; organic brain damage caused by advanced age or other physical degeneration in connection therewith; or due to conditions incurred at any age which are the result of accident, organic brain damage, mental or physical illness, or continued consumption or absorption of substances."[11]

9. G.S. 108A-101(i).
10. G.S. 108A-101(d).
11. *Id.*

EXAMPLE

Two sisters retired from their professional careers and were living together. Scammers contacted the sisters by phone and convinced them to transfer significant amounts of money, rapidly depleting their assets. A report was made to DSS. Social workers visited the home and found it to be in terrible condition and found that the utilities had been disconnected due to non-payment. DSS took the following steps:

- *obtained a protective order and froze the sisters' remaining financial assets;*
- *contacted family members;*
- *filed petitions for incompetency and guardianship, which resulted in a family member being appointed guardian of the person and a local attorney being appointed guardian of the estate for each sister; and*
- *worked with family to identify community resources to assist the sisters, including helping to find a residential facility for them that was close to family.*[12]

There are limits on the types of assistance or intervention that DSS can provide. For example, unless APS staff has an emergency order from a court specifically directing it to do so, staff may not assume physical custody of the adult without the adult's consent.[13]

C. HOW DOES APS WORK?

APS involvement begins with a report to the county social services agency. In general, an APS case will follow the path outlined below.

- **Reporting.** A report of suspected abuse, neglect, or exploitation is received by DSS.
- **Screening.** DSS then screens the report to determine if it has authority to conduct an APS evaluation.
- **Evaluation.** If DSS has such authority, it is supposed to "screen in" the report and conduct an evaluation that will include meeting with the adult and, possibly, reviewing records and interviewing caretakers, family, and other contacts.
- **Freeze and inspect financial records.** If the case involves potential financial exploitation, the evaluation will likely include a review of the older adult's financial records.

12. Interview with Assistant District Attorney Lori Wickline, Alamance County District Attorney's Office, in Chapel Hill, North Carolina (June 28, 2018).

13. *See* G.S. 108A-101(h), (i) (definitions of "emergency services" and "essential services," respectively). These definitions indicate that DSS can take custody of an adult pursuant to an emergency order issued pursuant to G.S. 108A-106. Another option for assuming physical custody of an older adult is through an involuntary commitment proceeding pursuant to G.S. Chapter 122C, Article 5, Part 7.

- **Provision of services.** If DSS concludes that an older adult is in need of "protective services" and the adult has the capacity to consent to the provision of these services, APS staff will ask the adult to consent. If DSS concludes that the older adult is in need of protective services but does not have the capacity to consent, APS staff will seek a court order authorizing it to provide essential services.

KEY TERMS

- ***Protective services*** *means "services provided by the State or other government or private organizations or individuals which are* ***necessary to protect the disabled adult from abuse, neglect, or exploitation****. They shall consist of evaluation of the need for service and mobilization of essential services on behalf of the disabled adult."*[14]
- ***Essential services*** *are "those social, medical, psychiatric, psychological or legal services necessary to safeguard the disabled adult's rights and resources and to maintain the physical or mental well-being of the individual."*[15]

If, during the screening process, DSS determines that it does not have the legal authority under the APS laws to proceed, the abuse report will be "screened out," which means that the agency will not conduct an APS evaluation. The reporter will be notified of the agency's decision. Depending on the circumstances, DSS may reach out to the affected adult to offer other services it provides or it may try to connect the adult with appropriate services available in the community. For example, DSS may conclude that the adult is not disabled but that he or she may still benefit from assistance with meals, transportation, or in-home assistance. APS may offer to help the adult identify needs and locate resources, but the adult may always refuse.

Below are more details about each of the five steps in the path of an APS case: reporting, screening, evaluation, freezing and inspecting financial records, and provision of services.

1. REPORTING

There is one universal APS reporting requirement in state law: Any person who has reasonable cause to believe that a disabled adult is in need of protective services must make a report to DSS.[16] With one exception, this reporting requirement applies to everyone—including law enforcement officials, court officials, and health care providers. Regional staff working with the State Long-Term Care Ombudsman Program, which

14. G.S. 108A-101(n) (emphasis added).

15. G.S. 108A-101(i). The definition goes on to provide a non-exhaustive list of examples, including "the provision of medical care for physical and mental health needs, assistance in personal hygiene, food, clothing, adequately heated and ventilated shelter, protection from health and safety hazards, protection from physical mistreatment, and protection from exploitation." The term does "not include taking the person into physical custody without his consent except as provided for in G.S. 108A-106 and in Chapter 122C of the General Statutes."

16. G.S. 108A-102.

provides advocacy for long-term care facility residents, are excepted from the mandatory reporting requirement. They are allowed to report abuse, neglect, or exploitation to APS with the consent of the long-term care resident or the State Ombudsman (see Chapter 7 for an overview of the ombudsman program).[17]

RESOURCE

Call a county social services agency to file an APS report. Contact information for each agency is available online:

http://www.ncdhhs.gov/divisions/dss/local-county-social-services-offices

If it is not appropriate for the contacted county to respond, the case may be referred to another county.

In addition to this universal reporting requirement, there are two reporting requirements that apply to certain types of organizations and individuals.

1. **Financial institutions, including officers and employees.**[18] If any of these parties has reasonable cause to believe that a disabled adult or older adult is the victim or target of financial exploitation, they must report it to

   - any person identified by the customer as a "trusted person";
   - the appropriate local law enforcement agency; and
   - the appropriate county department of social services, if the adult is a disabled adult.

   This report can be oral or in writing. It must include the name and address of the disabled adult or older adult, the nature of the suspected financial exploitation, and any other pertinent information.

2. **Employees and volunteers at mental health, developmental disability, or substance abuse treatment facilities (MH/DD/SA).**[19] These employees and volunteers are subject to the reporting rules set out below.

   - If an employee or volunteer at such a facility witnesses another employee or volunteer knowingly causing pain or injury to a client (other than as a part of generally accepted medical or therapeutic procedure), under G.S. 122C-66, he or she must report the incident.[20] This particular statute requires that reports

17. G.S. 143B-181.20(f) ("If the subject of the complaint involves suspected abuse, neglect, or exploitation, the Regional Ombudsman shall only with the written informed consent of the resident or authorization by the State Ombudsman notify the Adult Protection Services section of the county department of social services. Except as provided herein, the State or Regional Ombudsman is not subject to the reporting requirements of Article 6 of Chapter 108A of the General Statutes.").
18. G.S. 108A-115.
19. G.S. 122C-3(14) (definition of "facility"); -66 (reporting requirements).
20. G.S. 122C-66(b).

be made to authorized personnel designated by the facility. It is important to remember, however, that the universal reporting requirement still applies and that, therefore, a report must also be made to DSS if the victim is a disabled adult and the action constitutes abuse or neglect.[21]

- If an employee or volunteer at such a facility witnesses a client becoming a victim of one of many specific crimes, most of which involve sexual violence or abuse, under G.S. 122C-66, he or she must report it within twenty-four hours.[22] See Table 2.1, below, for a list of the different crimes included within the scope of this reporting requirement. The statute allows the reports to be made to DSS, law enforcement, or the district attorney. Again, the universal reporting requirement still applies in these circumstances, so the employee must also file a report with DSS if the victim is a disabled adult.[23]

Reading these reporting laws together, an employee or volunteer in an MH/DD/SA facility should always report the types of incidents described above to DSS if a disabled adult is involved. By doing so, they will have satisfied both reporting laws. If they report only to law enforcement and the victim is a disabled adult, they will not have satisfied the universal reporting requirement.

A facility employee or volunteer could be charged with a crime (misdemeanor) for failing to make one of these required reports.[24]

21. G.S. 122C-66(e).

22. G.S. 122C-66(b1). Subsection (b1) refers to G.S. Chapter 14, Article 7A; all of the statutes in that Article were recodified into Article 7B, which lists rape and other sexual offenses.

23. G.S. 122C-66(e).

24. G.S. 122C-66(b) (Class 1 misdemeanor for failure to properly report abuse, exploitation, or accidental injury); -66(b1) (Class A1 misdemeanor for failure to properly report sexual violence or abuse).

Table 2.1. **Selected Crimes Subject to the Specific Reporting Requirement Applicable to MH/DD/SA Employees and Volunteers**[25]

CRIME	STATUTORY CITATION
Forcible rape	G.S. 14-27.21 (First-degree) G.S. 14-27.22 (Second-degree)
Forcible sexual offense	G.S. 14-27.26 (First-degree) G.S. 14-27.27 (Second-degree)
Sexual battery	G.S. 14-27.33
Crime against nature	G.S. 14-177
Incest	G.S. 14-178
Fornication and adultery	G.S. 14-184
Obscene literature and exhibitions	G.S. 14-190.1
Coercing acceptance of obscene articles or publications	G.S. 14-190.4
Preparation of obscene photographs, slides, and motion pictures	G.S. 14-190.5
Disclosure of private images	G.S. 14-190.5A
Indecent exposure	G.S. 14-190.9
Using profane, indecent, or threatening language to any person over telephone; annoying or harassing by repeated telephoning or making false statements over telephone	G.S. 14-196
Cyberstalking	G.S. 14-196.3
Secretly peeping into room occupied by another person	G.S. 14-202

Under all three reporting laws, reporters have some level of immunity from liability.[26] The immunity provisions are slightly different in scope, as illustrated in Table 2.2.

25. Because this manual is limited to older adults, Table 2.1 does not include several crimes subject to the reporting requirement because they involve child victims. For example, the table does not include statutory rape, but MH/DD/SA employees and volunteers are required to report those crimes.

26. G.S. 108A-102(c) ("Anyone who makes a report pursuant to this statute, who testifies in any judicial proceeding arising from the report, or who participates in a required evaluation shall be immune from any civil or criminal liability on account of such report or testimony or participation, unless such person acted in bad faith or with a malicious purpose."); -115(c) ("No financial institution, or officer or employee thereof, who acts in good faith in making a report under this section may be held liable in any action for doing so."); 122C-66(d) ("An employee who makes a report in good faith under this section is immune from any civil liability that might otherwise occur for the report. In any case involving liability, making of a report under this section is prima facie evidence that the maker acted in good faith.").

Table 2.2. **Immunity from Liability for Reporting**

REPORTING REQUIREMENT	PERSON WITH IMMUNITY	SCOPE OF IMMUNITY	LIMITATIONS
Universal reporting	Anyone who makes a report, testifies in a proceeding, or participates in an evaluation	Immune from civil or criminal liability	Person must not act in bad faith or for a malicious purpose
Financial institutions	Financial institution or officer or employee of that institution	May not be held liable in any action	Person must act in good faith
MH/DD/SA facilities	Employee of the facility	Immune from any civil liability	Person must act in good faith. Making a report under the statute is prima facie evidence that the reporter acted in good faith.

2. SCREENING

When DSS receives a report, APS staff is required to screen the report to determine whether it falls within the scope of DSS's authority. In some circumstances, DSS may screen out a report because the agency does not have legal authority under the protective services law to take action. Three types of situations in which DSS lacks the authority to proceed with the provision of protective services are discussed below.

a. Not a "Disabled Adult"

North Carolina's child protective services are available to every child in the state. Adult protective services, on the other hand, are available only to a limited population of adults—those who are "disabled" and are in need of protective services. Some older adults will satisfy the definition of "disabled" but many others will not. Social workers are thus encouraged to consider the level of an adult's functioning by asking themselves the following question: "Does [the adult's] non- or reduced functioning necessitate reliance on others to meet his or her basic needs[?]"[27] Age alone is not enough to authorize DSS to screen in a report. For example, a 50-year-old with dementia or significant physical limitations will be considered disabled but a person who is 80 years old and in good physical and mental health will not. Similarly, diagnosis alone is not sufficient to determine disability. As the *APS Manual* explains:

> A physical condition, disease, or diagnosis that limits one person may not limit another. For example, arthritis and heart disease in one person may not impair

27. *See* APS MANUAL, *supra* note 3, at III-3.

that individual's functioning while in another it keeps them confined to bed. Each person and situation is unique.[28]

Finally, DSS must not rely only on a person's health or physical status, or on his or her living conditions, when deciding whether the adult is disabled. For example, an adult who is homeless but generally healthy and able would not meet the definition of disabled.[29]

When DSS receives a report, the social work staff will gather as much information as possible from the reporter about the adult's situation and condition in order to determine whether the agency has the authority to follow up on the report. If DSS concludes that the adult is not disabled, the agency is not authorized to provide protective services. It may, however, provide other support services to the adult depending on his or her situation and needs.

b. Someone Else Available to Help

One of the initial questions DSS will explore with the reporter is whether the affected adult needs services to protect him or her from abuse, neglect, or exploitation. In order to move forward with the evaluation or provision of services, the agency must conclude that

- the adult is unable to perform or obtain essential services because of his or her physical or mental incapacity and
- no able, responsible, and willing person is able to perform or obtain the essential services for the adult.[30]

As stated above, a service is considered "essential" if it is necessary to safeguard the adult's rights and resources and maintain his or her physical or mental well-being. Essential services could include medical care, food, clothing, shelter, protection from physical mistreatment, and protection from exploitation.

In some situations, DSS will determine that an older adult needs essential services but that a family member or friend is willing to help obtain those services for the adult. Before ceding responsibility, DSS must determine that the volunteer is not only willing to help but also able to provide the required assistance and responsible enough to provide the needed services.

c. Abuse or Neglect by Someone Other Than a Caretaker

DSS's authority extends to allegations of abuse, neglect, and exploitation. For exploitation, this authority reaches and covers any alleged perpetrator. For abuse or neglect, however, DSS has authority to act only (1) if the alleged perpetrator is the disabled adult's "caretaker" or (2) in cases that may involve self-neglect.[31] In order to understand how this all fits together, it is important to understand a few key definitions.

---

28. *Id.* at III-17.

29. *See id.* at III-43 (stating that some clients, such as those who are homeless, may not reach true stability and that such cases "should not be kept open for APS indefinitely.").

30. G.S. 108A-101(e).

31. G.S. 108A-101(a) (definition of "abuse"); (m) (definition of "neglect").

- A "**caretaker**" is "an individual who has the responsibility for the care of the disabled adult as a result of family relationship or who has assumed the responsibility for the care of the disabled adult voluntarily or by contract."[32] The *APS Manual* further clarifies that the term "does not include individuals or organizations that provide specific, limited services to the adult voluntarily or by contract, such as an in-home aide and adult day care program, home health aide, or general hospital."[33]
- "**Abuse**" is "the willful infliction of physical pain, injury or mental anguish, unreasonable confinement, or the willful deprivation by a caretaker of services which are necessary to maintain mental and physical health."[34]
- " '**[N]eglect**' refers to a disabled adult who is either living alone and not able to provide for himself or herself the services which are necessary to maintain the person's mental or physical health or is not receiving services from the person's caretaker."[35]

If these three definitions are woven together with the scope of authority granted to DSS, it seems that one type of case that may fall outside DSS's authority is the willful infliction of pain, injury, or anguish upon, or the confinement of, a disabled adult by someone other than a caretaker. However, depending on the circumstances, DSS may be able to screen in these types of cases if they rise to the level of self-neglect. In other words, the agency may determine that the disabled adult is not able to protect him- or herself from the abuse and may therefore proceed with the protective services evaluation.

EXAMPLE

Nancy is 90 years old and disabled. She lives alone and is generally able to take care of her own needs. She gets into a dispute with her next-door neighbor about trashcans and the neighbor pushes Nancy down. This type of physical assault would not be considered abuse by a caretaker and, therefore, would fall outside the scope of DSS's authority.

Even though such cases may not be within DSS's authority, they may easily fall within the scope of generally applicable criminal laws, such as assault, embezzlement, and larceny.

3. EVALUATION

Once DSS has received a report and screened it in, a social worker will meet with the affected adult as soon as possible; confer with other people connected to the adult, such as family members, neighbors, friends, and medical professionals; and gather records from

32. G.S. 108A-101(b).
33. APS MANUAL, *supra* note 3, at III-4. The manual further explains that "[s]uch services may assist to a limited degree with the adult's care, but the individual or organization providing the services does not have comprehensive responsibility for the adult's well-being." *Id.*
34. G.S. 108A-101(a).
35. G.S. 108A-101(m).

providers and/or financial institutions in an effort to properly evaluate the report. The purpose of the evaluation is to determine whether the case should be "substantiated"—in other words, to answer the question, "Are protective services necessary and appropriate?" DSS must initiate and complete this evaluation within statutorily prescribed timeframes (see Table 2.3).

Table 2.3. **Statutory Timelines for APS Evaluation**[36]

INITIATE EVALUATION		COMPLETE EVALUATION	
WHEN?	**IN WHAT CIRCUMSTANCES?**	**WHEN?**	**IN WHAT CIRCUMSTANCES?**
Immediately	If complaint alleges danger of death in an emergency[37]	**Within 30 days**	For allegations of abuse or neglect
Within 24 hours	If complaint alleges danger of irreparable harm in an emergency	**Within 30 days**	For allegations of exploitation
Within 72 hours	If complaint does not allege either of the above		

In the course of this evaluation, DSS has the authority to interview the affected adult alone, to obtain records related to the adult's care, and to request assistance with the evaluation from the local public health department and other public and private providers.[38] DSS may also contract with private providers to conduct medical assessments.[39]

During this process, DSS will compile a wealth of information about the adult, ranging from the social worker's interview notes to medical and, possibly, financial records. In addition, the social worker is required to complete a detailed report about the evaluation.[40] While the information gathered by DSS in the course of the evaluation is confidential pursuant to state law,[41] this information may be extremely useful in a guardianship proceeding, a law enforcement investigation, or in other legal proceedings. Despite the strict confidentiality laws that apply, there are opportunities for others involved with protecting the adult to obtain access to these records.

a. No Need for Protective Services

If, after the evaluation, DSS concludes that the adult does not need protective services from the agency, it may not proceed any further with regard to such services under the protective services law. Staff may, however, decide to offer other DSS services to the adult or may look into whether DSS should connect the adult with other agencies that could provide support.

36. G.S. 108A-103(d).
37. G.S. 108A-101(g) (defining "emergency").
38. G.S. 108A-103(a), (b).
39. G.S. 108A-103(c).
40. G.S. 108A-103(a).
41. G.S. 108A-80; 10A N.C.A.C. Ch. 69 ("Confidentiality and Access to Client Records").

EXAMPLE

Andy's neighbor contacts DSS because she is worried that Andy is not taking care of himself (i.e., that self-neglect may be an issue). A DSS social worker conducts an evaluation and concludes that Andy has decisional capacity and seems to be caring for himself adequately. However, Andy's apartment is quite untidy and he is a little unkempt in appearance. And while he does not appear malnourished, he does not have a lot of food in his kitchen. He visited his primary care doctor recently for a check-up and received a good report. The social worker does not believe that Andy is neglecting his own care but does think he might benefit from some supports. She shares information with him about available community resources (e.g., meal delivery from a nonprofit organization, in-home aides to assist with food preparation and cleaning) and economic services (such as SNAP, or food stamp, benefits from DSS). The social worker also offers to help Andy sign up for any of the community resources of interest to him and to connect with an economic services specialist at DSS to determine if he is eligible for any economic services.

This example helps illustrate how APS is just a subset of the services that DSS can provide to older adults. Even if a situation does not meet the statutory threshold for APS, DSS may still offer assistance and support or it may be able to help identify other supports available in the community.

Figure 2.1. **Adult Protective Services (APS) as a Subset of Overall Community Social Services for Older Adults**

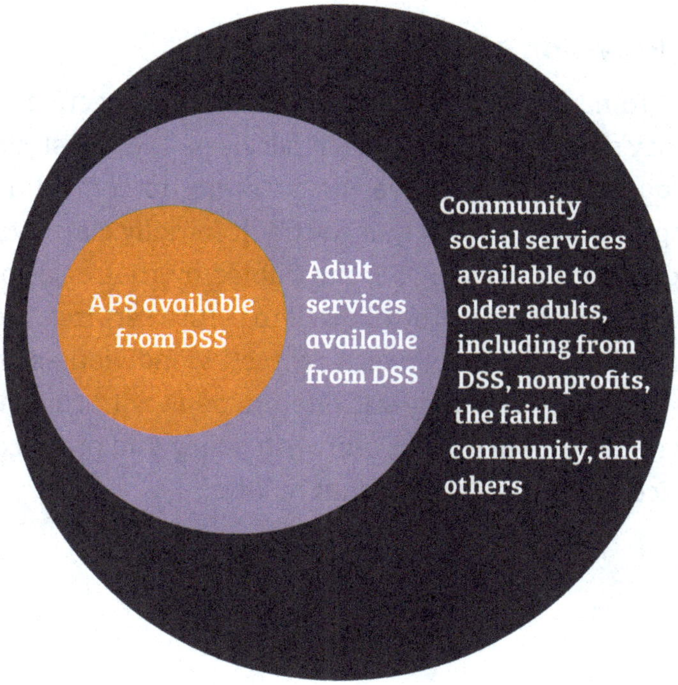

b. Need for Protective Services

If DSS concludes that an older adult needs protectives services (i.e., that the case is "substantiated"), the agency must then determine whether the disabled adult has capacity to consent to those services. The APS Manual provides some guidance for DSS staff when evaluating this type of capacity. It states that the focus should be on the adult's ability to perceive and understand his or her situation, including his or her physical limitations, the resources and assistance that are available to him or her, and the consequences of not getting such assistance.[42] It also emphasizes a few other points.

- **Capacity is different than competency.** The former is determined by DSS for the limited purpose of assessing ability to consent to services, while the latter is determined by a judicial official in the context of a guardianship case (see Chapter 4).[43]
- **Capacity may be intermittent**. Someone with an acute illness, such as a urinary tract infection, may temporarily lack decisional capacity. Once treated, the person's capacity may be restored, and DSS should recognize that change and adapt to it.[44]
- **Professional evaluations may be helpful but they are not determinative**. If DSS is unsure about an adult's capacity, it may consult with a medical or behavioral health professional. The decision about capacity, however, rests with DSS.[45]

If DSS concludes that an older adult has capacity, it must ask the adult for his or her consent to provide protective services.[46] If, on the other hand, DSS concludes that the older adult lacks capacity to consent, the agency must ask a court to order it to provide these services. DSS may choose to ask the court for a standard order or it may request an emergency ex parte order.

c. Capacity to Consent to Provision of Services

If an adult has been determined to have capacity to consent to DSS protective services and ultimately refuses the agency's offer to provide such services, DSS must close the protective services case.[47] The agency does not have the authority to compel an adult with decisional capacity to accept services. Similarly, if the adult initially consents to the services and then later withdraws that consent, DSS must abide by that decision.[48] By recognizing that an adult who has capacity must be allowed to refuse services, state law is clearly trying to find the appropriate balance between protecting individuals and preserving their independence and autonomy. DSS may still offer an adult with capacity who has refused its services other services that are consistent with policy and practice, but it may not provide protective services to that adult pursuant to law.

42. APS MANUAL, *supra* note 3, at III-28.
43. *Id.* at III-29.
44. *Id.*
45. *Id.*
46. G.S. 108A-104(a).
47. G.S. 108A-104(c).
48. *Id.*

d. Lacks Capacity to Consent to Provision of Services

If DSS concludes that an adult needs protective services but lacks the capacity to consent, the agency may file a petition in district court requesting permission to provide those services.[49] If the court finds by clear, cogent, and convincing evidence that the disabled adult (1) is in need of protective services and (2) lacks capacity to consent, under G.S. 108A-105, it will issue an order authorizing DSS to provide such services.[50] A determination by the court that the adult lacks capacity "shall in no way affect incompetency proceedings."[51]

G.S. 108A-106 allows for a more expedited process in emergency situations as well as for an ex parte order.[52] To issue one of these orders, the court must find that[53]

- the adult lacks capacity to consent,
- the adult is in need of protective services,
- an emergency exists, and
- no other person authorized by law or order to give consent for the adult is available and willing to arrange for emergency services.

The key to this type of order is the definition of "emergency." This term refers to a situation where

- the adult "is in **substantial danger of death or irreparable harm** if protective services are not provided immediately";[54]
- the adult is not able to consent to the provision of services;
- "no responsible, able, or willing caretaker is available to consent to emergency services";[55] and
- there is insufficient time to use the statutory procedure for obtaining a standard APS order.[56] (See Table 2.4, below, for a comparison of standard vs. emergency orders.)

If the court denies DSS's petition for either a standard or an emergency order, the agency may not proceed with its plan to provide protective services. Depending on the circumstances, DSS may still decide to offer some other services to the adult, such as referrals for nutrition programs or caregiver support, but it may not provide protective services.

---

49. G.S. 108A-105(a). If an adult lacks the capacity to consent to services and also has a guardian, the guardian could provide consent on the adult's behalf. See Chapter 4 for more details regarding the authority of a guardian.
50. G.S. 108A-105(c).
51. G.S. 108A-105(d). This subsection refers to incompetency proceedings as set forth in G.S. Chapters 33, 35, or 122. Note that all three chapters have been repealed and that the laws regarding incompetency proceedings are now codified in G.S. Chapter 35A.
52. G.S. 108A-106.
53. G.S. 108A-106(a).
54. G.S. 108A-101(g) (emphasis added).
55. *Id.*
56. *Id.*

Table 2.4. **Comparing Standard and Emergency APS Orders**

TYPE OF APS ORDER	TIMELINE	NOTICE TO CLIENT	DURATION OF AWARD
Standard[57]	Hearing must be held within 14 days of filing of petition	Affected adult must be given at least 5 days' notice of hearing	• No more than 120 days • Within 60 days, court must review to determine if there is a need to pursue guardianship or, for good cause shown, to extend APS order for an additional 60 days
Emergency[58]	Hearing must be held immediately	Affected adult, guardian, child, or next of kin must be given notice at least 24 hours prior to hearing OR No notice (ex parte) required if court makes certain findings	• Up to 14 days • Unless dissolved for good cause, ex parte order remains in effect until hearing is held on petition for emergency services • May order only such services as are necessary to remove the conditions creating the emergency

e. Freezing Assets and Inspecting Financial Records

EXAMPLE

Betty is a 90-year-old woman who has dementia. She owns a home and has significant monthly income from Social Security and retirement benefits. Her next-door neighbor, Stan, takes her to an attorney to complete a power of attorney granting Stan plenary authority. On the same day, Stan sells Betty's home and moves her to a skilled nursing facility. The proceeds from the sale of her home and her other assets are quickly depleted. The facility is never paid for providing Betty care and her taxes fall into arrears. If someone had made an APS report, DSS would have been able to take action quickly to freeze Betty's assets and conduct an evaluation.

If an APS report relates to financial exploitation, DSS will almost certainly need to obtain access to financial records. The older adult or the adult's guardian or agent may have some of the records available. If DSS needs to obtain access to records from a financial institution, such as a bank or credit union, it will need to either have valid written

57. G.S. 108A-105(b), (c).
58. G.S. 108A-106(b), (d).

consent from the adult or the adult's guardian or agent, or it will need to ask a court for permission to gain access. This is because financial institutions are subject to extraordinarily strict federal and state confidentiality laws.[59]

Table 2.5. **DSS Tools for Accessing a Disabled Adult's Financial Records**

TOOL	WHO CAN REQUEST?	WHAT DOES IT ALLOW?	WHEN IS IT ALLOWED?
Freeze and inspect order[60]	Social services officials	May ask a judge to issue an order (1) freezing the assets of a disabled adult who is a suspected victim of financial exploitation and (2) directing a financial institution to provide access to the adult's financial records	When social services has received a report of suspected financial exploitation of a disabled adult and a judge finds that (1) the adult is in need of protective services, (2) the adult lacks the capacity to consent to the release of financial records, and (3) the alleged exploitation was committed by the adult's caretaker
Subpoena for financial records[61]	Law enforcement and social services officials	May ask a judge to issue a subpoena directing a financial institution to provide access to the financial records of a disabled adult or older adult who may be the victim of financial exploitation	When a judge finds that (1) the official is investigating a credible report of financial exploitation, (2) financial records are needed for the investigation, and (3) time is of the essence in order to prevent further exploitation
Search warrant[62] (rare)	Any applicant may request but only a law enforcement official may execute[63]	May request a search warrant directing a law enforcement officer to seize financial records necessary to investigate suspected exploitation of a disabled adult or older adult	When the official issuing the warrant (1) finds probable cause to believe that the financial records constitute evidence of the crime of financial exploitation under G.S. 14-112.2 or (2) discovers the identity of a person participating in the crime

59. *See generally* G.S. Chapter 53B (Financial Privacy Act); 15 U.S.C. §§ 6801, 6803 (Gramm-Leach-Bliley Act).
60. G.S. 108A-106(f).
61. G.S. Ch. 108A, Art. 6A ("Protection of Disabled and Older Adults From Financial Exploitation"); 108A-116(a).
62. G.S. Ch. 15A, Art. 11 ("Search Warrants").
63. G.S. 15A-247. *See* Jeff Welty, *Non-Officers Applying for Search Warrants*, N.C. CRIM. L.: A UNC SCH. OF GOV'T BLOG (June 19, 2013), https://nccriminallaw.sog.unc.edu/non-officers-applying-for-search-warrants/.

It may be impractical to rely on the affected adult's consent in some situations involving access to financial records. For example, the adult's social worker may have concerns about

- the adult's capacity to consent,
- the adult being coerced by a caretaker who is benefiting from the suspected exploitation, or
- the guardian acting as the adult's exploiter.

If consent is impractical, DSS has three tools available for accessing financial records. The first is a freeze and inspect order authorized specifically for social services investigations. The second is a subpoena that is available for both social services and law enforcement investigations. The third is a traditional search warrant, which social services staff may apply for but not execute. While a search warrant would not be used to gather information for the APS investigation, DSS staff may nonetheless find it appropriate to apply for a warrant if it appears that a crime has been committed. This tool is rarely, if ever, used by DSS staff. Table 2.5, above, provides a brief overview of each of the three tools.[64]

There are several important differences between the two commonly used access tools, the freeze and inspect order and the subpoena for financial records. Some of these are set out below.

- **Differences as to the potential victim.** Law enforcement officials are authorized to investigate crimes involving both older adults and disabled adults. Social services officials may only investigate reports involving disabled adults. Under the applicable criminal law, an older adult is any person over 65 years of age.[65] Under the APS law, a disabled adult is any person 18 years of age or older (or a lawfully emancipated minor) who is physically or mentally incapacitated due to one more reasons, such as illness, accident, advanced age, and substance abuse.[66] Therefore, law enforcement officials using the subpoena tool have greater authority to act than does APS, as law enforcement is not limited to only using subpoenas for disabled adults. This difference may be a good reason to involve law enforcement early in the process if there is an emergency situation involving suspected financial exploitation of an older adult.
- **Differences as to the potential exploiter.** The freeze and inspect order is available only if the suspected exploitation is being committed by the disabled adult's caretaker.[67]
- **Differences as to notice.** The freeze and inspect order requires that notice of the order be provided to the adult and to his or her caretaker. With the subpoena,

64. For more details, see Aimee N. Wall, *Financial Exploitation of Older Adults and Disabled Adults: An Overview of North Carolina Law*, SOC. SERVS. L. BULL. No. 43 (Oct. 2014), https://www.sog.unc.edu/sites/www.sog.unc.edu/files/reports/sslb43_0.pdf.

65. G.S. 14-112.2(a)(2) (defining "older adult" as a person 65 or older).

66. G.S. 108A-101(d).

67. *See* G.S. 108A-101(b) (definition of "caretaker").

notice is required, but the investigating entity (law enforcement or social services) may request a delay in the notice in some circumstances.

- **Differences as to consent.** The freeze and inspect order is available only if the disabled adult lacks the capacity to consent. The laws governing the other two tools are silent in this regard.
- **Differences as to freezing the affected adult's assets.** The freeze and inspect order is the only tool that authorizes a judge to freeze the older adult's assets. In a criminal investigation, the district attorney may ask a judge to freeze the defendant's assets if the defendant is charged with a financial exploitation crime that involves assets valued at more than $5,000.[68]
- **Differences as to confidentiality of court records.** The law authorizing the subpoena provides that records of proceedings where a subpoena for access to a disabled or older adult's financial records is sought (1) are not a matter of public record, (2) must be maintained separately from other records, and (3) may be examined only pursuant to a court order.[69] Because of this heightened confidentiality requirement, the Administrative Office of the Courts (AOC) has established such a proceeding as a Special Proceeding Confidential.[70] The freeze and inspect order and search warrant tools are not subject to the same level of confidentiality protection.

D. PROVISION OF SERVICES

If DSS is authorized to provide protective services, pursuant to either consent or court order, the types of services that are appropriate will vary tremendously from person to person. As mentioned above, the law defines the term "essential services" broadly to include "those social, medical, psychiatric, psychological or legal services necessary to safeguard the disabled adult's rights and resources and to maintain the physical or mental well-being of the individual."[71]

1. EMERGENCY SERVICES

If a situation involving a disabled adult or an older adult rises to the level of an "emergency" as that term is defined above, and if DSS obtains an emergency ex parte order, the agency may provide only those services "necessary to maintain the person's vital functions and without which there is reasonable belief that the person would suffer irreparable harm or death."[72] In extraordinary circumstances, it may involve taking custody of the adult.

68. G.S. 14-112.2(f).
69. G.S. 108A-116(g).
70. *See* N.C. Admin. Off. of the Cts. (AOC), Form AOC-SP-630, "Petition and Order for Issuance of Subpoena Directing Release of Financial Records" (caption indicates that it is a special proceeding confidential), https://www.nccourts.gov/assets/documents/forms/sp630-en.pdf?yK8flemirJJ3YFWnwMVoB.260aDfJUZ4.
71. G.S. 108A-101(i).
72. G.S. 108A-101(h).

This narrowly defined service scope is trying to strike a balance, weighing the need to provide immediate protection to the older adult against the need to ensure that the adult and others are provided with appropriate due process. Because a court may issue this type of order quickly and with limited judicial proceedings, DSS must limit its response to addressing only the issue that gave rise to the emergency.[73] If additional protective services are necessary, DSS must petition the court for a non-emergency protective order.[74]

2. ENTERING PROPERTY

A social worker may need to enter a person's private property without the person's consent. There are two possible legal avenues for lawfully gaining entry to property without consent. First, after a court has issued an order directing DSS to provide short-term emergency services, staff members from the agency may enter property without consent if they determine that doing so is necessary to protect the affected adult.

Second, DSS may find it necessary to enter property without consent in the absence of an emergency order. For example, a social worker may want to enter an apartment to interview an adult who is the subject of a report but the adult's roommate may refuse to open the door. In such a situation, the social worker may ask a court to issue an administrative search and inspection warrant.[75] These warrants are not the same as the search warrants used by sworn law enforcement officers.[76] Instead, these are orders that authorize non-sworn public officials to enter property and conduct an inspection if

- the inspection is elsewhere authorized by law (such as DSS's authority to conduct an evaluation and interview the older adult);
- a warrant is constitutionally required to enter the property (which it would be, without the resident's consent); and
- there is probable cause to believe that there is a condition, object, activity, or circumstance that legally justifies the inspection (such as a report that the older adult has been abused or neglected).[77]

In order to obtain an administrative search and inspection warrant, DSS must file an affidavit.[78] The AOC has developed forms for both the affidavit and the warrant.[79] These

73. *See* G.S. 108A-106(b).

74. *Id.*; *id.* § 108A-105.

75. *See* G.S. 15-27.2 (administrative search and inspection warrants); 108A-106(e) (allowing entry into disabled adult's premises by DSS worker if necessary after entry of court order for emergency services).

76. G.S. 15-27.2(g) ("The warrants authorized under this section shall not be regarded as search warrants.").

77. G.S. 15-27.2(a), (c)(1). There is another type of administrative warrant that is available when there is a "legally authorized program of inspection which naturally includes that property." *See id.* § 15-27.2(c)(1).

78. G.S. 15-27.2(c).

79. AOC, Form AOC-CR-913M, "Affidavit to Obtain Administrative Inspection Warrant for Particular Condition or Activity," https://www.nccourts.gov/assets/documents/forms/cr913m-en.pdf?68gKaFqSOC3ASvY0bHvoFLgJvzdg1T7c.

types of warrants may be issued by a magistrate, judge, clerk, or an assistant or deputy clerk of court.[80] Once the administrative warrant is issued, the social worker who has obtained it will need to act quickly, as this warrant is valid for only twenty-four hours.[81]

3. DEVELOPMENT OF A SERVICE PLAN

Once a report is substantiated, DSS must develop a service plan for the disabled adult based on the findings from and recommendations made in its evaluation of the adult. The purpose of the plan is to establish goals and a time line for resolving the abuse, neglect, or exploitation identified in the evaluation, as well as to identify services needed by the disabled adult.[82] The *APS Manual* recommends that the service plan should

- flow from the evaluation,
- be client- and family-focused,
- contain function-oriented goals,
- be time-limited, and
- consider a wide range of services.[83]

The manual notes that the services "will vary according to factors such as community resources available and the client's personal needs and choices." It goes on to explain that protection may

> be provided on a continuum ranging from a very protective plan, such as placement, to a less protective plan, such as provision of in-home aide services several days per week. Often a compromise must be reached between the level of protection the worker considers optimal and the level of protection the client is willing to accept.[84]

In planning services, APS is expected to focus on identifying the least restrictive alternatives and respecting the adult's right to self-determination.[85]

80. G.S. 15-27.2(b).
81. G.S. 15-27.2(e).
82. APS MANUAL, *supra* note 3, at III-39.
83. *Id.*
84. *Id.*
85. *Id.* at III-39 through -40.

Table 2.6. **Available Adult Protective Services Forms**

FORM NO.	FORM NAME
CV-770	Petition for Order Authorizing Protective Services, Emergency Services, or Ex Parte Emergency Services and Appointment of a Guardian Ad Litem
CV-771	Certificate of Services (Adult Protective Services)
CV-772	Notice of Hearing in Adult Protective Services Proceedings
CV-773	Order Authorizing Protective Services
CV-774	Notice of Hearing in Emergency Protective Services Proceedings
CV-775	Order Authorizing Emergency or Ex Parte Emergency Protective Services
CV-776	Petition for Order to Inspect Financial Records and to Freeze Assets
CV-777	Order to Authorize Inspection of Financial Records and to Freeze Assets
CV-778	Notice of Order to Inspect Financial Records and Freeze Assets
CV-779	Certification to Financial Institution as Required by G.S. 53B-5
CV-781	Notice of Hearing to Enjoin Interference with Protective Services (Consenting Adult)
CV-782	Order to Enjoin Interference with Protective Services (Consenting Adult)
SP-630	Petition and Order for Issuance of Subpoena Directing Release of Financial Records

III. CHALLENGES FOR APS

A. DETERMINING WHICH COUNTY IS RESPONSIBLE

Sometimes multiple counties may be involved in an APS case. Consider the following example.

EXAMPLE

A disabled older adult owns a home in County A and has lived there independently for fifty years. The adult's grown child assists him with chores, shopping, and medication administration. The adult is hospitalized in County B after an injury and is discharged to a rehabilitation unit in County B; the adult may not be able to live independently in the future. An APS report is filed in County B related to potential abuse of the adult by his child.

In the example described above, both County A and County B have legal authority to take action with respect to this adult. The APS law grants authority to the director in the county in which the older adult resides (County A) and the one in the county in which the older adult is currently present (County B).[86]

86. The legal framework for APS grants authority to the DSS "director." In the context of the APS law, the term "director" is defined as "the director of the county [DSS] in the county in which the person resides or is present."

COMMUNICATE EARLY AND OFTEN AND REMAIN FLEXIBLE.

Because state statutes do not provide clear direction in these types of situations, counties rely primarily on state regulations and on guidance from the Division of Aging and Adult Services.[87] In most instances, the county in which the older adult is located (for purposes of our example, County B) will contact the county of residence (County A) after receiving a report about the adult. County A would then assume responsibility for the evaluation of the adult and for the provision of services to the adult. Exceptional circumstances may exist that make it more appropriate for County B to take the lead. Some examples are set out below.

- **Emergencies.** If there is an emergency and the older adult is in substantial danger, County B will likely try to obtain the adult's consent for protective services or pursue an emergency order. Once the older adult is out of danger, the two counties may decide that County A should assume responsibility going forward.
- **Residential facilities.** If an older adult moves into a residential facility, such as a nursing home, in a county other than the one in which he or she legally resides, a state regulation authorizes the county of residence to transfer responsibility to the county in which the adult is located.[88] This regulation provides that the county in which a residential facility is located has primary responsibility for providing protective services to adults in that facility. Questions may arise if an adult is in the facility for a short-term placement.
- **Conflicts of interest.** There are times when the DSS in an older adult's county of residence should not take the lead on an APS case because the agency has a conflict of interest. For example, a report could allege abuse, neglect, or exploitation of a disabled adult by a county commissioner or a DSS employee. Or the DSS director may be serving as the guardian of the disabled adult who is the subject of the report. In these instances, DSS will need to enlist assistance from a neighboring county to manage the adult's evaluation and possibly the provision of services to the adult.[89]

These situations and others require counties to communicate with one another regularly and remain flexible to meet the needs of the disabled adult.

B. DECIDING BETWEEN APS AND GUARDIANSHIP

Some may consider APS and guardianship, particularly interim guardianship, to be interchangeable tools available to help an older adult who may lack capacity and is in need of assistance. The APS tools available to DSS are unique and should be used carefully to

G.S. 108A-101(c). Therefore, both directors have the legal authority to act, and each director may delegate that authority to DSS staff. *Id.* § 108A-14(b).

87. 10A N.C.A.C. 71A, § .0504.

88. *Id.*

89. APS MANUAL, *supra* note 3, at III-2, III-7 to -8, III-24, III-37, and III-42.

carry out the purposes for which they are intended. The purposes of protective services, interim guardianship, and guardianship overlap to some extent, but they are also distinctive. Table 2.7, below, provides a high-level summary comparison of the essential elements and purposes of each APS tool.

One of the challenges facing DSS is that it may be more expedient to pursue interim guardianship if a disabled adult needs immediate assistance. This is, in part, because a clerk of superior court—the official who presides over guardianship proceedings—may be more readily accessible in some counties than a district court judge (who presides over APS proceedings).

MAKE CASE-SPECIFIC DECISIONS AFTER CAREFUL EVALUATION OF OBJECTIVES AND AVAILABLE OPTIONS.

Table 2.7. **Comparison: Protective Services, Interim Guardianship, and Guardianship**

	PROTECTIVE SERVICES	INTERIM GUARDIANSHIP	GUARDIANSHIP
Timeframe	Short-term	Short-term	Long-term
Function	Protection of a disabled adult from abuse, neglect, or exploitation; provision of essential services	Decision making and/or action on behalf of an adult who is probably incompetent	Decision making and/or action on behalf of an adult who has been adjudicated incompetent
Means of initiation	DSS can initiate following a report to APS	Petitioner, GAL, or clerk in a guardianship proceeding	Any person, including DSS, can initiate by filing a petition with clerk
Presiding official	District court judge	Elected clerk of superior court or an assistant clerk	Elected clerk of superior court or an assistant clerk
Standard of capacity applied	Lack capacity to consent to services (limited)	Inability to make or communicate decisions (more expansive)	Inability to make or communicate decisions (more expansive)

Table 2.7. *cont'd*

	PROTECTIVE SERVICES	INTERIM GUARDIANSHIP	GUARDIANSHIP
Duration of tool	Up to 120 days (initial order may be in effect for up to 60 days; may request additional 60 days)	Up to 90 days (initial order may be in effect for up to 45 days; may request additional 45 days)	Continues until death of the older adult or until clerk issues an order to restore competency

C. CARETAKER OR FAMILY INTERFERENCE

In some situations, an older adult's caretaker or family member may try to intervene or disrupt either the evaluation of the adult or the provision of services to him or her.

The law provides some options for addressing these challenges, but there may be times when DSS staff members will need to rely primarily on their social work skills to navigate such difficult situations.

CONSIDER WHETHER DSS SHOULD SEEK AN INJUNCTION TO PREVENT A CARETAKER FROM INTERFERING.

When an older adult has consented to the provision of protective services but his or her caretaker interferes with those services, DSS has the authority "to petition the district court for an order enjoining the caretaker from interfering."[90] Forms are available for both the petition and the order. If the caretaker continues to interfere after an order enjoining interference is issued, DSS may ask the court to hold the caretaker in contempt.[91]

Note that this type of court order is applicable only to a "caretaker," defined under statute to mean "an individual who has the responsibility for the care of the disabled adult as a result of family relationship or who has assumed the responsibility for the care of the disabled adult voluntarily or by contract."[92] If the person interfering is not a caretaker, options for DSS staff are more limited.

90. G.S. 108A-104(b).
91. G.S. 5A-21 (civil contempt).
92. G.S. 108A-101(b).

D. OBTAINING MEDICAL RECORDS FROM NON-CARETAKER MEDICAL PROVIDERS

In order to conduct a thorough evaluation in an APS case, social workers will often need to review medical records or talk with care providers. The state statute addressing the issue, G.S. 108A-103, is not entirely clear about DSS's right of access to otherwise confidential records. Subsection (a) of that law provides:

> When necessary for a complete evaluation of the report, the director shall have the authority to review and copy any and all records, or any part of such records, related to the care and treatment of the disabled adult that have been maintained by any individual, facility or agency acting as a caretaker for the disabled adult. This shall include but not be limited to records maintained by facilities licensed by the North Carolina Department of Health and Human Services.[93]

Some health care providers interpret this provision narrowly, arguing that it only allows DSS to have access to records if the involved provider was a "caretaker" of the adult. As discussed above, the term "caretaker" is defined in the law to mean someone who "has responsibility for the care of the disabled adult as a result of family relationship or who has assumed the responsibility for the care of the disabled adult voluntarily or by contract."[94] Some argue that the provision of medical services does not necessarily rise to the level of "assuming responsibility" for an adult's care. Others argue that such a narrow interpretation would defeat the purpose of the law and unnecessarily limit DSS's authority to conduct a thorough evaluation.

Subsection (b) of the same statute appears to support the latter argument. It states:

> The staff and physicians of local health departments, area mental health, developmental disabilities, and substance abuse authorities, and other public or private agencies shall cooperate fully with the director in the performance of his duties. These duties include immediate accessible evaluations and in-home evaluations where the director deems this necessary.[95]

Health care providers are subject to many different and complex confidentiality laws. Attorneys advising them may wish to see different language in the law to assure the providers that information-sharing is mandated. Typically, if a state law mandates disclosure, other medical confidentiality laws allow such disclosure.[96]

93. G.S. 108A-103(a).
94. G.S. 108A-101(b).
95. G.S. 108A-103(b).
96. *See, e.g.*, 45 C.F.R. § 164.512(a) (HIPAA Privacy Regulation allowing disclosures of protected health information if otherwise required by law). *But see* 42 C.F.R. pt. 2 (not allowing the disclosure of records from substance abuse treatment facilities when required by state law).

CONSIDER ALTERNATIVE APPROACHES FOR OBTAINING RECORDS.

If a provider refuses to share records in response to a request from DSS, the agency may consider asking the adult or the adult's legal representative to consent to the disclosure. If the adult lacks capacity to consent or consent is otherwise not a viable option, DSS could also consider asking the court to order disclosure. Procedurally, this would be feasible after DSS has already filed a protective services petition pursuant to G.S. 108A-105 or -106 or a guardianship action.

E. ADULT WITH CAPACITY REFUSES SERVICES

Older adults with decisional capacity have the right to refuse protective services. This fundamental concept can at times be frustrating for DSS because its social workers may recognize that an adult who has made such a refusal will suffer physical or financial harm if the agency does not intervene.

EXAMPLE

Jacob is 85 years old, is in a wheelchair, and has full decisional capacity. His son, along with his son's girlfriend, her children, and her children's spouses, all live in Jacob's large home. Jacob pays for all of the housing expenses and food for the entire group. Jacob primarily stays in one or two rooms in the house, while the group uses the rest of the space. His son's girlfriend provides Jacob with regular meals. Jacob's resources are being rapidly depleted but he tells DSS that he does not want anything to change because he wants to stay in his home and that this arrangement allows him to do so.

EXAMPLE

John is 85 years old, is homebound, is in a wheelchair, and has full decisional capacity. His son, David, serves as his representative payee for Social Security benefits. David uses about one-quarter of the money each month to buy his father a few groceries and pay for his father's utilities. He uses the rest of the money for his own purposes. John refuses DSS's offer to serve as his representative payee and to either (1) locate an in-home aide for him or (2) find him a placement in a facility. John explains that he knows exactly what his son is doing but that he does not mind. He believes that if he changes the arrangement, his son will stop visiting him.

TRAIN DSS STAFF TO CAREFULLY BALANCE THE NEED TO PROTECT AGAINST THE NEED TO PRESERVE THE ADULT'S RIGHT TO SELF-DETERMINATION.

In each of these two examples, a social worker is going to have to spend a significant amount of time explaining potential consequences to the older adult. The social worker will carefully evaluate each situation to determine whether the older adult is being coerced or threatened and, if coercion or threats are found, will take steps to intervene. But if the older adult's decision to refuse services is truly one that the adult is making freely and with full knowledge of the potential consequences, it is essential that the social worker respect that decision.

Figure 2.2. **APS Process Overview**

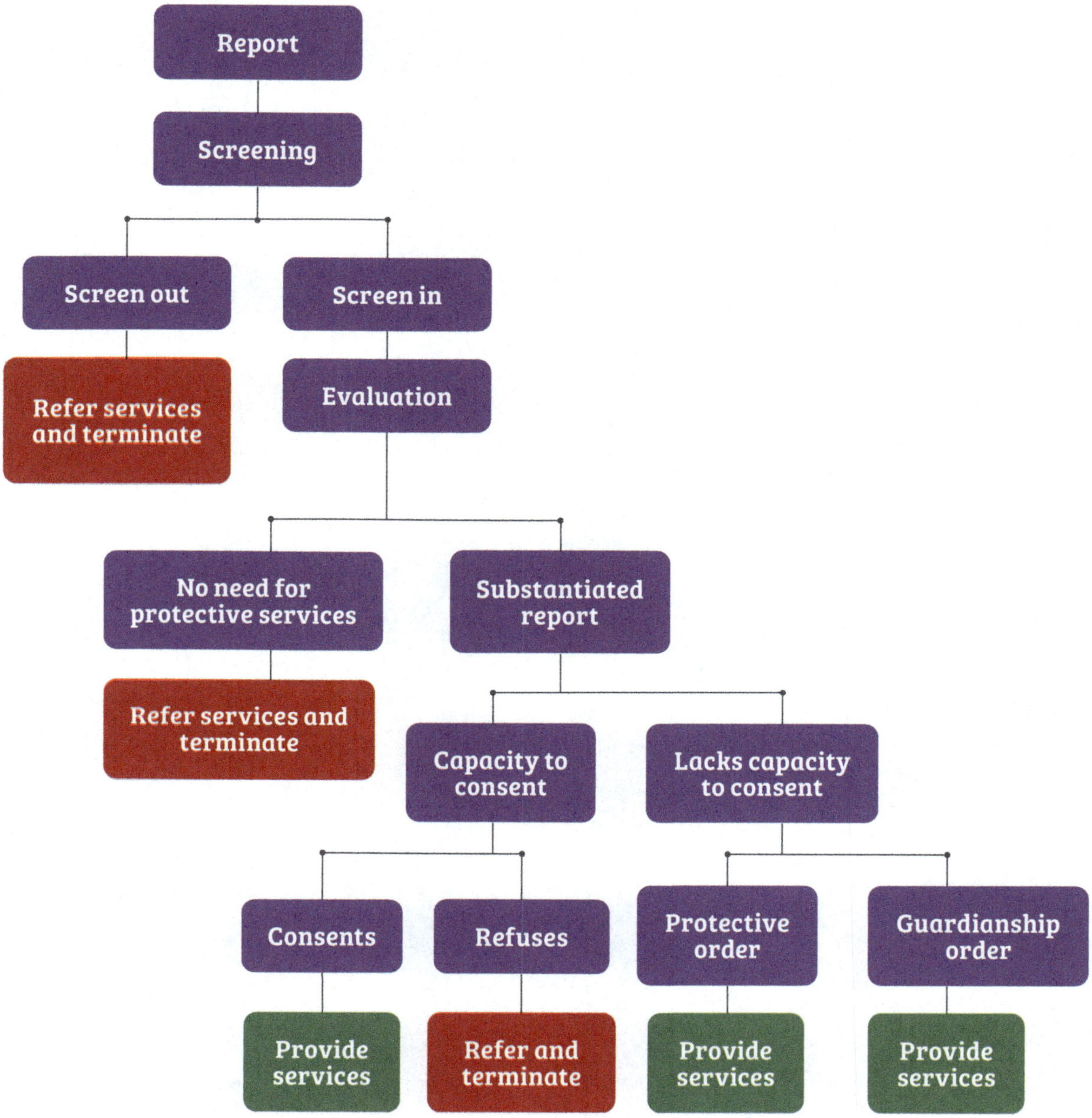

Chapter 3
Criminal Investigation and Prosecution

CONTENTS

I. SCOPE OF CHAPTER

This chapter provides an overview of the general landscape of criminal prosecution of elder abuse. It highlights some of the primary crimes implicated and provides an introduction to the actors involved in the prosecution of cases. Finally, it explores some of the challenges to prosecuting criminal cases involving older adults.

This chapter is not an in-depth guide to investigating and prosecuting an elder abuse case. Other resources have been developed specifically for law enforcement officials and prosecutors to support them in this work.[1] Rather, this chapter is designed to orient others involved with the elder protection system to the tools, processes, and challenges involved with criminal investigations and prosecutions.

In the context of crimes against older adults, criminal investigation and prosecution is unique in that it allows for the punishment of perpetrators. The other bodies of law discussed in this manual focus primarily on tools available through the civil legal system to protect an older adult or provide redress to the older adult or the adult's family. But criminal remedies are extremely important to the overall system of elder protection because they not only punish perpetrators but also possibly prevent further victimization of affected older adults and deter abuse of other older adults in the future.

North Carolina law does not establish a specific crime of "elder abuse." Instead, several crimes may be implicated if an older adult is being abused or exploited. While only two crimes focus specifically on older or disabled adults, many other generally applicable crimes—such as assault, rape, fraud, forgery, obtaining property by false pretenses, embezzlement, or robbery—may be applicable when a victim is an elder adult. A combination of local, state, and federal officials may be involved in both investigating and prosecuting these crimes.

II. OVERVIEW OF CRIMINAL INVESTIGATION AND PROSECUTION

This section provides some context for understanding the landscape for criminal investigation and prosecution of elder abuse cases. Why is it important? Who is involved in this work? What are they able to do?

1. AEQUITAS, THE PROSECUTOR'S RESOURCE: ELDER ABUSE (current as of Apr. 2017), https://aequitasresource.org/wp-content/uploads/2018/09/Prosecutors-Resource-on-Elder-Abuse.pdf; Lori A. Stiegel, ABA Comm'n on Law & Aging, Legal Issues Related to Elder Abuse: A Pocket Guide for Law Enforcement (2014), https://www.americanbar.org/content/dam/aba/administrative/law_aging/2014_ElderAbusePocketGuides.authcheckdam.pdf; Ctr. for Elders and the Cts., *Toolkits for Prosecutors and Courts*, "Elder Abuse Toolkit for Prosecutors," http://www.eldersandcourts.org/Elder-Abuse/Toolkits-for-Prosecutors-and-Courts.aspx (last visited July 17, 2019); NAT'L CTR. FOR STATE CTS., PROSECUTING ELDER ABUSE CASES: BASIC TOOLS AND STRATEGIES (2012), https://www.bja.gov/Publications/NCSC-Prosecuting-Elder-Abuse-Cases-Basic-Tools-and-Strategies.pdf; U.S. Dep't of Justice, *Elder Justice Initiative (EJI)*, https://www.justice.gov/elderjustice (including resources for law enforcement and prosecutors) (last visited July 17, 2019); EAGLE (Elder Abuse Guide for Law Enforcement), http://eagle.trea.usc.edu/.

A. HOW DOES CRIMINAL INVESTIGATION AND PROSECUTION PROTECT ELDERS?

Criminal investigation and prosecution plays several important roles in the elder protection system, including

- gathering essential information during the course of the investigation that may be useful in the criminal proceeding as well as in other proceedings necessary to help the adult, such as protective services, guardianship, and other civil proceedings;
- taking immediate action to protect an adult in an emergent or urgent situation, such as taking a perpetrator into custody;
- holding perpetrators accountable;
- protecting the community by deterring perpetrators from targeting other victims;
- preserving and possibly restoring assets taken from victims of exploitation by obtaining an order to freeze assets of the perpetrator and seeking court-ordered restitution; and
- treating or otherwise rehabilitating perpetrators.[2]

B. WHAT ARE SOME OF THE POTENTIAL CRIMES THAT MAY BE INVOLVED WITH ELDER ABUSE?

Two criminal statutes, Chapter 14, Sections 32.3 and 112.2 of the North Carolina General Statutes (hereinafter G.S.), focus specifically on harms caused to disabled and older adults. The first addresses domestic abuse and neglect and the second addresses exploitation. Many other criminal statutes that apply regardless of the age of the victim, such as assault, theft, and embezzlement, may also be implicated in a particular case. Below is a detailed review of the specific crimes that focus on older adults and a general overview of the other potential crimes that may be appropriate to consider.

1. G.S. 14-32.3: DOMESTIC ABUSE AND NEGLECT OF DISABLED OR ELDER ADULTS

There are two separate crimes under G.S. 14-32.3: (1) abuse and (2) neglect. Previously the law addressed exploitation as well, but that crime has been moved to a separate statute (G.S. 14-112.2, discussed below). However, the title of G.S. 14-32.3 was not amended to conform to the change and still includes the word "exploitation."

2. *See* Arlene M. Markarian, "Protecting Elder Abuse Victims: Building the Case, Building the Team," presentation at National Center for Victims of Crime 2012 National Conference (2012), https://victimsofcrime.org/docs/Toolkit%20 Bulletins/natl-center-for-victims-of-crime-conf-ea-handouts.pdf?sfvrsn=0.

A person may be guilty of **abuse** if

- the person is a caretaker of a disabled[3] or elder adult who is residing in a domestic setting;
- the person, with malice aforethought, knowingly and willfully
  - assaults the adult,
  - fails to provide the adult with medical or hygienic care, or
  - confines or restrains the adult in a place or under a condition that is cruel or unsafe, and
- the adult suffers mental or physical injury as a result.[4]

A person may be guilty of **neglect** if

- the person is a caretaker of a disabled or elder adult who is residing in a domestic setting;
- the person wantonly, recklessly, or with gross carelessness
  - fails to provide the adult with medical or hygienic care or
  - confines or restrains the adult in a place or under a condition that is unsafe; and
- the adult suffers mental or physical injury as a result.[5]

For both of these crimes—abuse and neglect—the statute includes some definitions that are key to establishing a sound case.

3. Chapter 14, Section 32.3(d)(2) of the North Carolina General Statutes (hereinafter G.S.) (This statute defines "disabled adult" as someone who is "18 years of age or older or a lawfully emancipated minor who is present in the State of North Carolina and who is physically or mentally incapacitated as defined in G.S. 108A-101(d)." G.S. 108A-101(d) defines physical or mental incapacitation as being caused by "an intellectual disability, cerebral palsy, epilepsy or autism; organic brain damage caused by advanced age or other physical degeneration in connection therewith; or due to conditions incurred at any age which are the result of accident, organic brain damage, mental or physical illness, or continued consumption or absorption of substances." Some older adults will satisfy the definition of "disabled," but many others will not.).

4. G.S. 14-32.3(a).

5. G.S. 14-32.3(b).

KEY TERM

Caretaker *is defined in the law as a "person who has the responsibility for the care of a disabled or elder adult as a result of family relationship or who has assumed the responsibility for the care of a disabled or elder adult voluntarily or by contract."*[6] *If the perpetrator of the abuse is a stranger, family member, or friend who is not actually responsible for the care of the older adult, prosecutors will not be able to charge this crime.*

KEY TERM

Elder adult *is defined as a "person 60 years of age or older who is not able to provide for the social, medical, psychiatric, psychological, financial, or legal services necessary to safeguard the person's rights and resources and to maintain the person's physical and mental well-being."*[7] *In some cases, older adults may be subject to abuse or neglect but they may still be able to provide for their own needs. If so, prosecutors will not be able to charge this crime.*

KEY TERM

Domestic setting *is defined as "any residential setting except for a health care facility or residential care facility. . . ."*[8] *This means that prosecutors will not be able to charge this particular crime if the abuse occurred in places such as hospitals, nursing homes, or rehabilitation or assisted living facilities. The crime also does not apply to abuse or neglect by staff of home health agencies.*

While these definitions are somewhat limiting, it is important to remember that other crimes of general applicability may be options for prosecutors. For example, abuse or neglect by a home health worker or a staff person in an assisted living facility is subject to a separate criminal law governing patient abuse and neglect.[9]

G.S. 14-32.3 requires a different state of mind for each of the two crimes it covers. Abuse requires the prosecutor to prove that the perpetrator acted "with malice aforethought, knowingly and willfully."[10] Neglect, on the other hand, will likely be easier to establish because it requires the prosecutor to prove that the perpetrator acted wantonly, recklessly, or with gross carelessness, a lower standard of proof than malice aforethought.[11] Briefly, a malicious state of mind may be proved by showing that a perpetrator's conduct

6. G.S. 14-32.3(d)(1).
7. G.S. 14-32.3(d)(4).
8. G.S. 14-32.3(d)(3).
9. G.S. 14-32.2.
10. *See* JESSICA SMITH, NORTH CAROLINA CRIMES: A GUIDEBOOK ON THE ELEMENTS OF CRIME 3–10 (7th ed. 2012) (discussing states of mind from intentional to negligent conduct).
11. *See id.*

was intentional and done with ill will or hatred, while wanton, reckless, or gross carelessness is indicated by conduct exhibiting a thoughtless disregard of consequences or an indifference to the harm that may be done to others.[12]

Both crimes require that the older adult suffer mental or physical injury. The consequences of conviction will be more severe if the injury suffered by the older adult was *serious.* (See Table 3.1, below.) According to the pattern jury instructions used by judges and attorneys, an injury is "serious" if it "causes great pain and suffering."[13] A mental injury may be sufficient to meet the definition of a "serious personal injury" if (1) it extends for an "appreciable" period of time beyond the circumstances of the crime and (2) it is a mental injury beyond that normally experienced in other crimes of the same type.[14] Examples of evidence of mental injuries that were found to have risen to the level of a "serious personal injury" include nightmares, difficulty sleeping, severe disruption to normal life activities, and the victim's need for therapy to overcome the lingering trauma from the crime.[15]

Both crimes—abuse and neglect—include an exception for situations in which a caretaker acted or failed to act in a manner that was consistent with state law related to a "natural death."[16] In this context, a natural death is one resulting from the withholding or discontinuation of life-prolonging measures. North Carolina has two separate laws that govern situations involving a natural death—one law addresses when a person has declared his or her wishes related to natural death and the second addresses when a person has not made a specific declaration.[17]

12. *See* State v. Sexton, 357 N.C. 235, 237–38 (2003) (discussing malice); State v. Jones, 353 N.C. 159, 165 (2000) (defining criminal negligence in terms of reckless and careless conduct).

13. N.C.P.I.—CRIM. 120.12; State v. Boone, 307 N.C. 198 (1982), *overruled on other grounds by* State v. Richmond, 347 N.C. 412, *cert. denied,* 525 U.S. 843 (1998).

14. State v. Baker, 336 N.C. 58, 64 (1994); *Boone,* 307 N.C. at 590.

15. *See, e.g.,* State v. Lilly, 117 N.C. App. 192 (1994), *aff'd per curiam,* 342 N.C. 409 (1995); State v. Davis, 101 N.C. App. 12 (1990). *See also* State v. Ackerman, 144 N.C. App. 452 (2001) (involving a combination of physical and mental injuries).

16. G.S. 14-32.3(a), (b) (both subsections provide that a caretaker is not guilty of a crime if the act or failure to act is in accordance with G.S. 90-321 or -322, which describe procedures for withholding or discontinuing life-prolonging measures).

17. G.S. 90-321 (declaration); -322 (no declaration).

Table 3.1. **Comparing Abuse and Neglect under G.S. 14-32.3**

	ABUSE	NEGLECT
Is perpetrator a caretaker of a disabled or elder adult in a domestic setting?	Yes	Yes
State of mind	With malice aforethought, knowingly and willfully	Wantonly, recklessly, or with gross carelessness
Acts or omissions	The perpetrator assaults the adult, fails to provide the adult with medical or hygienic care, or confines or restrains the adult in a place or under a condition that is cruel or unsafe.	The perpetrator fails to provide the adult with medical or hygienic care or confines or restrains the adult in a place or under a condition that is unsafe.
Did adult suffer mental or physical injury as a result of perpetrator's actions?	Yes	Yes
Exception for health care facilities and residential facilities?	Yes	Yes
Exception for acts complying with laws related to natural death?	Yes	Yes
Penalty[18]	• Class H (not serious injury) • Class F (serious injury)	• Class I (not serious injury) • Class G (serious injury)

See Section III.H. of this chapter for more discussion of the limitations of the abuse and neglect statutes.

In addition to the elder-specific abuse crimes set out in G.S. 14-32.3 and described above, several other crimes may be relevant when an older adult is physically abused. See Section II.B.3, below, for a list of possible crimes and Appendix C for more detailed summaries of

18. A number of factors determine the type and length of punishment a perpetrator may receive, including the class of offense, the perpetrator's prior record level, and possible enhancements or aggravating or mitigating factors. A perpetrator could receive an active sentence or a suspended sentence with either supervised or unsupervised probation. In addition, a perpetrator may be required to pay fines, costs, other fees, or restitution to the victim. For more information on sentencing factors and guidelines, see JAMES M. MARKHAM & SHEA RIGGSBEE DENNING, NORTH CAROLINA SENTENCING HANDBOOK (2018 ed.).

each. Two crimes in particular focus on specific populations that may be relevant in a case involving an older adult.

- **Assault on an individual with a disability (G.S. 14-32.1).** Under this law, the term "individual with a disability" is defined so broadly that it likely encompasses many older adults. The term refers to any individual who has a physical disability, a mental disability, or an infirmity "that would substantially impair the ability to defend oneself."[19] A simple assault under this law is a Class A1 misdemeanor.[20] The penalty increases to a Class F felony if the assault was aggravated (i.e., if the person used a deadly weapon or force likely to inflict serious injury or serious damage, inflicted serious injury or serious damage to the victim, or intended to kill the victim).[21]

- **Patient abuse or neglect (G.S. 14-32.2).** Under this law, it is a crime to physically abuse a patient when that abuse results in death or bodily injury.[22] "Abuse" is defined broadly enough to capture neglect in some circumstances because it includes conduct that is "culpably negligent," which means the conduct was "of a willful, gross and flagrant character, evincing reckless disregard of human life."[23] This law applies (1) to patients in medical facilities, such as hospitals and skilled nursing facilities (nursing homes), or in residential care facilities, such as adult care homes, and (2) to care by home health agencies.[24] Penalties range from Class C to Class H felonies, depending on the perpetrator's state of mind and the harm caused.[25]

Because the specific crime related to abuse and neglect of an older adult is somewhat narrow in scope, it is essential to think creatively about other possible crimes that may be involved in these cases.

2. G.S. 14-112.2: EXPLOITATION OF AN OLDER ADULT OR DISABLED ADULT

G.S. 14-112.2 includes two separate crimes of exploitation of an elder: one requires a specific relationship with the disabled or older adult and the other does not. At the outset, it should be noted that this law applies to adults who are 65 years of age or older, which is different from the other "elder adult" criminal law (G.S. 14-32.3), which applies to adults 60 years of age or older.[26]

A person may be guilty of **relationship-based exploitation** if

- the person either
  - stands in a position of trust and confidence with the adult or
  - has a business relationship with the adult;

19. G.S. 14-32.1(a).
20. G.S. 14-32.1(f). Note that a simple assault on a non-disabled person is a Class 2 misdemeanor. *Id.* § 14-33(a).
21. G.S. 14-32.1(e).
22. G.S. 14-32.2(a).
23. G.S. 14-32.2(e).
24. G.S. 14-32.2(a), (c), (c1).
25. G.S. 14-32.2(b).
26. G.S. 14-112.2(a)(2).

- the person
  - knowingly,
  - by deception or intimidation,
  - obtained, used, or endeavored to obtain or use
  - the adult's funds, assets or property; and
- the person intended to
  - temporarily or permanently deprive the adult or
  - benefit someone other than the adult.[27]

A person may otherwise be guilty of **exploitation** under this statute if

- the person
  - knowingly,
  - by deception or intimidation,
  - obtained, used, endeavored to obtain or use, or conspired to obtain or use
  - the adult's funds, assets, or property;
- the person intended to
  - temporarily or permanently deprive the adult or
  - benefit someone other than the adult; and
- the person was not acting within the scope of his or her lawful authority as agent for the adult.[28]

Table 3.2. **Comparing Penalties for Exploitation**[29]

VALUE OF FUNDS, ASSETS, OR PROPERTY	RELATIONSHIP-BASED EXPLOITATION	OTHER EXPLOITATION
< $20,000	Class H felony	Class I felony
$20,000 to $100,000	Class G felony	Class H felony
$100,000+	Class F felony	Class G felony

27. G.S. 14-112.2(b).
28. G.S. 14-112.2(c).
29. G.S. 14-112.2(d), (e).

If a person (defendant) is charged with either of the two exploitation crimes listed in G.S. 14-112.2 and the amount involved is valued at more than $5,000, the prosecutor may ask the court to freeze or seize enough of the defendant's assets to preserve them for potential restitution to the victim.[30] Key points to consider about "freeze and seize" orders are set out below.

PRACTICE NOTE

"Freeze and Seize" Orders

- Only the prosecutor has the authority to request this type of order.
- Procedurally, the prosecutor must file a petition in the pending criminal proceeding consistent with state rules governing injunctions as well as the specific rules governing these particular types of orders.[31]
- In order to succeed, the prosecutor must prove by clear and convincing evidence that the defendant is about to or intends to "divest himself or herself of assets in a manner that would render the defendant insolvent for purposes of restitution."[32]
- The court may issue an order affecting the defendant's assets in an amount equal to up to 150 percent of the value of the victim's potentially exploited assets.[33]

In practice, it is still somewhat unusual for prosecutors to rely on this tool for preserving assets. According to a recent elder abuse prosecution manual produced by the North Carolina Conference of District Attorneys, the requirement that the prosecutor prove that the defendant "is about to or intends to divest" the assets may be so difficult to establish that it serves as a significant deterrent for prosecutors.

3. OTHER CRIMES THAT MAY BE APPLICABLE IN ELDER ABUSE CASES

There are many other crimes that may be appropriate for prosecutors to consider in cases involving elder abuse. While a full summary and analysis of every possible law is beyond the scope of this manual, Table 3.3, below, includes a list of some of the potentially relevant crimes and Appendix C includes a more detailed review of each crime, including the elements associated with each.

30. G.S. 14-112.2(f).
31. G.S. 14-112.3(b) (referencing G.S. 1A-1, Rule 65, regarding injunctions).
32. G.S. 14-112.3(d).
33. G.S. 14-112.2(f).

Table 3.3. **Crimes That May Be Charged in Elder Abuse Cases**

RAPE AND OTHER SEX OFFENSES	
Crime	**Statute (G.S.)**
First-Degree Forcible Rape	14-27.21
Second-Degree Forcible Rape	14-27.22
First-Degree Forcible Sexual Offense	14-27.26
Second-Degree Forcible Sexual Offense	14-27.27
Sexual Battery	14-27.33
Crime Against Nature	14-177
ASSAULTS	
Crime	**Statute (G.S.)**
Assault with a Deadly Weapon with Intent to Kill Inflicting Serious Injury	14-32(a)
Assault with a Deadly Weapon Inflicting Serious Injury	14-32(b)
Assault with a Deadly Weapon with Intent to Kill	14-32(c)
Assault on an Individual with a Disability	14-32.1
Patient Abuse or Neglect	14-32.2
Assault Inflicting Serious Bodily Injury	14-32.4(a)
Assault by Strangulation	14-32.4(b)
Simple Assault	14-33(a)
Assault Inflicting Serious Injury	14-33(c)(1)
Assault on a Female	14-33(c)(2)
Habitual Misdemeanor Assault	14-33.2
KIDNAPPINGS	
Crime	**Statute (G.S.)**
First-Degree Kidnapping	14-39
Second-Degree Kidnapping	14-39
False Imprisonment	Common law
Felonious Restraint	14-43.3
BURGLARY AND OTHER HOUSEBREAKINGS	
Crime	**Statute (G.S.)**
First-Degree Burglary	14-51
Second-Degree Burglary	14-51
Breaking or Entering a Building with Intent to Commit Felony or Larceny	14-54(a)
Breaking or Entering a Building with Intent to Terrorize or Injure Occupant	14-54(a1)
Misdemeanor Breaking or Entering	14-54(b)
Break or Enter Motor Vehicle with Intent to Commit Felony or Larceny	14-56

Table 3.3. *cont'd*

LARCENY AND ROBBERY	
Crime	**Statute (G.S.)**
Felony Larceny	14-72
Misdemeanor Larceny	14-72
Larceny, Concealment or Destruction of Wills	14-77
Robbery with a Dangerous Weapon	14-87
Common Law Robbery	Common law; *see* 14-87.1
Extortion	14-118.4
OTHER FINANCIAL AND RELATED CRIMES	
Crime	**Statute (G.S.)**
Embezzlement by an Agent or Fiduciary	14-90
Obtain Property by False Pretenses	14-100
Obtain Signature by False Pretenses	14-101
Obtain Advance by False Promise to Work	14-104
Financial Transaction Card Theft	14-113.9(a)(1)
Forgery of Financial Transaction Card	14-113.11
Financial Transaction Card Fraud	14-113.13
Financial Identity Theft	14-113.20
Common Law Forgery	See 14-119, -120
Common Law Uttering	See 14-120
Forgery and Counterfeiting of Instruments	14-119
Uttering Forged Instruments	14-120
Forging an Endorsement on Checks and Securities	14-120
MISCELLANEOUS	
Crime	**Statute (G.S.)**
Indecent Exposure	14-190
Using Threatening Language on the Telephone	14-196(a)(2)
Repeated Telephone Calls to Harass, etc.	14-196(a)(3)
Using Electronic Mail or Communication to Threaten or Extort	14-196(b)(1)
Communicating Threats	14-277.1
Stalking	14-277.3A
Interfering with Emergency Communication	14-286.2
Violation of a Domestic Violence Protective Order	50B-4.1

C. WHO IS RESPONSIBLE FOR CRIMINAL INVESTIGATION OF ELDER ABUSE?

Many agencies and officials are involved in the investigation of potential criminal activity involving elder abuse, including

- local law enforcement officials, such as police officers and sheriff's deputies;
- state law enforcement officials, such as the N.C. Department of Justice and the N.C. Secretary of State; and
- federal law enforcement officials, such as the U.S. Department of Justice, the Internal Revenue Service, and the U.S. Postal Service.

Law enforcement officials will become involved in elder abuse cases only if their agencies have jurisdiction. An agency will have jurisdiction in certain geographic areas and in certain types of cases. Occasionally, jurisdiction is limited to one type of agency, but most often agencies have overlapping and concurrent authority. (See Table 3.4.)

Table 3.4. **Law Enforcement Officials Involved with Elder Abuse Investigations—Territorial Jurisdiction**

LAW ENFORCEMENT OFFICER	JURISDICTION TO ARREST	AUTHORIZING STATUTE (G.S.)
State officers	At any place within the state	15A-402(a)
County and city officers	Within the officer's particular city or county and on any property and rights-of-way owned by the city or county outside its territorial limits	15A-402(b)
	May pursue someone outside the territory for a crime committed within the territory if arrest is made during the person's immediate and continuous flight from that territory	15A-402(d)
City officers	If outside the city: within one mile or less from the nearest point in the boundary of that city	15A-402(c)
County officers[34]	At any place within the state for a felony committed within the officer's territory	15A-402(e)
Federal officer[35]	May enforce criminal laws anywhere in the state when a state or local law enforcement agency or officer has asked for temporary assistance and the request is within the scope of that agency's or officer's subject matter and territorial jurisdiction	15A-406(a)–(b)

34. For felonies, the term "county officer" includes officers of consolidated city-county law enforcement agencies. G.S. 15A-402(e).

35. Includes certain types of law enforcement officers if they are employed full-time by the federal government.

EXAMPLE

An older adult receives a call. The caller tells the adult that she must pay a fine because she purchased prescription medication over the Internet. The older adult suspects this is a scam and calls 911. The 911 operator routes the call to local law enforcement (police or sheriff, depending on the adult's location). Local law enforcement may conduct an investigation. Local law enforcement may also contact the Drug Enforcement Agency (DEA), which is part of the U.S. Department of Justice (US DOJ). The DEA has the authority to investigate as well.

EXAMPLE

An older adult purchased some securities and later realized that the securities were fake. The adult calls the municipal police to report the fraud. The police have the authority to investigate the fraud. The police may also contact the Securities Division of the North Carolina Secretary of State (NC SOS), which has authority to investigate.

Typically, municipal and county law enforcement officials work closely together to refer cases to each other and to federal or state agencies when it is appropriate to do so. Chapter 7 describes many of the state and federal agencies that could be involved in an elder abuse case and their respective areas of authority.

PRACTICE NOTE

If a person suspects that a crime has been committed, he or she should contact *local* law enforcement first. They can be the gateway to the other agencies and officials that may be able to assist with or assume responsibility for an investigation into the matter.

Examples include Federal Bureau of Investigation special agents, Drug Enforcement Administration special agents, United States Customs Service officers, United States Postal Service inspectors, Internal Revenue Service special agents, United States Marshals Service marshals and deputies, and Immigration and Naturalization Service officers. G.S. 15A-406(a).

Figure 3.1. **N.C. Prosecutorial Districts**

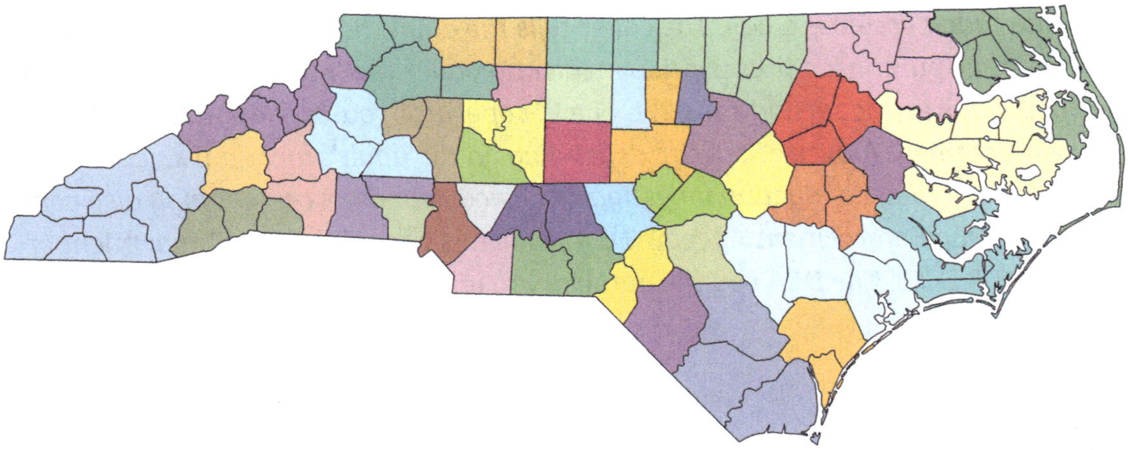

D. WHO IS RESPONSIBLE FOR CRIMINAL PROSECUTION IN ELDER ABUSE CASES?

District attorneys (DAs) are elected public officials who are responsible for prosecuting all state criminal actions in their respective prosecutorial districts.[36] While North Carolina has one hundred counties, the state is divided into forty-three prosecutorial districts, meaning that some district attorney offices have jurisdiction in more than one county.[37] (See Figure 3.1.)

Each DA's office employs a number of assistant district attorneys (ADAs), who typically are involved with the daily work of prosecuting elder abuse cases. The offices also have their own investigators, victim witness legal assistants, and other administrative staff who support the office's work.

The DA's office prosecutes criminal matters on behalf of the State. DAs work closely with the local law enforcement officials in their districts, who refer cases to the DA for prosecution and coordinate with the DA's office on case management. Because the DA represents the State rather than the individual victims of crime, the office may proceed with a case without the express cooperation of the victim.

With regard to federal law, the United States Attorney's Office serves as the prosecutor.[38] North Carolina has three federal prosecutorial districts: Eastern, Middle, and Western.[39] Some state and federal agencies also have prosecutorial authority and often coordinate efforts for both investigations and prosecutions. For example, the U.S. Department of

36. N.C. CONST. art. IV, § 18; G.S. 7A-61 (describing general duties of district attorneys); -63 (describing general duties of assistant district attorneys).

37. G.S. 7A-60. Note that effective January 1, 2023, prosecutorial districts will increase by one, to forty-four districts. *Id.* § 7A-60 (a1) (this statute has multiple subsections designated as (a1), each with a different effective time period).

38. U.S. Dep't of Just., Offices of the U.S. Att'ys, *Mission* (updated Sept. 22, 2016), https://www.justice.gov/usao/mission.

39. *See* U.S. Cts., *Court Website Links*, USCOURTS.GOV, https://www.uscourts.gov/about-federal-courts/federal-courts-public/court-website-links (showing a map of geographic boundaries of all U.S. Courts of Appeals and U.S. District Courts) (last visited July 19, 2019); U.S. Dist. Ct., E. Dist. of N.C., *County List*, NCED.USCOURTS.GOV, http://www.nced.uscourts.gov/counties/Default.aspx (showing a map and a list of counties in this district) (last visited July 19, 2019).

Justice issued a press release in February 2018 highlighting a nationwide "sweep" of elder abuse cases.[40] The cases involved a wide range of federal authorities and state attorneys general. One case in North Carolina related to a lottery scam. The defendant was a mail carrier who accepted cash for diverting packages.[41]

E. HOW DOES CRIMINAL INVESTIGATION AND PROSECUTION WORK IN ELDER ABUSE CASES?

A criminal case involving elder abuse may begin in several different ways.

- **Reporting.** A member of the public, such as a victim or a family member of a victim, or a representative of an organization, such as a bank or health care provider, makes a report of suspected elder abuse directly to 911 or law enforcement.
- **Agency referral.** Another government agency, such as the county department of social services, notifies law enforcement officials of suspected abuse.
- **Other investigations.** Officers, investigators, or prosecutors uncover evidence of elder abuse when investigating another crime.

Below is a brief overview of each possible path for initiating a criminal elder abuse case.

1. REPORTING

In almost all situations, a person who suspects that an older adult is being abused, neglected, or exploited is allowed to report those suspicions to law enforcement directly. Some professionals, such as social workers and medical professionals, may be subject to confidentiality laws that limit voluntary reporting. In addition to voluntary reporting, North Carolina has four mandatory reporting laws that may come into play in an elder abuse case. (See Table 3.5, below.)

40. Press Release, U.S. Dep't of Just., Justice Department Coordinates Nationwide Elder Fraud Sweep of More Than 250 Defendants (Feb. 22, 2018), https://www.justice.gov/opa/pr/justice-department-coordinates-nationwide-elder-fraud-sweep-more-250-defendants.

41. Bill of Indictment, United States v. Brown, No. 3:17-cr-00047-RJC-DCK (W.D.N.C. Feb. 22, 2017), https://www.justice.gov/opa/page/file/1037356/download; Press Release, U.S. Att'y's Off., W. Dist. of N.C., Former Charlotte-Area Mail Carrier Pleads Guilty to Mail Theft in Connection with Jamaican-Based Lottery Fraud Scheme (Apr. 3, 2017), https://www.justice.gov/usao-wdnc/pr/former-charlotte-area-mail-carrier-pleads-guilty-mail-theft-connection-jamaican-based.

Table 3.5. **Selected North Carolina Mandatory Reporting Laws**

WHO REPORTS?	WHEN/WHAT TO REPORT?	WHO TO REPORT TO?
Any person[42]	Report if there is reason to believe that a disabled adult needs protection from potential abuse, neglect, or exploitation	County DSS DSS must share information with the district attorney in certain situations[43]
Financial institutions and their officers and employees[44]	Report if there is reason to suspect that a disabled or older adult (65 or over) is the target or the victim of financial exploitation	Local law enforcement County DSS if the adult is disabled
Physicians and hospitals[45]	Report if physicians/hospitals treat wounds, injuries, or illnesses that arise from a gunshot wound, poisoning, knife, or sharp instrument (1) if it appears that a criminal act was involved or (2) that cause grave bodily harm or grave illness if it appears that the harm or illness resulted from a criminal act of violence	Local law enforcement
Licensed adult care homes[46]	Report any incidents of abuse, neglect, or exploitation of a resident by a person certified as an assisted living administrator	Health Care Personnel Registry

If a report is made to law enforcement, it can go to either the police or the sheriff. The law enforcement agency responsible for responding to and following up on the report will vary depending on whether the older adult is within a city (police) or in an unincorporated area of a county (sheriff). It may be that other law enforcement officials, such as campus police or private security, receive the report or are involved in the response. These law enforcement agencies typically communicate and coordinate regularly to determine which agency will be primarily responsible for the initial investigation. For the reporter, it is a matter of simply getting the report submitted as fast as possible so that the appropriate unit can respond quickly.

---

42. G.S. 108A-102(a), (b). There is one exception to this reporting requirement. If the subject of a complaint filed with the Long Term Care Ombudsman Program relates to potential abuse, neglect, or exploitation, regional program staff may submit a report to the county DSS only with (1) permission from the state or (2) the written, informed consent of the adult. G.S. 143B-181.20(f).

43. G.S. 108A-109.

44. G.S. 108A-115.

45. G.S. 90-21.20.

46. G.S. 90-288.19.

2. AGENCY REFERRAL

As mentioned above, state law requires every person who has "reasonable cause to believe that a disabled adult is in need of protective services" to report that belief to the county social services agency (DSS).[47] The agency will then screen and act on such a report in accordance with the adult protective services (APS) law. See Chapter 1 for more details about APS. While APS is subject to many confidentiality laws, those laws also recognize the importance of sharing information with law enforcement officials. The statutes address this exchange of information in several ways.

- **Immediate notification.** APS may contact the district attorney or law enforcement officials immediately after receiving a report if there is reason to believe that physical harm to the disabled adult may occur. In this situation, APS may share information that would otherwise be confidential, including most health information.[48]
- **After an evaluation.** If the county social services agency finds evidence of abuse, neglect, or exploitation of a disabled (possibly older) adult, it is required to notify the district attorney in writing.[49] The notification is required to include
  - the name, address, age, and condition of the adult;
  - the allegations (excluding the identity of the reporter);
  - the agency's evaluation, including findings and supporting documents such as medical records;
  - the agency's conclusions and recommendations for action.[50]

  While conducting a criminal investigation or prosecution, law enforcement officials may want to know the identity of the person who made the report or the identities of other people who provided information to DSS in the course of the protective services evaluation. In this situation, DSS may share this information with law enforcement officials or prosecutors upon request.[51]

In some jurisdictions, a single individual or unit within the DA's office may be responsible for coordinating with APS or receiving these agency referrals. Once received, staff with the DA's office will likely then follow a protocol for initiating potential criminal investigations.

---

47. G.S. 108A-102.

48. Title 10A, Chapter 71A, Section .0201(c) of the North Carolina Administrative Code (N.C.A.C.). DSS would not be able to share information subject to the Federal Substance Abuse Confidentiality regulation. 42 C.F.R. pt. 2 ("Confidentiality of Substance Use Disorder Patient Records").

49. G.S. 108A-109 (requires reporting); 10A N.C.A.C. 71A, § .0906 (requires that the report be in writing).

50. 10A N.C.A.C. 71A, § .0901.

51. 10A N.C.A.C. 71A, § .0802(2).

3. OTHER INVESTIGATIONS

As discussed in Chapter 1, one of the most challenging issues facing the professionals involved in elder protection is underreporting. Fortunately, law enforcement officials and prosecutors may be able to look for clues of elder abuse, neglect, or exploitation in other reports and cases to which they have access.

EXAMPLE

A case involving an 80-year-old widowed woman first came to the attention of the DA's office when a man was charged with obtaining property by false pretenses after stealing the woman's lawnmower. As part of the criminal case, the victim's daughter offered a five-page impact statement detailing how the man had exploited her mother, who was suffering from dementia. He had insinuated himself into her life by doing chores for her. Over the course of two years, he ended up obtaining $140,000 in loans and a land transfer from the victim, which required her to take out two mortgages on her home. The man was successfully prosecuted and sentenced to five years for exploitation of an elder.[52]

With this access and with increased awareness of elder abuse generally, law enforcement officials and prosecutors can take the time to dig deeper and ask questions that will help identify these difficult and sometimes hidden crimes.

Once potential elder abuse comes to the attention of law enforcement, local officers (police, sheriff) will typically conduct an investigation. A full review of the investigatory process is beyond the scope of this manual. In 2019, the North Carolina Conference of District Attorneys was finalizing an elder abuse manual for prosecutors. Once available, it should be able to provide additional information and support for law enforcement officials. Some key concepts for others involved with the elder protection system to understand about the investigatory process are listed below.

- Local law enforcement officials have expansive authority to investigate suspected criminal violations. Other components of the elder protection system have more narrowly tailored authority. For example, APS focuses on serving adults who are disabled, guardianship is limited to those who are found to be incompetent by a court, and legal aid is typically available to lower-income clients. The broader authority of law enforcement serves as an essential safeguard for older adults.
- While law enforcement officials have expansive authority to investigate criminal activity, they are somewhat limited in their ability to provide direct assistance to the older adults who have been harmed or are at risk.

52. Interview with Lori Wickline, Assistant District Attorney, Alamance County District Attorney's Office, in Chapel Hill, N.C. (June 28, 2018).

- Victim assistance advocates will be able to provide support and services to any older adult who has been the victim of or who witnesses a violent crime.
- Law enforcement may reach out to other components of the system for help. For example, APS may be able to help the affected adult find alternative housing or residential care. A private attorney may need to help the older adult obtain a protective order.
- Some communities have a "Family Justice Center" that serves as a coordinating hub for many of the services and supports an older adult may need after experiencing abuse. (See sidebar below.)

- Information-sharing and collaboration at the early stages of an investigation involving an older adult can be especially important. For example, a law enforcement official may have concerns that an older adult is being financially exploited. The official may reach out to APS to ask the agency to take immediate steps to freeze the adult's assets. Each component of the elder protection system should have a clear understanding of the laws and policies that govern the sharing of information with law enforcement officials to minimize delay and maximize cooperation.

RESOURCE

Family Justice Centers in North Carolina

At least three counties in North Carolina have established Family Justice Centers that incorporate supports and services for elder abuse.

- Family Justice Center of Alamance County, https://www.alamance-nc.com/fjc/
- Buncombe County Family Justice Center, https://www.buncombecounty.org/law-safety/family-justice-center/
- Guilford County Family Justice Center, https://www.guilfordcountync.gov/our-county/family-justice-center

While there are differences between the centers, they are all designed to provide centralized access to coordinated services from a wide array of professionals, such as law enforcement officials, social workers, health care providers, victim advocates, and attorneys.

Once law enforcement officials have investigated a case alleging elder abuse, neglect, or exploitation, they refer it to the DA's office for prosecution. A law enforcement officer explained that "[i]t's like a hand off in a football play. . . . We developed the investigation, collected the evidence and the facts. Once we hit that point and established probable cause exists, we charge the appropriate charges and hand it over to the prosecution."[53]

53. Abigail Margulis, *Cases of Elder Abuse Hard to Prosecute*, BLUERIDGENOW.COM (Times-News Online) (Jan. 31,

The DA's office decides whether to prosecute a named person criminally and, if so, with what charges.[54] As the North Carolina Supreme Court has stated,

> District attorneys have wide discretion in performing the duties of their office. This encompasses the discretion to decide who will or will not be prosecuted. In making such decisions, district attorneys must weigh many factors such as "the likelihood of successful prosecution, the social value of obtaining a conviction as against the time and expense to the State, and his own sense of justice in the particular case."[55]

Perhaps the most important issue a prosecutor will wrestle with is the last one that arises: How will justice best be served in this particular case?

EXAMPLE

A young man was charged with financial card theft after taking his grandmother's credit card and using it for his own purposes. The grandmother asked the prosecutor to dismiss the charges, arguing that he didn't mean to do it. Taking the matter at face value, the prosecutor could have simply charged the grandson with a misdemeanor. However, having received elder abuse training, she spent a little extra time, no more than fifteen to twenty minutes, asking the grandmother for more information. She discovered that the grandson had forcefully stolen the credit card by throwing the victim down and taking the card out of her back pocket. The grandmother admitted that her grandson had also assaulted her in the past and that he had drug problems. She was afraid of anything bad happening to her grandson, though, noting that she had mostly raised him since his mother had committed suicide and that his father was a drug addict who abandoned the family. The prosecutor considered the situation and allowed some time for the grandson to attend rehab and look for work. He followed through on both of these things, and the prosecutor considered proceeding with a misdemeanor, thereby avoiding subjecting the grandson to a felony, which would have more serious collateral consequences for him throughout his life. Taking into account the twin goals of victim safety and offender accountability, the prosecutor considers the matter to be a rare success in trying to achieve justice for all involved.[56]

If a prosecutor elects to proceed with an elder abuse case, the decisions he or she makes (e.g., with regard to strategy, witnesses, evidence, plea deals, etc.) could have a significant impact on the potential outcomes.

2016), https://www.blueridgenow.com/news/20160131/cases-of-elder-abuse-hard-to-prosecute.

54. State v. Spicer, 299 N.C. 309, 311 (1980). A prosecutor also has an ethical duty not to bring charges he or she knows are not supported by probable cause. N.C. R. PROF'L CONDUCT. 3.8 (N.C. State Bar 1997) (last amended Mar. 16, 2017), https://www.ncbar.gov/for-lawyers/ethics/rules-of-professional-conduct/rule-38-special-responsibilities-of-a-prosecutor/.

55. *Spicer*, 299 N.C. at 311.

56. Interview with Lori Wickline, *supra* note 52.

While a detailed review of the process of prosecuting a criminal case is beyond the scope of this manual, other resources tailored to prosecutors and other participants in the criminal justice system are available.[57]

PRACTICE NOTE

The state of North Carolina has a special fund dedicated to reimbursing crime victims for medical expenses and lost wages associated with certain crimes such as assault and rape.[58] In order to be eligible for reimbursement, the crime must be reported to law enforcement within seventy-two hours and a claim must be filed within two years.[59] Applications are available online at https://www.ncdps.gov/DPS-Services/Victim-Services. Alternatively, a victim or a representative may contact Victim Services at the N.C. Department of Public Safety at 800-826-6200 or 919-733-7974.

III. CHALLENGES TO CRIMINAL INVESTIGATION AND PROSECUTION

A. NATURE OF THE VICTIM

Investigators and prosecutors may be deterred from pursuing an elder abuse case because the victim (and possibly some witnesses) are older. They may have concerns about the reliability of an older adult's memory or the ability of the adult to physically participate in an investigation or trial.[60] When these concerns are not grounded in reality but are generalized to the population of older adults as a whole, they are biases. The American Bar Association's Criminal Justice Standards for the Prosecution Function include an explicit prohibition on manifesting or exercising "by words or conduct, bias or prejudice based upon race, sex, religion, national origin, disability, age, sexual orientation, gender identity, or socioeconomic status." The Standards also direct the prosecutor's office to be "proactive in efforts to detect, investigate, and eliminate improper biases . . . ."[61] Therefore, it is essential that investigators and prosecutors avoid age-related biases and assumptions.

---

57. OFF. OF KY. ATT'Y GEN., PROSECUTION MANUAL FOR CRIMES AGAINST THE ELDERLY (2018); Lori A. Stiegel, ABA Comm'n on Law & Aging, Legal Issues Related to Elder Abuse: A Desk Guide for Law Enforcement (2015), available for download at https://www.americanbar.org/groups/law_aging/resources/elder_abuse/legal_issues_related_to_elder_abuse_guides/.

58. G.S. Ch. 15B, Art. 1 (Crime Victims Compensation Act).

59. G.S. 15B-11(a)(1), (3).

60. Paul R. Greenwood, *Our Graying Society: Issues of Elder Abuse and Age Bias*, 31(4)/32(1) PROSECUTOR'S BRIEF 40 (California District Attorneys Association, 2010), https://d3n8a8pro7vhmx.cloudfront.net/kasemcares/pages/70/attachments/original/1510772835/Our_Graying_Society_Issues_of_Elder__Abuse_and_Age_Bias_by_Paul_Greenwood.pdf?1510772835.

61. CRIM. JUST. STANDARDS FOR THE PROSECUTION FUNCTION STANDARD 3-1.6 (Am. Bar Ass'n, 4th ed., Nov. 2018), https://www.americanbar.org/groups/criminal_justice/standards/ProsecutionFunctionFourthEdition/.

It is certainly true that some older adults may have cognitive impairments resulting from age or disability. These impairments may make it difficult for the adult to participate in an interview, testify in court, or be productively involved with other aspects of an investigation. Some older adults may die before the case proceeds to trial. The vulnerability of these victims is one reason why they are targeted.

While age and cognitive or physical impairment may present real challenges in some cases, there are deliberate steps that can be taken in the course of an investigation to gather useful and credible information from older adults and preserve testimony for use in the criminal proceeding.

TIPS FOR INTERVIEWING OLDER ADULT VICTIMS OR WITNESSES IN ELDER ABUSE CASES.

- Avoid making assumptions based on a person's age. Older witnesses often make excellent and compelling witnesses.
- Be thoughtful about interviewing older adults. Appendix B includes a detailed discussion of general interviewing techniques for older adults.
- Consider developing a protocol for joint investigations and/or interviews by APS and law enforcement.[62]
- Record interviews throughout the investigation. A taped interview will likely not be admissible to prove the truth of the matter asserted; however, it may be used in some situations for other reasons.[63] For example, one prosecutor recorded an interview with an older adult immediately after a caretaker neglect investigation began and recorded another interview with the same elder several months later. If the older adult were to be unable to testify, the prosecutor was planning to use the recordings to demonstrate the victim's improved condition. In a case from California, recorded interviews were allowed to be admitted as evidence to demonstrate the mental capacity of the older adult who had been a victim of exploitation and was deceased at the time of trial.[64]

62. *See, e.g.*, SANTA CLARA CTY., CAL., ELDER AND DEPENDENT ADULT ABUSE PROTOCOL FOR SANTA CLARA COUNTY LAW ENFORCEMENT (July 2010), https://www.sccgov.org/sites/ssa/daas/aps/Documents/daas_elder_dependent_adult_protocol.pdf ("While an officer has a duty to cross report any known or suspected instance of abuse or neglect immediately or as soon as practically possible to the appropriate agency, the need for a joint investigation may not be immediately apparent. Therefore, the decision to conduct a joint investigation may be made prior to, in conjunction with or after cross reporting obligations are satisfied. In some instances, the elder/dependent adult may be in need of immediate emergency services. In such cases it will be clear that an agency such as APS [Adult Protective Services] or OMB [Ombudsman] should be immediately contacted for the dual purpose of providing a cross report and beginning a joint investigation. . . . Whenever possible, the investigating officer shall coordinate the investigation with the appropriate agency while mindful that the officer's investigative focus may differ from that of the other agency. For instance, while the officer is responsible for the criminal documentation of the crime, the APS social worker and/or OMB are there to provide supportive services and to ensure the elder is safe.").

63. ROBERT L. FARB, ARREST, SEARCH, AND INVESTIGATION IN NORTH CAROLINA 726–30 (5th ed. 2016) (discussing hearsay and exceptions to the hearsay rule).

64. People v. Cooper, 56 Cal. Rptr. 3d 6 (Cal. Ct. App. 2007). *See* AEQUITAS, *supra* note 1, at 45–47 (discussing the preservation of witness testimony).

- Take depositions from the victim and from older witnesses. While depositions may be unusual in criminal cases, they can be useful for preserving testimony that ultimately may be admissible as evidence for the truth of the matter asserted.[65] An important difference between a deposition and a taped interview is that the defendant and the defendant's attorney would have an opportunity to participate in the former.[66] Even though North Carolina lacks a statutory framework for pretrial depositions in criminal cases, one author recommends several key features to consider:
  - The defendant should have a right to be present, with counsel, when the deposition is taken.
  - The defendant should be afforded full discovery far enough in advance of the deposition so that there will be a meaningful opportunity for cross-examination at the deposition.
  - The deposition should be recorded using audio and visual equipment. The addition of a visual component will allow the fact-finder to observe the witness's demeanor, an observation that is not possible with a written transcript.
  - The recording of the deposition must be of sufficient quality for in-court presentation.
  - While objections may be made at the time of the deposition, the witness should be required to answer all questions. Or, as an alternative, a judge could attend by remote video connection and rule on objections as they arise.[67]

  The author further emphasizes the importance of allowing the defendant to be present during any such deposition.
- Gather as much information as possible from the victim and from older witnesses during the probable cause hearing or at other preliminary hearings.[68] If the victim or witness is later unavailable, the prosecutor may be able to introduce testimony from the hearing to support the State's case.[69]

---

65. *See* Jessica Smith, *Two-Way Remote Testimony: Will It Pass Muster? (Part III)*, N.C. CRIM. L.: A UNC SCH. OF GOV'T BLOG (Feb. 10, 2011), https://nccriminallaw.sog.unc.edu/two-way-remote-testimony-will-it-pass-muster-part-iii/ ("Although North Carolina does not have a statutory procedure for the State to take pretrial depositions in a criminal case, procedures for doing so exist in other jurisdictions. *See, e.g.*, FED. R. CRIM. PRO. 15 (authorizing depositions in 'exceptional circumstances'). Additionally, the procedure is not unheard of in North Carolina; in extreme situations, such as when a key witness is ill and cannot travel to trial or is not expected to survive until trial, North Carolina trial judges have exercised their inherent authority and ordered pretrial depositions.").

66. Jessica Smith, *Understanding the New Confrontation Clause Analysis: Crawford, Davis, and Melendez-Diaz*, ADMIN. OF JUST. BULL. No. 2010/2 (Apr. 2010), https://www.sog.unc.edu/sites/www.sog.unc.edu/files/reports/aojb1002.pdf.

67. Smith, *supra* note 66.

68. *See* G.S. 15A-611.

69. State v. Ross, 216 N.C. App. 337, 345 (2011). *See also* Jessica Smith, *Court Holds That Probable Cause Hearing Provides a Prior Opportunity to Cross Examine*, N.C. CRIM. L.: A UNC SCH. OF GOV'T BLOG (Nov. 7, 2011), https://nccriminallaw.sog.unc.edu/court-holds-that-probable-cause-hearing-provides-a-prior-opportunity-to-cross-examine/.

B. POWERS OF ATTORNEY

Many cases of financial exploitation involve a family member, friend, or acquaintance who has secured a power of attorney (POA) from the older adult. Law enforcement officials may find these cases frustrating to investigate and prosecute.[70] It can be challenging to evaluate the validity and scope of the POA documents involved in an exploitation case. For example, the documents may be drafted broadly enough to allow the agent to use the older adult's funds to give the agent and others gifts. An investigator may in such circumstances face the following questions:

- Did the older adult have capacity to sign the document(s)?
- Is the gifting clause valid?
- Did the agent's actions exceed the scope of his or her authority?

Fortunately, it is possible to find answers to these questions, which may allow a criminal case to proceed when appropriate. In February 2019, for example, the Chatham County Sheriff's Office charged an older man's daughter with felony embezzlement and other crimes related to her abuse of a power of attorney.[71]

Because many older adults are completing POAs, and because so many exploitation cases involve them, it is important for law enforcement officials and prosecutors to become comfortable with the law governing POAs and to develop strategies for investigating their misuse and abuse.

TIPS FOR APPROACHING ELDER ABUSE CASES INVOLVING POWERS OF ATTORNEY.

- Remember that the existence of a POA does not automatically preclude prosecution.
- Learn the foundational law governing POAs. Some deficiencies and abuses will be relatively easy to identify.
- Develop relationships with local elder law attorneys. They may be willing to review and advise on the scope and limitations of specific POAs.
- See Chapter 5 for a fuller discussion of POAs.

---

70. As one district attorney explained: "I can't help them when I see [a power of attorney document] . . . To prove a crime in a case like this is a real, real challenge. While these crimes appear suspicious on the face, it does not mean that I can prove a crime." Margulis, *supra* note 53.

71. Blake Hodge, *Chatham County Woman Accused of Embezzling from Elderly Victim*, CHAPELBORO.COM (Feb. 25, 2019), https://chapelboro.com/news/crime/chatham-county-woman-accused-of-embezzling-from-elderly-victim; Donaldson Funeral Home & Cremation, "Lindo Marion Webster," https://www.donaldsonfunerals.com/notices/Lindo-Webster (identifying daughter as Deborah Bowes) (last visited July 19, 2019).

C. LIMITED FINANCIAL HARM

Investigators or prosecutors may choose not to pursue a financial exploitation case because the victim ultimately recovered the funds at the root of the charge. For example,

- a bank or credit card company might have detected the criminal activity and refunded the stolen money to the older adult customer or
- a guardian of the estate might have misused a ward's funds but the ward's estate might have recovered on the guardian's bond, thereby making the estate whole.

Recoveries like these may indicate that the harm caused was minimal or that the exploitation case was resolved. Some may also be concerned that the investment of time and money required for a criminal investigation is not appropriate when the financial loss to the older adult is relatively minimal or the money has already been recovered or restored. However, one should be mindful of a greater community concern, namely, that without criminal consequences for the perpetrator, it seems likely that other older adults will be victimized.

TIPS FOR APPROACHING ELDER ABUSE CASES WHERE LIMITED FINANCIAL HARM RESULTED.

- Become familiar with the civil remedies for restoring assets in financial crimes cases and encourage victims and their families to pursue them.
- Consider using these civil recovery methods to support the criminal financial exploitation case. Gather detailed information from fraud investigation units in financial institutions and, in cases involving guardianship, gather from the clerk of superior court the incompetency and guardianship court files. This information will likely make the criminal case stronger.

D. RELUCTANT OR RECANTING VICTIMS

Victims are often protective of family members and caretakers who are abusing them. For example, a grandchild may be stealing money from a grandparent in order to support a drug habit. The grandparent may not want to get the grandchild in trouble so is reluctant to report the abuse or participate in an investigation.

TIPS FOR APPROACHING ELDER ABUSE CASES INVOLVING RELUCTANT VICTIMS.

- Work with APS to encourage other family members and friends to support the older adult's participation in the criminal investigation and prosecution. A broader network of support may reduce the older adult's perceived dependence on the abuser.
- If necessary, consider using prior inconsistent statements, 911 recordings, or other evidence to impeach the victim.[72]

E. OBTAINING MEDICAL, APS, AND FINANCIAL RECORDS

Compiling records to build a strong elder abuse case can be challenging because some of the most helpful records—medical, APS, and financial—are subject to confidentiality laws that may be interpreted by the record holders as prohibiting or limiting disclosure. The bottom line is that all three types of records may be shared with law enforcement officials, including prosecutors, who are investigating or prosecuting elder abuse. There may be procedures to follow or exceptions that apply but, in general, law enforcement officials should not be discouraged by the need to obtain these types of records.

BECOME FAMILIAR WITH CONFIDENTIALITY LAWS GOVERNING ALL COMPONENTS OF THE ELDER PROTECTION SYSTEM.

For a brief summary of the law governing information sharing between DSS, law enforcement, health care providers, and clerks of court in guardianship proceedings, review "Quick Reference: Information Sharing in Elder Abuse Cases," available at protectadults.sog.unc.edu.

F. COMPLEXITY OF FINANCIAL EXPLOITATION CASES

Cases involving financial exploitation are resource-intensive and sometimes require specific knowledge, such as of financial privacy laws, or expertise. For example, some law enforcement agencies employ or work with forensic accountants. These experts will review financial records to identify patterns and aberrations. The review typically will go back at least one year.[73] Law enforcement officials may find the investigatory demands too daunting when other demands on their time and resources are so high.

72. Greenwood, *supra* note 60, at 46.
73. OFF. OF KY. ATT'Y GEN., *supra* note 57, at, 66.

TIPS FOR HANDLING COMPLEX FINANCIAL RECORDS AND ISSUES IN EXPLOITATION CASES.

- Invest in specialized training for selected investigators and prosecutors.
- Consider developing a regional support model. This could be accomplished informally, by relying on others who have developed specialized expertise, or it could be done more formally through the development of regional centers or teams. Formalized regional initiatives could provide support to local law enforcement officials or, in some cases, assume responsibility for the investigation entirely.

G. FREEZING ASSETS

As discussed above in Section II.B.2, after a person (the defendant) is charged with financial exploitation of an older or disabled adult, the district attorney (DA) may ask the court to freeze the defendant's funds, assets, or property.[74] The goal is to preserve some assets so that the defendant can provide restitution to the victim if the court so orders. There are at least two reasons why this tool may not be used very often.

- The tool is available only after a person has been charged with financial exploitation. In many cases, a perpetrator will sell property or expend funds soon after exploiting an older or disabled adult or as soon as the perpetrator suspects an investigation is underway.
- The law requires the DA to prove that the defendant "is about to or intends to divest himself or herself of assets in a manner that would render the defendant insolvent for purposes of restitution."[75] It may be difficult for a DA to establish this by "clear and convincing" evidence, which is the standard the court will apply in these proceedings.[76]

74. G.S. 14-112.3.
75. G.S. 14-112.3(b).
76. *Id.*

DISCUSS WITH APS THE POTENTIAL BENEFITS OF FREEZING THE OLDER ADULT'S ASSETS EARLY IN AN EXPLOITATION INVESTIGATION.

Communicate early with APS about the possibility of freezing the older adult's assets during the investigation stage. If this step is appropriate and is taken early enough, it may protect the remaining assets of the older adult. For example, if the exploiter has the older adult's power of attorney and suspects that an investigation is underway, the exploiter may try to transfer or expend most or all of the older adult's assets. It may be difficult at this point to recover those funds even if the exploiter is later convicted. See Chapter 2 for more details about the authority of APS to request a court order to freeze the older adult's assets.

H. LIMITATIONS OF ABUSE AND NEGLECT STATUTES

While there is a specific statute addressing abuse and neglect of disabled and older adults (G.S. 14-32.3) and another addressing exploitation (G.S. 14-112.2), a few concepts and terms integral to the laws make them more difficult to use effectively in elder abuse cases.

- **Caretaker.** In order for a person to be guilty of abuse or neglect of an older or disabled adult, the person must be a "caretaker" for the adult. G.S. 14-32.3(d)(1) defines the term to mean a "person who has the responsibility for the care of a disabled or elder adult as a result of family relationship or who has assumed the responsibility for the care of a disabled or elder adult voluntarily or by contract."[77] If a prosecutor is not able to establish such a relationship, this statute will not be useful in addressing abuse or neglect. For example, a son is visiting his father from another state for the weekend. During that time, he slaps his father and his father falls down and breaks his hip. While the son could be charged under another criminal law, such as assault, he could not be charged under the statute specific to abuse of older adults because he is not a caretaker.

- **Injury.** In order for a person to be guilty of abuse or neglect of a disabled or older adult, the adult must have suffered an injury.[78] In some situations, the adult may have been abused but does not ultimately suffer an injury. For example, in one case an in-home nursing assistant was overmedicating an older woman in order to make the woman less alert and sleep more. The nursing assistant could not be charged with domestic abuse of an older adult because the woman did not suffer any injury.[79] In this situation, other crimes may be applicable, such as patient abuse, but the penalties may be less severe.

77. G.S. 14-32.3(d)(1).
78. G.S. 14-32.3(a) (abuse), (b) (neglect).
79. Interview with Lori Wickline, *supra* note 52.

- **Malice aforethought.** The portion of G.S. 14-32.3 addressing abuse, subsection (a), requires that the prosecutor show that the perpetrator had "malice aforethought." That is a high bar, requiring proof that the perpetrator's conduct was done intentionally, either with ill will or hatred or without just cause or excuse.[80]
- **Deception or intimidation.** In order for a person to be guilty of exploitation of an older or disabled adult, the prosecutor must be able to show that the person employed "deception or intimidation" when depriving the adult of funds, assets, or property. This element may be difficult to prove where family members or close friends insinuate themselves into the older adult's life, express love and concern for them, and promise to take care of them. The older adult may even agree to allow the other person to use their funds, assets, or property, not realizing the potential for misuse or exploitation. Often the exploiter does provide some benefit to the older adult, blurring the line between assistance and exploitation. While a situation may look like someone is manipulating or taking advantage of an older adult, there may be insufficient evidence of lying or intimidation to meet the requirements of G.S. 14-112.2.

EXPLORE ALL OPTIONS WHEN DECIDING WHAT KINDS OF CHARGES TO BRING IN CASES INVOLVING OLDER ADULTS.

Do not rely entirely on the elder-specific criminal statutes. Remember that there are many crimes of general applicability that may be more appropriate and useful in a particular case involving elder abuse, neglect, or exploitation. For a summary of some potentially relevant crimes, see Appendix C.

80. *See* State v. Sexton, 357 N.C. 235 (2003). For a discussion of malicious conduct, and other criminal states of mind, see SMITH, *supra* note 10, at 3–10.

I. SCAMS

Some consumer scams that target older adults are local in nature, such as those involving home improvement or storm recovery. These local scams can often be investigated and prosecuted successfully.[81] But many consumer scams originate in other states or countries, making them extremely difficult to investigate. They may involve an older adult wiring money or purchasing gift cards, which can be impossible to trace and recover. As a result, local law enforcement officials often find these investigations frustrating or even futile.

TIPS FOR HANDLING SCAMS INVOLVING OLDER OR DISABLED ADULTS.

- Work with community partners to educate the public and retail outlets about consumer scams.
- Seek assistance from state and federal law enforcement officials, especially for scams that may be multi-state or international. See Chapter 7 for more information about the roles played by other state and federal agencies.

81. *See, e.g.*, Dalisa Robles, *Man Accused of Obtaining $3,500 as Part of Roofing Scam*, WNCT.COM (Aug. 17, 2018), https://www.wnct.com/local-news/man-accused-of-obtaining-3500-as-part-of-roofing-scam/.

Chapter 4
Adult Guardianship

CONTENTS

I. SCOPE OF CHAPTER

This chapter describes adult guardianship, a component of the elder protection system in North Carolina that exists to help individuals who lack capacity to exercise their rights and remain free from abuse.[1] Guardianship is the legal relationship created by a state court that gives a person or entity (the guardian) the authority to make decisions for an individual who lacks capacity (the ward) with respect to the individual's personal affairs, financial affairs, or both.[2] Adult guardianship is governed by state law in G.S. Chapters 35A and 35B and is available for incompetent persons aged 17.5 or older. This chapter focuses on guardianship as it applies to older adults in cases involving elder abuse. It provides an overview of guardianship in North Carolina, including

A. how guardianship protects older adults,
B. who is responsible for guardianship,
C. how the legal process for appointment of a guardian for an older adult works,
D. the role of the guardian appointed by the court, and
E. the role of the court in overseeing the guardianship.

This chapter concludes by identifying some of the common challenges related to guardianship, including the fact that the guardian may be the perpetrator of elder abuse.

II. OVERVIEW OF GUARDIANSHIP

A. HOW DOES GUARDIANSHIP PROTECT OLDER ADULTS?

A family member who is a caregiver for an older adult gets access to the older adult's bank account and withdraws money for her own benefit. She also leaves the older adult alone for long periods of time and the older adult becomes dehydrated and malnourished. A person concerned for the older adult wants to take action to stop the abuse and support the older adult. Or a county department of social services (DSS) in response to an adult protective services report is required to take action to provide protective services to the older adult.[3] The older adult is unable to take action on his own behalf or consent to protective services because he lacks capacity. There is no other surrogate decision maker, such as an agent under a power of attorney, authorized to act on the older adult's behalf. Or the agent authorized to act on behalf of the older adult is the perpetrator of the abuse.

Guardianship is a tool that may be used to stop such ongoing abuse and safeguard against future abuse. To appoint a guardian for an older adult, two proceedings are filed before the court: an incompetency proceeding and a guardianship proceeding. In

1. Chapter 35A, Section 1201, of the North Carolina General Statutes (hereinafter G.S.).
2. JOHN L. SAXON, NORTH CAROLINA GUARDIANSHIP MANUAL § 1.3, at 4 (2008).
3. For further discussion of the role of the county department of social services (DSS) in providing protective services to disabled adults, including disabled older adults, refer to Chapter 2 of this manual.

the incompetency proceeding, the court[4] determines, based on the evidence presented, whether the older adult is incompetent.[5] The term "incompetent adult" is defined under North Carolina law as an adult or emancipated minor who lacks sufficient capacity to

1. manage his or her own affairs or
2. make or communicate important decisions concerning his or her person, family, or property.[6]

If the court finds that an older adult is incompetent, the court must appoint a guardian to act on his or her behalf.[7] The court's role during the guardianship proceeding is to determine (1) the type of guardianship needed by the older adult based on the older adult's capacity, assets, needs, and liabilities and (2) who can most suitably serve as guardian.[8] There are three main types of guardians under North Carolina law: a guardian of the person (GOP), a guardian of the estate (GOE), and a general guardian (GG).[9] (See Table 4.1.) If there is or reasonably appears to be an imminent or foreseeable risk of harm to the older adult or to the older adult's property that requires immediate intervention, and if there is reasonable cause to believe that the older adult is incompetent, the court may appoint a temporary guardian, known as an interim guardian, to act on the older adult's behalf while the incompetency proceeding is pending before the court.[10]

Table 4.1. **Primary Types of Guardians for Adults in North Carolina**

GUARDIAN TYPE	RELEVANT STATUTE (G.S.)	NATURE OF GUARDIANSHIP
Guardian of the Person	35A-1202(10)	A guardian appointed solely for the purpose of performing duties relating to the care, custody, and control of a ward.
Guardian of the Estate	35A-1202(9)	A guardian appointed solely for the purpose of managing the property, estate, and business affairs of a ward.
General Guardian	35A-1202(7)	A guardian of both the estate and the person.

4. While the older adult who is the subject of the incompetency proceeding has a right to a jury trial, in practice, the decision of whether the adult is incompetent or not is most frequently made by the court. G.S. 35A-1110 (establishing the right to a jury trial in an incompetency proceeding). The right to a jury trial is discussed further in Section II.C.1.g, *infra*.

5. G.S. 35A-1112(c), (d).

6. G.S. 35A-1101(7). The older adult's lack of capacity may be because of a condition such as dementia, mental illness, intellectual disability, autism, inebriety, or other cause or condition. *See id.* However, evidence of a specific condition or diagnosis is not required for a court to find that an older adult is incompetent, and evidence of a specific condition or diagnosis is not determinative of incompetency. JOAN G. BRANNON & ANN E. ANDERSON, NORTH CAROLINA CLERK OF SUPERIOR COURT PROCEDURES MANUAL 85.1 (2012) (hereinafter CSC MANUAL).

7. G.S. 35A-1120.

8. G.S. 35A-1212(a). If the court determines that the nature and extent of the older adult's capacity justifies ordering a limited guardianship, the court may do so. *Id.*

9. G.S. 35A-1202(10), (9), (7).

10. Refer to Section II.C.3.b, *infra*, for a discussion of interim guardianship.

Once a guardian is appointed, the guardian has a duty to take actions, depending on the type of guardianship created, to protect the older adult and the older adult's property from abuse.[11] The court oversees the guardianship to ensure that the guardian carries out his or her duties.[12] This includes reviewing and responding to reports filed with the court, such as status reports filed by a GOP or accountings filed by a GOE. If the court detects abuse based on information it receives, the court has legal tools available to stop the abuse and protect the older adult. Examples include holding a status report hearing, modifying the guardianship, or removing the guardian.[13]

PRACTICE NOTE

When an Older Adult May Need a Guardian to Protect against or Remedy Abuse

The older adult is **incompetent** and . . .

- has no power of attorney (POA), health care power of attorney, or other surrogate decision-maker authorized to act on the adult's behalf.
- is the victim of financial exploitation and continues to pay money over to perpetrators of scams.
- the adult's agent under a POA misuses the adult's property or fails/is unable to carry out the duties of the agent under the POA and there is no successor agent identified in the POA.
- the agent under a health care POA fails/is unable to act on the adult's behalf or acts in a way that is inconsistent with the health care POA.
- the family members or caretakers of the adult argue over the adult's care and subject the adult to emotional abuse, placing the adult in the middle of a push-and-pull of decision-making, and a guardian is needed to provide consistency and certainty to the decisions made on the adult's behalf.
- has the financial means to pay for care or services but is unable to consent to services or care that would help to rectify the abuse.
- is unable to maintain a safe and accessible home environment.
- is unable to manage medications and/or seek health care treatment and has no other supports available to help guide health care decisions and care.
- is the victim of physical, emotional, sexual, or verbal abuse and is unable to stop or report the abuse.

11. Refer to Section II.D, *infra*, for a discussion of the role of the guardian.
12. G.S. 35A-1203(b).
13. Refer to Section II.E, *infra*, for further discussion of court oversight of the guardian.

B. WHO IS RESPONSIBLE FOR GUARDIANSHIP?

Various actors have roles in the legal process of determining incompetency and appointing a guardian for an allegedly incompetent older adult, including

- the clerk of superior court,
- the petitioner,
- the respondent/ward,
- the guardian ad litem attorney,
- next of kin of the older adult and other interested persons,
- the applicant for appointment of guardian, and
- guardian(s).

Unlike civil actions, where the parties are frequently adversarial and focused on their own interests, incompetency and guardianship proceedings are about the older adult, the capacity of the older adult, and what is in the best interests of an incompetent older adult. Guardianship can be effective in protecting incompetent older adults from abuse when each actor fulfills his or her legally prescribed role. Below is a brief overview of each of these actors' roles in these proceedings.

1. CLERK OF SUPERIOR COURT

The clerk of superior court is the judicial official who presides over incompetency and adult guardianship proceedings in North Carolina.[14] The duties of clerks include both administrative as well as judicial functions.[15] These judicial functions include adjudicating incompetence and appointing and overseeing guardians for adults.[16] The clerk decides all issues of fact and law raised in the incompetency and adult guardianship proceedings, unless there is a jury trial in the incompetency proceeding (discussed more in Section II.C.1.g, *infra*) or the clerk is disqualified from hearing either proceeding.[17]

Each of North Carolina's 100 counties has an elected clerk of superior court. Each clerk has a staff of assistant and deputy clerks. Assistant clerks are authorized to perform all of the duties and functions of the clerk.[18] This is unlike deputy clerks, who, except in limited criminal matters, only perform ministerial acts of the clerk.[19] An assistant clerk has the same judicial authority as the clerk and may preside over and enter orders as the judge in incompetency and guardianship proceedings.[20]

---

14. G.S. 35A-1103(a); 35A-1203(a).
15. *See* G.S. 1-13 (jurisdiction of clerk); 7A-40 (judicial powers of clerk); -109 (record-keeping procedures); -103 (authority of clerk of superior court).
16. G.S. 35A-1103(a); -1203.
17. G.S. 1-301.2(d), (g)(1); 1-301.3(b); 7A-104.
18. G.S. 7A-102(b).
19. *Id.*
20. G.S. 7A-102(b), -103.

Figure 4.1. **Who May Hear a Guardianship Case in North Carolina?**

Clerk of Superior Court	√
Assistant Clerk of Superior Court	√
Deputy Clerk of Superior Court	X
Superior Court Judge*	X
District Court Judge	X
Magistrate	X

* A superior court judge may hear the case if the clerk is disqualified under G.S. 7A-104; also, a superior court judge hears an appeal of the clerk's decision.

Under North Carolina law, a clerk's office may have no fewer than five staff positions plus the elected clerk.[21] There is no statutory maximum. As a result, some small counties, such as Perquimans, may have six people in the clerk's office, while other larger counties, like Mecklenburg, may have more than 200 people in the office. The staff in smaller counties tends to be comprised of generalists who have to fulfill every role in the clerk's office. The staff in larger counties tends to be more specialized. A clerk in a smaller county may preside over an incompetency and adult guardianship hearing as the judge, accept papers for filing at the front counter, and staff the district or superior court courtroom all in the same day. In many larger counties, there are assistant clerks designated as hearing officers whose sole role it is to preside over court proceedings such as those involving incompetency and guardianship.

Practices with respect to incompetency and guardianship proceedings differ across the state depending on the needs and demands of a particular clerk's office. Hearings may be held in a courtroom, a conference room, or a clerk's office. The clerk may wear a robe or dress in business casual clothes when presiding over a hearing. Regardless, the clerk is the judge in the proceedings, and valid orders of the clerk have the full force and effect as if they were entered by a district or superior court judge.[22]

2. PETITIONER

The petitioner brings an incompetency proceeding by filing a petition. The petition may be filed by "any person."[23] "Person" in this context includes individuals such as family members, caregivers, friends, or neighbors. It also includes entities such as nursing homes, county departments of social services (DSS), hospitals, or financial institutions.

There is no requirement that a person have a certain degree of kinship or particular relationship with the older adult to file an incompetency petition. This means that a low barrier exists to getting these types of proceeding before the court, which may be particularly important in cases involving elder abuse. For example, a family member may be

21. G.S. 7A-102(a).
22. *See* G.S. 7A-103.
23. G.S. 35A-1105.

the one who is financially exploiting an older adult who lacks capacity. A neighbor, friend, or DSS could file an incompetency petition and seek the appointment of a guardian to cut off the financial exploitation by the family member.

The petitioner may, but is not required to, apply to be appointed as the guardian for the older adult. Someone may have concerns about the abuse of an older adult and seek the appointment of a guardian to protect the adult, but he or she may be unwilling or unable to serve as guardian. If the petitioner does not want to apply to be a guardian for the older adult, the petitioner may recommend another person or entity in the petition to serve as guardian.

KEY TERMS

*A **petitioner** files an incompetency proceeding against a **respondent**, who is the alleged incompetent person.*

3. RESPONDENT/WARD

The respondent is the person who is alleged to be incompetent in a proceeding filed before the clerk.[24] If the respondent is adjudicated incompetent and a guardian is appointed by a court, the respondent is then referred to as the ward.[25]

KEY TERM

*Once the respondent is adjudicated incompetent and a guardian is appointed on his or her behalf, the respondent is known as the **ward**.*

4. GUARDIAN AD LITEM ATTORNEY

Every older adult who is a respondent in an incompetency proceeding is entitled to be represented by counsel of his or her choice or by an appointed guardian ad litem attorney (GAL).[26] Upon the filing of a petition, the court appoints a GAL to represent the older adult.[27] Clerks typically use N.C. Administrative Office of the Courts (AOC) Form AOC-SP-201, "Notice of Hearing on Incompetence/Motion in the Cause and Order Appointing Guardian ad Litem," to do this. The GAL is required to personally visit the respondent as soon as possible after being appointed by the court.[28] The GAL represents the older adult until the GAL is discharged by the court, the petition is dismissed, or a guardian is appointed.[29]

24. G.S. 35A-1101(15).
25. G.S. 35A-1101(17).
26. G.S. 35A-1107(a).
27. *Id.*
28. G.S. 35A-1107(b).
29. G.S. 35A-1107(a), (b).

RESOURCE

The *North Carolina Guardianship Manual* is a free online resource available from the UNC School of Government. It discusses the role and responsibilities of the GAL. To access the manual, visit https://defendermanuals.sog.unc.edu/defender-manual/5.

The GAL serves a dual role. The GAL's primary role is to make every reasonable effort to determine the older adult's wishes regarding the incompetency proceeding and any proposed guardianship.[30] The GAL must present those wishes to the court at all relevant stages of the proceedings.[31] The GAL also makes recommendations to the clerk regarding the older adult's best interests to the extent those recommendations differ from the older adult's wishes.[32]

The appointment of the GAL does not preclude the older adult from hiring his or her own attorney.[33] If the older adult does choose to hire an attorney, the GAL may be discharged by the court.[34] In practice, the court rarely discharges the GAL.

The GAL, as the respondent's counsel, plays an important role in protecting against and preventing elder abuse. Through his or her representation of the respondent, the GAL may (1) identify and take action to protect the respondent if the respondent is the subject of abuse, such as filing a motion for interim guardianship, and (2) investigate and screen potential guardians to enable the court to appoint a guardian who will not later subject the older adult to abuse.

5. NEXT OF KIN OF THE OLDER ADULT AND OTHER INTERESTED PERSONS

Every petition filed initiating an incompetency proceeding must contain, to the extent known, the name, address, and county of residence of the older adult's next of kin[35] and other persons known to have an interest in the proceeding, such as neighbors, friends, employees at a care facility, or other persons who play an important role in the older adult's life.[36] Next of kin and other interested persons often play an important role in providing a complete picture of the older adult's capacity, assets, needs, and liabilities to the court. A petitioner may present only one side of the story or, in extreme cases, actually mislead or hide information from the court. Next of kin and other interested persons may have critical information the court needs to assess the older adult's capacity and ensure that a guardian is appointed who will keep the older adult safe from abuse.

30. G.S. 35A-1107(b).
31. *Id.*
32. *Id.*
33. G.S. 35A-1107(a). *See also* N.C. State Bar, Formal Ethics Op. 16, Representation of Client Resisting an Incompetency Petition (Jan. 15, 1999), https://www.ncbar.gov/for-lawyers/ethics/adopted-opinions/98-formal-ethics-opinion-16/?opinionSearchTerm=Copy%20file.
34. *Id.*
35. The term "next of kin" is not defined in the law related to incompetency and adult guardianship proceedings. However, it has been construed in other contexts to mean heirs or persons entitled to inherit property from a decedent who did not leave a will. CSC MANUAL, at 85.4.
36. G.S. 35A-1106(5).

6. APPLICANT FOR APPOINTMENT OF GUARDIAN

Any person or entity that files an application for guardianship is known as the applicant and is a party to the guardianship proceeding.[37] Frequently, the applicant is a family member, such as an adult child, or a friend of the older adult. There may be more than one applicant in the guardianship proceeding or there may be no applicants—or no suitable applicants—in the proceeding. In the absence of a suitable applicant, the clerk of superior court will likely appoint DSS or a corporation as the older adult's GOP and a local attorney or public guardian as GOE if the court determines that the older adult is incompetent and needs both a GOP and a GOE.

KEY TERMS

*An **applicant** files an application to be appointed as a guardian for the **respondent**.*

7. GUARDIAN(S)

The guardian is appointed by the court to make decisions on behalf of an incompetent older adult. After a petition is filed and before the formal adjudication of incompetence, the clerk may appoint an interim guardian of the person, an interim guardian of the estate, or an interim general guardian to immediately intervene if (1) there is or reasonably appears to be an imminent or foreseeable risk of harm to the older adult or to the older adult's property that requires immediate interverntion and (2) there is reasonable cause to believe that the older adult is incompetent.[38]

After an older adult is adjudicated incompetent, the court has the discretion to appoint a guardian of the person, guardian of the estate, or a general guardian, depending on the capacity, assets, needs, and liabilities of the older adult. If the older adult has capacity with regard to certain decisions, the court may order a limited guardianship.[39] A limited guardianship allows an older adult to retain certain rights and privileges.[40] For example, a clerk may order that the older adult retains the right to make decisions related to expenditures of up to $50 a week or that the older adult retains the right to make decisions about what church to attend or who may visit him or her. The court may appoint a limited guardian of the person, a limited guardian of the estate, or a limited general guardian for an incompetent older adult.

C. HOW DOES GUARDIANSHIP WORK?

There are two separate court proceedings involved in the appointment of a guardian: an incompetency proceeding and a guardianship proceeding. As a practical matter, however, the adjudication of incompetency and appointment of a guardian are often combined into

37. G.S. 35A-1210; SAXON, *supra* note 2, at § 4.1, p. 46.
38. G.S. 35A-1114.
39. G.S. 35A-1212(a).
40. *Id.*

Figure 4.2. **Overview of the Court Procedure to Appoint a Guardian for an Incompetent Adult**

Filing of **Petition for Adjudication of Incompetence and Application for Appointment of Guardian or Limited Guardian** (Form AOC-SP-200)
- If appropriate, file **Motion For Appointment of Interim Guardian** (Form SP-198)

Appointment of GAL attorney (Form SP-201)

Service of **Petition and Application** and, if applicable, Service of **Motion for Appointment of Interim Guardian**

Court hearing before the clerk on interim guardianship, if applicable

Entry of **Order on Motion for Appointment of Interim Guardian**, if applicable (Form AOC-SP-900)

Court hearing on **Petition and Application**

Court enters:
Order on Petition for Adjudication of Incompetence (Form AOC-SP 202)
and
Order on Application for Appointment of Guardian
(Form AOC-E-406)

Application for Letters of Guardianship for an Incompetent Person filed (Form AOC-E-206)

GOE or GG **posts bond** (Form AOC-E-401)

Guardian **takes an oath/affirmation** (Form AOC-E-400)

Court enters **order authorizing issuance of letters** (Form AOC-E-402)

Court issues **guardianship letters**
- **Letters of Appointment Guardian of the Person** (Form AOC-E-408)
- **Letters of Appointment Limited Guardian of the Person** (Form AOC-E-418)
- **Letters of Appointment Guardian of the Estate** (Form AOC-E-407)
- **Letters of Appointment Limited Guardian of the Estate** (Form AOC-E-417)
- **Letters of Appointment General Guardian** (Form AOC-E-413)
- **Letters of Appointment Limited General Guardian** (Form AOC-E-419)

one hearing before the clerk. The subsections below provide an overview of each of these proceedings, with particular emphasis placed on opportunities to protect older adults from abuse. While the process may vary from case to case, Figure 4.2 presents a snapshot of some of the key steps in the process for appointing a guardian.

1. INCOMPETENCY PROCEEDING

a. Filing the Petition

The incompetency proceeding is initiated by the filing of a verified petition.[41] Through this petition, a person (the petitioner) is asking the court to determine whether an older adult (the respondent) is incompetent.[42] Typically, the petitioner completes and files N.C. Administrative Office of the Courts (AOC) Form AOC-SP-200, "Petition for Adjudication of Incompetence and Application for Appointment of Guardian or Limited Guardian," to initiate the action. The form satisfies state law requirements for initiating an incompetency proceeding. A petitioner may also write his or her own petition and file it to initiate the proceeding, provided the writing meets minimum legal requirements. While the AOC form is not required, petitioners rarely initiate proceedings without using it.

b. Notice of Hearing; Timing of the Hearing

Within five days after the filing of a petition, the clerk of superior court must issue a written notice of hearing.[43] Clerks typically use Form AOC-SP-201, "Notice of Hearing on Incompetence/Motion in the Cause and Order Appointing Guardian ad Litem," to do this. The notice must include the date, time, and place for the hearing.[44]

The hearing must take place not less than ten but no more than thirty days from the service of the petition on the older adult/respondent, unless the clerk extends the time for good cause, such as to allow time for mediation or for the completion of a medical, mental health, social work, or other multidisciplinary evaluation.[45] This time frame (from the filing of the action to the hearing) is much shorter than other court proceedings, such as civil actions, that may take up to two years or more to complete. It ensures that where an older adult is incompetent and needs the assistance of a guardian, one can be appointed relatively quickly. This is particularly true where there is no dispute as to the older adult's incapacity, such as where the older adult has advanced dementia. In cases involving ongoing elder abuse, the ability to go from the filing of a petition to a hearing within a short period of time is critical. If the thirty-day deadline must be extended for good cause, there are other tools, such as interim guardianship, that may be employed to stop or protect an older adult from abuse while the incompetency proceeding is pending. Interim guardianship is discussed further below.

41. G.S. 35A-1105.
42. *Id.*
43. G.S. 35A-1108(a).
44. *Id.*
45. *Id.*

c. Service of the Petition

The incompetency petition and the notice of hearing must be served personally on the respondent.[46] Because the use of private process servers is very limited in North Carolina, personal service is completed on the respondent by the sheriff in most cases.[47] Service is not proper if the notice and petition are sent by FedEx, UPS, or regular mail or left with a family member at the respondent's home. This heightened requirement of service on the respondent ensures that the respondent knows of the proceeding and knows the location, date, and time of the hearing. It reflects the significant impact an adjudication of incompetency has on a person's rights to make decisions about his or her life and property. The return of service located on the back of the Form AOC-SP-201, "Notice of Hearing," is typically completed to show proof of service on the respondent.

PRACTICE NOTE

For an older adult who may never have had an interaction with the court system before the filing of the incompetency petition, service by the sheriff may cause fear or anxiety. The petitioner may wish to speak with the sheriff's office prior to service on the older adult/respondent so that the petitioner may be present when the petition is served. The petitioner may also request that the sheriff send a plain-clothes officer to serve the older adult. These practices may minimize the older adult's fear and anxiety upon being served by the sheriff.

The GAL appointed to represent the respondent in the proceeding must be served with copies of the petition and notice of hearing in accordance with Rule 4 of the N.C. Rules of Civil Procedure.[48] In practice, the GAL often accepts service by signing the back of the Form AOC-SP-201.

The petitioner is required to serve copies of the notice of hearing and the petition on the respondent's next of kin identified in the petition and on any other persons the clerk may designate.[49] If, for example, the GAL determines through the GAL's representation of the older adult that the petitioner left next of kin or other interested persons off the petition and did not serve them with the notice of hearing, the GAL may request that the clerk direct the petitioner to serve them with notice. The petitioner completes service by mailing the copies by first-class mail within five days after the filing of the petition, unless the next of kin or other interested person accepted notice.[50] The petitioner files proof of service by filing a certificate with the court.[51] Typically, the petitioner uses Form AOC-SP-207, "Certificate of Service (Incompetent Proceeding)." Subsequent notices to next of kin and other persons are sent by the clerk via first-class mail.[52]

---

46. G.S. 35A-1109.
47. *See* Locklear v. Cummings, 822 S.E.2d 587, 593 (N.C. Ct. App. 2018); N.C. State Bar v. Hunter, 217 N.C. App. 216, 224 (2011). *See also* G.S. 1A-1, Rule 4(h), (h1).
48. G.S. 35A-1109.
49. *Id.*
50. *Id.*
51. *Id.*
52. *Id.*

d. Evidence at the Hearing

At the hearing on the incompetency petition, the burden is on the petitioner to present testimony and other evidence regarding the older adult/respondent's incapacity.[53] Both the petitioner and the respondent are entitled to present evidence.[54] Evidence related to the respondent's capacity typically includes testimony from the respondent, the petitioner, next of kin, and other interested persons. Additional evidence may include medical, mental health, and substance abuse records; adult protective services (APS) records; and financial records. The guardian ad litem attorney (GAL) presents the older adult's express wishes and may make recommendations concerning the respondent's best interests if those interests differ from the older adult's express wishes.[55]

The evidence may include a court-ordered multidisciplinary evaluation (MDE).[56] Any party may request, and the court may order, an MDE of the older adult.[57] A request for an MDE must be made in writing and filed with the clerk of superior court within ten days after service of the incompetency petition on the older adult.[58] The court may order an MDE at any time.[59] An MDE is an important tool that assists the court in (1) determining the nature and extent of the older adult's disability and (2) developing an appropriate guardianship plan and program.[60] The MDE may contain a current psychological, social work, and medical evaluation or other evaluations as directed by the court.[61] The MDE may be helpful in identifying areas in which the older adult is vulnerable to abuse, such as if a decline in an older adult's cognitive capacity tends to make him or her less able to identify scams or renders the older adult dependent upon a perpetrator of abuse.[62]

e. Respondent's Presence at the Hearing

The older adult (the respondent in this context) has a right to attend the hearing, but the respondent's presence is not required.[63] Frequently, the respondent does not appear at the hearing. This may be due to a number of factors, including inability to travel to the courthouse due to incapacity or other disability; lack of access to transportation; or fear, given that it may be the first time the older adult has ever been involved in a court proceeding. If the respondent is unable to make it to the hearing, the court may inquire as to whether he or she wants to be at the hearing but is being prevented from being there by something or

53. CSC MANUAL, at 85.15.
54. G.S. 35A-1112(b).
55. G.S. 35A-1107(b).
56. G.S. 35A-1111(e).
57. G.S. 35A-1111(a).
58. *Id.*
59. *Id.*.
60. *Id.*
61. *See* G.S. 35A-1111(c).
62. For further discussion of MDEs in incompetency and adult guardianship proceedings, refer to Meredith Smith, *Ordering, Preparing, and Paying for Multidisciplinary Evaluations in Incompetency and Adult Guardianship Proceedings*, SOC. SERVS. L. BULL. No. 47 (Dec. 2016), https://www.sog.unc.edu/publications/bulletins/ordering-preparing-and-paying-multidisciplinary-evaluations-incompetency-and-adult-guardianship.
63. SAXON, *supra* note 2, at § 5.11, p.64.

someone. The court may continue the hearing to allow the respondent to be present. The court may make an accommodation to provide the older adult access to the courthouse. Each North Carolina courthouse has a disability access coordinator who can assist the public with questions about and requests for accommodations.[64] The court may, instead, hold the hearing where the older adult is located, such as a mental health facility or adult care home.

PRACTICE NOTE

A list of disability access coordinators in each county is available at https://www.nccourts.gov/documents/publications/disability-access-coordinator.

The respondent's appearance at the hearing is important because it enables the court to observe and hear from the respondent to help the court make a determination as to the respondent's capacity. Often a clerk will ask questions of the respondent to better understand the nature and extent of the respondent's lack of capacity.[65] At times an older adult with dementia may begin a conversation in a coherent manner but then start to repeat himself or herself and forget commonly known information or what he or she just told the court.

The respondent's presence also helps ensure that his or her express wishes are made known to the court. This includes, for example, where the respondent wants to live, activities in which the respondent wants to participate, the type of guardian needed, and who the respondent wants to be appointed as guardian.

Finally, the respondent's presence at the hearing can be helpful because it gives the court an opportunity to look for signs of elder abuse. For example, the court will look for bruises on the respondent or for other signs of physical abuse, such as sprains or burns; signs of emotional abuse, such as acting in a frightened or withdrawn manner; and signs of neglect, such as poor hygiene, dirty clothes, unkempt hair, or absence of necessary aids, such as a walker, a hearing aid, or an oxygen tank. Note that if the older adult has concerns about testifying in open court, the older adult, the older adult's counsel, or the GAL may request that the court close the hearing. Upon such request, the court must close the hearing to the public so that only those persons directly involved in or testifying at the hearing are present.[66] This may be particularly helpful in cases where the perpetrator of the abuse appears at the hearing as a means of intimidating the older adult or in order to continue exerting influence over the older adult.

64. N.C. Jud. Branch, *Disability Access*, NCCOURTS.GOV, https://www.nccourts.gov/help-topics/disability-and-special-needs/disability-access (describing how to request reasonable accommodation in court proceedings).

65. The court has the authority to call and interrogate witnesses. G.S. 8C-1, Rule 614.

66. G.S. 35A-1112(a).

f. Burden of Proof

The burden of proof, or standard the petitioner must meet to prove the claim that the respondent is incompetent, is *clear, cogent, and convincing evidence*.[67] This is a high standard. It is higher than a preponderance of the evidence, typically seen as 51 percent or more likely than not, but not quite as high as beyond a reasonable doubt, the standard most frequently applied in criminal proceedings.

Figure 4.3. **Burdens of Proof under North Carolina Law**

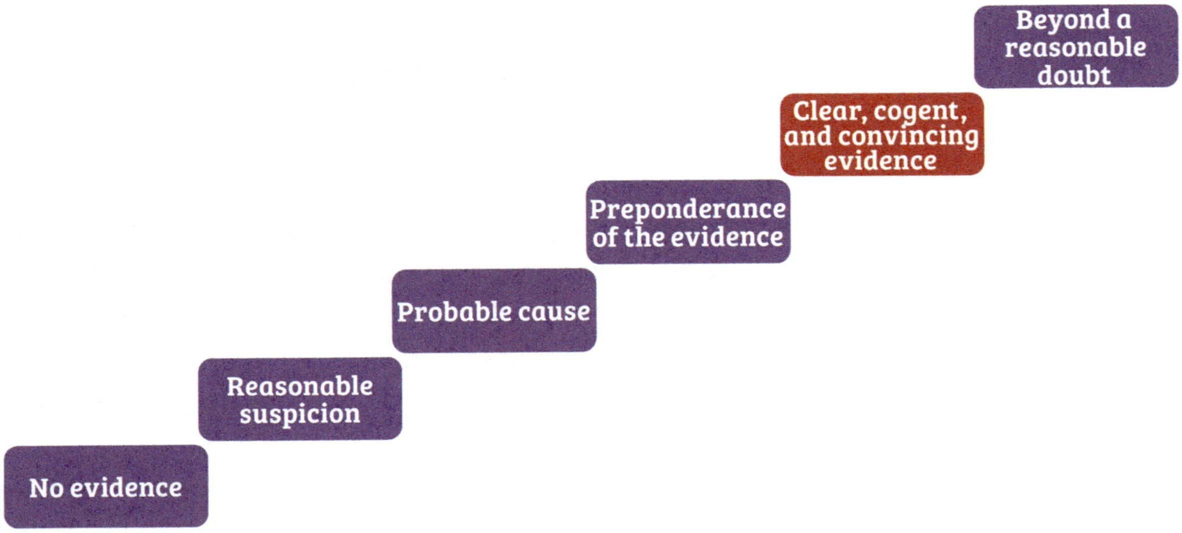

g. Right to Jury Trial

Typically, the decision about a respondent's competency is made by the clerk. However, a respondent has a right to a jury trial on the issue of his or her competency.[68] A jury trial may be requested by the respondent, the respondent's counsel, or the GAL.[69] Failure to request a jury trial constitutes a waiver of the right.[70]

h. Order

If the clerk or a jury does not find, based on the evidence presented, that the respondent is incompetent, then the court enters an order dismissing the proceeding.[71] If the court or a jury finds that the respondent is incompetent, then the court enters an order to that effect.[72] The court may also find that the respondent is incompetent to a limited extent and appoint a limited guardian.

67. CSC MANUAL, at 85.15; G.S. 35A-1112(d).
68. G.S. 35A-1110.
69. *Id.*
70. *Id.*
71. G.S. 35A-1112(c).
72. G.S. 35A-1112(d).

Figure 4.4. **Excerpt from Form AOC-SP-202, Order on Petition for Adjudication of Incompetence**

ORDER

☐ The clerk/the jury did not find the respondent to be incompetent by clear, cogent, and convincing evidence and it is ORDERED that the proceeding is dismissed.

☐ No hearing was held due to the death of the respondent and it is ORDERED that the proceeding is dismissed.

It is adjudged that:

☐ the respondent is incompetent.

☐ the respondent is incompetent to a limited extent.

☐ It is ORDERED that a guardian be appointed by this court.

2. GUARDIANSHIP PROCEEDING AND APPOINTMENT OF THE GUARDIAN

An incompetent older adult who is not able to act effectively on his or her own behalf has a right to a qualified, responsible guardian.[73] Once the court adjudicates an older adult incompetent or incompetent to a limited extent, it must appoint a guardian to act on the older adult's behalf.[74] The guardianship proceeding is initiated by an application and is in the nature of an estate matter.[75] The application may be joined with or filed subsequent to the petition for the adjudication of incompetence.[76] That petition and the application for the appointment of a guardian are, in practice, typically filed together. Form AOC-SP-200 is both a petition for adjudication of incompetence and an application for guardianship.[77]

During the guardianship proceeding, the court examines both the type of guardian needed by the older adult and who to appoint as a guardian. Once the guardian is appointed, the guardian must then qualify and obtain letters of appointment from the court. The "letters" evidence the guardian's authority to act on behalf of the older adult.

a. Type of Guardianship

In the guardianship proceeding, the court has a duty to make inquiries and to receive evidence necessary to determine the type of guardian to appoint.[78] This is different in each case and depends on the older adult's capacity, needs, assets, and liabilities. For example, if the older adult does not own any property and the only income he receives is from a federal benefit program, such as Social Security, then the clerk may decide to only appoint a guardian of the person because the adult's assets (or lack thereof) do not warrant appointing a guardian of the estate, who will have to post a bond and file annual accountings. The federal benefit may be managed by a representative payee appointed by the federal agency in charge of distributing the benefit, such as the Social Security

73. G.S. 35A-1201(a)(2).
74. G.S. 35A-1120.
75. *In re* Winstead, 189 N.C. App. 145, 151 (2008).
76. G.S. 35A-1210.
77. *See* N.C. ADMIN. OFF. OF THE CTS. (AOC), Form SP-200, "Petition for Adjudication of Incompetence and Application for Appointment of Guardian or Limited Guardian," available at https://www.nccourts.gov/assets/documents/forms/sp200-en_0.pdf?fENlxiBSNjB5NUdaKi9J.d4H04dFAjIU.
78. G.S. 35A-1212(a).

Administration. The three main types of guardians—guardian of the estate, guardian of the person, and general guardian—and the different roles of each are discussed further in Section II.D, *infra*.

b. Selection of a Suitable Guardian

The court has a duty to make inquiries and to receive evidence it deems necessary to determine who can most suitably serve as guardian for an older adult.[79] An individual, a corporation, or a county department of social services (DSS) director or assistant director (known as a disinterested public agent guardian) may be appointed as guardian for an older adult in North Carolina.[80] The clerk of superior court must by statute consider who to appoint in a certain order of priority. Specific preferences are given to certain recommendations made in a will, power of attorney, or health care power of attorney. Next, a general preference is given to individuals, then to corporations, and finally, as a last resort, to DSS.[81] Notwithstanding the priority set out in the statute, the clerk is always charged with basing the appointment of the guardian on the best interests of the ward.[82]

PRACTICE NOTE

Appointing a Guardian: Order of Priority

1. An individual recommended under certain wills (G.S. 35A-1212.1) or a nominee under a power of attorney (G.S. 32C-1-108(a)) or a health care power of attorney (G.S. 32A-22)
2. An individual
3. A corporation
4. A disinterested public agent (DSS)

To determine who can most suitably serve as guardian, the clerk may consider recommendations of next of kin and other persons. Even if it is clear that the older adult lacks capacity, the court may still order a multidisciplinary evaluation (see Section II.C.1.d, *supra*) to help with issues related to the guardianship proceeding, including a recommended guardianship plan and program, an evaluation of the suitability of a prospective guardian, and recommendations as to an appropriate party to serve as guardian.[83]

---

79. G.S. 35A-1212(a)(3). The clerk has exclusive authority to appoint the guardian; the issue may not be determined by a jury. *Id.* § 35A-1203. *See also id.* §§ 1-301.3(a), (b).

80. G.S. 35A-1213, -1214. The only disinterested public agent qualified to serve as a guardian in North Carolina is the director or assistant director of a county department of social services (DSS). *Id.* §§ 35A-1214; -1202(4). The DSS director or assistant director is appointed as guardian by the court in its order, but a social worker employed by the county DSS carries out the day-to-day powers and duties of guardian.

81. G.S. 35A-1214 (general order of priority); 35A-1212.1 (effect of a recommendation in a will); 32C-1-108(a) (effect of a nomination of a guardian in a power of attorney); 32A-22 (effect of a nomination of a guardian of the person in a health care power of attorney).

82. G.S. 35A-1214.

83. G.S. 35A-1111; -1212(b), (c).

The risk of abuse of an older adult under guardianship may be reduced by effective court screening of potential guardians.[84] This includes

1. appointing an effective GAL to represent the older adult who conducts civil and criminal background checks on potential guardians and takes other steps to screen potential guardians, such as interviewing the potential guardian prior to the hearing;
2. asking any potential guardian at the hearing questions similar to those questions set out in the *Preventing, Identifying, and Responding to Elder Abuse in Incompetency and Adult Guardianship Cases: A Bench Card for North Carolina Clerks of Superior Court*, available at protectadults.sog.unc.edu;
3. asking the older adult at the hearing who he or she wants to serve as guardian by employing interviewing techniques and tips similar to those set out in Appendix B; and
4. asking next of kin and other interested persons present at the hearing questions about the potential guardian's relationship with the older adult.

c. Qualification of a Guardian

After the clerk of superior court adjudicates incompetence and appoints a guardian, the guardian appointed by the clerk's order must then qualify with the court to obtain letters. The guardian initiates this process by submitting an application for letters (Form AOC-E-206). The form application contains a preliminary inventory—a listing/statement of the assets and liabilities of the ward—that is completed if a person is to act as a guardian with authority over the ward's property.[85]

Figure 4.5. **Steps to Qualify as a Guardian**

1. Guardian applies for letters (Form AOC-E-206) and submits bond, if GOE or GG (Form AOC-E-401)
2. Guardian takes an oath/affirmation (Form AOC-E-400)
3. Clerk enters order authorizing issuance of letters (Form AOC-E-402) and the clerk issues letters depending on the type of guardian appointed:
   - Letters of Appointment Guardian of the Person: Form AOC-E-408
   - Letters of Appointment Limited Guardian of the Person: Form AOC-E-418
   - Letters of Appointment Guardian of the Estate: Form AOC-E-407
   - Letters of Appointment Limited Guardian of the Estate: Form AOC-E-417
   - Letters of Appointment General Guardian: Form AOC-E-413
   - Letters of Appointment Limited General Guardian: Form AOC-E-419

84. U.S. GOV'T ACCOUNTABILITY OFF., GAO-17-33, ELDER ABUSE: THE EXTENT OF ABUSE BY GUARDIANS IS UNKNOWN, BUT SOME MEASURES EXIST TO HELP PROTECT OLDER ADULTS 19–20 (2016) (hereinafter GAO ELDER ABUSE REPORT).

85. AOC, Form E-206, "Application for Letters," available at https://www.nccourts.gov/documents/forms/application-for-letters-of-guardianship-for-an-incompetent-person.

A critical step in the qualification process involves the posting of a bond. If a guardian of the estate (GOE) or general guardian (GG) is appointed by the clerk, then the GOE or GG must post a bond before receiving any property and before the clerk will issue letters of appointment.[86] A guardian of the person (GOP) typically does not have to post a bond.[87] The amount of the bond is calculated based on the value of the ward's personal property and the rents and profits of the ward's real estate.[88] Typically, the guardian uses Form AOC-E-401 to post the bond, which contains forms for both a corporate surety bond and a personal surety bond.

PRACTICE NOTE

Critical Tool to Protect against Elder Abuse

A bond from an appropriate surety in the appropriate amount throughout the guardianship is a critically important tool to protect an older adult from financial exploitation by a guardian. The purpose of the bond is to protect the ward's estate and to compensate the ward if the ward suffers a financial loss as a result of the guardian's failure to properly exercise his or her duties to the ward.[89]

The bonding company will do a credit check on the potential guardian before issuing the bond. The ability to be bonded is often a challenge for potential guardians and may result in someone otherwise qualified to serve being unable to serve as a GOE or GG. The individual may still be appointed as GOP if otherwise qualified, and frequently the public guardian or a local attorney is appointed as GOE when no other suitable person qualifies.

The bond is conditioned on the guardian faithfully executing the trust placed in the guardian and obeying all lawful orders relating to the guardianship committed to the guardian.[90] If, for example, the guardian uses funds in the ward/older adult's bank account for the guardian's own personal purpose, the guardian may be removed and a successor guardian may make a claim against the bond on the older adult's behalf. If the surety company pays out on a bond claim, the surety company may then file a civil action against the former guardian for recovery of the amounts owed to the surety company.

After the bond is posted, to ensure that the older adult's property remains adequately protected, the guardian is charged with two critical responsibilities.

86. G.S. 35A-1230. There are exceptions to the guardian's duty to post a bond. For example, if a parent's will makes a recommendation for a guardian of an unmarried child adjudicated incompetent, the parent may also direct in the will that the guardian may qualify and serve without giving bond; the guardian may serve without a bond unless the clerk determines that the best interests of the ward require otherwise. *Id.* § 35A-1212.1.

87. G.S. 35A-1230. The clerk may require a nonresident guardian of the person to post a bond or other security. *Id.* The Secretary of the N.C. Department of Health and Human Services is required to purchase individual or blanket bonds that cover all disinterested public agents appointed as guardians of the estate, guardians of the person, and general guardians. *Id.* § 35A-1239. The bonds are conditioned on the faithful performance of their duties as guardians and are made payable to the State of North Carolina. *Id.* The premiums are paid by the State. *Id.*

88. G.S. 35A-1231(a).

89. CSC MANUAL, at 86.27.

90. G.S. 35A-1231(a).

1. **Renew the bond.** If the bond is from a personal surety, the guardian must renew the bond every three years.[91]
2. **Adjust the bond.** The guardian is required to increase the bond, as appropriate. The guardian must increase the amount of the bond before he or she receives the proceeds from the sale of real or personal property owned by the older adult if the value is believed to be greater than the value used in determining the amount of the bond.[92] The amount of the bond may be decreased in the discretion of the clerk if the amount of assets held by the guardian are reduced.[93]

While the duties to renew and adjust the bond fall on the guardian, the clerk may be liable to the ward's estate if the clerk fails to

- take a good and sufficient security for the bond,
- require an increase in the amount of the bond to cover an increase in the ward's assets, or
- compel the timely renewal of a personal surety bond.[94]

After the guardian submits an application for letters and the clerk approves the bond, the guardian takes an oath or affirmation (see Form AOC-E-400). In the oath, the guardian swears or affirms (1) to faithfully and honestly discharge the duties imposed on him or her to the best of his or her skill and abilities and according to law and (2) to support and maintain the laws of the United States and the State of North Carolina.[95] The clerk then enters an order authorizing the issuance of letters (see Form AOC-E-402) and issues letters.[96] The letters issued depend on the type of guardian appointed by the clerk. The N.C. Administrative Office of the Courts maintains the form letters referenced in Figure 4.5, *supra*. The letters attest to the authority granted to the guardian by the court and provide that the guardian's authority is in full force and effect. The letters also prescribe the nature and extent of the guardian's authority to act on the ward's behalf.

3. EMERGENCY CIRCUMSTANCES

Three tools are available under North Carolina guardianship law to address an emergency situation involving an older adult who lacks capacity. Examples of such emergency situations include (1) where someone has access to an older adult's bank accounts and is presently taking money from the account and (2) where an older adult is in need of an immediate medical procedure and is unable to consent to treatment. These tools are available prior to an adjudication of incompetency by the court. They may be critical to protecting an adult from ongoing elder abuse. The tools require a lower standard of proof, have truncated notice requirements, and enable the court to enter time-limited orders to respond to specific emergencies.

91. G.S. 35A-1236.
92. G.S. 35A-1231(b).
93. G.S. 35A-1233.
94. G.S. 35A-1238, -1231, -1236.
95. *See* G.S. 11-11.
96. G.S. 35A-1203, -1206, -1215.

Figure 4.6. **Emergency Guardianship, Special Protective Orders, and Interim Guardianship**

The first two tools fall under a court's "special jurisdiction" and are referred to in this manual as (1) emergency guardianship of the person and (2) special protective orders.[97] These types of emergency orders are appropriate when a North Carolina court's authority (jurisdiction) to decide a particular case is unclear, undetermined, or otherwise lacking because the respondent (the older adult) has contacts with multiple states. The third tool, interim guardianship, is available when a North Carolina court has the jurisdiction to hear the case.[98] It is available when there is or reasonably appears to be an imminent or foreseeable risk of harm to the respondent or the respondent's property.[99]

a. Emergency Guardianship of the Person and Special Protective Orders

An older adult may have lived in North Carolina for many years preceding the filing of a petition of incompetence in this state and may have few to no contacts with other states beyond visits for vacation or business. Under these circumstances, it is clear that North Carolina is the most appropriate state for the filing of an incompetency petition and the appointment and oversight of a guardian. There are no concerns about whether a North Carolina court has the authority to hear a particular case.

There may be other cases when an older adult has contacts with multiple states prior to the filing of the incompetency petition. This will most often be evidenced on the first page of the "Petition for Adjudication of Incompetence and Application for Appointment of Guardian or Limited Guardian," Form AOC-SP-200.

97. G.S. 35B-18(a).
98. G.S. 35A-1114(a).
99. G.S. 35A-1114(d).

Figure 4.7. **Excerpt from Petition for Adjudication of Incompetence and Application for Appointment of Guardian or Limited Guardian (Form AOC-SP-200)**

In support of this Petition, the undersigned states:

1. During the past twelve (12) months, the above-named respondent was physically present as follows:

Period of Physical Presence *(include up to the 12 months prior to the filing date of the petition; do not list periods of temporary absence)*		**Address**
From	**To**	
	Present	

For example, the older adult may live in North Carolina during the summer and Florida during the winter. Or the older adult may move from another state where he had lived his entire life to live with an adult child in North Carolina. There may also be more nefarious circumstances at play, such as when a family member or caregiver moves the older adult to North Carolina to isolate her from other family and friends and to take control of her finances through a guardianship proceeding (also known as "granny snatching"). Or one family member of an older adult may file a petition for guardianship in North Carolina and another may file a petition for guardianship in another state, creating dueling petitions in two different state courts. There may be confusion or conflict over which state is the most appropriate one to hear the incompetency proceeding and appoint a guardian to act on behalf of the older adult, if needed. The older adult is caught in the push and pull of the conflict and incurs unnecessary costs related to multiple proceedings or to a proceeding filed in an inappropriate state.

The Uniform Adult Guardianship and Protective Proceedings Jurisdiction Act (UAGPPJA) in G.S. Chapter 35B applies to North Carolina incompetency and adult guardianship proceedings. It provides the exclusive jurisdictional basis for a North Carolina court to adjudicate incompetence and appoint a guardian for an adult.[100] The purpose of UAGPPJA is to ensure that jurisdiction to hear a guardianship case exists in one and only one state, except when an emergency exists or an individual owns property in multiple states.[101]

100. G.S. 35B-16.
101. G.S. 35B-1(d)(1).

Before adjudicating incompetence and appointing a guardian for an older adult under G.S. Chapter 35A, a North Carolina court must first determine that it has jurisdiction under Chapter 35B to hear the case over other states because it is (1) the respondent's "home state," [102] (2) a "significant-connection state,"[103] or (3) an "other" state.[104]

RESOURCE

UAGPPJA and the related legal standards for each of the three grounds for jurisdiction listed above are discussed in more detail in Meredith Smith, *New Rules for Adult Guardianship Proceedings: Applying the Uniform Adult Guardianship and Protective Proceedings Jurisdiction Act (G.S. Chapter 35B) in North Carolina*, SOCIAL SERVICES LAW BULLETIN No. 46 (Nov. 2016), https://www.sog.unc.edu/sites/www.sog.unc.edu/files/reports/2016-11-29a%2020151134%20SSLB46_MSmith.pdf.

The North Carolina court may need to (1) communicate with a court in another state to determine which court will hear the case or (2) take additional evidence at a hearing on jurisdiction here in North Carolina.[105] While the North Carolina court sorts out the jurisdictional questions, there may be an emergency with regard to the older adult or the older adult's property.

i. Emergency Guardianship of the Person

UAGPPJA provides that a clerk of superior court has special jurisdiction to appoint a guardian of the person (GOP) in an emergency for a term not exceeding ninety days for a respondent/older adult who is physically present in North Carolina.[106]

KEY TERM

***Emergency** is defined as a circumstance that likely will result in substantial harm to a respondent's health, safety, or welfare, and for which the appointment of a guardian of the person is necessary because no other person has authority and is willing to act on the respondent's behalf.*[107]

102. G.S. 35B-15(a)(2) (defining "home state" as "[t]he state in which the respondent was physically present, including any period of temporary absence, for at least six consecutive months immediately before the filing of a petition for the adjudication of incompetence; or if none, the state in which the respondent was physically present, including any period of temporary absence, for at least six consecutive months ending within the six months prior to the filing of the petition for the adjudication of incompetence").

103. G.S. 35B-15(a)(3) (defining "significant-connection state" as "[a] state, other than the home state, with which the respondent has a significant connection other than mere physical presence and in which substantial evidence about the respondent is available"). Factors to consider when determining whether a respondent has a significant connection with a state are listed in G.S. 35B-15(b) and include location of the respondent's family members and property, the length of time the respondent was present in that state, and civic ties such as voter and motor vehicle registration.

104. G.S. 35B-17(3).

105. *See* G.S. 35B-5, -23(2).

106. G.S. 35B-18(a)(1).

107. G.S. 35B-15(a)(1).

An emergency GOP may make decisions related to the care, custody, and control of the respondent. There are no forms available for the petition for emergency guardianship, the court's order appointing the emergency GOP, or letters authorizing the emergency GOP to act on the respondent's behalf.

The appointment of an emergency GOP may provide a bridge to allow the court to resolve any jurisdictional questions while ensuring that the respondent's health, safety, and welfare are protected. An emergency guardianship of the person does not grant authority over the respondent's property.

EXAMPLE

Emergency Guardianship of the Person

Alice moves her 88-year-old mother, Jane, to North Carolina to live with her. Jane has lived her entire life in Georgia—her extended family and friends are there, as is her house, car, and personal property, except for a vacation home she owns in the North Carolina mountains. Jane was diagnosed with dementia and there has been a recent severe decline in her condition. Alice petitions to have Jane adjudicated incompetent and seeks to be Jane's appointed guardian in North Carolina. Jane's son, Tom, contests the petition in North Carolina and states that North Carolina does not have jurisdiction to hear the case; the appropriate state to hear the case is Georgia, he argues. There are allegations that Alice keeps the refrigerator and pantry in her house locked and that she has not taken Jane to see a doctor since moving her to North Carolina five months ago. The North Carolina court appoints Tom as emergency guardian of the person to allow him to seek treatment on behalf of his mother and move her to a stable residence while the jurisdictional questions are addressed by the court. Tom plans to file a petition for guardianship in Georgia.

ii. Special Protective Order for Certain Property

Similar to the appointment of an emergency guardian, a special protective order is available when there is a question as to a North Carolina court's jurisdiction to hear a case.[108] The North Carolina clerk of superior court always has the authority to issue a special protective order with respect to real or tangible personal property owned by a respondent located in North Carolina.[109] This is an important tool when an older adult who owns real or tangible personal property located in this state is the subject of financial exploitation. The clerk's order grants a GG or GOE the authority to take control of and protect the real and tangible personal property of the older adult located in North Carolina while the jurisdictional questions are sorted out between North Carolina and some other state or states.

108. G.S. 35B-18(a)(2).
109. *Id.*

b. Interim Guardianship

One of the most important tools available in guardianship to stop the abuse or exploitation of an older adult is interim guardianship.[110] An interim guardian is a temporary guardian appointed prior to an adjudication of incompetence.[111] The purpose of the interim guardianship is to provide temporary protection for a person who requires immediate intervention to address conditions that constitute imminent or foreseeable risk of harm to the person's physical well-being or to the person's estate.[112]

A verified motion for interim guardianship (Form AOC-SP-198) may be filed at the time of or subsequent to the filing of a petition for the adjudication of incompetence by the petitioner or the guardian ad litem.[113] The clerk may also appoint an interim guardian on his or her own motion at the incompetency hearing.[114] Unlike emergency guardianship of the person or special protective orders, the court must have jurisdiction of the underlying incompetency and guardianship proceeding as a home state, a significant connecting state, or other state to appoint an interim guardian.[115]

Upon the filing of a motion for an interim guardian, the clerk immediately sets a date, time, and place for a hearing on the motion.[116] The motion and notice of hearing on interim guardianship must be served promptly on the petitioner, respondent, guardian ad litem attorney, and anyone else designated by the clerk.[117]

If at the hearing the clerk finds that (i) there is reasonable cause to believe that the older adult is incompetent, and (ii) there is or reasonably appears to be an imminent or foreseeable risk of harm to the older adult's physical well-being or estate that requires immediate intervention, the clerk immediately enters an order appointing an interim guardian.[118] Once the court holds a hearing on the motion for appointment of an interim guardian, the petitioner may not voluntarily dismiss the petition for adjudication of incompetence.[119]

The clerk's order appointing an interim guardian sets forth the interim guardian's powers and duties.[120] These powers and duties are limited and extend only so far and so long as necessary to meet the conditions necessitating the appointment of an interim guardian.[121]

110. For additional information on interim guardianship, refer to Meredith Smith, *Some Things to Remember About Interim Guardianship*, ON THE CIVIL SIDE: A UNC SCH. OF GOV'T BLOG (May 4, 2016), https://civil.sog.unc.edu/some-things-to-remember-about-interim-guardianship/.

111. G.S. 35A-1101(11) (defining "interim guardian" as a guardian, appointed prior to adjudication of incompetence and for a temporary period, for a person who requires immediate intervention to address conditions that constitute imminent or foreseeable risk of harm to the person's physical well-being or to the person's estate").

112. G.S. 35A-1114(b).

113. G.S. 35A-1114(a).

114. G.S. 35A-1112(b1).

115. G.S. 35A-1114(a).

116. G.S. 35A-1114(c).

117. G.S. 35A-1114(c1).

118. G.S. 35A-1114(d).

119. G.S. 35A-1114(f).

120. G.S. 35A-1114(e).

121. *Id.*

An interim guardian's authority does not continue indefinitely. An interim guardianship terminates on the earliest of[122]

- the date specified in the clerk's order;
- forty-five days after entry of the clerk's order unless the clerk, for good cause shown, extends that period for up to forty-five additional days;
- when any guardians are appointed following an adjudication of incompetence; or
- when the incompetency petition is dismissed by the court.

As a practical matter, the longest period of time that an interim guardianship could possibly be in place is ninety days from entry of the clerk's order. After that time, the interim guardian no longer has authority to act because the interim guardianship terminates.

An interim guardian whose authority relates only to the person of the respondent does not have to post a bond.[123] However, an interim guardian of the respondent's estate must post a bond in an amount determined by the clerk and submit an account to the clerk.[124]

EXAMPLE

Interim Guardianship and Elder Abuse

Mary, an 89-year-old woman, fell in her yard one day. A younger man was driving by and stopped to help her up. He befriended Mary and began spending time with her by helping her with chores, paying bills, and administering her medication. After a few weeks, he had Mary sign a power of attorney (POA) naming him as her agent. Mary wrote several large checks for tens of thousands of dollars to the man, purportedly for home renovations that were only partially started but never completed, and Mary co-signed a car loan with him. After Mary's family became concerned about the nature of the relationship, her daughter filed an incompetency petition (AOC-SP-200) together with a motion for interim guardianship (AOC-SP-198). The interim guardian of the estate revoked the POA and put a freeze on Mary's accounts to stop further access to them by the man.

D. WHAT IS THE ROLE OF THE GUARDIAN?

A guardian is charged with making decisions for an older adult who lacks capacity. The guardian must make decisions that are in the best interests of the older adult.[125] This means that a guardian may first consider any express directions set out by the older adult on the issue underlying a particular decision. If there are no express directions,

122. *Id.*
123. *Id.*
124. *Id.*
125. G.S. 35A-1241(a)(3); *id.* § 35A-1251.

then the guardian may look to make a decision that aligns with the older adult's history of decision-making, including the adult's lifestyle, values, desires, and needs. Finally, if there are no express directions or guidance based on the adult's history, the guardian then makes a decision that the guardian determines is reasonable and prudent and in the older adult's best interests, which is the lodestar of guardianship decision-making.[126]

The extent of a guardian's decision-making powers and, thus, the guardian's duties, depends on the type of guardian appointed by the court. There are three primary types of guardians under North Carolina law: a guardian of the estate (GOE), a guardian of the person (GOP), and a general guardian (GG). For purposes of this section, references to a GOE and a GOP include a GG.

1. GUARDIAN OF THE ESTATE (GOE)

a. Powers of the GOE

A GOE's powers are broad. The GOE has the power to perform in a reasonable and prudent manner every act that a reasonable and prudent person would perform incident to the collection, preservation, management, and use of the older adult's estate to administer the older adult's estate (1) legally and (2) in the older adult's best interests.[127] These powers continue until the guardianship is terminated.[128]

North Carolina statutory law lists some of the specific powers of a GOE but makes clear that the list is not exhaustive.[129] The list includes the power to take possession of the older adult's estate, to receive assets, to maintain actions to recover property, to complete contracts, to abandon property, to renounce an interest in property, to insure property against loss, to pay necessary expenses of administering the older adult's estate, to employ professionals such as attorneys and accountants, and to pay taxes and expenses to protect the estate.[130] A GOE has the power to authorize a financial institution to provide access to the older adult's financial records and may also have the authority to place a security freeze with a credit reporting agency. Both actions are discussed in greater detail in Chapter 7.

126. G.S. 35A-1251, -1242(a2).
127. G.S. 35A-1251.
128. G.S. 35A-1295(a).
129. G.S. 35A-1251.
130. *Id.*

PRACTICE NOTE

It is important for the GOE to know what property the older adult owns so that the GOE can plan for the older adult's care and secure the older adult's real and personal property. The GOE is required to file an inventory with the court within three months of being appointed by the court but should begin taking action to identify and secure the older adult's property immediately after being appointed. This may include the following.

- Filing a change of address for the older adult to redirect mail to the GOE for at least six months to ensure that the GOE receives all bills and other notices related to the older adult's property. It also may help prevent consumer scam letters from reaching the older adult. The GOE should be sure to provide the older adult with any personal mail items received in a timely manner.
- Printing out copies of the older adult's bank and other financial statements for at least the last year and review what income has been coming in and what drafts have been going out to identify the scope of the older adult's property as well as whether there have been any suspicious transactions.

The default rule is that a GOE may exercise decision-making powers on behalf of the older adult without prior court approval.[131] There are exceptions to this rule. The GOE must initiate a proceeding before the court seeking court approval before taking any of the below-listed actions related to the older adult's property. Failure to obtain court approval of any of these actions may result in removal of the GOE.[132]

Actions by a GOE that require court approval include

- any action for which court approval is mandated by court order;
- expending estate principal;[133]
- selling, mortgaging, or exchanging real property;[134]
- leasing real estate for more than three years;[135]
- exercising certain powers with respect to revocable trusts;[136]
- selling, leasing, or exchanging any personal property in the aggregate value of more than $5,000 per accounting period (typically, one year);[137]

131. *See Id.*
132. *See* G.S. 35A-1290.
133. G.S. 35A-1251(12), (21).
134. *See generally* G.S. Ch. 35A, Art. 14 (Sale, Mortgage, Exchange or Lease of Ward's Estate).
135. G.S. 35A-1251(17)a. *See also id.* § 35A-1301(b).
136. G.S. 35A-1251(24).
137. G.S. 35A-1251(17)a.

- making gifts of the older adult's property;[138] and
- paying commissions to the guardian.[139]

A guardian may not receive a commission until the clerk enters an order allowing the commission and setting the amount of the commission. A GOE is entitled to receive commissions for the time and trouble spent in managing the older adult's estate, subject to court approval.[140] The commission may not exceed 5 percent of the receipts and expenditures of personal property made by the guardian.[141] In determining the amount of a commission, the clerk will consider the time, responsibility, trouble, and skill involved in the management of the older adult's estate.[142] The clerk may also take into account fees paid for professional services performed in the ordinary course of estate administration, including services performed by attorneys and accountants.[143] A petition for commissions is generally filed with an annual account so that the clerk may review the commissionable receipts and expenditures made by the guardian during the previous year.

A GOE may employ an attorney to advise or assist the guardian in the performance of the guardian's duties.[144] Attorneys' fees are a proper expense to be charged in the guardian's account if the fees are reasonable in amount and expended in connection with the proper administration of the estate.[145] The guardian may be individually liable for attorneys' fees not approved by the court.[146]

b. Duties of the GOE

A GOE is charged with certain duties, both as to the older adult and to the court. These include

- involving the older adult in decision-making to the extent possible;[147]
- permitting the older adult to exercise those rights within his or her comprehension and judgment, allowing for the possibility of error to the same degree as is allowed for persons who are not incompetent;[148]
- taking reasonable and prudent actions on the older adult's behalf;[149]
- administering the older adult's estate legally and in the older adult's best interests;[150]

138. *See generally* G.S. Ch. 35A, Art. 17 (Gifts from Income for Certain Purposes), Art. 18 (Gifts from Principal for Certain Purposes).

139. G.S. 35A-1269.

140. *Id.*

141. G.S. 28A-23-3(a) (G.S. 35A-1269 states that commissions shall be determined in the same manner and under the same rules and restrictions pursuant to G.S. 28A-23-3 and -4).

142. G.S. 28A-23-3(b).

143. G.S. 28A-23-3(a).

144. G.S. 35A-1251(14).

145. Md. Cas. Co. v. Lawing, 225 N.C. 103 (1945).

146. *Id.*

147. G.S. 35A-1201(a)(5).

148. *Id.*

149. G.S. 35A-1251.

150. *Id.*

- taking possession of the older adult's property and using it for the older adult's benefit;[151]
- diligently attempting to collect money and other obligations due to the older adult by lawful means;[152]
- paying taxes and other assessments owed by the older adult out of the older adult's estate;[153]
- observing "a standard of judgment and care under the circumstances then prevailing that an ordinarily prudent person of discretion and intelligence" would observe when serving as a fiduciary of the property of another person;[154]
- using any special skills or expertise for the benefit of the older adult;[155]
- obeying lawful court orders pertaining to the guardianship;[156]
- obtaining, renewing, and modifying any bond, as required by law;[157] and
- timely filing inventories and accountings with the court.[158]

The GOE's duties terminate when the guardianship is terminated, with one exception.[159] The GOE has a continued duty to file accountings after the guardianship is terminated until discharged by an order of the clerk.[160]

2. GUARDIAN OF THE PERSON (GOP)

a. Powers of the GOP

A GOP has far-reaching powers over an older adult, including custody.[161] Unless the court order appointing the GOP provides otherwise, the GOP has the power to make decisions relating to the following matters:

- Where the older adult lives. The GOP must give preference to locations in North Carolina that are not treatment facilities.[162] If the only available and appropriate location is a treatment facility, the GOP must give preference to community-based treatment facilities, such as group homes or nursing homes, over treatment facilities that are not community-based.[163]

151. G.S. 35A-1253(1).
152. G.S. 35A-1253(2).
153. G.S. 35A-1253(3).
154. G.S. 35A-1253(4).
155. *Id.*
156. G.S. 35A-1253(5).
157. G.S. 35A-1230, -1231, -1232.
158. G.S. 35A-1253(5).
159. G.S. 35A-1295(a).
160. G.S. 35A-1295(b).
161. G.S. 35A-1241 (listing powers and duties of a guardian of the person). *See also* Corbett v. Lynch, 251 N.C. App. 40 (2016).
162. G.S. 35A-1241(a)(2).
163. *Id.*

- Social interactions and visitation. This includes the power to impose limits if interactions would be deleterious to the older adult.
- Day-to-day needs. This includes arranging for the older adult's meals and grocery delivery, hygiene, and clothing, as necessary.
- Training, education, employment, rehabilitation, and habilitation for the older adult.[164]
- Consent to medical, psychological, or other professional care needed by the older adult.[165]
- Consent for the older adult to receive necessary legal or other professional counsel.[166]

The default rule is that the GOP may exercise decision-making powers on behalf of the older adult without prior court approval. There are exceptions to this rule. Decisions that require court approval include those involving

- any action for which court approval is mandated by court order; and
- consenting to sterilization of an older adult with a mental illness or intellectual disability, which requires a separate proceeding initiated pursuant to G.S. 35A-1245.[167]

Unlike a GOE, a GOP is not entitled to receive a fee for services performed and time spent carrying out guardianship duties.[168] The GOP is entitled to reimbursement from the older adult's estate for reasonable and proper expenses incurred in carrying out guardianship duties.[169]

There are legal limitations on the liability of the GOP to the older adult and to the older adult's estate. The GOP may not be held liable for damages to the older adult or to the older adult's estate if[170]

- the GOP authorizes or gives consent or approval for the older adult to receive legal, psychological, or other professional care and damages result from negligence or other acts of a third party or
- the GOP authorizes medical treatment or surgery for the older adult and does so acting in good faith and without negligence.

---

164. G.S. 35A-1241(a)(1).

165. G.S. 35A-1241(a)(3). Provided, however, that if the ward has a health care agent appointed under a valid health care power of attorney, the health care agent has the right to make medical decisions unless the clerk has suspended his or her authority. *Id. See also* Aimee Wall, *The Guardian's Role in Health Care Decision-Making*, ON THE CIVIL SIDE: A UNC SCH. OF GOV'T BLOG (Apr. 5, 2017), https://civil.sog.unc.edu/the-guardians-role-in-health-care-decision-making/.

166. G.S. 35A-1241(a)(3).

167. *Id.*

168. *See* G.S. 35A-1241(b).

169. *Id.*

170. G.S. 35A-1241(c).

b. Duties of the GOP

The GOP is charged with certain duties, both as to the older adult and to the court. These include

- involving the older adult in decision-making to the extent possible;[171]
- permitting the older adult to exercise those rights within his or her comprehension and judgment, allowing for the possibility of error to the same degree as is allowed for persons who are not incompetent;[172]
- acting in the older adult's best interests;
- making provision for the older adult's care, comfort, and maintenance;[173]
- arranging for training, education, employment, rehabilitation, or habilitation that are appropriate for the older adult;[174]
- taking reasonable care of the ward's clothing, furniture, vehicles, and other personal effects that are with the older adult;[175]
- obeying lawful court orders pertaining to the guardianship;[176] and
- timely filing status reports with the court, when required by law or court order.[177]

These duties continue until the guardianship is terminated.[178]

E. WHAT COURT OVERSIGHT EXISTS TO PROTECT OLDER ADULTS UNDER GUARDIANSHIP?

The court retains jurisdiction following the appointment of a guardian and oversees the guardianship as the "ultimate guardian" with the authority to take action to protect the interests of the incompetent older adult.[179] The risk of the abuse of an adult under guardianship may be mitigated, in part, by effective court oversight of the guardianship.[180] This includes ensuring timely and complete status reports, inventories, and accountings are filed with the court and taking actions to compel reports, which in extreme cases may result in holding the guardian in contempt of court. It also includes holding hearings to address information presented to the court about potential abuse of the older adult, modifying the guardianship when necessary to protect the older adult or better serve the older adult's interests, and, in extreme cases, removing the guardian for failing to protect an older adult from abuse or because the guardian is the perpetrator of abuse. For purposes of this section, references to a GOE or a GOP include a GG.

171. G.S. 35A-1201(a)(5).
172. *Id.*
173. G.S. 35A-1241(a)(1).
174. *Id.*
175. *Id.*
176. G.S. 35A-1241.
177. G.S. 35A-1242. The duty to file status reports is discussed in further detail in Section II.E.1.
178. G.S. 35A-1295(a).
179. *In re* Thomas, 290 N.C. 410, 424–25 (1976).
180. GAO ELDER ABUSE REPORT, at 19–20.

1. STATUS REPORTS AND STATUS REPORT HEARINGS

Certain GOPs are required to file status reports with the court. These reports must be filed

- in all cases where a corporation or disinterested public agent guardian (DSS) has been appointed as a GOP and
- when a court appoints an individual to serve as an older adult's GOP and orders the individual to file status reports.[181]

PRACTICE NOTE

The N.C. Department of Health and Human Services maintains a form status report that is used by many county departments of social services and by corporations. This form is available at https://policies.ncdhhs.gov/divisional/aging-and-adult/guardianship/manual/guardianship-status-report.

Instructions for the form are available at https://policies.ncdhhs.gov/divisional/aging-and-adult/guardianship/manual/guardianship-status-report-instructions.

If required by law or ordered by a court to file a status report, a GOP must file an initial report within six months after being appointed and then annually thereafter.[182] The status report should contain a summary of the work the guardian has performed on behalf of the ward and must include[183]

- a report or summary of recent medical and dental examinations of the ward by one or more physicians and dentists; if the guardian has made diligent but unsuccessful attempts to secure this information, the guardian must include an explanation and documentation of all actions taken to secure this information;
- a report on the guardian's performance of the duties imposed by law and in the clerk's order appointing the guardian;
- a report on the ward's residence, education, employment, and rehabilitation or habilitation;
- a report on the guardian's efforts to restore the ward's competency;
- a report on the guardian's efforts to seek alternatives to guardianship;
- a report on efforts to identify alternative guardians (if the guardian is a disinterested public agent or corporation);
- the guardian's recommendations for implementing a more limited guardianship, preserving for the ward the opportunity to exercise rights that are within the ward's comprehension and judgment;

181. G.S. 35A-1242(a).
182. *Id.*
183. G.S. 35A-1242(a1), (a2).

- any additional reports or information required by the clerk; and
- any additional information pertaining to the ward's best interests.

The status report must be filed with the court under the guardian's oath or affirmation or with the signature of a witness attesting that the report is complete and accurate so far as the guardian can determine.[184] The status report is not available for public inspection; it is only available to the guardian, the court, the ward, or the state or local human services agency providing services to the ward.[185]

After the report is filed with the court, the clerk, on his or her own motion, or on the motion of an interested party, may file a motion in the cause to request modification of the order appointing the guardian or guardians or for consideration of any matters contained in the status report.[186] The clerk may then hold a hearing on any matters contained in the motion and enter an order to address any issues in the status report, including ordering the guardian to take certain actions to remedy or address any deficiencies in the report.

EXAMPLE

A status report is filed by a corporate GOP for an older adult. The status report fails to include information about the older adult's residence, education, employment, and rehabilitation or habilitation. It also does not identify any doctor or dentist visits by the ward in the prior year. The clerk may, on his or her own motion, calendar a hearing and notice the guardian of the hearing. The clerk could then inquire about the deficiencies in the report to ensure that the guardian is not neglecting the older adult and is carrying out its duties as GOP.

2. INVENTORY AND ACCOUNTINGS

A GOE is required to file both an inventory and regular accountings with the court. These filings are critical to helping the court oversee the guardian and detect financial exploitation of the older adult, including whether the guardian is using the older adult's property for his or her own benefit. Some expenditures on an accounting, such as a $100 bill at a restaurant or a $500 cost for vacation travel when the incompetent adult is in a locked dementia unit, will raise red flags with the court and are not permissible uses of the incompetent adult's property by the guardian.[187]

a. Inventory

Within three months of being appointed guardian of the estate (GOE) for an older adult, a GOE must file an inventory, under oath, with the clerk of superior court listing the older

184. G.S. 35A-1242(b).
185. G.S. 35A-1242(c).
186. G.S. 35A-1242(d).
187. Note that some expenditures of the older adult's estate for the benefit of others are permissible, such as the expenditure of estate income for support, maintenance, and education of the ward's minor children, spouse, and dependents. G.S. 35A-1251(21).

adult's real and personal property.[188] Typically, the guardian uses Form AOC-E-510. The GOE must file a supplemental inventory when (1) the guardian becomes aware of property that was not included in the original inventory or (2) the value or description of any property or of the older adult's interest in the property is erroneous or misleading.[189] Common items on an inventory include real property, bank accounts, vehicles, household goods, jewelry, and income from benefit programs such as Social Security or veteran's benefits.

b. Accountings

The GOE has a duty to file annual accountings with the clerk for so long as any of the older adult's estate remains in the guardian's control.[190] The accounting is filed under oath with the clerk.[191] Typically, the guardian uses Form AOC-E-506. The accounting must include the amount of property received or invested by the GOE, as well as the receipts and disbursements for the preceding year.[192] The GOE is required to produce vouchers for all payments or verified proof for payments instead of vouchers.[193] The clerk has the authority to examine any person, including the guardian, on any matter related to the accounting or the estate.[194] The clerk carefully reviews and audits the account and, if the clerk approves the accounting, he or she then endorses approval on the accounting.[195]

3. CONTEMPT

If a guardian fails to file a satisfactory status report, inventory, or accounting, or if the guardian does not file a status report, inventory, or accounting at all, the clerk of court has the authority to compel the required filings.[196] This includes the authority after notice and hearing to hold a guardian in civil contempt and to imprison the guardian for so long as the deficiency exists or the filing is absent, for a period of up to one year.[197] The clerk may, in addition to or in lieu of holding the guardian in contempt, remove the guardian and appoint a new guardian.[198] Compelling timely filings is critical to ensure that any exploitation or other abuse of the older adult under guardianship does not go undiscovered or unaddressed. When a guardian fails to file required reports, inventories, and accountings, it is a warning sign for potential abuse.

4. MOTIONS IN THE CAUSE

An important mechanism for raising potential concerns about elder abuse to the court after the appointment of a guardian is through a motion in the cause. Any interested

188. G.S. 35A-1261. The clerk may extend the time to file the inventory to up to six months for good cause shown. *Id.*
189. G.S. 35A-1263.1.
190. G.S. 35A-1264.
191. *Id.*
192. *Id.*
193. *Id.*
194. *Id.*
195. *Id.*
196. G.S. 35A-1244 (status report); 35A-1262 (inventory or account); 35A-1265 (accounting).
197. *See* G.S. 5A-21(b2) (civil contempt statute).
198. G.S. 35A-1244; 35A-1262; 35A-1265. *See also id.* § 35A-1290 (removal by clerk).

person may file a motion in the cause in the guardianship proceeding before the clerk of superior court to ask the court to modify the guardianship or consider any matter pertaining to the guardianship.[199] The N.C. Administrative Office of the Courts (AOC) maintains a form "Motion in the Cause to Modify Guardianship" (Form AOC E-415).[200] However, an interested person is not required to use the form or to label the request to the court as a motion in the cause. The court is required to treat requests to modify the guardianship or to consider matters related to the guardianship, however labeled, as motions in the cause.[201] The clerk schedules a hearing on the motion and the movant serves the motion, together with a notice of hearing, on all other parties and any other persons on whom the clerk directs that service be made.[202]

After a guardian is appointed, if an emergency exists that threatens the physical well-being of an older adult under guardianship or constitutes a risk of substantial injury to an older adult's estate, the movant may include a request for ex parte relief in the motion.[203] If the clerk finds reasonable cause to believe that an emergency exists, the clerk may enter an ex parte order to address the emergency pending disposition of the matter at a hearing on the motion.[204]

A motion may be appropriate, in particular, if an interested person suspects that the guardian is not effectively protecting the adult against abuse or is a perpetrator of abuse.[205] In response to the motion, for example, the court could order an individual GOP to start filing regular status reports with the court to document the care, comfort, and maintenance the guardian is providing to the older adult or regarding anything else specifically requested by the court to be included in the report, such as medical visits, efforts to secure stable and appropriate housing, and efforts to secure an in-home aide. This could potentially result in the guardian taking more diligent steps to oversee the older adult's care if neglect by the guardian is a basis for the motion in the cause.

5. REMOVAL OF THE GUARDIAN

In extreme cases, when a guardian is a perpetrator of abuse or fails to take action to protect an older adult from abuse, removal of the guardian and the appointment of a successor guardian by the court may be necessary. There are two types of removal: removal in an emergency and removal after a hearing.[206]

a. Emergency Removal

The clerk may summarily remove a guardian without hearing if the clerk finds reasonable cause to believe that an emergency exists that threatens the physical well-being of the

199. G.S. 35A-1207(a).
200. AOC, Form E-415, "Motion in the Cause to Modify Guardianship," available at https://www.nccourts.gov/assets/documents/forms/e415-en.pdf?fY_pBR42JKVRtoiuMKdt5nBUb6BgNS3d.
201. G.S. 35A-1207(b).
202. G.S. 35A-1207(c).
203. G.S. 35A-1207(d).
204. *Id.*
205. G.S. 35A-1207; -1290.
206. G.S. 35A-1291 (summary removal); 35A-1290 (removal after a hearing).

older adult ward or constitutes a risk of substantial injury to the ward's estate.[207] This includes cases where there is evidence the guardian is subjecting the ward to ongoing abuse.

b. Removal after a Hearing

In the absence of an emergency, the clerk may remove a guardian after a hearing on the clerk's own motion or upon a motion or petition filed with the court.[208] The clerk has the authority to remove a guardian upon finding that removal will ensure the better care and maintenance of the older adult and the better management of the older adult's estate.[209] The clerk has a duty to remove the guardian or to take action necessary to protect the older adult's interests if the clerk finds that[210]

- the guardian has wasted the older adult's money or estate or converted it to the guardian's own use;
- the guardian has in any manner mismanaged the older adult's estate;
- the guardian has neglected to care for or maintain the older adult or the older adult's dependents in a suitable manner;
- the guardian or the guardian's sureties are likely to become insolvent or to become nonresidents of North Carolina;
- the original appointment was made on the basis of a false representation or mistake;
- the guardian has violated a fiduciary duty through default or misconduct;
- the guardian has a private interest, whether direct or indirect, that might tend to hinder or be adverse to carrying out his or her duties as guardian;
- the guardian has been adjudged incompetent by a court of competent jurisdiction and has not been restored to competence;
- the guardian has been convicted of a felony under the laws of the United States or of any state or territory of the United States or of the District of Columbia and the guardian's citizenship has not been restored;
- the guardian was originally unqualified for appointment and continues to be unqualified or the guardian would no longer qualify for appointment as guardian due to a change in residence, a change in the charter of a corporate guardian, or any other reason;

207. G.S. 35A-1291.
208. G.S. 35A-1290.
209. G.S. 35A-1290(a). *See also In re* Guardianship of Thomas, 183 N.C. App. 480, 484 (2007).
210. G.S. 35A-1290(b).

- the guardian is the older adult's spouse and has lost his or her rights under G.S. Chapter 31A;
- the guardian fails to post, renew, or increase a bond as required by law or by order of the court;
- the guardian refuses or fails without justification to obey any citation, notice, or process served on him or her in regard to the guardianship;
- the guardian fails to file required accountings with the clerk;
- the clerk finds the guardian unsuitable to continue serving as guardian for any reason;
- the guardian is a nonresident of North Carolina and refuses or fails to obey any citation, notice, or process served on the guardian or on the guardian's process agent; or
- the guardian is a licensed attorney, and the clerk is in receipt of an order entered pursuant to G.S. 84-28 enjoining, suspending, or disbarring the attorney.

Whether the guardian is removed in an emergency or after a hearing, the clerk must appoint a successor guardian to act on the older adult's behalf.[211] The clerk may, pending the resolution of any controversy regarding removal, make interlocutory orders and decrees as the clerk finds necessary for the protection of the older adult or the older adult's estate or as to the other party seeking relief through revocation.[212] For example, the clerk's order may direct the previous guardian to turn over the older adult's property to the successor guardian. The successor guardian should take steps to recover the older adult's property wrongfully conveyed or misappropriated by the previous guardian, including making a claim on the bond, and should make any necessary referrals to law enforcement for prosecution of the guardian removed by the court. If a guardian is removed and does not file a full and proper accounting with the court, the successor guardian must initiate a proceeding to compel an accounting by the former guardian.[213]

211. G.S. 35A-1293.
212. G.S. 35A-1291.
213. G.S. 35A-1294(a).

III. CHALLENGES OF GUARDIANSHIP

Guardianship may be an effective tool to protect an incompetent older adult from abuse. A guardian has the authority, as determined by the court, to make decisions for an older adult who lacks the capacity to make decisions. The guardian has a duty to stop ongoing abuse and to protect the older adult and the adult's property from future abuse. However, guardianship has its challenges. These challenges merit consideration before seeking guardianship on behalf of an older adult.

WARD AS A VICTIM OF ABUSE—CONNECTIONS BETWEEN ADULT PROTECTIVE SERVICES (APS) AND GUARDIANSHIP[214]

When a guardian is suspected of abusing an older adult under guardianship, it is appropriate to report the abuse to APS. The response from APS will vary depending on whether a county department of social services (DSS) is the ward's guardian and whether DSS is the alleged perpetrator.

DSS is the guardian and is not the alleged perpetrator. It is possible that DSS may "screen out" the case and not conduct a formal APS evaluation if DSS is the adult's guardian and is not the alleged perpetrator of the abuse. (See Chapter 2 of this manual for a detailed discussion of the screening process.) This is true even if there is evidence of abuse, neglect, or exploitation as defined in G.S. 108A-101. DSS will screen the case out because it is able, as the guardian of the ward, to act in an able, willing, and responsible manner to perform or obtain essential services for the adult. Therefore, the adult does not need protective services and fails to meet the criteria to be screened in as an APS report.

Where DSS is the guardian of the older adult and the alleged abuse is by a third party, such as a family member or other caregiver, DSS has the obligation as guardian to take necessary actions to protect the ward. As noted in the *Adult Protective Services, Division of Aging and Adult Services Manual* (*APS Manual*), this may include making reports to the district attorney, state Adult Home Specialists,[215] or other agencies regarding violations of laws or regulations; reviewing financial and/or medical records; authorizing and facilitating health care or mental health treatment; assisting the adult with personal hygiene; removing health and safety hazards; implementing more effective monitoring tools; and, if necessary, removing the adult from a setting where abuse may be taking place.[216]

214. For further discussion of adult protective services, refer to Chapter 2 of this manual.

215. N.C. Dep't of Health & Human Servs., *Adult Care Homes*, NCDHHS.GOV, https://www.ncdhhs.gov/assistance/adult-services/adult-care-homes (explaining that adult care homes are monitored by Adult Home Specialists within local DSS entities).

216. N.C. DIV. OF AGING & ADULT SERVS., ADULT PROTECTIVE SERVICES, DIVISION OF AGING AND ADULT SERVICES MANUAL III-7 (Apr. 1, 2011), https://files.nc.gov/ncdhhs/documents/files/APS_Manual.pdf (hereinafter APS MANUAL).

DSS is the guardian and is the alleged perpetrator. In some instances, DSS receives a report that meets the requisite screening criteria but the agency is the guardian of the suspected victim of elder abuse and the DSS director or a member of the director's staff or other county personnel is the alleged perpetrator of the abuse.[217] This may occur, for example, when there are allegations that DSS as the guardian has allowed the adult to live in an unsafe environment or failed to authorize medical treatment.[218] In these cases, the allegations are to be screened in as an APS report.[219] However, the county DSS that has been appointed as guardian has a conflict of interest and may not conduct the evaluation.[220] Another county is then engaged to conduct the evaluation in accordance with the APS Reciprocal Protocol.[221] An APS evaluation by another county must include an assessment of the director's performance of his or her duties as guardian.[222]

DSS is not the guardian and the guardian is not the alleged perpetrator. If the guardian is not the alleged perpetrator of the suspected abuse, DSS may screen in the case as an APS report if it is determined that the ward is a disabled adult in need of protective services because there are concerns that there is not an able, responsible, and willing person to perform or obtain essential services for the ward and thus protect the ward from such abuse. *The APS Manual* offers definitions and guidance on what it means to be an able, responsible, and willing person.[223]

It may be that the guardian is able and willing but is not responsible, in that the guardian has poor judgment, is unreliable, or does not demonstrate adequate oversight in making sure the ward's needs are met. By continuing to allow the ward to live in a possibly neglectful or exploitative situation and not taking the steps to remedy it, the guardian is not an "able, responsible, and willing person."[224]

If DSS screens in a report and substantiates an evaluation, the protective services provided to the ward may include working with the guardian to become an able, responsible, and willing person if the guardian expresses a desire to do so and consents to protective services on the ward's behalf. This could include providing planning and counseling to the guardian to assist the guardian in identifying, remedying, and preventing circumstances which result in abuse.[225] It is also possible that DSS may seek to remove the guardian and to be appointed itself as the ward's guardian.[226] After the guardian is removed and while DSS serves as guardian, the agency could work with the former guardian to improve

217. *Id.*
218. APS MANUAL, at III-7–8.
219. *Id.* at III-7.
220. *Id.*
221. *See* APS MANUAL app. U, at III-91–92.
222. *Id.*
223. *Id.* at III-18–19.
224. *See* G.S. 108A-101(e) (a disabled adult is in need of protective services, in part, if he or she is without an able, responsible, and willing person who can perform or obtain essential services for that person).
225. APS MANUAL, at III-19.
226. *Id.* at III-33.

the former guardian's ability to serve as guardian and to enable the former guardian to later file a motion requesting that the court re-appoint him or her as the ward's guardian if he or she becomes qualified to serve at a later date.

However, in the event the guardian does not consent to protective services on the ward's behalf and does not demonstrate a desire to become able, responsible, and willing, DSS may elect to file a motion to remove the guardian before the clerk of superior court due to the guardian's failure to protect the ward from abuse and suitably exercise his or her duties to care for the older adult.[227]

DSS is not the guardian and the guardian is the alleged perpetrator. If the guardian is the alleged perpetrator of the abuse and the report is screened in and an evaluation conducted by APS, the protective action taken by DSS may include filing a motion to remove the guardian.[228] This may be done on an emergency basis without a hearing if the clerk finds reasonable cause to believe that an emergency exists that (1) threatens the well-being of the ward or (2) constitutes a risk of substantial injury to the ward's estate.[229] If the clerk revokes a guardian's authority based on this emergency jurisdiction, the clerk may enter orders as he or she finds necessary to protect the older adult, which may include appointing DSS as guardian until such time as another individual is determined to be appropriate to serve as the older adult's guardian.[230]

A. GUARDIAN IS THE ABUSER

Just because an older adult has a guardian, it does not mean that the risks of elder abuse are eliminated. In fact, guardians may create circumstances that allow for such abuse by leaving the older adult in vulnerable situations and failing to monitor the adult's care. In addition, guardians may be the source of such abuse by taking advantage of and exploiting the authority they are given.

There are certain actions by a general guardian or guardian of the estate that are red flags for potential abuse. Some of these include when the guardian[231]

1. fails to file, or inadequately or incompletely files, inventories and accountings;
2. fails to respond to court notices or orders to complete such filings;
3. pays the older adult's bills late, irregularly, or not at all;
4. maintains a lifestyle that is more affluent than the one the guardian enjoyed prior to being appointed guardian;

227. *See* G.S. 35A-1290.
228. *See id.* Refer to Section II.E.5, *supra*, for further discussion of removal of the guardian.
229. G.S. 35A-1291.
230. *Id.*
231. Adapted from Nat'l Ass'n for Ct. Mgmt., Adult Guardianship Guide (2013-2014), https://nacmnet.org/sites/default/files/publications/AdultGuardianshipGuide_withCover.pdf.

5. fails to post, renew, or increase a bond or has a bond revoked;
6. has expenditures reflected on an accounting that are not appropriate for the older adult's lifestyle or setting;
7. refuses to pay for services and care the older adult is able to afford;
8. is the subject of complaints by the older adult's family or friends;
9. fails to secure the older adult's property;
10. executes transfers of the older adult's property to himself or herself as the guardian;
11. makes gifts or loans of the older adult's property without the approval of the court;
12. wastes the older adult's money; or
13. lists questionable entries on an accounting, including
    - utilities charges when the older adult is not living at home;
    - items purchased that are not present in the older adult's home, such as a television, cell phone, or other electronics;
    - checks written for cash;
    - unexplained ATM withdrawals;
    - vehicles purchased that are not appropriate for the older adult's transportation or not needed by the older adult;
    - a lack of entries for expected expenses, such as health insurance, property insurance, or taxes.

Other actions by a general guardian or guardian of the older adult's person are red flags for potential abuse by those guardians. Some of these include when the guardian

1. fails to file, or inadequately or incompletely files, any required status reports;
2. fails to respond to court notices or orders to complete such filings;
3. fails to visit the older adult regularly;
4. fails to oversee the older adult's care;
5. isolates the older adult from others;
6. induces fear of or submissiveness or unusual deference to the guardian by the older adult;
7. changes the older adult's residence without notifying the court or other family members or next of kin;
8. fails to take the older adult to necessary medical appointments;
9. refuses to allow the older adult to be interviewed alone;
10. treats the older adult like a child or in a dehumanizing way;
11. responds defensively when questioned;
12. blames the older adult for acts such as incontinence; or
13. fails to engage the older adult in decisions about the adult's day-to-day life.

WHAT TO DO IF YOU SUSPECT ELDER ABUSE BY A GUARDIAN.

- **Make an Adult Protective Services (APS) report.** Every person in North Carolina, with the singular exception of the long-term care ombudsman, must make an APS report if that person has reasonable cause to believe that a disabled adult needs protective services. This universal reporting requirement in North Carolina does not change simply because the adult has a guardian.[232] See Chapter 2 for a full discussion of the duty to report.
- **File a motion in the cause to modify the guardianship or a petition to remove the guardian.** As mentioned in Section II.E, *supra*, any interested person may file a motion in the cause before the clerk of superior court in the existing guardianship proceeding to modify the guardianship or a petition to remove the guardian if the guardian's actions (or lack thereof) result in elder abuse.
- **Make a report to law enforcement.** If there are concerns that the older adult is the victim of a crime, including one perpetrated by the guardian, the concerned person should make a report to law enforcement.
- **Make a claim on the bond.** If a guardian of the estate or a general guardian fails to perform his or her duties, the guardian may be removed and a new guardian appointed. The new guardian should make a claim on the bond (bonds are discussed in more detail in Section II.C, *supra*) with the bonding company to seek repayment for the older adult's loss due to the guardian's actions up to the amount recoverable under the bond.
- **File for civil damages.** A guardian may be held liable in civil court for breach of fiduciary duty, constructive fraud, or other offenses. Possible claims are set forth in Chapter 6. It may be necessary to seek civil damages in addition to any claim made on a bond. The bond may not cover the full amount of the damages to the older adult. Additional amounts may be recoverable through civil litigation.

232. *See* Aimee Wall, *Adult Protective Services: A New Reporting Requirement*, COATES' CANONS: N.C. LOC. GOV'T L. BLOG (June 23, 2015), https://canons.sog.unc.edu/adult-protective-services-a-new-reporting-requirement/.

B. LACK OF UNDERSTANDING OF GUARDIANSHIP

Most court-appointed individual guardians have had little training before taking on the responsibility of serving as someone else's guardian. This lack of understanding can leave the older adult open to abuse. Often, a spouse or family member of an older adult is told to "go get guardianship" by a hospital, a church, or some well-meaning person. Guardians are frequently unaware of the significance of their role and the breadth of decision-making they are charged with carrying out on the older adult's behalf.[233] People seeking guardianship for an incompetent adult often do not understand the scope of duties imposed on a guardian, including the duty to post a bond; maintain separate guardianship accounts; and file documents such as status reports, inventories, and accountings with the court. These filings may overwhelm an individual who has no history of managing and accounting for property or of documenting other actions taken on behalf of another person. This commonly occurs among spouses when one spouse is appointed as guardian for an incompetent spouse and the incompetent spouse was the one who handled the couple's finances prior to incompetency. In addition, the court proceedings can be costly, and costs are frequently charged against the estate of the older adult who is alleged to be incompetent.

233. *See* Meredith Smith, *Eight Common Mistakes Made by Guardians of an Incompetent Adult's Estate*, ON THE CIVIL SIDE: A UNC SCH. OF GOV'T BLOG (May 1, 2019), https://civil.sog.unc.edu/eight-common-mistakes-by-guardians-of-an-incompetent-adults-estate/.

RESOURCES FOR GUARDIANS.

The resources listed below will help guardians better understand the responsibilities, importance, and scope of their role.

- **Court files.** There are two court files produced when an older adult is adjudicated incompetent in North Carolina that are especially useful for guardians: the *incompetency special proceeding file* and the *guardianship estate file*. These files will contain copies of the court orders determining the type of guardian appointed and listing any limitations on the guardian's authority. In addition, the files will contain information related to the needs, assets, and liabilities of the older adult.
- ***Understanding Guardianship* video.** The North Carolina Administrative Office of the Courts (AOC) has created a video entitled "Understanding Guardianship." Guardians are advised to watch the video, which is available at https://www.nccourts.gov/about/nc-administrative-office-of-the-courts/training/understanding-guardianship.
- **Guardianship website and pamphlet.** The AOC maintains a help-topic webpage dedicated to providing information about the guardianship process in North Carolina (see https://www.nccourts.gov/help-topics/guardianship) and has created a form entitled "Responsibilities of Guardians in North Carolina" (see https://www.nccourts.gov/documents/forms/responsibilities-of-guardians-in-north-carolina).
- **Guardianship Services Manual (published for DSS and corporation guardians).** The N.C. Department of Health and Human Services' Division of Aging and Adult Services maintains a guardianship policy and procedures manual. It can be accessed at https://www.ncdhhs.gov/aging-and-adult-services-guardianship-services-policy-and-procedures-manual.
- **North Carolina Clerk of Superior Court Procedures Manual.** This manual, published by the School of Government, has two chapters on incompetency and guardianship proceedings. It is produced for clerks of superior court but is available for purchase by the public (see https://www.sog.unc.edu/publications/books/north-carolina-clerk-superior-court-procedures-manual-2012-edition-complete-set-volume-one-and).
- **Managing Someone Else's Money: Help for Court-Appointed Guardians of Property and Conservators.** The Consumer Financial Protection Bureau publishes guides to help people understand the role of a guardian of the estate or a general guardian (see https://files.consumerfinance.gov/f/documents/201310_cfpb_msem-help-for-court-appointed-guardians-of-property-and-conservators.pdf).

C. IMPACT ON AUTONOMY

Although guardianship serves an important function and may protect an older adult from abuse, it also limits the personal autonomy and legal rights of the affected older adult.[234] The law of guardianship attempts to strike a balance between preserving and protecting an older adult's legal rights, freedoms, and personal autonomy and the duty of the State to protect individuals who lack capacity, including the capacity to protect themselves or their property from harm, injury, or exploitation.[235]

It is important to note that not every older adult who lacks capacity needs a guardian. Guardianship should only be sought as a last resort when all other options, such as powers of attorney, trusts, and supportive decision-making, have failed or are not feasible. North Carolina law provides that placing limits on an older adult's rights by appointing a guardian for that adult should not be undertaken unless it is clear that a guardian will give the adult a fuller capacity for exercising his or her rights.[236]

IF NOT GUARDIANSHIP, THEN WHAT?

When an older adult appears to have some level of diminished capacity, rather than assuming that a full guardianship is needed, concerned individuals should

- consider seeking or granting a limited guardianship (Section II.C.2) or
- consider alternatives to guardianship. There are many alternatives to guardianship, such as a power of attorney, a representative payee, or a trust, that also may help protect an older adult from abuse. These alternatives empower a surrogate decision maker to act on behalf of the older adult and, in many cases, replace the need for a guardian. These and other alternatives are set out in Appendix A; powers of attorney are discussed in detail in Chapter 5.

D. INCREASING CASELOADS

The public guardianship system is dealing with increasing caseloads and limited resources to respond to the growing number of older adults in need of services. County departments of social services (DSS) are the only available disinterested public agent guardians in North Carolina and, if appointed by the court, they are required to serve.[237]

234. SAXON, *supra* note 2, at § 1.4, p. 8 (2008).
235. *Id.*
236. G.S. 35A-1201(a)(4).
237. G.S. 35A-1202(4); G.S. 35A-1213(d).

IDENTIFY AND CONSIDER OTHER POSSIBLE GUARDIANS.

- If DSS is not the party filing an incompetency petition for an older adult but it appears from the petition that DSS may be appointed as that adult's guardian, the court may direct the petitioner to serve of a copy of the petition and the notice of hearing on DSS at the time the incompetency petition is filed.[238] This will allow DSS to get involved in the case early to work to identify potential guardians (other than DSS) for the court to appoint.
- If DSS is appointed as an older adult's guardian, the agency will work to identify other potential guardians, such as family members and friends, and will work with those persons to prepare them to replace DSS as guardian with the approval of the court.[239]
- The clerk of superior court appoints DSS as an older adult's guardian only as a last resort.[240] The clerk, the petitioner, and the guardian ad litem each work diligently within their respective roles to identity an appropriate individual or corporation to serve as the older adult's guardian instead of DSS.

238. *See* G.S. 35A-1109 (allowing the clerk to designate other persons to receive notice of the incompetency petition and hearing).

239. G.S. 35A-1242(a1)(6).

240. G.S. 35A-1214.

Chapter 5
Powers of Attorney

CONTENTS

I. SCOPE OF CHAPTER

A power of attorney (POA) governed by Chapter 32C of the North Carolina General Statutes (hereinafter G.S.) grants authority to a person (the agent) to act on behalf of someone else (the principal) with respect to property and property interests. These POAs often make appearances in cases related to elder abuse. A POA may be used as a tool to protect against abuse; it also may be the source of abuse.

This chapter summarizes the parties responsible for POAs governed by G.S. Chapter 32C (also called the North Carolina Uniform Power of Attorney Act (NCUPOAA)), how these arrangements protect older adults, and how they work. It then discusses some common challenges that arise related to POAs when actors in the elder protection system seek to protect older adults from abuse. The chapter does not address health care powers of attorney (HCPOAs). G.S. Chapter 32A governs this type of POA, which is defined as "[a] written instrument . . . signed in the presence of two qualified witnesses, and acknowledged before a notary public, pursuant to which an attorney-in-fact or agent is appointed to act for the principal in matters relating to the health care of the principal."[1] The provisions of G.S. Chapter 32C specifically do not apply to a power to make health care decisions.[2]

II. OVERVIEW OF POWERS OF ATTORNEY (POAs)

A. WHO IS RESPONSIBLE?

1. PARTIES TO THE POA

Unlike guardianship, where a court appoints and oversees a guardian authorized to make decisions for someone else, a POA is a private arrangement. A POA is "[a] writing or other record that grants authority to an agent to act in the place of the principal."[3] An agent is sometimes called an "attorney-in-fact" (this is how now-repealed state law referred to agents). The term "agent" now includes an attorney-in-fact.[4] The agent may be an individual or any commercial or legal entity, such as a corporation or partnership.[5] The principal is the individual who executes the POA.[6]

1. Chapter 32A, Section 16(3), of the North Carolina General Statutes (hereinafter G.S.).
2. G.S. 32C-1-103(2).
3. G.S. 32C-1-102(9) (emphasis added). The term "power of attorney" does not have to be used for the writing or other record to be a power of attorney. *Id.*
4. G.S. 32C-1-102(1).
5. *Id.*; *id.* § 32C-1-102(8).
6. G.S. 32C-1-102(11).

Figure 5.1. **Parties to a POA**

The principal grants authority to the agent to act on the principal's behalf in the manner set forth in the POA with respect to some or all of the principal's property and property interests. An act by an agent under a POA has the same effect as, and binds the principal and the principal's successors in interest to the same extent as, if the principal had performed the act himself or herself.[7]

2. CAPACITY TO EXECUTE A POA

A principal must have capacity when he or she signs a POA. The standard of capacity applicable to the execution of a POA by a principal appears to be the same standard applicable to the capacity required to enter into a contract.[8] North Carolina courts have set the standard for competency to contract as follows:

> [A] person has mental capacity sufficient to contract if he knows what he is about, and that the measure of capacity is the ability to understand the nature of the act in which he is engaged and its scope and effect, or its nature and consequences, not that he should be able to act wisely or discreetly, nor to drive a good bargain, but that he should be in such possession of his faculties as to enable him to know at least what he is doing and to contract understandingly.[9]

In terms of a POA, this means that the principal must understand the nature of the act of executing a POA and the scope and effect of the POA on the agent's authority to handle the principal's property and other property interests.

3. OBTAINING A POA BY OR FOR AN OLDER ADULT

An older adult may draft and sign a POA or seek the assistance of an attorney who will prepare the POA for the older adult to sign. North Carolina law, in G.S. 32C-3-301, sets out a form POA that may be printed/duplicated and used free of charge.

7. G.S. 32C-2-201(h).

8. *See* Hedgepeth v. Home Sav. & Loan Ass'n, 87 N.C. App. 610, 611–12 (1987) (determining that a POA should be treated the same as a contract). *See also* O'Neal *ex rel.* Small v. O'Neal, 803 S.E.2d 184, 186-87 (N.C. Ct. App. 2017) (stating as a general matter that there is little reason to draw distinctions between POAs and contracts); 1 WIGGINS LAW OF WILLS AND TRUSTS IN NORTH CAROLINA § 20:3 (5th ed. 2020). *But see* RESTATEMENT (THIRD) OF AGENCY § 1.01 cmt. d (AM. LAW INST. 2006) (stating that an agency relationship does not always create an enforceable contract because many agents, such as family or friends of the principal, act or promise to act gratuitously).

9. Matthews v. James, 88 N.C. App. 32, 35 (1987) (quoting Sprinkle v. Wellborn, 140 N.C. 163, 181 (1905)). *See also* Ridings v. Ridings, 55 N.C. App. 630, 633, *discretionary review denied*, 305 N.C. 586 (1982).

RESOURCE

North Carolina Statutory Form POA

The statutory form POA is available online at https://www.ncleg.gov/Laws/GeneralStatuteSections/Chapter32C.

There are also groups, such as the N.C. Bar Foundation's Wills for Heroes program and Legal Aid of North Carolina's Senior Law Project, that provide free assistance in preparing POAs for certain eligible older adults. A private attorney will frequently charge fees for preparing a POA but may under certain circumstances draft a POA for a client pro bono (without charge). There are no generally available public funds to assist with the preparation and execution of POAs.

RESOURCE

Legal Aid of North Carolina—Senior Law Project

Legal Aid of North Carolina's Senior Law Project provides free civil legal help to North Carolinians who are 60 years of age or older.

Website

http://www.legalaidnc.org/about-us/projects/senior-law-project

Helpline:

- Toll-free: 1-877-579-7562
- Hours: Monday–Friday, 9–11 a.m. and 1–3 p.m.

There may be instances when an adult child contacts an attorney to prepare a POA for his or her parent and pays the attorney for the representation. The attorney may prepare the POA but the attorney must make clear that he or she represents the parent in that situation and has duties to the parent as the client.[10] The attorney must obtain the older adult's informed consent to the representation before accepting compensation for his or her services from the family member.[11] The attorney must determine whether the older adult wants or needs a POA; who the older adult, not the adult child, wants appointed as agent under the POA; and what powers the older adult wants the agent to be granted.[12] If the older adult has diminished capacity, Rule 1.14 of the N.C. Rules of Professional

10. N.C. State Bar, Preparation of Power of Attorney for Principal upon Request of Prospective Attorney-in-Fact, Formal Ethics Op. 7 (Jan. 16, 2004) (hereinafter 2003 FEO 7). Note that this rule does not apply to commercial or business transactions. *Id. See also* N.C. State Bar, Preparation of Legal Documents at the Request of Another, Formal Ethics Op. 11 (July 21, 2006) (hereinafter 2006 FEO 11). The attorney may meet with the adult child alone to discuss the representation of the parent, but the attorney must explain, in a timely and clear manner, that the attorney represents the parent and not the adult child. 2003 FEO 7. Statements given by the adult child in the initial interview may later be used by the attorney in the representation of the parent, including to defend a guardianship proceeding filed against the parent by the child. *Id.*

11. 2003 FEO 7, 2006 FEO 11, *supra* note 10.

12. 2003 FEO 7, *supra* note 10. *See also* 2006 FEO 11, *supra* note 10.

Conduct applies to guide the attorney in the representation of the older adult.[13] It requires the attorney to try to maintain a normal client-lawyer relationship, as far as this is reasonably possible, and to keep the client's interests foremost, looking to the older adult/client—and not the family member—when making decisions on the client's behalf.[14]

B. HOW DO POAs PROTECT OLDER ADULTS?

POAs empower an older adult (the principal) to grant authority to a trusted person (the agent) to act on the older adult's behalf. An older adult may execute a POA authorizing an agent to act on the older adult's behalf while the older adult has capacity or only after the adult becomes incapacitated and is unable to act. Examples of some of the different reasons why an older adult may execute a POA are provided below.

- An older adult has mental capacity but is homebound. He executes a POA granting a caregiver authority to access his bank accounts to pay bills, shop for groceries and household items, and manage other aspects of his property.
- An older adult is unavailable to attend the closing on the sale of property she owns. She executes a limited POA authorizing a family member to sign a deed on her behalf.
- An older adult executes a POA together with a will, an HCPOA, and a living will to prepare for future incapacity and death, naming his two children as co-agents.

POAs also protect older adults by preserving their autonomy and self-determination to a greater extent than more restrictive options for surrogate decision-making, such as guardianships, do.[15] Under a POA arrangement, an older adult retains legal ownership of his or her assets, as well as the authority to act when he or she has capacity. The older adult, not a court, selects the person authorized to act on his or her behalf and determines the nature and extent of an agent's authority under the POA. The agent can act without court oversight, unlike in a guardianship, and the principal's property and property interests are generally kept private. A POA may prevent the need for a court-appointed guardian of the estate or general guardian[16] if the older adult lacks capacity to make decisions or manage his or her property.

The benefits and protections provided to older adults by POAs may be outweighed in some cases by the risk of abuse. Abuse by the agent is discussed in Section III, *infra*.

---

13. N.C. R. PROF'L CONDUCT 1.14 (N.C. State Bar 1997, amended 2003, 2014). *See generally* ABA Comm'n on Law & Aging & Am. Psychol. Ass'n, *Assessment of Older Adults with Diminished Capacity: A Handbook for Lawyers* (2006), http://www.apa.org/pi/aging/resources/guides/diminished-capacity.pdf.

14. N.C. R. PROF'L CONDUCT 1.14(a) & cmt. [3]. The attorney may consult with individuals, including family members, who have the ability to take action to protect the client when the attorney reasonably believes that a client with diminished capacity is at risk of substantial physical, financial, or other harm unless action is taken and that the client cannot adequately act in his or her own interest. *Id.* at r. 1.14(b).

15. UNIF. POWER OF ATT'Y ACT, prefatory note (UNIF. LAW COMM'N 2006) (noting that a primary goal of the uniform law is to protect the principal's freedom to choose both the extent of the agent's authority and the principles to govern the agent's conduct).

16. Defined and discussed further in Chapter 4.

To ensure that a POA functions to protect an older adult and does not become a source of abuse, the older adult/principal may consider[17]

- selecting a trustworthy agent that will carry out the principal's expectations, values, and preferences and communicating those expectations, values, and preferences to the agent;
- clearly stating the agent's duties and authority, along with any limitations on the agent's authority, in the POA, including a limit on making gifts;
- including a statement in the POA that a third party may refuse to accept the POA if that party has a good faith belief that the principal is subject to abuse;
- requiring the agent, after the principal's incapacity, to account or submit regular financial statements to a third party who serves as a check on the agent's actions; and
- appointing a special fiduciary in the POA to approve any gifts made by the agent.

RESOURCE

The Consumer Financial Protection Bureau published a guide to assist family and friends serving as agents under POAs better understand the role of fiduciary. The guide, titled *Managing Someone Else's Money: Help for Agents under a Power of Attorney*, is available at https://files.consumerfinance.gov/f/documents/201310_cfpb_msem-help-for-agents-under-a-power-of-attorney.pdf.

C. HOW DO POAs WORK?

POAs are used often—and are often misunderstood. This section summarizes some of the basic aspects of POAs under North Carolina law, including

- what is required for a POA to be valid in North Carolina,
- when registration (recording) of the POA is required,
- third party protections for POAs accepted in good faith,
- the effect of the principal's incapacity on a POA,
- termination of the POA and an agent's authority,
- the meaning and effect of terms in a POA,

17. Linda S. Whitton, *Durable Powers as An Alternative to Guardianship: Lessons We Have Learned*, 37 STETSON L. REV. 7 (2007). *See generally* LORI A. STIEGEL & ELLEN VANCLEAVE KLEM, AARP PUB. POL'Y INST., POWER OF ATTORNEY ABUSE: WHAT STATES CAN DO ABOUT IT Exec. Summary, at vii–viii (2008), https://assets.aarp.org/rgcenter/consume/2008_17_poa.pdf (summarizing key provisions of the Uniform Power of Attorney Act that protect people who execute powers of attorney).

- when a POA is effective,
- the authority of an agent under a POA, and
- an agent's duties under a POA.

North Carolina passed the NCUPOAA, which took effect on January 1, 2018, and created G.S. Chapter 32C.[18] There are many POAs still in use that were created under the old law. Those POAs are still valid. The provisions of G.S. Chapter 32C discussed in this chapter generally apply to those POAs created before January 1, 2018, except in limited circumstances, such as a clear contrary intent expressed in the POA.[19]

1. REQUIREMENT FOR A POA TO BE VALID IN NORTH CAROLINA

As discussed in Section II.A.2, *supra*, in order for a POA to be valid in North Carolina, a principal must have capacity when he or she signs the POA. In addition, a POA must meet certain other technical requirements to be valid under North Carolina law. Those requirements are different depending on when and where the principal executed the POA.[20] An agent is not required to sign a POA for the POA to be valid.

A POA executed in this state on or after January 1, 2018, is valid if it is

a. signed[21] by the principal or by another individual directed by the principal to sign the principal's name on the POA in the principal's conscious presence[22] and
b. acknowledged.[23]

PRACTICE NOTE

A principal's signature on a POA is **presumed to be genuine** if it is acknowledged before a notary or other individual authorized to take acknowledgments.[24]

---

18. S.L. 2017-153. The General Assembly subsequently amended provisions of G.S. Chapter 32C in S.L. 2018-142 and S.L. 2019-243.

19. G.S. 32C-4-403 (setting out the effect of G.S. Chapter 32C on POAs executed prior to January 1, 2018).

20. G.S. 32C-1-105, -106. The purpose of these provisions is to promote the portability and use of POAs across jurisdictions. *See id.* § 32C-1-106, Official Cmt.

21. "Sign" means "[w]ith the present intent to authenticate or adopt a record, (i) to execute or adopt a tangible symbol or (ii) to attach to or logically associate with the record an electronic sound, symbol, or process." G.S. 32C-1-102(14).

22. "Conscious presence" under the Uniform Probate Code for the execution of wills generally requires that the signing by the person directed by the principal take place within the range of the principal's senses, such as sight or hearing; the signing need not have occurred within the testator's line of sight. Unif. Probate Code § 2-502 cmt. a (UNIF. LAW COMM'N 2010). North Carolina has not adopted the Uniform Probate Code. North Carolina probate law does not use or define the term "conscious presence," which is more expansive than the requirement under state law that the witnesses to an attested written will sign in the "presence" of the testator. G.S. 31-3.3; 32C-1-105, N.C. Cmt. To satisfy the requirement under North Carolina law that the witnesses sign in the presence of the testator, it is not necessary that the testator actually see the witnesses sign. *In re* Pridgen's Will, 249 N.C. 509, 512–14 (1959). It is sufficient if the signing was in the view of the testator and the testator would be capable of seeing the attesting witnesses sign the will. *Id.*; *In re* Cherry's Will, 164 N.C. 363 (1913); Graham v. Graham, 32 N.C. 219 (1849). *See also* G.S. 32C-1-105, N.C. Cmt.

23. G.S. 32C-1-105; 32C-1-106(a).

24. G.S. 32C-1-105 (emphasis added).

If a POA was executed in North Carolina prior to January 1, 2018, it is valid as long as it complied with North Carolina law at the time of its execution.[25] Under the law in effect in this state prior to January 1, 2018, a POA did not have to be acknowledged or witnessed to be valid.[26] It did have to be in writing and contain a grant of authority by the principal to an agent to act on the principal's behalf.[27]

If a POA was executed at any time in another state, it is valid in North Carolina if, when it was executed, it

- complied with the law of the jurisdiction indicated in the POA,
- without an indication of jurisdiction in the POA, complied with the law of the jurisdiction where it was executed, or
- complied with the requirements for a military POA under 10 U.S.C. § 1044b.[28]

The law of the jurisdiction indicated in a non-military POA controls over the place of execution. For example, if a POA is executed in Georgia but states that it is executed under North Carolina law, then North Carolina requirements for execution of a valid POA apply.[29]

Table 5.1. **Requirements for a POA to be Valid in North Carolina**

WHERE POA EXECUTED	WHEN POA EXECUTED	POA VALID IN NORTH CAROLINA IF IT COMPLIES WITH . . .
North Carolina	On or after January 1, 2018	G.S. 32C-1-105 (signed + acknowledged)
North Carolina	Before January 1, 2018	North Carolina law in effect at time of execution
Another state*	Before, on, or after January 1, 2018	Either 1. The law of the jurisdiction indicated in the POA; 2. If no jurisdiction is indicated in the POA, the law where the POA was executed; or 3. 10 U.S.C § 1044b (military POAs).

* The term "state" includes a state of the United States, the District of Columbia, Puerto Rico, the U.S. Virgin Islands, or "any territory or insular possession subject to the jurisdiction of" the U.S. G.S. 32C-1-102(15).

25. G.S. 32C-1-106(b).
26. *See generally* G.S. Ch. 32A, Arts. 1, 2 (repealed).
27. *See* N.C. Nat'l Bank v. Hammond, 298 N.C. 703, 713 (1979) (noting that G.S. 47-115.1 (which was later replaced by G.S. Chapter 32A) codified a particular subset of POAs which continued to be effective after the incapacity or mental incompetence of the principal but did not change the requirement that written authority is necessary for a POA); Howard v. Boyce, 266 N.C. 572, 577 (1966).
28. G.S. 32C-1-106(c), -107.
29. *See* G.S. 32C-1-106(c), -107.

2. WHEN REGISTRATION (RECORDING) OF THE POA IS REQUIRED

A POA does not have to be registered in a register of deeds office or with the clerk of superior court to be valid in North Carolina subsequent to a principal's incapacity.[30] This rule is stated in the NCUPOAA, which went into effect on January 1, 2018, and represents a change from prior law. Under the law previously in effect in North Carolina, no POA was valid after a principal's incapacity unless it was registered in the county register of deeds office.[31] In addition, within thirty days after registration, the agent under the POA had to file a copy of the POA with the clerk of superior court.[32] As a result of this prior law, there are many people who, in practice, may expect a POA to be recorded in order for it to be valid. But, as noted above, G.S. Chapter 32C does not require (1) registration of a POA after a principal's incapacity or incompetence or (2) later filing of the registered POA with the clerk in order for the POA to be valid.

The one exception to this rule applies when an agent desires to transfer real property under the POA. Before any transfer of real property executed by an agent under a POA, the POA, or a certified copy of it, must be registered in the register of deeds office in the county in which the principal is domiciled or where the real property lies.[33] If the principal is not a resident of North Carolina, the POA, or a certified copy of it, may be recorded in any county in this state in which the principal owns real property or has a significant business reason for registering the POA.[34]

3. THIRD-PARTY PROTECTIONS FOR POAs ACCEPTED IN GOOD FAITH

There are legal protections for third parties, such as financial institutions, who accept POAs in good faith, whether they are acknowledged or unacknowledged.[35] A third party can claim these protections provided that party does not have actual knowledge that

- the POA is void, invalid, or terminated;
- the purported agent's authority is void, invalid, or terminated; or
- the agent is exceeding or improperly exercising the agent's authority.[36]

A third party without actual knowledge of any of the circumstances listed above

- may rely on the POA as if
  - the POA were genuine, valid, and still in effect;
  - the agent's authority was genuine, valid, and still in effect; and

30. G.S. 32C-1-104, N.C. Cmt.
31. G.S. 32A-9(b) (repealed).
32. G.S. 32A-11(a) (repealed). Note that a principal or agent may present a POA for filing with the clerk under the misapprehension that it is still required. If a POA is presented for filing with the clerk and no related proceeding or request for relief is filed, the clerk opens an "E" file and places the POA in the file. *See* N.C. ADMIN. OFF. OF THE CTS., RULES OF RECORDKEEPING r. 6.1(g).
33. G.S. 47-28(a). The necessity to produce a POA in connection with the transfer of title dates far back into North Carolina law. *See* Yarborough v. Beard, 1 N.C. 117, Tay. 25 (1799) (holding that whenever a deed was executed by virtue of a POA, the POA or a copy of it must be produced).
34. G.S. 47-28(a).
35. G.S. 32C-1-119, N.C. Cmt.
36. G.S. 32C-1-119(c).

- the agent is not exceeding and had properly exercised the authority and
- shall not be held responsible for any breach of fiduciary duty by the agent.[37]

The purpose of these protections is to promote the acceptance of POAs by third parties. These protections would apply, for example, to a forged POA without an acknowledgment that was accepted by a person in good faith, unless that person has actual knowledge that (1) the POA or the agent's authority is void, invalid, or terminated or (2) the agent is exceeding or improperly exercising the agent's authority.[38]

EXAMPLE

An adult son forges his 85-year-old mother's signature and the acknowledgment on a POA. The mother is incapacitated and has a substantial 401K account. The son meets with the 401K account manager, who accepts the POA and allows the son to withdraw the total amount available from his mother's account, as is allowed under the terms of the POA.

- *Provided that the account manager did not have actual knowledge that the POA, or the agent's authority, was void and accepted the POA in good faith, the company for whom the account manager works may be protected against liability for allowing the son to withdraw the funds from the mother's retirement account.*
- *The mother may have a civil cause of action against the son to recover the money or to seek monetary damages, but likely not against the company that allowed the withdrawal. Civil actions are discussed in Chapter 6.*
- *The son may be subject to criminal prosecution for a crime such as common law forgery, obtaining property by false pretenses, or exploitation of an older adult. Criminal actions are discussed in Chapter 1.*
- *A friend, family member, or other person may file (1) a civil action to set aside the POA, (2) a POA proceeding to remove the agent for breach of fiduciary duty, or, if necessary, (3) a guardianship proceeding to appoint a guardian to terminate the POA. These are discussed in Section III.A, infra. Civil actions are discussed in detail in Chapter 6.*

37. *Id.*

38. Andrew H. Hook & Thomas D. Begley, Jr., *Uniform Power of Attorney Act: Protecting Third Parties Too Much?*, 37 EST. PLAN. 36, 37 (2010). The NCUPOAA places the risk that the POA is forged on the principal rather than on a third party. G.S. 32C-1-119, Official Cmt. This includes when someone forges the principal's signature on a POA and presents an unacknowledged POA to a third party, who then accepts the POA in good faith and without actual knowledge that it is invalid. G.S. 32C-1-119(c), N.C. Cmt. (providing protections to third parties for both acknowledged and unacknowledged POAs).

4. EFFECT OF THE PRINCIPAL'S INCAPACITY ON THE POA

A POA that is durable is a POA that is not terminated by the incapacity of the principal.[39] This means that the POA continues to remain in effect and the agent may act on the principal's behalf after the incapacity of the principal. A POA is durable unless it expressly states that it is terminated by the incapacity of the principal.[40] If the POA was created prior to January 1, 2018, and it is silent regarding durability, it is durable unless such an interpretation would substantially impair the rights of a party.[41]

EXAMPLE

An older adult executes a POA for the limited purpose of authorizing a family member, John, to sign a deed conveying property owned by the older adult. The older adult will be out of town when the closing is scheduled to occur and thus unable to attend the closing in person. The POA expressly states it is not durable and terminates upon the incapacity of the principal. A year later, the older adult suffers significant cognitive decline due to dementia. The county department of social services (DSS) receives a report that the adult is the subject of financial abuse. During the investigation, John tells DSS that the older adult appointed him as agent under a POA and he can take action as agent to protect the older adult from further financial abuse. DSS should obtain a copy of the POA and review it. John's statements are not consistent with the actual authority granted to him as agent under the POA. Because the POA is not durable, it terminated upon the older adult's incapacity. Therefore, John no longer has authority to act as agent under the POA. DSS risks leaving the adult without someone to act on the adult's behalf if it relies simply on John's statements about the POA and screens the case out on the mistaken belief that John has the authority to act on behalf of the older adult under the POA when, in reality, the POA terminated upon the principal's incapacity.

5. TERMINATION OF THE POA AND THE AGENT'S AUTHORITY

a. Termination of the POA

A POA terminates when any of the following occurs:[42]

1. The principal dies.
2. The POA is not durable and the principal becomes incapacitated.
3. The principal revokes the POA.
4. The POA provides that it terminates.

39. G.S. 32C-1-102(2).
40. G.S. 32C-1-104.
41. G.S. 32C-4-403(a)(4).
42. G.S. 32C-1-110(a).

5. The purpose of the POA is accomplished.
6. The principal revokes the agent's authority or the agent dies, becomes incapacitated, or resigns, and the POA does not provide for another agent to act under the POA.
7. A guardian of the principal's estate or general guardian terminates the POA.

b. Termination of the Agent's Authority

An agent's authority under a POA terminates when any of the following occurs:[43]

1. The principal revokes the agent's authority in writing.
2. The agent dies, becomes incapacitated, resigns, or is removed.
3. The court enters a decree of divorce between the principal and the agent. (Note: If the POA provides that divorce does not terminate the agent's authority, then that authority is not terminated by a divorce decree.)
4. The POA terminates.
5. A guardian of the principal's estate or general guardian terminates the agent's authority.

c. Effect of Termination on the Agent

If an agent does not have actual knowledge of the termination of (1) a POA or (2) the agent's authority under the POA, then the termination is not effective as to that agent, so long as the agent acts in good faith.[44] Any acts performed after termination by the agent in good faith and without actual knowledge of the termination bind the principal and the principal's successors in interest.[45] This is true unless the agent's act is otherwise invalid or unenforceable, such as any act that exceeds the scope of authority granted in the POA.[46]

EXAMPLE

John, the principal under a POA, dies at the age of 65. The agent under the POA is a local credit union. No one alerts the credit union that John died. Any acts conducted by the credit union, as agent under the POA, on behalf of John after his death still bind John's estate, so long as the acts are conducted in good faith and are not otherwise invalid or unenforceable.

43. G.S. 32C-1-110(b)
44. G.S. 32C-1-110(d).
45. *Id.*
46. *Id.*

d. Effect of Termination on a Third Party

If a third party does not have actual knowledge of the termination of (1) a POA or (2) the agent's authority under the POA, then the termination is not effective as to the third party, so long as the third party acts in good faith and the transaction is not otherwise invalid or unenforceable.[47] The principal and the principal's successors in interest are bound by such transactions.[48] This is true even if the agent has actual knowledge of the termination, as long as (1) the third party acts in good faith, (2) the third party does not have actual knowledge of the termination, and (3) the transaction is not otherwise invalid or unenforceable.[49]

EXAMPLE

Sally, the principal under a non-durable POA, becomes incapacitated (note that this terminates a POA under G.S. 32C-1-110(a)(2), as discussed above). Sally's agent under the POA is her son, Frank. Frank knows that Sally is incapacitated but continues to conduct transactions on Sally's behalf as agent under the POA. Frank sells Sally's car to a third-party purchaser for value. The non-durable POA authorizes Frank to sell Sally's car while Sally has capacity. Frank does not alert the third-party purchaser that Sally is now incapacitated and that the non-durable POA is therefore terminated. The sale of the car by Frank to the third-party purchaser binds Sally and Sally's successors in interest, provided that the sale is conducted by the third-party purchaser in good faith and is not otherwise invalid or unenforceable.[50]

6. MEANING AND EFFECT OF TERMS IN A POA

To analyze and construe the terms of a POA, it is necessary to first determine what law applies to the POA—whether the law of North Carolina applies to give meaning and effect to the POA or whether the law of another jurisdiction controls. This is first determined by looking at the POA itself.[51] If the POA expressly indicates that the law of a certain jurisdiction applies to give meaning and effect to the POA, then that law applies.[52] If the POA lacks an indication of jurisdiction, then the law of the jurisdiction in which the POA was executed applies.[53]

---

47. *Id.*
48. *Id.*
49. G.S. 32C-1-110, Official Cmt. (citing RESTATEMENT (THIRD) OF AGENCY § 3.11 (2006), which provides that termination of actual authority does not end any apparent authority held by the agent). *See also* G.S. 32C-1-119(c) (providing protections for any third party who accepts a POA in good faith without actual knowledge that the POA is terminated, including the protection that the third party may rely on the POA and the agent's authority as if they were genuine, valid, and still in effect).
50. G.S. 32C-1-110(e).
51. G.S. 32C-1-107.
52. *Id.*
53. *Id.*

EXAMPLE

A POA grants an agent the authority "to make gifts" on behalf of the principal, an older adult. The principal's in-home aide is the agent under the POA. The aide makes gifts of the older adult's property to the aide's wife in the amount of $335,000. A friend of the older adult makes a report to law enforcement that the aide is "stealing" from the older adult. To determine whether the gift by the aide is authorized by the POA or whether it exceeds the scope of his authority, the investigator will need to review the POA to determine what law—North Carolina law or the law of another state—applies to give meaning and effect to the term "make a gift."

Under North Carolina law, an agent may make a gift of the principal's property only if the POA expressly states that the agent has the authority to make a gift.[54] *The nature and extent of the agent's gifting authority depends on what is set out in the POA. If the POA only states that the agent has the authority to "make a gift," then the nature and extent of the agent's authority to make a gift is limited by North Carolina statute.*[55] *Under those circumstances, an agent may not make a gift that exceeds the greater of (1) the amount determined to be in accordance with the principal's history of making or of joining in the making of gifts or (2) the annual dollar limit of the federal gift tax exclusion.*[56] *If North Carolina law gives the POA meaning and effect, and if the aide's gift exceeds the scope of authority granted to the agent in the POA, then the aide may be guilty of a crime, such as embezzlement or exploitation of an older adult or disabled adult (discussed in more detail in Chapter 3).*

7. WHEN A POA IS EFFECTIVE

The default rule is that a POA is effective when it is executed.[57] This reflects the idea that any agent that can be trusted to act as an agent should be trusted enough to hold an immediate power, even if the principal still retains the desire and capacity to manage his or her own property and business affairs.[58] This rule also ensures that an agent can act immediately when needed by the principal. But a principal may instead desire to make a POA effective upon a future date or upon the occurrence of a future event or contingency,[59] such as the principal's incapacity.

54. G.S. 32C-2-201(a)(1)a.
55. G.S. 32C-2-217(b).
56. G.S. 32C-2-217(b)(1)a.
57. G.S. 32C-1-109(a). Note that although the POA may be effective, an agent does not accept appointment under a POA, and thus the agency relationship does not commence, until the agent exercises authority, performs duties, takes some other act, or makes some other assertion that indicates acceptance, unless the POA states otherwise. *Id.* § 32C-1-113. There is no statutory requirement that the POA must be actually delivered to the agent for the agent to have the authority to act on the principal's behalf. *See id.*
58. G.S. 32C-1-109, Official Cmt.
59. G.S. 32C-1-109(a).

KEY TERM

A POA effective upon the occurrence of a future event or contingency is often called a ***springing POA****.*

If the POA is effective upon a future event or contingency, the principal may authorize one or more persons in the POA to determine in a writing or other record that the event or contingency has occurred.[60] For example, the POA may state that it becomes effective upon the principal's incapacity. Once the principal becomes incapacitated, the authorized person(s) designated in the POA may write, date, and sign a statement that the principal is incapacitated and indicate that the agent's authority under the POA is activated or "sprung" into effect.[61]

KEY TERM

Incapacity *under the North Carolina Uniform Power of Attorney Act (NCUPOAA) is defined as the inability of an individual to manage his or her property or business affairs because he or she*

a. has "[a]n impairment in the ability to receive and evaluate information or make or communicate decisions even with the use of technological assistance"[62] *or*

b. "[i]s missing, detained, including incarcerated in a penal system, or outside the United States and unable to return."[63]

If the POA is effective upon the principal's incapacity and the principal has not authorized a person to determine whether the principal is incapacitated, or if the person authorized is unable or unwilling to make the determination, the POA becomes effective upon a determination in a writing or other record by either

- two individuals, who are either a physician, a licensed psychologist, or both, and after a personal examination, that the principal is unable to manage his or her property or business affairs because he or she has an impairment in the ability to receive and evaluate information or make or communicate decisions, even with the use of technological assistance, or[64]
- an attorney-at-law, a judge, or an appropriate governmental official[65] that the principal is unable to manage his or her property or business affairs because he or

60. G.S. 32C-1-109(b).

61. There is no requirement in G.S. Chapter 32C that the statement signed by the designated person be in the form of an affidavit or otherwise made under oath.

62. G.S. 32C-1-102(6)a.

63. G.S. 32C-1-102(6)b.

64. G.S. 32C-1-109(c)(1), -102(6)a.

65. If the principal is incarcerated in North Carolina, for example, the appropriate governmental official is likely the district or superior court judge who presided over the principal's case. If the principal is detained, such as by

she is missing; detained, including incarcerated in a penal system; or outside the United States and unable to return.[66]

EXAMPLE

Joan executes a POA appointing her son, Frank, as her agent. The POA states that it does not become effective until Joan is incapacitated, as determined in writing by her personal doctor, Dr. Betty Smith. Two years later, Joan is struggling with some of her day-to-day activities due to a stroke. Frank takes Joan to see Dr. Smith, but Dr. Smith refuses to state in writing that Joan is incapacitated, in part because she does not trust Frank. Frank then takes Joan to an urgent care clinic and gets the nurse practitioner there to put in writing that Joan is incapacitated. Frank then uses the POA to change the beneficiaries on Joan's retirement accounts, to sell Joan's home and move her to an assisted living facility, and to open a new credit card in Joan's name and make charges on the card. Each action may have been authorized under the POA but, because Frank did not obtain a letter from Joan's personal doctor, the POA never "sprung" into effect. Frank therefore lacked the authority to act as agent under the POA. Frank may be subject to civil or criminal liability for his unauthorized acts.

8. THE AUTHORITY OF AN AGENT UNDER A POA

The nature and extent of the agent's authority are set by the principal in the POA and will vary from POA to POA. When the court or a third party is presented with a POA, it is important to read the POA to determine the scope of and any limitations on an agent's authority.[67] An agent under one POA likely does not have the same authority as an agent under another POA. Furthermore, an agent may have the authority to act with respect to some areas of an older adult's property and property interests but not as to all areas. Granting one type of authority to an agent does not mean that the older adult has consented to all acts by the agent.

The NCUPOAA sets out various kinds of authority a principal may grant to an agent under a POA, which fall into four different categories:

1. general authority,
2. specific authority,
3. the authority to make a gift, and
4. incidental authority.

---

immigration officials, or precluded from entering the United States, then a statement from the federal officials with custody of the principal would seem appropriate. If the principal is missing, the appropriate governmental official may be a federal or state law enforcement officer. If the principal is unavailable due to military service, then the appropriate governmental official may be a person in the uniformed services of the United States. *See* G.S. 32C-1-109, Official Cmt.

66. G.S. 32C-1-109(c)(2); 32C-1-102(6)b.

67. *See* SunTrust v. C & D Custom Homes, LLC, 223 N.C. App. 347, 350–51 (2012).

a. General Authority

If a POA states that an agent has the authority "to do all of the acts a principal could do" or that the agent has general authority to act on the principal's behalf, then the agent has general authority to act/enter into transactions in the areas listed below, as set forth in the corresponding provisions of G.S. Chapter 32C.[68]

AREA	STATUTE (G.S.)
Real property	32C-2-204
Tangible personal property	32C-2-205
Stocks and bonds	32C-2-206
Commodities and options	32C-2-207
Banks and other financial institutions	32C-2-208
Operation of entity	32C-2-209
Insurance and annuities	32C-2-210
Estates, trusts, and other beneficial interests	32C-2-211
Claims and litigation	32C-2-212
Personal and family maintenance	32C-2-213
Benefits from governmental programs or civil or military service	32C-2-214
Retirement plans	32C-2-215
Taxes	32C-2-216

The drafter of a POA may incorporate by reference all or some of these provisions of general authority when establishing an agent's authority in the POA. The drafter may choose to grant the general authority to the agent by listing a descriptive term, such as "real property," or the related statutory citation, such as "G.S. 32C-2-204."[69] A reference in a POA to either a descriptive term for a subject or a citation to G.S. 32C-2-204 through -216 incorporates the entire section as if it were set out in full in the POA.[70] The drafter of a POA may modify in the POA any authority incorporated by reference.[71] Note that if a POA was created before January 1, 2018, using the statutory short form authorized under the now-repealed G.S. 32A-1, the powers conferred by the former G.S. 32A-2 apply.[72]

If the POA references some but not all of the descriptive terms or statutory citations listed above, then it does not incorporate all of the areas of general authority, and the agent only has general authority with regard to the areas listed. For example, if a POA

68. G.S. 32C-2-201(d).
69. G.S. 32C-2-202(a).
70. G.S. 32C-2-202(b). Note that inclusion of the descriptive term "make a gift" or the citation G.S. 32C-2-217 also incorporates the entire section as if it were set out in full in the POA. *Id.* Gifting authority is treated as both specific and general authority under the POA and is discussed separately in Section II.C.8.c, *infra*.
71. G.S. 32C-2-202(c).
72. G.S. 32C-4-403(d).

states that the agent has only general authority over real property, then the agent has all of the authority set out in G.S. 32C-2-204 but lacks the authority over any of the other areas of general authority, such as taxes, insurance, or any of the other subjects set out in G.S. 32C-2-205 through -216.

b. Specific Authority

Specific authority is authority that must be expressly granted in the POA in order for the agent to act; it may not be inferred from a general grant of authority.[73] The actions by an agent that require an express grant of specific authority in the POA under G.S. 32C-2-201(a)(1) include the authority to

- create or change rights of survivorship;
- create or change a beneficiary designation;
- delegate authority granted under the POA;
- waive the principal's right to be a beneficiary of a joint and survivor annuity, including a survivor benefit under a retirement plan;
- exercise fiduciary powers that the principal has authority to delegate;
- renounce or disclaim property, including a power of appointment; and
- exercise authority over the content of electronic communication, as defined in 18 U.S.C. § 2510(12), sent or received by the principal.

Furthermore, an agent may do the following only if the POA or the terms of a trust expressly grant such authority to the agent:

- exercise the powers of the principal as settlor of a revocable trust in accordance with G.S. 36C-6-602.1[74] or
- exercise the powers of the principal as settlor of an irrevocable trust to consent to the trust's modification or termination in accordance with G.S. 36C-4-411(a).[75]

These actions require a specific grant of authority because of the risk they pose to the principal's property and estate plan.[76] Despite the risk, it may be necessary to grant the agent the authority in order to effectuate the principal's property management and estate-planning objectives.[77] These areas of specific authority are often called "hot powers" because of the risks associated with them. A principal may further define or limit the specific authority granted in a POA.[78] For example, if a principal grants an agent the specific

73. UNIF. POWER OF ATTY ACT, Authority, General Cmt. (UNIF. LAW COMM'N 2006).
74. G.S. 32C-2-201(a)(2)a.
75. G.S. 32C-2-201(a)(2)b.
76. G.S. 32C-2-201, Official Cmt. The Official Comment also notes that these are areas where the principal would ideally seek advice before granting authority to the agent. *Id.*
77. *Id.*
78. *Id.*

authority to change survivorship rights or beneficiary designations, the principal may choose to restrict that authority to specifically-identified property interests, accounts, or contracts.[79]

c. Authority to Make a Gift

i. POA Is Silent Regarding Gifts

Gifting authority is in a category all its own because it is referred to throughout G.S. Chapter 32C as requiring general and specific authority.[80] If a POA is silent about gifts, then the agent lacks the authority to make gifts without a court order authorizing the particular gift.[81] This rule applies even when a POA states that the agent has the general authority to "do all of the acts a principal could do" or otherwise states that the agent has the broad authority to manage the principal's property.[82] This broad language does not confer gifting authority on the agent.

ii. POA Grants General Authority to Make a Gift

If the POA (1) expressly states that the agent is authorized to make a gift, (2) grants the agent general authority with respect to gifts, or (3) grants the agent only the authority under G.S. 32C-2-217, then the agent's gifting authority is not unlimited.[83] The agent may only make gifts under G.S. 32C-2-217, which provides, in part, that the agent may not make a gift to an individual that exceeds the greater of the amount determined to be in accordance with the principal's history of making or of joining in making of gifts or the annual dollar limit of the federal gift tax exclusion.[84]

iii. POA Grants Specific Authority to Make a Gift

Any authority that enlarges, modifies, or limits the agent's general authority to make a gift under G.S. 32C-2-217 requires specific, express language in the POA.[85] For example, if the goal is for the agent to be able to make unlimited gifts to a trust but the principal does not have a history of making such gifts, then the POA must expressly state this authority.

---

79. *Id.*

80. *See* G.S. 32C-2-201(a)(1)a (the specific authority to make a gift), -217 (gifts authorized by general authority).

81. G.S. 32C-2-218. *See also id.* §§ 32C-2-201(a), (d), -217.

82. G.S. 32C-2-201(d). This is unlike prior law under G.S. 32A-14.1 (repealed), which was enacted in 1995 and stated in subsection (a) that an express grant of power was not required to make gifts to individuals or charitable organizations in accordance with the principal's history of making gifts. *Id.* § 32C-2-201, N.C. Cmt.

83. G.S. 32C-2-201(a)(1)a; -217; -217, Official Cmt.

84. G.S. 32C-2-217(b)(1).

85. G.S. 32C-2-217, Official Cmt.

Table 5.2. **An Agent's Authority to Make a Gift under the NCUPOAA**

LANGUAGE IN THE POA	AGENT'S GIFT AUTHORITY
POA is silent or says that the agent has all of the powers of the principal	No authority to make a gift
POA only says that the agent has the authority to make a gift or references G.S. 32C-2-217	Agent ONLY has the authority to make gifts set forth in G.S. 32C-2-217, subject to G.S. 32C-2-201(b) and (c)
Any other authority to make gifts	Must be specifically set forth in the POA, subject to G.S. 32C-2-201(b) and (c), unless the POA states otherwise

Author's Note: The court may authorize any gift that is reasonable under the circumstances, including a gift that is in addition to or different from a gift authorized by the POA. G.S. 32C-2-218.

iv. Gifts Must Be Made in Accordance with the Principal's Objectives, if Known

Unless the POA states otherwise, the agent has a duty to make gifts in accordance with the principal's objectives, if these are known by the agent.[86] If the principal's objectives are not known by the agent, then the agent has a duty to make gifts consistent with the principal's best interests based on all relevant factors, which may include, but are not limited to,

- the value and nature of the principal's property;
- the principal's foreseeable obligations and need for maintenance;
- minimization of taxes, including income, estate, inheritance, generation-skipping transfer, and gift taxes;
- eligibility for a benefit, a program, or assistance under a statute or regulation;
- the principal's personal history of making or of joining in the making of gifts; and
- the principal's existing estate plan.[87]

Furthermore, under G.S. 32C-2-201(c), unless the POA states otherwise, the agent may not exercise authority under a POA to create in the agent, or in an individual to whom the agent owes a legal obligation of support, an interest in the principal's property, whether by gift or otherwise.

86. G.S. 32C-2-201(b).
87. G.S. 32C-2-201(b), (e).

d. Incidental Authority

Incidental authority is the authority that comes with or "tags along" when the principal executes a POA that (1) grants the agent any general authority, (2) grants the agent the authority to make a gift, or (3) states that the agent may do all of the acts the principal could do.[88] By granting an agent one of these types of authority, a principal also authorizes the agent to do the other "incidental acts" to exercise or implement that authority. Areas of incidental authority are set out below.[89]

1. Demand, receive, and obtain by litigation or otherwise, money or another thing of value to which the principal is, may become, or claims to be entitled, and conserve, invest, disburse, or use anything so received or obtained for the purposes intended.
2. Contract in any manner with any person, on terms agreeable to the agent, to accomplish a purpose of a transaction and perform, rescind, cancel, terminate, reform, restate, release, or modify the contract or another contract made by or on behalf of the principal.
3. Execute, acknowledge, seal, deliver, file, or record any instrument or communication the agent considers desirable to accomplish a purpose of a transaction, including creating at any time a schedule listing some or all of the principal's property and attaching it to the POA.
4. Initiate, participate in, submit to alternative dispute resolution, settle, oppose, or propose or accept a compromise with respect to a claim existing in favor of or against the principal or intervene in litigation relating to the claim.
5. Seek on the principal's behalf the assistance of a court or other governmental agency to carry out an act authorized in the POA.
6. Engage, compensate, and discharge an attorney, accountant, discretionary investment manager, expert witness, or other advisor.
7. Prepare, execute, and file a record, report, or other document to safeguard or promote the principal's interest under a statute or regulation.
8. Communicate with any representative or employee of a government or governmental subdivision, agency, or instrumentality, on behalf of the principal.
9. Access communications intended for, and communicate on behalf of the principal, whether by mail, electronic transmission, telephone, or other means.
10. Do any lawful act with respect to the subject and all property related to the subject.

---

88. G.S. 32C-2-203.
89. *Id.*

9. THE AGENT'S DUTIES UNDER A POA

An agent under a POA is a fiduciary concerning matters that are within the scope of the agency.[90] A fiduciary relationship is one of trust and confidence and carries with it certain legal responsibilities or duties.[91] To determine whether an agent has violated a duty under a POA and whether, as a result, the older adult/principal may have a claim for civil damages or a court should remove the agent for breach, it is necessary to identify the agent's duties to the principal under the POA. There are three sources for an agent's duties under a POA: (1) the POA, (2) statutory law, and (3) the common law of agency.[92]

The statutory duties imposed on an agent under G.S. Chapter 32C fall into two categories: (1) mandatory duties that may not be altered by the principal in a POA and (2) default duties that may be altered or eliminated by the principal in the POA.[93]

The agent's duties apply only when the agent exercises authority under a POA.[94] An agent has no affirmative duty to exercise powers or to continue to exercise powers granted to the agent by the POA, unless the POA states otherwise.[95]

Because a POA may expressly alter or omit any of the default duties of an agent, it is important to review every POA to determine the nature and extent of the agent's duties, particularly in a proceeding before a court alleging breach of an agent's duty. The principal may impose certain duties on the agent in the POA beyond what is set forth in G.S. Chapter 32C, such as the duty to account to the principal or to another person designated in the POA.

90. Albert v. Cowart, 219 N.C. App. 546, 554 (2012) ("The relationship created by a power of attorney between the principal and the attorney-in-fact is fiduciary in nature . . . ."); SNML Corp. v. Bank of N.C., 41 N.C. App. 28, 37 (1979); Honeycutt v. Farmers & Merchs. Bank, 126 N.C. App. 816, 820 (1997); G.S. 32C-1-114, Official Cmt. *See also* Meinhard v. Salmon, 249 N.Y. 458, 464 (1928) (stating that many forms of conduct permissible for those acting at arm's length are forbidden to those bound by fiduciary ties; a fiduciary "is held to something stricter than the morals of the market place").

91. Estate of Graham v. Morrison, 168 N.C. App. 63, 74 (2005); Dallaire v. Bank of Am., N.A., 367 N.C. 363, 367 (2014) (discussing different fiduciary relationships and providing that common to all fiduciary relationships is a heightened level of trust).

92. Linda S. Whitton, *Understanding Duties and Conflicts of Interest—A Guide for the Honorable Agent*, 117 PENN. ST. L. REV. 1037, 1040–41 (2013) (noting that the drafters of the uniform law "chose to enumerate specific duties because neither the common law nor existing state statutes provided a cohesive fiduciary standard for the [POA] relationship"). *See also In re* Skinner, 370 N.C. 126, 144 (2017) (noting that the question of whether a fiduciary violated a duty is a broader question than simply whether the fiduciary violated the written instrument governing the relationship, and that additional duties may be imposed by law).

93. G.S. 32C-1-114.

94. The duties imposed on an agent under G.S. Chapter 32C do not apply until the agent accepts the appointment as agent and exercises authority under the POA. G.S. 32C-1-114(a), (b).

95. G.S. 32C-1-114(b).

Table 5.3. **Mandatory and Default Duties of an Agent under G.S. Chapter 32C-1-114(a) and (b)**

MANDATORY DUTIES (May NOT Be Altered in the POA)	DEFAULT DUTIES (May Be Altered or Eliminated in the POA)
1. Act in accordance with the principal's reasonable expectations, to the extent they are actually known by the agent; otherwise, act in the principal's best interests.	1. Act loyally for the principal's benefit.
2. Act in good faith.	2. Act so as not to create a conflict of interest that impairs the agent's ability to act impartially in the principal's best interests.
3. Act only within the scope of authority granted in the POA.	3. Act with the care, competence, and diligence ordinarily exercised by agents in similar circumstances.
	4. Keep a record of all receipts, disbursements, and transactions made on behalf of the principal.
	5. Cooperate with any person who has authority to make health care decisions for the principal to carry out the principal's reasonable expectations, to the extent they are actually known by the agent; otherwise, act in the principal's best interests.
	6. Attempt to preserve the principal's estate plan, to the extent it is actually known by the agent, if preserving the plan is consistent with the principal's best interests based on all relevant factors.

III. CHALLENGES FOR POAs

A. ABUSE BY THE AGENT UNDER A POA

POAs are often recommended to older adults because of their flexibility, convenience, low cost, and lack of court involvement.[96] But POAs may also be a source of abuse against older adults. They have been referred to by some commentators as a "license to steal."[97] Common categories of abuse related to POAs include when a POA is improperly obtained and when an agent exceeds the scope of authority granted in a POA.

1. COMMON TYPES OF ABUSE

a. POA Improperly Obtained

Because POAs are private arrangements, an unscrupulous individual may write a POA and present it to an older adult to sign. The individual may use the older adult's lack of capacity or fraud, duress, undue influence, or misrepresentation to induce the older adult to sign the POA.

EXAMPLE

Jane Smith was a 98-year-old woman who lived alone in Florida after her husband died. She had no children. She had dementia and needed assistance with her care. A distant relative of Mrs. Smith appeared and offered to help her with her day-to-day needs. He moved Mrs. Smith from Florida to Alabama and had her sign a POA appointing him as her agent. He told her that she needed to sign the POA to lease her new apartment in Alabama. The POA was drafted by the relative's girlfriend. The relative then proceeded to exploit Mrs. Smith by using her money to gamble, to buy a house for himself, and to purchase large items such as motorcycles, a bulldozer, and a convenience store. In total, the relative spent around $53,000 per month and a total sum of $2.3 million.[98]

b. Agent Exceeds Scope of Authority

The agent has only the authority granted in the POA. If the agent exceeds the scope of that authority, the agent may be subject to civil or criminal liability.

---

96. *See* STIEGEL & VANCLEAVE KLEM, *supra* note 17, at 5.

97. *Id.*

98. Adapted from a May 16, 2015, story by Kym Klass in the *Montgomery Advertiser* describing the case of Virginia Freck that is available here: https://www.montgomeryadvertiser.com/story/life/project7/2015/05/17/project-elder-abuse/27479125/.

EXAMPLE

Tom executes a POA that gives the agent, Sarah, general authority over "real property." This means that Sarah has all of the authority set out in G.S. 32C-2-204, including the authority to sell, mortgage, and lease all real property owned by Tom. Sarah then cashes out Tom's retirement accounts, life insurance, and bank accounts. Sarah has exceeded the scope of her authority under the POA.

EXAMPLE

Fred executes a POA stating that his agent, John, has the authority to do all of the acts Fred could do. This means that John has all of the general authority set out under G.S. 32C-2-204 through -216 related to real property, personal property, taxes, insurance, retirement plans, and other areas described in those statutes. John then makes a gift of Fred's property and changes the beneficiary designations on Fred's retirement accounts. John exceeded the scope of his authority under the POA because the authority to make a gift and the authority to change beneficiary designations are not expressly set forth in the POA, which is required for an agent to have those types of specific authority.

WHAT TO DO IF YOU SUSPECT THAT AN AGENT FOR AN OLDER ADULT IS ABUSING AUTHORITY GRANTED UNDER A POA.

In such circumstances, the older adult, or someone acting with or on behalf of the older adult, could consider taking the following actions:

a. get a copy of the POA,
b. gather information/evidence,
c. refuse to accept the POA,
d. make a report to APS or law enforcement,
e. terminate the POA or the agent's authority, and
f. seek judicial relief.

Each of these actions is discussed in detail below.

2. POSSIBLE WAYS TO RESPOND TO ABUSE

a. Get a Copy of the POA

There is no standardized form POA that every individual who executes a POA must use. Although there is a form POA set out in statute, that form may be modified or ignored completely by the drafter of a POA. Each POA is unique. A POA is drafted to reflect the needs and wishes of a particular principal. It is imperative for any person who seeks to understand the authority granted to an agent by a principal in a POA to have a copy of the POA. This includes a law enforcement officer investigating a crime, a county social worker investigating reports of elder abuse, and a court seeking to determine whether an agent under a POA committed a breach of fiduciary duty.

PRACTICE NOTE

1. **Treat each POA as unique**—it is not a requirement that the available statutory form be used; if the form is used, it may be modified.
2. **Get a copy of the POA**—ask the principal, check with family and friends, and search the county register of deeds office for a recorded copy of the POA (note that the POA does not have to be recorded to be valid; see Section II.C.1, *supra*).
3. **Review the POA for the agent's authority to act and the extent of the agent's duties**—determine what acts are authorized by the POA and what duties it imposes on the agent (see Sections II.C.8 and 9, *supra*).

Reviewing the POA will enable the law enforcement officer, the county social worker, or the court to begin to answer key questions about whether the agent's actions on behalf of the principal were authorized or whether the agent's actions constitute elder abuse.

b. Gather Information/Evidence

There may be instances in which abuse of an older adult by an agent under a POA is suspected but not confirmed. Unless the POA states otherwise, the agent must keep a record of all receipts, disbursements, and transactions made on behalf of an older adult/principal.[99] The agent must disclose receipts, disbursements, or transactions conducted on behalf of the principal when

1. ordered to do so by a court or
2. a request to do so is made by
   a. the principal or a person designated by the principal in the POA;
   b. a guardian of the estate (GOE);
   c. a general guardian (GG); or,
   d. upon the death of the principal, by the personal representative or successor in interest of the principal's estate.[100]

99. G.S. 32C-1-114(b)(4).
100. G.S. 32C-1-114(h).

Any interested person may file a petition with the court asking it to enter an order compelling an accounting by the agent that includes the production of evidence substantiating any expenditure by the agent of the principal's assets.[101] The proceeding is commenced before the clerk of superior court as prescribed for in, and conducted in accordance with, estate proceedings under G.S. 28A-2-6.[102] There is no form available to initiate the proceeding.[103] There is a fee collected by the court to file the action unless the costs are waived because the petitioner is indigent (see Chapter 6 for discussion of suing as indigent).[104]

c. Refuse to Accept the POA

A person, including, in this context, a financial institution, is never required to accept and is not liable for refusing to accept a POA that is not duly acknowledged.[105]

If a POA is acknowledged, a person may refuse to accept the POA, for example, if the person

- believes in good faith that the POA is not valid;
- believes in good faith that the agent under the POA does not have the authority to perform the act requested;
- has reasonable cause to question the authenticity or validity of the POA or the appropriateness of its exercise by the agent; or
- makes, or has actual knowledge that another person has made, a report to adult protective services (APS) or law enforcement stating a good faith belief that the principal may be subject to physical or financial abuse, neglect, exploitation, or abandonment by the agent or a person acting for or with the agent.[106]

d. Make a Report

i. Adult Protective Services (APS)

Every person in North Carolina, with the singular exception of the long-term care ombudsman, must make an APS report if that person has reasonable cause to believe that a disabled adult needs protective services, including as a result of abuse by an agent under a POA.[107] Refer to Chapter 2 for a full discussion of the duty to report and the steps APS will take in response to a report.

---

101. G.S. 32C-1-116(a)(1), (c).
102. G.S. 32C-1-116(c).
103. For a discussion of the procedure applicable to estate proceedings before the clerk, refer to Ann M. Anderson, *Estate Proceedings in North Carolina*, EST. ADMIN. BULL. No. 1, 8–18 (Dec. 2012), https://www.sog.unc.edu/sites/www.sog.unc.edu/files/reports/eab01.pdf.
104. G.S. 7A-307(a).
105. G.S. 32C-1-120(a).
106. G.S. 32C-1-120(c) (listing the circumstances when a person is not required to accept an acknowledged POA).
107. G.S. 108A-102; 143B-181.20(f). *See* Aimee Wall, *Adult Protective Services: A New Reporting Requirement*, COATES' CANONS: NC LOC. GOV'T L. BLOG (June 23, 2015), https://canons.sog.unc.edu/adult-protective-services-a-new-reporting-requirement/.

ii. Law Enforcement

An agent under a POA is not immune from prosecution; a report or referral to law enforcement may be appropriate if the agent engaged in criminal activity. Possible crimes that may apply to abuse by an agent under a POA include

- obtaining property by false pretenses (G.S. 14-100),
- obtaining signature by false pretenses (G.S. 14-101),
- common law forgery (G.S. 14-119 and -120),
- embezzlement by an agent or fiduciary (G.S. 14-90), and
- exploitation of an older adult or disabled adult (G.S. 14-112.2).

e. Terminate the POA or the Agent's Authority

An older adult, as principal under a POA, has the authority to revoke the POA or the agent's authority under it.[108] If the older adult seeks to revoke the agent's authority, the revocation must be in writing, unless the POA states otherwise.[109] The termination of the agent's authority is not effective until the agent has actual knowledge of it.[110] If the older adult is incapacitated, then judicial action may be necessary to terminate the POA or the agent's authority.

f. Seek Judicial Relief

There are various types of judicial relief that may be available to protect an older adult in the event of abuse by an agent under a POA. The type of judicial action filed will depend upon the facts of a particular case. Possible judicial actions include (1) a POA proceeding, (2) a civil action, or (3) a guardianship proceeding.

108. G.S. 32C-1-110(a)(3), (b)(1).
109. G.S. 32C-1-110(b)(1), (c).
110. G.S. 32C-1-110(d).

Table 5.4. **Judicial Relief Available Related to POAs in Elder Abuse Cases**

TYPE OF ACTION	WHO PRESIDES?	POSSIBLE REMEDIES
POA proceeding	Clerk of superior court or superior court judge (on transfer from the clerk under G.S. 32C-1-116(a)(4))	• Compel an accounting by the agent • Remove the agent • Suspend the agent's authority • Reduce or deny the agent's compensation • Other relief set forth in G.S. 32C-1-117, except as limited by G.S. 32C-1-116(b)
Civil action	District or superior court judge or magistrate (in certain small claims)	• Set aside or rescind the POA based on undue influence or lack of capacity • Modify or amend the POA • Monetary damages • Recovery of property conveyed by an agent with the intent to hinder, delay, or defraud the principal's creditors • Other civil remedies (discussed in Chapter 6)
Guardianship proceeding	Clerk of superior court	For an older adult who lacks capacity, the appointment by the court of a guardian of the estate or general guardian who • takes action to terminate the POA and the agent's authority, • takes control of and secures the older adult's property, and • takes action to recover the older adult's property and seeks civil damages or other relief on behalf of the older adult.

i. POA Proceeding to Remove an Agent or Seek Other Relief before the Clerk

The term "POA proceeding" includes proceedings under G.S. Chapter 32C. Examples of POA proceedings that may be filed when an older adult is the subject of abuse include a proceeding to terminate a POA after the appointment of a guardian of the estate or a general guardian, a proceeding to determine compensation for an agent, and a proceeding to determine whether and to what extent a POA must be accepted by a third party.[111]

POA proceedings are commenced before the clerk and conducted in accordance with the procedures for estate proceedings under G.S. 28A-2-6.[112] Some POA proceedings initiated before the clerk will be transferred to superior court upon the request of a party.[113]

The person who files the petition and brings the POA proceeding is called the *petitioner*.

111. G.S. 32C-1-116(a).

112. G.S. 32C-1-116(c). The procedures for estate proceedings are set out in G.S. 28A-2-6. For further discussion of estate proceedings, refer to Anderson, *supra* note 103.

113. G.S. 32C-1-116(a)(4).

The following persons have standing to bring a POA proceeding:

- the principal under a POA;
- the agent under a POA;
- the principal's general guardian, guardian of the estate, or guardian of the person;
- the personal representative of the estate of a deceased principal;
- a person authorized to make health care decisions for the principal; and
- any other interested person, including a person asked to accept a POA.[114]

The term "interested person" is not defined in the statutes governing POA proceedings. Examples of persons who may qualify as interested persons are an heir or beneficiary under a will or trust, a caregiver, or a county department of social services (DSS) that has the authority to protect a principal from financial exploitation. A county DSS, for example, may choose to file a proceeding to compel an accounting from an agent to determine whether and to what extent an incapacitated adult is subject to financial exploitation by the agent. The county would likely have standing to file such an action as an interested person.[115]

Notwithstanding the broad authority of the clerk to hear POA proceedings, certain actions are carved out of the clerk's jurisdiction and must be filed in superior court. These are civil actions by nature or are otherwise matters traditionally adjudicated before the superior court.[116] They include any action[117]

- to modify or amend a POA;
- by or against creditors or debtors of an agent or a principal;
- involving claims for monetary damages;
- to set aside a POA based on undue influence or lack of capacity; or
- to recover property transferred or conveyed by an agent on behalf of a principal with the intent to hinder, delay, or defraud the principal's creditors.

It may be appropriate in some cases involving abuse by an agent of a principal/older adult to file a POA proceeding before the clerk of superior court rather than a civil action. A civil action in district or superior court may take longer to reach a final judgment and be more expensive than a POA proceeding initiated before the clerk. The relief sought to protect the older adult may be available through a more expeditious POA proceeding.

114. G.S. 32C-1-116(c).

115. G.S. 32C-1-116, Official Cmt. (noting that the uniform law sets forth broad categories of persons who have standing to petition the court for the primary purpose of protecting vulnerable or incapacitated principals against financial abuse). *But see id.* § 32C-1-116, N.C. Cmt. (stating that a "person that demonstrates sufficient interest in the principal's welfare" should be disregarded from the broad category of persons identified in the Official Comment as having standing to bring an estate proceeding).

116. Anderson, *supra* note 103.

117. G.S. 32C-1-116(b).

For example, it may be that instead of monetary damages, a principal/older adult's family member or friend, or another interested person, wants to compel an accounting, remove an agent, or compel an agent to return property to the principal, which can be done through a POA proceeding.[118]

A POA proceeding may also stop ongoing abuse of an older adult and prevent the need for a guardianship proceeding under G.S. Chapter 35A. In some cases where an older adult has a POA that is subject to abuse by an agent, the older adult may also lack capacity to make decisions or to manage his or her affairs. Family, friends, or other persons may consider seeking a court-appointed guardian who will take action to terminate the agent's authority.[119] However, the older adult may not need a guardian if the POA names a willing, responsible successor agent to act.[120] The family member, friend, or other interested person may instead choose to file a POA proceeding to remove an agent and stop abuse by the agent.[121] Once the agent is removed, the successor agent may act on behalf of the older adult, including taking steps to secure the older adult's property and recover any property improperly taken by the agent if authorized under the POA.[122]

EXAMPLE

Fran appointed her son, John, as her agent under a POA. Her other son, Jeff, is named as the successor agent. Jeff learns that John gifted much of Fran's property to John's wife, in violation of the authority granted to John under the POA, which restricts gifts and self-dealing. Jeff files a POA proceeding to remove John as agent. The clerk finds that John breached his fiduciary duty and removes him as the agent. The order removing John as agent then allows Jeff, as successor agent named in the POA, to act on Fran's behalf.

ii. Civil Action to Rescind a POA and for Civil Damages and Other Relief

If a POA is improperly obtained or an agent exceeds the scope of his or her authority, there are a number of civil remedies that may be obtained by initiating a civil action. For example, an older adult, or an authorized person acting on his or her behalf, may file a civil action in superior court to rescind, or set aside the POA, if the POA was signed when the older adult lacked capacity or as a result of undue influence.[123] Civil actions, including an action to set aside a document, are explained in Chapter 6.

A civil action may be the appropriate action to file when an older adult seeks monetary damages from an agent. The clerk of superior court in a POA proceeding lacks the

---

118. G.S. 32C-1-116(a) (stating that proceedings under G.S. Chapter 32C fall under the original jurisdiction of the clerk, except as set forth in G.S 32C-1-116(c)); 32C-1-117(b) (listing the types of relief the court may grant when an agent violates G.S. Chapter 32C).

119. Guardianship is discussed further in Chapter 4.

120. G.S. 32C-1-111(b).

121. G.S. 32C-1-116(a); 32C-1-117(b)(6).

122. G.S. 32C-1-111(b).

123. G.S. 32C-1-116(b)(4).

authority over claims for monetary damages.[124] Claims that do not involve monetary damages related to a POA, including claims that otherwise fall under the exclusive jurisdiction of the clerk, may be joined in the civil action by a party.[125] Furthermore, when there is a civil action before the superior court and a POA proceeding before the clerk that involve a common question of law or fact, on the court's motion or the motion of a party, the superior court judge may order consolidation of the POA proceeding and the civil action and decide all matters.[126]

iii. Proceeding to Appoint a Guardian; Termination of POA by Guardian

When an older adult lacks capacity and is subject to abuse by an agent under a POA, it may be necessary to seek the appointment of a guardian for the older adult, particularly where other supports, services, or alternatives to guardianship will not enable the adult to remain free from abuse. Guardianship is discussed in Chapter 4. A guardian of the estate (GOE) and a general guardian (GG) appointed by the court have the authority to terminate a POA without any further order from the court.[127] A guardian of the person (GOP) lacks the authority to terminate a POA.[128]

(a) Process for Termination of POA by GOE or GG

The process for terminating a POA by a GOE or GG appointed by the court is different depending on whether the POA was previously registered in a North Carolina register of deeds office.

(1) Termination by GOE or GG of POA Previously Registered in a North Carolina Register of Deeds Office

If a POA was previously registered in a North Carolina register of deeds office, the GOE or GG can terminate the POA by registering an instrument of revocation in the same office where the POA is registered.[129] The GOE or GG must execute and acknowledge the instrument of revocation.[130] The instrument must be registered along with proof of service on the agent under the POA being revoked.[131] Service of the instrument of revocation on the agent must be completed pursuant to Rule 5 of the state Rules of Civil Procedure, which requires

- handing a copy of the revocation to the agent,
- mailing a copy to the agent at the agent's last known address, or
- filing a copy with the clerk of court if the agent's address is not known.[132]

124. G.S. 32C-1-116(b)(3).
125. G.S. 32C-1-116(c); 28A-2-6(g).
126. G.S. 32C-1-116(c); 28A-2-6(f).
127. G.S. 32C-1-110(a)(7). The GOE and GG also have the authority to terminate the agent's authority under a POA. *Id.* § 32C-1-110(b)(5).
128. *See* G.S. 32C-1-110(a)(7).
129. G.S. 32C-1-110(h).
130. *Id.*
131. *Id.*
132. *Id.*; *id.* § 1A-1, Rule 5. Rule 5 allows for service on a party's attorney of record in some cases. The GOE or GG is not required to file a court action to terminate the POA, therefore Rule 5 service discussed herein addresses service on the agent.

Service by mail is complete once a copy of the revocation is placed in a pre-paid envelope or other wrapper, properly addressed, and deposited with the U.S. Postal Service.[133]

Typically, a certificate of service accompanies any paper served pursuant to Rule 5 and suffices for purposes of showing proof of service; a certificate of service is a way to show that service was effected in order to satisfy the requirements of G.S. 32C-1-110(h).[134] A certificate must

- include the date and method of service or the date of acceptance of service,
- include the name and service address of the agent served with the revocation, and
- be signed in accordance with and subject to Rule 11 of the N.C. Rules of Civil Procedure.[135]

The statute governing the termination of POAs requires proof of service of the revocation on "the agent."[136] An agent as defined in G.S. Chapter 32C includes an original agent, co-agent, successor agent, and any person to whom an agent's authority is delegated.[137]

PRACTICE NOTE

Steps to Revoke a Previously Registered POA by a GOE or GG

1. The GOE or GG executes and acknowledges an instrument of revocation.
2. The GOE or GG serves the instrument of revocation on the agent under Rule 5 of the N.C. Rules of Civil Procedure.
3. The GOE or GG registers the instrument of revocation along with proof of service on the agent (i.e., the certificate of service) with the register of deeds in the same county where the POA being revoked is registered.

(2) Termination by GOE or GG of POA Not Registered in a North Carolina Register of Deeds Office

G.S. Chapter 32C does not provide a procedure for a court-appointed GOE or GG to follow to terminate a POA if the POA was not previously registered with a North Carolina register of deeds office. The GOE or GG may choose to execute and acknowledge a written instrument of revocation and then serve a copy of that revocation on the agent, any co-agent, and any successor agents named in the POA. The GOE or GG could then file a copy of the written revocation along with proof of service on the agent(s) in the court's guardianship "E" file. This would make clear to the agent(s) and the court that the GOE or GG terminated the POA, and it would make the date of termination clear as well. A termination of a POA

133. G.S. 1A-1, Rule 5(b)(2) ("Service by mail shall be complete upon deposit of the pleading or paper enclosed in a post-paid, properly addressed wrapper in a post office or official depository under the exclusive care and custody of the United States Postal Service").

134. G.S. 1A-1, Rule 5(b1).

135. *Id.*

136. G.S. 32C-1-110(h).

137. G.S. 32C-1-102(1).

is not effective as to any agent(s) or third parties who, without actual knowledge of the termination, act in good faith under the POA.[138]

(b) Termination of POA by Interim Guardian

After a petition for adjudication of incompetence is filed but before the appointment of a GOE, GG, or GOP under G.S. Chapter 35A, the clerk may appoint an interim GOE, GG, or GOP on the clerk's own motion or on the motion of the petitioner or guardian ad litem.[139] An interim guardian is a guardian appointed when (1) there is or reasonably appears to be an imminent or foreseeable risk of harm to the older adult/respondent's physical well-being (interim GOP), estate (interim GOE), or both (interim GG) that requires immediate intervention and (2) there is reasonable cause to believe that the older adult is incompetent.[140] Interim guardians are discussed in detail in Chapter 4.

G.S. Chapter 32C does not expressly state that a G.S. Chapter 35A interim GOE or GG has the authority to terminate a POA. Because the powers of a plenary GOE and GG include the power to terminate a POA, it is likely that the clerk may specifically authorize an interim GOE or interim GG to terminate a POA in the clerk's order appointing an interim guardian.[141] It is advisable for the clerk to specifically state that termination authority in the order appointing the interim guardian.[142] It may be necessary for an interim GOE or GG to have that authority where there is an imminent risk of harm to an older adult/respondent's estate that arises from abuse or exploitation by an agent under a POA.

Unlike a GOE or GG, the powers of a GOP do not include the power to terminate a POA. Therefore, an interim GOP lacks the authority to terminate a POA.

B. LACK OF UNDERSTANDING ABOUT POAs

Law enforcement and others who work in criminal law may be inclined to view a report involving a POA as a "civil matter" or one where there is not criminal activity because the principal gave the agent consent to act. But just as in other, more familiar criminal cases like sexual assault, consent to one act does not mean consent to all acts. The principal may have granted the agent authority with regard to some of the principal's property but not all of it, and a criminal charge, such as embezzlement, may be appropriate against the agent under a POA. A list of crimes that may be implicated in elder abuse cases is available in Appendix C.

138. G.S. 32C-1-110(d).

139. G.S. 35A-1112(b1) (appointment on the clerk's own motion); 35A-1114(a) (appointment pursuant to a motion of the petitioner or the guardian ad litem).

140. G.S. 35A-1114(b), (d).

141. *See* G.S. 32C-1-110(a)(7).

142. *See* G.S. 35A-1114(e) (requiring the court to set forth the interim guardian's powers and duties in the order appointing the interim guardian). The court typically uses Form AOC-SP-900, "Order on Motion for Appointment of Interim Guardian," when appointing an interim guardian. The form is available at https://www.nccourts.gov/assets/documents/forms/459.pdf?Sf_GqOc97Vu6lMNzyFOP5UHCVSO8qlrg.

TIPS FOR HANDLING REPORTS OF ELDER ABUSE INVOLVING POAS.

1. Learn the foundational law governing POAs. Some abuses will be relatively easy to identify once a person has a basic understanding of the law governing POAs.
2. Always obtain a copy of a POA and review it to determine the nature and extent of the agent's authority to act under it.
3. Avoid making assumptions about POAs, including that a POA gives an agent unlimited authority to act for the principal or that if a person acted under a POA there is nothing law enforcement or APS can do to prosecute the agent or protect the older adult's property.
4. Develop relationships with local elder law attorneys. They may be willing to review and advise on the scope and limitations of specific POAs.

C. DIFFICULT TO DETECT ABUSE

POAs are private arrangements when they are executed and are likely to remain private during the time the agent acts on the principal's behalf. The agent does not have a duty to account to the principal, the court, or any other person, unless the POA provides otherwise or the court orders an accounting. Abuse under a POA can go undetected for long periods of time, as shown by the case of Virginia Freck, one of the most extreme examples of elder abuse and exploitation in recent years.[143] A distant relative of the 98-year-old appeared when Mrs. Freck started showing signs of dementia and needing assistance with her care. She had no children and lived alone. The relative moved Mrs. Freck from Florida to Alabama and had Mrs. Freck sign a POA appointing him as her agent. The POA was drafted by the relative's girlfriend. The relative then proceeded to exploit Mrs. Freck by using her money to gamble, to buy a house for himself, and to purchase large items, such as motorcycles, a bulldozer, and a convenience store. In total, he spent around $53,000 per month and a total sum of $2.3 million. The abuse did not come to light until Mrs. Freck's bank account was overdrawn and she was almost evicted from her apartment.

143. Klass, *supra* note 98.

TIPS FOR EARLY DETECTION OF ABUSE UNDER A POA.

- **Learn the signs of financial abuse or exploitation.** Individuals who work with older adults should be aware of the different types of abuse and remain alert to potential signs of financial abuse and exploitation. A list of signs of abuse is presented in Chapter 1.
- **Promote and use trusted persons lists.** Financial institutions are encouraged (but not required) by law to offer older adult customers the opportunity to submit and periodically update a list of trusted persons to be contacted in case of suspected abuse.[144] Adult protective services (APS) and others working with older adults should encourage them to submit such a list to financial institutions so that there is someone in place for the financial institution to reach out to if there is any indication of abuse.
- **Make an APS report.** Every person in North Carolina, with the singular exception of long-term care ombudsmen, must make an APS report if there is reasonable cause to believe that a disabled adult needs protective services, including as a result of abuse by an agent under a POA.[145] Refer to Chapter 2 for a full discussion of the duty to report and the steps APS will take in response to a report.

144. G.S. 108A-114.
145. G.S. 108A-102. *See* Wall, *supra* note 107.

Chapter 6
Civil Actions, Domestic Violence, and Housing

CONTENTS

I. SCOPE OF CHAPTER

The district attorney may criminally prosecute a perpetrator of elder abuse. An adult protective services (APS) investigation may lead to the mobilization of essential services to protect an older adult from abuse. A court may appoint a guardian for an older adult who lacks capacity and needs a surrogate decision-maker to take action to protect him or her from abuse. But the older adult still may not be made financially whole or may require additional legal protections to stop the abuse.

There are other remedies available through North Carolina courts to protect the older adult and his or her property. This chapter identifies some of these other civil judicial remedies, including remedies available (1) through civil litigation, (2) in cases involving domestic violence or unwanted contact, and (3) related to housing. It begins with a summary of how these remedies protect older adults. It then identifies who is responsible for bringing these types of actions. Next it provides details about each category of remedy and how it may provide compensation or relief for older adults in cases involving elder abuse. The chapter concludes with a discussion of some of the key challenges to seeking these civil remedies to address elder abuse and possible ways to tackle those challenges.

II. OVERVIEW OF CIVIL REMEDIES

A. HOW DO CIVIL LEGAL REMEDIES PROTECT OLDER ADULTS?

A door-to-door home repairman defrauds an older adult out of her life savings. A friend gets an older adult who lacks capacity to sign a deed conveying the older adult's property to the friend. A grandchild pushes an older adult to the ground trying to get the older adult's debit card. A caregiver refuses to move out of the older adult's home when asked. The civil remedies described in this chapter protect older adults in these types of situations by enabling the older adult to

- recover money or property or seek civil damages or other relief—for example, rescission of documents such as a will, a power of attorney, or a deed;
- obtain a civil protective order, such as a domestic violence protective order or a civil no-contact order; and
- remove someone from his or her residence, such as through summary ejectment or civil trespass.

B. WHO IS RESPONSIBLE?

1. WHO FILES THE ACTION?

In civil actions in North Carolina, claims and defenses must be brought in the name of the real party in interest.[1] A real party in interest is a party who has benefited or been injured by the judgment in a case and who by substantive law has the legal right to enforce the claim in question.[2] A person with a general interest in, or someone who will be indirectly impacted by, the outcome of a case is typically not a real party in interest.[3] Generally, the real party in interest is "the one entitled to receive the fruits of the litigation," such as damages.[4]

a. When the Older Adult Has Capacity

If an older adult is the aggrieved party and has capacity, then the older adult files the civil action and prosecutes the claim(s) as the real party in interest.[5] The older adult is the named plaintiff or petitioner in the action and has the right to prosecute the action with or without the assistance of an attorney.

b. When the Older Adult Is Incompetent

If an older adult is the aggrieved party and is incompetent, the general rule is that (1) claims may be prosecuted in the name of the older adult as the real party in interest or (2) if the older adult has a guardian, claims may be brought by the guardian in the guardian's own name without joining the older adult as a party subject to certain limitations discussed below.[6]

i. Older Adult Is the Real Party in Interest

If the claim is brought in the name of the incompetent older adult as the real party in interest, then, under Rule 17(b) of the North Carolina Rules of Civil Procedure, the older adult must appear by either

- a general guardian (GG)[7] appointed by the clerk pursuant to G.S. Chapter 35A or
- a guardian ad litem (Rule 17 GAL).[8]

---

1. Chapter 1, Section 57, of the North Carolina General Statutes (hereinafter G.S.); G.S. 1A-1, Rule 17(a) (N.C. Rules of Civil Procedure). *See* Reliance Ins. Co. v. Walker, 33 N.C. App. 15, 18 (1977) (stating that although Rule 17 by its terms applies only to "parties plaintiff," the rule is applicable to "parties defendant" as well (citing 3A MOORE'S FEDERAL PRACTICE § 17.07, at 226–27)).
2. *See Reliance*, 33 N.C. App. at 18–19; Energy Inv'rs Fund, L.P. v. Metric Constructors, Inc., 351 N.C. 331, 337 (2000) (quoting Parnell v. Nationwide Mut. Ins. Co., 263 N.C. 445, 448–49 (1965)).
3. *See* John L. Saxon, *Who Are the Parties in IV-D Child Support Proceedings? And What Difference Does it Make?* FAM. L. BULL. No. 22, at 5 (Jan. 2007). The concept of real party in interest is closely related to the concept of standing to commence and prosecute an action or proceeding before a court. *Id. See also* G. GRAY WILSON, NORTH CAROLINA CIVIL PROCEDURE § 17-1 (3d ed. 2007).
4. WILSON, *supra* note 3, at § 17-1.
5. G.S. 1A-1, Rule 17(a).
6. *Id.*
7. A general guardian is both a guardian of the person and a guardian of the estate. G.S. 35A-1101(7).
8. G.S. 1A-1, Rule 17(b)(1).

The appointment of a Rule 17 GAL must be made at any time prior to, or at the time of, the commencement of the action.[9] The appointment is made on the application of any relative or friend of the incompetent older adult or by the court on its own motion.[10] The written application is generally filed, and the appointment is typically made, by the clerk at the time the complaint initiating the action is presented for filing with the court. If the claim is brought in the name of the incompetent older adult as the real party in interest and the older adult has a GG, the court may still appoint a Rule 17 GAL if the court deems it expedient to have the older adult represented by a Rule 17 GAL.[11]

PRACTICE NOTE

Things to Keep in Mind about a Rule 17 GAL

- Any "relative or friend" may file a written application seeking the appointment of a Rule 17 GAL for an older adult who is (1) the plaintiff in a civil action or special proceeding and (2) incompetent.[12]
- A court may appoint a Rule 17 GAL on its own motion.[13]
- The Rule 17 GAL appointed by the court does not have to be an attorney and is not the older adult's lawyer.[14] Any competent adult may serve as a Rule 17 GAL.
- The Rule 17 GAL either serves pro bono or the Rule 17 GAL's fees may be taxed to a party as part of the costs if allowed by law.[15]

The role of the Rule 17 GAL, appointed when the incompetent older adult is the named party to the action, is one of substitution.[16] The North Carolina Court of Appeals has stated that the "[a]ppointment of a GAL under Rule 17 for an incompetent person 'will divest the [incompetent party] of their fundamental right to conduct his or her litigation according to their own judgment and inclination.'"[17] The Rule 17 GAL has a duty to file and timely serve pleadings.[18] If a party has a Rule 17 GAL, the court may proceed to final judgment, order, or decree as if the party had been under no legal disability.[19]

9. G.S. 1A-1, Rule 17(c)(1).
10. *Id.*
11. G.S. 1A-1, Rule 17(b)(3).
12. G.S. 1A-1, Rule 17(c)(1).
13. *Id.*
14. *See* N.C. State Bar, Formal Ethics Op. 11 (2004) (discussing the difference in ethical duties owed to the ward by a lawyer representing the ward as a client versus a lawyer who is appointed solely as a GAL). An exception to this rule is a GAL appointed to represent a respondent in a G.S. Chapter 35A incompetency and guardianship proceeding. The GAL is appointed pursuant to Rule 17 but is also the respondent's lawyer in the proceeding unless the respondent retains his own counsel, in which event the GAL may be discharged. G.S. 35A-1101(6); 35A-1107.
15. *See* N.C. OFF. OF INDIGENT DEF. SERVS. & ADMIN. OFF. OF THE CTS., NORTH CAROLINA PROCEEDINGS THAT INVOLVE GUARDIANS AD LITEM (GALs) (revised Oct. 2014), http://www.ncids.org/Rules%20&%20Procedures/GAL_Chart.pdf (hereinafter IDS GAL CHART).
16. *In re* P.D.R., 224 N.C. App. 460, 467 (2012) (quoting *In re* J.A.A. & S.A.A., 175 N.C. App. 66, 71 (2005)).
17. *J.A.A. & S.A.A.*, 175 N.C. App. at 71.
18. G.S. 1A-1, Rule 17(e).
19. *Id.*

ii. Guardian Sues in His or Her Own Name

Under Rule 17(a) of the North Carolina Rules of Civil Procedure, a claim may be brought by a guardian in the guardian's own name on behalf of the incompetent older adult without joining the older adult as a party.[20] The clerk of superior court appoints a guardian in a separate proceeding under G.S. Chapter 35A after a judicial determination of incompetency (discussed in more detail in Chapter 4).[21] The clerk may appoint

- a guardian of the person (GOP), who is a guardian with authority over the care, custody, and control of the incompetent older adult;
- a guardian of the estate (GOE), who is a guardian with authority over the property, estate,[22] and business affairs of the incompetent older adult; or
- a general guardian (GG), who is a guardian of the estate and the person.[23]

A GOP does not have authority to initiate an action on behalf of the older adult in the GOP's own name.[24] Both a GOE and a GG have the authority to initiate actions related to the incompetent older adult's estate in their own names without joining the older adult as a party.[25] A GOE generally may not initiate an action in his or her own name that relates to the care, custody, or control of the older adult, such as one to obtain a domestic violence protective order (DVPO).[26]

If there is any doubt as to whether a GOE or GG may commence the action in the guardian's own name without joining the incompetent older adult as a party, such as in the case of a DVPO or other action that does not involve the estate of the older incompetent adult, the action may be filed in the name of the older adult as the real party in interest, as discussed above, and the GG could appear on behalf of the incompetent older adult in the proceeding or a "relative or friend" could seek the appointment of a Rule 17 GAL to appear

20. G.S. 1A-1, Rule 17(a).

21. G.S. 35A-1120; 35A-1203(a); 35A-1210.

22. "Estate" means "[a]ny interest in real property, choses in action, intangible personal property, and tangible personal property, and includes any interest in joint accounts or jointly held property." G.S. 35A-1202(5).

23. G.S. 35A-1202(10), (9), (7). A clerk in a G.S. Chapter 35A proceeding may also appoint a limited GOP, GOE, or GG or an interim GOP, GOE, or GG. These types of guardians are discussed in more detail in Chapter 4. If the clerk appoints a limited GOE or GG or an interim GOE or GG, that guardian's authority to initiate an action in the guardian's own name on behalf of the incompetent older adult may be limited by the clerk's order appointing the limited or interim guardian.

24. G.S. 35A-1241 (listing the powers of the guardian of the person, which include the duty to give consent or approval to enable the incompetent adult to receive legal counsel but do not include the power to initiate legal action). *See* Clawser v. Campbell, 184 N.C. App. 526, 529 (2007) (holding that the guardian of the person lacks the power to maintain an action); Granville v. Yeddo, 199 N.C. App. 318 (2009) (unpublished) (stating that "[t]he power to initiate legal action lies with the general guardian, guardian of the estate, or guardian ad litem" and not with the guardian of the person).

25. G.S. 35A-1251(3) ("[A] general guardian or guardian of the estate has the power to perform . . . every act . . . incident to the collection, preservation, management, and use of the ward's estate . . . including but not limited to the . . . specific powers . . . [t]o maintain any appropriate action or proceeding to recover possession of any of the ward's property, to determine the title thereto, or to recover damages for any injury done to any of the ward's property; also, to compromise, adjust, arbitrate, sue on or defend, abandon, or otherwise deal with and settle any other claims in favor of or against the ward"); Stern v. Cinoman, 221 N.C. App. 231, 233–34 (2012) (stating that a guardian of the estate has the authority to bring a medical malpractice suit in his own name as guardian).

26. G.S. 35A-1251 (describing the authority of the guardian of the estate as limited to "the collection, preservation, management, and use of the ward's estate" and listing specific powers under that umbrella of authority as including the power to sue on or defend any claims in favor of or against the ward).

on his or her behalf.[27] If the relief granted does not relate to the older adult's estate, such as the relief in a DVPO proceeding, significant confusion may arise in the enforcement of the order or judgment if the action is brought in the name of the guardian rather than the older adult.[28]

c. Effect of the Death of the Older Adult on the Action

After the death of an older adult, the personal representative (PR) or collector of the adult's estate may bring an action as the real party in interest if the cause of action survives the death of the older adult.[29] Causes of action that do not survive death include those alleging libel and slander (except slander of title) or false imprisonment, and those where the relief sought could not be enjoyed, or where the granting of relief would be of no value or importance, after the older adult's death.[30]

If the action is pending at the time of the older adult's death and the cause of action survives, the action may be continued by the PR or collector of the adult's estate.[31] However, substitution of the PR or the collector is not automatic.[32] First, a PR or a collector must be appointed by the clerk of superior court as part of the administration of the older adult's estate.[33] Once a PR or a collector is appointed by the clerk, the court where the action is pending may, in response to a motion, order the PR or collector substituted in as the real party in interest.[34] The motion for substitution must be made within the time specified for the presentation of claims in the estate under G.S. 28A-19-3, which generally is around ninety days, as specified in the notice to creditors of the estate to file claims.[35]

d. Child's Right to Bring an Action on Behalf of a Parent

An adult child does not have the right to bring an action on behalf of a parent unless the parent is incompetent and the child brings the action as the parent's legal representative, as discussed in Section II.B.1.b, *supra*.[36]

There may be instances when an older adult changes a long-held estate plan later in life. This may include when the older adult revokes a will and executes a new will naming new beneficiaries who are not the adult's children. This may be a result of, for example, undue influence or fraud perpetrated by a caregiver, distant relative, or other person

---

27. G.S. 1A-1, Rule 17(b).
28. *See* Cheryl Howell, *Minor Parties in 50B Cases*, ON THE CIVIL SIDE: A UNC SCH. OF GOV'T BLOG (Mar. 13, 2015), https://civil.sog.unc.edu/minor-parties-in-50b-cases/ (explaining that, in cases involving minors, the child's name should be listed as plaintiff rather than the GAL's name).
29. G.S. 1A-1, Rule 17(a); 28A-18-1(a); 1-22.
30. G.S. 28A-18-1(b).
31. G.S. 28A-18-1(a); 1A-1, Rule 25(a).
32. Purvis v. Moses H. Cone Mem'l Hosp. Serv. Corp., 175 N.C. App. 474, 483 (2006).
33. Refer to G.S. Chapter 28A, related to the administration of decedents' estates, for the law governing the appointment of a personal representative and a collector. *See* Ragan v. Hill, 337 N.C. 667, 674 (1994) (noting that once a personal representative was appointed, the action could proceed); Pierce v. Johnson, 154 N.C. App. 34, 40 (2002) (explaining that at death the deceased person no longer had legal standing because the person transformed into the estate of the decedent).
34. G.S. 1A-1, Rule 25(a).
35. *Id.*; *id.* § 28A-19-3(a).
36. G.S. 1A-1, Rule 17; Hauser v. Hauser, 252 N.C. App. 10, 14 (2017).

who recently became involved in the older adult's life. A child who is disinherited by these changes may have a claim as a plaintiff in a civil action for wrongful interference with an expected inheritance *after* the death of his or her parent. North Carolina law recognizes a right of action, after the death of a person who makes a will (testator), when a third party wrongfully interferes with the beneficiary's expected inheritance through, for example, fraud or undue influence.[37] But an expected beneficiary such as a child of an older adult has no claim *during* the lifetime of the older adult who makes a will.[38] The North Carolina Supreme Court has stated that this is because a child has no interest in the property of a living parent, only an intangible hope of succession.[39] The child's right to inherit does not exist during the parent's lifetime.[40] A parent has an absolute right to dispose of property as he or she pleases and may make distributions or no distributions to children, with or without reason.[41]

Another legal ground to challenge changes to an older adult's will after the death of the older adult is through a caveat proceeding. A child or other interested person may challenge the validity of a will admitted to probate by the clerk of superior court by entering a caveat to the will.[42] The purpose of a caveat is to determine whether the will admitted to probate is in fact the last will and testament of the decedent.[43] Possible grounds for a caveat include undue influence, duress, fraud, forgery, mistake, revocation, and lack of testamentary capacity.[44]

2. TIME TO BRING THE ACTION

There are limits imposed by law on how long from the time of the events giving rise to the cause of action or from the discovery of such events a plaintiff has to file a civil lawsuit.[45] This is known as a statute of limitations. Once the statute of limitations expires, the plaintiff is time-barred from filing the lawsuit.

If an older adult is under a disability when the cause of action accrues, the statute of limitations is tolled (meaning, essentially, that the time for bringing suit is paused).[46] An older adult is under a disability if he or she is "insane" or "incompetent" as defined in G.S. Chapter 35A.[47] An adjudication of incompetency by the court under G.S. Chapter 35A is not required to toll the statute of limitations.[48] The statute of limitations is tolled until the

37. Bohannon v. Wachovia Bank & Tr. Co., 210 N.C. 679 (1936).
38. *Hauser*, 252 N.C. App. at 14.
39. *Id.* (quoting Holt v. Holt, 232 N.C. 497, 500–01 (1950)).
40. *Id.*
41. *Id.*
42. G.S. 31-32.
43. Wilder v. Hill, 175 N.C. App. 769, 772 (2006).
44. *See* Ann Anderson, *Will Caveats*, *in* NORTH CAROLINA SUPERIOR COURT JUDGES' BENCHBOOK (Sept. 2012), https://benchbook.sog.unc.edu/sites/default/files/pdf/Will%20Caveats.pdf.
45. G.S. 1-15(a).
46. G.S. 1-17(a).
47. *Id.* An "incompetent adult" is defined in G.S. 35A-1101(7) as an adult or emancipated minor who "lacks sufficient capacity (1) to manage his or her own affairs or (2) to make or communicate important decisions concerning his or her person, family, or property, regardless of whether the lack of capacity is due to mental illness, intellectual disability, epilepsy, cerebral palsy, autism, inebriety, senility, disease, injury, or similar cause or condition."
48. Ragsdale v. Whitley, 257 N.C. App. 336, 341–42, *review denied*, 371 N.C. 447 (2018).

disability is removed.[49] A disability may be removed generally, as to all causes of action. This happens, for example, if the older adult has a general guardian (GG) when the cause of action accrues or upon the appointment of a GG by the clerk of superior court in a Chapter 35A proceeding.[50] A disability may be removed as to a specific cause of action, for example, upon the appointment of a guardian ad litem (GAL) in the action.[51]

If the older adult is under a guardianship, and the guardian is the perpetrator of financial exploitation or other abuse against the older adult, the statute of limitations may be tolled with respect to claims the older adult has against the guardian until a successor guardian is appointed.[52] This is because both the GG and a guardian of the estate (GOE) have the authority to initiate actions related to the incompetent older adult's estate.[53] An exploitative or abusive guardian would not sue himself or herself, and the incompetent adult could not reasonably be expected to bring a lawsuit.[54]

If an older adult dies before the statute of limitations runs for an action and the cause of action survives the death of the older adult, the action may be commenced by the personal representative or collector of the older adult's estate up until the statute of limitations runs.[55] If the statute of limitations expires within one year after the death of the older adult, the statute of limitations is extended to one year from the date of death of the older adult.[56]

3. WHERE THE SUIT IS FILED

With limited exceptions, the district and superior courts in North Carolina generally have concurrent (shared) authority to hear matters of a civil nature.[57] This means that a plaintiff could file a civil action in either court. For judicial efficiency, however, state statutes prescribe the proper divisions for bringing civil actions.[58] For example, the district court is the proper division for the trial of all civil actions in which the amount in controversy is $25,000 or less, while the superior court is the proper division where the amount exceeds $25,000.[59]

---

49. G.S. 1-17(a).

50. *See* King *ex rel.* Small v. Albemarle Hosp. Auth., 370 N.C. 467, 472 (2018); Teele v. Kerr, 261 N.C. 148, 150 (1964); Fox v. Health Force, Inc., 143 N.C. App. 501, 507 (2001) (holding that once the general guardian was appointed to represent the plaintiff's interests, the limitation period began to run).

51. Jefferys v. Tolin, 90 N.C. App. 233, 235 (1988); *Teele*, 261 N.C. at 150. Note that the scope of the authority of the GAL is determined by the terms of the complaint, which means that those terms determine whether a GAL can join or bring a particular suit, which, in turn, will affect the operation of a statute of limitations. Genesco, Inc. v. Cone Mills Corp., 604 F.2d 281, 286 (4th Cir. 1979). *See also* Rowland v. Beauchamp, 253 N.C. 231, 234–36 (1960) (appointing a new GAL did not restart the statute of limitations, which began to run at the appointment of the first GAL).

52. *See* State *ex rel.* Duckett v. Pettee, 50 N.C. App. 119, 124–25 (1980).

53. *Id.* at 124. *See* note 25, *supra*.

54. *Id.*

55. G.S. 1-22.

56. *Id. See also* 2 JAMES B. MCLAUGHLIN, JR. & RICHARD T. BOWSER, WIGGINS WILLS & ADMINISTRATION OF ESTATES IN N.C. § 20:7 (4th ed.).

57. G.S. 7A-240.

58. G.S. 7A-242.

59. G.S. 7A-243.

Small claims are a subset of civil actions; these claims are heard by magistrates.[60] A special set of statutes governs the trial of small claims. A small claim is any civil action in which

1. the amount in controversy does not exceed $10,000;
2. the principal relief sought is money, the recovery of specific personal property, summary ejectment, or some combination of these things; and
3. the plaintiff (the person who files the civil action) requests that the action be assigned to a magistrate.[61]

The plaintiff initiates a small claims action by filing a complaint.[62] The clerk of superior court then issues a magistrate summons, which is served on the defendant. The N.C. Administrative Office of the Courts (AOC) maintains a number of small claims forms, including three complaint forms and a magistrate summons; all are available for free online at nccourts.gov.

Table 6.1. **Select AOC Small Claims Complaint Forms**

FORM	NAME
CVM-100	Magistrate Summons
CVM-200	Complaint for Money Owed
CVM-201	Complaint in Summary Ejectment
CVM-202	Complaint to Recover Possession of Personal Property

The small claims complaint must be filed in the county where at least one of the defendants (the persons being sued) resides.[63] The chief district court judge ultimately determines whether cases are assigned to a magistrate by a specific order or by a general rule.[64] The chief typically does this by a general administrative order directing the clerk to calendar specified cases to be heard by a magistrate.[65] Based on this order, the clerk calendars the case to be heard by a magistrate as soon as it is filed. The procedure for small claims is intended to be simpler than the procedural rules governing claims heard in district or superior courts. The small claims procedures are largely set out in G.S. Chapter 7A, Article 19.[66] Many litigants in small claims proceedings are not represented by attorneys. There are a number of free resources available to assist parties to small claims actions.

60. G.S. 7A, Article 19.
61. G.S. 7A-210. A request for claim and delivery as a remedy or an order from the clerk for relinquishment of property subject to a lien pursuant to G.S. 44A-4(a) does not prevent an action that otherwise qualifies as a small claim from qualifying. *Id.*
62. G.S. 7A-213.
63. *Id.*
64. G.S. 7A-211.
65. JOAN G. BRANNON, NORTH CAROLINA SMALL CLAIMS LAW 13 (2009) (hereinafter SMALL CLAIMS LAW).
66. *Id.*

RESOURCE

Small Claims

- **Legal Aid of N.C.** has an abundance of helpful information on its website (www.legalaidnc.org), including information about how to bring a lawsuit in small claims court.
- **The North Carolina Department of Justice** provides several brochures on its website related to consumer protection for tenants, as well as a guide to small claims court. *See* https://ncdoj.gov/protecting-consumers/home-repair-and-products/renting-a-home/.
- The website of **the N.C. Administrative Office of the Courts** (www.nccourts.gov/help-topics) includes information on topics such as housing and lawsuits and small claims.

C. HOW DO CIVIL LEGAL REMEDIES WORK?

This section provides a basic overview of how three types of civil legal remedies may provide relief or protection to older adults who are subject to elder abuse: (1) causes of action and remedies available through traditional civil litigation, including remedies available before a final judgment is entered by a court; (2) remedies available to protect an older adult from domestic violence or unwanted contact; and (3) remedies available when the older adult wants to remove an unwanted occupant from a home owned by the older adult, as well as remedies available when an older adult is a tenant of property owned by someone else.

1. CAUSES OF ACTION AND REMEDIES THROUGH CIVIL LITIGATION

An older adult, or an older adult's legal representative (as discussed above), may file a civil lawsuit against the perpetrator of abuse seeking monetary damages or other relief, such as the reformation or rescission of a deed or contract or an order for the return of personal property. Unlike other states, North Carolina does not have a specific civil private right of action for elder abuse and exploitation.[67] Many of these elder abuse and financial exploitation civil actions in other states have "heightened remedies and penalties to encourage enforcement and deter abuse."[68]

This section begins by providing examples of pre-judgment remedies that may be available to stop ongoing elder abuse while a civil action is pending and before a judgment is entered. It then catalogues common civil causes of action, together with the elements of each action, that may be relevant in cases of elder abuse.

67. *See, e.g.*, UTAH CODE ANN. § 62A-3-314; ARIZ. REV. STAT. ANN. § 46-455 and -456; CAL. WELF. & INST. CODE §§ 15657–15657.8 ("Civil Actions for Abuse of Elderly or Dependent Adults"); CONN. GEN. STAT. ANN. § 17b-462.
68. Jeff Aidikoff & Ashley Rivkin, *States with A Civil Private Right of Action for Financial Elder Abuse and Exploitation*, 24 PIABA B.J. 29 (2017).

PRACTICE NOTE

When an older adult is the victim of financial exploitation, it is likely that the perpetrator will attempt to hide the older adult's property or cause it to disappear. The faster the older adult or someone assisting the older adult is able to locate the property and seek a pre-judgment remedy, such as freezing a bank account through an attachment, the better the chances are for the older adult to be made whole through a final judgment in a civil action.

a. Pre-Judgment Civil Remedies to Stop Ongoing Abuse/Exploitation

Certain remedies may be sought while a civil action is pending and before a final judgment related to the alleged abuse of the older adult is entered. An underlying civil action must have been commenced in order for any of these remedies to be sought. A *temporary restraining order* or *injunctive relief* may be necessary to preserve the status quo while litigation is pending. An *attachment* may be necessary to secure the defendant's property to ensure that there will be assets available to satisfy any judgment ultimately entered against the defendant. A *claim and delivery action* may be sought to obtain possession of personal property while the litigation is pending. The older adult may file a *lis pendens* to restrain the defendant from transferring real property and to notify third parties that there is litigation pending related to the real property. Each of these pre-judgment remedies is detailed below, along with examples about how each may apply in a case involving elder abuse.

i. Preliminary Injunction; Temporary Restraining Order[69]

A preliminary injunction is an order of the court preventing a party from doing specified acts. Its purpose is to preserve the status quo or, far less commonly, to direct a party to take certain action(s), during an underlying litigation.[70] A request for a preliminary injunction may be included in the original complaint initiating the civil action or made as a separate motion filed with the court.[71] A prerequisite of a preliminary injunction is notice to the party to be restrained.[72] To obtain a preliminary injunction, the person seeking the injunction (the movant) must show that

1. there is a likelihood of success on the merits of the underlying case and
2. the movant will likely suffer "irreparable loss unless the injunction is issued"[73] or that issuance of the injunction "appears reasonably necessary to protect [the] plaintiffs' rights during the litigation."[74]

69. For more information on preliminary injunctions and TROs, refer to Ann Anderson, *Temporary Restraining Orders and Preliminary Injunctions (Rule 65)*, *in* NORTH CAROLINA SUPERIOR COURT JUDGES' BENCHBOOK (Feb. 2011) (hereinafter *TRO Chapter*).
70. *Id.* at 1.
71. *Id.* at 2.
72. G.S. 1A-1, Rule 65(a).
73. Ridge Cmty. Inv'rs, Inc. v. Berry, 293 N.C. 688, 701 (1977).
74. Setzer v. Annas, 286 N.C. 534, 537 (1975).

The movant must post a bond in an amount the judge finds proper.[75] The purpose of the bond is to protect the restrained party against costs and damages it may suffer if the injunction is dissolved or otherwise found to have been wrongful.[76]

A temporary restraining order (TRO) is an emergency measure that *precedes* a hearing on a preliminary injunction and serves the same function.[77] It may be granted without notice (oral or written) to the restrained party, which may be important in a case involving ongoing financial abuse of an older adult.[78] A party seeking a preliminary injunction does not have to also seek a TRO but may choose to do so at the start of litigation to prevent being harmed while waiting for a hearing on a preliminary injunction.[79]

Figure 6.1. **Relative Order of a TRO to a Preliminary Injunction**

To obtain a TRO, the person seeking the TRO (the applicant) must show to the court

1. that it clearly appears from specific facts shown by affidavit or by verified complaint that immediate and irreparable injury, loss, or damage will result to the applicant before the adverse party or that party's attorney can be heard in opposition and
2. a written certification from the applicant's attorney to the court detailing (a) the efforts, if any, that have been made to give notice to the other party or (b) the reasons supporting the claim that notice should not be required.[80]

A TRO granted without notice to the restrained party must expire within the time after entry as the judge sets in the TRO, not to exceed ten days.[81] The TRO may be extended before the original duration expires (1) for a like period for good cause shown or (2) for longer if the restrained party consents.[82] If the court issues a TRO without notice, the matter must be set for hearing at the earliest possible time.[83] At the hearing, the restraining party "shall proceed with a motion for a preliminary injunction."[84] If the restraining party does not

75. G.S. 1A-1, Rule 65(c). The amount of the bond is in the court's discretion. Schulz v. Ingram, 38 N.C. App. 422, 430 (1978).
76. G.S. 1A-1, Rule 65(c).
77. *TRO Chapter*, at 2.
78. G.S. 1A-1, Rule 65(b).
79. *TRO Chapter*, at 2.
80. G.S. 1A-1, Rule 65(b).
81. *Id.*
82. *Id.*
83. *Id.*
84. *Id.*

proceed, the judge "shall dissolve the temporary restraining order."[85] If the restraining party proceeds, the judge may grant a preliminary injunction or dissolve or modify the TRO.[86]

With limited exceptions, just as with a preliminary injunction, the party seeking a TRO must post a bond "in such sum as the judge deems proper" to protect the restrained party against costs and damages it may suffer if the TRO is dissolved or otherwise found to have been wrongful.[87]

EXAMPLE

Injunctive Relief

Frank is 75 years old and a retired farmer. He was diagnosed with dementia. Frank owns farm equipment worth more than $50,000. He let a former employee borrow the equipment. When Frank's daughter, who is his agent under a power of attorney, asks the employee to return the equipment, he refuses and asserts that Frank sold him the equipment. Frank's daughter applies to be appointed as guardian ad litem for Frank (see Section II.B.1.b, supra) and files a civil action to recover personal property (discussed in Section II.C.1.b.i.(b), infra) on Frank's behalf. Frank's daughter also includes in her verified civil complaint a request for both a TRO and a preliminary injunction preventing the employee from selling the property during the litigation. Frank's daughter has evidence that the employee listed the property for sale on a farming equipment auction site.

ii. Attachment

If an older adult has concerns that the defendant in a civil action will transfer, assign, or dispose of his or her property before entry of a final money judgment to avoid paying the judgment, the older adult could seek an attachment.[88] An attachment is an order entered by the court directing the sheriff to seize and hold the defendant's property pending the outcome of a lawsuit so that the property, should the plaintiff win a judgment, will be available to satisfy that judgment.[89]

All of a defendant's real or personal property in North Carolina that is subject to levy under an execution or that can be reached through a supplemental proceeding is subject to being attached.[90] A key feature of this remedy is that the property subject to being attached does not have to be related to the lawsuit.[91] Attachment is ancillary to an underlying pending action; the purpose of the underlying action must be, in whole or in part,

85. *Id.*

86. *Id.*

87. G.S. 1A-1, Rule 65(c).

88. Procedures for attachment may be found in G.S. Chapter 1, Article 35.

89. G.S. 1-440.1. For additional information on attachments, see JOAN G. BRANNON & ANN M. ANDERSON, NORTH CAROLINA CLERK OF SUPERIOR COURT PROCEDURES MANUAL ch. 34 (2012) (hereinafter CSC MANUAL).

90. G.S. 1-440.4.

91. *Id.*

to secure a money judgment, alimony, or child support.[92] Attachment is not available in a small claims action.[93] An attachment order is typically entered by the clerk of superior court.[94]

The clerk may enter an attachment order when it is shown by affidavit or by a verified complaint that the defendant is

1. a North Carolina resident with an intent to avoid service of summons who has departed or is about to depart the state or who is keeping himself or herself concealed;
2. a person or domestic corporation with an intent to default creditors that has removed or is about to remove property from North Carolina or has assigned, disposed of, or secreted property, or is about to do the same;
3. a nonresident.[95]

The plaintiff must furnish a bond before the clerk enters an order of attachment.[96] The clerk sets the bond amount at an amount necessary to afford reasonable protection to the defendant for the property to be taken.[97]

EXAMPLE

Attachment

Jane is 82 years old and lives alone in North Carolina. Thomas, a handyman who lives in Virginia, came to her home and offered to repair her leaky roof. Jane wrote him a check for $10,000 up front, and Thomas left and did not return. Jane filed a civil action in North Carolina against Thomas for fraud. Jane may consider filing an affidavit of attachment when she files the complaint against Thomas if Thomas has property in North Carolina, including bank accounts. (In practice, it will be necessary to know which bank Thomas uses in order to seize bank accounts.) If he does not have property in this state, then a North Carolina sheriff will not be able to seize any property.

92. G.S. 1-440.1(a); 1-440.2.
93. G.S. 7A-231.
94. G.S. 1-440.5. The trial judge may also enter the order. *Id.*
95. G.S. 1-440.3.
96. G.S. 1-440.10.
97. G.S. 1-440.10(1).

Table 6.2. **AOC Attachment Forms**[98]

FORM	NAME
CV-300	Affidavit in an Attachment Proceeding
CV-301	Order of Attachment
CV-901M	Defendant's Motion to Discharge Attachment
CV-302	Summons to Garnishee and Notice of Levy

iii. Claim and Delivery

If an older adult files an action to recover personal property, then the adult may consider filing a claim and delivery action in the underlying lawsuit.[99] A civil action to recover personal property is discussed in detail in Section II.C.1.b.i.(b), *infra*. Claim and delivery allows a plaintiff to get immediate possession of personal property pending the outcome of an underlying lawsuit.[100] The underlying lawsuit determines the right of permanent possession.[101] A claim and delivery order gives the plaintiff the right to possess the property until the lawsuit is decided.[102]

The claim and delivery action may be filed at any time after the complaint is filed and before judgment is entered in the principal action related to the property.[103] The clerk of superior court typically presides over the claim and delivery hearing. A claim and delivery action may be filed in connection with a civil action for recovery of personal property before a district or superior court judge or before a magistrate in a small claims action.[104] It may be more likely to be filed in a district or superior court civil action. It is rarely used in small claims actions because the trial before the magistrate on the underlying action may be heard more quickly than the claim and delivery before the clerk.[105]

A plaintiff initiates a claim and delivery action by filing an affidavit.[106] The affidavit must show

1. facts showing that the plaintiff is the owner of the property claimed (and the property must be particularly described) or is entitled to possession of it;
2. that the property is being wrongfully detained by the defendant;
3. the alleged cause(s) of the detention, according to the plaintiff's best knowledge, information, and belief;

98. The N.C. Judicial Branch's website features a "Forms" page where users may search for or download forms. *See* https://www.nccourts.gov/documents/forms.

99. Procedures for claim and delivery may be found in G.S. Chapter 1, Article 36. For additional information on claim and delivery, see CSC MANUAL, at ch. 35.

100. G.S. 1-472.

101. CSC MANUAL, at ch. 35, § 35.1.

102. *Id.*

103. *Id.*

104. G.S. 7A-231.

105. CSC MANUAL, at ch. 35, § 35.1.

106. G.S. 1-473.

4. that the property has not been
   a. taken for tax, assessment, or fine, pursuant to a statute;
   b. seized under an execution or attachment against the property of the plaintiff; or
   c. if so seized, that it is, by statute, exempt from the seizure; and
5. the actual value of the property.[107]

EXAMPLE

Claim and Delivery

Molly is 75 years old and was diagnosed with dementia this year. She owns a diamond ring and necklace worth $40,000. While visiting Molly, her daughter, Sara, notices that the jewelry is no longer in Molly's home. Sara confronts Molly's neighbor, Patricia, about the jewelry. Patricia says that Molly gave her the jewelry two years ago to show how grateful she was that Patricia cared for and checked on her each day. Patricia says that Molly told her that she was her "real daughter" when she gave her the jewelry. Sara is appointed as Molly's guardian ad litem and files a lawsuit to recover possession of the jewelry. Sara includes in the suit an action for claim and delivery.

After the affidavit is filed, the clerk will issue a notice of hearing.[108] The plaintiff may request that the clerk include an order in the notice enjoining the defendant (1) from willfully disposing of the property in any way, (2) from removing or permitting the removal of the property from North Carolina, or (3) from causing or permitting willful damage or destruction of the property.[109] If the defendant violates the order and the plaintiff is entitled to possession of the property, then the defendant may be held in contempt and fined or imprisoned by the court.[110]

The hearing date may not be less than ten days from the date the notice is served; service of the notice and a copy of the affidavit must be made on the defendant pursuant to Rule 4 of the N.C. Rules of Civil Procedure.[111] If the clerk finds that probable cause[112] exists to enter an order for seizure of the property, then he or she will enter an order of seizure.[113] The plaintiff must give a bond for double the value of the property to be recovered.[114] The defendant, within certain time limits, may object to the surety on the plaintiff's bond or

107. *Id.*
108. G.S. 1-474.1(a).
109. *Id.*
110. *Id.*
111. *Id.*
112. CSC MANUAL, at ch. 35, § 35.6. Note that G.S. Chapter 1, Article 36, regarding claim and delivery does not refer to the standard of proof.
113. *See* G.S. 1-474(a).
114. G.S. 1-475.

post a bond to allow the defendant to keep the property until the underlying lawsuit to recover possession of the personal property is decided.[115]

Table 6.3. **AOC Claim and Delivery Forms[116]**

FORM	NAME
CV-200	Affidavit and Request for Hearing in Claim and Delivery
CV-201	Notice of Hearing in Claim and Delivery
CV-202	Findings on Application for Claim and Delivery Order
CV-203	Order of Seizure in Claim and Delivery
CV-900M	Defendant's Bond in Claim and Delivery
CV-901M	Voluntary Waiver of Hearing in Claim and Delivery

iv. Lis Pendens

A lis pendens is a notice of pending litigation filed by a party to a civil action with the clerk of superior court in cases affecting title to real property.[117] A lis pendens may also be filed where an order of attachment is issued and real property is attached.[118] The lis pendens is cross-indexed by the clerk in a record called the "Record of Lis Pendens."[119] Once the lis pendens is cross-indexed, it provides constructive notice to any future purchaser or creditor seeking to secure a debt with the real property.[120] Any person who takes title to or a lien on the real property after the indexing of the lis pendens takes it subject to the outcome of the underlying civil action as if the person was a party to the civil action.[121] The lis pendens restricts the transfer or encumbrance of the real property during the litigation and ensures that the real property is available post-judgment; it preserves the status quo during the litigation.

EXAMPLE

Lis Pendens

Mary Jones is 85 years old. She has an adult son, John Jones, who is 45. John goes to Mary with three deeds transferring unencumbered real property owned by Mary to the "Jones Family Trust." John tells Mary that the purpose of the transfer is to create tax savings for Mary. John is the only one of Mary's children who visits her often, and she is afraid that if she does not sign the deeds, he will stop

115. G.S. 1-475; -477.
116. *See* note 98, *supra*
117. G.S. 1-116(a)(1). Procedures for lis pendens may be found in G.S. Chapter 1, Article 11.
118. G.S. 1-116(a)(3). Other cases where a lis pendens is permissible are (1) actions to foreclose any mortgage or deed of trust or to enforce any lien on real property, (2) actions seeking injunctive relief under G.S. 113A-64.1 or -65 regarding sedimentation and erosion control for any land-disturbing activity that is subject to the requirements of Article 4 of G.S. Chapter 113A, and (3) actions for asset freezing or seizure under G.S. 14-112.3. *Id.* § 1-116(a).
119. G.S. 1-117.
120. G.S. 1-118.
121. *Id.*

visiting her. John tells Mary that she is the beneficiary of the trust when in reality, John is the trustee and the sole beneficiary of the trust. After the deeds are recorded, John immediately takes out a loan on all three properties in the amount of $250,000. Mary's daughter, Jill, becomes suspicious and does some investigating. Jill helps Mary hire an attorney, who files a civil action to undo the transactions conducted by John and recover the real property. During the litigation, Mary may consider filing a lis pendens with the court to put third parties on constructive notice that the real property is the subject of a pending lawsuit and to hinder further transfers or encumbrances by John.

b. Civil Causes of Action

There are numerous civil causes of action that may be available to an older adult seeking redress for elder abuse or exploitation. This section does not provide an exhaustive list but instead provides a basis for thinking about what may be available depending on the facts of a particular case. If the action relates to personal property, the older adult may seek recovery of the value of the property wrongfully taken or of the property itself. The older adult may seek monetary damages based on other claims, such as breach of fiduciary duty, constructive fraud, actual fraud, negligent misrepresentation, unfair and deceptive trade practices, breach of contract, unjust enrichment, breach of trust, or civil torts. If a deed, power of attorney, trust, will, or other document was obtained from an older adult based on undue influence, duress, fraud, or lack of mental capacity on the part of the older adult, there may be a cause of action for rescission of the document. Each of these types of actions are discussed below.

i. Actions Related to Personal Property

(a) Conversion

If an item of personal property is wrongfully taken from an older adult who is the owner of the property, or taken with permission and then wrongfully detained, the older adult may bring either an action for conversion or an action to recover the personal property, discussed in more detail, *infra.*

The **elements** of an action for conversion are as follows.

1. The plaintiff is the lawful owner of personal property that has been taken and is entitled to repossess it immediately.
2. The defendant converted the property by
    a. wrongfully taking it from the plaintiff or
    b. rightfully taking it from the plaintiff but wrongfully retaining it after a demand was made to return it.
3. The fair market value of the property at the time it was wrongfully taken or wrongfully retained is ascertainable.[122]

122. SMALL CLAIMS LAW, at 122. *See also* Variety Wholesalers, Inc. v. Salem Logistics Traffic Servs., LLC, 365 N.C. 520,

Conversion is sometimes called a "forced sale" because if the plaintiff succeeds in the lawsuit, the defendant is effectively forced to buy the property from the plaintiff.[123] The plaintiff does not recover the property but recovers the fair market value of the property from the defendant plus interest from the date of the wrongful taking.[124]

A plaintiff is generally not required to demand return of his or her property from a defendant who has wrongfully taken possession of it.[125] But if the defendant took possession lawfully but failed to return the property, the property is not deemed converted until the plaintiff demands return of the property.[126] This is true even if the defendant was supposed to return the property at a specific time.

The **statute of limitations** for conversion is three years from when the unauthorized assumption and exercise of ownership occurs.[127]

EXAMPLE

Conversion

While 83-year-old Susie is in a rehabilitation facility recovering from a fall she suffered at home, her caregiver, Frank, goes to her house and takes the keys to her car (worth more than $15,000). He uses the car for months while Susie is in rehab. While using the car, Frank gets in an accident and causes $1,000 worth of damage to the car. When Susie returns home, she has to rent a car while her car is being repaired. Susie could sue Frank for conversion. If successful, she would recover damages equal to $15,000 (the value of the car when it was taken) plus interest from the time it was taken until judgment is entered.

(b) Action to Recover Personal Property

If an item of personal property is wrongfully taken from an older adult who is the owner of the property, or taken with permission and then wrongfully detained, instead of filing a claim for conversion, the older adult may bring an action to recover the personal property.

The **elements** of an action to recover personal property are as follows.

1. Plaintiff is the lawful owner of personal property and is entitled to repossess it immediately.
2. The property was wrongfully taken from the plaintiff or was lawfully taken but wrongfully retained after a demand was made for its return.

523 (2012) (citing Peed v. Burleson's, Inc., 244 N.C. 437, 439 (1956)) (stating that conversion is "an unauthorized assumption and exercise of the right of ownership over goods or personal chattels belonging to another, to the alteration of their condition or the exclusion of an owner's rights").

123. SMALL CLAIMS LAW, at 121.

124. *Id.* Fair market value is measured at the time the property was taken or not returned. *Id.*

125. *Id.* at 122.

126. *Id.*

127. G.S. 1-52(4); Stratton v. Royal Bank of Canada, 211 N.C. App. 78 (2011). As a general rule, the statute of limitations begins to accrue when the unauthorized assumption and exercise of ownership occurs—not when the plaintiff discovers the conversion. *Stratton*, 211 N.C. App. at 83. G.S. 1-52(9), which states that the cause of action shall not be deemed to have accrued until the discovery by the aggrieved party of the facts constituting the fraud or mistake, does not apply to a claim for conversion. *Id.*

3. The defendant is in possession of the property.
4. The amount of damages, if any, for loss of use of the property and physical damage to it are ascertainable.[128]

In this action, the plaintiff asks the court to order the return of the personal property, pay the plaintiff for damage done to the property while in the defendant's possession, and compensate the plaintiff for loss of use of the property while in the defendant's possession.[129] The plaintiff may file a separate action for damages once the property is returned and the plaintiff can assess the damages to it.[130] A form "Complaint to Recover Possession of Personal Property (Small Claims)" (CVM-202) is available from the N.C. Administrative Office of the Courts (AOC).[131] The form is designed for use in small claims court, discussed in Section II.B.3, *supra*.

The action is filed against the person in possession of the property.[132] If the person who wrongfully took or kept the property is no longer in possession of it, the plaintiff may consider an action for conversion instead of an action to recover possession.[133] The older adult may be entitled to payment of costs by the defendant, including reasonable attorneys' fees, in an action to recover possession of personal property.[134]

The **statute of limitations** for an action to recover personal property is three years from the taking or wrongful retention of the property.[135]

EXAMPLE

Action to Recover Personal Property

Rather than bring an action for conversion, Susie (see example immediately above) could bring an action to recover personal property (the car). If she prevails, her relief will be return of the property plus damages ($1,000 to repair the car and $500 to rent a car).

ii. General Claims Involving Monetary Damages

An older adult may have a claim against a perpetrator of abuse that could yield monetary damages and compensate the older adult for a loss resulting from the actions of the perpetrator. Damages may be strictly compensatory or, in some cases, may also include punitive damages.[136] Punitive damages (damages exceeding compensation and intended to punish and deter the defendant) may be available if the older adult can show

128. SMALL CLAIMS LAW, at 123.
129. *Id.* at 122.
130. *Id.*
131. *See* note 98, *supra*.
132. *Id.*
133. *Id.*
134. G.S. 6-18(2).
135. G.S. 1-52(4).
136. *See* Watson v. Dixon, 352 N.C. 343, 347–48 (2000) (discussing the different purposes of compensatory versus punitive damages).

that the defendant is liable for compensatory damages and there is an aggravating factor (as shown by clear and convincing evidence).[137] Aggravating factors include fraud, malice, and willful or wanton conduct.[138] Punitive damages are unavailable in cases solely for breach of contract.[139]

(a) Breach of Fiduciary Duty

The **elements** of a claim for breach of fiduciary duty are as follows.

1. The defendant owed the plaintiff a fiduciary duty.
2. The defendant breached that fiduciary duty.
3. The breach of fiduciary duty was a proximate cause of injury to the plaintiff.[140]

The existence of a fiduciary relationship is an essential element of a claim for breach of fiduciary duty. There are certain legal fiduciary relationships recognized by North Carolina law, including

- attorney-client,[141]
- spouse-spouse,[142]
- executor-beneficiary (decedent's estate),
- administrator-heir (decedent's estate),[143]
- guardian-ward (guardianship),[144]
- principal-agent (power of attorney),[145] and
- trustee-beneficiary (trust).[146]

In each relationship, there is a heightened level of trust and a duty imposed on the fiduciary to act in the best interests of the other party.[147]

137. G.S. 1D-1; -15(a), (b). Punitive damages may not exceed three times the amount of compensatory damages or $250,000, whichever is greater. *Id.* § 1D-25(b). If a trier of fact returns a verdict for punitive damages in excess of the maximum amount, the trial court must reduce the award and enter judgment for punitive damages in the maximum amount. *Id.*

138. G.S. 1D-15(a). The aggravating factor must be present and related to the injury for which the compensatory damages were awarded. *Id. See* Collier v. Bryant, 216 N.C. App. 419 (2011) (awarding punitive damages for constructive fraud); Lacey v. Kirk, 238 N.C. App. 376 (2014), *writ denied, review denied*, 368 N.C. 250 (2015) (awarding punitive damages in case of breach of fiduciary duty).

139. G.S. 1D-15(d).

140. Green v. Freeman, 367 N.C. 136, 141 (2013).

141. Fox v. Wilson, 85 N.C. App. 292, 299 (1987).

142. Eubanks v. Eubanks, 273 N.C. 189, 195–96 (1968) ("[t]he relationship between husband and wife is the most confidential of all relationships, and transactions between them, to be valid, must be fair and reasonable."); Dallaire v. Bank of Am., N.A., 367 N.C. 363, 367 (2014).

143. Collier v. Bryant, 216 N.C. App. 419, 432 (2011).

144. *In re* Estate of Armfield, 113 N.C. App. 467, 474 (1994).

145. *See* G.S. 32C-1-117(a); -114(a), (b) (duties of an agent to a principal).

146. Wachovia Bank & Trust Co. v. Johnston, 269 N.C. 701, 711 (1967).

147. *Dallaire*, 367 N.C. at 367. *See also* Hager v. Smithfield E. Health Holdings, LLC, ___ N.C. App. ___, ___, 826 S.E.2d 567, 571–74 (2019) (discussing fiduciary relationships generally and declining to find that a fiduciary relationship exists as a matter of law between assisted living facilities with memory wards and their residents).

A fiduciary relationship may also arise in other relationships, such as between an older adult and a caregiver, where "there has been a special confidence reposed in one who in equity and good conscience is bound to act in good faith and with due regard to the interests of the one reposing confidence[.]"[148] Such a relationship "extends to any possible case in which a fiduciary relationship exists in fact, and in which there is confidence reposed in one side, and resulting domination and influence on the other."[149] But "[o]nly when one party figuratively holds all the cards—all the financial power or technical information, for example—have North Carolina courts found that the special circumstance of a fiduciary relationship has arisen."[150]

The **statute of limitations** applicable to a claim for breach of fiduciary duty is three years from when the plaintiff either discovers the facts giving rise to the claim or with reasonable diligence could have discovered the facts.[151]

EXAMPLE

Breach of Fiduciary Duty

Sam is 78, a widower, and lives alone. He has two children who live outside North Carolina. Sam meets a young woman at church, Anna, who offers to run errands for him and help him out around the house. Sam is showing early signs of cognitive impairment but has not been diagnosed. After a few months of helping Sam out, Anna tells Sam it would be easier for her to keep helping him if he signs a power of attorney (POA) naming her as his agent, which Sam then does. The POA gives Anna broad authority but does not give her the authority to make gifts or to change rights of survivorship. Anna then executes a deed granting an 11-acre tract of land owned by Sam to herself. She then executes a second deed conveying another tract of land to her son, Brandon. The combined value of the properties is more than $500,000. This set of facts likely meets the requirements for breach of fiduciary duty. Anna owed Sam a fiduciary duty as agent under the POA. She breached that duty by conveying the land to herself and to her son without any consideration (payment). Sam lost significant assets as a result of her breach. Even if Anna were to argue that the transfers were made as consideration for her caregiving services, the value of the services likely would not reflect a fair and reasonable price for the properties.[152]

148. Dalton v. Camp, 353 N.C. 647, 651 (2001) (internal quotation marks omitted) (quoting Abbitt v. Gregory, 201 N.C. 577, 598 (1931). *See also* Meinhard v. Salmon, 249 N.Y. 458, 464 (1928) (describing fiduciaries as being held to a standard "stricter than the morals of the market place" and adding that "[n]ot honesty alone, but the punctilio of an honor the most sensitive, is then the standard of behavior").

149. *Dalton*, 353 N.C. at 651 (internal quotations and emphasis omitted) (quoting *Abbitt*, 201 N.C. at 598).

150. Lockerman v. S. River Elec. Membership Corp., 250 N.C. App. 631, 636 (2016) (internal quotation marks omitted) (quoting S.N.R. Mgmt. Corp. v. Danube Partners 141, LLC, 189 N.C. App. 601, 613 (2008). *See also Hager*, ___ N.C. App. at ___, 826 S.E.2d at 572.

151. Toomer v. Branch Banking & Tr. Co., 171 N.C. App. 58, 66 (2005) (holding that allegations of breach of fiduciary duty that do not rise to the level of constructive fraud are governed by the three-year statute of limitations applicable to contract actions contained in G.S. 1-52(1)).

152. *See* Estate of Graham v. Morrison, 168 N.C. App. 63, 69 (2005).

(b) Constructive Fraud

The **elements** of a claim for constructive fraud are as follows.

1. A relationship of trust and confidence existed between the plaintiff and the defendant.
2. The defendant took advantage of that position of trust to benefit himself or herself.
3. The plaintiff was, as a result, injured.[153]

Constructive fraud and breach of fiduciary duty are often pled together in the same complaint. Constructive fraud is similar to, but is a separate claim from, breach of fiduciary duty.[154] The primary difference between a claim for constructive fraud and one for breach of fiduciary duty is that constructive fraud requires that the defendant benefit himself or herself.[155] For example, if the actions by the defendant lead to a loss to the plaintiff but do not ultimately benefit the defendant, then there may be claim for breach of fiduciary duty but not a claim for constructive fraud.

Fraud may be *actual* or *constructive*. The elements of actual fraud are set out below. Constructive fraud differs from actual fraud in that "it is based on a confidential relationship rather than a specific misrepresentation."[156] It is the relationship between the parties that enables the defendant to take advantage of his or her position of trust to hurt the plaintiff.[157] An intent to deceive, an element of actual fraud, is not an element of constructive fraud.[158]

When the superior party obtains a possible benefit through the alleged abuse of the confidential or fiduciary relationship, the aggrieved party is entitled to a presumption that constructive fraud occurred.[159] The alleged fiduciary may rebut the presumption by showing, for example, that the confidence placed in the fiduciary was not abused.[160]

The **statute of limitations** applicable to a claim for constructive fraud is ten years after the cause of action accrues or ten years from when the aggrieved party either discovers the fraud or with reasonable diligence could have discovered it.[161] While there is no duty to investigate, a plaintiff may not remain willfully ignorant.[162]

---

153. Hauser v. Hauser, 252 N.C. App. 10, 16 (2017).

154. White v. Consol. Planning, Inc., 166 N.C. App. 283, 293 (2004).

155. *Id.* at 294.

156. Barger v. McCoy Hillard & Parks, 346 N.C. 650, 666 (1997) (internal quotation marks omitted) (quoting Terry v. Terry, 302 N.C. 77, 85 (1981).

157. Forbis v. Neal, 361 N.C. 519, 528 (2007).

158. *Id.* at 529.

159. *Id.*; Collier v. Bryant, 216 N.C. App. 419, 432 (2011).

160. *Forbis*, 361 N.C. at 529.

161. NationsBank of N.C., N.A. v. Parker, 140 N.C. App. 106, 113 (2000); Shepherd v. Shepherd, 57 N.C. App. 680, 682 (1982) ("An action for fraud accrues when the aggrieved party discovers the facts constituting the fraud, or when, in the exercise of due diligence, such facts should have been discovered.").

162. Honeycutt v. Weaver, 257 N.C. App. 599, 606 (2018) (quoting Vail v. Vail, 233 N.C. 109, 116–17 (1951) ("[w]here a confidential relationship exists between the parties, the aggrieved party 'is under no duty to make inquiry until something occurs to excite his suspicions, so long as he does not purposefully remain ignorant of such facts' ").

EXAMPLE

Constructive Fraud

Along with a claim for breach of fiduciary duty, Sam (see example immediately above) may also have a claim for constructive fraud against Anna for transferring the property to herself. Sam had a relationship of trust and confidence with Anna, his caregiver and agent under the POA. Anna exploited her position to benefit herself by transferring the property for no/inadequate consideration to herself. As a result, Sam incurred an injury, which was loss of a valuable asset without receiving adequate consideration.

(c) Fraud

The **elements** of a claim for actual fraud are

- false representation or concealment of a material fact
- that was reasonably calculated to deceive,
- made with intent to deceive,
- that did in fact deceive an injured party, and
- resulted in damage to that party.[163]

The proof required for an actual fraud claim is more exacting than that required in constructive fraud cases, and thus these types of claims are often harder to win.[164] Fraud must be pled with particularity.[165] The claim is not based on the relationship between the parties but, rather, on an intent to deceive. To prove fraud, a plaintiff must show that the defendant made a specific misrepresentation, the defendant intended to deceive the plaintiff and the plaintiff was in fact deceived, and as a result, the plaintiff was damaged. The plaintiff's reliance on the allegedly false representations must be reasonable.[166] Damages in a fraud case "is the amount of loss caused by the difference between what was received and what was promised through a false representation."[167]

The **statute of limitations** applicable to an action for actual fraud is three years after the cause of action accrues or three years from when the aggrieved party either discovers the fraud or with reasonable diligence could have discovered it.[168]

163. Jones v. Harrelson & Smith Contractors, LLC, 194 N.C. App. 203, 229 (2008), *aff'd*, 363 N.C. 371 (2009).
164. Watts v. Cumberland Cty. Hosp. Sys., Inc., 317 N.C. 110, 115–16 (1986).
165. Terry v. Terry, 302 N.C. 77, 84 (1981).
166. *Forbis*, 361 N.C. at 527.
167. First Atl. Mgmt. Corp. v. Dunlea Realty Co., 131 N.C. App. 242, 256 (1998).
168. *Forbis*, 361 N.C. at 524.

EXAMPLE

Fraud

Along with conveying property to herself and her son, Anna (see the example immediately above) also transferred the money in Sam's checking account to a joint account with a right of survivorship with Anna and Sam as the owners of the account. Anna had the authority to manage Sam's account as agent under the POA but lacked the authority to change ownership and survivorship rights. Anna told Sam that she needed access to his account to help pay for things she purchased for him when she ran errands for him and that the new account had a better rate of return than his sole checking account and carried fewer penalties. Anna did not tell Sam that she added herself to the account and made it a survivorship account. Anna then used the funds in the account for her own personal needs. She concealed the true nature of the account from Sam to deceive him about her rights to the account and ownership in the account. She then used the account funds for her own benefit and not Sam's benefit, causing him injury.[169] *As a result, Sam may also have a claim for fraud.*

(d) Negligent Misrepresentation

The **elements** of a claim for negligent misrepresentation are that

- a party justifiably relies
- to his or her detriment
- on information prepared without reasonable care
- by one who owed the relying party a duty of care.[170]

Unlike fraud, which requires an intent to deceive, negligent misrepresentation only requires justifiable reliance by the plaintiff on information prepared without reasonable care by someone who owed the plaintiff a duty of care. To succeed in a claim for negligent misrepresentation, a plaintiff must show that the defendant owed a duty to provide "complete and accurate information" and that such duty was breached.[171] In addition, the plaintiff must have actually relied, justifiably, on the false information supplied by the

169. *See Forbis*, 361 N.C. at 527.

170. Simms v. Prudential Life Ins. Co. of Am., 140 N.C. App. 529, 532 (2000) (quoting Raritan River Steel Co. v. Cherry, Bekaert & Holland, 322 N.C. 200, 206 (1988), *rev'd on other grounds*, 329 N.C. 646 (1991)), *discretionary review denied*, 353 N.C. 381 (2001).

171. *Simms*, 140 N.C. App. at 533 (2000). North Carolina courts have described a breach by a defendant of a duty of care as involving a situation where "[o]ne who, in the course of his business, profession or employment, or in any other transaction in which he has a pecuniary interest, supplies false information for the guidance of others in their business transactions, [and thus] is subject to liability for pecuniary loss caused to [those others] by their justifiable reliance upon the information, if [that person] fails to exercise reasonable care or competence in obtaining or communicating the information." *Id.* at 534 (emphasis omitted).

defendant.[172] A plaintiff cannot establish justified reliance on an alleged misrepresentation if the plaintiff fails to make reasonable inquiry regarding the alleged statement.[173]

The **statute of limitations** applicable to an action for negligent misrepresentation is three years after the cause of action accrues or three years from when the aggrieved party either discovers the misrepresentation or with reasonable diligence could have discovered it.[174]

(e) Unfair and Deceptive Trade Practices

The **elements** of a claim for unfair and deceptive trade practices (UDTP) are as follows.

1. The defendant committed an unfair or deceptive act or practice.
2. The action in question was in or affected commerce.
3. The act proximately caused injury to the plaintiff.[175]

A claim for UDTP may be appropriate in the case of elder abuse, particularly when asserted together with other claims, such as breach of fiduciary duty and/or constructive fraud.[176] A trade practice is *unfair* "when the practice is immoral, unethical, oppressive, unscrupulous, or substantially injurious to consumers."[177] A trade practice is *deceptive* if it "possessed the tendency or capacity to mislead or created the likelihood of deception."[178] A plaintiff must show that the defendant's misrepresentation proximately caused him or her to suffer injury.[179] "A party may be guilty of unfair or deceptive acts or practices when it engages in conduct that amounts to an inequitable assertion of its power or position."[180]

One of the benefits of a UDTP claim to a victim of elder abuse is that a successful claim will result in an award of automatic treble (triple) damages to the plaintiff.[181] Furthermore, the judge may award reasonable attorneys' fees, which are taxed as part of the costs to the defendant.[182]

---

172. Walker v. Town of Stoneville, 211 N.C. App. 24, 31 (2011); Brinkman v. Barrett Kays & Assocs., P.A., 155 N.C. App. 738, 742 (2003).

173. Pinney v. State Farm Mut. Ins. Co., 146 N.C. App. 248, 256 (2001) (citation omitted) ("It has also been held that when a party relying on a 'misleading representation could have discovered the truth upon inquiry, the complaint must allege that he was denied the opportunity to investigate or that he could not have learned the true facts by exercise of reasonable diligence.'"), *discretionary review denied*, 356 N.C. 438 (2002).

174. Carlisle v. Keith, 169 N.C. App. 674, 684 (2005) (referencing G.S. 1-52).

175. Capital Res., LLC v. Chelda, Inc., 223 N.C. App. 227, 239 (2012).

176. Compton v. Kirby, 157 N.C. App. 1, 20 (2003) (noting that North Carolina case law has held that conduct which constitutes a breach of fiduciary duty and constructive fraud is sufficient to support a UDTP claim).

177. Marshall v. Miller, 302 N.C. 539, 548 (1981).

178. *Capital Res.*, 223 N.C. App. at 239 (internal quotation marks omitted) (quoting Overstreet v. Brookland, Inc., 52 N.C. App. 444, 425–53 (1981).

179. Tucker v. Blvd. at Piper Glen LLC, 150 N.C. App. 150, 154 (2002).

180. *Compton*, 157 N.C. App. at 20 (quoting Edwards v. West, 128 N.C. App. 570, 575, *cert. denied*, 348 N.C. 282 (1998)).

181. G.S. 75-16.

182. G.S. 75-16.1. To award attorneys' fees, the judge must find that (1) the party charged with the violation has willfully engaged in the act or practice and that there was an unwarranted refusal by such party to fully resolve the matter which constitutes the basis of such suit; or (2) the party instituting the action knew, or should have known, the action was frivolous and malicious. *Id.*

The applicable **statute of limitations** requires that the UDTP claim must be commenced within four years after the cause of action accrues or within four years of the date the plaintiff discovers or should have discovered the defendant's wrongful conduct.[183]

EXAMPLE

Unfair and Deceptive Trade Practices

John is 89 and owns a home in a desirable neighborhood in an urban area. He has owned the home for sixty years. John suffers from memory loss. He has no family who lives close by and is pretty lonely on a day-to-day basis. One day, a real estate broker knocks on his door and John invites him in. The broker says that he has clients who would like to purchase the house. He tells John that he can also serve as his agent for the sale. The broker tells John that he has conducted an appraisal of the house and that it is worth $50,000. In reality, the house is worth more than $250,000. The broker handles the closing and conveys the property to himself. There was no third-party purchaser of the house. As a result, John may have a claim for UDTP against the broker.

(f) Other Possible Claims

There are other claims that might be appropriate for an older adult to bring depending on the facts of his or her case. Such claims can be brought either separate from or along with other claims.

(1) Breach of Contract

If the older adult enters into a valid contract and the other party to the contract breaches the contract, then the older adult may have a claim for breach of contract. A claim for breach of contract requires the showing of a valid contract and breach of that contract.[184] For example, assume that an older adult enters into a contract with a man who knocked on her door and claimed she needed a new roof. The older adult may assert breach of contract if the man fails to complete the project according to the contract.

(2) Unjust Enrichment

A claim for unjust enrichment might be available when a plaintiff has rendered services or made expenditures for someone else without an express contract to pay. When the other party was enriched by the plaintiff's actions, the law will imply a promise to pay a fair compensation for the services or expenditures. It is a claim for a contract that the law implies.[185] If there is a contract that governs the claim, then the appropriate claim would be for breach of contract, not for unjust enrichment.[186] The elements of a claim for unjust

183.G.S. 75-16.2; Hunter v. Guardian Life Ins. Co. of Am., 162 N.C. App. 477, 485 (2004).
184. Poor v. Hill, 138 N.C. App. 19, 26 (2000).
185. *See* Shelter Corp. v. BTU, Inc., 154 N.C. App. 321, 330–31 (2002).
186. *Id.* at 331.

enrichment are (1) the plaintiff conferred a benefit on another party, (2) the other party consciously accepted the benefit, and (3) the benefit was not conferred gratuitously or by an interference in the affairs of the other party.[187]

(3) Breach of Trust

If an older adult has a trust in place and the trustee breaches a duty the trustee owes under the trust, the older adult may have a claim for breach of trust.[188] The trustee may be held liable for the greater of: (1) the amount required to restore the value of the trust property and trust distributions to what they would have been had the breach not occurred or (2) the profit the trustee made because of the breach.[189] A proceeding against a trustee for breach of trust may be commenced up to five years after the earliest of the date on which

- the trustee is removed, resigns, or dies;
- the beneficiary's interest in the trust is terminated; or
- the trust is terminated.[190]

(4) Torts

A tort is a civil wrong for which a remedy may be obtained, usually in the form of damages.[191] Torts include cases resulting from intentional acts, such as assault, battery, and intentional infliction of emotional distress, and from the failure to observe a standard of care, such as negligent infliction of emotional distress and negligence. These civil claims may be brought in addition to any criminal action related to the same conduct.

(A) CIVIL ASSAULT AND BATTERY. An older adult may have a claim against a perpetrator of physical or sexual abuse for civil assault and battery. The tort of assault occurs when a person is put in reasonable apprehension of imminent harmful or offensive contact.[192] Words alone generally are not enough to constitute assault unless they are coupled with other acts or circumstances that put the older adult in reasonable fear of such contact.[193] Battery occurs when an older adult is offensively touched against his or her will.[194]

(B) INFLICTION OF EMOTIONAL DISTRESS. There are two types of infliction of emotional distress: intentional and negligent. Either may be an appropriate cause of action for an older adult to bring in the event of emotional abuse. The elements of intentional infliction of emotional distress (IIED) are

187. *Id.* at 330.
188. G.S. 36C-10-1001(a).
189. G.S. 36C-10-1002(a).
190. G.S. 36C-10-1005(a).
191. *Tort*, BLACK'S LAW DICTIONARY (11th ed. 2019).
192. *See* Dickens v. Puryear, 302 N.C. 437, 445 (1981); McCraney v. Flanagan, 47 N.C. App. 498, 499 (1980). "Imminent" in this context has been found to not mean immediate. *Dickens*, 302 N.C. at 445–46. Rather, it means "that there will be no significant delay." *Id.* at 446.
193. *Id.* at 446.
194. Lynn v. Burnette, 138 N.C. App. 435, 439 (2000).

(1) extreme and outrageous conduct by the defendant/perpetrator, (2) that is intended to cause severe emotional distress to the victim, and (3) that does in fact cause such severe emotional distress.[195]

The elements of a claim for negligent infliction of emotional distress (NIED) are (1) the defendant negligently engaged in conduct, (2) it was reasonably foreseeable that the conduct would cause the plaintiff severe emotional distress (often called mental anguish), and (3) the conduct did in fact cause the plaintiff severe emotional distress.[196] Unlike IIED, a claim for NIED does not require a showing of extreme and outrageous conduct.

For both IIED and NIED, *severe emotional distress* means "any emotional or mental disorder, such as, for example, neurosis, psychosis, chronic depression, phobia, or any other type of severe and disabling emotional or mental condition" which a professional may diagnose.[197] Punitive damages may be available for a claim for intentional or negligent emotional distress if the older adult can show that the actions of the perpetrator were done with malice or willful or wanton conduct.[198]

(C) FALSE IMPRISONMENT. False imprisonment is an intentional tort. The elements of false imprisonment are (1) the illegal restraint of the plaintiff by the defendant, (2) by force or by an implied threat of force, and (3) against the plaintiff's will.[199] Even a brief restraint of the plaintiff's freedom is sufficient for this tort.[200] This cause of action may be appropriate, for example, against a caregiver who moves an older adult who requires the use of a wheelchair to a second floor bedroom against the older adult's will. The caregiver may be trying to prevent the older adult from leaving the home and reporting the caregiver's abusive actions to others.

(D) NEGLIGENCE; GROSS NEGLIGENCE. The elements of negligence in the context of a situation involving an older adult are (1) the defendant owes a duty of care to the older adult, (2) the defendant breaches that duty of care, and (3) the breach proximately causes injury to the older adult.[201] Negligence may be easier to prove than a breach of fiduciary duty claim, and a negligence cause of action can be applied to more relationships than just fiduciary relationships. For example, if an adult care home fails to provide adequate care or to keep the premises reasonably safe and an older adult is

195. Holleman v. Aiken, 193 N.C. App. 484, 501 (2008) (citation omitted).
196. Wilkerson v. Duke Univ., 229 N.C. App. 670, 675 (2013).
197. *Id. at* 675–76 (internal quotation marks omitted).
198. G.S. 1D-15(a); Burgess v. Busby, 142 N.C. App. 393, 409–10 (2001) (intentional infliction of emotional distress); Shaw v. Goodyear Tire & Rubber Co., 225 N.C. App. 90, 94–95 (2013) (discussing what constitutes "willful or wanton" negligence and stating that the jury was properly instructed on what to find before punitive damages could be awarded in claim for negligent infliction of emotional distress).
199. *Wilkerson*, 229 N.C. App. at 674.
200. *Id.*
201. Lynn v. Burnette, 138 N.C. App. 435, 439 (2000).

injured as a result, the older adult may have a claim against the adult care home for negligence. Recovery in a negligence action is limited to compensatory damages.[202] Gross negligence requires the same showing as a negligence action but also requires the added element of "wanton conduct done with conscious or reckless disregard for the rights and safety of others."[203] A successful claim for gross negligence would entitle the older adult to punitive damages along with compensatory damages.[204]

iii. Rescission of Documents

An older adult may sign or modify a document such as a will, trust, deed, or contract as a result of undue influence,[205] duress, or fraud imposed by another person, or the older adult may lack capacity when the document was signed. As a result, the older adult, or a person legally acting on behalf of the older adult (discussed in Section II.B.1, *supra*), can seek a court order to rescind the document or the changes made to the document.[206] If the action involves the rescission of a deed, the older adult may also be entitled to payment of costs by the defendant, including reasonable attorneys' fees.[207]

(a) Undue Influence

The **elements** required to show undue influence are as follows.

1. A person is subject to influence.
2. The perpetrator has an opportunity to exert influence.
3. The perpetrator has a disposition to exert influence.
4. There is a result that indicates undue influence.[208]

To show undue influence in the execution of a document, a party must show that something operated on the mind of the older adult subject to influence that had "a controlling effect sufficient to destroy the person's free agency and to render the instrument not properly an expression of the person's wishes, but rather the expression of the wishes of

202. *See, e.g.*, King v. Britt, 267 N.C. 594, 597–98 (1966) (stating that in personal injury cases resulting from negligence, the plaintiff is entitled to recover damages resulting from the negligence).

203. Clayton v. Branson, 170 N.C. App. 438, 445 (2005) (internal quotation marks omitted).

204. G.S. 1D-15.

205. "Undue influence" is defined by North Carolina law as a "fraudulent influence over the mind and will of another to the extent that the professed action is not freely done but is in truth the act of the one who procures the result." *In re* Loftin's Estate, 285 N.C. 717, 722 (1974).

206. *See* Hinson v. United Fin. Servs., Inc., 123 N.C. App. 469, 473–74 (1996) (discussing statute of limitations for claim for rescission based on duress); Matthews v. James, 88 N.C. App. 32 (1987) (involving action for rescission based on lack of mental capacity and undue influence); Caudill v. Smith, 117 N.C. App. 64 (1994) (involving undue influence in the execution of a deed by a 90-year-old man; deed was set aside).

207. G.S. 6-18(1).

208. *In re* Will of Smith, 158 N.C. App. 722, 726 (2003).

another or others."[209] Undue influence may be shown by proving several factors, including

- the old age and physical and mental weakness of the person executing the instrument,
- that the person signing the paper is in the home of the beneficiary of the paper and is subject to his or her constant association and supervision,
- that others have little or no opportunity to see the person signing the paper,
- that the newly signed instrument is different from and revokes a prior instrument,
- that the new instrument has been made in favor of one with whom the signing party has no ties of blood,
- that the paper disinherits the natural objects of the signer's bounty, or
- that the beneficiary of the document has procured its execution.[210]

Undue influence is generally shown by several facts that, were they to be asserted individually, would not be enough to make a case but that, taken together, may be sufficient evidence of undue influence.[211] Undue influence need not be due to bad motives; even good motives may result in undue influence.[212]

EXAMPLE

Undue Influence

James was 73 years old and a chronic alcoholic with bipolar disorder. He originally named his wife and son as beneficiaries of his pension and profit-sharing plans administered by his employer. He then changed the beneficiary to his caregiver. Less than one month prior to the change, he attempted to take his own life, and two weeks after the change he did just that. James lived in his own home but for two months before signing the forms was subject to the constant association and supervision of the caregiver. Prior caregivers noted that James could not care for himself—he could not use the bathroom unassisted or care for his other personal hygiene needs. When anyone had contact with James, he was always accompanied by the caregiver.[213] *James depended on the caregiver for his basic needs and was lonely because the caregiver isolated him from others most of the time. These facts likely support a claim to rescind the beneficiary designations based on undue influence of James by the caregiver.*

209. Matthews v. James, 88 N.C. App. 32, 37 (1987) (quoting Hardee v. Hardee, 309 N.C. 753, 756 (1983)) (internal quotation marks omitted) (civil action to rescind change in beneficiary designations on pension and profit-sharing plans administered by an employer).

210. Hardee v. Hardee, 309 N.C. 753, 756–57 (1983).

211. *See In re* Will of Jones, 362 N.C. 569, 575 (2008) (stating that a determination of undue influence is highly fact-specific and inherently subjective).

212. *Id.* at 574.

213. *See Matthews*, 88 N.C. App. at 38–39 (similar facts sufficient to allow the question of undue influence to go to the jury).

(b) Duress

An older adult may have grounds to rescind a contract, deed, will, or other document based on duress. The **elements** required to show duress are that

- by the unlawful act(s) of another,
- an older adult is induced to make a contract or to perform or forego some act
- under circumstances that deprive the adult of his or her free will.[214]

A wrongful act or threat is a key element of duress. Whereas fraud rests on deception by misrepresentation or concealment, duress results from coercion and may exist even though the older adult is fully aware of all of the material facts of the situation.[215]

(c) Fraud

The elements of a fraud claim are set out in Section II.C.1.b.ii.(c), *supra*. Rather than seek compensatory damages for fraud, the older adult alleging fraud in connection with the execution of documents may elect the remedy of rescission.[216] This prevents double redress for a single wrong.[217] The election of rescission rather than damages does not preclude an award for punitive damages.[218]

(d) Lack of Mental Capacity

An older adult may have grounds to rescind an agreement or other document for lack of capacity.

(1) Mental Capacity to Contract

"[A] person has mental capacity sufficient to contract if he knows what he is about, and that the measure of capacity is the ability to understand the nature of the act in which he is engaged and its scope and effect, or its nature and consequences, not that he should be able to act wisely or discreetly, nor to drive a good bargain, but that he should be in such possession of his faculties as to enable him to know at least what he is doing and to contract understandingly."[219]

(2) Mental Capacity to Make a Will

The standard for capacity to make (or modify) a will (known as testamentary capacity) is different from the capacity to contract.[220] Testamentary capacity requires that a person be of *sound mind*, meaning that the person understands the natural objects of his or her bounty; understands the kind, nature, and extent of his or her property; knows the manner in which he or she desired the act to take effect; and realizes the effect that the act would have upon his or her estate.[221]

---

214. Radford v. Keith, 160 N.C. App. 41, 43–44 (2003), *aff'd*, 358 N.C. 136 (2004).
215. Link v. Link, 278 N.C. 181, 191 (1971).
216. Mehovic v. Mehovic, 133 N.C. App. 131, 135 (1999).
217. *Id.*
218. *Id.* at 135–37.
219. Sprinkle v. Wellborn, 140 N.C. 163 (1905) (internal citations omitted).
220. *In re* Will of Maynard, 64 N.C. App. 211, 224–25 (1983).
221. *Id.* at 224.

2. PROTECTION FROM DOMESTIC VIOLENCE OR UNWANTED CONTACT

There may be situations when an older adult is the victim of domestic violence perpetrated by someone with whom the adult has a personal relationship, such as a child, grandchild, or intimate partner. The older adult may also be the victim of sexual misconduct or stalking by someone with whom he or she does not have a personal relationship, such as an adult care home worker.

Two types of civil protective orders are available under North Carolina law to protect older adults in these situations. G.S. Chapter 50B authorizes the court to enter civil domestic violence protective orders (often referred to as DVPOs, 50B orders, or restraining orders) to protect victims of domestic violence. Chapter 50C authorizes the court to enter civil no-contact orders (no-contact or 50C orders) to protect victims of sexual misconduct and stalking who do not have the personal relationship with the perpetrator required for DVPOs. Actions to secure these orders may be initiated by an older adult himself or herself or by the older adult's authorized legal representative (persons authorized to act on behalf of an older adult are discussed in Section II.B, *supra*).

RESOURCES

- If the adult is in immediate danger, call 911.
- The telephone number of the National Domestic Violence Hotline is 1-800-799-7233 (SAFE); for TTY accessibility: 1-800-787-3224.
- Text HOME to 741741 at any time and from anywhere in the United States to talk by text about any type of crisis, including domestic violence.
- The N.C. Coalition Against Domestic Violence maintains a list of local domestic violence service providers in the state. The list can be accessed on the organization's website at https://nccadv.org/get-help.

A DVPO or 50C order may be obtained instead of or along with a criminal prosecution.[222] Neither type of order is tantamount to a criminal conviction, but a criminal conviction may result from the violation of a DVPO (but not from the violation of a 50C order). Similarly, obtaining a DVPO or 50C order does not preclude an older adult from obtaining relief through a civil lawsuit for tort claims, such as assault, battery, or intentional infliction of emotional distress.[223] A victim of domestic violence/unwanted contact may not, however, obtain both a DVPO and a 50C order. The two actions are mutually exclusive because, to obtain a DVPO, the victim and perpetrator must have a personal relationship with one another. By contrast, to obtain a 50C order, the parties need not have a personal relationship.

222. G.S. 50B-7; 50C-11.
223. *Id.*

a. Domestic Violence Protective Order

A DVPO is a court order that requires a perpetrator of domestic violence to stop committing domestic violence.[224] Domestic violence is defined[225] as

1. causing or attempting to cause bodily injury to someone;
2. putting someone in fear of imminent serious bodily injury;
3. putting someone in fear of continued harassment that inflicts substantial emotional distress; or
4. committing rape, sexual offense, sexual battery, or another act defined in G.S. 14-27.21 through -27.33.

RESOURCE

The North Carolina Administrative Office of the Courts maintains information on its website about how to get a protective order. See https://www.nccourts.gov/help-topics/domestic-violence/how-to-get-a-protection-order.

To obtain a DVPO, an older adult must have a personal relationship with the perpetrator of domestic violence.[226] If the older adult does not have a personal relationship with the perpetrator, the older adult may be able to obtain a 50C civil no-contact order in some cases (discussed in more detail below).[227] A "personal relationship" in the DVPO context means that the parties

- are current or former spouses,
- are persons of the opposite sex who live together or have lived together,
- are related as parents and children or as grandparents and grandchildren (a parent or grandparent may not obtain a protective order against a child or grandchild under the age of 16),
- have a child in common,
- are current or former household members, or
- are persons of the opposite sex who are in or have been in a dating relationship (defined as "romantically involved over time and on a continuous basis during the course of the relationship").[228]

224. G.S. 50B-1(c) (defining "protective order"); 50B-3 (describing the relief available in an order as directed by the court).

225. G.S. 50B-1.

226. G.S. 50B-1(a), (b).

227. G.S. 50C-1(8) (defining "victim" for purposes of civil no-contact orders as a person against whom an act of unlawful conduct, as defined by statute, has been committed by someone not involved in a personal relationship with that person).

228. G.S. 50B-1(b). A dating relationship does not include a casual acquaintance or ordinary fraternization between persons in a business or social context. *Id.* § 50B-1(b)(6).

i. Filing for a DVPO

Any person residing in North Carolina may seek a DVPO by filing a civil action or by filing a motion in any existing G.S. Chapter 50 action; the act of violence does not have to occur in North Carolina.[229] A form "Complaint and Motion for DVPO" (CV-303) is available from the N.C. Administrative Office of the Courts (AOC).[230] The form includes instructions on how to initiate and maintain a DVPO action. There are several local domestic violence agencies that will help victims with the process of filing for DVPOs. A list of these agencies is available at https://nccadv.org/get-help.

If an older adult is the aggrieved party in a domestic violence situation, and if the adult has capacity, then he or she files for the DVPO himself or herself and prosecutes the action as the real party in interest.[231] If the older adult in such circumstances lacks capacity, then he or she is named as the real party in interest to the proceeding but appears in the action through a general guardian or through a guardian ad litem (GAL) appointed by the court.[232] This process is explained in Section II.B.1.b, *supra*.

An older adult may file for a DVPO without the assistance of legal counsel.[233] The clerk of superior court of each county in the state must provide to any person without legal counsel who is seeking a DVPO all forms that are necessary or appropriate to enable the person to proceed without counsel.[234] The clerk must, whenever feasible, provide a private area for complainants to fill out forms and make inquiries.[235] No court costs or attorneys' fees are assessed for a DVPO.[236]

After the DVPO complaint is filed, a summons will be issued by the court and served by the sheriff. The summons requires the defendant to answer the complaint within ten days of the date of service.[237] The law does not specify the time within which the hearing on the order must be held, unless an ex parte DVPO has been entered. In any case, the hearing may be held only when the defendant has been served. If an ex parte DVPO has been entered, the hearing must be held within ten days of the issuance of the ex parte order or within seven days of the date of service of process on the defendant, whichever is later.[238] The hearing may be continued by consent of the parties or by the court for good cause.[239]

ii. Ex Parte DVPO Hearing and Order

Between the time the complaint or motion is filed in a DVPO matter and the hearing on the request for a DVPO, an older adult victim of domestic violence may seek a temporary

229. G.S. 50B-2(a).
230. *See* note 98, *supra*.
231. G.S. 1A-1, Rule 17(a).
232. G.S. 1A-1, Rule 17(a), (b)(1).
233. G.S. 50B-2(a).
234. G.S. 50B-2(d).
235. *Id.*
236. G.S. 50B-2(a). There is an exception to this rule for costs and attorneys' fees pursuant to G.S. 1A-1, Rule 11.
237. *Id.* This time period may be shortened by G.S. 50B-2(c)(5) if there is the issuance of an ex parte DVPO, which requires a hearing to be held within ten days from the date of issuance of the order or within seven days from the date of service of process on the other party, whichever occurs later, unless the hearing is continued by consent or for good cause. *Id.* § 50B-2(c)(5).
238. G.S. 50B-2(c)(5).
239. *Id.*

order, known as an *ex parte DVPO*, to protect himself or herself while the matter is pending. The older adult may request ex parte relief any time before the hearing on the DVPO complaint.[240] An ex parte order is relief granted by the court without the defendant being present and typically before service has been made on the defendant.

The hearing on the ex parte order is conducted by a judge or a magistrate in person or through a video conference.[241] The hearing is typically held at or shortly after the time the complaint is filed.[242] If the judge determines that there is a danger of acts of domestic violence being committed against the older adult, the judge may grant an ex parte DVPO, deeming it necessary for the protection of the older adult (this includes the relief available for a DVPO set forth below, including, in certain circumstances, surrender of firearms, ammunition, and permits after asking the older adult about the presence of or the defendant's access to or ownership of these items).[243]

If the ex parte DVPO is entered by a judge, as opposed to a magistrate, it will not expire unless the order includes a specific expiration date.[244] An ex parte order entered by a magistrate expires by the end of the next day that the district court is in session in the county in which the action was filed.[245] The magistrate must schedule a second ex parte hearing before a district court judge before the order expires.[246] In practice, the ex parte DVPO typically remains in effect for a brief time—until either the entry or denial of the DVPO.[247]

iii. DVPO Hearing and Order

The hearing for a DVPO is held before a district court judge who will either grant or deny the DVPO. The parties may also consent to the entry of a DVPO. For the court to enter a DVPO, it must find that the parties had a personal relationship and that an act of domestic violence has occurred.[248] If the court grants the DVPO, its order must dictate that the defendant must not commit further acts of domestic violence.[249] The DVPO may also include any of the following types of relief:[250]

1. granting a party possession of the residence or household of the parties and excluding the other party from the residence or household;

240. G.S. 50B-2(c)(1).
241. G.S. 50B-2(e).
242. If the older adult seeking the DVPO does not have an attorney, the clerk must schedule the ex parte hearing within seventy-two hours of the filing for relief or by the end of the next day on which the district court is in session, whichever occurs first. G.S. 50B-2(c)(6). If the district court is not in session, the older adult may contact the clerk in any other county in the judicial district, who then must schedule an ex parte hearing by the end of the next day with the district court in that county. *Id.*
243. G.S. 50B-2(c)(1).
244. G.S. 50B-2(c) does not specify a date or time for expiration of an ex parte order issued by a district court judge. For further discussion, see CHERYL D. HOWELL & JAN S. SIMMONS, NORTH CAROLINA TRIAL JUDGES' BENCHBOOK 7-22 (2019 ed.) (hereinafter BENCHBOOK).
245. G.S. 50B-2(c1).
246. *Id.*
247. BENCHBOOK, at 7-11.
248. G.S. 50B-1, -3(a).
249. G.S. 50B-3(a).
250. For a complete list, refer to G.S. 50B-3(a).

2. requiring a party to provide a spouse and his or her children suitable alternate housing;
3. ordering the eviction of a party from the residence or household and providing assistance to the victim in returning to it;
4. ordering either party to make payments for the support of a spouse as required by law;
5. providing for the possession of personal property of the parties, including the care, custody, and control of any animal owned, possessed, kept, or held as a pet by either party or any minor child residing in the household;
6. ordering a party to refrain from doing any or all of the following:
   a. threatening, abusing, or following the other party;
   b. harassing the other party, including by telephone, visiting the other party's home or workplace, or by some other means;
   c. cruelly treating or abusing any animal owned, possessed, kept, or held as a pet by either party or any minor child residing in the household;
   d. otherwise interfering with the other party;
7. awarding attorneys' fees to either party;
8. prohibiting a party from purchasing a firearm for a time fixed in the order;
9. ordering any party the court finds is responsible for acts of domestic violence to attend and complete an abuser treatment program if the program is approved by the Domestic Violence Commission; or
10. including in the order any additional prohibitions or requirements the court finds necessary to protect any party or any minor child.

Under certain circumstances, the court must order the defendant to surrender to the sheriff all firearms, ammunition, and permits that are in the care, custody, possession, ownership, or control of the defendant.[251] At the DVPO hearing, the court must ask the defendant about (1) the presence of, the defendant's ownership of, or the defendant's access to firearms, ammunition, or permits to purchase firearms or to carry concealed firearms and (2) identifying information for those items, such as a description of each item, the total number owned, and the location of each.[252] If the court orders the defendant to surrender firearms, ammunition, and permits, it must inform the plaintiff and the defendant of the terms of the DVPO and include these terms on the face of the order, including that the defendant is prohibited from possessing, purchasing, or receiving a firearm (or attempting to do any of these things) for so long as the protective order or any successive protective order is in effect.[253]

251. G.S. 50B-3.1. The court must order the defendant to surrender firearms, ammunition, and permits if it finds any of the following: (1) the use or threatened use of a deadly weapon by the defendant or a pattern of prior conduct involving the use or threatened use of violence with a firearm against any person(s), (2) threats made by the defendant to seriously injure or kill the aggrieved party or a minor child, (3) threats by the defendant to commit suicide, or (4) serious injuries inflicted upon the aggrieved party or a minor child by the defendant. G.S. 50B-3.1(a).

252. G.S. 50B-3.1(c).

253. G.S. 50B-3.1(d)(1).

The protective order may not exceed one year.[254] Before expiration of the current order, the court may renew a DVPO for good cause for a fixed period not to exceed two years, including an order that has previously been renewed.[255]

Table 6.4. **AOC G.S. Chapter 50B Domestic Violence Forms[256]**

FORM	NAME
CV-303	Complaint and Motion for Domestic Violence Protective Order; Instructions for Domestic Violence Forms
CV-304	Ex Parte Domestic Violence Order of Protection
CV-305	Notice of Hearing on Domestic Violence Protective Order
CV-306	Domestic Violence Order of Protection
CV-307	Motion for Order to Show Cause Domestic Violence Protective Order
CV-308	Order to Appear and Show Cause for Failure to Comply with Domestic Violence Protective Order
CV-309	Contempt Order Domestic Violence Protective Order
CV-311	Notice of Ex Parte Hearing before District Court Judge
CV-312	Identifying Information about Defendant Domestic Violence Action
CV-313	Motion to Renew/Modify/Set Aside Domestic Violence Protective Order Notice of Hearing
CV-314	Order Renewing Domestic Violence Protective Order; Order Setting Aside Domestic Violence Protective Order
CV-315	Request and Affidavit to Register and Registration of Out-of-State Domestic Violence Protective Order
CV-316	Order Continuing Domestic Violence Hearing and Ex Parte Order
CV-317	Civil Summons Domestic Violence
CV-319	Motion for Return of Weapons Surrendered under Domestic Violence Protective Order and Notice of Hearing
CV-320	Order Upon Motion to Return Weapons Surrendered under Domestic Violence Protective Order
CV-321	Motion and Notice of Hearing for Disposal of Weapons Surrendered under Domestic Violence Protective Order
CV-322	Order Upon Motion for Disposal of Weapons Surrendered under Domestic Violence Protective Order
CV-323	Victim Information Sheet
CV-326	Modified Domestic Violence Order of Protection

254. G.S. 50B-3(b).
255. *Id.*
256. *See* note 98, *supra*.

iv. Enforcement of a DVPO

A valid protective order, including a DVPO and an ex parte DVPO, must be enforced by all North Carolina law enforcement agencies without further order of the court.[257] Violation of a DVPO is a crime and may be reported to law enforcement. The defendant may be prosecuted for the crime of violating a protective order.[258] In the alternative, the protective order may be enforced through a motion filed with the court for contempt.[259] A form "Motion for Order to Show Cause DVPO" (CV-307) is available from the N.C. Administrative Office of the Courts (AOC). An older adult may use this form to initiate a contempt proceeding.

b. G.S. Chapter 50C Civil No-Contact Order

When an older adult who is subject to domestic violence does not have the type of personal relationship with the perpetrator that is defined in G.S. Chapter 50B, the older adult may be able to obtain a Chapter 50C civil no-contact order against a perpetrator. Chapter 50C allows the court to enter a civil no-contact order when an older adult proves that he or she is a victim of "unlawful conduct."[260] Unlawful conduct in this context means an act by a person who is 16 years or older of

- nonconsensual sexual conduct or
- stalking.[261]

PRACTICE NOTE

1. The statutory definition of "stalking" does not require the victim to give prior notice to the perpetrator to stop the behavior before the action may be legally considered stalking.
2. The definition of stalking in G.S. Chapter 50C does not exactly mirror the criminal definition of stalking in G.S. 14-277.3A.

To obtain a 50C order, the act of unlawful conduct must occur in North Carolina.[262]

257. G.S. 50B-4(c).
258. G.S. 50B-4.1(b).
259. G.S. 50B-4(a).
260. G.S. 50C-2(a).
261. G.S. 50C-1(7). "Sexual conduct" is defined as "[a]ny intentional or knowing touching, fondling, or sexual penetration by a person, either directly or through clothing, of the sexual organs, anus, or breast of another, whether an adult or a minor, for the purpose of sexual gratification or arousal." G.S. 50C-1(4). "Stalking" is defined as, "[o]n more than one occasion, following or otherwise harassing, as defined in G.S. 14-277.3A(b)(2), another person without legal purpose with the intent to do any of the following: (a) [p]lace the person in reasonable fear either for the person's safety or the safety of the person's immediate family or close personal associates[, or] (b) [c]ause that person to suffer substantial emotional distress by placing that person in fear of death, bodily injury, or continued harassment and that in fact causes that person substantial emotional distress." *Id.* § 50C-1(6). More than one incident of following or harassing is needed to constitute stalking. *Id.*
262. G.S. 50C-2(a).

i. Filing for a No-Contact Order

An older adult who is the victim of unlawful conduct may seek a 50C order by filing a verified complaint in district court or by a filing a motion in any existing civil action.[263] A competent adult who resides in North Carolina may file a complaint or motion for a 50C order on behalf of an incompetent adult.[264] A form "Complaint for No-Contact Order for Stalking or Nonconsensual Sexual Conduct" (Form AOC-CV-520) is available from the AOC.[265]

Once the 50C complaint is filed, the court will issue a summons, and the summons, the complaint, a notice of hearing, and any temporary civil no-contact order must then be served personally on the respondent/perpetrator by the sheriff.[266] If the respondent fails to answer the complaint or fails to appear after having been served, the court may enter a 50C order by default.[267]

ii. Entry of a No-Contact Order

If the court finds that an older adult who has filed a 50C complaint has suffered unlawful conduct committed by the respondent named in the complaint, the court may issue a permanent or temporary no-contact order.[268] Physical injury to the victim is not required to enter either order.[269] A temporary order may not exceed ten days' duration; it may be extended during the time the original temporary order is in effect, upon good cause, for ten days or for a longer period if the respondent consents.[270]

The court may issue an ex parte temporary order, meaning without notice to the respondent, in limited instances.[271] If an ex parte temporary order is entered, the hearing for the permanent order must be set for hearing within ten days from the date of the motion for the permanent order.[272]

If the court enters a no-contact order, whether temporary or permanent, it may also enter any or all of the following forms of relief:[273]

1. ordering the respondent not to visit, assault, molest, or otherwise interfere with the victim;
2. ordering the respondent to cease stalking the victim, including at the victim's workplace;

---

263. G.S. 50C-2(a)(1).
264. G.S. 50C-2(a)(2).
265. *See* note 98, *supra*.
266. G.S. 50C-3(a), (b). If the respondent cannot with due diligence be served by the sheriff by personal delivery, the respondent may be served by publication by the complainant in accordance with Rule 4(j1) of the Rules of Civil Procedure. *Id.*
267. G.S. 50C-3(c).
268. G.S. 50C-5(a).
269. *Id.*
270. G.S. 50C-8(a).
271. G.S. 50C-6(a). To enter an ex parte temporary no-contact order, the court must find (1) that it clearly appears that immediate injury, loss, or damage will result to the victim before the respondent can be heard in opposition and (2) either, (a) that the older adult certifies to the court in writing the efforts, if any, that have been made to give the notice and the reasons supporting the claim that notice should not be required or (b) that the older adult certified to the court that there is good cause to grant the remedy because the harm that the remedy is intended to prevent would likely occur if the respondent were given any prior notice of the complainant's efforts to obtain judicial relief. *Id.*
272. G.S. 50C-6(b)(4); 50C-8(a).
273. G.S. 50C-5(b).

3. ordering the respondent to cease harassment of the victim;
4. ordering the respondent not to abuse or injure the victim;
5. ordering the respondent not to contact the victim by telephone, written communication, or electronic means;
6. ordering the respondent to refrain from entering or remaining present at the victim's residence, school, place of employment, or other specified places at times when the victim is present; or
7. ordering other relief deemed necessary and appropriate by the court, including assessing attorneys' fees to either party.

iii. Enforcement of a No-Contact Order

A violation of a civil no-contact order is punishable as contempt of court, which may lead to a fine or imprisonment.[274] A form "Motion for Order to Show Cause" (CV-528) is available from the AOC. An older adult may use this form to initiate a contempt proceeding.[275]

Table 6.5. **AOC G.S. Chapter 50C Civil No-Contact Forms**[276]

FORM	NAME
CV-520	Complaint for No-Contact Order for Stalking or Nonconsensual Sexual Conduct
CV-522	Notice of Hearing on No-Contact Order for Stalking or Nonconsensual Sexual Conduct
CV-523	Temporary No-Contact Order for Stalking or Nonconsensual Sexual Conduct
CV-524	No-Contact Order for Stalking or Nonconsensual Sexual Conduct
CV-525	Motion to Renew/Set Aside No-Contact Order for Stalking or Nonconsensual Sexual Conduct
CV-526	Order Renewing No-Contact Order for Stalking or Nonconsensual Sexual Conduct
CV-527	Order Continuing No-Contact Hearing and Temporary Order
CV-528	Motion and Order to Show Cause for Failure to Comply with No-Contact Order for Stalking or Nonconsensual Sexual Conduct
CV-529	Contempt Order No-Contact Order for Stalking or Nonconsensual Sexual Conduct

274. G.S. 50C-10; *see also id.* § 50C-5(c).
275. *See* note 98, *supra.*
276. *See* note 98, *supra.*

3. HOUSING[277]

a. The Older Adult Is the Homeowner

The overwhelming majority of older adults are homeowners. A recent study showed that the homeownership rate for individuals in their early 70s was 81 percent.[278] This was higher than the national rate of 64 percent for all ages.[279] It is expected that homeowner households headed by a person age 80 or older will more than double—from 6 to 12 million—by 2035.[280]

It is a fairly common scenario, in cases involving elder abuse, for an older adult to have agreed to allow another person to live in the adult's home, only to later regret that decision. These situations are sometimes complicated. The older adult may be afraid or unwilling to change the status quo because he or she relies on the person living with him or her for food, companionship, or other assistance. The older adult (and those who support him or her) may face the difficult choice of whether to pursue judicial action to remove the person from the home or to continue living in an abusive situation because of fear, reliance, or a desire not to upset the person living with the older adult.

If the older adult decides that legal action is necessary to remove an unwanted occupant, the next step is to identify the correct legal procedure. In almost all cases, the occupant will be either a guest or a live-in paid companion or caregiver. In either situation, the available procedures include (1) seeking criminal charges for unlawful trespass and/or (2) filing a civil lawsuit for trespass in which the relief sought is a court order directing the occupant to leave. Both of these procedures will be discussed below.

Rarely, the unwanted occupant is a tenant, rather than a guest or current or former employee. When the occupant is a tenant, the procedure for removal is entirely different: the older adult, or someone legally authorized to act on the older adult's behalf,[281] must file a summary ejectment action, typically in small claims court.[282] Summary ejectment is an action by a landlord asking the court to terminate the lease of a tenant in breach and award possession of the premises to the landlord.[283] This lawsuit is available only when parties are involved in a landlord-tenant relationship. A summary ejectment action filed by a homeowner against an occupant other than a tenant, such as a guest or employee, will be dismissed,[284] with the homeowner losing time and court costs with no corresponding benefit. On the other hand, a residential tenant who refuses to vacate rental premises when legally obligated to do so may be evicted only by summary ejectment.[285] Landlords who change the locks or otherwise try to oust a tenant without going to court violate

277. This subsection was written by UNC School of Government faculty member Dona Lewandowski.

278. Joint Ctr. for Hous. Studies of Harvard Univ., Projections & Implications for Housing a Growing Population: Older Households 2015–2035, 7 (2016), https://www.jchs.harvard.edu/sites/default/files/harvard_jchs_housing_growing_population_2016_1_0.pdf

279. *Id.*

280. *Id.*

281. See Section II.B.1, *supra*, for a discussion of who is authorized to bring an action on behalf of an older adult.

282. G.S. 7A-210(2).

283. G.S. 42-26(a).

284. Marantz Piano Co., Inc. v. Kincaid, 108 N.C. App. 693 (1993).

285. G.S. 42-25.6.

the law and may themselves be civilly liable as a result.[286] Consequently, even though unwanted occupants are more often guests or employees than tenants, the first step in the process of forcing them to leave is to evaluate whether the law classifies them as tenants.

i. Is the Occupant a Tenant?

When a person entitled to possession of property agrees to transfer possession to another person temporarily in exchange for compensation such as money or services, a lease agreement is created between a landlord and a tenant.[287] Most of the time, the answer to whether the parties are involved in a lease is quite clear, but there are a few situations that sometimes cause confusion.[288]

One common misconception is that summary ejectment is required if the unwanted occupant is a legal resident. In fact, there is no legal relationship between tenancy and residency.[289] A person may receive mail at the residence, be registered to vote based on the address of the premises, obtain a library card on that basis, or even have children enrolled in school in that district—none of these facts are related to whether the occupant is a tenant.[290]

A second misconception is that a landlord-tenant relationship is created automatically if the occupant helped pay household expenses or provided services such as routine household maintenance. Such contributions may indeed be suggestive of a landlord-tenant relationship, but they occur in other contexts as well.[291] An appreciative guest, grateful for the generosity of a host, will often return that generosity, with neither party having any intention of establishing a contractually binding landlord-tenant relationship. People involved in romantic relationships or an older adult and an adult child sometimes decide to live together in a home owned by one of them with no notion of creating a landlord-tenant relationship, even if they agree to share expenses. The agreement between the parties in these cases lacks two requirements for a valid lease: first, the parties' agreement is usually indefinite, rather than for a specific period of time or an agreed-upon notice period for termination.[292] Second, the agreement between the parties is not to accomplish transfer

---

286. G.S. 42-25.9.

287. Carolina Helicopter Corp. v. Cutter Realty Co., 263 N.C. 139, 143–44 (1964).

288. When the parties have entered into a written lease agreement, the relationship is clear. Confusion arises, when it does, because the parties have entered into an oral agreement or, quite often, never had a frank, clear discussion about their expectations related to the person's occupancy. For more information on interpreting leases, see Dona Lewandowski, *A Lease Is a Contract*, ON THE CIVIL SIDE: A UNC SCH. OF GOV'T BLOG (Aug. 23, 2017), https://civil.sog.unc.edu/a-lease-is-a-contract/.

289. *See, e.g.*, Jones v. Swain, 89 N.C. App. 663 (1988) (although woman and son resided in plaintiff's home for a year, there was no landlord-tenant relationship where she had never been required to pay rent and there was no evidence of any contract or lease, actual or implied, between the parties).

290. *See id.*

291. *See* Jackson v. United States, 357 A.2d 409 (D.C. 1976) (boyfriend's evidence that he contributed furniture and food to his girlfriend's apartment not sufficient to establish a tenancy where he admitted he paid no rent and that there was no agreement to share the expenses of the apartment). *See also* Young v. District of Columbia, 752 A.2d 138 (D.C. 2000) (eviction upheld of man who argued that he was a subtenant because he occasionally paid some expenses despite not paying rent and having no agreement beyond a temporary stint as a guest).

292. For information on types of leases, see JOAN G. BRANNON, NORTH CAROLINA SMALL CLAIMS LAW 155–57 (2009).

of a property interest to the occupant for the occupant's exclusive possession and enjoyment but, to the contrary, is aimed at sharing the home.[293] In situations such as these, the occupant's right to occupy the premises is based on the homeowner's permission and ends when that permission is withdrawn.[294]

A third—and especially challenging—fact situation arises when the occupant is a live-in employee. A misconception in this situation is that an employee's right to live on the premises ends when the employment ends. In fact, the answer depends on whether the employee is also a tenant.[295] North Carolina appellate courts have established a test for categorizing the occupant in situations such as these. If residing on the premises is (1) reasonably necessary for the effective performance of the employee's job, (2) inseparable from the job, or (3) required by the employer, occupancy is assumed to be incidental to employment.[296] On the other hand, if the employee could perform the responsibilities of the job just as well while residing off premises, a landlord-tenant relationship is assumed, and summary ejectment is the required method of forcing the employee to leave.[297]

ii. The Occupant Is Not a Tenant

When an occupant who is not a tenant refuses to leave an older person's home after being asked to do so, there are two legal actions for removing the occupant from the adult's home: (1) seeking criminal charges for criminal trespass and (2) filing a civil action for civil trespass.

To pursue **criminal trespass**, an older adult would have to make a report to law enforcement or, in the alternative, visit the local magistrate's office in the county where the property is located to request that criminal charges be filed.

> **PRACTICE NOTE**
>
> Law enforcement officers sometimes believe that criminal charges are not appropriate under the circumstances and advise the homeowner to seek summary ejectment instead. An older adult who believes that the evidence does not support a landlord-tenant relationship and that, therefore, summary ejectment is not appropriate, might consider going directly to a magistrate to ask for a determination of whether probable cause exists to charge the occupant with trespass.

If the older adult visits the magistrate's office, the older adult should bring any written or other evidence related to the agreement between the parties. The magistrate will consider any such evidence in addition to the sworn testimony of the older adult in deciding whether criminal charges are appropriate. If the magistrate does find probable cause, the magistrate will issue either a warrant for the occupant's arrest or a summons requiring

293. *See, e.g., Young*, 752 A.2d at 143 (evicted man had been invited to live in apartment temporarily as a guest).
294. *See id. See also Jackson*, 357 A.2d at 411–12.
295. Simons v. Lebrun, 219 N.C. 42 (1941).
296. *Id.*
297. *Id.*

the occupant to appear at trial on the offense charged. The older adult's testimony at trial is likely to be required as evidence supporting a conviction of the criminal charge.

Whether a report is made to law enforcement or the action is initiated by visiting the magistrate, the failure of a person to leave the premises of another when told to do so may lead to a conviction for first-degree trespass under G.S. 14-159.12, which prohibits a person from entering or remaining in a building belonging to another without authorization.[298] Even when the person initially enters the property with the owner's consent, that person becomes a trespasser if the owner withdraws consent and tells the person to leave.[299]

To pursue a claim for **civil trespass** against an unwanted occupant, an older adult or someone legally authorized to act on the older adult's behalf[300] would file a civil complaint in district or superior court for civil trespass, asking the court to order the defendant to vacate the premises.[301] In addition to the order requiring the defendant to leave, the older adult is entitled to recover money damages resulting from the defendant's actions.[302] This lawsuit is not eligible for small claims court.

The elements of a claim for civil trespass to real property are

1. possession of the property by the older adult when the alleged trespass was committed,
2. an unauthorized entry that interferes with the older adult's ownership or possession of that property, and
3. damage to the older adult from the trespass.[303]

Similar to criminal trespass, just because an older adult consented to a person's initial entry onto the older adult's premises does not automatically defeat a claim for civil trespass.[304] If the person later commits wrongful acts that abuse or are in excess of his or her authority to enter the premises, the person may be held liable for civil trespass if the other elements set out immediately above are met.[305] Furthermore, actual damages do not have to be proven; any unauthorized entry entitles the property owner to, at minimum, nominal damages.[306]

iii. The Occupant Is a Tenant

When an unwanted occupant is a tenant, the tenant's right to continue living in the older adult's home is governed by the lease agreement. If the tenant violates the lease in a way that justifies eviction according to the lease, or if the tenant breaches in certain other ways, such as by failing to pay rent or engaging in criminal activity, summary ejectment is

298. G.S. 14-159.12. For further information, refer to Chapter 18 of *North Carolina Crimes: A Guidebook on the Elements of Crime* by Jessica Smith (7th ed., UNC School of Government, 2012).

299. Miller v. Brooks, 123 N.C. App. 20, 27–28 (1996) (citing Blackwood v. Cates, 297 N.C. 163, 167 (1979)).

300. *See* Section II.B.1, *supra*, for the process for seeking civil relief by someone acting on the older adult's behalf.

301. *See* Singleton v. Haywood Elec. Membership Corp., 357 N.C. 623 (2003).

302. Matthews v. Forrest, 235 N.C. 281, 283 (1952).

303. Keyzer v. Amerlink, Ltd., 173 N.C. App. 284, 289 (2005), *aff'd*, 360 N.C. 397 (2006). *See also* Batts v. Batts, 219 N.C. App. 650 (2012) (unpublished) (affirming a trial court's order entering a judgment finding that the defendant was a trespasser against the plaintiff's land).

304. *Keyzer*, 173 N.C. App. at 290.

305. *Id.*

306. Taha v. Thompson, 120 N.C. App. 697, 704 (1995).

the appropriate remedy.[307] This lawsuit may be filed in small claims court by filing a complaint.[308] A form "Complaint in Summary Ejectment" (Form AOC-CVM-201) is available from the N.C. Administrative Office of the Courts (AOC) in summary ejectment actions.[309] In cases involving residential leases, landlords may not use self-help remedies (e.g., forcibly removing a tenant, padlocking the premises, or rendering the premises uninhabitable by cutting off electricity or water).[310]

b. The Older Adult Is the Tenant

The previous section of this chapter focuses on situations when an older adult is a homeowner. In other cases, the older adult may be a tenant. One study estimates that by 2035, the number of households headed by renters age 65 and older will increase by 80 percent, up to 11.5 million.[311] Tenants have rights and protections under both federal and North Carolina law.

i. Federal Law: The Federal Fair Housing Act[312]

The federal Fair Housing Act does not provide protections based on age.[313] It does, however, prohibit discrimination based on physical or mental disability.[314] As applied to older adults, this means that a landlord may not[315]

1. refuse to rent a dwelling to an older adult with a disability;
2. require different lease terms because of an older adult's disability;
3. refuse to permit reasonable modification to the premises, such as the installation of a wheelchair ramp or grip rails in a bathroom, if the modification is necessary to allow a disabled older adult's full use of the dwelling; or
4. refuse to make reasonable exceptions to rules, policies, practices, or services when doing so may be necessary to afford an older adult with a disability equal opportunity to occupy and enjoy the full use of the dwelling.

ii. North Carolina Law

(a) The N.C. Residential Rental Agreement Act (RRAA)[316]

North Carolina law requires a landlord to provide residential tenants with fit and habitable premises.[317] This obligation is not subject to waiver or modification by the

307. G.S. 42-26(a); G.S. Chapter 42, Article 7 ("Expedited Eviction of Drug Trafficking and Other Criminals").
308. G.S. 7A-210(2); -213.
309. *See* note 98, *supra*.
310. Dona Lewandowski, *A Judgment for Possession Is Only Step 1 in Summary Ejectment Cases*, ON THE CIVIL SIDE: A UNC SCH. OF GOV'T BLOG (May 31, 2018), https://civil.sog.unc.edu/a-judgment-for-possession-is-only-step-1-in-summary-ejectment-cases/; G.S. 42-25.6 (stating that a residential tenant may only be evicted by the procedures set forth in Article 3 or 7 of G.S. Chapter 42).
311. Joint Ctr. For Hous. Studies of Harvard Univ., *supra* note 278, at 34.
312. 42 U.S.C. Ch. 45. See also G.S. Chapter 41A, the North Carolina Fair Housing Act, which provides similar protections.
313. 42 U.S.C. § 3604.
314. *Id.* The FHA uses the term "handicap." "Handicap" means a physical or mental impairment that substantially limits one or more major life activities of a person. 42 U.S.C. § 3602(h). This includes a person with a record of an impairment or a person who is regarded as having an impairment. *Id.* This manual uses the term "disability" to replace the term "handicap" to align with common practice.
315. 42 U.S.C. § 3604(f).
316. G.S. Ch. 42, Art. 5.
317. G.S. 42-42(a)(2).

tenant's agreement and is not affected by a landlord's agreement to lower the rent to reflect the fair rental value of the premises in their noncompliant condition.[318] Furthermore, under the RRAA, the landlord[319] must

1. comply with current applicable building and housing codes;
2. make all repairs and do whatever is necessary to put and keep the premises in a fit and habitable condition;
3. keep all common areas of the premises in safe condition;
4. maintain in good and safe working order and promptly repair all electrical, plumbing, sanitary, heating, ventilating, air conditioning, and other facilities and appliances supplied or required to be supplied by the landlord, provided that notification of needed repairs is made to the landlord in writing by the tenant, except in emergency situations; and
5. comply with the other requirements set forth in G.S. 42-42(a)(5) through (8).

(b) Other Tenant Consumer Protections under N.C. Law[320]

North Carolina law provides tenants with other protections as well. G.S. 42-46 regulates late fees in residential rental agreements. A landlord's obligations regarding security deposits is governed by G.S. Chapter 42, Article 6.

Several statutes regulate eviction of residential tenants. Landlords are prohibited from changing the locks, cutting off utilities, or otherwise rendering the premises uninhabitable to force tenants to leave.[321] Instead, a landlord must file a summary ejectment lawsuit. Landlords are not allowed to retain possession of tenants' personal property in an attempt to coerce payment of overdue rent,[322] and they must follow legal procedures before disposing of property belonging to evicted tenants.[323] Residential tenants may not be evicted in retaliation for making a good faith complaint or request for repairs, or because of other grounds set forth in G.S. Chapter 42, Article 4A ("Retaliatory Eviction," sections 42-37.1 through -37.3). If the older adult is a tenant of publicly assisted housing, including public housing and Section 8 housing, the older adult is entitled to additional protections and may only be evicted for good cause.[324] Finally, G.S. 42-46 restricts fees a landlord may assess connected with eviction.

318. G.S. 42-42(b). *See also* Mendenhall-Moore Realtors v. Sedoris, 89 N.C. App. 486 (1988).

319. "Landlord" is defined in G.S. 42-40(3) as any owner and any rental management company, rental agency, or any other person having the actual or apparent authority of an agent to perform the duties imposed by Article 5 of G.S. Chapter 42.

320. Dona G. Lewandowski, *A Lease Is a Contract, But . . .*, ON THE CIVIL SIDE: A UNC SCH. OF GOV'T BLOG (Oct. 11, 2017), https://civil.sog.unc.edu/a-lease-is-a-contract-but/.

321. G.S. 42-25.6. *See also* Dona G. Lewandowski, *Don't Try This at Home: Self-Help Evictions*, ON THE CIVIL SIDE: A UNC SCH. OF GOV'T BLOG (Apr. 25, 2018), https://civil.sog.unc.edu/dont-try-this-at-home-self-help-evictions/.

322. G.S. 42-25.7.

323. G.S. 42-36.2; 42-25.9.

324. *See* BRANNON & ANDERSON, *supra* note 89, at 184–86.

III. CHALLENGES TO PURSUING PRIVATE CIVIL REMEDIES

A. COST OF CIVIL LITIGATION

Litigation can be expensive. While an older adult may file a civil action without an attorney, matters are often complicated and challenging without an attorney's assistance. Filing fees start with the cost of filing a civil complaint—$96 for certain proceedings before a magistrate, $150 for certain ones before the district court, and around $200 in superior court—and add up from there. The cost of litigation may—and often does—prevent older adults from seeking civil legal remedies.

RESOURCES FOR OLDER ADULTS WHO WISH TO PURSUE CIVIL REMEDIES.

1. Seek advice from and/or representation by an attorney.

An older adult (or someone legally acting on his or her behalf) who is thinking about filing a civil suit may choose to seek legal advice from an attorney. The North Carolina Bar Association has a lawyer referral system that will help older adults find local attorneys with whom they can consult. Contact information is provided below.

N.C. Bar Association Lawyer Referral Service (LRS)

Website: http://www.ncfindalawyer.org/

LRS by phone:

1-800-662-7660 (toll-free) or 919-677-8574

*Note that there is a charge for an initial consultation.

If an older adult cannot afford an attorney, he or she may be eligible for legal services through a local office of Legal Aid, an organization that assists people free of charge with various legal problems, provided they meet certain eligibility guidelines based on household income and type of legal issue involved. Legal Aid maintains a Senior Law Project, which focuses specifically on assisting people age 60 and older.[325] Contact information is provided below.

325. Legal Aid of North Carolina, *Senior Law Project*, LEGALAIDNC.ORG, http://www.legalaidnc.org/about-us/projects/senior-law-project (last visited Aug. 6, 2019).

Legal Aid of North Carolina—Senior Law Project

Website: http://www.legalaidnc.org/about-us/projects/senior-law-project

Legal Aid of North Carolina—Senior Legal Helpline:

Toll-free: 1-877-579-7562

Hours: Monday–Friday, 9–11 a.m. and 1–3 p.m.

Several law schools in North Carolina operate elder law clinics that accept cases involving older adults and allow law students to obtain practical experience under the supervision of a licensed attorney. Two of these clinics, along with contact information, are listed below.

Wake Forest University Elder Law Clinic

Services are available to any person age 60 or older with a monthly household income of less than $2,200 for a household of one or $2,900 for a household of two.

This clinic serves Forsyth County and surrounding counties.

Website: http://elder-clinic.law.wfu.edu/

Phone: 336-758-5061

Senior Law Clinic, Campbell University

Services are available to any person age 60 and above with a monthly household income below $1,897 if single and $2,572 if married.

This clinic serves the greater Raleigh area.

Website: https://law.campbell.edu/advocate/clinical-programs/the-senior-law-clinic/

Phone: 919-865-4693

2. Use the free court forms provided by the state court system.

A number of forms are available online at no charge from the N.C. Administrative Office of the Courts (AOC) at https://www.nccourts.gov/documents/local-rules-and-forms. Using AOC forms is not a legal requirement, but it may help ensure compliance with law and established standards of practice. Using these forms also may help reduce the cost of litigation for an older adult, as the court is often familiar with AOC forms and may be able to process them more efficiently than litigant-drafted documents. Applicable civil forms are referenced throughout this chapter.

If an older adult (or any other person) is seeking a DVPO but cannot afford to hire an attorney, the clerk of superior court of each county in North Carolina must provide the adult with all of the forms that are necessary or appropriate to enable the adult to proceed without counsel.[326] The clerk must also, whenever feasible, provide a private area for DVPO complainants to fill out forms and make inquiries.[327] No court costs or attorneys' fees are assessed in connection with filing for a DVPO.[328]

3. Petition to sue as indigent.

While a person seeking a DVPO will not be assessed court costs or attorneys' fees, as mentioned above, for other civil matters a judge or clerk may authorize the person filing the claim to sue as indigent in the appropriate court.[329] To sue as indigent, a person must file an affidavit with the court stating that he or she is unable to advance court costs.[330] Typically, a person filing an action who is seeking an indigency classification will use the AOC's Form "Petition to Proceed as an Indigent" (G-106).[331] The clerk of superior court must authorize a person to sue as indigent if the person makes the required affidavit and

- receives electronic food and nutrition benefits, such as those offered through the Supplemental Nutrition Assistance Program (SNAP/food stamps);
- receives Work First Family Assistance, such as Temporary Assistance for Needy Families (TANF);
- receives Supplemental Security Income (SSI); or
- is represented by a legal services organization, such as Legal Aid of North Carolina, that has as its primary purpose the furnishing of legal services to indigent persons or by private counsel working on behalf of such an organization.

For all other persons, it is up to the discretion of the judge or the clerk whether to authorize a person to sue as an indigent based on the information presented in the affidavit.[332]

4. Seek recovery of attorneys' fees.

The default rule in North Carolina is that each party to a civil action is responsible for his or her own attorneys' fees. But there are exceptions to this rule. For example, where specifically authorized by statute, a court may award reasonable attorneys' fees to one party as costs taxed against the other party. This exception permitting the recovery of attorneys' fees applies to some of the civil actions referenced in this chapter, including

- actions for the recovery of personal property (*see* Section II.C.1.b.i.(b), *supra*),
- claims for unfair and deceptive trade practices (*see* Section II.C.1.b.ii.(e), *supra*), and
- claims for rescission of a deed (*see* Section II.C.1.b.iii, *supra*).

326. G.S. 50B-2(d).
327. *Id.*
328. G.S. 50B-2(a). There is an exception to this rule for costs and attorneys' fees pursuant to G.S. 1A-1, Rule 11.
329. G.S. 1-110(a).
330. *Id.*
331. This form is available at https://www.nccourts.gov/documents/forms/petition-to-proceed-as-an-indigent.
332. G.S. 1-110(a). For further discussion of determining indigency, refer to John Rubin, Phil Dixon Jr., and Allison Grine, *North Carolina Defender Manual* vol. 1 (2d edition 2013), at Section D, pages 12-26 to 12-27.

B. PERPETRATOR HAS NO MONEY OR OTHER PROPERTY TO SATISFY A JUDGMENT

By the time elder abuse is discovered, a perpetrator may have already spent (or hidden) the money or other property taken from the older adult. An often-heard refrain is that it is not worth the time and effort to file a civil action to go after the perpetrator because he or she "doesn't have anything anyway."

ADVICE FOR OLDER ADULT VICTIMS IN CASES WHERE RECOVERY AGAINST A PERPETRATOR MAY NOT BE POSSIBLE.

1. Make a report to adult protective services (APS).

Even if a perpetrator has already moved on to another victim and is no longer in the affected older adult's life, the adult may fall prey to abuse again. In response to a report, APS may be able to connect the older adult with community supports and services that will enable the adult, or those acting on his or her behalf, to be free from abuse in the future.

2. Make a report to law enforcement.

Although the older adult may not be able to recover from the perpetrator in a particular case, the perpetrator may move on to other victims. If a report is made to law enforcement, this may lead to a decision by law enforcement to investigate the perpetrator and take appropriate action against him or her—including criminal prosecution—to stop the perpetrator from committing more acts of elder abuse. Furthermore, if the perpetrator is found guilty in criminal court, he or she may be ordered to pay restitution to the older adult. "[C]ivil settlement agreements and restitution awards are separate and distinct remedies."[333] A civil settlement does not bar criminal restitution, and vice versa.[334] The civil settlement is intended to compensate the victim for a civil wrong, while criminal restitution serves the additional "rehabilitative, deterrent, and retributive goals of the criminal justice system" by "forc[ing] the defendant to confront, in concrete terms, the harm his actions have caused."[335] Criminal restitution in excess of $250 must be docketed as a civil judgment for offenses covered under the N.C. Crime Victims' Rights Act (G.S. 15A-830).[336]

---

333. State v. Williams, No. COA18-994, 2019 WL 2344858, at *3 (N.C. Ct. App. June 4, 2019).

334. G.S. 15A-1340.37(a); *Williams*, 2019 WL 2344858, at *3.

335. *Williams*, 2019 WL 2344858, at *3 (quoting Kirby v. Florida, 863 So. 2d 238 (Fla. 2003)). For further discussion, refer to Jamie Markham, *Civil Settlements and Criminal Restitution*, N.C. CRIM. L.: A UNC SCH. OF GOV'T BLOG (June 6, 2019), https://nccriminallaw.sog.unc.edu/civil-settlements-and-criminal-restitution/.

336. For further discussion of docketing a criminal monetary obligation as a civil judgment, refer to Jamie Markham, *I'm Just a Civil Judgment*, N.C. CRIM. L.: A UNC SCH. OF GOV'T BLOG (Oct. 19, 2017), https://nccriminallaw.sog.unc.edu/im-just-civil-judgment/.

3. Consider the nature of a civil money judgment.

Given the nature of civil money judgments, it may still be helpful for an older adult to obtain a judgment even if the perpetrator does not currently have assets.

- **A judgment draws interest.** Money judgments draw interest at the legal rate on the principal.[337]
- **A judgment is good for ten years (longer if extended).** An older adult may win a case against a perpetrator/defendant and obtain a money judgment. Once the judgment is entered, the older adult has ten years to try to collect on it. If the defendant does not have sufficient property to satisfy the judgment when it is entered, the judgment does not go away. Instead, it is docketed for any amount unpaid. If the defendant later comes into property, the judgment may attach to the property and the older adult, or someone acting on his or her behalf, including the older adult's estate after the older adult's death, could execute on the judgment at that time. Furthermore, the judgment may be extended for an additional ten years. The legal mechanism for obtaining an extension is for the older adult to bring a second lawsuit for the amount remaining due on the original judgment.[338]
- **A judgment attaches generally to real and personal property owned by the defendant.** A monetary judgment attaches to more than the specific property taken by the defendant from the older adult. It may attach to other real and personal property. Note, however, that a judgment debtor may claim certain property he or she owns as exempt (or free) from the enforcement of a monetary judgment or a judgment for possession of household goods.[339]

C. UNABLE TO LOCATE THE PERPETRATOR

Financial scams against older adults may be committed by perpetrators located outside the United States or across state lines.[340] The perpetrator may travel door to door offering bogus or unnecessary services, such as home repairs, to older adults. As soon as the perpetrator has drained the older adult's accounts, or if there is a hint of skepticism from a neighbor or friend of the older adult, the perpetrator takes off. The task of trying to track down the perpetrator, or the feeling that it would be impossible to locate him or her, may prevent an older adult (or someone legally acting on his or her behalf), from seeking civil remedies.

---

337. G.S. 24-1, -5. The one exception to this rule is for money judgments arising out of a contract that is not for consumer purposes. *Id.* Then it draws interest at the contract rate if the contract specifically provides that the contract rate applies after judgment. *Id.*

338. Dona Lewandowski, *Action to Renew a Judgment—But Not Really*, ON THE CIVIL SIDE: A UNC SCH. OF GOV'T BLOG (Feb. 24, 2017), https://civil.sog.unc.edu/action-to-renew-a-judgment-but-not-really/.

339. CSC MANUAL, at ch. 37, § 37.1; G.S. Chapter 1C.

340. David Kirkman, *Fraud, Vulnerability, and Aging – When Criminals Gang Up on Mom and Dad*, N.C. STATE BAR J., 15 (Winter 2013) (noting that the elder fraud industry is "diverse and global" and includes mobsters from the former Soviet Union; Caribbean criminal gangs; groups from the Middle East, South Asia, and western Africa; and groups in the western United States who target seniors with home-based Internet marketing programs), https://www.ncbar.gov/media/121117/journal-18-4.pdf.

WHAT TO DO WHEN THE PERPETRATOR CANNOT BE LOCATED.

1. **Make a report to federal and state agencies.**

Certain federal and state agencies receive and respond to cases of elder abuse, particularly cases that impact commerce and more than one victim. Many of these agencies and their roles related to elder abuse, including how to make a report, are explained in Chapter 7. Two specific tools are available through the U.S. Department of Justice to assist people with reporting and connecting to resources related to financial abuse and fraud, including scams where the perpetrator cannot be located.

- The **Elder Abuse Resource Roadmap** is designed to help victims of financial abuse identify the proper agencies to contact to report, and to receive assistance in connection with, abuse. It is available at https://www.justice.gov/elderjustice/roadmap.
- The **National Elder Fraud Hotline** is available for people to report fraud against anyone age 60 or older and to connect to a case manager who will provide assistance with the reporting process. The phone number for the hotline is **833-FRAUD-11 (833-372-8311)**. It is open seven days a week, from 6 a.m. to 11 p.m.

2. **Act to protect the adult from repeat offenders.**

It may not be possible for a victim of elder abuse to seek civil remedies if the perpetrator of the abuse cannot be found. Older adults who are victims of elder abuse may (and likely will) be scammed more than once.[341] Once an older adult falls prey to elder abuse, particularly financial fraud and exploitation, it is crucial that the adult (or others acting on his or her behalf) try to protect the adult from further abuse. This may include, for example, adding the older adult's phone number to the National Do Not Call Registry (https://www.donotcall.gov/). A number of other steps are outlined in the guide, Money Smart for Older Adults, available at https://www.consumerfinance.gov/practitioner-resources/resources-for-older-adults/protecting-against-fraud/.

D. RELATIONSHIP TO THE PERPETRATOR

The relationship between an older adult and a perpetrator of abuse on the adult may cause the adult to resist seeking civil remedies such as a monetary judgment, a protection order, or summary ejectment. This may be because the older adult is protective of family members or caretakers who are abusing them. In such situations, the older adult wants some relief but does not want his or her loved one to be the defendant in a court proceeding or "to get them in trouble." The older adult may be lonely and want the continued

341. Kirkman, *supra* note 340, at 15.

attention and contact from a phone scammer. The older adult may be unwilling to recognize that the transaction he or she has engaged in is a scam and that the perpetrator committed abuse against him or her.

TIPS FOR HELPING A VICTIM OF ELDER ABUSE WHO HAS A RELATIONSHIP WITH THE PERPETRATOR OF THE ABUSE.

- **Engage adult protective services and other family and friends to support the older adult's participation in a civil action.** A broader network of support may reduce the older adult's perceived dependence on the abuser.
- **Contact ombudsman.** If the older adult lives in a state-licensed adult care home or other facility, contact the ombudsman who serves as the facility's patient advocate. The role of the ombudsman is discussed in Chapter 7.
- **Connect with community services and supports that will engage the older adult in activities and connect with others in the community.** An area authority on aging serving the older adult's community may be able to assist the adult in getting plugged into community networks. Area authorities are discussed in Chapter 7. The Eldercare Locator is a nationwide service that connects older adults and caregivers to local support resources. It is available at https://eldercare.acl.gov/Public/Index.aspx or **1-800-677-1116**.

E. NATURE OF THE VICTIM AND THE ROLE OF CONSENT

A defense often raised in civil proceedings involving property brought by older adults is that the adult had capacity and consented to the transfer of his or her property, either as a gift or as consideration for caregiving services or for property of the defendant. Either the older adult lacked capacity at the time of the incident or the older adult's capacity declines so significantly between the incident and the trial on the civil claim that the older adult is unable to testify and refute the defense of consent.

TIPS FOR HANDLING CASES WHERE AN OLDER ADULT'S CONSENT IS ASSERTED AS A DEFENSE BY THE PERPETRATOR.

- **Gather evidence to refute capacity to consent.** Evidence that might help show an older adult's inability to consent at the time of a disputed transaction may include medical records and witness testimony.
- **Obtain a professional evaluation of the older adult's cognitive abilities.** An older adult's medical records may not include a recent cognitive assessment. It may be critical to litigation brought by the adult (or brought on the adult's behalf) to have evidence of the adult's lack of capacity at the time of the disputed transaction in order to refute the defense of consent. This lack of capacity could be documented through a geriatric psychiatric or other cognitive evaluation of the older adult.
- **Take the older adult's deposition as soon as possible after the incident at issue.** Depositions are used in civil actions to obtain evidence in preparation for trial.[342] An older adult's condition may decline between the time of the incident at the heart of the abuse claim and the trial. The older adult may be unavailable to testify at the trial as a witness. Live witness testimony is "more desirable" at trial and, generally speaking, witness testimony must be taken orally in open court, unless otherwise provided by law.[343] In "sharply limited" circumstances, some of which are set out in Rule 32 of the N.C. Rules of Civil Procedure, deposition testimony may be used at trial.[344] Under Rule 32, deposition testimony may be used at trial if it meets the following three criteria:
  - it is being used against a party who was present or represented at, or who had reasonable notice of, the deposition;
  - it falls within one of the categories set out in Rule 32(a)(1) through (a)(4), including that the deposition is of a witness who is unavailable because the witness is dead or is unable to testify due to age, illness, infirmity, or imprisonment;[345] and
  - it is admissible under the Rules of Evidence (applied as though the witness were present and testifying).[346]

Depending on the facts of the particular case, Rule 32 may provide an avenue for admitting the older adult's deposition testimony at the civil trial.

342. Ann Anderson, *Use of Deposition Testimony at Trial*, ON THE CIVIL SIDE: A UNC SCH. OF GOV'T BLOG (Nov. 9, 2016), https://civil.sog.unc.edu/use-of-deposition-testimony-at-trial/.

343. Investors Title Ins. Co. v. Herzig, 330 N.C. 681, 690 (1992); G.S. 1A-1, Rule 43. Anderson, *supra* note 342.

344. Warren v. City of Asheville, 74 N.C. App. 402, 408-10 (1985). Anderson, *supra* note 342.

345. If the witness is unavailable due to death, age, illness, infirmity, imprisonment, or some other category in G.S. 1A-1, Rule 32(a)(4), the deposition testimony must also comply with N.C. Rule of Evidence 804(b)(1), which states that the party against whom it is used "had an opportunity and similar motive to develop the testimony by direct, cross, or redirect examination." Pleasant Valley Promenade v. Lechmere, Inc., 120 N.C. App. 650, 659 (1995); *see also Investors Title*, 330 N.C. at 692 (opposing party had been given requisite opportunity). Anderson, *supra* note 342.

346. G.S. 1A-1, Rule 32. Anderson, *supra* note 342.

Chapter 7
Other Critical Components of the Elder Protection System

CONTENTS

I. SCOPE OF CHAPTER

The term "elder protection system" encompasses not only the agencies, individuals, and options identified in the first several chapters of this manual. It extends to many other public and private actors who are essential to preventing abuse; providing protection, care, and services; and enforcing other applicable laws. This chapter provides an overview of several of the components that play a major role in this system. It is not intended to be comprehensive but, rather, representative. There are certainly many other essential partners involved with protecting older adults in North Carolina.

II. OVERVIEW OF OTHER COMPONENTS

A. HEALTH CARE PROVIDERS

Health care providers play an important role in identifying and reporting elder abuse. This includes primary care physicians, hospitals, mental health providers, dentists, pharmacists, chiropractors, nurses, home health providers, physical therapists, and any other person providing medical care. Health care providers may be the first people to interact with an older adult after an incident and, possibly, the only people outside of family who the older adult sees regularly.[1]

A health care provider is mandated to report suspected elder abuse if the provider has reasonable cause to believe that a disabled adult is in need of protective services.[2] This duty to report is described in detail in Chapter 2 of this manual. Despite this mandatory duty, studies show underreporting by health care providers.[3] This lack of reporting may be due to a reluctance to acknowledge abuse, lack of protocols for acknowledging abuse, lack of protocols for identifying abuse, fear of liability, and limited services to respond to abuse.[4] Physicians specifically may be concerned about the impact on patient rapport and trust, patient quality of life, and physician control.[5] Studies suggest that cases go undetected because of a lack of knowledge about elder abuse, the prevalence of elder abuse, signs and symptoms, risk factors, and information on perpetrators.[6]

1. *See* Amy N. Schmeidel et al., *Healthcare Professionals' Perspectives on Barriers to Elder Abuse Detection and Reporting in Primary Care Settings*, 24(1) J. ELDER ABUSE & NEGLECT 17–36 (2012), https://www.ncbi.nlm.nih.gov/pmc/articles/PMC3298114/.
2. Chapter 108A, Section 102, of the North Carolina General Statutes (hereinafter G.S.).
3. Schmeidel et al., *supra* note 1.
4. *Id.*
5. *Id.*
6. *Id.*

B. N.C. DEPARTMENT OF HEALTH AND HUMAN SERVICES

The North Carolina Department of Health and Human Services (DHHS) is a state agency with an expansive mission that encompasses many programs, divisions, and offices that are involved with providing services to and protecting older adults.[7] Of the sixteen service divisions within the agency, five have a significant role in supporting older adults.

Table 7.1. **Overview of Selected DHHS Divisions Involved with Elder Protection**

DHHS DIVISION	ROLE
Aging and Adult Services	Oversees adult protective services (APS) and other aging programs provided by county departments of social services and area agencies on aging; administers the long-term care ombudsman program and the state-county special assistance program
Health Service Regulation	Responsible for regulation and oversight of health care facilities such as hospitals, nursing homes, and adult care homes
Medical Assistance (Medicaid)	Manages administration of health insurance program that is available to many low-income and disabled adults
Mental Health, Substance Abuse, and Developmental Disabilities	Oversees regional managed care program providing publicly funded services, primarily funded through Medicaid
Social Services	Oversees administration of economic services programs relied upon by older adults, such as food and nutrition services (e.g., food stamps, energy assistance)

Other divisions and offices involved with protecting the safety and welfare of older adults include public health, rural health, services for the deaf and hard of hearing, and services for the blind. Rather than provide detailed information about the roles of each of these divisions within DHHS, the discussion below highlights several specific and important functions that may overlap or intersect regularly with other components of the state's elder protection system.

Each area of work comes equipped with different bodies of law, including different tools and processes designed to support compliance with laws and policies. For example, a particular agency may, in the case of elder abuse, be able to impose a fine or other financial penalty, take action on a facility or individual license or permit, or require a regulated

7. The agency's mission statement provides: "In collaboration with our partners, DHHS provides essential services to improve the health, safety and well-being of all North Carolinians." Its vision statement goes further to explain that the agency intends to advance "innovative solutions that foster independence, improve health and promote well-being for all North Carolinians." N.C. Dep't of Health & Human Servs., *Mission Vision*, NCDHHS.GOV, https://www.ncdhhs.gov/about/dhhs-mission-vision-values-and-goals/mission-vision.

entity or person to take corrective action within a specified period. Many types of inspection reports and penalties are public record and may be available upon request.

1. SUPERVISION OF COUNTY SOCIAL SERVICES AGENCIES

North Carolina operates a state-supervised, county-administered system to deliver social service programs, including adult services. In this model, local social services agencies take on the primary role of day-to-day program administration. The state provides supervision, direction, and support to the local agencies.[8] For adult services, including adult protective services (APS) and guardianship by a county department of social services (DSS), the state's Division of Aging and Adult Services (DAAS) provides oversight and supervision for the county departments providing direct services. Supervision includes developing policies and forms, offering training, collecting data, and compliance monitoring. In most situations, other components of the elder protection system will work directly with a county DSS but occasionally it may be appropriate and necessary to contact the DAAS for assistance as well.

2. REGULATION OF LONG-TERM CARE FACILITIES

An older adult may be the subject of physical, emotional, or sexual abuse or neglect while a resident in a long-term care facility. Consider the following examples.

- A resident with Alzheimer's disease may be seriously injured after leaving the facility unsupervised.
- A resident may be sexually or physically abused by another resident or by a member of the staff.
- Staff may not administer pain medication as ordered or provide appropriate wound care, causing the resident to suffer unnecessarily.

DHHS has a role in both (1) trying to prevent this type of harm and (2) investigating and penalizing facilities where such harm has or may have occurred.

On the prevention side, DHHS's Division of Health Service Regulation (DHSR) is responsible for licensure and certification of nursing homes, adult care homes, and facilities for individuals with intellectual disabilities, developmental disabilities, mental illness, and substance abuse issues. These facilities must apply for a license, pass inspections, and be approved before serving patients. During this process, the government agency's role is to determine whether the facility complies with all applicable federal and state laws and policies, including the applicable resident "bill of rights." (See resource below.) After a license is issued, the facility remains subject to regular inspections and oversight by the government.[9] For example, DHSR has the authority to inspect most adult care homes at any time

8. *See* SOC. SERVS. REG'L SUPERVISION & COLLABORATION WORKING GROUP, STAGE ONE FINAL REPORT (UNC School of Government, Mar. 2018), https://www.sog.unc.edu/resources/microsites/social-services/reports.

9. G.S. 131D-2.11(a).

and is required to do so at least annually.[10] County departments of social services (DSS) are required to work with DHSR to support this oversight function.[11] If problems are identified in the course of standard oversight and monitoring, the agency will work with the facility to remedy the problem, impose fines, or take action on the facility's license.[12]

KEY TERMS

Key Terms: Adult Care Home vs. Nursing Home

Term	*Definition*
Adult Care Home[13]	A facility that provides twenty-four-hour personal care services, such as eating, dressing, bathing, toileting, and grooming, to two or more residents Medical care is usually occasional or incidental, with supervised administration of medication[14] Adult care homes that provide care to two to six unrelated residents are referred to as "family care homes"
Nursing Home[15]	A facility that provides nursing or convalescent care for three or more persons Nursing homes generally provide care for people who are not sick enough to require general hospital care but who require nursing care to address chronic or rehabilitative needs The general term "nursing home" encompasses more specific types of facilities, such as skilled nursing and intermediate care facilities
Combination Home[16]	A facility may be a "combination home" that offers various levels of care, including both adult care home services and nursing home services

If DHSR or DSS receives a complaint regarding a licensed facility, an investigation must be initiated within certain timeframes.[17] For adult care homes, the county DSS will be responsible for conducting the investigation. This investigation is in addition to any adult protective services (APS) process that DSS may initiate (see Chapter 2 for more details about APS). If DSS finds a violation, the agency will inform both the facility and DHSR

10. G.S. 131D-2.11(a), (a1). DHSR may waive an annual inspection for an adult care home that achieved the highest performance rating the previous year; however, the agency must inspect the adult care home at least once every two years. *Id.* § 131D-2.11(a1).

11. G.S. 131D-2.11(b).

12. *See* G.S. 131D-34(a).

13. G.S. 131D-2.1(3) (definition of "adult care home" in the context of adult care home regulation); 131E-101(1) (definition of "adult care home," in contrast to definition of "nursing home").

14. G.S. 131D-2.2(a). There is an exception for when a physician certifies that appropriate care can be provided on a temporary basis to meet the resident's needs and prevent unnecessary relocation. *Id.* Adult care homes also do not care for (1) individuals who are dependent on ventilators, (2) individuals whose physician certifies that placement is no longer appropriate, (3) individuals whose health needs cannot be met in the specific adult care home as determined by the residence, and (4) such other medical and functional care needs as the Medical Care Commission determines cannot be properly met in an adult care home. *Id.*

15. G.S. 131E-101(6).

16. G.S. 131E-101(1a).

17. G.S. 131D-26(a1) (adult care homes); 131E-124(a1) (nursing homes).

of the violation, what corrective action must be taken, and a date by which the violation must be corrected.[18] DSS may request assistance from DHSR in resolving complaints.[19] If the complaint involves a nursing home, DHSR rather than the county DSS will be responsible for conducting the investigation.[20] DHSR must reply to the complaint within a reasonable time, which must not exceed sixty days.[21]

RESOURCE

Long-Term Care Residents' Bill of Rights

Adult care homes and nursing homes are required by law to treat their residents in accordance with a residents' bill of rights.[22] The facilities may not require residents to waive these rights.[23] For example, residents have the right

- to be treated with consideration and respect;
- to be free of mental and physical abuse;
- to be free of neglect and exploitation (adult care homes);
- except in emergencies, to be free from chemical and physical restraint, unless authorized for a specified period of time by a physician according to clear and indicated medical need; and
- to be encouraged to exercise their rights as residents and citizens and to be permitted to make complaints and suggestions without fear of coercion or retaliation (adult care homes).

For a more detailed comparison of the bills of rights for adult care homes and nursing homes, see Comparing Residents' Bills of Rights, available at protectadults.unc.edu.

DHSR has the authority to take action if it finds that a facility is out of compliance with applicable laws, including the residents' bill of rights.[24] The penalty DHSR may impose depends on the severity of the violation committed.[25] For example, in the context of adult care homes, the agency has the authority to

- revoke, suspend, or summarily suspend a license;[26]

18. G.S. 131D-26(b).
19. G.S. 131D-26(c).
20. G.S. 131E-124(a).
21. *Id.*
22. G.S. 131D-21 (adult care homes); 131E-117 (nursing homes).
23. G.S. 131D-23 (adult care homes); 131E-119 (nursing homes).
24. G.S. 131D-34 (adult care homes); 131E-124 (nursing homes).
25. G.S. 131D-34.
26. G.S. 131D-2.7; -29.

- require a court-appointed temporary manager for the facility;[27] and
- impose an administrative penalty, which may include a corrective action plan and fines up to $20,000 for each violation and up to $1,000 each day the violation continues beyond the specified deadline.[28]

Penalties will vary based on the severity of the violation. The most severe violations (known as Type A violations) are those that result in or create a substantial risk[29] of death or serious physical harm, abuse, neglect, or exploitation.[30] Less severe violations (known as Type B violations) include those that are detrimental to the health, safety, or welfare of any resident but do not create a substantial risk that death or serious physical harm, abuse, neglect, or exploitation will occur.[31]

Table 7.2. **Examples of Violations in Adult Care Homes**

VIOLATION	EXAMPLE
Type A	"A confused resident who is not properly supervised, wanders away from the facility and as a result, his or her safety is endangered or the resident suffers serious physical harm." "A wrong medication is given to a resident by facility staff which has the strong potential of adversely affecting the resident or the resident suffers serious physical harm."
Type B	"Several resident[s] have orders to receive over the counter pain medications every morning but on one morning, staff forget to give the residents the medication. The residents suffer no ill consequence from the missed doses and subsequent doses are given as ordered." "The facility's pest management program is not effective and insects are noted in a couple of resident rooms on one out of two halls in the facility."

Source: N.C. Div. of Health Serv. Regulation (DSHR), Adult Care Licensure Sec., *Adult Care Home Violations and Penalties*, "Regarding Adult Care Home Inspections," NCDHHS.GOV, https://info.ncdhhs.gov/dhsr/acls/adultcarehomefines.html.

27. G.S. 131D-34(a)(3).
28. G.S. 131D-34(a) (adult care homes); 131E-129 (nursing homes).
29. Substantial risk means the risk of an outcome that is substantially certain to materialize if immediate action is not taken. G.S. 131D-34(2b).
30. G.S. 131D-34(a)(1), (1a).
31. G.S. 131D-34(a)(2).

PRACTICE TIP

Find information about particular facilities, including the facts listed below.

- **Adult care homes.** Investigate "star ratings" (rankings of homes based on one to four stars), penalties imposed, and information gathered by the state Department of Health and Human Services in the course of inspections of family care homes and adult care homes. For more information on star ratings, see DSHR, *Star Rating Program*, NCDHHS.GOV, https://www2.ncdhhs.gov/dhsr/acls/star/search.asp#search.
- **Nursing homes.** Nursing homes certified by Medicare or Medicaid are listed in a comparison tool developed by the U.S. Department of Health and Human Services that includes star ratings, staffing information, and quality of care information. For more on this tool, see U.S. Dep't of Health & Human Servs., *Nursing Home Compare*, "Find a Nursing Home," MEDICARE.GOV, https://www.medicare.gov/nursinghomecompare/search.html?.

In addition to filing a complaint with DHSR, a resident of a facility (or the resident's legal representative) may file a civil action for injunctive relief to enforce the applicable bill of rights.[32] See Chapter 6 for further discussion of private civil actions.

3. LONG-TERM CARE OMBUDSMAN PROGRAM

The Long-term Care Ombudsman Program provides another avenue for promoting the well-being of older adults who are residents in long-term care facilities, including both nursing homes and adult care homes.[33] One purpose of the Ombudsman Program is to advocate on behalf of residents of long-term care facilities.[34] There is a State Ombudsman located within the DHHS Division of Aging and Adult Services and Regional Ombudsmen throughout the state in each of the Area Agencies on Aging.[35] In 2016, the state's program reported receiving 3,769 complaints and closing almost 2,000 cases.[36]

Upon receiving a complaint, the ombudsman will typically attempt to resolve the problem using informal techniques such as mediation, conciliation, and persuasion.[37] If those

32. G.S. 131D-28 (adult care homes); 131E-123 (nursing homes).
33. G.S. 143B, Art. 3, Pt. 14D.
34. G.S. 143B-181.15. *See also* DHHS, ADULT HOME AND NURSING HOME LONG TERM CARE ADVISORY COMMITTEES (CACS): THE ESSENTIAL GUIDE 1 (June 2009), https://files.nc.gov/ncdhhs/documents/files/CAC_Essential_Guide.pdf. A list of State and Regional Ombudsman contact information may be accessed online. *See* DHHS, *Long Term Care Ombudsman (Advocacy for Residents in Long Term Care Facilities)*, NCDHHS.GOV, https://www.ncdhhs.gov/assistance/adult-services/long-term-care-ombudsman (last visited Aug. 12, 2019).
35. G.S. 143B-181.17; -181.18(3a).
36. Data is from U.S. Department of Health and Human Services, Administration for Community Living's *AGing Integrated Database* (AGID), "State Profiles," https://agid.acl.gov/StateProfiles/Profile/Compare/?id=35&compareid=109&variable=7&years=2016 (last visited Aug. 12, 2019).
37. G.S. 143B-181.21(a).

methods are unsuccessful, the ombudsman will refer the matter to DHSR if the complaint relates to an adult care home or nursing home.[38] The ombudsman has the authority to[39]

- enter any long-term care facility at any time during regular visiting hours, or at any other time when access may be required by the circumstances to be investigated, and may have related authority to obtain access to any resident;
- communicate privately and confidentially with residents of the facility, individually or in groups; and
- access residents' files, records, and other information.[40]

The ombudsman must identify himself or herself as such to the resident about whom a complaint was filed. The resident may be unable to or may refuse to communicate with the ombudsman, but that does not diminish the authority of the ombudsman to gather information about the complaint.[41] The resident has the right to participate in planning any actions proposed by the ombudsman and ultimately retains the right to approve or disapprove any proposed action.[42]

If the subject of the complaint involves suspected abuse, neglect, or exploitation, the Regional Ombudsman may only notify the Adult Protection Services (APS) section of the county department of social services (DSS) after obtaining either the written informed consent of the resident or authorization by the State Ombudsman.[43] This is an exception to the general APS reporting obligations discussed in Chapter 2.

Another way the State Ombudsman works to promote quality of care in both nursing homes and adult care homes is through community advisory committees (CACs).[44] Members of each CAC serve as representatives of the State Ombudsman.[45] A CAC exists in each county where there is an adult care home or nursing home.[46] The CAC works to serve the best interests of the residents, assist persons who have grievances with the facility, and attempt to facilitate the resolution of grievances at the local level.[47]

---

38. G.S. 143B-181.21(b).
39. G.S. 143B-181.20(a).
40. Access is allowed as permitted under the Older Americans Act of 1965, as amended, 42 U.S.C. §§ 3001 *et seq.*, and regulations promulgated thereunder, and under procedures established by the State Ombudsman pursuant to G.S. 143B-181.18(6).
41. G.S. 143B-181.20(b).
42. G.S. 143B-181.20(c).
43. G.S. 143B-181.20(f).
44. G.S. 131D-31 (adult care home CAC); 131E-128 (nursing home CAC).
45. G.S. 131D-31 (adult care home CAC); 131E-128 (nursing home CAC).
46. G.S. 131D-31(b)(1) (adult care homes); 131E-128(b)(1) (nursing homes).
47. G.S. 131D-32(e) (adult care homes); 131E-128(h)(1) (nursing homes).

Table 7.3. **Contacting Agencies about Concerns Related to a Long-Term Care Facility**

GOVERNMENT AGENCY	INVESTIGATIVE AUTHORITY	CONTACT INFORMATION
Department of Health Services Regulation (DHSR)	• Investigate complaints related to nursing homes • Refer complaints related to adult care homes to local DSS • Assist local DSS with adult care home investigations as necessary	• (800) 624-3004 (N.C. calls only) • (919) 855-4500 • https://www2.ncdhhs.gov/dhsr/
Local DSS	• Investigate complaints related to adult care homes in the county or region	Local DSS directory: https://www.ncdhhs.gov/divisions/social-services/local-dss-directory
State Ombudsman	• Refer complaints related to long-term care facilities to regional offices • Assist regional ombudsman with complaint investigations as necessary	• (919) 855-3400 • http://www.ncdhhs.gov/aging/ombud.htm
Regional Ombudsman	• Investigate complaints related to long-term care facilities in the region	Regional office directory: https://files.nc.gov/ncdhhs/Ombudsman-Contact%20List_2.pdf

4. HEALTH CARE PERSONNEL REGISTRY

Doctors, nurses, and some other health care personnel are subject to regulation by their professional licensing boards. Any suspected misconduct can be reported directly to those boards, which have the authority to take disciplinary action.[48] In addition, an individual may be charged with a crime for failing to comply with the standards that apply to his or her profession.[49]

Many staff working in health care facilities are not licensed and not subject to the same type of oversight as the personnel listed above. Therefore, DHHS maintains a registry of "health care personnel" who have been found by the agency to have committed certain types of misconduct in a health care facility.[50] The term "health care facility" is defined

48. *See, e.g.*, G.S. 90-14 (Medical Board); -171.37 (Board of Nursing); *see also* N.C. Med. Bd., *Resources & Information*, "Filing a Complaint with the NC Medical Board," NCMEDBOARD.ORG, https://www.ncmedboard.org/resources-information/consumer-resources/complaint-process (last visited Aug. 12, 2019).

49. *See, e.g.*, G.S. 90-18 (crime to practice medicine or surgery without a license); -171.45 (crime to fail to comply with the Nursing Practice Act).

50. G.S. 131E-256; Title 10A, Subchapter 13O, of the North Carolina Administrative Code (N.C.A.C.).

broadly to include hospitals, adult care homes, nursing homes, home health care agencies, and agencies providing in-home aide. Examples include

- neglect or abuse of a resident in a health care facility or upon a person who is receiving home care or hospice care;
- misappropriation of a resident's property, including home care and hospice care patients;
- diversion of drugs belonging to a patient or client of a health care facility; and
- fraud against a patient or client for whom the employee is providing services.[51]

In addition, the registry includes any personnel who have been accused of misconduct if DHHS "has screened the allegation and determined that an investigation is required."[52] The law provides opportunities for personnel to challenge their placement on the registry and, in limited circumstances, request removal from the registry.

This registry includes "health care personnel," which is defined to mean "any unlicensed staff of a health care facility that has direct access to residents, clients, or their property."[53] It also includes nurse aides, who are also included on a separate registry.[54] Health care facilities are required to (1) notify DHHS of potential misconduct within twenty-four hours of the facility becoming aware of it, (2) investigate the circumstances, and (3) promptly report to DHHS about the findings of the investigation.[55] Facilities are also required to check the Health Care Personnel Registry before hiring health care personnel.[56] Federal and state law prohibit facilities from hiring a nurse's aide or medication aide who has a substantiated finding against him or her on a registry.[57]

PRACTICE NOTE

Identifying information on a registry is not a public record,[58] but the information may be disclosed pursuant to a subpoena or court order. Prosecutors, clerks of court, social services staff, and others may want to request information from a registry in the course of an elder abuse investigation.

51. G.S. 131E-256(a)(1).
52. G.S. 131E-256(a)(2).
53. G.S. 131E-256(c).
54. G.S. 131E-255.
55. G.S. 131E-256(g); 10A N.C.A.C. 13O, § .0102.
56. G.S. 131E-256(d2).
57. 42 U.S.C. § 1395i-3(g)(1)(C); *id.* § 1396r(g)(1)(C); 42 C.F.R. § 483.35(d)(4) (nurse aides); G.S. 131E-270 (medication aides).
58. G.S. 131E-256(g1).

KEY TERM

Health care personnel, *in the context of the health care personnel registry, is defined to mean "any unlicensed staff of a health care facility that has direct access to residents, clients, or their property."*

C. OTHER STATE AGENCIES

In addition to the N.C. Department of Health and Human Services (DHHS), there are several other state agencies involved with elder protection. Each has a unique area of emphasis and different powers and duties. It is helpful for other components of the elder protection system to have an understanding of the scope of authority for each agency because it may be necessary to collaborate with one or more in order to provide the best possible protection to an older adult. Below is a brief overview of the elder protection role played by three key state agencies: the Department of Justice, the Secretary of State, and the Department of Insurance.

1. DEPARTMENT OF JUSTICE

A key civil function of the North Carolina Department of Justice (DOJ) is protecting consumers, including older adults, from frauds and scams. DOJ does this primarily through public education and responding to consumer complaints. In 2018, one-fifth of the approximately 20,000 consumer complaints received related to elder fraud.

DOJ has the authority to investigate corporations and persons who do business in the state in violation of law, such as those related to unfair competition and unfair and deceptive trade practices. In response to a complaint, the agency will typically contact the business for a response and may work to resolve the dispute directly. It may also refer the complaint to another state or federal agency or to a local prosecutor. In some cases, DOJ may suggest that the consumer consult a private attorney or file a small claims action. See Chapter 6 for more details on these types of civil actions.

If DOJ identifies a pattern of illegal business practices, it may file a civil lawsuit in the name of the State on behalf of all North Carolina consumers against a corporation and any of the corporate officers, agents, and employees. In the civil action, DOJ may seek to recover money and property for victims, cancellation of contracts, civil money damages, and attorneys' fees.

Table 7.4. **Common Scams Targeting Older Adults under DOJ Authority**

TYPE	THE SCAMMER . . .
Sweetheart	• Creates a fake online profile, posing as someone working out of state or overseas • Develops a friendship with the older adult which, in turn, develops into a romantic relationship and, in some cases, a marriage proposal • Asks the older adult to wire money immediately to help with a financial crisis
Home repair	• Comes to the older adult's house • Identifies unnecessary repairs that need to be made to the roof, driveway, or other parts of the house • After starting the work, may identify more and more repairs or problems, such as toxic mold • Collects series of payments from the older adult • Disappears before the work is complete or completes shoddy repairs
IRS	• Calls the older adult demanding payment of a bogus tax bill • States that the adult will be sent to jail unless the payment is made immediately through a wire transfer or debit card • May require the adult to stay on the phone while completing the wire transfer
Grandparent	• Calls the older adult claiming to be a grandchild or a friend of a grandchild • Asks the older adult to wire money immediately to pay for medical care or get the grandchild out of jail
Lottery	• Calls the older adult and says that the adult won the lottery or a contest • Asks the older adult to wire money to cover fees and taxes so that the adult can claim the winnings

In addition to this role in consumer protection, DOJ also takes the lead on investigating potential fraud involving the Medicaid program. Examples of potential signs of this type of fraud include

- a patient being pressured to receive unnecessary or excessive services,
- a patient's medical records being altered,
- a medical provider claiming to provide services for free, and
- a medical provider dispensing excessive amounts of controlled substances.[59]

DOJ is able to both criminally prosecute those involved with fraud and also pursue a civil suit to recover program funds.

59. N.C. Dep't of Just., Att'y Gen., *How to Spot Medicaid Fraud & Abuse*, NCDOJ.GOV, http://ncdoj.gov/responding-to-crime/health-fraud (last visited Oct. 16, 2019).

Information maintained by DOJ may be useful to assist other components of the elder protection system, such as local prosecutors and adult protective services.

2. SECRETARY OF STATE

The N.C. Secretary of State (SOS) has specific authority related to the regulation and oversight of the securities industry and of charities.

> **EXAMPLE**
>
> *Bob, an 82-year-old widower, receives a call from an unknown investment broker. The broker explains that he is reaching out to a small group of people to offer an opportunity to get in on a new investment. He describes it as a "once-in-a-lifetime opportunity." Bob thinks the broker sounds really bright and trustworthy. He's excited about growing his retirement nest egg. The broker persuades Bob to transfer $5,000 to an investment account the same day.*

> **EXAMPLE**
>
> *Linda receives a letter asking her to donate money to raise funds to feed local children. She writes a check for $200 and mails it to the organization. She later finds out that the charity does not exist.*

The SOS plays a role in trying to prevent the types of fraud discussed in the examples above through education. The agency also registers investment salespersons, advisors, securities, and charities. A consumer who has questions about a particular opportunity may contact the SOS to learn about the organization or individual offering the opportunity.

If someone has a negative experience with a regulated individual, organization, or entity, he or she can file a consumer complaint with the SOS. While the agency is not able to represent individuals or recover money for private persons, it does have the authority to enforce the state laws regulating these activities and individuals.

The SOS also maintains a voluntary online registry of advance health care directives. The registry is password-protected and allows a family member or doctor to access the directives of an individual once the individual has given the family member/doctor the correct file number and password. Alternatively, an individual may keep a registry card containing that information in a location where it can be found in the event it is needed by a family member, caregiver, or medical professional.

3. DEPARTMENT OF INSURANCE

The N.C. Department of Insurance (DOI) regulates the insurance industry, which encompasses all types of insurance, such as health, life, long-term care, disability, homeowners, and auto insurance, and oversees collection agencies, among other duties. The DOI assists consumers with questions about insurance and the filing of claims. It also investigates complaints and allegations of insurance fraud. In 2016, the agency's Criminal Investigation Division handled more than 4,500 cases and recovered in excess of $4.8 million.

EXAMPLE

After a big hailstorm, a roofing company representative knocks on Dan's door. The representative explains that his company can inspect the roof, repair it, and get reimbursed from Dan's homeowner's insurance. Dan, who is 85 years old, signs paperwork authorizing the company to collect directly from his insurer. The company never repairs his roof.

EXAMPLE

An insurance agent contacts Mary, who is 82 years old, and explains that she can use her existing insurance policy's cash value to pay for a newer policy. In order to generate a commission, the agent "may 'twist' the truth and 'churn' a new, 'better' or 'cheaper' policy to the customer. This new policy may, in fact, have less favorable terms or fewer benefits. This is illegal."[60]

60. N.C. DEP'T OF INS. CRIM. INVESTIGATIONS UNIT, INSURANCE FRAUD: RECOGNIZE IT. REPORT IT. PROTECT YOURSELF, http://ncdoi.com/_Publications/Insurance%20Fraud%20in%20North%20Carolina_CIF1.pdf.

RESOURCE

Which State Agency Should an Older Adult Call for Assistance?

TYPE OF COMPLAINT	AGENCY	CONTACT
Consumer fraud or scam	DOJ	• (919) 716-6000 • (877) 5-NO-SCAM (only N.C. calls) • (919) 716-0058 (Spanish) • www.ncdoj.gov
• Securities (investment) professionals • Securities (investment) offerings • Charities	SOS	• (800) 688-4507 • www.sosnc.gov
Insurance fraud	DOI	• (919) 807-6840 • (888) 680-7684 (only N.C. calls) • reportfraud@ncdoi.gov • www.ncdoi.gov
Medicaid recipient fraud	DHHS	• (800) 862-7030 • (877) DMA-TIP1 (362-8471)
Medicaid provider fraud	DOJ	• (919) 881-2320
Tax fraud	Revenue	• (800) 232-4939 • www.ncdor.gov

D. AREA AGENCIES ON AGING

The federal government provides funding to the states to establish Area Agencies on Aging (AAA). North Carolina has sixteen of these regional agencies in place, which are co-located with the regional Councils of Government. Each agency is home to a regional Long-Term Care Ombudsman, described above. In addition, each agency plays an important role in its community by working with local officials and others to identify needs of older adults in the community and then contracting with service providers to meet those needs. The Land of Sky AAA describes its role as promoting

> the highest level of well being of older adults and their families by partnering with organizations to provide a comprehensive system of opportunities, services, and protective services. The AAA is a leader and catalyst in helping older adults in our four county region lead more independent, vibrant lives. As part of a national network of aging agencies established by the Older Americans Act, we work to strengthen home and community care for older adults.[61]

61. LAND OF SKY REGIONAL COUNCIL, http://landofsky.org/aaa.html (last visited Aug. 12, 2019).

An AAA may have contracts with organizations that provide home meal delivery or congregate meals, transportation services, adult day care services, recreation, or wellness activities. AAAs are also involved with advocacy for older adults in the community, both individually and collectively. Except for the ombuds program, each agency is involved with different types of programs and services.

Agency staff or contractors who interact with older adults may identify suspected elder abuse and report it to adult protective services and law enforcement. The agency may also be able to help other components of the elder protection system identify resources and supports within the community to improve the quality of life for an older adult who has been abused.

RESOURCE

Identify the AAA in your region and determine what services and supports it may have available. If there are service gaps for older adults in your community, share those with the AAA. This will help the staff to integrate those needs into the regional planning efforts and advocate for them in the community. A list of agency locations can be found at https://files.nc.gov/ncdhhs/documents/files/aging/AAA-Locations.pdf

E. FEDERAL AGENCIES

In 2010, Congress enacted a law that established the Elder Justice Coordinating Council (EJCC).[62] The EJCC is housed in the U.S. Department of Health and Human Services (DHHS) and is required to include representatives from "each Federal department or agency or other governmental entity identified by [DHHS] as having responsibilities, or administering programs, relating to elder abuse, neglect, and exploitation."[63] The EJCC includes representation from approximately sixteen different federal agencies and programs[64] (see sidebar for the complete list).

62. 42 U.S.C. § 1397k(b)(1).

63. *Id.*

64. U.S. Dep't of Health & Human Servs., Admin. for Cmty. Living, Fall 2018 EJCC Meeting, "Elder Justice Coordinating Council Membership List" (last modified Mar. 29, 2019), https://acl.gov/programs/elder-justice/fall-2018-ejcc-meeting.

Membership of the Federal Elder Justice Coordinating Council

- Department of Health and Human Services (chair of council)
- Consumer Financial Protection Bureau
- Corporation for National and Community Service
- Federal Trade Commission
- Department of Agriculture
- Department of Housing and Urban Development
- Department of the Interior
- Department of Justice
- Postal Inspection Service
- Department of Labor
- Social Security Administration
- Department of the Treasury
- Department of Veterans Affairs
- Securities and Exchange Commission

A full overview of the role of each agency is beyond the scope of this manual, but below are brief overviews of the roles played by six key agencies that may interact more frequently with components of North Carolina's elder protection system.

1. U.S. DEPARTMENT OF HEALTH AND HUMAN SERVICES

The U.S. Department of Health and Human Services (US DHHS) is involved in funding and supporting quite a few initiatives focused on elder abuse. For example, the agency provides support and funding to

- states for training, education, and coalition-building;
- the National Center for Elder Abuse, which provides information, training, and consultation for professionals involved with elder protection;
- the National Center on Law and Elder Rights, which provides tools and support for legal and aging provider organizations;
- organizations providing legal services to older adults;
- states, in the form of grants, to support adult protective services (APS) programs;
- states for the operation of their long-term care ombudsman programs; and
- researchers examining topics related to elder abuse.[65]

In 2016, US DHHS worked with a wide range of professionals to develop "Voluntary Consensus Guidelines for State APS Systems."[66] The guidelines are intended to "provide

65. U.S. DEP'T OF HEALTH & HUMAN SERVS. (DHHS), ELDER JUST. COORDINATING COUNCIL, 2014–2016 REPORT TO CONGRESS 6–15, https://acl.gov/sites/default/files/programs/2017-11/2017%20EJCC%20Report.pdf.

66. U.S. DHHS, Admin for Cmty. Living, *Voluntary Consensus Guidelines for State APS Systems* (2016), https://acl.gov/programs/elder-justice/final-voluntary-consensus-guidelines-state-aps-systems.

a core set of principles and common expectations for APS programs, and to encourage consistency in the policies and practices of APS across the country."[67]

US DHHS also recently started gathering data from states on adult mistreatment on a voluntary basis. The new database is called the National Adult Mistreatment Reporting System (NAMRS) and it began receiving data submissions from states in 2017. It is described as "aspirational" because many states, including North Carolina, do not have robust electronic APS systems and therefore are not able to contribute some or all of the data elements.[68]

2. U.S. DEPARTMENT OF JUSTICE

The U.S. Department of Justice (US DOJ) has focused significant resources on disseminating information; providing training, education, and technical assistance; and, in conjunction with US DHHS, supporting the provision of direct legal services to older adults. The Elder Justice Initiative website includes a tremendous amount of information for public agencies involved with elder protection and citizens, including

- written materials, videos, and websites specifically designed for law enforcement officials and prosecutors;
- webinars and other training materials for other types of elder abuse professionals;
- community outreach materials;
- tools and resources for multidisciplinary teams; and
- curated research on elder abuse topics.

The website includes an "Elder Abuse Resource Roadmap" for victims of financial exploitation.[69] The roadmap is a tool that walks users through a series of questions and answers that ultimately guide them to the government agency or connection that may be able to receive a report or provide assistance. Through the Office for Victims of Crime, the US DOJ also maintains the National Elder Fraud Hotline. The hotline allows people to report fraud against anyone age 60 or older and to connect to case managers who will provide assistance with the reporting process at the federal, state, and local levels. The phone number for the hotline is 833-FRAUD-11 (833-372-8311).

The US DOJ also has a role in leading, coordinating, and assisting with investigations and prosecutions when federal laws are violated. For example, in 2018, the department worked with state and local law enforcement to conduct an elder fraud "sweep."

> The cases involve more than two hundred and fifty defendants from around the globe who victimized more than a million Americans, most of whom were elderly.

---

67. ELDER JUST. COORDINATING COUNCIL, *supra* note 65, at 8.

68. U.S. DHHS., Admin. for Cmty. Living, *NAMRS (Nat'l Adult Maltreatment Reporting Sys.)*, "FAQ: What Else Do I Need to Know?," https://namrs.acl.gov/FAQ.aspx (last visited Aug. 12, 2019).

69. U.S. Dep't of Just., *Elder Abuse Resource Roadmap: Financial*, JUSTICE.GOV, https://www.justice.gov/elderjustice/roadmap (last visited Aug. 12, 2019).

The cases include criminal, civil, and forfeiture actions across more than 50 federal districts. Of the defendants, 200 were charged criminally.[70]

A map of the federal prosecutions resulting from the sweep is also available online, including available court documents.[71]

3. CONSUMER FINANCIAL PROTECTION BUREAU

This agency focuses entirely on consumer financial protection.[72] It has the authority to adopt rules and enforce federal consumer financial laws. It also receives consumer complaints, promotes financial education, researches consumer behavior, and monitors financial markets for risks to consumers.[73] One office within the agency is dedicated to protecting older adults. It generates outreach and educational materials for consumers and financial institutions and conducts research on issues that impact older adults (such as reverse mortgages).[74]

4. FEDERAL TRADE COMMISSION

One role of the Federal Trade Commission (FTC) is to "combat unfair, deceptive, abusive and fraudulent practices that impact older adults."[75] Like many of the other federal agencies, the FTC has developed outreach and training materials for both consumers and professionals. The agency also plays an active role in enforcement. For example, it prosecutes scams, such as those involving international sweepstakes, government imposters, and unnecessary computer technical support. It also accepts consumer complaints.

Additionally, the FTC plays a central role in the federal government's identity theft–prevention efforts and in helping victims build "personal recovery plans" that are tailored to their circumstances.[76] These plans help victims (1) determine who they need to call and what steps they should take to protect their assets going forward and (2) possibly recover assets that may have been lost.

5. U.S. DEPARTMENT OF THE TREASURY

The charge of the Financial Crimes Enforcement Network (FinCEN) within the U.S. Department of the Treasury is to safeguard "the financial system from illicit use, combat money laundering, and promote national security through the strategic use of financial authorities and the collection, analysis, and dissemination of financial intelligence."[77]

---

70. U.S. Dep't of Just., *Justice News*, "Justice Department Coordinates Nationwide Elder Fraud Sweep of More Than 250 Defendants," JUSTICE.GOV (Feb. 22, 2018), https://www.justice.gov/opa/pr/justice-department-coordinates-nationwide-elder-fraud-sweep-more-250-defendants.

71. U.S. Dep't of Just., *February 22, 2018 Elder Fraud Sweep Map*, JUSTICE.GOV, https://www.justice.gov/opa/february-22-2018-elder-fraud-sweep/map (last visited Aug. 12, 2019).

72. Consumer Fin. Prot. Bureau, CONSUMERFINANCE.GOV, https://www.consumerfinance.gov/ (last visited Aug. 12, 2019).

73. ELDER JUST. COORDINATING COUNCIL, *supra* note 65, at 21.

74. Research reports are available on the Consumer Financial Protection Bureau's website at https://www.consumerfinance.gov/data-research/research-reports/ (last visited Aug. 12, 2019).

75. ELDER JUST. COORDINATING COUNCIL, *supra* note 65, at 24.

76. U.S. Fed. Trade Comm'n, *Report Identity Theft and Get a Recovery Plan*, IDENTITYTHEFT.GOV, https://Identity-Theft.gov (last visited Aug. 12, 2019).

77. U.S. Dep't of Treasury, Fin. Crimes Enf't Network, *Mission*, FINCEN.GOV, https://www.fincen.gov/about/mission (last visited Aug. 12, 2019).

In this role, FinCEN provides support for financial institutions, such as banks and credit unions, collects data from those institutions, and links the data from various sources to provide system oversight. Since 2013, financial institutions have been required to submit "Suspicious Activity Reports" (SARs) to FinCEN. With these reports, federal and state law enforcement officials are able to both investigate individual cases and identify trends. A financial institution may be required to file a SAR if it knows, suspects, or has reason to suspect that a transaction conducted or attempted by, at, or through the financial institution

- involves funds derived from illegal activity or attempts to disguise funds derived from illegal activity,
- is designed to evade regulations promulgated under the Bank Secrecy Act (BSA),
- lacks a business or apparent lawful purpose, or
- involves the use of the financial institution to facilitate a criminal activity.[78]

There has been significant growth in the reporting of SARs related to elder financial exploitation since the reporting mandate went into effect. See Figure 7.1.

Figure 7.1 **Number of Suspicious Activity Reports (SARs) Submitted by Financial Institutions in North Carolina Identified by the Institution as Involving "Elder Financial Exploitation," 2012–2018[79]**

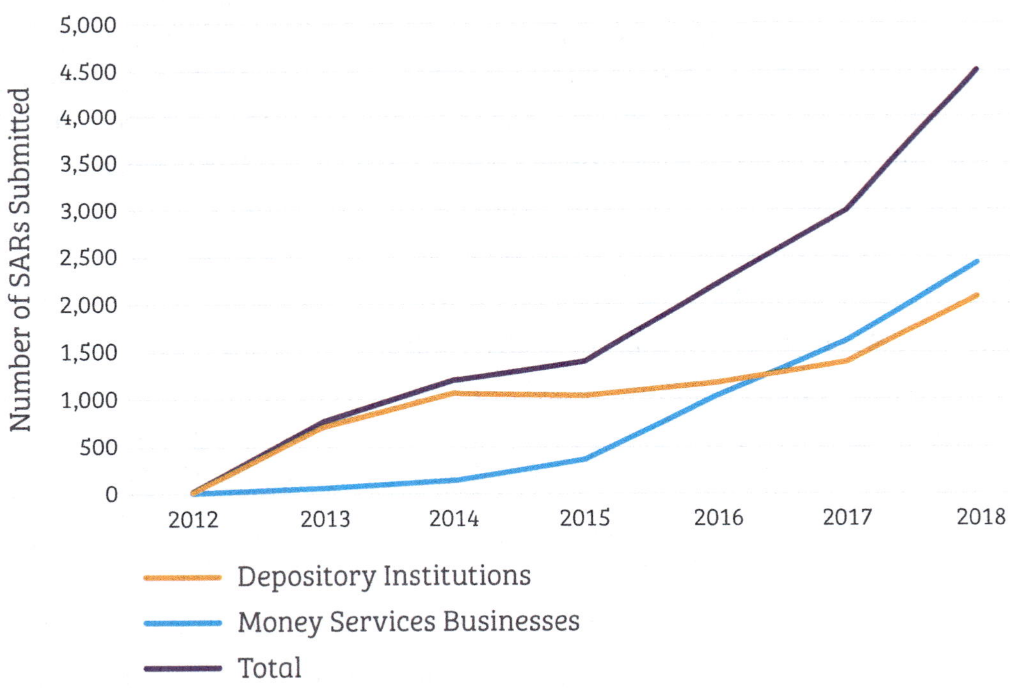

78. CONSUMER FIN. PROT. BUREAU & U.S. DEP'T OF TREASURY, FIN. CRIMES ENF'T NETWORK, MEMORANDUM ON FINANCIAL INSTITUTION AND LAW ENFORCEMENT EFFORTS TO COMBAT ELDER FINANCIAL EXPLOITATION (Aug. 30, 2017), https://files.consumerfinance.gov/f/documents/201708_cfpb-treasury-fincen_memo_elder-financial-exploitation.pdf.

79. U.S. Dep't of Treasury, Fin. Crimes Enf't Network, *Suspicious Activity Report Statistics (SAR Stats)*, https://www.fincen.gov/ (searchable database) (last visited Aug. 12, 2019).

The federal Consumer Financial Protection Bureau (see Section II.E.3, *supra*) studied the SARs data for elder financial exploitation and identified patterns. For example,

- the majority (51 percent) of the suspects listed in the reports were strangers;
- financial losses were greater if the suspect was known to the older adult victim; and
- more than half of the reports related to a money transfer.

Information collected by FinCEN through SARs reporting is protected by federal confidentiality laws, but law enforcement officials can initiate a FinCEN query after a criminal investigation has been opened or in connection with reviews conducted by a task force or group charged with proactively reviewing SARs to identify potential exploitation.[80]

PRACTICE NOTE

The SARs reporting requirement is based in federal law. The financial institution must still comply with reporting requirements under ***state*** law. See Chapter 2, Section II.C.I, for more details regarding the APS reporting obligations.

6. SOCIAL SECURITY ADMINISTRATION

Many older adults receive Social Security income every month. The federal Social Security Administration (SSA) is responsible for paying these benefits and has a strong interest in ensuring that payments are received and used by or on behalf of the older adults who have earned them. One of the best tools available from SSA to help older adults who may be cognitively impaired is the representative payee program.[81]

In short, the program allows another individual to apply to the SSA to serve as a recipient's representative payee. If SSA approves the application, benefit payments will go directly to the payee, and the payee is expected to spend them only for the benefit of the recipient. In some instances, it may be appropriate to appoint an organization, such as a nursing home, or an agency, such as DSS, to serve as the representative payee. The payee is required to keep records of how the benefits are used and saved and to provide an accounting to SSA upon request.[82]

80. 31 C.F.R. § 1010.950(b) ("The Secretary may make any information set forth in any report received pursuant to this chapter available to another agency of the United States, to an agency of a state or local government or to an agency of a foreign government, upon the request of the head of such department or agency made in writing and stating the particular information desired, the criminal, tax or regulatory purpose for which the information is sought, and the official need for the information."); *id.* § 1010.950(e) (placing restrictions on redisclosure of information received). *See also* U.S. Dep't of Just., *Suspicious Activity Reports (SARs) and Their Role in Investigations of Elder Financial Exploitation*, JUSTICE.GOV (Nov. 2, 2017), https://www.justice.gov/elderjustice/video/suspicious-activity-reports-sars-and-their-role-investigations-elder-financial.

81. *See, e.g.*, Soc. Sec. Admin., *Frequently Asked Questions (FAQs) for Representative Payees*, SSA.GOV, https://www.ssa.gov/payee/faqrep.htm (describing the role of a representative payee) (last visited Aug. 12. 2019).

82. Justice in Aging, *Fact Sheet: SSA's Representative Payee Program*, JUSTICEINAGING.ORG (2016), https://www.justiceinaging.org/our-work/economic-security/rep-payee-program/.

Unfortunately, this program has the potential to be abused. If a payee has misused benefits, SSA has the authority to pursue both civil and criminal penalties.[83]

RESOURCE

The federal government has invested significant resources in developing training materials and other resources related to elder protection. Some of the most comprehensive materials include the following:

- DOJ Elder Justice Initiative (EJI): https://www.justice.gov/elderjustice
- National Center on Elder Abuse: https://ncea.acl.gov/
- Consumer Financial Protection Bureau: https://www.consumerfinance.gov/
- Federal Trade Commission: https://www.ftc.gov/ and https://IdentityTheft.gov
- National Center on Law and Elder Rights: https://ncler.acl.gov/

F. FINANCIAL INSTITUTIONS

Banks, credit unions, and other financial institutions are critical components of the elder protection system with respect to financial exploitation.[84] They have expertise in identifying irregular financial activity and offer tools to monitor accounts and transactions when necessary. These institutions (1) identify potential exploitation and make reports, (2) provide access to records, and (3) freeze accounts. Below is a brief overview of their connection to the system in each of these three areas.

1. IDENTIFY AND REPORT

Financial institutions are subject to several federal and state confidentiality laws that can at times be perceived as barriers to information-sharing (see further discussion below). Even with these rigorous laws in place, financial institutions, and their officers and employees, are clearly allowed to comply with the reporting requirements for adult protective services (APS), law enforcement, "trusted persons," and the federal government (SARs).

- **Duty to report all abuse, neglect, and exploitation to APS.** Financial institutions must comply with the universal mandated APS reporting law, which requires all individuals who have reasonable cause to believe that a *disabled* adult is in need of services to provide protection from abuse, neglect, or exploitation.[85]

- **Duty to report financial exploitation to APS.** Financial institutions are also subject to a more specific (and likely redundant) law that requires them to report to

83. 42 U.S.C. § 408(a)(5); *id.* § 405(j)(7).
84. CONSUMER FIN. PROT. BUREAU & U.S. DEP'T OF TREASURY, FIN. CRIMES ENF'T NETWORK, *supra* note 79. *See also* Quick Reference: Legal Framework for the Role of Financial Institutions in Elder Protection, available at protectadults.sog.unc.edu.
85. G.S. 108A-102.

APS if they have reasonable cause to believe that a *disabled* adult is the victim or target of financial exploitation.[86] See Chapter 2 for further discussion of APS reporting laws.

- **Duty to report to law enforcement.** If a financial institution has reasonable cause to believe that a *disabled adult or older adult* (65 years and older) is the victim or target of financial exploitation, the institution must make a report to local law enforcement.[87]
- **Trusted persons list.** Under state law, financial institutions are encouraged to offer disabled adults and older adults an opportunity to submit to the institutions a list of "trusted persons" and to update the lists periodically.[88] If the institution has reasonable cause to believe that the adult is the victim or target of financial exploitation, it must report the suspicion to any "trusted person" identified by the customer, unless the institution "suspects that [the trusted person is] financially exploiting the disabled adult or older adult."[89]
- **Duty to report to federal government (SARs).** As discussed above, financial institutions are required to file Suspicious Activity Reports with the U.S. Department of the Treasury in some circumstances.

2. PROVIDE ACCESS TO RECORDS

As mentioned above, financial institutions are subject to several complex federal and state confidentiality laws.[90] While strict confidentiality is a high priority, these laws also recognize the need to share information in order to protect older adults from exploitation. A financial institution may, in some circumstances, provide access to an older adult's financial records to (1) APS, (2) law enforcement, and (3) a party to a court proceeding.

A full review of the confidentiality laws governing financial institutions is beyond the scope of this manual, but a brief overview is important to help orient the other components of the elder protection system to the legal framework.

The first thing to keep in mind is that an older adult with capacity, or an adult's legal representative (such as a general guardian, guardian of the estate, or interim guardian), may authorize a financial institution to provide access to an official, agency, or individual at any time.[91] If the older adult lacks capacity or there is a need to obtain access without asking for the older adult's authorization, there are some tools and processes available to the three entities listed above to obtain access to information from financial institutions.

---

86. G.S. 108A-115(a)(3).
87. G.S. 108A-115(a)(2).
88. G.S. 108A-114.
89. G.S. 108A-115(a)(1).
90. *See* 15 U.S.C. § 6801(a) ("It is the policy of the Congress that each financial institution has an affirmative and continuing obligation to respect the privacy of its customers and to protect the security and confidentiality of those customers' nonpublic personal information."); G.S. 53B-3 ("It is the public policy of this State that financial records should be treated as confidential and that no financial institution may provide to any government authority and no government authority may have access to any financial records except in accordance with the provisions of [Chapter 53].").
91. 15 U.S.C. § 6802(e)(2); 12 C.F.R. § 332.15(a)(1); G.S. 35B-4(1); *id.* § 35A-1251. Note that an interim guardian of the estate (GOE) or general guardian (GG) has only the authority set forth in the order appointing the interim guardian. G.S. 35A-1114(e).

- **APS.** In the course of an APS investigation, social services officials have three tools available to obtain information from a financial institution: subpoenas, freeze and inspect orders, and search warrants. See Chapter 2 for an overview of each of these tools.

- **Law enforcement.** In a criminal investigation, law enforcement officials may use search warrants, court orders, or subpoenas[92] to obtain information from financial institutions. See Chapter 2 for an overview of each of these options.

- **Party to a court proceeding.** A party to a court proceeding, such as a petitioner in a guardianship proceeding, may rely on traditional discovery under the rules of civil procedure to gain access to an older adult's financial records. This includes a request for production of documents. The downside to relying on civil discovery is that it can be costly and time-consuming. If an older adult is the subject of financial exploitation, quick action may be necessary to protect the adult, and civil discovery may be an inadequate tool to stop ongoing exploitation.

As a general rule, a financial institution is required to (1) provide every customer with notice that it plans to disclose the customer's information to a third party and (2) provide the customer with an opportunity to opt out of the disclosure.[93] This requirement is based on both federal and state law, although the parameters for each body of law are slightly different.

A governmental authority requesting access to records from a financial institution may request that the notice to the customer be delayed. A judge (not the clerk or magistrate) may order delayed notice to the customer if the request is relevant to a legitimate governmental inquiry and if notice to the customer will

- endanger the life or physical safety of any person,
- result in flight from prosecution,
- lead to intimidation of a witness,
- result in destruction of or tampering with evidence, or
- otherwise seriously jeopardize the governmental inquiry or an official proceeding or investigation.[94]

If the disclosure is being made pursuant to a subpoena issued by a district court judge, that judge has the authority to authorize the delay.[95] If the disclosure is being made pursuant to other process, such as a court order or search warrant, the order delaying notice must be issued by a superior court judge (not a clerk or magistrate).[96]

92. G.S. 108A-116 (authorizing law enforcement to request a subpoena for financial records).
93. 15 U.S.C. §§ 6803(a), (b); 6802(a), (b).
94. G.S. 53B-6.
95. G.S. 108A-117(b).
96. G.S. 53B-6.

3. FREEZE ACCOUNTS

If government officials find it necessary to freeze the assets of either an older adult or a defendant in a criminal case, then the involvement of financial institutions will be necessary.

- **Assets of an older adult.** In the course of investigating potential financial exploitation, adult protective services (APS) is authorized to petition a district court judge to issue an order freezing the adult's assets and allowing APS to inspect them.[97] See Chapter 2 for more details about this process.
- **Assets of a criminal defendant.** A district attorney may ask the court to freeze the assets of a defendant if "it appears by clear and convincing evidence that [the] defendant is about to or intends to divest himself or herself of assets in a manner that would render the defendant insolvent for the purposes of restitution."[98] See Chapter 3 for more details about this process.

G. CREDIT REPORTING AGENCIES

An older adult, like anyone else, may be the victim of identity theft. Some common identity theft scams targeting older adults involve (1) telephone calls that persuade the adult to share personal or financial information in exchange for the promise of time-limited, too-good-to-be-true deals and (2) emails asking the adult to confirm account information by clicking on a link.[99]

If an older adult's identity is stolen, one of the most important steps the adult or the adult's representative can take is to freeze the victim's credit temporarily. All consumers have the authority to put a security freeze on credit accounts.[100] Once the freeze is in place, a credit reporting agency may not release the consumer's credit report or information to a third party without the express authorization of the consumer.[101] The effect of a freeze is that it stops someone from opening a new account in the consumer's name or increasing an existing credit line.[102] A credit freeze is a tool that helps lessen the impact of identity theft.

97. G.S. 108A-106(f).
98. G.S. 14-112.3(b).
99. FBI, *Scams and Safety*, "Common Fraud Schemes," FBI.GOV, https://www.fbi.gov/scams-and-safety/common-fraud-schemes/telemarketing-fraud (last visited Aug. 13, 2019).
100. G.S. 75-63(a). *See* N.C. Att'y Gen., *Free Security Freeze*, NCDOJ.GOV, https://ncdoj.gov/protecting-consumers/protecting-your-identity/free-security-freeze (providing instructions for placing a security freeze) (last visited Aug. 13, 2019).
101. G.S. 75-63(a). Note that an agency may notify a third party that a freeze is in place. *Id.*
102. *See* N.C. Att'y Gen., *supra* note 100.

An older adult may be incapacitated and, as a result, unable to place a credit freeze without assistance. State law allows a representative of a "protected consumer" to place a security freeze with a credit reporting agency.[103] A protected consumer includes both

- an incapacitated adult (note that the adult does not first have to be adjudicated incompetent to qualify as a protected consumer) and
- an adult for whom a guardian or guardian ad litem has been appointed.[104]

To be authorized to place the freeze, the representative must be able to document his or her authority to act on behalf of the protected consumer.[105] Acceptable documentation includes

- a court order;
- a valid power of attorney; and
- a written, notarized statement signed by the protected consumer that expressly describes the authority of the representative to act on behalf of the consumer.[106]

The representative places the freeze by contacting the credit reporting agency by mail, phone, or through a secure website.[107] The three nationwide credit reporting agencies are Equifax, TransUnion, and Experian. [108] To place the freeze, the representative must do all of the following:[109]

- follow the instructions for submitting the report specified by the agency;
- provide sufficient identification for both himself or herself and for the protected consumer;
- provide sufficient proof of authority to act on the protected consumer's behalf; and
- pay a reasonable fee, not to exceed $5.00, for placement or removal of the freeze.[110]

Charging a fee is prohibited if the protected consumer is over age 62 or if the representative submits a copy of a report or complaint to law enforcement about the unlawful use of the consumer's identifying information by another person.[111]

---

103. G.S. 75-63.1. For a detailed discussion of this law and some of the practical questions raised by it, see Kate Mewhinney, *The Protected Consumer Credit Freeze: A New Tool to Prevent and Stop Financial Exploitation of Incapacitated Adults*, Wake Forest University School of Law Elder Law Clinic (2016), http://elder-clinic.law.wfu.edu/files/2016/09/Protected-Consumer-Security-Freeze-.pdf.

104. G.S. 75-61(11a). The statute does not make clear what type of guardian may place the freeze—a general guardian, a guardian of the estate, or a guardian of the person.

105. G.S. 75-61(13a) (defining "representative"), (16) ("sufficient proof of authority").

106. G.S. 75-61(16)b.

107. G.S. 75-63.1(a)(1).

108. *See* N.C. Att'y Gen., *Children's Security Freezes*, NCDOJ.GOV, https://www.ncdoj.gov/protecting-your-identity/childrens-security-freezes/ (providing contact information for each of the three national credit bureaus) (last visited Aug. 13, 2019).

109. G.S. 75-63.1(a)(2).

110. G.S. 75-63.1(d).

111. G.S. 75-63.1(d)(2)a., c.

Once these requirements are satisfied, the credit reporting agency must place the freeze within thirty days.[112] The freeze remains in effect until the protected consumer (or his or her representative) submits a request to the agency to remove the freeze and pays the fee (unless the consumer is over age 62 or submits a law enforcement report or complaint of unlawful use of identifying information, in which case no fee can be charged).[113] If a protected consumer himself or herself asks for the freeze to be removed, he or she must provide identification and proof that the representative no longer has valid authority to act on his or her behalf.[114] If the representative asks for the removal of the freeze, he or she must provide identification and proof of authority to act on the protected consumer's behalf.[115] The credit reporting agency has up to thirty days to remove the freeze.[116]

III. CHALLENGE FOR OTHER ELDER PROTECTION SYSTEM COMPONENTS

Perhaps the greatest challenge facing these other players in the elder protection system is the one that underlies the system as a whole: fragmentation. Each component has limited resources, knowledge, and legal authority. With these limitations, it is difficult to develop the resource-intensive connections and collaborations that are often needed to provide adequate services and supports to victims of elder abuse.

TIPS FOR COMBATTING SYSTEM FRAGMENTATION.

- Develop a list of contact people in your jurisdiction who are involved with elder protection. Update the list regularly.
- Develop multidisciplinary teams and convene information-sharing meetings and other types of collaborative initiatives.[117] See Chapter 1 for more information about multidisciplinary teams.
- Participate in online forums, either through protectadults.unc.edu or locally. These types of virtual communities can support collaboration and communication and help the overall elder protection system become more consistent and cohesive.

112. G.S. 75-63.1(a).
113. G.S. 75-63.1(c), (d).
114. G.S. 75-63.1(c)(1)b.
115. G.S. 75-63.1(c)(1)c.
116. G.S. 75-63.1(c).
117. CONSUMER FIN. PROT. BUREAU, OFF. FOR OLDER AMERICANS, REPORT AND RECOMMENDATIONS: FIGHTING ELDER FINANCIAL EXPLOITATION THROUGH COMMUNITY NETWORKS (2016), https://files.consumerfinance.gov/f/documents/082016_cfpb_Networks_Study_Report.pdf.

With tremendous demographic shifts on the horizon, agencies, organizations, and individuals involved with the protection of older adults have an opportunity to take critical steps now to build an effective elder protection system. Components of the system identify partners, develop relationships, and work together. As demonstrated throughout this manual, the "elder protection system" depends on meaningful and productive connections across disciplines, borders, and authority.

Appendix A
Alternatives to Guardianship

Every older adult who lacks capacity does not need a guardian. Guardianship removes fundamental rights, inhibits autonomy, and is indefinite and difficult to terminate, particularly for older adults with a condition like dementia that will continue to decline over time. There are legal and practical alternatives to guardianship of the person and of the estate that empower surrogate decision makers to act on an older adult's behalf (guardianship is discussed in detail in Chapter 4). The most effective of these alternatives may be powers of attorney, which require advance planning and are discussed in detail in Chapter 5. But, even without advance planning, there are supports that may be put in place for an older adult after a cognitive decline occurs that may prevent or, at the very least, delay the need for a guardian.

I. HEALTH AND PERSONAL CARE DECISION-MAKING ALTERNATIVES TO A GUARDIANSHIP OF THE PERSON (GOP)

A. HEALTH CARE POWER OF ATTORNEY (HEALTH CARE POA)

A health care POA is a written instrument, signed in the presence of two qualified witnesses and acknowledged before a notary public, pursuant to which an attorney-in-fact or agent is appointed to act for an older adult in matters relating to health care.[1] This may include the power to authorize withholding or discontinuing life-prolonging measures and to authorize providing or withholding mental health treatment.[2] Any person who is 18 years of age or older and has an understanding and capacity to make and communicate health care decisions may make a health care POA.[3] If a court appoints a guardian of the person or general guardian for an older adult, the agent's authority under a health care POA continues until suspended by court order for good cause.[4] The order suspending the health care POA should direct whether the guardian must act consistently with the health care POA and whether and to what extent the guardian may deviate from it.[5] A form health care POA is set forth in G.S. 32A-25.1.

B. LIVING WILL

A living will is a type of health care advanced directive that allows an individual to give future instructions to health care providers to withhold or withdraw life-prolonging measures, such as a feeding tube, in certain situations.[6] A living will states the choices an individual would make if the individual were able to communicate. It must be signed in

1. Chapter 32A, Section 16(3), of the North Carolina General Statutes (hereinafter G.S.).
2. G.S. 32A-19(a).
3. G.S. 32A-17.
4. G.S. 32A-22(a).
5. *Id.*
6. G.S. 90-321.

the presence of two qualified witnesses and acknowledged before a clerk, assistant clerk, or notary public.[7] A form living will is set forth in G.S. 90-321.

C. ADVANCE INSTRUCTION FOR MENTAL HEALTH TREATMENT

An advance instruction for mental health treatment is a written instruction signed in the presence of two qualified witnesses and acknowledged before a notary public.[8] In an advance instruction, a principal makes a declaration of instructions, information, and preferences regarding mental health treatment to be followed when the principal is incapable of giving or refusing consent.[9] It may include the authority to administer medications, to deliver shock treatment, and to admit the individual to a facility for care.[10] A form advance instruction is set forth in G.S. 122C-77.

D. INFORMED CONSENT STATUTE

A health care provider may not treat a patient without consent in most non-emergency situations.[11] Consent must be voluntarily given by a person with the legal authority and the decisional capacity to make health care decisions.[12] In addition, consent must be informed.[13] When a person lacks capacity to make or communicate health care decisions, North Carolina law sets out a list of persons who may consent to medical treatment on the person's behalf.[14] Priority is first given to a guardian of the person or a general guardian, then to a health care agent under a health care POA, and then an agent with powers to make health care decisions for the patient.[15] If there is no guardian or agent authorized to make decisions, the patient's spouse is first in line.[16] The list continues with other relatives and involved individuals.[17]

E. ADULT PROTECTIVE SERVICES (APS)

An APS unit exists in every county in North Carolina and serves to protect disabled adults, including older adults who lack capacity, who are abused, neglected, or exploited.[18] APS may help an older adult resolve a crisis situation and avoid the need for a more permanent guardianship by connecting the older adult to essential services in the community or initiating court action to protect the adult under G.S. Chapter 108A. A more in-depth discussion of APS is presented in Chapter 2.

7. G.S. 90-321(c)(3), (4).
8. G.S. 122C-72(1).
9. *Id.*
10. G.S. 122C-72(5).
11. *See* G.S. 90-21.13 (describing the standards a health care provider must meet in obtaining informed consent).
12. *Id.*
13. *Id.*
14. G.S. 90-21.13(c).
15. *Id.* Note that if a patient has a health care POA and a general guardian or guardian of the person, the health care agent under a valid health care POA has the right to exercise the authority in the health care POA unless the clerk suspends the authority of the health care agent. *Id.* § 90-21.13(c)(1).
16. *Id.*
17. *Id.*
18. *See* G.S. Ch. 108A, Art. 6 (Protection of the Abused, Neglected, or Exploited Disabled Adult Act).

F. SUPPORTS AND SERVICES

There may be a number of public and private supports and services that can be put in place to help older adults who lack capacity navigate their day-to-day needs. This includes meal delivery programs, such as Meals on Wheels; transportation services;[19] in-home aides and home health managers; housing locators;[20] and placement services[21] and technologies that are geared toward older adults, such as medical alert systems, smart pillboxes, and remote patient monitoring devices.

II. FINANCIAL DECISION-MAKING ALTERNATIVES TO A GUARDIAN OF THE ESTATE (GOE)

A. DURABLE POWER OF ATTORNEY (POA)

A POA is a common planning tool that is employed when an individual with capacity, the principal, wants to authorize another person, the agent, to act on his or her behalf.[22] It is typically used with regard to property and property affairs. An individual may execute a POA for any reason, including for convenience or mental or physical incapacity. The POA may become effective immediately or upon the occurrence of a future event, such as the mental or physical incapacity of an individual.[23] A POA subject to G.S. Chapter 32C is durable by default, meaning that it survives the incapacity of the principal unless it expressly states otherwise.[24] The principal determines the nature and extent of the agent's authority under the POA.[25] The principal may give the agent the authority over just a certain tract of real property or over all of his or her financial affairs. A POA is not typically subject to court oversight and is susceptible to abuse, particularly where the agent exceeds the scope of the agent's authority or conducts transactions under the POA for the agent's own benefit or otherwise not in the best interests of the principal. A form POA is set forth in G.S. 32C-3-301. POAs are discussed further in Chapter 5.

B. TRUST

A trust is a fiduciary relationship in which one person (the trustee) holds a property interest subject to an obligation to keep or use that interest for the benefit of another (the beneficiary).[26] Typically, there is a trust instrument that sets out the terms of the

19. *See* N.C. Dep't of Health & Human Servs. (DHHS), *Transportation Services for Older Adults*, NCDHHS.GOV, https://www.ncdhhs.gov/assistance/adult-services/transportation-services-for-older-adults (last visited Aug. 13, 2019).
20. DHHS, *Elder Housing Locator*, NCDHHS.GOV, https://www.ncdhhs.gov/assistance/adult-services/elder-housing-locator (last visited Aug. 13, 2019).
21. DHHS, *Adult Placement Services*, NCDHHS.GOV, https://www.ncdhhs.gov/assistance/adult-services/adult-placement-services (last visited Aug. 13, 2019).
22. G.S. 32C-1-102(9) (defining "power of attorney").
23. G.S. 32C-1-109.
24. G.S. 32C-1-104.
25. G.S. Chapter 32C, Article 2.
26. *See* G.S. 36C-4-402(a). The North Carolina Uniform Trust Code is contained in G.S. Chapter 36C and applies to any express trust no matter how created. *Id.* § 36C-1-102.

trust.[27] A common type of trust used to avoid guardianship for an older adult is a revocable living trust, which may be modified or revoked by the older adult.[28] The older adult may create the trust naming himself or herself as the trustee but then name a successor trustee to take over the management of the trust in the event of the adult's incapacity.

C. REPRESENTATIVE PAYEE

A representative payee is a person or an organization appointed by a federal governmental agency to receive benefits for a person who is unable to manage or direct the management of his or her benefits.[29] A representative payee may be appointed after an individual loses capacity. The payee must use the benefits to pay for the current and future needs of the beneficiary and save any benefits not required to meet current needs. A payee must keep records of expenses and provide an accounting upon request by the agency. Federal agencies with representative payee programs include the Social Security Administration (for Social Security benefits such as Medicaid and Medicare and supplemental Social Security benefits (commonly referred to as disability benefits)), the Veteran's Administration, the Department of Defense, and the Office of Personnel Management.

D. CLERK ADMINISTRATION OF FUNDS

A clerk of superior court may receive $5,000 or less from any person for an incapacitated adult who does not have a guardian and is domiciled in the clerk's county.[30] In addition, if an incapacitated adult is entitled to insurance proceeds that do not exceed $5,000, the proceeds may be paid to the clerk in the county of the adult's domicile.[31] The clerk may receive, administer, and, upon finding that it is in the best interest of the incapacitated adult, disburse the funds to a creditor, relative, or some "discreet and solvent neighbor" or friend for the purpose of handling the property and affairs of that adult.[32] The clerk will require receipts or paid vouchers showing that the money disbursed was used for the exclusive benefit of the incapacitated adult.[33]

E. JOINT PROPERTY

An older adult may own property, such as a house, car, or bank accounts, jointly with a spouse or other family member or friend. The joint ownership allows continued use of the assets for the older adult's benefit after one joint owner's incapacity. This type of ownership may prevent the need for a guardian, particularly in those situations involving one

27. G.S. 36C-1-103(21).
28. *See* G.S. Ch. 36C, Art. 6 (Revocable Trusts).
29. *See, e.g.*, Soc. Sec. Admin., *Frequently Asked Questions (FAQs) for Representative Payees*, SSA.GOV, https://www.ssa.gov/payee/faqrep.htm (describing the role of a representative payee).
30. G.S. 7A-111(b).
31. *Id.*
32. *Id.*
33. *Id.*

spouse with capacity who is a joint owner with a spouse who lacks capacity. If spouses hold property as tenants by the entirety and one or both of the spouses is/are mentally incompetent to execute a conveyance of the property when it is necessary or desirable that the property be mortgaged or sold, a special proceeding may be brought to authorize a sale or mortgage of the property.[34] This process is available when a spouse has not been adjudicated incompetent but is not competent to convey property.

F. SUPPORTS AND SERVICES

An older adult who lacks capacity may avoid the need for guardianship through supports and services, such as a daily money management (DMM) program. A DMM helps older adults with personal household finances, and services can range from comprehensive financial management to maintaining financial records to reminders to pay bills.[35] These types of services may be most helpful in situations where one spouse dies and the living spouse has not had a history of or experience with managing finances and needs some assistance and support.

34. G.S. 35A-1310.

35. Lynnette Khalfani-Cox, *Need Help Managing Day-to-Day Finances?*, AARP.ORG (July 1, 2016), https://www.aarp.org/money/budgeting-saving/info-2016/money-management-on-a-budget.html/.

Appendix B
Techniques and Tips for Interviewing Older Adults

A law enforcement officer interviews an older adult who is the victim of a crime. An adult protective services (APS) social worker interviews an older adult as part of an APS investigation. An attorney interviews an older adult as part of the attorney's representation of the adult in a guardianship case or civil litigation.

This appendix provides information for these professionals and others to consider when interviewing older adults in connection with elder abuse cases.

I. SELECTING THE INTERVIEW LOCATION

The interviewer may

- conduct the interview in the older adult's home or at a location that is comfortable to the older adult (note: conducting interviews in the homes of older adults allows interviewers to assess living conditions and ask questions about what they see around them);
- ensure that the location is free from distractions for both the older adult and the interviewer; and
- ask about and be aware of any physical limitations the older adult might have, such as hearing or sight impairment, and make sure that the older adult has access to accommodations that will empower him or her to participate meaningfully in the interview.

II. CONDUCT OF THE INTERVIEWER

The interviewer may

- provide his or her name and contact information to the older adult;
- explain the role of the interviewer and the purpose of the interview to the adult;
- develop a rapport with the older adult by asking about the adult's life and daily routine;
- ask the older adult whether he or she has any questions, needs, or concerns before going into the substance of the interview;
- make sure that cell phones, televisions, and other electronic devices that will distract from the interview are turned off and/or put away;
- treat the older adult with respect;
- ask the older adult how he or she prefers to be addressed;
- refrain from stereotyping the older adult; and
- be prepared to offer the older adult referrals to supports and services in the community, including protective services against further abuse.

III. SPECIAL CONSIDERATIONS FOR OLDER ADULTS WITH COGNITIVE IMPAIRMENTS

The interviewer may

- remember that a cognitive impairment does not always prevent an older adult from relaying what happened (i.e., don't discount what the older adult has to say because of a cognitive impairment);
- ask short, open-ended but specific questions;
- ask about one thing at a time, building on what the older adult has already disclosed;
- give the older adult time to answer each question without interrupting the adult but redirect as necessary;
- speak slowly and clearly but not condescendingly;
- speak at eye level with the older adult and maintain eye contact;
- NOT correct the older adult; and
- consider the timing of the interview, asking, for example, whether the older adult is more or less alert because the interview is occurring
  - after a meal,
  - after the adult has taken medication(s),
  - after physical exercise, or
  - earlier in the day.

Older adults with dementia may experience "sundowning," which is a restlessness, agitation, and confusion that worsens later in the day as the sun goes down. A caregiver may be able to provide information about the best time of day to conduct the interview with the older adult.

IV. JOINT INTERVIEWS WITH OTHER PROFESSIONALS

There are advantages and disadvantages of conducting joint interviews of older adults with other professionals. For example, consider the case of law enforcement joining an APS social worker to interview an older adult.

A. ADVANTAGES

- The older adult only has to give a statement once.
- The interview may be more comprehensive; one interviewer may ask a question another interviewer had not thought to ask.

B. DISADVANTAGES

- APS and law enforcement serve different societal purposes. APS provides protection to older adults who are victims of elder abuse, while law enforcement conducts investigations to prosecute perpetrators.
- An older adult may be wary of sharing information needed by APS to provide protective services to the adult if law enforcement is present, particularly if the perpetrator is a family member or caregiver of the older adult.
- The presence of law enforcement may be intimidating to the older adult and could make the adult afraid that he or she did something wrong.

V. PRESENCE OF FAMILY, FRIEND, OR CAREGIVER

It may be necessary, for confidentiality purposes or for other legal reasons, to conduct an interview of an older adult alone. Doing so also helps build trust with the older adult and ensures that the adult's story, and not another person's version of it, is told to the interviewer. It may be necessary for the older adult to have a support person present for some of the interview, until the adult feels comfortable. The support person may leave after introducing the older adult to the interviewer, so that the older adult may be interviewed alone.

VI. RESOURCES

- Elder Abuse Guide for Law Enforcement (EAGLE): Interviewing Older Adults, available at http://eagle.trea.usc.edu/law-enforcement-resources/interviewing-older-adults/.
- American Bar Association & American Psychological Association, Assessment of Older Adults with Diminished Capacity: A Handbook for Lawyers, available at https://www.apa.org/pi/aging/resources/guides/diminished-capacity.pdf.
- San Diego Elder and Dependent Adult Abuse Blueprint 2018, main document without addenda available at https://www.sdcda.org/helping/elder-abuse-blueprint.pdf.

- National Institute on Aging, Alzheimer's Care: Tips for Coping with Sundowning, available at https://www.nia.nih.gov/health/tips-coping-sundowning.
- Sheri Gibson, U.S. Dep't of Justice, Elder Justice Initiative, Forensic Interviewing of Older Adults (Dec. 8, 2017), webinar presentation slides available at https://www.justice.gov/file/1064541/download.
- Kay de Vries, Communicating with Older People with Dementia, 25(4) Nursing Older People 30–37 (May 2013), available for purchase at https://www.ncbi.nlm.nih.gov/pubmed/23789241.
- Gerontological Society of America, Communicating with Older Adults: An Evidence-Based Review of What Really Works (2012), see https://geron.org/publications/communicating-with-older-adults.

Appendix C
Crimes That May Be Implicated in Elder Abuse Cases

The table below identifies some of the crimes that may be charged in cases involving elder abuse. It is a more detailed version of Table 3.3 in Chapter 3.

CRIMES SPECIFIC TO ELDER AND DISABLED ADULTS

CRIME	STATUTE (G.S.)	ELEMENTS
Assault on Handicapped Person	14-32.1	(1) The defendant commits an assault or battery (2) on a handicapped person (3) knowing or having reason to know that the person is handicapped • No age requirement for victim • "Handicapped person" has definition specific to this crime
Aggravated Assault on a Handicapped Person	14-32.1(e)	(1) The defendant commits an assault or battery (2) on a handicapped person (3) knowing or having reason to know that the person is handicapped and (4) (a) uses a deadly weapon or other means of force likely to cause serious injury or serious damage to a handicapped person, (b) inflicts serious injury on a handicapped person, or (c) intends to kill a handicapped person
Patient Abuse and Neglect There are four levels of conduct, resulting in different felony classifications depending on the nature of the conduct and the harm to the victim: (1) Willful or Culpably Negligent Pattern of Conduct Causing Bodily Injury (2) Willful or Culpably Negligent Conduct Causing Serious Bodily Injury (3) Culpably Negligent Conduct Causing Death (4) Intentional Conduct Causing Death	14-32.2	(1) The defendant physically abuses (2) (a) a patient of a health care facility or (b) a resident of a residential care facility and **Lowest level of offense:** (3) the abuse evinces a pattern of conduct (4) that is (a) willful or (b) culpably negligent and (5) proximately causes (6) bodily injury to a patient or resident **Next-higher levels of offense:** (3) the abuse is (a) willful or (b) culpably negligent and (4) proximately causes (5) serious bodily injury/death to a patient or resident **Highest level of offense:** (3) the abuse constitutes intentional conduct (4) that proximately causes (5) the death of the patient or resident • No age requirement for victim

CRIMES SPECIFIC TO ELDER AND DISABLED ADULTS, ***cont'd***

CRIME	STATUTE (G.S.)	ELEMENTS
Abuse of a Disabled or Elder Adult	14-32.3	(1) The defendant is a caretaker of (2) (a) a disabled adult or (b) an elder adult (3) who is residing in a domestic setting and (4) with malice, knowingly and willfully (5) (a) assaults the adult, (b) fails to provide medical care or hygienic care to the adult, or (c) confines or restrains the adult in a place or under a condition that is cruel or unsafe and (6) as a result the adult suffers mental or physical injury • If the mental or physical injury is serious, the crime is elevated from a Class H to a Class F felony
Neglect of a Disabled or Elder Adult	14-32.3(b)	(1) The defendant is a caretaker of (2) (a) a disabled adult or (b) an elder adult (3) who is residing in a domestic setting and (4) wantonly, recklessly, or with gross carelessness (5) (a) fails to provide medical or hygienic care to the adult or (b) confines or restrains the adult in a place or under a condition that is unsafe and (6) as a result, the adult suffers mental or physical injury • If the mental or physical injury is serious, the crime is elevated from a Class I to a Class G felony
Exploitation of a Disabled or Elder Adult through a Position of Trust or Business Relationship	14-112.2(b)	(1) The defendant (a) stands in a position of trust and confidence or (b) has a business relationship (2) with an elder or disabled adult and (3) knowingly (4) by deception or intimidation (5) obtains, uses, or endeavors to obtain or use an elder or disabled adult's funds, assets, or property (6) with the intent to (a) deprive temporarily or permanently the elder or disabled adult of the use, benefit, or possession of the funds, assets, or property or (b) benefit someone other than the elder or disabled adult
Exploitation of a Disabled or Elder Adult Lacking Capacity	14-112.2(c)	(1) The defendant knows or reasonably should know that (2) an elder or disabled adult lacks the capacity to consent and (3) obtains, uses, endeavors to obtain or use, or conspires with another to obtain or use an elder or disabled adult's funds, assets, or property (4) with the intent to (a) deprive temporarily or permanently the elder or disabled adult of the use, benefit, or possession of the funds, assets, or property or (b) benefit someone other than the elder or disabled adult

RAPE AND OTHER SEX OFFENSES

CRIME	STATUTE (G.S.)	ELEMENTS
First-Degree Forcible Rape	14-27.21	(1) The defendant has vaginal intercourse (2) with a person (3) by force and (4) against that person's will and (5) the defendant (a) uses, threatens to use, or displays a dangerous or deadly weapon (or what reasonably appears to be a dangerous or deadly weapon), (b) inflicts serious personal injury on the victim, (c) inflicts serious personal injury on another person, or (d) is aided and abetted by one or more other persons
Second-Degree Forcible Rape	14-27.22	(1) The defendant has vaginal intercourse (2) with a person (3) and the intercourse is (a) by force and against the person's will or (b) with someone who is (i) mentally disabled, (ii) mentally incapacitated, or (iii) physically helpless and (4) the defendant knew or should have known that the victim was mentally disabled, mentally incapacitated, or physically helpless
First-Degree Forcible Sexual Offense	14-27.26	(1) The defendant engages in a sexual act other than vaginal intercourse (2) with a person (3) by force and (4) against that person's will and (5) the defendant (a) uses, threatens to use, or displays a dangerous or deadly weapon (or what reasonably appears to be a dangerous or deadly weapon), (b) inflicts serious personal injury on the victim, (c) inflicts serious personal injury on another person, or (d) is aided and abetted by one or more other persons
Second-Degree Forcible Sexual Offense	14-27.27	(1) The defendant engages in a sexual act other than vaginal intercourse (2) with a person and (3) the act is (a) by force and against the person's will or (b) with someone who is (i) mentally disabled, (ii) mentally incapacitated, or (iii) physically helpless and (4) the defendant knew or should have known that the victim was mentally disabled, mentally incapacitated, or physically helpless
Sexual Battery	14-27.33	(1) The defendant, for the purpose of sexual arousal, sexual gratification, or sexual abuse (2) engages in sexual contact with another person (3) (a) by force and against the will of the other person or (b) who is mentally disabled, mentally incapacitated, or physically helpless and the defendant knows or should reasonably know that the other person is mentally disabled, mentally incapacitated, or physically helpless
Crime Against Nature	14-177	(1) Commits a crime against nature • This crime requires penetration of, or by, a sexual organ, as illustrated by examples from case law

ASSAULTS*

CRIME	STATUTE (G.S.)	ELEMENTS
Assault with Deadly Weapon with Intent to Kill Inflicting Serious Injury	14-32(a)	(1) The defendant commits an assault (2) on another (3) with a deadly weapon and (4) with intent to kill and (5) inflicts serious injury
Assault with Deadly Weapon Inflicting Serious Injury	14-32(b)	(1) The defendant commits an assault (2) on another (3) with a deadly weapon and (4) inflicts serious injury
Assault with Deadly Weapon with Intent to Kill	14-32(c)	(1) The defendant commits an assault (2) on another (3) with a deadly weapon (4) with intent to kill
Assault Inflicting Serious Bodily Injury	14-32.4(a)	(1) The defendant commits an assault (2) on another and (3) inflicts serious bodily injury
Assault by Strangulation	14-32.4(b)	(1) The defendant commits an assault (2) on another and (3) inflicts physical injury (4) by strangulation
Simple Assault	14-33(a)	(1) The defendant commits an assault (2) on another
Assault Inflicting Serious Injury; Assault with Deadly Weapon	14-33(c)(1)	(1) The defendant commits an assault (2) on another and (3) inflicts serious injury
Assault with a Deadly Weapon	14-33(c)(1)	(1) The defendant commits an assault (2) on another (3) with a deadly weapon
Assault on Female	14-33(c)(2)	(1) The defendant is a male, (2) at least 18 years old, and (3) commits an assault (4) on a female
Habitual Misdemeanor Assault	14-33.2	(1) The defendant (a) (i) violates G.S. 14-33 and (ii) causes physical injury or (b) violates G.S. 14-34 and (2) has two or more prior felony or misdemeanor assault convictions and (3) the earlier of the convictions occurred no more than fifteen years before the date of the offense in Element (1)

* The term "assault" is defined by common law.

KIDNAPPING

CRIME	STATUTE (G.S.)	ELEMENTS
First-Degree Kidnapping	14-39	(1) The defendant (a) confines, (b) restrains, or (c) removes from one place to another (2) a person (3) (a) without the person's consent or, (b) if the person is under 16, without consent of the person's parent or guardian (4) for the purpose of (a) holding the victim as hostage, (b) holding the victim for ransom, (c) using the victim as a shield, (d) facilitating the commission of a felony, (e) facilitating flight following the commission of a felony, (f) doing serious bodily harm to the victim or any other person, (g) terrorizing the victim or any other person, (h) holding the victim in involuntary servitude, (i) trafficking another person, or (j) subjecting or maintaining the victim for sexual servitude and (5) (a) does not release the victim in a safe place, (b) seriously injures the victim, or (c) sexually assaults the victim
Second-Degree Kidnapping	14-39	Consists of elements (1) through (4) from First-Degree Kidnapping
False Imprisonment	Common law	(1) The defendant intentionally and unlawfully (2) (a) restrains or (b) detains (3) a person (4) without the person's consent
Felonious Restraint	14-43.3	(1) The defendant unlawfully restrains (2) a person (3) (a) without the person's consent or, (b) if the person is under 16, without consent of the person's parent or guardian and (4) transports the person by motor vehicle or other conveyance from the place of the initial restraint

BURGLARY AND OTHER HOUSEBREAKINGS

CRIME	STATUTE (G.S.)	ELEMENTS
First-Degree Burglary	14-51	(1) The defendant breaks and (2) enters (3) without consent (4) the dwelling house or sleeping apartment (5) of another (6) while it is actually occupied (7) at night (8) with the intent to commit any felony or larceny therein
Second-Degree Burglary	14-51	(1) The defendant breaks and (2) enters (3) without consent (4) the dwelling house or sleeping apartment, or any building within the curtilage of the dwelling, (5) of another (6) at night (7) with the intent to commit any felony or larceny therein
Breaking or Entering Building with Intent to Commit Felony or Larceny	14-54(a)	(1) The defendant breaks or (2) enters (3) without consent (4) any building (5) with the intent to commit any felony or larceny therein
Breaking or Entering Building with Intent to Terrorize or Injure Occupant	14-54(a1)	Consists of elements (1) through (4) of Breaking or Entering Building with Intent to Commit Felony or Larceny, plus (5) with the intent to terrorize or injure an occupant of the building
Misdemeanor Breaking or Entering	14-54(b)	(1) The defendant breaks or (2) enters (3) without consent (4) any building
Break or Enter Motor Vehicle with Intent to Commit Felony or Larceny	14-56	(1) The defendant breaks or (2) enters (3) without consent (4) any railroad car, motor vehicle, trailer, aircraft, boat, or other watercraft (5) containing goods, wares, freight, or anything of value (6) with the intent to commit any felony or larceny therein

LARCENY AND ROBBERY

CRIME	STATUTE (G.S.)	ELEMENTS
Felony Larceny	14-72	(1) The defendant takes (2) personal property (3) in the possession of another and (4) carries it away (5) without the consent of the possessor and (6) with the intent to deprive the possessor of its use permanently, (7) knowing that he or she was not entitled to it and (8) the larceny was (a) of property worth more than $1,000; (b) from the person; (c) committed pursuant to burglary, breaking out of a dwelling, breaking or entering a building, breaking or entering a building that is a place of religious worship, or burglary with explosives; (d) of an explosive or incendiary device; (e) of a firearm; (f) of a record or paper in the custody of the N.C. State Archives; or (g) of a horse, mule, swine, cattle, or dog
Misdemeanor Larceny	14-72	(1) The defendant takes (2) personal property (3) in the possession of another and (4) carries it away (5) without the consent of the possessor and (6) with the intent to deprive the possessor of its use permanently, (7) knowing that he or she was not entitled to it
Larceny, Concealment, or Destruction of Wills	14-77	"If any person, either during the life of the testator or after his death, shall steal or, for any fraudulent purpose, shall destroy or conceal any will, codicil or other testamentary instrument, he shall be guilty of a Class 1 misdemeanor."
Robbery with a Dangerous Weapon	14-87	(1) The defendant commits or attempts to commit larceny (2) from the person or from the person's presence (3) by the possession, use, or threatened use of a firearm or other dangerous weapon (4) that endangers or threatens the life of a person
Common Law Robbery	Common law; *see* 14-87.1	(1) The defendant commits larceny (2) from the person or from the person's presence (3) by violence or intimidation
Extortion	14-118.4	(1) The defendant threatens or communicates a threat to another (2) with the intent to obtain wrongfully (3) anything of value, any acquittance, any advantage, or any immunity

OTHER FINANCIAL AND RELATED CRIMES

CRIME	STATUTE (G.S.)	ELEMENTS
Embezzlement by an Agent or Fiduciary	14-90	(1) The defendant fraudulently or knowingly and willingly (2) uses for a purpose other than that for which the defendant received it (3) the property of another (4) held by the defendant under his or her care • Applies to fiduciaries, including a guardian, administrator, executor, trustee, or any receiver • Requires that the property be entrusted to the defendant; if no entrustment, the taking is larceny or obtaining property by false pretenses
Obtain Property by False Pretenses	14-100	(1) The defendant makes a representation about a past or existing fact or a future event (2) that is false and (3) is calculated and intended to deceive, and (4) the representation does in fact deceive another person, and (5) the person thereby obtains, or attempts to obtain, money, goods, property, services, choses in action, or any other thing of value from that other person
Theft of Financial Transaction Card	14-113.9 (a)(1)	(1) The defendant (a) takes, (b) obtains, or (c) withholds (2) a financial transaction card (3) from another (4) without the cardholder's consent and (5) with the intent to use it
Forgery of Financial Transaction Card	14-113.11	(1) The defendant (a) falsely makes or embosses a purported financial transaction card or utters a falsely-made or falsely-embossed financial transaction card; (b) falsely encodes, duplicates, or alters existing encoded information on a financial transaction card or utters a falsely-encoded, -duplicated, or -altered card; or (c) not being the cardholder or a person authorized by the cardholder, signs a financial transaction card (2) with the intent to defraud
Financial Transaction Card Fraud	14-113.13	(1) The defendant, with the intent to defraud, (2) uses a financial transaction card (3) (a) obtained or retained, or received with knowledge that it was obtained or retained, in violation of 14-113.9 or 14-113.11; (b) that he or she knows is forged, expired, revoked, or altered; or (c) that he or she knows was obtained by a fraudulent application in violation of 14-113.13(c) (4) for the purpose of obtaining money, goods, services, or anything else of value

OTHER FINANCIAL AND RELATED CRIMES, *cont'd*

CRIME	STATUTE (G.S.)	ELEMENTS
Financial Identity Theft	14-113.20	(1) The defendant knowingly (2) (a) obtains, (b) possesses, or (c) uses (3) identifying information of another person, living or dead, (4) with the intent to fraudulently represent the person is the other person (5) for the purpose of (a) making financial or credit transactions in the other person's name; (b) avoiding legal consequences; or (c) obtaining anything of value, benefit, or advantage
Common Law Forgery	*See* 14-119, -120	Common law elements: (1) The defendant makes a false writing (2) that is apparently capable of effecting a fraud (3) with the intent to defraud
Common Law Uttering	See 14-120	Common law elements: (1) The defendant utters as true (2) a false writing (3) that is apparently capable of effecting a fraud (4) with the intent to defraud and (5) knowing that the writing is false
Forgery and Counterfeiting of Instruments	14-119	(1) The defendant (a) forges or (b) counterfeits (2) an instrument (3) with the intent to injure or defraud (4) a person, financial institution, or governmental unit
Uttering Forged Instruments	14-120	(1) The defendant utters, publishes, passes, delivers, or attempts to pass or deliver (2) an instrument (3) (a) that is false, forged, or counterfeit or (b) that contains a false, forged, or counterfeit endorsement (4) (a) for the sake of gain or (b) with the intent to defraud or injure another and (5) knowing that (a) it was falsely forged or counterfeited or (b) falsely endorsed
Forging an Endorsement on Checks and Securities	14-120	(1) The defendant falsely makes, forges, or counterfeits (2) an endorsement (3) on an instrument (4) (a) for the sake of gain or (b) with the intent to defraud or injure another

MISCELLANEOUS

CRIME	STATUTE (G.S.)	ELEMENTS
Communicating Threats	14-277.1	(1) The defendant, without lawful authority, (a) willfully threatens to physically injure (i) another person or (ii) that person's child, sibling, spouse, or dependent or (b) willfully threatens to damage another's property and (2) communicates that threat to the other person (3) in a manner that would make a reasonable person believe it is likely to be carried out and (4) the threat is believed by the threatened person
Using Threatening Language on the Telephone	14-196(a)(2)	(1) The defendant, in a telephonic communication, (2) uses words or language (3) (a) threatening to inflict bodily harm to any person, (b) threatening physical injury to another's property, or (c) for the purpose of extorting something of value from another
Repeated Telephone Calls to Harass, etc.	14-196(a)(3)	(1) The defendant telephones (2) another (3) repeatedly (4) for the purpose of (a) abusing, (b) annoying, (c) threatening, (d) terrifying, (e) harassing, or (f) embarrassing (5) a person at the called number
Using Electronic Mail or Communication to Threaten or Extort	14-196(b)(1)	(1) The defendant uses, in (a) electronic mail or (b) electronic communication, (2) words or language (3) (a) threatening to inflict bodily harm to any person, (b) threatening physical injury to the property of another, or (c) for the purpose of extorting money or other things of value from any person

MISCELLANEOUS, *cont'd*

CRIME	STATUTE (G.S.)	ELEMENTS
Stalking	14-277.3A	(1) The defendant, willfully and (2) without legal purpose, (3) (a) harasses another person on more than one occasion or (b) engages in a course of conduct directed at a specific person (4) when the defendant knows or should know that the harassment or course of conduct would cause a reasonable person to (a) fear for the safety of (i) him or herself, (ii) his or her immediate family, or (iii) his or her close personal associates or (b) suffer substantial emotional distress by placing that person in fear of (i) death, (ii) bodily injury, or (iii) continued harassment • This constitutes a misdemeanor • A repeat offense is punishable as a felony
Interfering with Emergency Communication	14-286.2	(1) The defendant (a) intentionally interferes (i) with an emergency communication, (ii) knowing that the communication is an emergency communication, and (iii) while not making an emergency communication himself or herself and (b) interferes (i) with a communication instrument or other emergency equipment (ii) with the intent to prevent an emergency communication
Violation of a Domestic Violence Protective Order	50B-4.1	(1) The defendant knowingly (2) violates a valid protective order entered pursuant to (a) Chapter 50B of the General Statutes, (b) a court of another state, or (c) a court of an Indian tribe • This constitutes a misdemeanor • A repeat offense is punishable as a felony

Note: The list of crimes in this appendix is from the *Alamance County Elder A/N/E Legal Resources and Remedies Booklet*. The elements are from Jessica Smith, *North Carolina Crimes: A Guidebook on the Elements of Crime* (7th ed. 2012).

Volkswagen EuroVan

Repair Manual
1992, 1993, 1994, 1995, 1996, 1997, 1998, 1999

Gasoline, Diesel, TDI, 5-cylinder and VR6, including MultiVan and CV Camper

Volkswagen EuroVan

Repair Manual
1992, 1993, 1994, 1995, 1996, 1997, 1998, 1999

Gasoline, Diesel, TDI, 5-cylinder and VR6, including MultiVan and CV Camper

[B] BentleyPublishers®
.com

BENTLEY PUBLISHERS® | Automotive Reference™

Bentley Publishers, a division of Robert Bentley, Inc.
1734 Massachusetts Avenue
Cambridge, MA 02138 USA
800-423-4595 / 617-547-4170

Information that makes the difference®

BentleyPublishers®.com

Technical contact information

We welcome your feedback. Please submit corrections and additions to our Volkswagen technical discussion forum at:

`http://www.BentleyPublishers.com`

Updates and Corrections

We will evaluate submissions and post appropriate editorial changes online as updates or tech discussion. Appropriate updates and corrections will be added to the book in future printings. Check for updates and corrections for this book before beginning work on your vehicle. See the following web address for additional information:

`http://www.BentleyPublishers.com/updates/`

WARNING—Important Safety Notice

Do not use this manual unless you are familiar with automotive repair procedures and safe workshop practices. This manual illustrates workshop procedures required for service work; it is not a substitute for full and up-to-date information from the vehicle manufacturer or for proper training as an automotive technician. Note that it is not possible for us to anticipate all of the ways or conditions under which vehicles may be serviced or to provide cautions as to all of the possible hazards that may result.

We have endeavored to ensure the accuracy of the information in this manual. Please note, however, that considering the vast quantity and the complexity of the service information involved, we cannot warrant the accuracy or completeness of the information contained in this manual.

FOR THESE REASONS, NEITHER THE PUBLISHER NOR THE AUTHOR MAKES ANY WARRANTIES, EXPRESS OR IMPLIED, THAT THE INFORMATION IN THIS BOOK IS FREE OF ERRORS OR OMISSIONS AND WE EXPRESSLY DISCLAIM THE IMPLIED WARRANTIES OF MERCHANTABILITY AND OF FITNESS FOR A PARTICULAR PURPOSE, EVEN IF THE PUBLISHER OR AUTHOR HAVE BEEN ADVISED OF A PARTICULAR PURPOSE, AND EVEN IF A PARTICULAR PURPOSE IS INDICATED IN THE MANUAL. THE PUBLISHER AND AUTHOR ALSO DISCLAIM ALL LIABILITY FOR DIRECT, INDIRECT, INCIDENTAL OR CONSEQUENTIAL DAMAGES THAT RESULT FROM ANY USE OF THE EXAMPLES, INSTRUCTIONS OR OTHER INFORMATION IN THIS BOOK. IN NO EVENT SHALL OUR LIABILITY WHETHER IN TORT, CONTRACT OR OTHERWISE EXCEED THE COST OF THIS MANUAL.

Before attempting any work on your Volkswagen, read the **WARNINGS** and **CAUTIONS** on page vii and viii, and any **WARNING** and **CAUTION** that accompanies a procedure in the service manual. Review the **WARNINGS** and **CAUTIONS** on page vii and viii each time you prepare to work on your Volkswagen.

Your common sense and good judgment are crucial to safe and successful service work. Read procedures through before starting them. Think about whether the condition of your car, your level of mechanical skill, or your level of reading comprehension might result in or contribute in some way to an occurrence which might cause you injury, damage your car, or result in an unsafe repair. If you have doubts for these or other reasons about your ability to perform safe repair work on your car, have the work done at an authorized Volkswagen dealer or other qualified shop.

Part numbers listed in this manual are for identification purposes only, not for ordering. Always check with your authorized Volkswagen dealer to verify part numbers and availability before beginning service work that may require new parts.

Special tools required to perform certain service operations are identified in the manual and are recommended for use. Use of tools other than those recommended in this service manual may be detrimental to the car's safe operation as well as the safety of the person servicing the car.

The vehicle manufacturer will continue to issue service information updates and parts retrofits after the editorial closing of this manual. Some of these updates and retrofits will apply to procedures and specifications in this manual. We regret that we cannot supply updates to purchasers of this manual.

Copies of this manual may be purchased from authorized Volkswagen dealers, most automotive accessories and parts dealers specializing in Volkswagen automobiles, from selected booksellers, or directly from the publisher.

ISBN 978-0-8376-1681-0 (3-Volume Set)
ISBN 978-0-8376-1682-7 (Volume 1)
ISBN 978-0-8376-1683-4 (Volume 2)
ISBN 978-0-8376-1684-1 (Volume 3)

Bentley Stock No. VV99 **Job code: VV99-10** **VWoA, Inc. Part No. LPV 800 149**

Library of Congress Cataloging-in-Publication Data
Volkswagen EuroVan: official factory repair manual 1992,1993, 1994, 1995, 1996, 1997, 1998, 1999: gasoline, diesel, TDI, 5-cylinder, and VR6, including multivan and CV camper
p. cm.
ISBN 978-8376-0335-3 (alk. paper)
1. EuroVan van --Maintenance and repair--Handbooks, manuals, etc.
I. Robert Bentley, inc.
TL230.5.E92V55 1997
629.28'722--DC21 97-31787
CIP

Manufactured in the United States of America.

202510R003

Foreword

Service to Volkswagen owners is a top priority of the Volkswagen organization that has always included the continuing development and introduction of new and expanded services. In line with this purpose, Bentley Publishers in cooperation with Volkswagen of America, Inc. has introduced this Volkswagen Official Factory Repair Manual.

This Volkswagen EuroVan manual covers the model years 1992, 1993, 1994, 1995, 1996, 1997, 1998, and 1999. It includes Volkswagen EuroVan models equipped with gasoline and diesel engines. This manual was created specifically to cover only those models built for sale in the United States and Canada.

This manual has been prepared from the information that the Volkswagen organization provides to its own factory-trained technicians. It has been developed primarily with the Volkswagen dealership technician in mind. The aim throughout has been clarity and completeness, with step-by-step procedures and factory specifications.

For the automotive service professional, this manual includes the specifications and procedures that were available in an authorized Volkswagen dealer service department as this manual went to press. The Volkswagen owner who has no intention of working on his or her car will find that owning and referring to this manual will make it possible to be better informed and to more knowledgeably discuss repairs with a professional automotive service technician.

Disclaimer

We have endeavored to ensure the accuracy of the information in this manual. When the vast array of data presented in the manual is taken into account, however, no claim to infallibility can be made. We therefore cannot be responsible for the result of any errors that may have crept into the text. Please also read **WARNING–Important Safety Notice** on the copyright page.

Prior to starting a repair procedure, read the procedure, **Warnings and Cautions** on page vii and viii and the **warnings** and **cautions** that accompany the procedure. Reading a procedure before beginning work helps you determine in advance the need for specific skills, identify hazards, prepare for appropriate capture and handling of hazardous materials, and the need for particular tools and replacement parts such as gaskets.

For those intending to do maintenance and repair on their Eurovan, it is essential that safety equipment be used and safety precautions observed when working on your vehicle. A minimum safety equipment list includes hand protection, eye protection, and a fire extinguisher. A selection of good quality hand tools is also needed. This includes a torque wrench to ensure that fasteners are tightened in accordance with specifications.

Special tools that may be required for a particular repair procedure are usually identified by their Volkswagen special tool number and illustrated. A thorough review of each procedure is recommended to determine in advance the complexity of the repair work and the need for particular tools and replacement parts such as gaskets.

Some of the information in this manual applies only to cars of a particular model year or range of years. For example, "m.y. 1993" refers to the 1993 model year. The model year does not necessarily match the calender year in which the car was manufactured or sold. To be sure of the model year of a particular car, check the vehicle identification number (VIN) on the car. Technical changes made in production within a model year are identified in this manual by listing the VIN for the first car produced with this change.

The VIN is a unique sequence of 17 characters assigned by Volkswagen to identify each individual car. WV2MC0709PH016886 is an example. Each of the 17 letters and numbers indicates certain facts about the car and its manufacture. The characters in the 7th and 8th spaces are Volkswagen's model designation. The letter in the 10th space indicates model year. The last six digits are the unique sequential production number. References to VIN in this manual will often include only the last several characters, such as 709PH016886 or 70_P_016886 from the sample VIN above.

The Volkswagen VIN can be found on a plate mounted on the top of the instrument panel, on the driver's side where the number can be seen through the windshield, and on an identification label on the left door jamb. This manual covers Volkswagen EuroVan from model years 1992 through 1999, with these VINs:

position	1	2	3	4	5	6	7	8	9	10	11	12	13	14	15	16	17		1	2	3	4	5	6	7	8	9	10	11	12	13	14	15	16	17
1992:							7	0		N		0	0	0	0	0	1	to							7	0		N		9	9	9	9	9	9
1993:							7	0		P		0	0	0	0	0	1	to							7	0		P		9	9	9	9	9	9
1994:							7	0		R		0	0	0	0	0	1	to							7	0		V		9	9	9	9	9	9
1995:							7	0		S		0	0	0	0	0	1	to							7	0		S		9	9	9	9	9	9
1996:							7	0		T		0	0	0	0	0	1	to							7	0		T		9	9	9	9	9	9
1997:							7	0		V		0	0	0	0	0	1	to							7	0		V		9	9	9	9	9	9
1998:							7	0		W		0	0	0	0	0	1	to							7	0		W		9	9	9	9	9	9
1999:							7	0		X		0	0	0	0	0	1	to							7	0		X		9	9	9	9	9	9

Parts of this manual apply only to certain models or components. Notice especially that the Fuel Injection and Ignition, Engine, and Transmission Repair Group numbers are repeated, each Group covering a particular engine, fuel and ignition system, or transmission type. Most pages are clearly labeled to indicate the systems or components to which the information applies.

Bentley Publishers encourages comments from the readers of this manual with regard to errors, and/or suggestions for improvement of our product. These communications have been and will be carefully considered in the preparation of this and other manuals. If you identify inconsistencies in the manual, you may have found an error. Please contact the publisher and we will endeavor to post applicable corrections on our website. Posted updates and corrections should be reviewed before beginning work. Please see the following web address:

`http://www.BentleyPublishers.com/updates/`

Volkswagen continues to issue service information and parts retrofits after the editorial closing of this manual. Some of this updated information may apply to procedures and specifications in this manual. For the latest information, please see the following web address:

`http://www.ebahn.com/vw`

Volkswagen offers extensive warranties, especially on components of the fuel delivery and emission control systems. Before deciding to repair a car that may be covered wholly or in part by any warranties issued by Volkswagen of America, Inc., consult an authorized Volkswagen dealer. You may find that the dealer can make the repair either without charge or at minimal cost. Regardless of its age, or whether it is covered by warranty, a Volkswagen is an easy car to get serviced. If at any time a repair is too difficult, or requires special equipment that is not available, a trained Volkswagen dealer service technician is ready to do the job for you.

Bentley Publishers

Please read these WARNINGS and CAUTIONS before proceeding with maintenance and repair work.

WARNING—

• Some repairs may be beyond your capability. If you lack the skills, tools and equipment, or a suitable workplace for any procedure described in this manual, we suggest you leave such repairs to an authorized Volkswagen dealer service department, or other qualified shop.

• Volkswagen is constantly improving its cars. Sometimes these changes, both in parts and specifications, are made applicable to earlier models. Therefore, before starting any major jobs or repairs to components on which passenger safety may depend, consult an authorized Volkswagen dealer about Technical Bulletins that may have been issued since the editorial closing of this manual.

• Do not re-use any fasteners that are worn or deformed in normal use. Some fasteners are designed to be used only once, and are unreliable and may fail if used a second time. This includes, but is not limited to, nuts, bolts, washers, circlip and cotter pins. Always replace these fasteners with new parts.

• Never work under a lifted car unless it is solidly supported on stands designed for the purpose. Do not support a car on cinder blocks, hollow tiles or other props that may crumble under continuous load. Never work under a car that is supported solely by a jack. Never work under the car while the engine is running.

• If you are going to work under a car on the ground, make sure that the ground is level. Block the wheels to keep the car from rolling. Disconnect the battery negative terminal (ground strap) to prevent others from starting the car while you are under it.

• Never run the engine unless the work area is well ventilated. Carbon monoxide (CO) kills.

• Do not attempt to work on a vehicle if you do not feel well. You increase the danger of injury to yourself and others if you are tired, upset or have taken medication or any other substance that may impair you or keep you from being fully alert.

• Disconnect the battery negative (–) terminal (ground strap) whenever you work on the fuel system or the electrical system. Do not smoke or work near heaters or other fire hazards. Keep an approved fire extinguisher handy.

• Batteries produce explosive hydrogen gas. Keep sparks, lighted matches and open flame away from the top of the battery. If hydrogen gas escaping from the cap vents is ignited, it will ignite gas trapped in the cells and cause the battery to explode.

• Connect and disconnect battery cables, jumper cables or a battery charger only with the ignition switched off, to prevent sparks. Do not quick-charge the battery (for boost starting) for longer than one minute and do not allow charging voltage to exceed 16.5 volts. Wait at least one minute before boosting the battery a second time.

• Illuminate your work area adequately but safely. Use a portable safety light for working inside or under the car. Make sure the bulb is enclosed by a wire cage. The hot filament of an accidentally broken bulb can ignite spilled fuel or oil.

• Tie long hair behind your head. Do not wear a necktie, a scarf, loose clothing, or a necklace when you work near machine tools or running engines. If hair, clothing, or jewelry were to get caught in the machinery, severe injury could result.

• Finger rings, bracelets and other jewelry should be removed so that they cannot cause electrical shorts, get caught in running machinery, or be crushed by heavy parts.

• Catch draining fuel, oil, or brake fluid in suitable containers. Do not use food or beverage containers that might mislead someone into drinking from them. Store flammable fluids away from fire hazards. Wipe up spills at once, but do not store the oily rags, which can ignite and burn spontaneously.

• Always observe good workshop practices. Wear goggles when you operate machine tools or work with battery acid. Gloves or other protective clothing should be worn whenever the job requires working with harmful substances.

• The Air-Conditioning (A/C) system is filled with chemical refrigerant, which is hazardous. The A/C system should be serviced only by trained technicians using approved refrigerant recovery/recycling equipment, trained in related safety precautions, and familiar with regulations governing the discharging and disposal of automotive chemical refrigerants.

• Do not expose any part of the A/C system to high temperatures such as open flame. Excessive heat will increase system pressure and may cause the system to burst.

• Some aerosol tire inflators are highly flammable. Be extremely cautious when repairing a tire that may have been inflated using an aerosol tire inflator. Keep sparks, open flame or other sources of ignition away from the tire repair area. Inflate and deflate the tire at least four times before breaking the bead from the rim. Completely remove the tire from the rim before attempting any repair.

• Friction materials such as brake or clutch discs may contain asbestos fibers. Do not create dust by grinding, sanding, or by cleaning with compressed air. Avoid breathing asbestos fibers and asbestos dust. Breathing asbestos can cause serious diseases such as asbestosis or cancer, and may result in death.

• Greases, lubricants and other automotive chemicals contain toxic substances, many of which are absorbed directly through the skin. Read manufacturer's instructions and warnings carefully. Use hand and eye protection. Avoid direct skin contact.

• An airbag is an explosive device. Handled improperly or without adequate safeguards, it can be accidently activated and cause serious personal injury. To prevent personal injury or airbag system failure, **only trained Volkswagen dealer service technicians** should test, disassemble or service airbag system.

WARNINGS and CAUTIONS continued on next page ▶

Please read these WARNINGS and CAUTIONS before proceeding with maintenance and repair work.

WARNING (continued) —

• ALWAYS disconnect the power supply before working on the airbag system, or when doing repairs that require removing airbag system components. Disconnect the battery negative (–) terminal and cover the battery.

• The airbag unit should not be removed, nor should any work be performed on the airbag system, without first reviewing the warnings and cautions that accompany the airbag system repair information in this manual.

• Never apply stickers or any other coverings on the steering wheel. Do not let chemical cleaners, oil or grease come into contact with vinyl covering of the airbag unit.

• Never open or otherwise attempt to repair airbag system parts. Always use new parts. Never leave airbag parts or the partially disassembled airbag system unattended.

• Never use a test light or volt meter to conduct electrical tests on the airbag system. The airbag system must only be tested by trained Volkswagen Service technicians using special airbag tester equipment. The airbag system must only be tested while it is installed in the car.

• Do not expose an airbag unit to temperatures above 194°F (90°C), even for a brief period, while handling it during the repair process. Keep the unit clear of heat sources such as hot plates, soldering irons, heat lamps, welding equipment, or the like.

• Always replace airbag system components that have been mechanically damaged (bubbles, cracks, etc.).

• Always set down a removed airbag unit so that the horn pad is facing upward.

• The storage, transportation and disposal of airbag units are subject to the laws for flammable solids.

• When driving or riding in an airbag-equipped vehicle, never hold test equipment in your hands or lap while the vehicle is in motion. Objects between you and the airbag can increase the risk of injury in an accident.

CAUTION—

• If you lack the skills, tools and equipment, or a suitable workshop for any procedure described in this manual, we suggest you leave such repairs to an authorized Volkswagen dealer or other qualified shop. We especially urge you to consult an authorized Volkswagen dealer before beginning repairs on any car that may still be covered wholly or in part by any of the extensive warranties issued by Volkswagen of America, Inc.

• Volkswagen is constantly improving its cars and sometimes these changes, both in parts and specifications, are made applicable to earlier models. Therefore part numbers in this manual are listed for reference only. Always check with an authorized Volkswagen dealer parts department for the latest information.

• Before starting a job, make certain that you have all the necessary tools and parts on hand. Read all the instructions thoroughly, do not attempt shortcuts. Use tools that are appropriate to the work and use only replacement parts meeting Volkswagen specifications. Makeshift tools, parts and procedures will not make good repairs.

• Use pneumatic and electric tools only to loosen threaded parts and fasteners. Never use these tools to tighten fasteners, especially on light alloy parts. Always use a torque wrench to tighten fasteners to the tightening torque specification listed.

• Be mindful of the environment and ecology. Before you drain the crankcase, find out the proper way to dispose of the oil. Do not pour oil onto the ground, down a drain, or into a stream, pond or lake. Consult local ordinances that govern the disposal of wastes.

• When connecting cables or ground straps, all connections must be cleaned to bare metal. Be sure mounting bolts are tight.

• Do not replace fuse links with fuse links of other gauge or with standard wire. Always replace the entire length of the fuse link.

• Before doing any electrical welding on vehicles equipped with Anti-lock Brakes (ABS), disconnect the battery negative terminal (ground strap) and the ABS Control Module connector.

• On cars equipped with ABS, the ABS control unit cannot withstand temperatures from a paint-drying booth or a heat lamp in excess of 203°F (95°C) and should not be subjected to temperatures in excess of 185°F (85°C) for more than two hours.

• On cars equipped with anti-theft radios, make sure you know the correct radio activation code before disconnecting the battery or removing the radio. If the wrong code is entered into the radio when power is restored, that radio may lock up and be rendered inoperable, even if the correct code is then entered.

• When boost-charging the battery, first remove the fuses for the Engine Control Module (ECM), the Transmission Control Module (TCM), the ABS Control Module, and the On-Board computer. In cases where one or more of these components is not separately fused, disconnect the Control Module connector(s).

• Do not quick-charge the battery (for boost starting) for longer than one minute. Wait at least one minute before boosting the battery a second time.

◀ **WARNINGS and CAUTIONS continued from previous page**

You are now in ▶ Volume 1

Maintenance

Section

A

WARNING!
Before proceeding with any work, please read the warnings and cautions immediately following this index. Also read any warning and caution that accompanies a procedure in the manual.

Page

Maintenance **Page**

Please read these WARNINGS and CAUTIONS before proceeding with maintenance and repair work.

WARNING—

- Some repairs may be beyond your capability. If you lack the skills, tools and equipment, or a suitable workplace for any procedure described in this manual, we suggest you leave such repairs to an authorized Volkswagen dealer service department, or other qualified shop.

- Volkswagen is constantly improving its cars. Sometimes these changes, both in parts and specifications, are made applicable to earlier models. Therefore, before starting any major jobs or repairs to components on which passenger safety may depend, consult your authorized Volkswagen dealer about the Technical Bulletins that may have been issued since the editorial closing of this manual.

- Do not re-use any fasteners that are worn or deformed in normal use. Many fasteners are designed to be used only once and become unreliable and may fail when used a second time. This includes, but is not limited to, nuts, bolts, washers, self–locking nuts or bolts, circlips and cotter pins. Always replace these fasteners with new parts.

- Never work under a lifted car unless it is solidly supported on stands designed for the purpose. Do not support a car on cinder blocks, hollow tiles or other props that may crumble under continuous load. Never work under a vehicle that is supported solely by a jack. Never work under the car while the engine is running.

- If you are going to work under a car on the ground, make sure that the ground is level. Block the wheels to keep the car from rolling. Disconnect the battery negative terminal (ground strap) to prevent others from starting the vehicle while you are under it.

- Never run the engine unless the work area is well ventilated. Carbon monoxide (CO) kills.

- Do not attempt to work on your vehicle if you do not feel well. You increase the danger of injury to yourself and others if you are tired, upset or have taken medicine or any other substance that may impair you or keep you from being fully alert.

- Disconnect the battery negative (–) terminal (ground strap) whenever you work on the fuel system or the electrical system. Do not smoke or work near heaters or other fire hazards. Keep an approved fire extinguisher handy.

- Batteries produce explosive hydrogen gas. Keep sparks, lighted matches and open flame away from the top of the battery. If hydrogen gas escaping from the cap vents is ignited, it will ignite gas trapped in the cells and cause the battery to explode.

- Connect and disconnect battery cables, jumper cables or a battery charger only with the ignition switched off, to prevent sparks. Do not quick–charge the battery (for boost starting) for longer than one minute, and do not allow charging voltage to exceed 16.5 volts. Wait at least one minute before boosting the battery a second time.

- Illuminate your work area adequately but safely. Use a portable safety light for working inside or under the car. Make sure the bulb is enclosed by a wire cage. The hot filament of an accidentally broken bulb can ignite spilled fuel or oil.

- Tie long hair behind your head. Do not wear a necktie, a scarf, loose clothing, or a necklace when you work near machine tools or running engines. If your hair, clothing, or jewelry were to get caught in the machinery, severe injury could result.

- Finger rings, bracelets and other jewelry should be removed so that they cannot cause electrical shorts, get caught in running machinery, or be crushed by heavy parts.

- Catch draining fuel, oil, or brake fluid in suitable containers. Do not use food or beverage containers that might mislead someone into drinking from them. Store flammable fluids away from fire hazards. Wipe up spills at once, but do not store the oily rags, which can ignite and burn spontaneously.

- Always observe good workshop practices. Wear goggles when you operate machine tools or work with battery acid. Gloves or other protective clothing should be worn whenever the job requires working with harmful substances.

- The Air-Conditioning (A/C) system is filled with a chemical refrigerant, which is hazardous. The A/C system should be serviced only by trained technicians using approved refrigerant recovery/recycling equipment, trained in related safety precautions, and familiar with regulations governing the discharging and disposal of automotive chemical refrigerants.

- Do not expose any part of the A/C system to high temperatures such as an open flame. Excessive heat will increase system pressure and may cause the system to burst.

- Some aerosol tire inflators are highly flammable. Be extremely cautious when repairing a tire that may have been inflated using an aerosol tire inflator. Keep sparks, open flame or other sources of ignition away from the tire repair area. Inflate and deflate the tire at least four times before breaking the bead from the rim. Completely remove the tire from the rim before attempting any repair.

- Friction materials such as brake or clutch discs may contain asbestos fibers. Do not create dust by grinding, sanding, or by cleaning with compressed air. Avoid breathing asbestos fibers and asbestos dust. Breathing asbestos can cause serious diseases such as asbestosis or cancer, and may result in death.

- Greases, lubricants and other automotive chemicals contain toxic substances, many of which are absorbed directly through the skin. Read manufacturer's instructions and warnings carefully. Use hand and eye protection. Avoid direct skin contact.

- An airbag is operated by an explosive device. Handled improperly or without adequate safeguards, it can be accidently activated and cause serious personal injury. To prevent personal injury or airbag system failure, **only trained Volkswagen dealer service technicians** should test, disassemble or service the airbag system.

WARNINGS and CAUTIONS continued on next page ▶

Please read these WARNINGS and CAUTIONS before proceeding with maintenance and repair work.

WARNING (continued) —

- ALWAYS disconnect the airbag power supply before using a computer memory saver. Failure to disconnect the airbag power supply may result in accidental activation of the airbag.
- The airbag unit should not be removed, nor should any work be performed on the airbag system, without first reviewing the warnings and cautions that accompany the airbag system repair information in this manual.
- Never apply stickers or any other coverings on the steering wheel. Do not let chemical cleaners, oil or grease come into contact with the vinyl covering of the airbag unit.
- Never open or otherwise attempt to repair airbag system parts. Always use new parts. Never leave airbag parts or the partially disassembled airbag system unattended.
- Never use a test light or volt meter to conduct electrical tests on the airbag system. The airbag system must only be tested by trained Volkswagen Service technicians using special airbag tester equipment. The airbag system must only be tested while it is installed in the car.
- Do not expose an airbag unit to temperatures above 194°F (90°C) even for a brief period, while handling it during the repair process. Keep the unit clear of heat sources such as hot plates, soldering irons, heat lamps, welding equipment, or the like.
- Always replace airbag system components that have been mechanically damaged (bubbles, cracks, etc.).
- Always set down a removed airbag unit so that the horn pad is facing upward.
- When driving or riding in an airbag-equipped vehicle, never hold test equipment in your hands or lap while the vehicle is in motion. Objects between you and the airbag can increase the risk of injury in an accident.
- The storage, transportation and disposal of airbag units are subject to the laws for flammable solids.

CAUTION—

- If you lack the skills, tools and equipment, or a suitable workshop for any procedure described in this manual, we suggest you leave such repairs to an authorized Volkswagen dealer or other qualified shop. We especially urge you to consult an authorized Volkswagen dealer before beginning repairs on any car that may still be covered wholly or in part by any of the extensive warranties issued by Volkswagen of America, Inc.
- Volkswagen is constantly improving its cars and sometimes these changes, both in parts and specifications, are made applicable to earlier models. Therefore, part numbers listed in this manual are for reference only. Always check with your authorized Volkswagen dealer parts department for the latest information.
- Before starting a job, make certain that you have all the necessary tools and parts on hand. Read all the instructions thoroughly, do not attempt shortcuts. Use tools that are appropriate to the work and use only replacement parts meeting Volkswagen specifications. Makeshift tools, parts and procedures will not make good repairs.
- Use pneumatic and electric tools only to loosen threaded parts and fasteners. Never use these tools to tighten fasteners, especially on light alloy parts. Always use a torque wrench to tighten fasteners to the tightening torque specification listed.
- Be mindful of the environment and ecology. Before you drain the crankcase, find out the proper way to dispose of the oil. Do not pour oil onto the ground, down a drain, or into a stream, pond, or lake. Consult local ordinances that govern the disposal of wastes.
- When connecting cables or ground straps, all connections must be cleaned to bare metal. Be sure mounting bolts are tight.
- Do not replace fuse links with fuse links of other gauge or with standard wire. Always replace the entire length of the fuse link.
- Before doing any electrical welding on vehicles equipped with Anti-lock Brakes (ABS), disconnect the battery negative terminal (ground strap) and the ABS Control Module connector.
- On cars equipped with ABS, the ABS control unit cannot withstand temperatures from a paint–drying booth or a heat lamp in excess of 203°F (95°C) and should not be subjected to temperatures in excess of 185°F (85°C) for more than two hours.
- On cars equipped with anti-theft radios, make sure you know the correct radio activation code before disconnecting the battery or removing the radio. If the wrong code is entered when power is restored, the radio may lock up and be rendered inoperable, even if the correct code is then entered.
- When boost-charging the battery, first remove the fuses for the Engine Control Module (ECM), the Transmission Control Module (TCM), the ABS Control Module, and the On-Board computer. In cases where one or more of these components is not separately fused, disconnect the Control Module connector(s).
- Do not quick-charge the battery (for boost starting) for longer than one minute, and do not exceed 16.5 volts at the battery with the boosting cables attached. Wait at least one minute before boosting the battery a second time.

◀ **WARNINGS and CAUTIONS continued from previous page**

Engine overview

Engine code		AAB	AAF	AES
Manufactured	from to	09.90	12.90	01.96
No. of cylinders		5	5	6
Displacement	liters	2.4	2.5	2.8
Output	kW at rpm (hp @ rpm)	57/3700 77/3700	81/4500 109/4500	103/4750 139/4750
Torque	Nm at rpm (ft lb @ rpm)	164/1800 ... 2200	190/2200	240/3200
Bore dia.	mm	79.5	81.0	81.0
Stroke	mm	95.5	95.5	90.3
Compression ratio		22.5	8.5	10.0
Exhaust turbocharger		–	–	–
Hydraulic valve lifters		X	X	X
Fuel injection		Diesel	Digifant	Motronic
RON	min.	–	91 unleaded[1)]	95 unleaded[1)]
CN	min.	45	–	–
Ignition system		–	Digifant	Motronic
Exhaust gas recirculation		–	–	X
On Board Diagnostic (OBD) with Diagnostic Trouble Code (DTC) Memory		–	X	X

Engine code	AAB	AAF	AES
Exhaust Emission control	–	Three way catalytic converter	Three way catalytic converter
Oxygen Sensor (O2S) control	–	X	X

[1)] RON of at least 91 can be used but performance is reduced.

Pre-delivery Inspection

Under hood checks – check, install, remove or adjust:	Page
– Check battery positive voltage (including additional battery); recharge if necessary (min. 12.5 volts)	A 85
– Battery cables: check tightness	–
– Engine oil level: fill if necessary	A 33
– Engine coolant level: fill if necessary	A 42
– Windshield washer fluid level: fill if necessary	–
– Power steering fluid level: fill if necessary	A 68
– Brake fluid level: fill if necessary	A 74

Exterior checks – check, install, remove or adjust:	Page
– Transportation wiper blades: replace with standard wiper blades (48 hours before delivery)	–
– Windshield washer jets	A 86
– Torque wheel bolts: re-torque if necessary	A 71
– Spare tire, spare tire pressure, tool kit; stow towing hook (if applicable)	
– Wheel covers	–
– All painted surfaces: check for imperfections, scratches, dents, transportation coatings and environmental damage	–
– All windows: check for chips and scratches	–
– All exterior lights: high-beam and low beam headlights, fog lights/driving lights, turn signals, luggage compartment, brake lights, taillights, back-up lights and emergency flashers	–
– Front license plate bracket (if required)	–

Interior checks – check, install, remove or adjust:	Page
– Transportation protective pieces: remove from interior and doors	–
– Fuses (as required)	A 84
– Safety belts and retractors: check for proper operation	–
– Clock: check operation and set to local time	A 91
– Radio and cassette player: check operation; pre-set radio buttons to local stations	–
– Radio anti-theft code: (LED must blink when ignition key is removed from ignition lock); attach radio sticker with serial number and code number to radio card	–
– Inventory maintenance sticker: attach to inside of windshield	–
– VAG 1551 Scan Tool: check Diagnostic Trouble Code (DTC) Memory and re-establish basic settings	A 44
– Readiness code: check (if readiness code is not set, establish during road test)	–
– Door locks and child safety locks: check for proper operation	–

On hoist checks – check, install, remove or adjust:	Page
– Engine and transmission: check for leaks and/or damage	A 39
– Axles, CV joint boots, suspension and steering: check for leaks and/or damage	–
– Brake system: check for leaks and/or damage	A 73
– Underbody: check for damage	A 79
– Tires: check condition and tire pressure	A 70
– Oval plugs (4) in tie-down openings (where applicable)	–

Road test – check and/or adjust:	Page
– Engine cold-start, idle and performance during warm-up	–
– Clutch operation	–
– Manual transmission operation	–
– Automatic transmission operation, including automatic shift lock and kickdown function	A 92
– Engine performance	–
– Steering: check steering wheel alignment; check for pulling	–
– Brake system including ABS and parking brake: check function; check for pulling, pulsating and squeaking	A 92
– Wheels and tires: check for proper balance	–
– Engine, transmission, steering, drive axles, wheel bearings and exhaust system: check for noises	–
– Wind noises, squeaks, rattles	–
– All electrical instruments, gauges and switches: check for proper function and illumination	–
– Horns	–
– Engine: check hot-start and idle performance	–

30 day inventory maintenance – US vehicles only

Exterior checks:	Page
– Windows, doors, trunk, hood and sunroof fully closed	–
– Body surfaces clean and free of environmental damage, scratches, etc.	–
– Engine compartment clean	–
– Tire inflation pressure correct (50 – 58 psi during inventory storage)	–
– Battery positive voltage (B+) minimum 12.5 volts; recharge if necessary[1]	A 85

[1] If battery is dead (disconnected or static charge less than 10 volts), VAG 1551 Scan Tool must be used to re-establish basic settings for the Engine Control Module (ECM) and, on vehicles with automatic transmission, Transmission Control Module (TCM).

Interior checks:	Page
– All accessories and lights switched OFF	–
– Interior surfaces clean and free of damage	–
– Verify that disposable floor mats are in place	–
– Attach next 30 day sticker to windshield	–

Road test:	Page
– Start engine, check idle and A/C operation	–
– Check automatic transmission shifting operation and shiftlock function	–
– Drive vehicle minimum one mile and apply brakes several times at approx. 20 mph (32 km/h) to clean brake rotors	–

Emissions/lubrication/vehicle maintenance

First 5,000 miles (8,000 kilometers)

Vehicles with gasoline engine produced from 01.96	Page
– Engine: change oil and replace oil filter	A 34

Every 7,500 miles (12,000 kilometers)[1]

Vehicles with gasoline or Diesel engine produced up to 12.95	Page
– Engine: change oil and replace oil filter	A 34
– Brake pads: check thickness	A 72
– Automatic shift lock: check operation including park/neutral position switch (automatic transmission)	–
– Wheels: rotate front to rear (adjust tire inflation pressures accordingly)	–

[1] See Owner's Maintenance book for time intervals

Every 10,000 miles (15,000 km)

Every 7,500 miles (12,000 km) – Vehicles with Diesel engine

Vehicles with gasoline engine or Diesel engine produced from 01.96	Page
– Engine: change oil and replace oil filter	A 34
– Water separator: drain water (Diesel engine)	A 38
– Brake pads: check pad thickness	A 72
– Brake system: check for damage and leaks; check brake fluid level	A 73
– Automatic shift lock: check operation including park/neutral switch (automatic transmission)	–
– Wheels: rotate front to rear (adjust tire pressures accordingly)	–
– Windshield washer: check fluid level, add if necessary	–

Every 15,000 miles (24,000 km)[1)]

Vehicles with gasoline or Diesel engine produced up to 12.95	Page
– Engine: change oil and replace oil filter	A 34
– Engine idle speed: check (gasoline engine)	–
– Water separator: drain water (Diesel engine)	A 38
– Battery: check electrolyte level, add if necessary	A 85
– Dust/pollen filter: replace	A 90
– Cooling system: check coolant level, add if necessary	A 42
– Automatic shift lock: check operation including park/neutral position switch	–
– Manual transmission: check for leaks	–
– Automatic transmission final drive: check fluid level, add if necessary	A 65
– Wheels: rotate front to rear	–
– Tires and spare: check condition and inflation pressure	A 70
– Brake system: check for damage and leaks; check brake pad thickness; check brake fluid level	A 73
– Drive axle shafts: check boots	–
– On Board Diagnostic system: check Diagnostic Trouble Code (DTC) Memory with VAG 1551 Scan Tool and erase if necessary	A 45

During road test:	Page
– Check kickdown, braking, steering, heating, ventilation, air conditioning, power accessories and electrical systems	

[1)] See Owner's Maintenance book for time intervals

Every 15,000 miles (24,000 km) continued[1)]

After road test:	Page
– Engine: check for leaks	A 39
– Automatic transmission: check ATF [2)]	A 57
– Power steering: check fluid level	A 68
– Exhaust system: check for damage and/or leaks	–
– On Board Diagnostic system: check Diagnostic Trouble Code (DTC) Memory with VAG 1551 Scan Tool and erase if necessary	A 44

[1)] See Owner's Maintenance book for time intervals

[2)] In the case of severe conditions such as extremely high temperatures, continuous mountain driving, trailer towing, predominantly stop-and-go traffic conditions, it is necessary to change the ATF every 30,000 miles (48,000 km).

Every 20,000 miles (30,000 km)

Vehicles with gasoline engine produced from 01.96	Page
– Engine: change oil and replace oil filter	A 34
– Water separator: drain water (Diesel engine)	A 38
– Battery: check electrolyte level, add if necessary	A 85
– Dust/pollen filter: replace (where applicable)	A 90
– Cooling system: check coolant level, add if necessary	A 42
– Automatic shift lock: check operation including park/neutral position switch	–
– Manual transmission: check fluid level, add if necessary; check for leaks	A 67
– Automatic transmission final drive: check fluid level, add if necessary	A 65
– Wheels: rotate front to rear	–
– Tires and spare: check condition and inflation pressures	A 70
– Brake system: check for damage and leaks; check brake pad thickness; check brake fluid level	A 72
– Drive axle shafts: check boots	–
– Door check straps: lubricate	A 79
– On Board Diagnostic system: check Diagnostic Trouble Code (DTC) Memory with VAG 1551 Scan Tool and erase if necessary	A 45
– Windshield washer: check fluid level, add if necessary	–

Every 20,000 miles (30,000 km) continued

During road test:	Page
– Check kickdown, braking, steering, heating, ventilation, air conditioning, power accessories and electrical systems	A 92

After road test:	Page
– Engine: check for leaks	A 39
– Power steering: check fluid level	A 68
– Exhaust system: check for damage and/or leaks	–
– On Board Diagnostic system: check Diagnostic Trouble Code (DTC) Memory with VAG 1551 Scan Tool and erase if necessary	A 45

Additionally every 30,000 miles (48,000 km)[1]

Vehicles with gasoline or Diesel produced up to 12.95	Page
– Air cleaner: replace filter element[2]	A 43
– V-belts: check tension and condition, adjust if necessary	–
– Fuel filter: replace (Diesel engine)	A 37
– Spark plugs: replace (gasoline engine)	–
– Engine idle speed: check and adjust if necessary (Diesel engine)	A 46
– Timing belt: check tension and condition, adjust if necessary (Diesel engine)	A 50
– Front axle: check dust seals of ball joints and tie rod ends, check tie rods	A 69

[1]See Owner's Maintenance book for time intervals
[2] Replace filter element at this mileage or at least every two years.

Additionally every 40,000 miles (60,000 km)

Vehicles with gasoline or Diesel engine produced from 01.96	Page
– Engine: change oil and replace oil filter	A 34
– Fuel filter: replace (Diesel engine)	A 37
– Battery: check electrolyte level, add if necessary	A 85
– Water separator: drain water (Diesel engine)	A 38
– Air cleaner: replace filter element[1]	A 43
– Cooling system: check coolant level and add if necessary	A 42
– Dust/pollen filter element: replace (where applicable)	A 90
– Timing belt: check tension and condition, adjust if necessary. Replace at 60,000 miles (96,000 km) (Diesel engine)	A 50
– V-belts: check tension and condition, adjust if necessary	–
– Ribbed belt: check condition at 60,000 miles (96,000 km)	A 47
– Spark plugs: replace (gasoline engine)	–
– Windshield washer: check fluid level, add if necessary	–
– Door check straps: lubricate	A 79
– Automatic shift lock: check operation including park/neutral position switch	–
– Manual transmission: check for leaks; check oil level, add if necessary	A 67
– Automatic transmission: check final drive oil level, add if necessary; check for leaks	A 65
– Wheels: rotate front to rear	–
– Tires/spare: check condition and inflation pressures	A 70
– Brake system: check for damage/leaks; check brake pad thickness; check brake fluid level	A 72

Vehicles with gasoline or Diesel engine produced from 01.96 (continued)	Page
– Brake system: replace brake fluid every two years regardless of mileage	A 76
– Drive axle shafts: check boots	–
– Front axle: check dust seals on ball joints, tie rod ends and check tie rods	A 69
– On Board Diagnostic system: check Diagnostic Trouble Code (DTC) Memory with VAG 1551 Scan Tool and erase if necessary	A 45

[1] Replace filter element at this mileage or every two years.

During road test:	Page
– Check kickdown, braking, steering, heating, ventilation, air conditioning, power accessories and electrical systems	A 92

After road test:	Page
– Engine: check for leaks	A 39
– Automatic transmission: replace ATF	A 63
– Power steering: check fluid level	A 68
– Exhaust system: check for damage and/or leaks	–
– On Board Diagnostic system: check Diagnostic Trouble Code (DTC) Memory with VAG 1551 Scan Tool and erase if necessary	A 45

Additionally every 60,000 miles (90,000 km)

Vehicles with gasoline or Diesel engine – all model years	Page
– Ribbed V-belt: check condition (vehicles with automatic belt tensioning); check condition and adjust if necessary (vehicles without automatic tensioning)	A 47

Every 2 years regardless of mileage (km)

Vehicles with gasoline or Diesel engine – all model years	Page
– Brake fluid: replace	A 76
– Air cleaner: replace air filter element – required at 30,000 miles (48,000 km) or 40,000 miles (60,000 km) depending on production date of vehicle	A 43

Vehicles with gasoline or Diesel engine – from 01.96	Page
– Airbag: check airbag system for function and damage (after initial inspections at 4 and 8 years)	A 80

At 4 years and 8 years regardless of mileage (km), and every 2 years thereafter

Vehicles with gasoline or Diesel engine – from 01.96	Page
– Airbag: check airbag system for function and damage	A 80

Emission and idling test

Gasoline engine

Note:

Before performing the emission and idling test, note the following:

- *Test and adjustment conditions, specifications and spark plugs ⇒ appropriate Repair Manual booklet.*
- *Malfunctions recognized when checking the Diagnostic Trouble Code (DTC) Memory must have been repaired.*
- *DTC Memory must be erased.*

> ***Warning!***
>
> ***Do not disconnect or connect the cables of the ignition system – also not HT cables – unless the ignition is switched OFF, in order to avoid injury to persons and/or damage to the ignition and fuel injection systems.***

The following operations should be performed in the order stated:

Visual inspection

– Make sure all components that influence exhaust (e.g. vacuum lines, crankcase ventilation, air cleaner, catalytic converter, oxygen sensor, restricted filler neck) are installed and connected, and that exhaust system is free of leaks.

Description of work according to engine codes:

AAF ⇒ page A 20

AES ⇒ page A 25

Engine code: AAF

Connecting test equipment

VAG 1551 Scan Tool must be connected.

Note:

Some vehicles have a TDC sender installed as standard. On these vehicles the ignition tester can be connected without removing the distributor cap even with the engine at operating temperature. Use adapter cable VAG 1367/9 or VAG 1767/4 to connect to TDC sender.

- Remove distributor cap from distributor.

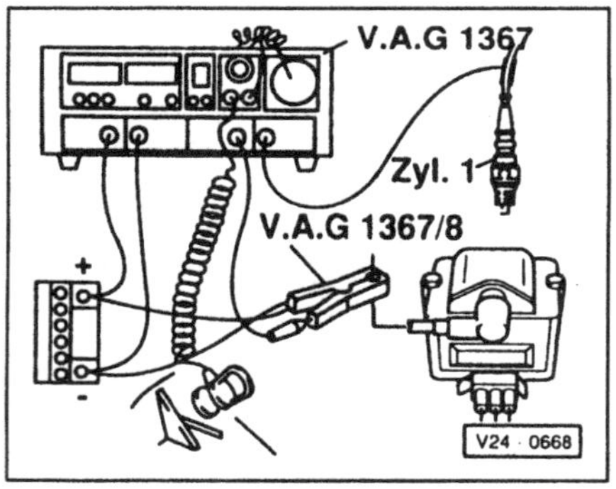

- Connect ignition tester VAG 1367 with HT pick-up VAG 1367/8 or ignition tester VAG 1767 with ignition switched off.
- Install distributor cap.
- Connect CO test unit VAG 1363 A or 4 gas emission tester VAG 1788 or equivalent to exhaust tail pipe.

Only for vehicles up to 12.92:

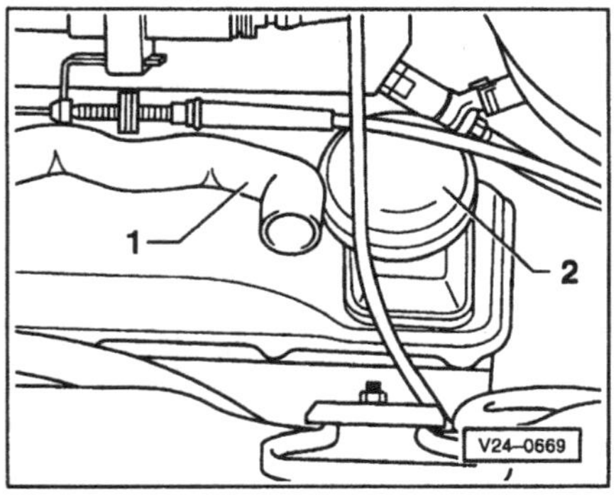

- Pull crankcase breather hose -1- off pressure regulating valve -2- and place so that only fresh air is drawn in.

Test sequence (for all vehicles)

– Start engine and run at idle speed.

Note:

If the engine stops, it is possible after restarting the engine will run at an increased idle speed for up to 4 minutes. Continue only when the rpm has reduced.

On VAG 1551:

– Press button -1- to select "Rapid data transfer" mode.

– Press buttons -0- and -1- for address word "Engine electronics" and confirm entry with -Q- button.

– Press → button.

– Press buttons -0- and -4- for function "Introduction of basic setting" and confirm entry with -Q- button.

Initiate basic setting	HELP
Enter display group number XX	

◄ Indicated on display:

– Press buttons -0- and -0- for enter "Display group number" and confirm entry with -Q- button.

System in basic setting									→
1	2	3	4	5	6	7	8	9	10

◄ Indicated on display:

The figures indicated in display are of no consequence for this test.

Function is unknown/or cannot be carried out at the moment.

◄ Indicated on display:

♦ Coolant temperature of at least 80° C (176°F) not reached.

♦ Idle speed over 1500 rpm.

or

♦ Function "Initiating basic setting" with VAG 1551 not possible.

Basic setting not possible:

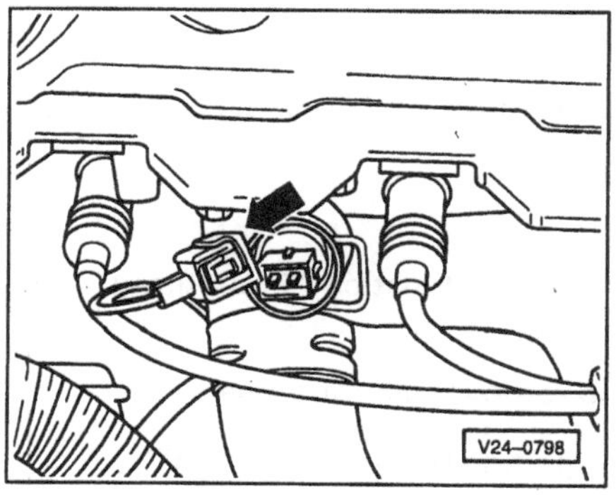

◄ – With throttle valve closed and after fan has run once, pull coolant temperature sensor connector (2-pin) off -arrow-.

Note:

If the engine stops, before restarting it reconnect the temperature sensor connector or the control module will begin an emergency program and a correct check/setting is not possible.

– Check ignition timing at 2000 – 2500 rpm, adjust timing if necessary by turning distributor.

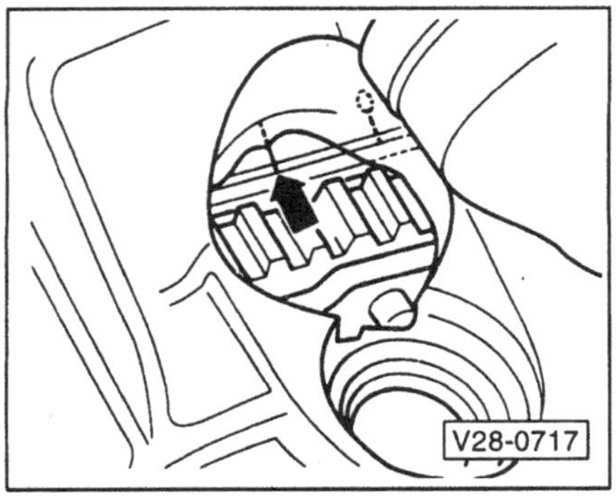

Notes:

- *With TDC sender the ignition timing is displayed direct on ignition tester.*
- *With strobe lamp the strobe must be directed at the ignition timing marks.*

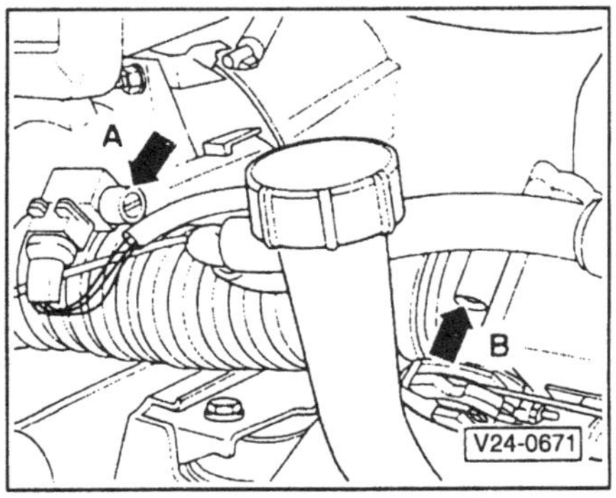

Only on vehicles up to 12.92:

– If necessary, adjust by alternately turning adjustment screws.

A - CO adjustment screw

B - Idling speed adjustment screw

If it is not possible to set CO content to relevant test values then perform repair measures.

– Seal CO adjustment screw with new anti-tamper plug.

– Install connector to coolant temperature sensor.

On VAG 1551 (for all vehicles):

– Press → button.

– Press buttons -0- and -2- for function "Read DTC Memory" and confirm entry with -Q- button.

– Press → button.

– Press buttons -0- and -5- for function "Erase DTC Memory" and confirm entry with -Q- button.

– Press → button.

– Press buttons -0- and -6- for the function "End output" and confirm entry with -Q- button.

– Allow engine to cool and remove distributor cap.

– Remove TDC sender for ignition tester 1367 or 1767.

– Install distributor cap.

After completing emissions test:

Note:

- *Operate assemblies e.g. power steering, automatic transmission, air conditioning system and check that the engine operates smoothly under these load conditions.*
- *Reconnect all hoses, connections that have been disconnected or separated for checking and adjusting purposes.*

Engine Code: AES

Required special tools

- VAG 1551 Scan Tool with harness VAG 1551/3

Note:

- *All test data and data for exhaust test: =>Repair Manual, General – Engine, Fuel Injection and Ignition.*
- *Idle speed, ignition timing point and CO content are not adjustable.*
- *Idle speed is controlled by the throttle kicker in connection with the DLS-Function for specified value.*
- *The CO–content is controlled by the Oxygen sensor system for specified value. Interferences to this system are obtained by the On Board Diagnostic and stored in the Diagnostic Trouble Code (DTC) Memory.*
- *When activating the DTC Memory recognized malfunctions must be eliminated (engine electronics) and the DTC Memory erased.*

Warning!

Do not disconnect or connect the cables of the ignition system – also not HT cables – unless the ignition is switched OFF, in order to avoid injury to persons and/or damage to the ignition and fuel injection systems.

Test sequence

– Start engine and let idle.

On VAG 1551:

– Push button -1- for operating mode "Rapid Data Transfer".

– Push buttons -0- and -1- for the code word "Engine Electronics" and input with -Q- button.

– Push –> button.

Rapid Data Transfer	HELP
Select Function XX	

Display shows:

– Push buttons -0- and -8- for the function "Read measuring value block" and input with -Q- button.

Read Measuring Value Block	HELP
Input display group number XX	

Display shows:

– Push button -0- and -1- for "Display Group Number" and input with -Q- button.

Read	Measuring	Value	block	1
→				
1	2	3		4

Display shows:
(1...4 = display fields)

Continue with the test, if the engine oil temperature is over 80°C (176°F) –display field 2.

– Increase engine RPM (fuel push) and then let engine idle another 2 minutes.

– Check idle RPM in display field 1.

– Check ignition timing point in display field 4.

– Push –> button.

– Push button -0- and -6- for the function "End data transfer" and input with -Q- button.

– Switch off ignition.

If the actual value deviates from the specified value: repair as necessary.

After ending the exhaust test:

Note:

- *Actuate auxiliary components, e.g. power steering, automatic transmission, air conditioning and check if the engine runs properly with this load.*
- *Reconnect all hoses and connectors which were removed or disconnected for testing and adjusting.*

Emission and idling test

Diesel engine

Testing idle speed, maximum engine speed (rpm) and exhaust for particulate.

Engine code: AAB

Oil capacity:	
With filter	5.5 Liters (5.8 qt)
Idle speed:	
Specified value	850 ± 50 rpm
Maximum RPM (no load)	4800 ±100 rpm
Start of injection, dynamic[1]	
Test value	11.5 – 13.5°
Adjustment value	12.5 ± .02°

[1] with VAG 1543, impulse clamp before inlet injector cylinder 1

Start of injection, static (with dial indicator)	
Test value	0.93 – 1.07 mm stroke
Adjustment value	1.00 ± 0.02 mm stroke
Exhaust test for particle percentage:	
Opaqueness value	10% maximum

Note:

- *Tests should be performed following a road test and in the open if possible.*
- *To minimize the noise level, close the hood to the first detent during the measurement.*
- *Engine speed can be measured with VAG 1500 or with VAG 1367 ignition tester via the TDC sensor.*

Visual check

- Make sure all components that influence the exhaust are installed and connected, and that the exhaust system is free of leaks.

Test sequence

Do not place the combustion tester probe into the exhaust pipe for idle speed and RPM test or adjustment procedures.

Test and adjustment requirements

Idle speed and maximum RPM:

- ♦ Engine oil temperature 60°C (140°F) minimum
- ♦ Cold start accelerator knob pushed fully in
- ♦ Electrical consumers switched off

Start of program (feed):

- ♦ Engine oil temperature 60°C (140°F) minimum

- ♦ Belt tension OK
- ♦ Idle RPM OK

Exhaust check for particle percentage:

- ♦ Engine oil temperature 80°C (176°F) minimum
- ♦ Cold start accelerator knob pushed fully in
- ♦ VAG 1500 or equivalent combustion tester connected according to operating instructions

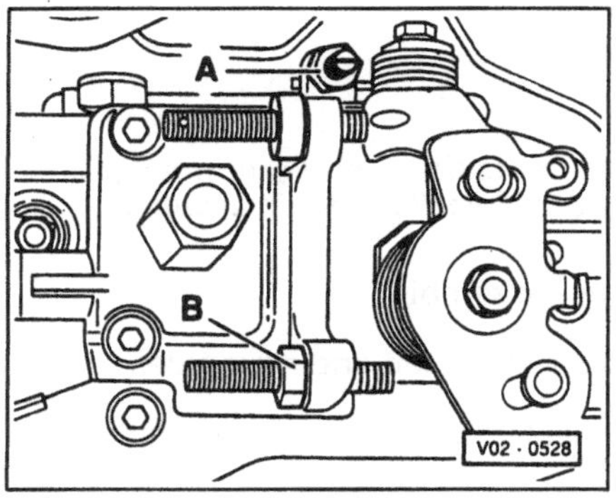

- (For vehicles through 03.96 prod.) Check idle speed and, if necessary, adjust by turning idle speed adjustment screw -A- .Check maximum engine speed (not under load) and, if necessary, adjust by turning maximum engine speed adjustment nut -B-

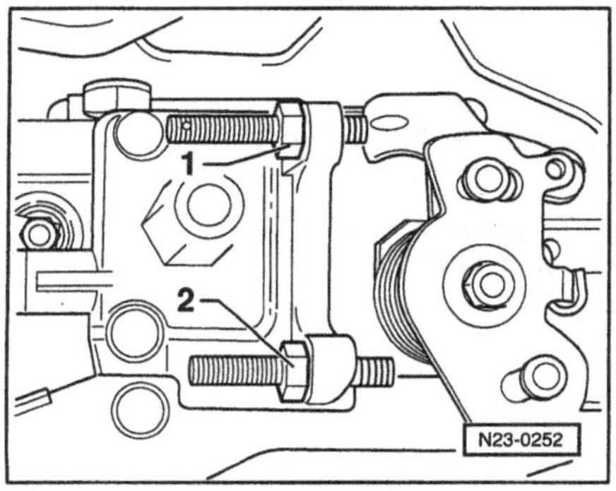

- (For vehicles from 04.96 prod.) Check idle speed and, if necessary, adjust by turning idle speed adjustment nut -1- .Check maximum engine speed (not under load) and, if necessary, adjust by turning maximum engine speed adjustment nut -2-
- After adjustment, lock adjustment screw.
- Place test probe onto exhaust pipe.
- Blip throttle at least 2 x 5 times, but not more than 5 x 5 times.

- ● If after 2 x 5 throttle bursts the opacity figures are equal to or less than the prescribed figures then end measurement.
- ● If after 5 x 5 throttle bursts the determined opacity figures are over the prescribed figures, determine cause and repair.

Engine compartment pan (sound dampening), removing and installing

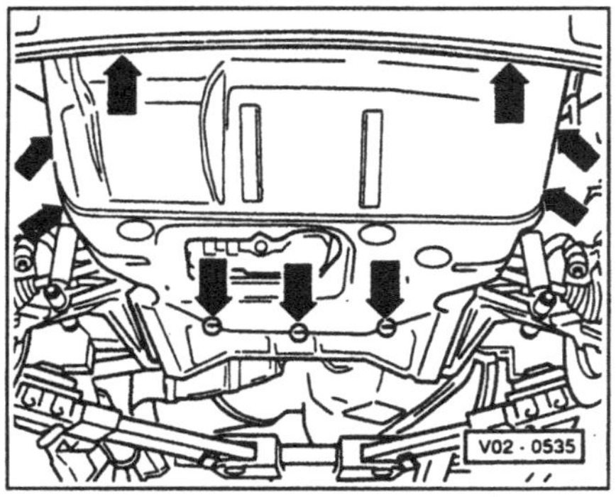

◄ – Remove bolt/washer assemblies and nuts -arrows-.

– Disengage locking lever, swing pan down and unhook retainer brackets.

– When installing tighten nuts and bolts to 9 Nm (7 ft lb)

Radiator, tilting forward

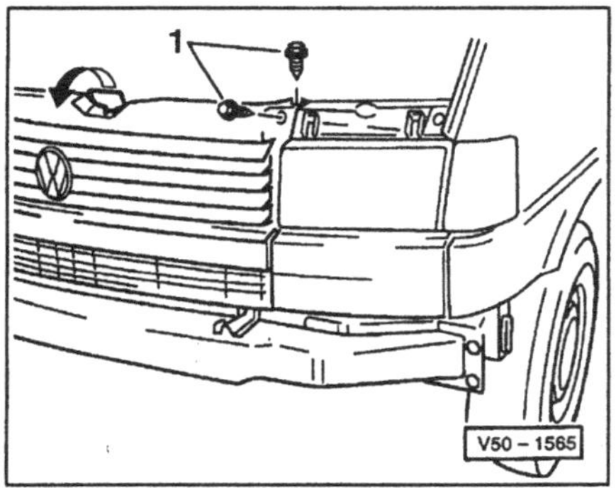

Vehicles up to 08.94:

◄ – Remove mounting bolts -1- on left and right.

– Swing radiator and upper radiator support out forward -arrow-.

Vehicles from 09.94 ➤ 12.95:

Note:

For vehicles from 01.96 ➤ ⇒ Radiator grille, removing and installing, Body–Exterior/ Body–Interior, Repair Group 66.

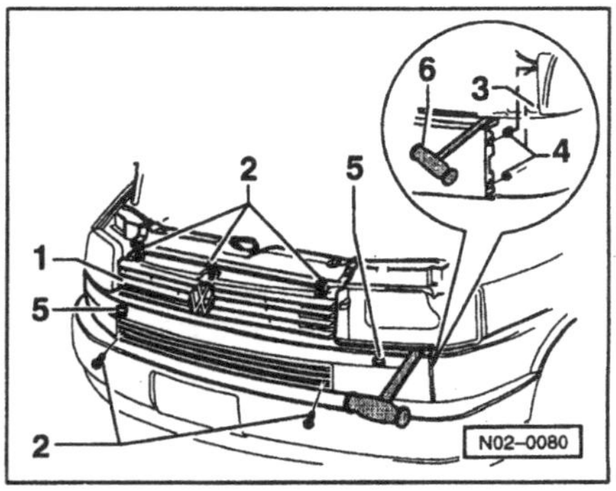

◄ – Remove screw and washer assemblies -2-.

– Remove spray jet (if equipped) on left and right sides.

– Hook tool 3370 -6- underneath headlight and trim frame.

– Remove radiator grille with trim frame -1- on left and right side of T-bolt -3-.

Note:

- *Damaged mounting clips -4- must be replaced before installing the radiator grille and trim frame.*
- *When installing the radiator grille and trim frame, clip it in simultaneously on the left and right sides.*

Engine oil level, checking

Switch off the engine and allow it to stand for a short time (at least 3 minutes) so that the oil can flow back into the oil pan.

- Pull out dipstick, wipe with clean cloth and re-insert as far as stop

- Pull dipstick out again and observe oil level.

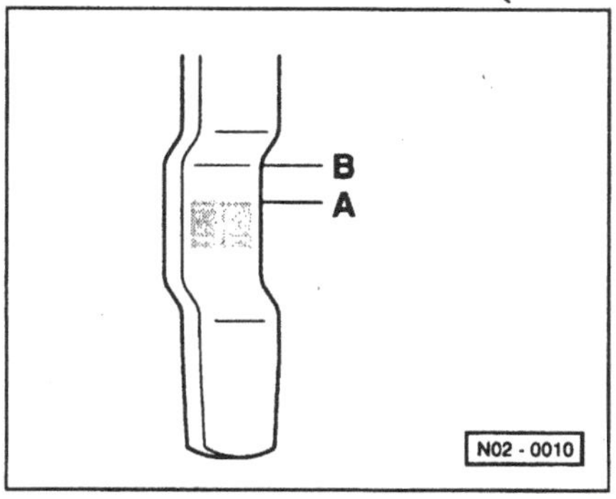

◄ The oil level must be in the area between -A- and -B- but never above -B-.

> ***Caution!***
>
> ***A danger exists that the catalytic converter will be damaged when the oil level is above -B-.***

- If oil level is below -A-, top up to, but not above, mark -B-.

Engine oil, changing

Notes:

- ♦ *If the engine oil is drained and not extracted with fluid extractor VAG 1307, VAG 1358 or equivalent then replace the drain plug seal.*
- ♦ *Observe oil and filter disposal recommendations.*

Oil capacities and specifications, with filter change:

- ♦ 5-cylinder gasoline: 5.5L (5.8 qt.) API service SF or SG
- ♦ 5-cylinder diesel: 5.5L (5.8 qt.) API service CF4 or CG4
- ♦ 6-cylinder gasoline: 6.0L (6.3 qt.) API service SF or SG

Tightening torque for drain plug:

- ♦ 5-cylinder and 6-cylinder engines: 50 Nm (37 ft lb)

- After topping up with oil wait at least 3 minutes then check oil level again using dipstick.

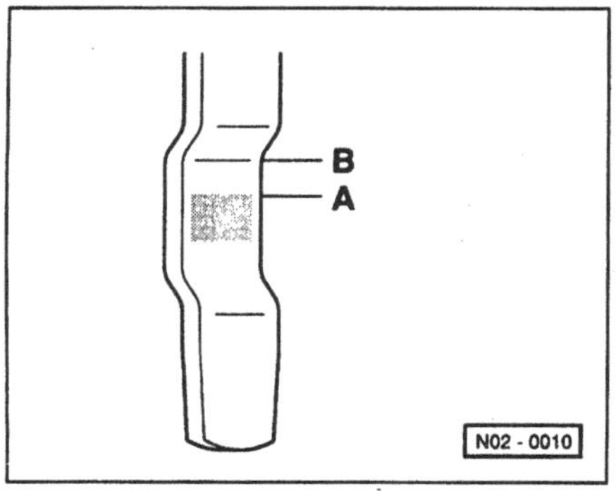

> ***Caution!***
>
> ***A danger exists that the catalytic converter will be damaged when the oil level is above -B-.***

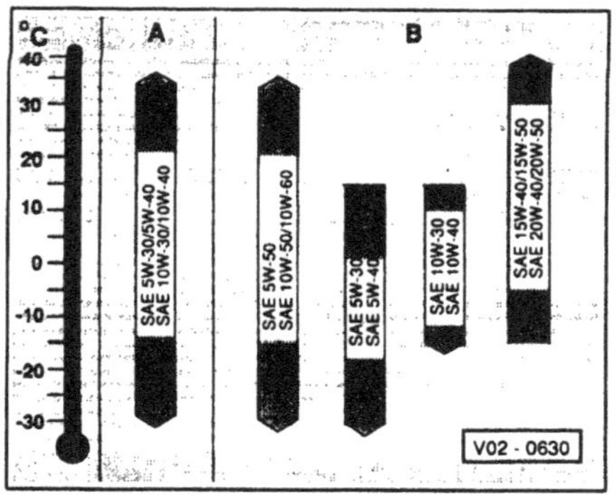

◄ **Gasoline engine oil specifications:**

A - Energy-conserving oil

B - Multi-grade oil

For gasoline engines use multi-grade oils, API-SF or SG

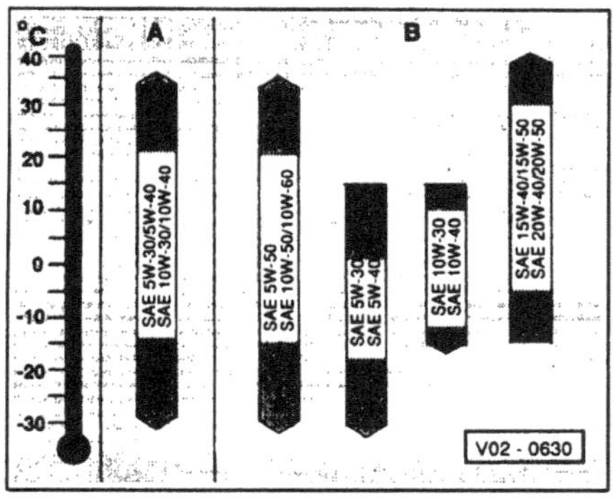

◄ **Diesel engine oil specifications:**

A - Energy-conserving oil

B - Multi-grade oil

For Diesel engines use multi-grade oils, API-CD (not for turbo-diesel engines)

Oil filter, changing

Note:

Observe oil and filter disposal recommendations.

Location:

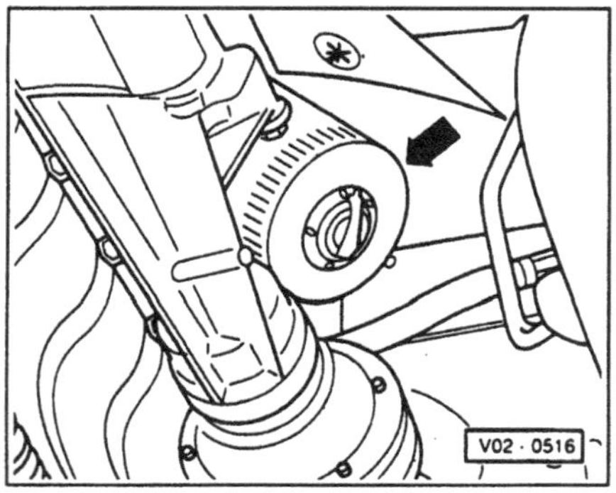

◄ 5-cylinder engines, on engine rear -arrow-.

- Loosen oil filter with filter strap (e.g. Hazet 217-1) and remove oil filter.
- Clean engine sealing surface.
- Lightly oil rubber seal on filter.
- Screw on new filter and tighten hand-tight.

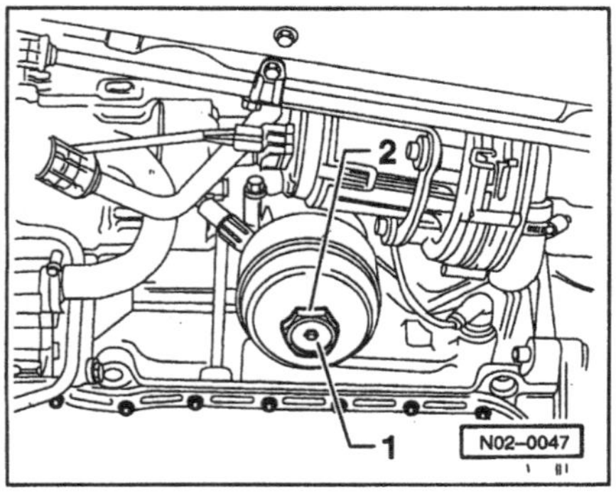

◄ 6-cylinder engines

- Drain oil at drain plug -1-.
- Remove lower part of filter -2- with tool.
- Coat new O-ring with engine oil.
- Install new filter insert and O-ring.
- Tighten lower part of filter -2- to 25 Nm (18 ft lb)
- Install new drain plug -1- with new seal.

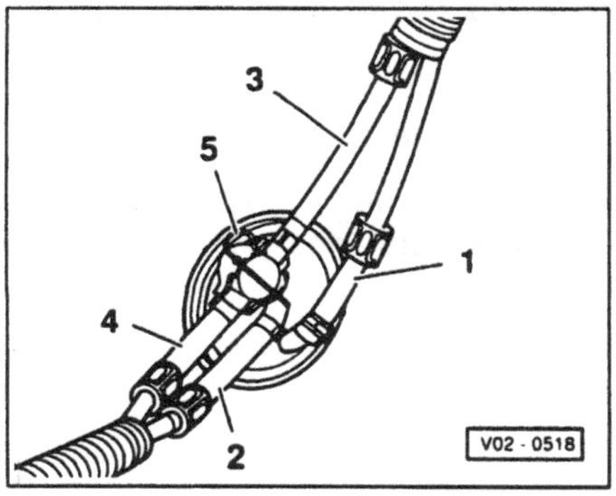

Fuel filter, replacing (Diesel engine)

Notes:

- *Ensure no Diesel fuel contacts coolant hoses. If necessary, clean hose immediately.*
- *Observe fuel and filter disposal recommendations.*

Removing:

- Remove retaining clip -5-.
- Remove control valve with fuel lines connected.

Installing:

- Place new O-ring on control valve, install, lines connected
- Install retaining clip -5-.
- Secure new filter with clamp -A-.
- Secure all fuel hoses with hose clamps.

Note:

Flow direction is marked by arrows (do not interchange connections).

- Check fuel system for leaks (visual check).
- Operate throttle repeatedly.
- ● When engine is at idling speed fuel must flow bubble-free through the transparent hoses.

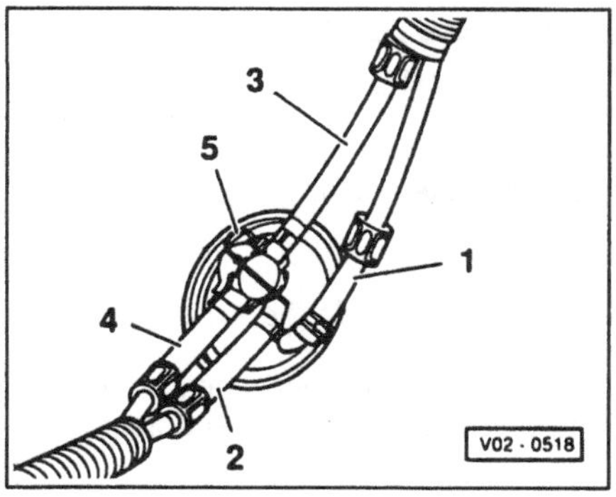

Fuel filter (Diesel engine), draining water

Notes:

- *Ensure that no Diesel fuel comes in contact with coolant hoses. If necessary clean hoses immediately.*
- *Observe fuel and filter disposal recommendations.*

- Remove retaining clip -5- and take control valve off with fuel lines connected.

- Drain approx. 100 cm^3 (6.1 cu. in.) of fluid via water drain screw -arrow-.
- Install control valve and connect retaining clip.
- Tighten drain screw.
- Check fuel system for leaks (visual check).
- Operate throttle repeatedly.
- ● When engine is at idling speed fuel must flow bubble-free through the transparent hoses.

Visual check of engine for leaks and damage, from below/above

- Check engine for leaks and damage.
- Check fuel system, cooling and heating systems, hoses, lines and connections for leaks, abrasions, porosity and brittleness.

Cooling system, anti-freeze protection and coolant level, checking

Vehicles produced from 07.96 are filled with colant additive -G12-. If coolant has to be topped up only use coolant additive -G12-.

Note:

- *You can recognize -G12- by the red color in the expansion tank.*

Vehicles produced through 06.96 are filled with coolant additive -G11-. If coolant has to be topped up only use -G11- coolant.

Note:

- *You can recognize -G11- by the green color in the expansion tank.*
- *If vehicles produced through 06.96 were filled with -G12- after repairs, only -G12- may be used for topping up.*

WARNING!

- *The coolant additives -G11- and -G12- should never be mixed.*
- *If the additive in the expansion tank is brown, this indicates improper mixing of the two coolant types. The coolant must be changed immediately or severe engine damage can occur!*

- Check concentration of coolant anti-freeze with a commercial anti-freeze tester or VW special tool T10007 (refractometer).

If a greater freeze protection is required for climatic reasons, the amount of -G11- or -G12- can be increased, but only up to 60% (freeze protection to about -40 °C), as otherwise freeze protection is reduced again and cooling effectiveness is also reduced.

Freeze protection table

Freeze protection to °C (°F)		Required quantity in Liters (quarts)	
Actual fig.	Specified fig.	gas and diesel engines 5-cyl.	6-cyl.
0 (32)	-25 (-13)	3.5 (3.7)	4.0 (4.2)
	-35 (-31)	4.0 (4.2)	5.0 (5.3)
-5 (23)	-25 (-13)	3.0 (3.2)	3.5 (3.7)
	-35 (-31)	3.5 (3.7)	4.5 (4.75)
-10 (14)	-25 (-13)	2.0 (2.1)	3.0 (3.2)
	-35 (-31)	3.0 (3.2)	4.0 (4.2)
-15 (5)	-25 (-13)	1.5 (1.6)	2.0 (2.1)
	-35 (-31)	2.0 (2.1)	3.0 (3.2)
-20 (-4)	-25 (-13)	1.0 (1.05)	1.5 (1.6)
	-35 (-31)	1.5 (1.6)	2.0 (2.1)
-25 (-13)	-35 (-31)	1.0 (1.05)	1.5 (1.6)
-30 (-22)	-35 (-31)	0.5 (0.53)	1.0 (1.05)
-35 (-31)	-40 (-40)	0.5 (0.53)	0.5 (0.53)

– After test drive check coolant additive concentration.

Coolant level, checking and topping up if necessary

– Check coolant level in expansion tank with engine cold.

- Delivery inspection: Coolant level at MAX marking.
- Inspection service: Coolant level between MAX and MIN marking.

– If coolant too low, add according to mixture ratio:

Freeze protection to:	Coolant additive G 11 V8 C	Water
-25 °C	approx. 40 %	approx. 60 %
-35 °C	approx. 50 %	approx. 50 %
-40 °C	approx. 60 %	approx. 40 %

Notes:

- *G 11 V8 C and coolant additives marked "In accordance with TL VW 774 C" prevent freeze and corrosion damage, scaling and also raise the boiling point of coolant. For this reason the system must be filled all year round with freeze and corrosion protection additives.*
- *The coolant additive ratio must be at least 40 %.*
- *Particularly in countries with tropical climates, the coolant improves engine operating safety during high loads with a raised boiling point.*

Air filter element, replacing

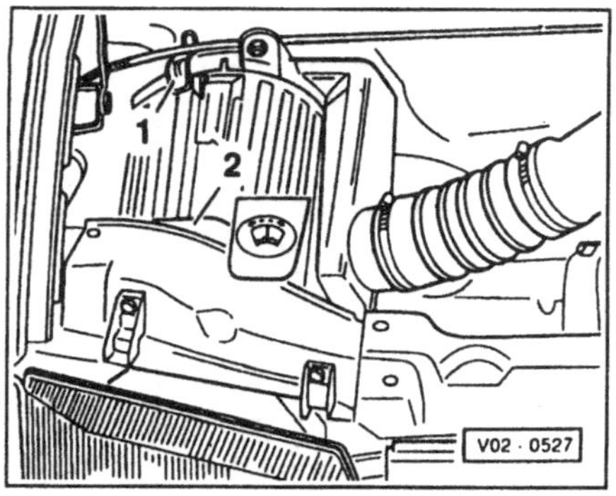

5-cylinder engines:

- Loosen spring retainers -1- and press locking tab -2- down and unhook.
- Remove filter housing upward and remove filter element.
- Clean filter housing and install new filter element.
- Install filter housing. The plastic tab on end of filter element must locate in retainer cut-out.
- Secure spring retainers -1- and pull locking tab -2- up until it engages.

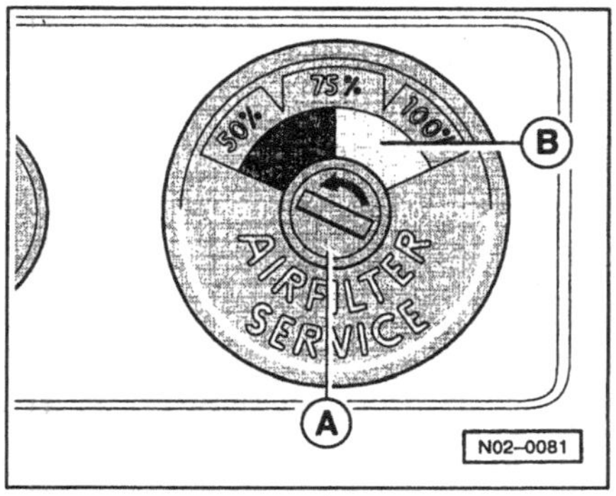

6-cylinder engines with saturation indicator:

The display is located in a console underneath the ashtray on the instrument panel.

- Ask customer if air filter element had been replaced between specified change intervals.

The amount of dirt in the filter element is indicated as follows:

- ♦ If the red area in the display field shows a 75% marking, the filter must be cleaned or replaced.

- Reset indicator by turning button -A- to left until red area is out of display field -B-.

On Board Diagnostic system, reading/erasing Diagnostic Trouble Code (DTC) Memory with VAG 1551 Scan Tool

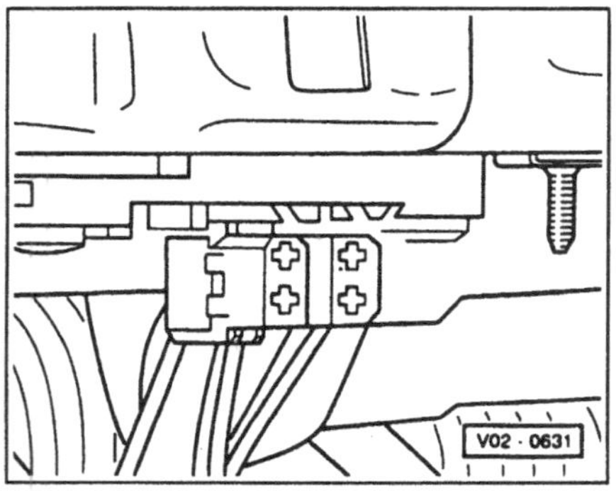

- Move selector lever to position "P" or "N" and engage parking brake (automatic transmission).

Vehicles produced up to 12.95:

- Fold relay plate cover down.
- With ignition switched off connect VAG 1551 Scan Tool to Data Link Connectors (DLC) above relay plate using diagnostic cable VAG 1551/1:
- Connect black connector (for voltage supply) to black DLC socket.

Note:

Do not connect white connector if there is no indication on display! Check Scan Tool voltage supply.

- Connect white connector to white DLC socket only when display reads "VAG ON BOARD DIAGNOSTIC".

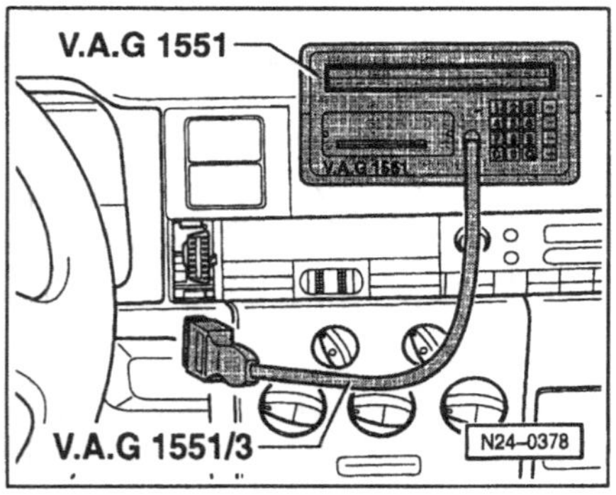

Vehicles produced from 01.96:

- Unclip cover for DLC next to instrument cluster.
- With ignition switched off, connect VAG 1551 Scan Tool to DLC with diagnostic cable VAG 1551/3.

Diagnostic Trouble Code (DTC) Memory, reading

- Start engine and let idle.
- Switch A/C on.
- Switch printer on with print button (indicator lamp lights up).
- Press button -1- for "Rapid data transfer" operating mode.
- Press button -0- twice for address word "automatic test sequence" and acknowledge input with -Q- button.

The Scan Tool transmits all known address words in sequence.

A control module responds with its identification and "no DTC recognized" or the number of malfunctions stored in the system is shown on the display.

Any malfunctions that are stored are displayed and printed out in sequence. The Scan Tool then sends the next address word.

VAG ON BOARD DIAGNOSTIC	HELP
1 – Rapid data transfer*	
2 – Blink code output*	

◄ The automatic test sequence has ended when following is indicated on display:

* Appears alternately

- Switch ignition off.

If malfunctions are stored then repair measures are required. The DTC print-out usually follows the repair order.

Idle speed (Diesel engine), checking and adjusting if necessary

Note:

Checking and adjustment conditions and specifications ⇒ Repair Manual, Diesel engine.

- Connect ignition tester VAG 1367 or VAG 1767 or equivalent.
- Check idle speed and, if necessary, adjust by turning idle speed adjustment screw -A-.

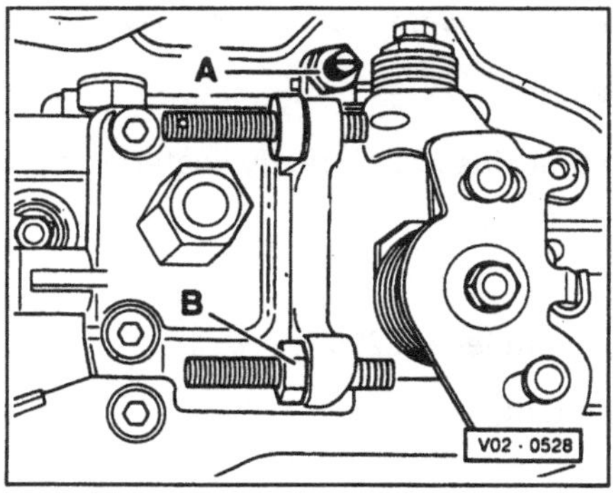

◄ 5-Cyl. engine

Ribbed belt, checking condition

- Check condition of ribbed belts for following conditions and replace if necessary:
  - ♦ Sub-surface deterioration (cracks, broken core, diagonal breaks)
  - ♦ Layer separation
  - ♦ Fraying of draw strands
  - ♦ Edge wear (material wear, frayed flanks, flank brittleness glassy flanks, surface cracks)
  - ♦ Traces of oil and grease

Ribbed belt, removing and installing

Before removing ribbed belt:

- Mark running direction of belt using a felt tipped marker.

When installing ribbed belt:

- Center belt and ensure that ribs are correctly seated in belt pulley grooves.

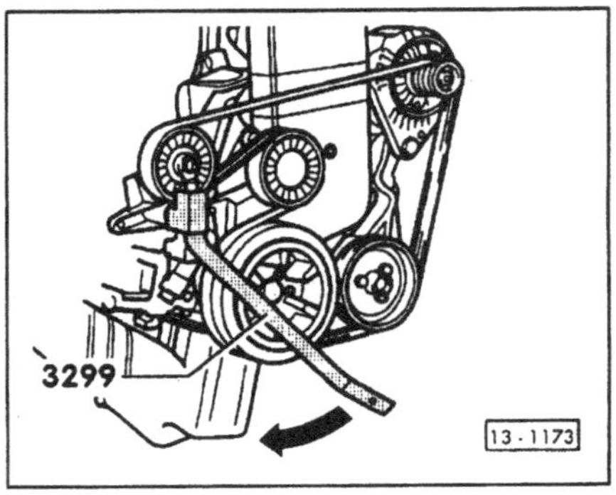

◄ Belt drive without A/C

- Loosen tensioner pulley with lever 3299
- Remove or install ribbed belt.

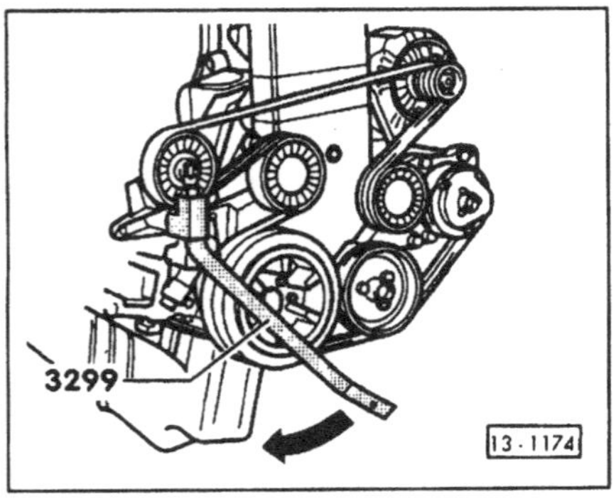

◄ Belt drive with A/C

- Loosen tensioner pulley with lever 3299
- Remove or install ribbed belt.

Camshaft drive toothed belt, checking condition (Diesel and 5-cylinder gasoline engines)

Toothed belt condition, checking

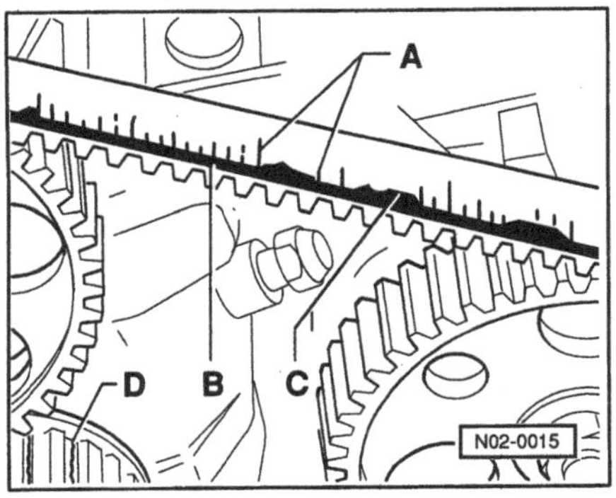

- Check toothed belt for:

A - Cracks, cross sectional breaks

B - Side contact

C - Fraying of draw strands

D - Surface cracks (synthetic coating)

Traces of oil and grease

- Replace the toothed belt if any of the above conditions are found.

Notes:

- *It is essential to replace the toothed belt if faults are found. This will avoid possible break-downs or operating problems.*
- *The engine must never under any circumstances be turned over using the camshaft when checking and making adjustments. Not observing this can lead to severe engtine damage.*

Toothed belt tension, adjusting

5-Cyl. Diesel engine with manual toothed belt adjustment:

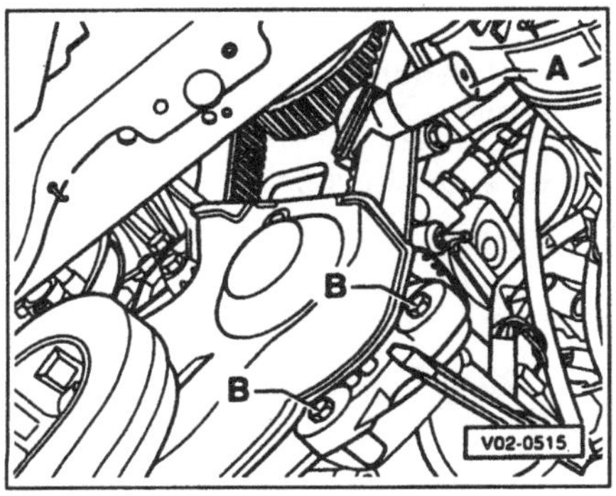

- Remove toothed belt cover.
- Loosen all tensioning arm and generator securing bolts at least one turn.
- Remove tensioning arm from coolant pump and press generator upward.
- Measure toothed belt tension between camshaft sprocket and coolant pump sprocket with tension checker VW 210 -A- and note values.
- Turn crankshaft one complete turn further and repeat measurement.
- Compare average of both measurements with specification.

● Specification: Scale value = 12 - 13

If actual value is outside tolerance then tension toothed belt as follows:

- Loosen bolts -B- and tension toothed belt by turning coolant pump (e.g. with screwdriver) to specification.
- Tighten securing bolts to 20 Nm (15 ft lb).

- Bolt tensioning arm to coolant pump.
- Install toothed belt cover.

5-Cyl. Diesel engine with semi automatic tensioning system:

- Loosen spring loaded tensioning roller securing nut on cylinder head approx. one turn. This will automatically set toothed belt tension.
- Turn engine approx. quarter to half turn (90° - 180°) in direction of rotation.
- Tighten securing nut to 15 Nm (11 ft lb) .

Camshaft drive toothed belt, replacing

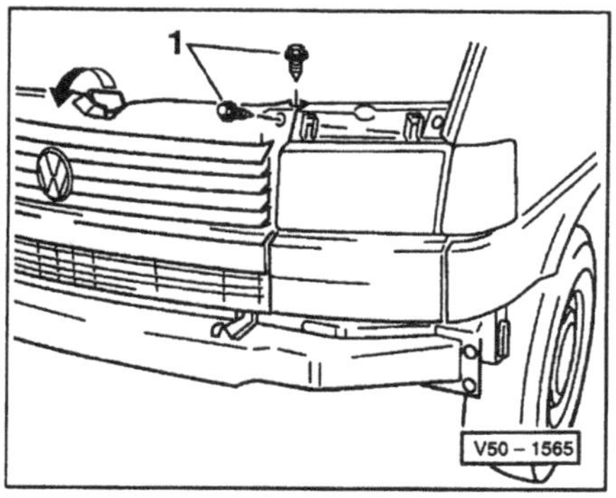

5-Cyl. Diesel engine

- Remove engine sound dampening pan.
- Remove left and right-hand securing bolts -1-.
- Fold radiator and upper radiator support out forward -arrow-.
- Remove belts for generator and power steering pump.

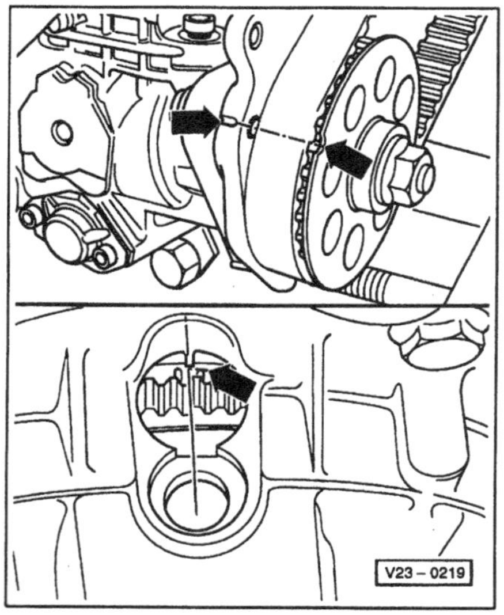

- Pivot generator up completely and tighten.
- Remove guard for both toothed belts and cylinder head cover.
- Turn crankshaft to TDC No. 1 Cylinder
- Align markings on flywheel/clutch bell housing and injection pump sprocket/mounting -arrows-.
- Hold injection pump sprocket with pin 2064.

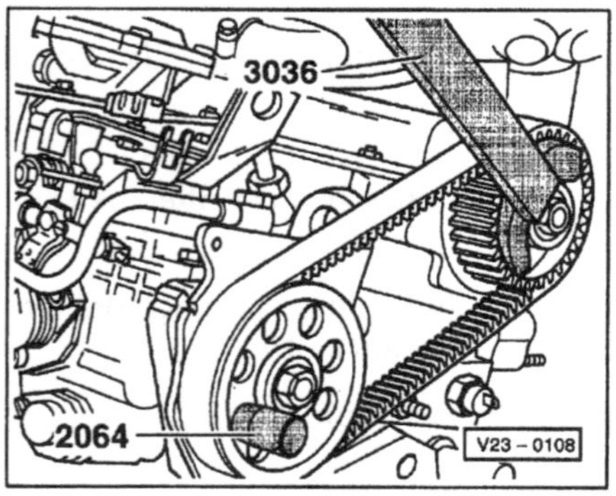

- Secure drive sprocket for injection pump with lever 3036 or equivalent.
- Remove securing bolt and take toothed belt and sprocket off.

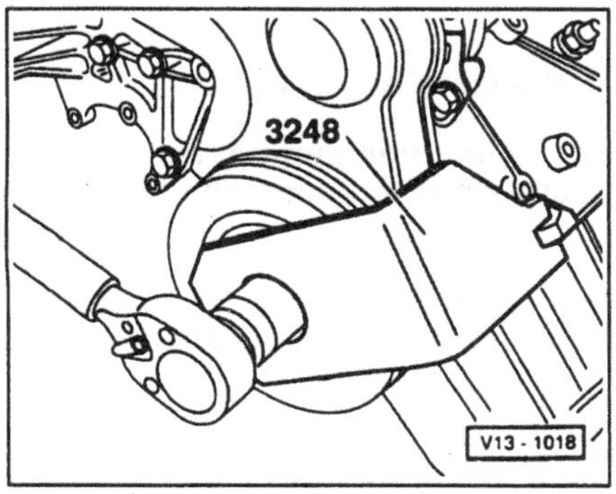

- Install counter-hold device 3248 as illustrated and loosen center bolt on vibration damper.
- Remove four M8 securing bolts on vibration damper/toothed belt sprocket.
- Remove vibration damper.
- Release toothed belt tension (loosen coolant pump).
- Remove lower toothed belt guard and toothed belt.

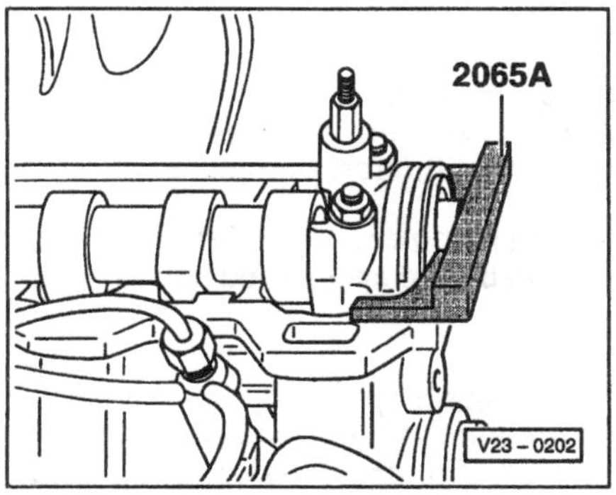

Installing

- Hold camshaft with setting bar 2065 A.
- Loosen camshaft sprocket securing bolt approx. 1 turn.
- Release camshaft sprocket from camshaft taper by tapping with hammer and drift through opening in cover plate.
- Install toothed belt for camshaft drive.
- Install lower toothed belt guard and insert M8 bolt for coolant pump.
- Tension toothed belt by turning coolant pump:

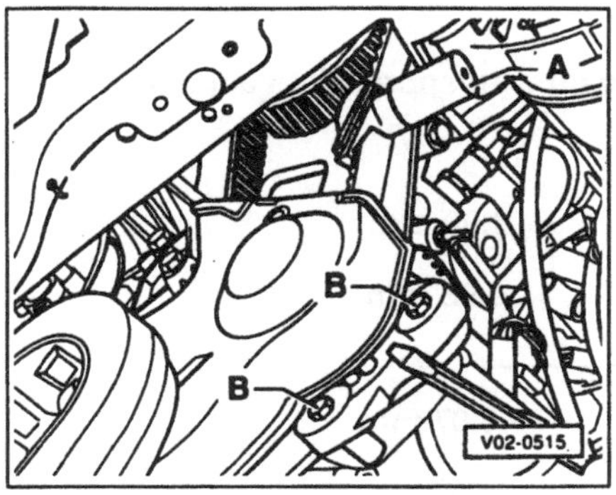

- Tension toothed belt using tension gauge VW 210.
- Specification: Scale value 12 ... 13.
- Securely tighten lower toothed belt guard.
- Check crankshaft TDC setting for No. 1 cylinder.
- Tighten camshaft sprocket securing nut to 45 Nm (33 ft lb) and remove setting bar.
- Install vibration damper.

Tightening torque:

M8 bolts	20 Nm (15 ft lb)
Center bolt	460 Nm (339 ft lb)

- Install drive sprocket for injection pump and toothed belt for injection pump drive. Tighten drive sprocket securing bolt only far enough to allow sprocket to be turned by hand.
- Check toothed belt tension and adjust if necessary, ⇒ removing and installing injection pump toothed belt, 2.4 Liter Diesel, Fuel Injection and Glow Plug, Group 23.
- Remove holding pin from injection pump sprocket.

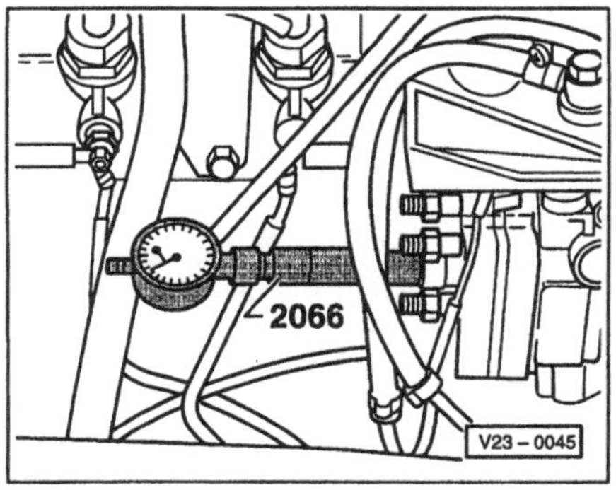

- Install adapter 2066 and gauge (scaled 0...3 mm) with approx. 2.5 mm preload in place of sealing plug.
- Check crankshaft TDC setting for No. 1 cylinder.

Injection pump timing, checking and adjusting:

When the vehicle is raised, the injection pump drive sprocket must be turned from below allowing the gauge to be read while turning the sprocket.

When checking the injection timing by turning the crankshaft forward and back, a second technician is required to check the markings on the flywheel.

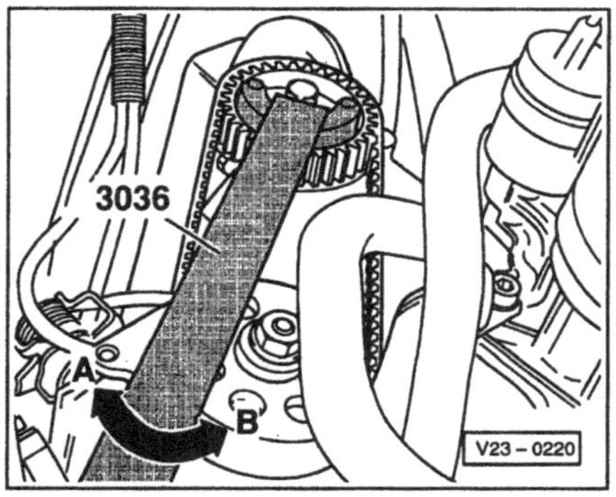

◄

- Turn injection pump drive sprocket against engine direction of rotation using counter-hold lever -arrow direction A- until gauge pointer no longer moves.
- Set gauge to "0".
- Turn injection pump drive sprocket in engine direction of rotation using counter-hold lever -arrow direction B- until gauge reads 1.00 ± 0.02 mm of lift (start of injection).
- Hold injection pump sprocket using counter-hold lever in this position and tighten securing bolt to approx. 50 Nm (37 ft lb).

Note:

The start of injection is checked again by turning the crankshaft back at the vibration damper until the gauge reads "0" and then turning again onto "TDC". The check values differ from the set values because of toothed belt slippage.

- Set start of injection again with appropriate adjustment.

	First adjusted value	= 1.00 mm
–	Checked value	= 0.93 mm
	Difference	= – 0.07 mm
	Second adjustment figure	= 1.07 mm

- Tighten injection pump drive sprocket after second adjustment to 100 Nm (74 ft lb).
- Install cylinder head cover, V-belts, toothed belt guard, radiator, lock carrier and engine insulation tray.

ATF level, checking and topping up (automatic transmission)

098 Transmission

Conditions for performing check

- Vehicle on level surface
- Parking brake pulled on
- Selector lever in "P"
- Engine running at idling speed

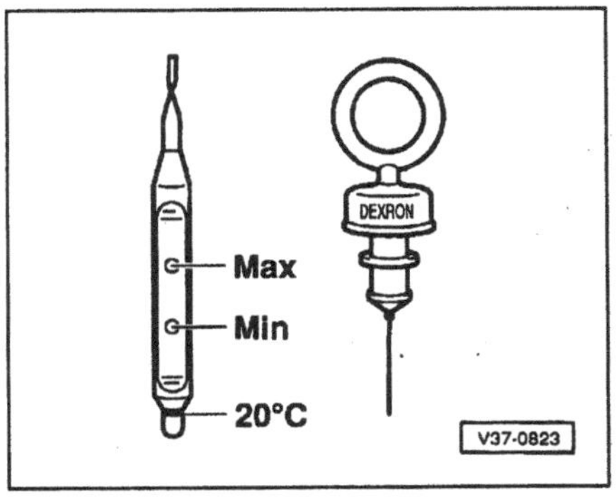

- ATF must be up to normal operating temperature of approx. 60°C (140°F)
- ◄ When cold, the ATF must be filled up to 20 °C marking, otherwise top up ATF.

Checking

Note:

- *Use non-fluffy cloth to wipe off dipstick.*
- *Do not use any lubricant additives.*
- *The MIN and MAX markings on the dipstick relate to an ATF temperature of 60°C (140°F).*

– Bring ATF temperature up to 50 ... 70 °C (122 ... 158°F). Temperature is measured using VAG 1551 Scan Tool as follows:

– Connect VAG 1551 Scan Tool ⇒ Page A 44

– Press button -1- for "Rapid data transfer" mode.

– Press buttons -0- and -2- for address word "Transmission electronics" and confirm entry with -Q- button

– Press → button.

– Press buttons -0- and -8- for the function "Reading measuring value block" and confirm entry with -Q- button.

– Press buttons -0- and -5- for "Display group number" and confirm entry with -Q- button.

Reading measured value block			1
1	2	3	4

◄ The ATF temperature appears in zone 1 in °C (precise figures begin at 50 °C).

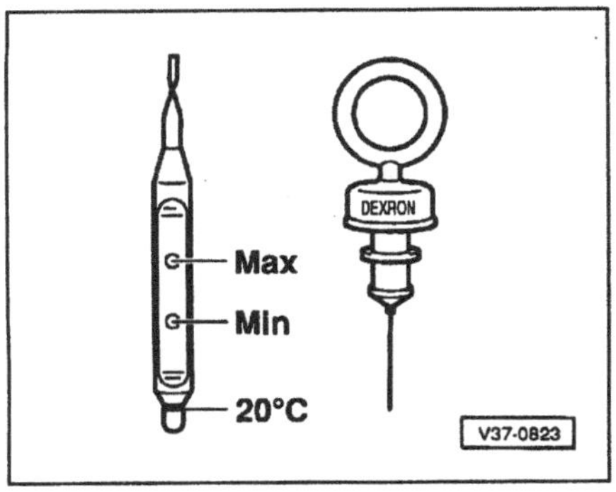

◄ – Check ATF level on dipstick at a temperature of between 50 ... 70 °C.

- ATF level must be between MIN and MAX marking on dipstick.

– If ATF level too low, top up ATF via funnel.

> ***Caution!***
>
> - ***Too much ATF will cause transmission malfunctions and must therefore be extracted.***
> - ***Only ATF with the designation Dexron (or VW ATF) may be used. Do not use any lubricant additives.***

- If ATF level too high, extract ATF with VAG 1358/A extraction system, EZ1 Fluid Extractor or equivalent.

Note:

Observe prescribed ATF disposal recommendations.

- Press → button on VAG 1551 Scan Tool.
- With engine running but vehicle standing still move through all selector lever positions once.
- Check ATF level again (between 50 ... 70 °C)

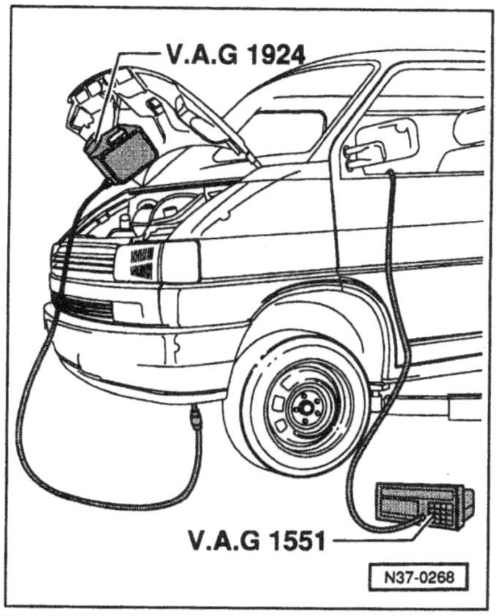

01P Transmission

Conditions for performing check

- Transmission not in emergency running mode
- ATF temperature not above 30°C
- Vehicle level
- Selector lever at "P"

- Secure reservoir of ATF filling system VAG 1924 to vehicle.
- Connect VAG 1551 Scan Tool and enter address word 02 for "Transmission electronics" and advance until "Select function XX" is indicated on display.

- Start engine
- Raise vehicle

Rapid data transfer	HELP
08 – Reading measuring value block	

◄ Indicated on display:

- Press buttons -0- and -8- (The function "Read measuring value block" is selected with 08).

Rapid data transfer	Q
08 – Reading measuring value block	

◄ Indicated on display:

- Confirm entry with -Q- button.

Reading measuring value block
Enter display group number XX

◄ Indicated on display:

- Press buttons -0- and -5- (05 selects display group number 05).
- Confirm entry with -Q- button.

Reading measuring value block			5 →
40°C	0011011	0	900 rpm

◄ Indicated on display:

The first display zone shows the ATF temperature.

Note:

The ATF temperature must not be more than approx. 30°C.

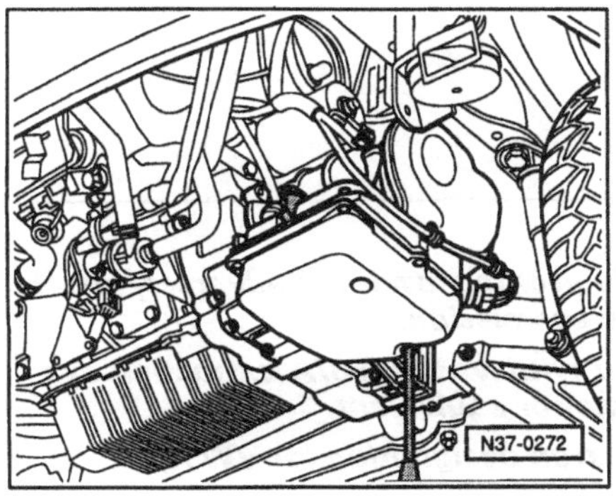

- Remove ATF level plug from oil pan -arrow-.

- ATF present in overflow tube runs out.

- Bring ATF to test temperature.

- ATF test temperature: 35 to 45°C

If ATF continues to drip out of plug hole:

ATF need not be topped up.

- Install new seal to plug and tighten to 15 Nm (11 ft lb). The ATF level check is completed.

If only the ATF present in the overflow tube runs our of the hole (no further dripping):

- Top up ATF level.

ATF level, topping up

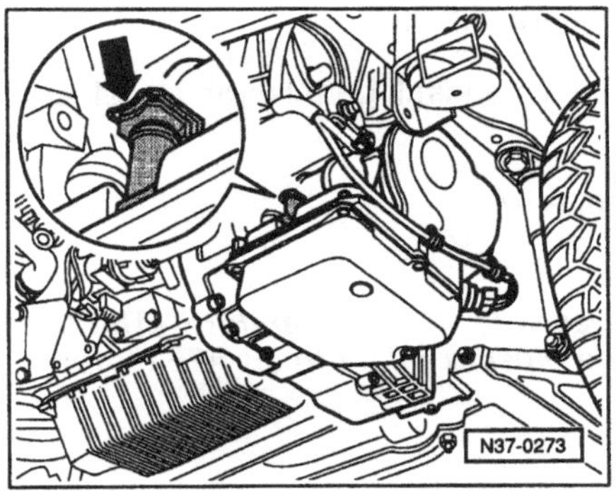

- Remove cap -arrow- from filler pipe.

Note:

Some transmissions have a plug with a cap. The cap is destroyed during removal and must always be replaced.

- Pry cap out with a screwdriver and remove plug.

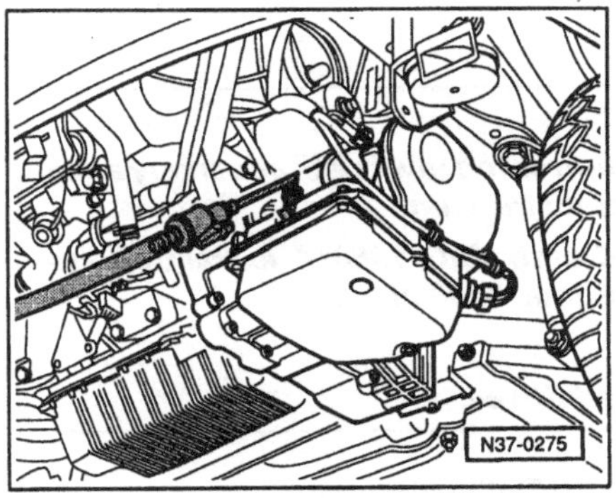

- Fill with ATF using VAG 1924 until ATF runs out of level hole -arrow-.

> ***Caution!***
>
> ***If the ATF level is too high or too low it will adversely affect the operation of the transmission.***

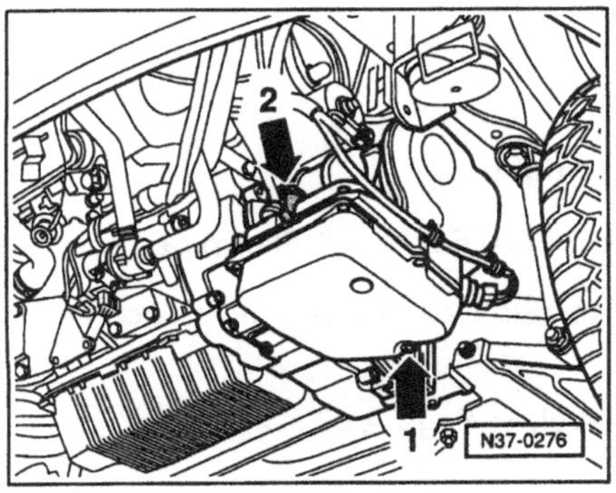

- Install new seal to level plug -arrow 1- and tighten to 15 Nm (11 ft lb).

- Push cap -arrow 2- onto filler pipe until spring retainer locates correctly.

Note:

Some transmissions have a plug with a cap. The cap is destroyed during removal and must always be replaced.

ATF, replacing

098 Transmission

> ***Caution!***
> - ***If the ATF level is too high or too low it will adversely affect the operation of the transmission.***
> - ***ATF can be suctioned with VAG 1358/A extraction system, EZ1 Fluid Extractor or equivalent.***
> - ***Use only ATF with Dexron designation (or VW ATF).***
> - ***Do not use lubricant additives.***

– Drain ATF and refill.

- For refill use approx. 3 Liters (3.2 qt).

– Start engine and while at a standstill go through all selector positions once.

– Check ATF level, ⇒ Page A 57

Note:

The ATF fluid level changes with ATF temperature. The MIN and MAX markings on the dipstick relate to an ATF temperature of 60°C (140°F).

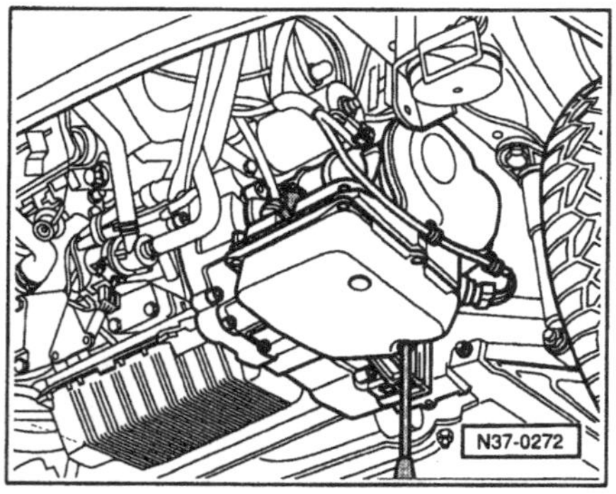

01P Transmission

> ***Caution!***
> - ***If the ATF level is too high or too low it will adversely affect the operation of the transmission.***
> - ***ATF can be suctioned with VAG 1358/A extraction system, EZ1 Fluid Extractor or equivalent.***
> - ***Use only VW ATF.***
> - ***Do not use lubricant additives.***

◄ – Remove ATF level plug from oil pan -arrow-.

– Remove overflow tube through ATF level hole.

– Drain ATF.

– Install overflow tube

– Screw level plug in hand-tight.

– Refill with 3 Liters (3.2 qt) of ATF through filler pipe.

– Start engine and shift through all selector lever positions with vehicle stationary.

– Check and top up ATF level, ⇒ Page A 57

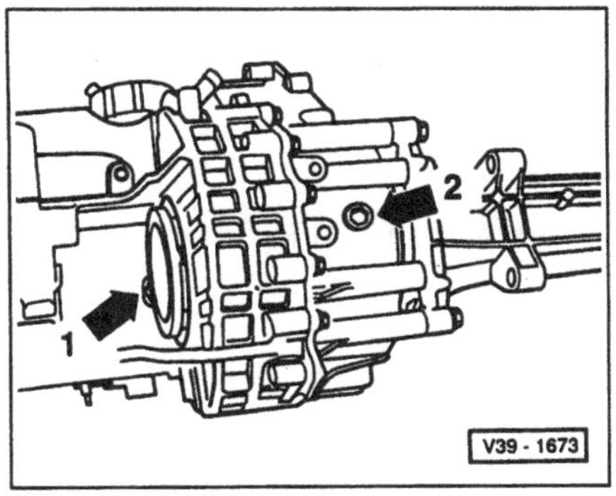

Checking final drive oil level and topping up (automatic transmission)

Note:

Observe prescribed gear oil disposal recommendations.

098 Transmission

◄ – Remove plug to check gear oil level, top up to lower edge of hole, if necessary

Note:

The plug next to the flange shaft -arrow 1- or the plug in the torque converter housing -arrow 2- can be removed to check the gear oil level.

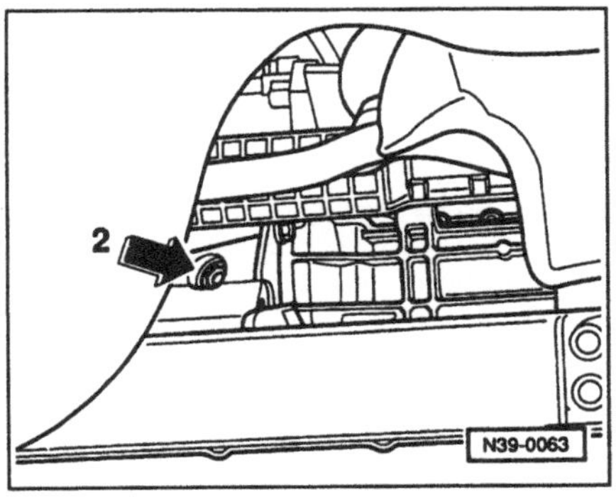

Vehicles from 08.92 with modified assembly carrier (subframe)

◄ – Remove bolt -arrow 2- through hole in the assembly carrier.

– Check gear oil level, top up to lower edge of hole, if necessary

– Install bolt.

- Tightening torque: 20 Nm (15 ft lb)
  - ♦ Specification: SAE 75W90 (synthetic)
  - ♦ Refill capacity: Filled for life. No change necessary

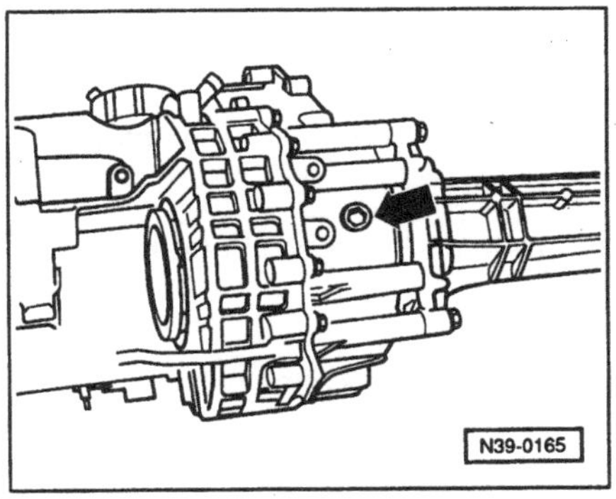

01P Transmission

◄ – Remove plug -arrow- to check gear oil level.

– Top gear oil up to lower edge of hole if necessary.

- ♦ Specification: SAE 75W90 (synthetic)
- ♦ Refill capacity: Filled for life. No change necessary.

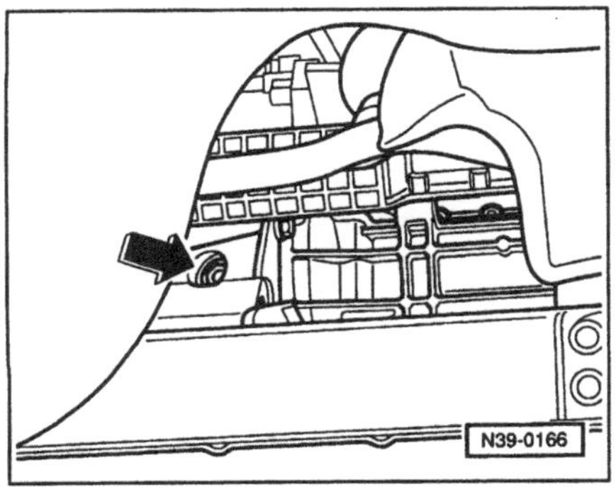

◄ – Remove and install plug -arrow- through hole in subframe.

- Tightening torque: 20 Nm (15 ft lb)

Final drive oil level, checking and topping up (manual transmission)

– Remove oil filler plug.

– Check oil level.

● Oil level must be to lower edge of filler plug hole.

– If necessary top up gear oil level.

♦ Specification G 50 SAE 75W90 (synthetic oil)

– Install oil filler plug.

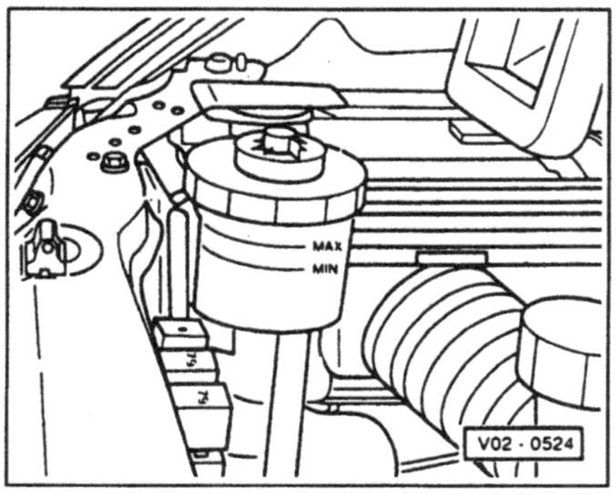

Power steering fluid level, checking

Check fluid level with engine running and front wheels in the straight-ahead position.

◄ ● Oil level must be between min. and max. markings.

– Top up with oil if necessary.

♦ Specification: Part No. G 002 000 or G 002 000 A8

Note:

If fluid level has sunk to MIN marking check power steering for possible repair. It is not sufficient to only top up fluid level.

Tie rod ends/tie rods, checking

- With vehicle raised (wheels hanging free), check play by moving tie rods and wheels.

- Specification: Zero play

- Check mountings.

- Check that boots are not damaged and are correctly seated.

Tires, checking condition (including spare)

Note:

For reasons of safety only tires of the same type and profile are to be used on vehicle.

Delivery inspection:

- Check tire tread and side walls for damage; remove any foreign objects, such as nails or glass splinters.

Maintenance service:

- Check tires for scuffing, one-sided or other unusual wear, porous side walls, cuts and punctures. Inform customer of any faults found.

- Check tire tread depth
- Minimum depth: 1.6 mm (1/16 in.)

This figure may vary in accordance with local regulations.

If tread depth is approaching legal permissible minimum, i.e. if the 1.6 mm high wear indicators around the tire circumference no longer have any tread pattern, inform the customer.

- Check tire pressures.

Note:

- *The recommended cold tire inflation pressures are found on label on driver's side B-pillar.*
- *When using winter tires, inflation pressures should be increased by approximately 3 psi.*

Wheel mounting bolts, tightening

Tightening torque:

Wheel bolt to wheel hub for all vehicles: 170 Nm (125 ft-lb)

Changed lug bolts from m.y. 2001

From m.y. 2001 changed lug bolts have been installed. The dimensions and tightening torques of the previous and changed lug bolts are the same.

WARNING!

- *Changed lug bolts are not permissible on vehicles produced up to m.y. 2000.*
- *Wheel rims of vehicles which were produced up to m.y. 2000 are not permissible on vehicles from m.y. 2001.*

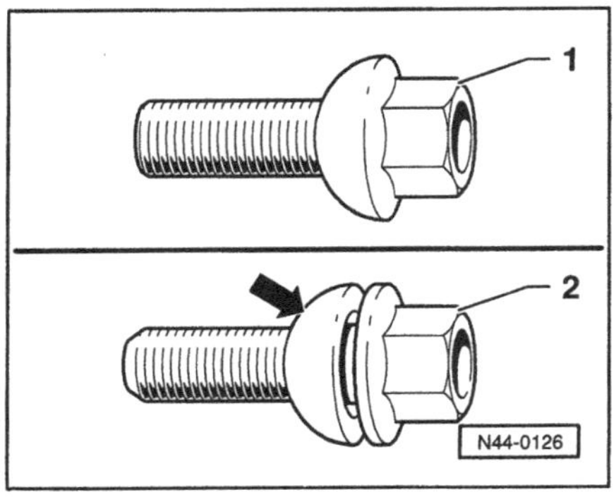

◄ **1. Previous wheel bolt**

For vehicles up to m.y. 2000

Surface coated in black, part number 701 601 139B

2. Wheel bolt for vehicles as of m.y. 2001

Collar (arrow) is not tightly connected to the hex head.

Suface is layered in silver, part number 7M3 601 139B

Disc brake pads, checking thickness

Front disc brakes

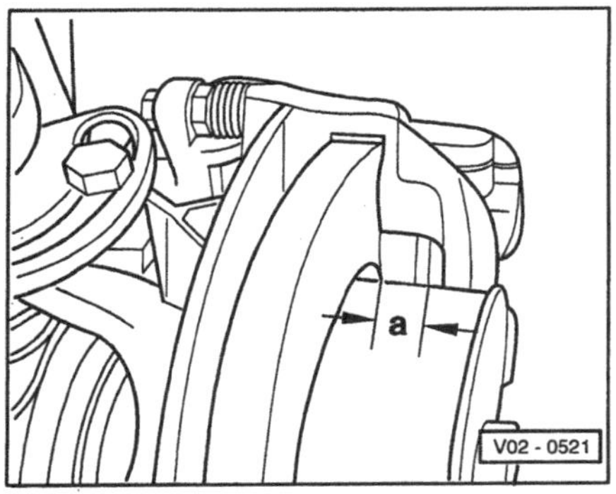

- Mark position of wheel in relation to disc and remove wheel.
- ◄ Measure inner and outer pad thickness
- ● Pad thickness (a) including backing plate: wear limit 7mm
- Replace pads when they have reached the wear limit.

Rear disc brakes (m.y. 1997 and later)

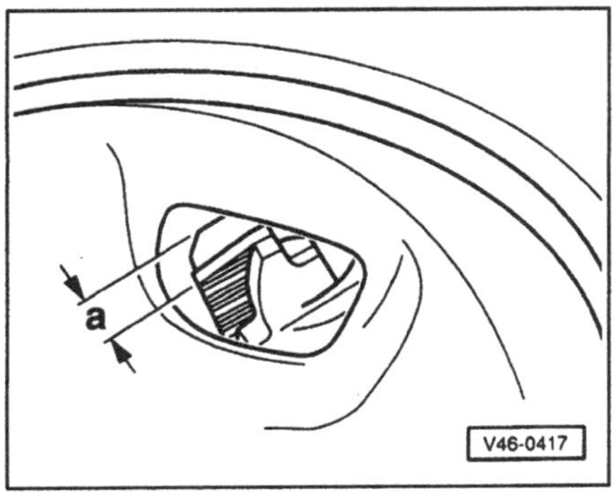

- ◄ Determine thickness of outer pad by visual inspection through opening in wheel using a flashlight.
- Determine thickness of inner pad by visual inspection using a flashlight and a mirror or using a vernier gauge.
- ● Pad thickness (a) including backing plate: wear limit 7mm
- Replace pads when they have reached the wear limit.

Rear drum brakes, checking lining thickness (m.y. 1992-1996)

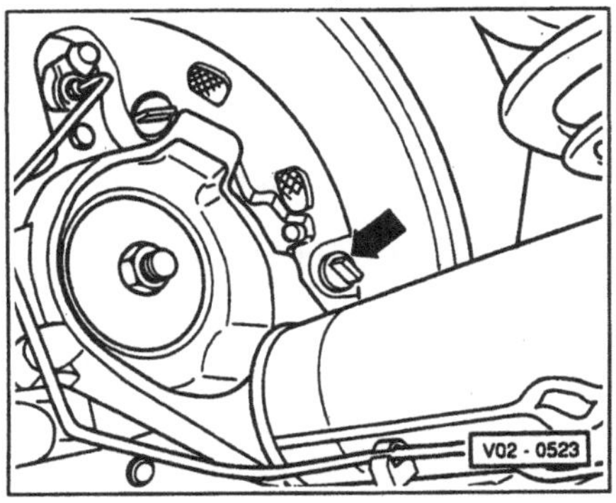

Drum brake linings:

- Check brake lining thickness through inspection hole in backing plates -arrow-.

• Wear limit: 1.0 mm (lining only)

- Replace pads when they have reached the wear limit.

Note:

Check linings for brake fluid or grease contamination.

Brake system, checking for leaks and damage

- Check brake master cylinder, brake booster (hydraulic unit on vehicles with ABS), brake pressure regulator, and brake calipers for leaks and damage.
- Ensure that brake hoses are not twisted or do not touch any vehicle components when steering is turned to full lock.
- Check brake hoses/lines for porosity, brittleness and chafing.
- Check brake connections and mountings for correct fit, for leaks and corrosion.

Caution!

Faulty components must be replaced.

Brake fluid level, checking

Use only new genuine VW/Audi brake fluid in accordance with US standard FMVSS 116 DOT 4.

Warning!

- ***Brake fluid is poisonous. DO NOT siphon by mouth. If brake fluid contacts skin, wash thoroughly.***
- ***If brake fluid contacts eyes, flush with running water for 15 minutes. If taken internally, drink water and induce vomiting. Get medical attention immediately.***

Caution!

- ***Brake fluid is caustic. Because of its etching effect it must not come in contact with paint.***
- ***Brake fluid is hygroscopic. It absorbs water from the ambient air and must be stored in tightly closed containers.***

Delivery inspection:

The brake fluid level must be at the MAX marking.

Note:

Do not exceed the MAX marking or brake fluid could overflow.

Inspection service:

- The fluid level must always be evaluated in relationship to brake pad wear. When the vehicle is in use, the fluid level tends to drop slightly due to lining wear and automatic adjustment.

- When the fluid level is at the MIN marking or just above, the fluid level must not be topped up if the linings are almost at the wear limit.
- If the linings are new or well above the wear limit then the fluid level must be between MIN and MAX markings.
- If the fluid level is below the MIN marking, the brake system must be checked before fluid is added.

Brake fluid, changing

Use only new, genuine VW/Audi brake fluid in accordance with US standard FMVSS 116 DOT 4.

Warning!

- ***Brake fluid is poisonous. DO NOT siphon by mouth. If brake fluid contacts skin, wash thoroughly.***
- ***If brake fluid contacts eyes, flush with running water for 15 minutes. If taken internally, drink water and induce vomiting. Get medical attention immediately.***

Caution!

- ***Brake fluid must on no account come into contact with fluids containing minerals (oil, gasoline, cleaning materials). Oils containing minerals damage plug and seals in brake systems.***
- ***Observe prescribed disposal instructions!***
- ***Brake fluid is caustic. Because of its etching effect it must not come in contact with paint.***
- ***Brake fluid is hygroscopic. It absorbs water from the ambient air and must be stored in tightly closed containers.***

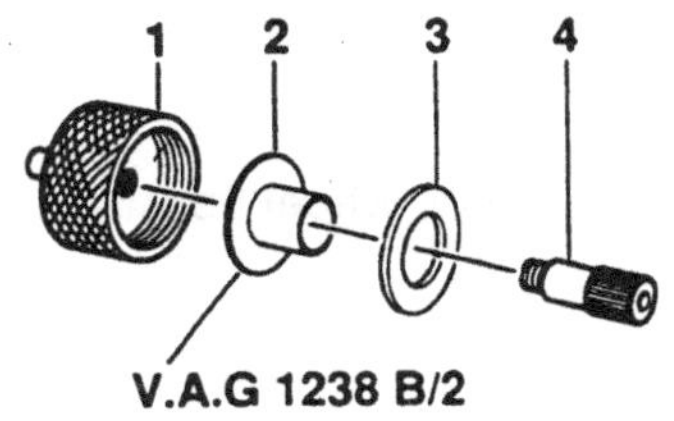

◄ – Connect brake filling and bleeding device US 1116 to brake fluid reservoir. Use adapter -1- including synthetic filler union -2-, seal -3- and metal connection -4-.

> ***Caution!***
>
> ***Do not use cloths containing minerals to clean filling and bleeding device.***

– Use suction bottle (equipped with a strainer) to extract as much brake fluid as possible from brake fluid reservoir.

> ***Caution!***
>
> ***Do not reuse extracted (used) brake fluid.***

– Position brake pedal depressor between driver's seat and brake pedal. Pretension pedal depressor.

– Open bleed screws and allow corresponding fluid quantity to flow out. Used brake fluid is pushed out of system by pumping in new fluid.

Sequence: Wheel cylinder/ Brake caliper	Brake fluid quantity which must flow out of wheel cylinders/brake calipers:
Right rear	400 ... 500 cm^3
Left rear	400 ... 500 cm^3

Sequence: Wheel cylinder/ Brake caliper	Brake fluid quantity which must flow out of wheel cylinders/brake calipers:
Right front	400 ... 500 cm^3
Left front	400 ... 500 cm^3

Total quantity: 2 Liters (2.1 qt)

– Take connections off reservoir and remove pedal depressor.

– Check pedal pressure and brake pedal free play.

- Free play: max. $^1/_3$ of pedal travel.

Underbody sealant, checking visually for damage

During visual check, observe floor pan, wheel housings and sills.

Faulty areas found must be repaired.

Door check straps and securing pins, lubricating

◄ – Grease door checks -arrow A- with grease, Part No. G 000 400.

– Grease securing pins -arrow B- with lock cylinder lubricant spray, Part No. G 000 400 01.

Airbag unit, inspection

Models equipped with driver and front passenger airbags have the inscription "AIRBAG" on the steering wheel and right-hand side of the instrument panel.

The following inspection must be performed, independent of the running performance of the vehicle, after 4 years from the date on the safety compliance sticker, again after 8 years and every 2 years thereafter:

♦ Check airbag system for function and inspect for damage.

Inspection service procedure

– Conduct visual check of cushioned pad (driver airbag) and surface of right-side instrument panel (passenger side) for damage done from the outside.

Note:

♦ *The cushioned pad of the steering wheel and the foamed surface of the airbag unit on the passenger side must not be glued, covered or show signs of having been worked on in any way.*

♦ *The lettering "Airbag" must be visible on the cushioned pad of the steering wheel and on the right side of the instrument panel (passenger side).*

– Ensure customer is aware that adhesive and other residues or unauthorized work on airbag units can affect airbag function.

– Visually inspect all deployment points of driver and passenger airbag units for crack formation or mechanical damage.

– Conduct visual and functional check of warning light for airbag system:

  ♦ The warning light must light for 3 seconds when the ignition is switched on.

  ♦ The warning light must switch off after 3 seconds and then not light again or flicker during a test drive.

If either or both of the above functions are not observed, repairs to the airbag system are required.

– Check that airbag control module is securely installed.

⇒ Tightening torque and procedure – Airbag control module, removing and installing, ⇒ Repair Manual, Group 69

Headlights, adjusting

Requirements:

♦ Tires inflated to correct pressure.

♦ Lenses clean and not damaged.

♦ Reflectors in proper condition.

♦ Springs settled. Load vehicle with approx. 75 kg (165 lb) on driver's seat and roll several meters (yards).

♦ Vehicle standing on level ground.

Vehicles through 12.95 production

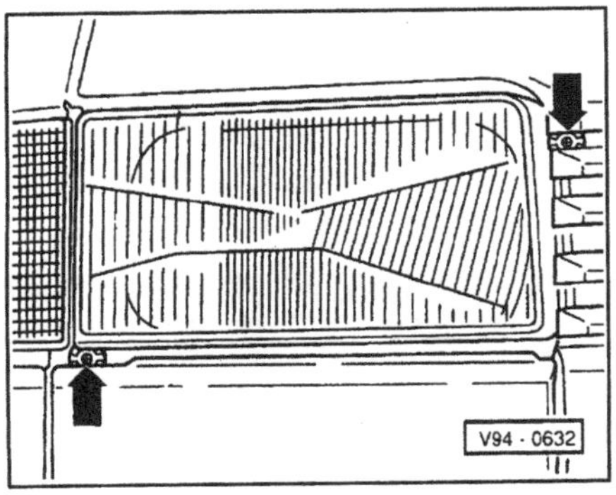

◄ - Adjust headlights using a Phillips screwdriver

Upper adjustment screw = lateral adjustment
Lower adjustment screw = height adjustment

Note:

Right side headlight adjustment screws are shown. The left side headlight screws are a mirror image.

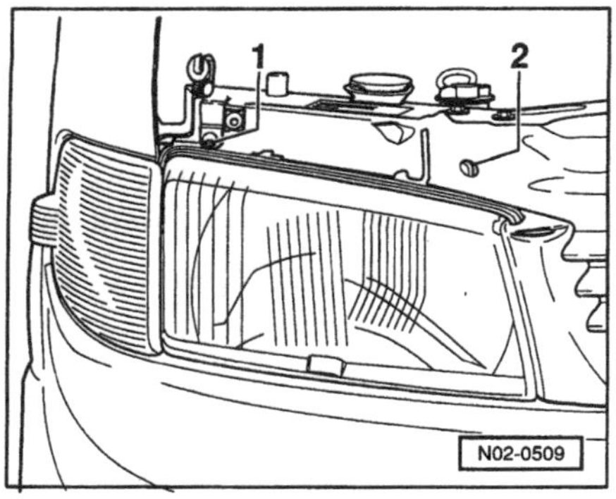

Vehicles from 01.96 production

- Release hood and open.
- ◄ Adjust headlights using a suitable screwdriver

1 = height adjustment
2 = lateral adjustment

Note:

Right side headlight adjustment screws are shown. The left side headlight screws are a mirror image.

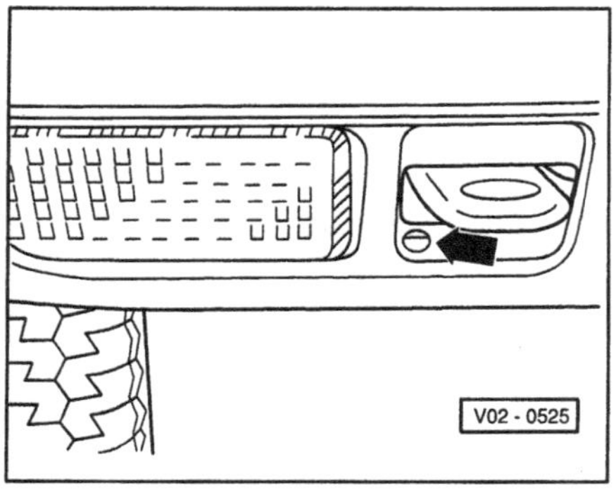

Adjusting foglights

- Using a long shaft screwdriver, turn adjusting wheel through opeining in bumper (arrow). Lateral adjustment is not possible.

Note:

On vehicles without a spoiler the adjustment wheel can also be turned by hand.

Fuses, installing

California vehicles:

The fuse box for the camping equipment is installed on the side wall behind the driver's seat. The following three fuses are to be installed (from top to bottom):

Fuse 1 – (central electrics) / 5 A

Fuse 4 – (auxiliary heater) / 25 A

Fuse 6 – (cooler) / 15 A

Battery no-load voltage, checking

- Battery must be in a no-load situation for at least two hours (no starting, charging or discharging).

The following procedure applies to measure battery voltage in no-load condition (after at least two hours):

- Check voltage using digital multimeter Flluke 83 (US 1119) between pole terminals with battery installed (ignition switched off).

- If instrument reads 12.5 volts or above, battery is OK.
- If voltage is below 12.5 volts. determine cause and repair.

Battery electrolyte level, checking

If the electrolyte level has dropped below the MIN mark, the affected battery cells must be filled to the MAX mark with distilled water.

Windshield washer system, adjusting nozzles

Note:

- *Never use a needle or similar object or water passages in the nozzles will be damaged!*
- *The windshield washer reservoir must be filled completely with washer solvent.*

- Check nozzle setting, if necessary adjust with tool 3125 A.

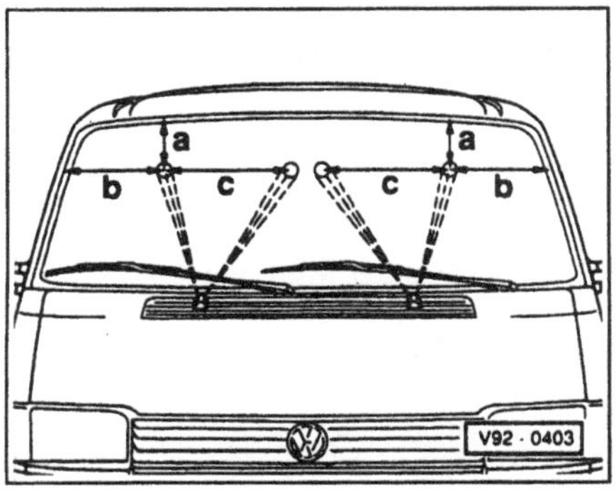

◄ Windshield washer nozzle setting figures:

a	400 mm (15.7 in.)	c	520 mm (20.5 in.)
b	300 mm (11.8 in.)	d	600 mm (23.6 in.)

Tolerance: ± 20 mm (0.80 in.)

Note:

Preadjusted spray nozzles (identified by a white dot under the nozzles) are not adjustable.

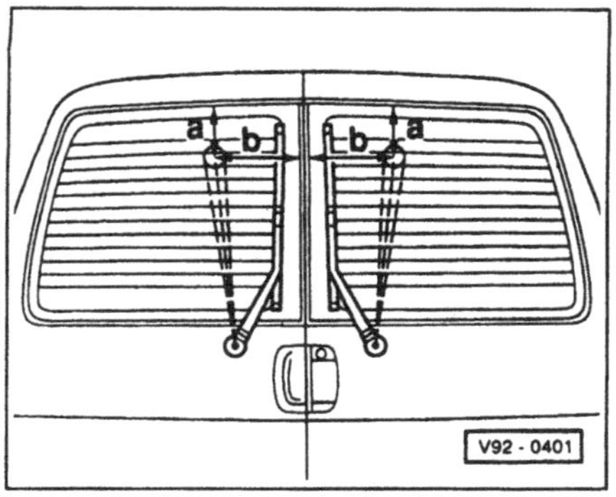

Rear window washer nozzle setting figures:

♦ Tailgate

Washer nozzle in center of wiped area

◄ ♦ Wing doors

Left-hand side (right-hand side is mirror image)

a	150 mm (5.9 in.)
b	250 mm (9.8 in.)

Note:

If jet of water is irregular or cannot be adjusted to prescribed figures, then replace nozzle.

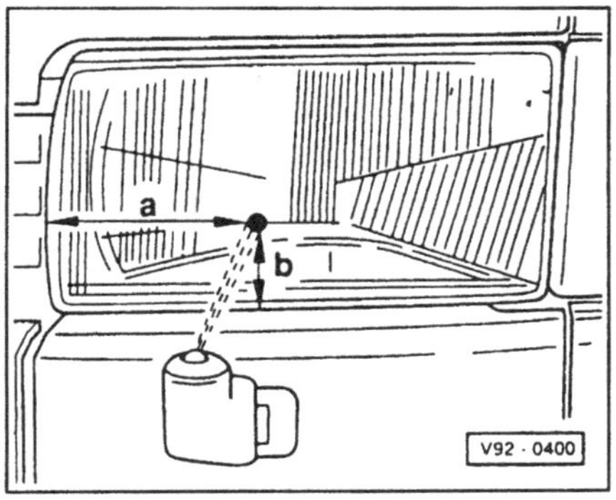

Headlight washer system, adjusting nozzles

– Check nozzle settings, if necessary adjust with tool 3019 A or equivalent.

◄ – Pull washer nozzles out onto stop.

a	120 mm (4.7 in.)
b	50 mm (1.9 in.)

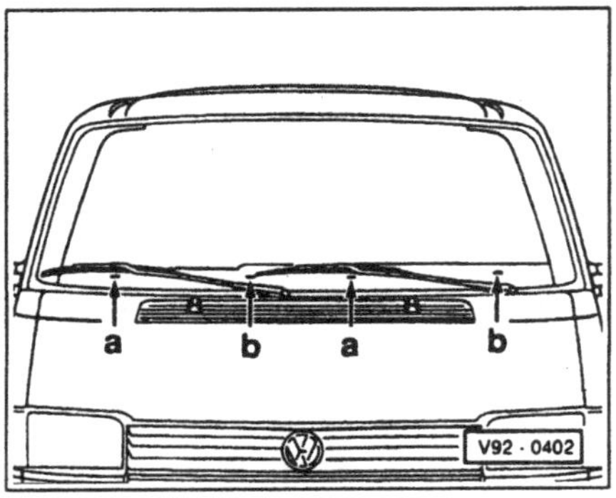

Wiper blades, adjusting park position

Windshield:

◄ – Set wiper blades on markings in windscreen.

a = Mark for left-hand drive vehicles

b = Mark for right-hand drive vehicles

Wiper arm tightening torque: 19 Nm (14 ft lb)

Rear window:

♦ Tailgate

◄ – Set wiper blade on markings at height of lower heater element in heated rear window.

a = 45 mm (1.7 in.)

Wiper arm tightening torque: 19 Nm (14 ft lb)

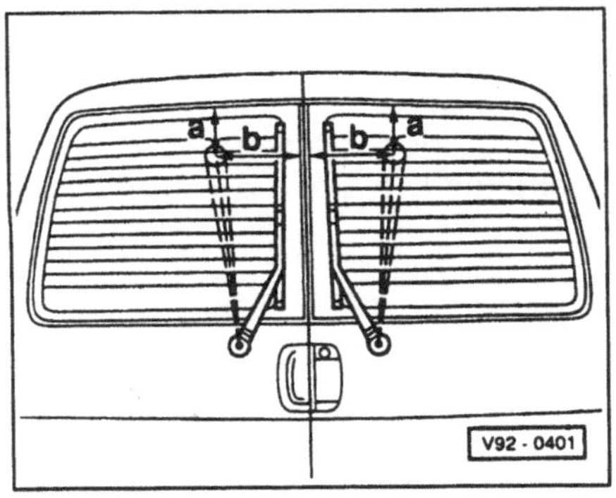

♦ Wing doors

– Set left and right-hand wiper blades vertical

Wiper arm tightening torque: 19 Nm (14 ft lb)

Dust and pollen filter insert, replacing

In engine compartment

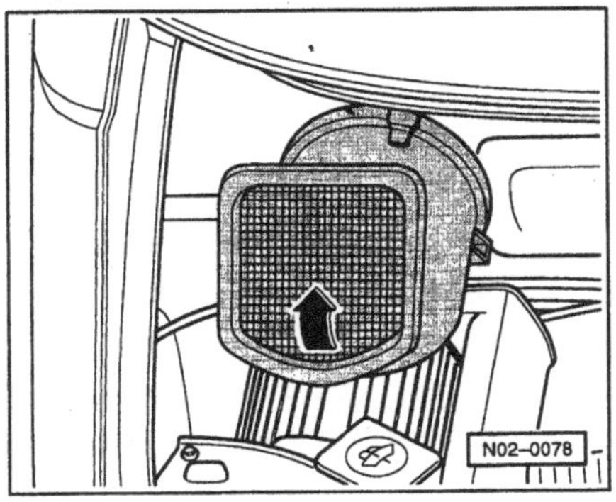

– Loosen three spring brackets and pull out upper part of filter.

– Pull out filter insert

– Separate filter from seal by compressing both connections.

Note:

When installing, be sure that the filter can be heard latching to the sealing ring and the outer rubber lip is pushed onto the offset in the upper part of the filter.

In passenger compartment

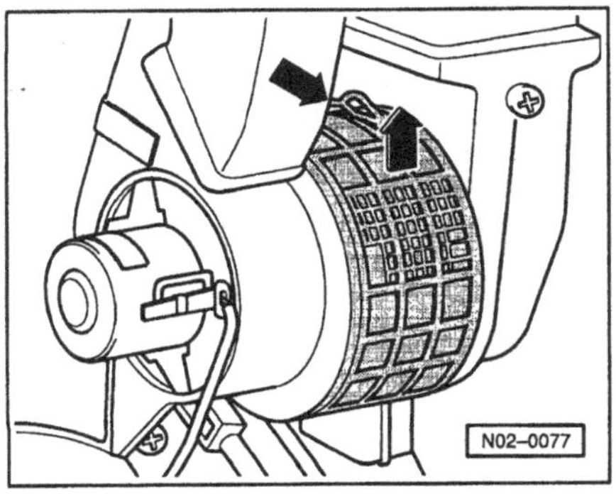

– Remove cover.

– Loosen upper wire bracket and lower lid

– Remove vertical filter bracket and change felt pad, or -

– Remove dust and pollen filter by compressing both connectors to the right and inward.

Note:

♦ In order to avoid damage to the system, the blower should only be running if a filter has been installed.

Clock, setting

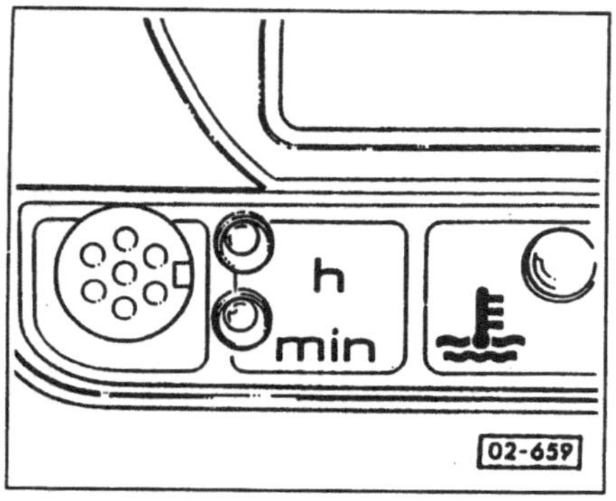

◄ Two buttons located below and to the left of the clock display are used to set the clock time.

h = hours
m = minutes

– Press buttons briefly with tip of ball pen to advance time one hour or one minute.

Note:

Press and hold the buttons to advance the hours or minutes continuously.

Setting time to exact second:

– Press "min" button until time is one minute before time to be set.

– Press "min" button again at moment when seconds indicator of an accurate clock shows a full minute or when time signal is heard on radio.

Road test

– Check brake pedal and parking brake for free play and operation.

- Brake pedal free play: max. $^1/_3$ of total pedal travel
- Parking brake free play: 2 notches

– Check operation of gear selector mechanism.

– Check operation of steering.

– Check steering play with vehicle stationary and on wheels by turning steering wheel back and forth (wheels in straight-ahead position).

- Steering play: Zero play (engine running)

– Check kickdown operation: Depress accelerator pedal fully beyond the pressure point. Depending on vehicle speed and engine speed, upshift is either retarded or transmission shifts down into next lower gear.

– Check operation of air conditioner: cold or warm air must flow out of vents.

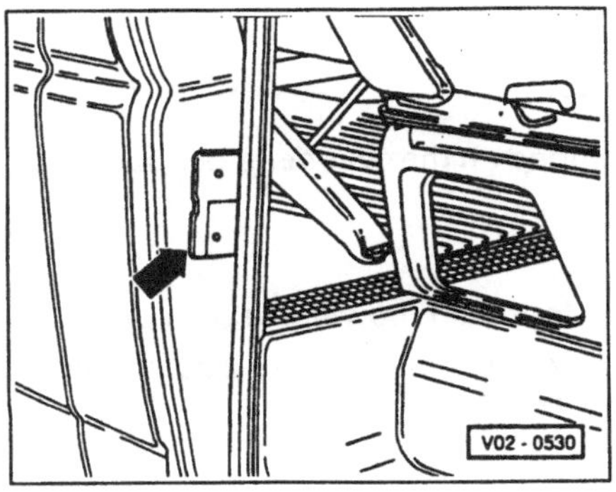

Identification plate, vehicle identification number (chassis number)

◄ A - Identification plate:
located on passenger door lock column -arrow-.

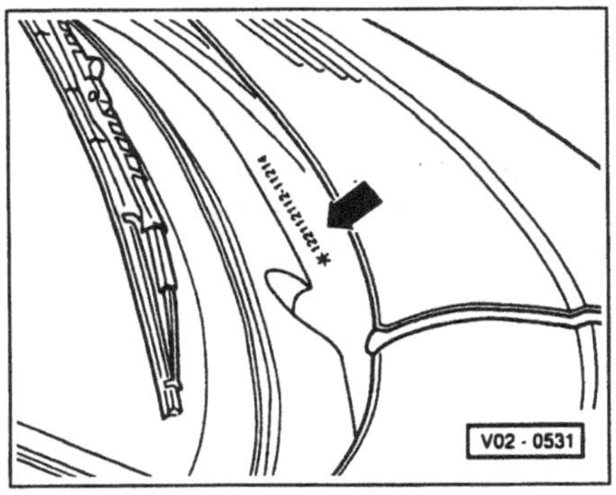

◄ B - Vehicle identification number (chassis number)
located below windshield -arrow-.

Breakdown of vehicle identification number:

WV2	ZZZ	70	Z	R	H	000 001
Manufacturer's character	Filler characters	Type	Filler character	Model year (e.g. 1994)	Production plant	Serial number

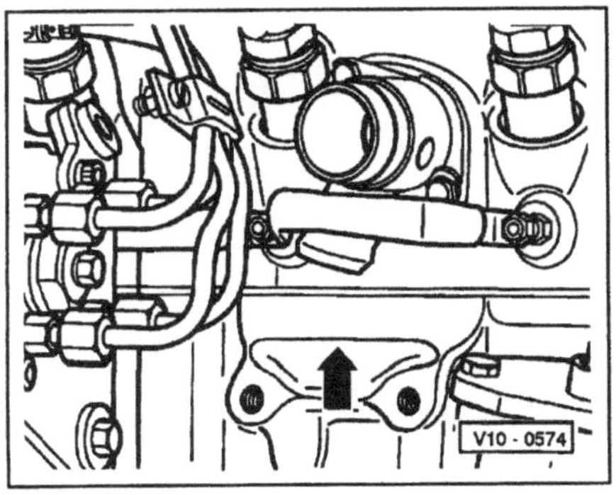

Engine code letters and engine number

◄ 5-cylinder Diesel engine:

The engine number is stamped on the left-hand side of cylinder block next to the injection pump.

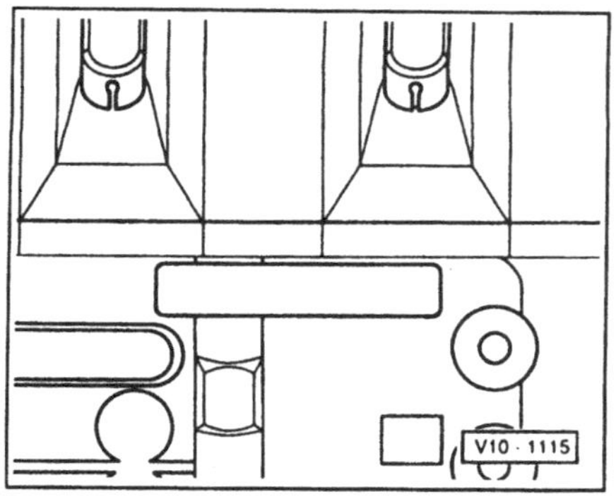

5-cylinder gasoline engines:

The engine number is stamped on the cylinder block above the oil filter.

Note:

- *The engine code is also found on the vehicle data plate.*
- *The engine code and the engine number are also shown on a sticker on the toothed belt guard.*

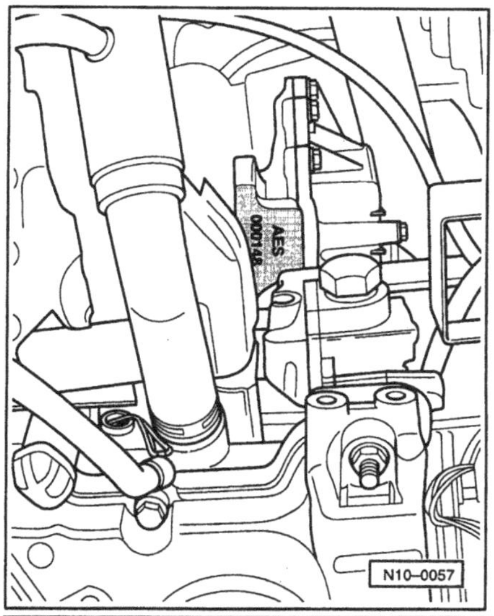

6-cylinder gasoline engines:

The engine number (engine code and sequence number) is located on the left side of engine block behind the cylinder head cover.

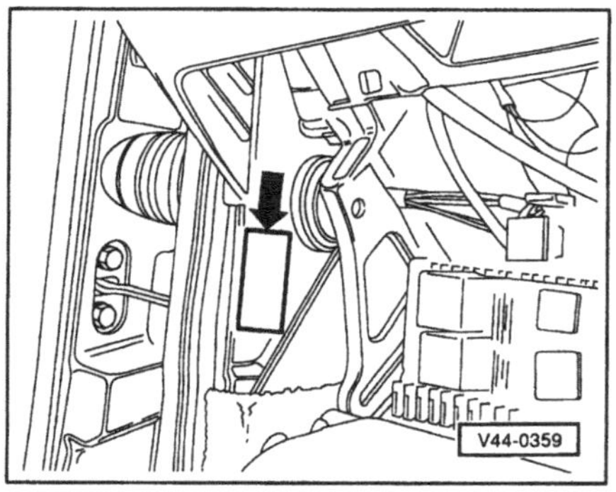

Vehicle data plate is located on the A-pillar next to central electric.

On left-hand drive vehicles - left-hand side

On right-hand drive vehicles - right-hand side

Lifting vehicle

Workshop hoist:

Caution!

- ***Before driving onto a hoist, make sure that the weight of the vehicle does not exceed the permissible bearing capacity of the hoist.***
- ***Only two-pillar, two-column or double strut hoist with sufficiently long supporting arms may be used.***
- ***A single-column hoist may be used — but only as an exception — for short wheelbase vehicles in an unloaded condition.***
- ***Hoists with liquid cushions must not be used to raise the vehicle.***
- ***Before driving onto a hoist, make sure there is sufficient clearance between low-lying vehicle components and the hoist.***
- ***The vehicle may only be lifted at the points indicated to avoid damaging the vehicle underbody and to prevent the vehicle from tipping.***

Floor jack:

Caution!

- ***The vehicle may only be lifted with a trolley jack at the same points indicated for use with a workshop hoist.***
- ***To prevent damage to the vehicle underbody, always use a suitable rubber or wood liner.***
- ***Never lift the vehicle under the engine oil pan, transmission, rear axle, front axle or on the bottom sill as this may cause serious damage.***
- ***Never start the engine and engage a gear with the vehicle raised if even one drive wheel is touching the ground.***
- ***If work is to be performed under the vehicle it must be securely supported by suitable stands.***

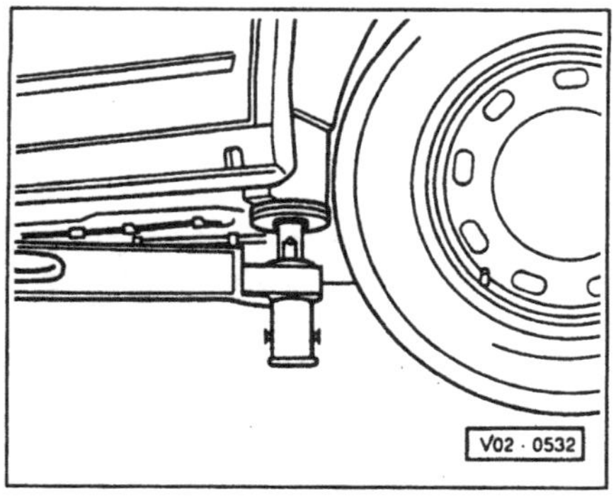

Lifting points for workshop hoists and floor jacks:

The vehicle may only be lifted at the points indicated to avoid damaging the vehicle underbody and to prevent the vehicle from tipping.

◄ **Front:**

On front cross member

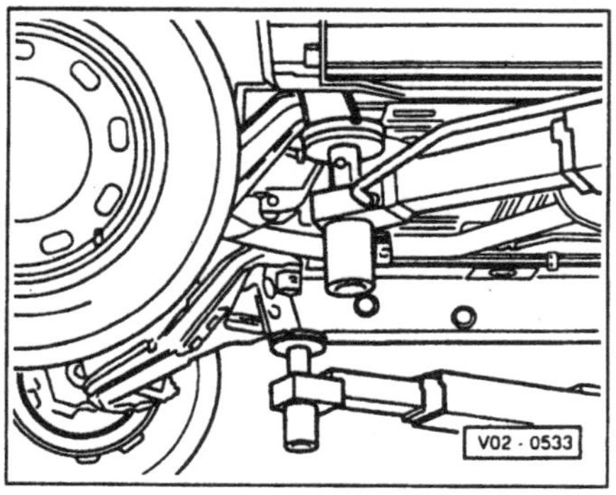

◄ **Rear:**

On rear control arm mounting

Note:

Unloaded short wheelbase vehicles may be lifted with a single-column hoist as an exception to the recommended two-column hoist. The lifting point is then located on the long member reinforcing plate, ⇒ next illustration.

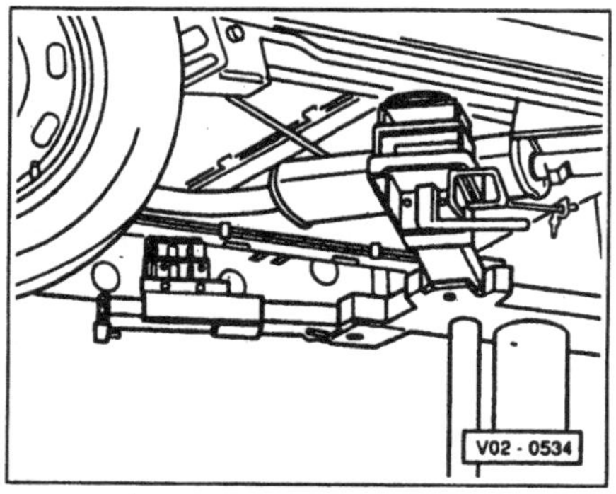

◄ The alternate rear lifting point for single-column hoists is the long member reinforcing plate.

Towing

Note:

- *Tow vehicle with the drive wheels lifted whenever possible.*
- *Vehicles with automatic transmissions cannot be started by pushing or towing.*
- *Vehicles with manual transmissions must not be started by pushing or towing. Damage to the catalytic converter and/or other parts of the vehicle may result from tow or push starting.*

Front towing

> ***Caution!***
>
> ***The EuroVan cannot be towed with conventional sling-type equipment or non-self-loading wheel dollies. Towing with this type of equipment will cause bumper and body panel damage.***

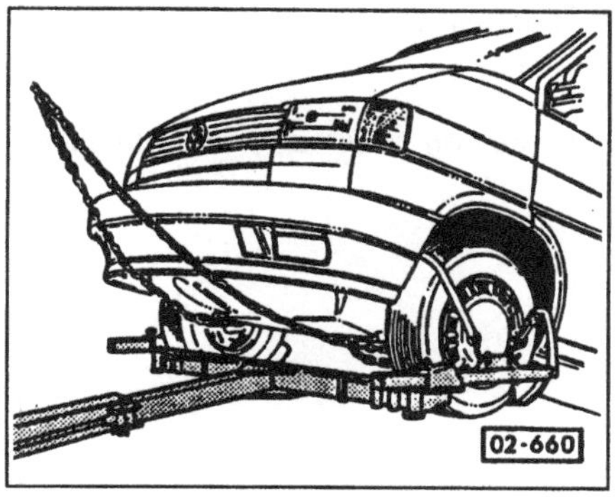
02-660

◄ **Front hook-up procedure:**

– Attach wheel lift equipment to wheels.

– Attach safety straps to wheels.

– Attach safety chains to lower control arms.

Towing clearance: 15 – 30 cm (6 – 12 in.) between tires and ground.

Rear towing

> ***Caution!***
>
> - ***The EuroVan cannot be towed with conventional sling-type equipment or non-self-loading wheel dollies. Towing with this type of equipment will cause bumper and body panel damage.***
> - ***If an automatic transmission vehicle cannot be towed with wheel lift equipment in combination with self-loading dollies, it must be transported on a flat bed to avoid damage to the transmission due to the lack of lubrication.***

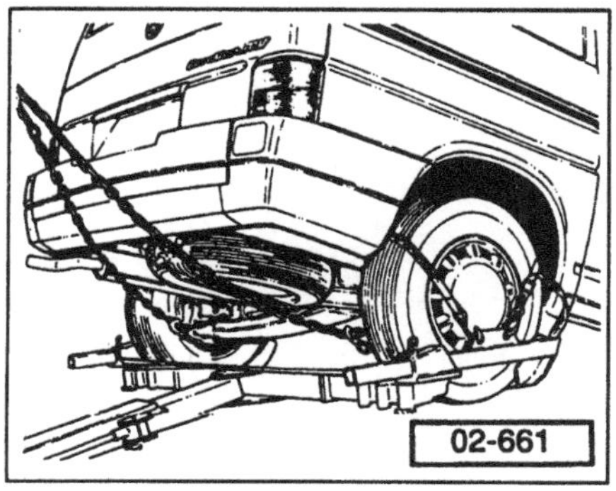
02-661

◄ **Rear hook-up procedure:**

– Attach wheel lift equipment to wheels.

– Attach safety straps to wheels.

– Attach safety chains to axle beam.

Towing clearance: 15 – 30 cm (6 – 12 in.) between tires and ground.

Towing speed/distance

Manual transmission: 50 mph / 50 miles (80 km/h / 80 km)

Automatic transmission: If an automatic transmission vehicle cannot be towed with wheel lift equipment in combination with self-loading dollies, it must be transported on a flat bed to avoid damage to the transmission due to the lack of lubrication.

Spark plugs, replacing

Special tools and epuipment

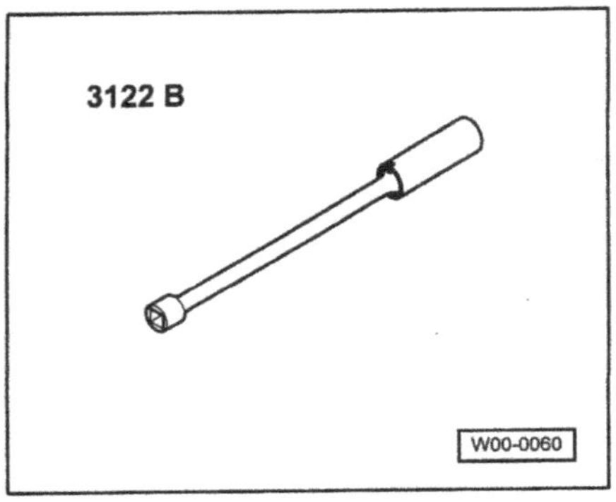

- ♦ 3122B Spark plug wrench

6-cylinder vehicles

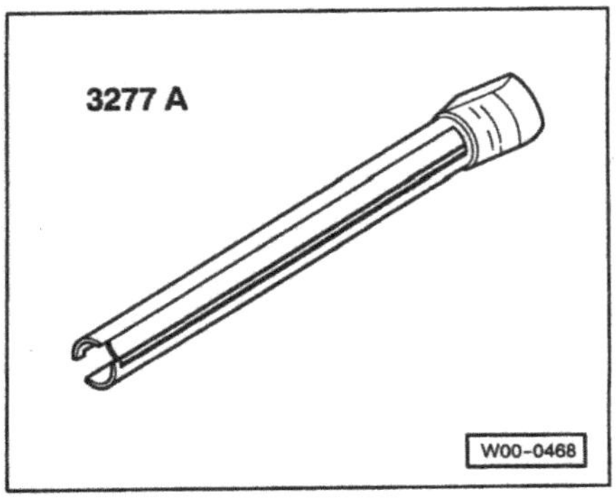

- ♦ 3277A Spark plug connector tool

- Use tool 3277A to pull off and push on spark plug connectors.

Note:

Spark plug designation and tightening torques: ⇒ Fuel Injection and Ignition.

2.4 Liter Diesel, General Engine (Engine Codes: AAB, ACV)

Section **B**

> ***WARNING!***
> ***Before proceeding with any work, please read the warnings and cautions immediately following this index. Also read any warning and caution that accompanies a procedure in the manual.***

Introduction

This Repair Manual booklet covers the EuroVan Diesel: General - Engine Repair
Groups: 00, 10, 13, 15, 17, 19, 20, 21, 26
Engine Codes: **AAB** and **ACV**.

Important!

Engine Code ACV (**TDI**) is covered in this Repair Manual booklet. This vehicle was not available in the North American market at the time of printing.

Please read these WARNINGS and CAUTIONS before proceeding with maintenance and repair work.

WARNING—

- Some repairs may be beyond your capability. If you lack the skills, tools and equipment, or a suitable workplace for any procedure described in this manual, we suggest you leave such repairs to an authorized Volkswagen dealer service department, or other qualified shop.

- Volkswagen is constantly improving its cars. Sometimes these changes, both in parts and specifications, are made applicable to earlier models. Therefore, before starting any major jobs or repairs to components on which passenger safety may depend, consult your authorized Volkswagen dealer about the Technical Bulletins that may have been issued since the editorial closing of this manual.

- Do not re-use any fasteners that are worn or deformed in normal use. Many fasteners are designed to be used only once and become unreliable and may fail when used a second time. This includes, but is not limited to, nuts, bolts, washers, self–locking nuts or bolts, circlips and cotter pins. Always replace these fasteners with new parts.

- Never work under a lifted car unless it is solidly supported on stands designed for the purpose. Do not support a car on cinder blocks, hollow tiles or other props that may crumble under continuous load. Never work under a vehicle that is supported solely by a jack. Never work under the car while the engine is running.

- If you are going to work under a car on the ground, make sure that the ground is level. Block the wheels to keep the car from rolling. Disconnect the battery negative terminal (ground strap) to prevent others from starting the vehicle while you are under it.

- Never run the engine unless the work area is well ventilated. Carbon monoxide (CO) kills.

- Do not attempt to work on your vehicle if you do not feel well. You increase the danger of injury to yourself and others if you are tired, upset or have taken medicine or any other substance that may impair you or keep you from being fully alert.

- Disconnect the battery negative (–) terminal (ground strap) whenever you work on the fuel system or the electrical system. Do not smoke or work near heaters or other fire hazards. Keep an approved fire extinguisher handy.

- Batteries produce explosive hydrogen gas. Keep sparks, lighted matches and open flame away from the top of the battery. If hydrogen gas escaping from the cap vents is ignited, it will ignite gas trapped in the cells and cause the battery to explode.

- Connect and disconnect battery cables, jumper cables or a battery charger only with the ignition switched off, to prevent sparks. Do not quick–charge the battery (for boost starting) for longer than one minute, and do not allow charging voltage to exceed 16.5 volts. Wait at least one minute before boosting the battery a second time.

- Illuminate your work area adequately but safely. Use a portable safety light for working inside or under the car. Make sure the bulb is enclosed by a wire cage. The hot filament of an accidentally broken bulb can ignite spilled fuel or oil.

- Tie long hair behind your head. Do not wear a necktie, a scarf, loose clothing, or a necklace when you work near machine tools or running engines. If your hair, clothing, or jewelry were to get caught in the machinery, severe injury could result.

- Finger rings, bracelets and other jewelry should be removed so that they cannot cause electrical shorts, get caught in running machinery, or be crushed by heavy parts.

- Catch draining fuel, oil, or brake fluid in suitable containers. Do not use food or beverage containers that might mislead someone into drinking from them. Store flammable fluids away from fire hazards. Wipe up spills at once, but do not store the oily rags, which can ignite and burn spontaneously.

- Always observe good workshop practices. Wear goggles when you operate machine tools or work with battery acid. Gloves or other protective clothing should be worn whenever the job requires working with harmful substances.

- The Air-Conditioning (A/C) system is filled with a chemical refrigerant, which is hazardous. The A/C system should be serviced only by trained technicians using approved refrigerant recovery/recycling equipment, trained in related safety precautions, and familiar with regulations governing the discharging and disposal of automotive chemical refrigerants.

- Do not expose any part of the A/C system to high temperatures such as an open flame. Excessive heat will increase system pressure and may cause the system to burst.

- Some aerosol tire inflators are highly flammable. Be extremely cautious when repairing a tire that may have been inflated using an aerosol tire inflator. Keep sparks, open flame or other sources of ignition away from the tire repair area. Inflate and deflate the tire at least four times before breaking the bead from the rim. Completely remove the tire from the rim before attempting any repair.

- Friction materials such as brake or clutch discs may contain asbestos fibers. Do not create dust by grinding, sanding, or by cleaning with compressed air. Avoid breathing asbestos fibers and asbestos dust. Breathing asbestos can cause serious diseases such as asbestosis or cancer, and may result in death.

- Greases, lubricants and other automotive chemicals contain toxic substances, many of which are absorbed directly through the skin. Read manufacturer's instructions and warnings carefully. Use hand and eye protection. Avoid direct skin contact.

- An airbag is operated by an explosive device. Handled improperly or without adequate safeguards, it can be accidently activated and cause serious personal injury. To prevent personal injury or airbag system failure, **only trained Volkswagen dealer service technicians** should test, disassemble or service the airbag system.

WARNINGS and CAUTIONS continued on next page ▶

Please read these WARNINGS and CAUTIONS before proceeding with maintenance and repair work.

WARNING (continued) —

- ALWAYS disconnect the airbag power supply before using a computer memory saver. Failure to disconnect the airbag power supply may result in accidental activation of the airbag.
- The airbag unit should not be removed, nor should any work be performed on the airbag system, without first reviewing the warnings and cautions that accompany the airbag system repair information in this manual.
- Never apply stickers or any other coverings on the steering wheel. Do not let chemical cleaners, oil or grease come into contact with the vinyl covering of the airbag unit.
- Never open or otherwise attempt to repair airbag system parts. Always use new parts. Never leave airbag parts or the partially disassembled airbag system unattended.
- Never use a test light or volt meter to conduct electrical tests on the airbag system. The airbag system must only be tested by trained Volkswagen Service technicians using special airbag tester equipment. The airbag system must only be tested while it is installed in the car.
- Do not expose an airbag unit to temperatures above 194°F (90°C) even for a brief period, while handling it during the repair process. Keep the unit clear of heat sources such as hot plates, soldering irons, heat lamps, welding equipment, or the like.
- Always replace airbag system components that have been mechanically damaged (bubbles, cracks, etc.).
- Always set down a removed airbag unit so that the horn pad is facing upward.
- When driving or riding in an airbag-equipped vehicle, never hold test equipment in your hands or lap while the vehicle is in motion. Objects between you and the airbag can increase the risk of injury in an accident.
- The storage, transportation and disposal of airbag units are subject to the laws for flammable solids.

CAUTION—

- If you lack the skills, tools and equipment, or a suitable workshop for any procedure described in this manual, we suggest you leave such repairs to an authorized Volkswagen dealer or other qualified shop. We especially urge you to consult an authorized Volkswagen dealer before beginning repairs on any car that may still be covered wholly or in part by any of the extensive warranties issued by Volkswagen of America, Inc.
- Volkswagen is constantly improving its cars and sometimes these changes, both in parts and specifications, are made applicable to earlier models. Therefore, part numbers listed in this manual are for reference only. Always check with your authorized Volkswagen dealer parts department for the latest information.
- Before starting a job, make certain that you have all the necessary tools and parts on hand. Read all the instructions thoroughly, do not attempt shortcuts. Use tools that are appropriate to the work and use only replacement parts meeting Volkswagen specifications. Makeshift tools, parts and procedures will not make good repairs.
- Use pneumatic and electric tools only to loosen threaded parts and fasteners. Never use these tools to tighten fasteners, especially on light alloy parts. Always use a torque wrench to tighten fasteners to the tightening torque specification listed.
- Be mindful of the environment and ecology. Before you drain the crankcase, find out the proper way to dispose of the oil. Do not pour oil onto the ground, down a drain, or into a stream, pond, or lake. Consult local ordinances that govern the disposal of wastes.
- When connecting cables or ground straps, all connections must be cleaned to bare metal. Be sure mounting bolts are tight.
- Do not replace fuse links with fuse links of other gauge or with standard wire. Always replace the entire length of the fuse link.
- Before doing any electrical welding on vehicles equipped with Anti-lock Brakes (ABS), disconnect the battery negative terminal (ground strap) and the ABS Control Module connector.
- On cars equipped with ABS, the ABS control unit cannot withstand temperatures from a paint–drying booth or a heat lamp in excess of 203°F (95°C) and should not be subjected to temperatures in excess of 185°F (85°C) for more than two hours.
- On cars equipped with anti-theft radios, make sure you know the correct radio activation code before disconnecting the battery or removing the radio. If the wrong code is entered when power is restored, the radio may lock up and be rendered inoperable, even if the correct code is then entered.
- When boost-charging the battery, first remove the fuses for the Engine Control Module (ECM), the Transmission Control Module (TCM), the ABS Control Module, and the On-Board computer. In cases where one or more of these components is not separately fused, disconnect the Control Module connector(s).
- Do not quick-charge the battery (for boost starting) for longer than one minute, and do not exceed 16.5 volts at the battery with the boosting cables attached. Wait at least one minute before boosting the battery a second time.

◀ **WARNINGS and CAUTIONS** continued from previous page

General

Engine number

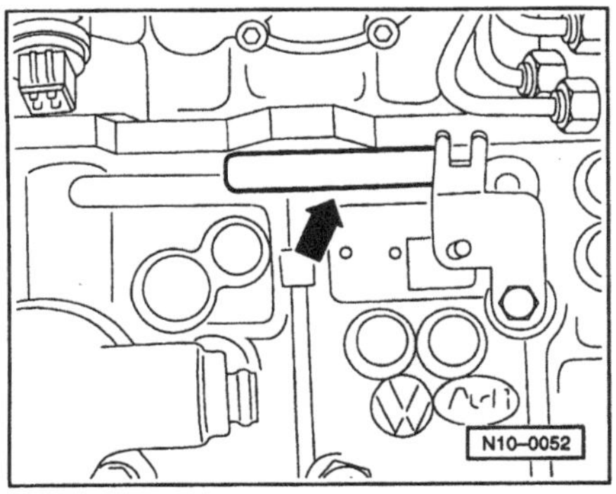

◄

- The "engine number" (Engine Code letters plus serial number) is stamped on the left side of cylinder block next to injection pump
- There is also an "engine number" sticker attached to the toothed belt guard.
- The engine code is also displayed on the vehicle data plate.

Technical data

Code letters		AAB	ACV
Manufactured		09.90 ➤	08.95 ➤
Capacity	liters	2.4	2.5
Output	kW at rpm	57/3700	75/3500
Torque	Nm at rpm	164/1800...2200	250/2300
Bore	mm ∅	79.5	81
Stroke	mm	95.5	95.5
Compression ratio		23:1	20.5:1
Octane Rating	minimum	45	45
Firing order	cyl nos.	1-2-4-5-3	1-2-4-5-3
Catalytic converter		NO	YES
Exhaust Gas Recirculation		NO	YES
Turbocharged		NO	YES
Charge Air cooler		NO	YES

Engine / Transmission, removing and installing

Special tools, testers and auxiliary items

- VAG 1921 spring clip pliers
- 3227 engine stand
- VAG 1383A engine/transmission jack
- VW 540 engine/transmission support
- 2024 A Lifting appliance with 2024 A/1 extension
- VW 540 engine/transmission support with VW 540/1A supplementary kit
- G 000 100 Grease
- VAG 1331 Torque wrench: 5 to 50 Nm (3.7 to 37 ft lb)
- VAG 1332 Torque wrench: 40 to 200 Nm (30 to 148 ft lb)
- Cable ties

Engine / Transmission, removing

- Remove engine/transmission assembly from below
- Ensure that ignition is switched OFF
- Disconnect battery ground strap

CAUTION!

Obtain the radio anti-theft code before disconnecting the battery negative cable!

- When installing, replace all cable ties (which were opened or cut to remove the engine) in their original position
- Remove sound dampening pan
⇒ Repair Group 50
- Remove front exhaust pipe
⇒ Repair Group 26
- Drain coolant
⇒ Repair Group 19

Vehicles 09.94 ➤

- Remove radiator grille
⇒ Repair Group 66

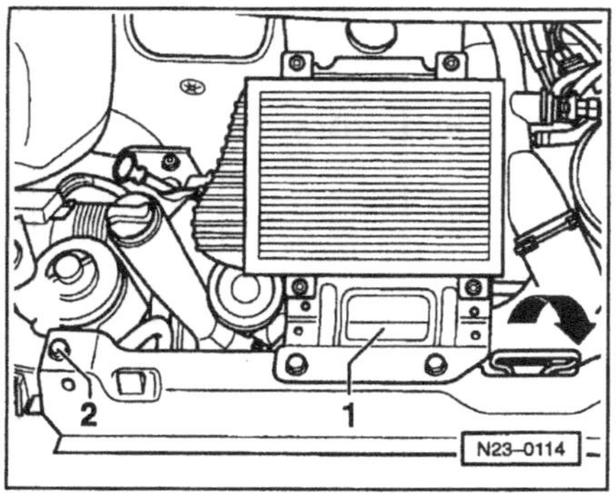

Engine code ACV

– Remove charge air cooler bracket -1-

– Remove charge air cooler with air hoses
⇒ Repair Group 21

All Engine Codes

– Unfasten left and right-hand mounting bolts -2-

Note:

Vehicles ➤ 08.94: there are 2 mounting bolts on each side of the lock carrier.

– Tilt forward the lock carrier and radiator -arrow-

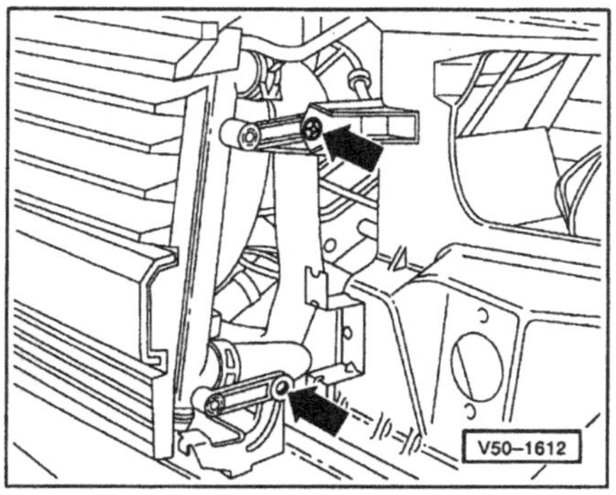

– Remove radiator coolant hoses from engine using VAG 1921 hose clip pliers

– Pull connectors off thermal switch and radiator fan

– Push pins out from left and right hand spreader clips -arrows- and unclip spreader clips form radiator bracket

– Lift out radiator complete with fan, air guide and lock carrier

– Detach speedometer drive at transmission

Vehicles with A/C

> ***CAUTION!***
> ***Do NOT open the A/C refrigerant circuit.***

– Observe additional information and removal instructions
⇒ page B 10-7

Engine Code AAB

– Disconnect throttle cable at injection pump lever, remove securing clip on support bracket and remove throttle cable from injection pump
⇒ Repair Group 20

– Disconnect Cold Start Accelerator cable
⇒ Repair Group 20

– Remove mechanical clutch control cable or hydraulic clutch control slave cylinder
⇒ Repair Group 30, 5-Speed manual transmission 02B

– Disconnect Transmission Range selector mechanism
⇒ Repair Group 34, 5-Speed manual transmission 02B

Engine Code ACV

– Disconnect hose/metal pipe from hydraulic clutch slave cylinder on transmission
⇒ Repair Group 30, 5-Speed manual transmission 02G

– Disconnect transmission range selector mechanism
⇒ Repair Group 30, 5-Speed manual transmission 02G

All Engine Codes

– Remove fuel supply and return lines at injection pump

– Remove inter-connecting, coolant, vacuum and intake hoses on engine

– Disconnect all wiring from engine, transmission, generator and starter and move clear to one side

– Disconnect power steering pump hydraulic lines from engine and drain hydraulic fluid
⇒ Repair Group 48

– Remove left-hand drive shaft and disconnect right-hand drive shaft at transmission
⇒ Repair Group 40

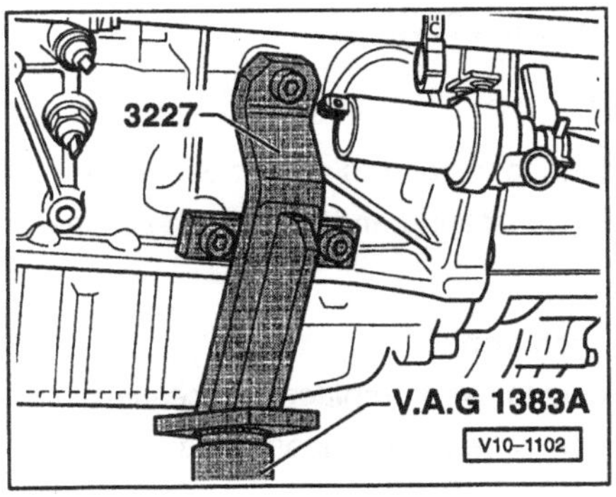

◄ – Bolt engine mount 3227 to cylinder block

♦ 20 Nm (15 ft lb)

– Gently lift engine and transmission using VAG 1383 A engine/transmission jack

– Remove transmission mounts

♦ Engine code AAB
⇒ Repair Group 34, 5-Speed manual transmission 02B

♦ Engine code ACV
⇒ Repair Group 34, 5-Speed manual transmission 02G

– Remove engine mount center bolt (in engine compartment)

– Remove engine/transmission assembly from below, while guiding the power steering return hose out of the way

CAUTION!
Carefully guide the engine/transmission assembly while lowering to prevent damage to the bodywork!

Vehicles with A/C, additional removal notes

CAUTION!

Do NOT open the A/C refrigerant circuit.

Note:

To prevent damage to the condenser and refrigerant lines/hoses, ensure that the lines and hoses are not stretched, kinked or bent.

– Remove A/C fluid reservoir and allow to hang free

– Remove retaining clamp(s) from refrigerant lines

– Detach A/C compressor and condenser and secure to body so that refrigerant lines and A/C hoses are not stressed

Engine / Transmission, installing

Versions with clutch cable

– Check clutch release bearing for wear, replace if necessary

– Lightly lubricate clutch release bearing and input shaft splines

♦ G 000 100 grease

Vehicles with hydraulic clutch control

– Check clutch release bearing for wear, replace if necessary

– Lightly lubricate clutch release bearing, release bearing guide sleeve and input shaft splines

♦ G 000 100 grease

All vehicles

– Verify that engine/transmission centering dowels are installed in cylinder block, install if necessary

– Ensure sufficient clearance between drive shafts during assembly installation

– Install drive shafts
⇒ Repair Group 40

– Install power steering pump hydraulic lines
⇒ Repair Group 48

– Electrical connections and routing
⇒ Repair Group 97

– Rock the engine and transmission mounts to align stress-free

Engine Code AAB

– Install transmission mounts.
⇒ Repair Group 34, 5-Speed manual transmission 02B

– Adjusting accelerator cable
⇒ Repair Group 20

– Adjust CSA operating cable
⇒ Repair Group 20

– Installing mechanical clutch control clutch cable or hydraulic clutch control slave cylinder
⇒ Repair Group 30, 5-Speed manual transmission 02B

– Connecting selector mechanism to transmission.
⇒ Repair Group 34, 5-Speed manual transmission 02B

Engine Code ACV

– Install transmission mounts
⇒ Repair Group 34, 5-Speed manual transmission 02G

– Install hose/metal pipe from hydraulic clutch slave cylinder to (manual) transmission
⇒ Repair Group 30, 5-Speed manual transmission 02G

– Connect transmission range selector mechanism
⇒ Repair Group 34, 5-Speed manual transmission 02G

All Engine Codes

– Install front exhaust pipe
⇒ Repair Group 26

– Fill system with coolant
⇒ Repair Group 19

– Check headlight adjustment and adjust if necessary
⇒ Maintenance booklet

Fastener connections, torque values

Fastener connection		Tightening torque
Engine to transmission	M12	80 Nm (59 ft lb)
	M10	60 Nm (44 ft lb)
	M8	25 Nm (18 ft lb)
Engine mount center bolt	M10	65 Nm (48 ft lb)
Drive shaft to flange shaft		80 Nm (59 ft lb)

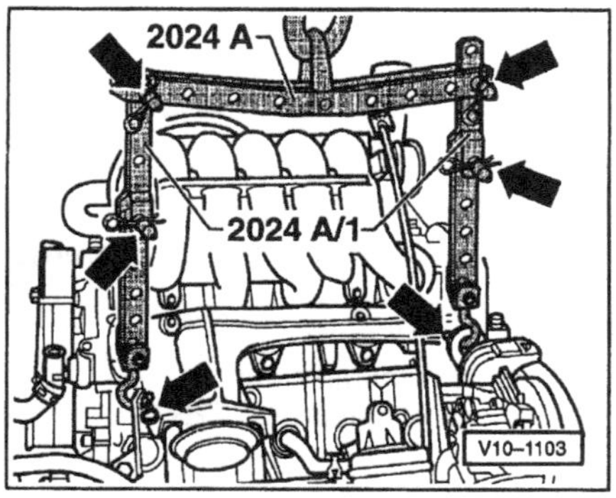

Engine stand, mounting engine

– When working on engine, secure engine stand to VW 313 support clamp using VW 540 engine/transmission bracket

Work sequence

– Remove transmission

◄ – Attach lifting tackle 2024A with extension 2024 A/1 as follows:

- lift from VAG 1383 engine/transmission jack using workshop crane

> ***CAUTION!***
>
> ***Always secure hooks and locating pins with lock pins.***

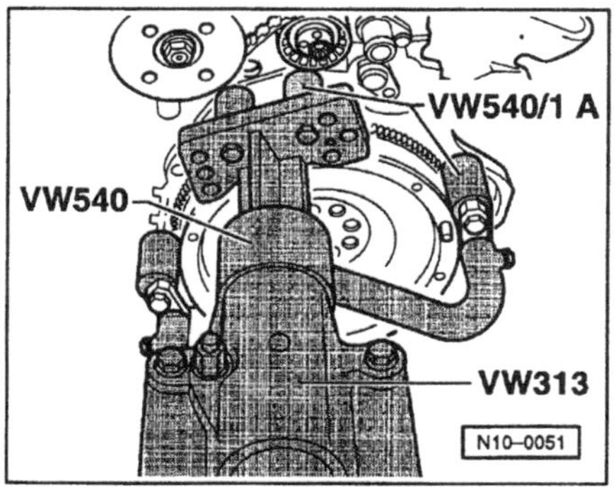

◄ – Mount engine to VW 313 support clamp using VW 540 engine/transmission bracket and VW 540/1 supplementary kit

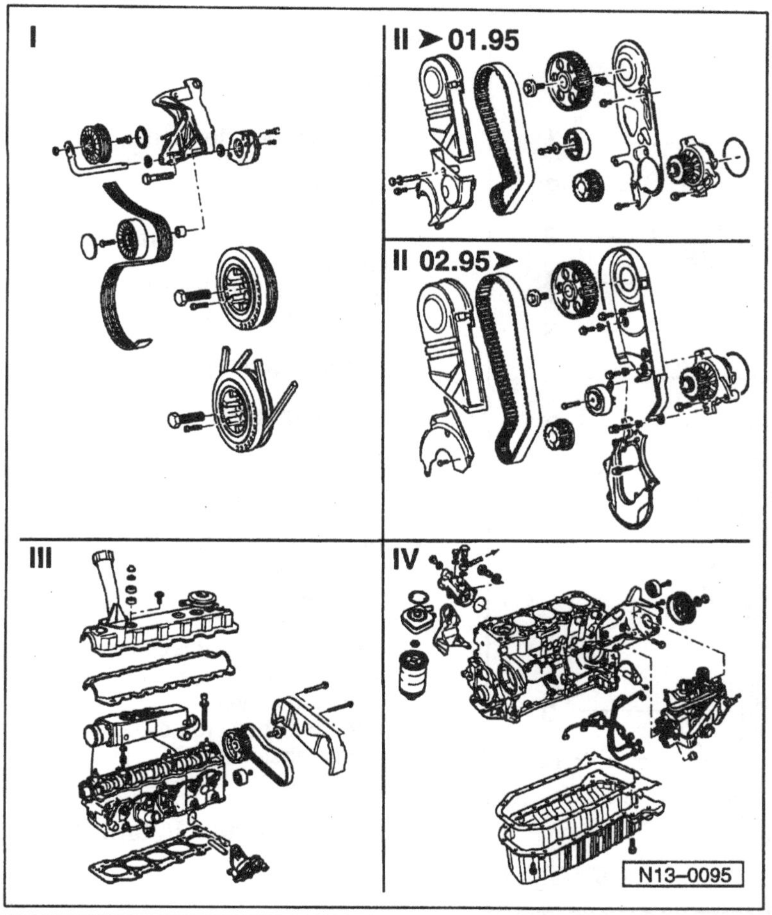

Engine, disassembling and assembling

Notes:

- *If during repairs, metal shavings or quantities of small metal particles are found in the engine oil; caused, for example, by partial seizure of the crankshaft and connecting rod bearings - then, beside cleaning out the oil passages, you must also replace the oil cooler.*
- *Faulty injectors can cause violent knocking noises in the engine which can also sound like faulty bearings. If this occurs; run the engine at idle and loosen the injector lines one after the other. If the knocking stops when a line has been loosened, it indicates that the respective injector is faulty.*

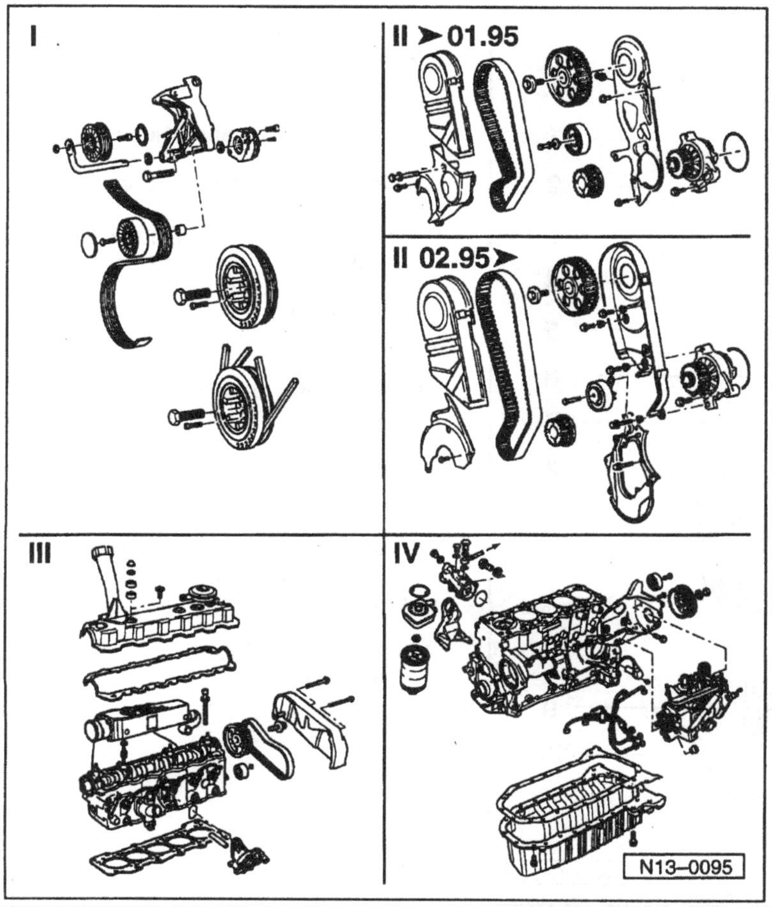

Fuel injector servicing:
Engine codes AAB and ACV:
⇒ Repair Group 23

Part I
⇒ page B 13-3

Part II ➤ 01.95
⇒ page B 13-7

Part II 02.95 ➤
⇒ page B 13-9

Part III
⇒ page B 13-11

Part IV
⇒ page B 13-15

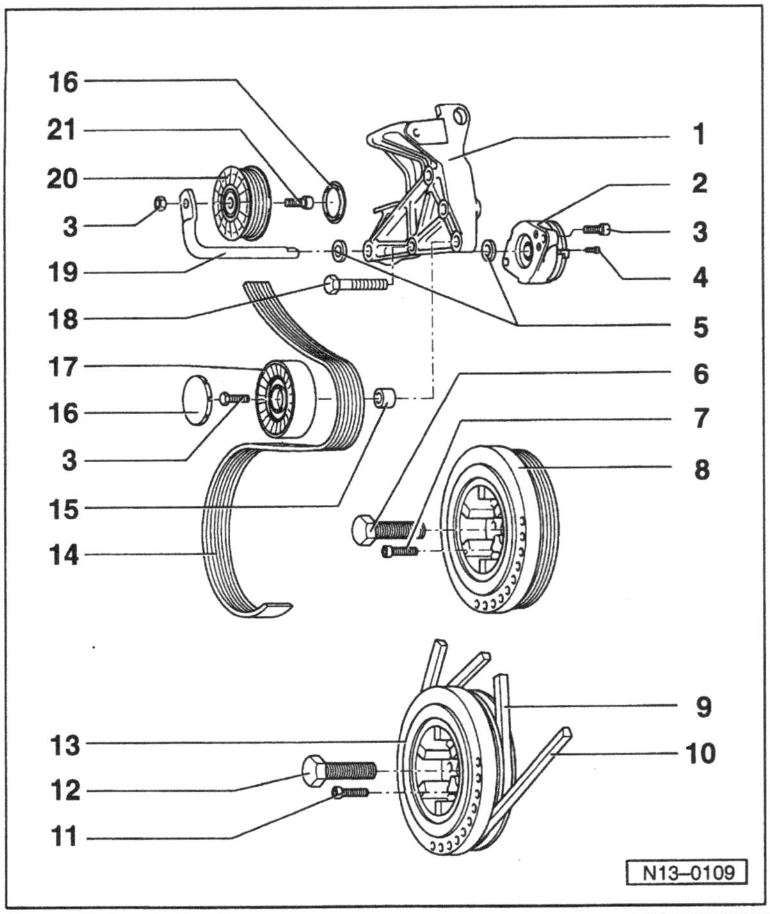

Part I

1 - Bracket
02.95 ➤
- ♦ ribbed belt tensioner, removing and installing:

⇒ page B 13-22

2 - Tensioning roller tensioner element
- ♦ can only be installed one way, holes are offset

3 - 20 Nm (15 ft lb)

4 - 10 Nm (7 ft lb)

5 - Oil seal
- – Replace if damaged

6 - 160 Nm (118 ft lb) + $^{1}/_{2}$ turn (180 °) additional
02.95 ➤
- – Replace
- – Oil threads and contact surfaces
- – Counter-hold using 3248 A to loosen and tighten
- ♦ toothed belt, removing, installing and tensioning:

⇒ page B 13-36

7 - 20 Nm (15 ft lb) + $^{1}/_{4}$ turn (90°) additional
02.95 ➤

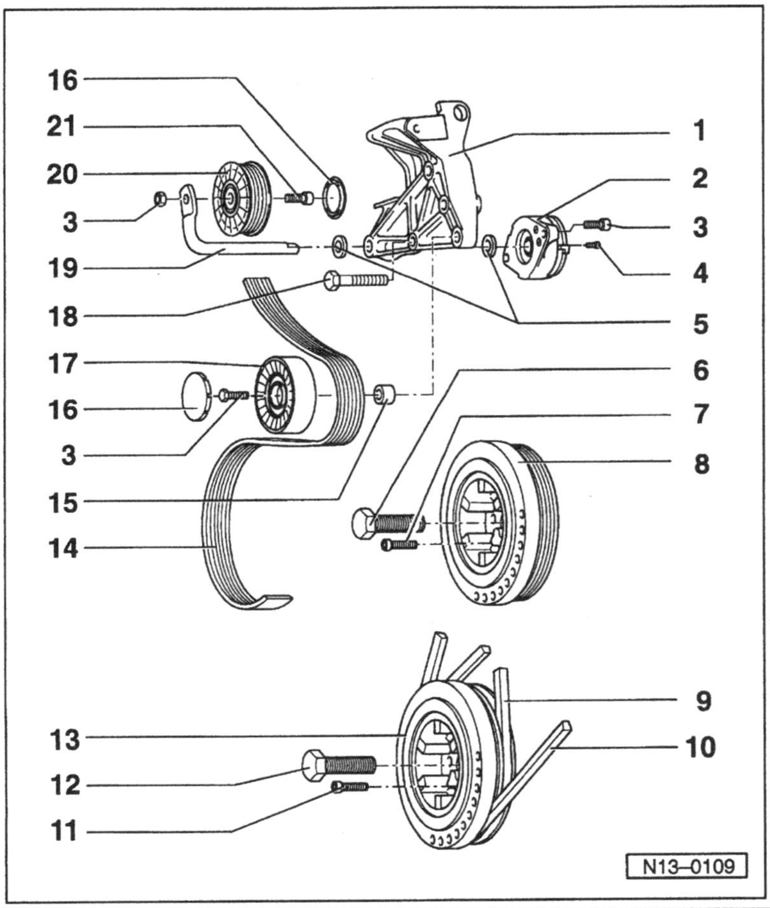

8 - Vibration damper with ribbed belt pulley
02.95 ➤
- – Note orientation when installing

9 - Power steering pump V-belt
➤ 01.95
- – Check tension via thumb pressure deflection: new and used V-belts approx. 5 mm
- ♦ V-belt tension, adjusting:

⇒ Repair Group 48

10 - Generator V-belt
➤ 01.95
- – Check tension by thumb pressure max. deflection:
  "new" ribbed belt approx. 2 mm
  "used" ribbed belt approx. 5 mm
- ♦ vehicles with toothed rack tensioner, V-belt tension, checking:

⇒ page B 13-19

11 - 20 Nm (15 ft lb)
➤ 01.95

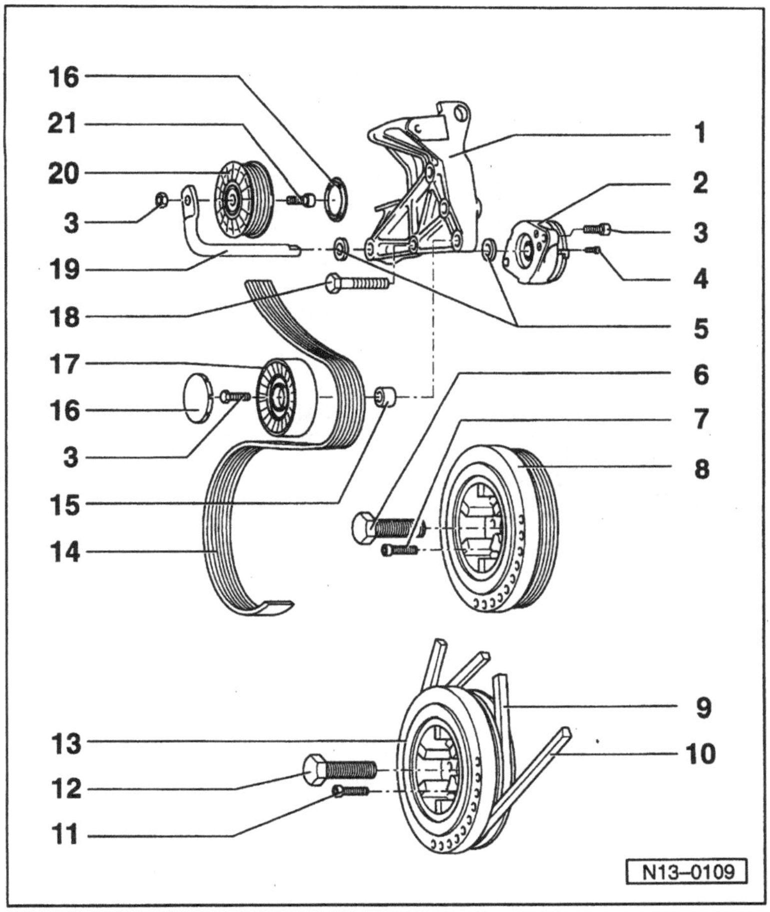

12 - 460 Nm (339 ft lb)

➤ 01.95

– Coat threads and bolt head contact surfaces with sealing paste: AMV 188 001 02

– Loosen and tighten using 3248 A counter-hold tool

♦ camshaft toothed belt: removing, installing, tensioning

⇒ page B 13-26

13 - Vibration damper w/ V-belt pulley

➤ 01.95

– Note orientation of parts

14 - Ribbed belt

02.95 ➤

– Mark direction of rotation before removing

– Check for wear

♦ remove and install with 3299 lever

⇒ page B 13-20

15 - Spacer bushing

16 - Dust cap

17 - Idler roller

18 - 40 Nm (30 ft lb)

19 - Tensioning lever

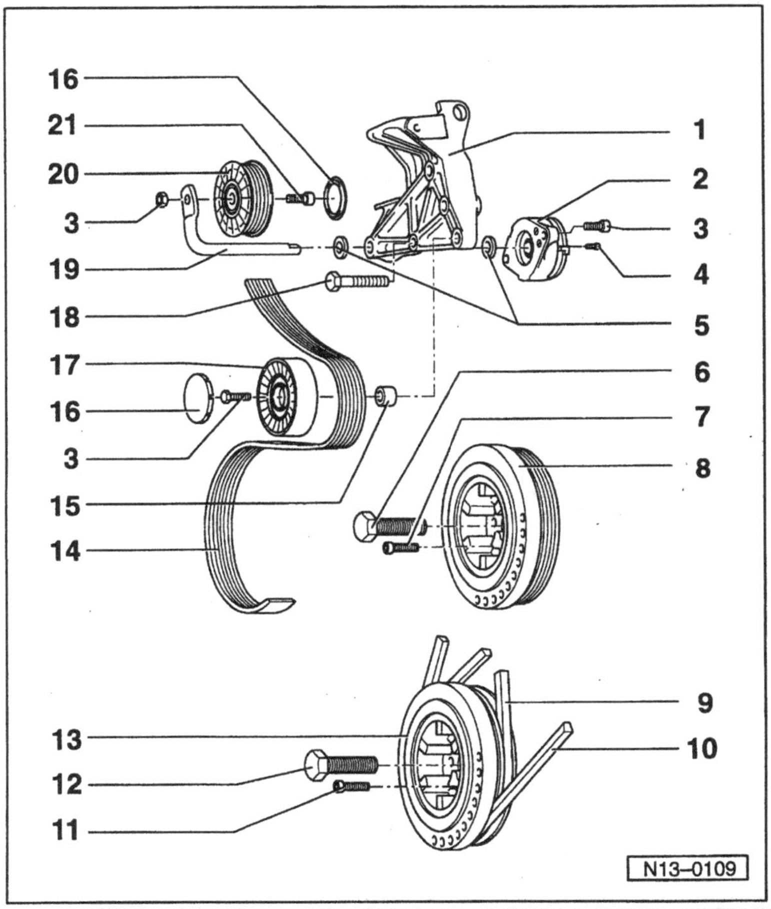

20 - Tensioner

21 - Tensioning roller mounting bolt

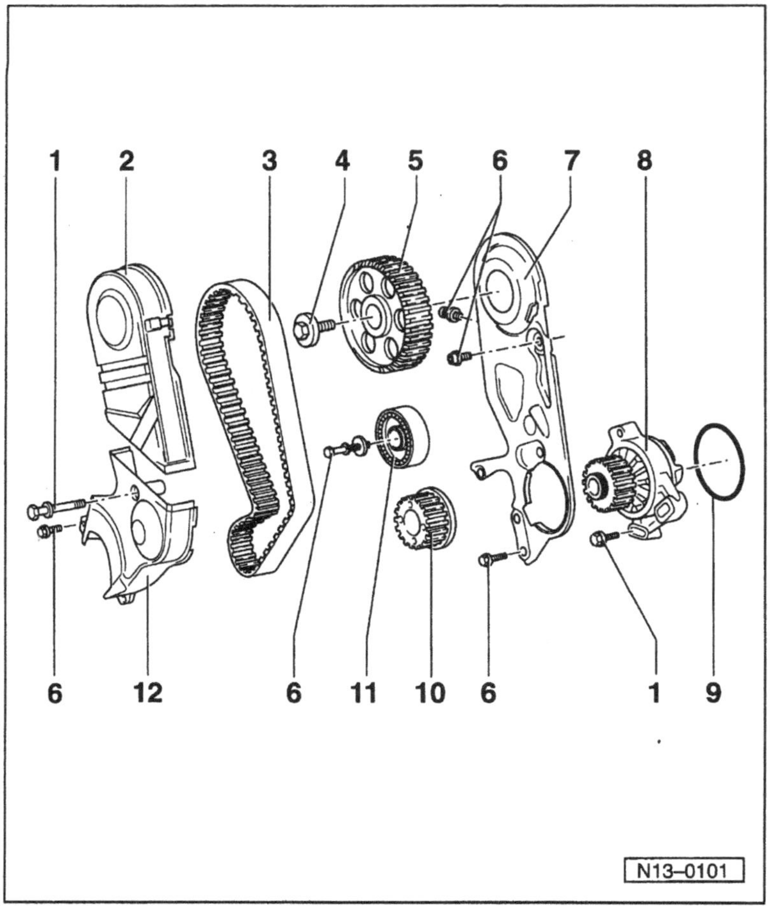

Part II ➤ 01.95

1 - 20 Nm (15 ft lb)

2 - Toothed belt guard – upper part

3 - Toothed belt
- mark direction of rotation before removing
- check for wear
- do not kink
- ♦ removing, installing and tensioning

⇒ page B 13-26

4 - Camshaft sprocket mounting bolt
- ♦ observe coding on bolt head:
  - 8.8 = 85 Nm (63 ft lb)
  - 10.9 = 100 Nm (74 ft lb)
- Counter-hold with 3036 to loosen and tighten

5 - Camshaft sprocket
- Knock off camshaft taper using hammer and drift through toothed belt guard openings
- Note position when installing toothed belt
- ♦ removing, installing and tensioning toothed belt

⇒ page B 13-26

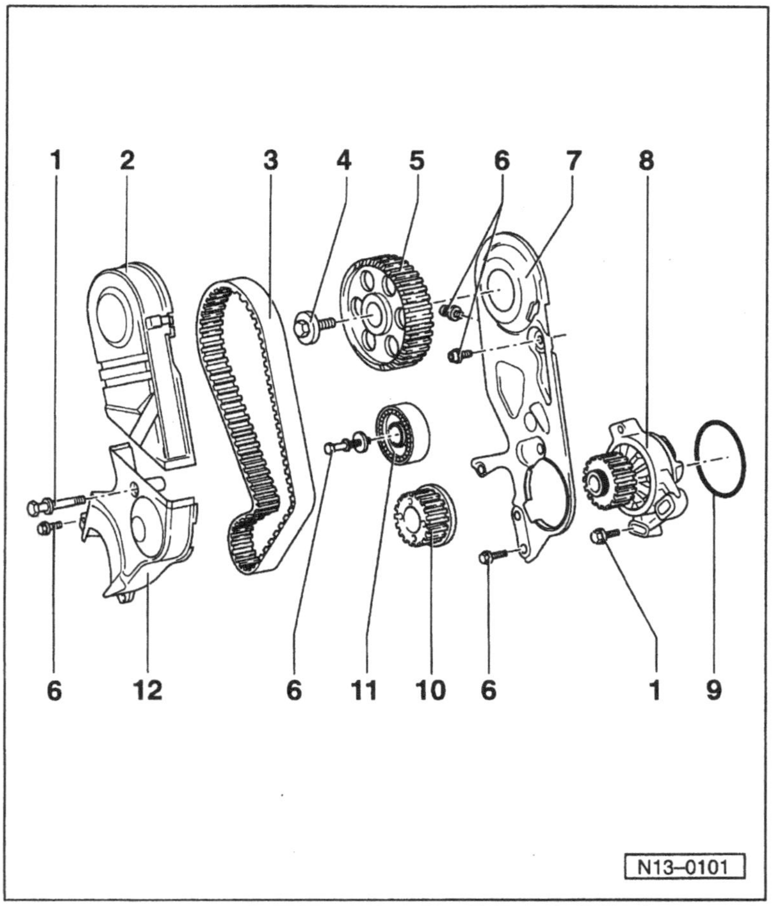

6 - 10 Nm (7 ft lb)

7 - Rear toothed belt guard

8 - Coolant pump
- ♦ with elongated holes
- check shaft for ease of movement
- if leaking and damaged, replace as an assembly
- loosen slightly and turn with screwdriver to tension toothed belt
- ♦ removing, installing, tensioning toothed belt

⇒ page B 13-26

9 - O-ring
- Replace if leaking or damaged

10 - Crankshaft sprocket
- ♦ removing, installing, tensioning toothed belt

⇒ page B 13-26

11 - Idler roller
- Remove using 3034 puller and 3034/1 bolt

12 - Lower toothed belt guard

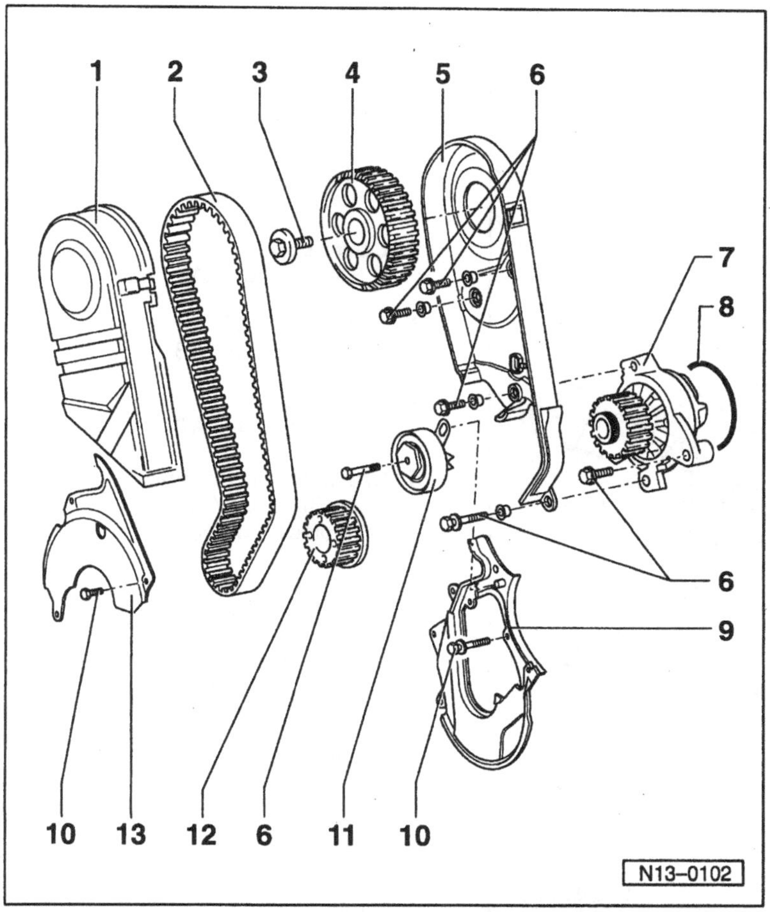

Part II, 02.95 ➤

1 - Upper toothed belt guard

2 - Toothed belt
- Mark direction of rotation before removing
- Check for wear
- Do not kink
- ♦ removing, installing and tensioning

⇒ page B 13-36

3 - Camshaft sprocket mounting bolt
- Observe coding on bolt head:
  8.8 = 85 Nm (63 ft lb)
  10.9 = 100 Nm (74 ft lb)
- Counter-hold with 3036 to loosen and tighten

4 - Camshaft sprocket
- Drive off camshaft taper using hammer and drift through toothed belt guard openings
- Note position when installing toothed belt

⇒ page B 13-36

5 - Rear toothed belt guard

6 - 20 Nm (15 ft lb)

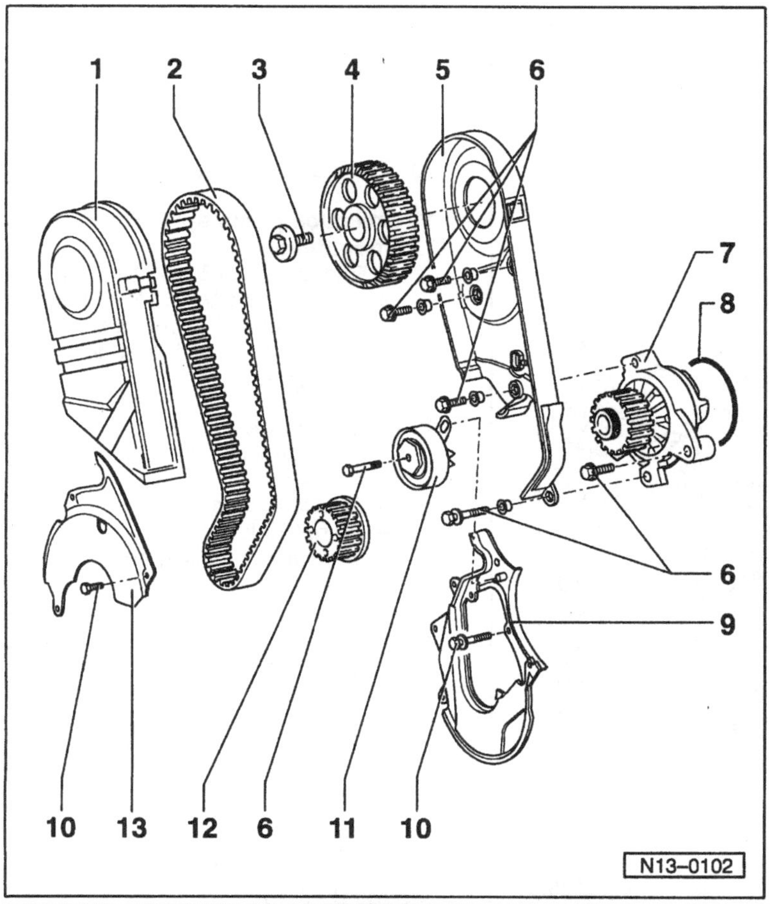

7 - Coolant pump
- ♦ without elongated holes
- Check shaft for ease of movement
- Replace complete, if damaged and leaking

8 - O-ring
- Replace if leaking or damaged

9 - Lower toothed belt guard

10 - 10 Nm (7 ft lb)

11 - Tensioning roller

12 - Crankshaft sprocket
- ♦ removing and installing:

⇒ page B 13-36

13 - Toothed belt guard

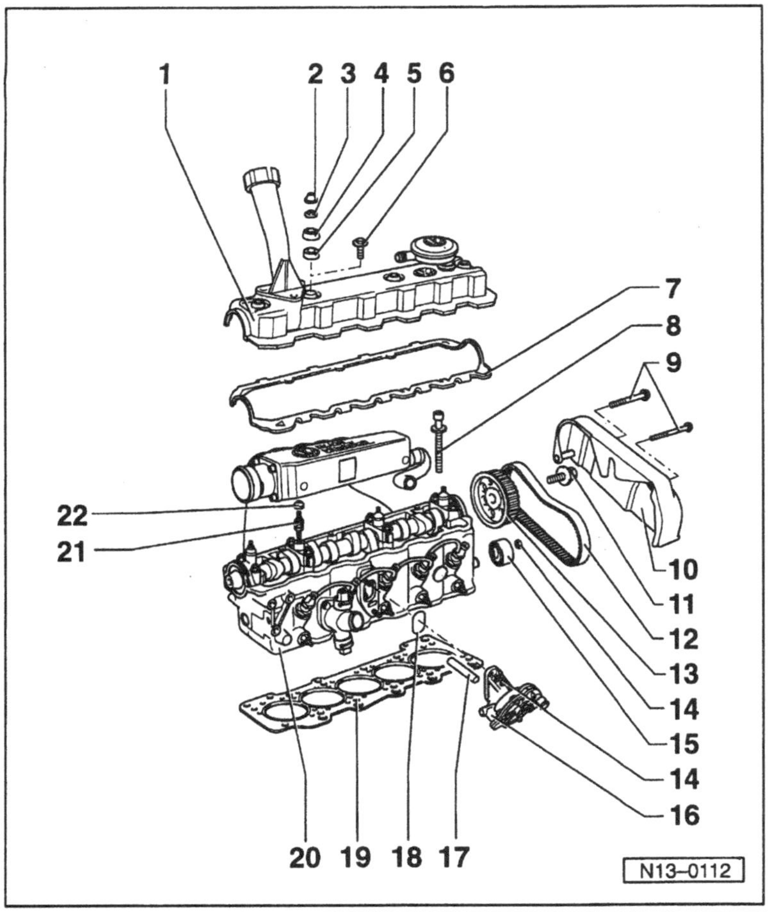

Part III

1 - Valve cover (Engine code: AAB)
- ♦ Engine code ACV: valve cover attached to bearing cap with hex bolts

2 - Cover cap
- ♦ Engine code AAB

3 - 10 Nm (7 ft lb)
- ♦ Engine code AAB

4 - Cup washer
- ♦ Engine code AAB

5 - Upper sealing washer
- ♦ Engine code AAB
- – Replace if damaged

6 - 10 Nm (7 ft lb)
- ♦ Engine code ACV

7 - Valve cover gasket
- – Replace if damaged
- – Insert into groove on valve cover

8 - Cylinder head bolt
- – Replace
- – Note sequence when loosening and tightening

⇒ page B 15–8

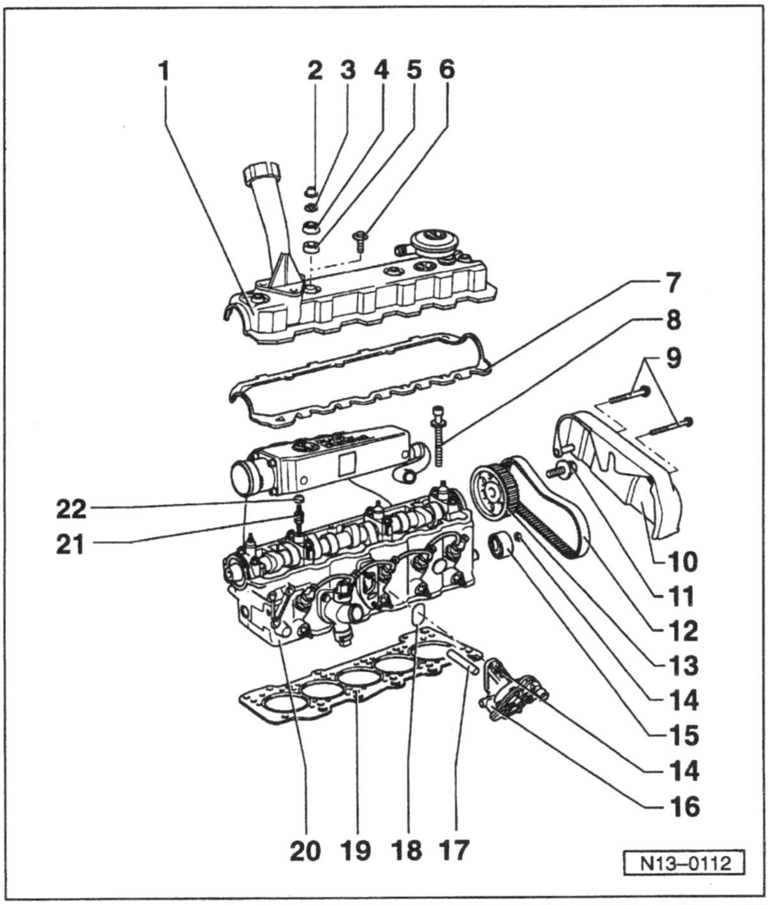

9 - Toothed belt guard mounting bolt
- ♦ M6 = 10 Nm (7 ft lb)
- ♦ M8 = 20 Nm (15 ft lb)

10 - Toothed belt guard

11 - Injection pump sprocket mounting bolt
- ♦ Eng. code AAB: 100 Nm (74 ft lb)
- ♦ Eng. code ACV: 160 Nm (118 ft lb)
- – Oil threads and contact surfaces
- – Counter-hold with 3036 to loosen and tighten

12 - Toothed belt
- – Mark direction of rotation before removing
- – Check for wear
- – Do not kink
- ♦ removing, installing and tensioning:

Engine code AAB
⇒ page B 13-42
Engine code ACV
⇒ page B 13-48

13 - Injection pump sprocket
- – Note position when installing toothed belt:

Engine code AAB
⇒ page B 13-42
Engine code ACV
⇒ page B 13-48

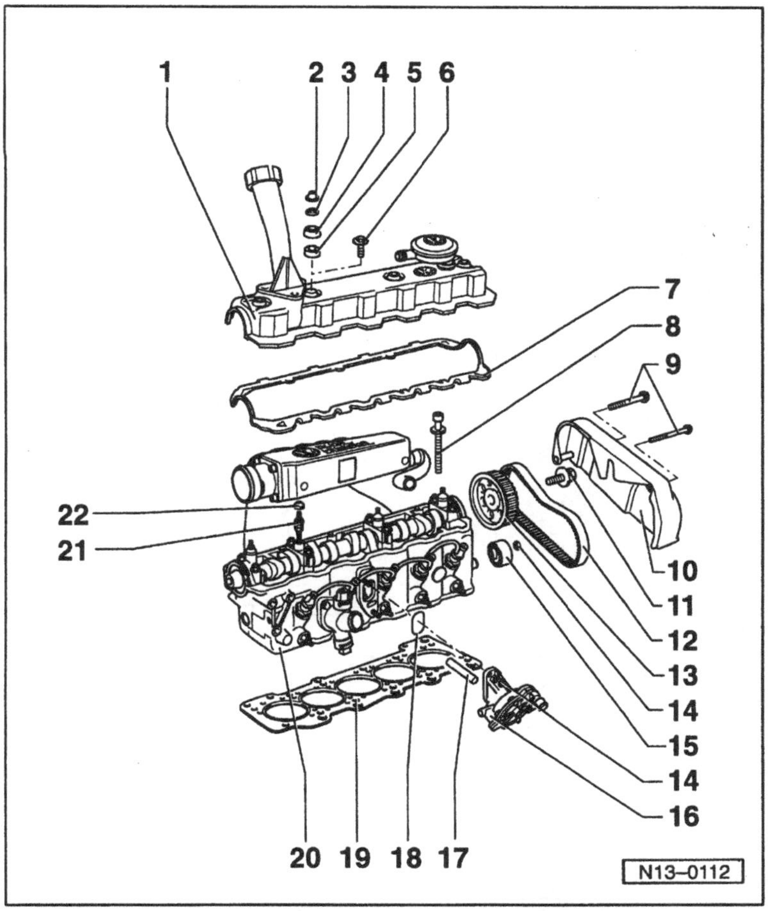

14 - 20 Nm (15 ft lb)

15 - Idler roller
- ♦ Engine code ACV
- – Note installation position

⇒ page B 13-48

16 - Vacuum pump

17 - Plunger

18 - O-ring
- – Replace

19 - Cylinder head gasket
- – Replace
- – Note marking

⇒ page B 15–7
- – If replaced, completely replace engine coolant

20 - Cylinder head
- ♦ installing:

⇒ page B 15–8
- – If replaced, completely replace engine coolant
- ♦ removing and installing injectors:

⇒ Repair Group 23

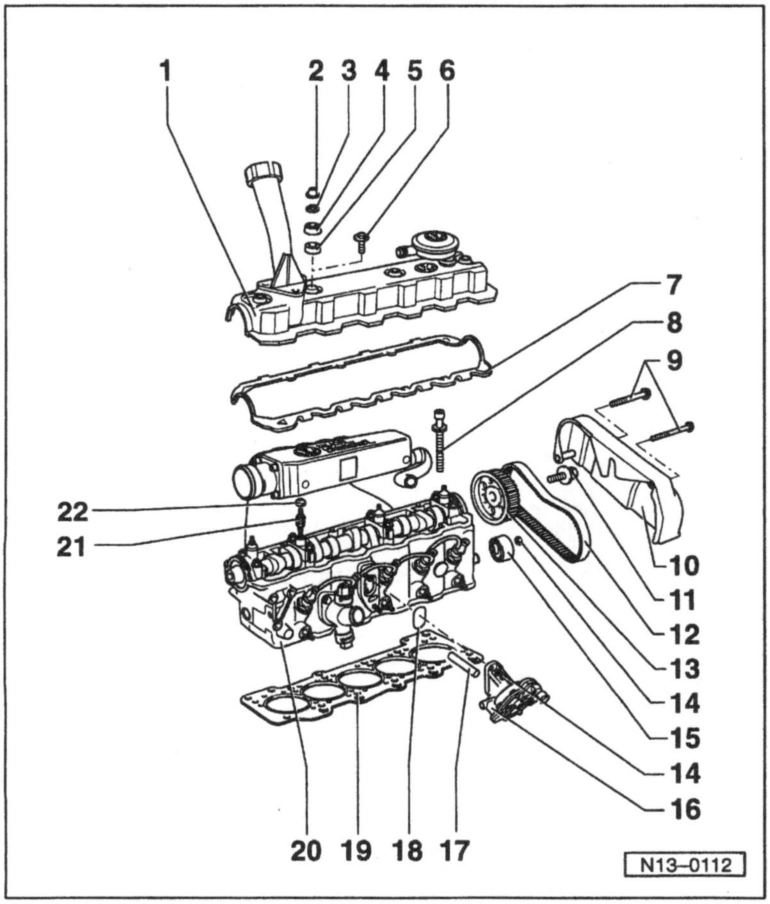

21 - 15 Nm (11 ft lb)
- ♦ Engine code AAB

22 - Lower sealing cone
- ♦ Engine code AAB
- – Replace if damaged

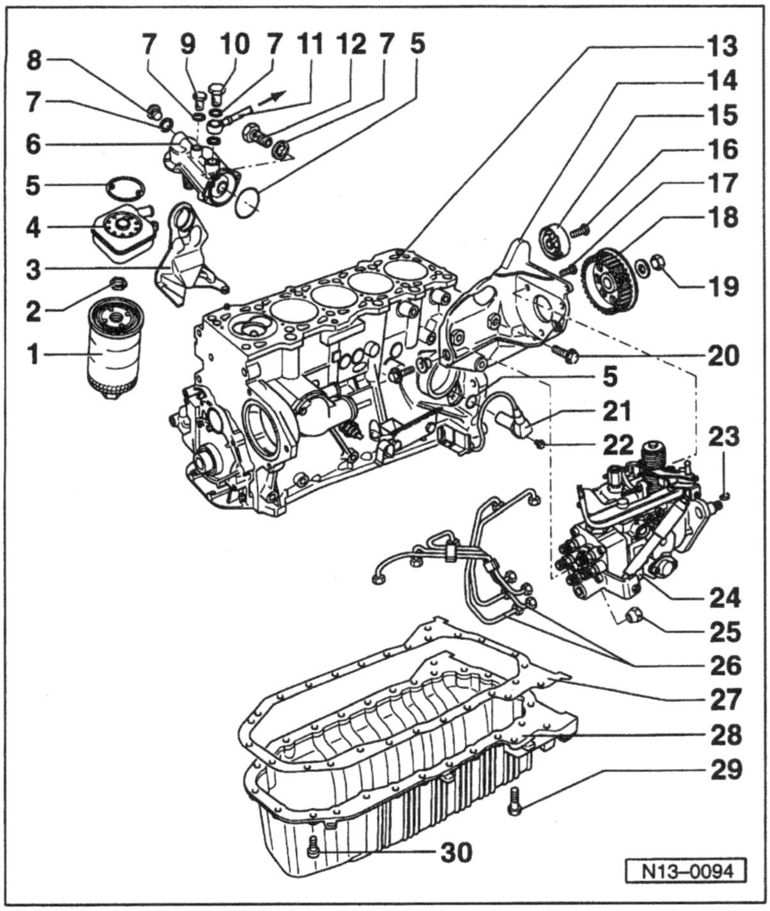

Part IV

1 - Oil filter
- Loosen with strap wrench
- Tighten by hand
- Note instructions on filter when installing

2 - 25 Nm (18 ft lb)

3 - Oil collector

4 - Oil cooler
- Coat contact area to flange, outside seal, using AMV 188 100 02
- Ensure clearance to adjacent components
- ♦ see note

⇒ page B 13-1

5 - O-ring
- ♦ Replace if damaged

6 - Oil filter bracket
- ♦ installed position determined by pin

7 - Sealing ring
- Replace

8 - Sealing plug
- ♦ 40 Nm (30 ft lb)

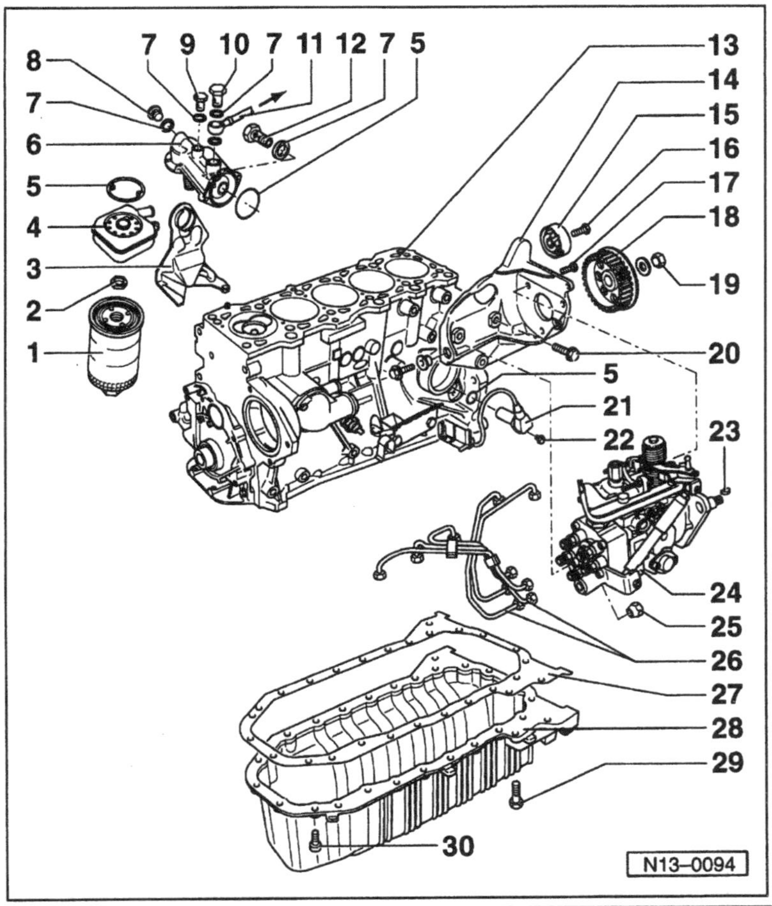

9 - Sealing plug
- ♦ 20 Nm (15 ft lb)

10 - Banjo bolt
- ♦ 30 Nm (22 ft lb)

11 - Oil supply line
- ♦ Engine code ACV
- ♦ to turbocharger

⇒ page B 21–4 (item 24)

12 - Banjo bolt
- ♦ 70 Nm (52 ft lb)

13 - Cylinder block
- ♦ removing and installing sealing flange and flywheel:

⇒ page B 13-55

- ♦ removing and installing crankshaft:

⇒ page B 13-58

- ♦ disassembling and assembling pistons and connecting rods:

⇒ page B 13-67

14 - Console

15 - Tensioner
- ♦ Engine code ACV
- ♦ removing and installing

⇒ page B 13-48

16 - 15 Nm (11 ft lb)

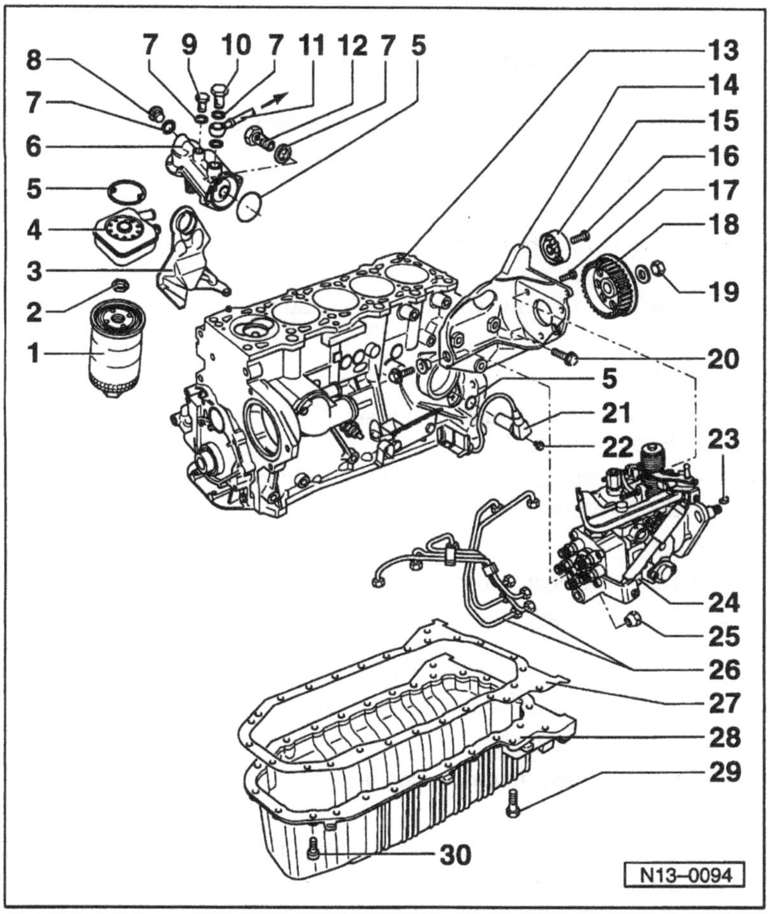

17 - 30 Nm (22 ft lb)

18 - Injection pump sprocket
- ♦ Engine code AAB, Engine code ACV, removing and installing:

⇒ Repair Group 23

19 - Injection pump sprocket mounting bolt
- ♦ Engine code AAB: 50 Nm (37 ft lb)
- ♦ Engine code ACV: 90 Nm (66 ft lb)
- – Counter-hold with 3036 to loosen and tighten

20 - Console mounting bolt
- ♦ Engine code AAB 50 Nm (37 ft lb)
- ♦ Engine code ACV 45 Nm (33 ft lb)

21 - Engine speed sensor G28
- ♦ checking:

⇒ *2.4 Liter Diesel, Fuel Injection and Glow Plug*, Repair Group 01

22 - 10 Nm (7 ft lb)

23 - Woodruff key
- – Check for tight fit

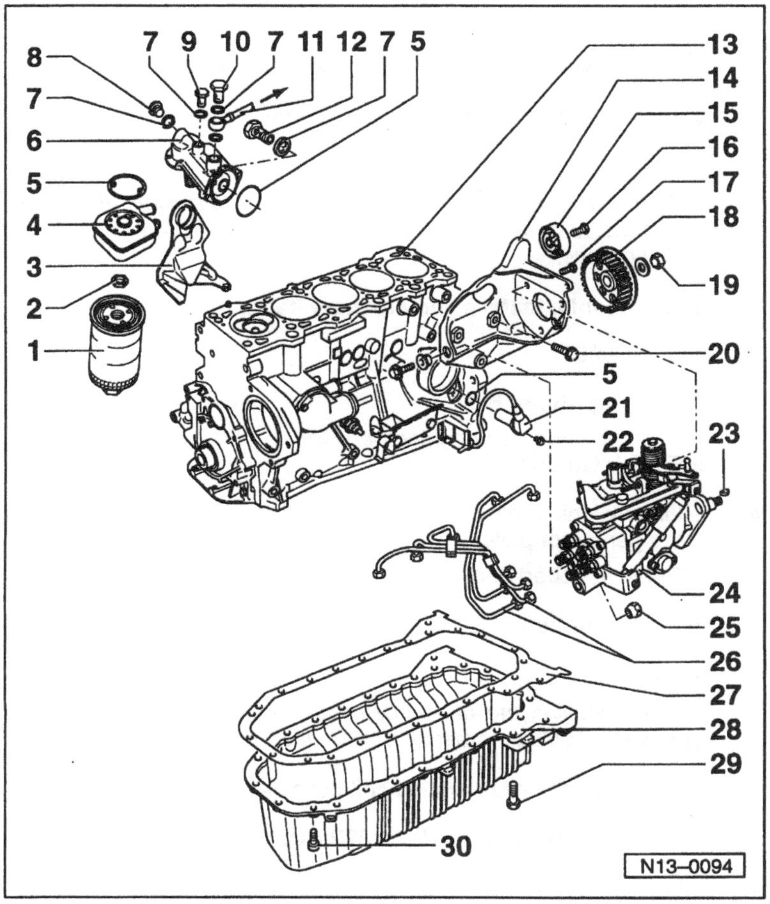

24 - Injection pump
- ♦ Engine code AAB, Engine code ACV, removing and installing

⇒ Repair Group 23

25 - 25 Nm (18 ft lb)
- ♦ with cone

26 - Injector lines
- – 25 Nm (18 ft lb)
- – Remove with 3035 box wrench
- – Always remove the fuel line cluster as an assembly
- ♦ Do not alter the fuel line shapes!

27 - Oil pan gasket
- – Replace
- – Install M8 bolts with hex head toward transmission

28 - Oil pan
- – Clean sealing surfaces before installing

29 - 20 Nm (15 ft lb)
- – Install M8 bolts with hex head toward transmission

30 - 10 Nm (7 ft lb)
- – Remove and install with tool 3249
- – Turn flywheel so that cut-outs align with bolts (with flywheel installed)

Generator V–belt tension, adjusting

Vehicles ➤ 01.95 with toothed rack tensioner only

Special tools, testers and auxiliary items

- SW 22 -VAG 1410/2 Ring insert
- VAG 1410 Torque wrench (4 to 20 Nm) (3 to 15 ft lb)
- VAG 1331 Torque wrench (5 to 50 Nm) (3.7 to 37 ft lb)

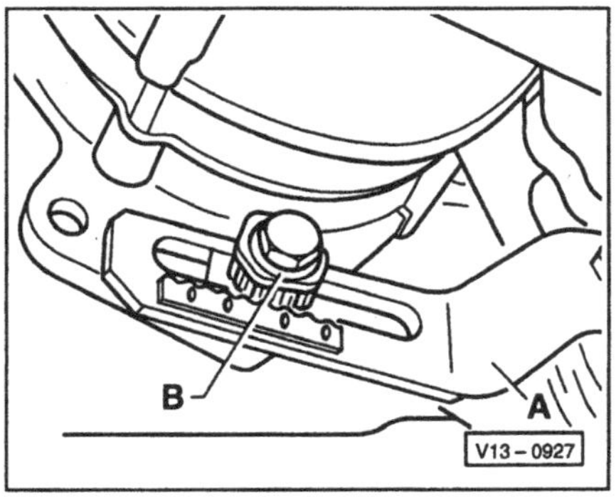

Work sequence

– Remove sound dampening pan
⇒ Repair Group 50

◄ – Loosen all mounting bolts for tensioning bracket -A- and turn generator at least one turn

Note:

It must be possible to easily turn the generator by hand.

– Tension V-belt by turning tensioning nut -B- with torque wrench
Specification: New V-belt 8 Nm (71 in. lb)
Used V-belt 4 Nm (35 in. lb)

– Tighten tensioning nut mounting bolt

- 30 Nm (22 ft lb)

– Tighten generator mounting bolt

- 35 Nm (26 ft lb)

– Attach tensioning bracket to cylinder head lifting eye

- 25 Nm (18 ft lb)

Ribbed belt, removing and installing

Vehicles 02.95 ➤ with tensioning roller only

Note:

Before removing the ribbed belt, mark the direction of rotation. When installing the belt ensure that it is correctly seated in the pulley groove.

Special tools, testers and auxiliary items

- Lever 3299

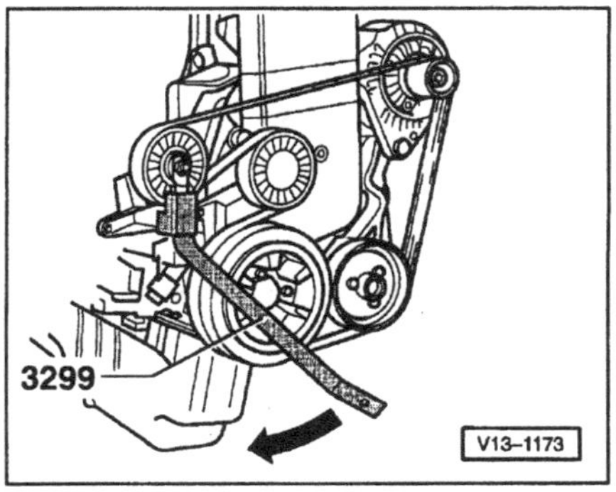

Removing ribbed belt

– Remove sound dampening pan
⇒ Repair Group 50

◄ – Lift tensioning roller with lever 3299 and remove ribbed belt from the generator pulley

– Remove ribbed belt

Installing ribbed belt

Note:

Before installing the ribbed belt, ensure that all sub-assemblies (generator, A/C compressor, power steering pump) are tight.

– Place ribbed belt on ribbed belt pulley/vibration damper

– Lift tensioning roller with lever 3299, install ribbed belt and tension

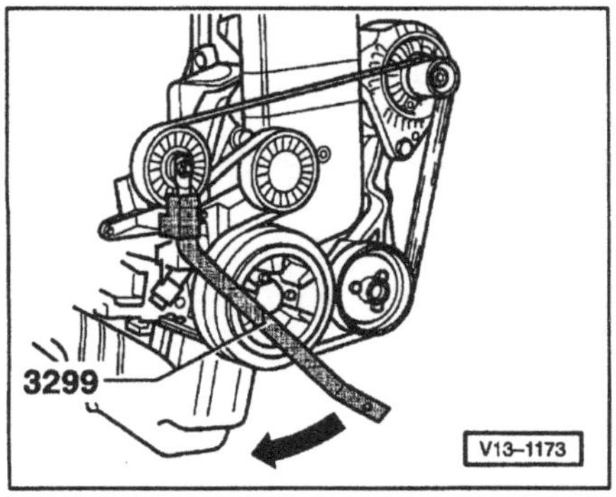

◄ Belt drive without A/C compressor

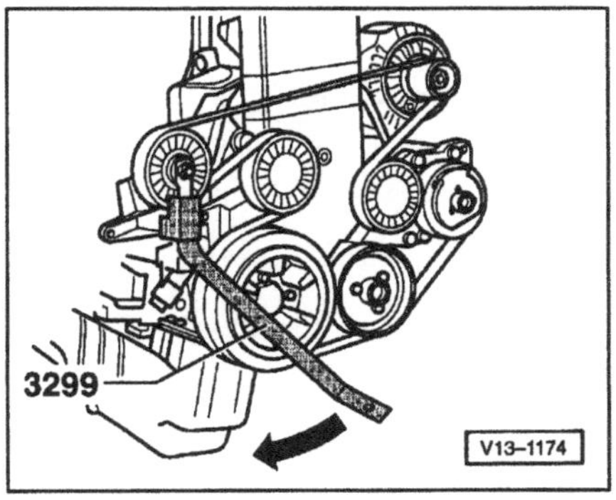

◄ Belt drive with A/C compressor

– Start engine and check belt running

Ribbed belt tensioner, removing and installing

Vehicles 02.95 ➤ with tensioning roller only

Notes:

♦ *When lowering engine; ensure that front exhaust pipe does not rest on the steering rack.*

♦ *When pushing engine forwards ensure that cables, pipes and hoses are not overstretched.*

Special tools, testers and auxiliary items

♦ VAG 1921 Pliers for spring type clips

♦ 3227 Engine stand

♦ VAG 1383 A Engine/transmission jack

♦ Wooden wedge

Removing

– Remove ribbed belt
⇒ page B 13-20

– Remove radiator grille
⇒ Repair Group 66

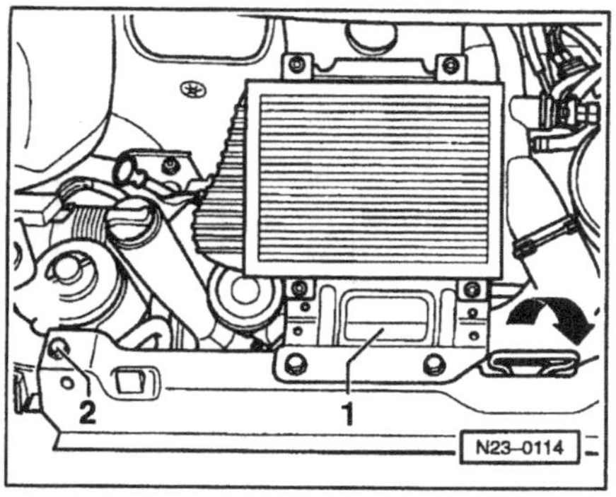

Engine Code ACV

– Remove Charge Air cooler bracket -1-

– Remove Charge Air cooler with air hoses
⇒ Repair Group 21

All Engine Codes

– Remove left and right-hand mounting bolts -2-

– Tilt lock carrier and radiator forward -arrow-

– Disconnect power steering pump hydraulic lines from engine
⇒ Repair Group 48

– Unbolt right-hand drive shaft at transmission
⇒ Repair Group 40

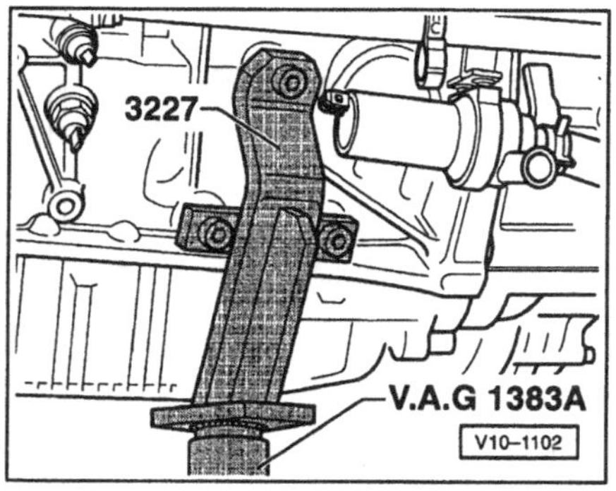

– Bolt engine stand 3227 to cylinder block and tighten

♦ 20 Nm (15 ft lb) approx.

– Slightly lift engine/transmission using VAG 1383 A engine / transmission jack

– Remove transmission mounts:

♦ Engine code AAB
⇒ *Manual Transmission 02B*, Repair Group 34

♦ Engine code ACV
⇒ *Manual Transmission 02G*, Repair Group 34

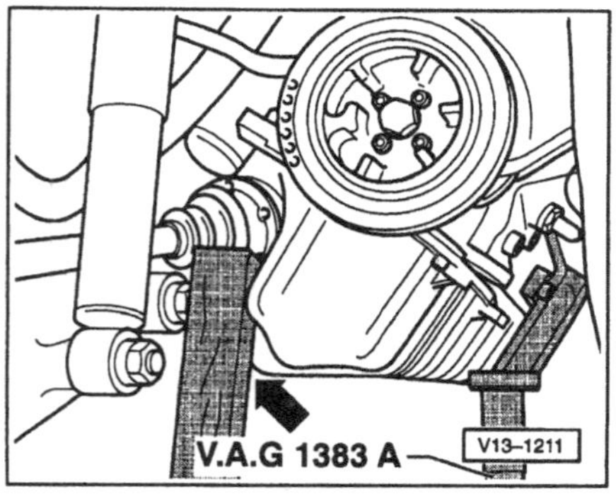

– Remove right-hand engine mount center bolts

– Lower engine/transmission using VAG 1383 A jack as far as possible, push forward and prevent from swinging back by mounting with wooden wedge -arrow-

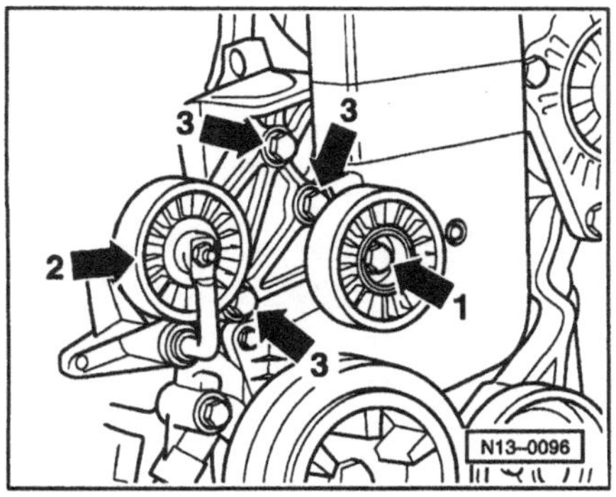

◄ – Remove ribbed V-belt idler roller -arrow -1-

– Remove ribbed V-belt tensioning roller -arrow -2-

– Remove tensioner bracket -arrow -3-

Disassembling and assembling tensioner:
⇒ page B 13-3

Installing

– Install ribbed V-belt tensioner in reverse of removal sequence

Tightening torques

Fastener connection	Tightening torque
Bracket to cylinder block	70 Nm (52 ft lb)
Tensioning roller to tensioning lever	20 Nm (15 ft lb)
Idler roller to bracket	20 Nm (15 ft lb)
Center engine mounting bolt M10x60	65 Nm (48 ft lb)

Toothed belt (camshaft), removing, installing and tensioning

Vehicles ➤ 01.95 with elongated holes in coolant pump for toothed belt tensioning

Vehicles 02.95 ➤ with tensioning roller for tensioning toothed belt: ⇒ page B 13-36

Special tools, testers and auxiliary items

- 3248 A Counter-hold tool
- 2064 Pin
- 3036 Counter-hold tool
- 2065 A Setting bar
- Feeler gauge
- 2068 A TDC setting device
- VW 210 Vee and toothed belt tension tester
- Dial gauge (measuring range 0 to 3 mm)
- Adapter for dial gauge 2066
- VAG 1331 Torque wrench (5 to 50 Nm) (3.7 to 37 ft lb)
- VAG 1332 Torque wrench (40 to 200 Nm) (30 to 148 ft lb)
- VAG 1601 Torque wrench (150 - 800 Nm) (111 to 590 ft lb)

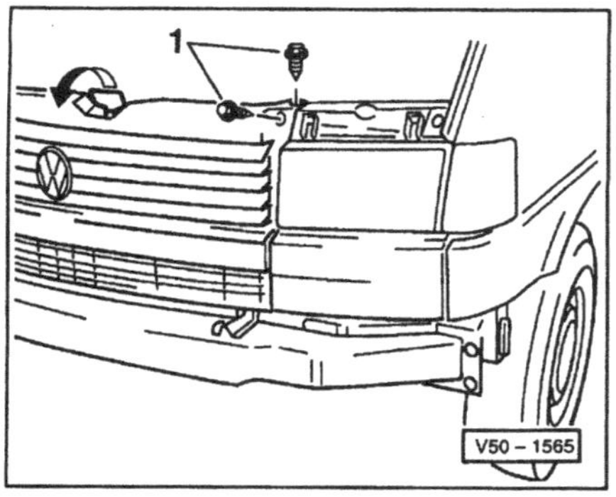

Removing

– Remove sound dampener pan
⇒ Repair Group 50

Vehicles 09.94 ➤

– Remove radiator grille:
⇒ Repair Group 66

All vehicles

◄ – Unbolt left and right-hand mounting bolts -1-

Note:

Vehicles 09.94 ➤ one mounting bolt is located on each left and right-hand side on lock carrier.

– Tilt lock carrier (with radiator) forward and out -arrow-

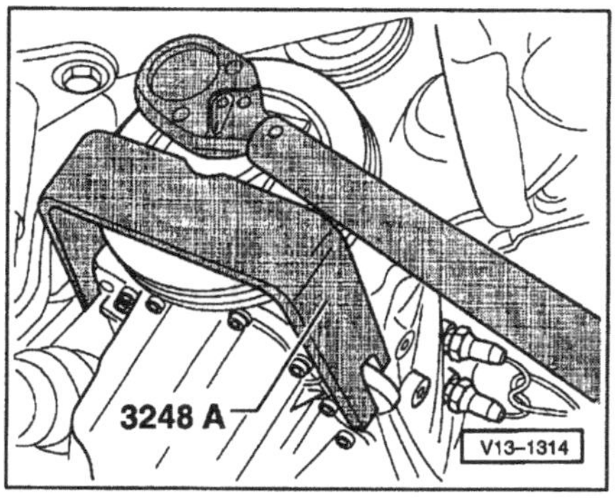

– Remove generator V-belt:
⇒ Repair Group 27

– Pull generator up as far out of way as possible and tie off

– Remove V-belt for power steering pump:
⇒ Repair Group 48

– Remove valve cover and toothed belt guard for both toothed belts

◄ – Insert 3248 A counter-hold tool and loosen vibration damper/crankshaft pulley by loosening center bolt

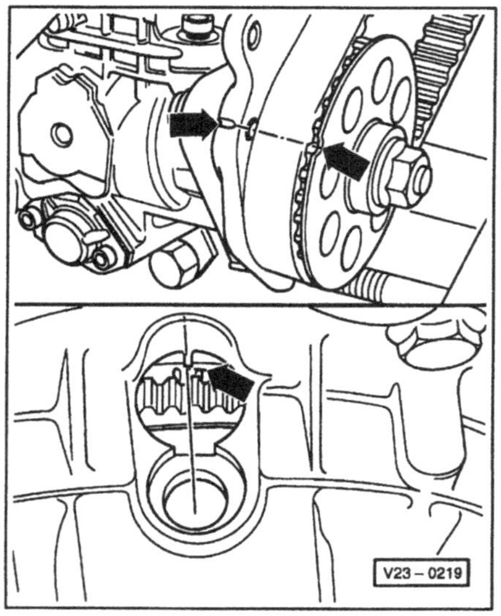

Note:

Counter-hold tool 3248 can be used if counter-hold tool 3248 A cannot be inserted.

– Turn crankshaft to TDC No. 1 cylinder -arrow-

♦ Marks on injection pump sprocket/console and on flywheel/clutch bell housing -arrows- must align

◄ Engine installed

Note:

This condition is only possible every 2nd TDC position.

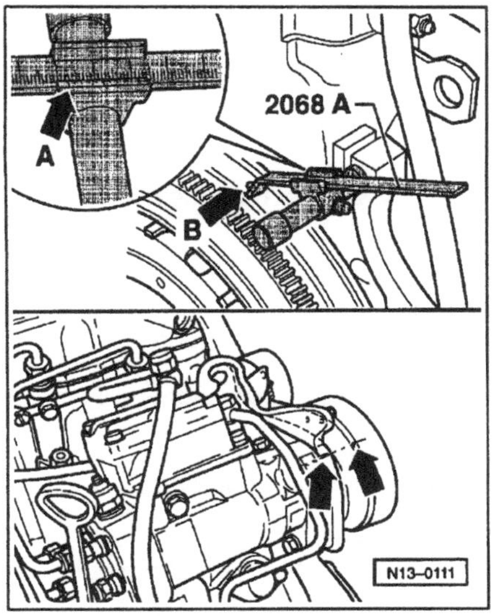

Engine removed

- Set TDC setting device 2068 A to 82 mm -arrow A-
  - ♦ left-hand mark on scale is reference point
- Install setting device as shown
- Turn crankshaft until TDC mark on flywheel aligns with edge of setting device -arrow B-
  - ♦ marks on injection pump sprocket and console must align

Note:

This condition is only possible every 2nd TDC position.

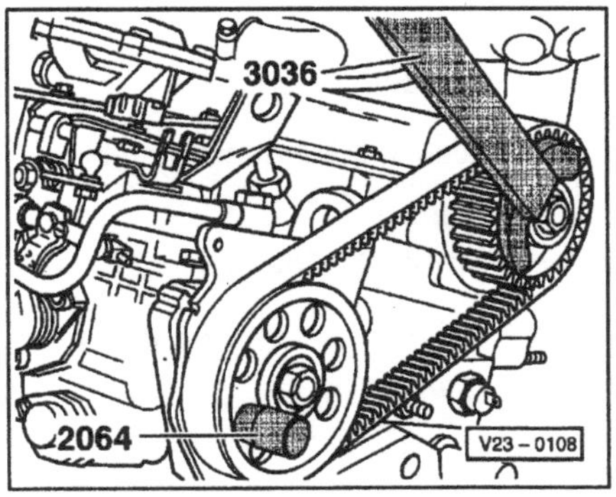

- Lock injection pump sprocket using 2064 pin
- Mark direction of rotation on toothed belt
- Hold injection pump drive sprocket using 3036 counter-hold tool
- Remove mounting bolt then remove drive sprocket/toothed belt
- Remove vibration damper center bolt

- Remove 4 x M8 crankshaft vibration damper/toothed belt pulley mounting bolts
- Remove vibration damper
- Relieve toothed belt tension (loosen coolant pump)
- Remove lower toothed belt guard
- Mark direction of rotation on toothed belt
- Remove toothed belts

Installing, tensioning

- Ensure that flywheel TDC mark and reference mark are aligned

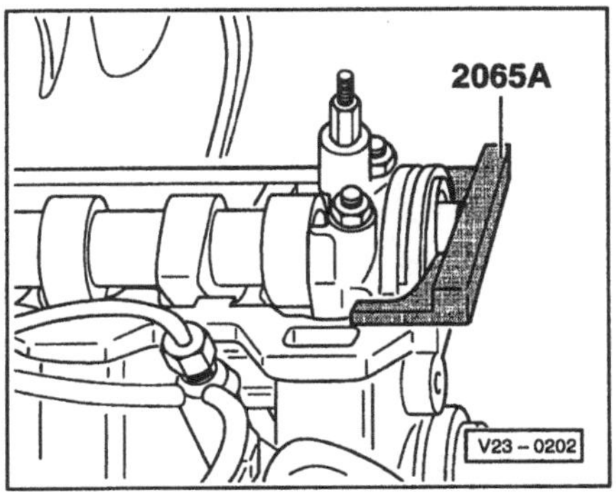

- Lock camshaft in place using 2065 A setting bar

- Centralize setting bar as follows:
- Turn camshaft so one end of setting bar contacts cylinder head

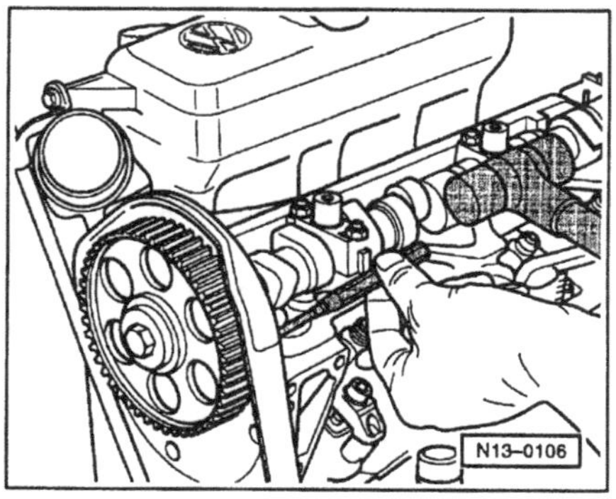

- Using feeler gauge establish gap at other end of setting bar
- Place feeler gauge (corresponding to half the gap) between setting bar and cylinder head
- Turn camshaft until setting bar contacts feeler gauge
- Place 2nd feeler gauge, of same thickness, at other end between setting bar and cylinder head
- ◄ Loosen camshaft sprocket mounting bolt a half turn
- Release camshaft sprocket from camshaft taper by tapping with a hammer (using a drift through rear toothed belt guard opening)

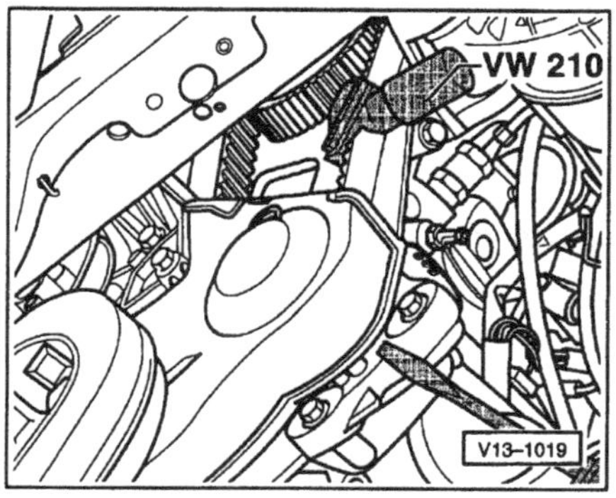

- Fit toothed belt for camshaft drive
  - ♦ Note direction of rotation for used belts
- Fit lower toothed belt guard and also fit M8 mounting bolt for coolant pump
- ◄ Adjust toothed belt tension by turning coolant pump using VW 210
  - ♦ Scale value: 12 to 13, measured between coolant pump and camshaft sprocket

- Tighten coolant pump mounting bolts
  - ♦ 20 Nm (15 ft lb)

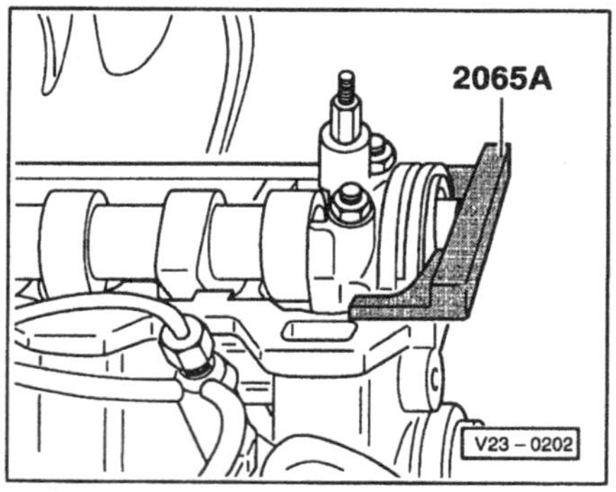

- Tighten lower toothed belt guard
- Ensure crankshaft is still at cyl. 1 TDC, correct if necessary
- Tighten camshaft sprocket mounting bolt using 3036 counter-hold tool
  - ♦ Observe coding embossed on bolt head:
    8.8 = 85 Nm (63 ft lb)
    10.9 = 100 Nm (74 ft lb)
- ◄ Remove 2065 A setting bar from camshaft

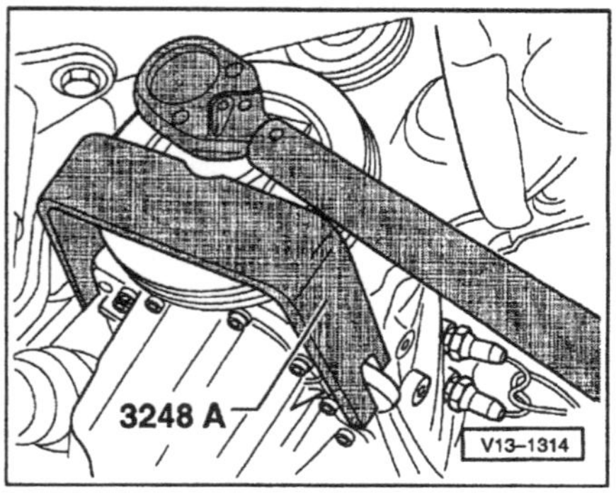

- ◄ Attach 3248 A counter-hold tool and tighten crankshaft vibration damper/toothed belt pulley center bolt
  - ♦ 460 Nm (340 ft lb)

Note:

3248 Counter-hold tool can be used if tool 3248 A cannot be attached.

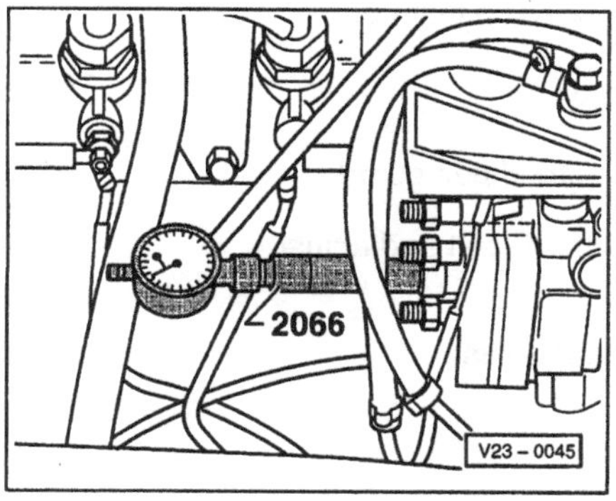

– Tighten 4 x M8 crankshaft vibration damper/toothed belt pulley mounting bolts

- ♦ 20 Nm (15 ft lb)

– Install injection pump toothed belt/injection pump drive sprocket

– Tighten mounting bolt until drive sprocket can still be hand turned

- ♦ note direction of rotation (hand marked) on used toothed belts

– Check toothed belt tension, adjust if necessary ⇒ page B 13-42

– Remove 2064 pin from injection pump sprocket

◄ – Install 2066 gauge adaptor and gauge

- ♦ measuring range 0 to 3 mm, with 2.0 mm preload in place of sealing plug

– Ensure crankshaft is still on cyl. 1 TDC and adjust "start of injection" as follows:

Notes:

- ♦ *Vehicle must be raised and readings taken from below to enable the gauge to be read while turning injection pump drive sprocket.*
- ♦ *A second technician is required to observe the flywheel/clutch bell housing markings when checking the "start of injection" while the crankshaft is turned back and forth.*

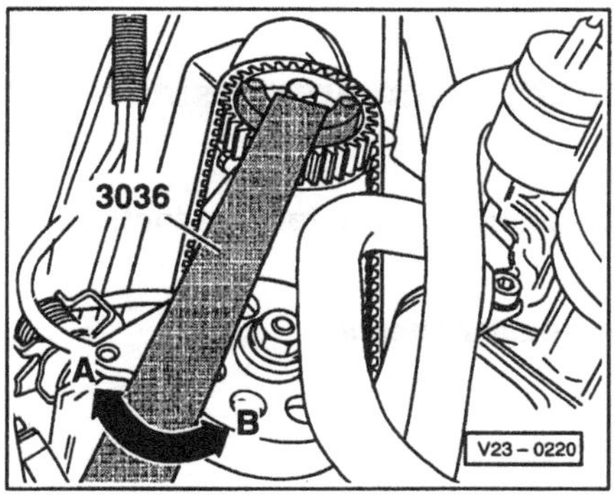

◄ – Turn injection pump drive sprocket against engine direction of rotation -direction of arrow A- using counter-hold 3036 until the gauge needle does not move any more

– "Zero" the gauge

– Turn injection pump drive sprocket in direction of engine rotation (direction of arrow B) using counter-hold 3036 until gauge reads:

- ♦ 1.00 ± 0.02 mm lift ("start of injection")

– Hold injection pump drive sprocket in position with 3036 counter-hold tool and pre-tighten

- ♦ 50 Nm (37 ft lb)

Note:

The "start of injection" must be checked again by turning crankshaft back to gauge reading "0" (via vibration damper) and then forward again to TDC. The reading will deviate due to toothed belt step.

– Reset "start of injection" a second time, take deviation into account

Example

	First value	1.00 mm
–	Checked value	0.93 mm
=	Deviation	0.07 mm
	Value for second adjustment	1.07 mm

– Hold injection pump drive sprocket using 3036 counter-hold tool after second adjustment and tighten

♦ Observe coding embossed on bolt head:

8.8 = 85 Nm (63 ft lb)

10.9 = 100 Nm (74 ft lb)

– Install valve cover and toothed belt guard

– Install power steering pump V-belt and adjust ⇒ page B 13-4 (item 9)

– Install generator V-belt and adjust ⇒ page B 13-19

– Install sound dampener

– Install radiator/lock carrier

Toothed belt (camshaft), removing, installing and tensioning

Vehicles 02.95 ➤ with tensioning roller to tension toothed belt

Special tools, testers and auxiliary items

♦ 3355 Box wrench

♦ 3036 Counter-hold tool

♦ 3248 A Counter-hold tool

♦ 2065 A Setting bar

♦ 2068 A TDC setting device

♦ Feeler gauge

♦ VAG 1332 Torque wrench (40 to 200 Nm) (30 to 148 ft lb)

♦ VAG 1601 Torque wrench (150 to 800 Nm) (111 to 590 ft lb)

Removing

– Remove ribbed belt ⇒ page B 13-20

– Remove radiator grille ⇒ Repair Group 66

Engine Code ACV

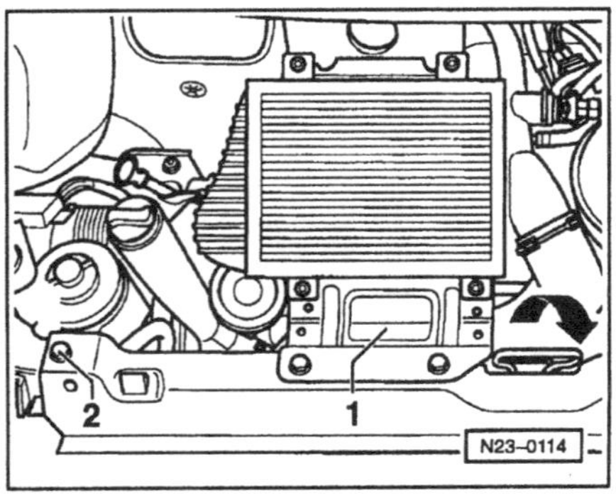

◄ – Remove Charge Air cooler bracket -1-

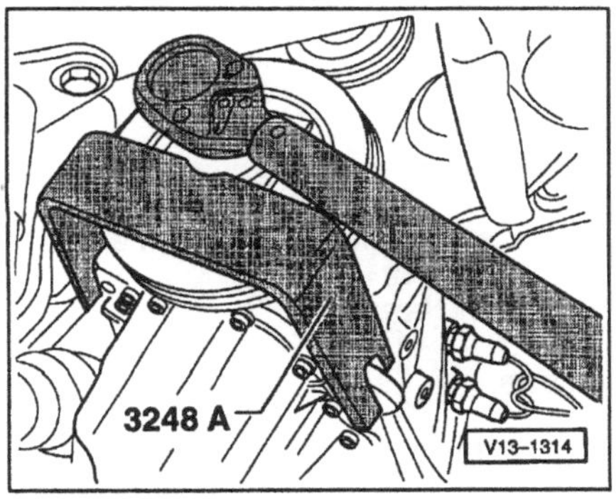

All vehicles

– Remove left and right-hand mounting bolts -2-

– Tilt lock carrier and radiator out and forward -arrow-

– Remove both toothed belt guards and valve cover

◄ – Insert 3248 A counter-hold tool and loosen vibration damper / crankshaft pulley center bolt

Note:

Counter-hold tool 3248 can be used if 3248 A counter-hold tool cannot be inserted.

– Turn crankshaft to cyl. 1 TDC -arrow-

- ♦ Marks on injection pump sprocket/console and on flywheel/ clutch bell housing -arrows- must align

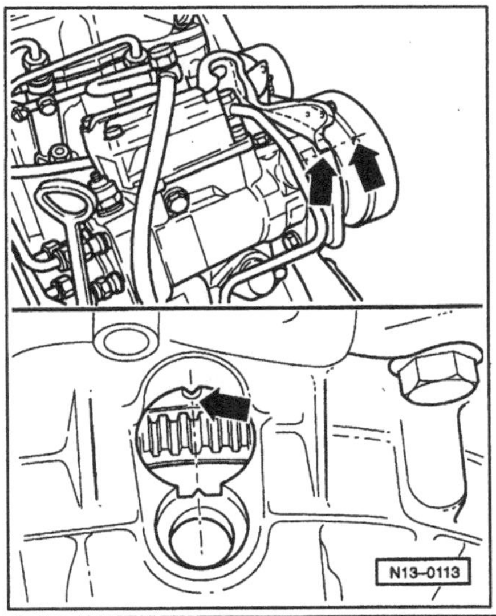

◄ Engine installed

Note:

This condition is only possible every 2nd TDC position.

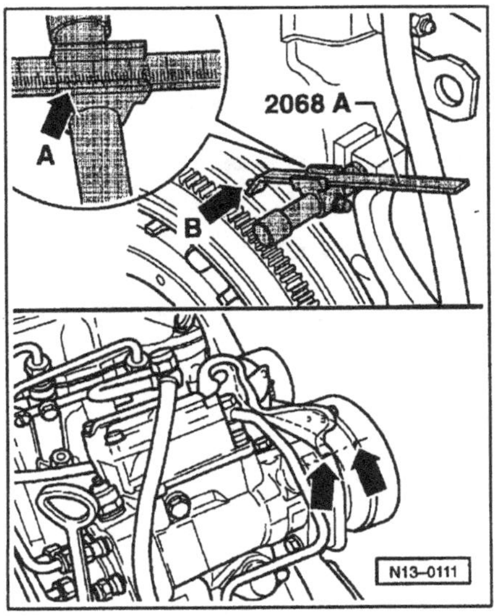

◄ Engine removed

– Set TDC setting device 2068 A to 82.5 mm -arrow A-

- ♦ left-hand mark on scale is the reference point

– Install setting device as shown, turn crankshaft until TDC mark on flywheel aligns with edge of setting device -arrow B-

- ♦ marks on injection pump sprocket and console must also align

Note:

This condition is only possible every 2nd TDC position.

– Remove (injection pump) toothed belt

♦ Engine code AAB
⇒ page B 13-42

♦ Engine code ACV
⇒ page B 13-48

– Remove vibration damper center bolt

– Remove the 4 x M8 crankshaft vibration damper/toothed belt pulley mounting bolts

– Remove vibration damper

– Mark direction of engine rotation on toothed belt

– Relieve toothed belt tension using 3355 box wrench

– Remove toothed belts

Installing, tensioning

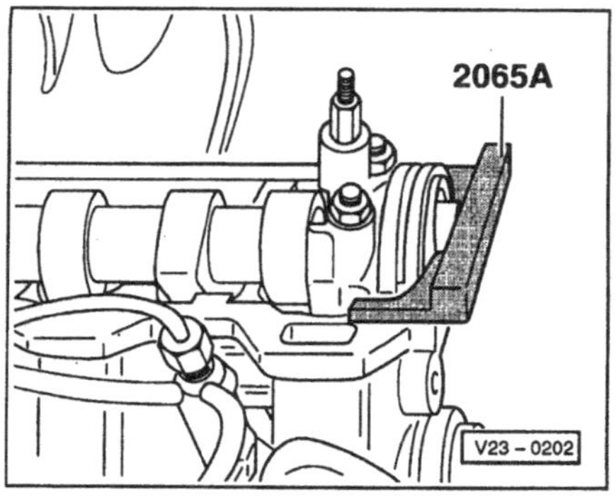

- Remove injection pump drive sprocket
- Ensure that flywheel TDC mark and reference mark are aligned
- ◄ Lock camshaft using 2065 A setting bar
- Centralize setting bar as follows:
- Turn camshaft so one end of setting bar contacts cylinder head
- Using feeler gauge establish gap at other end of setting bar
- Place feeler gauge (corresponding to half the gap) between setting bar and cylinder head
- Turn camshaft until setting bar contacts feeler gauge

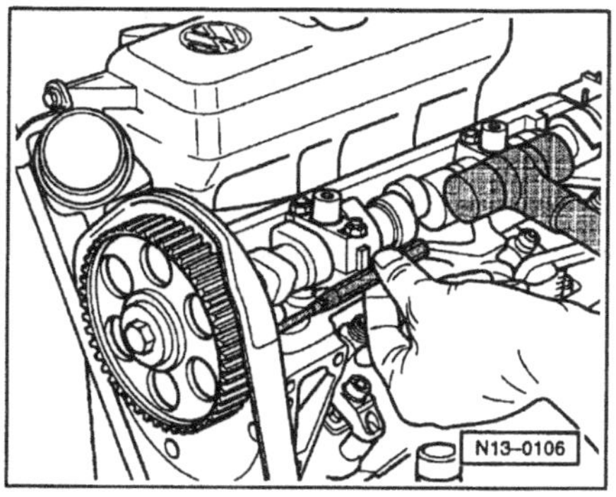

- Place 2nd feeler gauge, of same thickness, at other end between setting bar and cylinder head
- ◄ Loosen camshaft sprocket mounting bolt a half turn
- Release camshaft sprocket from camshaft taper by tapping with a hammer (using a drift through rear toothed belt guard opening)

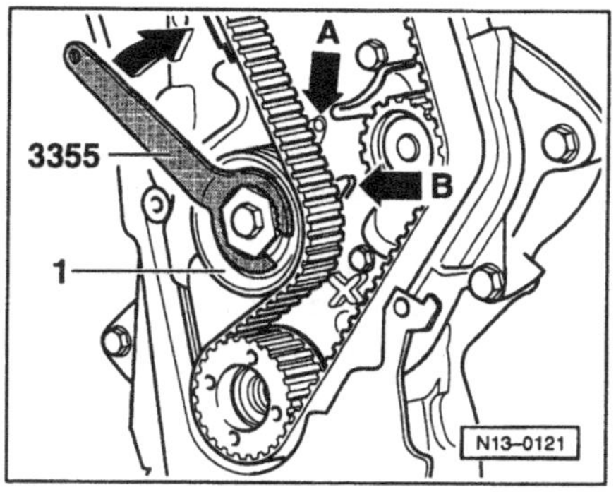

- ◄ Install tensioning roller -1- so the tensioning roller tab seats in the lower toothed belt guard part moving pin -arrow A-
- Fit toothed belt for camshaft drive. For used belts note direction of rotation
- Tighten tensioning roller mounting bolt hand tight
- Turn tensioning roller clockwise with ring spanner 3355 onto inner tensioning roller stop. Then turn tensioning roller back until both indicators align -arrow B-
- Tighten tensioning roller mounting bolt
  - ♦ 20 Nm (15 ft lb)
- Check if crankshaft is still on cyl. 1 TDC, correct if necessary
- Tighten camshaft sprocket mounting bolt using 3036 counter-hold tool
  - ♦ Observe coding embossed on bolt head:
    8.8 = 85 Nm (63 ft lb)
    10.9 = 100 Nm (74 ft lb)

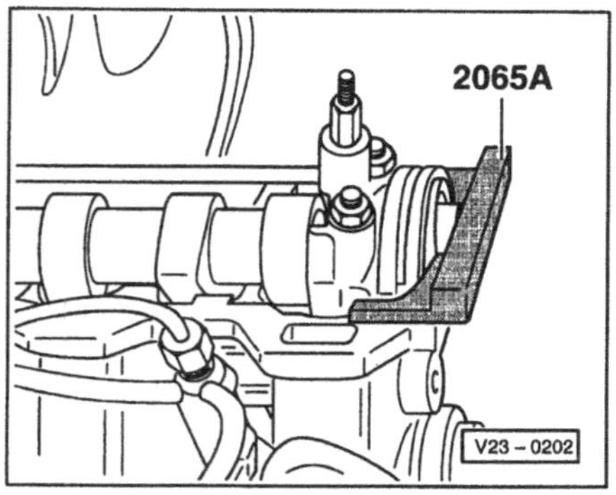

- ◄ Remove setting bar 2065A from camshaft

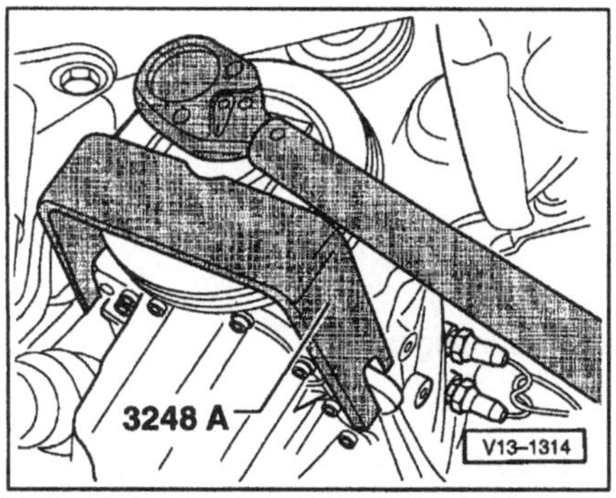

◄ – Insert 3248 A counter-hold tool and tighten crankshaft vibration damper/toothed belt pulley center bolt

◆ 160 Nm (118 ft lb) plus an additional 90° (1/4 turn)

Note:

Counter-hold 3248 can be used if counter-hold 3248 A cannot be inserted. Also note, the additional quarter turn can be completed in several stages.

– Tighten the 4 x M8 crankshaft vibration damper/toothed belt pulley mounting bolts

◆ 20 Nm (15 ft lb) plus an additional 90° (1/4 turn)

Note:

The additional quarter turn can be completed in several stages.

– Install injection pump toothed belt

◆ Engine code AAB
⇒ page B 13-42

◆ Engine code ACV
⇒ page B 13-48

– Install both toothed belt guards and valve cover

– Install radiator with lock carrier

– Install ribbed belt
⇒ page B 13-20

– Install sound dampener

Toothed belt (injection pump), removing, installing and tensioning (Engine Code: AAB)

Engine Code AAB, without toothed belt tensioning roller

Engine code ACV with tensioning roller
⇒ page B 13-48

Special tools, testers and auxiliary items

◆ 2064 Pin

◆ 3036 Counter-hold tool

◆ VW 210 Vee and toothed belt tension tester

◆ Dial gauge (range 0 to 3 mm)

◆ 2066 Adapter for dial gauge

◆ 2068 A TDC setting device

◆ VAG 1331 Torque wrench (5 to 50 Nm) (3.7 to 37 ft lb)

◆ VAG 1332 Torque wrench (40 to 200 Nm) (30 to 148 ft lb)

Removing

– Remove sound dampening pan
⇒ Repair Group 50

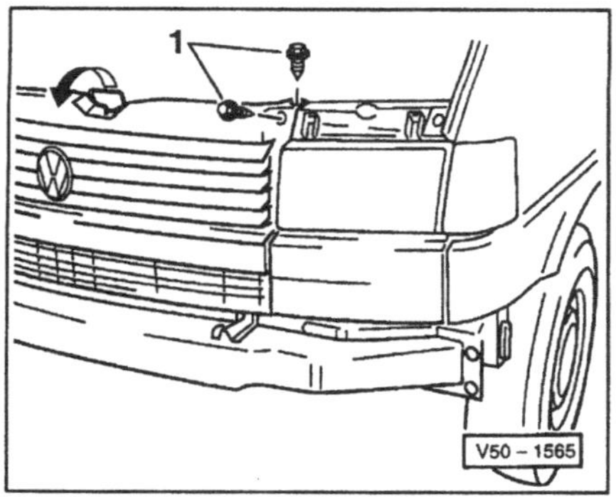

Vehicles 09.94 ➤

- Remove radiator grille
  ⇒ Repair Group 66

All vehicles

◄ – Remove left and right-hand mounting bolts -1-

Note:

Vehicles 09.94 ➤ there is 1 mounting bolt on each left and right hand side of lock carrier.

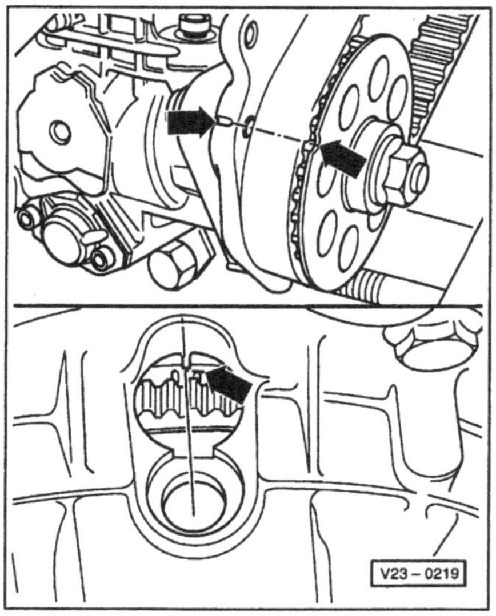

- Tilt lock carrier with radiator out and forward -arrow-
- Remove injection pump toothed belt guard
- Turn crankshaft in direction of engine rotation to cyl. 1 TDC

◄ Engine installed

- Ensure that injection pump sprocket/console and flywheel/clutch bell housing marks -arrows- are aligned

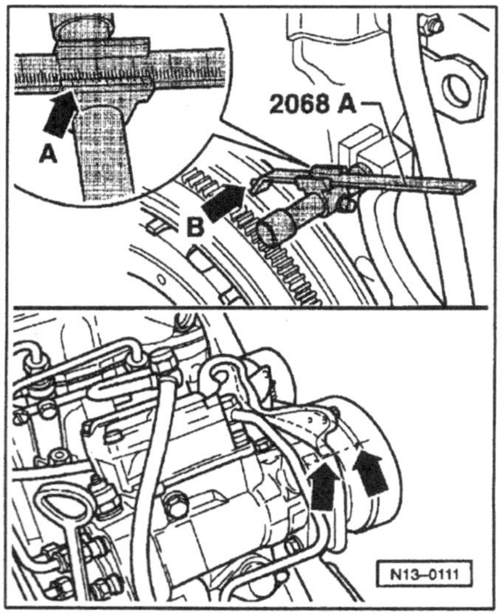

◄ Engine removed

- Set TDC setting device 2068 A to 82 mm -arrow A-
  - left scale mark is reference point
- Attach setting device as illustrated
- Turn crankshaft until TDC mark on flywheel aligns with edge of setting device -arrow B-
  - marks on injection pump sprocket and console must align

Note:

This condition is only possible every 2nd TDC position.

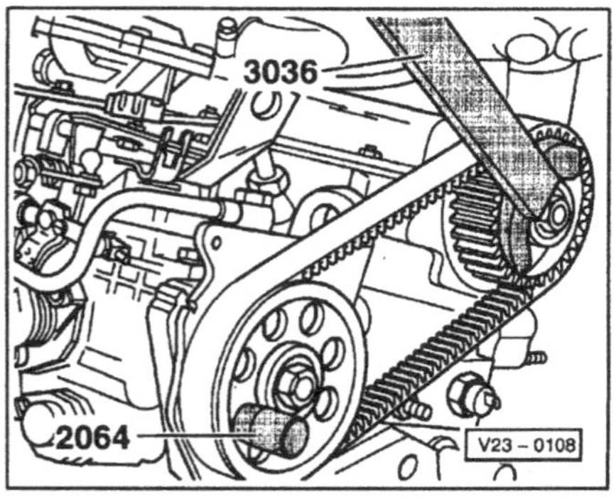

◄ – Lock injection pump sprocket with pin 2064

- Mark direction of engine rotation on toothed belt
- Hold injection pump drive sprocket using 3036 counter-hold tool
- Remove mounting bolt and take off drive sprocket w/ toothed belt

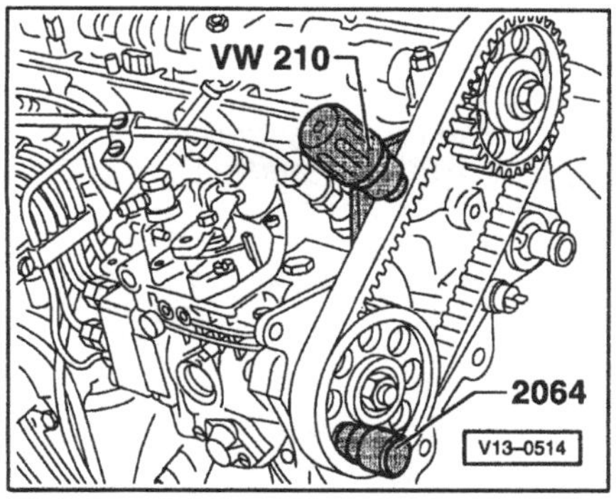

Installing, tensioning

– Check whether TDC mark on flywheel and reference mark are aligned

– Install injection pump drive toothed belt with injection pump drive sprocket

– Tighten mounting bolt until drive sprocket can just barely be turned by hand

– Mark direction of engine rotation on used toothed belts

◄ – Check toothed belt tension using VW 210 tension tester

♦ scale value: 12 to 13

If scale value not obtained

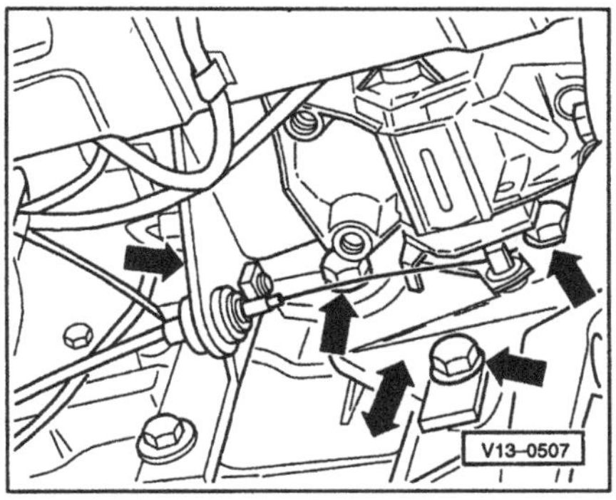

◄ – Adjust toothed belt tension to scale value after loosening mounting bolts -arrows- and moving console (with injection pump)

If scale value is obtained

– Remove pin 2064 from injection pump sprocket

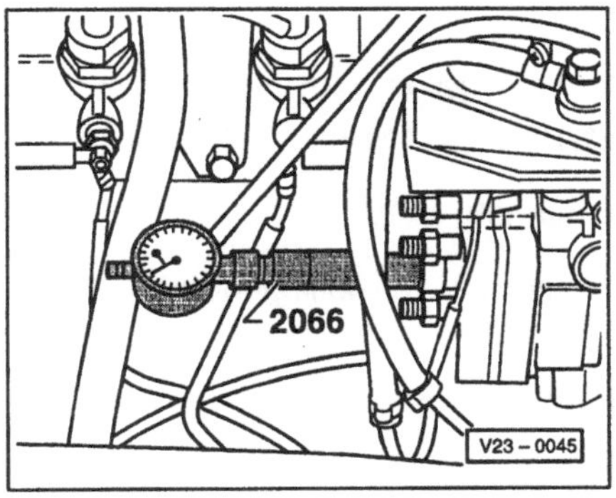

◄ – Install 2066 gauge and gauge adapter with 2.0 mm preload in place of sealing plug

♦ measuring range 0 to 3 mm

– Check that crankshaft is still on cyl. 1 TDC and adjust "start of injection" as follows

Notes:

♦ *Vehicle must be raised and readings made from below to enable the gauge to be read while turning injection pump drive sprocket.*

♦ *A second technician is required to observe the flywheel/clutch bell housing markings when checking the "start of injection" while turning crankshaft back and forth.*

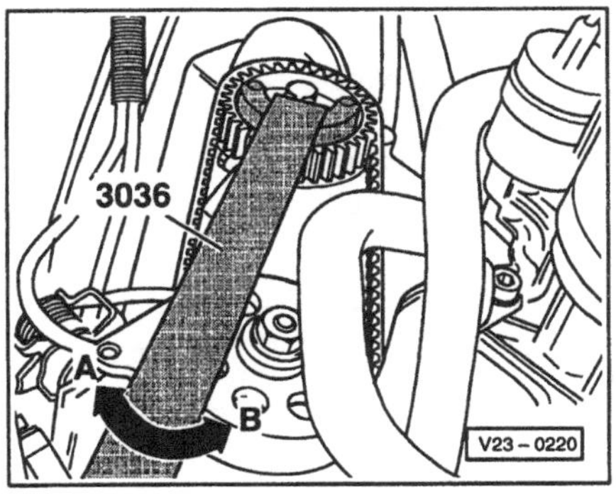

◄ – Turn injection pump drive sprocket against direction of engine rotation (direction of arrow A) using 3036 counter-hold tool until gauge needle stops moving

– "Zero" gauge

– Turn injection pump drive sprocket in direction of engine rotation (direction of arrow B) using counter-hold 3036 until gauge reads:

♦ 1.00 ± 0.02 mm lift "start of injection"

– Hold injection pump drive sprocket in this position using 3036 counter-hold tool and pre-tighten

♦ 50 Nm (37 ft lb)

Note:

The "start of injection" must be checked again by turning crankshaft back via vibration damper to gauge reading "0" and forward to TDC. The value will deviate due to the toothed belt step.

– Reset "start of injection" again, taking deviation into account

Example:

	First value	1.00 mm
–	Checked value	0.93 mm
=	Deviation	0.07 mm
	Value for second adjustment	1.07 mm

– Hold injection pump drive sprocket (after second adjustment) using 3036 counter-hold tool and tighten

♦ 100 Nm (74 ft lb)

– Install toothed belt guard for injection pump

– Install radiator with lock carrier

– Install sound dampener

Toothed belt (injection pump), removing, installing and tensioning (Engine Code: ACV)

Engine Code ACV with tensioning roller

Engine code AAB without toothed belt tensioning roller ⇒ page B 13-42

Special tools, testers and auxiliary items

- ♦ 3036 Counter-hold tool
- ♦ Adapter for 3313 dial gauge
- ♦ 2068 A TDC setting device
- ♦ Dial gauge (range 0 to 3 mm)
- ♦ VAG 1331 Torque wrench (5 to 50 Nm) (3.7 to 37 ft lb)
- ♦ VAG 1332 Torque wrench (40 to 200 Nm) (30 to 148 ft lb)

Removing

– Remove sound dampening pan ⇒ Repair Group 50

– Remove radiator grille ⇒ Repair Group 66

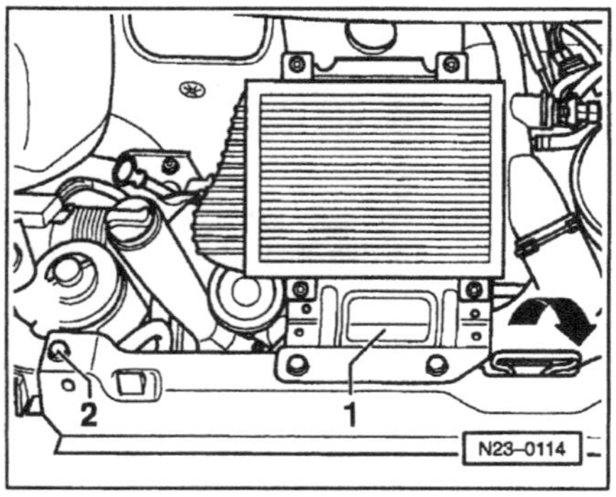

– Remove Charge Air cooler -1-

– Remove left and right mounting bolts -2-

– Tilt lock carrier with radiator out and forward -arrow-

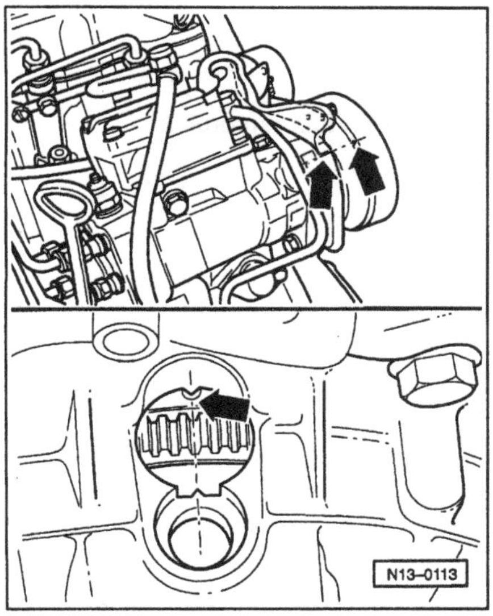

- Remove injection pump toothed belt guard
- Turn crankshaft in direction of engine rotation to cyl. 1 TDC -arrow-
  - ♦ Injection pump sprocket/console and flywheel/clutch bell housing marks -arrows- must align

◄ Engine installed

Note:

This condition is only possible every 2nd TDC position.

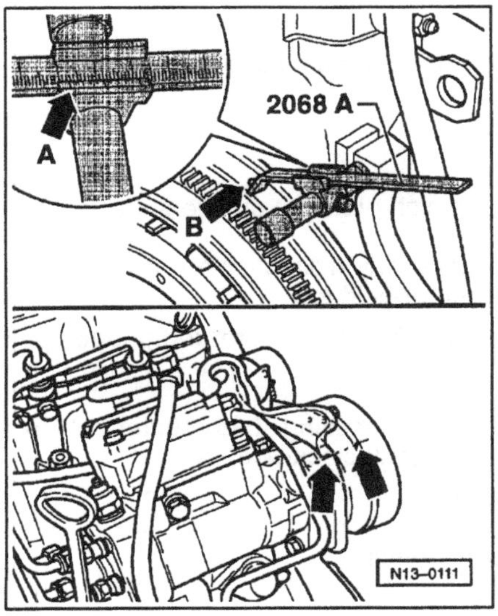

◄ Engine removed

- Set TDC setting device 2068 A to 82.5 mm -arrow A-, the left scale mark is the reference point
- Attach setting device as shown
- Turn crankshaft until TDC mark on flywheel aligns with edge of setting device -arrow B-
  - ♦ marks on injection pump sprocket and console must align

Note:

This condition is only possible every 2nd TDC position.

- Mark direction of engine rotation on toothed belt
- Hold injection pump drive sprocket using 3036 counter-hold tool
- Remove mounting bolt and take off drive sprocket w/ toothed belt
- Remove toothed belt tensioning roller

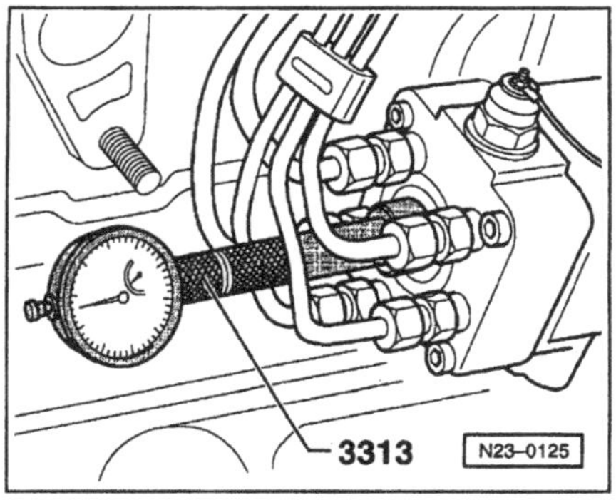

Installing, tensioning

◄ – Install 3313 gauge and adapter with 2.0 mm preload (in place of sealing plug)

♦ measuring range 0 to 3 mm

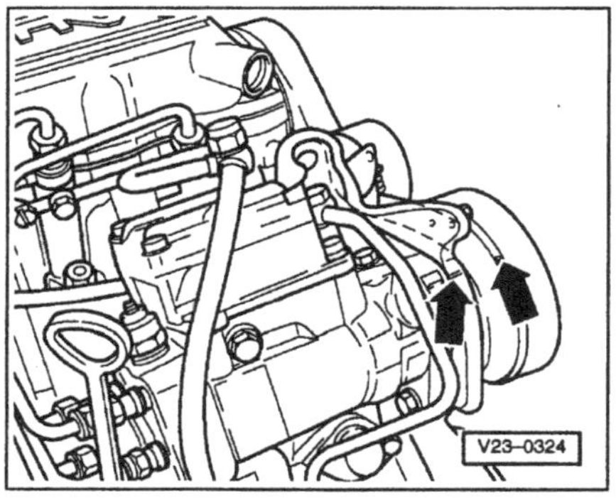

◄ – Ensure that marks on injection pump sprocket and injection pump -arrows- align

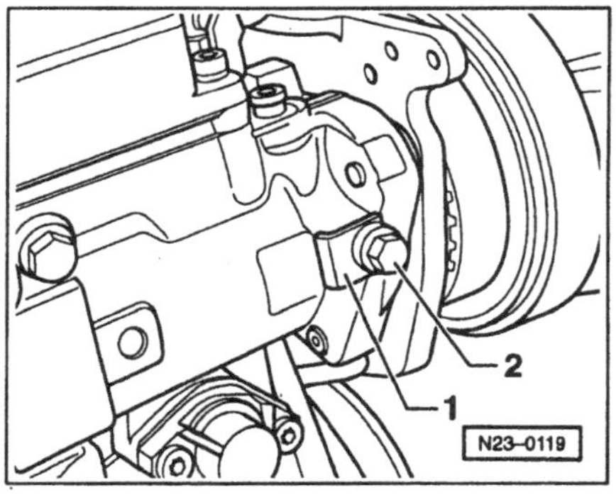

◄ – Loosen locking bolt -2- on injection pump and remove intermediate plate -1-

– “Zero” gauge

To ensure that injection pump high pressure plungers are at TDC

– Turn injection pump sprocket slowly in direction of engine rotation (clockwise) using 3036 counter-hold tool

♦ Gauge needle must remain on “0” or “Zero” the gauge upon reaching TDC

– Slowly turn injection pump sprocket using 3036 counter-hold tool in direction of engine rotation (anti-clockwise) until

♦ 55 mm lift “start of injection”

– Tighten lock bolt on injection pump

♦ 30 Nm (22 ft lb)

– Ensure that TDC mark on flywheel and reference are aligned

– Install toothed belt with injection pump drive sprocket

– Tighten mounting bolt until drive sprocket can just barely be hand-turned

– Mark direction of rotation on used toothed belts

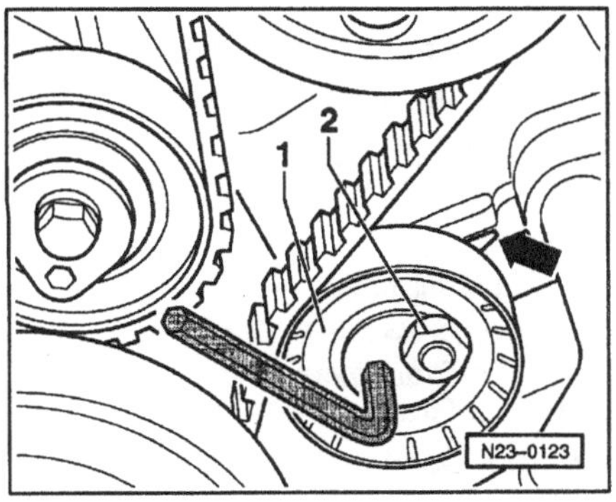

- Check idler roller installation position
  - ♦ Idler roller indicator -1- must align with cylinder head flange contour -arrow-
- Loosen mounting nut -2- and adjust idler roller -1-, if necessary
- Tighten idler roller mounting nut
  - ♦ 20 Nm (15 ft lb)

- Install tensioning roller -1- and adjust so tensioning roller tab is positioned in console cut-out -arrow B-
- Tighten mounting bolt hand tight
- Turn tensioning roller anti-clockwise onto inner tensioning roller stop, then turn tensioning roller back until both pointers align -arrow A-
- Tighten mounting bolt
  - ♦ 15 Nm (10 ft lb)

- Hold injection pump drive sprocket using 3036 counter-hold tool and tighten
  - ♦ 160 Nm (118 ft lb)

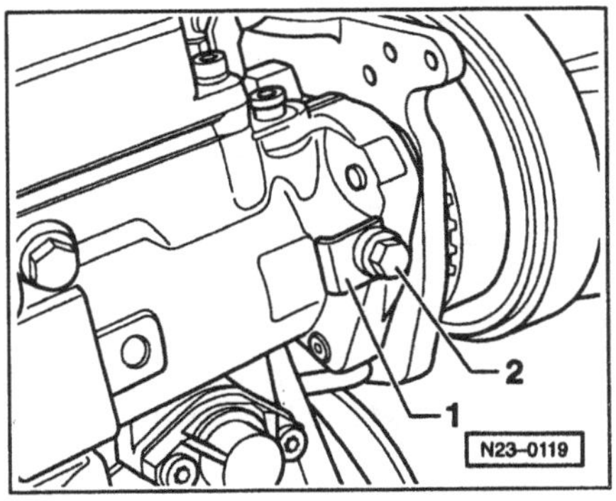

- Loosen injection pump lock bolt -2-
- Fit intermediate plate -1- and tighten locking bolt
  - ♦ 25 Nm (18 ft lb)
- Install toothed belt guard for injection pump
- Dynamically check “start of injection”; adjust if necessary ⇒ Repair Group 23

Note:

If toothed belt must be removed/installed; first install ribbed V-belt. *⇒ page B 13-20*

- Install radiator with lock carrier
- Install sound dampening pan

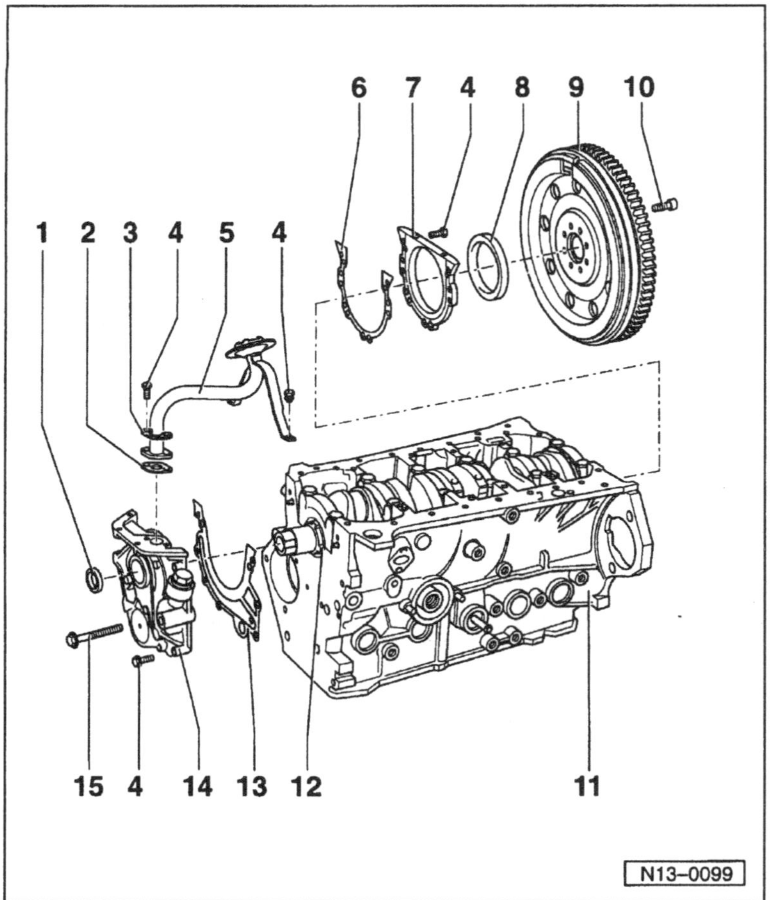

Crankshaft sealing flange and flywheel, removing and installing

Note:

For clutch repairs:

- *Engine Code AAB*

⇒ *Manual Transmission 02B,* Repair Group 30

- *Engine Code ACV*

⇒ *Manual Transmission 02G,* Repair Group 30

1 - Oil seal
- replacing

⇒ page B 13-59

2 - Gasket
- Replace

3 - Securing plate
- Engine Code AAB
- Replace

4 - 10 Nm (7 ft lb)

5 - Suction pipe

6 - Gasket
- Replace

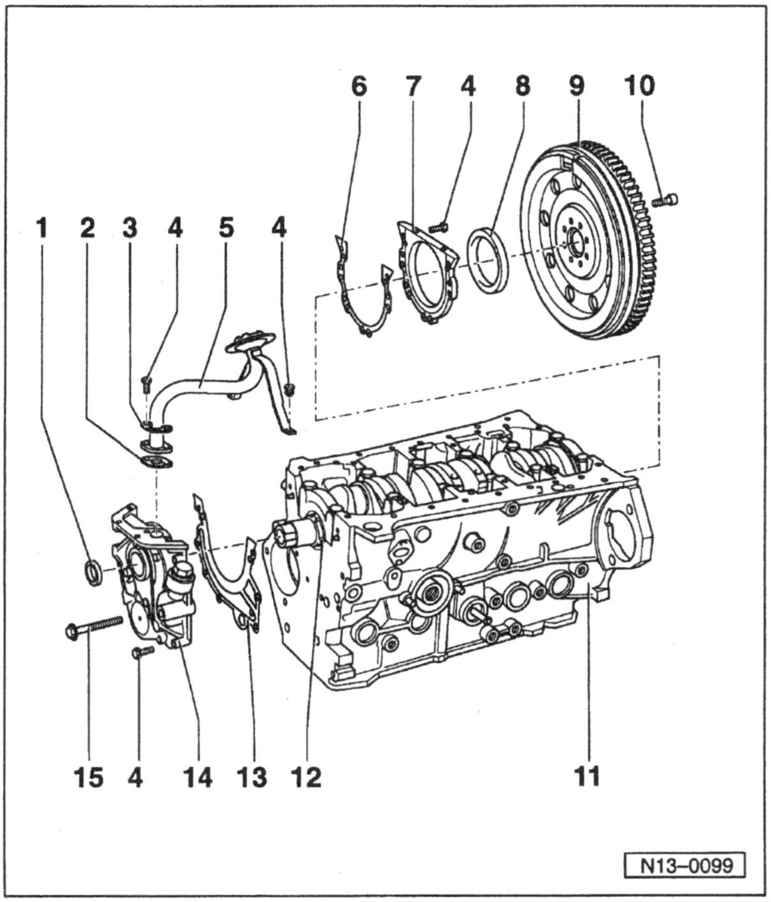

7 - Sealing flange
- must be located on dowel sleeves

8 - Oil seal
- replacing

⇒ page B 13-61

9 - Flywheel (dual mass)
- Engine Code ACV
- Remove and install flywheel using 3067 counter-hold tool
- removing and installing:

⇒ Fig. B 13-58

10 - 60 Nm (44 ft lb) + $^{1}/_{4}$ turn (90°) further
- Replace
- dual mass flywheel, removing and installing

⇒ Fig. B 13-58

11 - Cylinder block
- crankshaft removing and installing

⇒ page B 13-63
- Disassembling and assembling pistons and connecting rods

⇒ page B 13-67

12 - Oil pump coupling ring
- with four drive lugs
- Break open to pull off
- Heat new coupling ring to 200 °C (392°F) max. before installing

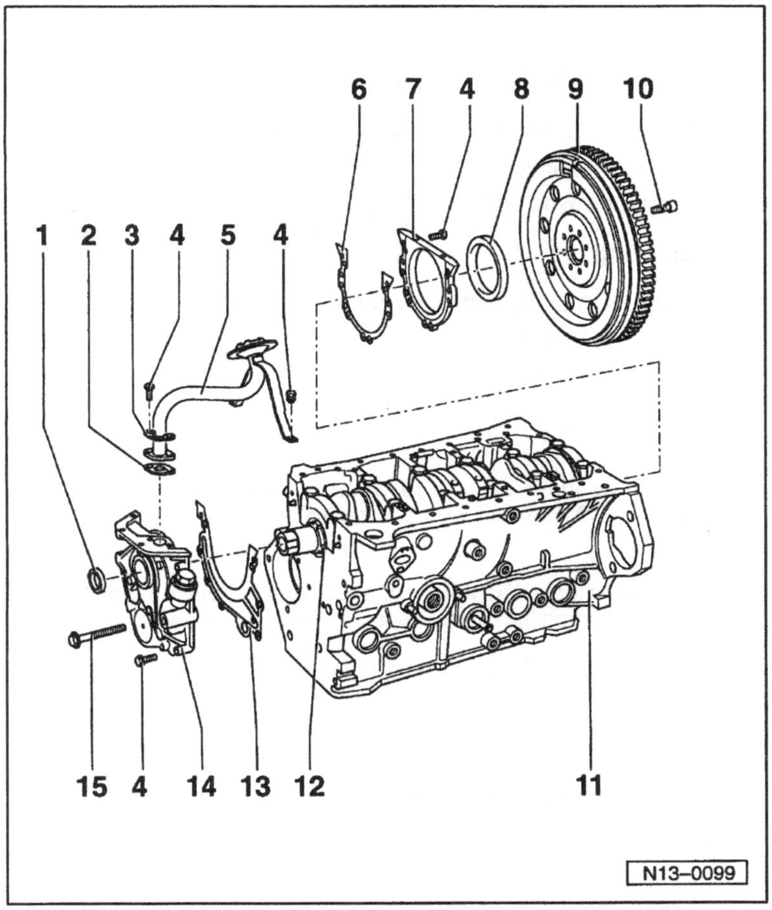

13 - **Gasket**
- Replace

14 - **Oil pump**
- When installing note coupling ring (item 12) on crankshaft
- Only replace as an assembly
  - ♦ must sit on dowels
  - ♦ disassembling and assembling

⇒ Repair Group 17

15 - 20 Nm (15 ft lb)

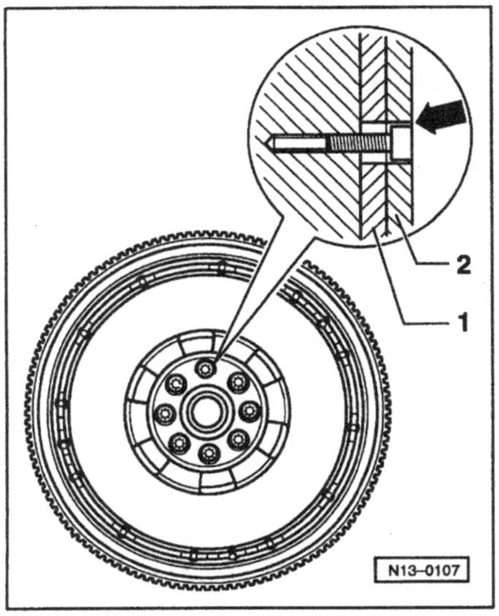

◄ **Fig. 1 Dual mass flywheel, removing and installing**

Engine code ACV

Special tools, testers and auxiliary items

- ♦ 3067 Counter-hold tool
- ♦ VAG 1332 Torque wrench, 40 to 200 Nm (30 to 148 ft lb)

Removing

- First remove one mounting bolt ensuring that the bolt head does not contact the primary flywheel mass -1-

Note:

To remove the remaining mounting bolts, screw out the bolts until they are flush -arrow- with secondary flywheel -2-.

Installing

- Tighten new mounting bolts
  - ♦ 60 Nm (44 ft lb) plus an additional 1/4 turn (90°)

Note:

The additional quarter turn can be accomplished using more than one step.

Crankshaft oil seal (pulley end), replacing

Special tools, testers and auxiliary items

- ♦ Oil seal extractor 3203
- ♦ Fitting sleeve 2080 A

Removing

- Remove toothed belt (camshaft):

♦ Vehicles ➤ 01.95
⇒ page B 13-26

♦ Vehicles 02.95 ➤
⇒ page B 13-36

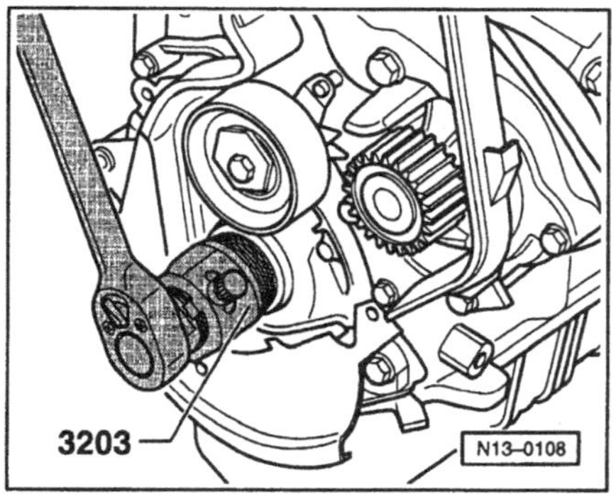

- Unscrew inner section of 3203 oil seal extractor two turns (approx. 3 mm) out of the outer section and lock with knurled screw

◄ – Lubricate threaded head of oil seal extractor, place in position and while exerting firm pressure, screw as far as possible into oil seal

- Loosen knurled screw and turn inner section against crankshaft until oil seal is pulled out

Installing

- Lightly oil sealing lip of oil seal.

- Slide oil seal over guide sleeve from 2080 A.

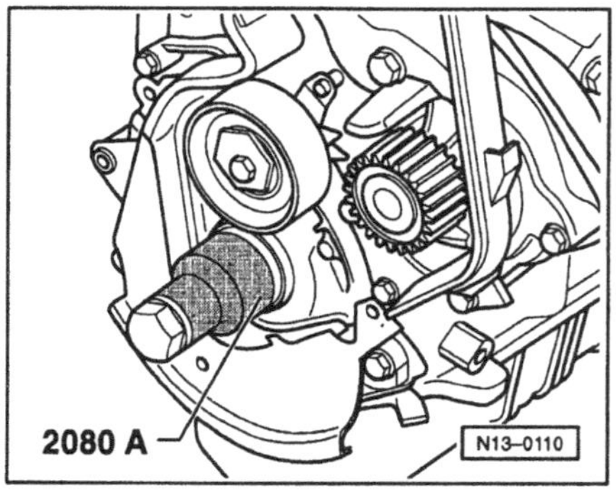

◄ – Press in oil seal up to stop with press sleeve from 2080 A and vibration damper center bolt

- Install toothed belt and tension

♦ Vehicles ➤ 01.95
⇒ page B 13-26

♦ Vehicles 02.95 ➤
⇒ page B 13-36

Crankshaft oil seal (flywheel end), replacing

Special tools, testers and auxiliary items

- Extractor hook 10-221
- Insertion ring 2003/1

Removing

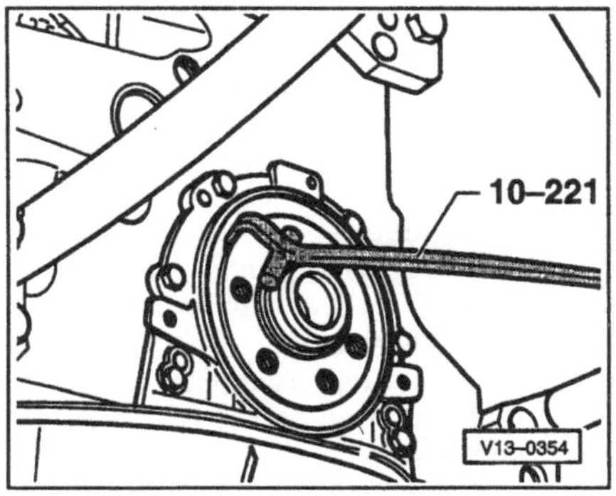

– Remove transmission

- Engine code AAB
⇒ *Manual Transmission 02B*, Repair Group 34
- Engine code ACV
⇒ *Manual Transmission 02G*, Repair Group 34

– Remove flywheel
⇒ page B 13-58

◄ – Remove seal with 10-221 extractor hook

Installing

– Clean sealing flange mounting holes with a cloth

Note:

The new seal has an assembly aid and a slide rail. The seal must not be oiled or greased.

– Slide seal on evenly by hand using the assembly aid and then carefully remove assembly aid.

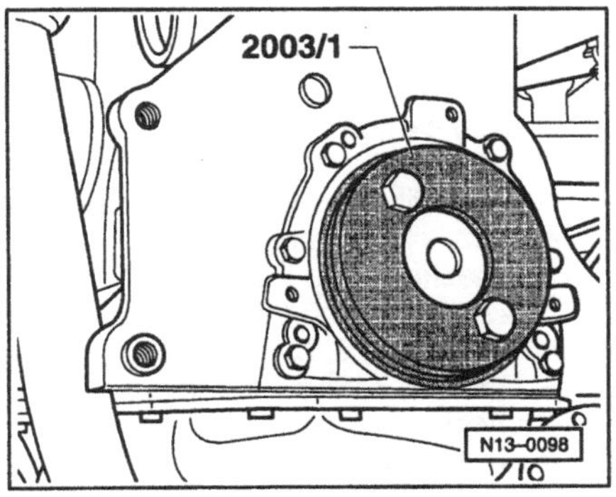

◄ – Press seal onto stop with 2003/1 insertion ring

– Install transmission

- Engine code AAB:
⇒ *Manual Transmission 02B*, Repair Group 34
- Engine code ACV:
⇒ *Manual Transmission 02G*, Repair Group 34

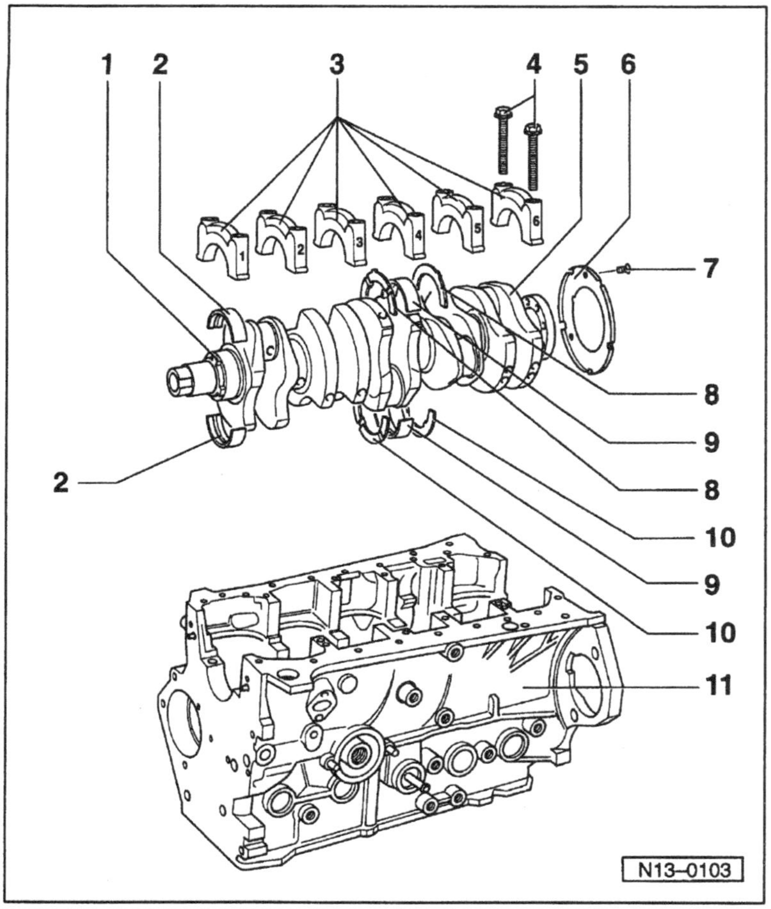

Crankshaft, removing and installing

1 - Oil pump coupling ring
- ♦ with four drive lugs
- – Break open to pull off
- – Heat new coupling ring to 200°C (392°F) max. before fitting

2 - Bearing shell 1, 2, 3, 5 and 6
- ♦ for bearing caps without oil groove
- ♦ for cylinder block with oil groove
- – Do not interchange used bearing shells (mark accordingly)

3 - Bearing cap
- ♦ bearing cap 1: pulley end
- ♦ bearing cap 4 with recesses for thrust washers
- ♦ bearing shell retaining lugs cyl. block/bearing cap must be on the same side

4 - 65 Nm (48 ft lb)

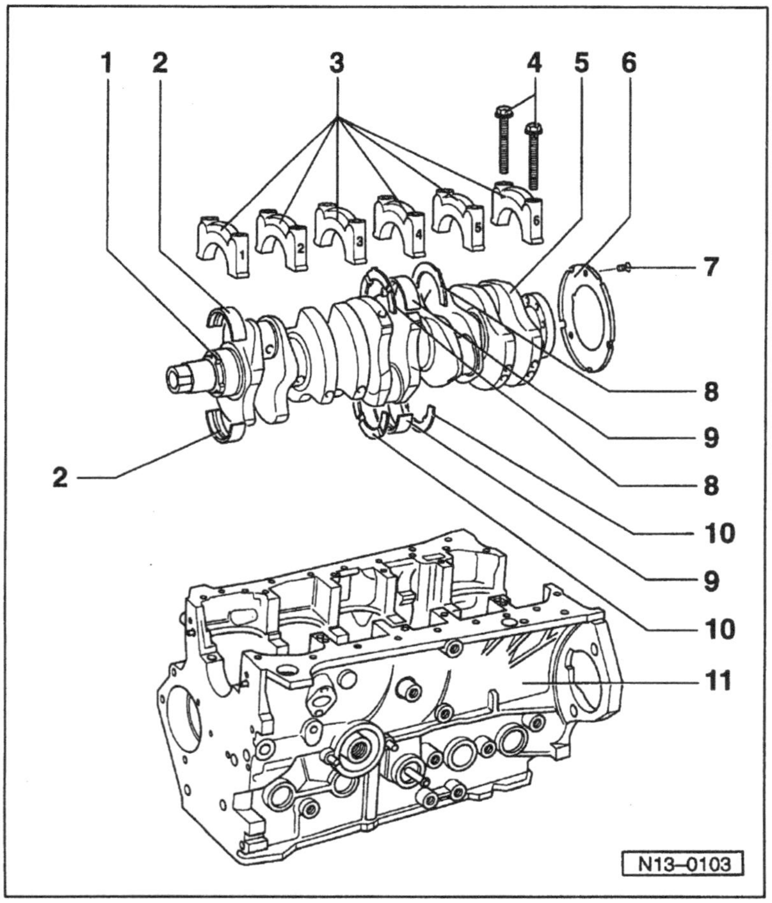

5 - Crankshaft
- ♦ axial clearance:
  "new": 0.07 to 0.18 mm
  "Wear limit": 0.25 mm
- – radial clearance:
  (checking with Plastigage®):
  New: 0.016...0.075 mm
  Wear limit: 0.16 mm
- – Do not rotate crankshaft while checking radial clearance
- ♦ crankshaft dimensions:

⇒ page B 13-66

6 - Sensor wheel
- ♦ Engine Code: ACV
- ♦ for engine speed sensor G28

7 - 25 Nm (18 ft lb)
- ♦ Engine Code: ACV
- – Replace

8 - Thrust washer
- ♦ for bearing cap 4
- – Note installation orientation

9 - Bearing shell 4
- ♦ for bearing cap without oil groove
- ♦ for cylinder block with oil groove

10 - Thrust washer
- ♦ for cylinder block, bearing 4

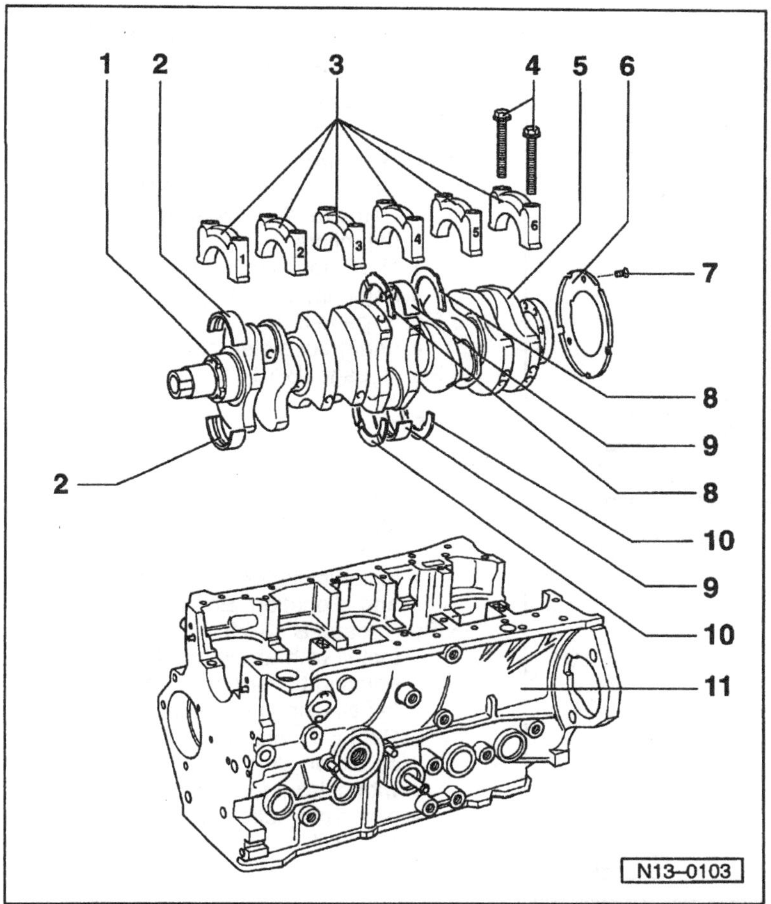

11 - Cylinder block

- Disassembling and assembling pistons and connecting rods

⇒ page B 13-67

Crankshaft, dimensions (mm.)

Honing dimension	Main journal ∅	Connecting rod journal ∅
Basic dimension	58.00 −0.022 −0.042	47.80 −0.022 −0.042
1st undersize	57.75 −0.022 −0.042	47.55 −0.022 −0.042
2nd undersize	57.50 −0.022 −0.042	47.30 −0.022 −0.042
3rd undersize	57.25 −0.022 −0.042	47.05 −0.022 −0.042

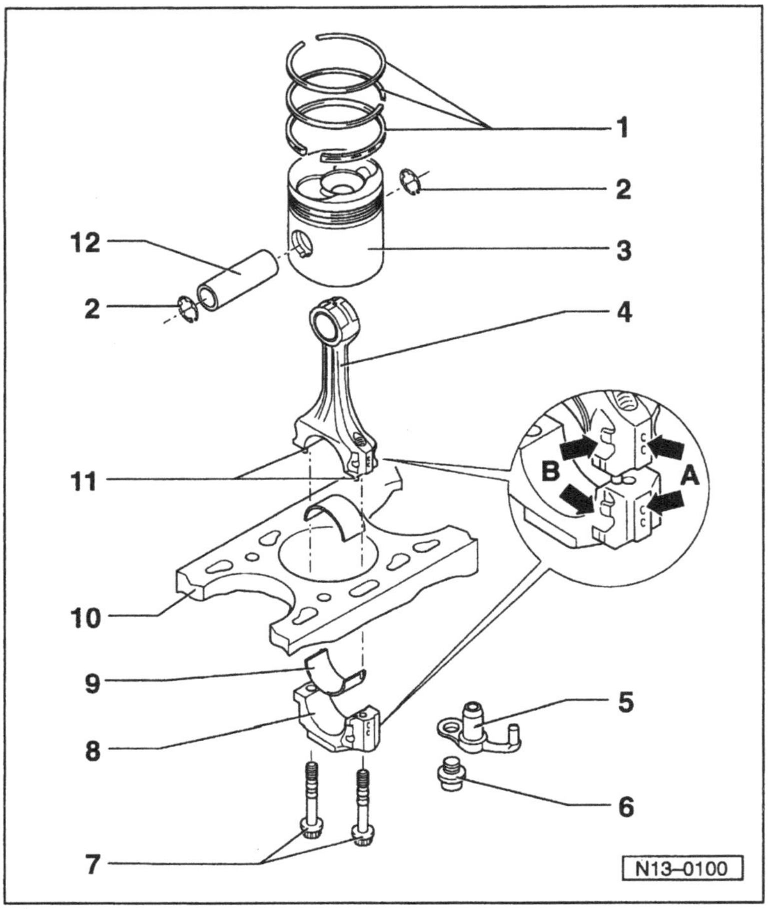

Pistons and connecting rods, disassembling and assembling

1 - Piston ring
- Offset ring gaps by 120°
- Remove and install using piston ring pliers
- ♦ "TOP" faces towards piston crown
- ♦ ring gap, checking:

⇒ Fig. 1, page B 13-70
- ♦ ring/groove clearance, checking:

⇒ Fig. 2, page B 13-71

2 - Circlip

3 - Piston
- ♦ Engine code ACV
- Mark installation position and cyl. number
- ♦ piston/cylinder installed position and allocation, Engine Code ACV

⇒ Fig. 4, page B 13-73
- Install with arrow on piston crown pointing toward pulley end
- Install using piston ring clamp
- Replace piston if cracks are found on piston skirt
- ♦ with cut-out for oil jet
- ♦ piston projection at TDC, checking

⇒ page B 13-74

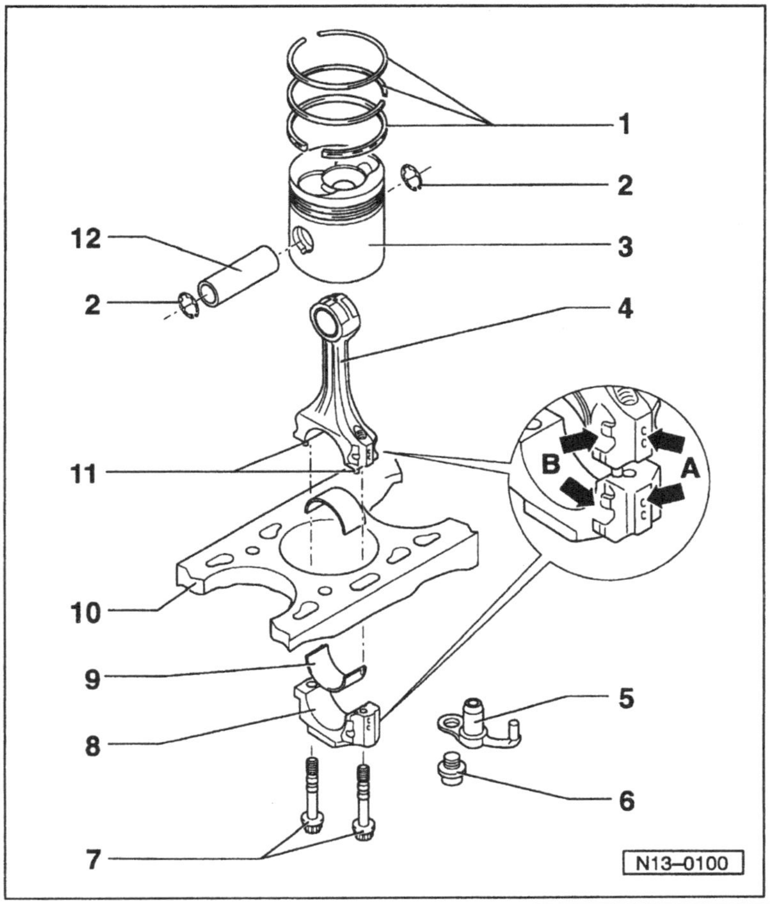

4 - Connecting rod
- Only replace as a set
- Mark cylinder number -A-
- ♦ installed position: Mark -B- faces towards pulley end

5 - Oil spray jet
- ♦ for piston cooling

6 - 10 Nm (7 ft lb)
- Install with AMV 188 100 02

7 - Connecting rod bolt
- ♦ 30 Nm (22 ft lb) + 1/4 turn further
- Replace
- Oil threads and contact surfaces
- Use old bolts to measure radial clearance

8 - Connecting rod bearing cap
- Mark cylinder number -A-
- ♦ installed position: Mark -B- faces toward pulley end

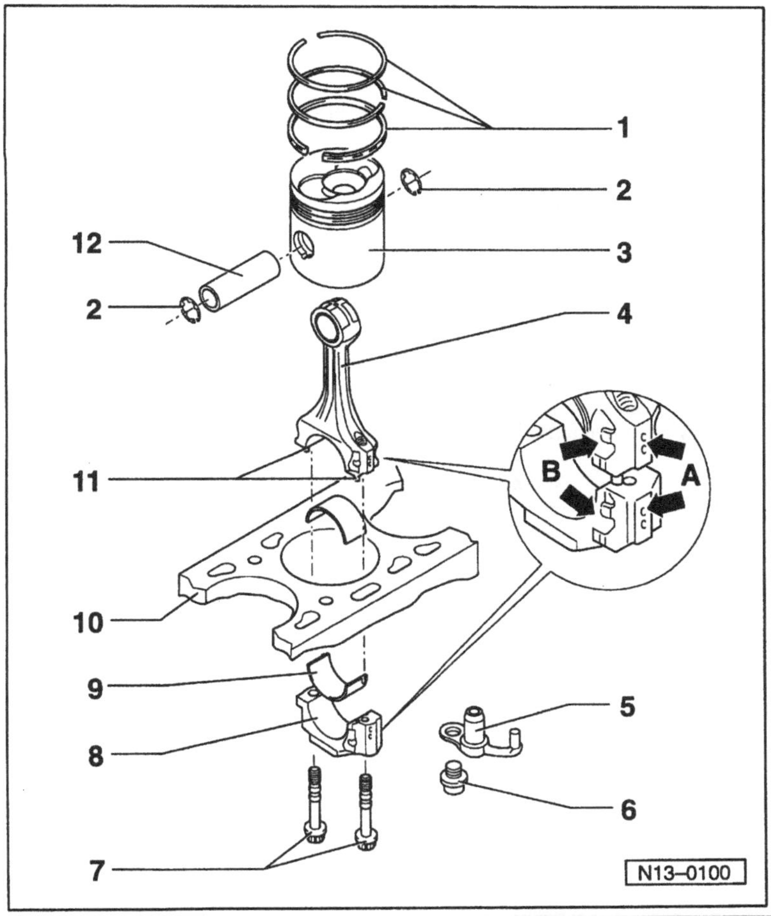

9 - **Bearing shell**
- Note installed position
- Do not interchange used bearing shells
- Ensure that retaining lugs fit tightly into recesses
- ♦ axial clearance
  Wear limit: 0.40 mm
- ♦ radial clearance, check using Plastigage :
  Wear limit: 0.08 mm
  Do not rotate crankshaft while checking radial clearance

10 - **Cylinder block**
- ♦ cylinder bores, checking:

⇒ pageB 13-76
- ♦ piston and cylinder dimensions:

⇒ pageB 13-76

11 - **Fitted pin**
- ♦ Engine Code AAB
- Seat fitted pin securely into connecting rod, not in bearing cap

12 - **Piston pin**
- ♦ If difficult to remove, heat piston to 60 °C (140 °F)
- ♦ Remove and install using VW 222a drift

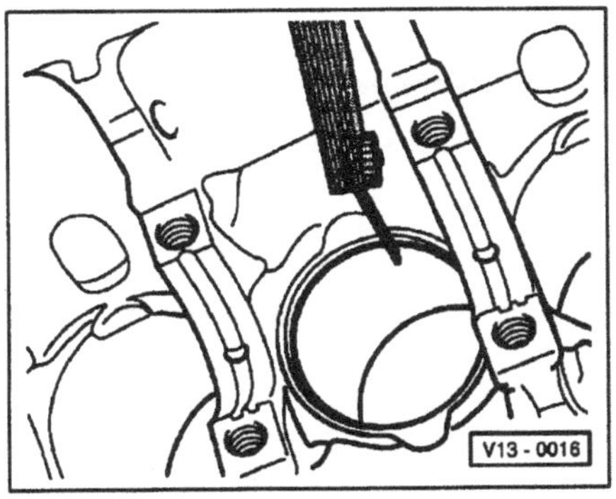

◄ **Fig. 1 Piston ring gap, checking**

Special tools, testers and auxiliary items

♦ Feeler gauge

Test sequence

- Squarely insert ring from top of block and push down to approx. 15 mm from lower end of cylinder

Piston ring Dimensions in mm	**New**	**Wear limit**
1st compression ring		
AAB	0.20...0.40	1.2
ACV	0.25...0.45	1.0
2nd compression ring		
AAB	0.20...0.40	0.6
ACV	0.20...0.40	1.0
Oil scraper ring		
AAB	0.25...0.50	1.2
ACV	0.25...0.50	1.0

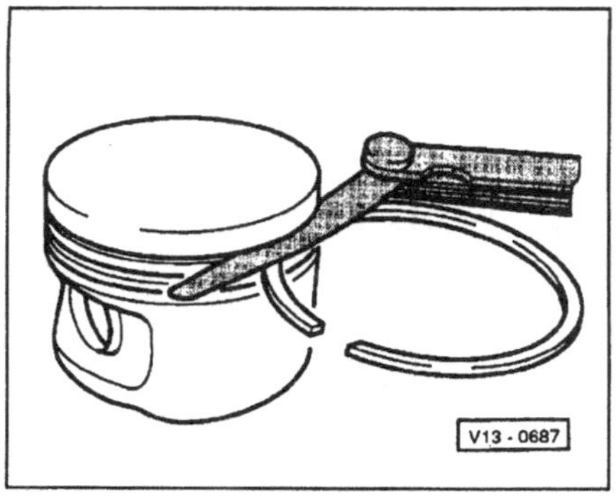

Fig. 2 Piston ring to groove clearance, checking

Special tools, testers and auxiliary items

♦ Feeler gauge

Test sequence

– Clean ring groove before checking

Piston ring Dimensions in mm	**New**	**Wear limit**
1st compression ring AAB ACV	0.09...0.12 0.07...0.11	0.25 0.25
2nd compression ring	0.05...0.08	0.25
Oil scraper ring	0.03...0.06	0.15

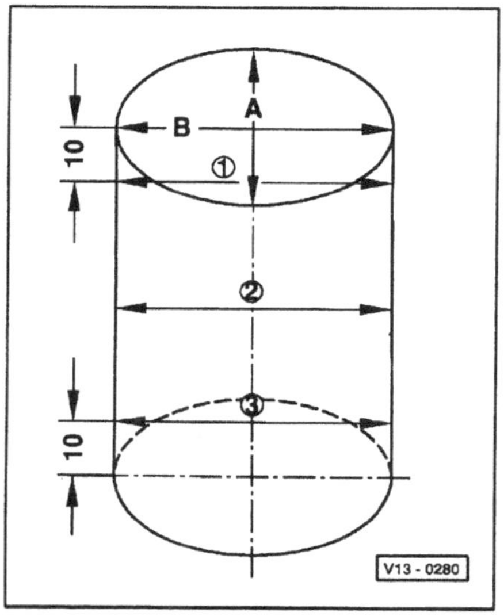

Fig. 3 Cylinder bores, checking

Special tools, testers and auxiliary items

♦ Internal dial gauge 50 to 100 mm

Test sequence

– Take measurements from 3 positions in both lateral -A- and longitudinal -B- directions

Deviation from nominal dimension:

Engine code Dimensions in mm	**Deviation from nominal dimension**
AAB	0.10
ACV	0.08

Note:

Measuring the cylinder bores must not be done when the cylinder block is mounted on a repair stand with adapter bracket VW 540, as incorrect measurements would then be possible.

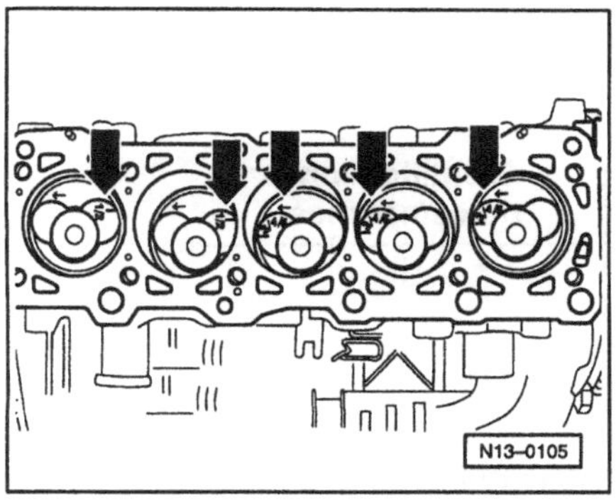

Fig. 4 Piston installed position and piston / cylinder allocation

Engine code: ACV

Pistons in cylinders 1 and 2:

Larger intake valve chamber towards flywheel -arrows-

Pistons in cylinders 3, 4 and 5:

Larger intake valve chamber towards belt pulley side -arrows-

Note:

New piston allocation to cylinders is shown by a colored mark on piston crown.

- *Piston for cylinder 1 and 2: marked 1/2*
- *Piston for cylinder 3, 4 and 5: marked 3/4/5*

Piston crown projection, checking

Special tools, testers and auxiliary items

- VW 382/7 Measuring bridge
- VW 385/17 End plate
- Dial gauge

Test sequence

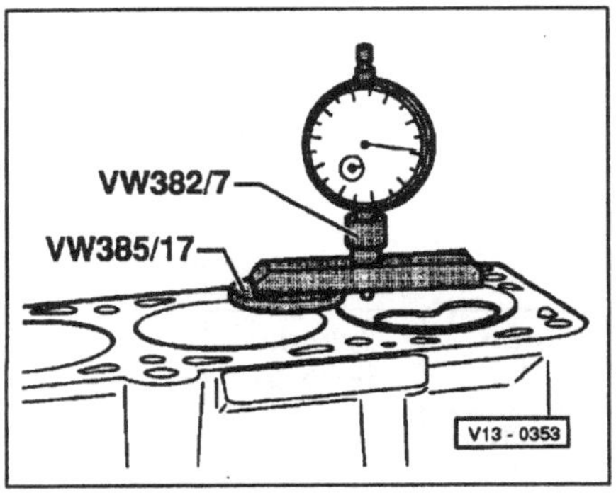

Note:

Measure piston crown projection at TDC whenever installing new pistons or a short block. Based on the piston projection dimension; install the corresponding gasket using the following table:

Engine code: AAB

Piston projection	Identification Holes/notches
0.66 mm to 0.86 mm	1
0.87 mm to 0.90 mm	2
0.91 mm to 1.02 mm	3

Engine code: ACV

Piston projection	Identification Holes/notches
0.76 mm to 1.01 mm	1
1.02 mm to 1.05 mm	2
1.06 mm to 1.13 mm	3

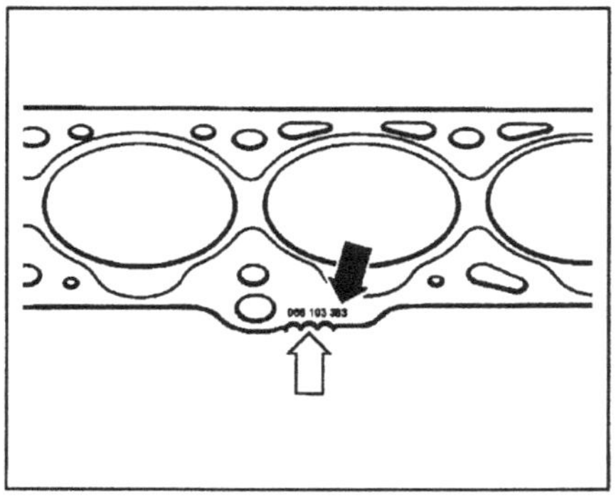

◄ **Cylinder head gasket identification**

- Part No. = black arrow
- Holes/notches = white arrow

Note:

If differing values are obtained when measuring piston projection, use the highest value to select the gasket.

Pistons and cylinders, dimensions

Engine code: AAB

Honing dimension		Piston ∅	Cylinder bore ∅
Basic dimens.	mm	79.48	79.51
1st oversize	mm	79.73	79.76
2nd oversize	mm	79.98	80.01

Engine code: ACV

Honing dimension		Piston ∅	Cylinder bore ∅
Basic dimens.	mm	80.96	81.01
1st oversize	mm	81.21	81.26

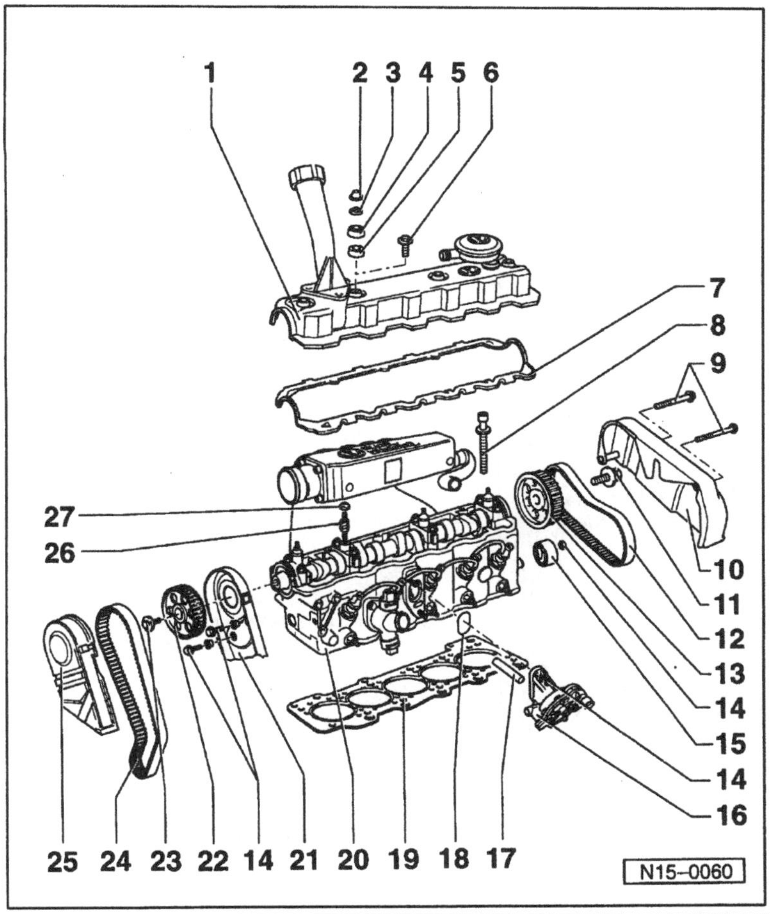

Cylinder head components, removing and installing

Cylinder compression, checking
⇒ page B 15–10

Notes:

- *When installing an exchange cylinder head (with camshaft installed), after installation, the contacting surfaces between the hydraulic lifter and the camlobe must be oiled.*
- *Plastic protectors fitted to protect the open valves should only be removed just before installing the cyl. head.*
- *When replacing the cylinder head, also replace the complete engine coolant*

1 - Cylinder head cover
- Engine code: AAB
- Engine code ACV, cylinder head cover mounted with hex bolts to the bearing caps

2 - Cover cap
- Engine code AAB

3 - 10 Nm (7 ft lb)
- Engine code AAB

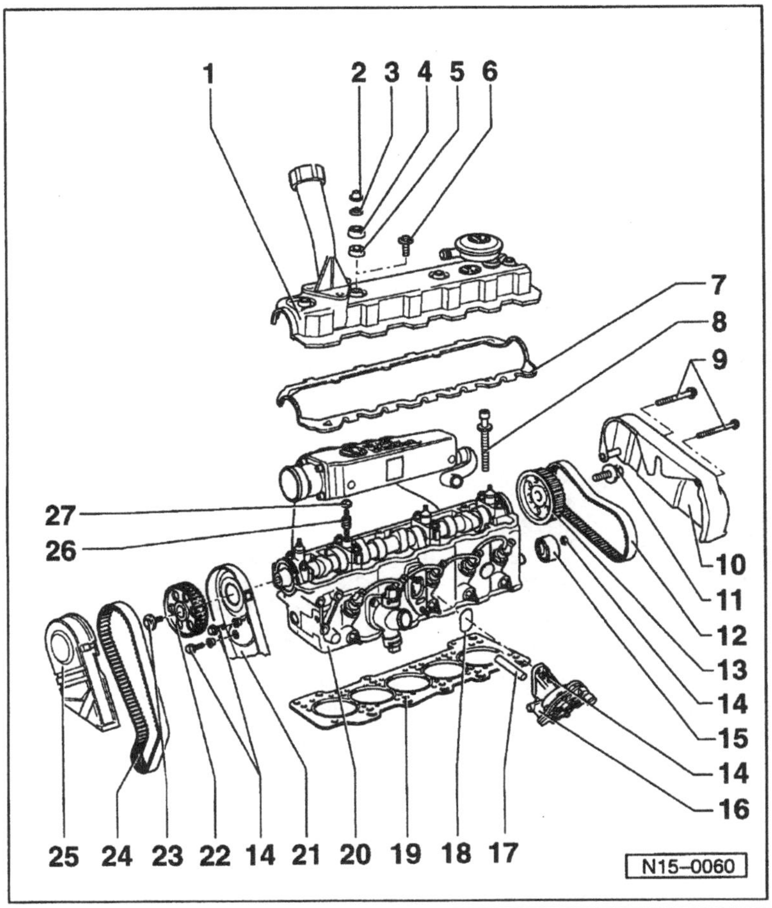

4 - Cup washer
- Engine code AAB

5 - Upper sealing washer
- Engine code AAB
- – Replace if damaged

6 - 10 Nm (7 ft lb)
- Engine code ACV

7 - Cylinder head cover gasket
- – Replace if damaged
- – Insert into groove on cylinder head cover

8 - Cylinder head bolt
- – Replace
- – Note sequence when loosening and tightening

⇒ page B 15–8

9 - Toothed belt guard mounting bolt
- M6 = 10 Nm (7 ft lb)
- M8 = 20 Nm (15 ft lb)

10 - Toothed belt guard

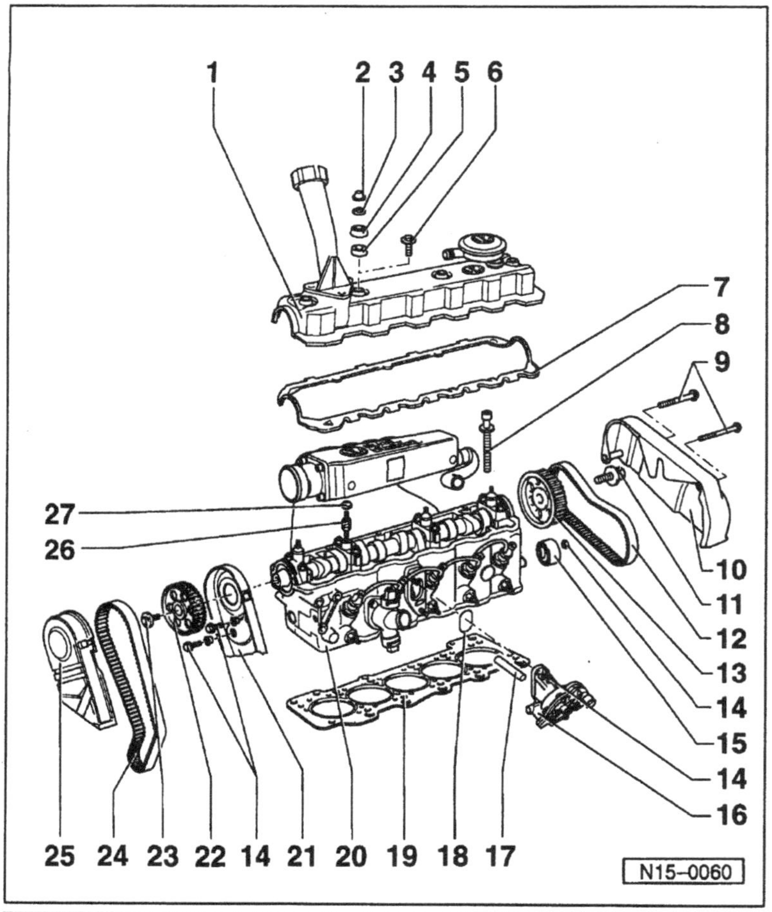

11 - Injection pump drive sprocket mounting bolt
- ♦ Engine code AAB: 100 Nm (74 ft lb)
- ♦ Engine code ACV: 160 Nm (118 ft lb)
- – Oil threads and contact surfaces
- – Use 3036 counter-hold tool to loosen and tighten

12 - Injection pump toothed belt
- – Mark direction of engine rotation before removing
- – Check for wear
- – Do not kink
- ♦ removing, installing, tensioning:

Engine code AAB
⇒ page B 13-42
Engine code ACV
⇒ page B 13-48

13 - Injection pump drive sprocket
- – Note position when installing toothed belt:

Engine code ACV:
⇒ page B 13-48
Engine code AAB:
⇒ page B 13-42

14 - 20 Nm (15 ft lb)

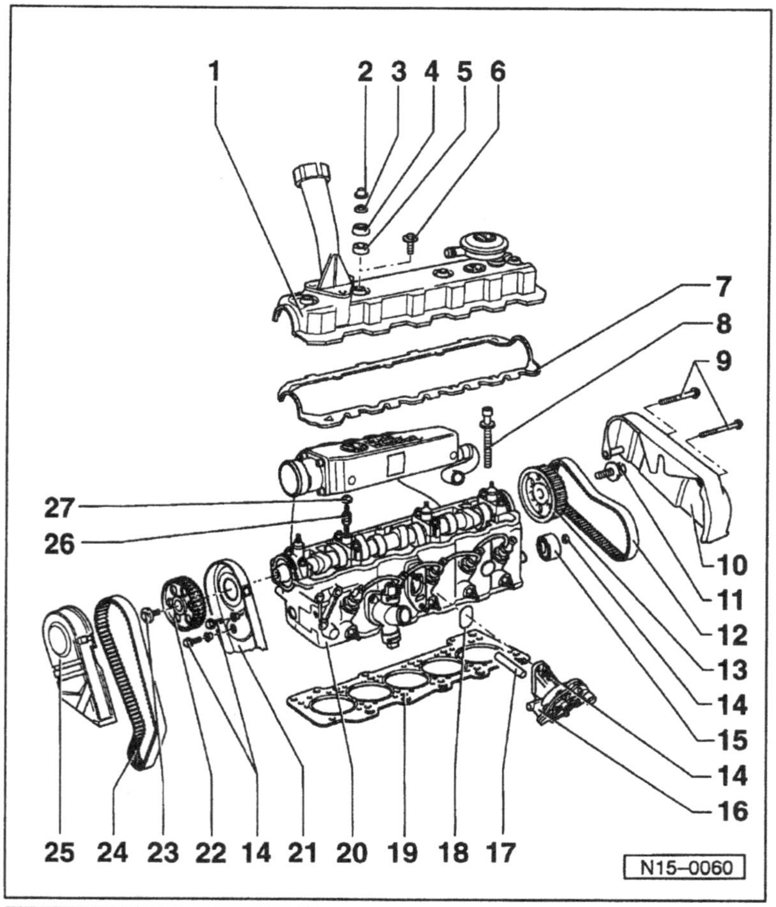

15 - Idler roller
- ♦ Engine code ACV
- ♦ note installation position

⇒ page B 13-48

16 - Vacuum pump

17 - Plunger

18 - O-ring
- – Replace

19 - Cylinder head gasket (2 types)
- – Replace
- ♦ Note marking

⇒ Fig. 2
- ♦ If replaced, also replace complete engine coolant

20 - Cylinder head
- – Check for distortion

⇒ Fig. 1, page B 15–7
- ♦ installing:

⇒ page B 15–8
- ♦ if replaced, completely replace engine coolant
- ♦ fuel injectors, removing and installing

⇒ Repair Group 23

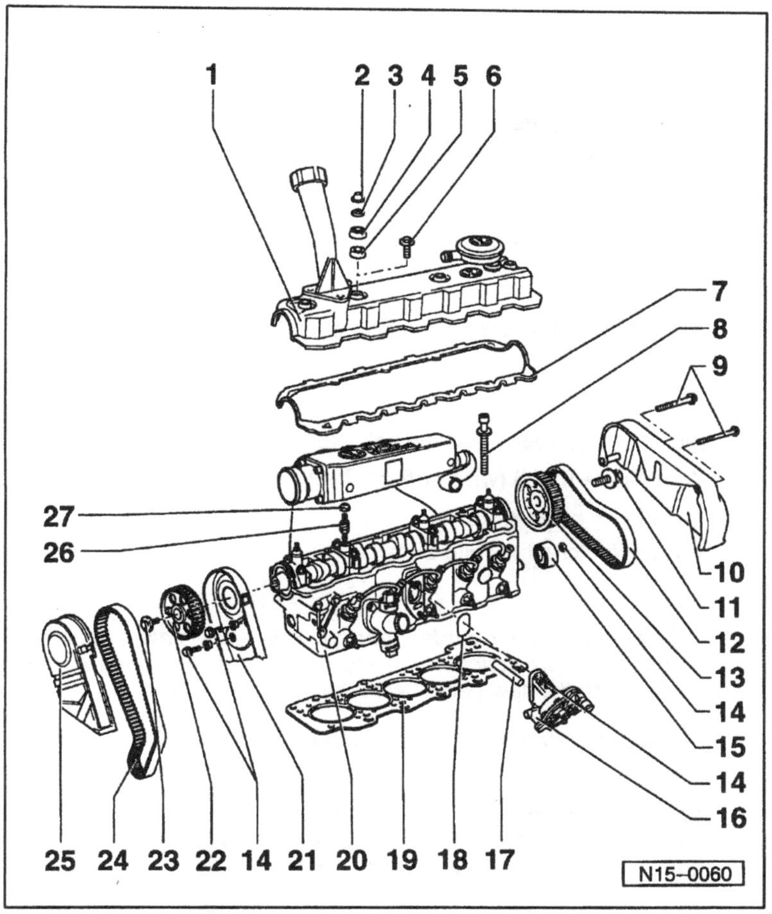

21 - Rear toothed belt guard
02.95 ➤
➤ 01.95
⇒ page B 13-8 (item 7)

22 - Camshaft sprocket
– Drive off camshaft taper using hammer and drift through toothed belt guard openings
– Note position when installing toothed belt:
Vehicles ➤ 01.95
⇒ page B 13-26
Vehicles 02.95 ➤
⇒ page B 13-36

23 - Camshaft sprocket mounting bolt
♦ Observe coding on bolt head:
8.8 = 85 Nm (63 ft lb)
10.9 = 100 Nm (74 ft lb)
– Use 3036 counter-hold tool to loosen and tighten

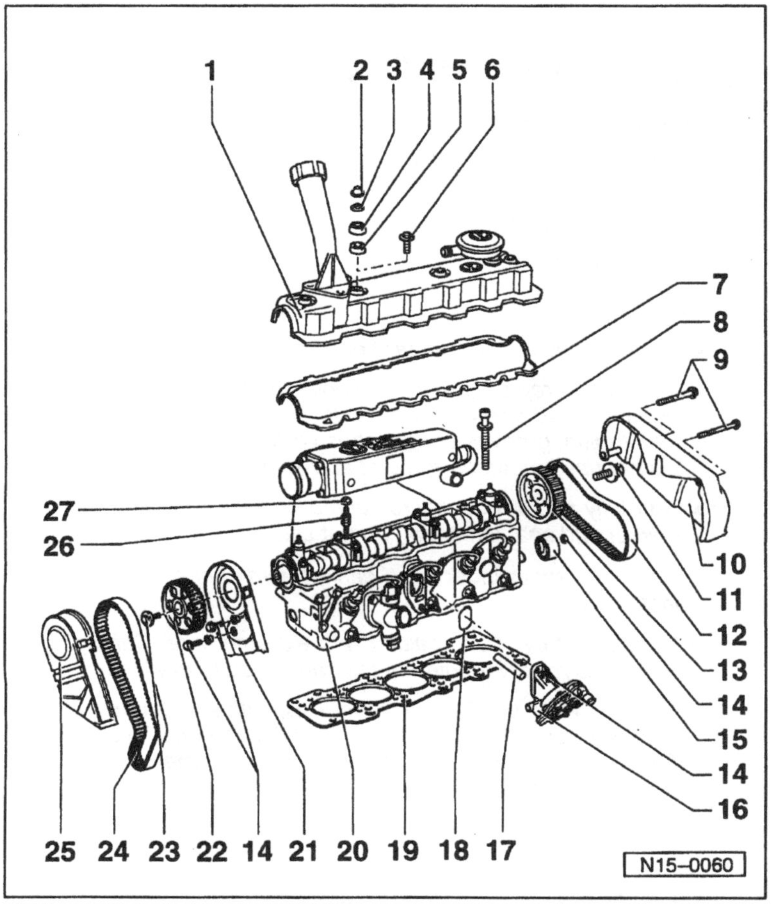

24 - Camshaft toothed belt
– Mark direction of engine rotation before removing
– Check for wear
– Do not kink
♦ removing, installing, tensioning:
Vehicles ➤ 01.95
⇒ page B 13-26
Vehicles 02.95 ➤
⇒ page B 13-36

25 - Upper toothed belt guard

26 - 15 Nm (11 ft lb)
♦ Engine code AAB

27 - Lower sealing cone
♦ Engine code AAB
– Replace if damaged

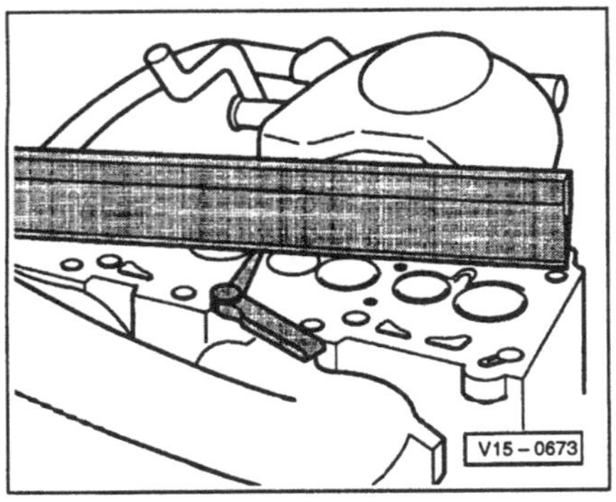

◄ **Fig. 1 Cylinder head distortion, checking**

Special tools, testers and auxiliary items

- Knife edge / straight edge
- Feeler gauge

Max. permissible distortion: 0.2 mm

Note:

Reworking Diesel cylinder heads is not permissible.

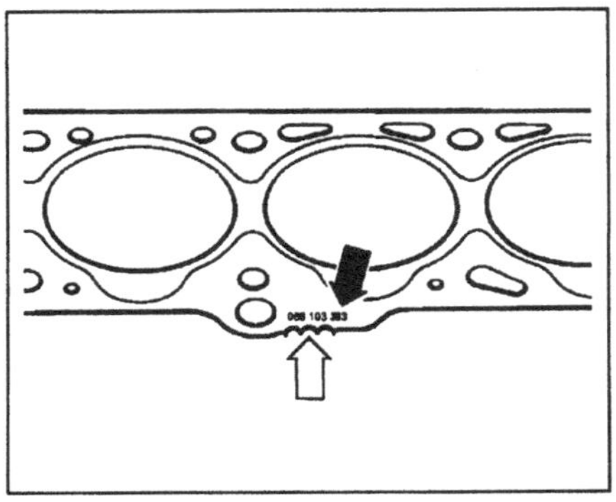

◄ **Fig. 2 Cylinder head gasket, identification**

Vehicles ➤ 01.95 (with soft gasket)

- Part No. = black arrow
- Holes/notches = white arrow

Note:

Different thickness cylinder head gaskets are installed depending on the piston projection. When replacing the cylinder head gasket, always install a new gasket with the same identification.

Vehicles 02.95 ➤ (with metal gasket)

Note:

Starting 02.95 ➤ *Metal cylinder head gaskets installed.*
It is no longer necessary to re-tighten the cylinder head bolts an additional quarter turn with these gaskets!

Cylinder head, installing

Special tools, testers and auxiliary items

- VAG 1332 Torque wrench
  40 to 200 Nm (30 ft lb to 148 ft lb)
- 3070 Guide pins
- Emery paper

Notes:

- *Always replace the cylinder head bolts.*
- *In cases of repair, carefully remove seal/gasket remnants from cylinder head and cylinder block. Ensure that you don't create longitudinal grooves or scratches while cleaning the surfaces. Do not use a coarser grade of abrasive paper than 100.*
- *Carefully and thoroughly remove all abrasive particles, dust, gasket and seal remnants, do not allow to enter engine interior!*
- *Remove new cylinder head gasket from packaging, just before installation.*
- *Handle soft cyl. head gasket with extreme care. Damaging the silicone layer or indented areas can cause future leaks.*
- *Vehicles ➤ 01.95 (Engine Code AAB) with soft material cylinder head gasket: in cases of repair, install metal head gasket. Replace the swirl chambers before installing metal head gasket (Engine Code AAB)*

⇒ page B 15–32

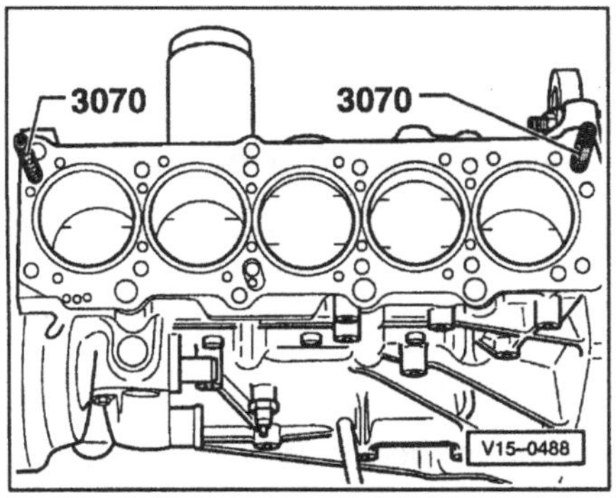

– Turn crankshaft to TDC mark before installing cylinder head
– Turn crankshaft in direction of rotation until no piston is at TDC
– Fit cylinder head gasket into place
◄ – Center by screwing 3070 guide pins into outer holes (intake side)
– Install cylinder head
– Thread in head bolts (10) finger-tight
– Remove guide pins using 3070 removal tool and install remaining head bolts where guide pins had previously been installed

Cylinder head bolts, tightening

All Vehicles

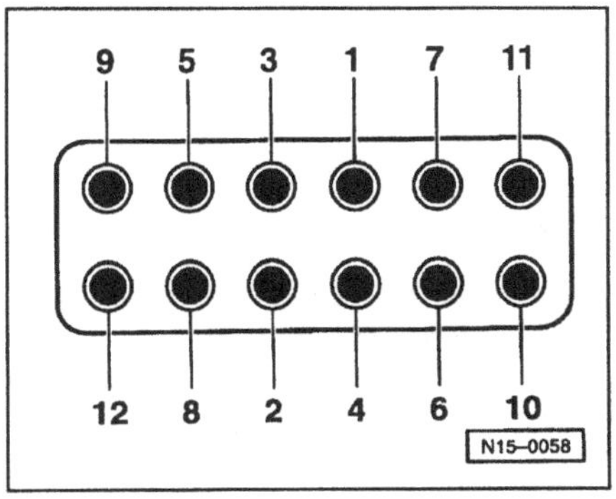

◄ – Tighten using torque wrench:
Stage I = 40 Nm (30 ft lb)
Stage II = 60 Nm (44 ft lb)

Vehicles ➤ 01.95 ONLY (with soft head gasket)

– In addition to above, tighten half turn further using normal wrench
Stage III = $^{1}/_{4}$ turn (90 °)
Stage IV = $^{1}/_{4}$ turn (90 °)

Notes:

- *Loosening cylinder head: reverse of installation sequence.*
- *Re-torquing cylinder head after repairs is not required.*

– After tightening cylinder head, turn camshaft so cyl. 1 cam-lobes point evenly upwards
– Turn crankshaft to TDC (in direction of engine rotation) before installing toothed belt

Cylinder compression, checking

Special tools, testers and auxiliary items

- Compression tester VAG 1381 or VAG 1763

Engine code AAB

- VAG 1323/2A adaptor
- 3035 Box wrench

Engine code ACV

- VAG 1381/12 adaptor
- 3220 flexible wrench

Test conditions

- Engine oil temperature 30 °C (86 °F) minimum

Test sequence

Engine code: AAB

– Pull wiring off engine limiter on injection pump, insulate and lay to one side
– Remove injection lines using 3035 tubing wrench
– Unscrew all injectors and remove all heat shields

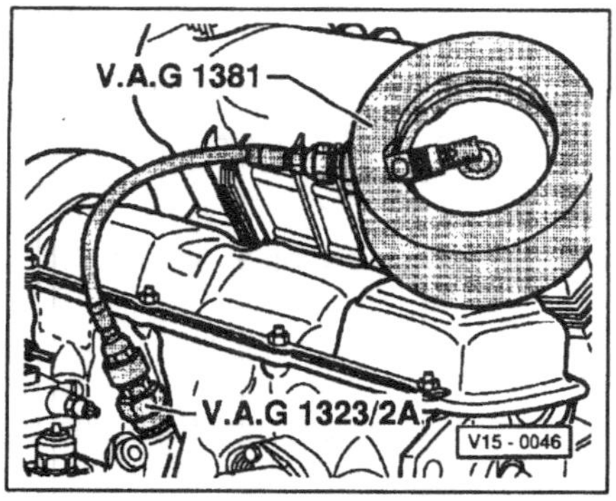

- Screw in VAG 1323/2A adaptor in place of the fuel injectors
- Insert old heat shield between adaptor and cylinder head
- Screw VAG 1381 or VAG 1763 compression tester finger tight into adaptor

To use compression tester
⇒ Manufacturers operating instructions

- Operate starter until tester shows no additional pressure increase

Compression specifications

New: 34 bar (493 psi)
Wear limit: 26 bar (377 psi)

Permissible difference between all cylinders: 5 bar (73 psi)

Note:

Always replace the heat shield seals between the cylinder head and fuel injectors.

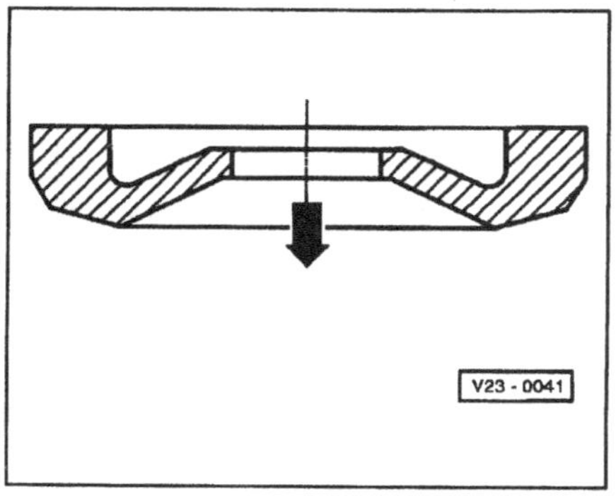

Installed position of heat shield: arrow points toward cylinder head

- ♦ tightening torques:
  - Fuel injector lines = 25 Nm (18 ft lb)
  - Fuel injectors = 70 Nm (52 ft lb)

Engine code ACV

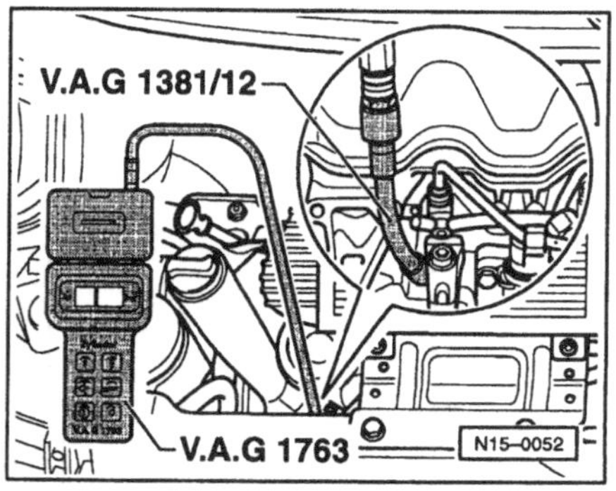

- Disconnect fuel cut-off valve/start of injection valve on pump
- Disconnect quantity adjuster on injection pump
- Remove all glow plugs using 3220 flexible wrench
- Screw in adapter VAG 1381/12 in place of the glow plugs
- Check compression using VAG 1381/1763 compression tester

To use compression tester
⇒ Manufacturers operating instructions

- Operate starter until tester shows no further pressure increase

Compression pressure:

New: 25...31 bar (362...450 psi)
Wear limit: 24 bar (348 psi)

Permissible difference between all cylinders: 5 bar (73 psi)

- Install glow plugs using 3220 flexible wrench
  - ♦ tightening torque: 15 Nm (11 ft lb)
- Check DTC memory

⇒ Repair Group 01

Note:

A Diagnostic Trouble Code will be stored because the injection pump connector was disconnected. To eliminate, check DTC memory then erase.

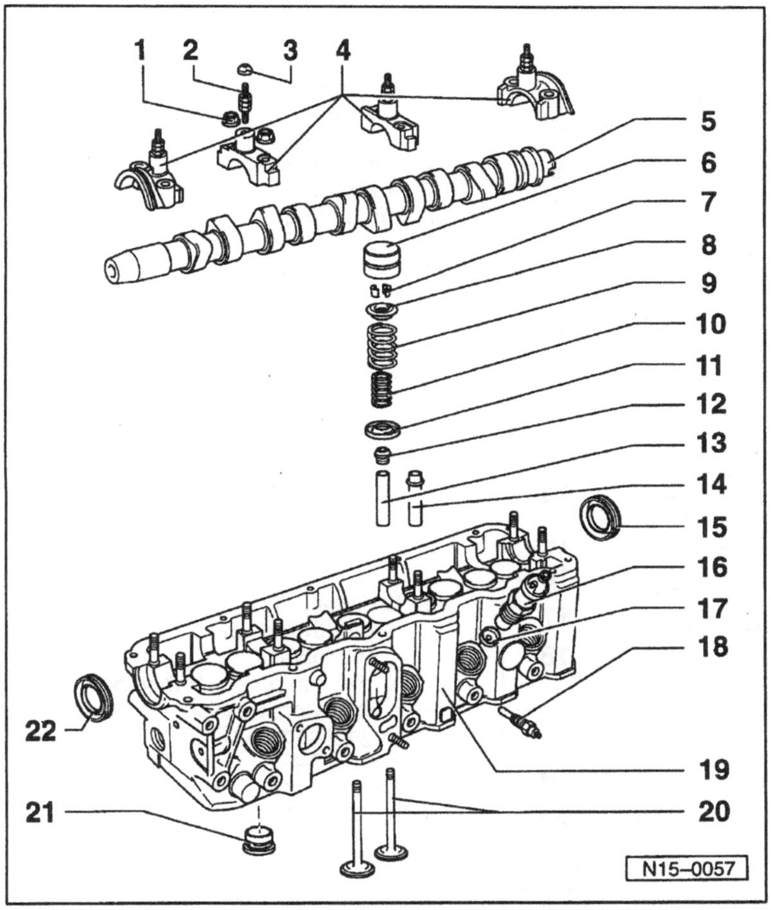

Valvetrain, servicing

Cylinder heads with cracks between the valve seats may be used without reducing engine life, provided the cracks are small and not more than 0.5 mm wide (0.02 in.).

1 - 20 Nm (15 ft lb)

2 - 15 Nm (11 ft lb)
- ♦ Engine code AAB

3 - Lower sealing cone
- ♦ Engine code AAB
- – Replace if damaged

4 - Bearing cap
- ♦ installed position:

⇒ Fig. 2, page B 15–18
- ♦ camshaft, removing and installing:

⇒ page B 15–28

5 - Camshaft
- ♦ axial clearance, checking:

⇒ Fig. 1, page B 15–18
- ♦ removing and installing:

⇒ page B 15–28
- ♦ radial clearance, checking using Plastigage : Wear limit: 0.11 mm Run-out: max. 0.01 mm
- ♦ identification and valve timing

⇒ Fig. 4, page B 15–20

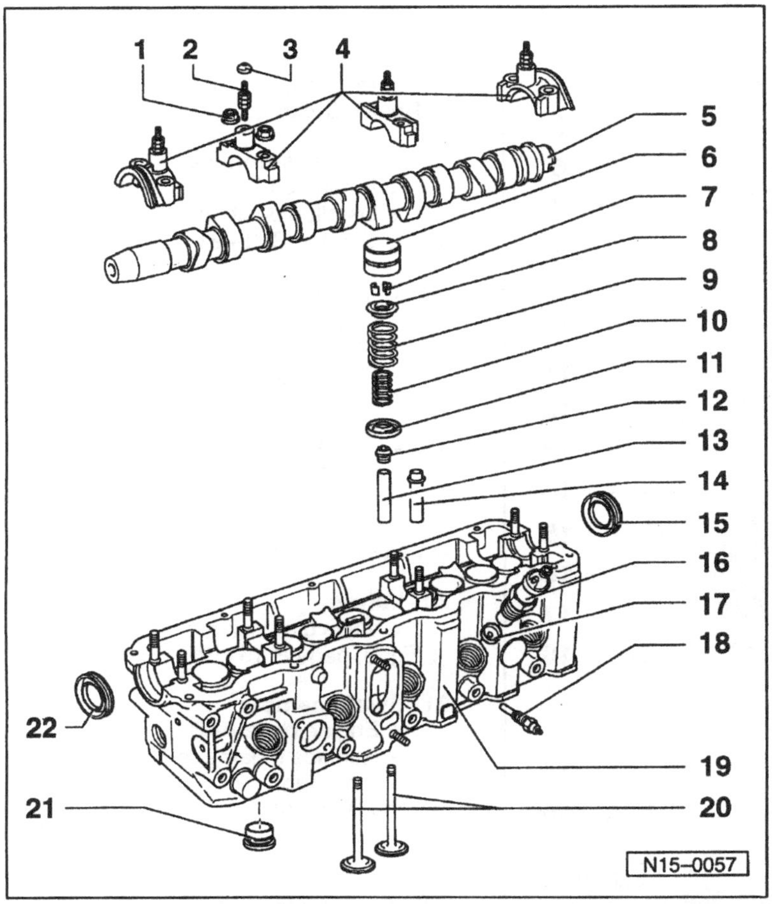

6 - Hydraulic lifter
- ♦ do not interchange
- ♦ with hydraulic valve clearance compensation
- ♦ checking:

⇒ page B 15–30
- – Store with cam contacting surfaces downwards
- – Before installing check camshaft axial clearance

⇒ Fig. 1, page B 15–18
- – Oil contacting surfaces

7 - Retainers

8 - Upper valve spring plate

9 - Outer valve spring
- ♦ removing and installing: w/ Cylinder head removed: use 2037 valve spring compressor w/ Cylinder head installed:

⇒ page B 15–26

10 - Inner valve spring
- ♦ Engine code AAB ➤ 11.94
- ♦ removing and installing: w/ Cylinder head removed: use 2037 valve spring compressor w/ Cylinder head installed:

⇒ page B 15–26

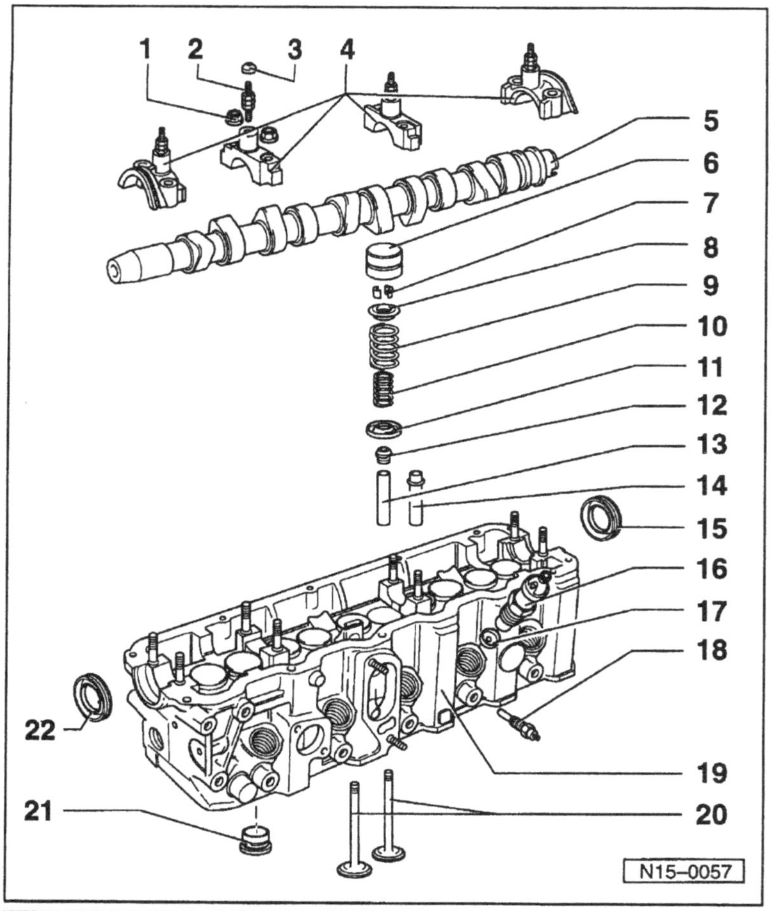

11 - Lower valve spring plate

– Remove and install using 3047A puller

12 - Valve stem seal

♦ replacing:

⇒ page B 15–26

13 - Valve guide

♦ checking:

⇒ page B 15–24

♦ replacing:

⇒ page B 15–25

14 - Valve guide w/ collar

♦ service version

♦ checking:

⇒ page B 15–24

♦ replacing:

⇒ page B 15–25

15 - Oil seal

– Remove bearing cap to remove and install,

♦ injection pump toothed belt, removing, installing, tensioning:

Engine code AAB

⇒ page B 13-42

Engine code ACV

⇒ page B 13-48

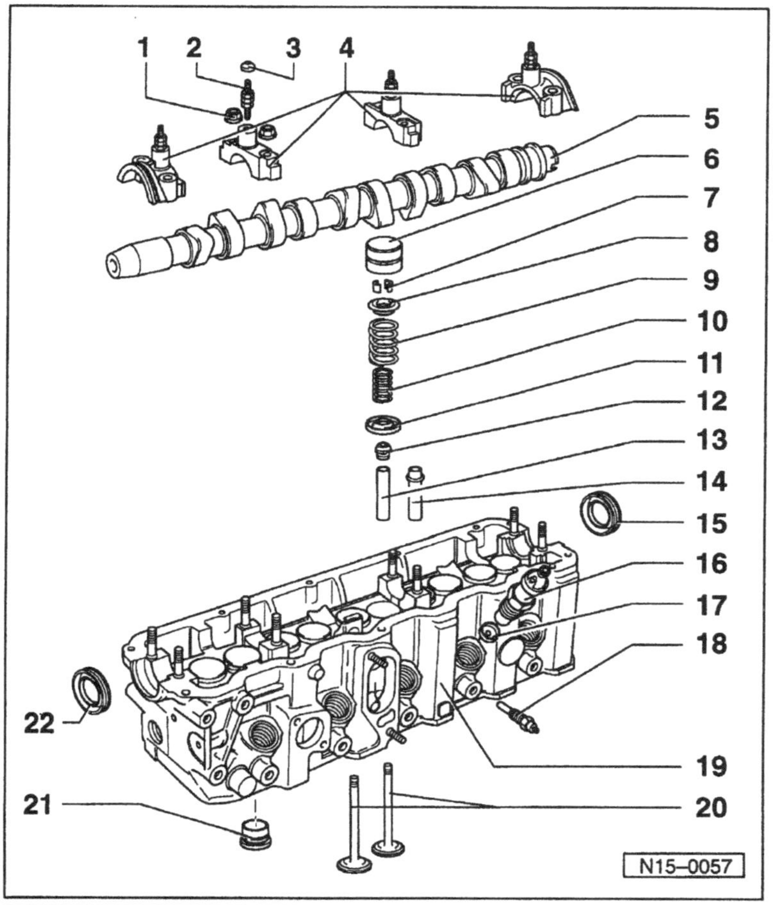

16 - Fuel injector

♦ removing and installing injectors

⇒ Repair Group 23

17 - Heat insulation seal

♦ Engine code AAB

♦ installed position:

⇒ Fig. 5, page B 15–21

18 - Glow plug

♦ Engine Code AAB

♦ removing, installing, checking glow plugs

⇒ Repair Group 28

19 - Cylinder head

♦ see note:

⇒ page B 15–13

♦ reworking valve seats:

⇒ page B 15–22

20 - Valves

♦ valve dimensions:

⇒ Fig. 3, page B 15–19

21 - Swirl chamber

♦ Engine code AAB

– Replace if damaged

♦ replacing:

⇒ page B 15–32

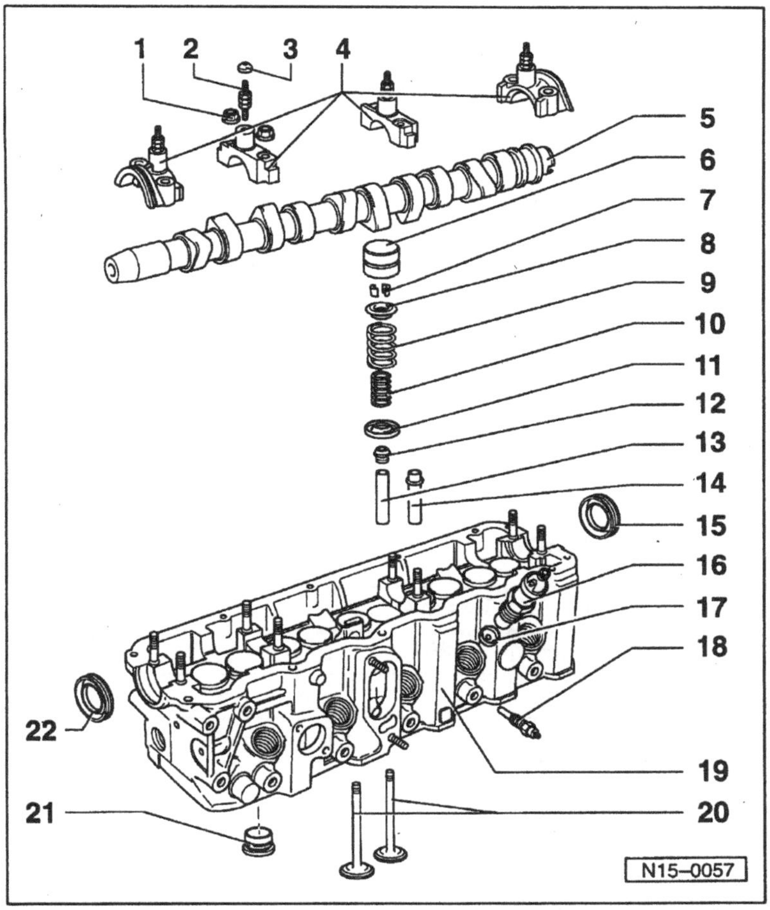

22 - Oil seal

- remove bearing cap to remove and install
  - ♦ camshaft toothed belt, removing, installing, tensioning: ➤ 01.95

⇒ page B 13-26

02.95 ➤

⇒ page B 13-36

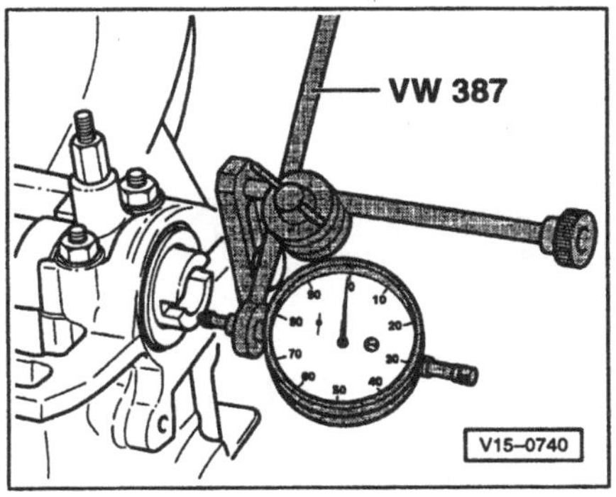

◄ **Fig. 1 Camshaft axial clearance, checking**

Special tools, testers and auxiliary items

- ♦ VW 387 Universal dial gauge bracket
- ♦ Dial gauge

Wear limit: max. 0.15 mm

- Check with hydraulic lifters removed and with first and last bearing caps installed

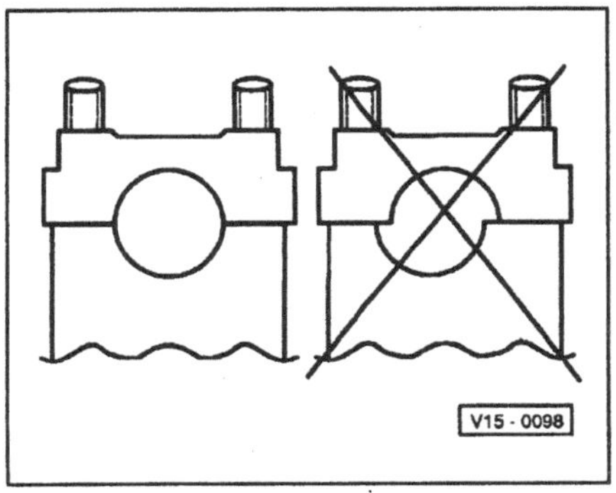

◄ **Fig. 2 Camshaft bearing caps, installed position**

- Note offset, before installing camshaft, fit bearing caps and determine final installed position

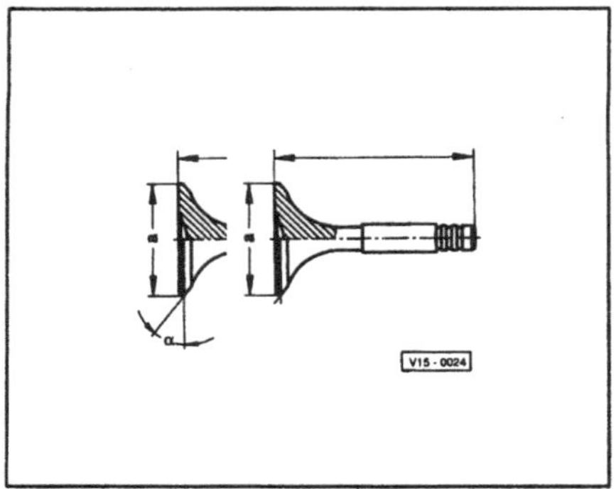

◄ **Fig. 3 Valve dimensions**

Note:

Valves must not be reworked! Only lapping-in is permissible!

Engine code AAB

Dimension		Intake valve	Exhaust valve
Ø a	mm	36.00	31.00
Ø b	mm	7.97	7.95
c	mm	95.00	95.00
α	∠°	45	45

Engine code ACV

Dimension		Intake valve	Exhaust valve
Ø a	mm	36.00	31.50
Ø b	mm	7.97	7.95
c	mm	96.85	96.85
α	∠°	45	45

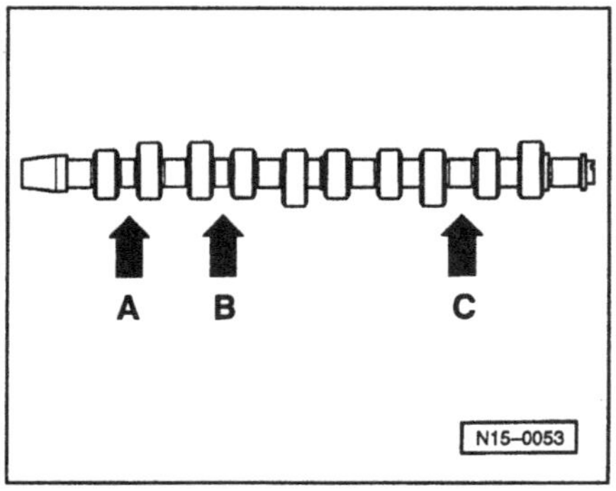

◄ **Fig. 4 Camshaft identification, valve timing**

Identification

- Cam base diameter: a = 38 mm Ø
- Identification via numbers and letters stamped between intake and exhaust cams:

Engine codes	AAB	ACV
No. 1 cylinder -arrow A-	W	WZO
No. 2 cylinder -arrow B-	–	046
Between No. 4 and 5 cylinders -arrow C-	074B	–

Valve timing at 1 mm valve lift

Engine codes	AAB	ACV
Intake opens after TDC	6.0 °	8.0 °
Intake closes after BDC	20.0 °	28.0 °
Exhaust opens before BDC	25.5 °	37.0 °
Exhaust closes before TDC	6.5 °	10.0 °

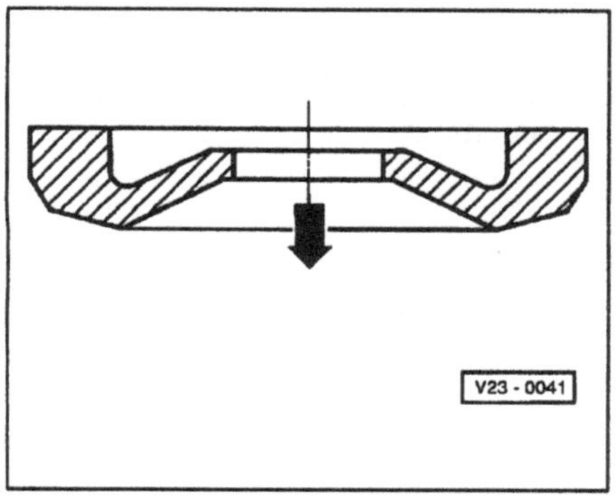

Fig. 5 Heat insulation seal, installation position

Engine code AAB

- ♦ arrow points toward cylinder head

Valve seats, reworking

Special tools, testers and auxiliary items

- ♦ Depth gauge
- ♦ Valve seat refacing tool

Notes:

- ♦ *When repairing engines with leaking valves, it is not always sufficient to replace or renew valve seats and valves. It is also necessary to check the valve guides for wear. This is particularly important on high mileage engines.*
- ♦ *The valve seats should only be reworked just enough to produce a perfect seating pattern. The maximum permissible reworking dimension must be calculated before reworking commences. If the reworking dimension is exceeded, the function of the hydraulic lifters can no longer be guaranteed and the cylinder head should be renewed.*

Calculating max. permissible working dimension

– Insert valve and press firmly against seat

Note:

If the valve is to be renewed as part of a repair, use a new valve for the calculation.

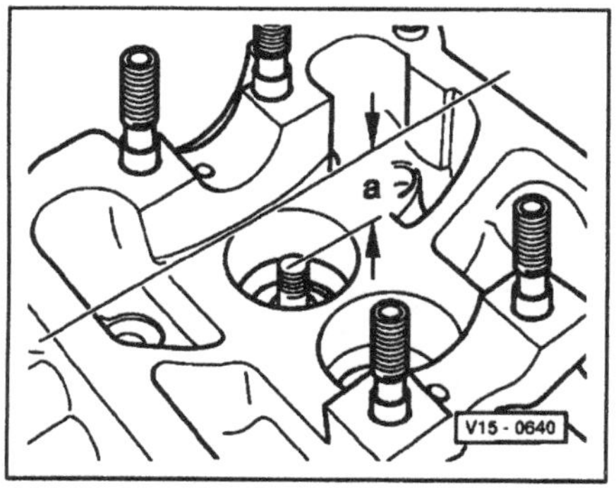

– Measure distance -a- between end of valve stem and upper edge of cylinder head

– Calculate max. permissible reworking dimension from measured distance -a- and minimum dimension

Minimum dimension:

Intake valve 35.8 mm

Exhaust valve 36.1 mm

Measured distance minus minimum dimension
= max. permissible reworking dimension

Example:

Measured distance	36.5 mm
– Minimum dimension	35.8 mm
= max. perm. rework dimension	0.7 mm

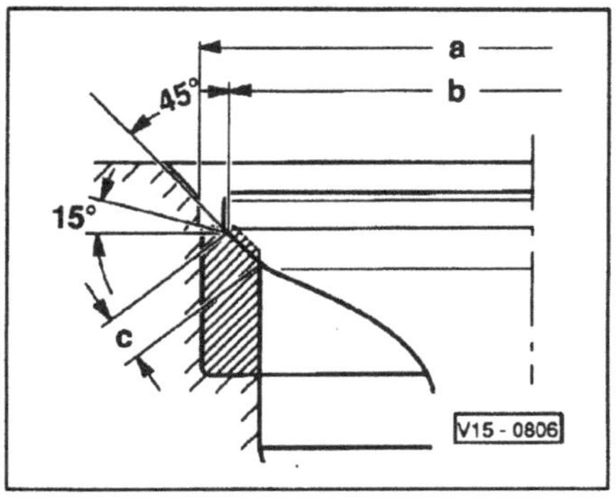

Reworking valve seats

Dimension		Intake valve seats	Exhaust valve seats
∅ a	mm	37.20[1)]	33.20[1)]
∅ b	mm	34.80	30.40
c	mm	2.70	2.05
45°		Valve seat angle	
15°		Correction angle	

1) max. external diameter of correction cutter

Valve guides, checking

Special tools, testers and auxiliary items

- Universal dial gauge bracket VW 387
- Dial gauge

Test sequence

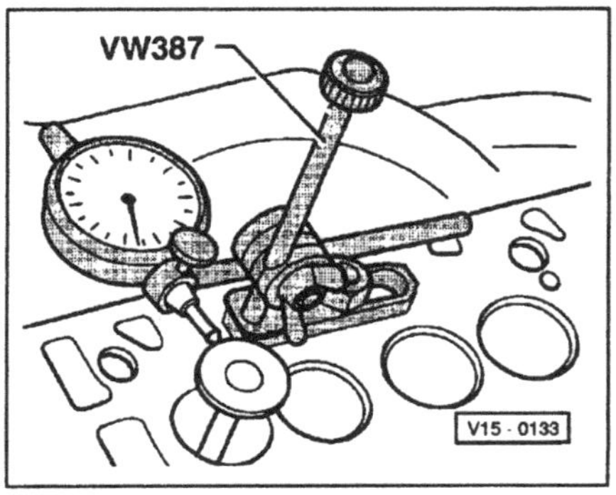

– Insert new valve into guide until end of valve stem is flush with end of guide. Due to the slight difference in stem dimensions, ensure that only an inlet valve is used in the inlet guide and an exhaust valve in the exhaust guide.

- Valve rock: 1.3 mm max.

Valve guides, replacing

Special tools, testers and auxiliary items

- ♦ 10-206 drift
- ♦ 10-215 hand reamer and cutting fluid

Removing

– Clean and check cylinder head

> ***CAUTION!***
> ***Do not replace valve guides in cylinder heads where valve seats can no longer be reworked, or in cylinder heads which have already been machined to the minimum dimension***

– Press out worn valve guides with drift 10-206 from camshaft side

- ♦ valve guides with shoulder (service version) from combustion chamber side

Installing

– Coat new guides with oil and press in with 10-206 drift from camshaft side (cylinder head cold) until shoulder makes contact

> ***CAUTION!***
> ***When the guide shoulder makes contact, ensure that the applied hydraulic pressure does not exceed 2000 psi, otherwise; the guide shoulder could shear off.***

– Ream guides using 10-215 hand reamer and plenty of cutting fluid

– Rework valve seats as necessary
⇒ page B 15–22

Valve stem seals, replacing

With cylinder head installed

Special tools, testers and auxiliary items

- ♦ 3047A Puller
- ♦ 2036 Assembly tool
- ♦ VW 541/1A Valve lever with press piece
- ♦ 10-204 Installation tool

Removing

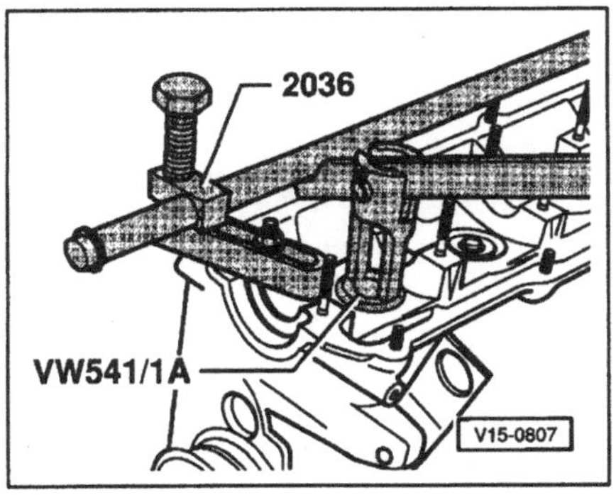

– Remove camshaft
⇒ page B 15–28

– Remove hydraulic lifters (do not interchange)

- ♦ store lifters with the cam contact surface facing downward

– Set piston of respective cylinder to TDC

◄ – Install 2036 assembly tool and adjust mounts to stud height

– Remove springs using VW 541/1A valve lever and press piece

Note:
The valves are supported by the piston crown.

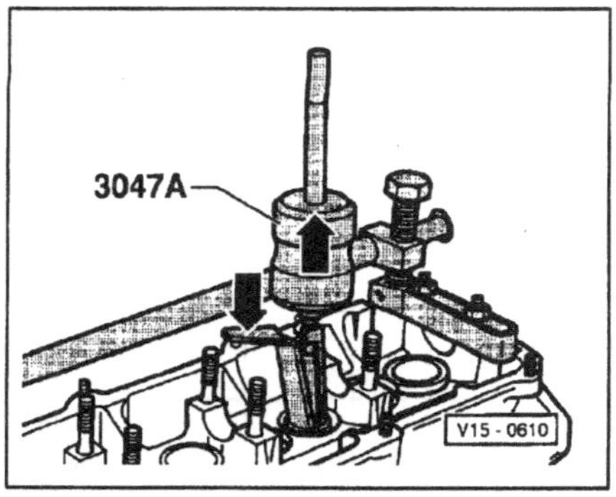

◄ – Remove valve stem seals using 3047A puller

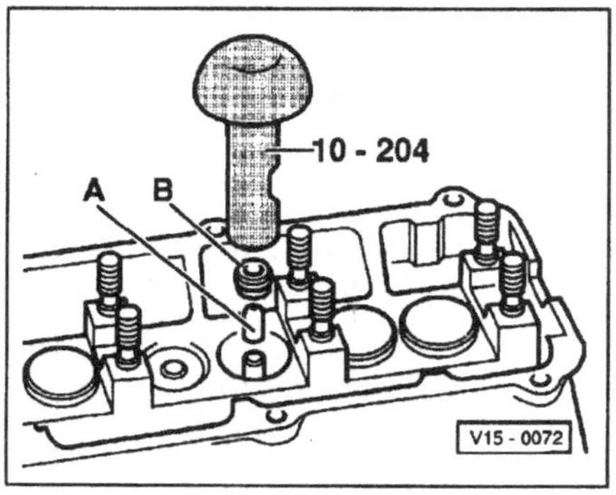

Installing

◄ – Place plastic sleeve -A- on valve stem to prevent damage to the new valve stem seals

– Oil valve stem seal -B-, place it in 10-204 tool and carefully push onto valve guide

Camshaft, removing and installing

Special tools, testers and auxiliary items

♦ VAG 1331 Torque wrench: 5 to 50 Nm (3.7 to 37 ft lb)

Removing

– Remove camshaft toothed belt:

♦ Vehicles ➤ 01.95
⇒ page B 13-26

♦ Vehicles 02.95 ➤
⇒ page B 13-36

– Removing injection pump toothed belt:

♦ Engine code AAB
⇒ page B 13-42

♦ Engine code ACV
⇒ page B 13-48

– Remove vacuum pump with plunger
⇒ page B 15–4, items 16, 17

– First remove bearing caps 1 and 3, then loosen bearing caps 2 and 4 alternately and diagonally

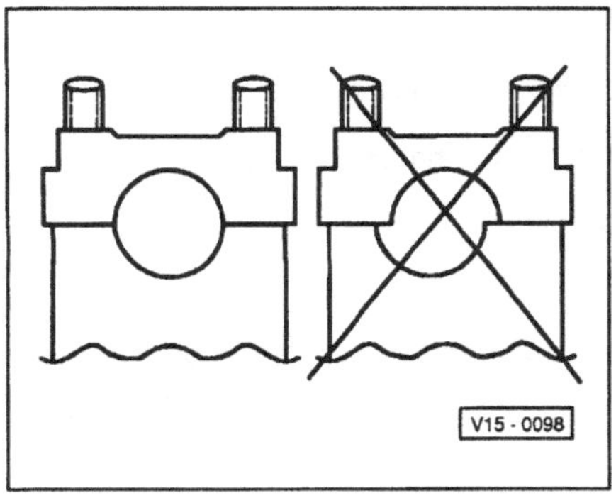

Installing

Notes:

◄

- *When installing bearing caps, note the offset. Before installing camshaft, fit bearing caps to determine installed position.*
- *When installing camshaft, cyl. 1 cam-lobes must point upwards.*

– Oil camshaft contacting surfaces

– Tighten bearing caps 2 and 4 alternately and diagonally
  - 20 Nm (15 ft lb)

– Install bearing caps 1 and 3 and tighten
  - 20 Nm (15 ft lb)

– Install camshaft toothed belt and tension:

- Vehicles ➤ 01.95
⇒ page B 13-26
- Vehicles 02.95 ➤
⇒ page B 13-36

– Install injection pump toothed belt and tension:

- Engine code AAB
⇒ page B 13-42
- Engine code ACV
⇒ page B 13-48

Note:

When new lifters have been installed, the engine must not be started for about 30 minutes. Hydraulic compensation elements must settle (otherwise valves will strike pistons).

Hydraulic lifters, checking

Special tools, testers and auxiliary items

- Feeler gauge
- Wood or plastic wedge

Notes:

- *Replace faulty lifter (cannot be adjusted or repaired).*
- *Irregular valve noises when starting engine are normal.*

Test sequence

– Start engine and run until radiator fan has switched on once

– Increase engine speed to about 2500 rpm for 2 minutes

If lifters still noisy, locate faulty lifter as follows:

– Remove valve cover

– Rotate crankshaft clockwise, until cam for lifter to be checked is pointing upward

– Measure clearance between cam and hydraulic lifter

If clearance is in excess of 0.1 mm

– Replace faulty hydraulic lifter

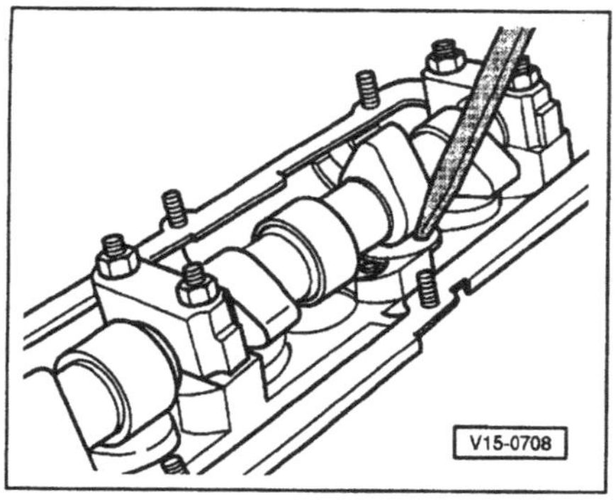

If clearance is less than 0.1 mm or no play

– Proceed with check as follows

◄ – Press lifter down with wooden or plastic wedge

If free travel in excess of 1 mm is felt before lifter contacts valve

– Replace faulty hydraulic lifter

Note:

After installing new lifters the engine must not be started for approx. 30 minutes. Hydraulic compensation elements must settle, otherwise valves will strike pistons.

Swirl chambers, replacing

Engine Code AAB

Notes:

- *Vehicles ➤ 01.95 (with soft material cylinder head gasket) in cases of repair, install a metal head gasket and new swirl chambers.*

Special tools, testers and auxiliary items

- 3035 box wrench
- Drift
- Synthetic head hammer
- VW 382/7 Measuring bridge
- VW 385/17 End plate
- Dial gauge

Requirement

- Cylinder head removed

Work sequence

– Remove fuel injectors ⇒ Repair Group 23

– Remove glow plugs using 3035 box wrench

– Drive swirl chamber out using suitable drift inserted through fuel injector opening

- Carefully and thoroughly clean off combustion material from swirl chamber contact surfaces (and on cylinder head)
- Fit new swirl chamber into position
  - ♦ installation position is determined by guide lug and groove

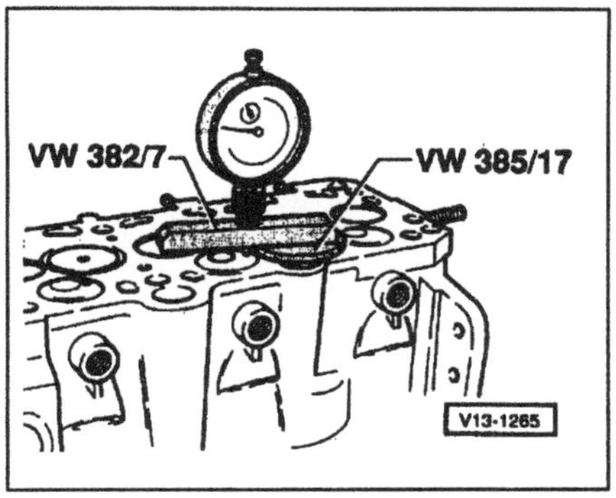

- Drive swirl chamber into head using synthetic head hammer
- ◄ Measure swirl chamber projection above deck height
  - ♦ Specification: 0.05 mm max.

If specification exceeded

- Replace cylinder head

Lubrication system components, removing and installing

Oil pressure, checking
⇒ page B 17–13

To prevent consequential damage if metal shavings or small metal particles (in quantity) are found in the engine oil during repairs, (caused for example by bearing seizure):

– Thoroughly clean all oil passages

– Replace oil cooler

> ***CAUTION!***
> ***Do NOT allow the oil level above the max. mark! This could lead to catalyst damage!***

Lubrication system, capacity

Without oil filter 5.0 liters (5.3 quarts)

With oil filter 5.5 liters (5.8 quarts)

Engine oil, specifications

Engine oil specifications:

♦ Only use "API Service CD" engine oil

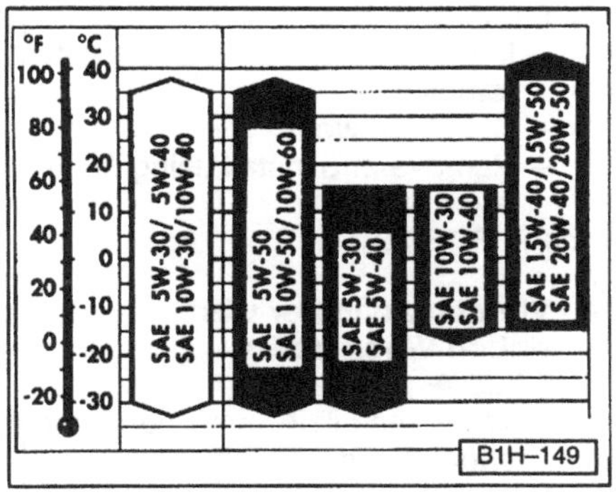

◄ – Choose proper viscosity grade based on environmental temperatures and conditions in which vehicle will be operated

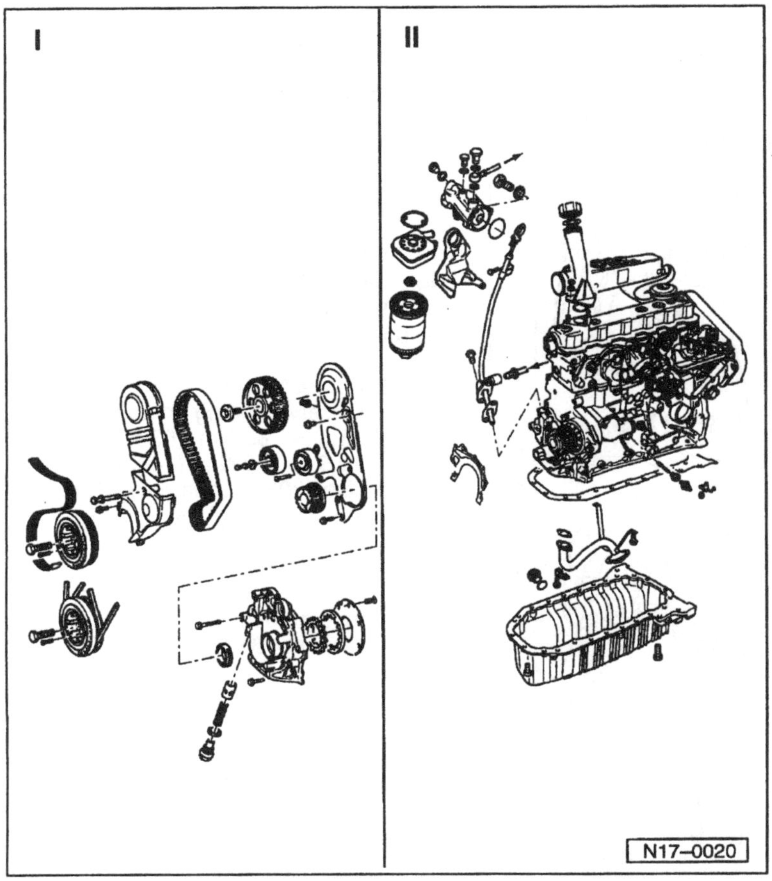

View I:
⇒ page B 17–3

View II:
⇒ page B 17–8

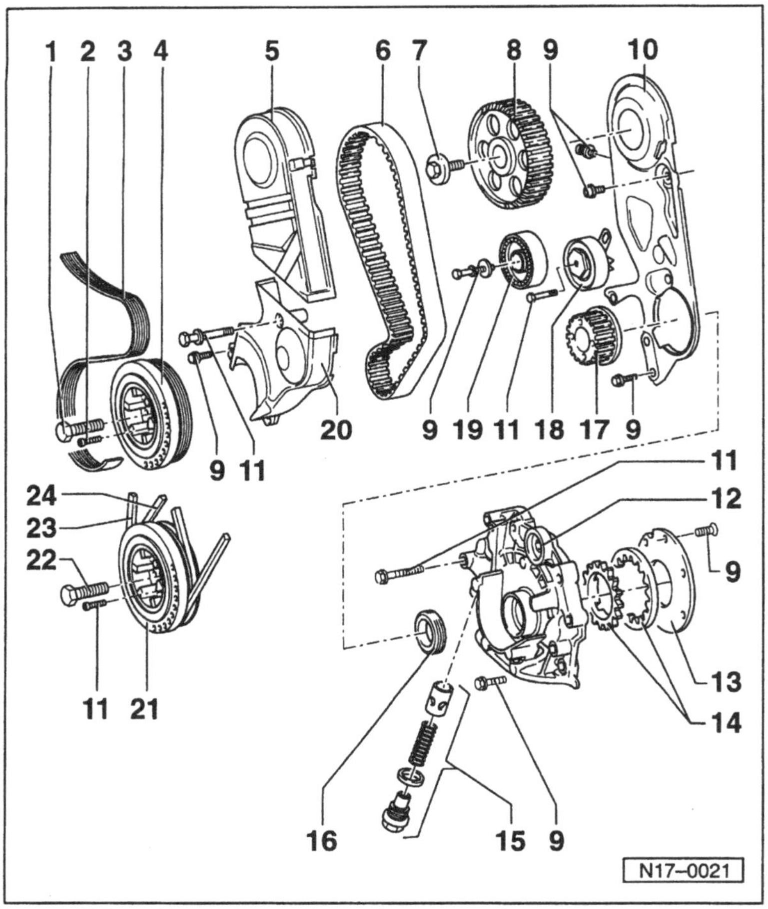

View I:

1 - 160 Nm (118 ft lb) + $^1/_2$ turn (180°) further
02.95 ➤
- Replace
- Oil threads and contact surfaces
- Loosen and tighten using 3248 A Counter-hold tool
- ♦ camshaft toothed belt, removing, installing and tensioning:

⇒ page B 13-36

2 - 20 Nm (15 ft lb) + $^1/_4$ turn (90°) further
02.95 ➤

3 - Ribbed belt
02.95 ➤
- Mark direction of rotation before removing
- Check for wear
- Remove and install using 3299 lever

⇒ page B 13-20

4 - Vibration damper with ribbed V-belt pulley
02.95 ➤
- ♦ When installing, note component orientations and relationships

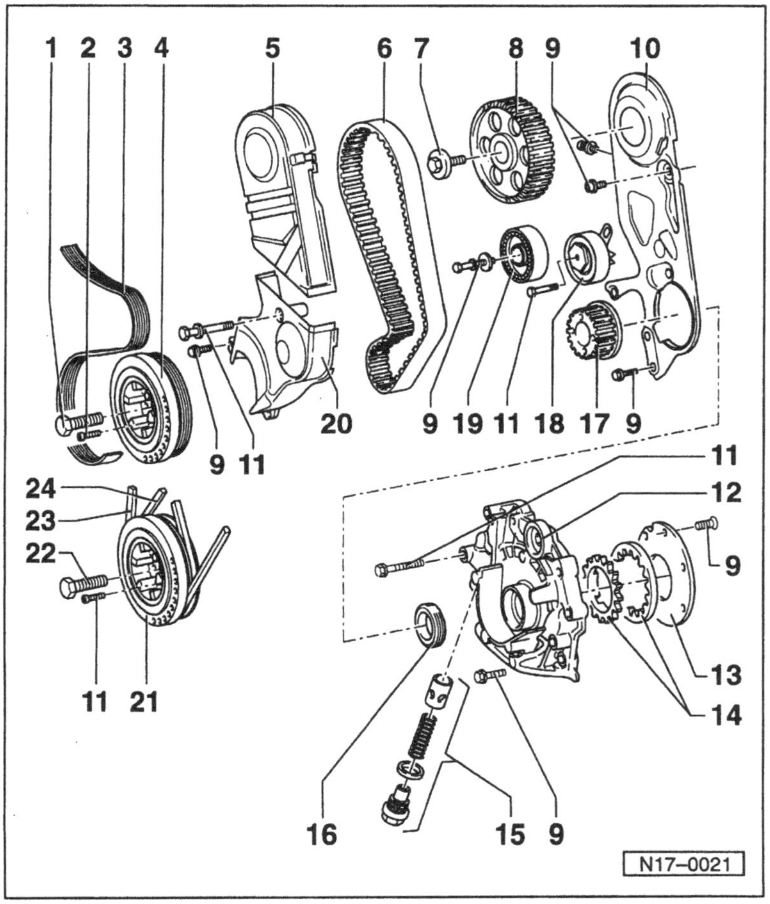

5 - Upper toothed belt guard

6 - Camshaft toothed belt
- Mark direction of engine rotation before removing
- Check for wear
- Do not kink
- ♦ removing, installing, tensioning:

Vehicles ➤ 01.95
⇒ page B 13-26
Vehicles 02.95 ➤
⇒ page B 13-36

7 - Camshaft sprocket mounting bolt
- Observe coding on bolt head:
  8.8 = 85 Nm (63 ft lb)
  10.9 = 100 Nm (74 ft lb)
- Use 3036 counter-hold tool to loosen and tighten

8 - Camshaft sprocket
- Note position when installing toothed belt:

Vehicles ➤ 01.95
⇒ page B 13-26
Vehicles 02.95 ➤
⇒ page B 13-36

9 - 10 Nm (7 ft lb)

10 - Rear toothed belt guard ➤ 01.95
02.95 ➤
⇒ page B 13-9 (item 5)

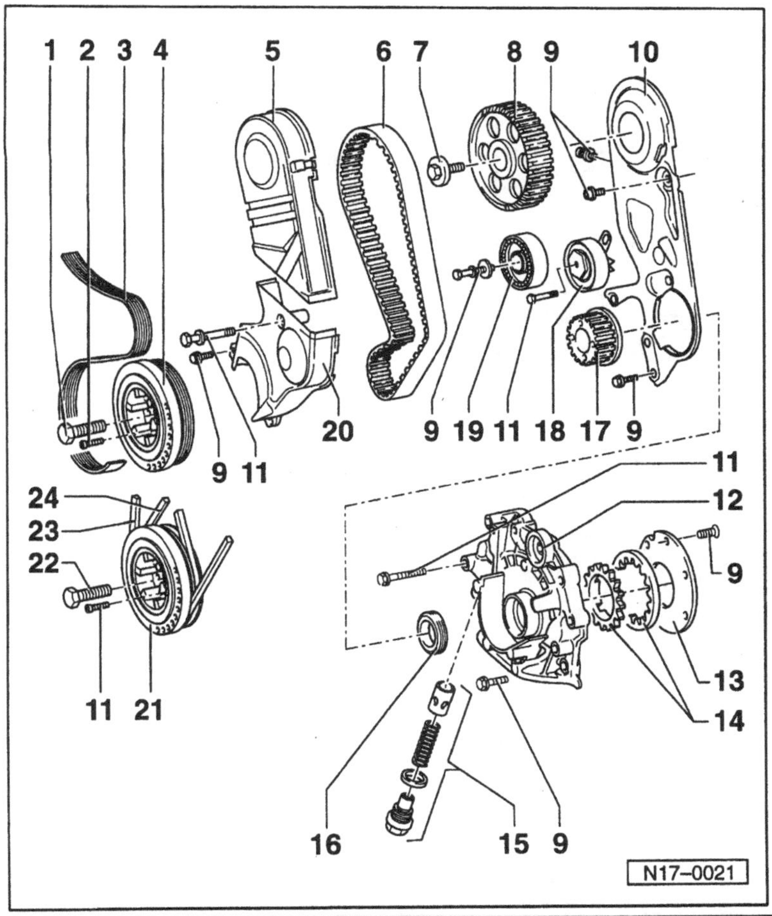

11 - 20 Nm (15 ft lb)

12 - Oil pump
- When installing, note coupling ring on crankshaft

⇒ page B 17–11 (item 32)
- ♦ only replace as an assembly
- ♦ must be located on dowel sleeves

13 - End plate

14 - Oil pump
- ♦ "D" identification mark, points in direction of end plate

15 - Pressure relief valve
- ♦ 40 Nm (30 ft lb)
- ♦ opening pressure: 5.3 to 6.3 bar (77 to 91 psi)

16 - Oil seal
- ♦ replacing:

⇒ Repair Group 13

17 - Crankshaft sprocket

18 - Tensioner
02.95 ➤

19 - Idler roller
➤ 01.95
- Remove using 3034 puller and 3034/1 bolt

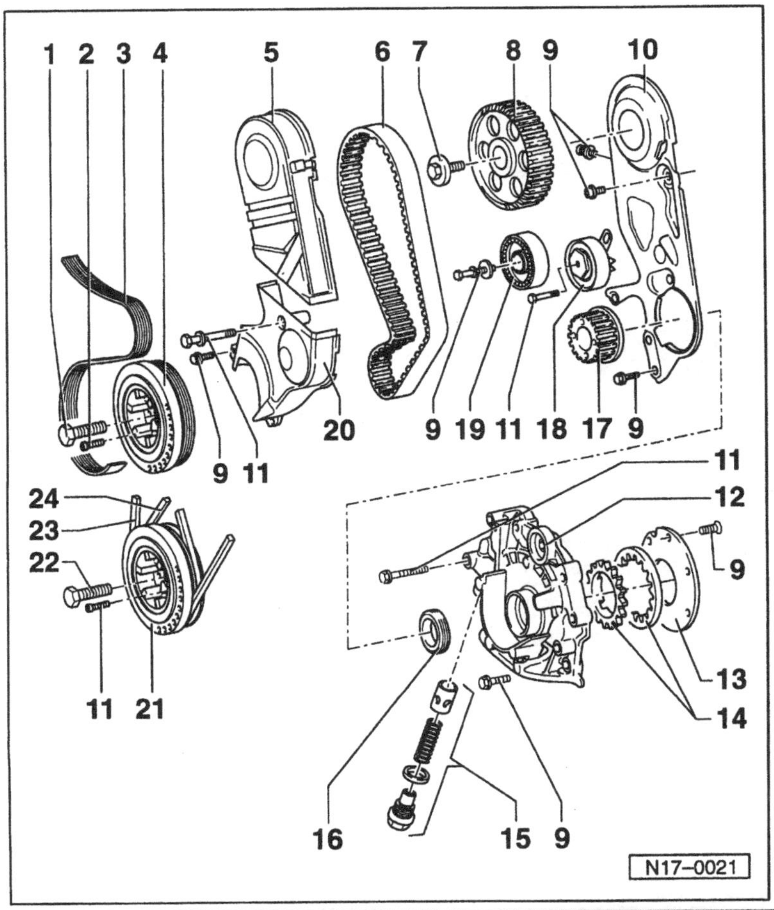

20 - Lower toothed belt guard
➤ 01.95

21 - Vibration damper with V-belt pulley
➤ 01.95
- When installing, note component orientations and relationships

22 - 460 Nm (340 ft lb)
➤ 01.95
- Coat threads and bolt head contact surfaces with sealing paste: AMV 188 001 02
- Loosen and tighten using 3245 counter-hold tool
- ♦ removing, installing, tensioning camshaft toothed belt:

⇒ page B 13-26

23 - V-belt
- ♦ for Generator

➤ 01.95
- Check tension by thumb pressure:

max. deflection:
new V-belt approx. 2 mm
used V-belt approx. 5 mm
- ♦ V-belt tension (vehicles with toothed rack tensioner), checking:

⇒ page B 13-19

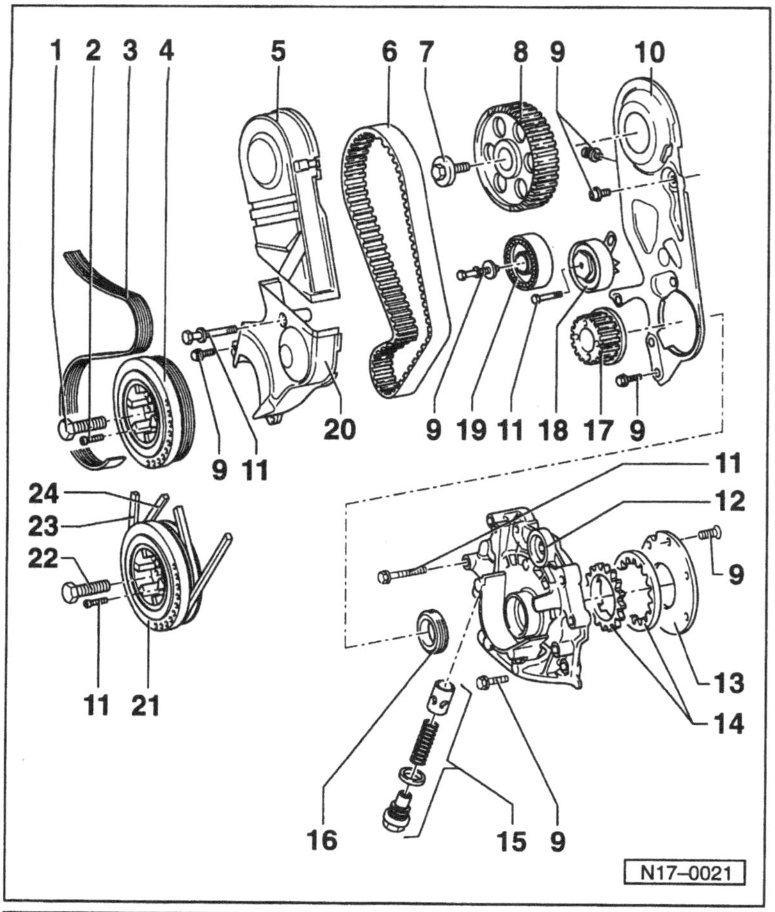

24 - V-belt

- for power steering pump
  - Check tension by thumb pressure:

    max. deflection:

    new and used V-belts approx. 5 mm
- V-belt tension, adjusting:

⇒ Repair Group 48

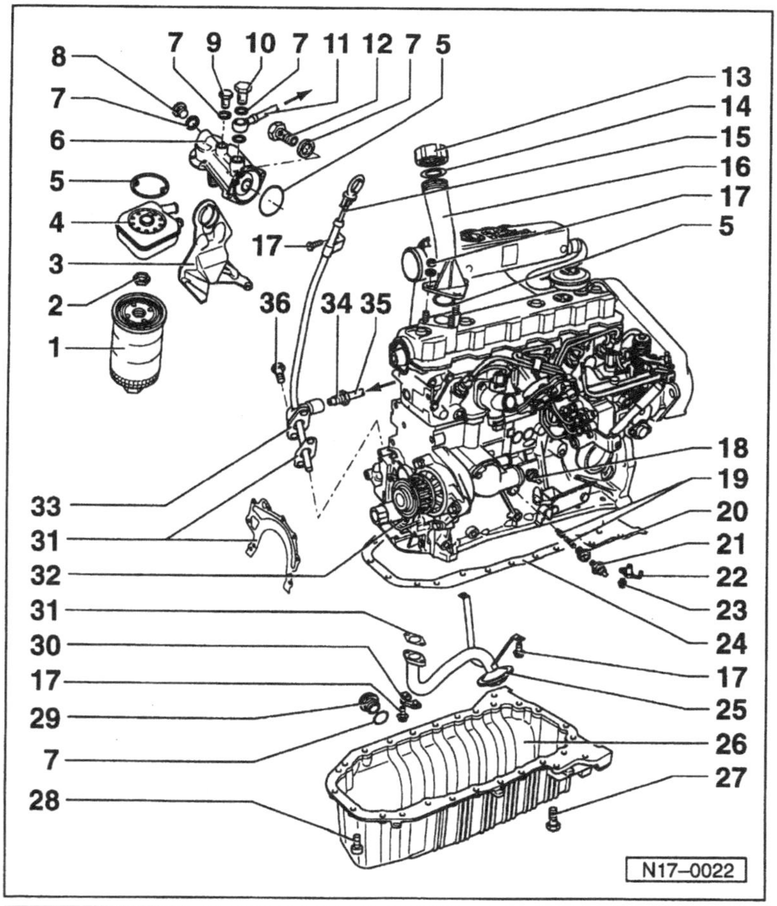

View II:

1 - Oil filter

- Loosen using strap wrench
- Tighten by hand
- Note instructions on filter when installing

2 - 25 Nm (18 ft lb)

3 - Oil collector

4 - Oil cooler

- Coat the contact area to flange, outside of the seal, using AMV 188 100 02
- Ensure clearance between adjacent components
- See note

⇒ page B 17–1

5 - O-ring

- Replace if damaged

6 - Oil filter bracket

- installed position determined by dowel pin

7 - Sealing ring

- Replace

8 - Sealing plug

- 40 Nm (30 ft lb)

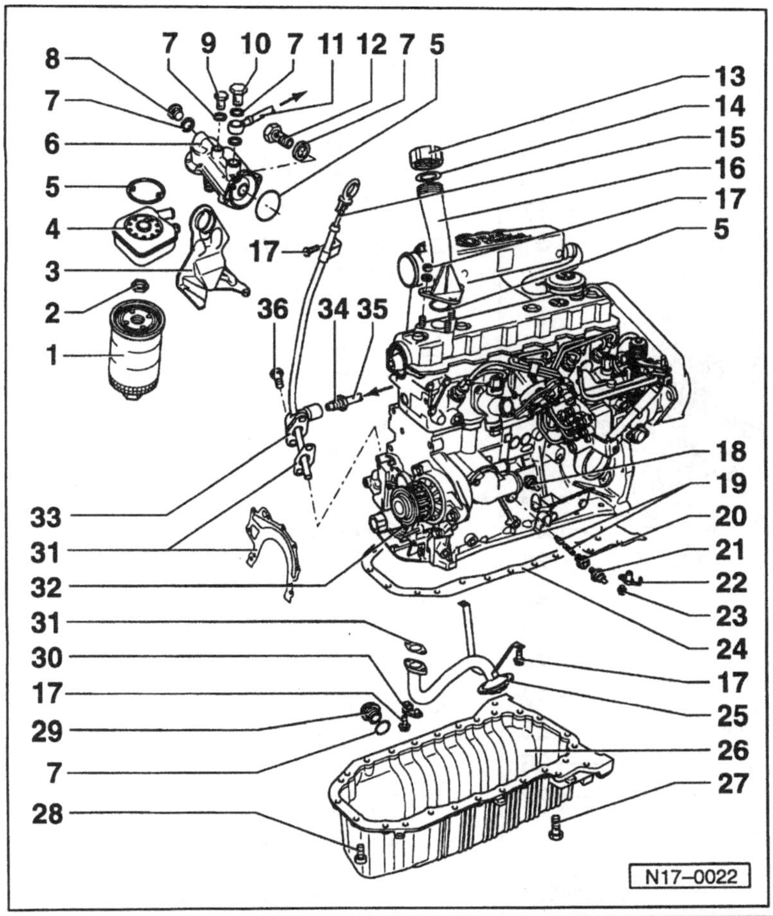

9 - **Sealing plug**
- ♦ 20 Nm (15 ft lb)

10 - **Banjo bolt**
- ♦ 30 Nm (22 ft lb)

11 - **Oil supply line**
- ♦ Engine Code ACV
- ♦ to exhaust turbocharger

⇒ page B 21–4 (item 24)

12 - **Banjo bolt**
- ♦ 70 Nm (52 ft lb)

13 - **Cap**

14 - **Gasket**
- – Replace if damaged

15 - **Dipstick**
- ♦ Oil level must NOT be above the max. mark!

16 - **Oil filler tube**
- ♦ Engine Code AAB
- ♦ Engine Code ACV with crankcase breather valve

17 - **10 Nm (7 ft lb)**

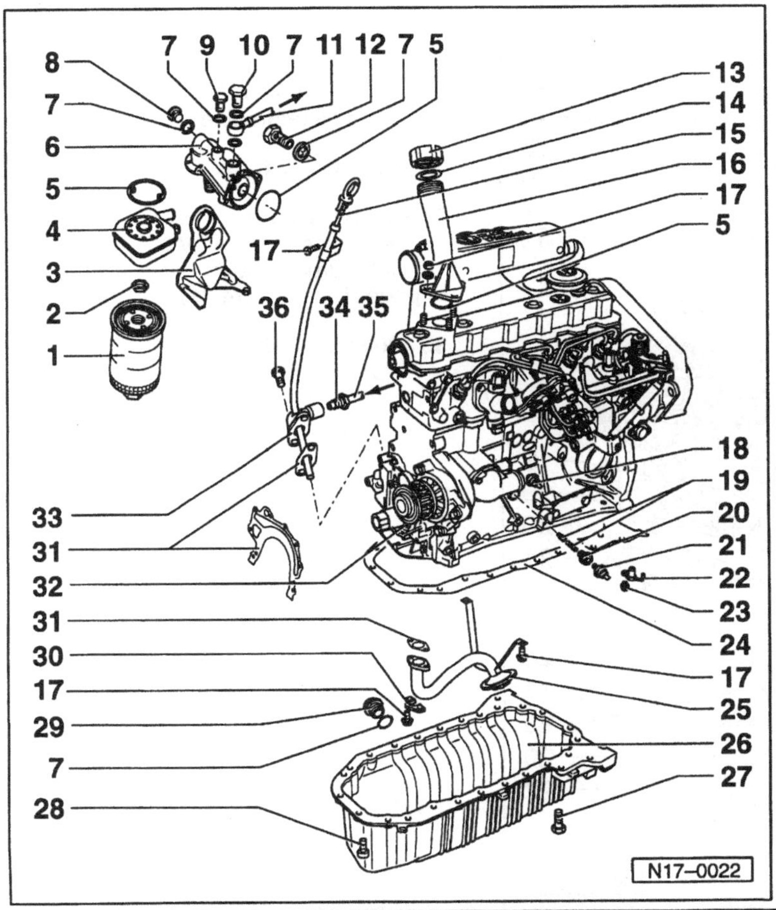

18 - **0.9 bar oil pressure switch F1**
- ♦ 25 Nm (18 ft lb)
- ♦ grey
- – If sealing ring is leaking, nip open and replace
- ♦ checking:

⇒ page B 17–13

19 - **Oil pressure retention valve**

20 - **Adaptor**
- ♦ 50 Nm (37 ft lb)
- – If sealing ring is leaking, nip open and replace

21 - **0.3 bar oil pressure switch F22**
- ♦ 25 Nm (18 ft lb)
- ♦ brown
- – If sealing ring is leaking, nip open and replace
- ♦ checking:

⇒ page B 17–13

22 - **Oil spray jet**
- ♦ for piston cooling

23 - **10 Nm (7 ft lb)**
- – Install using AMV 188 100 02

24 - **Oil pan gasket**
- – Replace

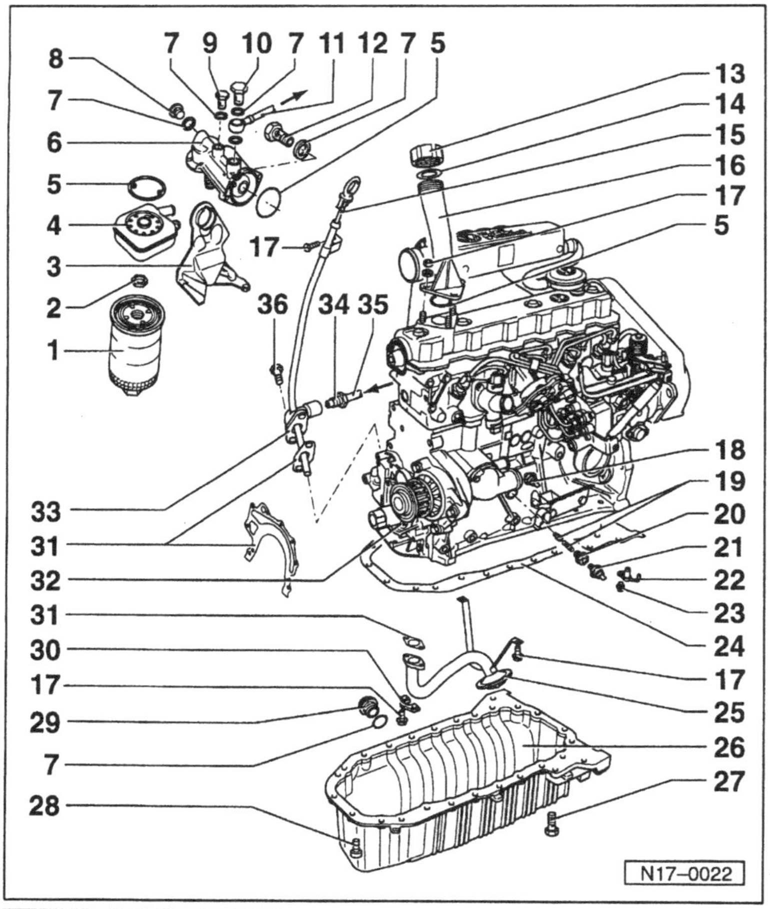

25 - Suction pipe
- Clean strainer if contaminated

26 - Oil pan
- Clean sealing surfaces before installing

27 - 20 Nm (15 ft lb)
- Install M8 bolt with hex head on transmission side

28 - 10 Nm (7 ft lb)
- Remove and install using 3249 socket

With flywheel installed
- Turn flywheel so that cut-outs align with bolts

29 - Oil drain plug
- ♦ 50 Nm (37 ft lb)

30 - Securing plate
- ♦ Engine Code AAB
- Replace

31 - Gasket
- Replace

32 - Coupling ring
- ♦ for oil pump
- ♦ with four drive lugs
- Heat new coupling ring to max. 200 °C (392 °F) before installing

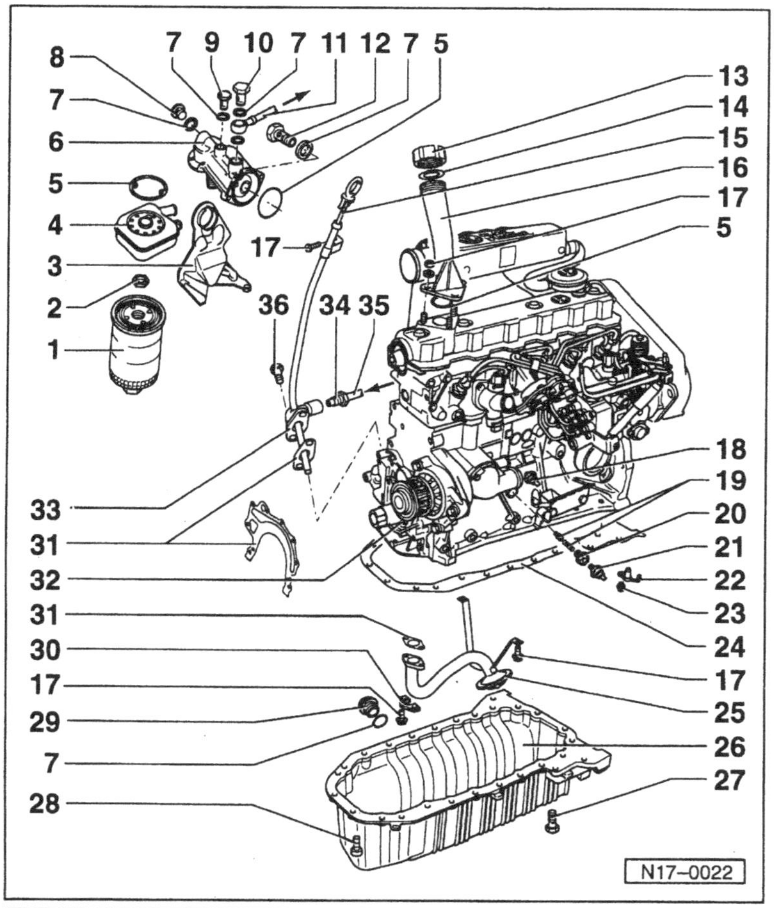

33 - Dipstick guide tube
- ♦ Engine Code ACV has connection for oil return line

34 - 40 Nm (30 ft lb)

35 - Oil return line
- ♦ Engine Code ACV
- ♦ to turbocharger

⇒ page B 21–4 (item 21)

36 - 20 Nm (15 ft lb)

Oil pressure and oil pressure switch, checking

Note:

For functional checking and servicing of the optical and acoustic oil pressure warning system:

⇒ Wiring diagrams, Electrical Troubleshooting and Component locations

Special tools, testers and auxiliary items

- ♦ VAG 1342 Oil pressure tester
- ♦ VAG 1527 B LED tester
- ♦ VW 1594 Adaptor kit

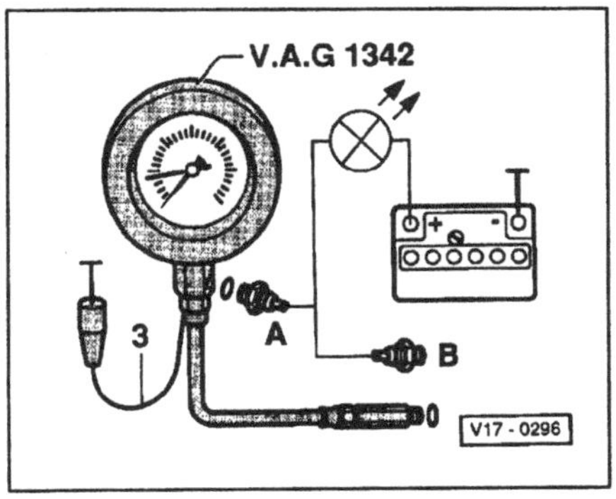

Test sequence

– Remove sound dampening pan
⇒ Repair Group 50

◄ – Remove 0.3 bar oil pressure switch (brown insulation) and screw into tester

– Screw VAG 1342 tester into position for oil pressure switch in cyl. head

– Connect brown tester wire -3- to Ground

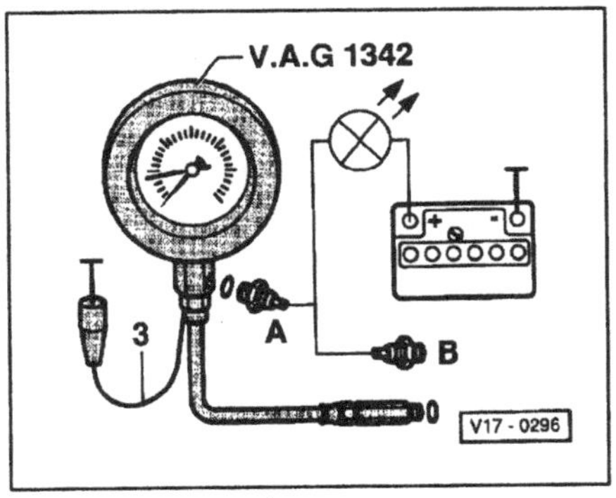

◄ – Connect VAG 1527B LED tester between battery positive and 0.3 bar oil pressure switch -A- using jumper wires from VW 1594 adaptor kit

- ♦ LED must light up

– Start engine and slowly increase speed

- ♦ At 0.15 to 0.45 bar (2.2 to 6.5 psi): LED must go out

If LED remains lit

– replace 0.3 bar oil pressure switch.

– Connect VAG 1527B LED tester to 0.9 bar oil pressure switch -B-

- ♦ At 0.75 to 1.05 bar (10.9 to 15.2 psi): LED must light up

If LED not lit up

– Replace 0.9 bar oil pressure switch

– Increase engine speed further

- ♦ at 2000 rpm and 80°C (176°F) oil temperature, oil pressure must be 2.0 (29 psi) minimum
- ♦ At higher engine speed, oil pressure must not exceed 7.0 bar (101.5 psi)

If pressure exceeds specification:

– Replace oil pressure relief valve
⇒ page B 17–5 (item 15)
or
– Replace oil pressure retention valve
⇒ page B 17–10 (item 19)

Cooling system components, removing and installing

Notes:

- *When the engine is warm the cooling system is under pressure. If necessary, release the system pressure before starting repairs.*
- *Hoses are secured with spring clips. When replacing, only use spring type clips.*

Special tools, testers and auxiliary items

- VAG 1274 cooling system tester
- VAG 1274/3 adaptor
- VAG 1921 spring clip pliers

Cooling system, body side components
⇒ page B 19–2

Cooling system, engine side components
⇒ page B 19–6

Cooling system. hose connections diagram
⇒ page B 19–9

Cooling system, draining and filling
⇒ page B 19–10

Coolant, mixture ratios
⇒ page B 19–10

Thermal switch and coolant pump, checking
⇒ page B 19–15

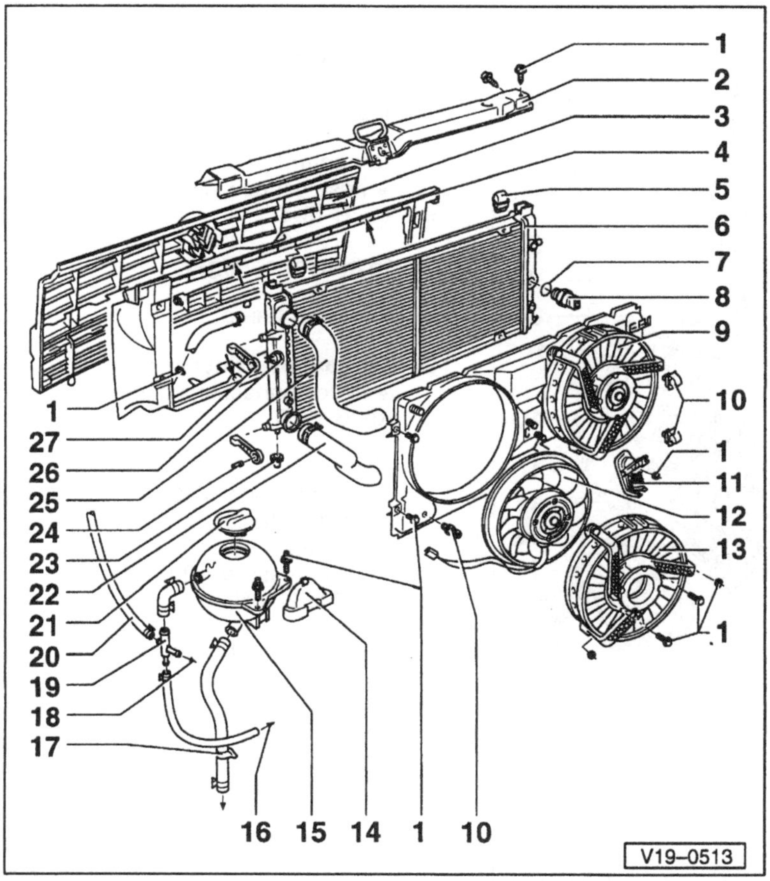

Cooling system, body side components

1 - 10 Nm (7 ft lb)

2 - Lock carrier

3 - Radiator grille

4 - Air intake

- mounted to radiator:
  Vertical: 4 screws
  Horizontal: 4 rivets -arrows-

5 - Mounting rubber

6 - Radiator

- removing and installing:
⇒ page B 19–12
  – After replacing, completely replace entire engine coolant

7 - Seal

- Replace

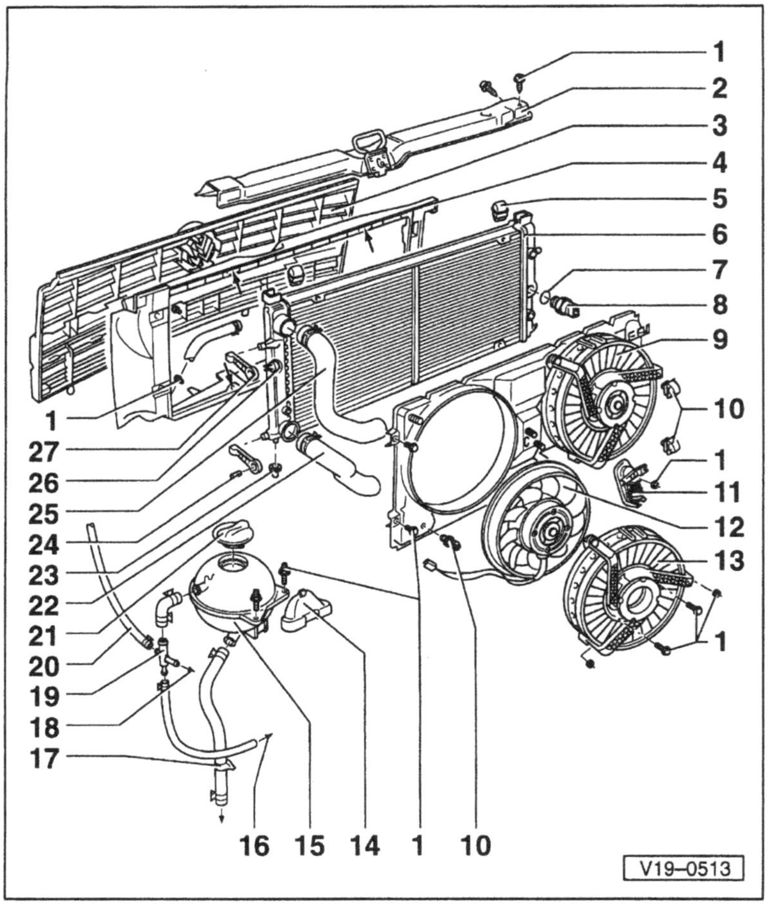

8 - Coolant Fan Control Thermal switch F18
- ♦ for electric fan
- ♦ 25 Nm (18 ft lb)
- ♦ switching temperatures:

1st speed
ON: 84 to 89 °C (183 to 192°F)
OFF: 76 to 83 °C (169 to 181°F)

2nd speed
ON: 90 to 95 °C (194 to 203°F)
OFF: 82 to 89 °C (180 to 192°F)

9 - Radiator cowling
- ♦ with electric fan and adjustable fan-shroud

10 - Cable clip

11 - Fan shroud adjuster
- ♦ checking with engine cold 25 °C (77 °F) max: Fan shroud (item 13) must be closed

12 - Radiator fan

13 - Fan shroud (adjustable)

14 - Cover

15 - Expansion tank

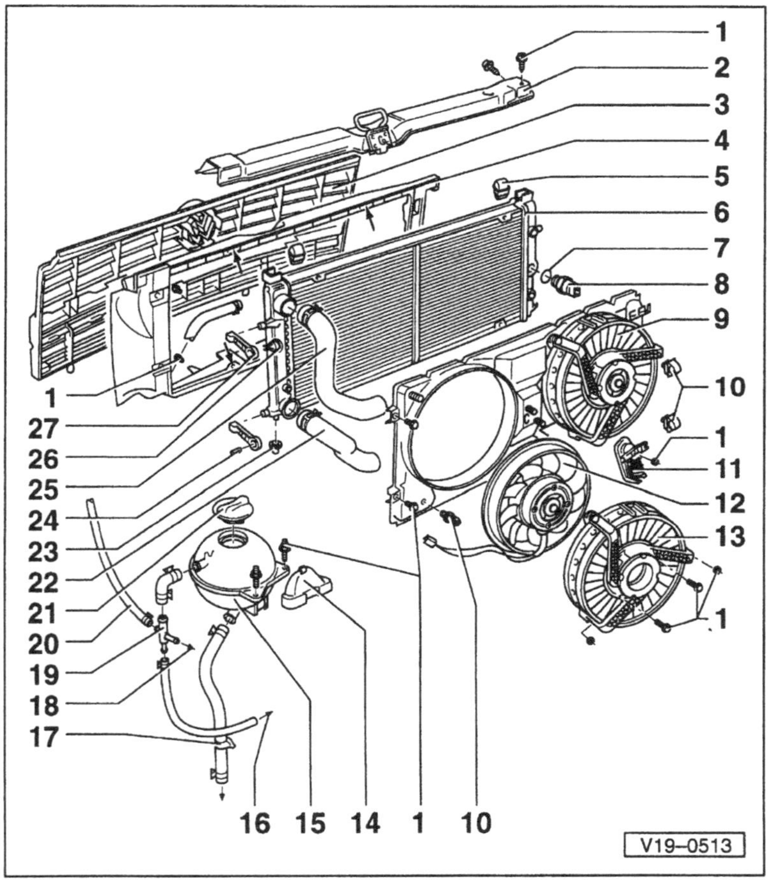

16 - to cylinder head
- ♦ hose connections diagram

⇒ page B 19–9

17 - to coolant pipe
- ♦ hose connections diagram

⇒ page B 19–9

18 - to heat exchanger

19 - Junction piece

20 - Coolant overflow hose
- ♦ hose connections diagram

⇒ page B 19–9

21 - Cap
- – Check using VAG 1274 cooling system tester and VAG 1274/4 adaptor
- ♦ Test pressure 1.2 to 1.5 bar (17 to 22 psi)

22 - Lower coolant hose
- ♦ hose connections diagram

⇒ page B 19–9

23 - Rubber washer

24 - Pin

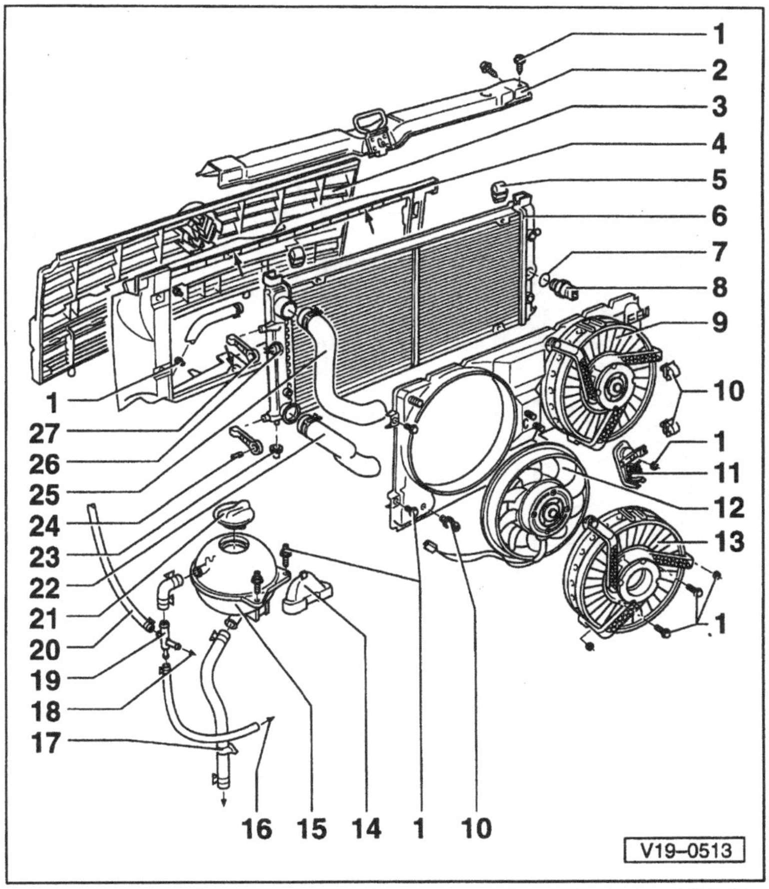

25 - Upper coolant hose
- hose connections diagram

⇒ page B 19–9

26 - Spreader clip

27 - Bracket

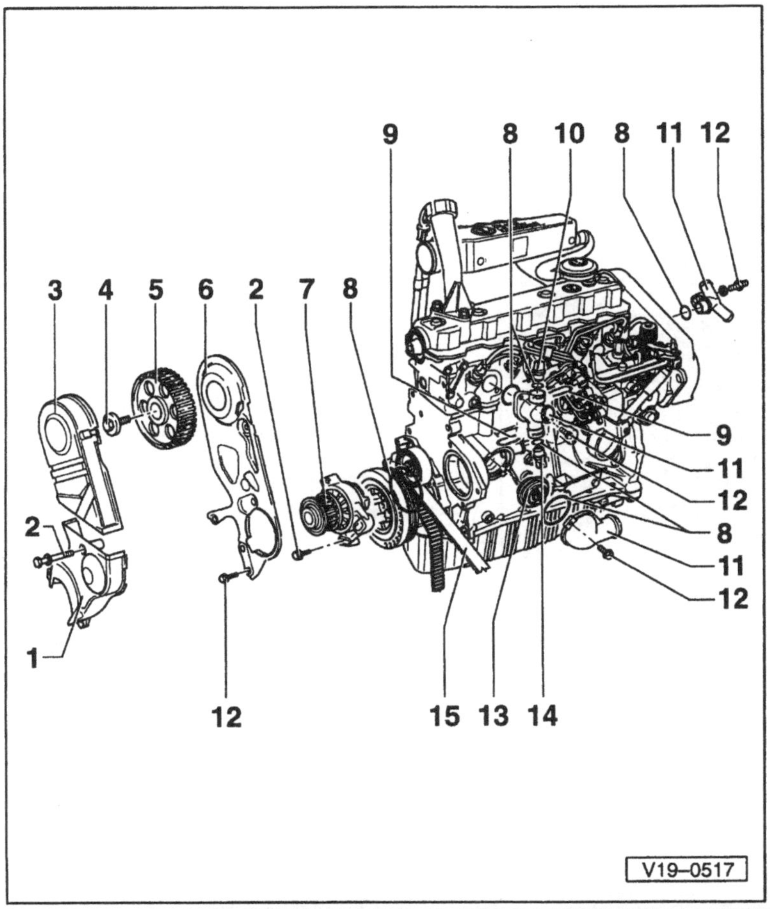

Cooling system, engine side components

1 - Lower toothed belt guard
- ➤ 01.95

2 - 20 Nm (15 ft lb)

3 - Upper toothed belt guard

4 - Camshaft sprocket mounting bolt
- Observe coding on bolt head:
  - 8.8 = 85 Nm (63 ft lb)
  - 10.9 = 100 Nm (74 ft lb)
- Loosen and tighten using 3036 Counter-hold tool

5 - Camshaft sprocket
- Note positioning when installing toothed belt:
  ➤ 01.95

⇒ page B 13-26

02.95 ➤

⇒ page B 13-36

6 - Rear toothed belt guard ➤ 01.95

02.95 ➤

⇒ page B 13-9 (item 5)

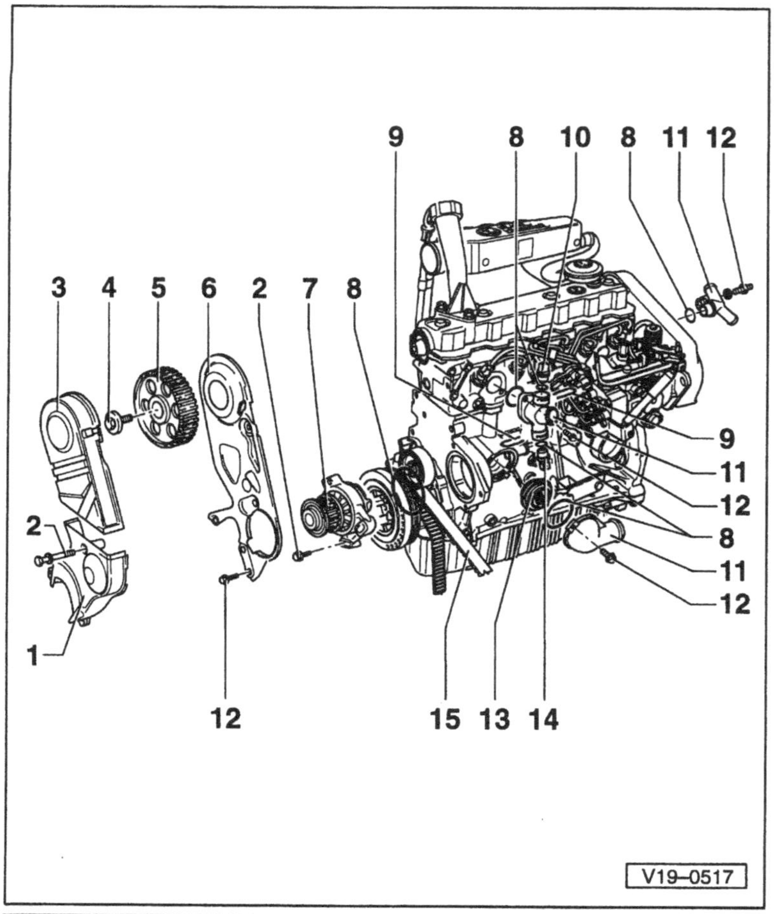

7 - Coolant pump

- Check shaft for ease of movement
- Replace as an assembly if damaged or leaking

➤ 01.95 with elongated holes:

- To tension toothed belt: loosen slightly and turn using screwdriver

⇒ page B 13-26

8 - O-ring

- Replace if leaking or damaged

9 - Retaining clip

- Ensure it is securely seated

10 - Temperature sensor

- ♦ Engine code AAB:
  Glow plug system, sensor for engine temperature G27
- ♦ Checking:

⇒ Wiring diagram, Electrical fault finding and Component locations binder

- ♦ Engine code ACV:
  Engine Coolant temperature sensor G62
- ♦ blue, 2-pin
- ♦ checking:

⇒ Repair Group 01

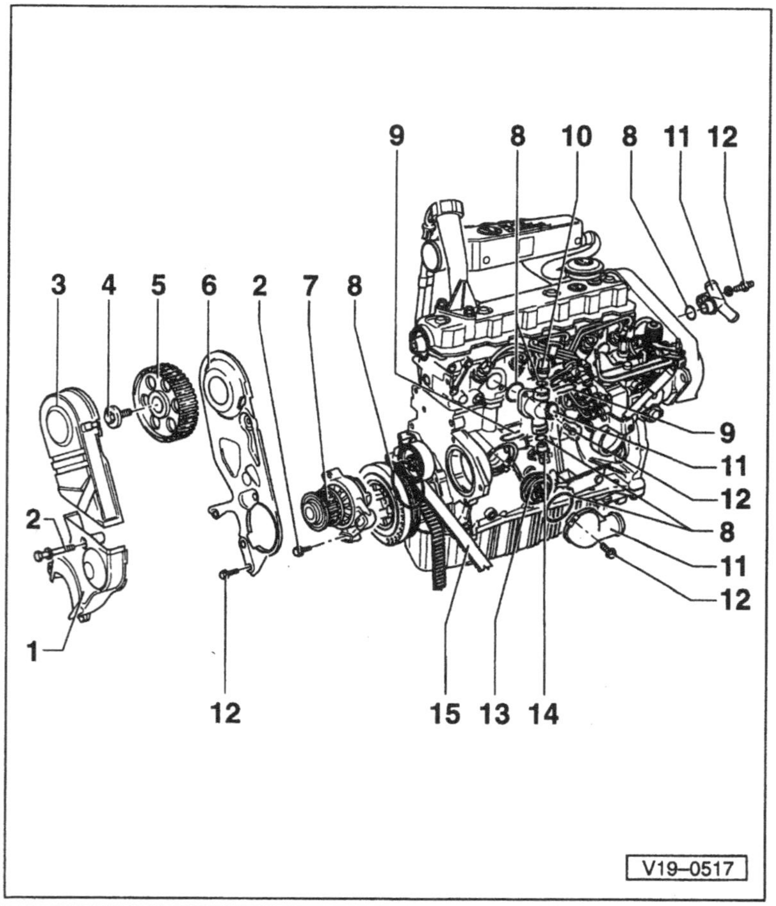

11 - Connection

12 - 10 Nm (7 ft lb)

13 - Coolant thermostat

- Checking: heat thermostat in water
- ♦ opening starts approx. 87 °C (189°F)
- ♦ ends approx. 102 °C (216°F)
- ♦ opening lift 7 mm (0.2755 in) min.

14 - Coolant circulation engine coolant temperature thermal switch F51 with engine coolant temperature sensor G2

- ♦ yellow, 4-pin
- ♦ F51 checking:

⇒ page B 19–15

15 - Camshaft toothed belt

- ♦ Mark direction of engine rotation before removing
- ♦ Check for wear
- ♦ Do not kink
- ♦ removing, installing, tensioning:

Vehicles ➤ 01.95

⇒ page B 13-26

Vehicles 02.95 ➤

⇒ page B 13-36

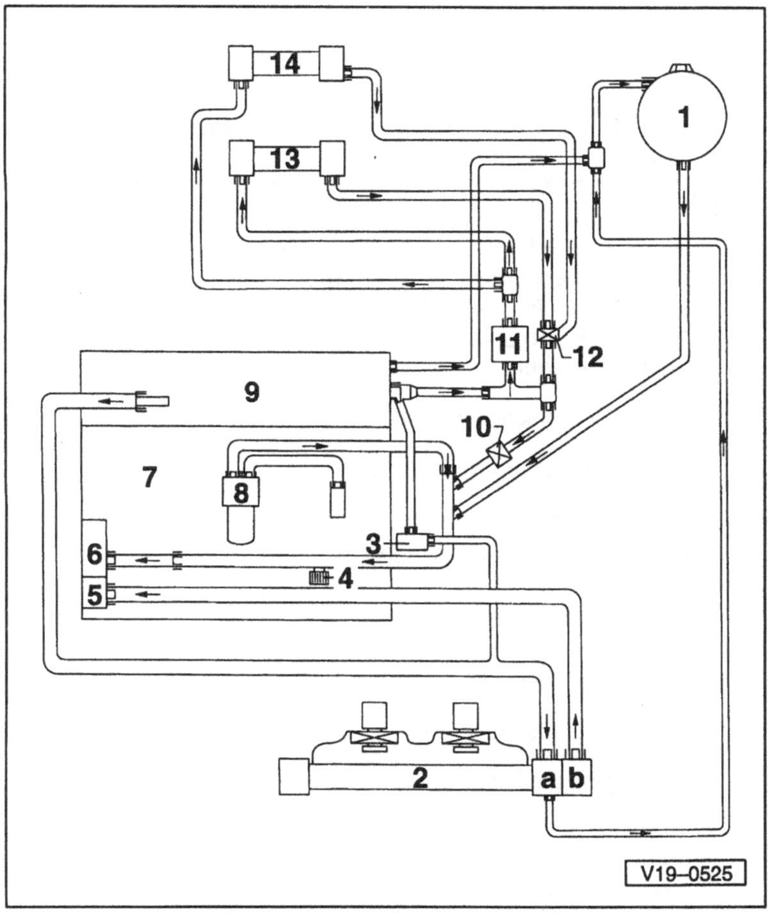

Cooling system, hose connections diagram

1 - **Expansion tank**

2 - **Radiator**
- a = top
- b = bottom

3 - **Coolant pump V50**
- checking:

⇒ page B 19–15

4 - **Drain screw**
- 10 Nm (7 ft lb)

5 - **Coolant thermostat**

6 - **Coolant pump**

7 - **Cylinder block**

8 - **Oil cooler**

9 - **Cylinder head**

10 - **Solenoid valve**

11 - **Auxiliary heater**

12 - **Control valve**

13 - **Heat exchanger for heating system**

14 - **Additional heat exchanger**

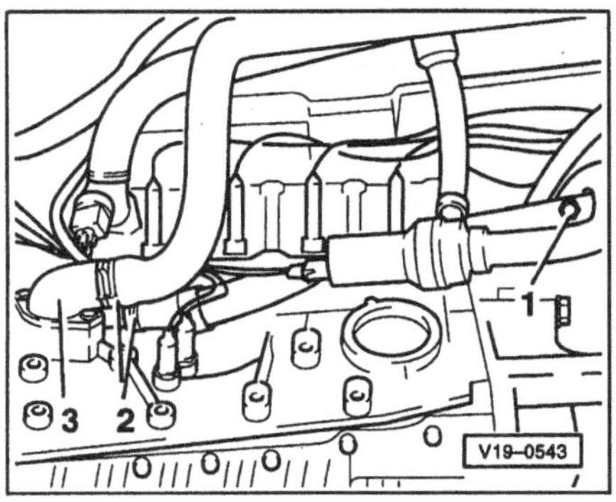

Cooling system, draining and filling

Special tools, testers and auxiliary items

- VAG 1921 spring clip pliers

Draining

– Remove cap from coolant expansion tank

– Remove sound dampener pan
⇒ Repair Group 50

◄ – Drain coolant either via drain plug -1- and coolant hose -2- or via thermostat connection -3-

Filling

Notes:

- *The cooling system is filled year-round with a mixture of water and anti-freeze plus G11 corrosion protection agent. G11 and coolant additives will prevent frost and corrosion damage, the formation of chalk and in addition, they raise the coolants' boiling point. For these reasons, the cooling system must be filled year round with anti-freeze and G11. Due to the higher boiling point, the mixture is also an aid to operational efficiency where engines operate at high loads, particularly in tropical climates.*
- *If radiator, heat exchanger, cylinder head or cylinder head gasket is replaced, do not reuse old coolant.*

Recommended mixture ratios:

Frost protection to	Anti-freeze amount[1)]	G 11[2)]	Water[2)]
–25 °C (–13°F) –35 °C (–31°F)	40 % 50 %	4.6 ltr. 5.75 ltr.	6.9 ltr. 5.75 ltr.

[1)] Amount of anti-freeze must not exceed 60 %. Frost protection and cooling effects will decrease if anti-freeze content is too high!

[2)] The quantity of coolant can vary depending upon specific vehicle equipment levels.

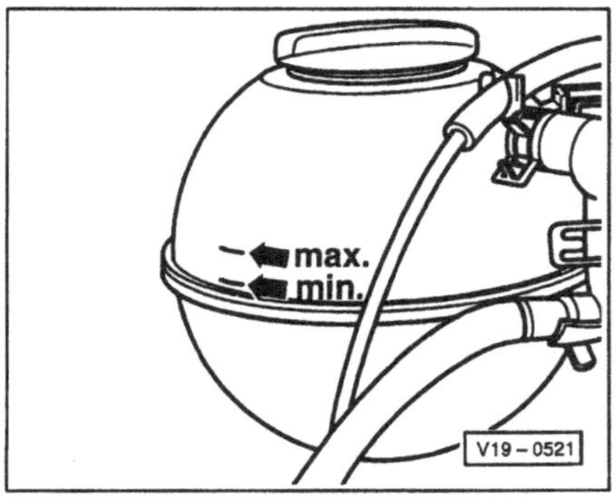

– Open bleeder screw in coolant hose (to heat exchanger)

– Press down on top radiator hose

◄ – Slowly fill with coolant up to max. mark on expansion tank
- ♦ filling time approx. 5 minutes

– Close bleeder screw

– Start engine and run at approx. 1500 rpm for 2 minutes max. at same time fill with coolant up to over-flow hole on expansion tank

– Install expansion tank cap

– Run engine until radiator fan comes on at least once

– Check coolant level and top-up if necessary
- ♦ When engine at normal operating temp, coolant level must be on max. mark. When cold, between min. and max. marks.

Radiator and radiator fan, removing and installing

Special tools, testers and auxiliary items

♦ VAG 1921 spring clip pliers

Removing

– Remove sound dampener pan
⇒ Repair Group 50

– Drain coolant
⇒ page B 19–10

Vehicles 09.94 ➤

– Remove radiator grille:
⇒ Repair Group 66

Engine code ACV

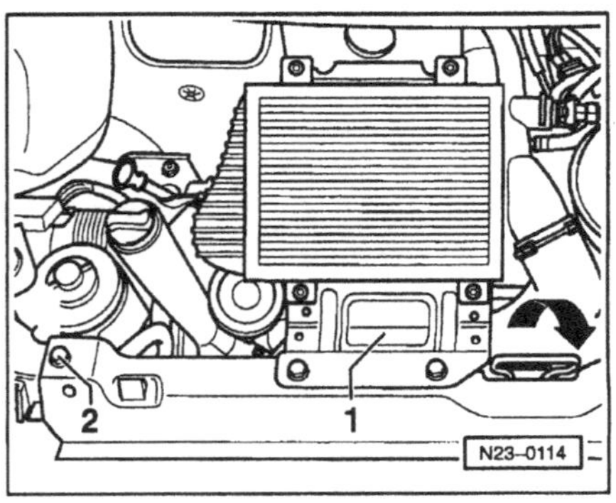

◄ – Remove bracket for Charge Air cooler -1-

All vehicles

– Remove left and right-hand mounting bolts -2-

Note:

Vehicles ➤ 08.94: 2 mounting bolts are attached to each left and right side of the lock carrier.

– Tilt lock carrier and radiator out and forward -arrow-

– Disconnect radiator coolant hoses using VAG 1921 spring clip pliers

– Disconnect thermoswitch and radiator fan connectors

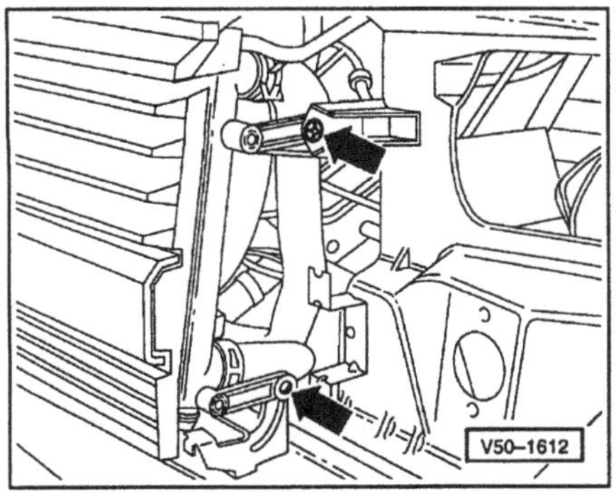

◄ – Push pin out of spreader clip (arrows) on left and right-hand sides and unclip spreader clip from radiator retainer

– Lift out radiator, fan and air-shrouding

Vehicles with A/C

– Observe additional information and removal work
⇒ page B 19–14

Installing

Installation is carried out in the reverse order of removal, when performing, note the following

– Filling with coolant
⇒ page B 19–10

– Electrical connections and routing:
⇒ Repair group 97

– Check headlight adjustment and adjust if necessary
⇒ Maintenance

Vehicles with A/C, additional information and removal work

CAUTION!
Do NOT open the A/C refrigerant circuit.

Note:

To prevent damage to the condenser, refrigerant lines, pipes and hoses; ensure that none of them are stretched, kinked or bent.

– Remove A/C fluid reservoir and allow to hang free

– Remove clamps from refrigerant lines

– Unfasten A/C compressor and condenser and secure to body such that refrigerant lines are not stressed

Thermal switch and coolant pump, checking

Special tools, testers and auxiliary items

- ♦ VW 1594 adaptor kit
- ♦ VAG 1527B LED tester
- ♦ Fluke 83 multimeter (or equivalent)
- ♦ Wiring diagram

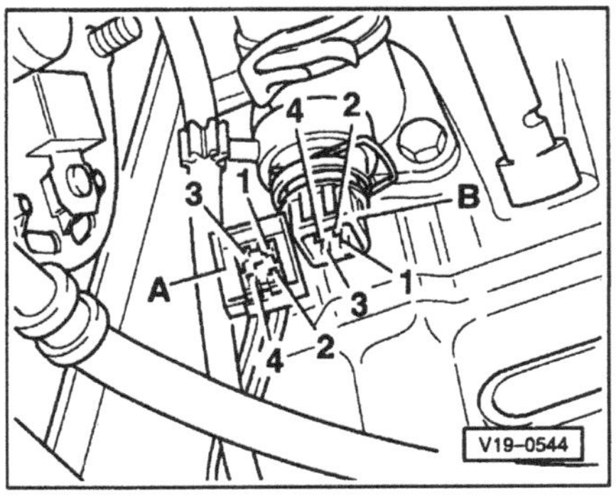

Test sequence

– Remove sound dampener pan
⇒ Repair Group 50

– Disconnect 4-pin harness connector from Coolant circulation Engine Coolant Temperature Thermal switch F51 (with integral Engine Coolant Temperature sensor G2 -yellow-)

◄ – Bridge connector -A- terminals -1- and -4- using jumper wires from VW 1594 adaptor kit

♦ Coolant pump must run

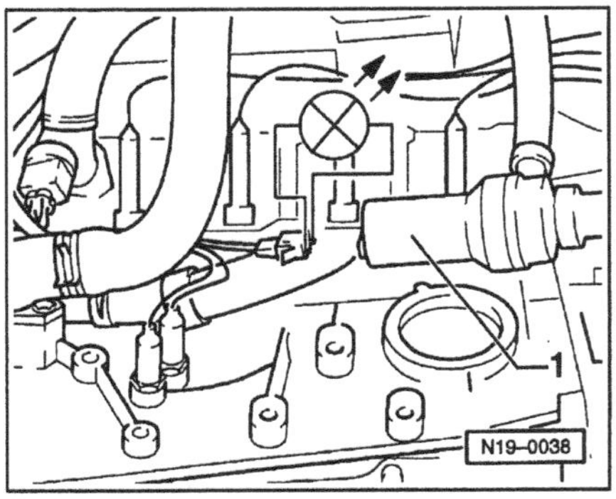

If coolant pump does not run

◄ – Disconnect 2-pin harness connector from coolant pump -1- and connect VAG 1527 B LED tester to disconnected connector using jumper wires from VW 1594 adaptor kit

♦ LED must flash

Note:

Vehicles with Engine Code ACV: Coolant pump is below radiator.

If LED flashes

– Replace coolant pump V50

If LED does NOT flash

– Locate and eliminate open circuit using wiring diagram
⇒ Wiring diagrams, Electrical Troubleshooting and Component locations binder

Thermal switch resistance, checking

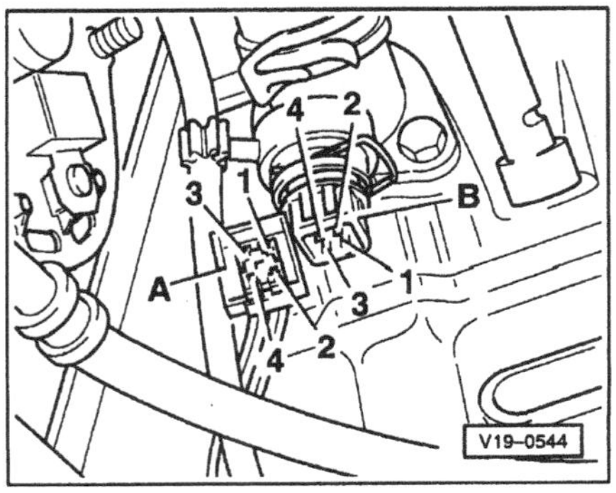

– Switch Fluke 83 multimeter to resistance range

◄ – Connect Fluke 83 multimeter between thermal switch -B- connector terminals -1- and -4- using jumper wires from VW 1594 adaptor kit

♦ Specifications: above approx.: 104 °C (219°F) = 0 Ω
below approx. 103 °C (217°F) = ∞ Ω

If specifications not obtained

– Replace F51/G2 switch/sensor

Fuel supply system components, removing and installing

Notes:

- *Observe Fuel system safety precautions!*
⇒ page B 20–4

- *Observe rules of cleanliness*
⇒ page B 20–5

- *Hose connections are secured using either screw clamps or spring clips.*

- *Always replace screw clamps with spring-type clips.*

- *Always use spring type clips for engine compartment fuel lines and hoses.*

- *Do NOT use screw clamps on fuel lines, it is not permissible!*

Special tools, testers and auxiliary items
- VAG 1921 spring clip pliers

Engine Code AAB:

Fuel filter, removing and installing
⇒ Repair Group 23

Fuel system leaks, checking
⇒ Repair Group 23

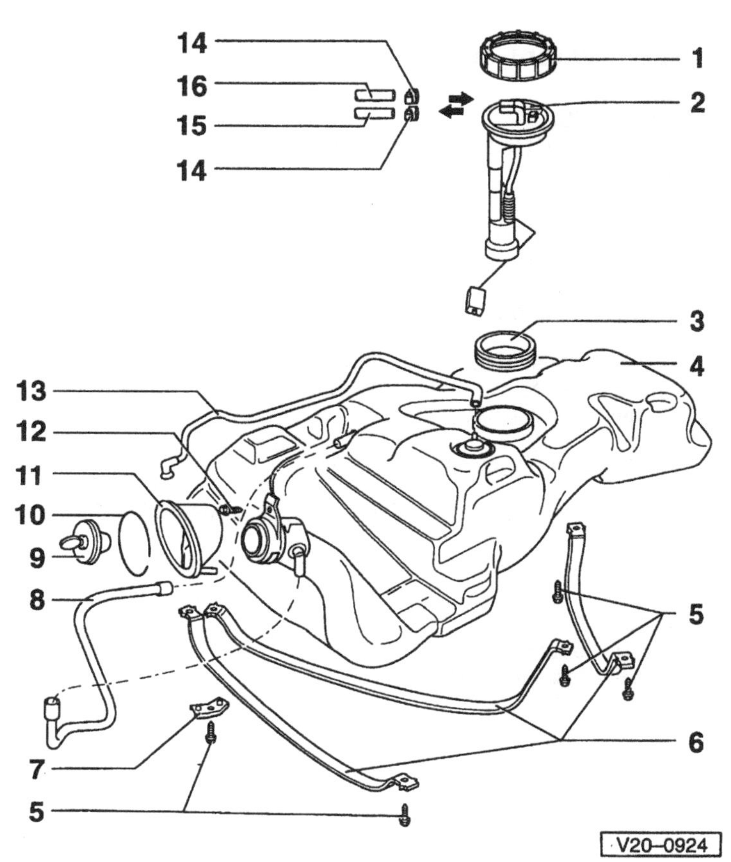

Fuel tank assembly, removing and installing

1 - **Collar nut**
- remove and install using 3217 collar nut wrench

2 - **Fuel gauge sending unit**
- note installation position
- removing and installing:

⇒ page B 20–8

3 - **Sealing ring**
- replace if damaged
- coat with fuel when installing

4 - **Fuel tank**
- when removing, support with VAG 1383 A engine/transmission jack
- removing and installing:

⇒ page B 20–6

5 - **25 Nm (18 ft lb)**

6 - **Mounting straps**
- note differing lengths

7 - **Bracket**
- for mounting straps

8 - **Vent pipe**
- for filler vent

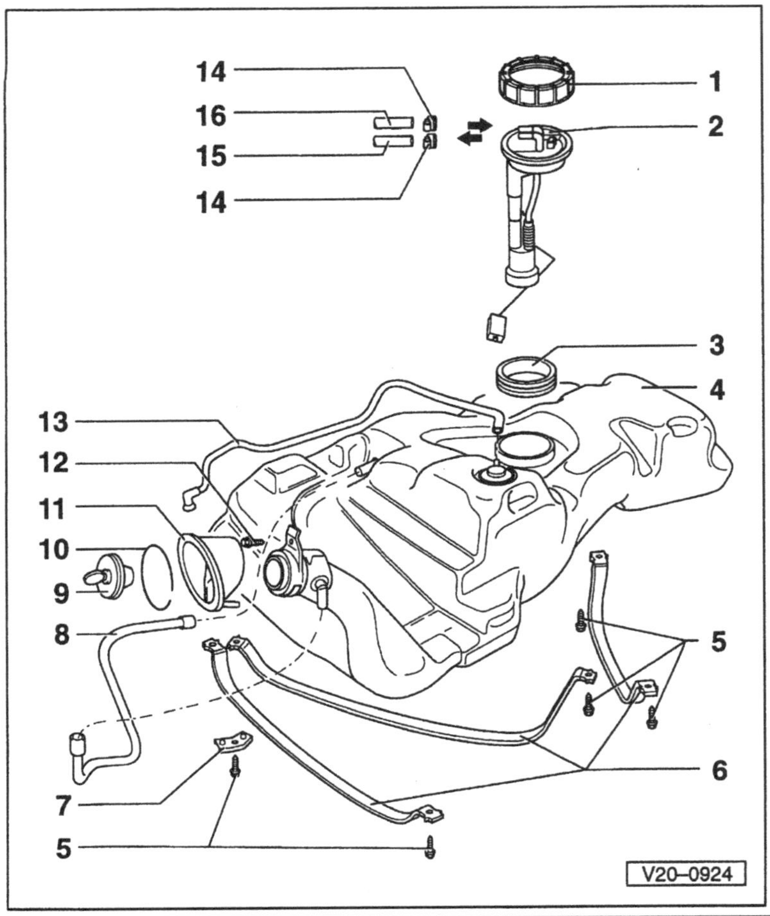

9 - **Cap**
- Replace seal if damaged

10 - **Retaining ring**

11 - **Splash shield**

12 - **10 Nm (7 ft lb)**

13 - **Vent pipe**
- ♦ operating vent

14 - **Screw clip**

15 - **Supply line**
- ♦ black

16 - **Return line**
- ♦ blue

Fuel system, safety precautions

> ***WARNING!***
> ***Fire Hazard! Do NOT have anything in the area that can ignite fuel!***

When removing/installing the fuel gauge sending unit from a full or partially full tank of fuel; observe the following :

Before starting the work

- Switch on exhaust extraction system and place an extraction hose close to the fuel gauge sender opening in the fuel tank to draw off any escaping fuel fumes.

If no extraction system is available

- Use a radial fan with a minimum displacement of 530 ft^3/hr
  - ♦ ensure that the fan is not in the air flow

> ***CAUTION!***
> ***Wear Diesel fuel resistant gloves, to prevent Diesel fuel from contacting your skin!***

Rules for cleanliness

When working on the fuel supply/injection system, pay careful attention to the following rules:

- Thoroughly clean all unions and adjacent areas before disconnecting
- Place parts that have been removed on a clean surface and cover them. Do not use fluffy cloths!
- Carefully cover opened components or seal them up if the repair can't be performed immediately
- Only install clean components
- Do not use parts that have been stored loose, in tool boxes etc.
- Only unpack replacement parts immediately prior to installation
- When the system is open:
  Do not use compressed air if it can be avoided.
  Do not move the vehicle unless absolutely necessary
- Ensure that Diesel fuel does NOT contact the coolant hoses! Immediately clean any hoses that have made contact with Diesel fuel. Always replace contaminated hoses.

Fuel tank, removing and installing

Special tools, testers and auxiliary items

- ♦ VAG 1383 A engine/transmission jack
- ♦ 3217 Collar nut wrench

Removing

Observe Fuel system safety precautions!
⇒ page B 20–4

- Switch OFF ignition
- Disconnect battery ground strap

> ***CAUTION!***
> ***First obtain radio anti-theft code BEFORE disconnecting the battery ground strap!***

- Drain fuel tank, clean fuel filler neck and surrounding area
- Remove retaining ring and splash shield from filler neck then remove mounting bolt
- Remove mounting straps
  - ♦ support fuel tank using VAG 1383 A engine/transmission jack
- Lower assembly using VAG 1383 A engine/transmission jack just enough to allow the supply and return lines and fuel gauge sending unit harness connector to be disconnected

Note:

On vehicles equipped with an additional heater, disconnect the fuel lines between the supply and return lines.

– Lower fuel tank

Installing

Observe Fuel system Safety precautions!
⇒ page B 20–4

Install in reverse order of removal procedure noting the following:

– Route the breather hose kink free

– Secure fuel hoses using spring clamps

– Do not interchange supply and return lines

♦ return line = blue

Fuel gauge sending unit, removing and installing

Special tools, testers and auxiliary items

♦ 3217 collar nut wrench

Observe Fuel system Safety precautions!
⇒ page B 20–4

Removing

– Cut carpet along perforations and remove cover plate

– Remove harness connector and supply and return lines from fuel gauge sending unit

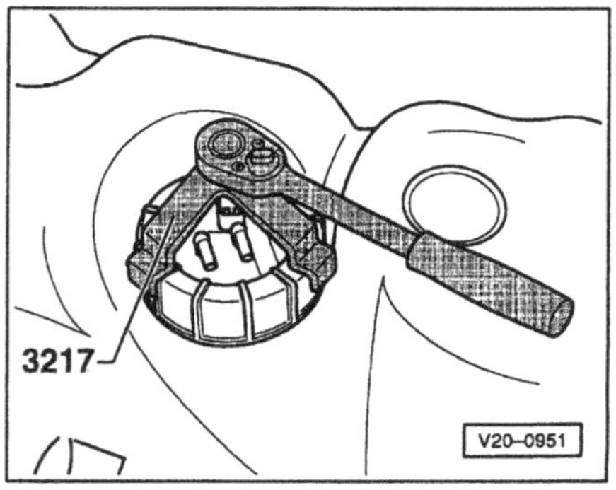

◄ – Remove collar nut using 3217 wrench

– Take out fuel gauge sending unit

Installing

– Installation is the reverse of the removal procedure

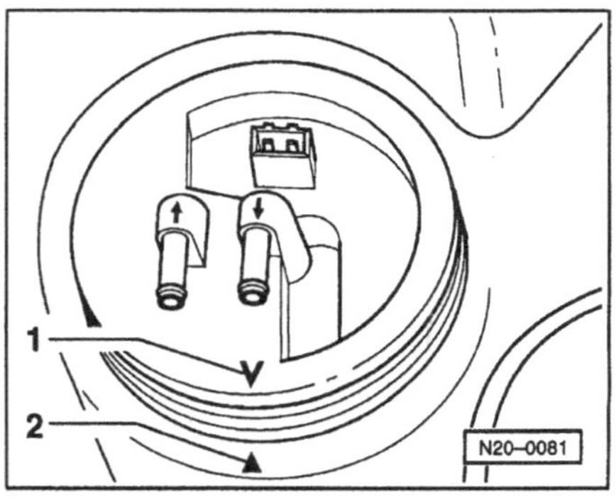

◄ – Note installation position

♦ mark on sending unit -1- must align with mark on fuel tank -2-

– Re-attach carpet after installing using glue or velcro

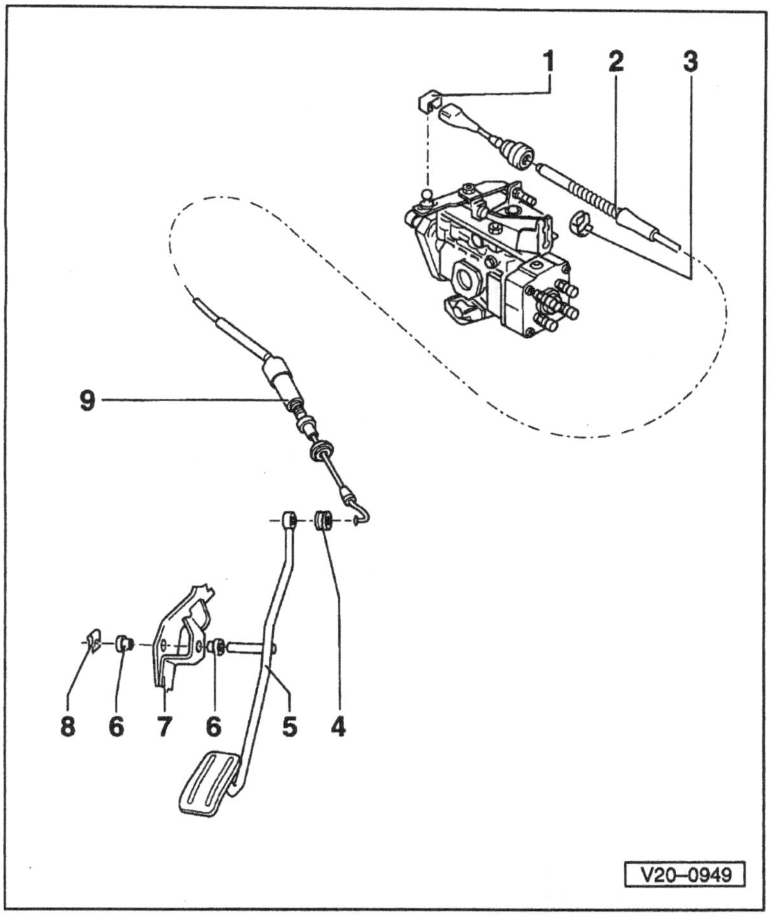

Accelerator mechanism assembly, servicing

Engine Code AAB

Engine Code ACV:
⇒ Repair Group 23
(Diesel direct injection)

1 - Retainer clip

2 - Accelerator cable

- Adjust by changing position of adjustment clip on cable grooves until proper play is obtained

⇒ page B 20–10

3 - Adjustment clip

4 - Rubber bushing

5 - Accelerator pedal

6 - Bushing

7 - Accelerator pedal carrier

8 - Shaft clip

9 - Load change damper

Accelerator pedal cable, adjusting

Engine Code AAB

Vehicles 09.94 ➤

– Remove radiator grille:
⇒ Repair Group 66

All vehicles

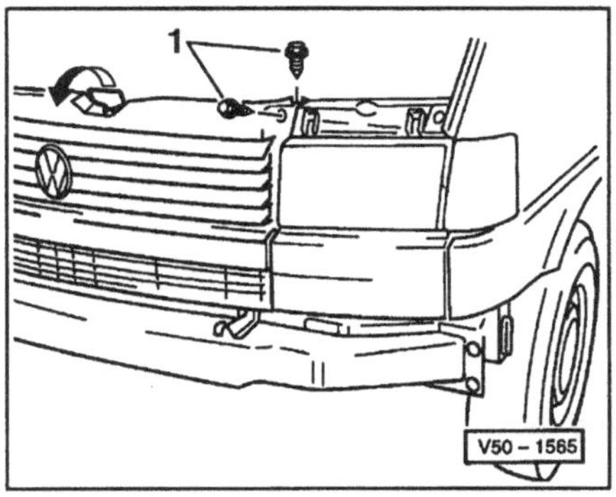

– Remove left and right-hand mounting bolts -1-

Note:

Vehicles 09.94➤ 1 mounting bolt located on each left and right side of lock carrier.

– Tilt lock carrier and radiator out and forward -arrow-

Note:

Adjust accelerator cable in Wide Open Throttle position

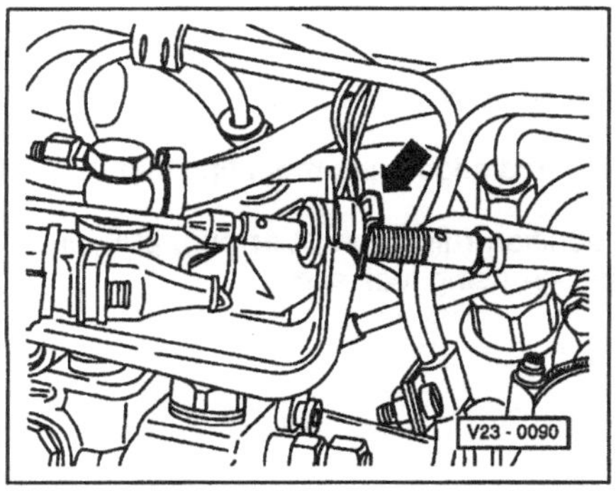

– Adjust cable by changing position of adjusting clip -arrow- on cable grooves so injection pump lever lies stress free on stop

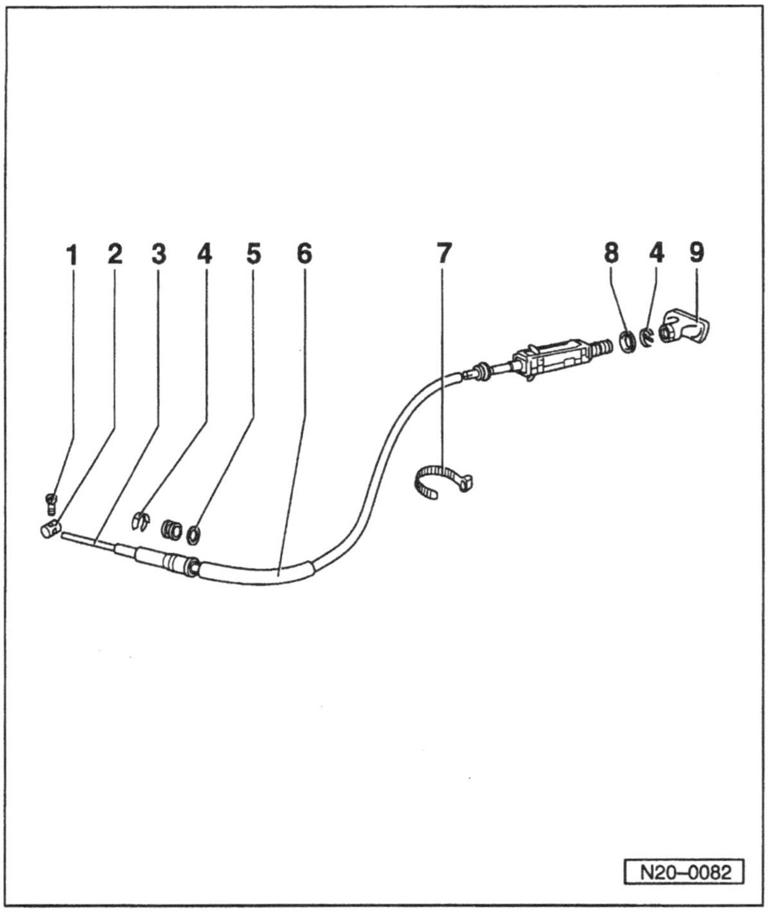

Cold Start Accelerator (CSA) cable, servicing

Engine Code AAB

1 - Lock screw

2 - Pivot ferrule

3 - Inner pull cable

4 - Clip

5 - Washer

6 - CSA cable (outer)
- ♦ adjusting:
⇒ page B 20–12

7 - Cable tie
- ♦ in engine compartment

8 - Nut

9 - Release lever

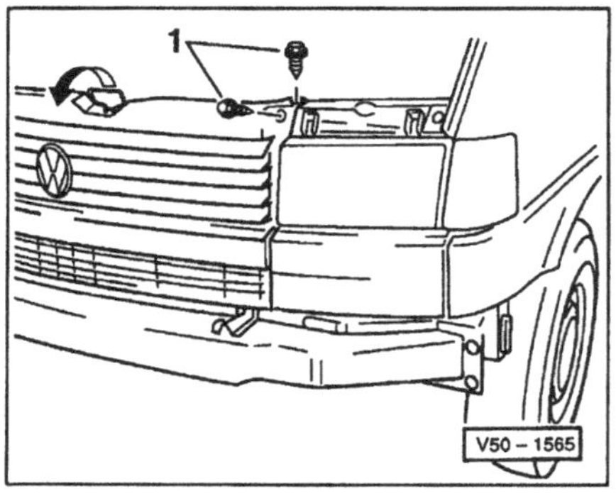

Cold Start Accelerator (CSA) cable, adjusting

Engine Code AAB

Vehicles 09.94 ➤

– Remove radiator grille:
⇒ Repair Group 66

All vehicles

◄ – Remove left and right-hand mounting bolts -1-

Note:

Vehicles 09.94 ➤ 1 mounting bolt located on each left and right side of lock carrier.

– Tilt lock carrier and radiator out and forward -arrow-

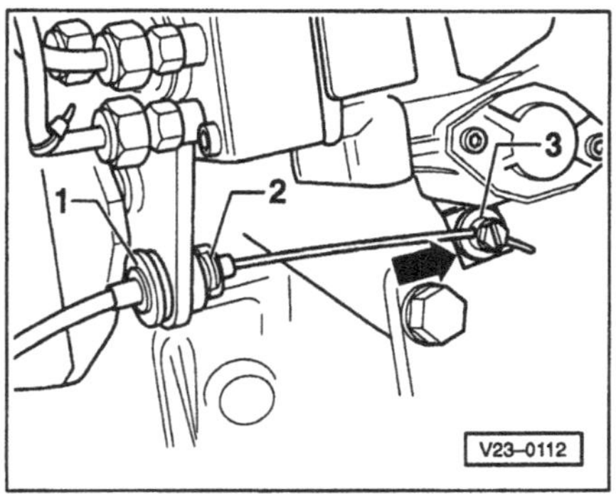

◄ – Slide washer -1- onto cable and secure via mounting clip -2-

– Set operating lever to 0 position (direction of arrow), pull inner cable taut and attach in pin -3- using lock screw

Turbocharger, boost system

Notes:

- *All hose connections are secured with clips.*
- *Boost system must be free of leaks*
- *Replace self-locking nuts*
- *Use VAG 1921 spring clip pliers to install spring clips*

Turbocharger component assembly, removing and installing
⇒ page B 21–2

Air-cooling components, removing and installing
⇒ page B 21–6

Observe Rules for cleanliness
⇒ page B 21–8

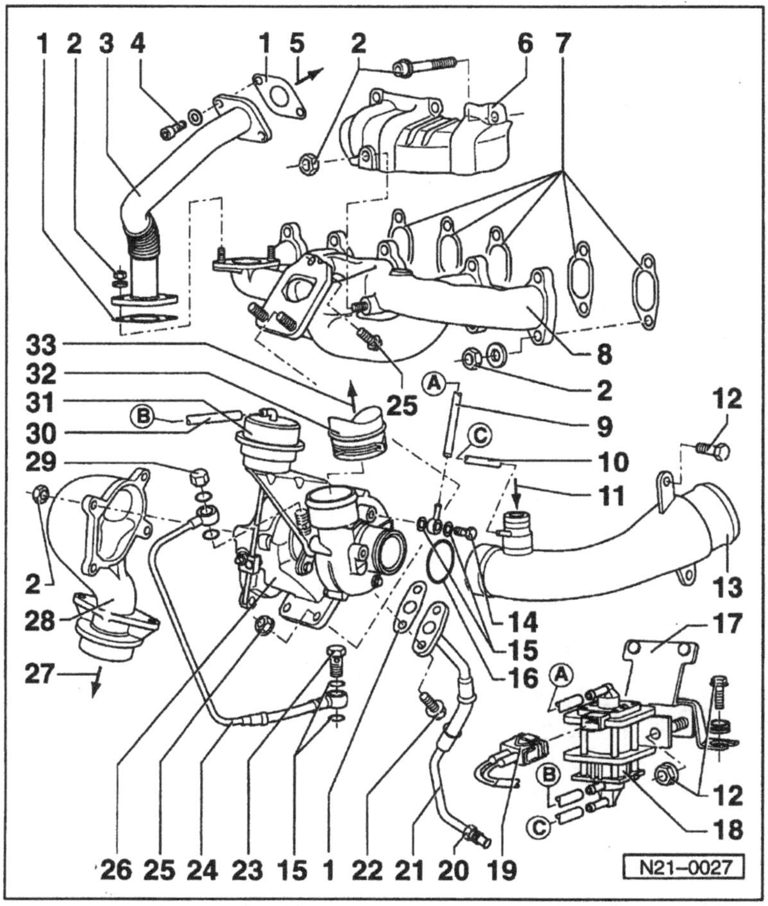

Turbocharger component assembly, removing and installing

1 - Gasket
- Replace

2 - 25 Nm (18 ft lb)

3 - Connecting pipe
- When installing, first snug all bolts (parts must be just free to move), then tighten stress free

4 - 15 Nm (11 ft lb)

5 - To Exhaust Gas Recirculation (EGR) valve
⇒ Repair Group 26

6 - Heat shield
- ♦ for intake pipe

7 - Gasket
- Replace
- ♦ note installation position

8 - Exhaust manifold

9 - Vacuum line
- ♦ red

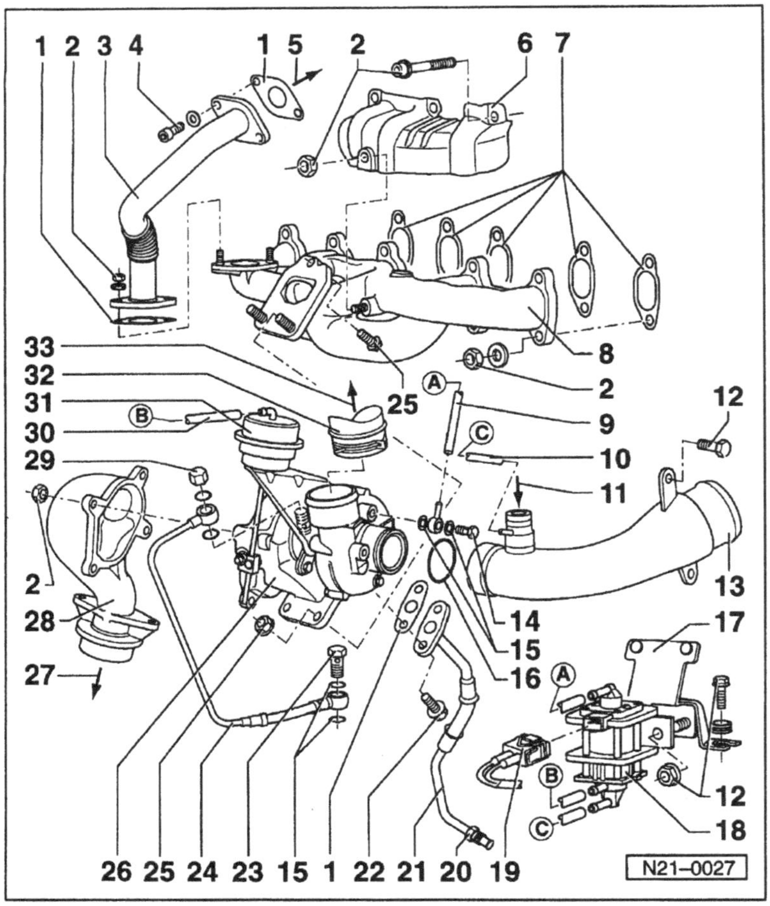

10 - Vacuum line
- black

11 - from Positive Crankcase Ventilation valve

12 - 10 Nm (7 ft lb)

13 - Connecting pipe
- between turbocharger and Mass Air Flow sensor connecting hose
- attached to intake pipe along with dipstick guide tube

14 - Banjo bolt
- 15 Nm (11 ft lb)

15 - Oil seal
- Replace

16 - O-ring
- Replace if damaged

17 - Mounting bracket
- for EGR vacuum regulator solenoid valve N18 and Wastegate bypass regulator valve N75

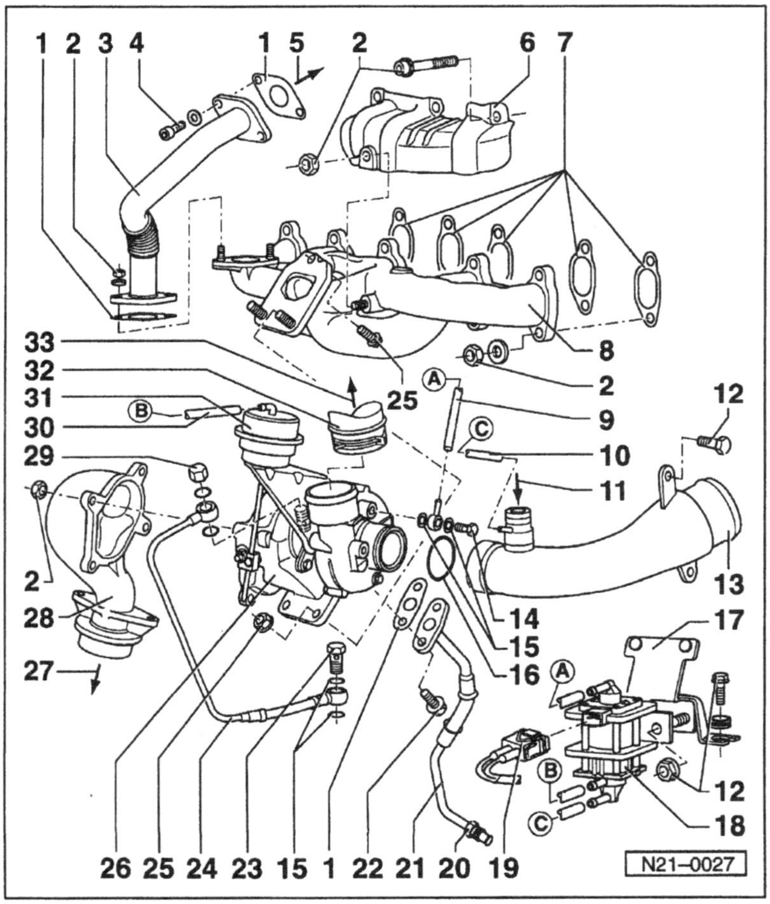

18 - Wastegate bypass regulator valve N75
- control, checking :

⇒ Repair Group 23

19 - 2-pin harness connector
- for Wastegate bypass regulator valve N75

20 - 40 Nm (30 ft lb)

21 - Oil return pipe
- to dipstick guide tube connection

⇒ Repair Group 17

22 - 30 Nm (22 ft lb)

23 - Banjo bolt
- 30 Nm (22 ft lb)

24 - Oil supply pipe
- Before installing, fill turbocharger with engine oil using oil supply pipe connection
- from oil filter bracket

⇒ Repair Group 17

25 - 45 Nm (33 ft lb)
- Replace
- Coat threads and bolt head contact surfaces with G 000 500 grease

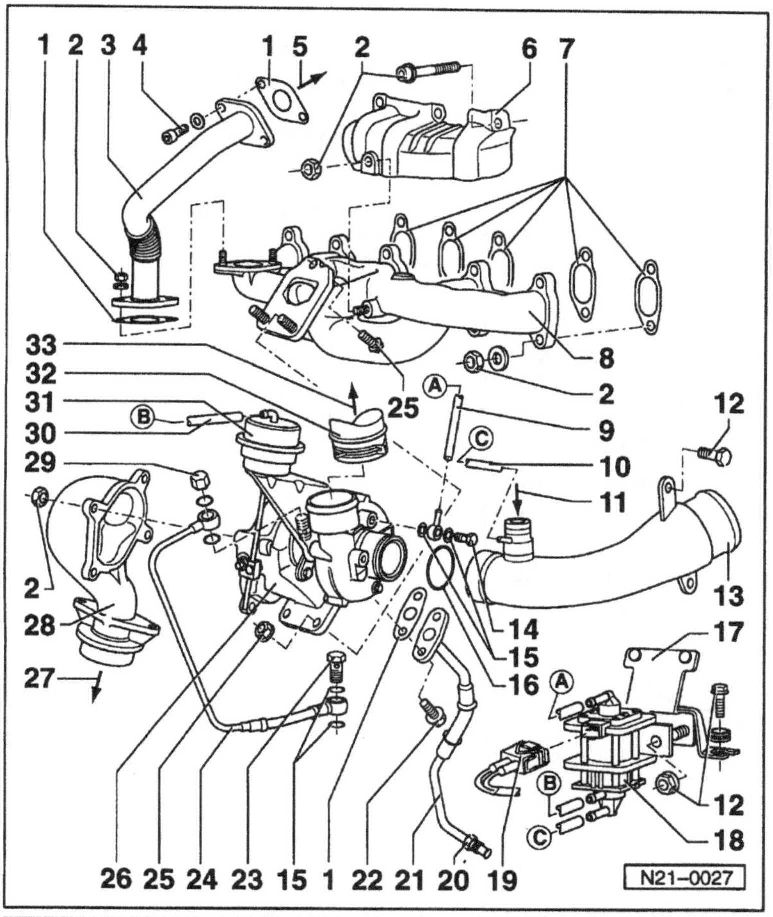

26 - **Turbocharger**
- removing and installing

⇒ page B 21–9
- boost pressure, measuring:

⇒ page B 21–14

27 - **to front exhaust pipe**
⇒ Repair Group 26

28 - **Pipe elbow**

29 - **Cap nut**
- 15 Nm (11 ft lb)

30 - **Control line**
- blue

31 - **Wastegate**
- integral part of turbocharger cannot be individually replaced
- boost pressure, checking

⇒ page B 21–14

32 - **Air hose**

33 - **to Charge Air cooler**
⇒ page B 21–6 (item 1)

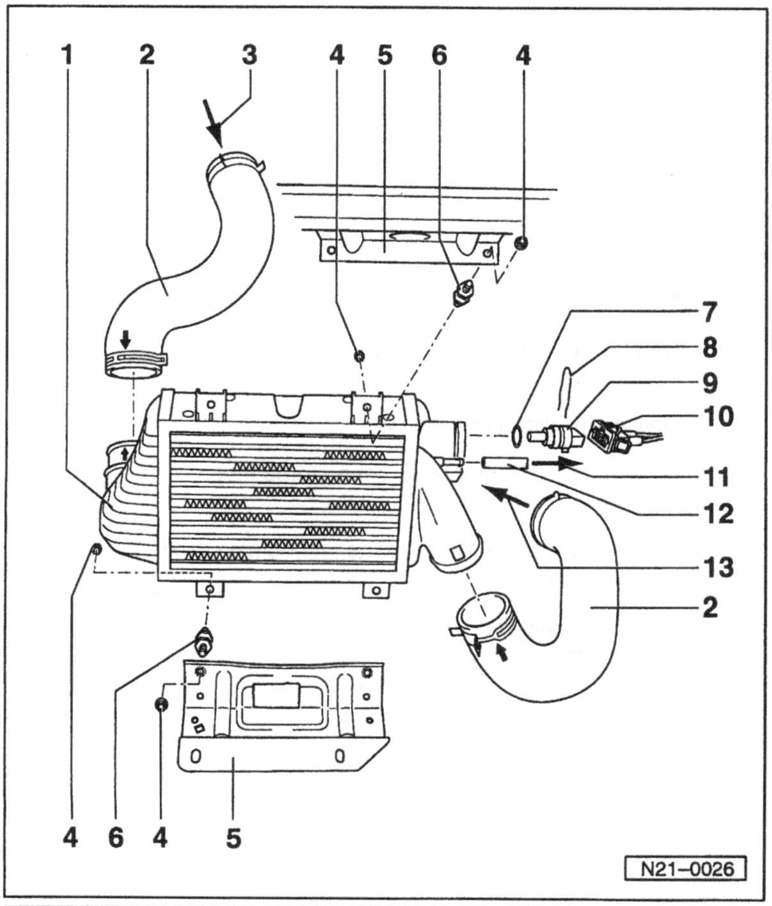

Air–cooling components, removing and installing

1 - **Charge Air cooler**

2 - **Air hose**
- note installation position

3 - **from turbocharger**
⇒ page B 21–5 (item 26)

4 - **10 Nm (7 ft lb)**

5 - **Mounting bracket**
- for Charge Air cooler

6 - **Bonded rubber mounting**

7 - **O-ring**
- Replace if damaged

8 - **Connector retaining clip**
- Ensure that it is seated securely

9 - **Intake Air Temperature sensor G72**
- checking:

⇒ Repair Group 01

10 - **2-pin harness connector**
- for Intake Air Temperature sensor G72

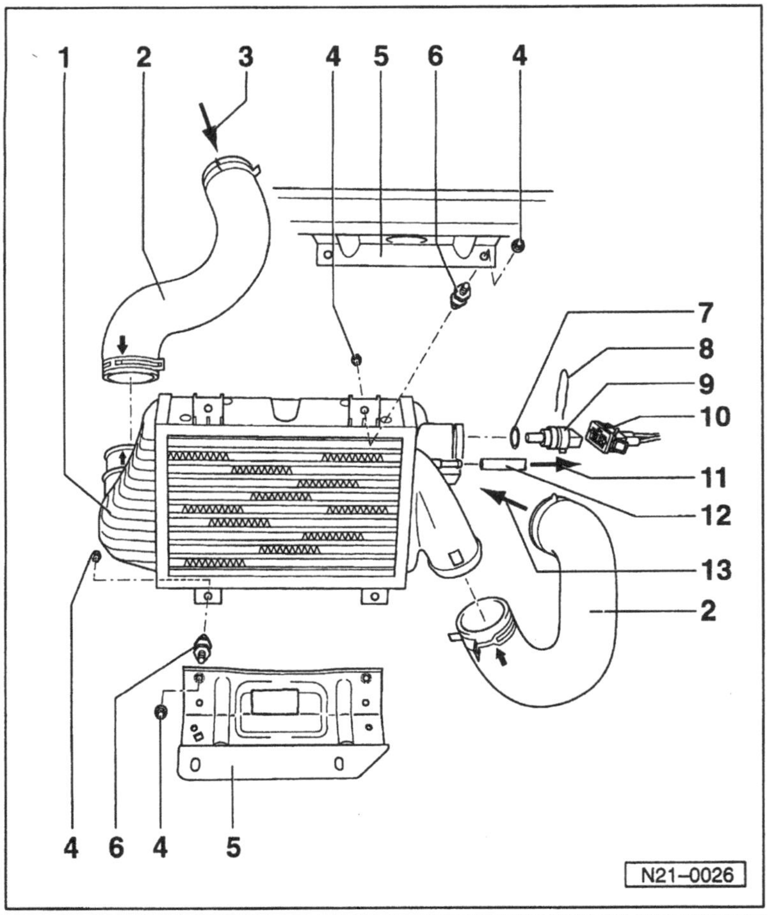

11 - to ECM J248 (Diesel direct injection system)

12 - Pressure hose

- Black

13 - to Exhaust Gas Recirculation valve

⇒ Repair Group 26

Rules for cleanliness

When working on the turbocharger system, pay careful attention to the following rules:

- Thoroughly clean all unions and adjacent areas before disconnecting
- Place parts that have been removed on a clean surface and cover them. Do not use fluffy cloths!
- Carefully cover opened components or seal them up if the repair can't be performed immediately
- Only install clean components
- Do not use parts that have been stored loose, in tool boxes etc.
- Only unpack replacement parts immediately prior to installation
- When the system is open:
  Do not use compressed air if it can be avoided.
  Do not move the vehicle unless absolutely necessary
- Ensure that Diesel fuel does NOT contact the coolant hoses! Immediately clean any hoses that have made contact with Diesel fuel. Always replace contaminated hoses.

Turbocharger, removing and installing

Special tools, testers and auxiliary items

- VAG 1331 Torque wrench 5 to 50 Nm (3.7 to 37 ft lb)
- G 000 500 grease

Removing

– Switch OFF ignition

– Disconnect battery Ground strap

CAUTION!
First obtain radio anti-theft code BEFORE disconnecting the battery ground strap!

– Remove sound dampening pan
⇒ Repair Group 50

– Remove front exhaust pipe
⇒ Repair Group 26

– Remove radiator grille:
⇒ Repair Group 66

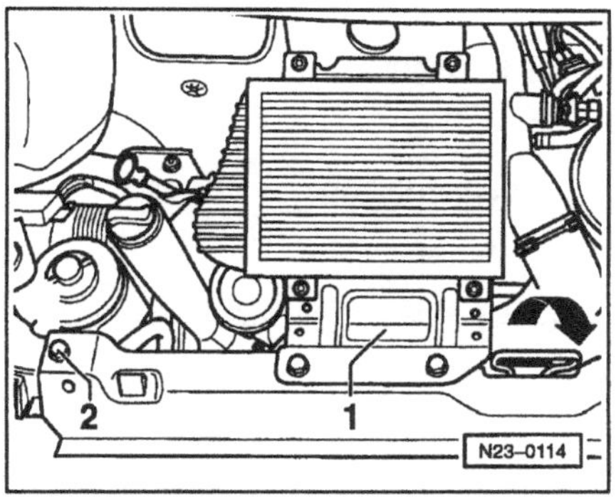

◄ – Remove Charge Air cooler mount -1-

– Remove left and right hand mounting bolts -2-

– Tilt lock carrier and radiator out and forward -arrow-

– Remove Charge Air cooler with air hoses
⇒ page B 21–6

– Pull off control pipe on Wastegate bypass regulator valve (blue)

– Pull off vacuum hoses on connecting pipe (black), turbocharger (red) and EGR vacuum regulator solenoid valve (black)

– Remove connecting hose between connecting pipe and Mass Air Flow sensor

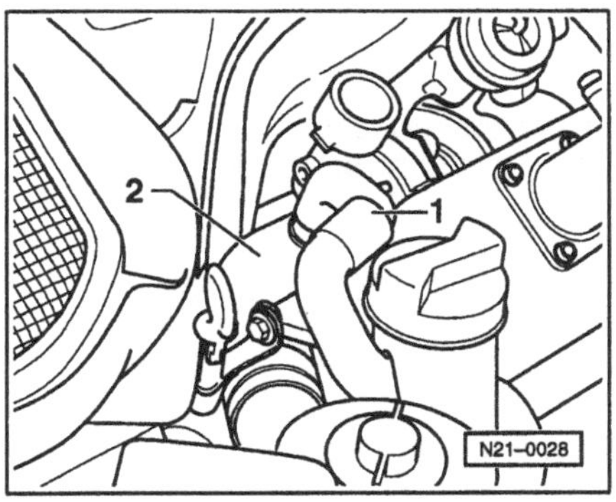

◄ – Remove breather hose -1- between Positive Crankcase Ventilation valve and connecting pipe

– Remove connecting pipe -2-

– Remove connecting pipe between EGR valve and exhaust manifold

– Remove intake pipe with heat shield and EGR valve

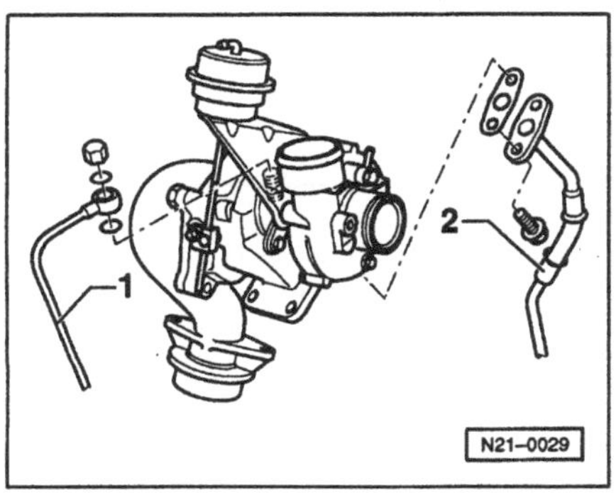

◄ – Remove oil supply pipe -1- and oil return pipe -2- on turbocharger

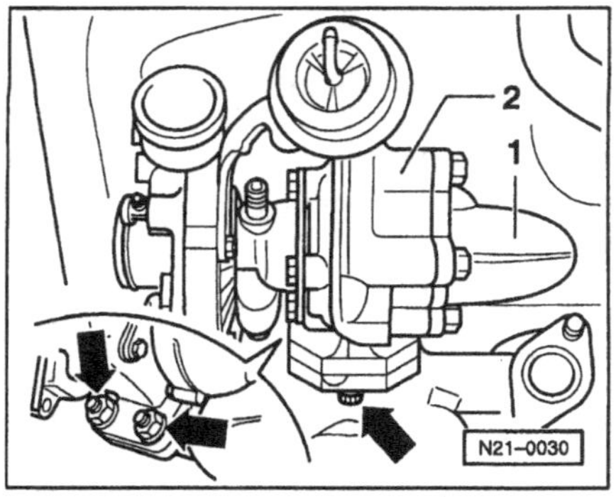

- Remove pipe elbow -1-
- Remove mounting bolts and nuts between exhaust manifold and turbocharger
- Lift turbocharger -2- out and upwards

Installing

Perform installation in reverse order of removal procedure, but note following:

- Coat threads and contact surfaces of nuts and bolts used between exhaust manifold and turbocharger with G 000 500 grease and tighten
  - ♦ 45 Nm (33 ft lb)
- Fit pipe elbow to turbocharger and tighten
  - ♦ 25 Nm (18 ft lb)
- Install oil return pipe with new seal and tighten
  - ♦ 30 Nm (22 ft lb)
- Fill the turbocharger with engine oil via the oil supply connection

- Install oil supply pipe with new seal and tighten cap nut
  - ♦ 25 Nm (18 ft lb)
- Fit intake pipe with heat shield and new seal (coating or seal bead points to intake pipe) and tighten
  - ♦ 25 Nm (18 ft lb)
- Install connecting pipe between EGR vacuum regulator solenoid valve and exhaust manifold

Note:

When installing, first snug all bolts (parts must be just free to move) then tighten stress free.

- Attach control line (blue) to EGR vacuum regulator solenoid valve and secure with a hose clamp
- Fit vacuum hose (red) to turbocharger and secure with hose clamp

> ***CAUTION!***
> ***After installing the turbocharger, run the engine at low rpm for approximately one minute to ensure it is properly lubricated before being subjected to higher loads.***

Turbocharger, checking

Special tools, testers and auxiliary items

- ♦ VAG 1397 A turbocharger tester
- ♦ VAG 1397 A/1 connecting hose (with Tee-piece)

Checking conditions

Note:

The turbocharger and wastegate consist of a single component. Faulty turbochargers must be replaced as an assembly because shop repairs using workshop equipment are not possible.

Prerequisites for perfect turbocharger function and attainment of prescribed boost pressure are:

- ♦ No malfunctions stored in DTC memory
⇒ Repair Group 01
- ♦ Output Diagnostic Test Mode performed:
⇒ Repair Group 01
- ♦ No leaks from intake or exhaust systems
- ♦ Control line (blue) between Wastegate bypass regulator valve N75 and pressure line (black) between Charge Air cooler and ECM J248 is not blocked, loose or leaking
- ♦ No engine or fuel injection system malfunctions, e.g. start of injection, fuel injectors and cylinder compression
- ♦ Engine oil temperature 80 °C (176 °F) minimum

Boost pressure, measuring

for turbocharger tester operation
⇒ *manufacturers operating instructions*

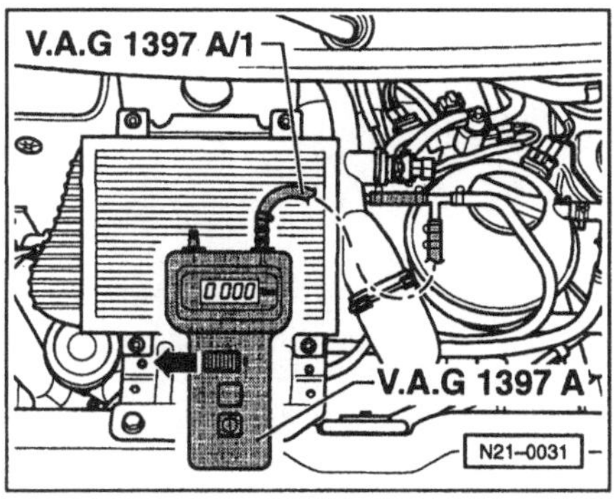

Note:

- ♦ *Measure boost pressure while driving on an open road (at Wide Open Throttle) or on a dynamometer.*
- ♦ *Allow 10 seconds maximum for each measurement.*

◄

- – Disconnect pressure line (black) between Charge Air cooler and ECM J248 at Charge Air cooler
- – Connect T-piece to Charge Air cooler and pressure hose
- – Use VAG 1397 A/1 connecting hose to connect T-piece to VAG 1397 A turbocharger tester (connection II)
- – Select measuring range II

Notes:

- ♦ *All hoses and lines must be securely connected so there is no possibility of leakage.*
- ♦ *If boost pressure is being measured on the road, you must use a second technician to operate the turbocharger tester.*
- ♦ *Ensure that the VAG 1397 A/1 connecting hose is not pinched between the hood and the body.*

– Measure boost pressure at Wide Open Throttle:

On a dynamometer:
3rd gear between 2500 and 3000 rpm
On open road:
In 2nd gear at Wide Open Throttle while watching vehicle tach

Note:

The brake pedal must not be operated while taking measurements. The ECM will reduce/compensate fuel quantity which will lead to incorrect measurements.

– Press "M" button on turbocharger tester at 2500 to 3000 rpm and record values
  - ♦ specification: (relative pressure) 0.60 to 0.80 bar (9 to 12psi)

If specifications not obtained

– Replace turbocharger
⇒ page B 21–9

If boost pressure is too high and if control line to Wastegate bypass regulator valve is not blocked, kinked, loose or leaking

– Replace turbocharger
  - ♦ because Wastegate bypass regulator valve is faulty
⇒ page B 21–9

Exhaust system components, removing and installing

Notes:

- *Replace self-locking nuts*
- *Observe specified torque values*

After working on the exhaust system:

- *Ensure that (at room temperature) the system is not stressed*
- *Ensure that sufficient clearance exists between the exhaust and bodywork, if necessary, loosen the required clamps and align the muffler and front exhaust pipe to achieve the needed clearance*
- *Ensure the various hangers are evenly loaded*

Exhaust system component overviews:

Engine Code AAB
⇒ page B 26–2

Engine Code ACV
⇒ page B 26–4

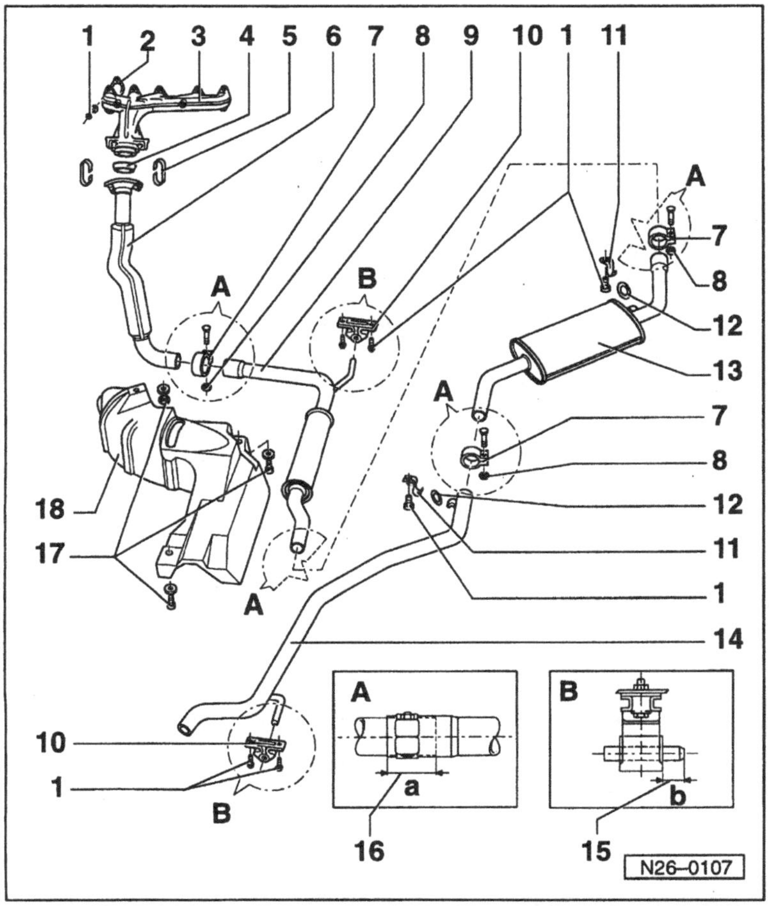

Engine Code AAB

Note:

Longitudinally align the exhaust system so dimensions -a- and -b- are maintained.

1 - 25 Nm (18 ft lb)

2 - Gasket
- Replace

3 - Exhaust manifold

4 - Pivoting exhaust seal
- Replace if damaged
- Pry off using screwdriver

5 - Spring clamp
- Remove and install using: 3140A wedge set

⇒ page B 26–6
- tensioning or relieving tension:

⇒ page B 26–7

6 - Front exhaust pipe

7 - Clamp

8 - 40 Nm (30 ft lb)

9 - Front muffler

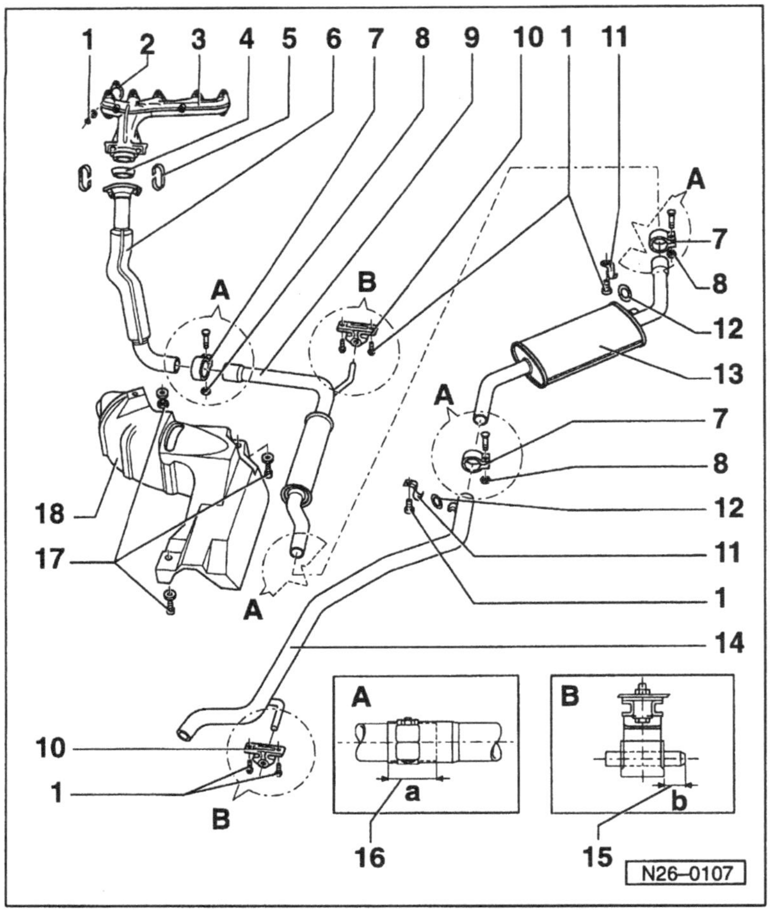

10 - **Mount**

11 - **Retainer**

12 - **Rubber hanger**
- Replace if damaged

13 - **Center muffler**

14 - **End pipe**

15 - **Dimension -b-**
- ♦ 10 mm (0.4 in.) minimum

16 - **Dimension -a-**
- ♦ 50 ± 5 mm (1.97 ± 0.2 in.)

17 - **5 Nm (44 in. lb)**

18 - **Heat shield**

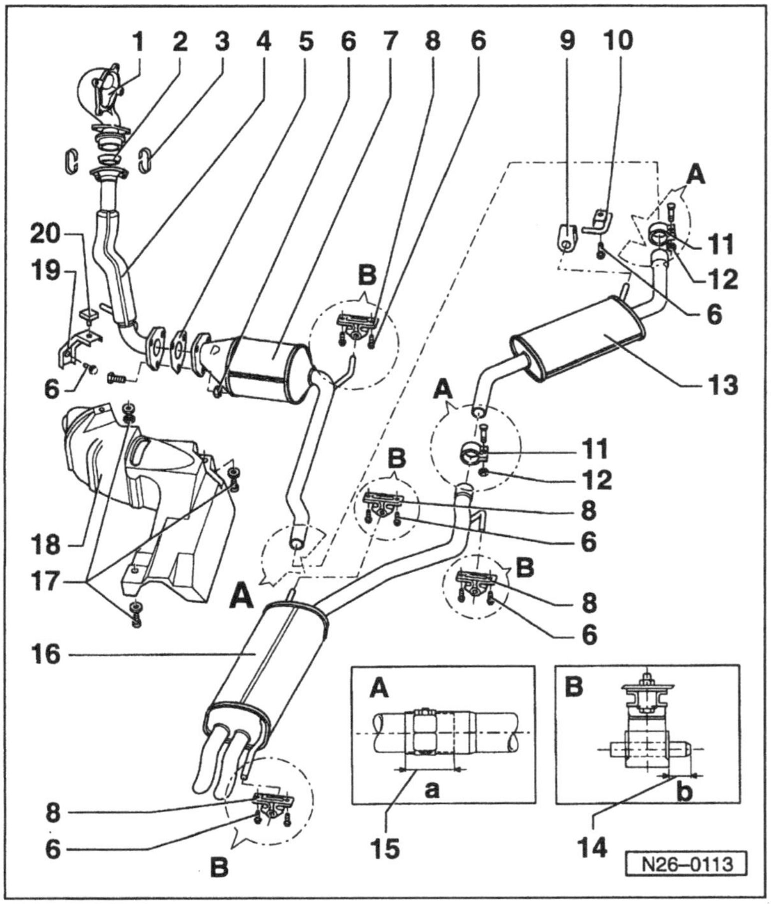

Engine Code ACV

Notes:

- ♦ *Align exhaust system longitudinally to ensure that dimensions -a- and -b- are maintained.*
- ♦ *Removing and installing the exhaust manifold:*

⇒ Repair Group 21

1 - **Pipe elbow**
- ♦ Between turbocharger and front exhaust pipe

2 - **Pivoting exhaust seal**
- Replace if damaged
- Pry off with screwdriver

3 - **Spring clamp**
- Remove and install using 3140A tensioning wedges

⇒ page B 26–6

- ♦ tensioning or relieving tension:

⇒ page B 26–7

4 - **Front exhaust pipe**

5 - **Gasket**
- Replace

6 - **25 Nm (18 ft lb)**

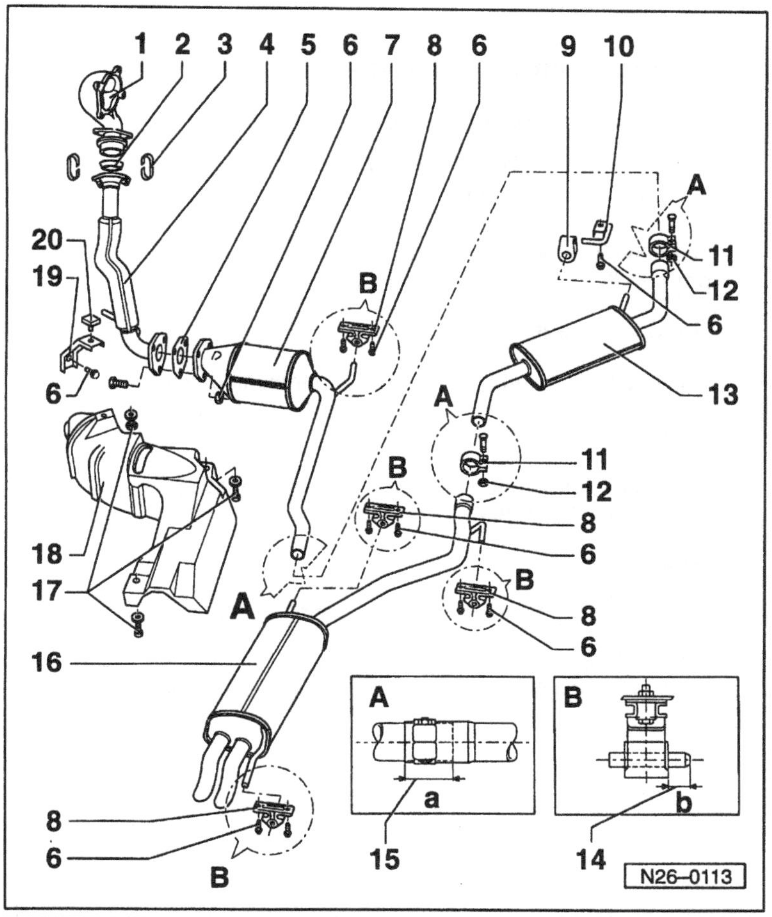

7 - **Catalytic converter**

8 - **Mounting**

9 - **Connector piece**
- Replace if damaged

10 - **Finger mount**

11 - **Clamp**

12 - **40 Nm (30 ft lb)**

13 - **Center muffler**

14 - **Dimension -b-**
- ♦ 10 mm (0.4 in.) minimum

15 - **Dimension -a-**
- ♦ 50 ± 5 mm (1.97 ± 0.2 in.)

16 - **Rear muffler**

17 - **5 Nm (44 in. lb)**

18 - **Heat shield**

19 - **Support bracket**
- ♦ for damper rubber

20 - **Damper rubber**
- ♦ for front exhaust pipe (item 4)

Spring clamps, removing and installing

Special tools, testers and auxiliary items

- ♦ 3140 A/2 wedge set

Requirement

- ♦ Exhaust system at room temperature

Engine Code AAB

- Separate exhaust system between front exhaust pipe and front muffler
  - ♦ in some cases it helps to release the exhaust system from its hangers

Engine Code ACV

- Separate exhaust system between front pipe and catalytic converter

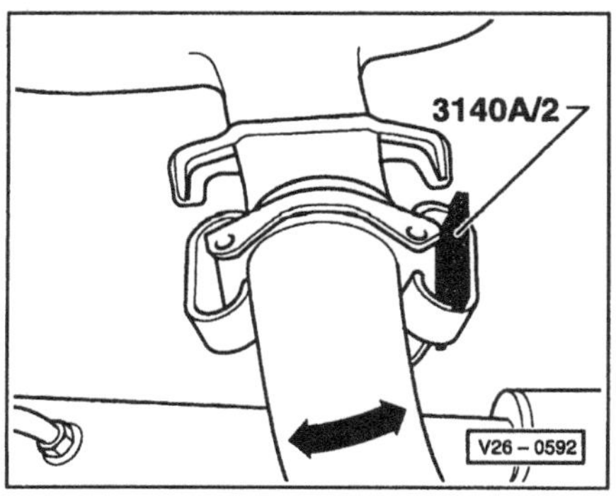

All Engine Codes

◄ – Open spring clamp by pressing sideways on exhaust pipe until short wedge 3140 A/2 can be inserted into clamp up to shoulder of wedge

To open spring clamps
- Grip front exhaust pipe with pipe wrench and push exhaust system to side in required direction

Installing

Installation is reverse order of removal, however;
- At end, ensure that spring clamps are seated in dimples

Spring clamps, tensioning and relieving

Special tools, testers and auxiliary items

- 3140 A/1 3140 A/2 and wedges
- Synthetic head hammer

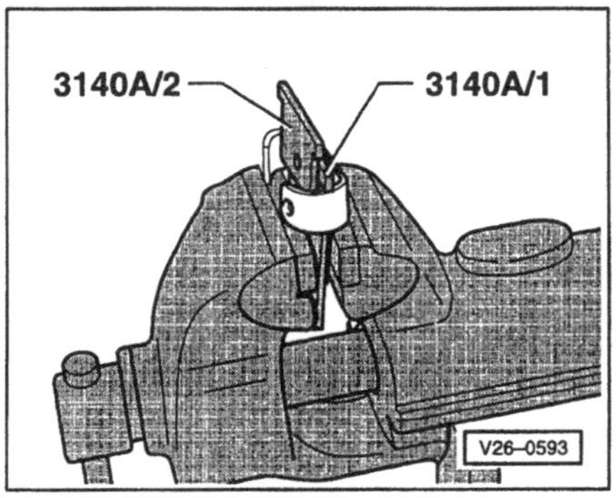

To relieve a removed spring clamp or to spread a new spring clamp perform the following vise operations:

Tension, relieving

◄

- Place spring clamp with 3140 A/2 tensioning wedge in vise pre-opened approx. 15 mm (0.6 in.), so hammered side of wedge is between vise jaws
- Carefully drive out wedge between gap in vise jaws using synthetic head hammer

Tensioning

- Place spring clamp in vise pre-opened to approx. 15 mm (0.6 in.)
- Drive long wedge through spring clamp (between vise jaws) up to wedge shoulder using synthetic head hammer

Note:

In instances where a spring clamp has the long wedge installed but still lacks sufficent spreading; install the short wedge as follows:

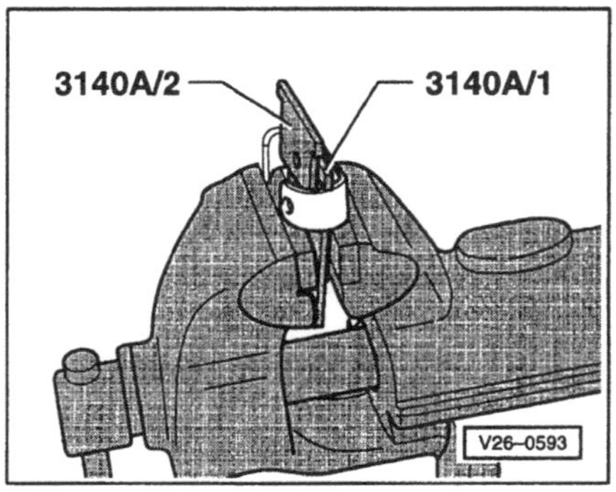

◄

- Drive short wedge (next to long wedge) into clamp up to shoulder of short wedge
- Hold clamp over opened vise so that only the short wedge (hammering side) lies on vise jaw
- Carefully drive out long wedge through gap between vise jaws using synthetic hammer

Exhaust Gas Recirculation (EGR) system, overview

Engine Code ACV

Notes:

- *The function/control of the Exhaust Gas Recirculation (EGR) system is under the management of the Diesel Direct Injection system Engine Control Module (ECM) J248 via EGR vacuum regulator solenoid valve N18 in final turn to the mechanical EGR valve (in manifold).*
- *EGR vacuum regulator solenoid valve N18, checking:*

⇒ Repair Group 01, Output Diagnostic Test Mode checks

- *The cone shaped plunger in the mechanical EGR valve ensures that a variety of cross sectional openings are possible at different plunger lengths.Every conceivable valve position is possible via pulsed control.*

– Replace self-locking nuts

– Install spring clips using VAG 1921 spring clip pliers

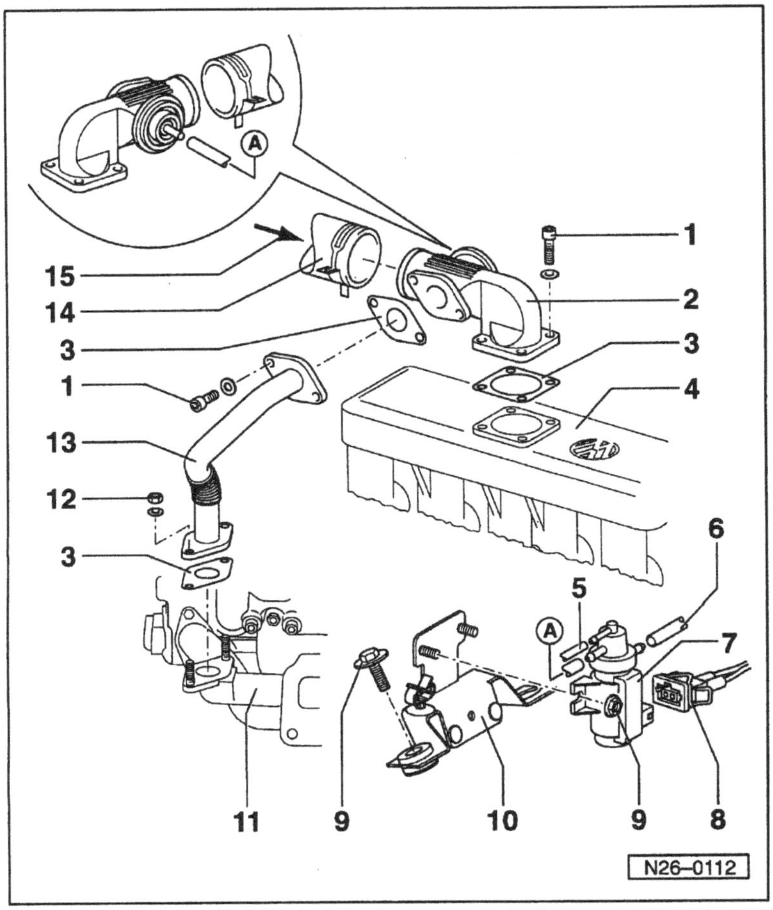

Exhaust Gas Recirculation (EGR) system, removing and installing

1 - 15 Nm (11 ft lb)

2 - EGR valve
- checking:

⇒ page B 26–12

3 - Gasket
- Replace

4 - Intake manifold

5 - Vacuum line
- black
- to check valve between vacuum pump and brake servo

6 - Vacuum line
- black
- from upper Air Cleaner section

7 - EGR vacuum regulator solenoid valve N18
- control, checking

⇒ Repair Group 01, Output Diagnostic Test Mode checks

2.5 Liter 5–Cylinder, General Engine (Engine Codes: AAF, ACU)

Section **C**

WARNING!
Before proceeding with any work, please read the warnings and cautions immediately following this index. Also read any warning and caution that accompanies a procedure in the manual.

15 Engine—Cylinder head, Valvetrain

17 Engine—Lubrication system

19 Engine—Cooling system

20 Fuel supply

26 Exhaust system/Emission controls

Please read these WARNINGS and CAUTIONS before proceeding with maintenance and repair work.

WARNING—

- Some repairs may be beyond your capability. If you lack the skills, tools and equipment, or a suitable workplace for any procedure described in this manual, we suggest you leave such repairs to an authorized Volkswagen dealer service department, or other qualified shop.

- Volkswagen is constantly improving its cars. Sometimes these changes, both in parts and specifications, are made applicable to earlier models. Therefore, before starting any major jobs or repairs to components on which passenger safety may depend, consult your authorized Volkswagen dealer about the Technical Bulletins that may have been issued since the editorial closing of this manual.

- Do not re-use any fasteners that are worn or deformed in normal use. Many fasteners are designed to be used only once and become unreliable and may fail when used a second time. This includes, but is not limited to, nuts, bolts, washers, self–locking nuts or bolts, circlips and cotter pins. Always replace these fasteners with new parts.

- Never work under a lifted car unless it is solidly supported on stands designed for the purpose. Do not support a car on cinder blocks, hollow tiles or other props that may crumble under continuous load. Never work under a vehicle that is supported solely by a jack. Never work under the car while the engine is running.

- If you are going to work under a car on the ground, make sure that the ground is level. Block the wheels to keep the car from rolling. Disconnect the battery negative terminal (ground strap) to prevent others from starting the vehicle while you are under it.

- Never run the engine unless the work area is well ventilated. Carbon monoxide (CO) kills.

- Do not attempt to work on your vehicle if you do not feel well. You increase the danger of injury to yourself and others if you are tired, upset or have taken medicine or any other substance that may impair you or keep you from being fully alert.

- Disconnect the battery negative (–) terminal (ground strap) whenever you work on the fuel system or the electrical system. Do not smoke or work near heaters or other fire hazards. Keep an approved fire extinguisher handy.

- Batteries produce explosive hydrogen gas. Keep sparks, lighted matches and open flame away from the top of the battery. If hydrogen gas escaping from the cap vents is ignited, it will ignite gas trapped in the cells and cause the battery to explode.

- Connect and disconnect battery cables, jumper cables or a battery charger only with the ignition switched off, to prevent sparks. Do not quick–charge the battery (for boost starting) for longer than one minute, and do not allow charging voltage to exceed 16.5 volts. Wait at least one minute before boosting the battery a second time.

- Illuminate your work area adequately but safely. Use a portable safety light for working inside or under the car. Make sure the bulb is enclosed by a wire cage. The hot filament of an accidentally broken bulb can ignite spilled fuel or oil.

- Tie long hair behind your head. Do not wear a necktie, a scarf, loose clothing, or a necklace when you work near machine tools or running engines. If your hair, clothing, or jewelry were to get caught in the machinery, severe injury could result.

- Finger rings, bracelets and other jewelry should be removed so that they cannot cause electrical shorts, get caught in running machinery, or be crushed by heavy parts.

- Catch draining fuel, oil, or brake fluid in suitable containers. Do not use food or beverage containers that might mislead someone into drinking from them. Store flammable fluids away from fire hazards. Wipe up spills at once, but do not store the oily rags, which can ignite and burn spontaneously.

- Always observe good workshop practices. Wear goggles when you operate machine tools or work with battery acid. Gloves or other protective clothing should be worn whenever the job requires working with harmful substances.

- The Air-Conditioning (A/C) system is filled with a chemical refrigerant, which is hazardous. The A/C system should be serviced only by trained technicians using approved refrigerant recovery/recycling equipment, trained in related safety precautions, and familiar with regulations governing the discharging and disposal of automotive chemical refrigerants.

- Do not expose any part of the A/C system to high temperatures such as an open flame. Excessive heat will increase system pressure and may cause the system to burst.

- Some aerosol tire inflators are highly flammable. Be extremely cautious when repairing a tire that may have been inflated using an aerosol tire inflator. Keep sparks, open flame or other sources of ignition away from the tire repair area. Inflate and deflate the tire at least four times before breaking the bead from the rim. Completely remove the tire from the rim before attempting any repair.

- Friction materials such as brake or clutch discs may contain asbestos fibers. Do not create dust by grinding, sanding, or by cleaning with compressed air. Avoid breathing asbestos fibers and asbestos dust. Breathing asbestos can cause serious diseases such as asbestosis or cancer, and may result in death.

- Greases, lubricants and other automotive chemicals contain toxic substances, many of which are absorbed directly through the skin. Read manufacturer's instructions and warnings carefully. Use hand and eye protection. Avoid direct skin contact.

- An airbag is operated by an explosive device. Handled improperly or without adequate safeguards, it can be accidently activated and cause serious personal injury. To prevent personal injury or airbag system failure, **only trained Volkswagen dealer service technicians** should test, disassemble or service the airbag system.

WARNINGS and CAUTIONS continued on next page ▶

Please read these WARNINGS and CAUTIONS before proceeding with maintenance and repair work.

WARNING (continued) —

- ALWAYS disconnect the airbag power supply before using a computer memory saver. Failure to disconnect the airbag power supply may result in accidental activation of the airbag.
- The airbag unit should not be removed, nor should any work be performed on the airbag system, without first reviewing the warnings and cautions that accompany the airbag system repair information in this manual.
- Never apply stickers or any other coverings on the steering wheel. Do not let chemical cleaners, oil or grease come into contact with the vinyl covering of the airbag unit.
- Never open or otherwise attempt to repair airbag system parts. Always use new parts. Never leave airbag parts or the partially disassembled airbag system unattended.
- Never use a test light or volt meter to conduct electrical tests on the airbag system. The airbag system must only be tested by trained Volkswagen Service technicians using special airbag tester equipment. The airbag system must only be tested while it is installed in the car.
- Do not expose an airbag unit to temperatures above 194°F (90°C) even for a brief period, while handling it during the repair process. Keep the unit clear of heat sources such as hot plates, soldering irons, heat lamps, welding equipment, or the like.
- Always replace airbag system components that have been mechanically damaged (bubbles, cracks, etc.).
- Always set down a removed airbag unit so that the horn pad is facing upward.
- When driving or riding in an airbag-equipped vehicle, never hold test equipment in your hands or lap while the vehicle is in motion. Objects between you and the airbag can increase the risk of injury in an accident.
- The storage, transportation and disposal of airbag units are subject to the laws for flammable solids.

CAUTION—

- If you lack the skills, tools and equipment, or a suitable workshop for any procedure described in this manual, we suggest you leave such repairs to an authorized Volkswagen dealer or other qualified shop. We especially urge you to consult an authorized Volkswagen dealer before beginning repairs on any car that may still be covered wholly or in part by any of the extensive warranties issued by Volkswagen of America, Inc.
- Volkswagen is constantly improving its cars and sometimes these changes, both in parts and specifications, are made applicable to earlier models. Therefore, part numbers listed in this manual are for reference only. Always check with your authorized Volkswagen dealer parts department for the latest information.
- Before starting a job, make certain that you have all the necessary tools and parts on hand. Read all the instructions thoroughly, do not attempt shortcuts. Use tools that are appropriate to the work and use only replacement parts meeting Volkswagen specifications. Makeshift tools, parts and procedures will not make good repairs.
- Use pneumatic and electric tools only to loosen threaded parts and fasteners. Never use these tools to tighten fasteners, especially on light alloy parts. Always use a torque wrench to tighten fasteners to the tightening torque specification listed.
- Be mindful of the environment and ecology. Before you drain the crankcase, find out the proper way to dispose of the oil. Do not pour oil onto the ground, down a drain, or into a stream, pond, or lake. Consult local ordinances that govern the disposal of wastes.
- When connecting cables or ground straps, all connections must be cleaned to bare metal. Be sure mounting bolts are tight.
- Do not replace fuse links with fuse links of other gauge or with standard wire. Always replace the entire length of the fuse link.
- Before doing any electrical welding on vehicles equipped with Anti-lock Brakes (ABS), disconnect the battery negative terminal (ground strap) and the ABS Control Module connector.
- On cars equipped with ABS, the ABS control unit cannot withstand temperatures from a paint–drying booth or a heat lamp in excess of 203°F (95°C) and should not be subjected to temperatures in excess of 185°F (85°C) for more than two hours.
- On cars equipped with anti-theft radios, make sure you know the correct radio activation code before disconnecting the battery or removing the radio. If the wrong code is entered when power is restored, the radio may lock up and be rendered inoperable, even if the correct code is then entered.
- When boost-charging the battery, first remove the fuses for the Engine Control Module (ECM), the Transmission Control Module (TCM), the ABS Control Module, and the On-Board computer. In cases where one or more of these components is not separately fused, disconnect the Control Module connector(s).
- Do not quick-charge the battery (for boost starting) for longer than one minute, and do not exceed 16.5 volts at the battery with the boosting cables attached. Wait at least one minute before boosting the battery a second time.

◀ **WARNINGS and CAUTIONS continued from previous page**

General

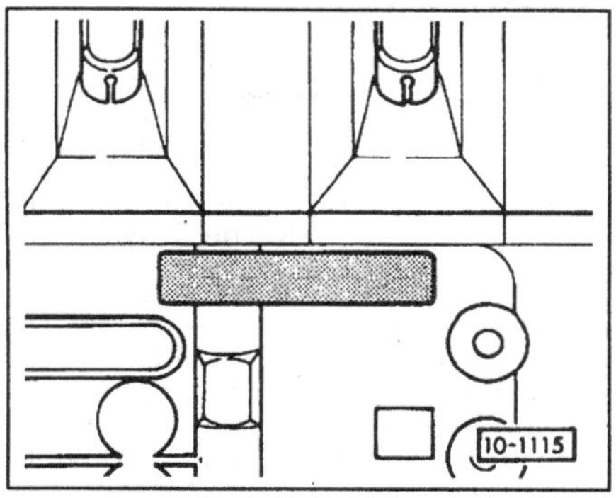

Engine number

- The "engine number" (Engine Code letters plus serial number) is stamped on the cylinder block between cylinders 1 and 3.
- There is also an "engine number" sticker attached to the toothed belt guard.
- The "engine number" is also displayed on the vehicle data plate.

Technical data, Engine Code AAF

Engine code		AAF
Manufactured		1993 m.y.
Displacement	ltr.	2.5
Output	kW at rpm	81/4500
Torque	Nm at rpm	190/2200
Bore	Ø mm	81
Stroke	mm	95.5
Compression ratio		8.5:1
RON (Octane)	min.	91 unleaded
Fuel Injection system		Digifant
Ignition system		Digifant
Firing order		1–2–4–5–3

Knock control system	NO
On Board Diagnostic system	YES
Three Way Catalytic converter	YES
Emission control system	YES

Technical data, Engine Code ACU

Engine code		ACU
Manufactured		03.94➤
Cylinder configuration		In-line 5 Cylinder
Displacement	ltr.	2.5
Output	kW at rpm SAE BHP at rpm	81/4500 105/4500
Torque	Nm at rpm SAE BHP at rpm	190[1]/2200 140/2200
Bore	∅ mm	81
Stroke	mm	95.5
Compression ratio		10.0:1
RON	minimum	91 unleaded [2]
Fuel Injection system		Digifant
Ignition system		Digifant
Firing order		1–2–4–5–3

[1] 195 Nm (144 ft lb) when using premium unleaded 95 RON

[2] RON 95 optional

Technical data, Engine Code ACU continued

Knock control system	YES
On Board Diagnostic system	YES
Oxygen sensor control system	YES
Three Way Catalytic converter	YES
Turbocharger	NO
Exhaust Gas Recirculation system	YES
Secondary Air Injection system	YES

Engine, removing and installing

Notes:

- *Remove the engine / transmission as an assembly, from below.*
- *All straps and wires that are removed or cut loose to remove the engine assembly must be replaced or re-used in the identical position and location as installed by production.*

Removing

– Switch OFF ignition

> ***CAUTION!***
> ***Obtain the radio anti-theft code BEFORE disconnecting the battery ground cable!***

– Disconnect battery ground cable

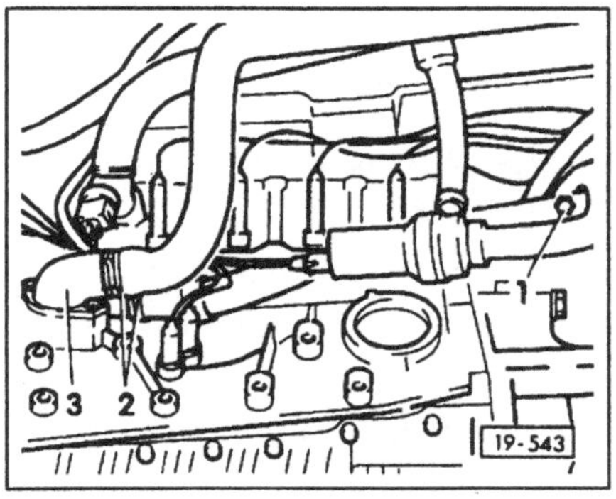

– Support the upper control arms by fitting 3250 left and right support wedges to the upper wishbones
⇒ Repair Group 40

– Remove sound–deadening pan

– Remove coolant expansion tank cap

◄ – Drain engine coolant, using either drain plug -1- and coolant hoses -2- or via thermostat connection -3-

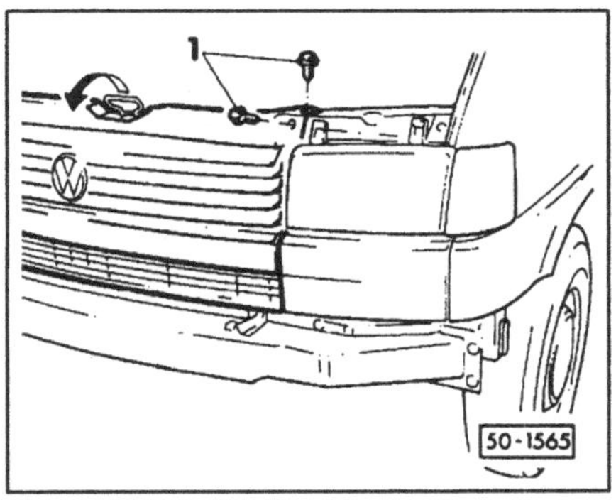

◄ – Remove mounting bolts -1- from left and right

– Tilt the radiator and lock carrier forward (arrow)

– Disconnect coolant fan and thermoswitch

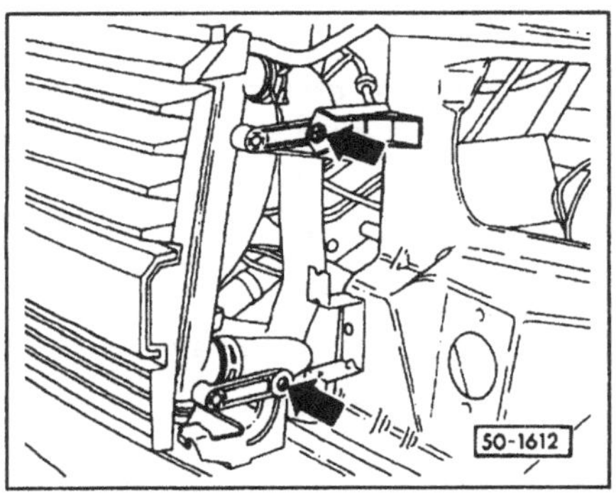

◄ – Drive pins out of right and left radiator bracket expansion clip (arrow)

– Remove radiator assembly complete with hood lock assembly/ coolant hoses

– Disconnect speedometer drive at transmission connection point

– Detach accelerator cable at throttle body and support bracket

– Disconnect clutch cable (or slave cylinder if hydraulic)
⇒ Repair Group 30

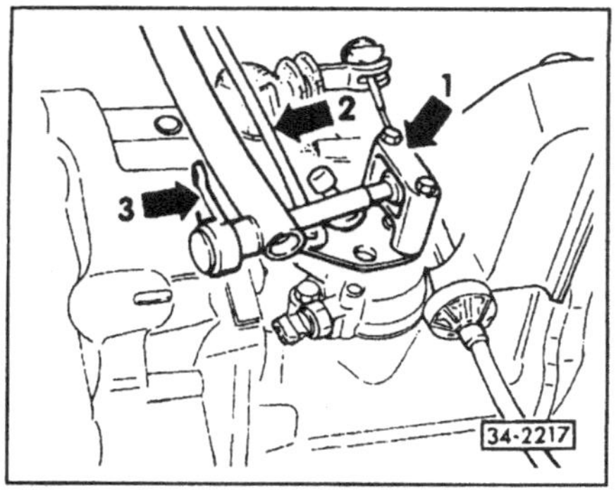

- Disconnect and neatly tuck away the engine, transmission, generator and starter wiring
- Disconnect all coolant, vacuum and intake hoses from the engine
- Disconnect fuel supply line (black) at the T-piece and return line (blue) at the fuel rail
- ◄ Disconnect shift mechanism from transmission as follows:
- Remove clevis -1- (arrow)
- Pry up shift lever at front from gear control lever (arrow 2)
- Disconnect selector rod from bearing block (arrow 3)
- Disconnect oil lines from power steering pump and allow hydraulic fluid to drain

Vehicles with A/C

> ***CAUTION!***
> ***The A/C refrigerant circuit must NOT be opened. Use extreme care when handling refrigerant hoses, they are sensitive to kinking.***

- Remove left-hand drive shaft and detach right-hand drive shaft at transmission
- Remove front exhaust pipe complete with oxygen sensor
- Disconnect supply and return lines from power steering pump

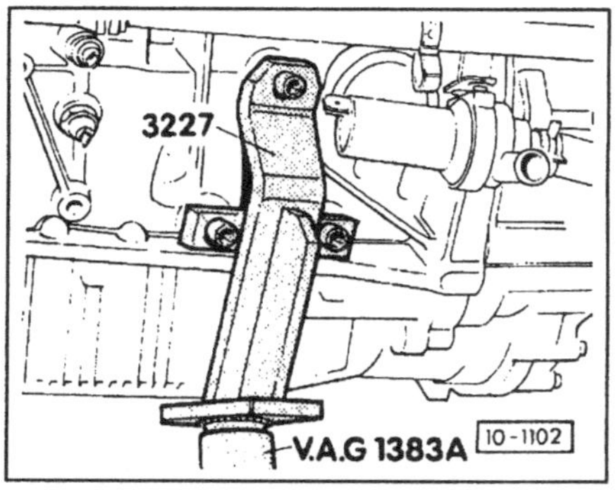

- ◄ Bolt 3227 engine takeup bracket to cylinder block
  - ♦ Approx. 20 Nm (15 ft lb)
- Slightly raise engine and transmission using VAG 1383A engine/transmission lift

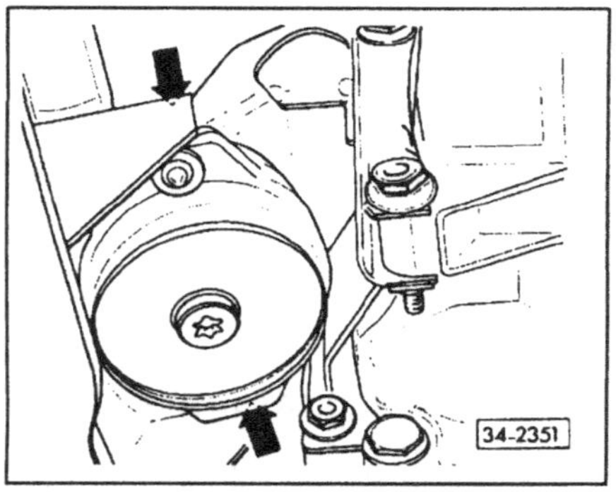

- ◄ Remove both mounting bolts (arrows) from transmission mounting bracket
- Remove central bolts for engine and transmission mounts on right and left side of engine compartment
- Remove engine/transmission assembly downwards while guiding power steering pump oil return line away

> ***CAUTION!***
> ***Carefully guide the engine and transmission assembly during removal, to avoid damage to the body.***

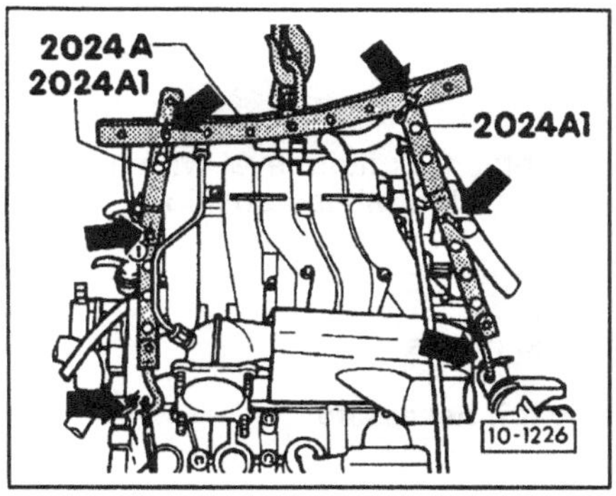

Mounting engine on repair stand

– Separate engine and transmission

◄ – Attach lifting tackle and extensions (two) as shown

– Lift engine using hoist

> ***CAUTION!***
> ***Use locking pins on the hooks and marking pins (arrows).***

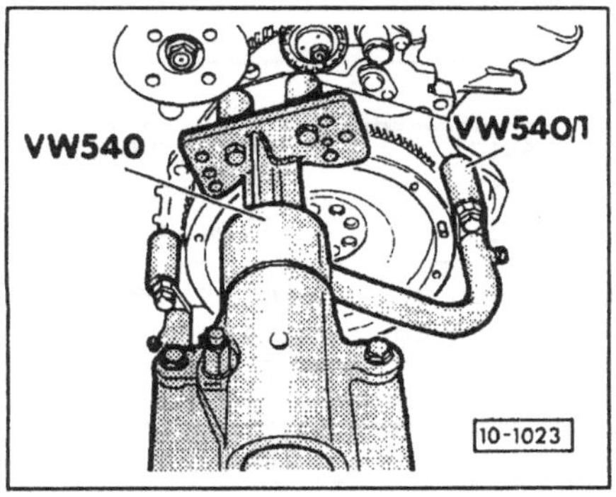

◄ – Attach VW 540 engine mounting bracket to engine, then attach engine to repair stand

Installing

Installation is the reverse of removal, note the following points:

– Check clutch release bearing for wear, replace if necessary

– Lightly lubricate clutch release bearing and input shaft using: G 000 100

♦ Do not lubricate the release bearing guide sleeve

– Check that centering dowels are properly positioned in cylinder block; install if necessary

– Fit intermediate plate onto lightly greased centering dowels and secure to cylinder block

– Align engine onto mounts without force, without tension, align by rocking if necessary

– Adjust throttle cable
⇒ Repair Group 20

– Do not confuse fuel supply line (black) on T-piece with return line (blue) on fuel rail

– Install front exhaust pipe (complete with oxygen sensor)

– Align exhaust system, free of tension
⇒ Repair Group 26

– Electrical connections and wire routing
⇒ Repair Group 97

– Fill (replace) system with coolant
⇒ Repair Group 19

– Check transmission shift operation and adjust if necessary
⇒ Repair Group 34

– Fill reservoir with hydraulic oil

♦ G 002 000

- Start engine and let idle
- Turn steering to left and right; check fluid level with engine running and front wheels in straight-ahead position
- Top up hydraulic oil if necessary
    - ♦ fill between min. and max. marks
- Check ignition timing, adjust if necessary
⇒ Repair Group 28
- Check idle speed
- Check headlight alignment, adjust as necessary

Tightening torques:		
Engine to transmission	M12 M10 M8	80 Nm (59 ft lb) 60 Nm (44 ft lb) 20 Nm (15 ft lb)
Bracket/transmission mount	M10 x 60 M10 x 28	65 Nm (48 ft lb) 45 Nm (33 ft lb)
Engine/transmission mount	M10	65 Nm (48 ft lb)
Cardan shaft at drive flange		55 Nm (41 ft lb)

Vehicles with A/C

CAUTION!

- ***The A/C refrigerant circuit must NOT be opened to the atmosphere***
- ***Refrigerant hoses are sensitive to kinking***
- ***The refrigerant circuit can only be opened in workshops with specially trained personnel and the required special tools and equipment***

If engine was removed/installed without opening refrigerant circuit

- Remove A/C compressor and secure to one side such that A/C hoses are not stressed

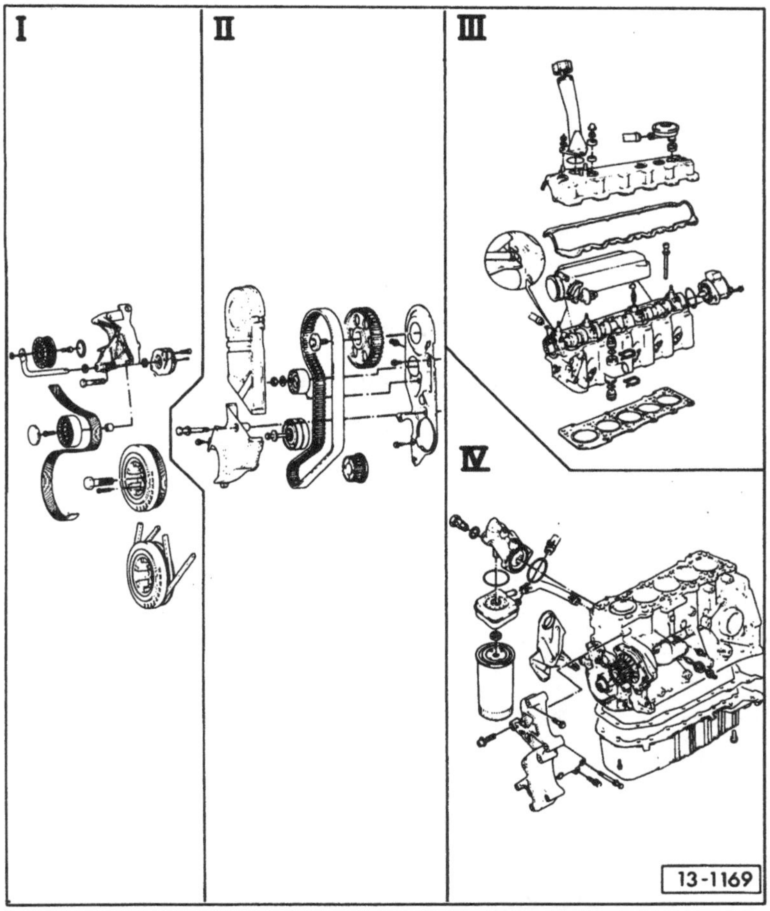

Engine, disassembling and reassembling

Engine assembly, section overview

> ***CAUTION!***
> ***If as a result of engine damage, metal chips or metal powder are observed in the engine oil; thoroughly clean all of the engine oil passages, then replace the oil cooler and oil filter.***

- Always replace all gaskets and seals

I - Page C 13-2

II - Page C 13-4

III - Page C 13-6

IV - Page C 13-9

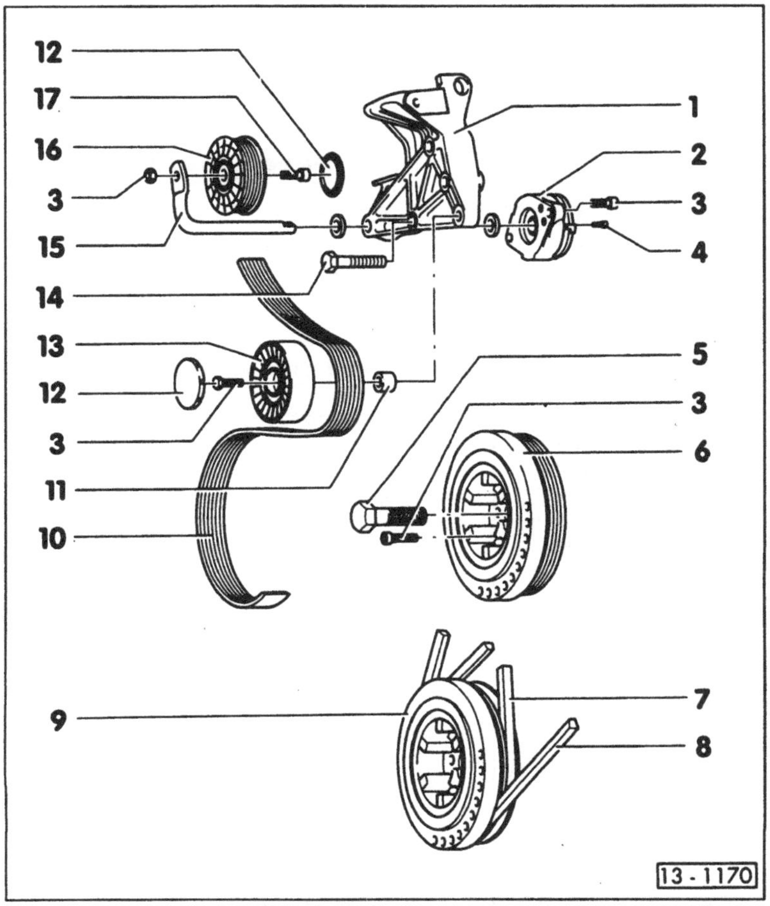

I - Engine pulleys, component layout

1 - Pulley mounting bracket
- for ribbed belt tension adjustment
- removing and installing:

⇒ page C 13-12

2 - Tensioner element for pulley

3 - 20 Nm (15 ft lb)

4 - 10 Nm (7 ft lb)

5 - 460 Nm (340 ft lb)
- coat threads and contact surfaces of bolt head with AMV 188 001 02
- use tool 3248 to loosen and tighten

⇒ page C 13-14

6 - Vibration damper
- damper and toothed belt pulley can only be mounted one way

7 - Not applicable to US vehicles

8 - Not applicable to US vehicles

9 - Not applicable to US vehicle

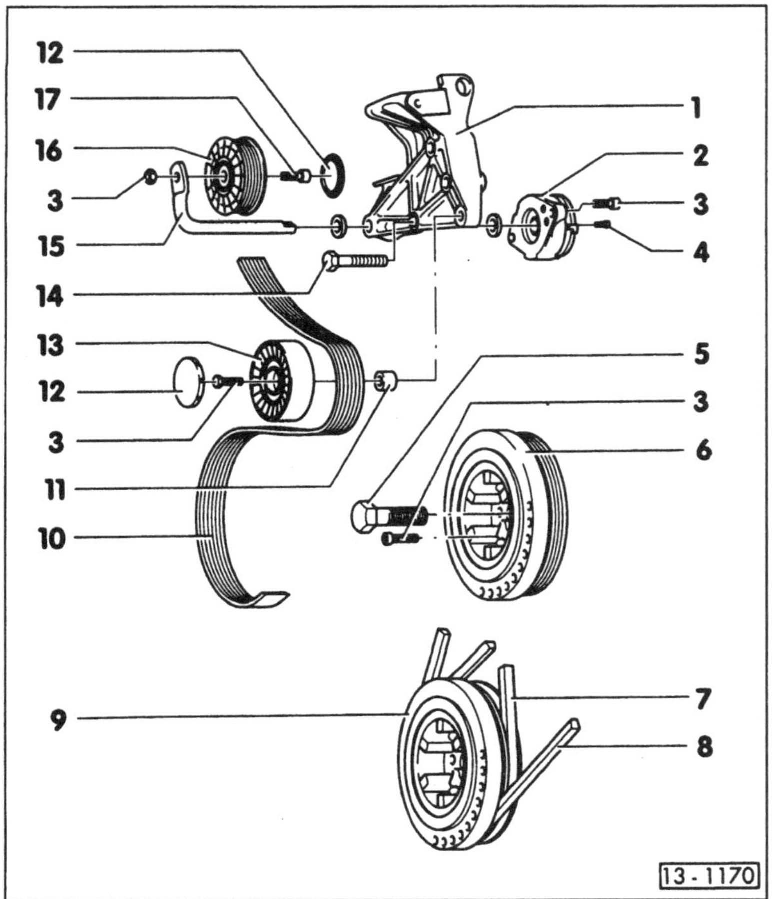

10 - Ribbed belt
- mark running direction with felt pen before removal
- remove and install using 3299 tool:

⇒ page C 13-12
- check for wear

11 - Spacer bushing

12 - Protective cap

13 - Idler pulley

14 - 40 Nm (30 ft lb)

15 - Tensioning lever

16 - Tensioner pulley

17 - Pulley mounting bolt

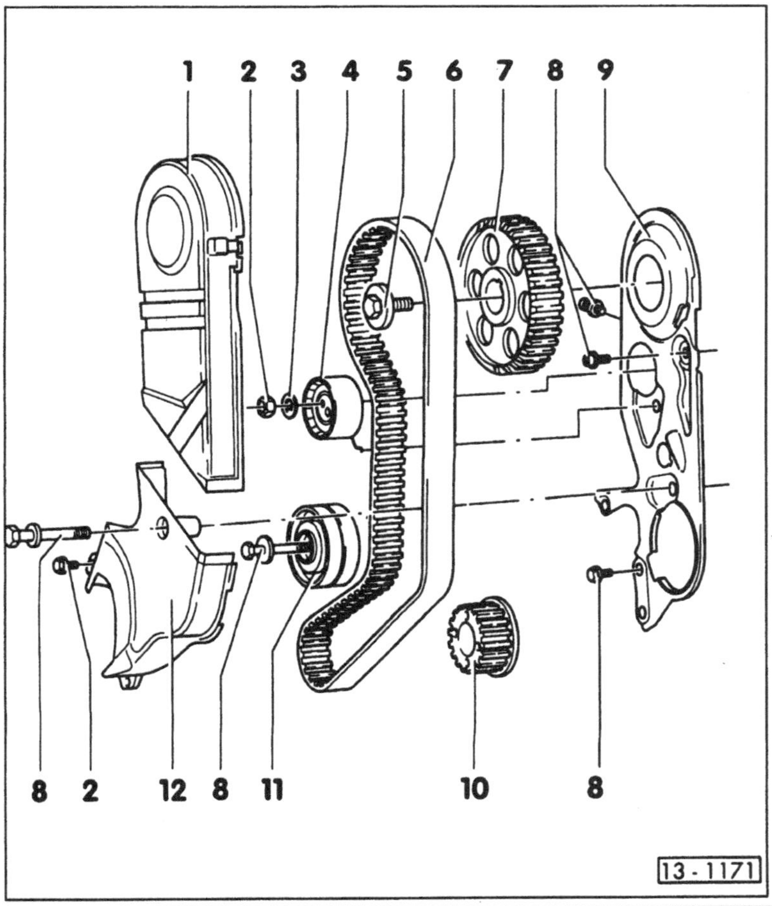

II - Toothed belt assembly, component layout

1 - Toothed belt cover, upper

2 - 20 Nm (15 ft lb)
- mounting nut for tensioner pulley
  15 Nm (11 ft lb)

3 - Washer
- with crimps to prevent rotation

4 - Tensioner pulley
- toothed belt, removing and installing:

⇒ page C 13-13

5 - Mounting bolt for camshaft drive sprocket
- note raised lettering on bolt head to determine tightening torque:
  8.8 = 85 Nm (63 ft lb)
  10.9 = 100 Nm (74 ft lb)
- use 3036 countering tool to loosen and tighten

6 - Toothed belt
- removing and installing:

⇒ page C 13-13
- tensioning:

⇒ page C 13-17

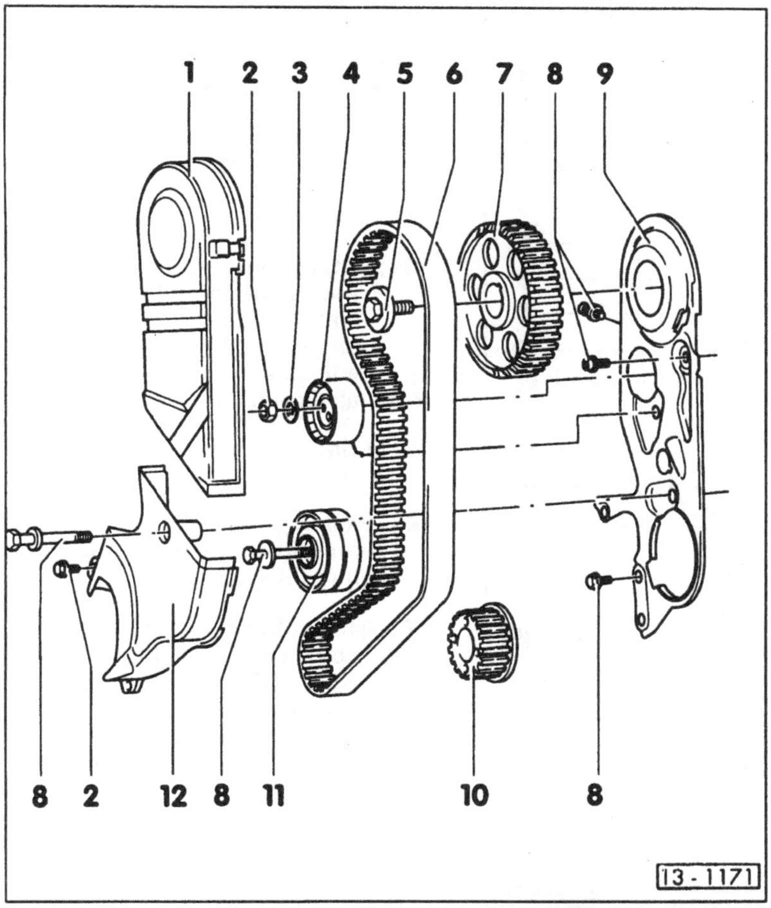

7 - **Camshaft drive sprocket**
- note orientation during toothed belt installation:

⇒ page C 13-17

8 - **10 Nm (7 ft lb)**

9 - **Rear toothed belt guard**
- to remove, take off vibration damper (if necessary)

10 - **Toothed belt sprocket (crankshaft)**

11 - **Idler pulley**

12 - **Lower toothed belt guard**
- removing:
- – remove vibration damper,if necessary

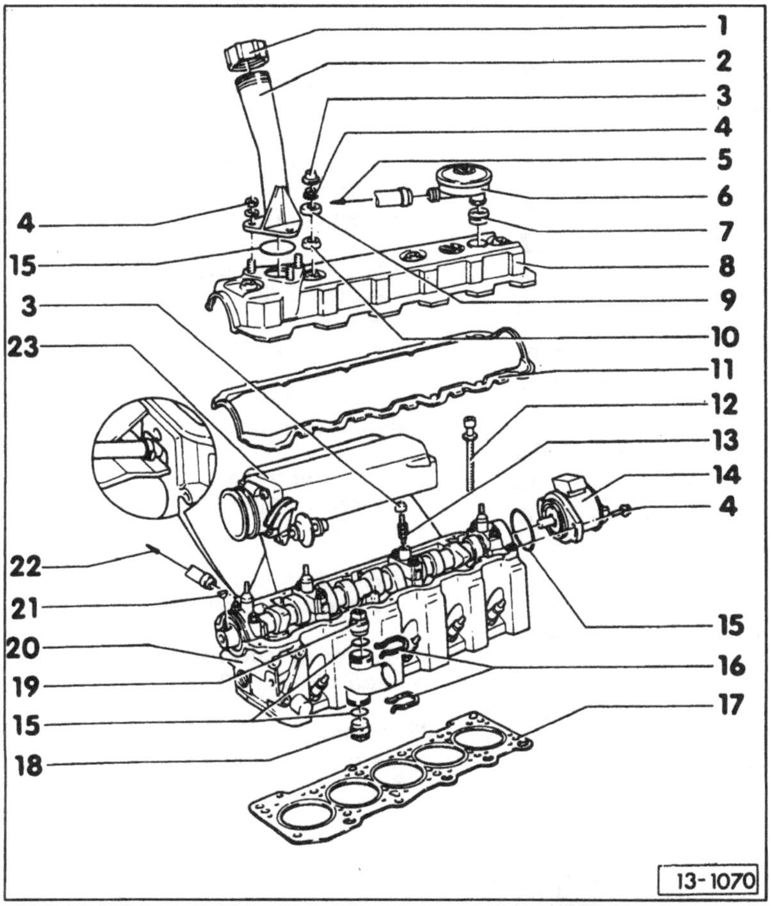

III - Cylinder head, component layout

1 - **Oil filler cap**

2 - **Oil filler pipe**

3 - **End cap**

4 - **10 Nm (7 ft lb)**

5 - **to intake hose**
- vent hose mounted to oil filler pipe (item 2) via bracket
- ensure sufficient clearance between throttle connection

6 - **Positive Crankcase Ventilation valve**

7 - **Seal**
- replace if damaged

8 - **Valve cover**
- with oil deflector

9 - **Dished washer**

10 - **Top sealing ring**
- replace if damaged

11 - **Valve cover gasket**
- replace if damaged

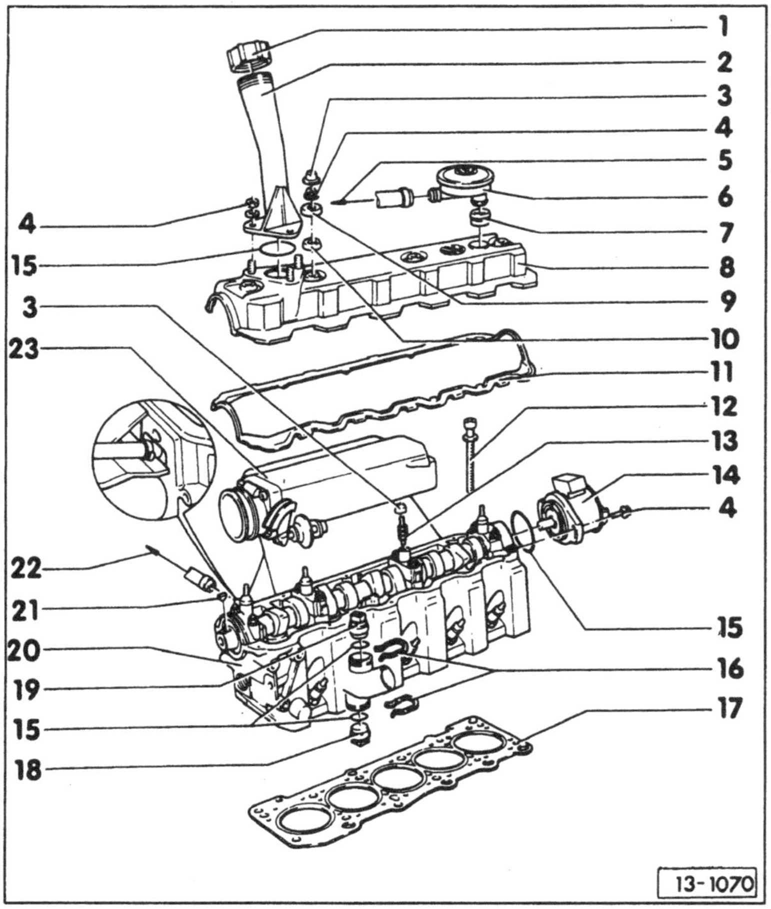

12 - **Cylinder head bolt**
- note loosening and tightening sequence in the installation instructions:

⇒ Repair Group 15

13 - **15 Nm (11 ft lb)**

14 - **Ignition distributor**
- note position of drive-shaft slot when installing
- ignition timing,checking and adjusting:

⇒ Repair Group 28

15 - **O-ring**
- replace if damaged

16 - **Retaining clip**
- for Engine Coolant Temperature (ECT) sensor

17 - **Cylinder head gasket**
- note installation position
- word "OBEN" must face toward cylinder head
- if gasket is replaced, completely replace coolant

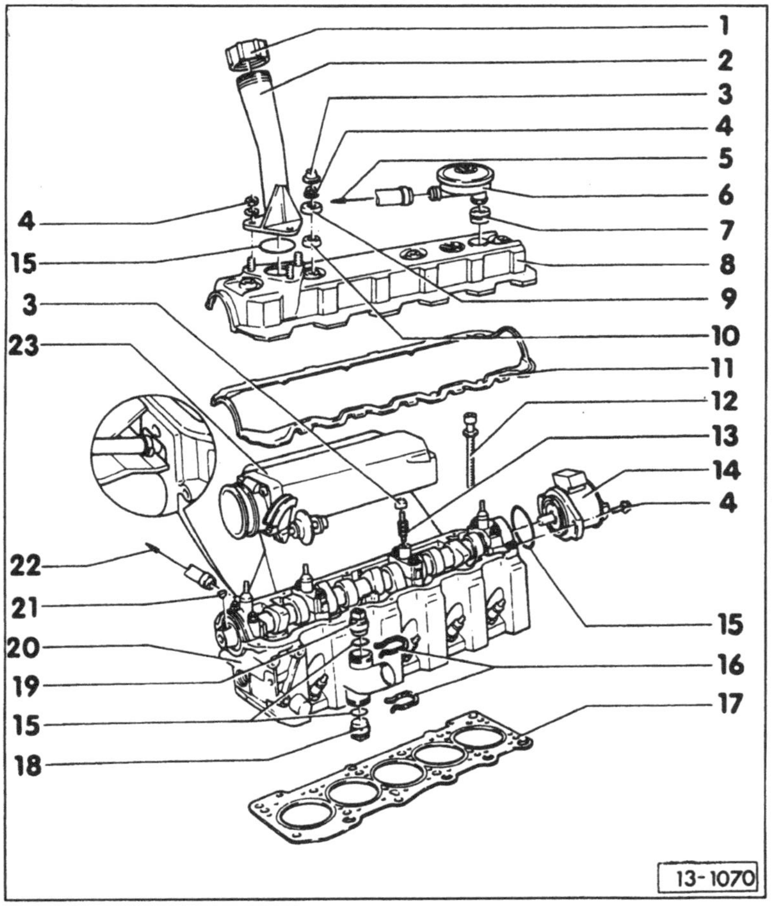

18 - **Coolant Circulation Engine Coolant Temperature Thermal switch F 51 and Engine Coolant Temperature sensor G2**
- yellow, 4-pin
- Thermal switch, checking:

⇒ Repair Group 19

19 - **Engine Coolant Temperature sensor G62**
- blue, 2-pin
- for Digifant fuel and ignition system
- checking:

⇒ Repair Group 24

20 - **Cylinder head**
- removing/installing:

⇒ Repair Group 15

21 - **Woodruff key**
- check for tight fit

22 - **to tee on coolant expansion tank**

⇒ Repair Group 19

23 - **Intake manifold**
- removing and installing:

⇒ Repair Group 24

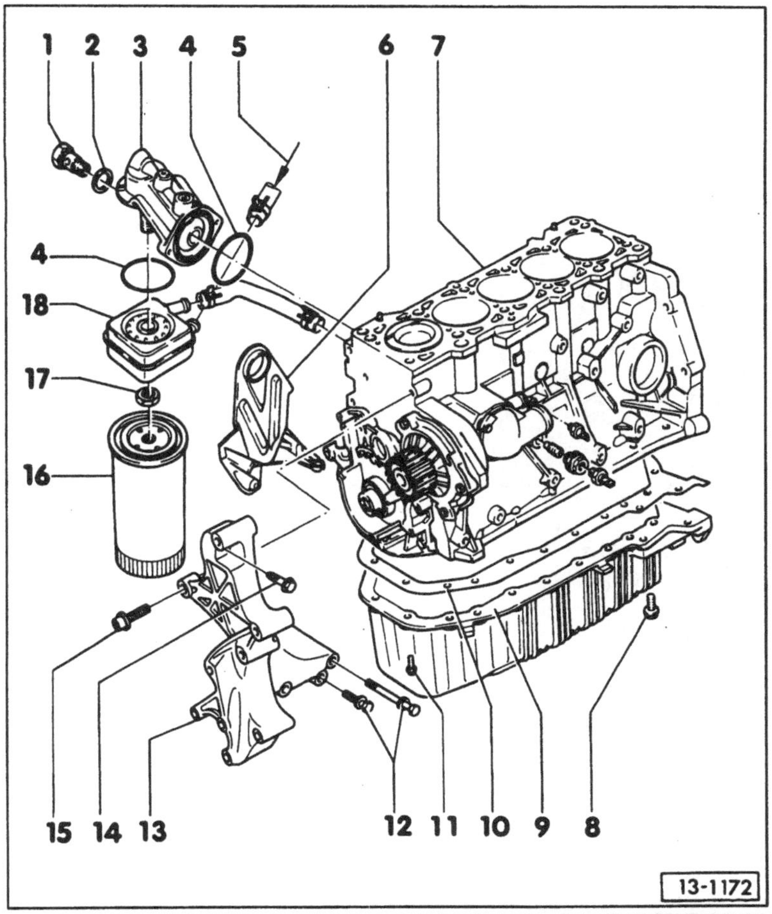

IV - Lubrication system, component layout

1 - 70 Nm (52 ft lb)

2 - Sealing ring
- ♦ replace

3 - Oil filter bracket
- ♦ positioning (during installation) determined by centering pins
- ♦ with oil return check valves to maintain oil supply/pressure to hydraulic valve lifters

4 - O-ring
- ♦ replace if damaged

5 - from coolant hose:

⇒ Repair Group 19

6 - Oil collecting tray

7 - Engine block
- ♦ cylinder block, crankshaft, flywheel, disassembly and reassembly:

⇒ page C 13-22

8 - 20 Nm (15 ft lb)
- ♦ install M8 bolts with hex head on transmission side

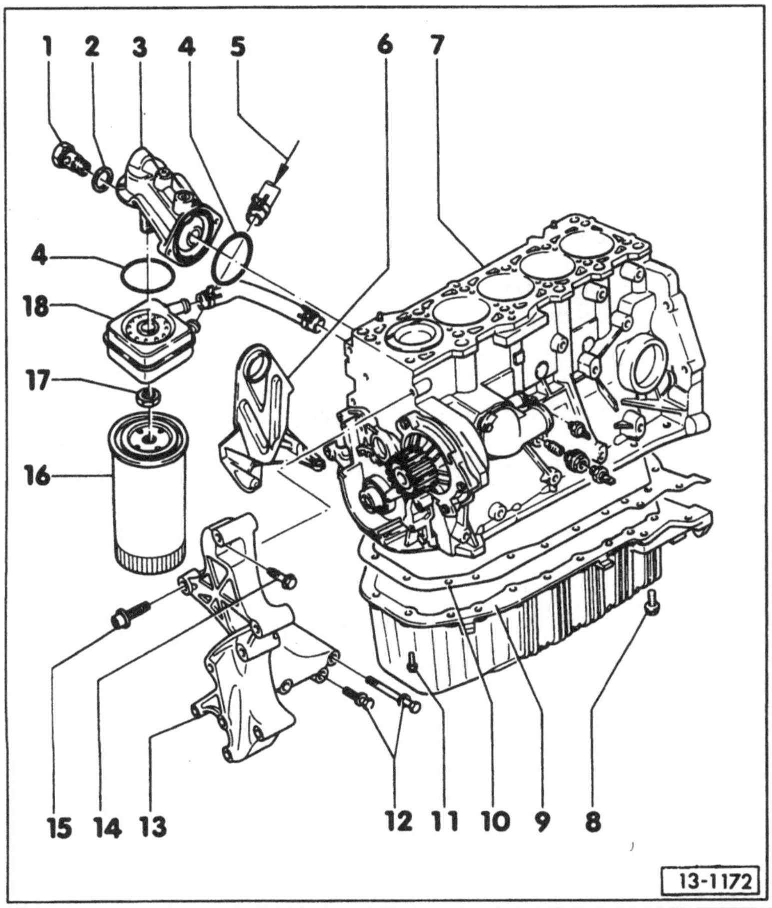

9 - Oil pan

10 - Gasket for oil pan
- ♦ replace
- ♦ do not bond with adhesives
- ♦ check for correct fit

11 - 10 Nm (7 ft lb)
- ♦ remove/install M6 bolts using 3249 insert
- ♦ with flywheel installed: rotate flywheel so that opening aligns with bolt

12 - 40 Nm (30 ft lb)

13 - Bracket

14 - 20 Nm (15 ft lb)
- ♦ attach to cylinder head

15 - 20 Nm (15 ft lb)

16 - Oil filter
- ♦ loosen using 2067
- ♦ follow manufacturers installation instructions printed on oil filter
- ♦ hand tighten only

17 - 25 Nm (18 ft lb)

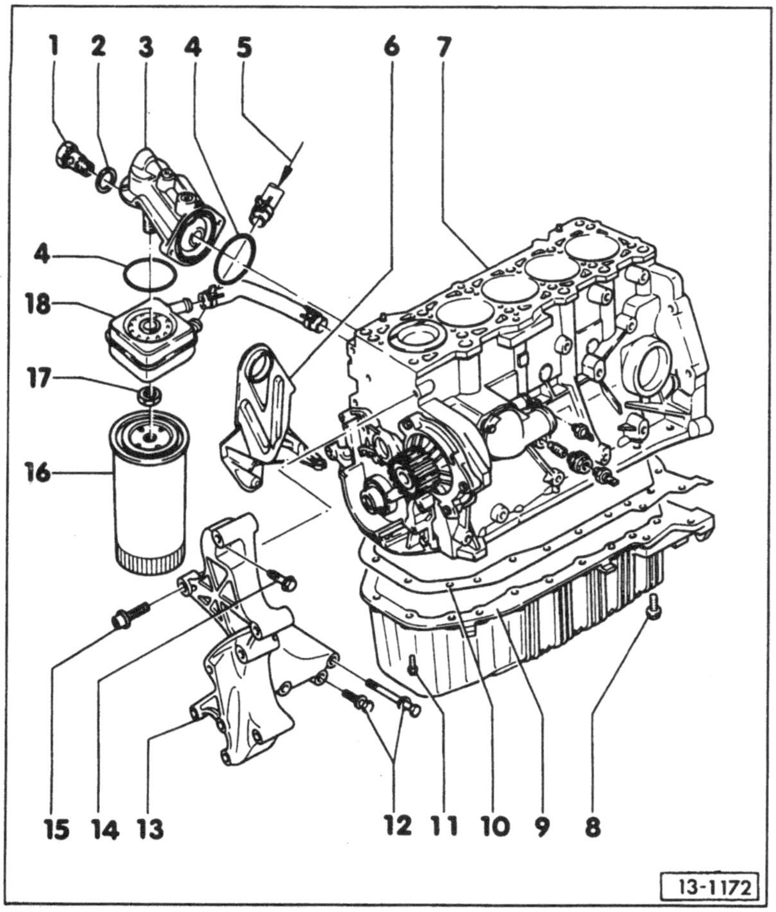

18 - Oil cooler

⇒ Caution page C 13-1

- coat contact surfaces of the flange outside of the sealing ring using: AMV 188100 02
- ensure sufficient clearance between adjacent components

Ribbed belt, removing and installing

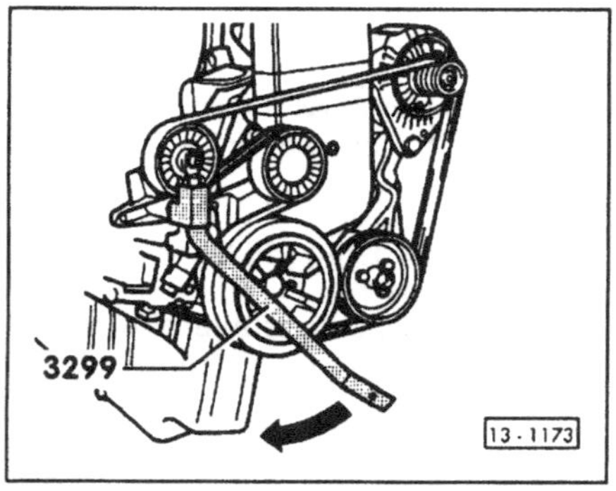

Before removing ribbed belt:

– Mark engine direction of rotation using felt tip marker

When installing ribbed belt:

– Ensure that belt is centered and ribs are correctly seated in belt pulley grooves

◄ Belt drive without A/C:

– Loosen tensioner pulley with 3299 lever

– Remove or install ribbed belt

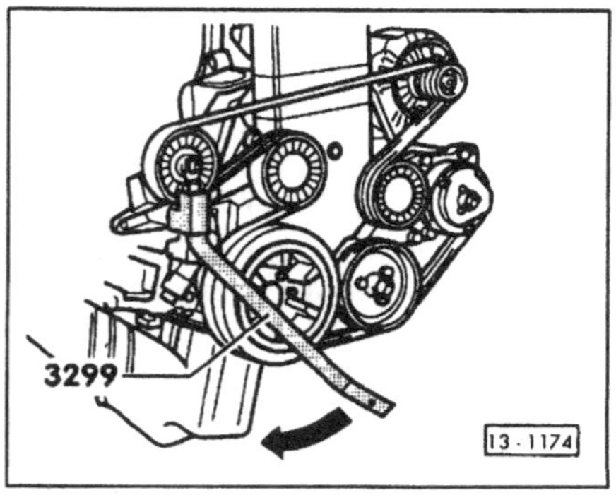

◄ Belt drive with A/C:

– Loosen tensioner pulley with 3299 lever

– Remove or install ribbed belt

Toothed belt, removing and installing

Removing

- Remove ribbed belt, vibration damper, upper and lower belt guards:
⇒ page C 13-12

- Mark running direction of toothed belt using felt tip marker

- Loosen tensioner pulley and/or coolant pump

- Remove toothed belt

Installing

- Ensure that crankshaft is at TDC

- Place belt on crankshaft sprocket, tensioner and coolant pump

  - ♦ Note running direction per previously–applied marking

- Install lower toothed belt guard

- Fit M8 securing bolt for coolant pump

  - ♦ If sprocket is present, tighten to 20 Nm (15 ft lb)

- Secure vibration damper with crankshaft sprocket

  - ♦ -4- M8 bolts, 20 Nm (15 ft lb)

- Coat center bolt threads and surface contacting portion of bolt head with: AMV 188 001 02

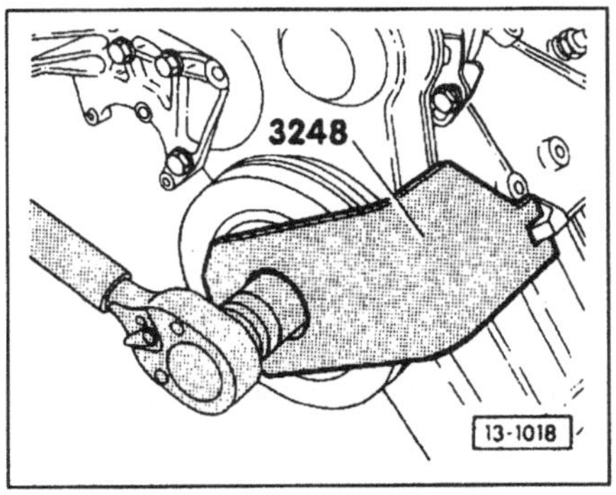

◄ - Fit tool 3248 and secure vibration damper/crankshaft sprocket

  - ♦ Tightening torque: 460 Nm (339 ft lb)

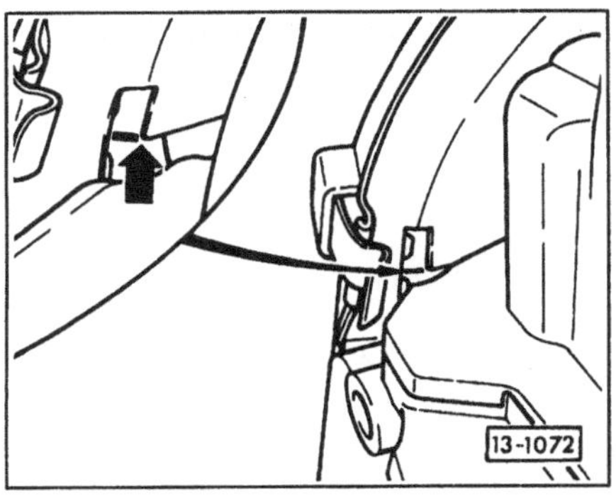

◄ - Align camshaft sprocket to cylinder 1 TDC mark

- Align mark on camshaft sprocket and mark on toothed belt guard at rear (arrow)

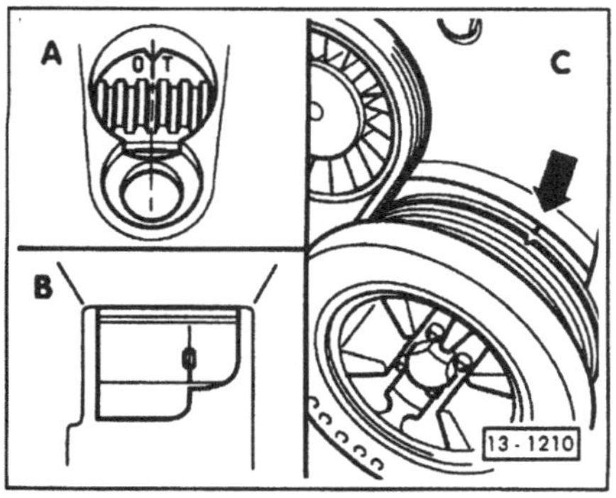

◄ A–With engine installed:

– Rotate flywheel -A- or drive plate -B- to TDC (No. 1 cylinder)

B–With engine removed:

– Align mark on vibration damper -C- with mark on bottom of toothed belt guard

Toothed belt, tensioning

Vehicles with tensioner pulley

Requirement

♦ Engine cold

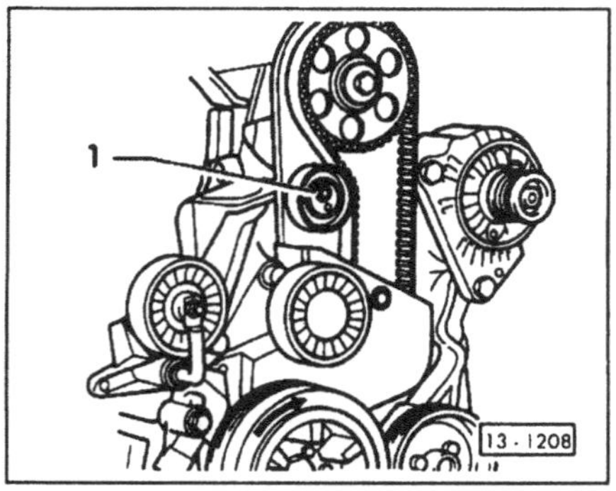

◄ – With nut 1 loosened, check tensioner pulley for ease of movement and place toothed belt on camshaft sprocket

– Rotate engine (manually) approx. 2 revolutions until just before TDC

– To tension toothed belt: continue to slowly turn crankshaft to TDC

♦ Crankshaft must not spring back

– Tighten tensioner pulley nut

♦ Tightening torque: 15 Nm (10 ft lb)

– Rotate crankshaft two complete revolutions and check adjustment

– Install upper belt guard

– Check ignition timing and adjust if necessary:
⇒ Repair Group 28

– Re-install ribbed belt:
⇒ page C 13-12

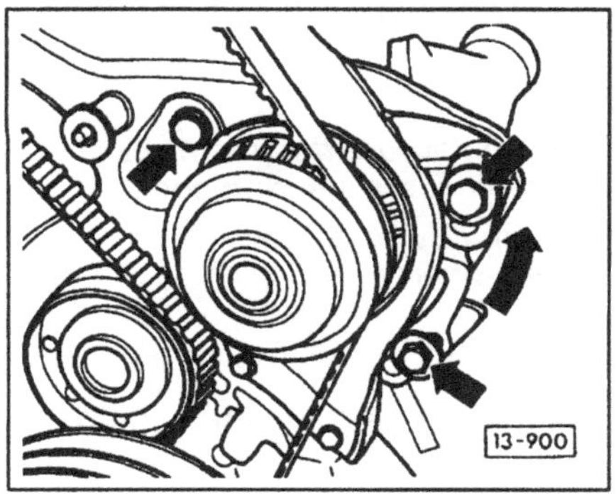

Vehicles without tensioner pulley

– Place toothed belt on camshaft sprocket

◄ – Tension toothed belt by turning loosened coolant pump upward and to the left

Engines with high mileage

– Remove coolant pump

– Clean sealing surfaces and replace O-ring

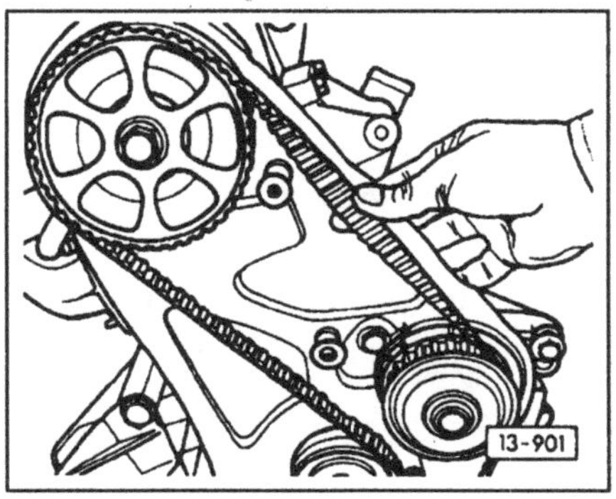

◄ – Check tension by twisting toothed belt (in middle, between camshaft sprocket and coolant pump) through a 90 degree angle using thumb and forefinger

– Tighten coolant pump

♦ -3- M8 bolts, 20 Nm (15 ft lb)

– Adjust power steering pump drive belt:
⇒ Repair Group 48

– Adjust generator drive belt tension

Generator V-belt, adjusting

For vehicles with toothed bracket adjusting mechanism

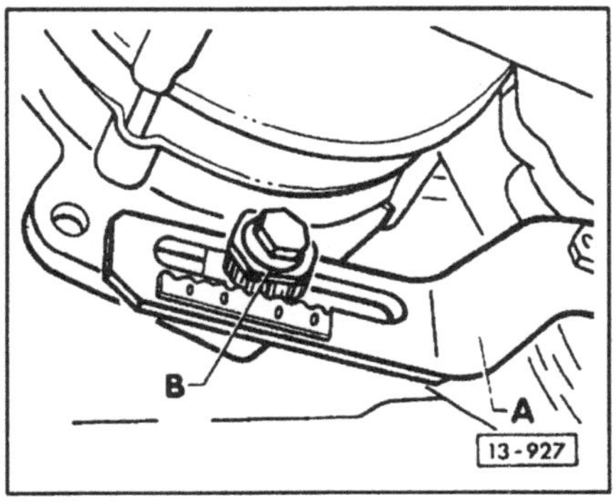

◄ – Loosen all mounting bolts for tension adjusting bracket -A- and for the generator by at least one extra turn

♦ The mounting bolts should be loose enough for the generator to swing freely under its own weight

– Tension V-belt by turning tensioning nut –B–

♦ 8 Nm (72 in. lb)

– Tighten tensioning nut mounting screw

♦ 35 Nm (26 ft lb)

– Tighten all mounting bolts for adjusting bracket -A- and generator

– Start engine and let idle for approx. 5 minutes

– Switch OFF ignition

– Tighten V-belt again

♦ 8 Nm (72 in. lb)

Note:

The VAG 1410 torque wrench in conjunction with the SW 22-VAG 1410/2 ring insert tool is especially adapted for these adjustments.

Ribbed belt tensioner, removing and installing

Note:

- *When lowering the engine, make sure that the front of the exhaust pipe does not lie against the steering gear*
- *When pushing the engine forward make sure that none of the wires and hoses are stretched too far*

- Remove left and right mounting bolts -1-
- Tilt radiator and upper radiator support forward (arrow)
- Remove Air Cleaner housing
- Remove power steering lines bracket screws from tensioner bracket and engine mount
- Remove noise damping pan
- Remove ribbed belt using 3299 wrench ⇒ page C 13-12
- Disconnect right drive shaft at transmission drive flange ⇒ Repair Group 40

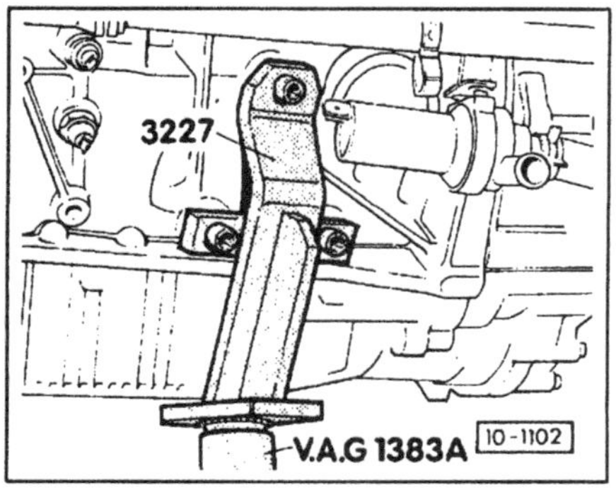

◄
- Attach 3327 engine support to cylinder block
  - Tighten to approx. 20 Nm (15 ft lb)
- Support engine and transmission using VAG 1383A support

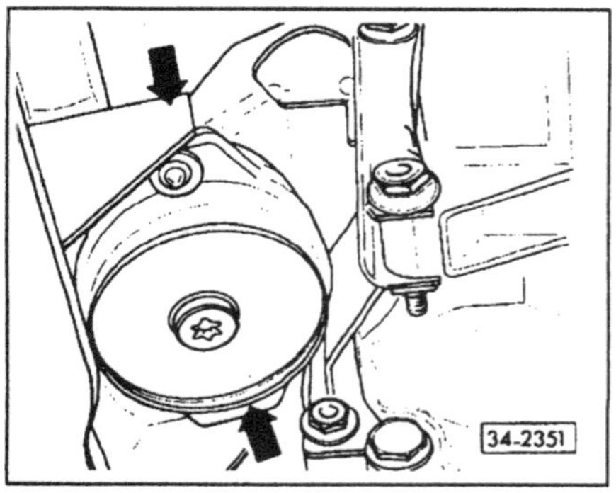

◄
- Remove 2 mounting bolts (arrows) from transmission bearing mount at subassembly
- Loosen center bolt for left engine/transmission bearing mount one turn
- Remove right center engine mount bolt

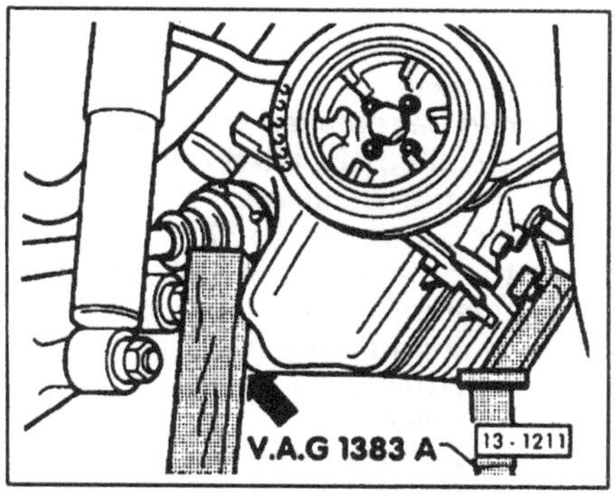

◄ – Lower engine as far as possible using VAG 1383A

– Push engine forward and secure to prevent swinging (arrow)

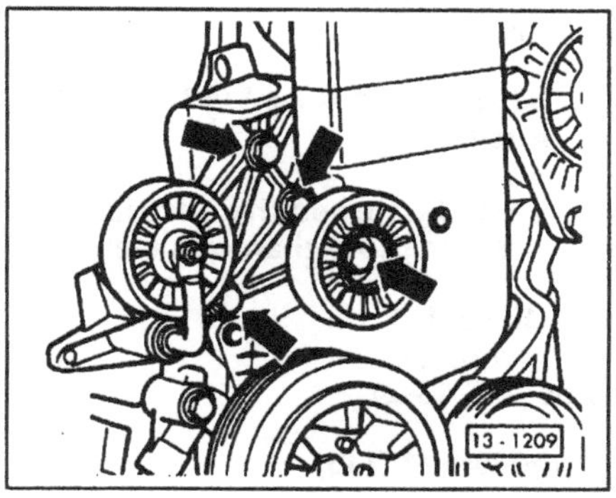

◄ – Remove ribbed belt idler pulley (arrow)

– Remove ribbed belt tensioner pulley

– Completely remove tensioner bracket (arrows)
⇒ page C 13-12

– Installation is reverse of removal sequence

Tightening torques:

Engine mount central bolts	65 Nm	(48 ft lb)
Drive shaft to flange	55 Nm	(41 ft lb)
Transmission mount to sub–assembly	45 Nm	(33 ft lb)
Tensioner/engine mount bracket to cylinder block	40 Nm	(30 ft lb)

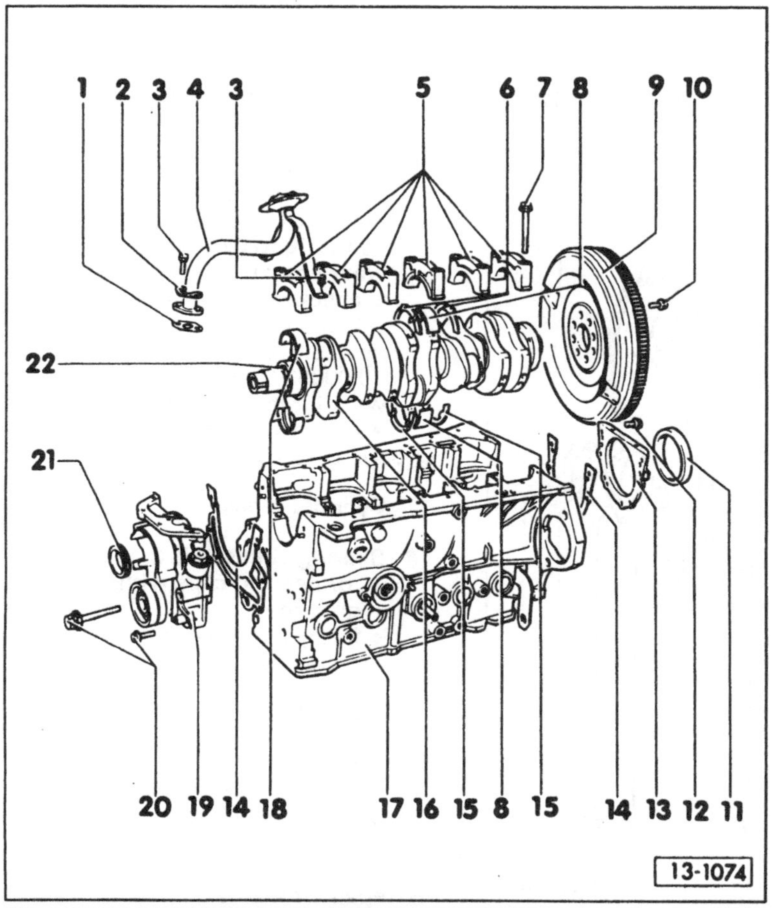

Engineblock,crankshaft, and flywheel, disassembling and assembling

For clutch repair procedures:
⇒ Repair Group 30

1 - Gasket
- replace

2 - Locking plate

3 - 10 Nm (7 ft lb)

4 - Intake pipe

5 - Bearing cap
- bearing cap 1 = pulley end
- bearing cap 6 = flywheel end
- retaining lugs on bearing shells must be opposite one another

6 - Thrust washer
- for bearing cap
- note retainer

7 - 65 Nm (48 ft lb)

8 - Bearing shell 4
- fitted bearing
- for cylinder block location with oil groove
- for bearing cap w/o oil groove

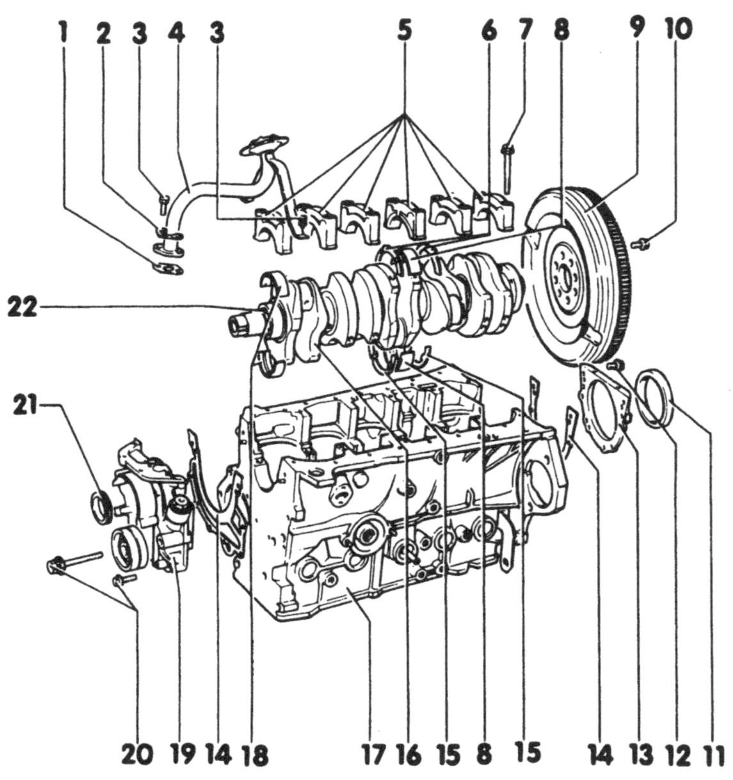

13-1074

9 - Flywheel
- can be replaced with the egine installed after first removing the transmission:

⇒ Repair Groups 34 or 37
- to remove and install: lock in position using 3067 tool
- ignition timing mark, inscribing:

⇒ page C 13-29
- drive plate removing and installing (vehicles with automatic transmission):

⇒ page C 13-30

10 - 30 Nm (22 ft lb) + 1/4 turn (90°) further
- replace
- can be turned the additional 90° in more than one step

11 - Oil seal
- replacing:

⇒ page C 13-27

12 - 10 Nm (7 ft lb)

13 - Oil seal mounting flange

14 - Gasket
- replace

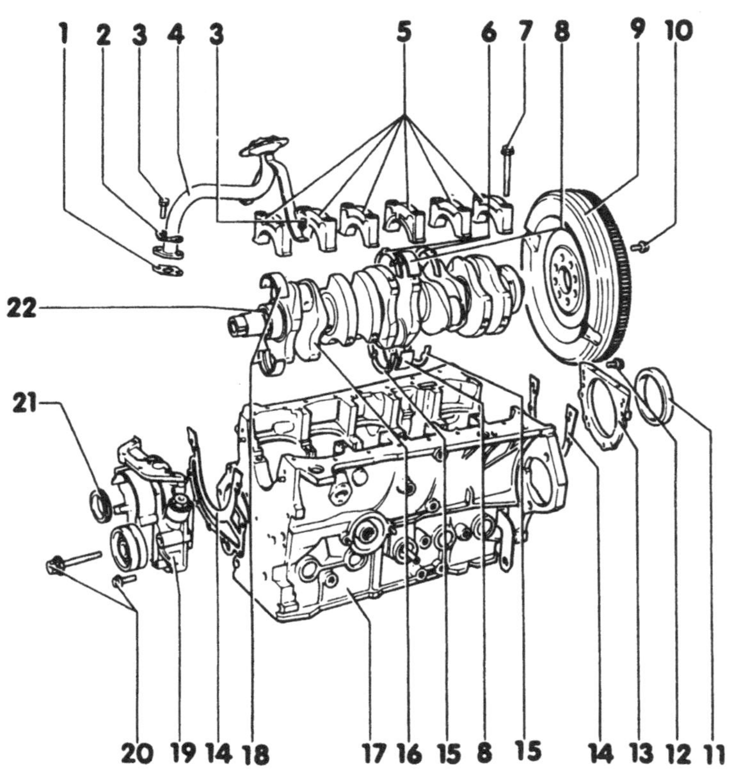

13-1074

15 - Thrust washer
- for cylinder block
- note retainers

16 - Crankshaft
- axial clearance

new: 0.07 to 0.18 mm (0.00276 to 0.00709 in.)
wear limit: 0.25 mm (0.00984 in.)
- check radial clearance with Plastigage

new: 0.016 to 0.075 mm (0.00063 to 0.00295 in.)
wear limit: 0.16 mm (0.00629 in.)
- crankshaft dimensions:

⇒ page C 13-28

17 - Cylinder block

18 - Bearing shells 1, 2, 3, 5 and 6
- for bearing caps without oil groove
- for cylinder block location with oil groove
- do not interchange used bearing shells

19 - Oil pump
- only replace as an assembly
- when installing, note drive dog on crankshaft (item 22 on illus.)
- removing and installing:

⇒ Repair Group 17

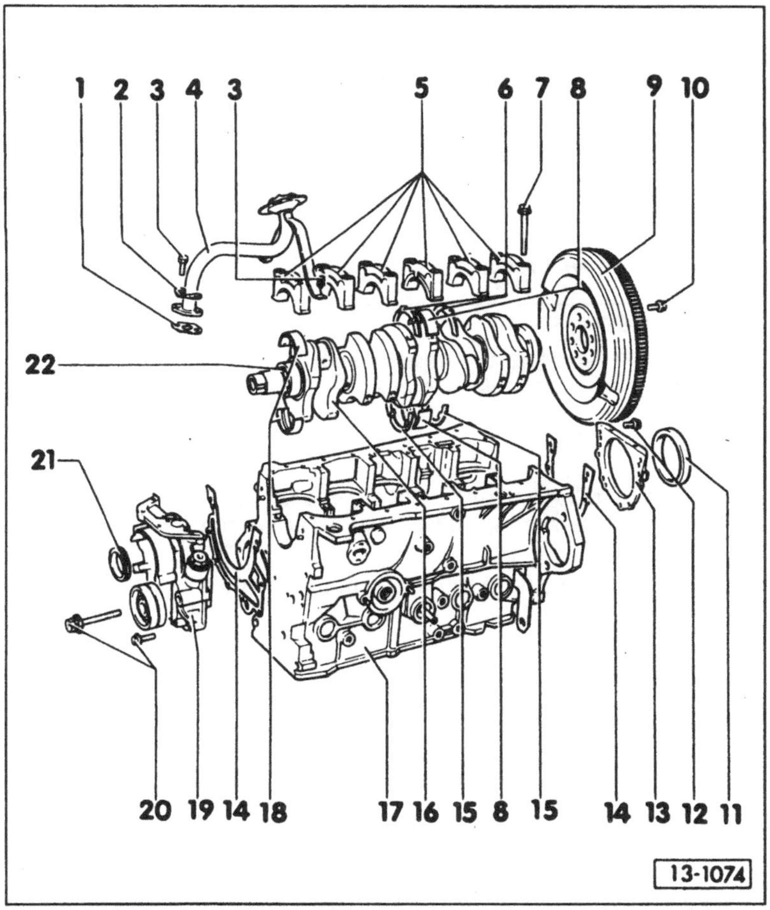

20 - M8 = 20 Nm (15 ft lb)
M6 = 10 Nm (7 ft lb)

21 - Oil seal
- replacing:

⇒ page C 13-26

22 - Drive dog for oil pump
- with 4 drive pins
- split to remove
- heat to 200°C (392 °F), maximum, before installing new drive dog

Crankshaft oil seal (pulley end), replacing

– Remove toothed belt
⇒ page C 13-13
⇒

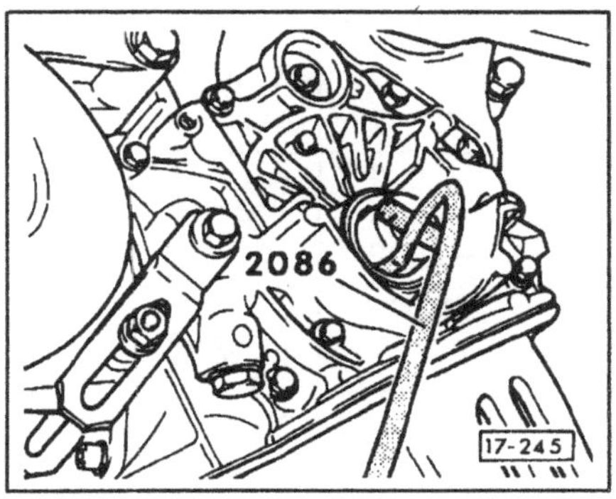

◄ – Remove vibration damper and toothed belt sprocket

- Counter-hold with tool 3248 to loosen the center bolt

– Press out oil seal using 2086

– Lightly oil sealing lip and outer edge of oil seal

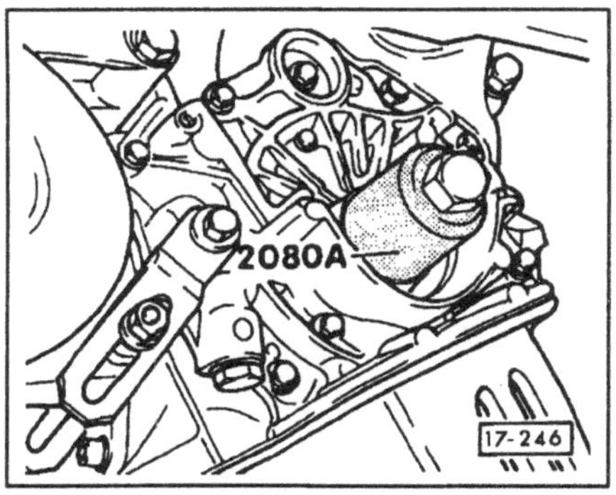

◄ – Fit oil seal over 2080A installation sleeve and press in as far as it will go, using pressure sleeve 2080A and vibration damper center bolt

– Install toothed belt (adjust valve timing)
⇒ page C 13-13

Crankshaft oil seal (flywheel end), replacing

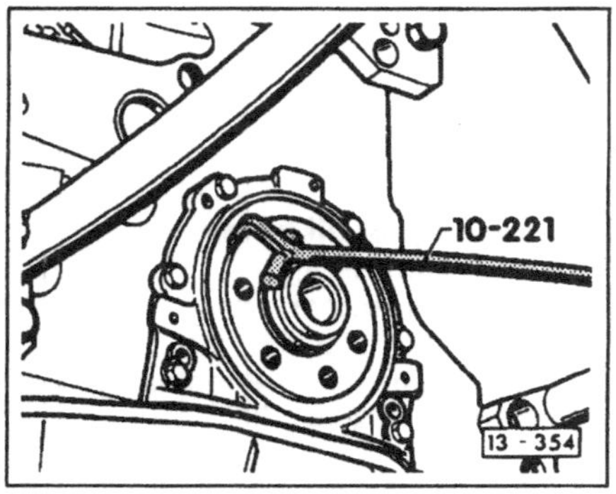

- Remove transmission and flywheel
⇒ Repair Groups 34 or 37

◄ - Remove oil seal using 10-221 tool

- Clean oil seal recess in sealing flange using a cloth

> *CAUTION!*
> ***DO NOT lubricate the new oil seal, it is provided with a fitting aid and a slip-coating.***

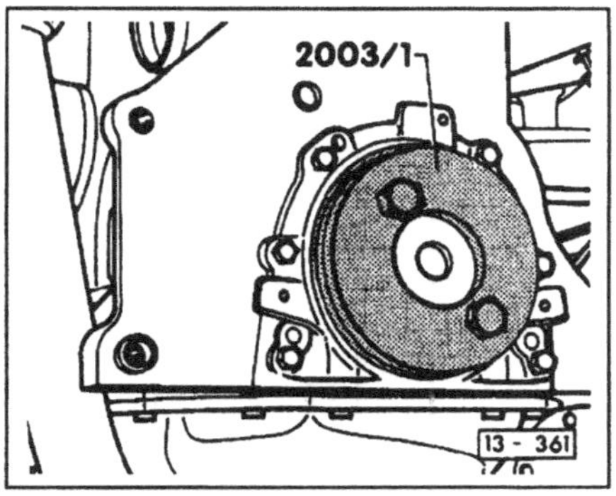

- With installation tool inserted, evenly push oil seal by hand onto rear sealing flange and carefully remove tool

◄ - Press in oil seal up to limit stop using 2003/1

Crankshaft, dimensions (mm)

Finishing dimension	Main journal ∅	Connecting rod journal ∅
Basic dimension	58.00 −0.022 / −0.042	47.80 −0.022 / −0.042
1st undersize	57.75 −0.022 / −0.042	47.55 −0.022 / −0.042
2nd undersize	57.50 −0.022 / −0.042	47.30 −0.022 / −0.042
3rd undersize	57.25 −0.022 / −0.042	47.05 −0.022 / −0.042

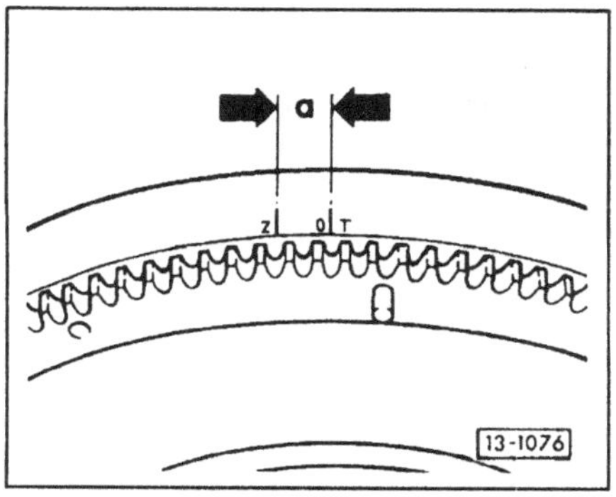

Ignition timing mark, inscribing

Note:

Replacement flywheels only come with the TDC mark inscribed. If the flywheel is replaced, the appropriate ignition timing mark must also be added (inscribed).

◄ – Inscribe ignition timing mark "a": 14.5 mm (0.571 in.) to left of TDC mark

- ♦ Measure length of arc for this purpose

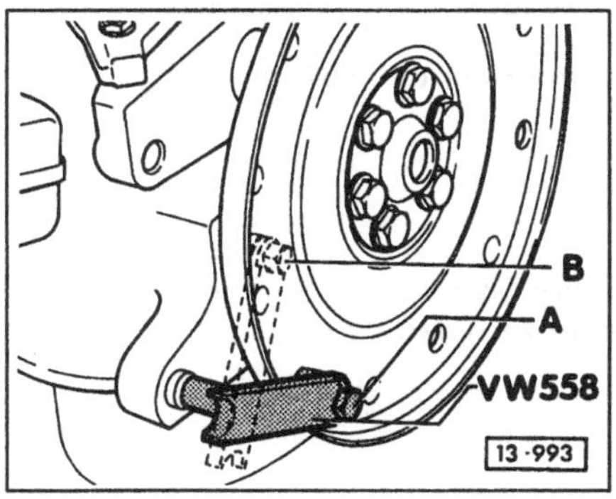

Drive plate, removing and installing

Loosening and tightening

◄ – Attach VW 558 retainer to the drive plate using hexagon bolt M8 x 45

– Insert two M10 hexagon nuts between retainer and drive plate

Installed position of retainer:

- ♦ A–when loosening
- ♦ B–when tightening

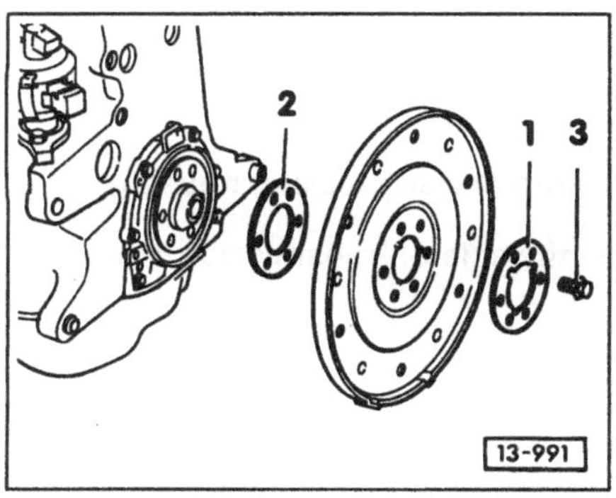

Installing

◄ – Fit drive plate into position together with notched washer

– Install new bolts -3- and tighten

- ♦ 30 Nm (22 ft lb)

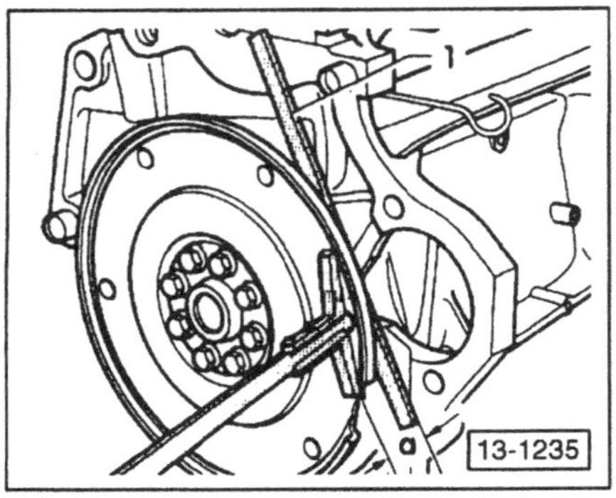

- Check dimension "a" at three locations and calculate the average
  - ♦ Must be 10.7 to 12.3 mm (0.421 to 0.484 in.)

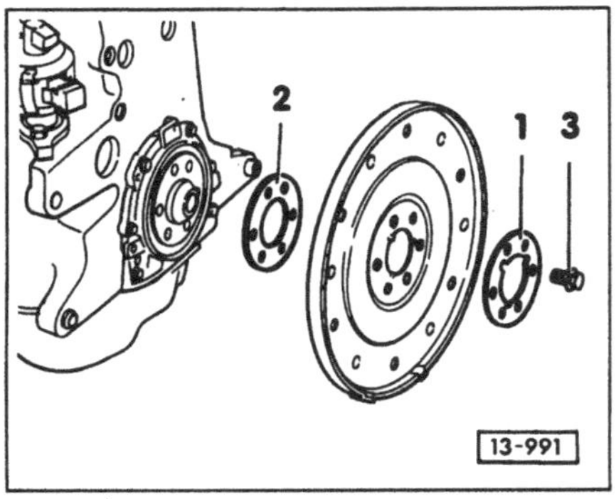

If dimension is not obtained:

- Remove drive plate again and insert shim -2-
- Re-install bolts -3- and tighten
  - ♦ 30 Nm (22 ft lb)

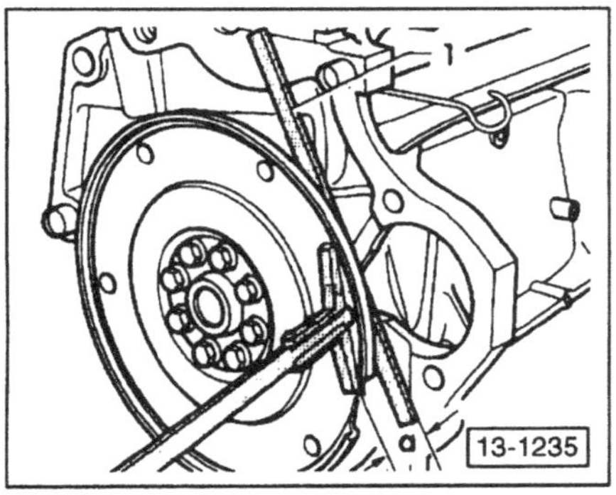

- Check dimension a at three locations and calculate average
  - ♦ Must be 10.7 to 12.3 mm (0.421 to 0.484 in.)

If dimension is now OK:

- Fully tighten bolts
  - ♦ 60 Nm (44 ft lb), then turn bolts –3– an additional 1/4 turn (the additional quarter turn can be obtained in several steps)

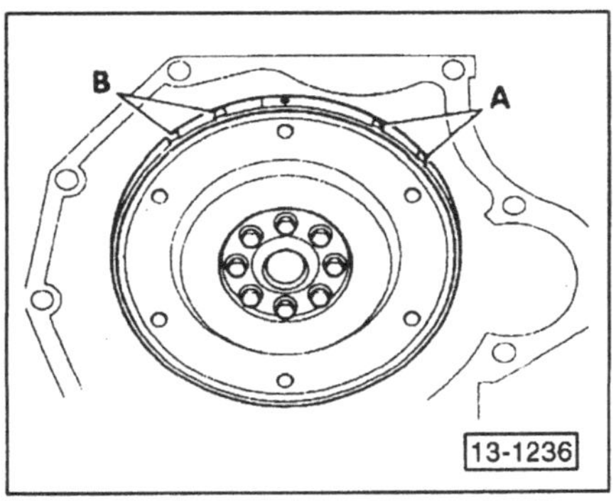

When replacing the driving plate:

- Note transmission type
  - ♦ Type A: TDC sensor on top of transmission housing
  - ♦ Type B: TDC sensor on the side of transmission housing

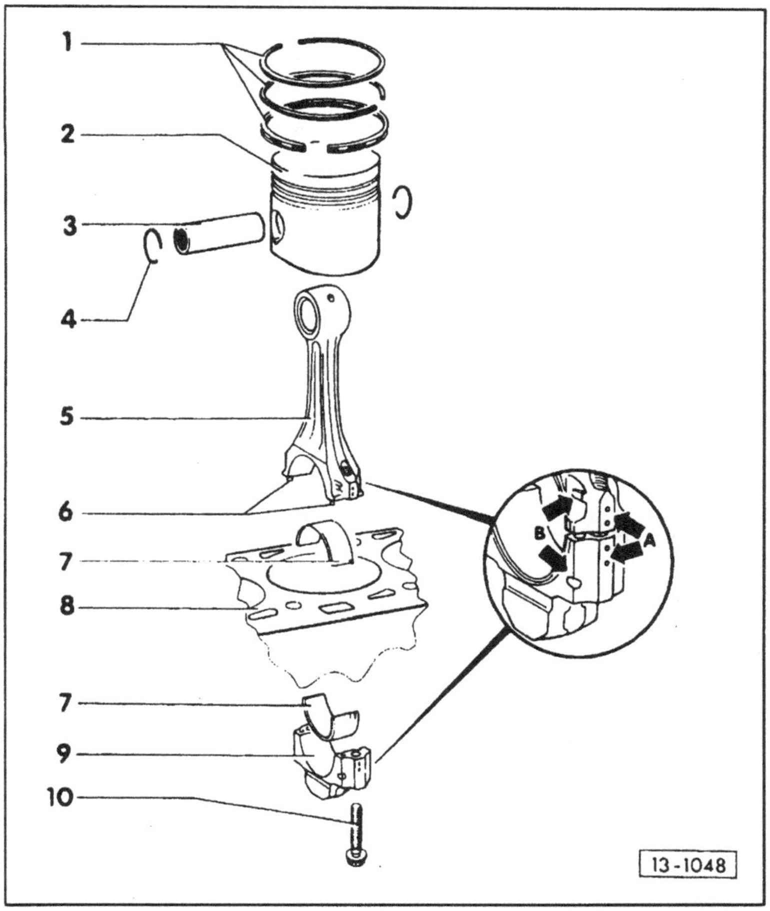

Pistons and connecting rods, disassembling and assembling

> ***CAUTION!***
>
> ***DO NOT allow crankshaft to turn while measuring radial clearance.***

1 - Piston ring
- ♦ offset gaps by 120°
- ♦ remove and install with piston ring pliers
- ♦ checking ring gap:

⇒ page C 13-36
- ♦ checking side clearance:

⇒ page C 13-36
- ♦ the word "OBEN" faces towards piston crown

2 - Piston
- ♦ checking:

⇒ page C 13-37
- ♦ mark installation position and cylinder number
- ♦ arrow on piston crown points to pulleys
- ♦ install using piston ring clamp

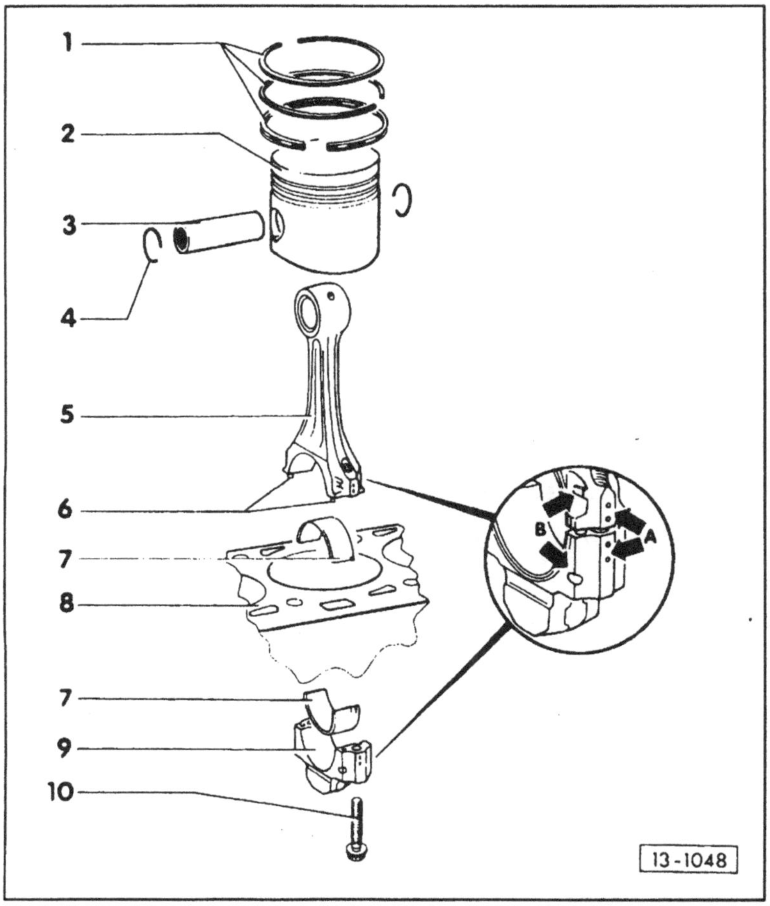

3 - Piston wrist pin
- ♦ if difficult to remove, heat piston to approx. 60°C (140 °F)
- ♦ remove/install using VW222a

4 - Circlip

5 - Connecting rod
- ♦ always replace as a set
- ♦ mark cylinder number A
- ♦ installed position: markings B face towards pulley end

6 - Dowel
- ♦ dowel must be tight in the connecting rod; not in the cap

7 - Bearing shells
- ♦ note installation position
- ♦ do not interchange
- ♦ ensure lugs fit tightly in recesses
- ♦ axial clearance

  new: 0.05 to 0.31 mm (0.00197 to 0.0122 in.)

  wear limit: 0.37 mm (0.01457 in.)
- ♦ check radial clearance using Plastigage®

  New: 0.01 to 0.06 mm (0.00039 to 0.00236 in.)

  Wear limit: 0.12 mm (0.00472 in.)
- ♦ do not turn crankshaft when measuring radial play

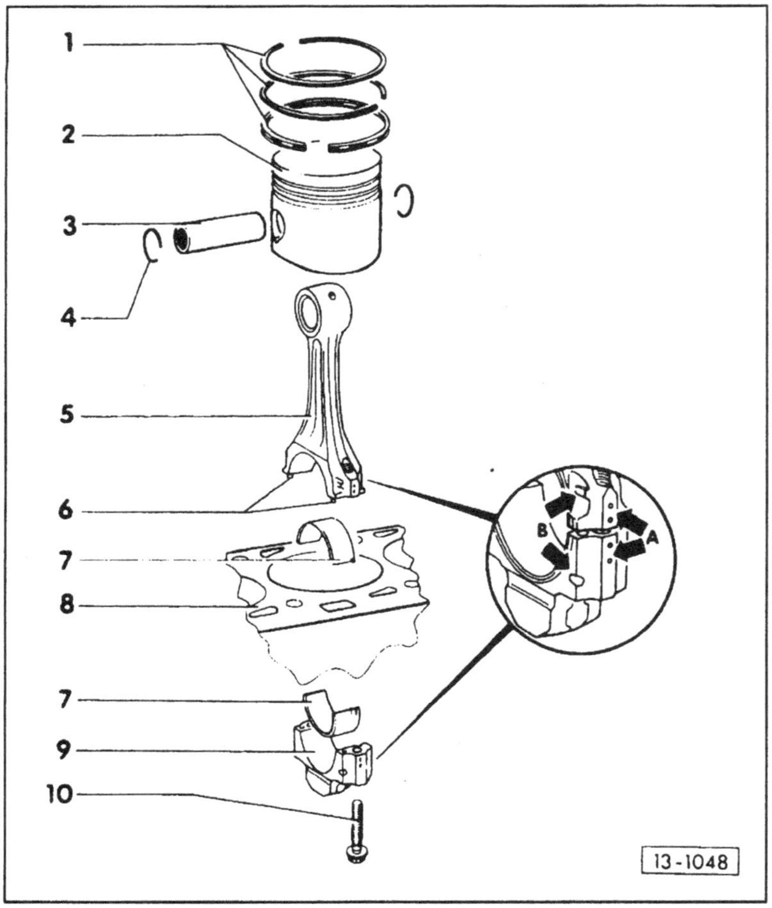

8 - **Cylinder block**
- checking cylinder bore diameter:

⇒ page C 13-37
- piston and cylinder dimensions:

⇒ page C 13-38

9 - **Connecting rod bearing cap**
- installed position: markings B face toward pulley end

10 - **Connecting rod bolt**
- replace
- oil the thread–and–contact surfaces
- 30 Nm (22 ft lb) + 1/4 additional turn (this further movement can be done in several steps)
- to check radial clearance, tighten old bolts to 30 Nm (22 ft lb) but no further

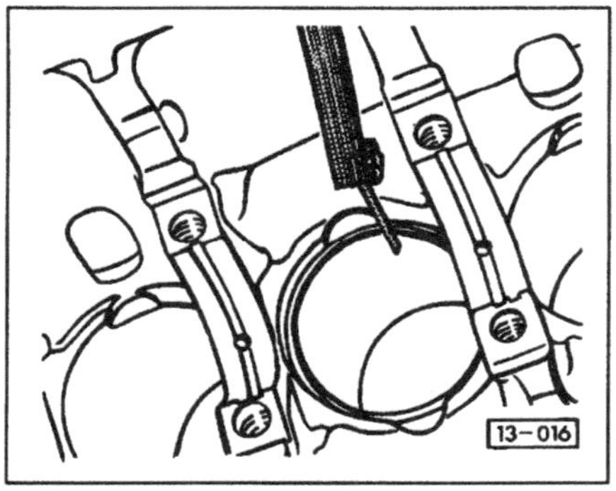

◄ **Piston ring gap, checking**

– Squarely install ring into lower end of cylinder, approximately 15 mm from bottom edge of cylinder

- New:

Compression rings	0.20 to 0.40 mm
Oil scraper ring	0.25 to 0.50 mm
Wear limit:	1.0 mm

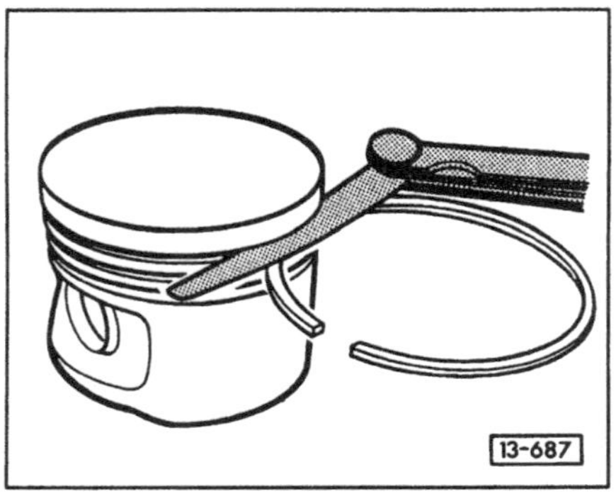

◄ **Side clearance, checking**

– Clean groove before checking

New:	0.02 to 0.05 mm
Wear limit:	0.15 mm

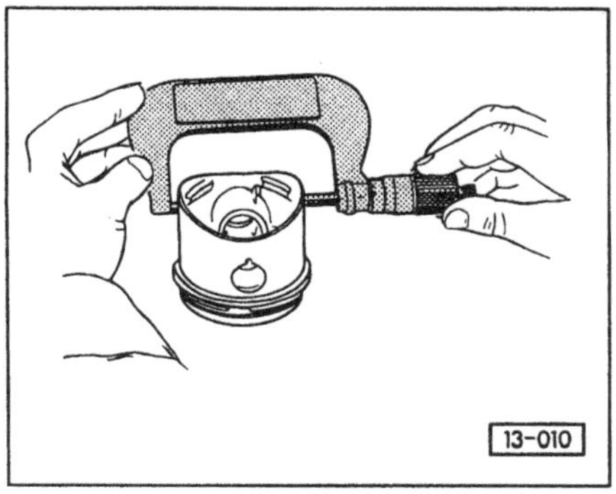

Piston, checking

– Measure pistons approx. 10 mm from lower edge of skirt, at 90° axis to piston pin

- ♦ 0.04 mm = max. allowable deviation from nominal dimension

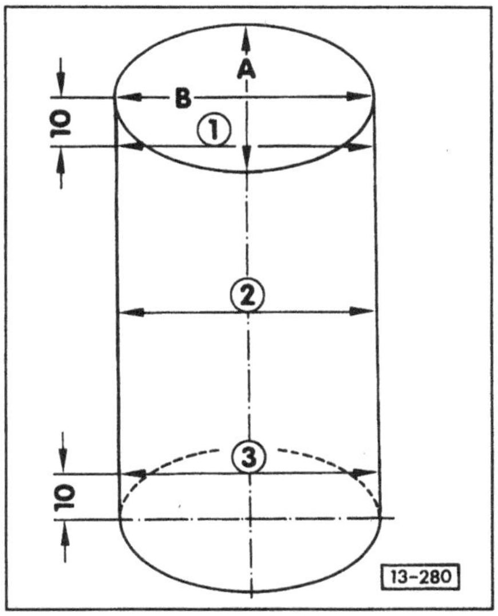

Cylinder Bores, checking

– Measure bore at three locations, in both directions, using a 50–to–100 mm inside micrometer

- ♦ "A" across engine block
- ♦ "B" in line with crankshaft
- ♦ 0.08 mm=max. allowable deviation from nominal dimension

> ***CAUTION!***
>
> ***DO NOT measure cylinder bores when cylinder block is mounted on repair stand with adaptor VW 540 because the hanging weight of the engine will change the shape of the block and distort the measurements.***

Piston and cylinders, dimensions (mm)

Engine Code AAF

Finishing dimension	Piston ∅	Bore size ∅
Basic dimension	80.985	81.01
1st oversize	81.235	81.26
2st oversize	81.485	81.51

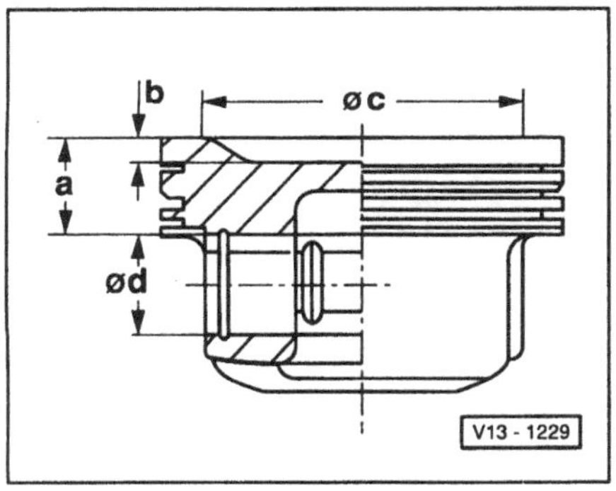

Engine Code ACU

Engine code		
Dimension "a"	mm	26.4
Dimension "b"	mm	4.6
Recess ∅ "c"	mm	62.0
Piston pin ∅ "d"	mm	24.0

When repairing an engine, only install pistons and rings of the same type and pistons within the same weight range.

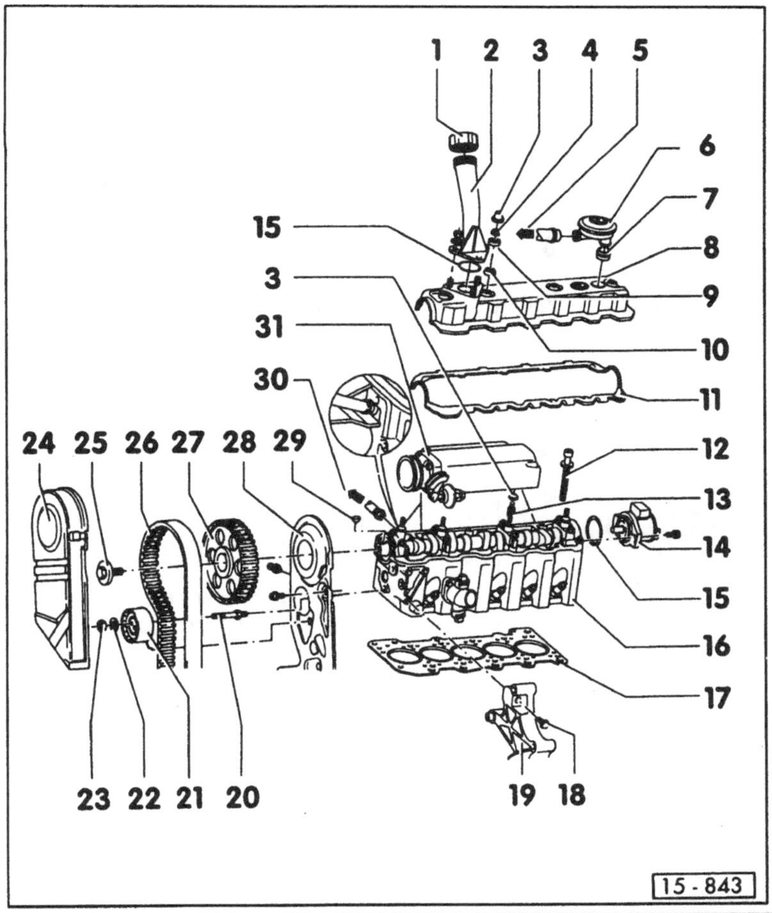

Cylinder head, removing and installing

- The cylinder head can be removed and replaced with the engine installed
- When installing a replacement cylinder head, lubricate the contacting surfaces between the hydraulic lifters and the cam lobes
- The plastic caps for protecting the open valves must not be removed until immediately before fitting the cylinder head
- When replacing the cylinder head, you must also completely replace the engine coolant mixture
- Compression pressure, checking:

⇒ page C 15-9

1 - Oil filler cap

2 - Oil filler pipe

3 - Cap

4 - 10 Nm (7 ft lb)

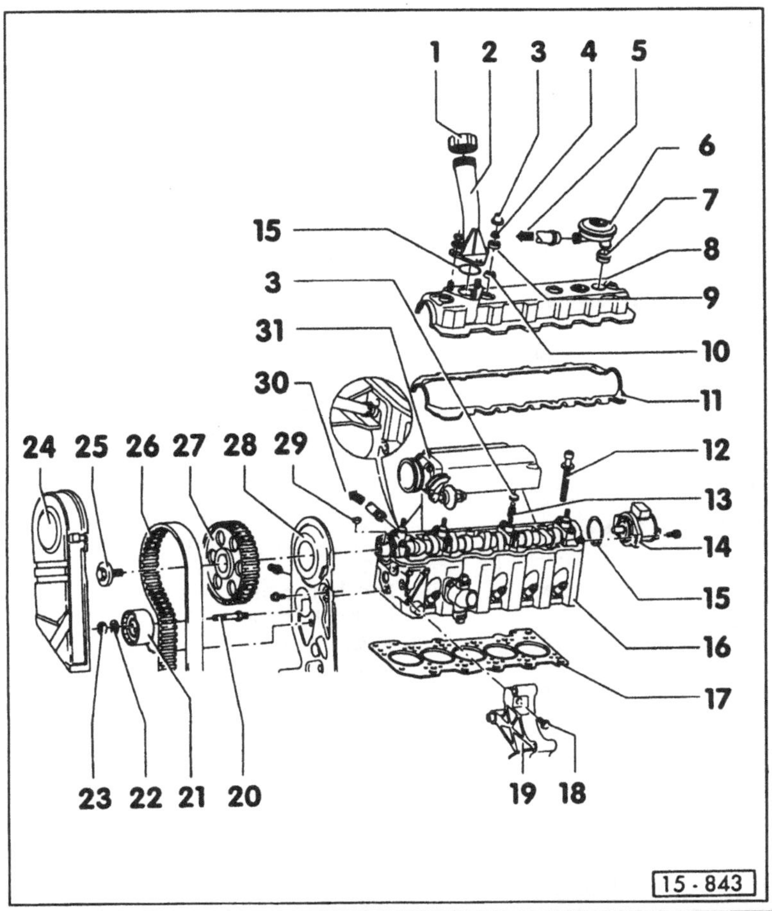

5 - to intake hose
- breather hose secured with bracket to oil filler pipe (item 2)
- ensure adequate clearance between throttle connection

6 - Positive Crankcase Ventilation valve

7 - Oil seal
- replace if damaged

8 - Valve cover
- with oil baffle

9 - Dished washer

10 - Sealing ring, top
- replace if damaged

11 - Cylinder head cover gasket
- replace if damaged

12 - Cylinder head bolt
- follow instructions and sequence when loosening and tightening:

⇒ page C 15-8

13 - 15 Nm (11 ft lb)

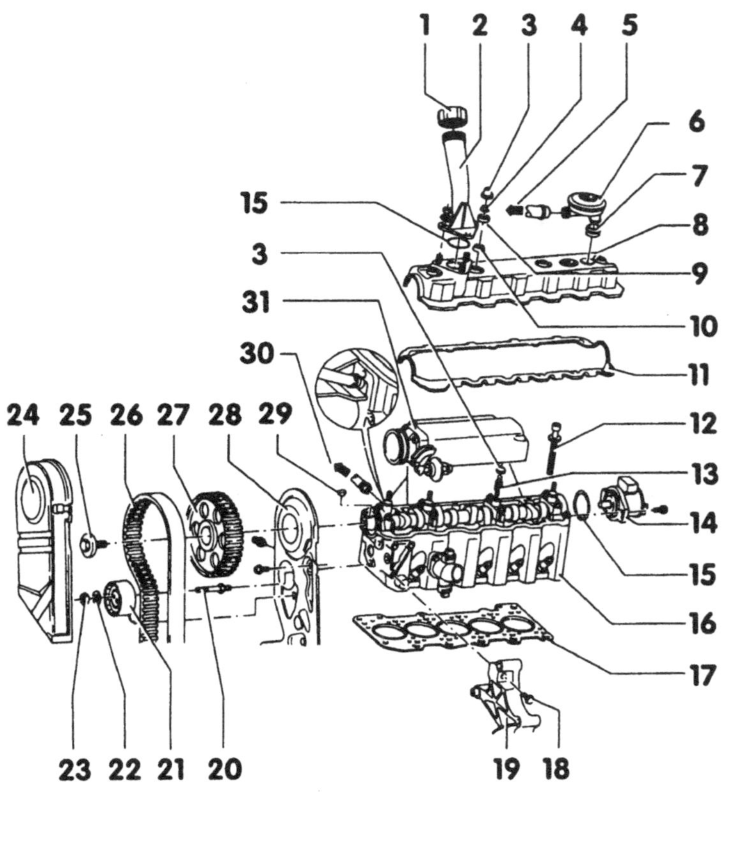

15 - 843

14 - Ignition distributor
- when installing, note position of drive dog
- ignition timing, checking/adjusting:

⇒ Repair Group 28

15 - O-ring
- replace if damaged

16 - Cylinder head
- installing:

⇒ page C 15-7
- check for distortion:

⇒ page C 15-6
- valve train, repairing:

⇒ page Repair Group 19
- after replacing, you must completely drain and replace the coolant mixture

17 - Cylinder head gasket
- note installed position
- replace
- after replacing, completely drain and replace the coolant mixture

18 - 20 Nm (15 ft lb)

19 - Bracket

20 - 20 Nm (15 ft lb)

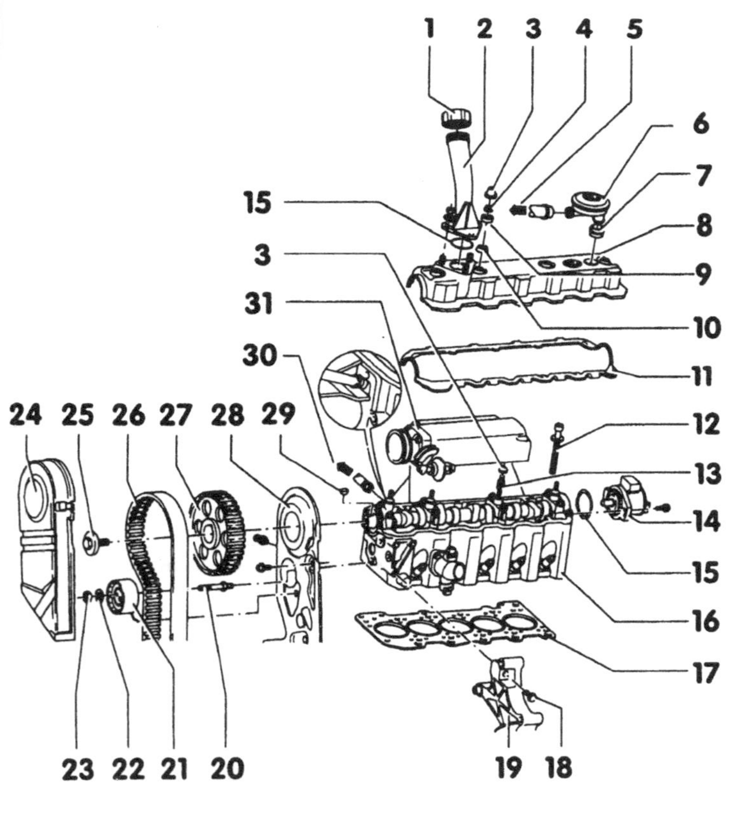

15 - 843

21 - Tensioner pulley
- toothed belt, removing/installing:

⇒ Repair Group 13

22 - Washer
- with crimps to prevent rotation

23 - 15 Nm (11 ft lb)

24 - Toothed belt guard, upper

25 - Camshaft drive sprocket mounting screw
- note identification for bolt steel on bolt head:
  - 8.8 = 85 Nm (63 ft lb)
  - 10.9 = 100 Nm (74 ft lb)
- use countering tool 3036 for loosening/tightening

26 - Toothed belt
- check for wear
- do not kink
- removing, installing, tensioning:

⇒ Repair Group 13

27 - Camshaft drive sprocket
- note position during toothed belt installation:

⇒ Repair Group 13

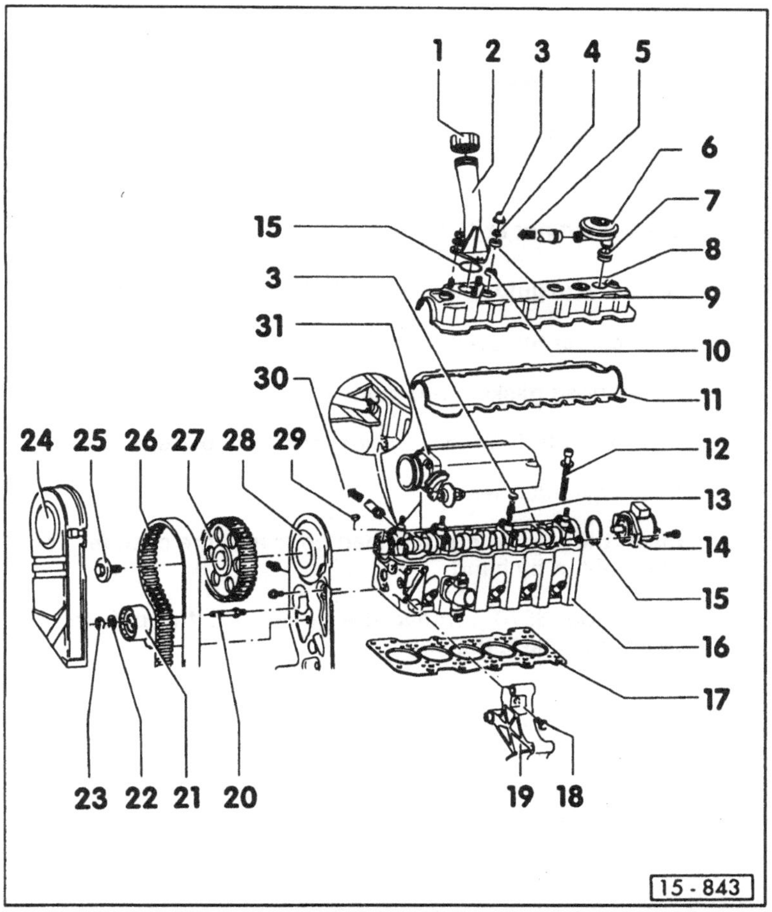

28 - Toothed belt guard, rear
- to remove cylinder head, loosen mounting screws on head and push toothed belt guard back slightly

29 - Woodruff key
- check for tight fit

30 - to T-connector on coolant expansion reservoir:
⇒ Repair Group 19

31 - Intake manifold
- removing and installing:
⇒ Repair Group 24

Cylinder head distortion, checking

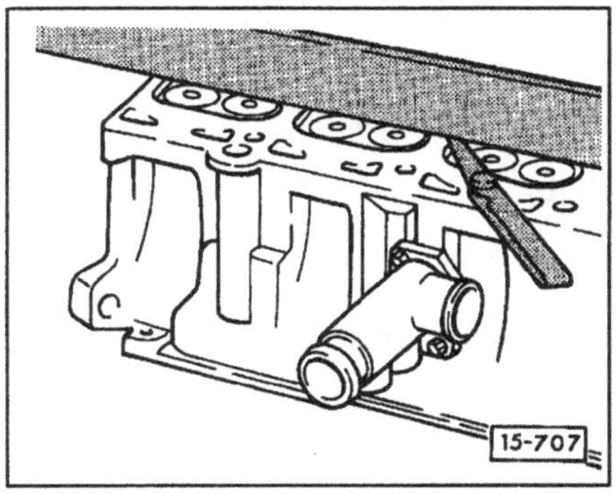

◄ **Maximum allowable distortion**

- 0.1 mm

Cylinder head, installing

Requirements

- ♦ Engine cold
- ♦ Crankshaft not at TDC

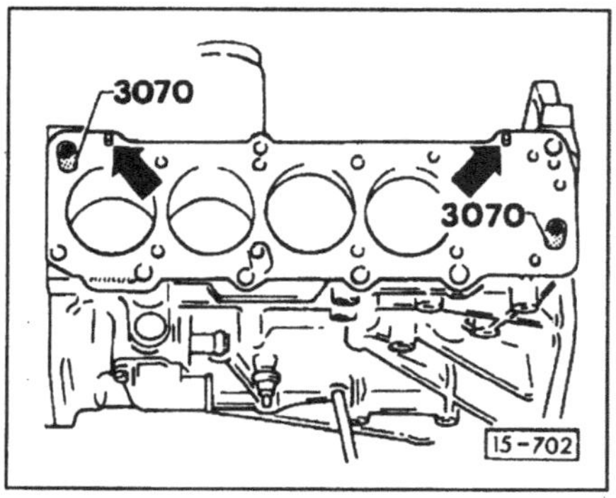

- Screw 3070 guide pins into cylinder head bolt holes 9 and 10
  - ♦ To center the cylinder head
- Install head gasket onto guide pins
  - ♦ Note centering pins (arrows) and hole pattern
- Install cylinder head
- Insert the remaining (10) head bolts into the cylinder head and tighten by hand
- Using tool 3070, remove the guide pins through the bolt holes and insert the bolts

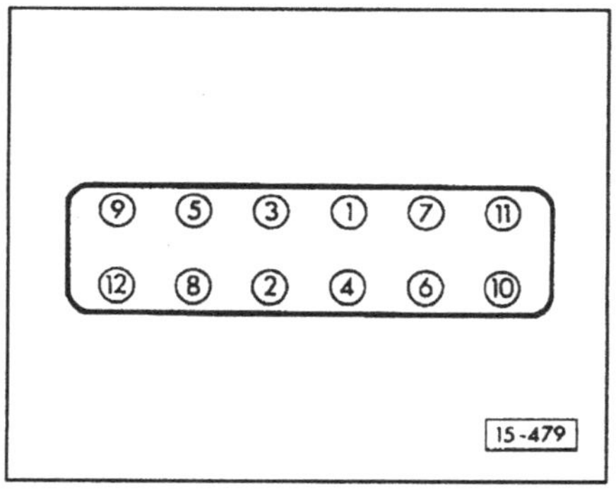

- Tighten cylinder head in four stages, using the following sequence:
- First, pre-tighten using torque wrench:
  - ♦ Stage I = 40 Nm (30 ft lb)
  - ♦ Stage II = 60 Nm (44 ft lb)
- Second, turn further using regular wrench
  - ♦ Stage III = 1/4 turn (90°)
  - ♦ Stage IV = 1/4 turn (90°)

Notes:

- ♦ *Cylinder head removal is reverse of installation sequence*
- ♦ *It is not necessary to re-torque the cylinder head bolts after repairs*

Cylinder compression pressure, checking

Requirements:

- ♦ Engine coolant temperature 30 °C (86 °F) minimum
- ♦ Throttle valve must be wide open during cranking
- ♦ Camshaft Position sensor disconnected at ign. distributor

– Check compression using VAG 1381 compression tester

- ♦ Follow tester manufacturer's instructions

– Operate starter until tester shows no additional pressure increase

Compression pressure specifications:

Engine Code AAF

- ♦ New: 9 to 12 bar (131 to 174 psi)
- ♦ Wear limit: 7.0 bar (102 psi)
- ♦ Permissible difference between all cylinders: 3 bar (44 psi)

Engine Code ACU

- ♦ New: 10 to 13 bar (145 to 189 psi)
- ♦ Wear limit: 7.5 bar (109 psi)
- ♦ Permissible difference between all cylinders: 3 bar (44 psi)

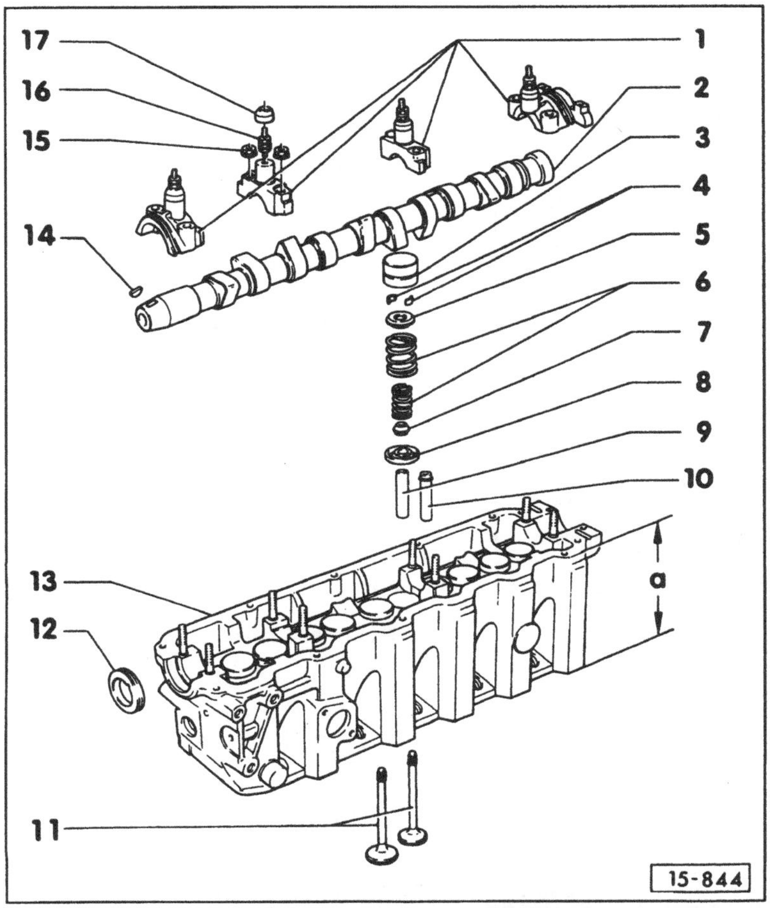

Valve train, servicing

Cylinder heads with small cracks between the valve seats or between the valve seat inserts and spark plug threads can continue to be used without reducing service life, provided the crack widths do not exceed 0.5 mm maximum, or when no more than the first spark plug thread is cracked.

1 - Bearing cap
- ♦ note bore offset:

⇒ page C 15-15

- ♦ installation sequence:

⇒ page C 15-23

2 - Camshaft
- ♦ axial clearance, checking:

⇒ page C 15-14

- ♦ removing and installing:

⇒ page C 15-22

- ♦ check the radial clearance using Plastigage®
- ♦ wear limit: 0.01 mm
- ♦ run-out: max. 0.01 mm
- ♦ camshaft identification:

⇒ page C 15-16

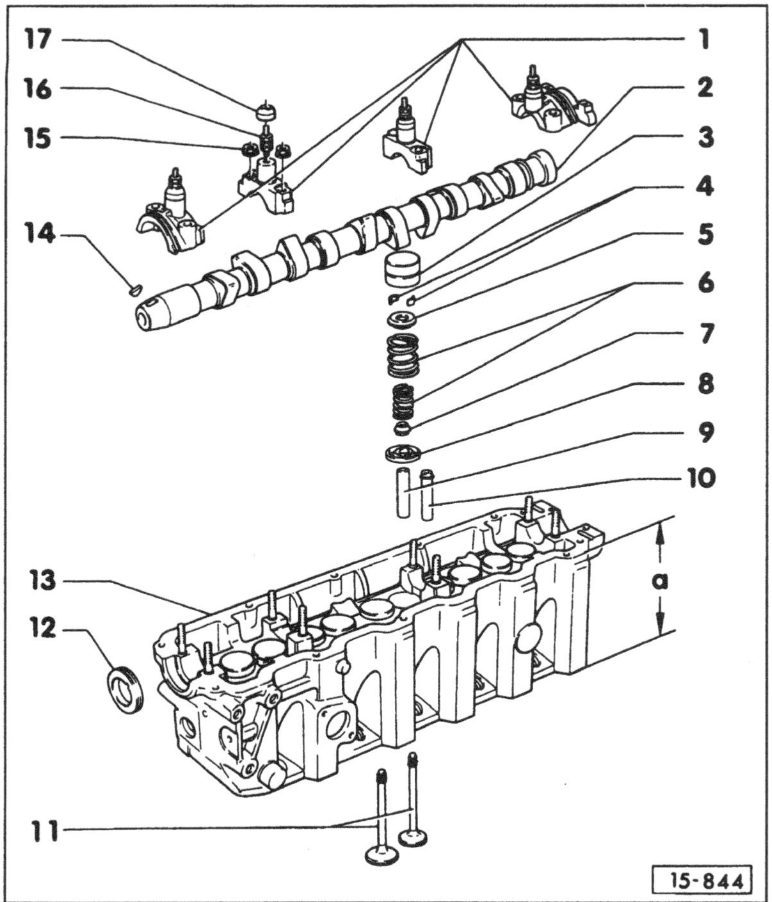

3 - **Hydraulic lifter**
- ♦ camshaft axial clearance, checking before installing:

⇒ page C 15-14
- ♦ lubricate contacting surfaces
- ♦ do not interchange lifters, due to critical wear patterns each lifter must always be returned to its original bore
- ♦ store with cam contacting surface facing downward
- ♦ checking:

⇒ page C 15-20

4 - **Valve spring keepers**

5 - **Spring retainer**
- ♦ identification:
- – wider chamfer to outside
- – internal chamfer

6 - **Outer valve spring (larger diameter) Inner valve spring (smaller diameter)**
- ♦ removing and installing:
- – with cylinder head removed, use tool 2036
- – with cylinder head installed:

⇒ page C 15-29

7 - **Valve stem seal**
- ♦ replacing:

⇒ page C 15-29

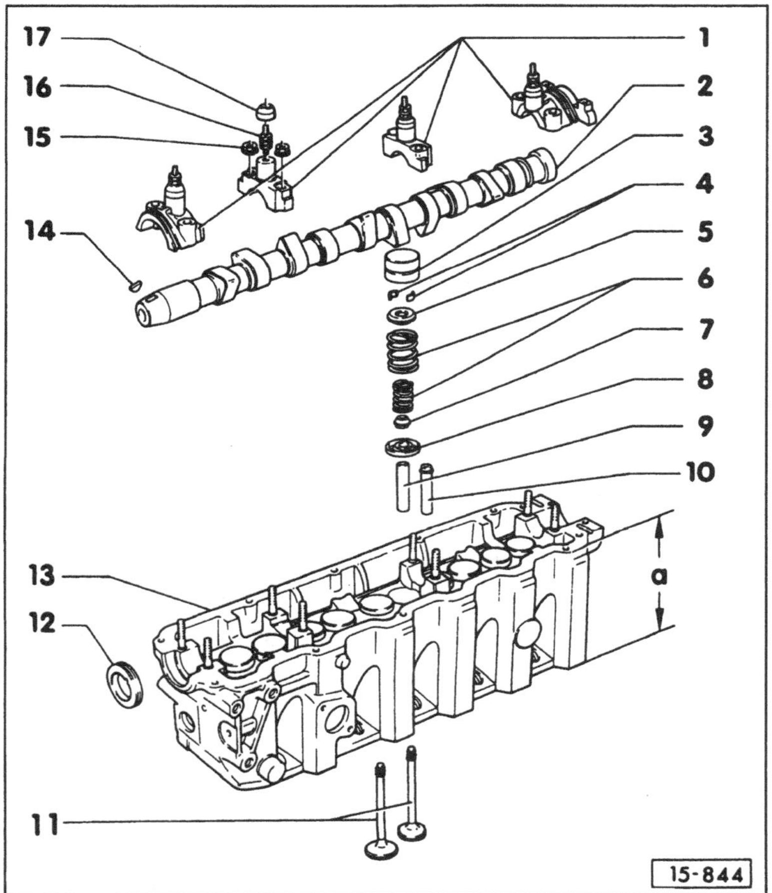

8 - **Valve spring seat**
- ♦ remove and install using tool 3047A

9 - **Valve guide**
- ♦ wear checking:

⇒ pageC 15-27
- ♦ replacing:

⇒ page C 15-27

10 - **Replacement valve guide**
- ♦ with collar

11 - **Valves**
- ♦ lap in only, do not re-work
- ♦ valve dimensions:

⇒ page C 15-17

12 - **Oil seal**
- ♦ replacing:

⇒ page C 15-25

13 - **Cylinder head**
- ♦ reworking dimension:

⇒ page C 15-18
- ♦ valve seats, reworking:

⇒ page C 15-18 and note, page C 15-10

14 - **Woodruff key**
- ♦ check for tight fit

15 - **20 Nm (15 ft lb)**

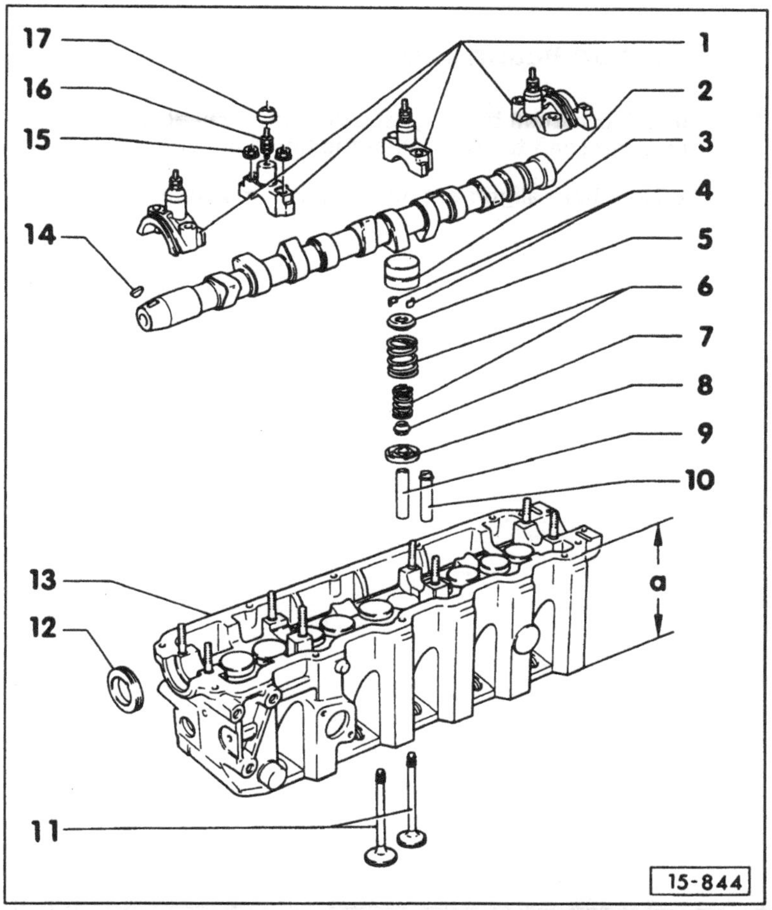

16 - 15 Nm (11 ft lb)

17 - Cap

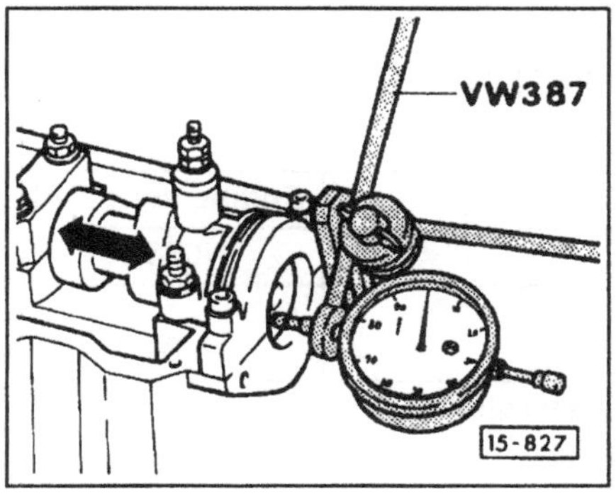

Camshaft axial clearance, checking

Requirement

- ♦ Measure with hydraulic lifters removed, and with first and last bearing cap installed

◄

- – Measure camshaft axial clearance using dial gauge fitted to VW 387 holder
- – Fully push camshaft longitudinally in either direction by hand
- – Zero dial gauge
- – Fully push camshaft longitudinally in other direction by hand
  - ♦ Wear limit: 0.15 mm

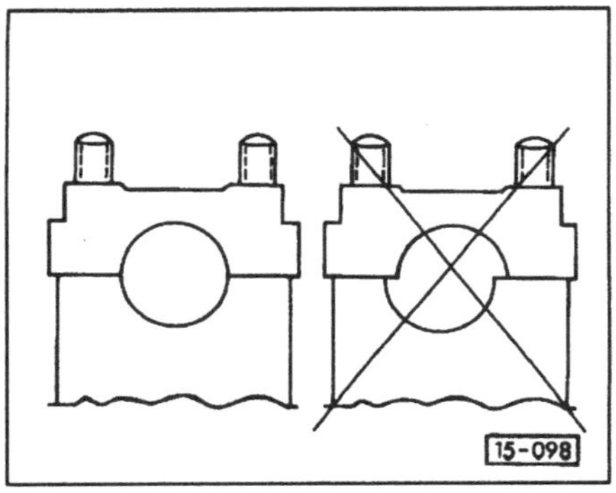

Camshaft bearing cap, installing

◄ – Install camshaft bearing caps on cylinder head before installing camshaft to ensure that the bores are concentric

- ♦ Note bore alignment off-set when improperly installed

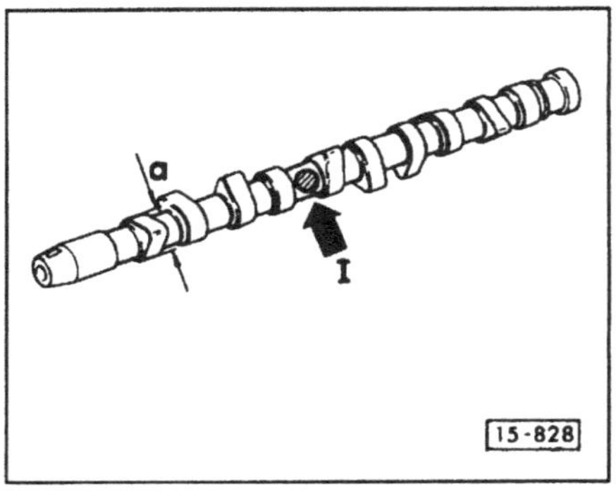

Camshaft, technical data

◄ – Note identification (arrow 1) between cam pairs for 2nd and 3rd cylinder

Camshaft	**Engine code AAF**
Identification	023E
Cam base circle a = mm	34
Cam timing with 1 mm of valve stroke:	
Intake opens after TDC	2.5°
Intake closes after BDC	32.5°
Exhaust opens before BDC	32.5°
Exhaust closed before TDC	2.5°

Intake and exhaust valves, dimensions

Valve dimensions			
Inlet valve		Exhaust valve	
a = ϕ	40.00 mm	a = ϕ	33.00 mm
b = ϕ	7.97 mm	b = ϕ	7.95 mm
c =	91.00–0.9 mm	c =	90.80–0.4 mm
∝ =	45°	∝ =	45°

CAUTION!
Valves cannot be reworked. Only lapping is permitted.

Reworking Valve Seats

Note:

Only rework the valve seats enough to produce an intimate contact surface. Before starting the rework, calculate the maximum permissible reworking dimension (⇒ page C 15-18).
If this dimension is exceeded, the cylinder head must be replaced because hydraulic lifter clearance cannot be guaranteed.

Maximum permissible reworking dimension, calculating

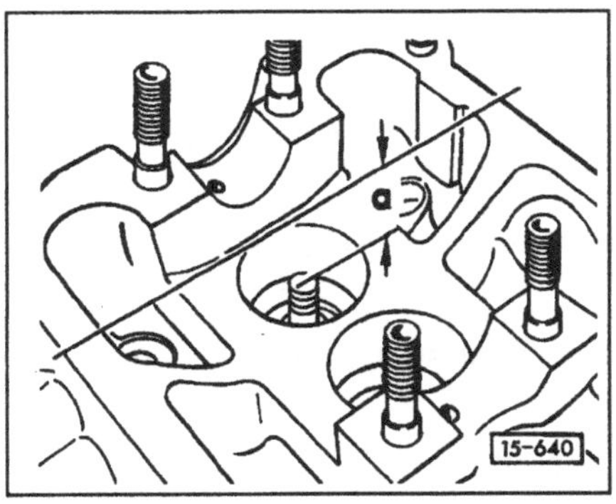

If a valve is replaced, make the following measurement to ensure there is adequate clearance:

– Insert valve and hold tight against the valve seat

– Measure distance "a" between valve stem end and top surface of cylinder head

– Compare measured distance with minimum dimensions:

- ♦ Intake valve 33.8 mm
- ♦ Exhaust valve 34.1 mm

The measured distance "a" minus the minimum dimension = the maximum permissible rework dimension

Example:

Measured distance	34.5 mm
– minimum distance	33.8 mm
= max. permissible rework dimension	0.7 mm

Note:

If measured distance "a" is less than the minimum dimension, repeat measuring process with new valve and, if necessary, use a shorter valve (⇒ page C 15-17, valve dimension "c") or replace cylinder head.

Valve seats, reworking

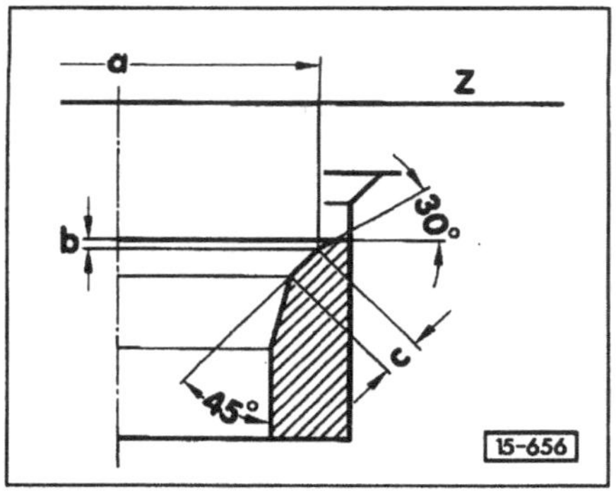

◄ **Intake valve seat, re-working**

a = ϕ 37.2 mm

b = Max. permissible reworking dimension

c = Approx. 2.0 mm

Z = Lower edge of cylinder head

30° = Upper correction angle

45° = Valve seat angle

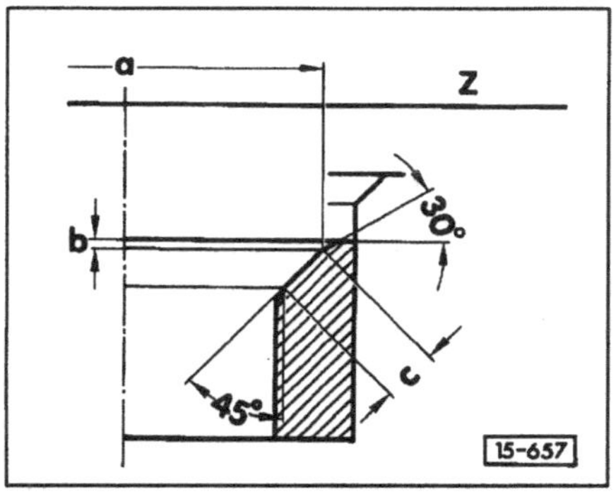

◄ **Exhaust valve seat, re-working**

a = ϕ 32.4 mm

b = Max. permissible reworking dimension

c = Approx. 2.4 mm

Z = Lower edge of cylinder head

30° = Upper correction angle

45° = Valve seat angle

Note:

Exhaust valve seat inserts have a reduced internal diameter. When reworking seats, great care should be taken to ensure that the radius is not damaged due to reduction.

Hydraulic lifters, checking

- Place removed lifters on a clean surface with cam contacting surface of lifter pointing downwards
- Lifters can only be replaced as complete assemblies, they cannot be adjusted or repaired
  - ♦ Irregular valve noises when engine is first started are normal
- Start engine and let idle until radiator cooling fan comes on at least once
- Increase engine speed to approx. 2500 RPM for 2 minutes
- Listen for irregular valve noise (mechanical)

If irregular valve noise continues

- Identify faulty lifter as follows:
- Remove valve cover
- Rotate crankshaft clockwise by hand until cam-lobe (for lifter to be checked) is pointing upward

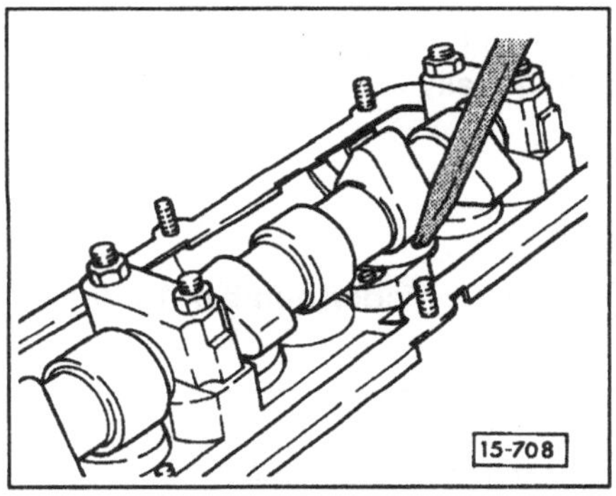

◄ – Push lifter down using a wooden or plastic wedge

- ♦ Must not be more than 0.1 mm of clearance before valve opens

If clearance exceeds 0.1 mm

– Replace that hydraulic lifter

> ***CAUTION!***
> ***If new lifters have been installed, DO NOT attempt to start the engine for at least 30 minutes. The valves could strike the pistons!***

Camshaft, removing and installing

Removing

– Remove upper belt guard

– Remove valve cover

– Loosen camshaft drive sprocket using 3036 countering tool

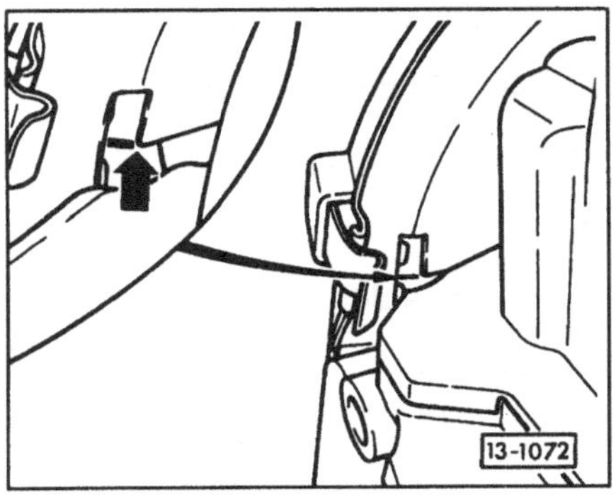

◄ – Locate camshaft drive sprocket to TDC for cylinder number 1 by manually rotating the crankshaft

- ♦ Marking on camshaft drive sprocket must align with marking on rear toothed belt guard (arrow)

– Loosen tensioning pulley and/or coolant pump and take off toothed belt

– Remove camshaft drive sprocket using suitable puller

– Remove Woodruff key from camshaft

– Remove ignition distributor

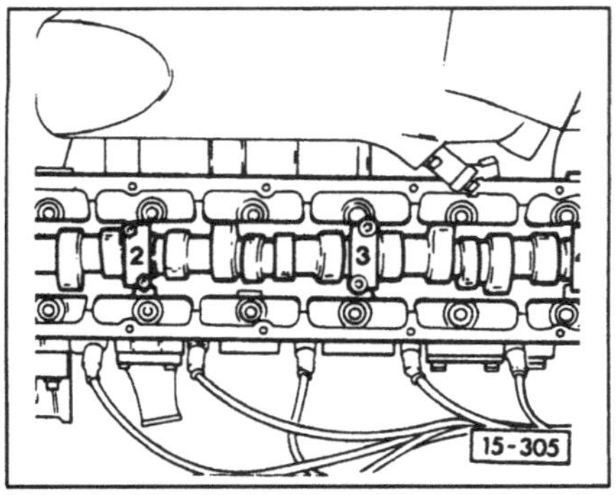

◄ – First remove bearing caps 1 and 3, then loosen bearing caps 2 and 4 alternately and diagonally in sequence

Installing

– Lubricate contact surfaces

– Install camshaft with lobes for cylinder number 1 pointing upward

> ***CAUTION!***
> ***The bearing caps must be oriented correctly!***
> ***⇒ page C 15-15.***

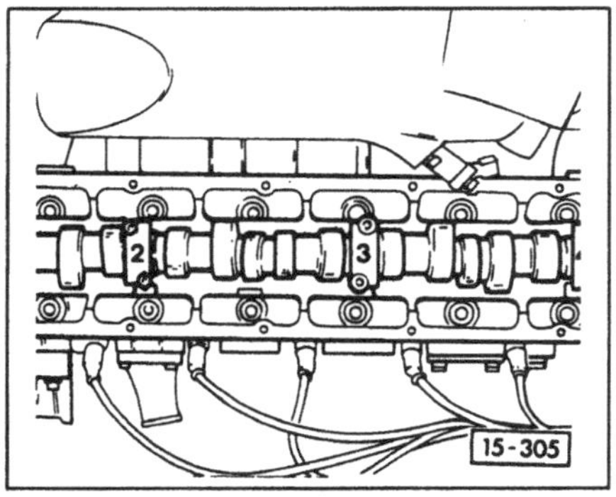

◄ – Tighten bearing caps 2 and 4 alternately and diagonally

♦ Tightening torque: 20 Nm (15 ft lb)

– Install bearing caps 1 and 3

♦ Tightening torque: 20 Nm (15 ft lb)

– Insert Woodruff key (for camshaft sprocket) in camshaft

– Install camshaft sprocket and tighten while counterholding with tool 3036

Tightening torques:

Examine bolt head for identification code (in raised letters):

♦ 8.8 = 85 Nm (63 ft lb)

♦ 10.9 = 100 Nm (74 ft lb)

– Install ignition distributor

♦ Note position of distributor drive dog and slot

♦ Tightening torque: 10 Nm (7 ft lb)

– Install toothed belt

– Adjust valve timing
⇒ Repair Group 13

> ***CAUTION!***
> ***If new lifters have been installed, DO NOT attempt to start the engine for at least 30 minutes. The valves could strike the pistons!***

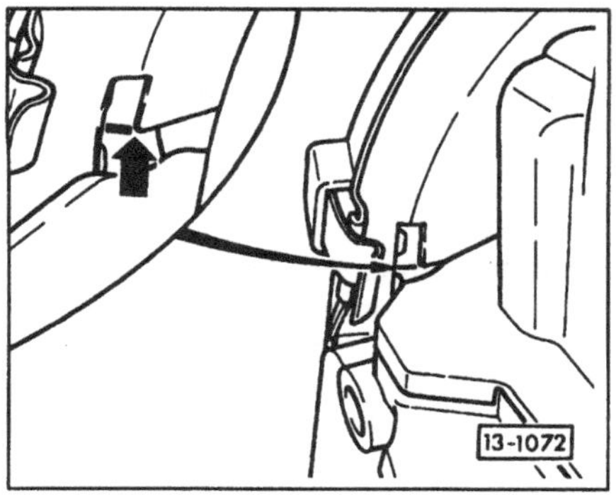

Camshaft oil seal, removing and installing

Removing

– Remove upper toothed belt guard

– Loosen camshaft drive sprocket using 3036 countering tool

◄ – Position camshaft drive sprocket at TDC for cylinder 1 by manually turning the crankshaft

♦ Marking on camshaft drive sprocket must align with marking on rear toothed belt guard (arrow)

– Loosen tensioning pulley and/or coolant pump

– Remove toothed belt

– Remove camshaft drive sprocket using suitable puller

– Remove Woodruff key from camshaft

– Insert camshaft drive sprocket mounting screw (with washer)into camshaft, up to stop

– Rotate inner part, sealing ring puller 2085, out two revs (approx. 3 mm) from outer part and stop with knurled screw

– Lubricate threaded head of oil seal extractor, place in position, screw into oil seal as far as possible, using pressure

– Loosen knurled screw and turn inner part of extractor against camshaft until oil seal is extracted

– Clamp extractor in vice (along flats)

– Remove oil seal using pliers

Installing

– Lightly lubricate sealing lip and outer edge of oil seal

– Install oil seal and press in flush using sleeve 10-203

– Install toothed belt

– Adjust valve timing
⇒ Repair Group 13

Valve guides, checking and replacing

- Insert a new valve into guide until end of valve stem is flush with end of guide

> ***CAUTION!***
> ***Due to the difference in stem diameters, ensure that only an inlet valve is used in the inlet guide and an exhaust valve is used in the exhaust guide during this check.***

Using dial gauge attached to edge of cylinder head:

- Lightly push valve against dial-gauge pushrod and zero gauge
- Push valve away from dial-gauge and calculate difference
  - ♦ Intake valve guide wear limit: 1.0 mm
  - ♦ Exhaust valve guide wear limit: 1.3 mm

Replacing

> ***CAUTION!***
> ***Cylinder heads in which the valve seats can no longer be reworked or which have already been machined to the minimum dimension should no longer be repaired!***

- Press worn valve guides out of cylinder head from the camshaft side using tool 10-206
  - ♦ Valve guides with collar = replacement guides to be installed from combustion chamber side
- Coat new guides with oil and press into cold cylinder head from camshaft side using tool 10-206 until guide shoulder makes contact

> ***CAUTION!***
> ***When the valve guide shoulder makes contact with the cylinder head, do not allow the applied pressure to exceed 1.0 ton or the guide shoulder could break off!***

- Ream valve guides out using hand reamer 10-215 and plenty of cutting fluid

Valve stem seals, replacing

With cylinder head installed

- Remove hood lock assembly mounting bolts
- Tilt radiator and hood lock assembly forward
- Support radiator with a workshop crane
  - ♦ VAG 1202 or VAG 1556/2

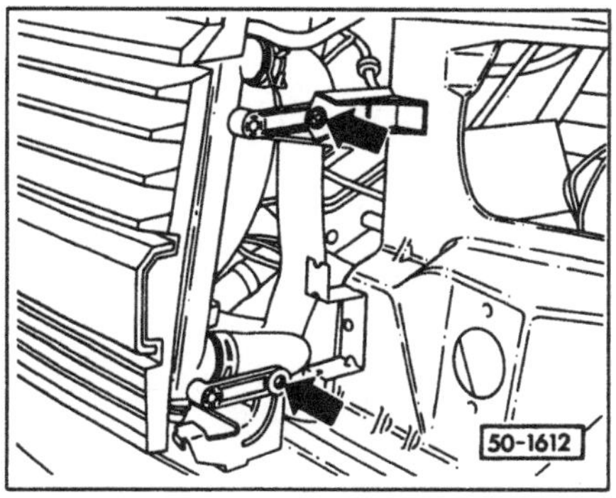

- Knock pins out of spring clips (arrows) on right and left
- Remove spring clips from radiator brackets
- Lift radiator using workshop crane
- Remove camshaft
  ⇒ page C 15-22
- Remove hydraulic lifters
- Remove spark plugs
- Set piston of appropriate cylinder to BDC

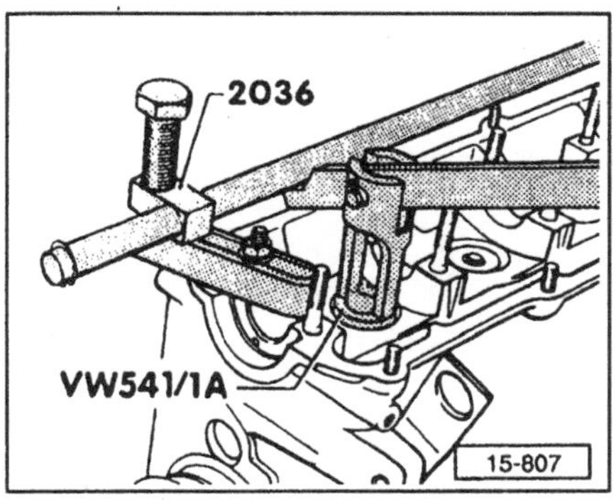

- Install compressor tool 2036 and adjust to height of studs
- Attach compressed air hose to adaptor VW 653/3
- Insert adaptor with seal into spark plug threads, hand tighten
- Apply a continuous pressure, 6 bar (87 psi) minimum, to the adaptor
- Remove valve springs using valve lever VW 541/1 and adaptor VW 541/5
  - ♦ Tight keepers can be loosened by lightly tapping valve lever with a hammer
- Remove valve stem seals using adaptor 3047 A

Installing

- Install valve stem seals as follows:

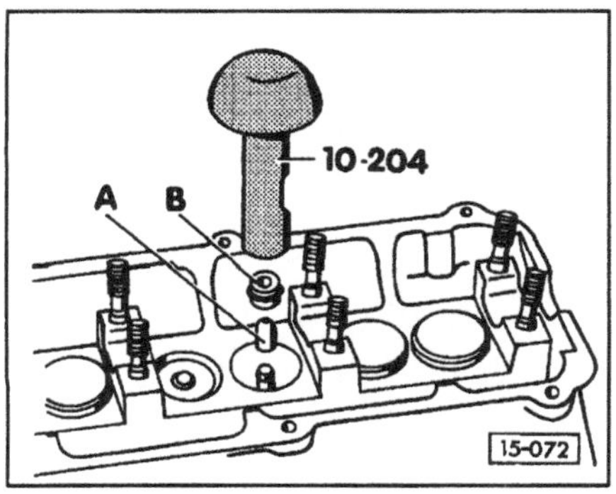

- Install plastic sleeve –A– onto valve stem
- Oil valve stem seal –B– and carefully slide it onto the valve guide
  - ♦ Always use plastic sleeve when installing valve stem seals

> ***CAUTION!***
> ***If new lifters have been installed, DO NOT attempt to start the engine for at least 30 minutes. The valves could strike the pistons!***

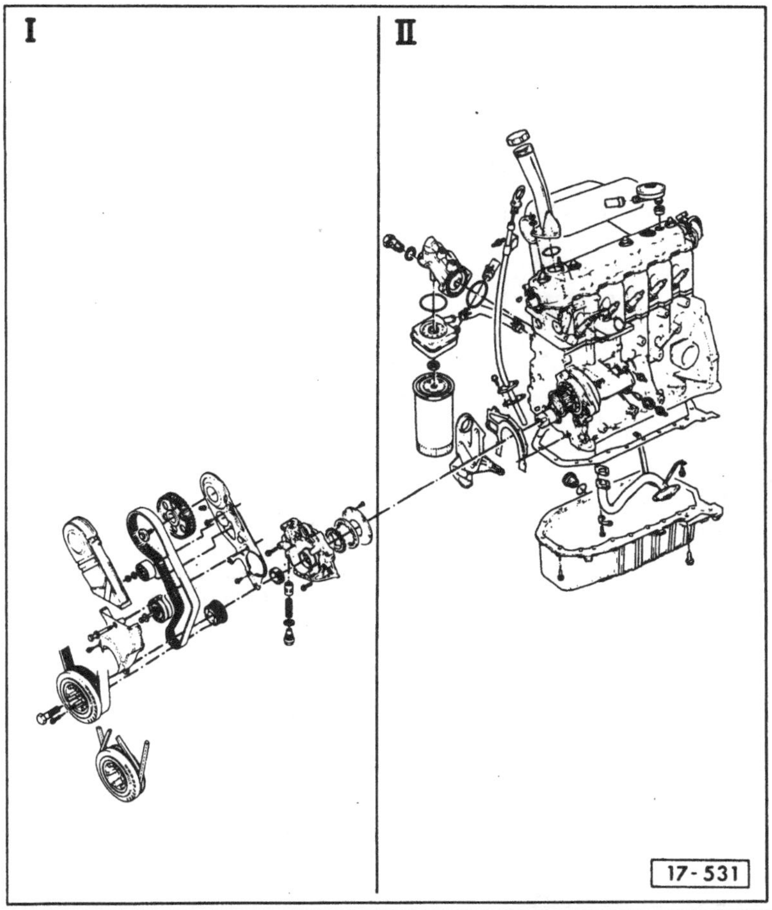

Lubrication system, component overview

I - ⇒ page C 17-3

II - ⇒ page C 17-6

- Always replace seals
- Oil pressure and oil pressure switch, checking

⇒ page C 17-10

- All components shown in illustration can be removed and installed with the engine installed
- If, when performing engine repairs, metal shavings or large quantities of metal particles, caused for example by partial seizure of crankshaft and connecting rod bearings, are found in the engine oil; thoroughly clean all of the oil passages and replace the oil cooler to prevent future damage.

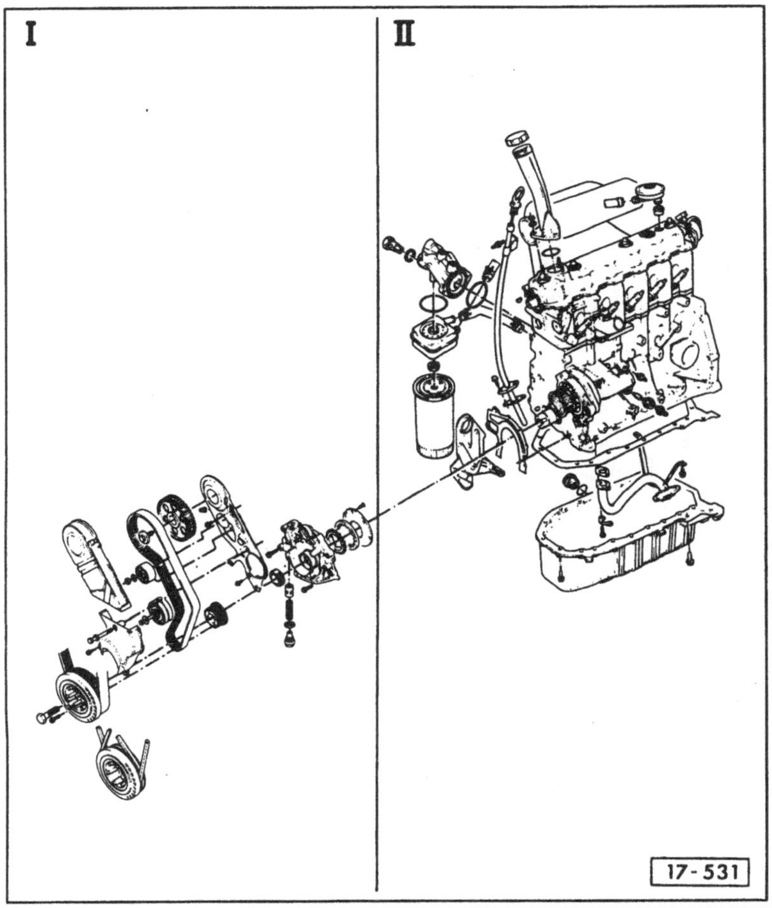

CAUTION!

DO NOT exceed the specified engine oil level as indicated on the dipstick, or damage to the catalytic converter could result.

Oil capacities:

- Without filter: 5.3 quarts (5.0 liter)
- With filter: 5.8 quarts (5.51 liter)

Engine oil specification:

- Use engine oils that comply with Owners Manual recommendations.

CAUTION!
Multi-grade or single grade oils corresponding to API-SF or SG, may be used, BUT only as an exception to the VW factory recommendation!

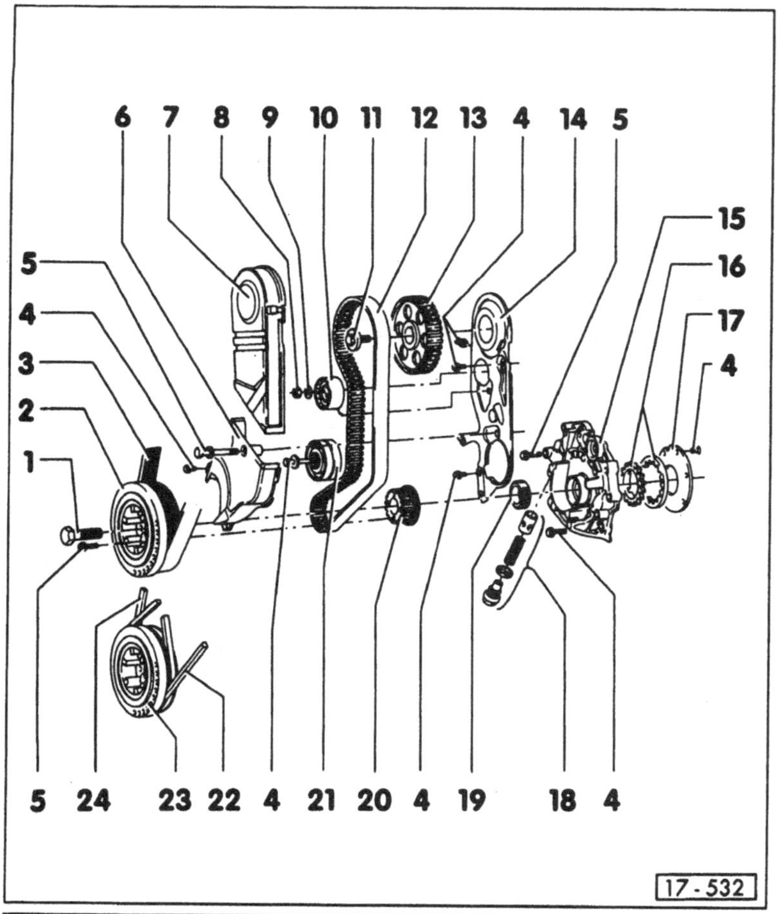

I - Lubrication system, drivebelts and pulleys

1 - 460 Nm (339 ft lb)
- coat threads and contact surfaces of the bolt head with: AMV 188 001 02
- to loosen and tighten, use 3248 countering tool

⇒ Repair Group 13

2 - Vibration damper for ribbed belt pulley
- vibration damper and crankshaft toothed belt sprocket can only be assembled one way

3 - Ribbed belt
- check for wear
- before removal, mark running direction using felt tipped marker
- remove and install using 3299 wrench

⇒ Repair Group 13

4 - 10 Nm (7 ft lb)

5 - 20 Nm (15 ft lb)

6 - Toothed belt guard, lower
- remove vibration damper –2–, if necessary for removal

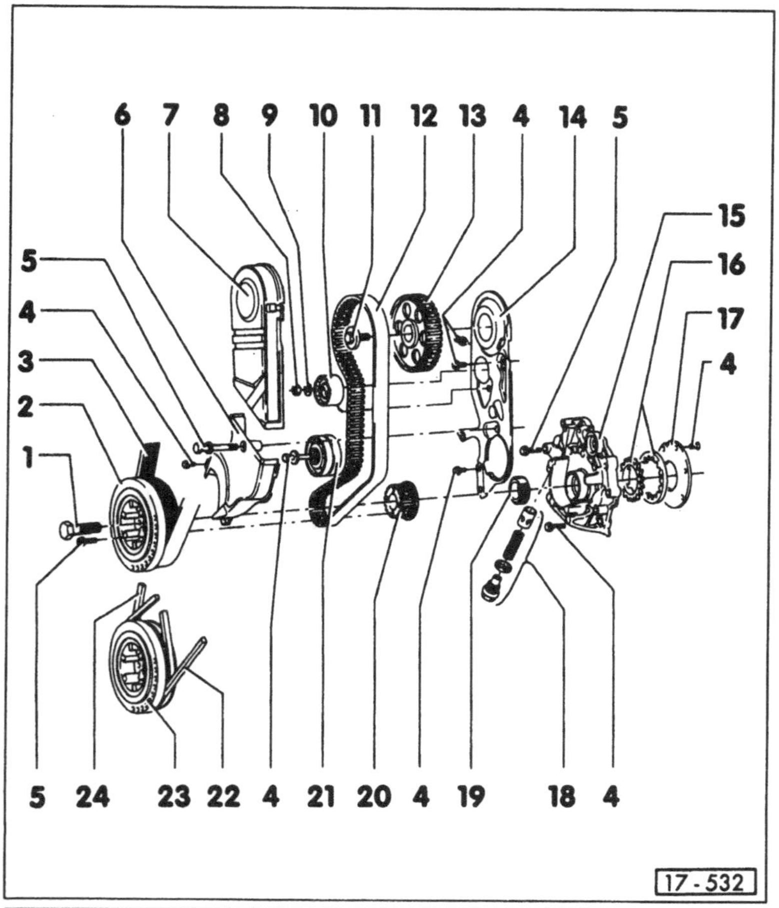

7 - Toothed belt guard, upper

8 - 15 Nm (11 ft lb)

9 - Washer
- with anti-rotation crimps

10 - Tensioner pulley
- toothed belt: removing/installing/tensioning

⇒ Repair Group 13

11 - Camshaft drive sprocket mounting screw
- observe raised letter coding on bolt head:
  8.8 = 85 Nm (63 ft lb)
  10.9 = 100 Nm (74 ft lb)
- use 3036 countering tool to loosen and tighten

12 - Toothed belt
- removing/installing/tensioning

⇒ Repair Group 13

13 - Camshaft drive sprocket
- note position while installing toothed belt

⇒ Repair Group 13

14 - Toothed belt guard, rear
- remove vibration damper, if necessary, for removal

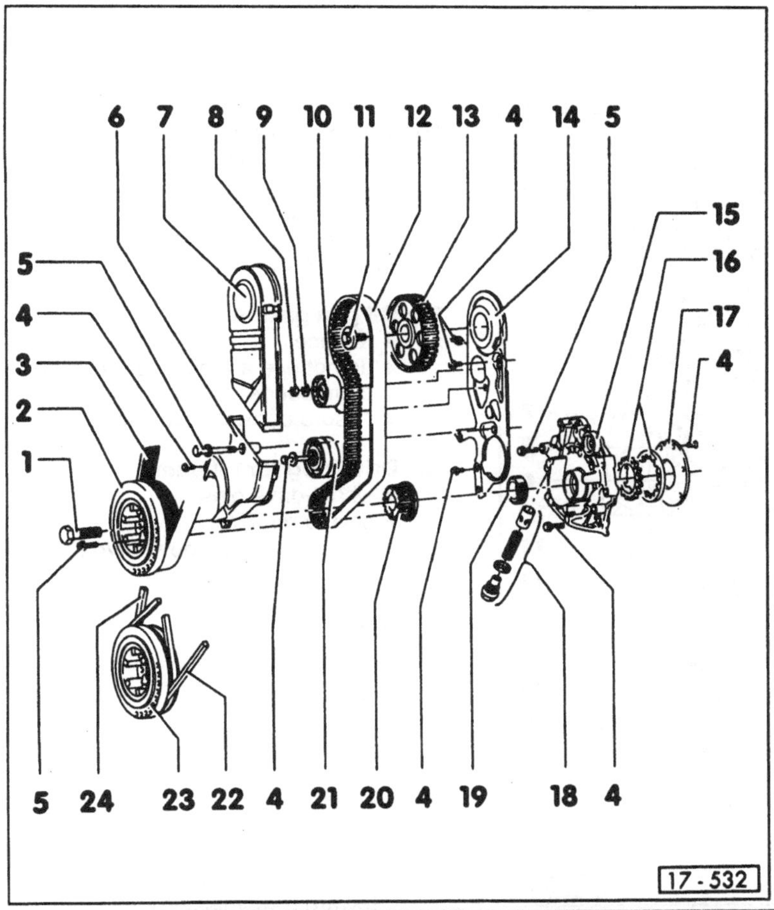

15 - **Oil pump**
- available only as an assembly
- note drive pin on crankshaft during installation

16 - **Oil pump gears**
- markings " " point in direction of cover

17 - **Cover**

18 - **Oil pressure relief valve**
- 40 Nm (30 ft lb)
- opening pressure: 5.3 - 6.3 bar (77 – 91psi)

19 - **Gasket**
- replacing

⇒ Repair Group 13

20 - **Crankshaft toothed belt drive sprocket**

21 - **Idler pulley**

22 - **Not for US vehicles**

23 - **Not for US vehicles**

24 - **Not for US vehicles**

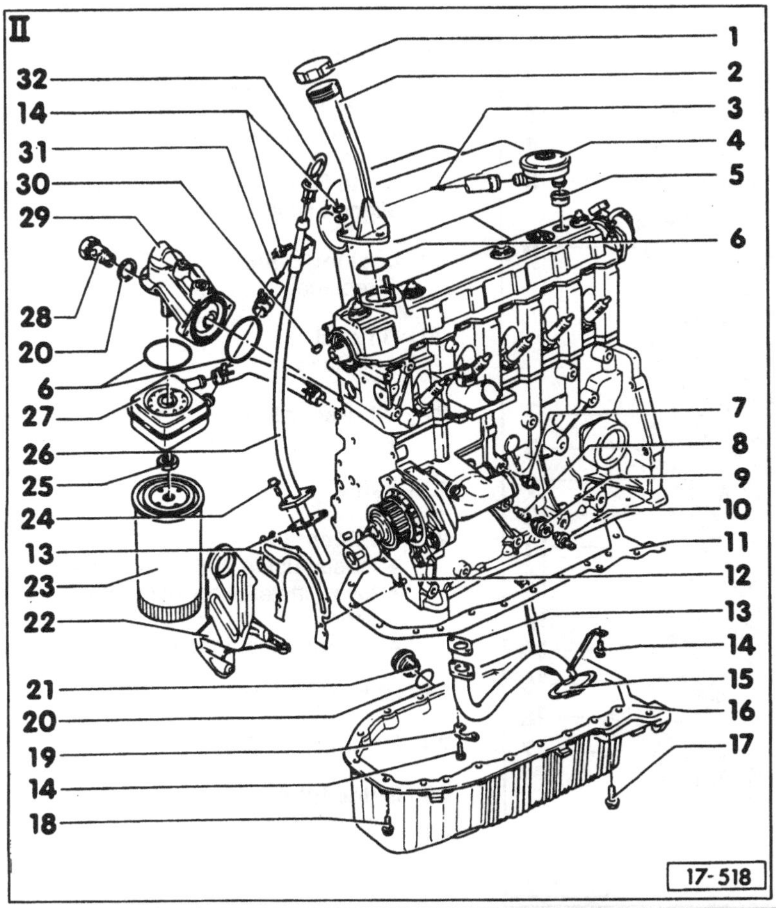

II - Lubrication system, engine mechanicals

1 - **Oil filler cap**

2 - **Oil filler pipe**

3 - **To intake hose**
- breather hose secured via bracket to oil filler pipe
- ensure adequate clearance between throttle body connection

4 - **Emission control valve**

5 - **Oil seal**
- replace if damaged

6 - **O-ring**
- replace if damaged

7 - **0.3 bar oil pressure switch (F 22)**
- 25 Nm (18 ft lb)
- brown
- blue/black wire
- checking:

⇒ page C 17-10

8 - **Oil pressure retaining valve**
- 6 Nm (53 inch lb)
- remove and install using 8 mm socket wrench
- install using D6 adhesive sealer

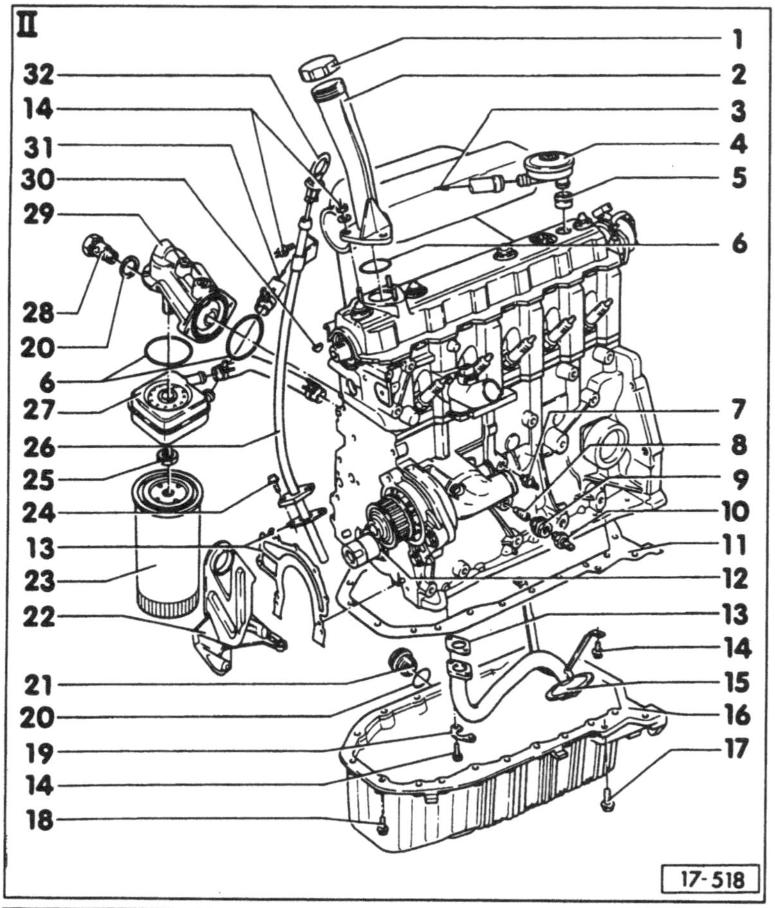

9 - **Adaptor**
- ♦ 50 Nm (37 ft lb)

10 - **1.8 bar oil pressure switch (F 1)**
- ♦ 25 Nm (18 ft lb)
- ♦ white
- ♦ yellow wire
- ♦ checking:

⇒ page C 17-10

11 - **Oil pan gasket**
- ♦ replace
- ♦ do not use adhesive or bonding compounds
- ♦ ensure correct install position

12 - **Drive dog for oil pump**
- ♦ with 4 drive pins
- ♦ split to remove
- ♦ before installing new drive dog, heat approx. 392°F (200°), max.

13 - **Gasket**
- ♦ replace

14 - **10 Nm (7 ft lb)**

15 - **Intake pipe**

16 - **Oil pan**

17 - **20 Nm (15 ft lb)**
- ♦ install M8 bolts with hex heads toward transmission

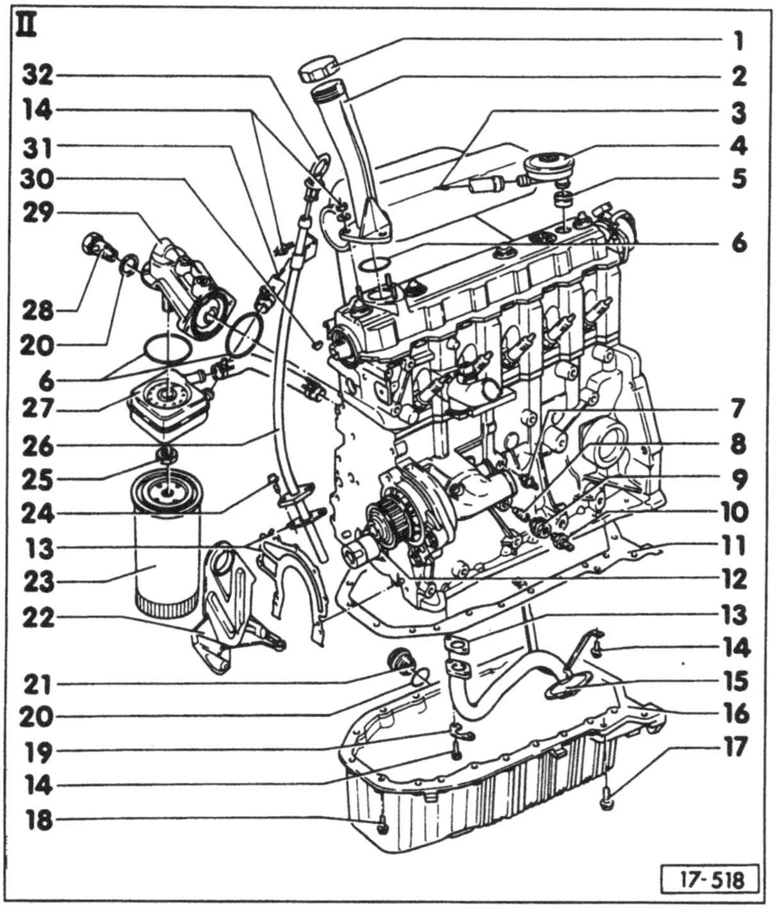

18 - **10 Nm (7 ft lb)**
- ♦ remove and install M6 bolts using 3249 socket wrench
- ♦ with flywheel installed:

– rotate flywheel so that recess is aligned flush with bolts

19 - **Locking plate**
- ♦ replace

20 - **Oil seal**
- ♦ replace

21 - **Oil drain plug**
- ♦ 40 Nm (30 ft lb)

22 - **Baffle**

23 - **Oil filter**
- ♦ loosen using 2067 box wrench
- ♦ follow installation instructions on filter
- ♦ tighten hand tight, only

24 - **20 Nm (15 ft lb)**

25 - **25 Nm (18 ft lb)**

26 - **Guide tube**
- ♦ for dipstick

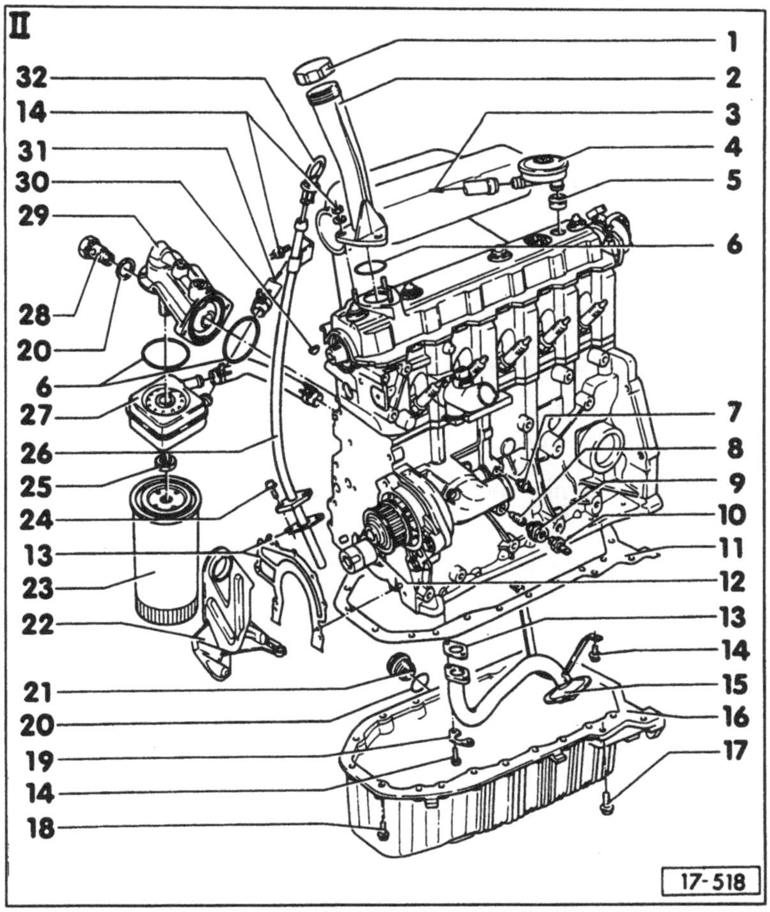

27 - Oil cooler
- coat oil seal flange contact surfaces with AMV 188100 02
- ensure clearance between adjacent parts
- see note page C 17-1

28 - 70 Nm (52 ft lb)

29 - Oil filter bracket
- installation position determined by dowel pins
- with oil check valves for hydraulic lifters

30 - Woodruff key
- check for tight fit

31 - From coolant pipe
⇒ Repair Group 19

32 - Dipstick
- quantity difference between minimum and maximum marks: 1.5 liters (1.6 quarts)

> ***CAUTION!***
> ***DO NOT exceed the specified engine oil level as indicated on the dipstick, or damage to the catalytic converter could result.***

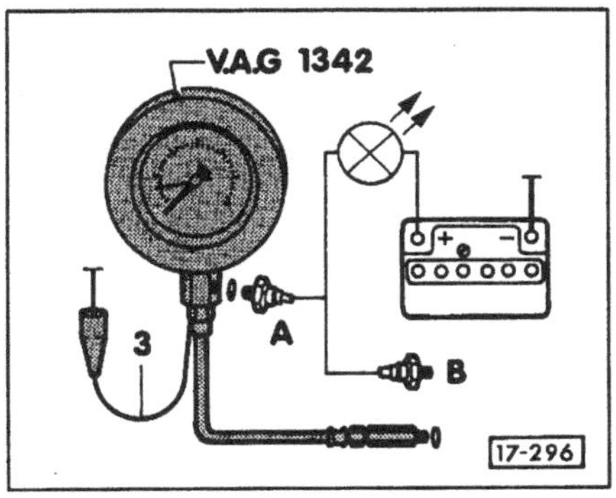

Oil pressure switch and oil pressure, checking

Visual and audible oil pressure warning

◄

– Remove 0.3 bar oil pressure switch (brown) and screw into tester

– Screw tester into cylinder block (substitute for removed oil pressure switch)

– Connect brown wire between tester and ground

– Connect VAG 1527B LED tester between B+ and 0.3 bar oil pressure switch (mounted in tester –A–), using VW 1594 adaptor kit

- LED should light up

– Start engine

– Slowly increase engine speed until a pressure of 0.15 to 0.45 bar (2.2 to 6.5 psi) is obtained

- LED must go out

If LED remains lit

– Replace 0.3 bar oil pressure switch

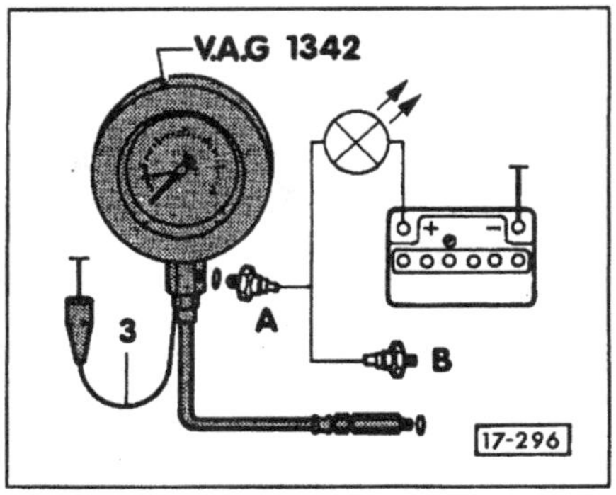

◄ – Connect LED tester to (white) 1.8 bar oil pressure switch B (on cylinder block)

- ♦ At a pressure of 1.6 to 2.0 bar (23.2 to 29 psi), the LED must light up

If NO

– Replace 1.8 bar oil pressure switch

– Raise and hold engine speed at slightly more than 2000 RPM

- ♦ At 2000 RPM and an oil temperature of 80°C (176°F), oil pressure must be 2.0 bar (29 psi) minimum

Oil pressure must not exceed 7.0 bar (101 psi) at higher engine speed

– If necessary, replace pressure relief valve (oil pump) or check valve

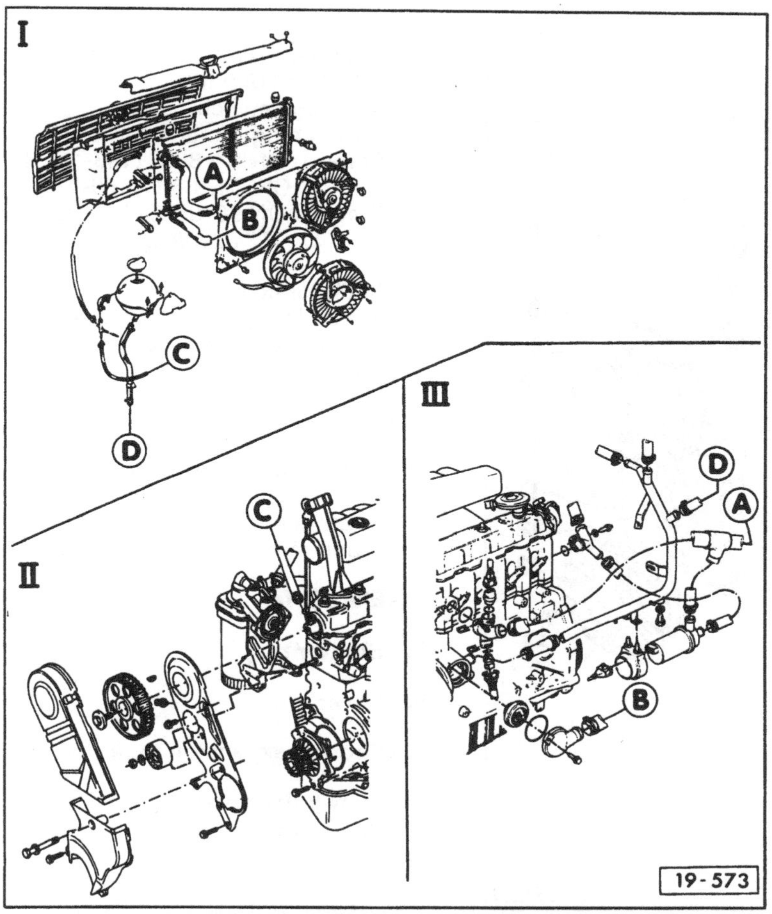

Cooling system, component overview

- When engine is hot, relieve cooling system pressure before starting repairs
- Hose connections are secured with either spring or screw type clamps. Spring clamps can be replaced with screw clamps
- Use commercial pliers such as Hazet 798-5 to install spring clamps
- All components shown in the illustration can be removed and replaced with the engine installed
- Coolant, draining and filling:

⇒ page C 19-10

- Coolant mixture ratios:

⇒ page C 19-11

- Perform cooling system leak testing using VAG 1274 and 1274/3

I - page C 19-2

II - page C 19-5

III - page C 19-7

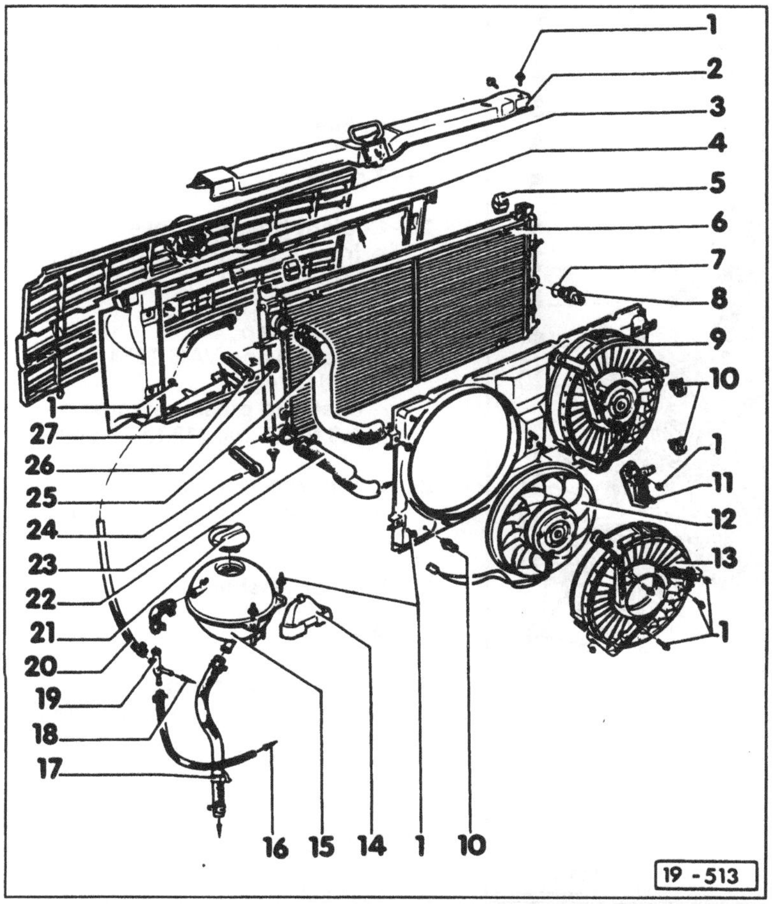

I - Engine coolant radiator, component overview

1 - 10 Nm (7 ft lb)

2 - Hood-lock carrier

3 - Radiator grille

4 - Air duct

- secured to radiator via 4 vertical bolts and 4 horizontal rivets or bolts (arrows)

5 - Rubber block

6 - Radiator

- if new radiator has been installed, completely replace engine coolant
- removing:

⇒ page C 19-13

7 - Seal

- replace

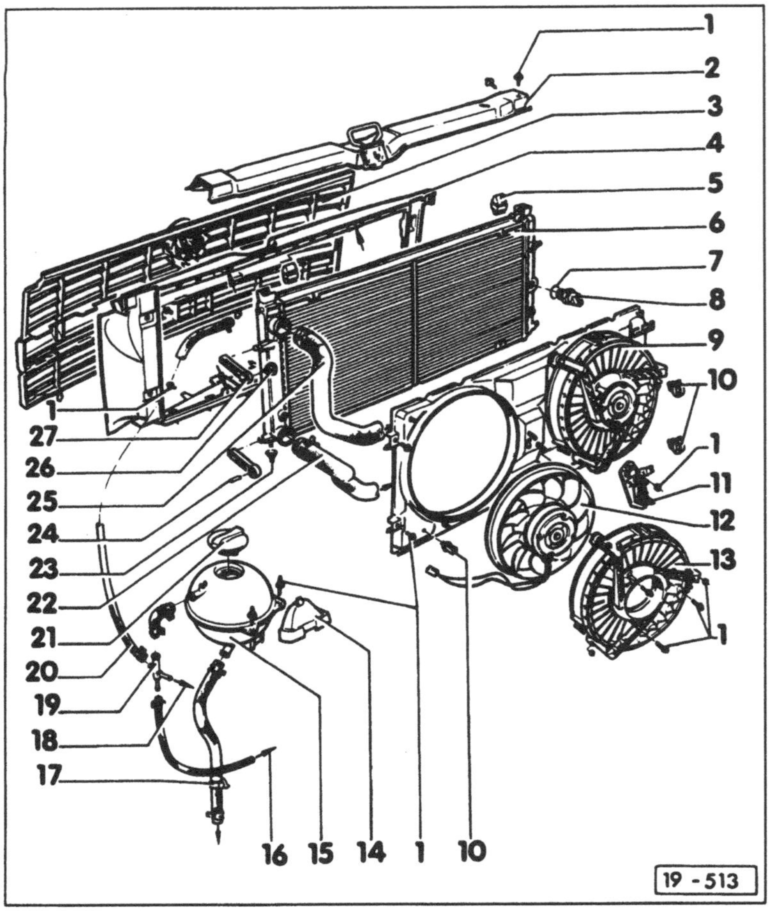

8 - Thermal switch
- 25 Nm (18 ft lb)
- 2-stage switch
- switching temperatures:

Stage 1: ON 84–89°C (183–192°F)
OFF 76–83°C (169–181°F)
Stage 2: ON 90–95°C (194–203°F)
OFF 82–89°C (180–192°F)

9 - Radiator cowl
- with integrated electric fan
- with thermostatically controlled shutters

10 - Cable clip

11 - Thermostat control for shutters
- checking: engine coolant temperature below 25°C (77°F) and shutters closed

12 - Electric fan

13 - Shutter ring

14 - Cover

15 - Coolant expansion tank

16 - to cylinder head
⇒ page C 19-5

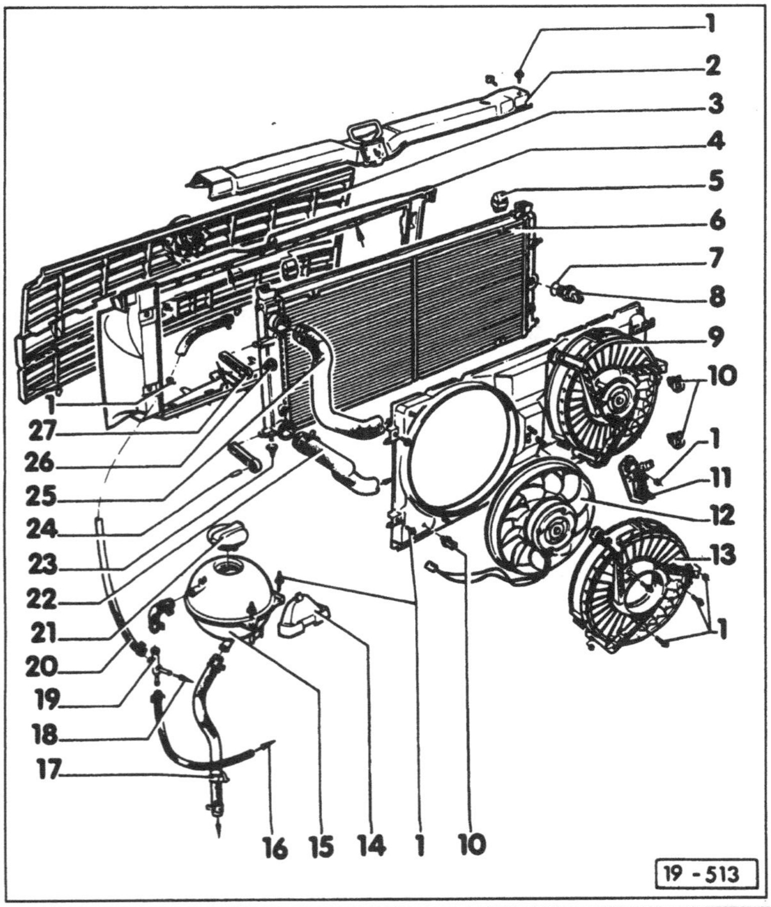

17 - to coolant hose
⇒ page C 19-7

18 - to heat exchanger

19 - T-piece

20 - Coolant breather hose
- from radiator to expansion tank

21 - Radiator cap
- check using VAG 1274 and1274/4
  checking pressure: must be 1.3 to 1.5 bar (19 to 22 psi)

22 - Lower radiator hose
- to connection, coolant pump:

⇒ page C 19-7

23 - Rubber washer

24 - Pin

25 - Upper radiator hose
- from connection on cyl. head:

⇒ page C 19-7
- with branch for coolant pump:

⇒ page C 19-7

26 - Spring clip

27 - Bracket

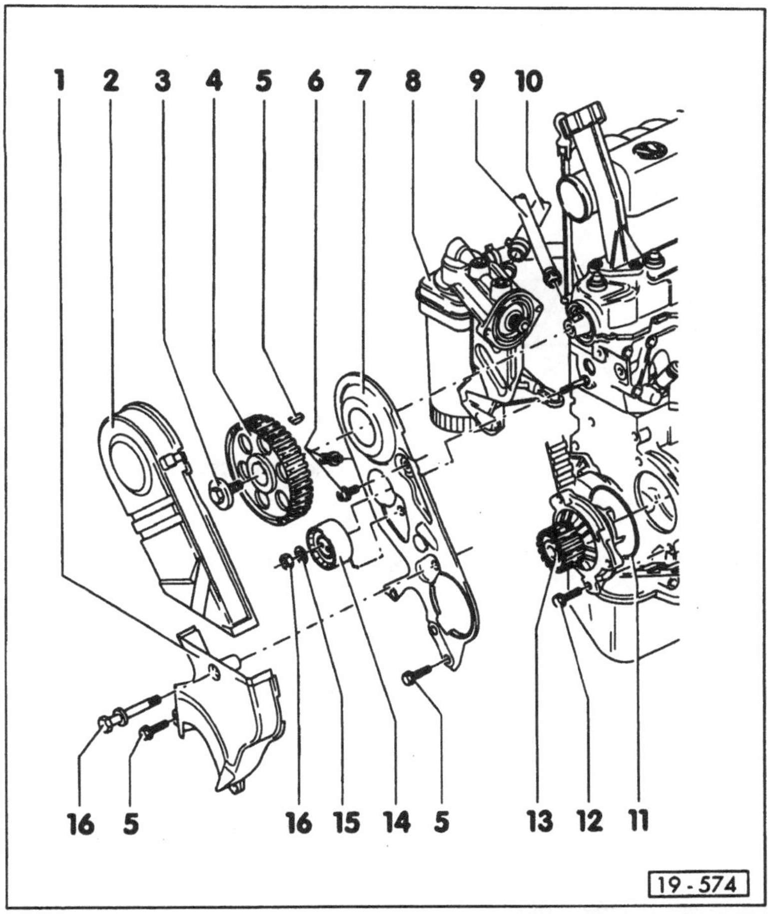

II - Cooling system, drivebelts and pulleys

1 - Belt guard, lower
- for removal, vibration damper may be removed if necessary

2 - Belt guard, upper

3 - Camshaft drive sprocket mounting screw
- note torque identification on bolt head:
  8.8 = 85 Nm (63 ft lb)
  10.9 = 100 Nm (74 ft lb)
- to loosen/tighten, use 3036 holding tool

4 - Camshaft drive sprocket
- note position when installing toothed belt

⇒ Repair Group 13

5 - Woodruff key
- ensure key is correctly seated on camshaft

6 - 10 Nm (7 ft lb)

7 - Belt guard, rear
- for removal, vibration damper may be removed if necessary

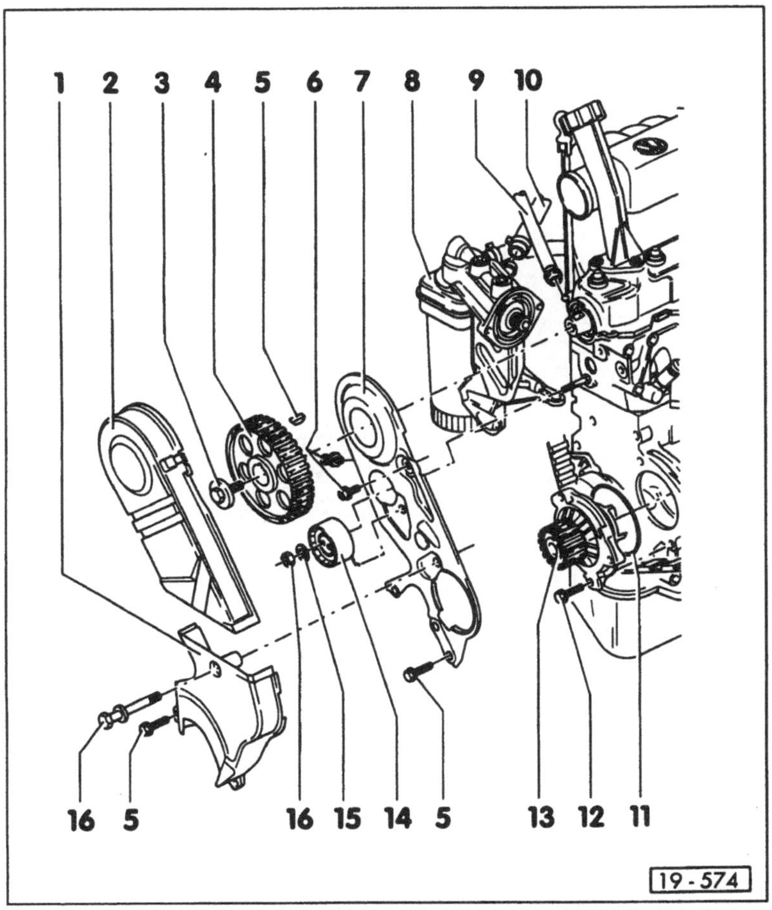

8 - Oil cooler
- removing and installing:

⇒ Repair Group 17

9 - to T-piece on coolant expansion tank

10 - to coolant pipe

⇒ page C 19-7

11 - O-ring
- replace if damaged

12 - 20 Nm (15 ft lb)

13 - Coolant pump
- ensure that shaft moves freely
- replace completely if there is damage or leakage

14 - Idler pulley
- toothed belt, removing/installing/tightening

⇒ Repair Group 13

15 - Crimped washer

16 - 20 Nm (15 ft lb)
- mounting nut for idler pulley: 15 Nm (11 ft lb)

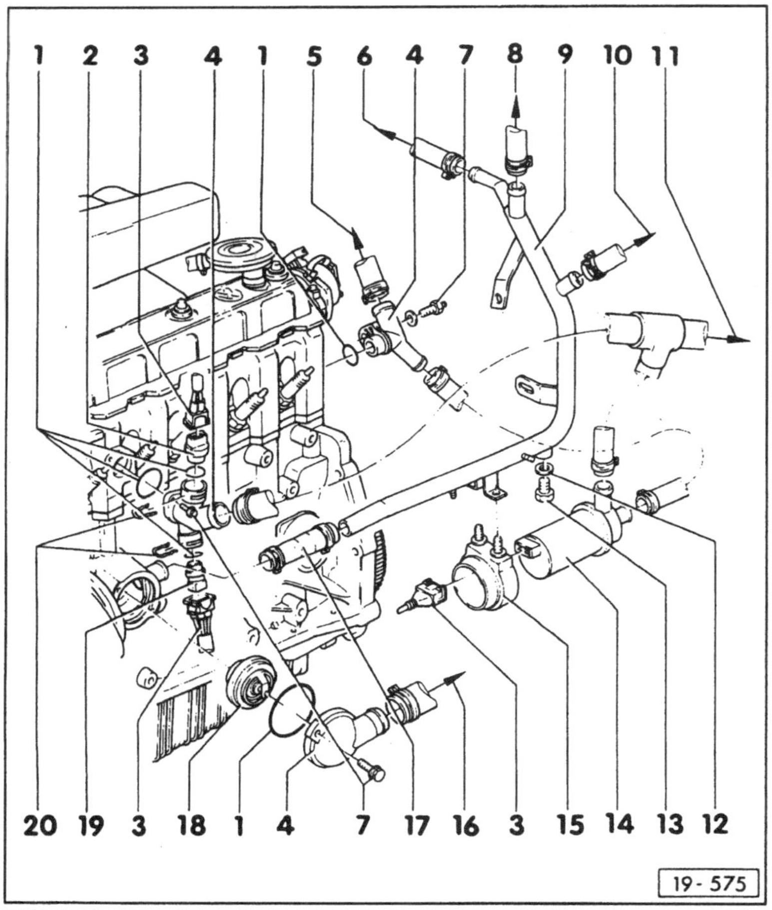

III - Cooling system, component overview

1 - O-ring
- replace if damaged

2 - Engine Coolant Temperature sensor (G62)
- blue
- 2-pin
- for Digifant fuel injection and ignition system
- checking:

⇒ Repair Group 24

3 - Harness connector

4 - Hose flange

5 - to heat exchanger

6 - to oil cooler

⇒ page C 19-6

7 - 10 Nm (7 ft lb)

8 - to heat exchanger regulator valve

9 - Coolant pipe
- mounted on starter

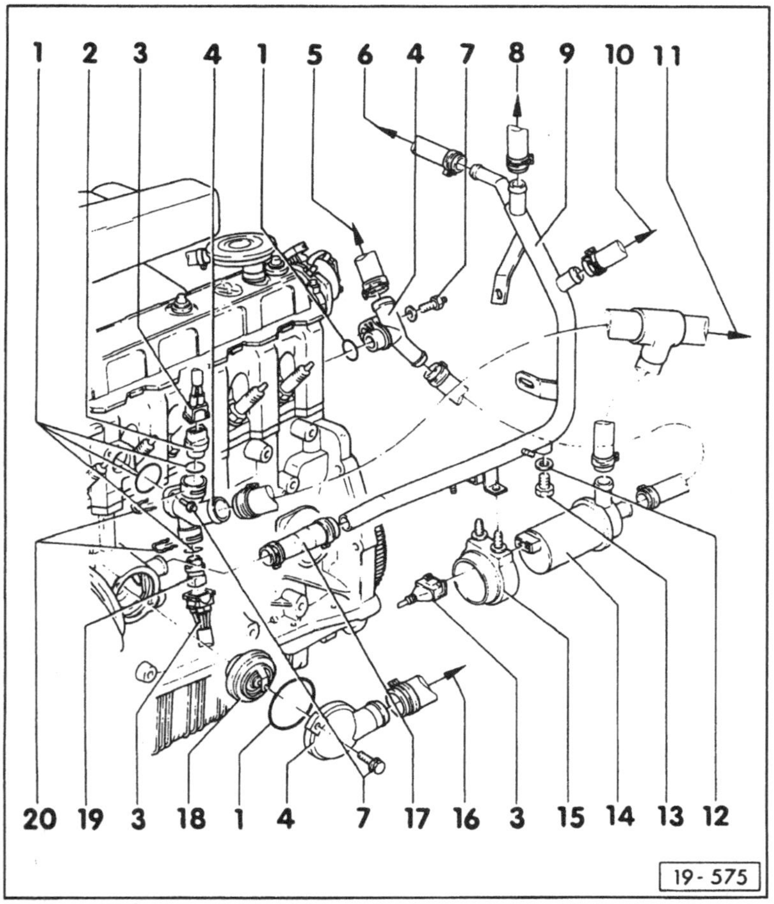

10 - to coolant expansion tank

⇒ page C 19-3

11 - to upper radiator

⇒ page C 19-2

12 - Sealing washer
- replace

13 - Drain plug
- 10 Nm (7 ft lb)
- draining coolant:

⇒ page C 19-10

14 - Coolant circulation pump V50
- checking:

⇒ page C 19-14

15 - Rubber retainer

16 - to lower radiator

⇒ page C 19-2

17 - Connecting hose

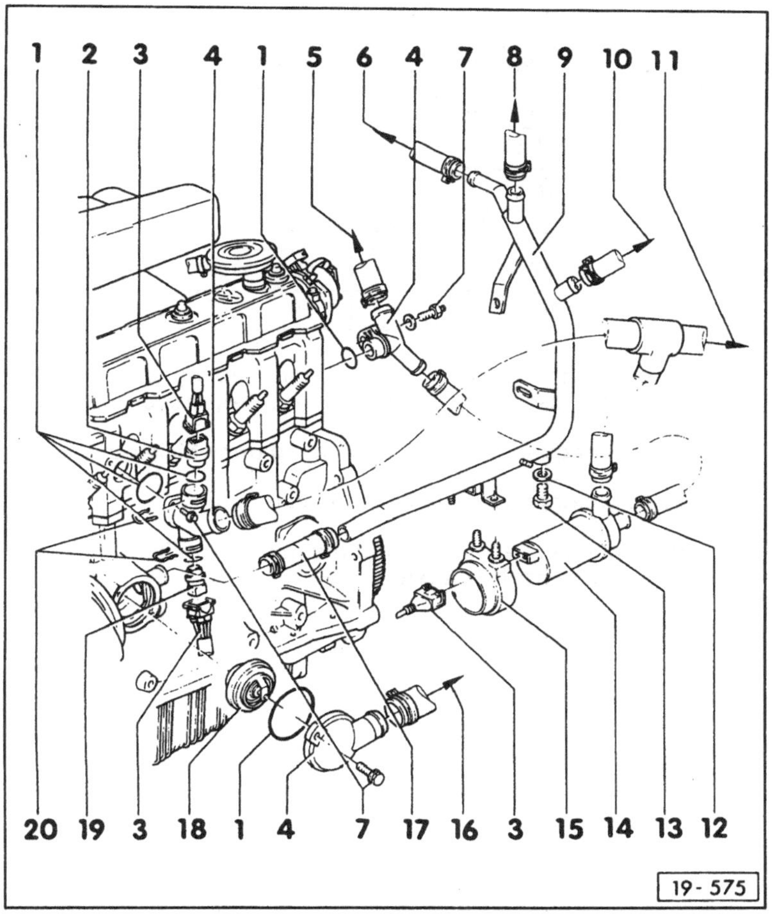

18 - Thermostat
- ♦ checking:

– heat thermostat in water
- ♦ starts to open approx. 87°C (189°F)
- ♦ completely open approx. 102°C (216°F)
- ♦ opening stroke 7 mm (0.28 in) minimum

19 - Coolant Circulation Engine Coolant Temperature (ECT) Thermal switch (F51) and Engine Coolant Temperature sensor (G2)
- ♦ yellow
- ♦ 4-pin
- ♦ Thermal switch (F 51) checking:

⇒ page C 19-14

20 - Retaining clips

Coolant, draining and filling

Draining

Requirement

- ♦ Heater temperature control on full warm position

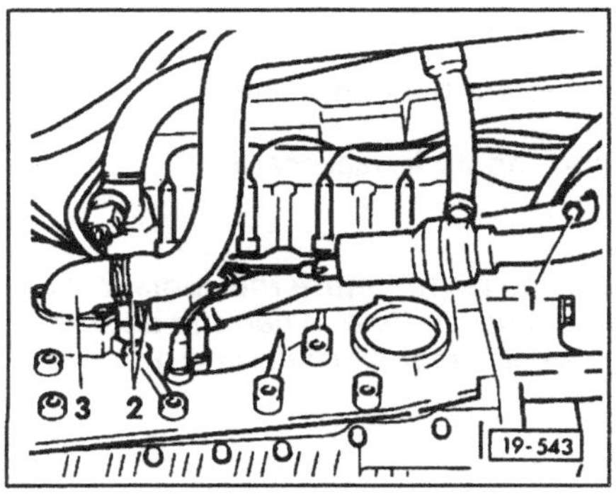

◄ – Open cap on coolant expansion tank

– Drain coolant using drain plug -1- and coolant hose -2- or via thermostat connector hose -3-

Filling

- ♦ The cooling system must be filled year round with the proper mixture of water and G11 antifreeze.
- ♦ G11 and coolant additives marked: "in accordance with TL VW 774 A" will prevent freezing, corrosion damage and scale formation and also raise the boiling point of the coolant.
- ♦ The high boiling point (higher than water) of the coolant mixture improves engine efficiency when the engine is operating at full load, particularly in tropical temperatures.
- ♦ If radiator, heat exchanger, cylinder head or head gasket are replaced, completely replace coolant with new G11 mixture.

Recommended mixture ratios:	
For protection down to –25°C (–13°F)	
% Water	% Anti-freeze
(60%) 5.4 : 1	(40%) 3.6 : 1
For protection down to –35°C (–31°F)	
% Water	% Anti-freeze
(50%) 4.5 : 1	(50%) 4.5 : 1

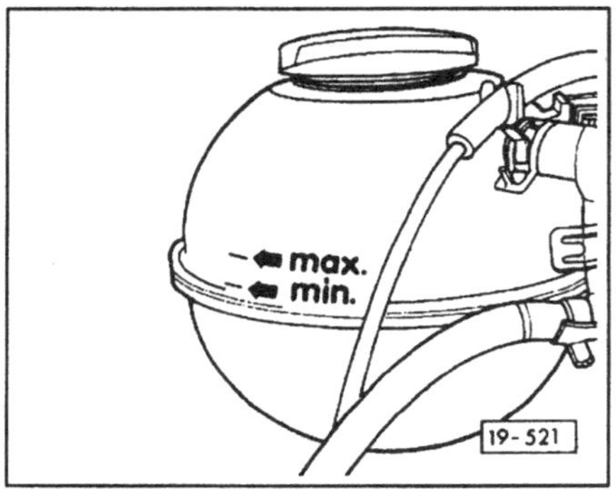

- ♦ Low–temperature protection and cooling effectiveness decreases if the percentage of anti-freeze exceeds 60%
- ♦ Coolant quantity varies depending on vehicle options

– Open breather screw in hose to heater core

◄ – Fill coolant expansion tank to the maximum line with appropriate coolant mixture

– Close breather screw

– Start engine and run at higher speed than idle (using accelerator pedal) for a few minutes

– Check coolant level and top up if necessary

– Install cap on coolant expansion tank

– Run engine until engine coolant fan comes on

– Re-check coolant level and top up if necessary

Note:

When the engine is at operating temperature the coolant level must be slightly above the maximum line, when the engine is cold; the level must fall between the maximum and minimum lines.

Radiator, removing

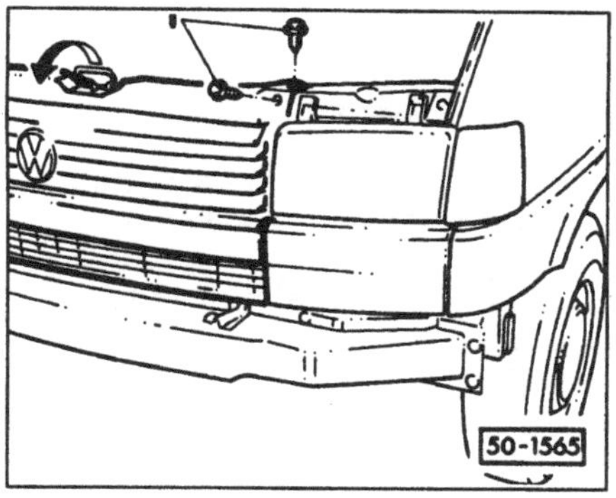

- Remove mounting bolts -1- from left and right
- Tilt the radiator and hood-lock assembly forward (arrow)
- Disconnect coolant fan and thermoswitch
- Remove sound deadening pan
- Drain coolant
⇒ page C 19-10
- Detach all coolant hoses from radiator

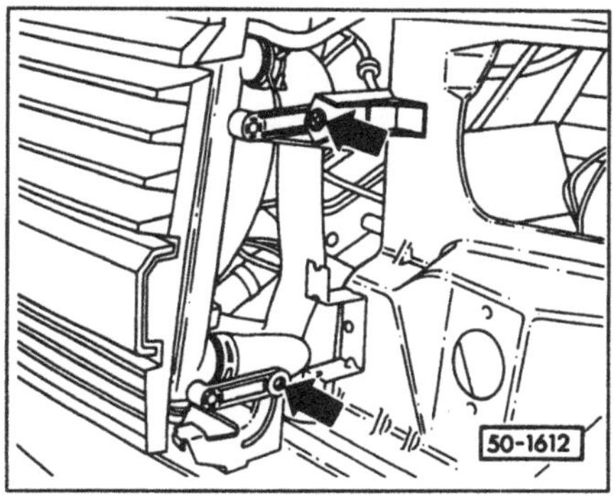

- Drive pins out of right and left radiator bracket expansion clips (arrow)
- Remove radiator assembly complete with hood-lock assembly and coolant hoses

Coolant pump and coolant circulation ECT thermal switch, checking

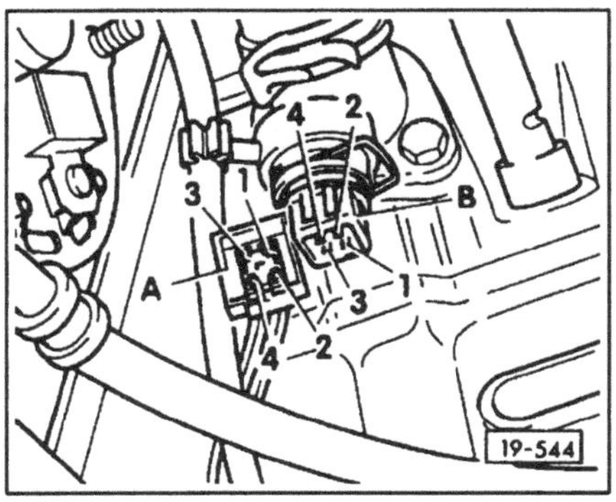

- Disconnect coolant pump V 50 from Coolant Circulation Engine Coolant Temperature Thermal switch F 51
- Disconnect Engine Coolant Temperature sensor G2 for Engine Coolant Temperature gauge
- Bridge terminals 1 and 4 on plug -A- using jumper wires from VW 1594 adaptor kit
- Coolant pump must run

If NO:

- Disconnect coolant pump harness connector

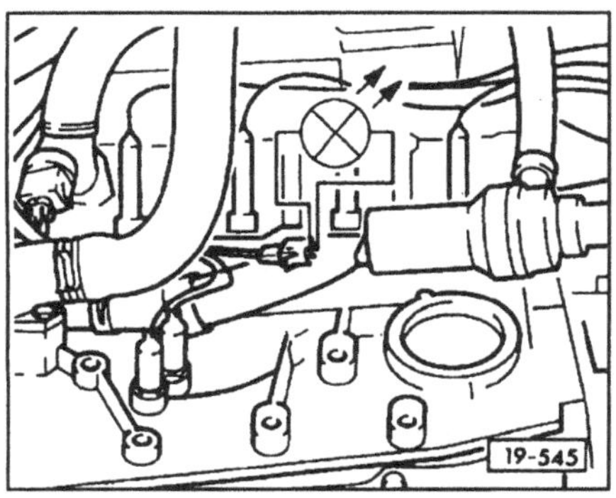

- Connect VAG 1527B LED tester between terminals of harness connector using jumper wires from VW 1594 adaptor kit
  - ♦ LED must light up (indicating voltage supply to pump is OK)

If voltage supply OK:

- Replace coolant pump V 50

If voltage supply NOT OK:

- Locate and eliminate open circuit using wiring diagram

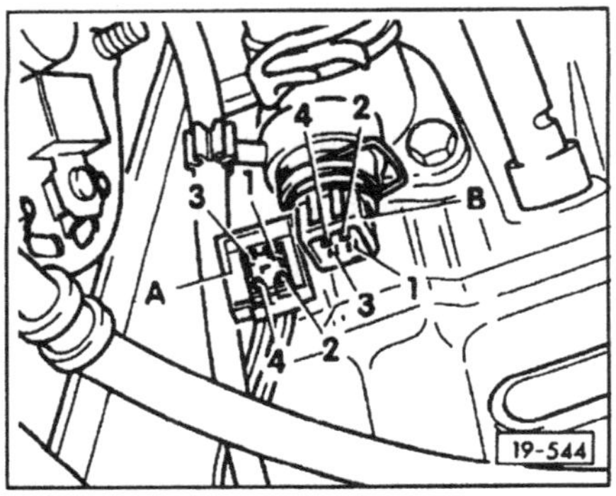

Thermal switch F51 resistance, checking

– Switch Fluke 83 multimeter to resistance range

◄ – Connect multimeter between terminals 1 and 4 of thermal switch -B- using jumper wires from VW 1594 adaptor kit

♦ Below approx. 103°C (217°F) = infinite Ohms (open)

♦ Above approx. 104°C (219°F) = 0 Ohms (continuity)

If resistance not within specified range:

– Replace thermal switch F 51

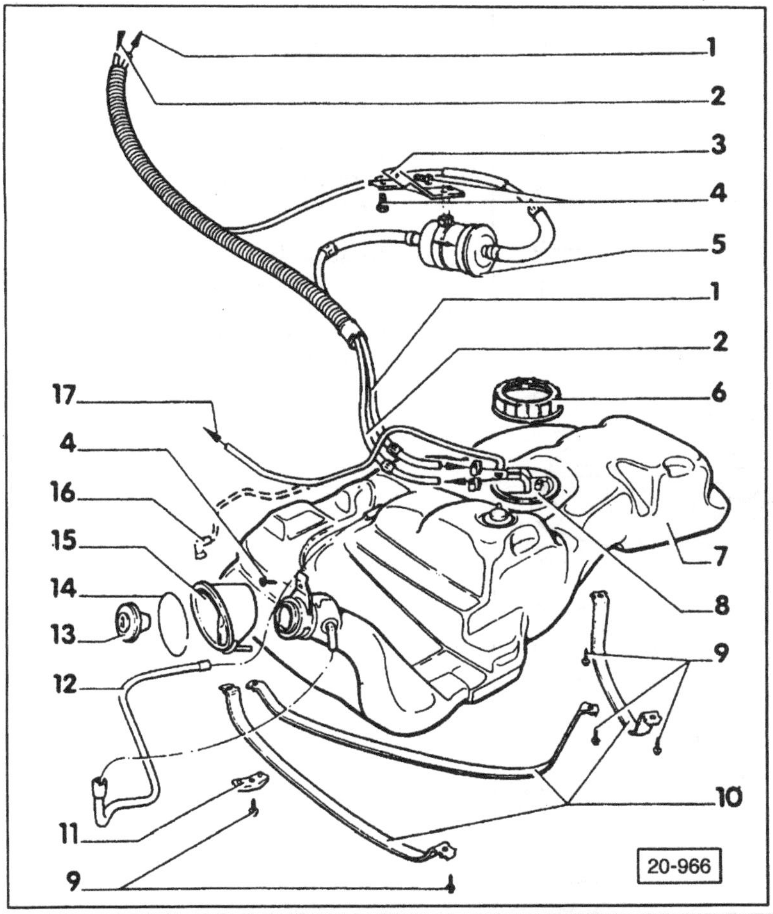

Fuel tank assembly, component layout

> ***WARNING!***
> ***Fire hazard. DO NOT smoke or have anything in area that can ignite fuel.***

- Fuel delivery unit servicing:
⇒ page C 20-14

- Observe safety precautions:
⇒ page C 20-7

- Observe Rules of Cleanliness:
⇒ page C 20-8

- Throttle linkage repairing:
⇒ page C 20-23

- Secure hose connections using either screw- or spring-type clips

- Always replace spring-type clips

1 - Fuel supply line
- black
- to fuel rail connector

⇒ Repair Group 24

2 - Fuel return line
- blue
- from fuel rail

⇒ Repair Group 24

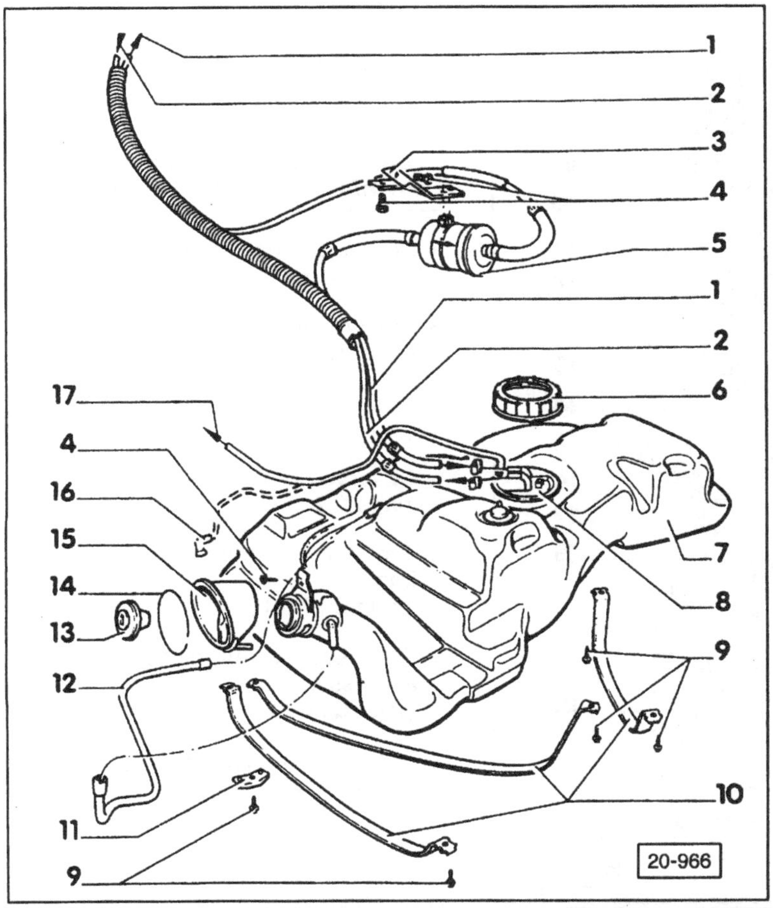

3 - Bracket

4 - 10 Nm (7 ft lb)

5 - Fuel filter
- note installed position; arrow points in direction of flow

6 - Collar nut
- Loosen and tighten using 3217

7 - Fuel tank
- removing and installing:

⇒ page C 20-21

8 - Flange
- note installed position:

⇒ page C 20-11

- fuel delivery unit, remove and install:

⇒ page C 20-10

- has additional fuel line connection for vehicles with auxiliary heater

9 - 25 Nm (18 ft lb)

10 - Support strap

11 - Retaining bracket

12 - Overflow hose

13 - Fuel filler cap

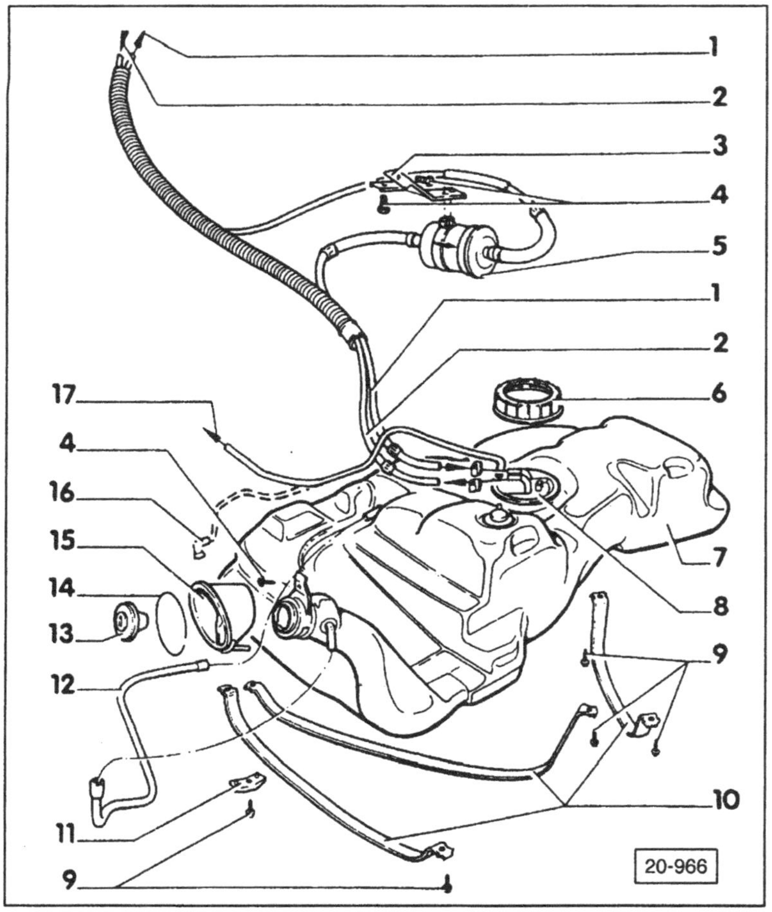

14 - **Retaining ring**

15 - **Splash shield**

16 - **Breather hose**
- for vehicles without EVAP emissions control system

17 - **Breather hose**
- for vehicles with EVAP emissions control system
- to EVAP canister:

⇒ page C 20-25, item 9

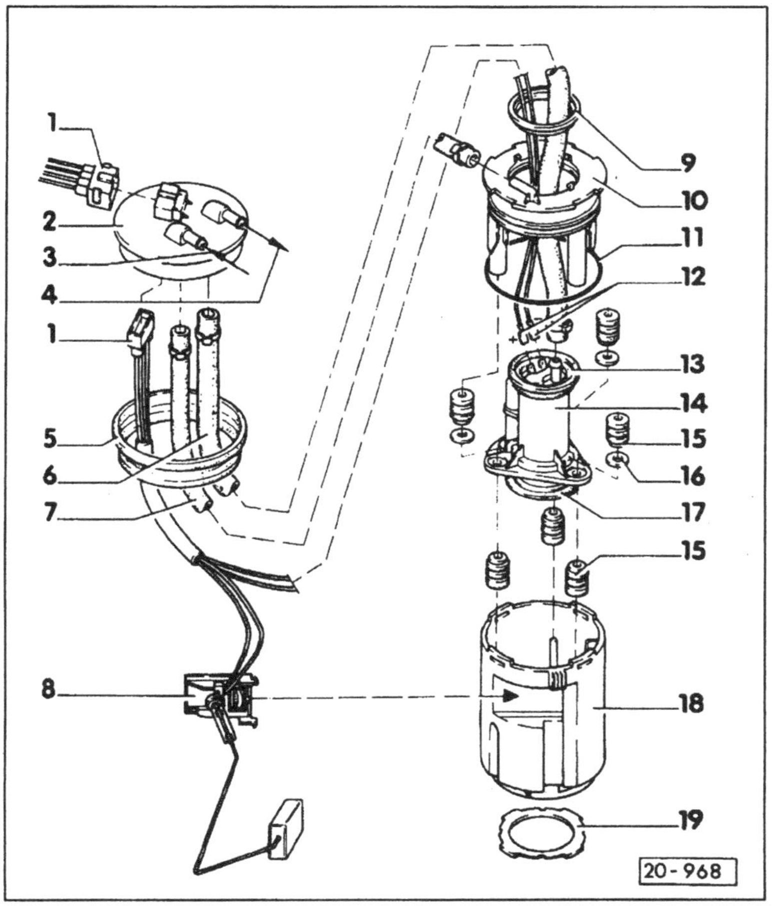

Fuel delivery unit, servicing

> ***WARNING!***
>
> ***Fire hazard. DO NOT smoke or have anything in area that can ignite fuel.***

- Secure all hose connections with either screw or spring-type clips
- Always replace spring-type clips, never re-use
- Observe safety precautions:

⇒ page C 20-7

- Observe Rules of Cleanliness:

⇒ page C 20-8

- Fuel delivery unit, removing/installing:

⇒ page C 20-10

- Fuel delivery unit, disassembling and assembling:

⇒ page C 20-12

- Fuel pump relay, checking

⇒ Repair Group 24

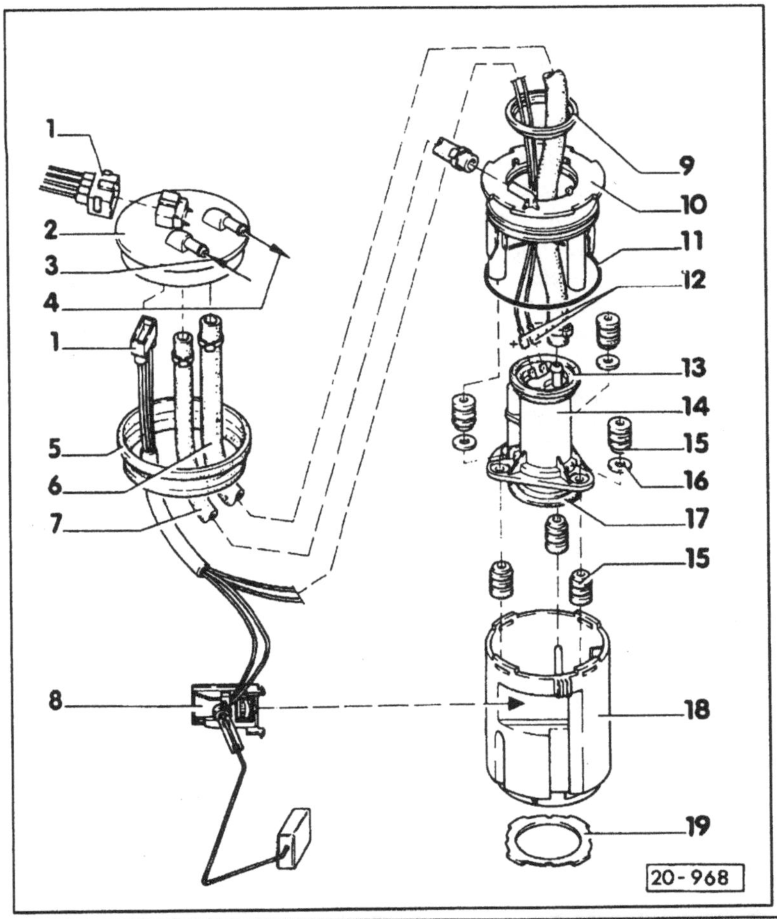

1 - Connector

2 - Flange
- note installed position on fuel tank:

⇒ page C 20-11
- note markings for supply and return hoses on underside of flange
- vehicles with an auxiliary heater will have an additional fuel line connection

3 - Return flow
- from fuel rail

⇒ Repair Group 24

4 - Supply flow
- to fuel filter:

⇒ page C 20-2, item 5

5 - Sealing ring
- lubricate before installing

6 - Fuel supply line

7 - Fuel return line

8 - Fuel gauge sending unit
- removing and installing:

⇒ page C 20-10

9 - Upper retaining ring
- unclip using screwdriver

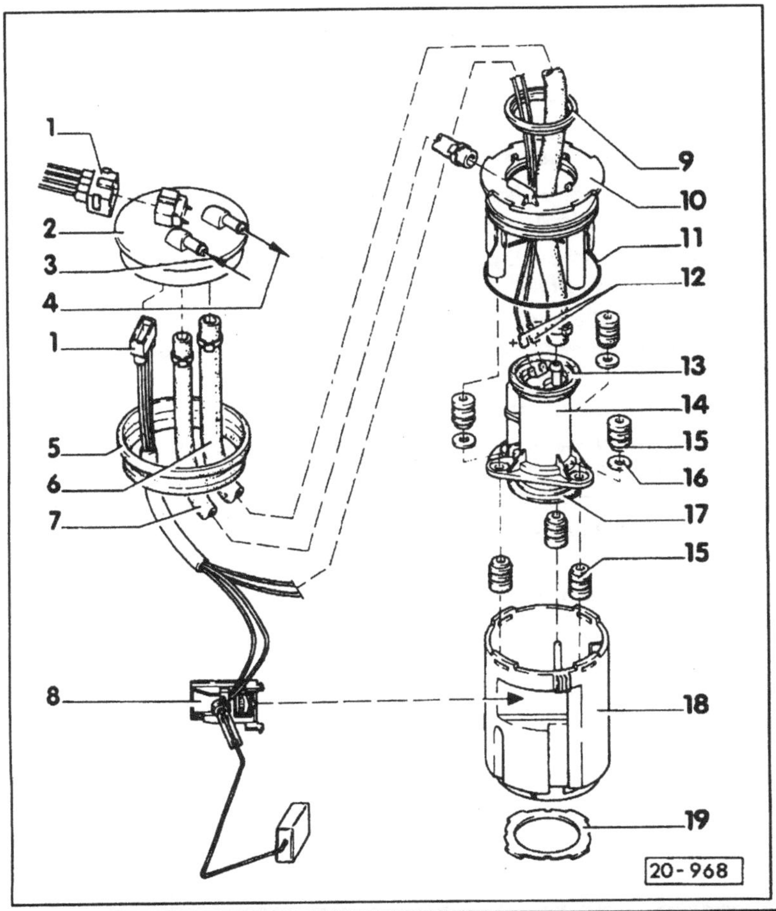

10 - Upper housing
- unclip using screwdriver

11 - O-ring
- lubricate with fuel before installing
- replace if damaged

12 - Fuel pump electrical connectors

13 - Upper sealing ring
- install, pull into upper housing

14 - Fuel pump
- has screen filter and check valve
- removing/installing:

⇒ page C 20-10
- checking:

⇒ page C 20-15

15 - Rubber mounting
- note installed position

16 - Washer

17 - Lower sealing ring
- install, pull into lower housing

18 - Lower housing

19 - Bayonet ring
- unclip using screwdriver

Safety precautions

CAUTION!

Observe the following points whenever removing or installing the fuel gauge sending unit or fuel delivery unit from a full or partially filled tank:

- ***Before starting work, provide exhaust extraction close to the inspection opening for the fuel delivery unit in the fuel tank to draw off escaping fumes. If no extraction system is available, use a fan (but DO NOT place fan in path of fumes)***
- ***Wear fuel-resistant disposable protective gloves whenever handling fuel.***

Rules of Cleanliness

CAUTION!

Carefully observe the following points:

- ***Thoroughly clean all connections and surrounding areas before disconnecting any fuel lines***
- ***Place removed parts on a clean surface and cover with paper or plastic but DO NOT use fluffy cloths (lint)***
- ***Carefully cover or seal any components that have been opened or dismantled if the repair cannot be carried out immediately***
- ***Only install clean components***
- ***Only unpack replacement parts immediately prior to installation***
- ***DO NOT use parts that have been stored loose or unpacked as in tool boxes etc.***
- ***When the fuel system is open, DO NOT work with compressed air if it can be avoided and DO NOT move the vehicle unless absolutely necessary***

Fuel delivery unit, installing

> ***WARNING!***
> ***Fire hazard. DO NOT smoke or have anything in the area that can ignite fuel.***

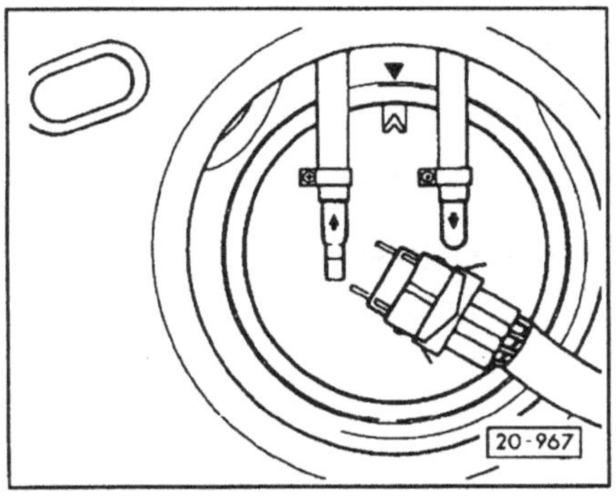

◄ – Align mark on flange with mark on fuel tank

Fuel delivery unit, removing and installing

Removing

– Observe safety precautions

⇒ page C 20-7

– Obtain radio anti-theft code from customer (write it down)

– Disconnect battery ground strap

– Pull out carpeting around perforation to right of handbrake lever

– Remove cover plate

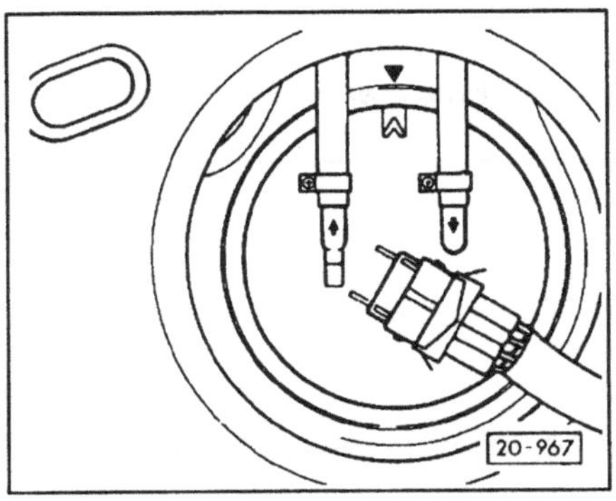

◄ – Disconnect harness connector, supply and return lines from flange on fuel tank

If vehicle has an auxiliary heater:

– Disconnect fuel line between supply and return lines

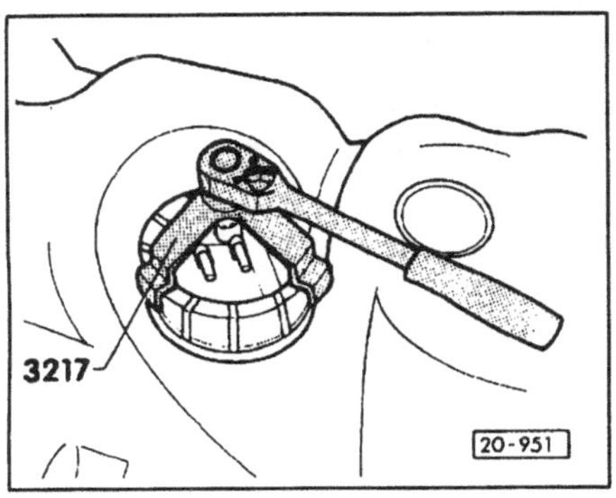

◄ – Loosen union nuts using 3217

– Pull flange and sealing ring out of fuel tank opening

– Loosen fuel delivery unit from bayonet connection by twisting left

– Withdraw fuel delivery unit from fuel tank

Installing

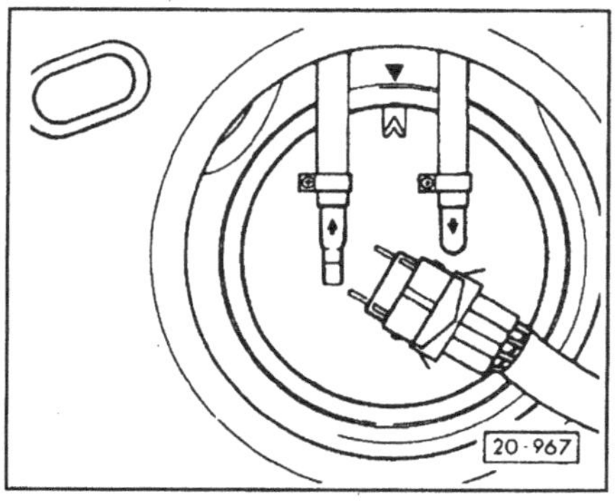

- Installation of fuel delivery unit is reverse of removal procedure
- Ensure that sending unit is installed with a frontal angle of approx. 30 degrees (and is not bent)
- Lubricate flange sealing ring before installing
- ◄ Align mark on flange with mark on fuel tank
- After installing fuel delivery unit, re-attach carpeting, either by bonding or with Velcro

Fuel delivery unit, disassembling and assembling

> ***WARNING!***
>
> ***Fire hazard. DO NOT smoke or have anything in area that can ignite fuel.***

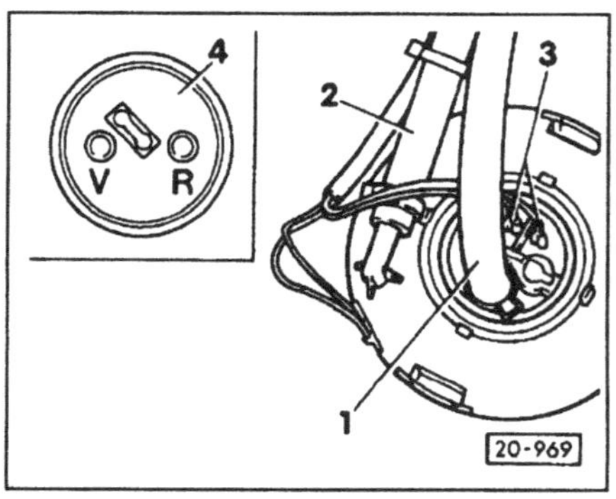

Requirement

♦ Fuel delivery unit removed

Disassembling

- Detach fuel gauge sending unit from lower housing
- ◄ Disconnect supply line -1-, return line -2-, and fuel pump harness connector -3-
- When re-assembling, use the markings for the fuel supply and return lines on the underside of flange -4-

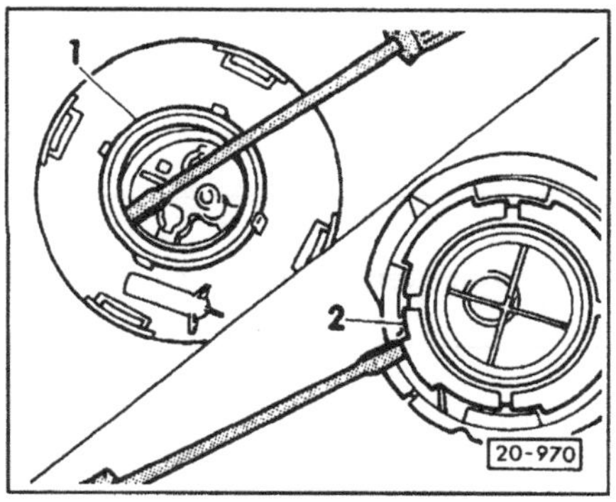

- Unclip upper retaining ring -1- and bayonet ring -2- on lower housing using screwdriver

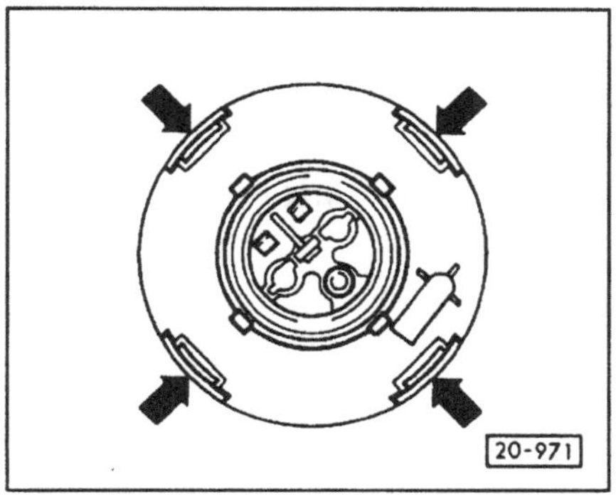

- Unclip upper housing using screwdriver (arrows)
- Pull upper housing out of lower housing
  - ♦ When re-assembling, lubricate upper housing O-ring
- Pull fuel pump out of lower housing

> ***WARNING!***
> ***Fire hazard. DO NOT smoke or have anything in area that can ignite fuel.***

Assembling

- Fuel delivery unit assembly is performed in the reverse order of the disassembly procedure

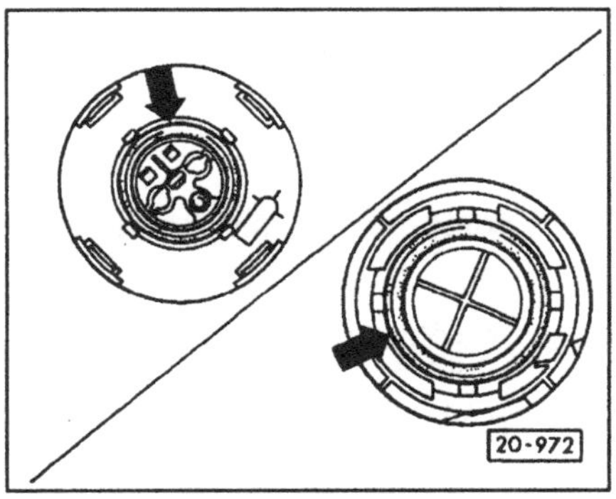

- Carefully pull the fuel pump top and bottom sealing rings (arrows) into the upper and lower housings
- Secure top housing with retaining ring
- Secure bottom housing with bayonet ring

Fuel pump, checking

> ***WARNING!***
> ***Fire hazard. DO NOT smoke or have anything in the area that can ignite fuel.***

Voltage supply, checking

Requirements

- ♦ Battery voltage OK
- ♦ Fuse number 18 OK

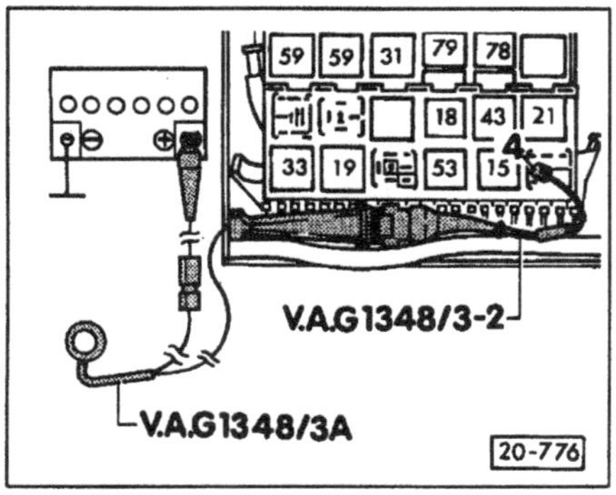

- Switch ON ignition
  - ♦ Fuel pump must activate for approximately 1 second

If fuel pump does NOT run:

- Remove storage shelf in front of fuse/relay panel
- Remove fuel pump relay J17 from relay panel position 12
- Plug adaptor cable VAG 1348/3-2 into terminal 4 of vacated relay socket
- Connect alligator clip of remote control VAG 1348/3A to B+
- Operate remote control
  - ♦ Fuel pump must run

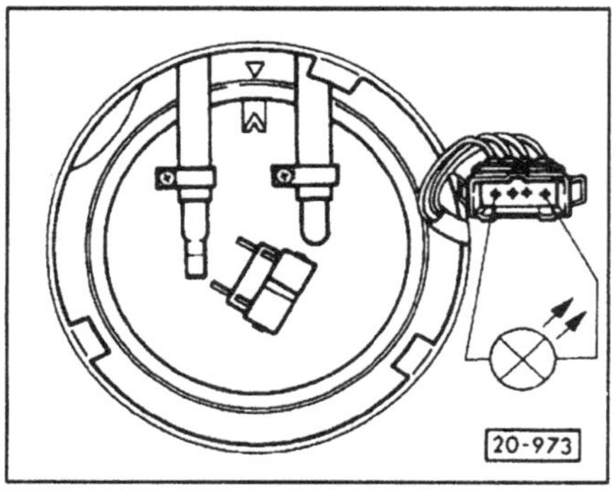

If YES:

- Check fuel pump relay control, see Repair Group 01 and perform Output Diagnostic Test Mode (DTM)

If fuel pump does NOT run:

- Cut out carpeting around perforations to right of handbrake lever
- Disconnect harness connector from fuel tank flange
- Connect VAG 1527B LED tester to outer terminals of connector using jumper wires from VW 1594 adaptor kit
- Operate remote control
  - ♦ LED must light up

If NO:

- Find open circuit using wiring diagram, repair or replace as necessary

If LED lights up:

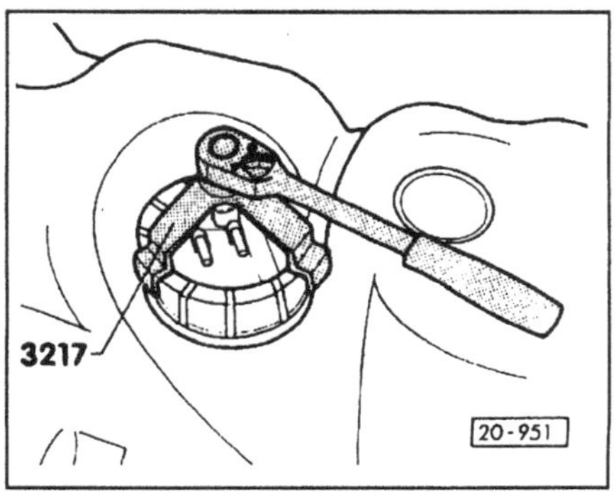

- Remove collar nut using 3217
- Ensure that wiring between flange and fuel pump is connected, correct if necessary

If wiring OK:

- Replace fuel pump

⇒ page C 20-10

Fuel pump delivery rate, checking

> ***WARNING!***
> ***Fire hazard. DO NOT smoke or have anything in area that can ignite fuel.***

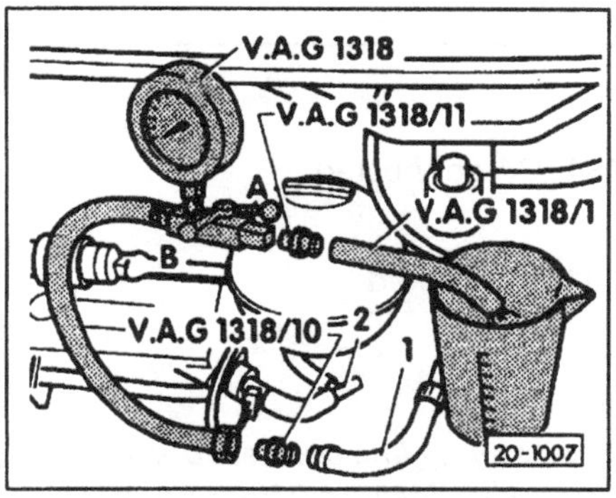

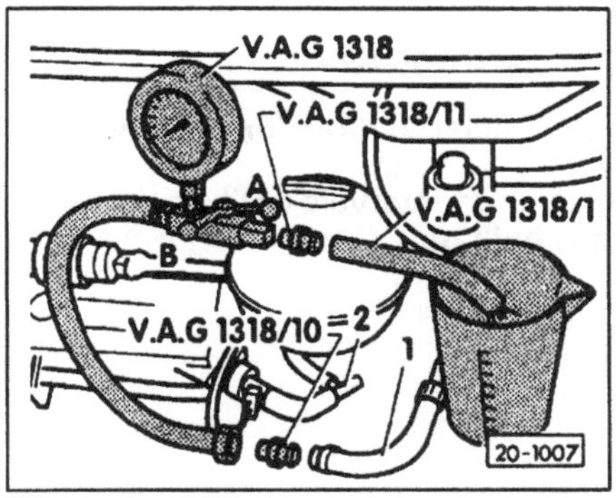

Requirements

- ♦ Voltage supply OK
- ♦ Remote control VAG 1348/3A connected
- – Remove fuel filler cap
- ◄ – Disconnect fuel supply line -1- from Tee-connector -2-
- – Connect pressure gauge VAG 1318 to fuel supply line -1- using VAG 1318/10 adaptor
- – Attach hose to pressure gauge adaptor VAG 1318/11 and hold in measuring glass
- – Open pressure gauge shut-off valve
  - ◄ ♦ Lever parallel with direction of flow (position A)
- – While operating remote control VAG 1348/3A, slowly close shut-off valve until pressure gauge indicates a reading of 3 bar (44 psi); once obtained, stop moving lever

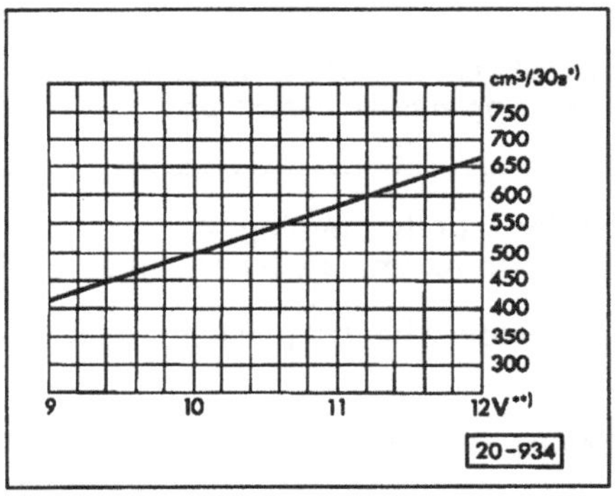

- – Empty measuring glass
- – Operate remote control switch for 30 seconds
- ◄ – Compare amount of fuel delivered with values shown in chart

*) Minimum delivery in cc's per 30 seconds

**) Voltage at fuel pump w/ engine stopped and fuel pump energized

- ♦ Must be approximately 2 Volts less than battery voltage

If minimum delivery is not obtained:

- – Check for kinked or blocked fuel lines
- – Check for plugged fuel filter, replace if necessary ⇒ page C 20-2, item 5
- – Check if fuel pump faulty, replace if necessary ⇒ page C 20-15

Fuel pump check valve, checking

> *WARNING!*
>
> ***Fire hazard. DO NOT smoke or have anything in area that can ignite fuel.***

Requirements

♦ Remote control VAG 1348/3A connected
⇒ page C 20-15

♦ Pressure gauge VAG 1318 connected
⇒ page C 20-17

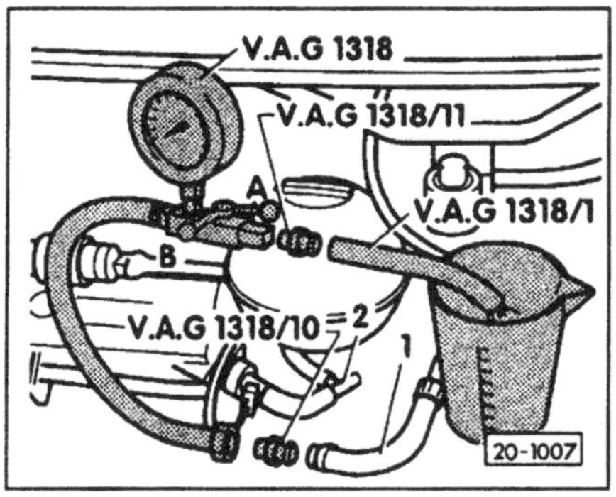

Note:

This test also checks the fuel supply line connections between the fuel pump and the VAG 1318 pressure gauge for leaks.

◄ – Close shut-off valve on pressure gauge

♦ Position B, lever perpendicular to direction of flow

– Operate remote control in short intervals until a pressure of approx. 3 bar (44 psi) has built up

> *CAUTION!*
>
> ***Danger of fuel spray when opening the shut-off valve! Cover the open end of the measuring gauge before opening the valve.***

– Relieve excess pressure by slightly opening shut-off valve until the pressure drops to approximately 3 bar (44psi)

♦ Pressure must not drop below 2 bar (29 psi) within 10 minutes

If after one minute a pressure of 3 bar (44 psi) has not been maintained:

– Check hose connections or fuel pump check valve for leakage, repair or replace as necessary, then re-check

Fuel tank, removing and installing

> ***WARNING!***
>
> ***Fire hazard. DO NOT smoke or have anything in area that can ignite fuel.***

Removing

– Observe safety precautions
⇒ page C 20-7

– Obtain and record anti-theft code for radio from customer

– Disconnect battery ground strap

– Drain fuel tank

– Clean area around fuel filler pipe

– Remove retaining ring and splash shield from top of filler neck

– Remove filler neck securing bolt

– Support fuel tank using VAG 1383A transmission jack

– Remove fuel tank support straps

– Lower transmission jack until the fuel supply, return, and breather lines can easily be removed from the flange

Vehicles with an auxiliary heater

– Also remove the fuel line between the supply and return lines

– Lower fuel tank

Installing

– Fuel tank installation is the reverse of the removal procedure

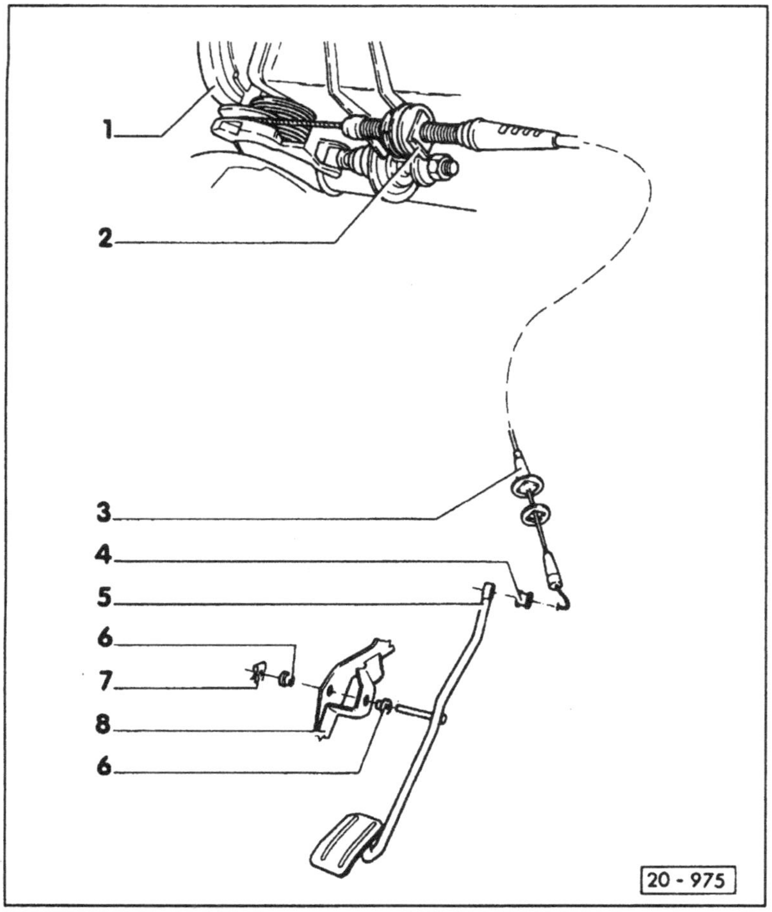

Throttle linkage, component layout, adjusting and removing

1 - Throttle body

2 - Retaining clip

3 - Accelerator cable

Adjusting

- Change position of retaining clip at support bracket so that throttle valve lever just reaches Wide Open Throttle position when pedal is fully depressed

♦ 1 mm (0.039 in) maximum clearance at throttle body lever

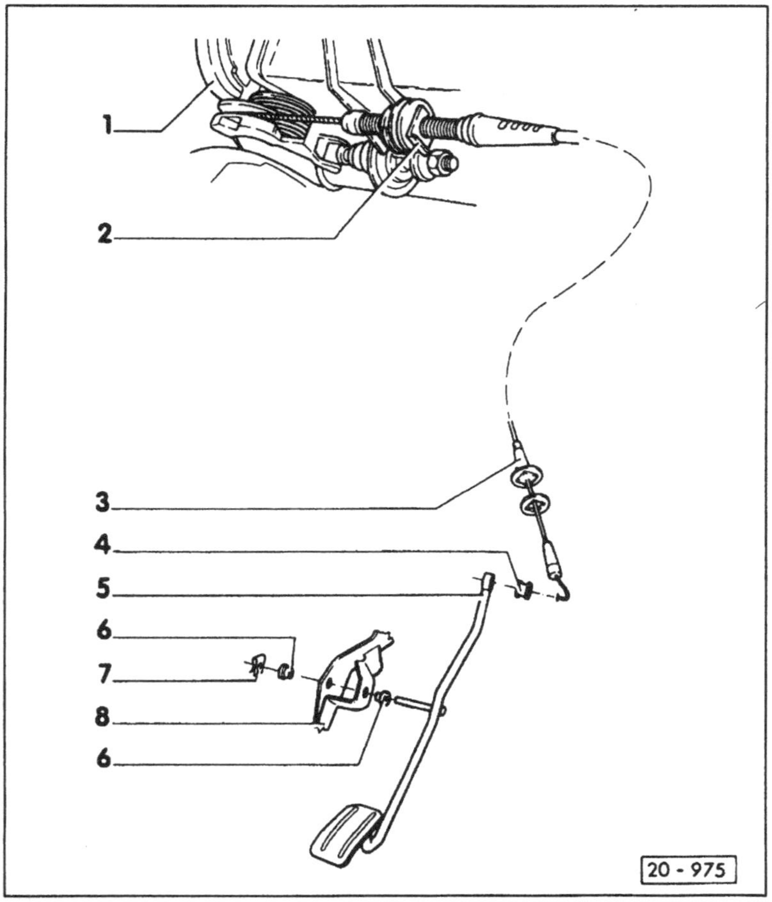

Removing

- Disconnect throttle cable at accelerator pedal, support bracket and at throttle body

- Break off the lugs on the interior side of the cable

- Remove cable through engine compartment and then discard

4 - Rubber bushing

5 - Accelerator pedal

6 - Pivot bushing

7 - Retaining clip

8 - Accelerator pedal bracket

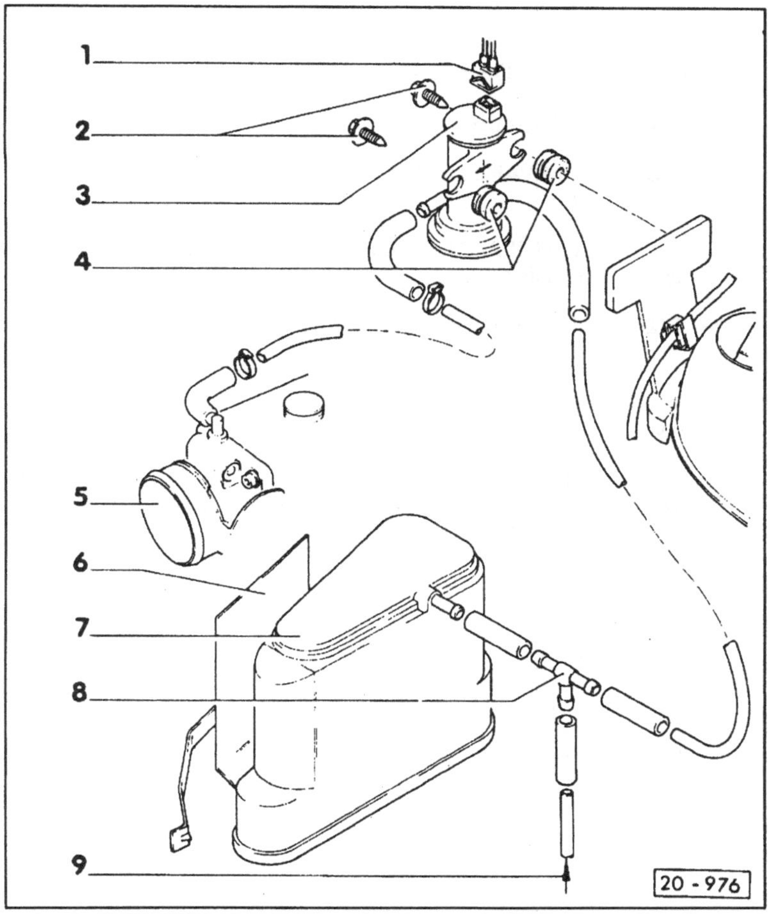

Evaporative emissions (EVAP) control system, component layout

> ***WARNING!***
>
> ***Fire hazard. DO NOT smoke or have anything in area that can ignite fuel.***

1 - Connector

2 - 10 Nm (7 ft lb)

3 - EVAP canister purge reg valve (N80)
- ♦ checking

⇒ page C 20-26
- ♦ controlled by ECM (J169)
- ♦ note installed position, arrow points in direction of flow

4 - Rubber bushing

5 - Throttle body

6 - Bracket

7 - EVAP canister
- ♦ on front left wheel housing

8 - Tee

9 - Breather hose
- ♦ from fuel tank

⇒ page C 20-3 (item 17)

Evaporative emissions system, control checking

Requirements

♦ Oxygen sensor and emission controls OK, checking
⇒ Repair Groups 24 and 26

♦ Engine coolant temperature 80°C (176°F) minimum

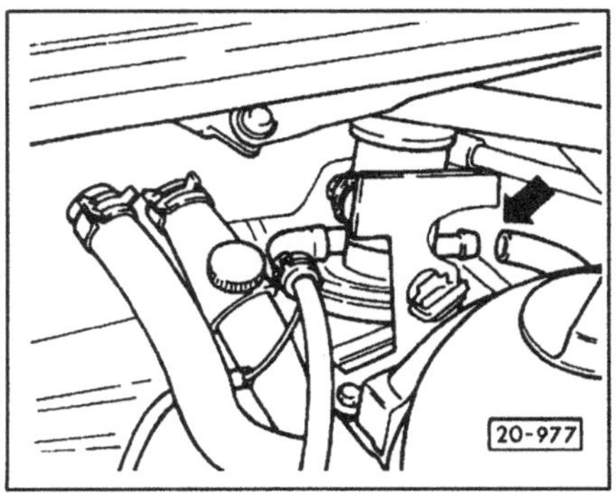

◄ – Disconnect hose (from EVAP canister) at EVAP canister purge regulator valve (arrow)

– Start engine and let idle

♦ Valve must not operate and no vacuum should be felt at the valve connection

– Raise engine speed

♦ Valve must open and close

♦ Vacuum must be felt at connection

If valve does NOT operate

– Perform Output Diagnostic Test Mode
⇒ Repair Group 01

Vehicles without On Board diagnostic capability

- Switch OFF ignition
- Disconnect EVAP canister purge regulator valve harness connector
- Connect VAG 1527B LED tester between terminals of harness connector using jumper wires from VW 1594 adaptor kit
- Start engine and raise engine speed
  - ♦ LED must flicker briefly

If NO:

- Locate and eliminate open circuit in wiring between EVAP canister purge regulator valve (N80) and ECM (J169) using wiring diagram, repair or replace as necessary

If wiring OK:

- Replace ECM (J169)

⇒ Repair Group 24

If valve still does NOT operate:

- Replace EVAP canister purge regulator valve N80

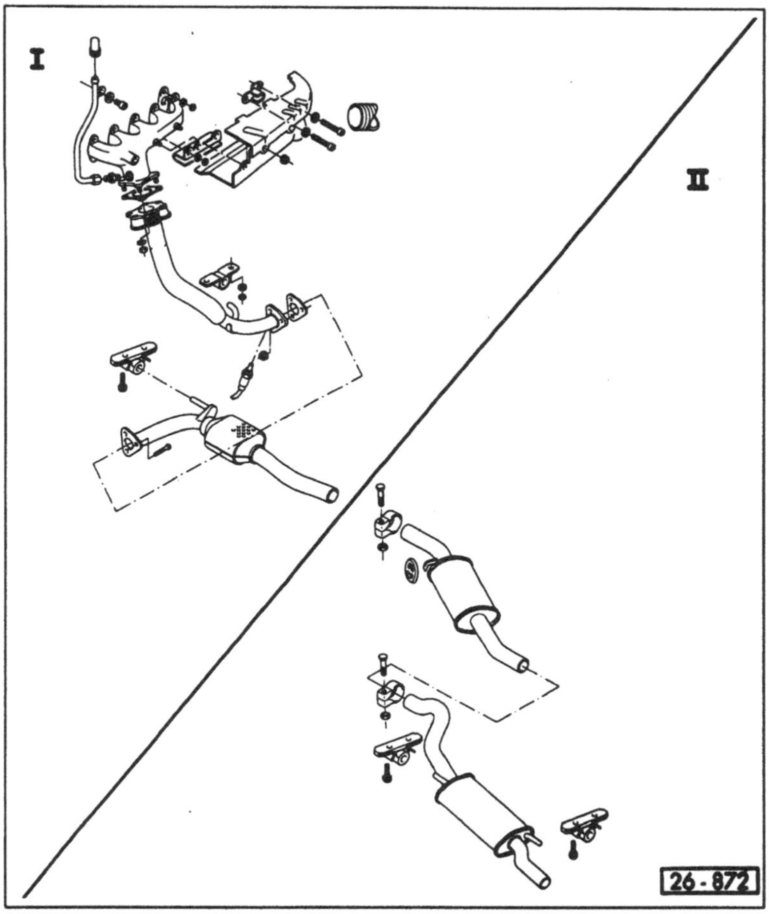

Exhaust system, component layout

- During exhaust system repairs, ensure that the system is not over-tightened
- Always ensure there is sufficient distance between the exhaust system and the body
- If necessary, loosen clamps and align muffler and exhaust pipe so that sufficient clearance between the body and the exhaust is present along the entire system and that the brackets and hangers are uniformly stressed
- Replace all self-locking nuts

I - page C 26-2

II - page C 26-4

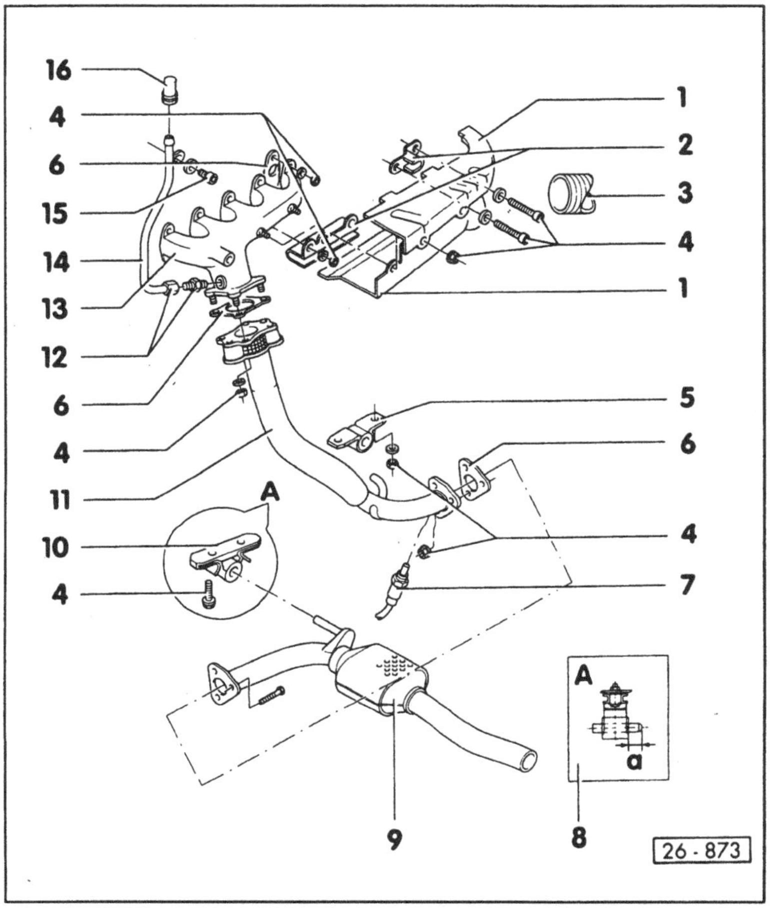

I - Exhaust system (front section from engine back), component layout

1 - Heat shield/stove

2 - Bracket
- for stove

3 - Hose
- to intake air hose on Air Cleaner housing

4 - Tightening torques:
- M6 - 10 Nm (7 ft lb)
- M8 - 25 Nm (18 ft lb)
- M10 - 40 Nm (30 ft lb)

5 - Bracket

6 - Gasket
- replace

7 - Oxygen sensor probe
- 50 Nm (37 ft lb)
- checking:

⇒ Repair Group 24
- lubricate threads with G5, do not allow G5 to enter slotted area of the Oxygen sensor probe

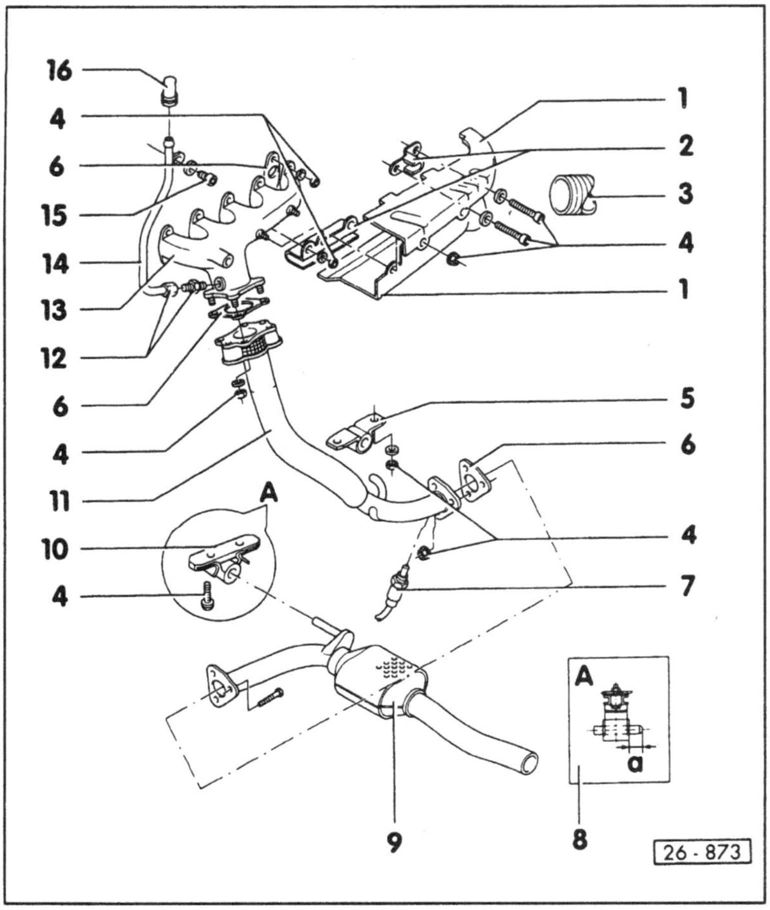

8 - **Dimension "a" = 15 to 25 mm (0.591 to 0.984 in.)**

9 - **Three Way Catalytic convertor**

10 - **Bracket**

11 - **Exhaust pipe, front**

12 - **30 Nm (22 ft lb)**

13 - **Exhaust manifold**

14 - **CO tap tube**
- also connected to intake manifold

15 - **15 Nm (11 ft lb)**

16 - **Cap**
- ensure it is properly installed and leak-tight

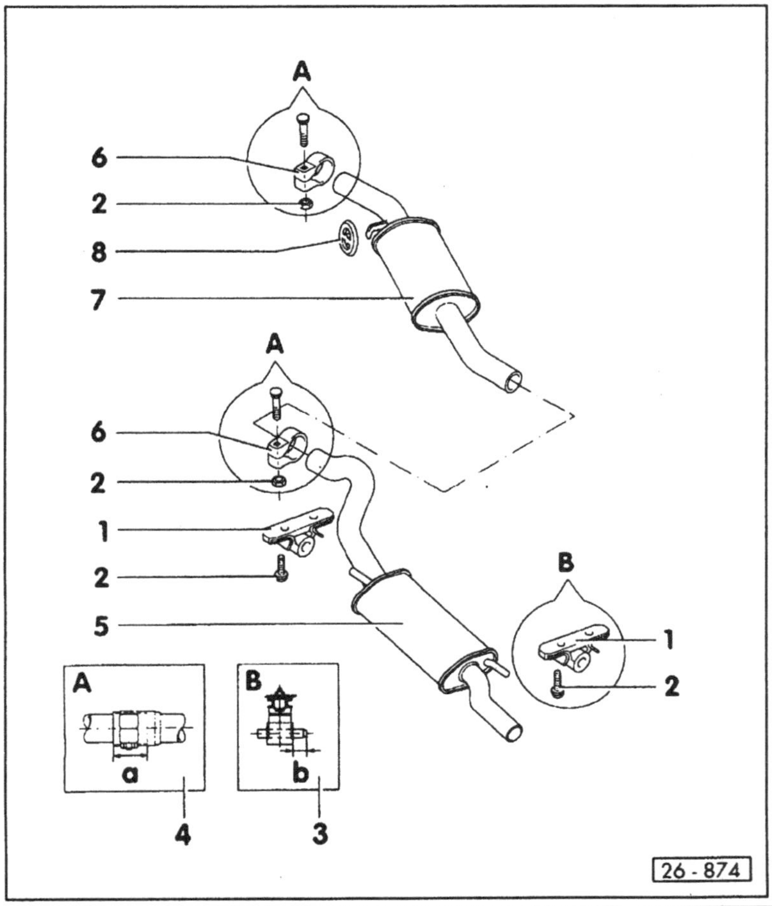

II - Exhaust system (center and rear muffler sections), component layout

1 - **Bracket**

2 - **Tightening torques:**
- M6 - 10 Nm (7 ft lb)
- M8 - 25 Nm (18 ft lb)
- M10 - 40 Nm (30 ft lb)

3 - **Dimension "b" = 25 to 35 mm (0.984 to 1.378 in.)**

4 - **Dimension "a" = 45 to 55 mm (1.772 to 2.165 in.)**

5 - **Rear muffler**

6 - **Clamp**
- align exhaust system in a lengthwise direction at the clamp so that dimensions (items -3- and -4-) are obtained

7 - **Center muffler**

8 - **Retaining ring**
- note style and type

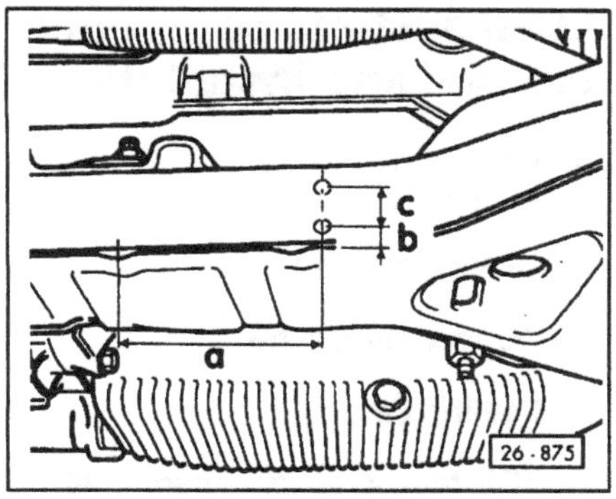

Exhaust pipe stop plate, installing

Note:

If the front exhaust pipe has to be replaced, it may be necessary to install a new stop plate. Use the following procedure where applicable:

– Drill holes for pop rivet nuts in the stop plate mount subassembly

♦ 11 mm (0.433 in.)diameter

Dimensions:

♦ "a"= 120 mm (4.724in.) from the center of the center rib

♦ "b"=24 mm (0.095in.) from lower edge of subassembly

♦ "c"=30 mm (1.181in.) hole spacing

– Install pop rivet nuts in holes using VAG 1765 pop rivet tool

– Install stop plate

♦ 20 Nm (15 ft lb)

Exhaust Gas Recirculation (EGR) system

Engine Code ACU

Notes:

♦ *The function/control of the EGR system is monitored by the On Board Diagnostic system of the Digifant Engine Control Module (J169)*
⇒ Repair Group 01

♦ *Components marked with ** are checked via Function 05: "Output Diagnostic Test Mode"*
⇒ Repair Group 01

♦ *Always replace all seals, O-rings and gaskets when assembling*

♦ *Vacuum lines and hose connections must be free of leaks*

♦ *Vacuum lines must not be blocked or kinked*

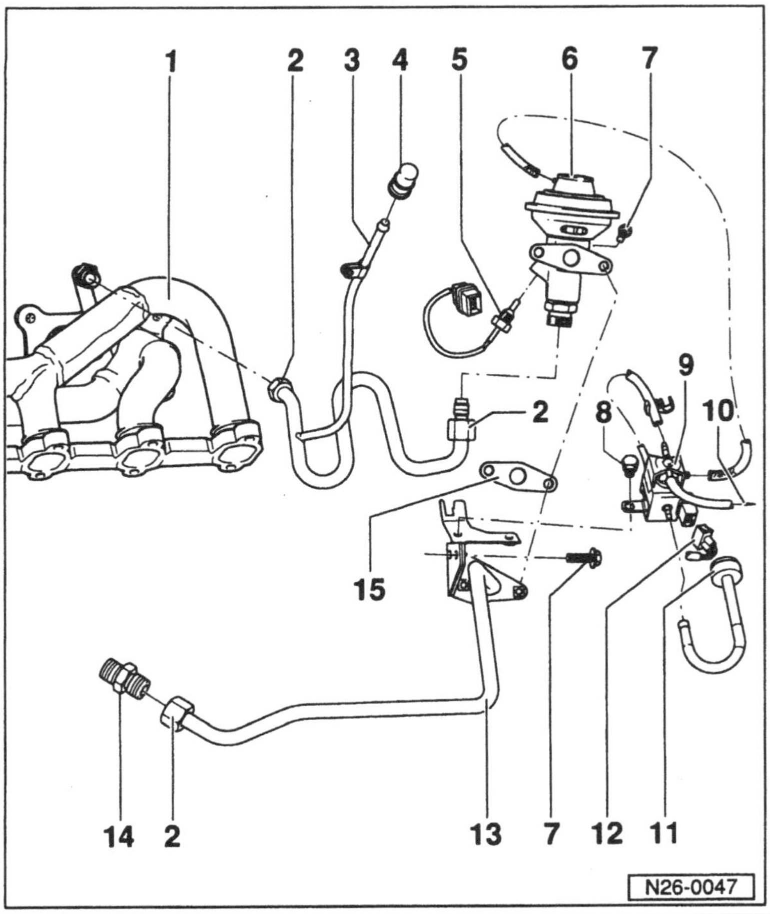

Exhaust Gas Recirculation (EGR) system, component removal and installation

1 - Exhaust manifold
- ♦ 2 sections

2 - 35 Nm (26 ft lb)

3 - CO sampling tube

4 - Sealing cap

5 - EGR temperature sensor G98
- ♦ 20 Nm (15 ft lb)
- ♦ with 2-pin connector
- ♦ checking:

⇒ Repair Group 01

6 - EGR valve
- ♦ checking:

⇒ page C 26-9

7 - 9 Nm (80 in lb)

8 - 10 Nm (7 ft lb)

9 - EGR vacuum regulator solenoid valve N18**
- ♦ two-way valve
- ♦ checking:

⇒ Repair Group 01

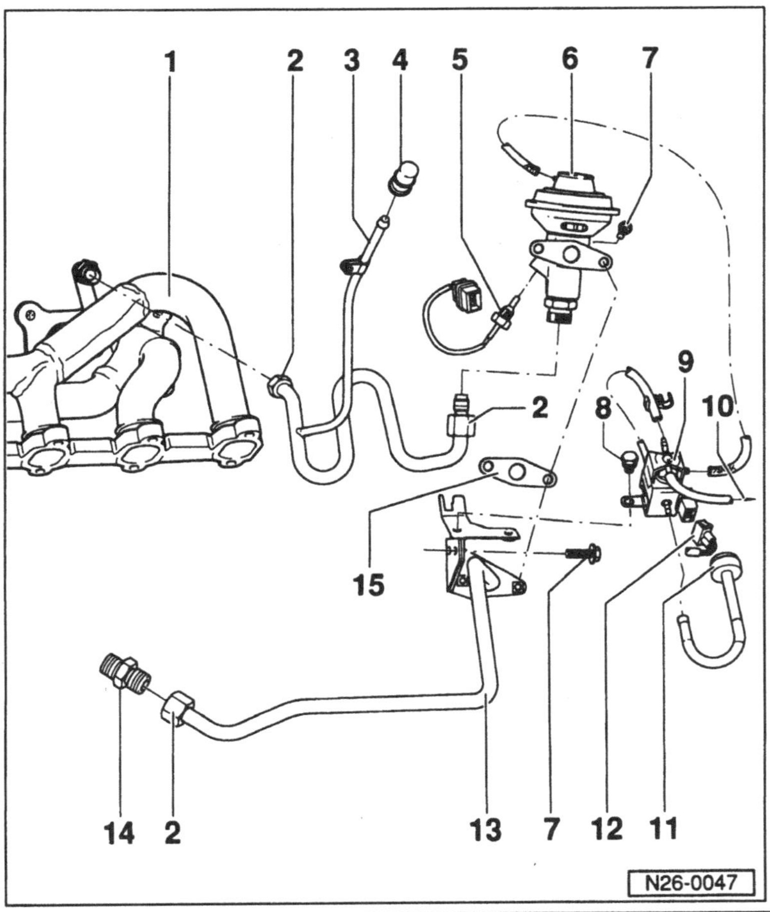

10 - Vacuum connection
- ♦ for intake manifold vacuum

11 - Check-valve

12 - Harness connector
- ♦ 2-pin
- ♦ to EGR vacuum regulator solenoid valve (N18)

13 - Hose

14 - Union fitting
- ♦ 34 Nm (25 ft lb)
- ♦ installed in the intake manifold

15 - Gasket
- ♦ replace

Exhaust Gas Recirculation (EGR) valve, checking

Special tools

- US 8026 Hand vacuum pump

Requirements

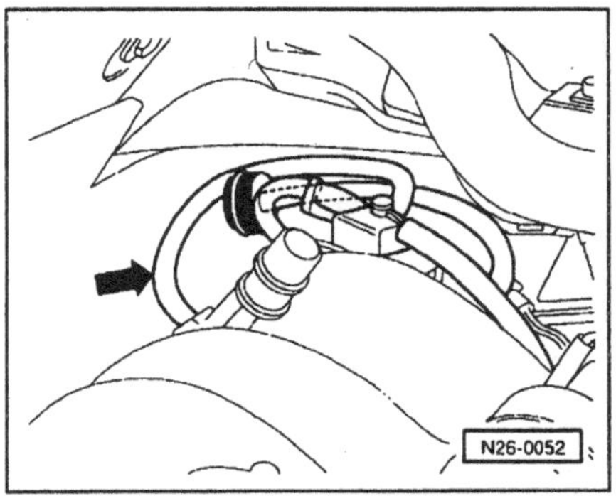

- Vacuum lines and hose connections leak tight
- Vacuum lines not blocked, pinched or kinked
- Engine oil temperature 50 °C (122 °F) minimum

Checking

◄ – **Disconnect vacuum hose (arrow) from EGR valve**

– Connect US 8026 hand vacuum pump to valve using auxiliary hose

– Start engine and let idle

– Operate hand vacuum pump

- Idle quality must noticeably deteriorate

If idle quality does not deteriorate

– Check lines and connections for blockage, clean as necessary, replace EGR valve if necessary

If the idle quality does deteriorate:
⇒ Repair Group 01, perform test steps 22, 23, 24

– Interrogate and erase DTC memory
⇒ Repair Group 01

Secondary Air Injection system

Secondary Air Injection system, function

The Secondary Air Injection system blows in air behind the exhaust valves for 97 seconds during cold starts (Engine Coolant Temperature between 15 – 35°C (59 – 95°F) . This action produces an Oxygen–rich exhaust, causes after-burning and reduces the heat-up time for the Three–Way Catalytic converter.

Secondary Air Injection system activation comes from the Digifant Engine Control Module (J169) via the Secondary Air Injection pump relay (J299) to the Secondary Air Injection solenoid valve (N112), check-valve and combi-valve.

In addition to operating during the cold start, the Secondary Air Injection system also switches on during idle until the Engine Coolant Temperature reaches a maximum of 60°C (140 °F).

The Secondary Air Injection system is monitored via the On Board Diagnostic system

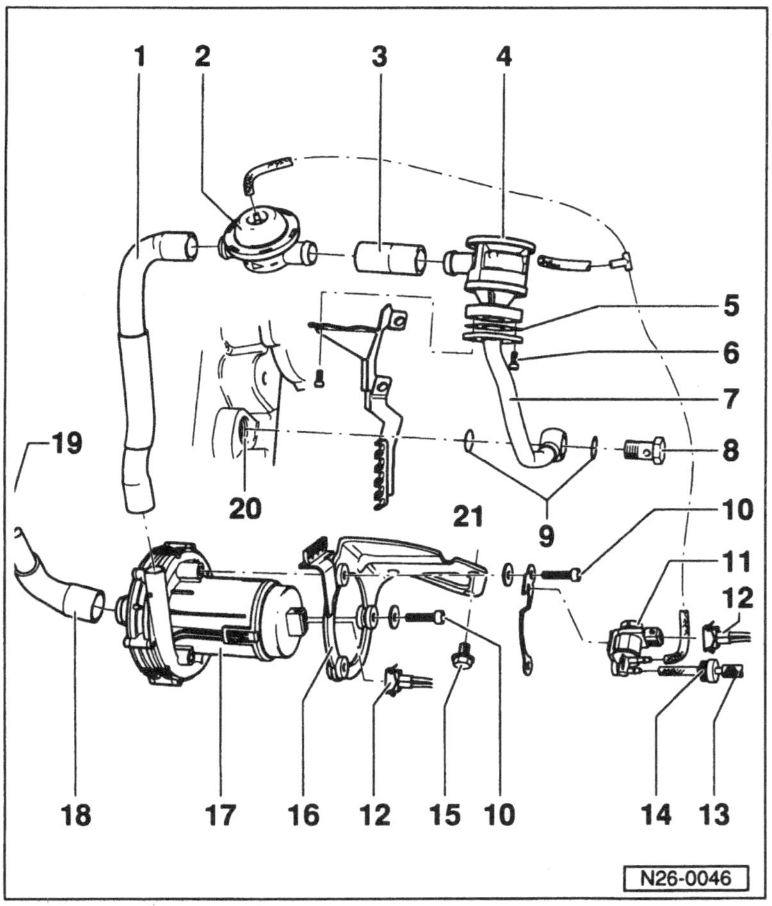

Secondary Air Injection system, removing and installing

Notes:

- *This system is monitored by the On Board Diagnostic system.*

⇒ Repair Group 01

- *Components marked with ** are checked via Output Diagnostic Test Mode*

⇒ Repair Group 01

1 - Pressure hose
- Ensure it is securely seated

2 - Check-valve

3 - Connecting hose
- Ensure it is securely seated

4 - Combi-valve
- Checking:

⇒ page C 26-18

5 - Gasket
- Replace

6 - 9 Nm (80 in lb)

7 - Connecting pipe

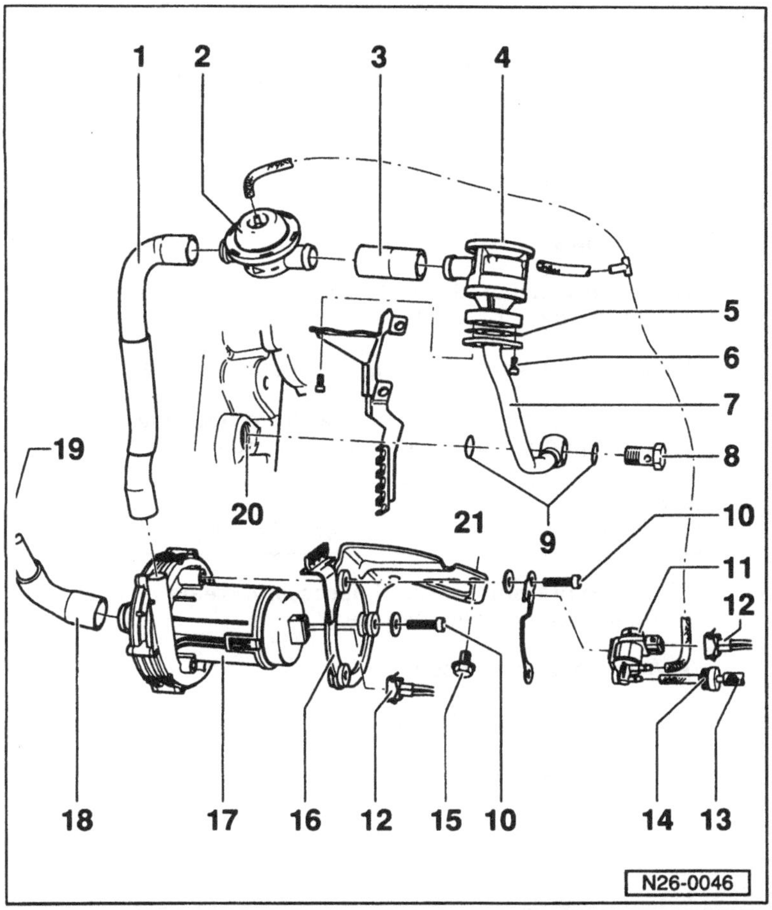

8 - 30 Nm (22 ft lb)

9 - Sealing washer
- replace

10 - 10 Nm (7 ft lb)

11 - Secondary Air Injection solenoid valve N112**
- checking:

⇒ page C 26-18

12 - Harness connector
- 2-pin

13 - Vacuum hose
- To brake booster check-valve connection

14 - Check-valve

15 - 40 Nm (30 ft lb)

16 - Bracket
- for Secondary Air Injection pump (item 17) and Secondary Air Injection solenoid valve (item 11)

17 - Secondary Air Injection pump**
- with motor V101
- checking:

⇒ page C 26-16

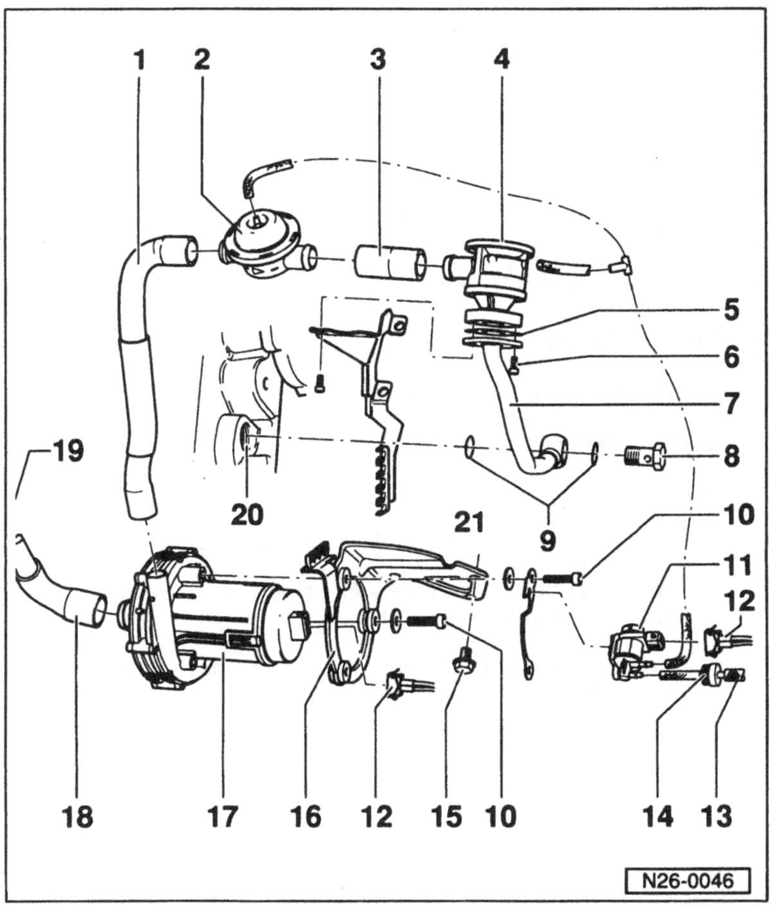

18 - Intake hose
- for Secondary Air Injection pump

19 - To Air Cleaner
- to air hose connection

20 - Air passage
- in cylinder head

21 - Bracket
- for combi-valve

Combi-valve and check-valve, checking

Special tools

- ♦ US 8026 Hand vacuum pump

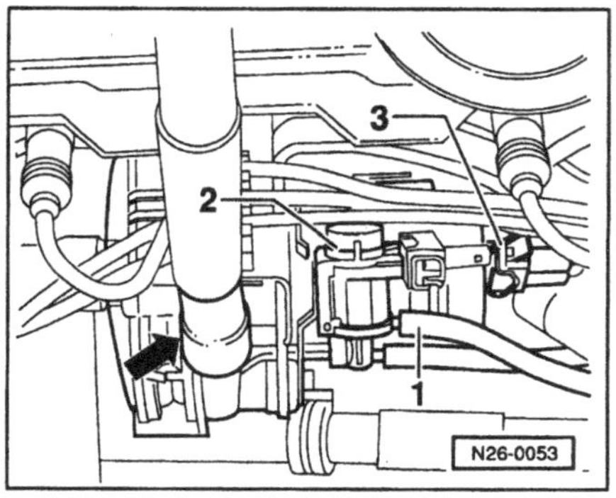

Test sequence

- Disconnect vacuum hose -1- from Secondary Air Injection solenoid valve -2- (N112)
- Connect hand vacuum pump to vacuum hose -1-
- ◄ Disconnect pressure hose (arrow) from Secondary Air Injection pump motor and route upwards

> ***CAUTION!***
> ***Do not use compressed air for the following check.***

- Blow into pressure hose. If necessary, create an extension using a piece of auxiliary hose
  - ♦ Valves must be closed
- Operate hand vacuum pump
  - ♦ Valves must be open

Secondary Air Injection pump, checking

Special tools, testers and auxiliary items

- ♦ VAG 1598/18 Test Box
- ♦ VW 1594 Adaptor kit
- ♦ VAG 1527B LED tester

Test conditions

- ♦ Fuse on Secondary Air Injection pump relay (J299) OK
- ♦ VAG 1598/18 Test box connected

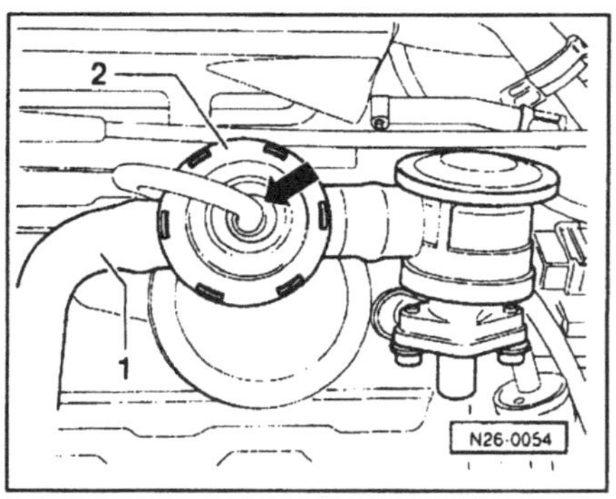

Test sequence

- ◄ Disconnect pressure hose -1- from check-valve -2-
- Bridge Test Box sockets 29 + 42 using jumper wires from the VW 1594 adaptor kit
  - ♦ The Secondary Air Injection pump motor must run, and air must exit the pressure hose

If no air exits from the hose

- Replace Secondary Air Injection pump

If pump motor does not run:

– Disconnect the 2-pin harness connector from the Secondary Air Injection pump motor (V101)

– Connect VAG 1527B LED tester using jumper wires from the VW 1594 to detached connector

- ♦ LED must light up

If YES (Voltage supply OK):

– Replace Secondary Air Injection pump

If LED does not light up:

– Connect 2-pin harness connector

– Check activation of Secondary Air Injection pump motor
⇒ *2.5 Liter 5–Cylinder, Fuel Injection and Ignition,* Repair Group 01; Output Diagnostic Test Mode (DTM) and Repair Group 01; Electrical checks

If Secondary Air Injection pump motor does not run during electrical check:

– Check Secondary Air Injection pump relay (J299)
⇒ Wiring diagrams

– Interrogate and erase DTC memory
⇒ Repair Group 01; On Board Diagnostic

Secondary Air Injection solenoid valve, checking

Special tools, testers and auxiliary items

- ♦ VW 1594 adaptor kit
- ♦ VAG 1527B LED tester

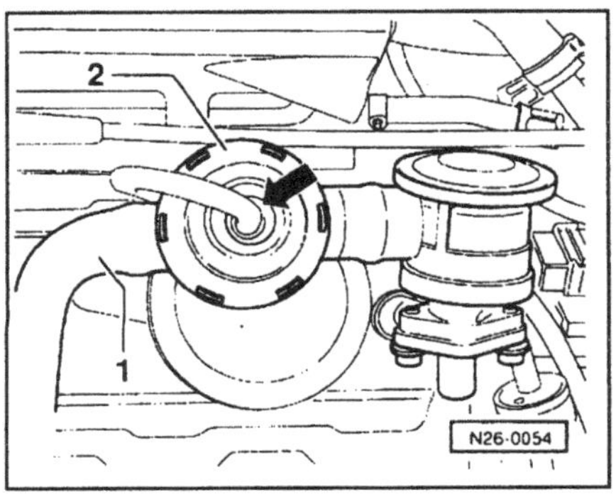

Test conditions

- ♦ Engine oil temperature 15 to 35 °C (59 to 95 °F)
- ♦ Secondary Air Injection pump OK

Test sequence

◄ – Disconnect vacuum hose (arrow) from check-valve -2-

– Start engine and let idle

When the Secondary Air injection pump motor runs, (intake manifold) vacuum must be present at the vacuum hose

If vacuum NOT present:

– Switch off ignition

– Disconnect 2-pin harness connector from Secondary Air Injection solenoid valve (N112)

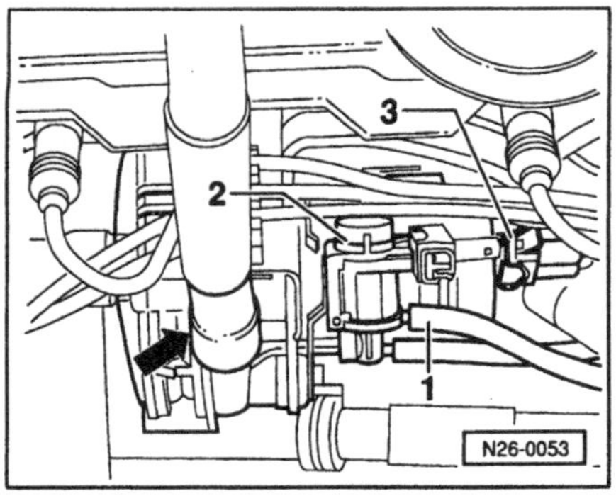

- Connect VAG 1527B LED tester to harness connector using jumper wires from the VW 1594 adaptor kit
- Start engine and let idle

LED must light up

If the LED lights up (Voltage supply OK):

◄ – Replace Secondary Air Injection solenoid valve -2-

If LED does not light up:

- Connect 2-pin harness connector
- Check activation of Secondary Air Injection solenoid valve ⇒ Repair Group 01; Electrical checks

If Valve cannot be felt to switch during electrical check:

- Check Secondary Air Injection pump relay J299 ⇒ Wiring diagrams
- Interrogate and erase DTC memory ⇒ Repair Group 01; On Board Diagnostic

2.8 Liter VR6, General Engine (Engine Code: AES)

Section D

> ***WARNING!***
> ***Before proceeding with any work, please read the warnings and cautions immediately following this index. Also read any warning and caution that accompanies a procedure in the manual.***

Please read these WARNINGS and CAUTIONS before proceeding with maintenance and repair work.

WARNING—

- Some repairs may be beyond your capability. If you lack the skills, tools and equipment, or a suitable workplace for any procedure described in this manual, we suggest you leave such repairs to an authorized Volkswagen dealer service department, or other qualified shop.

- Volkswagen is constantly improving its cars. Sometimes these changes, both in parts and specifications, are made applicable to earlier models. Therefore, before starting any major jobs or repairs to components on which passenger safety may depend, consult your authorized Volkswagen dealer about the Technical Bulletins that may have been issued since the editorial closing of this manual.

- Do not re-use any fasteners that are worn or deformed in normal use. Many fasteners are designed to be used only once and become unreliable and may fail when used a second time. This includes, but is not limited to, nuts, bolts, washers, self–locking nuts or bolts, circlips and cotter pins. Always replace these fasteners with new parts.

- Never work under a lifted car unless it is solidly supported on stands designed for the purpose. Do not support a car on cinder blocks, hollow tiles or other props that may crumble under continuous load. Never work under a vehicle that is supported solely by a jack. Never work under the car while the engine is running.

- If you are going to work under a car on the ground, make sure that the ground is level. Block the wheels to keep the car from rolling. Disconnect the battery negative terminal (ground strap) to prevent others from starting the vehicle while you are under it.

- Never run the engine unless the work area is well ventilated. Carbon monoxide (CO) kills.

- Do not attempt to work on your vehicle if you do not feel well. You increase the danger of injury to yourself and others if you are tired, upset or have taken medicine or any other substance that may impair you or keep you from being fully alert.

- Disconnect the battery negative (–) terminal (ground strap) whenever you work on the fuel system or the electrical system. Do not smoke or work near heaters or other fire hazards. Keep an approved fire extinguisher handy.

- Batteries produce explosive hydrogen gas. Keep sparks, lighted matches and open flame away from the top of the battery. If hydrogen gas escaping from the cap vents is ignited, it will ignite gas trapped in the cells and cause the battery to explode.

- Connect and disconnect battery cables, jumper cables or a battery charger only with the ignition switched off, to prevent sparks. Do not quick–charge the battery (for boost starting) for longer than one minute, and do not allow charging voltage to exceed 16.5 volts. Wait at least one minute before boosting the battery a second time.

- Illuminate your work area adequately but safely. Use a portable safety light for working inside or under the car. Make sure the bulb is enclosed by a wire cage. The hot filament of an accidentally broken bulb can ignite spilled fuel or oil.

- Tie long hair behind your head. Do not wear a necktie, a scarf, loose clothing, or a necklace when you work near machine tools or running engines. If your hair, clothing, or jewelry were to get caught in the machinery, severe injury could result.

- Finger rings, bracelets and other jewelry should be removed so that they cannot cause electrical shorts, get caught in running machinery, or be crushed by heavy parts.

- Catch draining fuel, oil, or brake fluid in suitable containers. Do not use food or beverage containers that might mislead someone into drinking from them. Store flammable fluids away from fire hazards. Wipe up spills at once, but do not store the oily rags, which can ignite and burn spontaneously.

- Always observe good workshop practices. Wear goggles when you operate machine tools or work with battery acid. Gloves or other protective clothing should be worn whenever the job requires working with harmful substances.

- The Air-Conditioning (A/C) system is filled with a chemical refrigerant, which is hazardous. The A/C system should be serviced only by trained technicians using approved refrigerant recovery/recycling equipment, trained in related safety precautions, and familiar with regulations governing the discharging and disposal of automotive chemical refrigerants.

- Do not expose any part of the A/C system to high temperatures such as an open flame. Excessive heat will increase system pressure and may cause the system to burst.

- Some aerosol tire inflators are highly flammable. Be extremely cautious when repairing a tire that may have been inflated using an aerosol tire inflator. Keep sparks, open flame or other sources of ignition away from the tire repair area. Inflate and deflate the tire at least four times before breaking the bead from the rim. Completely remove the tire from the rim before attempting any repair.

- Friction materials such as brake or clutch discs may contain asbestos fibers. Do not create dust by grinding, sanding, or by cleaning with compressed air. Avoid breathing asbestos fibers and asbestos dust. Breathing asbestos can cause serious diseases such as asbestosis or cancer, and may result in death.

- Greases, lubricants and other automotive chemicals contain toxic substances, many of which are absorbed directly through the skin. Read manufacturer's instructions and warnings carefully. Use hand and eye protection. Avoid direct skin contact.

- An airbag is operated by an explosive device. Handled improperly or without adequate safeguards, it can be accidently activated and cause serious personal injury. To prevent personal injury or airbag system failure, **only trained Volkswagen dealer service technicians** should test, disassemble or service the airbag system.

WARNINGS and CAUTIONS continued on next page ▶

Please read these WARNINGS and CAUTIONS before proceeding with maintenance and repair work.

WARNING (continued) —

- ALWAYS disconnect the airbag power supply before using a computer memory saver. Failure to disconnect the airbag power supply may result in accidental activation of the airbag.
- The airbag unit should not be removed, nor should any work be performed on the airbag system, without first reviewing the warnings and cautions that accompany the airbag system repair information in this manual.
- Never apply stickers or any other coverings on the steering wheel. Do not let chemical cleaners, oil or grease come into contact with the vinyl covering of the airbag unit.
- Never open or otherwise attempt to repair airbag system parts. Always use new parts. Never leave airbag parts or the partially disassembled airbag system unattended.
- Never use a test light or volt meter to conduct electrical tests on the airbag system. The airbag system must only be tested by trained Volkswagen Service technicians using special airbag tester equipment. The airbag system must only be tested while it is installed in the car.
- Do not expose an airbag unit to temperatures above 194°F (90°C) even for a brief period, while handling it during the repair process. Keep the unit clear of heat sources such as hot plates, soldering irons, heat lamps, welding equipment, or the like.
- Always replace airbag system components that have been mechanically damaged (bubbles, cracks, etc.).
- Always set down a removed airbag unit so that the horn pad is facing upward.
- When driving or riding in an airbag-equipped vehicle, never hold test equipment in your hands or lap while the vehicle is in motion. Objects between you and the airbag can increase the risk of injury in an accident.
- The storage, transportation and disposal of airbag units are subject to the laws for flammable solids.

CAUTION—

- If you lack the skills, tools and equipment, or a suitable workshop for any procedure described in this manual, we suggest you leave such repairs to an authorized Volkswagen dealer or other qualified shop. We especially urge you to consult an authorized Volkswagen dealer before beginning repairs on any car that may still be covered wholly or in part by any of the extensive warranties issued by Volkswagen of America, Inc.
- Volkswagen is constantly improving its cars and sometimes these changes, both in parts and specifications, are made applicable to earlier models. Therefore, part numbers listed in this manual are for reference only. Always check with your authorized Volkswagen dealer parts department for the latest information.
- Before starting a job, make certain that you have all the necessary tools and parts on hand. Read all the instructions thoroughly, do not attempt shortcuts. Use tools that are appropriate to the work and use only replacement parts meeting Volkswagen specifications. Makeshift tools, parts and procedures will not make good repairs.
- Use pneumatic and electric tools only to loosen threaded parts and fasteners. Never use these tools to tighten fasteners, especially on light alloy parts. Always use a torque wrench to tighten fasteners to the tightening torque specification listed.
- Be mindful of the environment and ecology. Before you drain the crankcase, find out the proper way to dispose of the oil. Do not pour oil onto the ground, down a drain, or into a stream, pond, or lake. Consult local ordinances that govern the disposal of wastes.
- When connecting cables or ground straps, all connections must be cleaned to bare metal. Be sure mounting bolts are tight.
- Do not replace fuse links with fuse links of other gauge or with standard wire. Always replace the entire length of the fuse link.
- Before doing any electrical welding on vehicles equipped with Anti-lock Brakes (ABS), disconnect the battery negative terminal (ground strap) and the ABS Control Module connector.
- On cars equipped with ABS, the ABS control unit cannot withstand temperatures from a paint–drying booth or a heat lamp in excess of 203°F (95°C) and should not be subjected to temperatures in excess of 185°F (85°C) for more than two hours.
- On cars equipped with anti-theft radios, make sure you know the correct radio activation code before disconnecting the battery or removing the radio. If the wrong code is entered when power is restored, the radio may lock up and be rendered inoperable, even if the correct code is then entered.
- When boost-charging the battery, first remove the fuses for the Engine Control Module (ECM), the Transmission Control Module (TCM), the ABS Control Module, and the On-Board computer. In cases where one or more of these components is not separately fused, disconnect the Control Module connector(s).
- Do not quick-charge the battery (for boost starting) for longer than one minute, and do not exceed 16.5 volts at the battery with the boosting cables attached. Wait at least one minute before boosting the battery a second time.

◀ **WARNINGS and CAUTIONS continued from previous page**

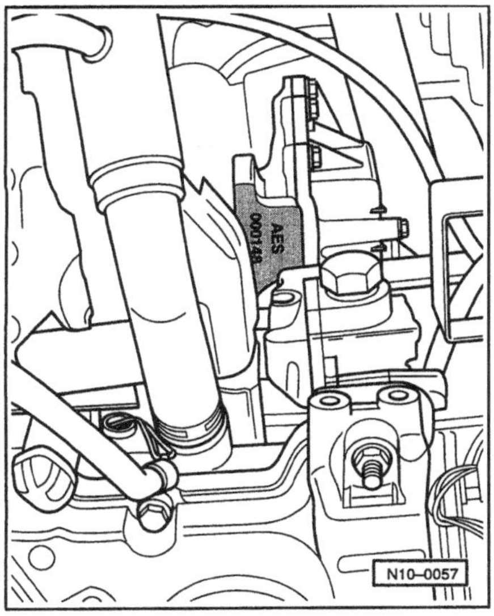

General

Engine number, location

◄ ♦ The engine number ("Engine Code letters" plus "Serial number") can be found on the left side of the engine behind the camshaft cover on the cylinder block.

♦ The engine number also appears on the adhesive sticker applied to the the cylinder head cover.

♦ The engine number also appears on the vehicle data plate.

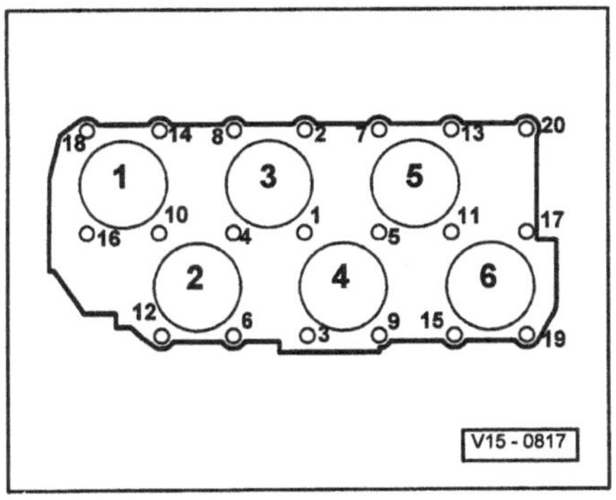

◄ ♦ Cylinder number 1 is located at right-rear of engine block. Cylinders 2, 4 and 6 are on front of the engine block toward front of vehicle.

Engine, technical data

Engine code		AES
Manufactured		01.96 ➤
Arrangement of cylinders		VR[1]
Cylinder angle		15°
Displacement	ltrs.	2.8
Output	kW at rpm	103/4750
Torque	Nm at rpm	240/3200
Bore	∅ mm	81
Stroke	mm	90.3
Compression ratio		10.0 : 1

[1] VR = 15° V-cylinder arrangement in a compact in-line design.

Engine technical data, continued

Engine code		AES
RON	minimum	95 unleaded[1]
Fuel Injection system		Motronic
Ignition system		Motronic
Firing order		1–5–3–6–2–4
Knock control		YES
On Board Diagnostic		YES
Oxygen sensor control		YES
Three-Way Catalytic converter		YES
Exhaust Gas Recirculation system		YES
Secondary Air Injection system		YES
Turbocharging		NO

[1] In an emergency, 91 RON (minimum) can be used, however; engine performance will be reduced.

Engine, removing and installing

Special tools, testers and auxiliary items

- ♦ VAG 1921 Spring-clip Pliers
- ♦ VAG 1306 Drip tray
- ♦ 3277 A Fitting tool
- ♦ 3408 Engine support
- ♦ VAG 1383 A Engine/transmission jack
- ♦ G 000 100 Grease (for vehicles with manual transmission)
- ♦ VAG 1331 Torque wrench (5 to 50 Nm)
- ♦ VAG 1332 Torque wrench (40 to 200 Nm)
- ♦ Cable tie

– Remove the engine/transmission assembly from below

CAUTION!
Obtain the radio anti-theft code before disconnecting the battery ground strap.

– Disconnect battery ground cable

♦ ignition must be switched OFF

– Always replace all cable ties (in the original position) which were opened or cut while removing the engine

– Drain coolant
⇒ page D 19-13

– Remove radiator and radiator cooling fan
⇒ page D 19-18

– Remove ribbed belt
⇒ page D 13-19

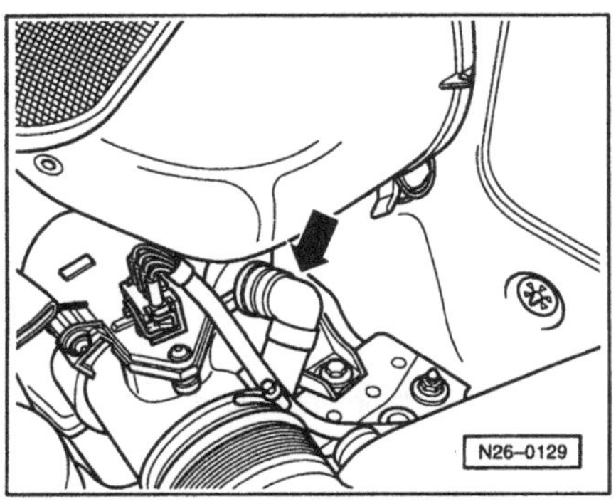

◄ – Detach hose from combi-valve at Air Cleaner upper section -arrow-

– Remove intake manifold complete with intake manifold, lower section and Throttle Valve Control Module
⇒ page D 15-8

– Disconnect power steering lines from right engine support

– Remove power steering pump with bracket and secure to body with wire (hoses remain connected)
⇒ Repair Group 48

– Remove front exhaust pipe
⇒ page D 26-2

– Disconnect wiring from transmission, generator and starter and move out of the way

– Disconnect all engine coolant, vacuum and breather hoses

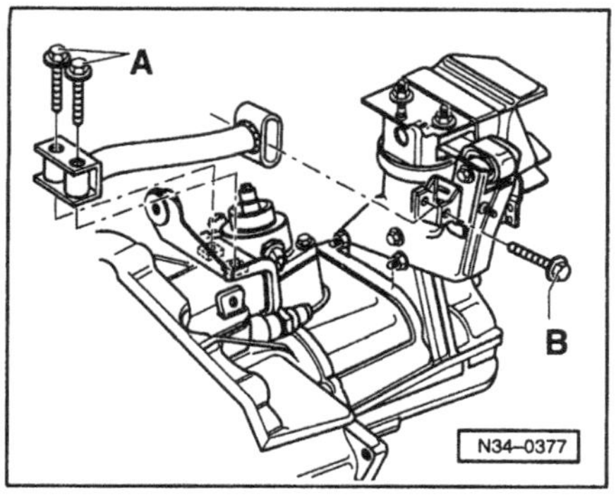

Vehicles with manual transmission:

– Pry off line/hose from slave cylinder on transmission
⇒ Repair Group 30

◄ – Remove transverse support mounting bolts -A- and -B-

– Remove transverse support

– Remove gear change mechanism from transmission:
⇒ Repair Group 34, 5-Speed manual transmission 02G

Vehicles with automatic transmission:

– Remove transmission range selector lever cable
⇒ Repair Group 37, Automatic transmission 099

Vehicles with A/C:

– Observe additional information and removal instructions
⇒ page D 10-14

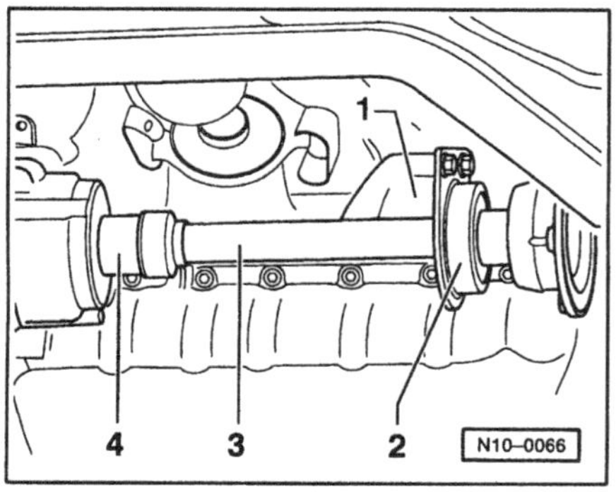

All vehicles:

– Remove drive shafts
⇒ Repair Group 40

◄ – Remove support bracket -1- from cylinder block and pull flange shaft -3- out of transmission shaft -4-

– Remove flange shaft -3- with flange shaft bearing -2-

– Fit 3408 engine support onto VAG 1383 A engine/transmission jack

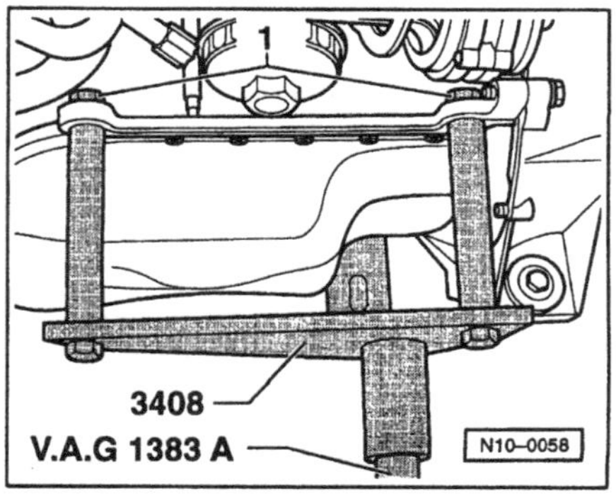

◄ – Fit 3408 engine support onto cylinder block and tighten mounting nuts -1-

- ♦ 40 Nm (30 ft lb)

– Remove pendulum support
⇒ Repair Group 40

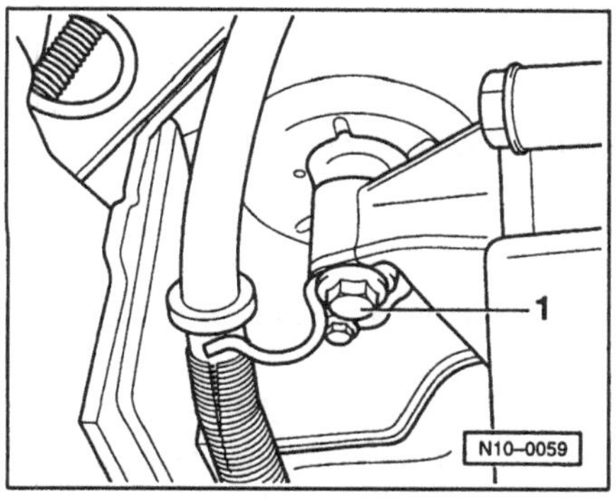

◄ – Remove right assembly mounting bolt -1-

◄ – Remove left assembly mounting bolts -arrows-

– Carefully lower assembly

> ***CAUTION!***
> ***Carefully guide the assembly out of the vehicle while lowering, do not allow the assembly to contact and damage the bodywork.***

Engine, mounting on engine stand

– Mount engine to VW 313 engine stand support clamp using 3269 engine bracket

Special tools, testers and auxiliary items

♦ VAG 1202 A Workshop crane

♦ 2024 A Lifting tackle

♦ 3269 Engine bracket

♦ VW 313 Support clamp

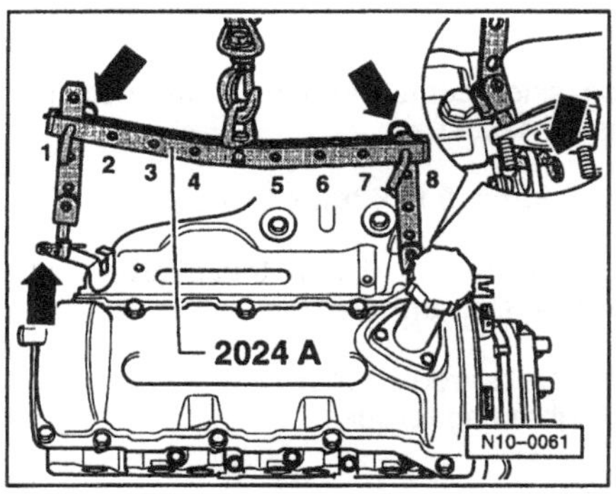

Work sequence

Vehicles with manual transmission

◄ – Attach 2024 A lifting tackle as follows

– Lift off of VAG 1383 A engine/transmission jack using workshop crane

♦ Vibration damper end: 3rd hole in hook at position 1

♦ Flywheel end: 4th hole in hook at position 8

> ***CAUTION!***
>
> ***The hooks and locating pins must be secured with locking pins.***

Notes:

- *Positions marked 1 to 4 on the bar must face towards the vibration damper.*
- *The holes in the hooks are counted up from the hook.*
- *If the engine is to be separated from the automatic transmission, the torque converter must first be separated from the drive plate (3 bolts). The torque converter must then be secured so that it cannot fall out.*

– Remove 3408 engine bracket from cylinder block

– Install 3269 engine bracket onto cylinder block and tighten mounting bolts

- 40 Nm (30 ft lb)

– Install engine in VW 313 support clamp using VAG 1202 A workshop crane

Installation notes:

Installation is performed in the reverse of disassembly, when installing; note the following:

Vehicles with manual transmission:

– Check clutch release bearing in slave cylinder for wear, if necessary. replace slave cylinder with release bearing

– Clean notched splines of input shaft and lightly grease using: G 000 100

All vehicles:

– Check if the engine/transmission centering dowels are installed in the cylinder block, install if necessary

– Install mounting hardware approx. 5 to 6 turns by hand

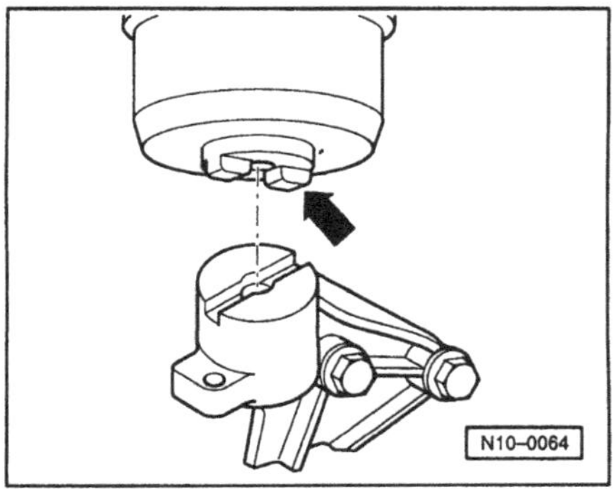

◄ – When installing right side engine mount, ensure that hydro mount lugs engage in engine bracket slot -arrow-

– Align assembly mountings stress-free by rocking
⇒ page D 10-13, assembly tightening torques

– Installing pendulum support
⇒ Repair Group 40

Vehicles with A/C:

– Installing A/C compressor
⇒ Repair Group 87

Vehicles with manual transmission:

– Connect line/hose on slave cylinder and secure with clip
⇒ Repair Group 30, 5-Speed manual transmission 02G

– Install Transmission Range Selector mechanism on transmission, adjust if necessary
⇒ Repair Group 34, 5-Speed manual transmission 02G

Vehicles with automatic transmission:

– Install Transmission Range selector cable on transmission, adjust if necessary
⇒ Repair Group 37, Automatic transmission 099

All vehicles:

– Install drive shafts
⇒ Repair Group 40

– Install power steering pump with bracket
⇒ Repair Group 48

– Install front exhaust pipe
⇒ Repair Group 26

– Install intake manifold complete with intake manifold lower section and Throttle Valve Control Module (note position of dowel sleeves in cylinder head when installing)
⇒ page D 15-8

– Install ribbed belt
⇒ page D 13-19

– Install radiator and radiator fan
⇒ page D 19-16

– Fill system with coolant
⇒ page D 19-13

– Adjust accelerator cable
⇒ page D 20-23

– Re-connect wiring and route as necessary
⇒ Wiring diagrams, Electrical troubleshooting and Component locations

– Interrogate Diagnostic Trouble Code (DTC) memory
⇒ Repair Group 01

– Check idle speed and ignition timing
⇒ Repair Group 24

– Check headlight adjustment; adjust if necessary
⇒ Maintenance booklet

Tightening torques

Bolted joint		Tightening torque
Engine to transmission	M8	25 Nm (18 ft lb)
	M10	60 Nm (44 ft lb)
	M12	80 Nm (59 ft lb)
Flywheel cover plate	M7	10 Nm (7 ft lb)
Pendulum support to transmission		80 Nm (59 ft lb) + 1/4 turn (90°) further
Pendulum support to sub-frame		200 Nm (148 ft lb)
Starter to engine and transmission		45 Nm (33 ft lb)
Front exhaust pipe to exh. manifold		40 Nm (30 ft lb)
Front exhaust pipe to catalyst		25 Nm (18 ft lb)

Bolted joint	Tightening torque
Transverse support to transmission and left mount	30 Nm (22 ft lb)
Drive shaft to wheel hub	150 Nm (111 ft lb) + 1/4 turn (90°) further
Drive shafts to flanged shafts	80 Nm (59 ft lb)

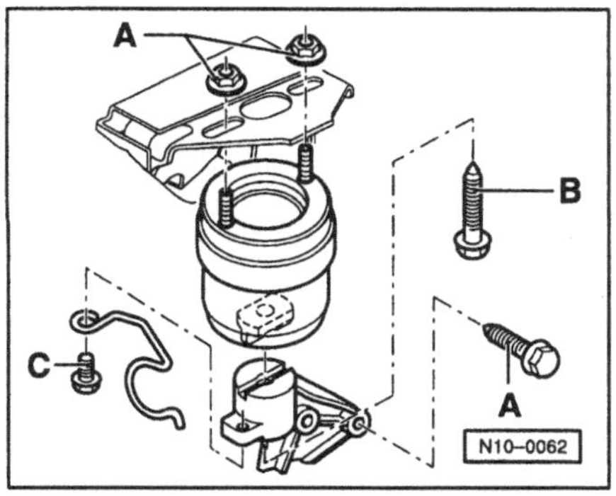

Assembly mountings

Tightening torques with bolts oiled

◄ Right side assembly mounting

- A = 55 Nm (41 ft lb)
- B = 60 Nm (44 ft lb)
- C = 10 Nm (7 ft lb)

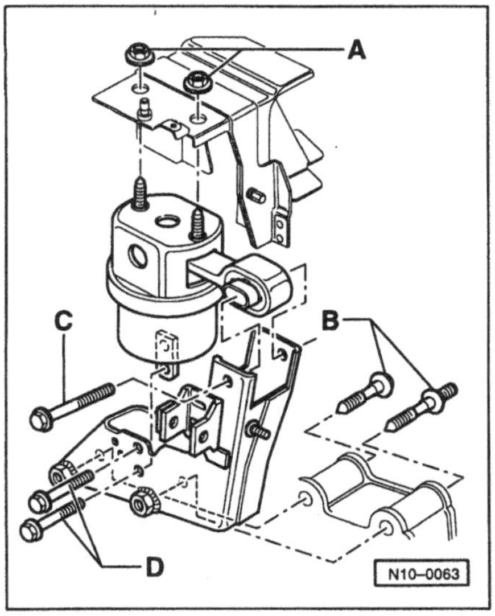

◄ Left side assembly mounting

- A = 55 Nm (41 ft lb)
- B = 50 Nm (37 ft lb) + 1/4 turn (90°) further
- C = 60 Nm (44 ft lb)
- D = 30 Nm (18 ft lb)

Vehicles with A/C, additional information and removal instructions

CAUTION!
Do not open the A/C refrigerant circuit!

Note:

Only break open A/C refrigerant circuit in workshops which have trained personnel and the necessary range of tools and workshop equipment.

To allow engine removal and installation without breaking open the refrigerant circuit:

– Detach refrigerant line retaining clamp(s)

– Remove generator
⇒ Repair Group 27

– Remove A/C compressor
⇒ Repair Group 87

– Secure A/C compressor to vehicle body to relieve any strain or stress to the refrigerant lines and hoses

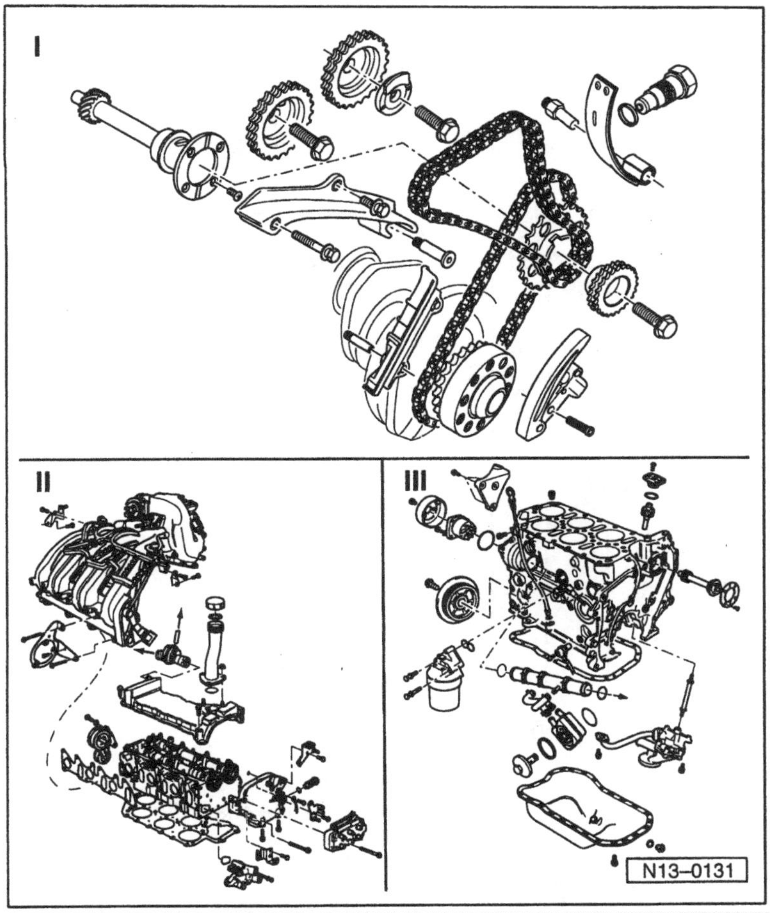

Engine, disassembling and assembling

Note:

When disassembling and assembling the engine, mount it on an engine stand using the 3269 engine bracket.

> ***CAUTION!***
>
> ***If as a result of engine damage, metal chips or metal powder is observed in the engine oil; thoroughly clean all of the engine oil passages then replace all of the oil spray jets, the oil check-valve and oil cooler.***

I ⇒ page D 13-2

II ⇒ page D 13-8

III ⇒ page D 13-13

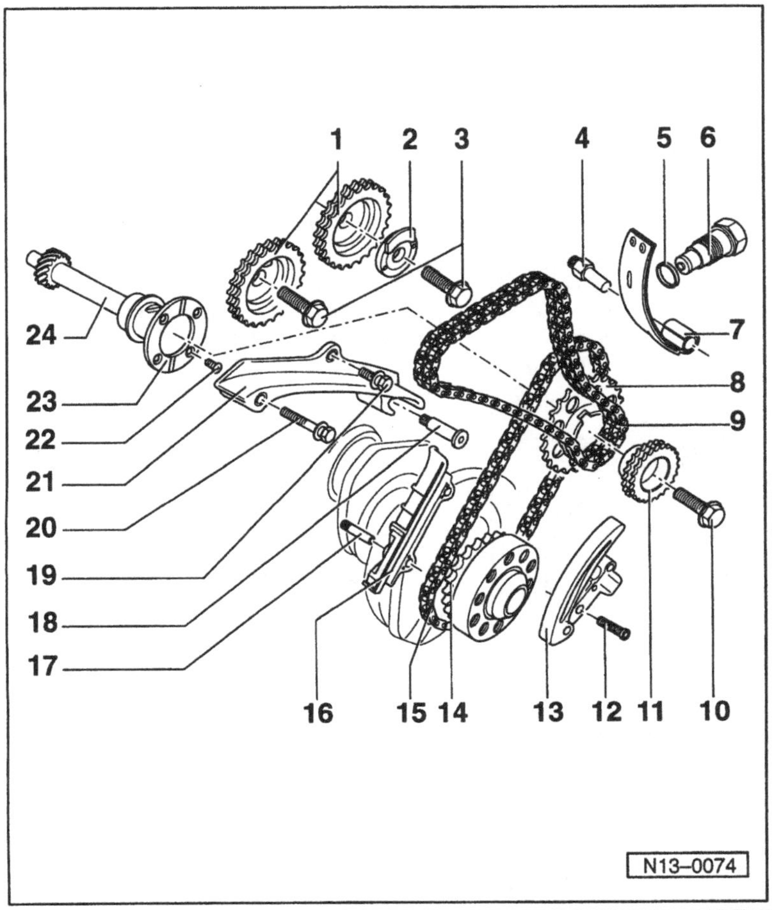

Part I

1 - Camshaft sprocket
- for double chain (item 9)
- removing and installing:

⇒ page D 15-29

2 - Sensor wheel
- for Camshaft Position sensor G40
- contact surfaces of timing chain and sensor wheel must be dry when installing
- removing and installing:

⇒ page D 15-29

3 - 100 Nm (74 ft lb)
- oil bolt head contacting surface when installing
- to remove and install: counter-hold with 24 mm open wrench on camshaft

⇒ page D 15-29

4 - Pivot pin
- 25 Nm (18 ft lb)
- for tensioning plate (item 7)

5 - Seal
- replace

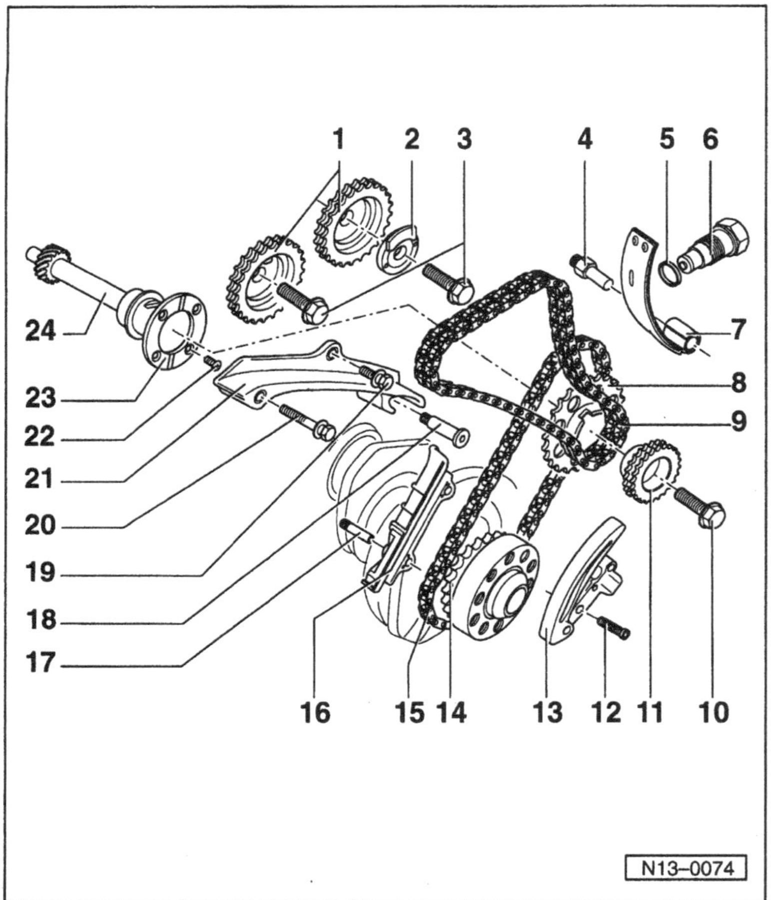

6 - Chain tensioner
- 30 Nm (22 ft lb)
- for double chain (item 9)
- bleed before installing

⇒ Fig. 2

> ***CAUTION!***
> ***Only turn the engine with chain tensioner installed!***

7 - Tensioning plate
- for double chain (item 9)

8 - Sprocket
- for single chain (item 15)
- installing

⇒ page D 13-22

9 - Double chain
- Mark direction of rotation before removing

⇒ Fig. 1
- installing

⇒ page D 13-22

10 - 100 Nm (74 ft lb)

11 - Sprocket
- for double chain (item 9)
- installing

⇒ page D 13-22

12 - 10 Nm (7 ft lb)

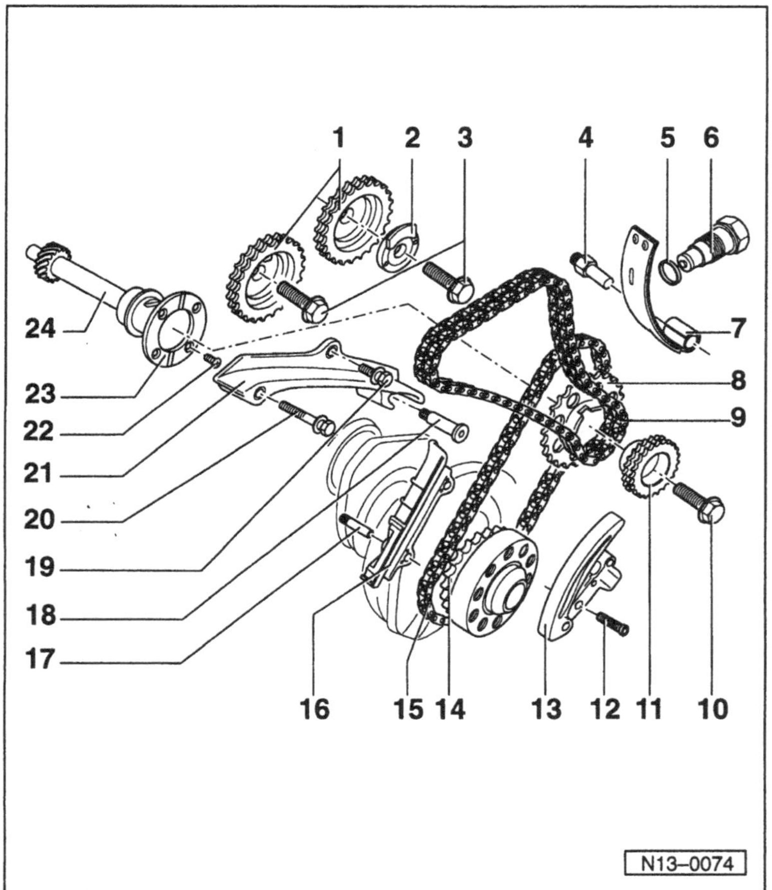

13 - Chain tensioner with tensioning plate
- for single chain (item 15)
- before installing: release locking spline in chain tensioner with a small screwdriver and press tensioning plate against tensioner

> ***CAUTION!***
> ***Only turn the engine with chain tensioner installed!***

14 - Crankshaft sprocket
- integral part of crankshaft
- ground down tooth aligned with main bearing joint:
  = TDC for Cyl No. 1

⇒ page D 13-22

15 - Single chain
- mark direction of rotation before removing

⇒ Fig. 1
- installing:

⇒ page D 13-22

16 - Guide rail
- for single chain (item 15)
- remove together with single chain

⇒ page D 13-22

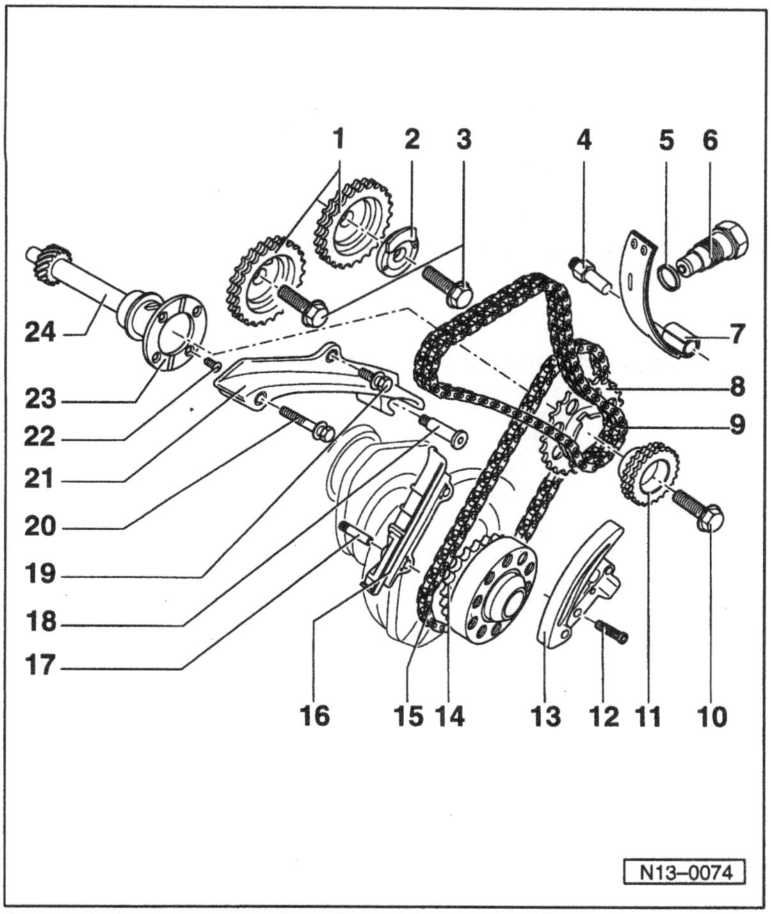

17 - locating pin w/out collar
- 25 Nm (18 ft lb)
- for guide rail (item 16)

18 - locating pin with collar
- 25 Nm (18 ft lb)
- for guide rail (item 21)

19 - 20 Nm (15 ft lb)
- insert using "D6" locking fluid

20 - 20 Nm (15 ft lb)

21 - Guide rail
- for double chain (item 9)

22 - 10 Nm (7 ft lb)
- insert using "D6" locking fluid

23 - Thrust washer

24 - Intermediate shaft

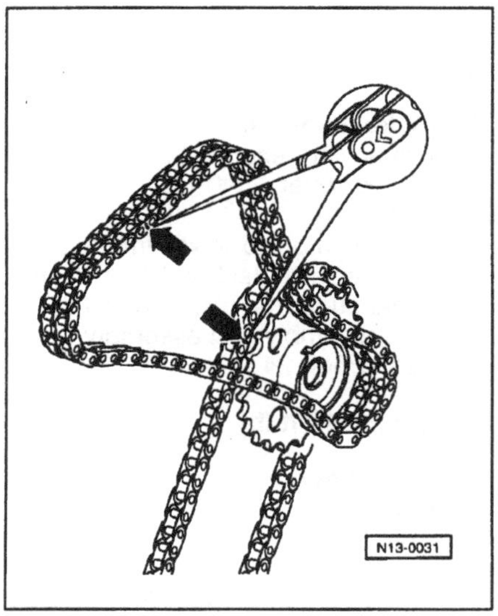

Fig. 1 Marking single and double chains

– Mark single and double chains before removing (e.g. with marked arrow pointing in direction of rotation)

> ***CAUTION!***
> ***Do NOT mark the timing chain using a punch or any other mechanical device that could weaken the chain.***

Note:

- *As of engine number AES 003279 only single–link chains are used. As a result, chain tensioner has no oil and does not have to be bled ⇒ Fig 2.*
- *Only use single link chain with tensioning bar.*

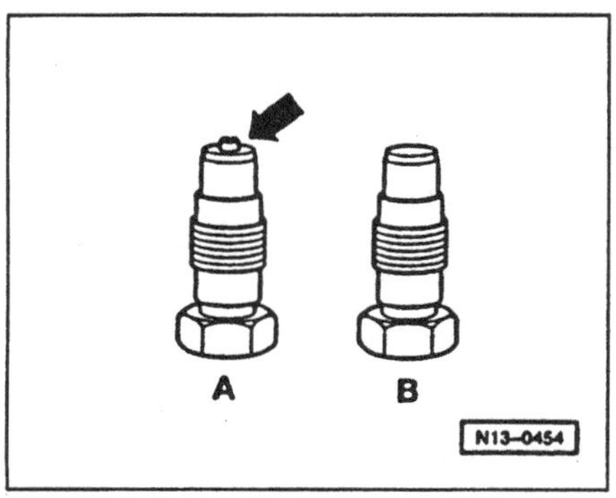

Fig. 2 Chain tensioner for camshaft chain

- Install chain tensioner –A– with oil hole (arrow) only with double link chain.
- Install chain tensioner –B– only with single link chain.

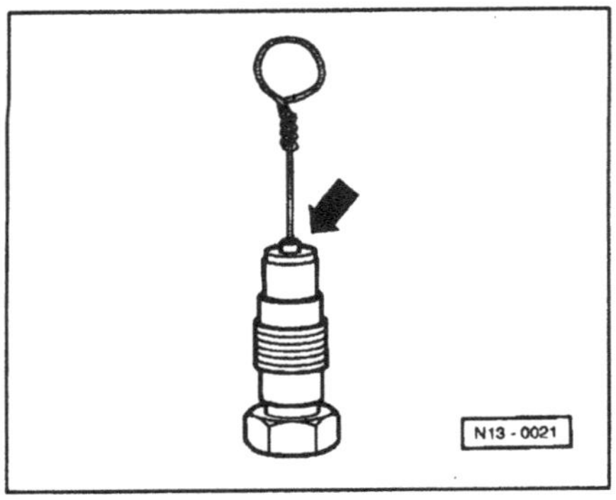

◄ **Fig. 3 Double chain tensioner, bleeding**

Special tools, testers and auxiliary items

♦ Wire (∅: 0.8 mm)

– Push piece of wire (∅: 0.8 mm) through pressure piston hole -arrow- up to ball valve and press piston and housing together onto stop

Note:

If the piston moves out again, repeat bleeding procedure.

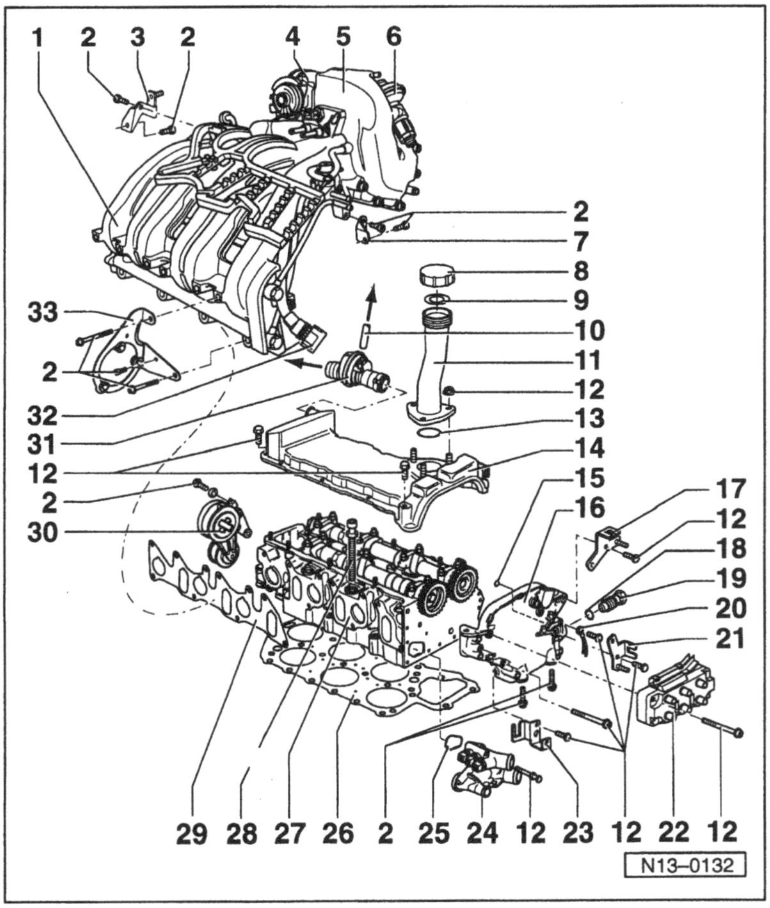

Part II

1 - Intake manifold

♦ removing and installing cylinder head cover

⇒ page D 15-8

♦ first tighten to lower intake manifold on cylinder head, then the two rear supports, (items 7 and 3)

♦ disassembly and assembly

⇒ Repair Group 24

2 - 25 Nm (18 ft lb)

3 - Rear right support

♦ between intake manifold and cylinder head

4 - Throttle Valve Control Module J338

♦ heated by coolant

♦ removing and installing:

⇒ Repair Group 24

5 - Connection

♦ removing and installing

⇒ Repair Group 24

6 - Exhaust Gas Recirculation (EGR) valve

♦ for EGR system

⇒ page D 26-8

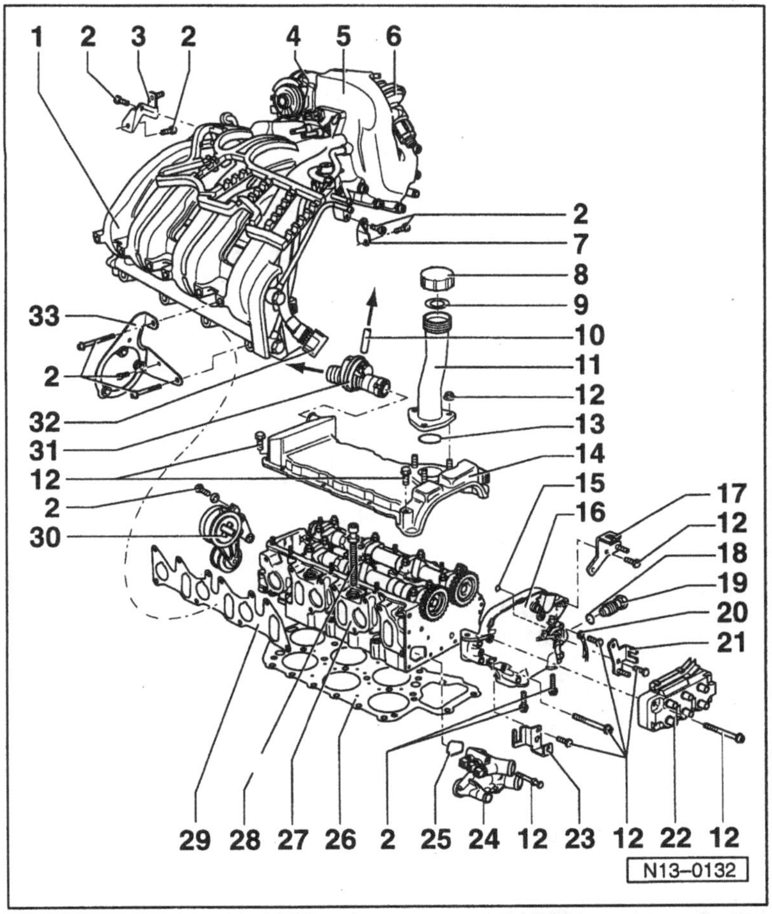

7 - Rear left support
- between intake manifold and cylinder head

8 - Cap

9 - Gasket
- replace if damaged

10 - Vacuum hose
- to EGR valve/intake manifold junction piece

⇒ page D 26-8

11 - Oil filler pipe

12 - 10 Nm (7 ft lb)

13 - O-ring
- replace if damaged

14 - Cylinder head cover
- removing and installing:

⇒ page D 15-8

- replace if damaged or leaking

15 - O-ring
- replace
- coat with oil before assembly
- – insert into camshaft sprocket cover (item 16)

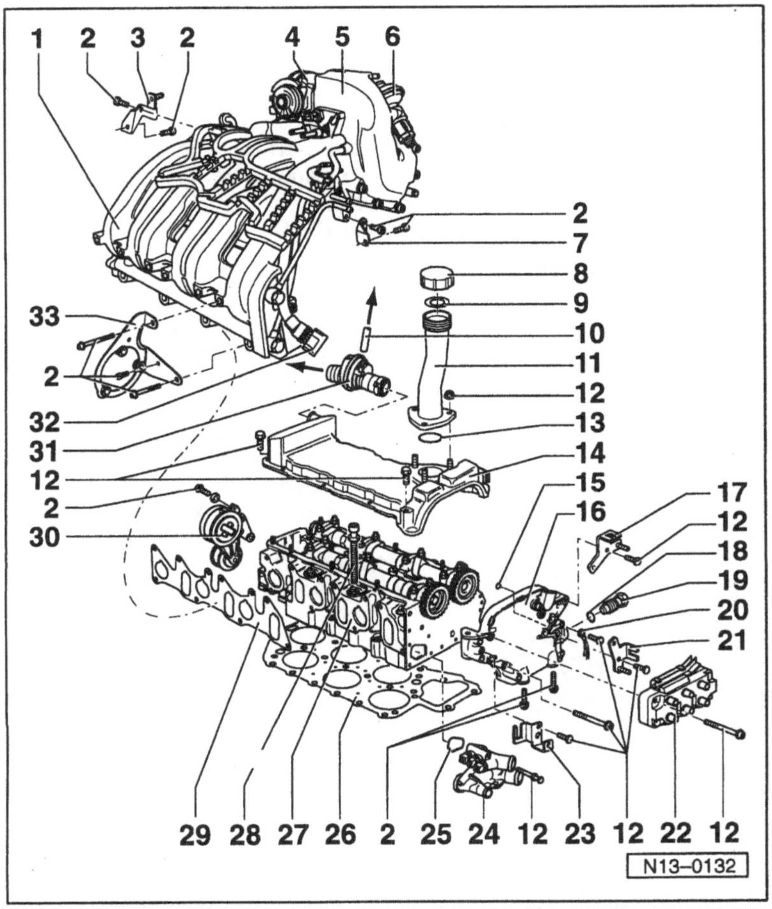

16 - Camshaft sprocket cover
- can be removed/installed with cylinder head installed
- coat sealing surfaces with AMV 188 001 02
- if only the camshaft sprocket cover has been removed; prepare cylinder head gasket for assembly

⇒ page D 15-7, Fig. 2

17 - Bracket
- for G98 2-pin EGR Temp. sensor harness connector

⇒ page D 26-8

18 - Seal
- replace

19 - Chain tensioner
- 30 Nm (22 ft lb)
- for double chain
- bleed before installing

⇒ page D 13-7, Fig. 2

- only turn engine if chain tensioner is installed!

20 - Ground connection

21 - Bracket

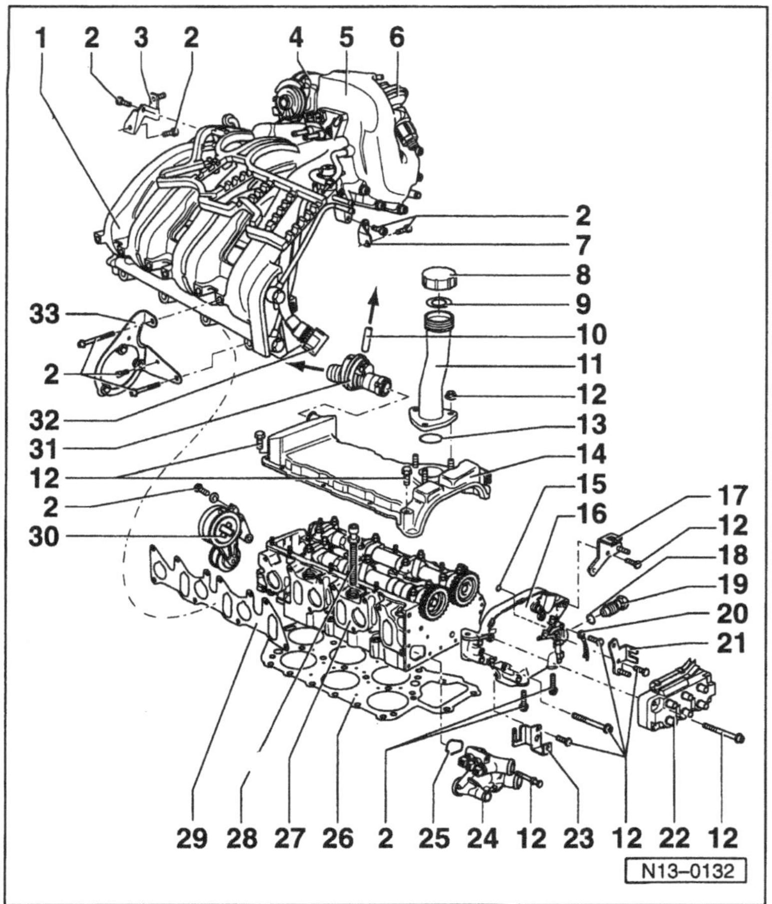

22 - Ignition coil N152*
- ♦ checking:

⇒ Repair Group 28

23 - Bracket
- ♦ for fuel injector connectors (item 32)

24 - Thermostat housing
- ♦ disassembly and assembly

⇒ page D 19-11

25 - O-ring
- ♦ replace

26 - Cylinder head gasket
- ♦ replace
- ♦ if replaced; completely replace the engine coolant

27 - Cylinder head
- ♦ removing and installing:

⇒ page D 15-1
- ♦ if replaced; completely replace the engine coolant

28 - Cylinder head bolt
- ♦ replace
- ♦ follow sequence when loosening and tightening

⇒ page D 15-16

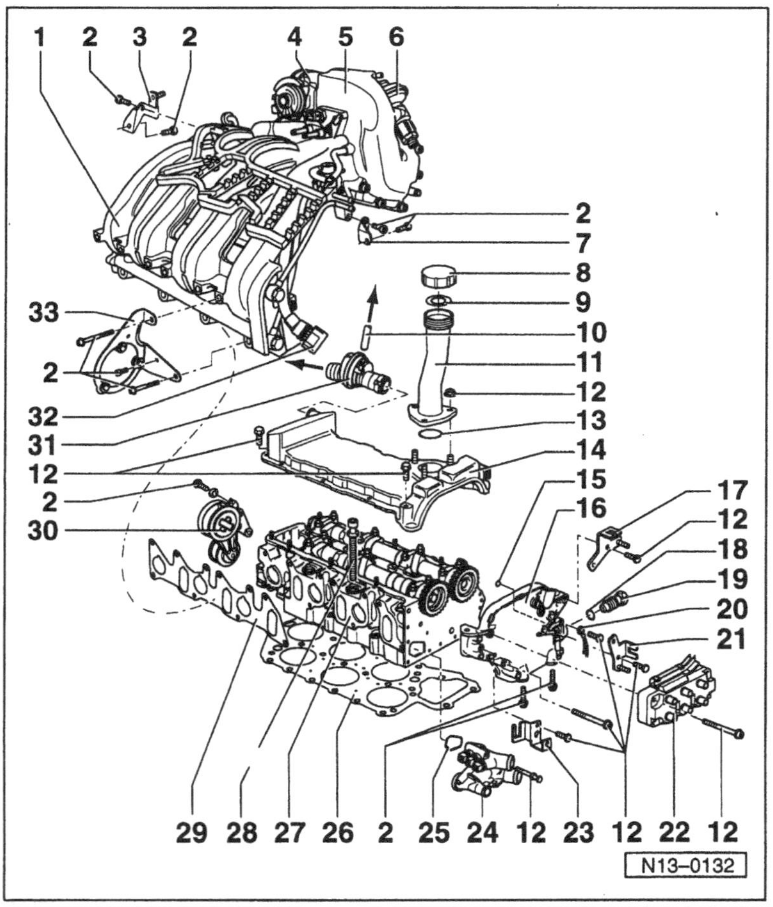

29 - Lower intake manifold gasket
- ♦ replace
- ♦ note installed position

30 - Ribbed belt tensioner
- ♦ removing and installing ribbed belts

⇒ page D 13-19

31 - Positive Crankcase Ventilation valve
- ♦ arrow on crankcase breather valve points to intake hose

⇒ Repair Group 24

32 - Harness connector
- ♦ for injectors N30, N31, N32, N33, N83, N84
- ♦ mounted to bracket (item 23)

33 - Retainer
- ♦ for Secondary Air Injection pump motor

⇒ page D 26-15

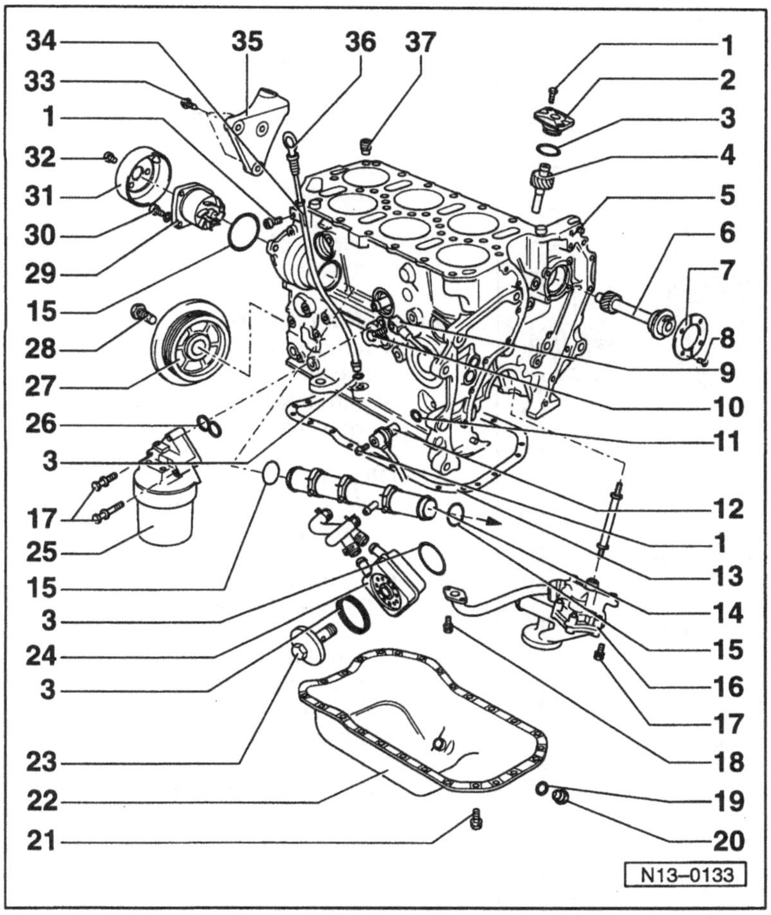

Part III

1 - 10 Nm (7 ft lb)

2 - Oil pump drive cover

3 - O-ring
- replace
- oil before assembling

4 - Oil pump drive

5 - Cylinder block
- removing and installing sealing flange and flywheel/drive plate:

⇒ page D 13-31
- removing and installing crankshaft:

⇒ page D 13-41
- disassembling and assembling pistons and conrods:

⇒ page D 13-44

6 - Intermediate shaft

7 - Thrust washer

8 - 10 Nm (7 ft lb)
- Install with D6 locking fluid

9 - Knock sensor 2 G66
- checking:

⇒ Repair Group 01

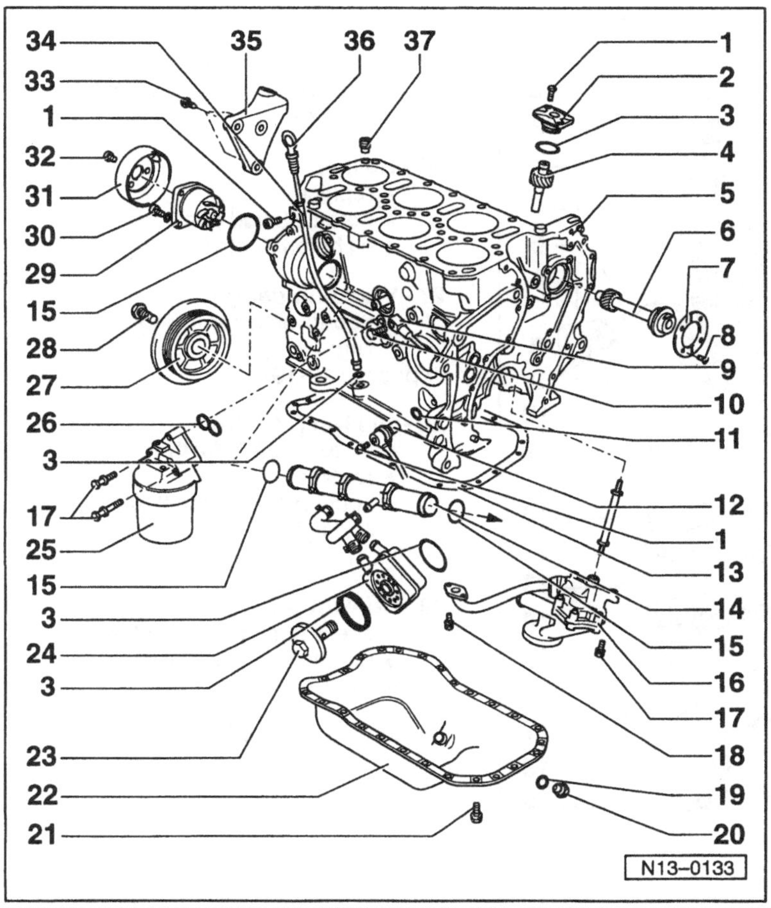

10 - 20 Nm (15 ft lb)
- tightening torque influences knock sensor function

11 - O-ring
- replace if damaged

12 - Engine Speed sensor G28
- checking:

⇒ Repair Group 01

13 - Gasket
- replace if damaged
- coat sump flange/cylinder block flange with "D2" before installing

14 - Coolant pipe
- to thermostat housing

⇒ page D 13-11, item 24
- removing and installing:

⇒ page D 19-5

15 - O-ring
- replace

16 - Oil pump
- disassembly and assembly:

⇒ page D 17-8
- coat oil pressure line on block and oil pump housing with AMV 188 001 02

17 - 25 Nm (18 ft lb)

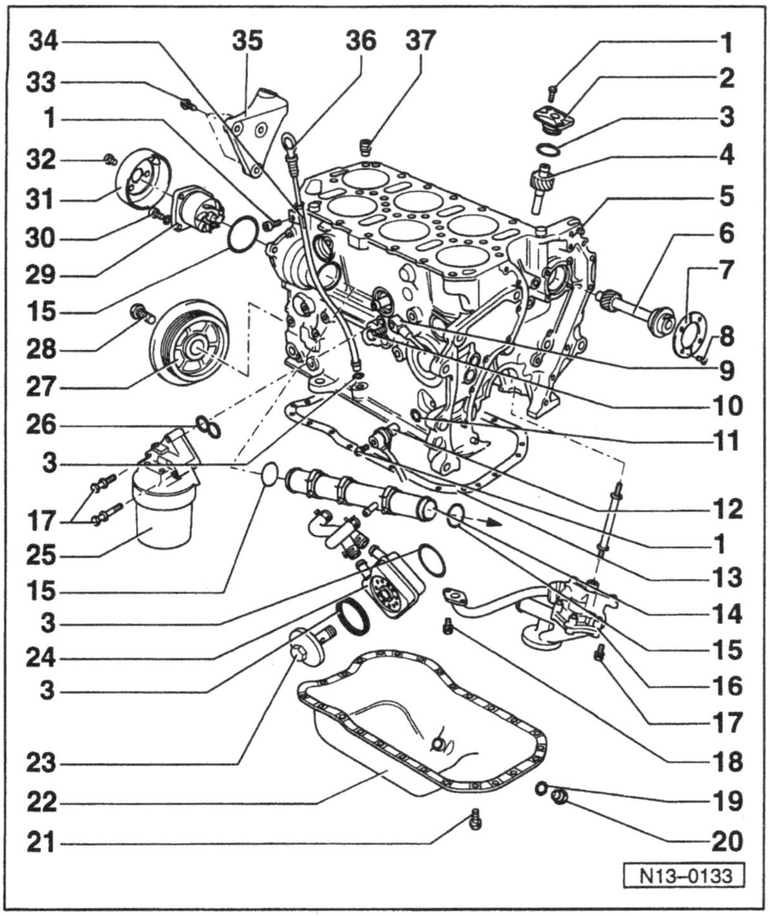

18 - 10 Nm (7 ft lb)

- replace
- install with D6 locking fluid

19 - Seal

- replace

20 - Oil drain plug

- 30 Nm (22 ft lb)

21 - 15 Nm (11 ft lb)

- remove and install using 3249 socket
- with flywheel installed: turn flywheel until recess aligns with bolts

22 - Oil pan

- clean sealing surfaces before installing

23 - Oil cooler cover

- 25 Nm (18 ft lb)

24 - Oil cooler

- coat contact area outside seal with AMV 188 100 02
- ensure clearance with any adjacent components
- see note ⇒ page D 13-1

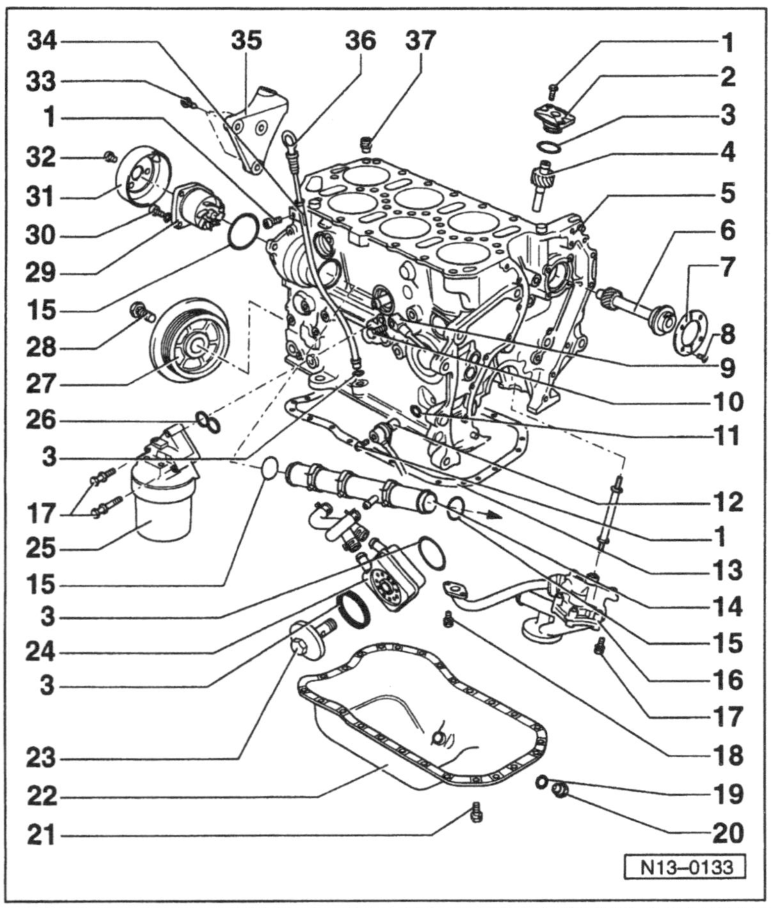

25 - Oil filter housing

- disassembly and assembly

⇒ page D 17-6

26 - Gasket

- replace
- note installed position
- oil before installing

27 - Vibration damper

- ribbed belt, removing and installing:

⇒ page D 13-19

28 - 100 Nm (74 ft lb) + $^1/_4$ turn (90 °) further

- replace
- counter-hold using 3406 to loosen and tighten

⇒ Fig. 1

29 - Coolant pump

- check shaft for ease of movement
- removing and installing:

⇒ page D 19-19

30 - 20 Nm (15 ft lb)

31 - Pulley

- for coolant pump

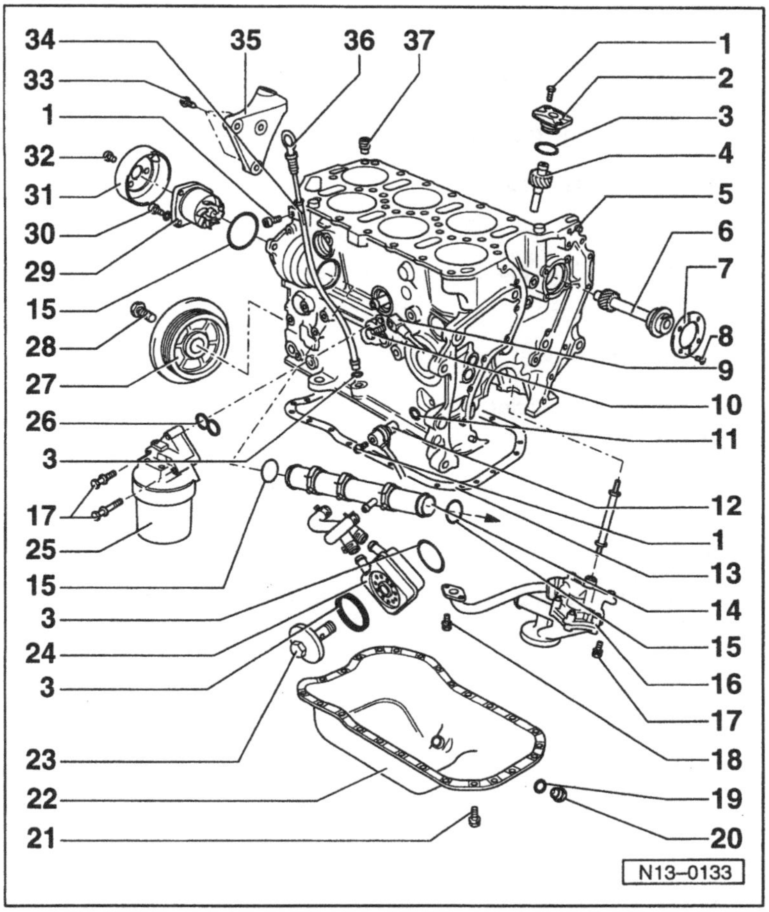

32 - 25 Nm (18 ft lb)
- loosening and tightening: counter-hold using a punch fed through the holes

33 - 55 Nm (41 ft lb)

34 - Guide tube
- for dipstick
- bolted to intake manifold

35 - Right engine bracket

36 - Dipstick

> ***CAUTION!***
> ***Oil must NOT be above MAX mark on dipstick!***

37 - Oil check valve
- 5 Nm (44 in. lb)
- note installed position
- clean if contaminated
- see note:

⇒ page D 13-1

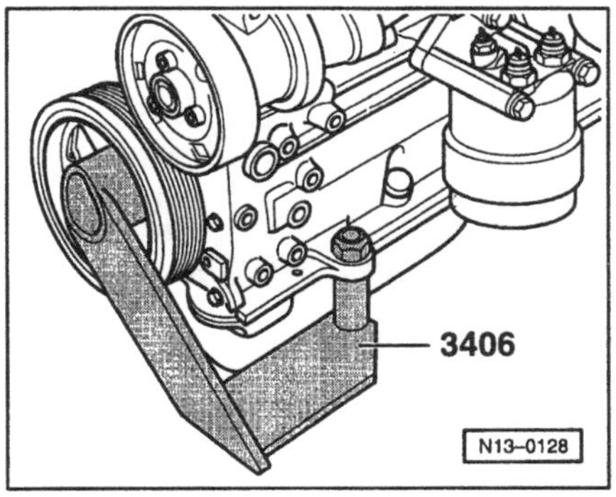

◄ **Fig. 1 Holding vibration damper using 3406 counter-hold tool to loosen or tighten mounting bolt**

– Replace mounting bolt

> ***CAUTION!***
> ***Do not allow the crankshaft to turn while tightening the mounting bolt!***

Ribbed belt, removing and installing

Special tools, testers and auxiliary items

♦ M8 x 80 hex bolt

Note:

When installing the belt, ensure that it is correctly seated in the pulley.

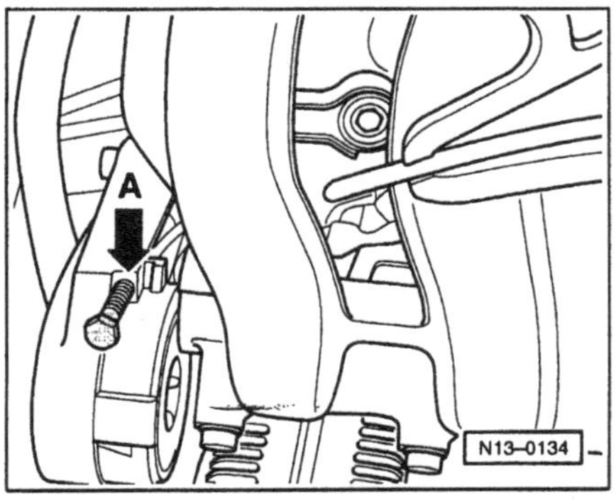

Removing

– Remove insulation tray
⇒ Repair Group 50

◄ – Screw M8 x 80 bolt into tensioner threaded hole -A- until ribbed belt is no longer under tension

> ***CAUTION!***
> ***Only thread in bolt until belt can be removed, otherwise tensioner housing can be damaged!***

– Remove ribbed belt

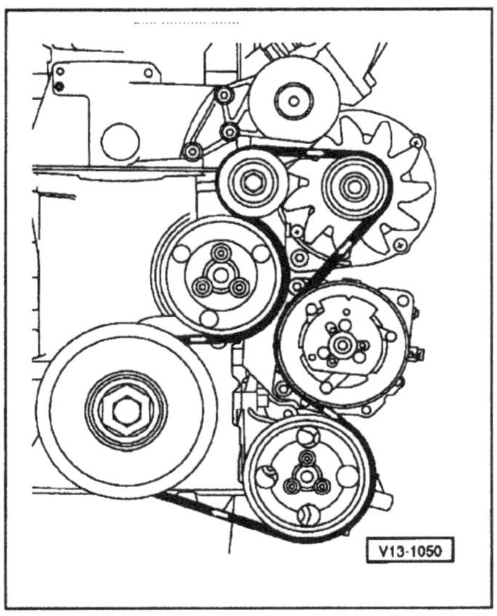

Installing

Note:

Before installing the ribbed belt, ensure that the generator, A/C compressor, and vane pump sub-assemblies are tight.

◄ – Install ribbed belt

– Remove M8 bolt from tensioner

– Start engine and check belt

Note:

Vehicles with A/C are equipped with a double ribbed belt.

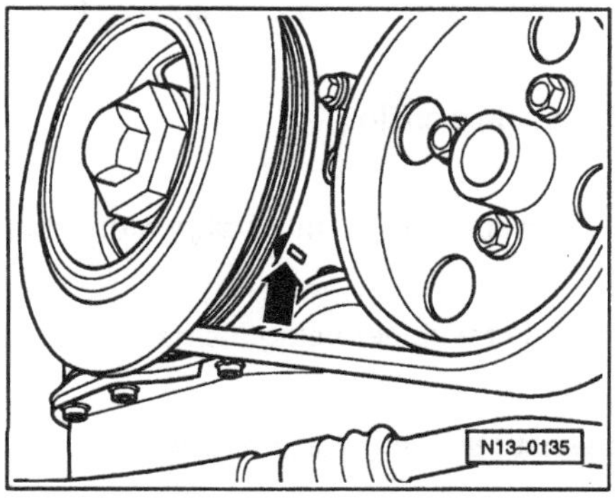

Valve timing, checking

Special tools, testers and auxiliary items

♦ 3268 Camshaft setting bar

Test sequence

– Remove insulation tray
⇒ Repair Group 50

◄ – Set crankshaft to TDC cyl. 1 mark -arrow- by turning the crankshaft in direction of engine rotation using the vibration damper bolt

– Remove cylinder head cover
⇒ page D 15-8

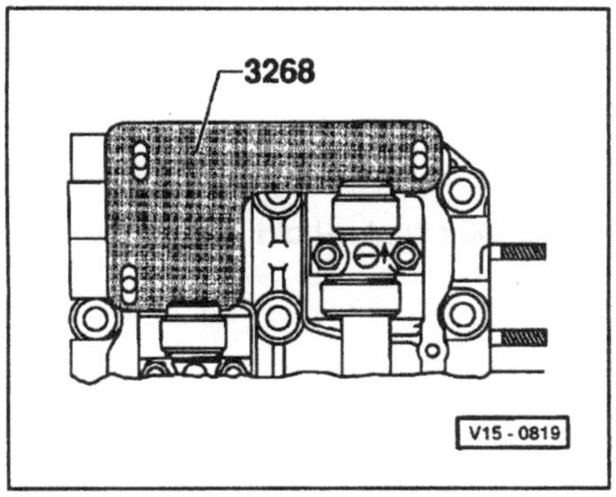

◄ ♦ 3268 Camshaft jig must fit into both shaft grooves

Note:

This orientation is only possible every 2nd TDC position.

Valve timing, adjusting (with timing chains removed)

Special tools, testers and auxiliary items

♦ 3406 Counter-hold tool

♦ 3268 Camshaft setting bar

♦ VAG 1331 Torque wrench (5 to 50 Nm)

♦ VAG 1332 Torque wrench (40 to 200 Nm)

Work sequence (with engine removed)

– Install single chain and chain tensioner with tensioning plate

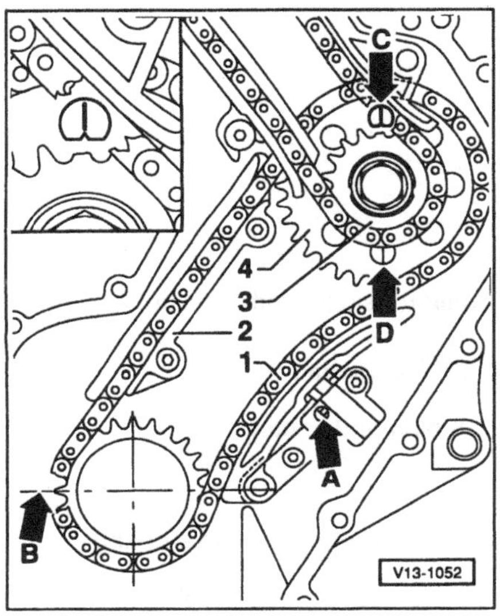

◄ – Set/check position of crankshaft to intermediate shaft

♦ Ground down tooth on crankshaft sprocket -B- must align with the main bearing joint (= TDC for cylinder 1)

– Install pin (without collar) for guide rail -2- and tighten

♦ 25 Nm (18 ft lb)

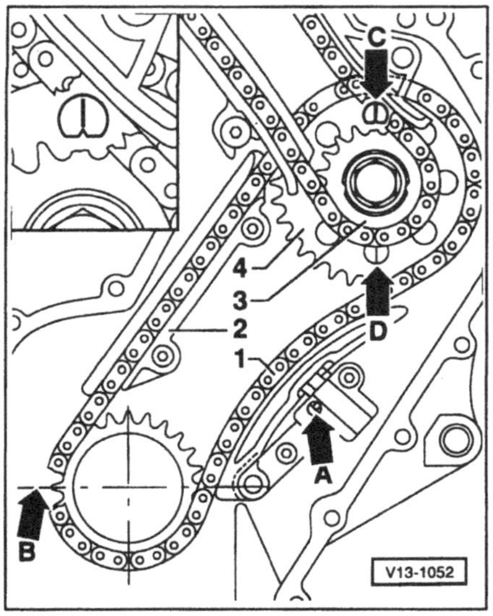

- Install guide rail -2- with single chain -1- and both sprockets -3- and -4-
- Note direction of rotation for single chain ⇒ page D 13-6, Fig. 1
    - ♦ The marking on single chain sprocket -4- must align with notch -C- or -D- on the thrust washer
- Release locking spline in chain tensioner using a small screwdriver -A-
- Press chain tensioner against tensioner plate and then tighten chain tensioner
    - ♦ 10 Nm (7 ft lb)

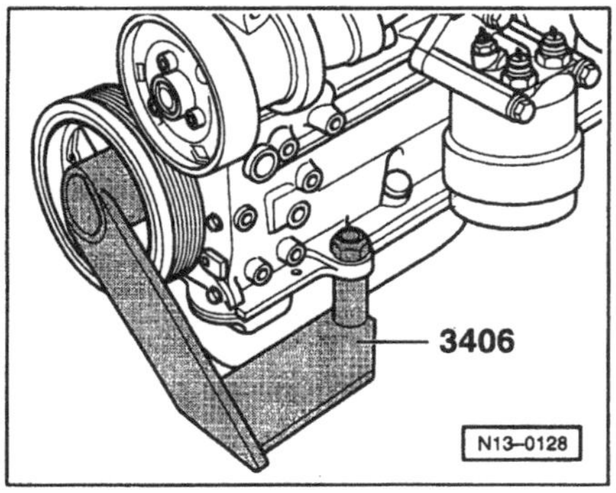

- Lock vibration damper using 3406 counter-hold tool

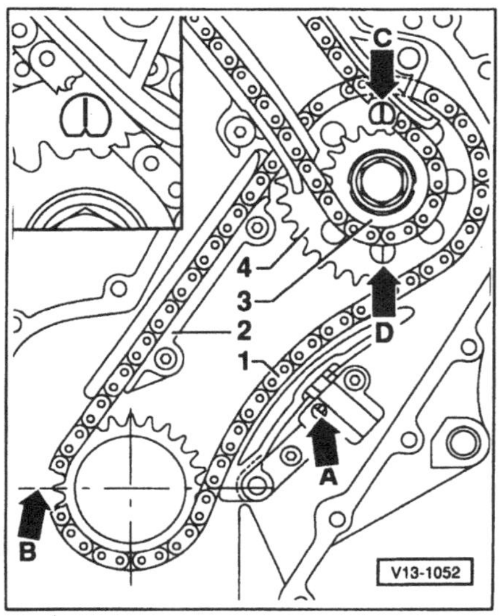

- Tighten intermediate shaft sprockets 3 and 4
    - ♦ 100 Nm (74 ft lb)
- Check position of crankshaft relative to intermediate shaft
    - ♦ Ground–down tooth on crankshaft sprocket -B- must align with the main bearing joint (= TDC for cylinder 1)

- Install double chain and chain tensioner with tensioning plate

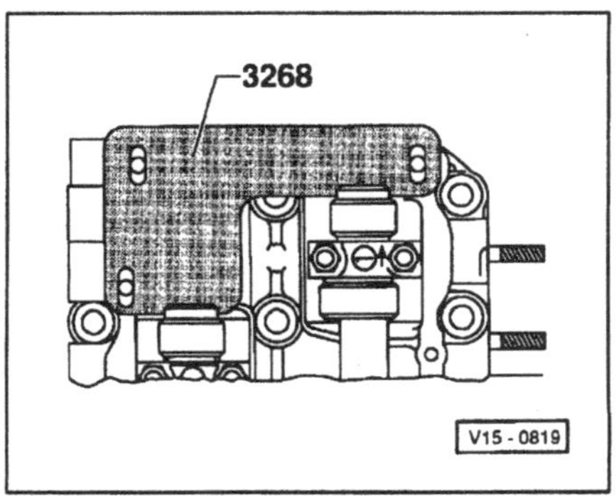

- Position camshafts using 3268 camshaft jig
- Install tensioning plate pivot pins and tighten
    - ♦ 25 Nm (18 ft lb)
- Install tensioning plate for chain tensioner (double chain)
- Install locating pin with collar for guide rail and tighten
    - ♦ 25 Nm (18 ft lb)

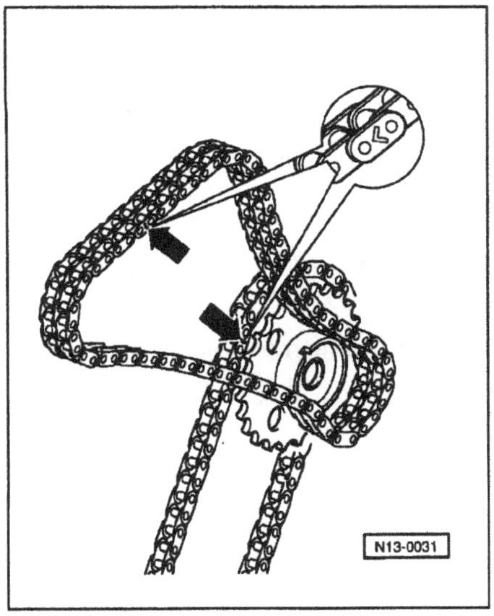

With cylinder head removed

Cylinder head, installing
⇒ page D 15-16

– Place guide rail on locating pin, insert short mounting bolt using "D6" locking fluid and tighten both bolts

  ♦ 20 Nm (15 ft lb)

◄ – Place double chain on intermediate shaft

  ♦ note direction of engine rotation for double chain

– Install camshaft sprocket and double chain to camshaft for cylinders 2, 4 and 6 (short camshaft) and hand tighten

– Install camshaft sprocket (with sensor wheel for Camshaft Position sensor) and double chain on camshaft for cylinders 1, 3 and 5 and tighten by hand

Notes:

♦ *Contact surfaces of timing chain and sensor wheel must be dry when installing*

♦ *Oil bolt head contact surfaces when installing*

– Remove 3268 camshaft jig

– Tighten camshaft sprocket mounting bolts

  ♦ 100 Nm (74 ft lb)

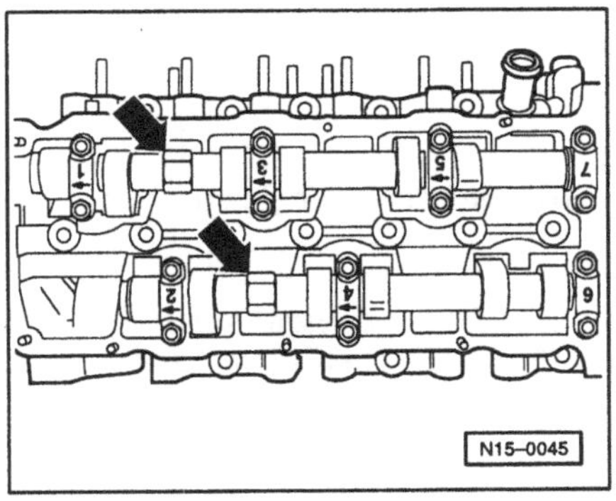

Note:

Only counter-hold using a 24–mm open end wrench on the camshaft -arrow-. The 3268 camshaft jig must not be installed when tightening or loosening the sprockets.

– Coat sealing surface of sealing flange with AMV 188 001 02 and install

– Tighten mounting bolt

  ♦ 10 Nm (7 ft lb)

– Replace sealing flange oil seal
⇒ page D 13-31

– Prepare cylinder head gasket for assembly
⇒ page D 15-7, Fig. 2

– Coat camshaft sprocket cover sealing flange w/AMV 188 001 02

– Oil O-ring and insert in camshaft sprocket cover
⇒ page D 13-9, item 15

– Install cylinder head cover, insert all mounting bolts and lightly tighten

– First tighten M8 mounting bolt

  ♦ 25 Nm (18 ft lb)

– Then tighten M6 mounting bolts

  ♦ 10 Nm (7 ft lb)

- Install chain tensioner and tighten

  - 30 Nm (22 ft lb)

Notes:

- *If the chain tensioner has been pulled apart, bleed before installing*
⇒ page D 13-7, Fig. 2
- *Only turn engine with chain tensioner installed! Otherwise the single or double chain will jump the sprockets.*

- Turn crankshaft two full turns in direction of engine rotation and check the valve timing
⇒ page D 13-21

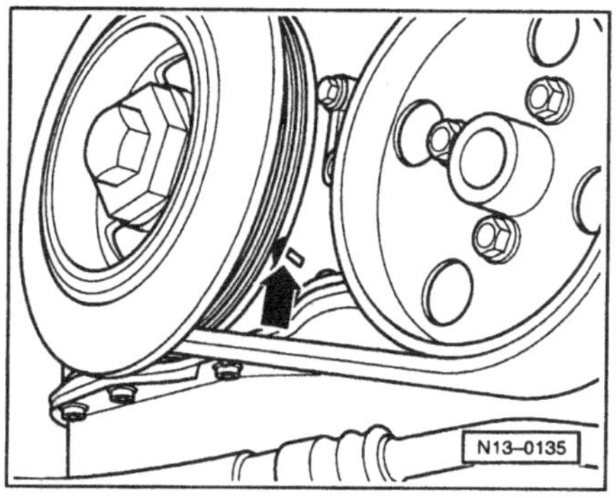

Engine installed, cylinder head removed

◄ - Set crankshaft to TDC (cylinder 1) marks -arrow- by turning crankshaft in direction of engine rotation using vibration damper mounting bolt

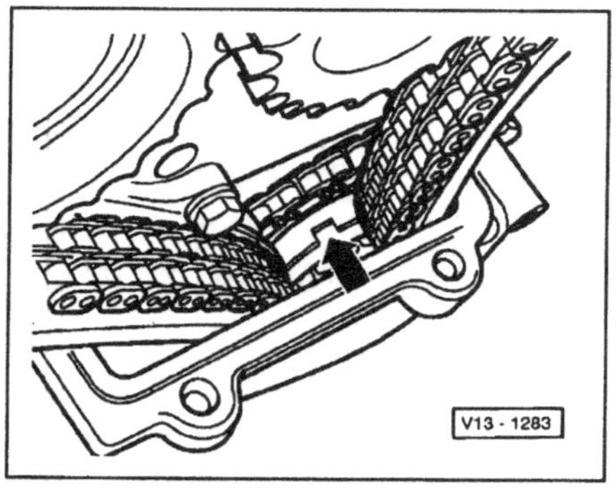

◄ If the TDC cylinder 1 setting is correct, it is possible to see a notch on the intermediate shaft sprockets -arrow-

If the notch can't be seen:

- Turn crankshaft one full turn in direction of engine rotation

Note:

If the crankshaft must be turned with the cylinder head removed, use a 2nd technician to guide the double chain by hand to prevent it from jamming.

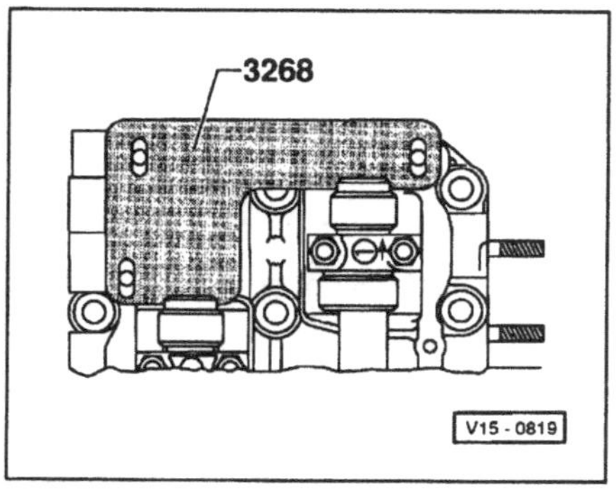

◄ - Position camshafts using 3268 camshaft jig

- Prepare cylinder head gasket for assembly
⇒ page D 15-7, Fig. 2

- Install cylinder head
⇒ page D 15-16

- Place guide rail on locating pin

- Insert short mounting bolt using D6 locking fluid and tighten

  - 20 Nm (15 ft lb)

- Install camshaft sprocket and double chain to camshaft for cylinders 2, 4 and 6 (short camshaft), hand-tighten

– Install camshaft sprocket (with trigger wheel for Camshaft Position sensor) and double chain on camshaft for cylinders 1, 3 and 5, hand-tighten

Notes:

♦ *Contact surfaces of timing chain and sensor wheel must be dry when installing*

♦ *Oil bolt head contacting surfaces when installing*

– Remove 3268 camshaft jig

– Tighten camshaft sprocket mounting bolts

♦ 100 Nm (74 ft lb)

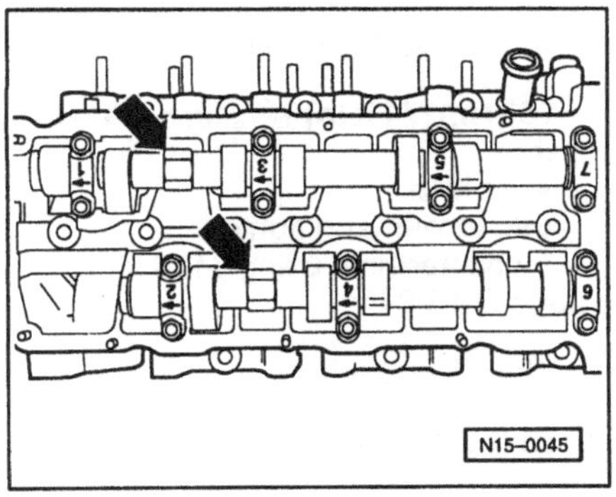

Note:

Only counter-hold using a 24–mm open end wrench on the camshaft -arrow-. The 3268 camshaft jig must not be installed when tightening or loosening the sprockets.

◄ – Coat sealing flange sealing surface with AMV 188 001 02

– Oil O-ring and insert in camshaft sprocket cover
⇒ page D 13-9 (item 15)

– Install camshaft cover

– install all mounting bolts and lightly tighten

– First tighten M8 mounting bolt

♦ 25 Nm (18 ft lb)

– Then tighten M6 mounting bolts

♦ 10 Nm (7 ft lb)

– Install double chain, chain tensioner and tighten

♦ 30 Nm (22 ft lb)

Notes:

♦ *If the chain tensioner has been pulled apart, bleed before installing*
⇒ page D 13-7, Fig. 2

> ***CAUTION!***
> ***Only turn engine with chain tensioner installed! Otherwise the chain (single or double) will jump time!***

– Turn crankshaft two full turns in direction of engine rotation and check the valve timing
⇒ page D 13-21

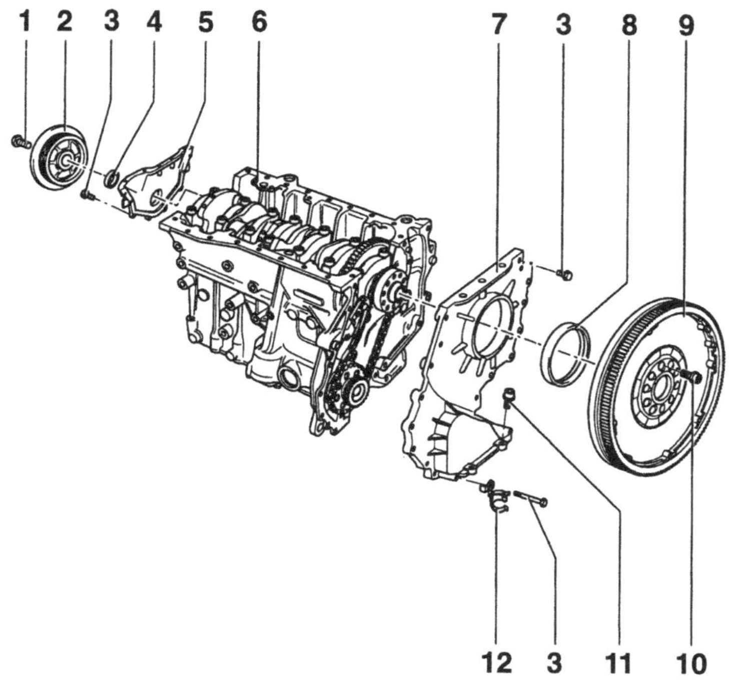

N13–0136

Sealing flange and flywheel/drive plate, removing and installing

Notes:

- *for repairs to the clutch:*

⇒ Repair Group 30, 02G 5 Speed manual transmission

- *The sealing flange (item 7) can be removed and installed with the cylinder head installed*
- *When stripping and assembling the engine, attach the block to an engine mount using 3269 bracket*

1 - 100 Nm (74 ft lb) + 1/4 turn (90 °) further

- replace
- to loosen and tighten: counter-hold using 3406 tool

⇒ page D 13-34

2 - Vibration damper

3 - 10 Nm (7 Ft lb)

4 - Oil seal

- replacing:

⇒ page D 13-34

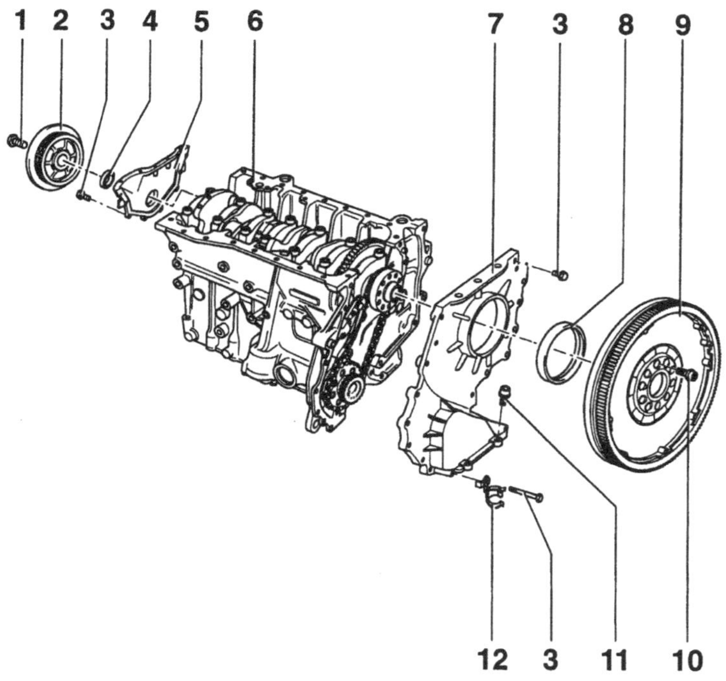

N13–0136

5 - Sealing flange

- coat sealing surfaces with AMV 188 001 02

6 - Cylinder block

- crankshaft, removing and installing:

⇒ page D 13-41

- pistons and conrods, disassembling and assembling:

⇒ page D 13-44

7 - Sealing flange

- coat sealing surfaces with AMV 188 001 02

8 - Oil seal

- remove using 2086 extractor hook
- lightly oil sealing lip
- install over 2003/2A sleeve
- pull into stop using: 2003/3 installation tool

9 - Flywheel/drive plate

- dual mass flywheel, removing and installing:

⇒ page D 13-37

- drive plate, removing and installing:

⇒ page D 13-39

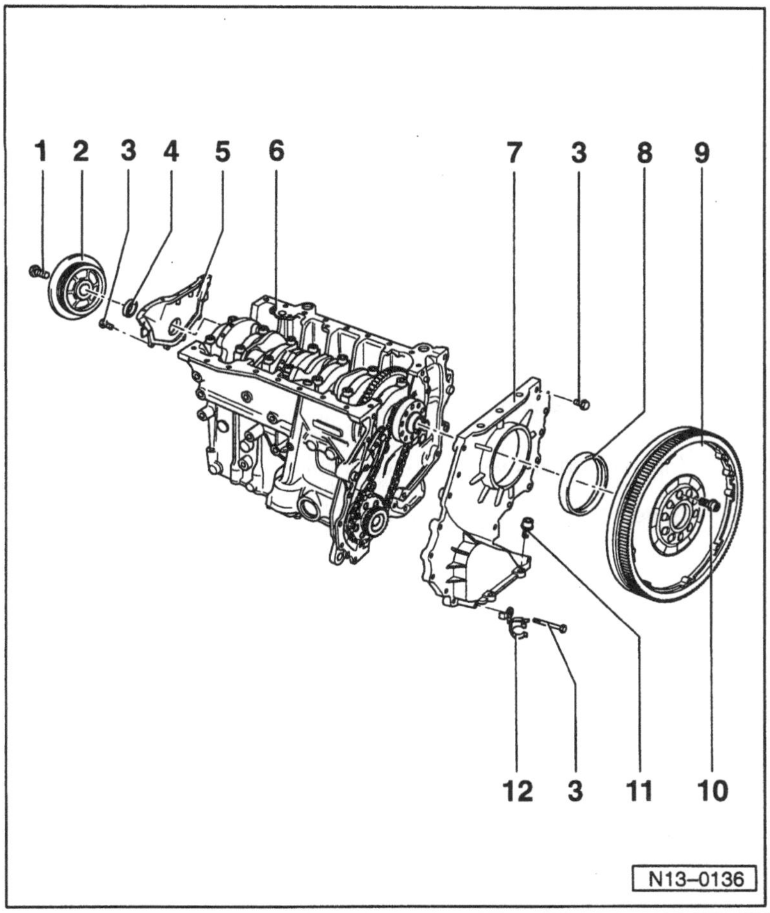

10 - 60 Nm (44 Ft lb) + 1/4 turn (90 °) further
- replace

11 - 25 Nm (18 Ft lb)

12 - Bracket
- for coolant hose

Crankshaft oil seal (vibration damper end), replacing

Special tools, testers and auxiliary items

- 3406 Counter-hold tool
- 3203 Oil seal extractor
- 3266 Pressure sleeve
- 3266/1 Guide sleeve
- VAG 1332 Torque wrench
40 - 200 Nm (30 to 148 Ft lb)

Removing

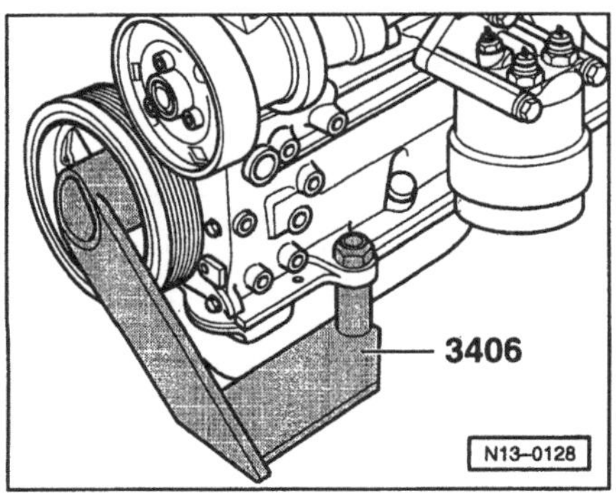

– Remove ribbed belt
⇒ page D 13-19

◄ – Remove vibration damper by locking vibration damper with counter-hold tool 3406

– Unscrew inner part of 3203 oil seal extractor three turns (approx. 4 mm) from the outer part and lock, using the knurled screw

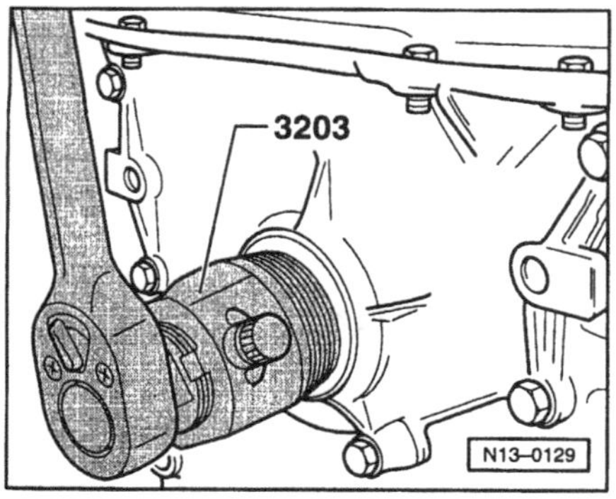

◄ – Lubricate threaded head of 3203 oil seal extractor, place in position and while exerting firm pressure, screw as far as possible into oil seal

– Loosen knurled screw and turn inner part against crankshaft until oil seal is pulled out

Installing

– Lightly oil sealing lip of oil seal

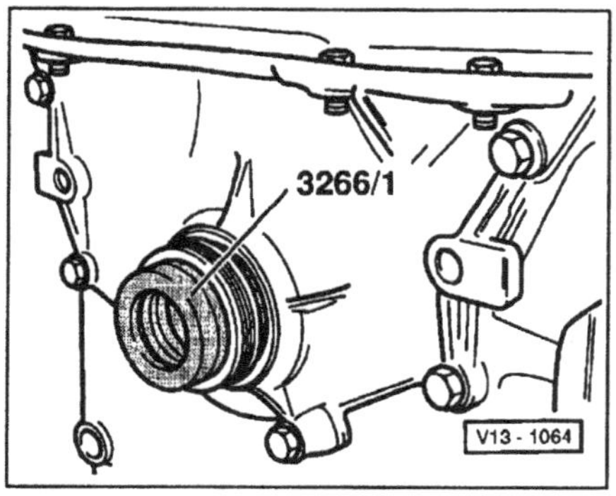

◄ – Place guide sleeve from 3266/1 onto crankshaft journal

– Slide oil seal over guide sleeve

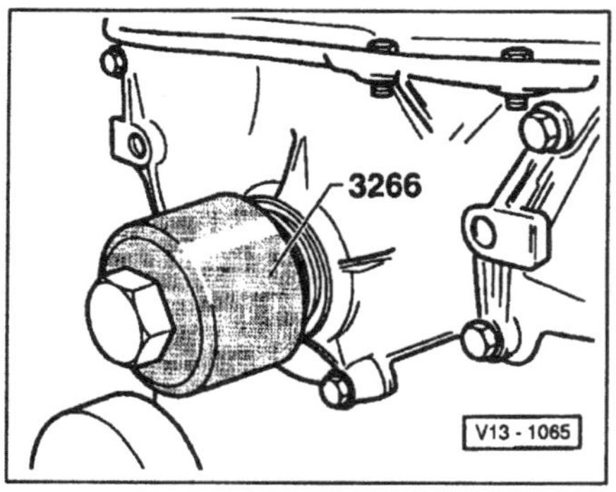

◄ – Using an old vibration damper mounting bolt, press in oil seal up to the stop, using press sleeve from 3266

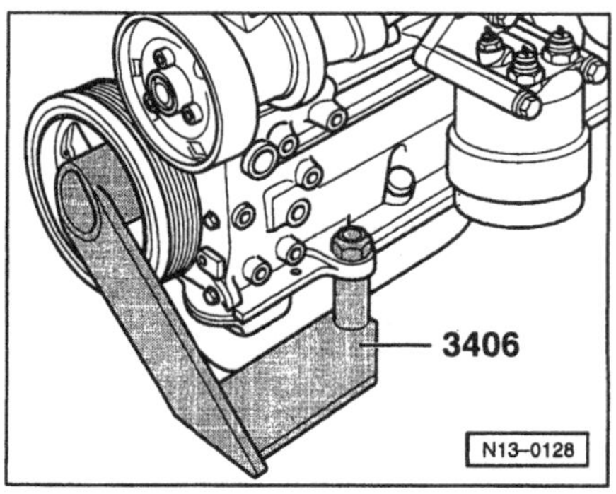

◄ – Install vibration damper and lock into place using 3406 counterhold tool

– Tighten new mounting bolt to 100 Nm (74 ft lb) and then turn 1/4 turn (90°) further

– Install ribbed belt
⇒ page D 13-19

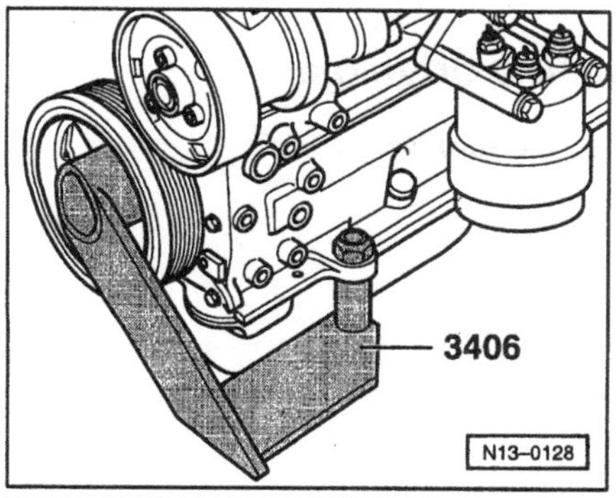

Flywheel (dual mass), removing and installing

Special tools, testers and auxiliary items

- ♦ 3406 Counter-hold tool
- ♦ VAG 1332 Torque wrench
  40 - 200 Nm (30 to 148 Ft lb)

Removing

◄ – Lock vibration damper with 3406 counter-hold tool

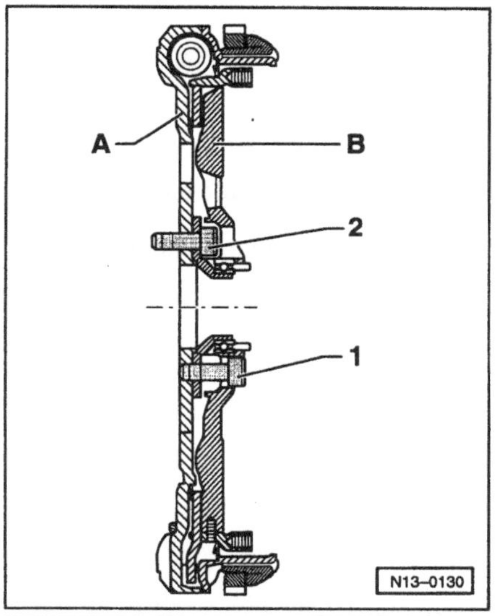

◄ – Turn secondary flywheel (mass -B- of dual mass flywheel) until the mounting bolt heads can be seen through the secondary flywheel holes

– Carefully loosen one mounting bolt -1- and unscrew until it sits in the hole of the secondary flywheel mass and prevents it from turning

– Loosen remaining dual mass flywheel mounting bolts -2- diagonally and remove

– Remove dual mass flywheel

Installing

– Fit dual mass flywheel to crankshaft

– Align bolt holes of primary flywheel mass -A- and secondary flywheel mass -B-

– Insert new mounting bolts and tighten by hand

– Tighten mounting bolts to 60 Nm (44 Ft lb) and then turn an additional 90° (1/4 turn)

- ♦ the additional 1/4 turn can be performed in more than one stage

Removing and installing drive plate

Special tools, testers and auxiliary items

- 3406 Counter-hold tool
- Depth gauge
- Straight edge
- VAG 1331 Torque wrench
  5 - 50 Nm (4 to 37 Ft lb)
- VAG 1332 Torque wrench
  40 - 200 Nm (30 to 148 Ft lb)

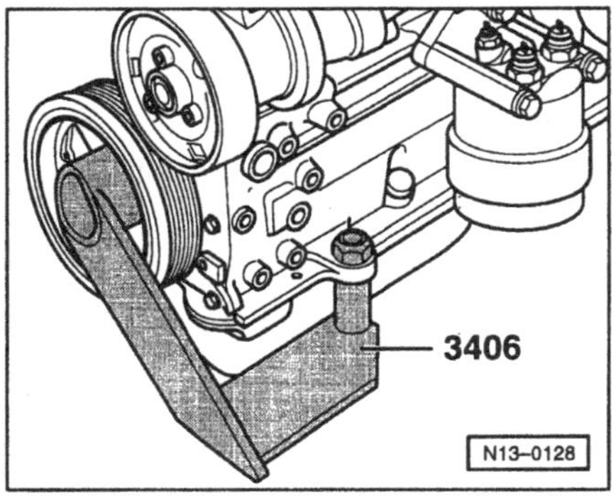

Removing

- Lock vibration damper using 3406 counter-hold tool
- Diagonally loosen (and remove) drive plate mounting bolts
- Remove drive plate

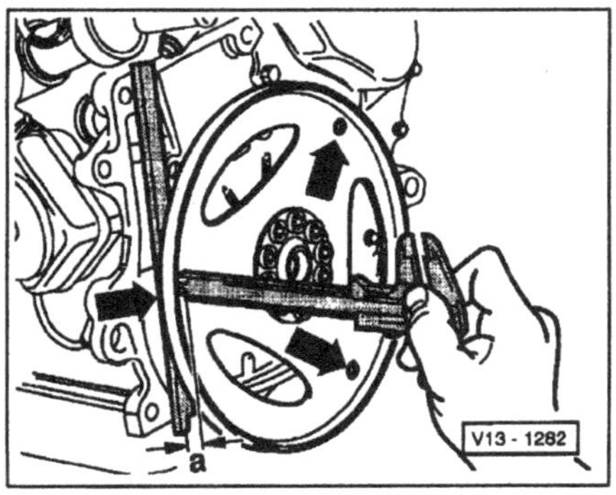

Installing

- Fit drive plate on crankshaft.
- Insert 3 (minimum) old mounting bolts and tighten
  - 30 Nm (22 Ft lb)
- Check dimension -a- through the three torque converter mounting holes using a straight edge and a depth gauge; calculate average
- Compare average with specification (measured distance + thickness of straight edge)
  - Specification: 15.7 to 16.5 mm (0.618 to 0.650 in.)

If specification not obtained

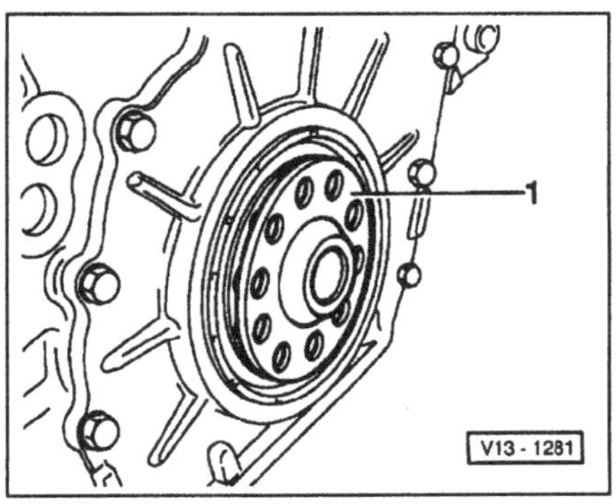

- Remove drive plate again and install appropriate shim -1-

Note:
Only one shim of the appropriate thickness may be used.

If the specification is obtained

- Insert new mounting bolts and tighten by hand
- Tighten mounting bolts to 60 Nm (44 Ft lb) and then turn an additional 90° (1/4 turn)
  - the additional 1/4 turn can be obtained using more than one step

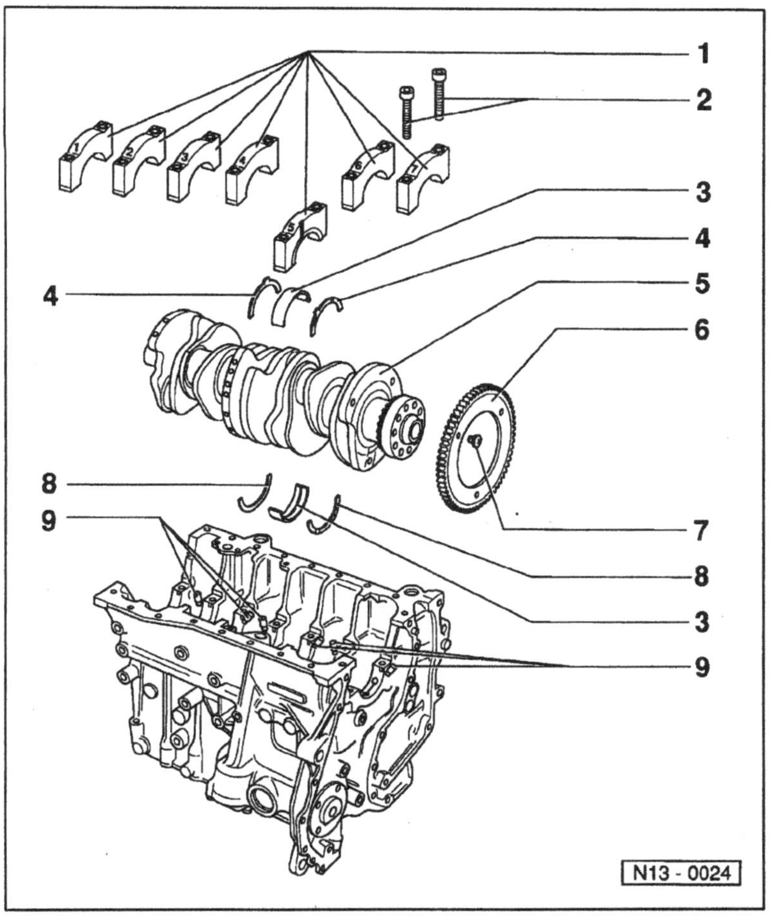

Crankshaft, removing and installing

Note:

When stripping and assembling the engine, mount it on an engine stand using 3269 engine bracket.

1 - Bearing cap
- bearing cap 1:
  vibration damper end
- bearing cap 5:
  with recesses for thrust washers
- bearing shell retaining lugs: cylinder block/bearing cap must be on the same side

2 - 30 Nm (22 ft lb) + 1/2 turn (180°) further
- replace
- 2 x 90° to achieve the extra 1/2 turn is permissible

3 - Bearing shells 1 to 7
- for bearing cap without oil groove
- for cylinder block with oil groove
- do not interchange used bearing shells (mark location)

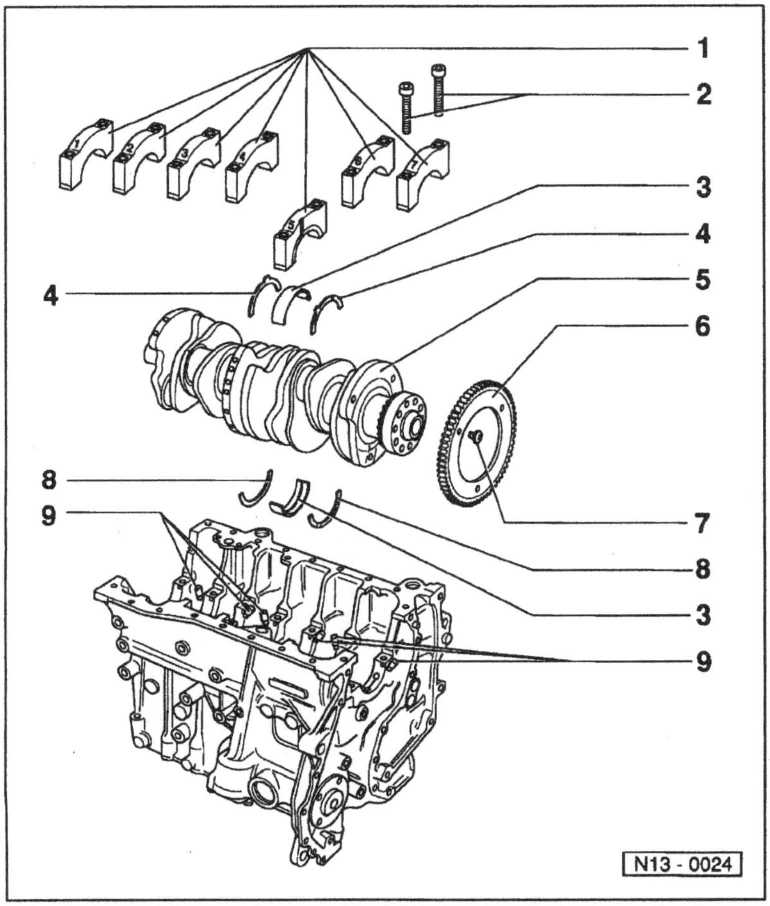

4 - Thrust washer
- for bearing cap 5
- note installed position

5 - Crankshaft
- axial clearance new:
  0.07 to 0.23 mm
  Wear limit: 0.30 mm
- check radial clearance with Plastigage ®
  New: 0.02 to 0.06 mm
  Wear limit: 0.10 mm
- do not rotate crankshaft while checking radial clearance
- crankshaft dimensions:
  Main journal:
  59.958 to 59.978 mm
  Crankshaft journal:
  53.958 to 53.978 mm
  Reworking is not permitted!

6 - Sensor wheel
- for Engine Speed sensor G28
- replace

7 - 10 Nm (7 ft lb) + 1/4 turn (90 °) further
- replace

8 - Thrust washer
- for engine block, bearing 5
- note installed position

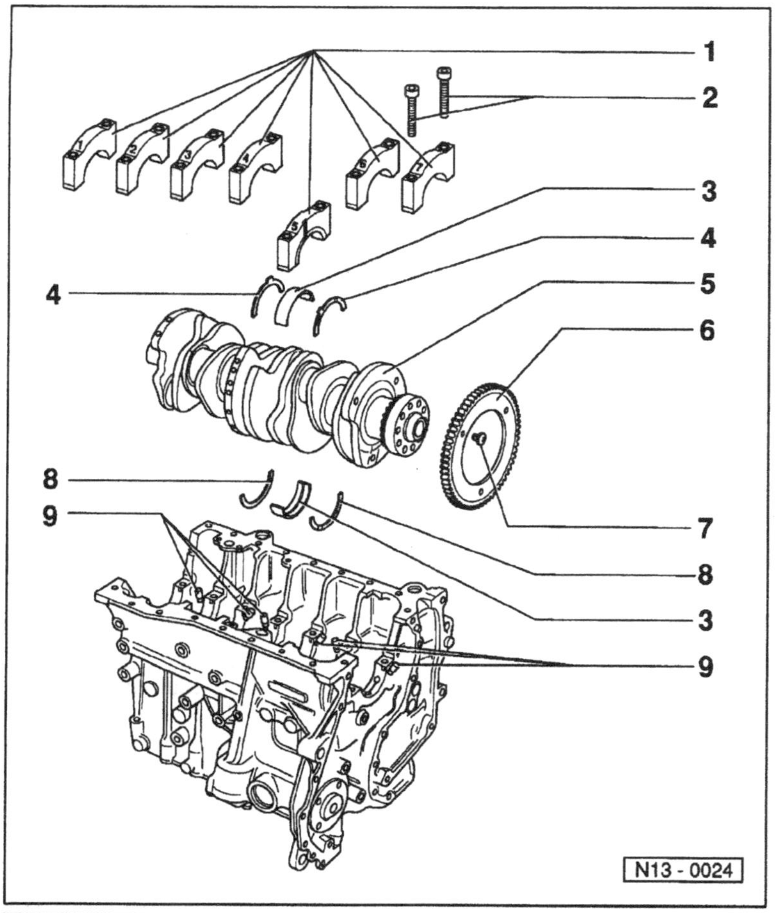

9 - Oil spray jet
- for crankshaft bearings 2 to 7
- for piston cooling
- opening pressure: 2.0 bar
- removing and installing:

⇒ page D 17-5, Fig. 1
⇒ also see note, page D 13-1

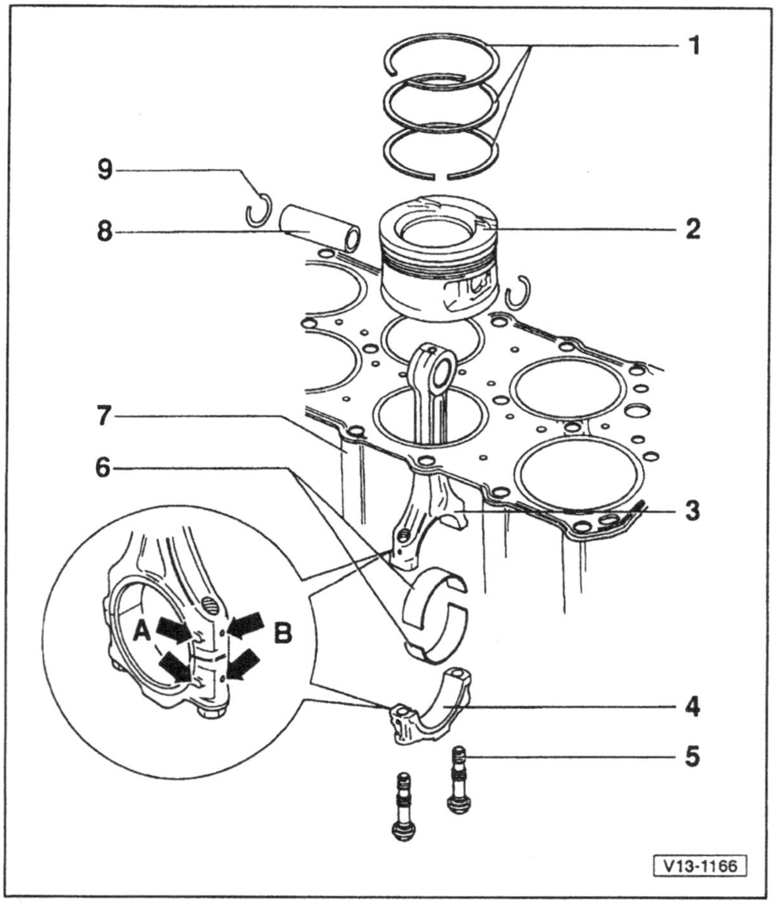

Pistons and connecting rods, disassembling and assembling

When stripping and assembling the engine, mount it on an engine stand using 3269 engine bracket.

1 - Piston ring
- offset ring gaps 120 °
- remove and install using piston ring pliers
- "TOP" faces towards piston crown
- ring gap, checking:

⇒ Fig. 1
- ring to groove clearance, checking:

⇒ Fig. 2

2 - Piston
- checking:

⇒ Fig. 3
- mark orientation to connecting rod and cylinder number using marking pen
- high point of piston crown faces centerline of cylinder block
- install using 3278 piston fitting tool

⇒ Fig. 5

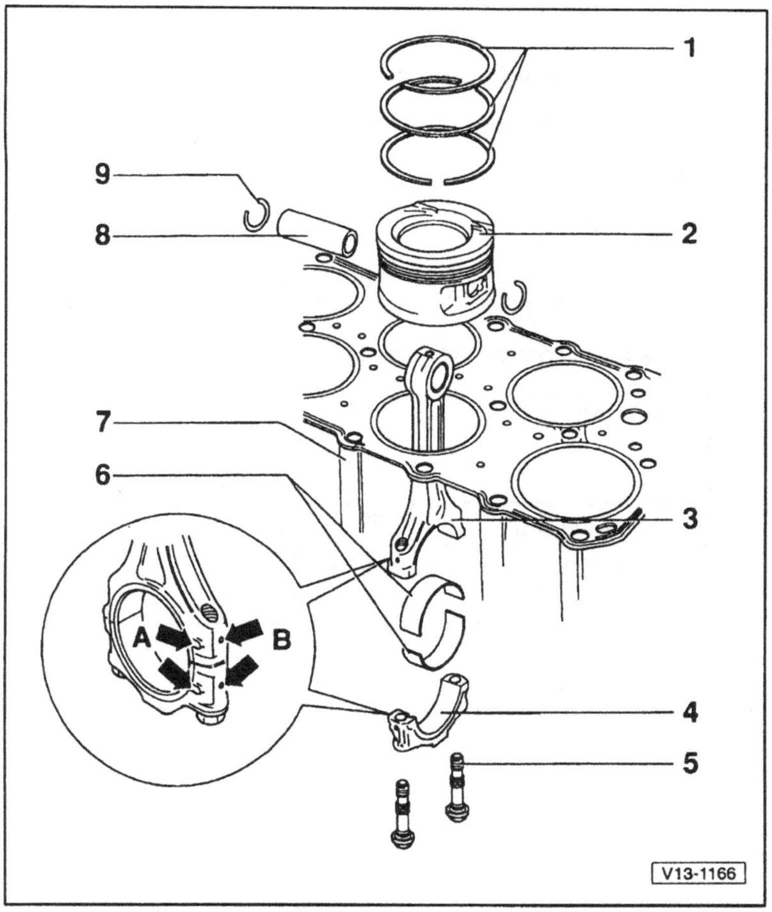

3 - Connecting rod
- only replace as a set
- mark cylinder number -B-
- Installation position: marks -A- must align above one another

4 - Connecting rod bearing cap
- note installation position

5 - 30 Nm + 1/4 turn (90 °) further
- replace
- oil threads and contacting surfaces
- measuring radial clearance: tighten to 30 Nm (22 ft lb) but no further

6 - Bearing shell
- note installation position
- do not interchange used bearing shells
- bearing shell lugs must fit tightly in the recesses
- axial clearance
  New: 0.05 to 0.31 mm
  Wear limit: 0.40 mm
- check radial clearance with Plastigage®:
  New: 0.02 to 0.07 mm
  Wear limit: 0.10 mm

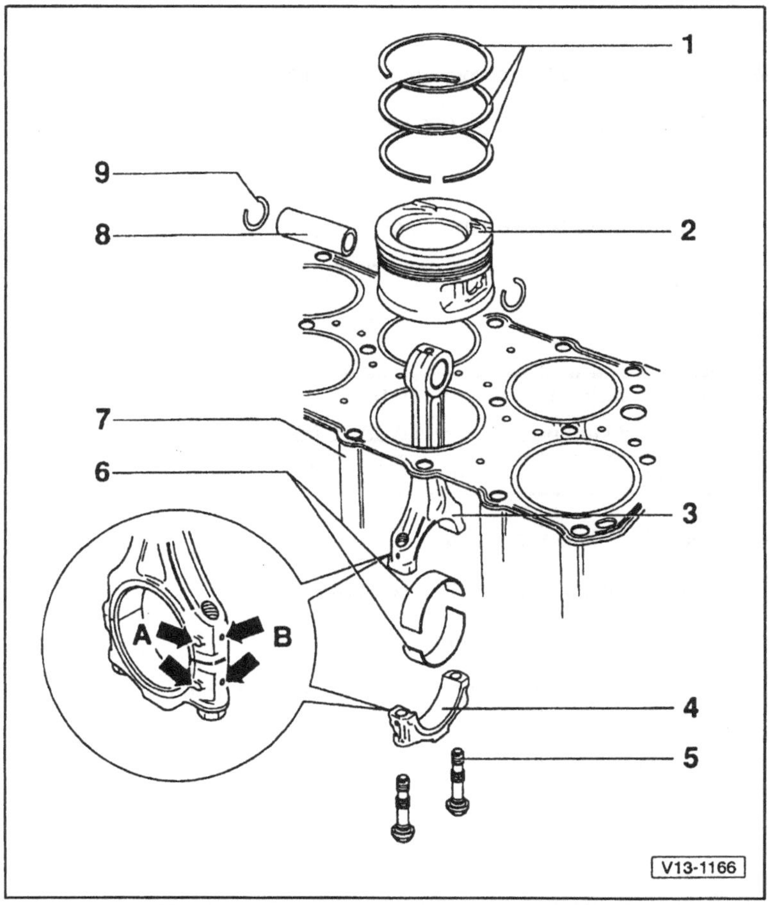

CAUTION!
Do not rotate crankshaft while checking radial clearance!

7 - Cylinder block
- cylinder bores, checking:

⇒ Fig. 4
- piston and cyl. dimensions:

⇒ page D 13-51

8 - Piston pin
If difficult to remove
- heat piston to 60 °C (140 °F)
- remove and install using VW 222a drift

9 - Circlip

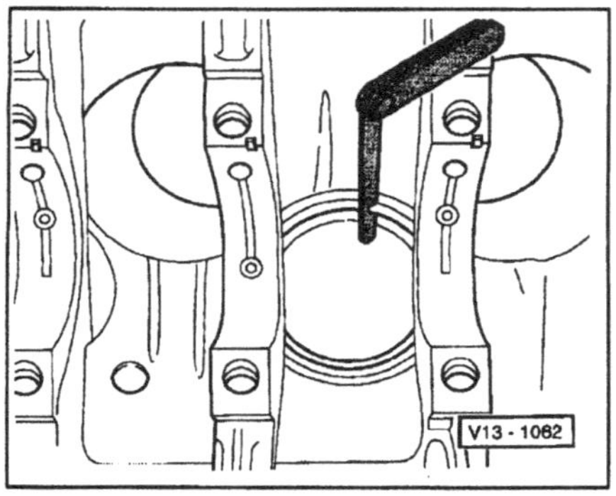

◄ **Fig. 1 Piston ring gap, checking**

Special tools, testers and auxiliary items

- ♦ Feeler gauges

Test sequence

- Using a piston without rings, squarely push ring down into cylinder to a depth of approx. 15 mm (0.6 in.) from lower end of cylinder
- Insert feeler gauges into ring gap to determine clearance value

Piston ring		Gap	
		New	Wear limit
Compression ring	mm	0.20...0.40	1.0
Tapered step ring	mm	0.20...0.40	1.0
Oil scraper ring	mm	0.25...0.50	1.0

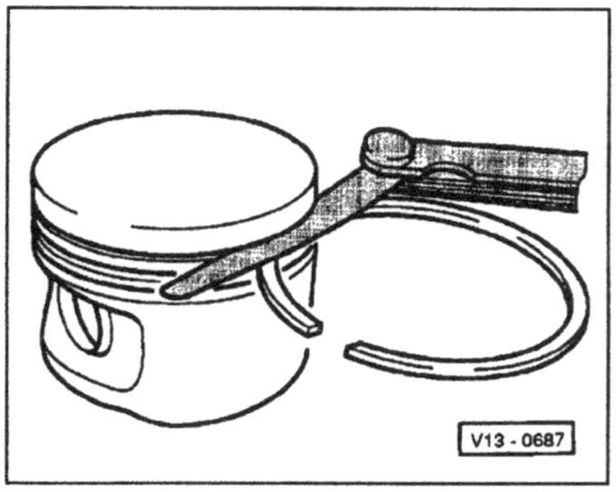

◄ **Fig. 2 Ring to groove clearance, checking**

Special tools, testers and auxiliary items

- ♦ Feeler gauges
- Clean ring grooves before checking

Piston ring		Clearance	
		New	Wear limit
Compression ring	mm	0.02...0.07	0.15
Tapered step ring	mm	0.03...0.06	0.15
Oil scraper ring	mm	0.02...0.06	0.15

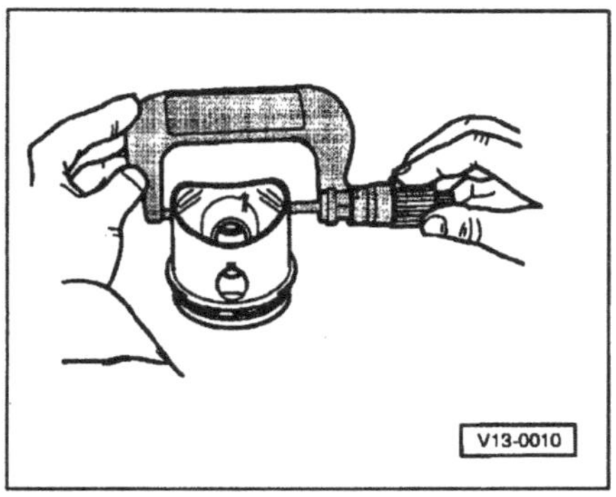

◄ **Fig. 3 Piston, checking**

Special tools, testers and auxiliary items

- ♦ 75 to 100 mm micrometer
- Measure pistons approx. 6 mm from lower edge of skirt, at 90° axis to piston pin
  - ♦ deviation from nominal dimension: 0.04 mm (max.)

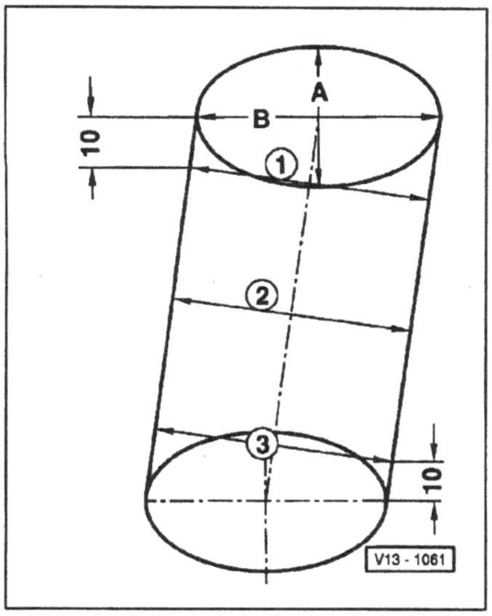

◄ **Fig. 4 Cylinder bore, checking**

Special tools, testers and auxiliary items

- 50 to 100mm Internal dial gauge

Test sequence

– Measure bore at 3 locations in both directions -A- across the block and -B- in line with crankshaft

  - Deviation from nominal dimension: 0.08 mm (max.)

CAUTION!
Do not measure cylinder bores with the block mounted on an engine stand. Natural distortions due to hanging weight will cause measurement errors!

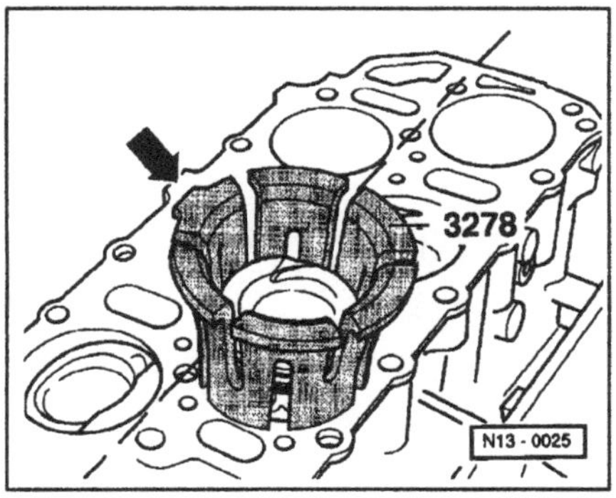

◄ **Fig. 5 Pistons, installing**

Special tools, testers and auxiliary items

- 3278 Piston installation tool

CAUTION!
Before using a new piston installation tool for the first time, first pass a piston (with oiled rings) twice through the tool. Then, thorougly clean any resulting metal shavings or dirty oil. Only then should the tool be brought into operation! Ensure that all tools and components involved in piston installation are clean.

– Offset piston ring gaps 120°

– Oil piston installation tool and insert piston by hand

  - high point on piston crown must face lug on tool -arrow-

– Hold tool (with piston inserted) on upper edge and press piston into tool using both thumbs

– Push piston in until it protrudes approx. 15 mm (0.591 in.) from the lower edge of the tool

– Orient piston to appropriate cylinder bore

  - Lug on tool -arrow- must face toward center of block

– Press tool firmly against cylinder block and push piston completely into the cylinder

Piston and cylinder dimensions

Honing dimension		Piston-∅	Cylinder bore-∅
Basic dimen.	mm	80.985	81.01
1st oversize	mm	81.485	81.51
2nd oversize	mm	81.985	82.01

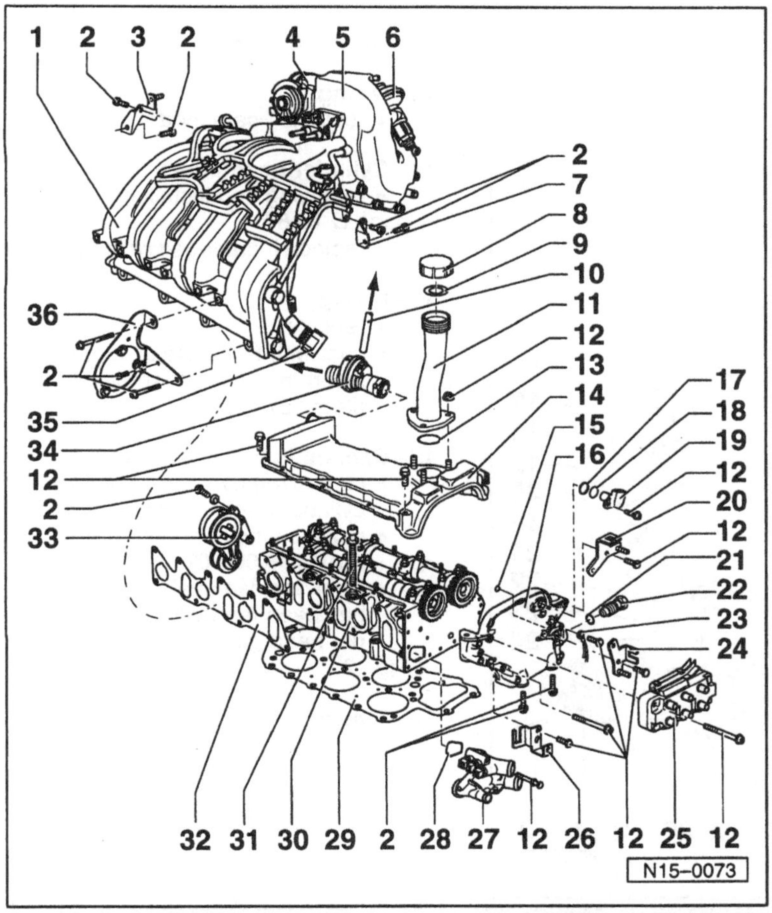

Cylinder head, removing and installing

Compression pressure, checking
⇒ page D 15-18

Notes:

- *When installing an exchange cylinder head (with camshaft), the contact surfaces between hydraulic lifter and cam must be oiled after installation.*
- *The plastic protectors (fitted to protect the open valves) should only be removed just before installing the cylinder head.*
- *If the cylinder head is replaced, completely replace the engine coolant*

1 - Intake manifold
- removing and installing
⇒ page D 15-8
- first tighten to lower intake manifold, then to the two rear supports (items 7 and 3)
- disassembly and assembly
⇒ Repair Group 24

2 - 25 Nm (18 ft lb)

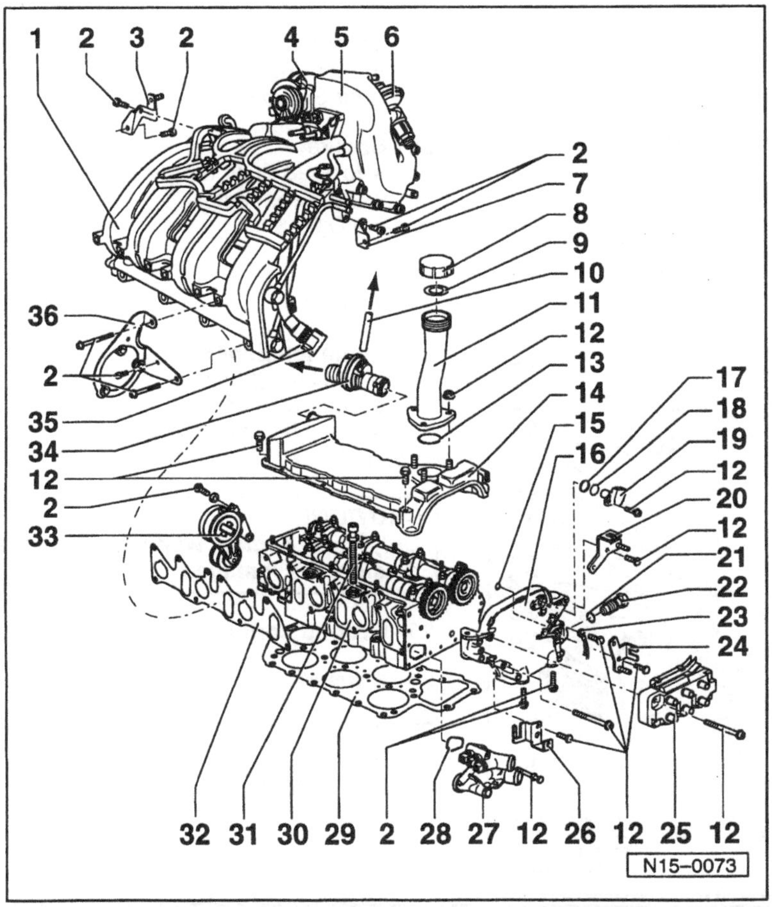

3 - Right rear support
- between intake manifold and cylinder head cover

4 - Throttle Valve Control Module
- heated by coolant
- removing and installing:
⇒ Repair Group 24

5 - Connection
- removing and installing:
⇒ Repair Group 24

6 - (EGR) Exhaust Gas Recirculation valve
⇒ page D 26-8

7 - Rear left support
- between intake manifold and cylinder head

8 - Cap

9 - Gasket
- replace if damaged

10 - Vacuum hose
- to EGR valve/intake manifold junction piece
⇒ page D 26-8

11 - Oil filler pipe

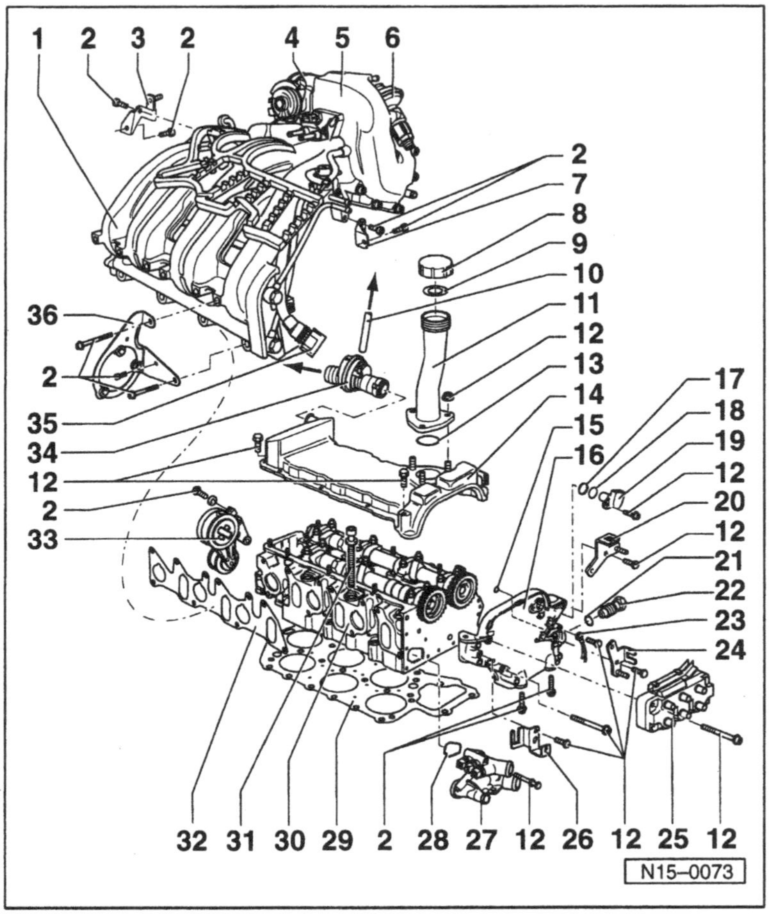

12 - 10 Nm (7 ft lb)

13 - O-ring
- ♦ replace if damaged

14 - Cylinder head cover
- ♦ removing and installing:

⇒ page D 15-8
- ♦ replace if damaged or leaking

15 - O-ring
- ♦ replace
- ♦ coat with oil before assembling, insert in camshaft sprocket cover (item 16)

16 - Camshaft sprocket cover
- ♦ can be removed and installed with cylinder head installed
- ♦ coat sealing surfaces with AMV 188 001 02
- ♦ if only the camshaft sprocket cover has been removed; prepare cylinder head gasket for assembly:

⇒ Fig. 2

17 - Spacer ring

18 - O-ring
- ♦ replace
- ♦ oil before installing

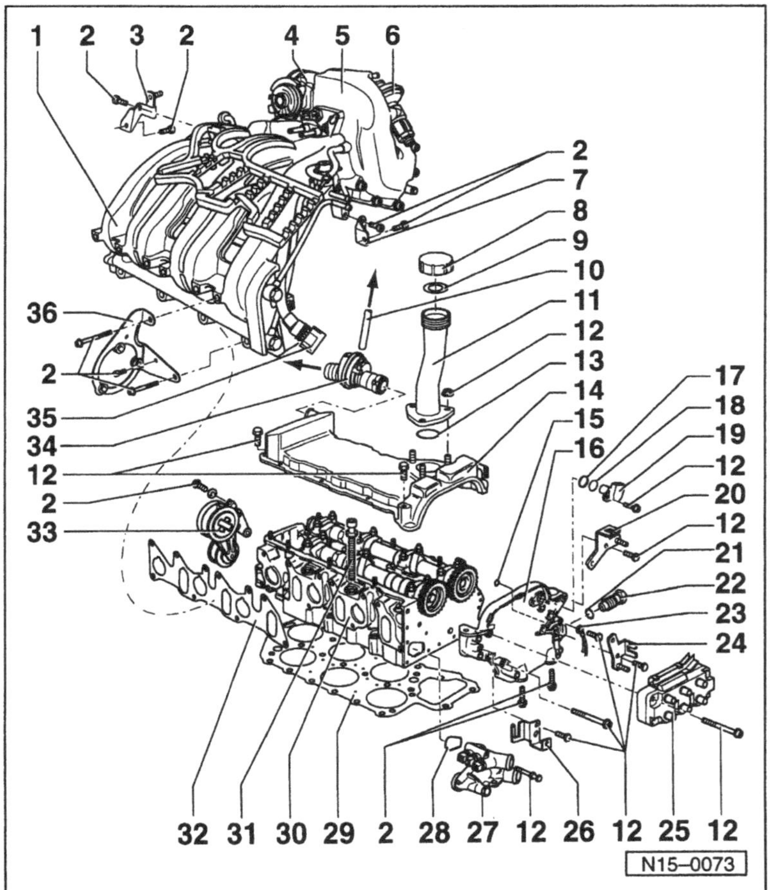

19 - Camshaft Position sensor G40
- ♦ checking:

⇒ Repair Group 01

20 - Bracket
- ♦ for G98 EGR Temperature sensor, 2-pin connector

⇒ page D 26-8

21 - Seal
- ♦ replace

22 - Chain tensioner
- ♦ 30 Nm (22 ft lb)
- ♦ for double chain
- ♦ bleed before installing

⇒ page D 13-7, Fig. 2

> ***CAUTION!***
> ***Only turn engine when the chain tensioner is installed***

23 - Ground connection

24 - Bracket

25 - Ignition coil N152*
- ♦ checking:

⇒ Repair Group 28

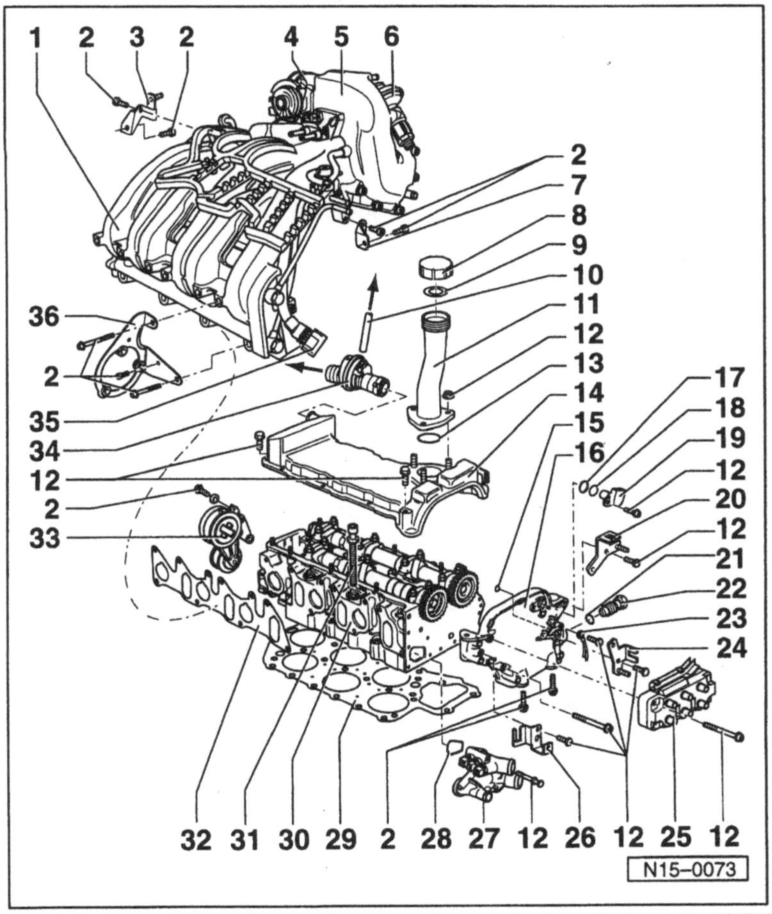

26 - Bracket
- for fuel injector connectors (item 35)

27 - Thermostat housing
- disassembly and assembly:

⇒ page D 19-11

28 - O-ring
- replace

29 - Cylinder head gasket
- replace
- if replaced, completely replace the engine coolant

30 - Cylinder head
- check for distortion

⇒ Fig. 1
- installing:

⇒ page D 15-16
- if replaced, completely replace the engine coolant
- note sequence when loosening and tightening

⇒ page D 15-16

31 - Cylinder head bolt
- replace
- note sequence when loosening and tightening

⇒ page D 15-16

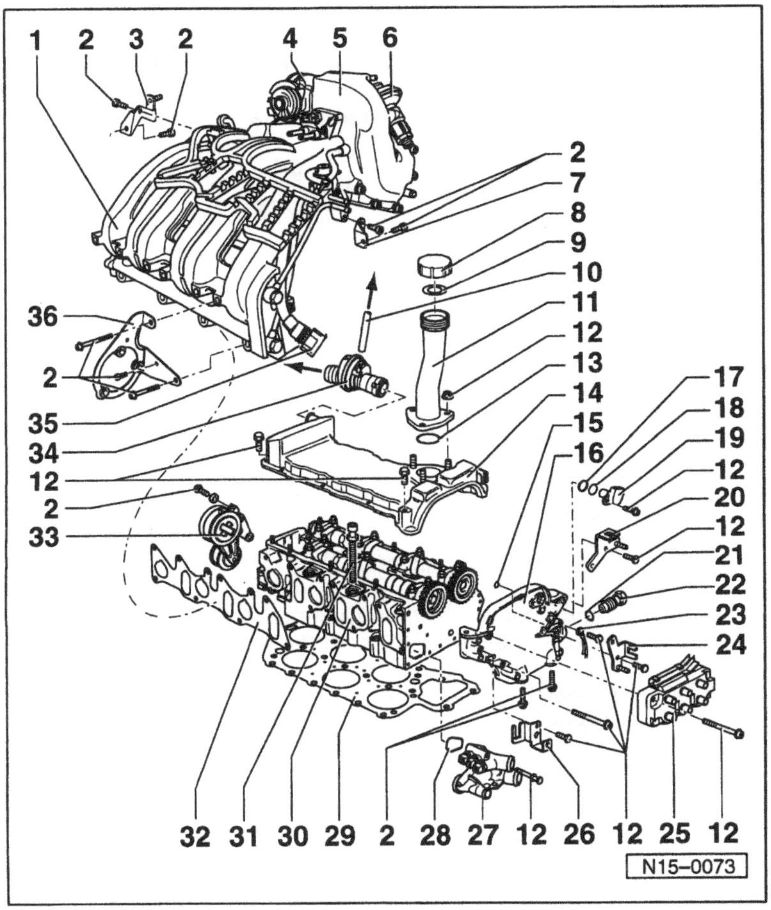

32 - Gasket for lower intake manifold
- replace
- note installed position

33 - Ribbed belt tensioner
- ribbed belts, removing and installing:

⇒ page D 13-19

34 - Positive Crankcase Ventilation valve
- arrow on valve points toward intake hose:

⇒ Repair Group 24

35 - Connector
- for injectors N30, N31, N32, N33, N83, N84
- mounted to bracket (item 26)

36 - Retainer
- for Secondary Air Injection pump motor

⇒ page D 26-15

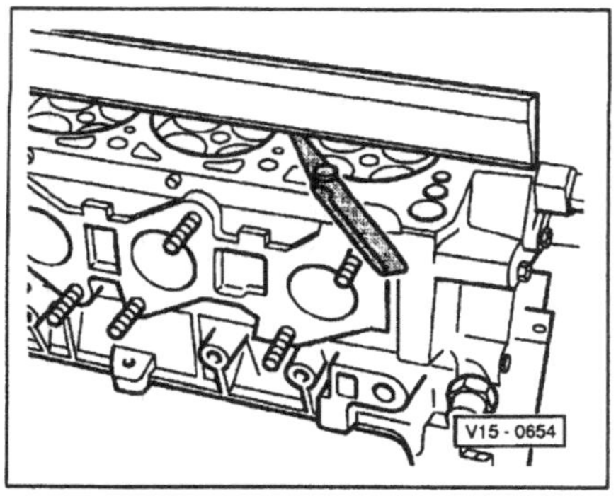

◄ **Fig. 1 Cylinder head, checking for distortion**

Special tools, testers and auxiliary items

- ♦ Feeler gauges

Max. permissible distortion: 0.1 mm

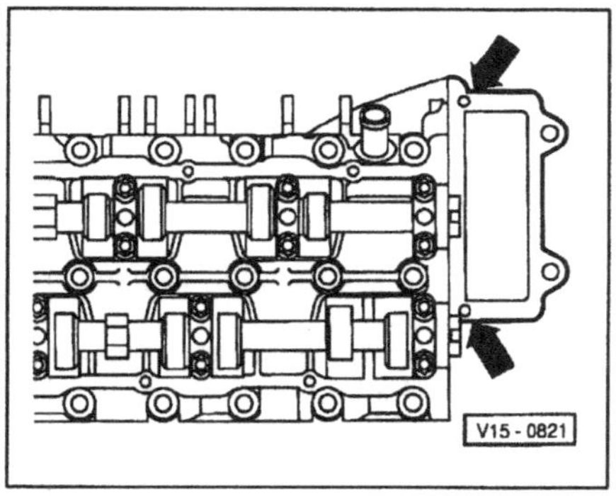

◄ **Fig. 2 Cylinder head gasket, preparing for assembly**

Special tools, testers and auxiliary items

- ♦ AMV 188 001 02 sealant

– Remove old sealant from 3 mm holes in the cylinder head gasket -arrows-

– Fill 3 mm holes in the cylinder head gasket using sealant AMV 188 001 02

Note:

When the cylinder head is installed, the holes are only half visible.

Cylinder head cover, removing and installing

Special tools, testers and auxiliary items

- ♦ 3277 A installing tool
- ♦ VAG 1331 Torque wrench 5 to 50 Nm (4 to 37 ft lb)
- ♦ VAG 1921 spring clip pliers

Removing

> ***CAUTION!***
> ***Obtain radio code before disconnecting battery ground strap.***

– Switch off ignition

– Disconnect battery ground strap

– Replace all cable ties which were opened or cut to remove the engine and replace them in their original position

– Remove noise insulation tray
⇒ Repair Group 50

– Remove radiator grille
⇒ Repair Group 66

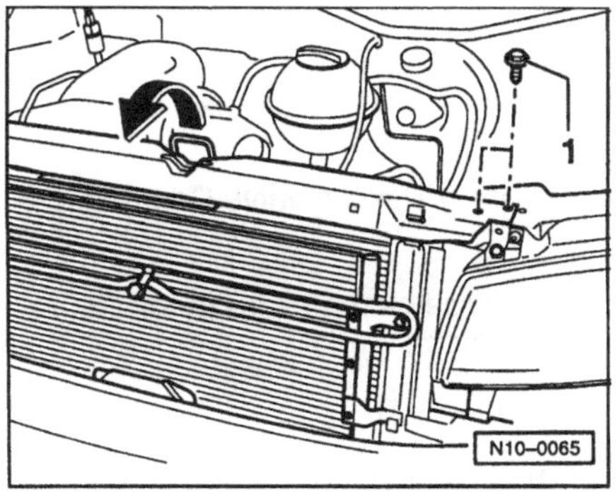

◄ – Remove lock carrier mounting bolts -1- on left and right side

– Hinge lock carrier forward (with radiator) -arrow-

– Disconnect heater element harness connector (on intake hose)

– Remove intake hose between upper Air Cleaner and Throttle Valve Control Module J338 together with the Positive Crankcase Ventilation valve
⇒ Repair Group 24

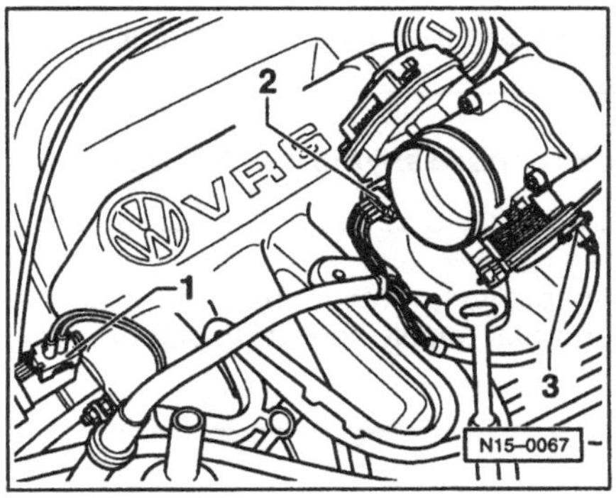

◄ – Disconnect harness connectors from EGR valve -1-, Throttle Valve Control module -2- and Intake Manifold Temperature sensor-3-

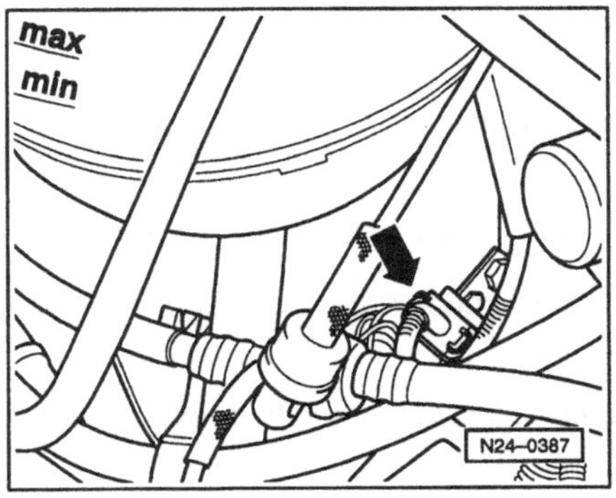

◄ – If installed, disconnect 2-pin harness connector from EGR Temperature sensor -arrow-

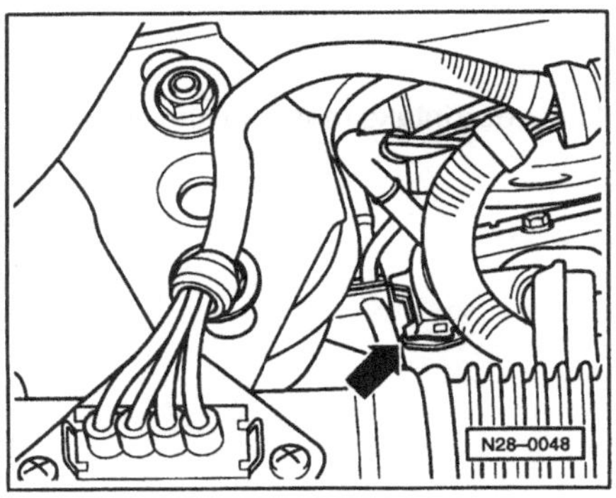

◄ – Disconnect white 3-pin harness connector from Knock sensor 1 -arrow-

– Release wiring from clips behind intake manifold and on EGR valve

– Remove spark plug connectors using 3277A release tool and unclip the ignition cables from the ignition cable guides
⇒ Repair Group 28

– Detach accelerator cable (do not remove locating clip) from support bracket and Throttle Valve Control Module

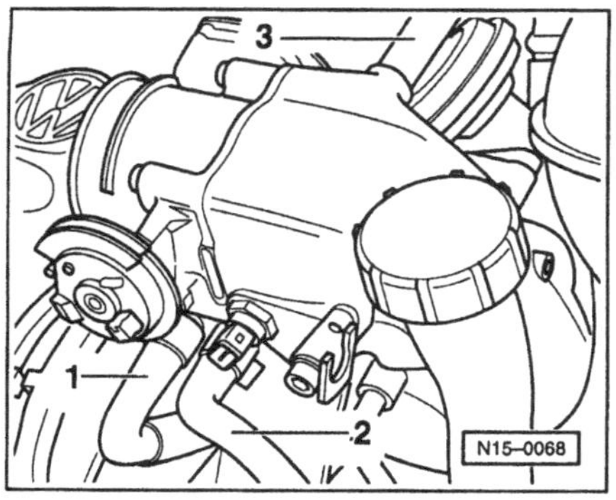

- Mark coolant hoses -1- and -2- from Throttle Valve Control Module
- Pull off hoses using VAG 1921 hose clamp pliers (after first releasing pressure from cooling system)
- Seal coolant hoses
- Pull off breather hose from EVAP canister purge regulator valve -3-
- Disconnect vacuum hose to brake servo from intake manifold

> ***CAUTION!***
> ***Fire Hazard. Do NOT smoke or have anything in the area that can ignite fuel.***

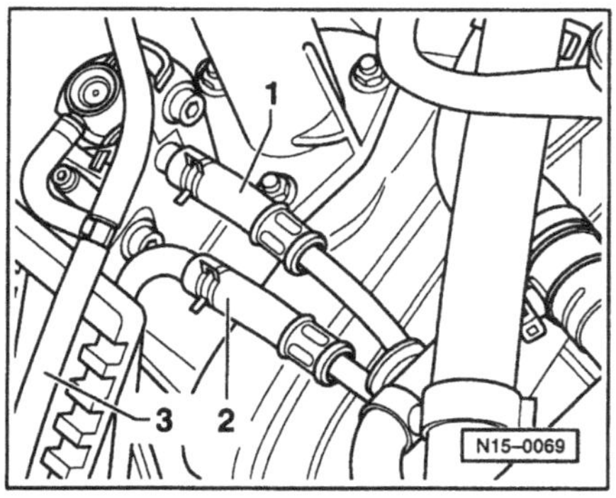

- Using VAG 1921 hose clamp pliers, remove fuel return line -1- (blue or blue markings) and fuel supply line -2- (black or black markings)

> ***CAUTION!***
> ***Fuel supply lines are under pressure! Before disconnecting line connections; wrap a cloth around the connection. Then release pressure by carefully pulling the hose off the connection.***

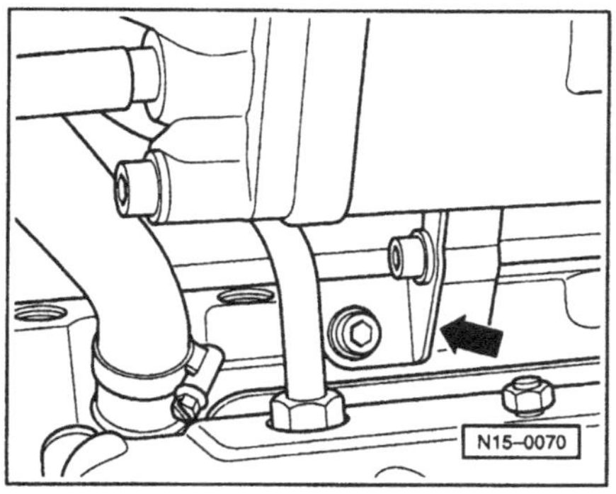

- Disconnect vacuum hose -3- from Secondary Air Injection valve off of junction piece
- Disconnect line from exhaust manifold at EGR valve connection
- Disconnect fuel injector harness connectors and remove connector from retaining bracket
- Remove left rear support between intake manifold and cyl. head -arrow-

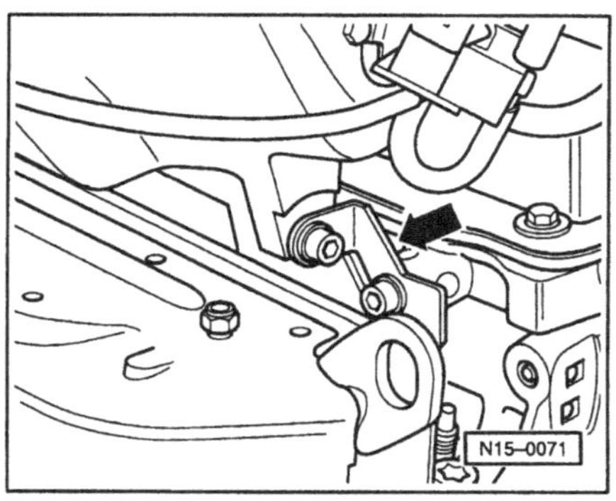

- Remove right rear support between intake manifold and cyl. head -arrow-

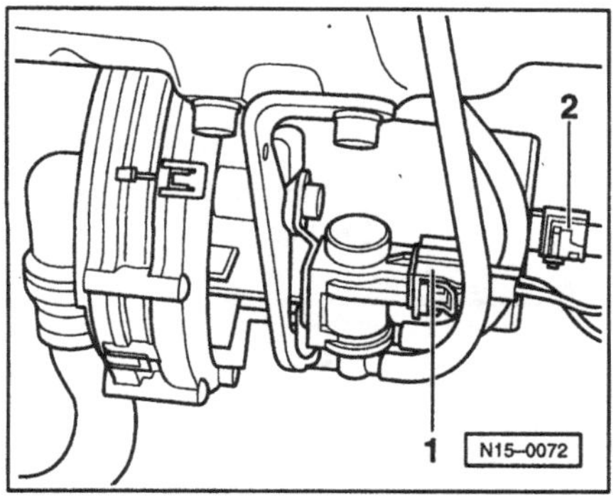

◄ – Disconnect Secondary Air Injection system valve -1- and Secondary Air Injection system pump motor -2-

– Remove Secondary Air Injection pump motor
⇒ page D 26-15

– Remove Secondary Air Injection combi-valve
⇒ page D 26-21

– Remove combi-valve connection at cylinder head
⇒ page D 26-15

– Remove dipstick guide tube

– Remove intake manifold mounting bolts

– Remove intake manifold assembly/Throttle Valve Control Module

♦ when installing, note position of dowel sleeves in cyl head

Note:

Seal the dipstick guide tube opening in the cylinder block and the intake ports in cylinder head using a clean cloth.

– Remove cylinder head cover

Cylinder head, installing

– Install components in reverse order of removal

Notes:

- *Replace cylinder head cover if damaged or leaking*
- *Replace gasket between lower intake manifold and cylinder head cover*
- *First tighten the intake manifold (including lower intake manifold) to cylinder head, then tighten both rear supports*
- *Ensure that fuel lines are tight*

– Top-up coolant
⇒ page D 19-13

– Adjust throttle cable
⇒ page D 20-23

– Interrogate Diagnostic Trouble Code (DTC) memory
⇒ Repair Group 01

Tightening torques

Bolted joint	Tightening torque
Cylinder head cover to cylinder head	10 Nm (7 ft lb)
Lower intake manifold to cylinder head	25 Nm (18 ft lb)
Right and left rear supports to intake manifold and cylinder head	25 Nm (18 ft lb)
Line to EGR valve connection	30 Nm (22 ft lb)

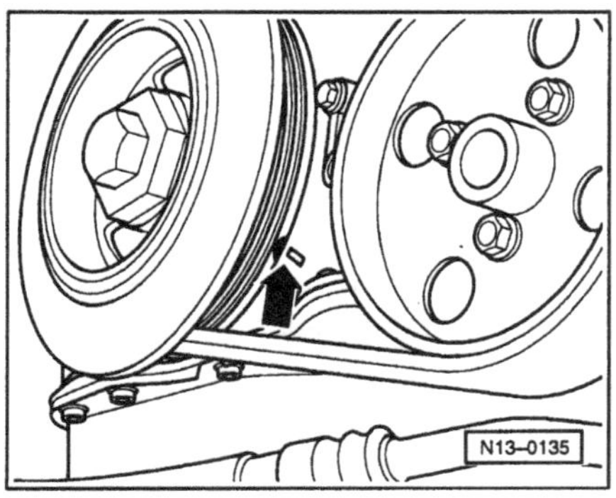

Cylinder head, installing

Special tools, testers and auxiliary items

- VAG 1332 Torque wrench 40 to 200 Nm (30 to 148 ft lb)
- 3268 Crankshaft setting bar

Work sequence

◄ – Set crankshaft to TDC cyl. 1 marks -arrow- by turning crankshaft (via vibration damper mounting bolt) in direction of engine rotation

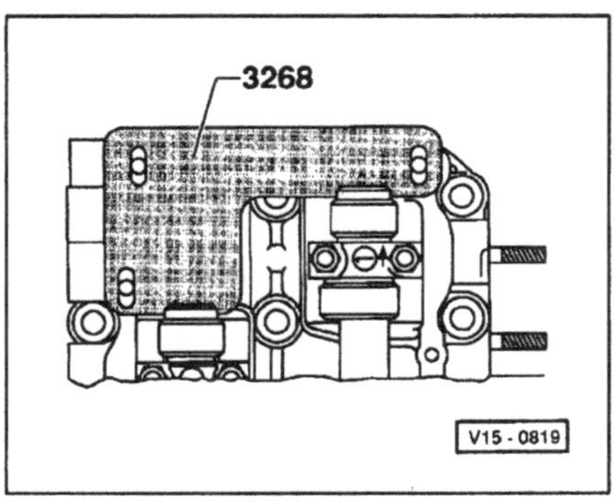

◄ – Position camshafts using 3268 camshaft jig

Note:
This orientation is only possible every 2nd TDC position.

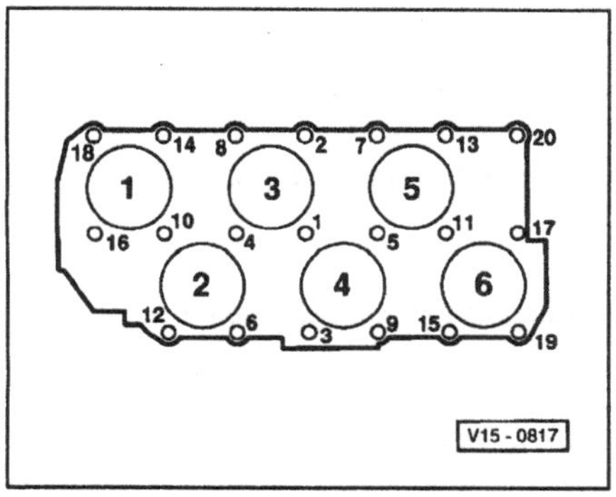

- Install cylinder head gasket
  - ♦ Note position of centering sleeves (in block holes 12, 20)
- Install cylinder head
- Insert cylinder head bolts and tighten by hand
- Tighten cylinder head using four stage sequence as follows:
- Tighten initially using torque wrench
  - ♦ Stage I = 40 Nm (30 ft lb)
  - ♦ Stage II = 60 Nm (44 ft lb)
- Turn further using ordinary wrench
  - ♦ Stage III = $^{1}/_{4}$ turn (90 °) additional
  - ♦ Stage IV = $^{1}/_{4}$ turn (90 °) additional

Notes:

- ♦ *Loosening cylinder head: reverse sequence*
- ♦ *Torquing cylinder head after repairs is not necessary*

Cylinder compression, checking

Special tools, testers and auxiliary items

- ♦ VAG 1763 Compression tester
- ♦ 3122 B Spark plug wrench
- ♦ 3277 Installing tool

Test conditions

- ♦ Engine oil temperature 30 °C (86 °F) minimum

Test sequence

- Remove radiator grille
⇒ Repair Group 66

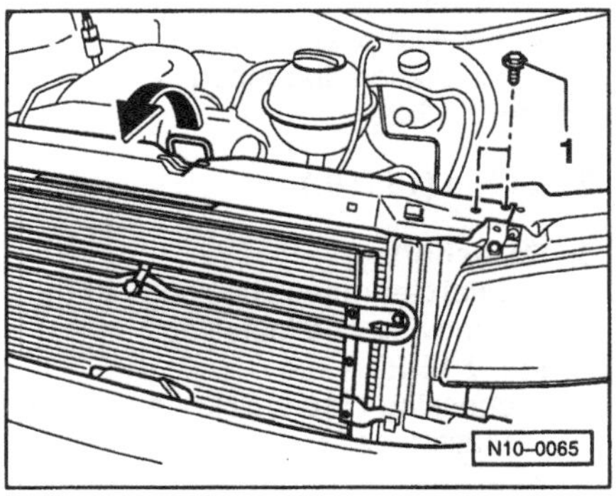

- Remove left and right mounting screws
- Hinge lock carrier forward (with radiator) -arrow-
- Disconnect heater element connector and remove intake hose between upper Air Cleaner and Throttle Valve Control Module J338 together with Positive Crankcase Ventilation valve
⇒ Repair Group 24
- Remove spark plug connectors using 3277 A tool and unclip ignition cables
⇒ Repair Group 28

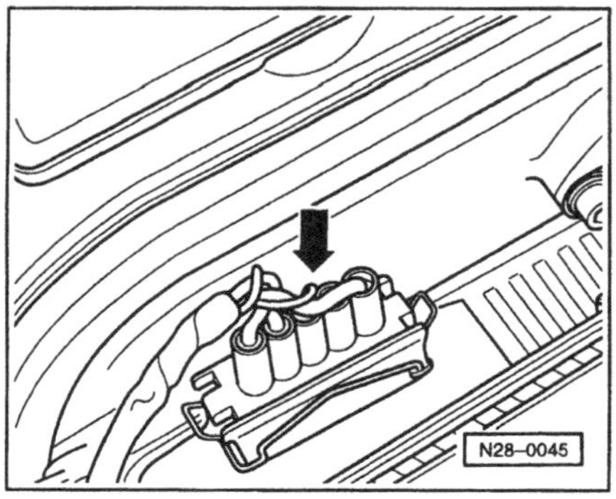

- Remove spark plugs using 3122 B spark plug wrench
- ◄ Disconnect 5-pin harness connector from ignition coil -arrow-
- Fully open throttle valve
- Check compression using VAG 1763 compression tester

Note:

See the manufacturers operating instructions for questions regarding compression tester specific usage.

- Operate starter until tester shows no further pressure increase

Compression checking specifications

- ♦ New: 10 to 13 bar (145 to 189 psi)
- ♦ Wear limit: 7.5 bar (109 psi)
- ♦ Permissible difference between all cylinders: 3 bar (44 psi)

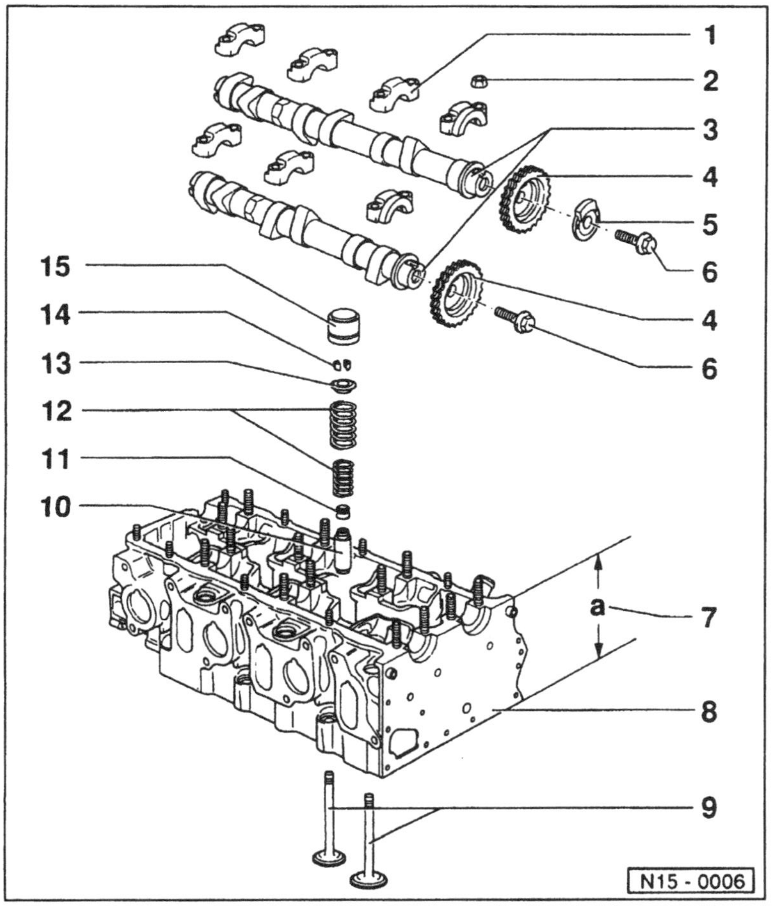

Valvetrain, servicing

Note:

Cylinder heads which have cracks between the valve seats or between valve seat inserts and the spark plug thread can continue to be used without reducing service life, provided the cracks do not exceed a maximum width of 0.5 mm.

1 - Bearing cap
- ♦ installed position ⇒ Fig. 2
- ♦ installation sequence

⇒ page D 15-29

2 - 20 Nm (15 ft lb)

3 - Camshafts
- ♦ axial clearance checking ⇒ Fig. 1
- ♦ removing and installing:

⇒ page D 15-29

- ♦ checking radial clearance with Plastigage®:

wear limit: 0.10 mm
run-out: max. 0.01 mm

- ♦ identification and valve timing ⇒ Fig. 4

4 - Camshaft sprocket
- ♦ removing and installing:

⇒ page D 15-29

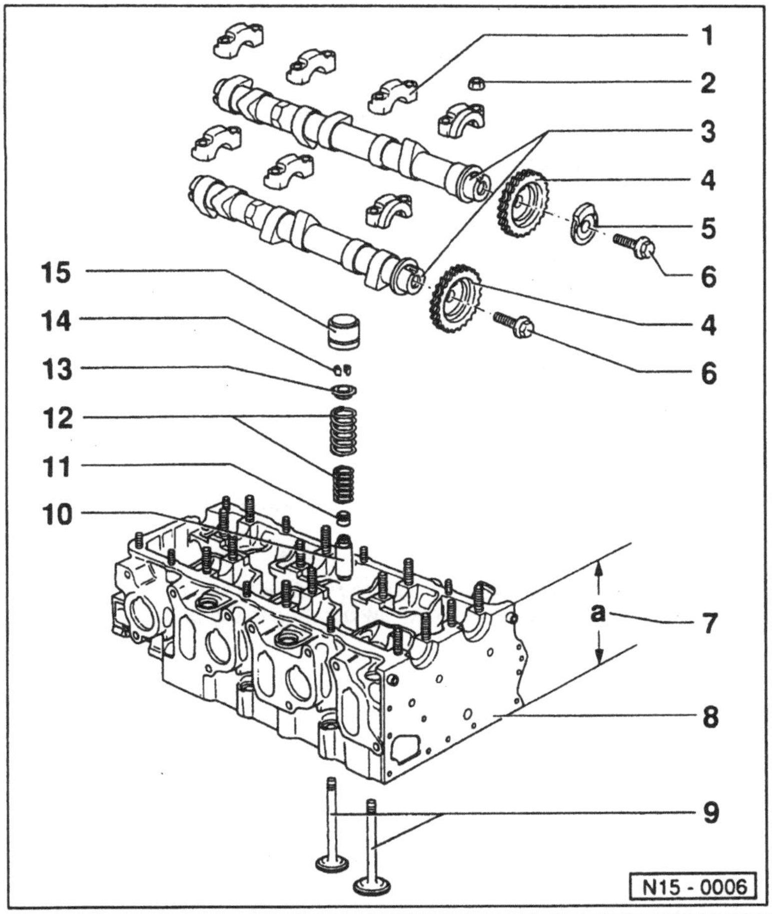

5 - Sensor wheel
- for Camshaft Position sensor
- when installing, contact surfaces on timing chain and sensor wheel must be dry
- removing and installing:

⇒ page D 15-29

6 - 100 Nm (74 ft lb)
- to remove and install: counter-hold with 24 mm open end wrench on camshaft

⇒ page D 15-29
- oil bulkhead contact surface when installing

7 - Cylinder head deck height
- minimum: a = 139.5 mm

8 - Cylinder head
- see note:

⇒ page D 15-20
- re-working valve seats

⇒ page D 15-26

9 - Valves
- do not rework; only lapping-in is permitted
- valve dimensions:

⇒ Fig. 3

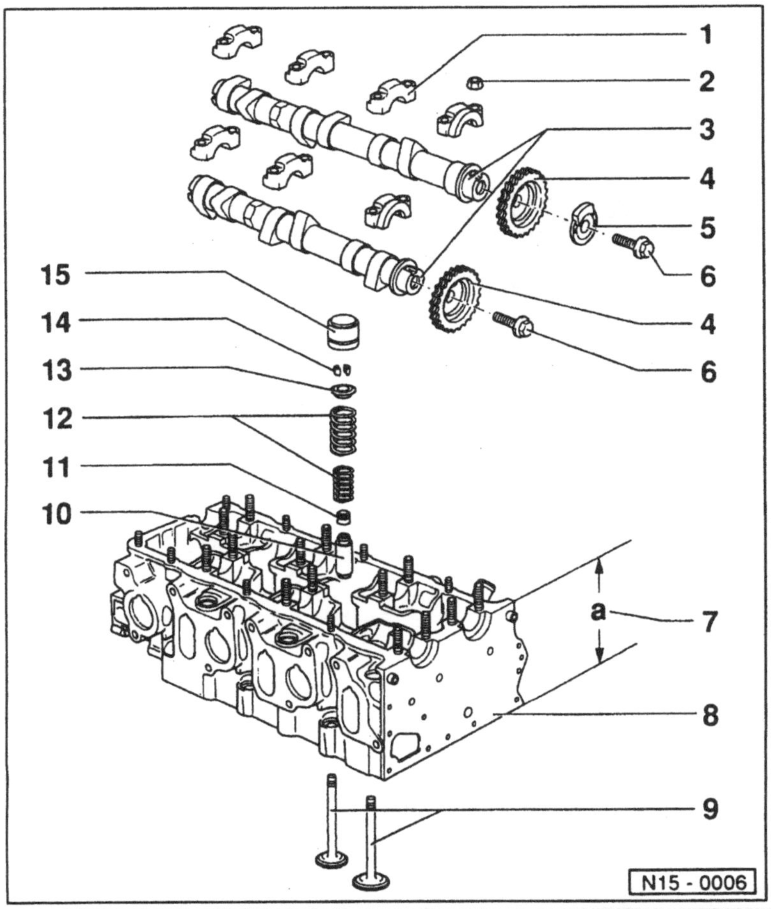

10 - Valve guide
- service version with collar
- checking:

⇒ page D 15-36
- replacing:

⇒ page D 15-37

11 - Valve stem seal
- replacing:

⇒ page D 15-38

12 - Valve springs
- removing and installing:
- cylinder head removed: use 2037 valve spring compressor
- cylinder head installed:

⇒ page D 15-38

13 - Valve spring plate

14 - Valve keepers

15 - Hydraulic lifter
- with hydraulic valve clearance compensation
- do not interchange
- store with cam contacting surface facing downwards
- oil contacting surfaces
- checking:

⇒ page D 15-34
- before installing; check camshaft axial clearance ⇒ Fig. 1

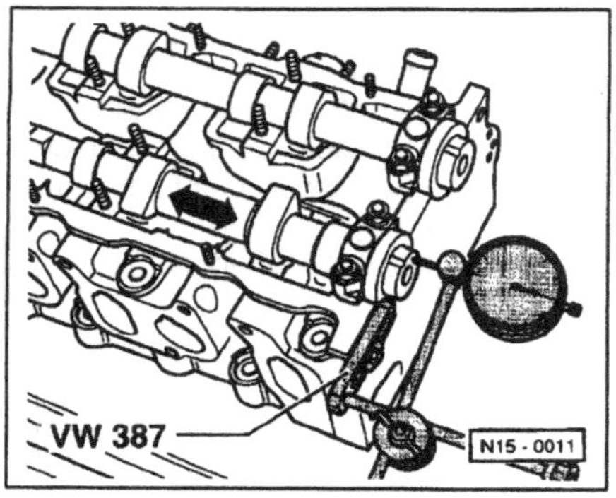

◄ **Fig. 1 Camshaft axial clearance, checking**

Special tools, testers and auxiliary items

- VW 387 Universal dial gauge bracket
- Dial gauge

Test sequence

Wear limit: max. 0.15 mm

– Perform check with hydraulic lifters removed and with first and last bearing caps installed on the appropriate camshaft

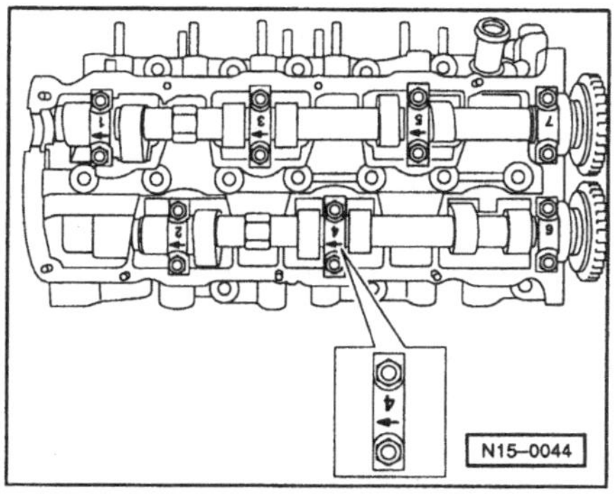

◄ **Fig. 2 Camshaft bearing caps, installed position**

Note:

Bearing cap identification must be readable from the exhaust side of the cylinder head and the arrow pointing to vibration damper end.

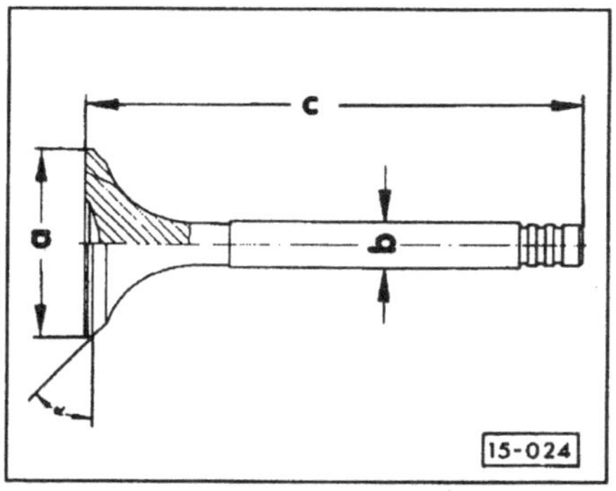

◄ **Fig. 3 Valve dimensions**

Note:

Valves may not be reworked. Only lapping-in is permitted.

Dimension		Intake valve	Exhaust valve
Ø a	mm	39.0	34.20
Ø b	mm	6.97	6.95
c	mm	105.95	106.95
α	∠°	45	45

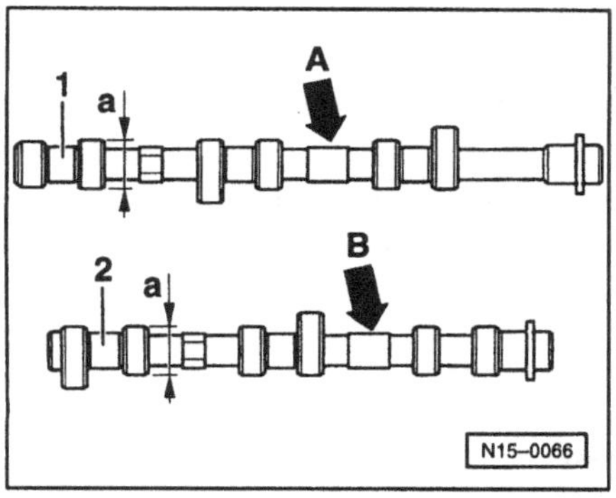

◄ **Fig. 4 Camshaft identification, valve timing**

Item 1 = Camshaft for cylinders 1, 3 and 5

Item 2 = Camshaft for cylinders 2, 4 and 6

Identification

- Cam base diameter: a = 34 mm Ø
- Identification by numbers and letters stamped on camshaft

Cylinders:	1, 3, 5	2, 4, 6
Between cylinders 3 and 5 -arrow A-	021 101 Q	–
Between cylinders 4 and 6 -arrow B-	–	021 102 D

Valve timing at 1 mm valve lift

Cylinders:	1, 3, 5	2, 4, 6
Intake opens ATDC	5.50 °	5.50 °
Intake closes ABDC	29.50 °	29.50 °
Exhaust opens BBDC	29.50 °	29.50 °
Exhaust closes BTDC	5.50 °	5.50 °

Valve seats, re-working

Special tools, testers and auxiliary items

- Depth gauge
- Valve seat refacing tool

Notes:

- *When repairing engines with leaking valves, it is not always sufficient to rework or replace valve seats and valves. It is also necessary to check the valve guides for wear. This is particularly important on high mileage engines.*
- *The valve seats should only be reworked the minimum amount to achieve a perfect seating pattern. The maximum permissible reworking dimension must be calculated before reworking commences. If the reworking dimension is exceeded, the function of the hydraulic lifters can no longer be guaranteed and the cylinder head should be replaced.*

Work sequence

Maximum permissible reworking dimension, calculating

– Insert valve and press firmly against seat

Note:

If a valve will be replaced as part of the repair, use the new valve for the calculation.

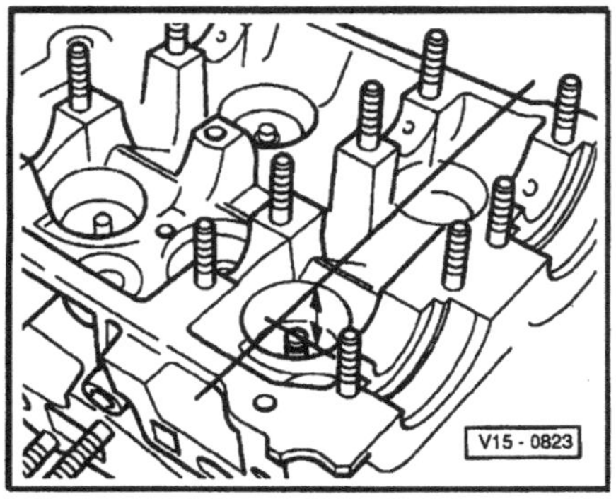

- Measure distance -a- between end of valve stem and upper edge of cylinder head
- Calculate max. permissible reworking dimension from the measured distance -a- and the minimum dimension

Minimum dimension:

- Intake valve: 33.9 mm
- Exhaust valve: 34.1 mm

Measured distance minus minimum dimension
= max. permissible reworking dimension

Example:

	Measured distance -a-	34.8 mm
–	Minimum dimension	34.1 mm
=	maximum permissible reworking dimension[1]	0.7 mm

[1] ⇒ page D 15-28

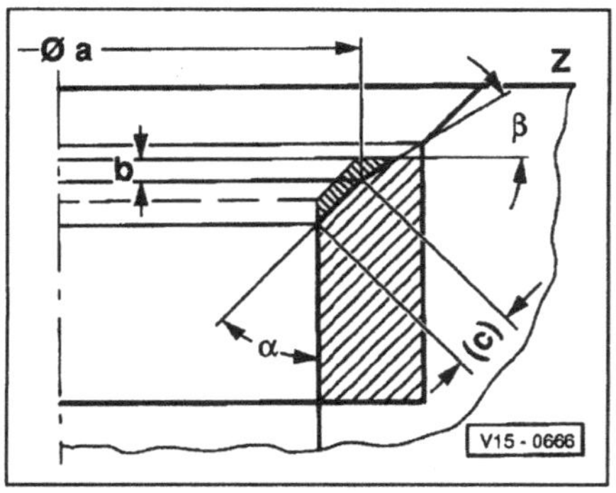

Intake valve seat, re-working

a	=	∅ 38.3 mm
b	=	Max. permissible reworking dimension[1]
c	=	1.4 mm to 2.0 mm if necessary rework valve seat insert using 75 ° correction reamer
Z	=	Cylinder head lower edge
α	=	45 ° valve seat angle
β	=	30 ° upper correction angle
γ	=	75 ° lower correction angle

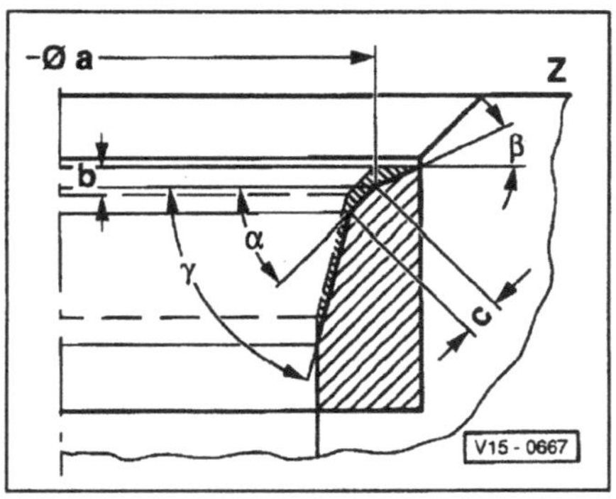

Exhaust valve seat, re-working

a	=	∅ 33.5 mm
b	=	Max. permissible reworking dimension[1]
c	=	2.0 mm to 2.5 mm if necessary rework valve seat insert with 75 ° correction reamer
Z	=	Cylinder head lower edge
α	=	45 ° valve seat angle
β	=	30 ° upper correction angle

Camshafts, removing and installing

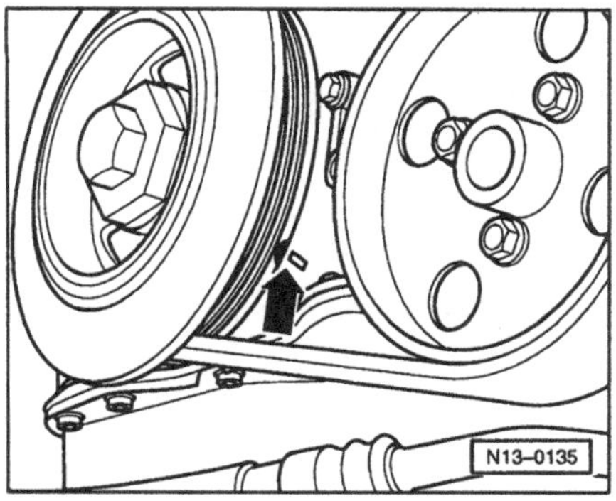

Special tools, testers and auxiliary items

- 3268 Camshaft setting bar
- VAG 1331 Torque wrench
  5 to 50 Nm (4 to 37 ft lb)

Removing

– Set crankshaft to TDC cyl. 1 marks -arrow- by turning crankshaft via vibration damper mounting bolt (in direction of engine rotation)

– Remove cylinder head cover
⇒ page D 15-8

– Remove ignition coil N152
⇒ Repair Group 28

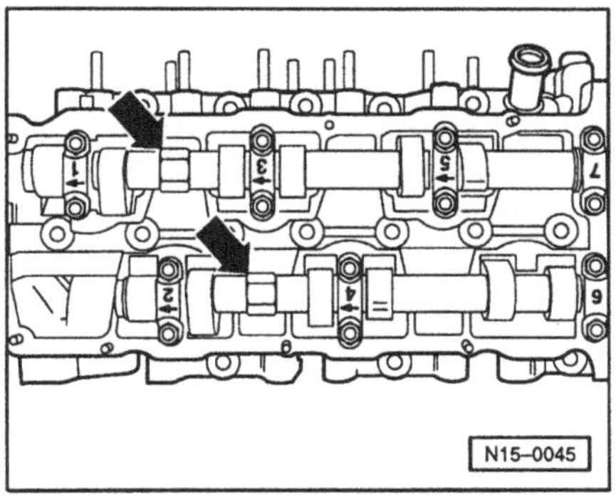

– Remove double chain tensioner

– Remove camshaft sprocket cover

– Loosen camshaft sprocket mounting bolts

Note:

Only counter-hold camshaft using 24–mm open end wrench -arrow-. The 3268 camshaft jig must not be in place when tightening or loosening the chain sprockets.

– Remove camshaft sprockets

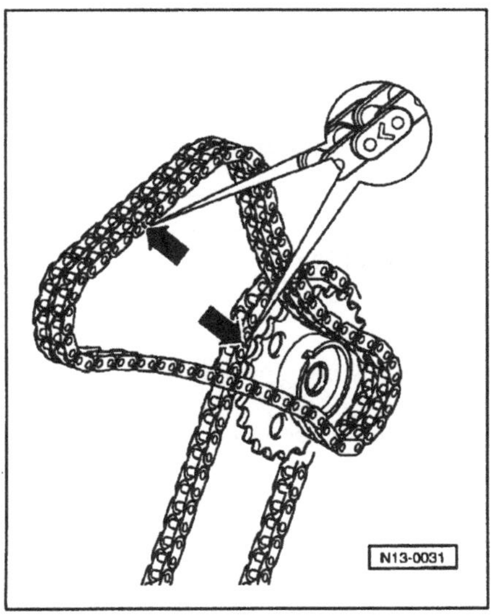

– Mark double chain before removing (e.g., with paint arrow pointing in direction of rotation)

> ***CAUTION!***
> ***Do NOT mark the timing chain using a punch or any other mechanical device that could weaken the chain.***

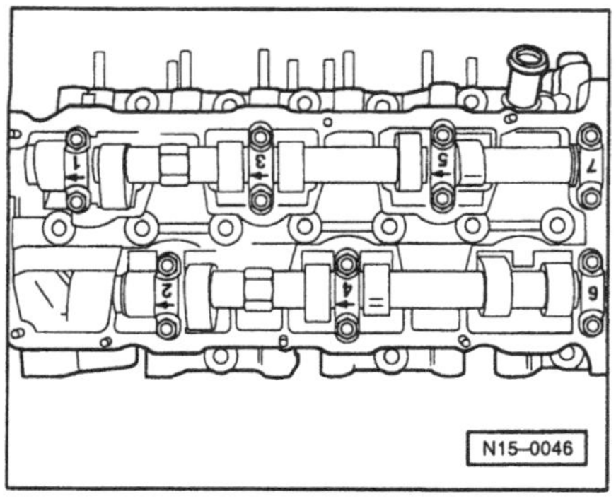

Camshaft for cylinders 1, 3 and 5

– First remove bearing caps 1 and 7

– Slacken off bearing caps 3 and 5 alternately and diagonally

Camshaft for cylinders 2, 4 and 6

– First remove bearing cap 4

– Slacken off bearing caps 2 and 6 alternately and diagonally

Installing

– Oil running surfaces of both camshafts

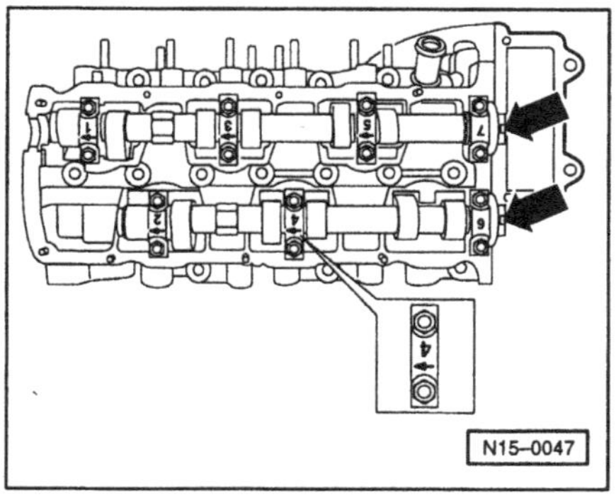

Notes:

- *Observe engine direction of rotation marking on double chain!*
- *When installing camshafts, the recess for the camshaft sprockets -arrows- must be at the top.*
- *When installing bearing caps, ensure that the identification mark is readable from the exhaust side of cylinder head and that the arrow points toward the vibration damper.*

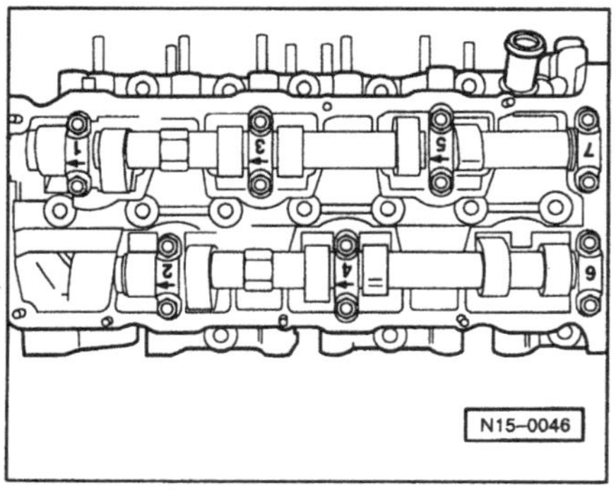

Camshaft for cylinders 1, 3 and 5

– Tighten bearing caps 3 and 5 alternately and diagonally

- 20 Nm (15 ft lb)

– Install bearing caps 1 and 7 and tighten

- 20 Nm (15 ft lb)

Camshaft for cylinders 2, 4 and 6

– Tighten bearing caps 2 and 6 alternately and diagonally

- 20 Nm (15 ft lb)

– Install bearing cap 4 and tighten

- 20 Nm (15 ft lb)

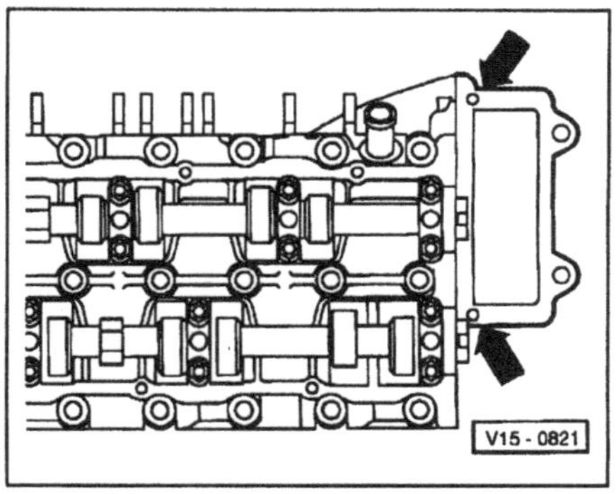

– Clean sealing surfaces of camshaft sprocket cover and cylinder head

– Remove old sealant from 3 mm holes in cylinder head gasket -arrows-

Note:

With the cylinder head installed, the holes in the cylinder head gasket are only half visible.

– Install camshaft sprockets (double chain) ⇒ page D 13-22

– Fill 3 mm holes in head gasket with AMV 188 001 02 sealant

– Coat camshaft cover sealing surfaces with AMV 188 001 02

– Oil O-ring and insert in cover for camshafts
⇒ page D 15-3 (item 15)

– Install cover for camshafts, insert old mounting bolts and lightly tighten

– First tighten M8 mounting bolts

- ♦ 25 Nm (18 ft lb)

– Tighten M6 securing bolts
⇒ 10 Nm (7 ft lb)

– Install chain tensioner for double chain and tighten

- ♦ 30 Nm (22 ft lb)

Notes:

♦ *If chain tensioner has been pulled apart, bleed before installing*
⇒ page D 13-7, Fig. 2

> ***CAUTION!***
> ***When new lifters have been installed, do NOT start the engine for at least 30 minutes; lifter hydraulics must settle (otherwise valves will strike pistons).***

Hydraulic lifters, checking

Special tools, testers and auxiliary items

♦ Feeler gauges

♦ Wood or plastic wedge

Test sequence

Notes:

♦ *Replace faulty lifters complete (cannot be adjusted or repaired).*

♦ *Irregular valve noises during engine warmup are normal*

– Start engine and run until radiator fan has switched on at least once

– Increase engine speed to about 2500 rpm for 2 minutes

If the hydraulic lifters are still noisy, isolate noise as follows:

– Remove cylinder head cover
⇒ page D 15-8

– Rotate crankshaft clockwise via vibration damper mounting bolt, until cam for lifter to be checked is pointing upward

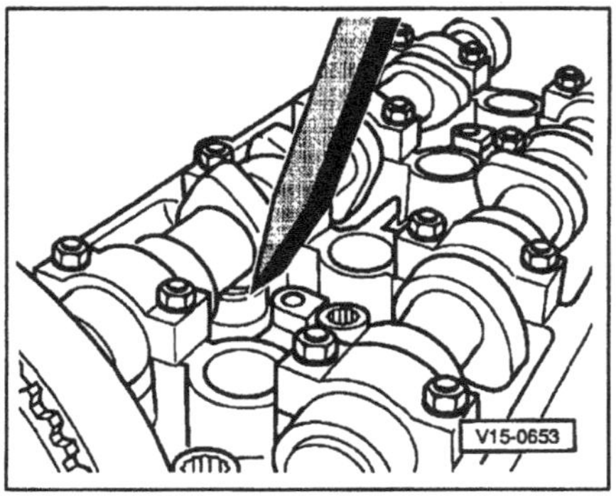

– Measure play between cam and hydraulic lifter

If play is in excess of 0.1 mm

– Replace lifter

If play is less than 0.1 mm or no play

– Proceed with check as follows

◄ – Press lifter down with a wooden or plastic wedge

If free travel in excess of 1 mm is felt before lifter contacts valve

– Replace lifter

> ***CAUTION!***
> ***When new lifters have been installed, do NOT start the engine for at least 30 minutes; lifter hydraulics must settle (otherwise valves will strike pistons).***

Valve guides, checking

Special tools, testers and auxiliary items

- VW 387 Universal dial gauge bracket
- Dial gauge

Test sequence

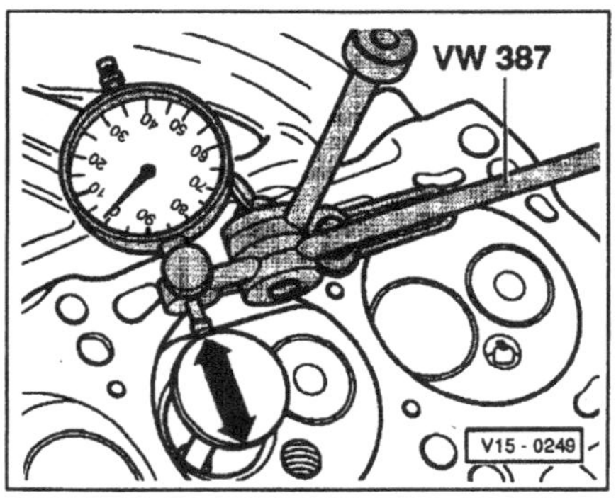

◄ – Insert new valve into guide until end of valve stem is flush with end of guide

- Due to slight difference in stem dimensions, ensure that intake valves only are used in intake guides and exhaust valves only in exhaust guides

– Measure rocking distance

Wear limit:

- Inlet valve guide = 1.0 mm
- Exhaust valve guide = 1.3 mm

Valve guides, replacing

- 3120 Hand reamer and cutting fluid
- 3121 Drift

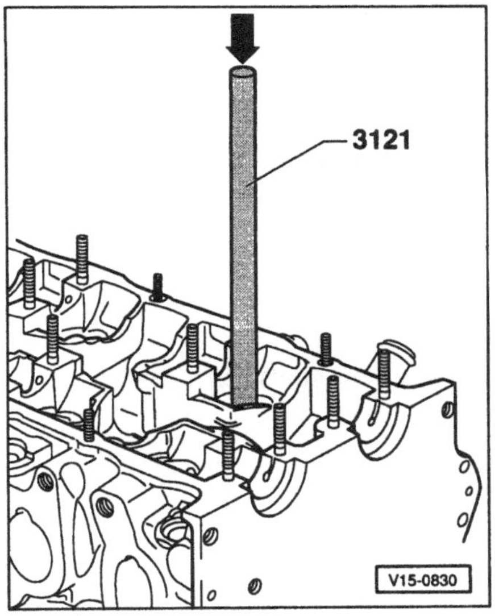

Removing

– Clean and inspect cylinder head

New valve guides cannot be installed in cylinder heads having valve seats that can no longer be reworked, or heads which have already been machined to the minimum dimension (height) ⇒ page D 15-21, item 7, or already have service version valve guides installed.

◄ – Press out worn valve guides using 3121 from the cam side

Installing

– Coat new guides with oil and press in (from camshaft side) with 3121 (cylinder head cold) until valve guide shoulder bottoms out. Cylinder head must lay flat during press operation.

> ***CAUTION!***
> ***When valve guide shoulder makes contact, do not exceed 1 ton hydraulic pressure, otherwise the guide shoulder (on service versions) could break.***

– Ream out guides using 3120 hand reamer and plenty of cutting fluid

– Rework valve seats ⇒ page D 15-26

Valve stem seals, replacing

(with cylinder head installed)

Special tools, testers and auxiliary items

- 3122 B Spark plug wrench
- 2036 Assembly tool
- 3047 A Puller
- 3129 Installing tool
- VW 541/1A Lever with VW 541/5 press tool
- VW 653/3 Pressure hose

Removing

– Remove camshafts
⇒ page D 15-29

– Remove hydraulic lifters (do not interchange) and store with the contact surface downwards.

– Remove spark plugs using 3122 B spark plug wrench

– Set piston of appropriate cylinder to "bottom dead center".

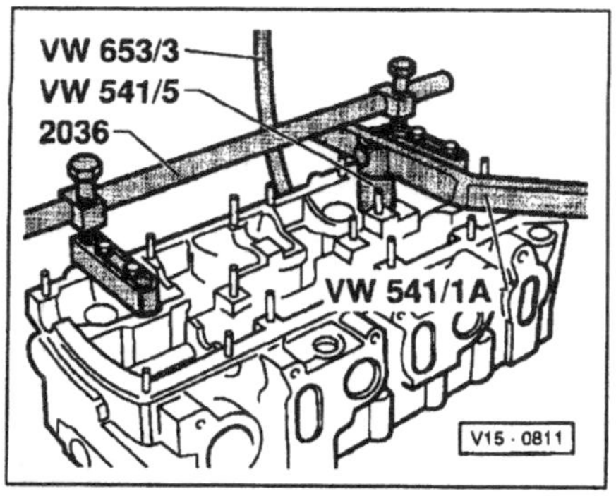

◄ – Install 2036 assembly tool and adjust mountings to height of studs

– Screw compressed air hose VW 653/3 into spark plug thread and apply a continuous pressure of 85 psi minimum (5.9 bar)

– Remove valve springs with lever VW 541/1A and press tool VW 541/5

Note:

Tight valve keepers can be loosened with a light hammer-tap on the lever.

– Remove valve stem seals using tool 3047 A

Installing

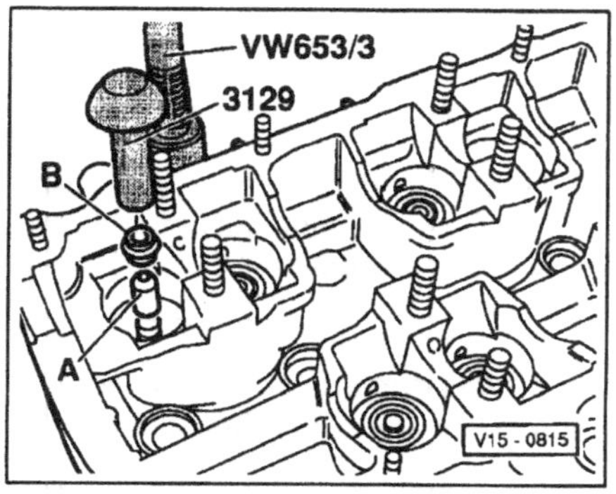

◄ – To avoid damaging the new valve stem seals, place plastic sleeve -A- on valve stem

– Oil valve stem seal -B-, place it on tool 3129 and carefully push it onto the valve guide

Lubrication system components, removing and installing

If metal shavings or large quantities of metal particles (possibly caused by partial seizure of crankshaft and connecting rod bearings) are found in the engine oil while performing engine repairs:

- Thoroughly clean all oil passages, replace all oil spray jets, the oil non-return valve and the oil cooler

Checking oil pressure and oil pressure switch
⇒ page D 17-10

Oil system capacity

- ♦ without oil filter: 5.5 ltrs. (5.8 quarts)
- ♦ with oil filter: 6.0 ltrs. (6.3 quarts)

> ***CAUTION!***
> ***Do NOT allow engine oil to be above the MAX. mark. This can lead to catalyst damage!***

Engine oil specifications

- ♦ Only use engine oil designated "API-SF or SG"

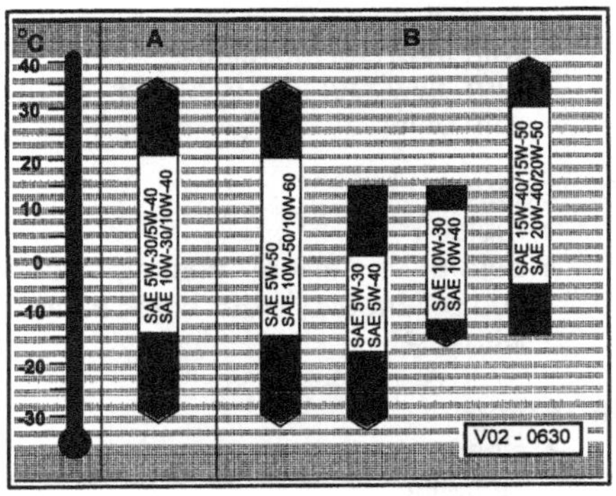

◄

- Choose the proper viscosity grade by considering the ambient temperatures and environment in which vehicle will be operated

A - energy conserving oil
B - multi-grade oil

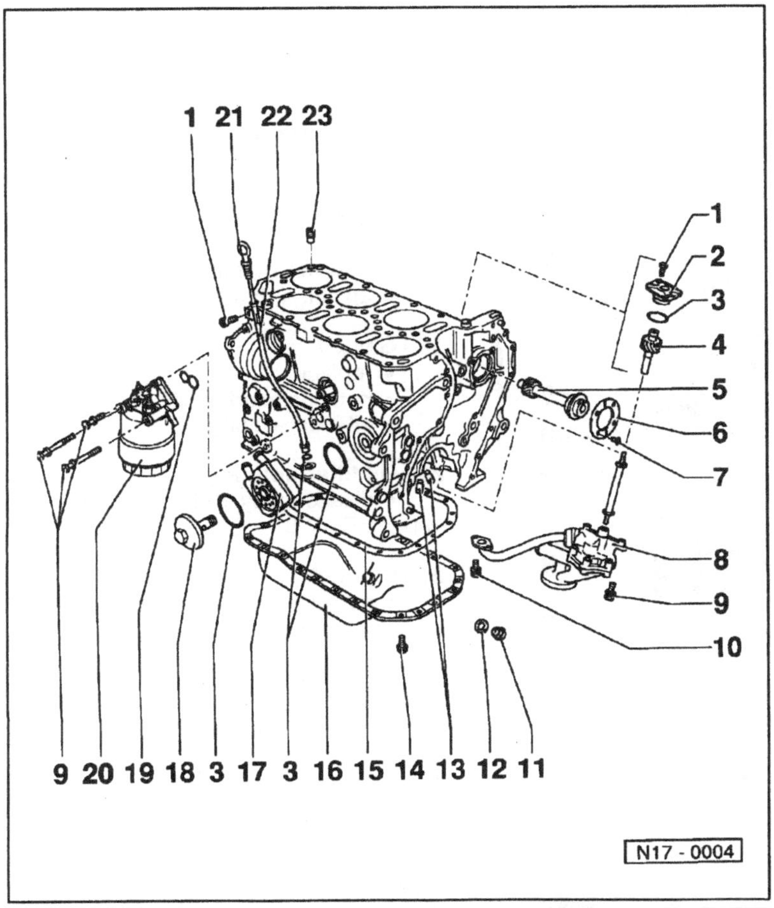

1 - 10 Nm (7 ft lb)

2 - Oil pump drive cover

3 - O-ring
- ♦ replace
- ♦ oil before installing

4 - Oil pump drive

5 - Intermediate shaft

6 - Thrust washer

7 - 10 Nm (7 ft lb)
- ♦ install with locking fluid "D6"

8 - Oil pump
- ♦ disassembly and assembly

⇒ page D 17-8
- ♦ Coat oil pump housing and oil pressure pipe at cylinder block using AMV 188 001 02

9 - 25 Nm (18 ft lb)

10 - 10 Nm (7 ft lb)
- ♦ replace
- ♦ install with "D6" locking fluid

11 - Oil drain plug
- ♦ 30 Nm (22 ft lb)

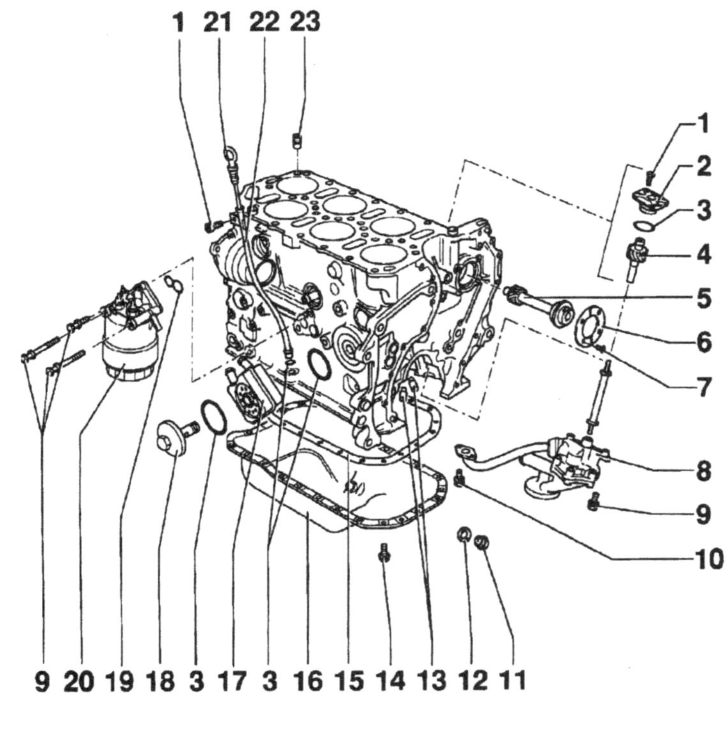

N17 - 0004

12 - Seal
- replace

13 - Oil spray jet
- for crankshaft bearings 2 to 7
- for piston cooling
- removing and installing:

⇒ Fig. 1
- opening pressure: 2.0 bar (29 psi)
- see note

⇒ page D 17-1

14 - 15 Nm (11 ft lb)
- remove and install using 3249 socket
- with flywheel installed:
  - turn flywheel so recesses align with bolts

15 - Gasket
- replace
- before installing gasket, coat sump flange/cylinder block flange with "D2"

16 - Sump
- clean sealing surfaces before installing

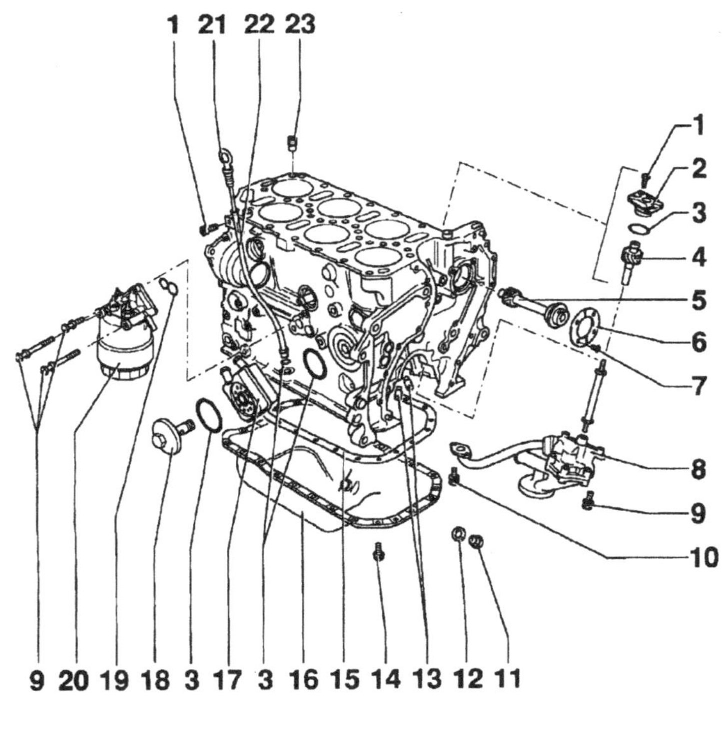

N17 - 0004

17 - Oil cooler
- coat contact area to flange, outside the seal, with AMV 188 100 02
- ensure clearance to adjacent components
- see note ⇒ page D 17-1

18 - Oil cooler cover
- 25 Nm (18 ft lb)

19 - Gasket
- replace
- note installed position
- oil before fitting

20 - Oil filter housing
- disassembly and assembly:

⇒ page D 17-6

21 - Dipstick
- oil level must not be above the max. mark!

22 - Guide tube
- for dipstick
- bolted to intake manifold

23 - Oil non-return valve
- 5 Nm (4 ft lb)
- note installed position
- clean if necessary, see note

⇒ page D 17-1

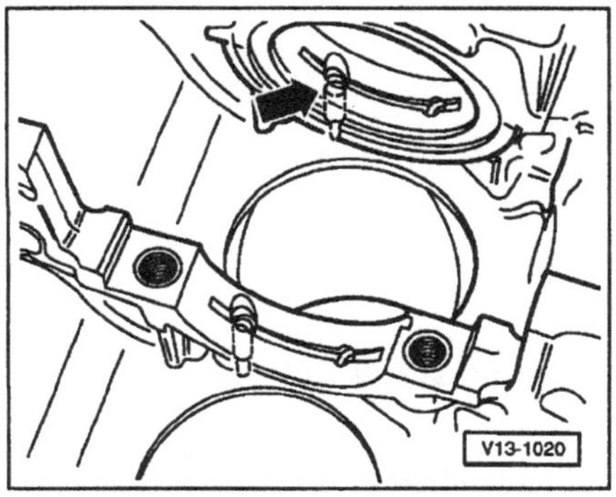

◄ **Fig. 1 Oil spray jet, removing and installing**

Special tools, testers and auxiliary items

- 4 mm Ø Punch
- 6 mm Ø Punch

Note:

Oil spray jets are installed in main bearings 2 through 7.

Requirement

- Crankshaft must be removed

Removing

– Remove using 4 mm Ø punch

Installing

– Install by hand using 6 mm Ø punch -arrow-

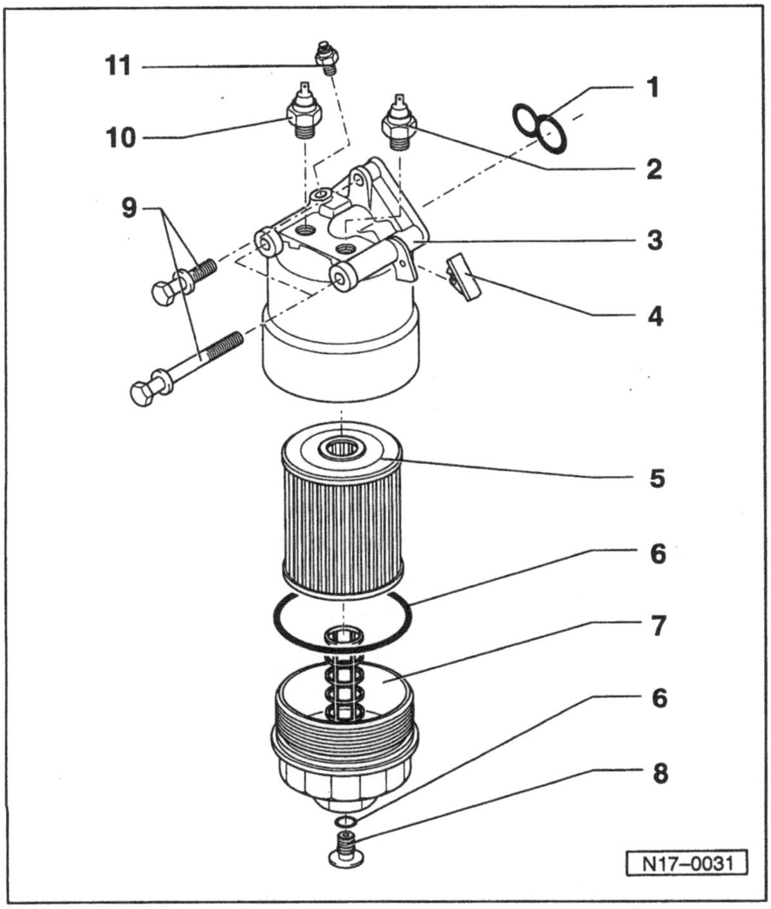

Oil filter housing, disassembling and assembling

1 - Gasket
- replace
- note installed position
- oil before installing

2 - Oil pressure switch (0.3 bar) F22
- 20 Nm (15 ft lb)
- brown body
- blue/black wiring
- checking:

⇒ page D 17-10

– If sealing ring is leaking, replace

3 - Oil filter bracket

4 - Stop plate
- for oil cooler
- mounted to oil filter bracket

5 - Oil filter element
- note replacement intervals
- with by-pass valve: opening pressure: 2.0 bar (29 psi)
- clip into lower oil filter section before installing

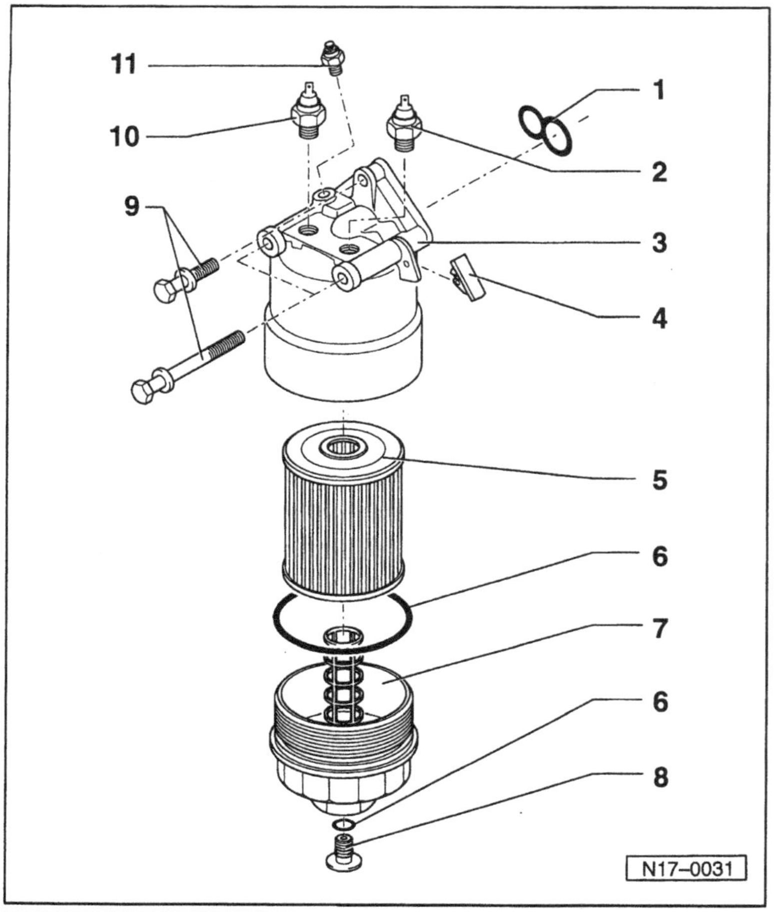

6 - O-ring
- replace
- oil before installing

7 - Lower oil filter section
- 30 Nm (22 ft lb)
- drain before removing

8 - Oil drain screw
- 10 Nm (7 ft lb)

9 - 25 Nm (18 ft lb)

10 - Oil pressure switch (1.4 bar) F1
- 20 Nm (15 ft lb)
- black body
- yellow wiring
- checking:

⇒ page D 17-10

  – if sealing ring is leaking, replace

11 - Engine Oil Temperature sensor G8
- 10 Nm (7 ft lb)
- green/black wiring

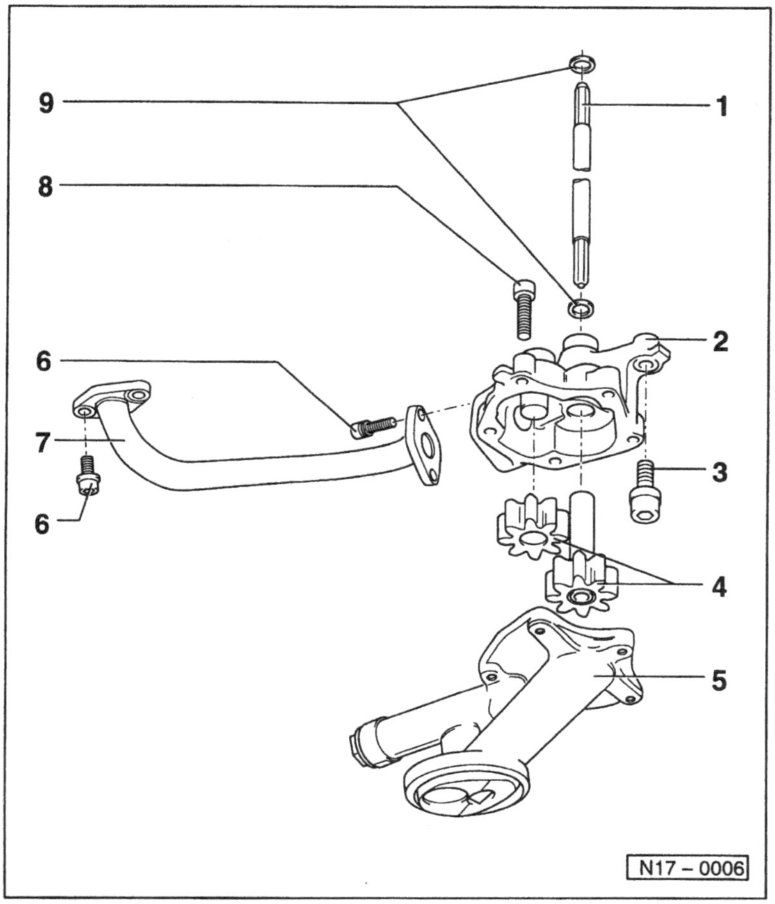

Oil pump, disassembly and assembly

1 - Drive shaft
- for oil pump drive

2 - Oil pump housing

3 - 25 Nm (18 ft lb)

4 - Gears◊
- backlash, checking: ⇒ Fig. 1
- axial clearance, checking: ⇒ Fig. 1

5 - Oil pump cover (with pressure relief valve)
- opening pressure: 5.3 to 5.7 bar (77 to 82 psi)
- clean strainer if dirty

6 - 10 Nm (7 ft lb)
- replace
- install with locking fluid "D6"

7 - Oil pressure pipe
- coat cylinder block and oil pump housing with AMV 188 001 02

8 - 10 Nm (7 ft lb)

9 - O-ring
- replace if damaged

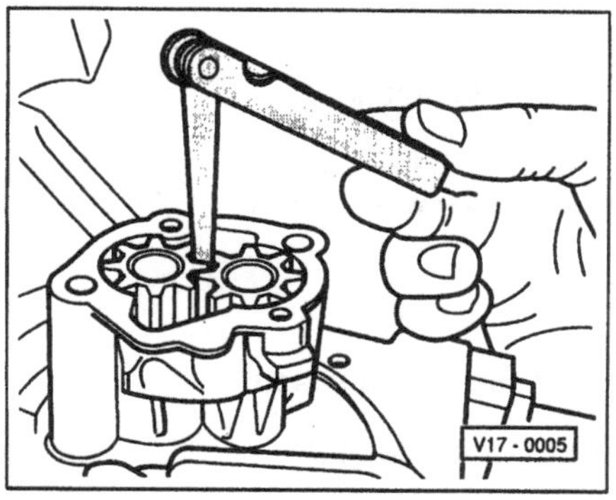

Fig. 1 Oil pump backlash, checking

Special tools, testers and auxiliary items

♦ Feeler gauge

Wear limit: 0.20 mm

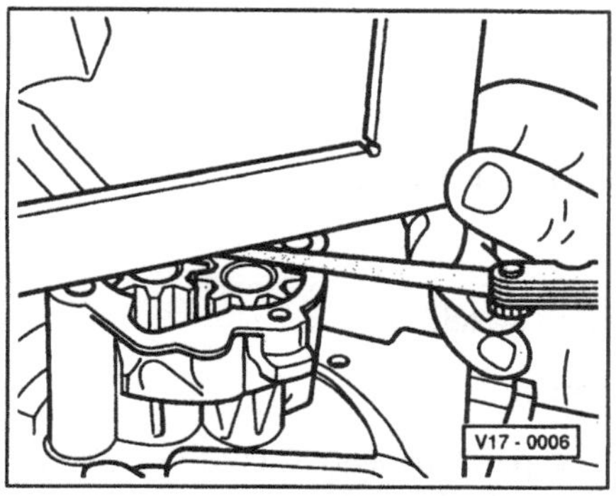

Fig. 2 Oil pump axial clearance, checking

Special tools, testers and auxiliary items

♦ Feeler gauge

Wear limit: 0.10 mm

Oil pressure and oil pressure switches, checking

Note:

Functional check and servicing the optical and acoustic oil pressure warning:
⇒ Wiring diagrams

Special tools, testers and auxiliary items

♦ VAG 1342 Oil pressure tester

♦ VAG 1527B LED tester

♦ VW 1594 Adaptor kit

♦ Wiring diagram

Test sequence

– Remove noise insulation tray:
⇒ Repair group 50

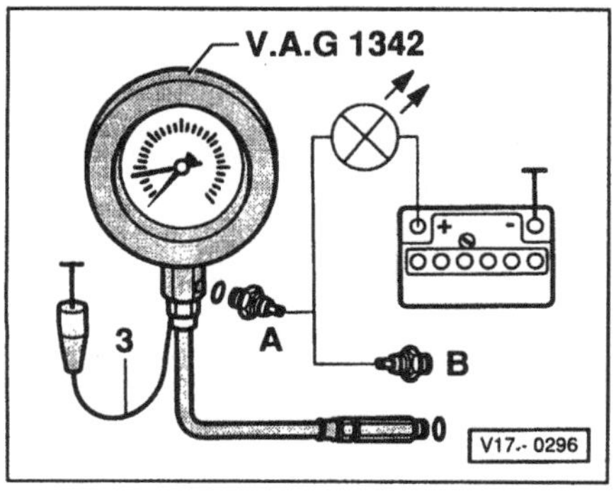

– Remove 0.3 bar oil pressure switch (brown body)

– Screw removed oil pressure switch into tester

– Screw tester into the oil filter bracket in place of oil pressure switch

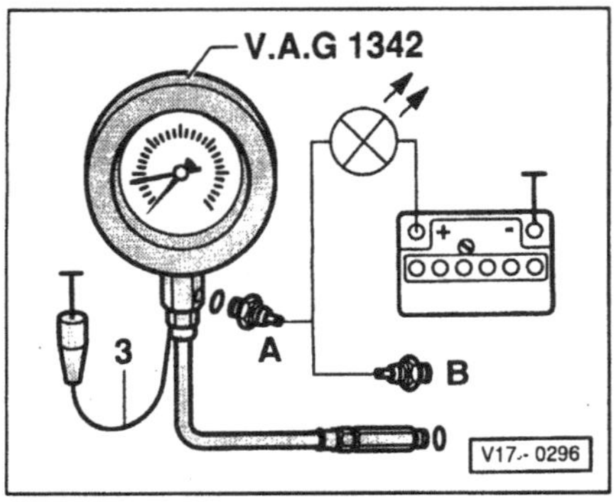

◄ – Connect tester wire -3- (brown) to ground

– Connect VAG 1527B LED tester to battery positive (+) and 0.3 bar oil pressure switch -A- using jumper wires from VW 1594 adaptor kit

♦ LED must light up

– Start engine and slowly increase engine speed

♦ at 0.15 to 0.45 bar, the LED must go out

If LED does not go out

– Replace 0.3 bar oil pressure switch

– Connect LED tester to 1.4 bar oil pressure switch -B- (black)

♦ at 1.2 to 1.6 bar, the LED must light up

If LED does not light up

– Replace 1.4 bar oil pressure switch

– Increase engine speed further

♦ At 2000 rpm and an oil temperature of 80 °C (176 °F), oil pressure must be 2.0 bar minimum (29 psi)

♦ At higher rpm, oil pressure must not exceed 7.0 bar (102 psi)

– Replace oil pump if necessary
⇒ page D 17-8

Cooling system components, removing and installing

Notes:

- *When the engine is warm, the cooling system is under pressure. Release any pressure before starting repair work.*
- *Hoses are secured with spring-type clips, when performing repairs; only use spring-type clips.*
- *VAG 1921 pliers are recommended for installing spring-type clips.*
- *When installing coolant hoses; always route them stress-free, so they don't come into contact with other components (observe markings on coolant connection and hose).*

Check cooling system for leakage using cooling system tester VAG 1274 and adapter VAG 1274/3.

Cooling system components (body side)
⇒ page D 19-2

Cooling system components (engine side)
⇒ page D 19-5

Coolant hose connections, diagram
⇒ page D 19-9

Coolant system, draining and filling
⇒ page D 19-13

Coolant mixing ratios
⇒ page D 19-13

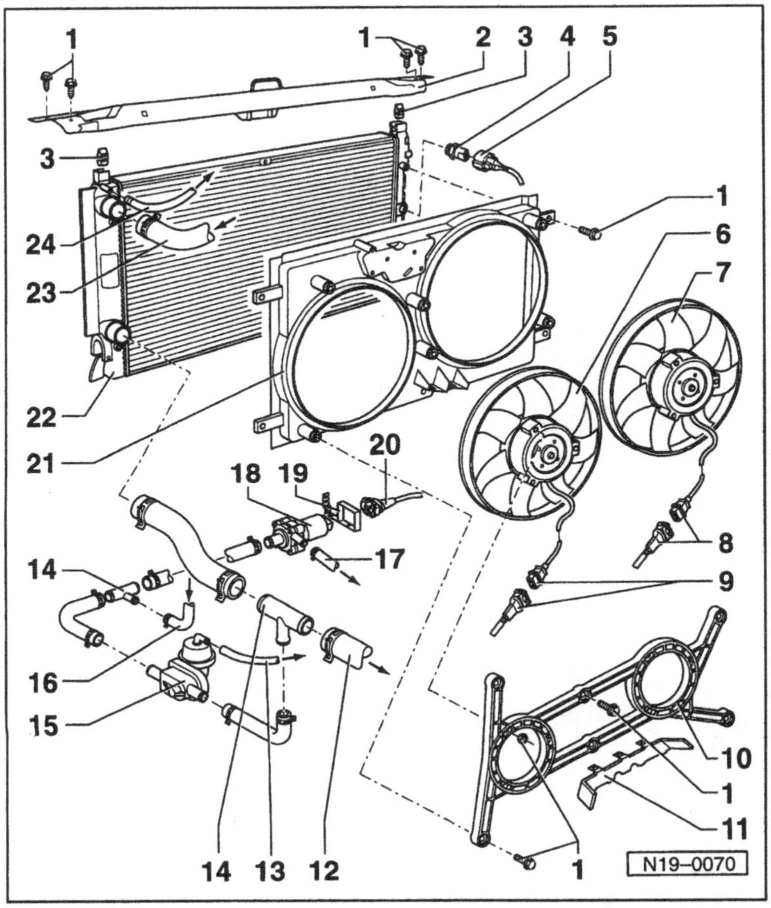

Cooling system components (body side)

1 - 10 Nm (7 ft lb)

2 - Lock carrier

3 - Mounting rubbers

4 - Coolant Fan Control Thermal switch F18

- 35 Nm (26 ft lb)
- switching temperatures:

Stage 1:
ON: 84 to 89°C (183 to192°F)
OFF: 76 to 83°C (169 to181°F)
Stage 2
ON: 90 to 95°C (194 to 203°F)
OFF: 82 to 89°C (180 to 192°F)

5 - 3-pin harness connector

- black
- for Coolant Fan Control Thermal switch F18

6 - Left Coolant fan V7

- removing and installing:

⇒ page D 19-16

7 - Right Coolant fan V35

- removing and installing:

⇒ page D 19-16

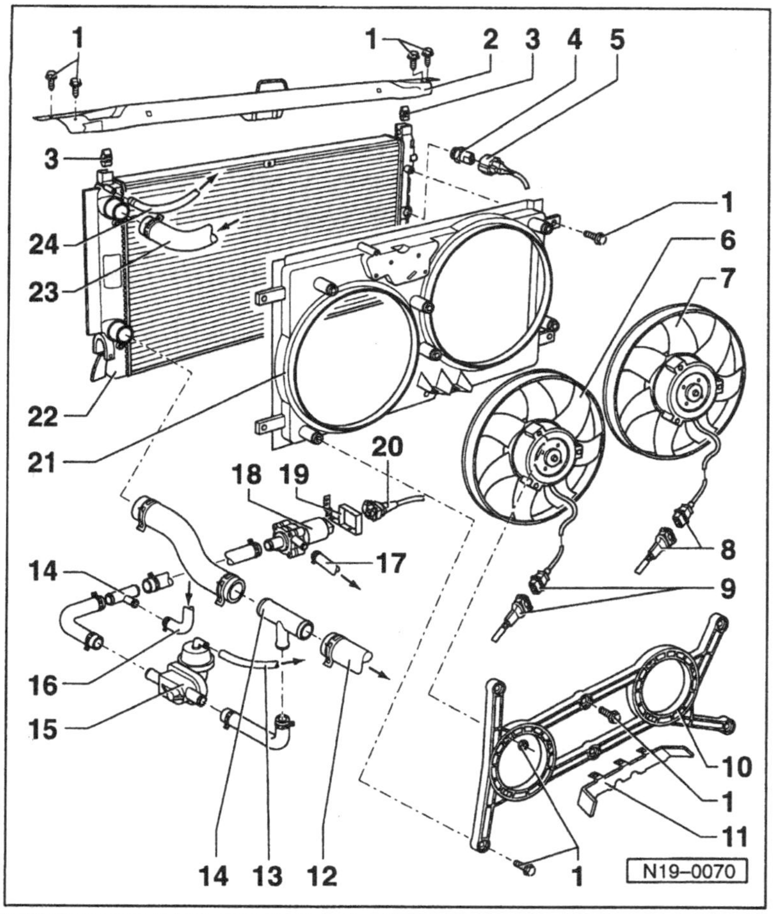

8 - 2-pin harness connector
- black
- for Right Coolant fan V35

9 - 2-pin harness connector
- black
- for Left Coolant fan V7

10 - Fan ring

11 - Cable guide

12 - Lower coolant hose
- coolant hose connections, diagram

⇒ page D 19-9

13 - Vacuum line
- to brake servo vacuum line

14 - Junction piece

15 - Vacuum unit
- arrow on vacuum valve points to the After-run Coolant pump
- checking:

⇒ page D 19-24

16 - Coolant hose
- coolant hose connections, diagram

⇒ page D 19-9

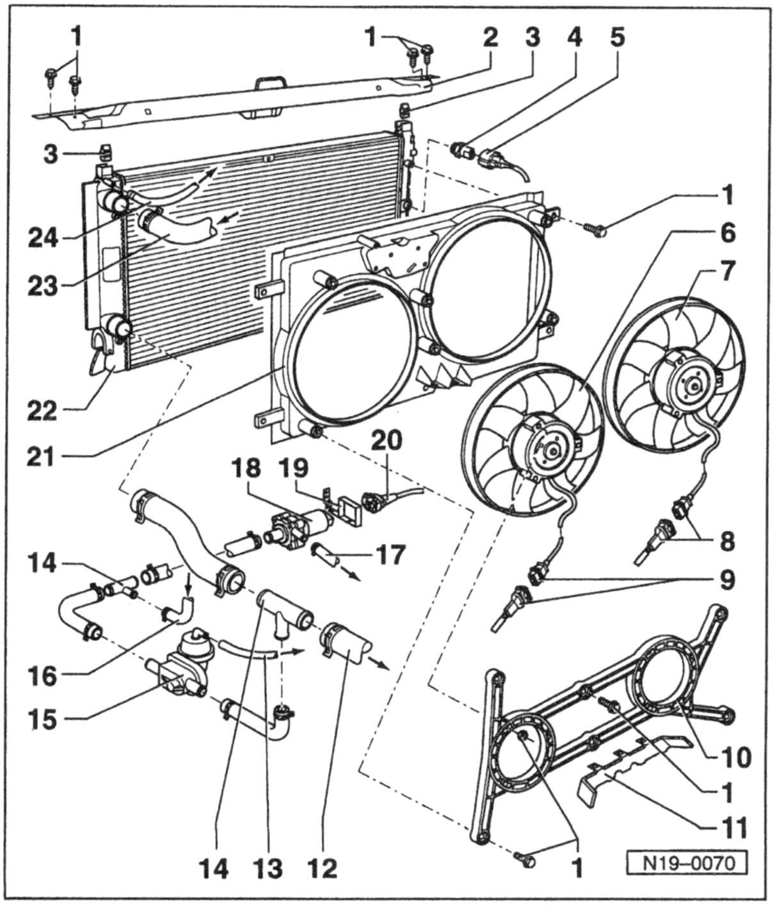

17 - Coolant hose
- coolant hose connections, diagram

⇒ page D 19-9

18 - After-run Coolant pump V51
- checking:

⇒ page D 19-21

19 - Retainer
- for After-run Coolant pump

20 - 2 pin harness connector
- black
- for After-run Coolant pump

21 - Air intake duct

22 - Engine Coolant radiator
- removing and installing:

⇒ page D 19-16

- if replaced; fill entire system with new coolant mixture

23 - Upper coolant hose
- coolant hose connections, diagram

⇒ page D 19-9

24 - Coolant overflow hose
- coolant hose connections, diagram

⇒ page D 19-9

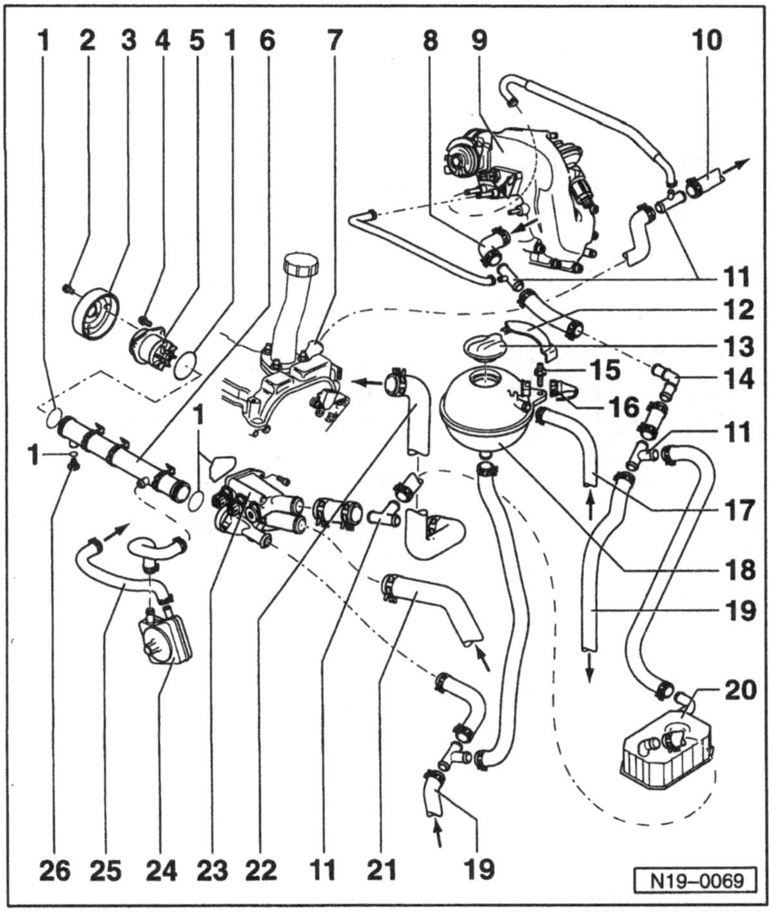

Cooling system components (engine side)

1 - O-ring
- ♦ replace

2 - 25 Nm (18 ft lb)
- ♦ to loosen and tighten pulley; counter-hold using a punch inserted through the holes

3 - Pulley
- ♦ for coolant pump

4 - 20 Nm (15 ft lb)

5 - Coolant pump
- ♦ check shaft for ease of movement
- ♦ removing and installing:

⇒ page D 19-19

6 - Coolant pipe

7 - Connection
- ♦ on cylinder head

8 - from heat exchanger
- ♦ coolant hose connections, diagram

⇒ page D 19-9

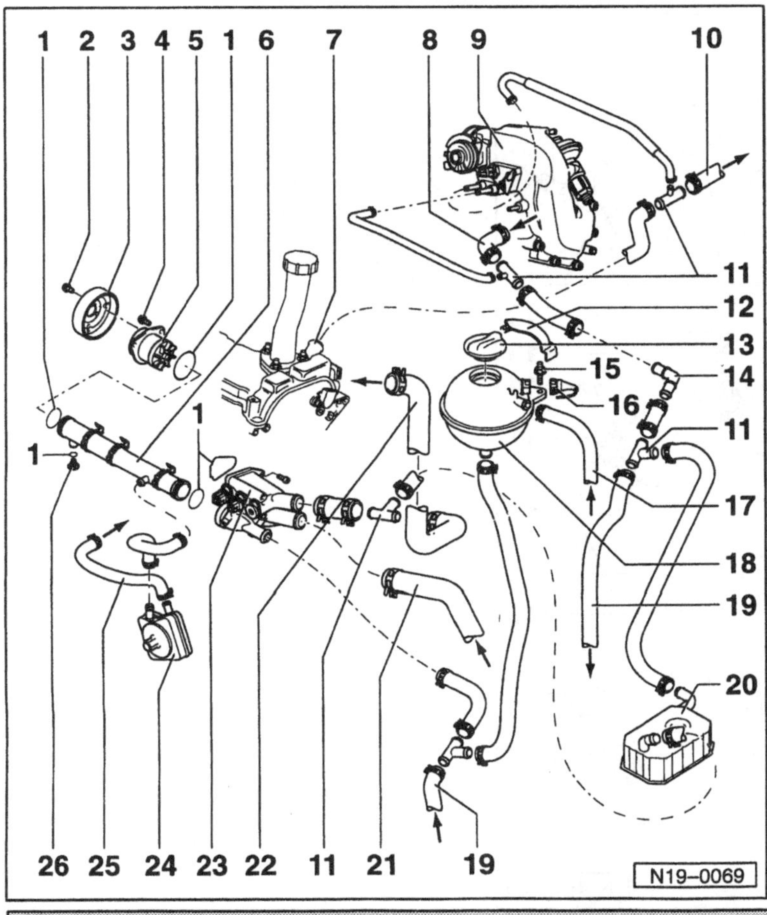

9 - Throttle Valve Control Module
- ♦ heated by coolant

10 - to heat exchanger
- ♦ coolant hose connections, diagram

⇒ page D 19-9

11 - Junction piece

12 - Cover

13 - Cap
- ♦ check cooling system using VAG 1274 tester and VAG 1274/4 adapter
- ♦ test pressure: 1.2 to 1.5 bar (17 to 22psi)

14 - Angle piece

15 - 10 Nm (7 ft lb)

16 - 2-pin harness connector
- ♦ black

17 - Coolant overflow hose
- ♦ coolant hose connections, diagram

⇒ page D 19-9

18 - Expansion tank

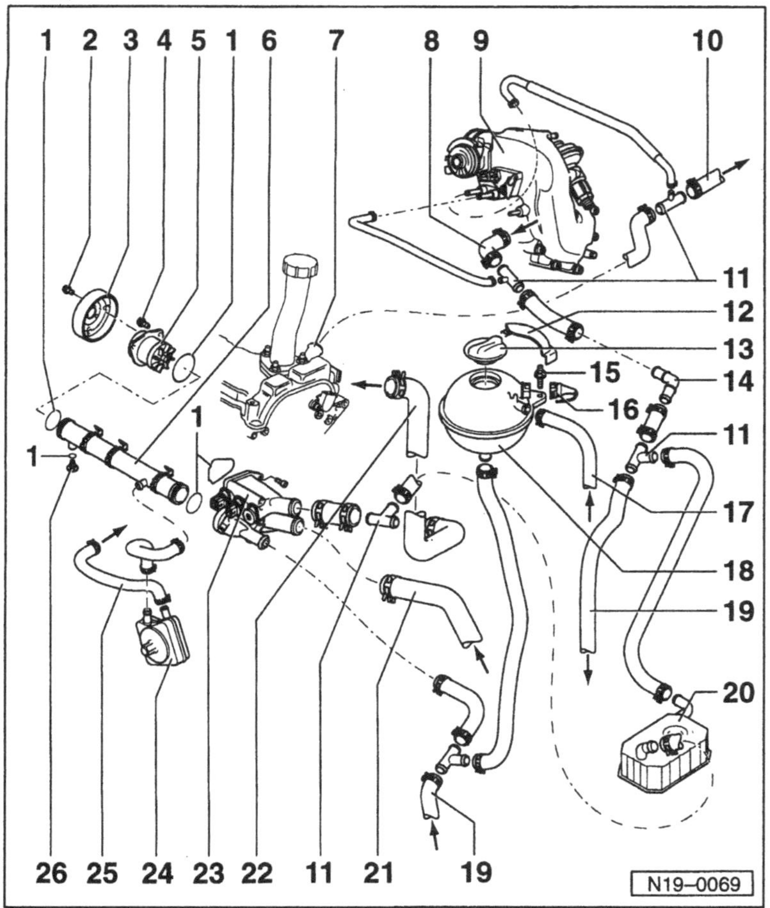

19 - Coolant hose

- coolant hose connections, diagram

⇒ page D 19-9

20 - ATF cooler

- only installed in vehicles with an Automatic transmission
- removing and installing:

⇒ Repair Group 37, 098/01P Automatic transmission

21 - Lower coolant hose

- from bottom of radiator
- coolant hose connections, diagram

⇒ page D 19-9

22 - Upper coolant hose

- to top of radiator
- coolant hose connections, diagram

⇒ page D 19-9

23 - Thermostat housing

- disassembly and assembly:

⇒ page D 19-11

24 - Oil cooler

- removing and installing:

⇒ page D 17-4 (item 17)

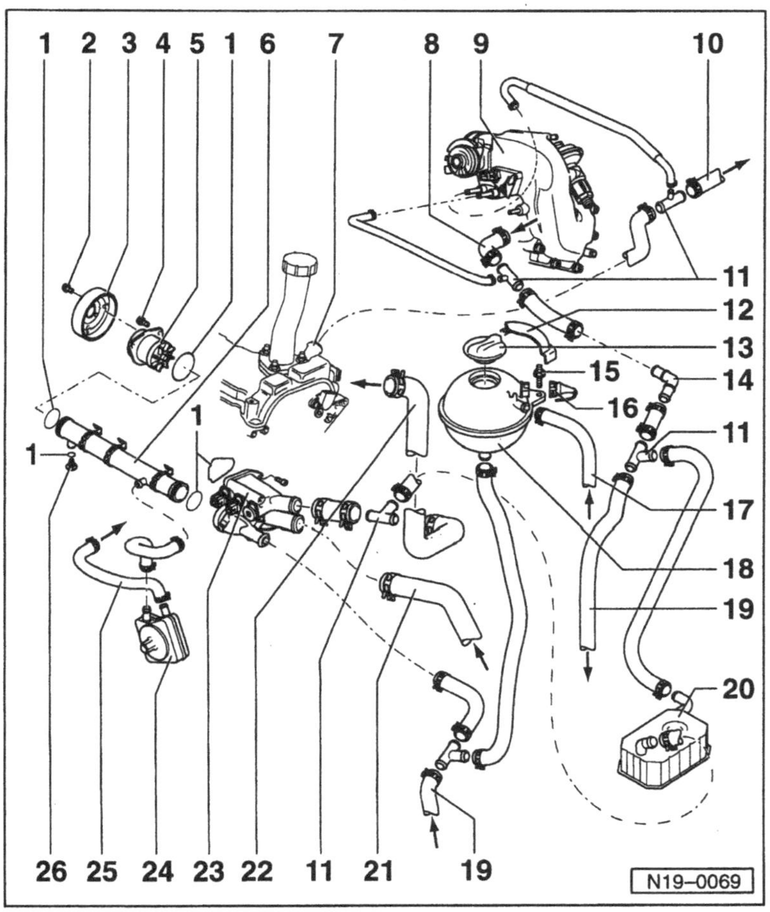

25 - to cylinder block

- coolant hose connections, diagram

⇒ page D 19-9

26 - Drain screw

- 10 Nm (7 ft lb)
- coolant, draining and filling:

⇒ page D 19-13

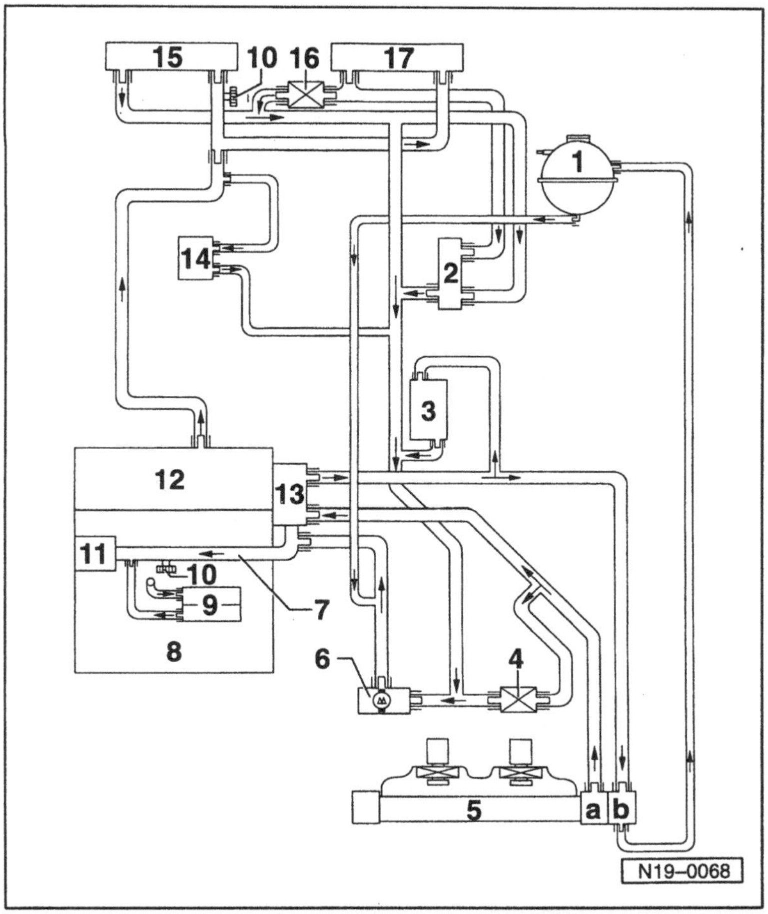

Coolant hose connections, diagram

1 - **Expansion tank**

2 - **Control valve**
- ♦ option

3 - **ATF cooler**
- ♦ only installed in vehicles with an Automatic transmission

4 - **Vacuum valve**

5 - **Radiator**
- ♦ b = Bottom
- ♦ a = Top

6 - **After-run Coolant pump V51**

7 - **Coolant pipe**

8 - **Cylinder block**

9 - **Oil cooler**

10 - **Drain screw**
- ♦ 10 Nm (7 ft lb)

11 - **Coolant pump**

12 - **Cylinder head**

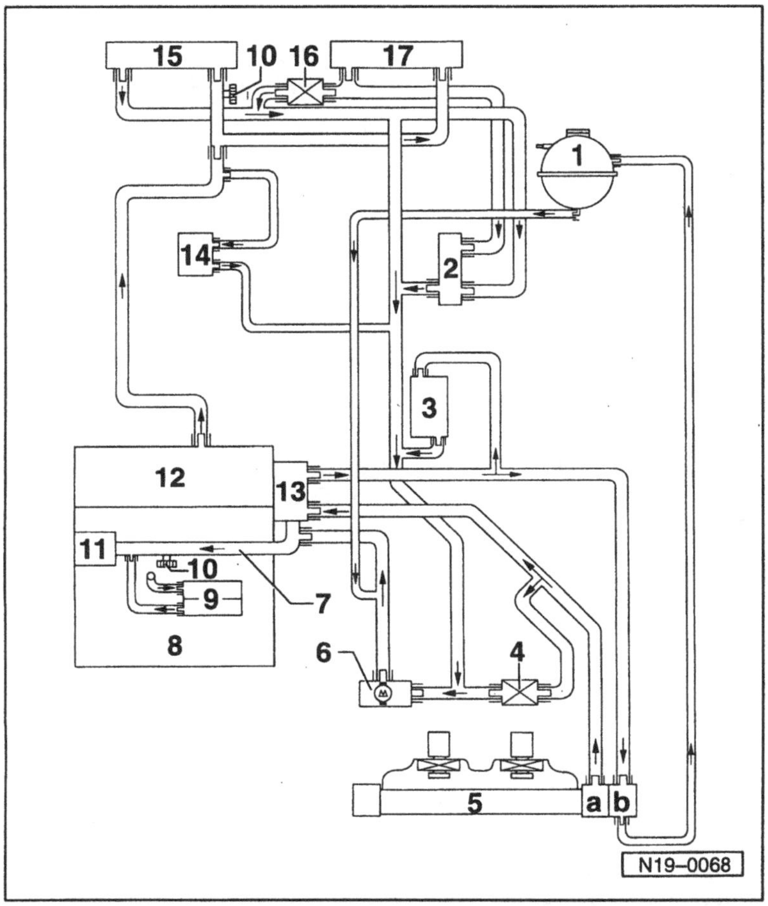

13 - **Thermostat housing**

14 - **Throttle Body/Throttle Valve Control Module J338**

15 - **Heat exchanger**
- ♦ for heating system

16 - **Solenoid valve**
- ♦ optional

17 - **Auxiliary heat exchanger**
- ♦ option

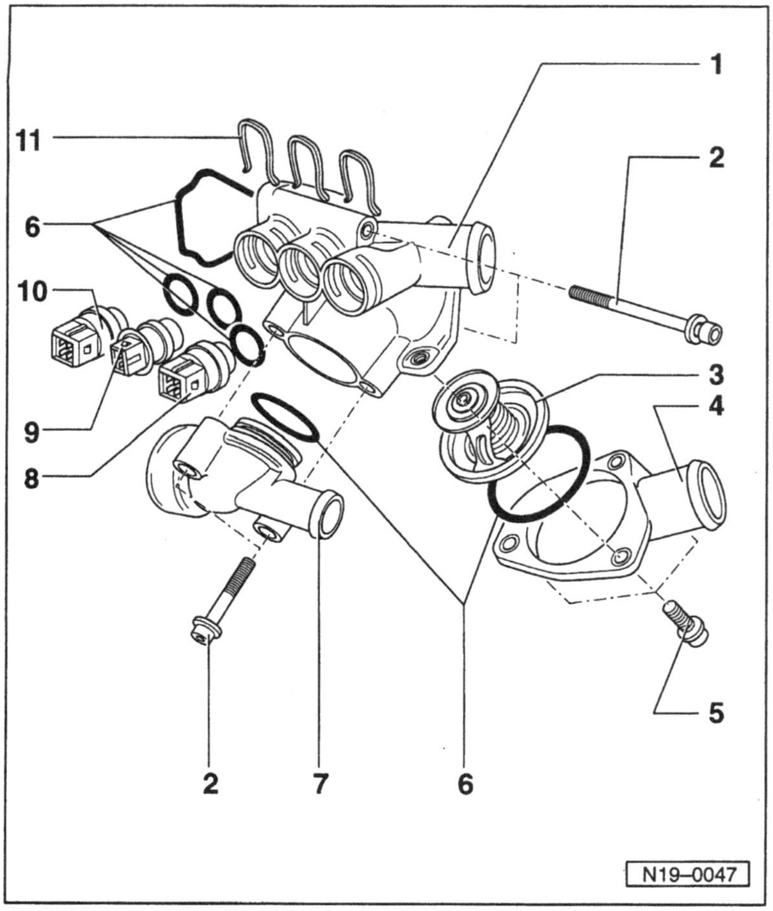

Engine coolant thermostat housing, disassembling and assembling

Connecting the coolant hoses to thermostat housing:
⇒ page D 19-5

1 - Thermostat housing

2 - 10 Nm (7 ft lb)

3 - Coolant thermostat
- ♦ installed position: breather slot/ valve uppermost
- ♦ checking:
- – heat-up thermostat in water
- ♦ opening starts approximately 80 °C (176°F)
- ♦ ends approx. 105 °C (221°F).
- ♦ opening lift 7 mm (0.276 in.) min.

4 - Connection

5 - 10 Nm (7 ft lb)

6 - O-ring
- ♦ replace

7 - Connection

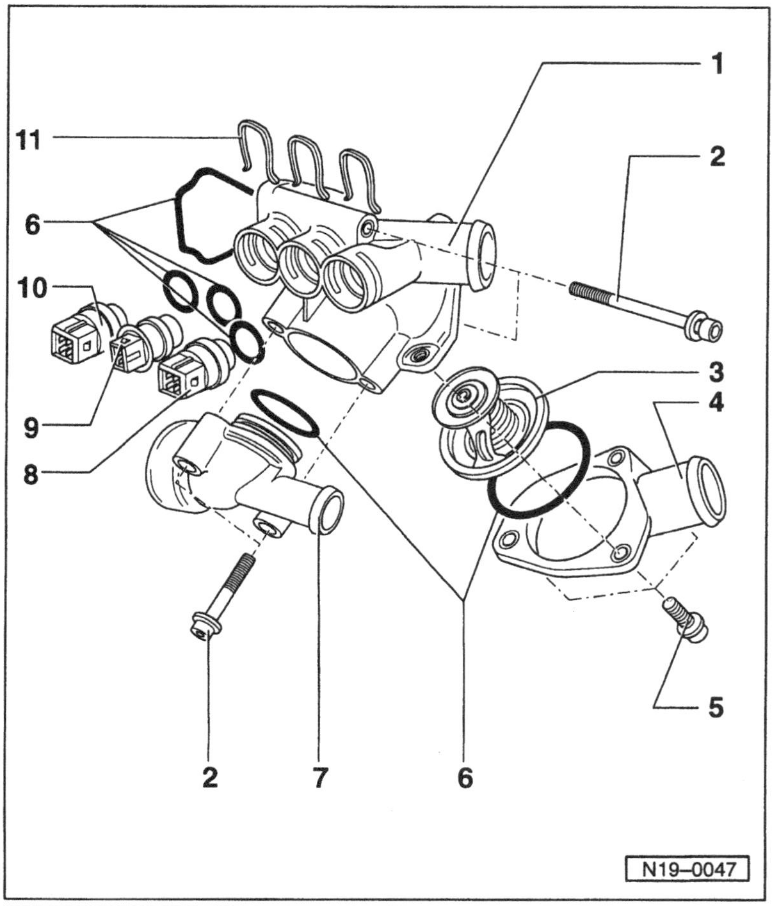

8 - A/C Cut-out Thermal switch F163 / Third Speed Coolant Fan Control

Thermal switch F165
- ♦ brown, 4-pin
- ♦ for vehicles with A/C

⇒ Repair Group 87
- ♦ vehicles w/o A/C are plugged

9 - Engine Coolant Temperature (ECT) sensor G62
- ♦ blue, 2-pin
- ♦ for Motronic system
- ♦ checking:

⇒ Repair Group 01

10 - After-run Coolant Thermal switch F95 / Engine Coolant Temperature

sensor G2
- ♦ yellow, 4-pin
- ♦ checking:

⇒ page D 19-21

11 - Retaining clip
- ♦ ensure proper seating

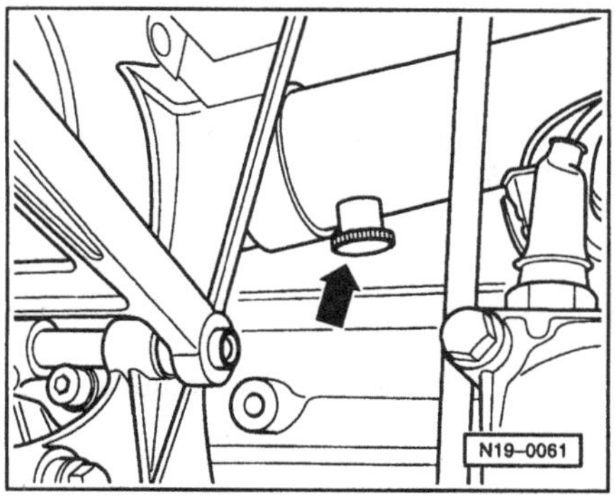

Cooling system, draining and filling

Special tools, testers and auxiliary items

- VAG 1306 Drip tray

Draining

– Remove coolant expansion tank cap

– Remove noise insulation tray
⇒ Repair Group 50

◄ – Remove coolant line drain screw -arrow-

Filling

Notes:

- *The cooling system is filled year-round with a mixture of water, anti-freeze and corrosion protection agent G 11. G 11 and coolant additives marked as being "in accordance with TL VW 774 C" prevent frost and corrosion damage, the formation of chalk and in addition, they raise the boiling point of the coolant. For these reasons, the cooling system must be filled year-round with an anti-freeze and corrosion protection agent. Due to the higher boiling point, the coolant is an aid to operational efficiency when the engine is operating at high loads, particularly in tropical climates.*
- *If radiator, heat exchanger, cylinder head or cylinder head gasket is replaced, completely replace engine coolant.*

Recommended mixture ratios:

Equipment:	**Protection to:**	**Anti-freeze quantity:** [1]	**G 11:** [2]	**H_2O**
One heat exchanger	–25 °C –35 °C	40 % 50 %	3.6 ltr. 4.5 ltr.	5.4 ltr. 4.5 ltr.
Two heat exchangers	–25 °C –35 °C	40 % 50 %	4.3 ltr. 5.4 ltr.	6.5 ltr. 5.4 ltr.
Two heat exchangers and additional water heater	–25 °C –35 °C	40 % 50 %	4.6 ltr. 5.7 ltr.	6.8 ltr. 5.7 ltr.

[1] The amount of anti-freeze must not exceed 60 %. Frost protection and cooling efficiency will decrease if the percentage of anti-freeze is too high.

[2] Coolant quantities shown are for vehicles with manual transmission. For vehicles with an automatic transmission, increase both G11 and water by 0.1 ltr.

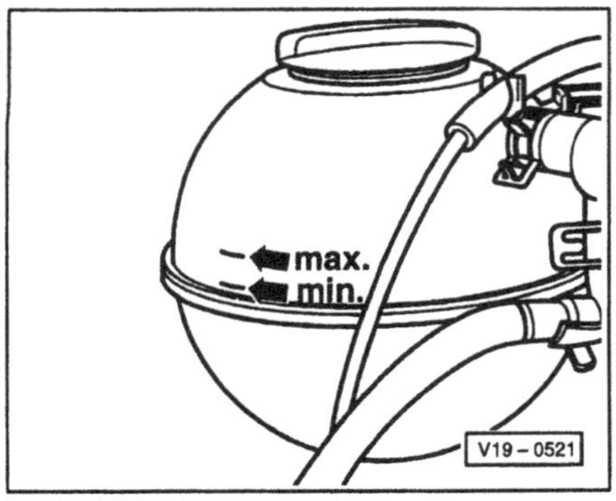

– Press down on top radiator hose

◄ – Fill expansion tank with coolant up to max. mark

– Start engine and run at approximately 2500 rpm while filling with coolant up to overflow hole on expansion tank

– Fit expansion tank cap

– Run engine until radiator fan starts running

– Run engine for an additional 10 minutes at approximately 2500 rpm

– Check coolant level and top-up if necessary

- ♦ With engine at normal operating temperature; coolant level must be on max. mark
- ♦ With engine cold, coolant level must be between the min. and max. marks

Radiator and radiator fan, removing and installing

Special tools, testers and auxiliary items

- ♦ VAG 1921 Pliers for spring type clips
- ♦ VAG 1306 Drip tray

Removing

– Remove noise insulation tray:
⇒ Repair Group 50

Vehicles with A/C

– Remove ribbed belt
⇒ page D 13-19

– Remove power steering pump with bracket and secure to body with wire; hoses remain connected
⇒ Repair Group 48, Running gear

– Remove A/C compressor:
⇒ Repair Group 87

CAUTION!
The A/C refrigerant circuit must not be opened!

– Observe additional information and removal work
⇒ page D 19-18

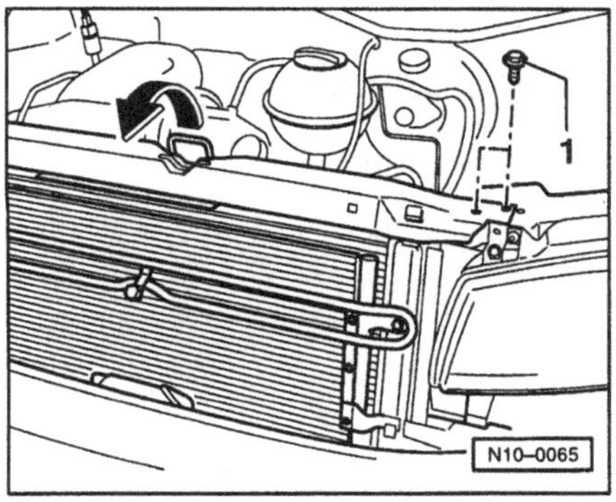

All vehicles

– Remove radiator grille
⇒ Repair Group 66

◄ – Remove lock carrier mounting bolts -1- on left and right

– Tilt lock carrier with radiator in forward direction -arrow-

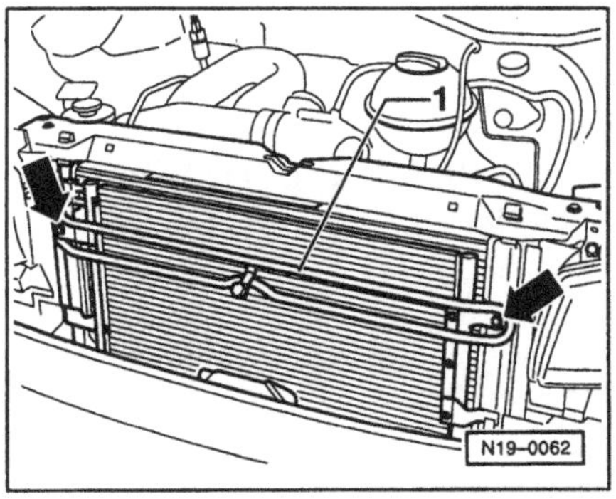

◄ – Disconnect power steering line -1- from radiator -arrows- and lay to one side

– Pull connectors off thermal switch and radiator fan

– Drain coolant
⇒ page D 19-13

– Disconnect coolant hoses from radiator

– Lift out radiator assembly (complete with fan cowl and fan) in upward direction

Installing

Installation is carried out in the reverse order of the removal procedure; when installing, note the following:

– Fill system with engine coolant
⇒ page D 19-13

– Route wiring and make electrical connections
⇒ Repair group 97

– Check headlight adjustment, adjust if necessary:
⇒ Maintenance booklet

Vehicles with A/C, additional information

> ***CAUTION!***
> ***The A/C refrigerant circuit must not be opened.***

> ***CAUTION!***
> ***To prevent damage to the condenser and the refrigerant lines/hoses; ensure that the lines and hoses are not stretched, kinked or bent.***

– Remove retaining clamp(s) from refrigerant lines

– Remove condenser from radiator, pull forward as far as possible

– Remove radiator in an upward direction

– Secure condenser to body so that refrigerant lines and hoses are not stressed

Coolant pump, removing and installing

Special tools, testers and auxiliary items

- ♦ VAG 1331 Torque wrench 5 to 50 Nm (4 to 37 ft lb)
- ♦ Punch
- ♦ VAG 1306 Drip tray

Removing

– Remove ribbed belt
⇒ page D 13-19

– Drain coolant
⇒ page D 19-13

– Unscrew coolant pump mounting bolts through the holes in the pulley and remove coolant pump

Installing

Installation is performed in the reverse order of the removal procedure, when installing, note the following:

– Replace coolant pump O-ring

– Install ribbed belt
⇒ page D 13-19

– Fill with coolant
⇒ page D 19-13

Tightening torques

Bolted joint:	Tightening torque:
Coolant pump to cylinder block	20 Nm (15 ft lb)
Coolant pump pulley	25 Nm (18 ft lb)
Drain plug in coolant line	10 Nm (7 ft lb)

After-run Coolant Thermal switch and After-run Coolant pump, checking

Special tools, testers and auxiliary items

- ♦ VW 1594 Adaptor kit
- ♦ VAG 1527B LED tester
- ♦ VAG 1526 multimeter
- ♦ Wiring diagram

Checking conditions

- ● Fuse 19 OK

Test sequence

– Remove insulation tray
⇒ Repair Group 50

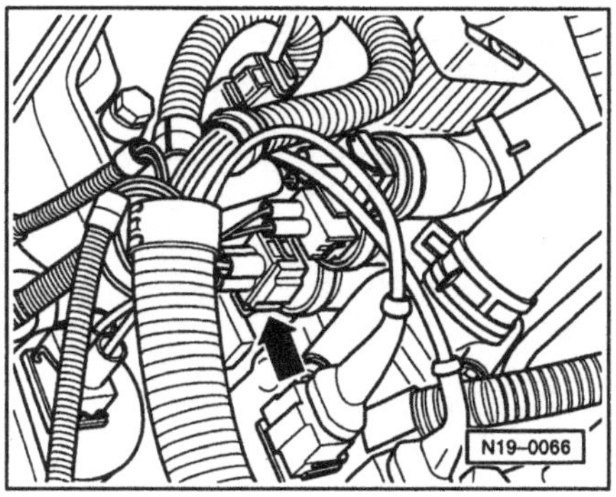

– Disconnect 4-pin harness connector -arrow- from: Engine Coolant Temperature sensor G2 -yellow- and After-run Coolant Thermal switch F95

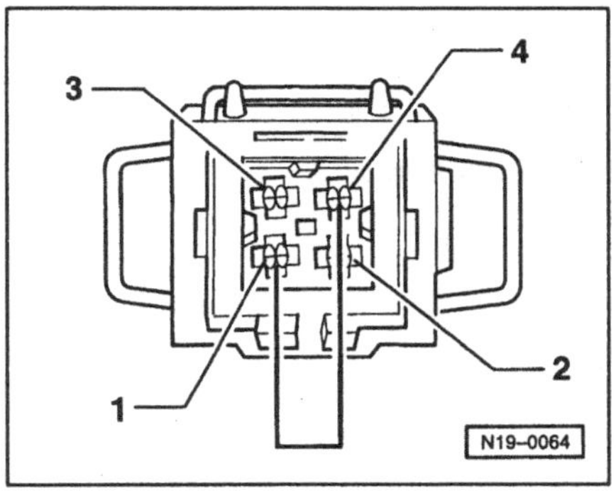

– Bridge connector terminals -1- (grey) and -4- (brown/green) using jumper wires from VW 1594 adaptor kit

- ♦ After-run Coolant pump must run

If pump does not run

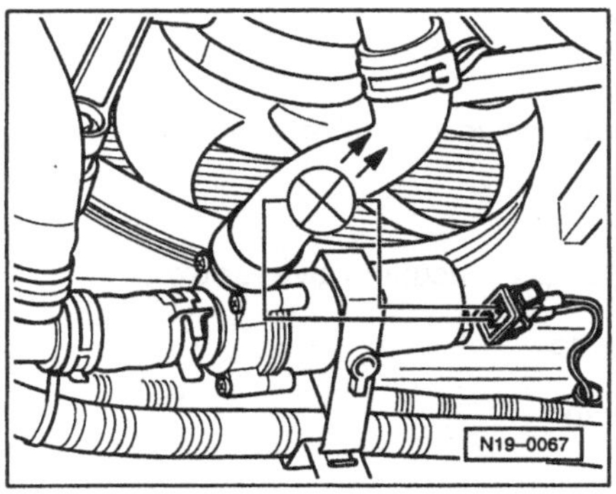

– Disconnect 2-pin harness connector from After-run Coolant pump V51 -1- and connect LED tester to disconnected harness connector using jumper wires from VW 1594 kit

- ♦ LED must light up

If LED lights up (voltage supply OK.):

– Replace After-run coolant pump

If LED does not light up:

– Locate and eliminate open circuit using wiring diagram

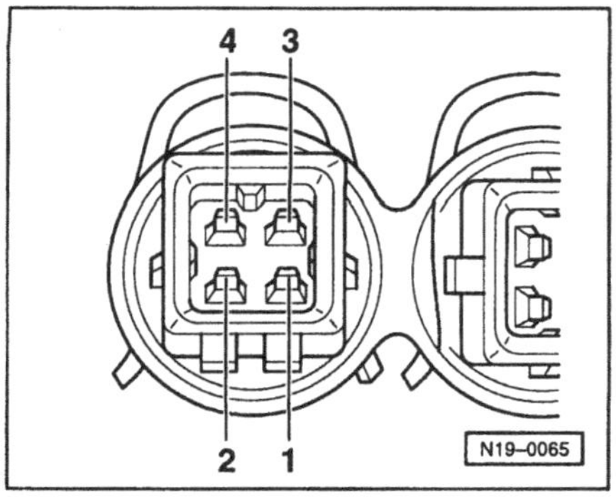

After-run Coolant Thermal switch, resistance checking

◄ – Connect VAG 1526 multimeter between terminals 1 and 4 of Thermal switch using jumper cables from the VW 1594 adaptor kit

♦ Specifications:

below approx. 103 °C (217°F) = ∞ Ω (open)

above approx.: 104 °C (219°F) = 0 Ω (closed)

If specifications are not obtained:

– Replace After-run Coolant Thermal switch F95 / Engine Coolant Temperature sensor G2

Vacuum valve, checking

Special tools, testers and auxiliary items

♦ VAG 1921 Pliers for spring type clips

♦ VAG 1306 Drip tray

♦ US 8012 Hand vacuum pump

– Remove insulation tray:
⇒ Repair group 50

– Drain coolant
⇒ page D 19-13

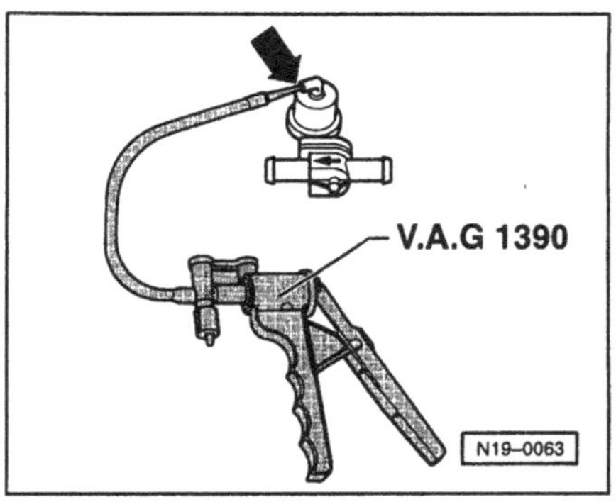

– Disconnect vacuum hose from vacuum valve

– Remove vacuum valve

◄ – Connect US 8012 hand pump to vacuum valve -arrow-

– Operate hand vacuum pump

♦ Vacuum valve must close

If the vacuum valve does not close:

– Replace vacuum valve

Note:

Note installed position (arrow on vacuum valve points to After-run coolant pump).

Fuel supply system components, removing and installing

Notes:

- *Hose connections are secured with either screw, spring or clamp-type clips*
- *Always replace clamp-type clips with screw or spring-type clips*
- *Fuel hoses in engine compartment must only be secured with spring-type clips. The use of clamp or screw-type clips is not permissible*
- *VAG 1921 pliers are recommended for installing spring-type clips*

Observe safety precautions
⇒ page D 20-8

Observe rules of cleanliness
⇒ page D 20-9

Accelerator mechanism, servicing
⇒ page D 20-23

Evaporative emissions system components, servicing
⇒ page D 20-27

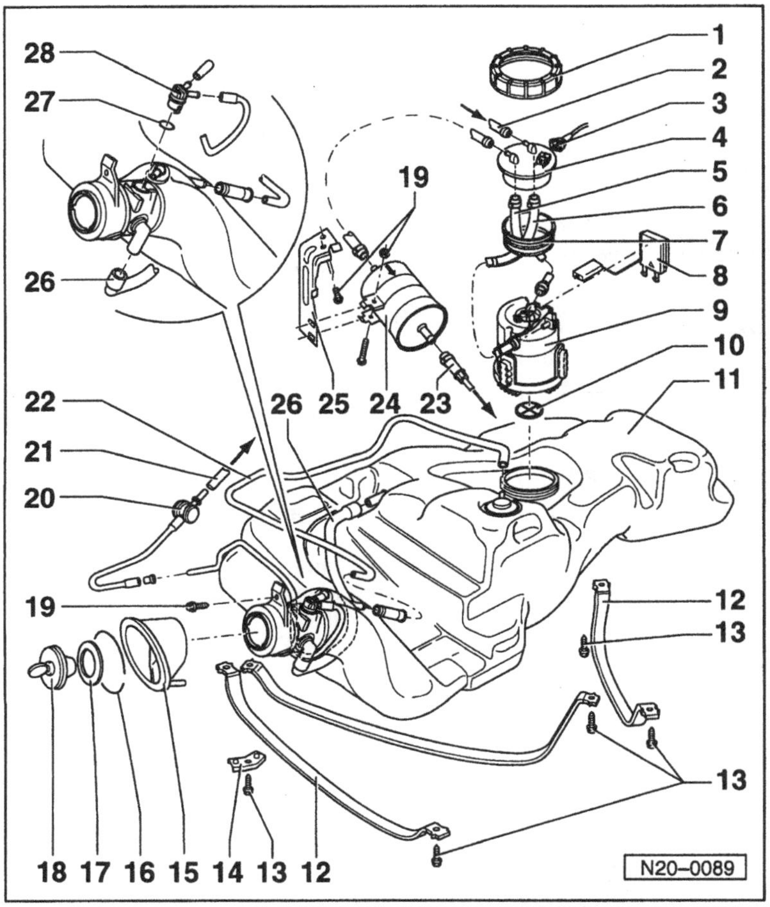

Fuel supply system components, removing and installing

Note:

After all repairs to the fuel supply unit or the fuel gauge sender unit have been carried out, ensure that supply/return hoses do not make contact with the fuel tank which could cause pump noise transference

1 - Collar nut
- remove and install using tool 3217

2 - Fuel return line
- blue
- secure with spring-type clips
- ensure it is securely seated
- from fuel pressure regulator bracket

⇒ Repair Group 24

3 - 4-pin harness connector
- black
- for Fuel Level sensor (G) and Fuel Pump (G6)

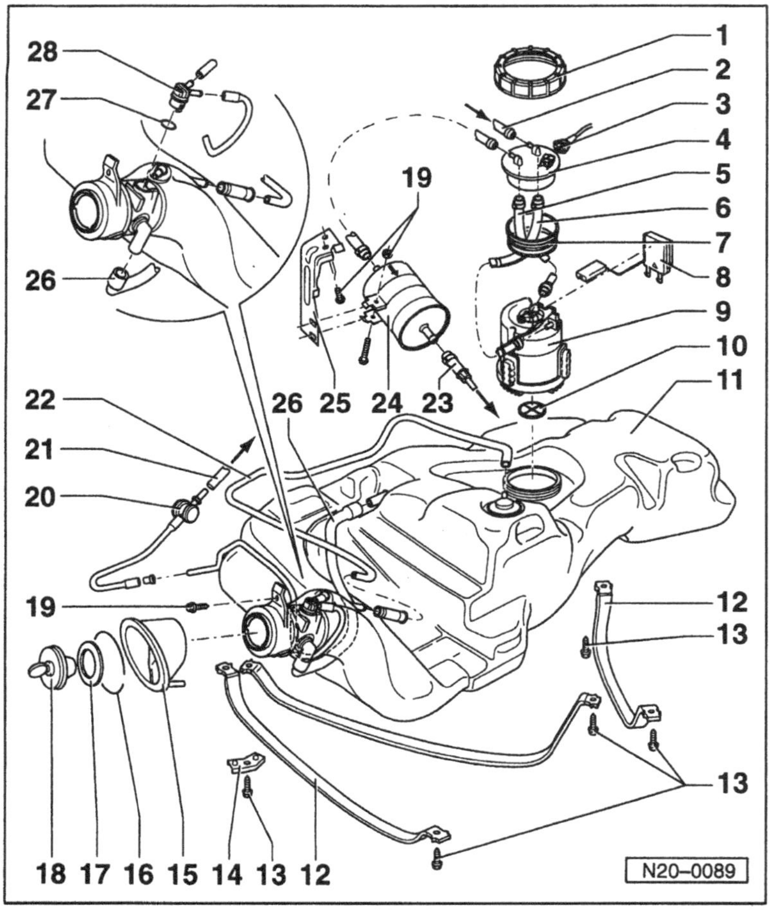

4 - Flange
- note installed position on fuel tank

⇒ page D 20-6, Fig. 1
- underside marked with a "V" (for supply) and an "R" (for return) hoses

5 - Supply hose

6 - Return hose

7 - Sealing ring
- coat with fuel when installing
- replace if damaged

8 - Fuel Level sensor (G)

9 - Fuel delivery unit
- removing and installing:

⇒ page D 20-10
- fuel pump, checking:

⇒ page D 20-15

10 - Strainer
- clean if contaminated

11 - Fuel tank
- removing and installing:

⇒ page D 20-13
- when removing, support using engine/transmission jack VAG 1383 A

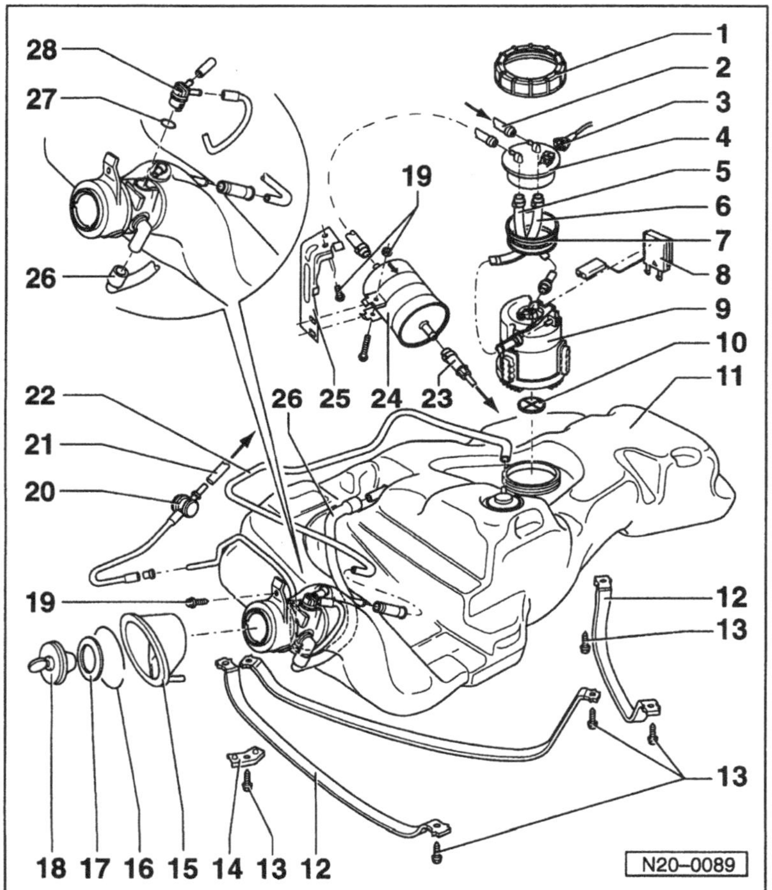

12 - Mounting straps
- note different lengths

13 - 25 Nm (18 ft lb)

14 - Bracket
- for mounting straps

15 - Splash shield

16 - Retaining ring

17 - Gasket
- if damaged; replace together with cap as an assembly

18 - Cap

19 - 10 Nm (7 ft lb)

20 - Check valve
- for fuel tank breathing
- checking:

⇒ page D 20-7, Fig. 3

21 - Breather tube
- to junction piece between EVAP canister and EVAP canister purge regulator valve

⇒ page D 20-28 (item 8)

22 - Breather tube

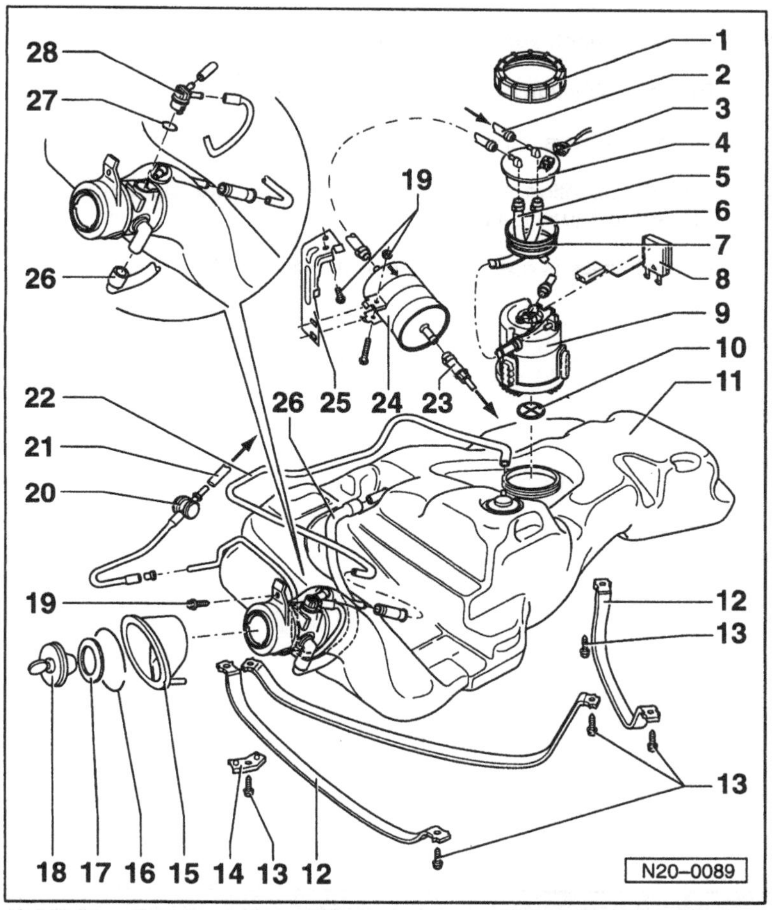

23 - **Supply line**
- black
- mount using spring clips
- ensure it is securely seated
- to fuel supply line on: lower intake manifold

⇒ Repair Group 24

24 - **Fuel filter**
- installed position: -arrow- points in direction of flow

25 - **Bracket**
- for fuel filter

26 - **Breather tube**
- fill vent

27 - **O-ring**

28 - **Gravity/vent valve**
- cannot be removed
  – replace as an assembly together with filler neck
- checking:

⇒ page D 20-6, Fig. 2

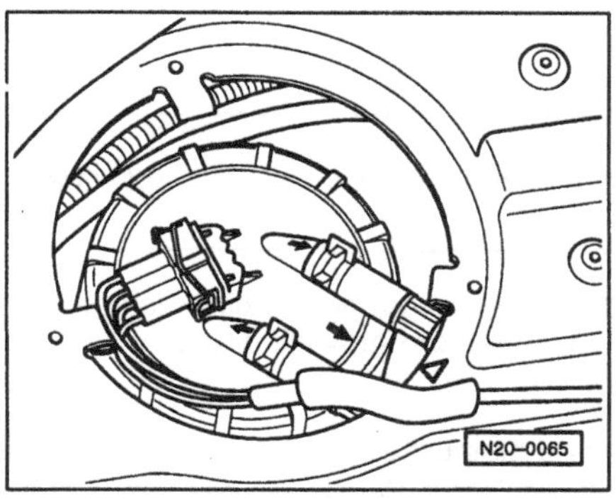

◄ **Fig. 1 Fuel delivery unit/flange, installed position**

Marking on flange must align with marking on fuel tank

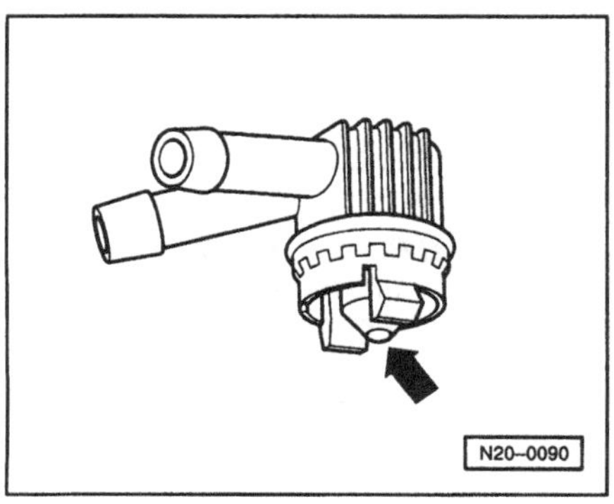

◄ **Fig. 2 Gravity/vent valve, checking**

- Lever in rest position: No Flow
- Lever pushed in direction of arrow: Flow

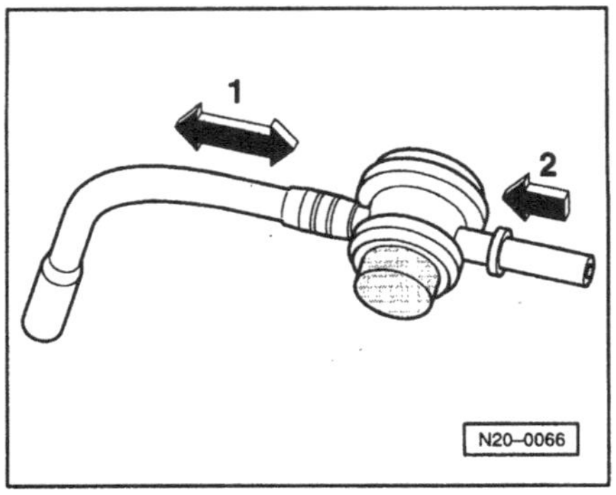

Fig. 3 Check valve, checking

From the direction of the gravity/vent valve:

- check valve is open in both directions of flow: arrow -1-

From the direction of the EVAP canister/EVAP canister purge regulator valve 1 junction piece:

- check valve is open in only one direction of flow: arrow -2-

Safety precautions

> ***WARNING!***
> ***Fire hazard! Do not smoke or have anything in the area that can ignite fuel.***

When removing and installing the fuel gauge sending unit or fuel pump (fuel delivery unit) from a filled or partly filled fuel tank; observe the following:

- Before starting work, provide exhaust extraction close to the inspection opening for the fuel delivery unit in the fuel tank to draw off escaping fumes. If no extraction system is available, use a fan (but DO NOT place fan in path of fumes)
- Wear fuel-resistant disposable protective gloves whenever handling fuel.

> ***CAUTION!***
>
> ***The fuel system is under pressure! Before opening the system, place a rag around the connection and release the pressure by slowly loosening the connection.***

Rules for cleanliness

> ***CAUTION!***
> ***When working on the fuel system, carefully observe the following "Rules for cleanliness".***

- Thoroughly clean the fuel system line and hose connections as well as the surrounding area before disconnecting fuel connections.
- Place removed components on a clean surface and cover them up with plastic sheeting or paper. Don't use fluffy rags or materials that could leave lint!
- If the repair can't be carried out immediately, carefully cover up any opened components or protectively seal them off.

Only install clean components:

- Only unpack replacement parts at the moment of installing
- Do not use parts that have been stored loose or without their protective packaging (e.g. in tool boxes, etc.)

When the fuel system is open:

- Do not work with compressed air if it can be avoided
- Do not move the vehicle if it can be avoided

Fuel delivery unit, removing and installing

Special tools, testers and auxiliary items

- 3217 Collar wrench

Removing

– Observe safety precautions
⇒ page D 20-8

– Switch off ignition

– Disconnect battery ground strap

> ***CAUTION!***
> ***Obtain Anti-theft radio code before disconnecting battery ground strap.***

– Remove driver's seat
⇒ Repair Group 72

– Lift carpeting above the hand brake lever

– Remove cover plate

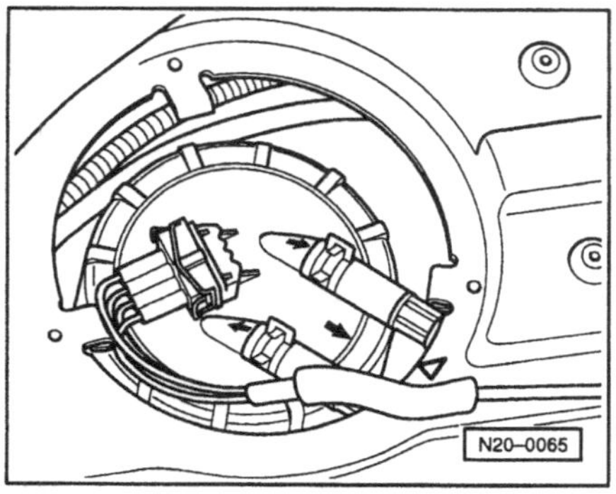

- Disconnect 4-pin harness connector from flange
- Disconnect supply and return lines from flange

> ***CAUTION!***
>
> ***The fuel system is under pressure! Before opening the system, place a rag around the connection and release the pressure by slowly loosening the connection.***

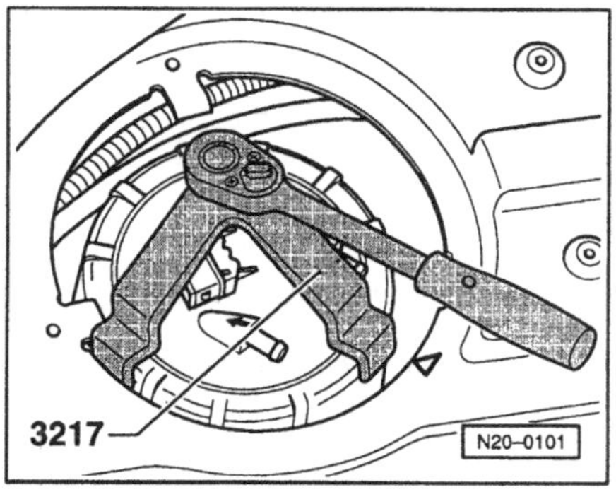

- Remove collar nut using tool 3217
- Pull flange and seal out of opening in fuel tank
- Release delivery unit by turning to the left and then out of the bayonet connection
- Remove the delivery unit

> ***CAUTION!***
>
> ***If the delivery unit contains any fuel, empty it before replacing.***

Installing

Note:

Fuel delivery unit installation is performed in the reverse order of the removal procedure

Installation notes:

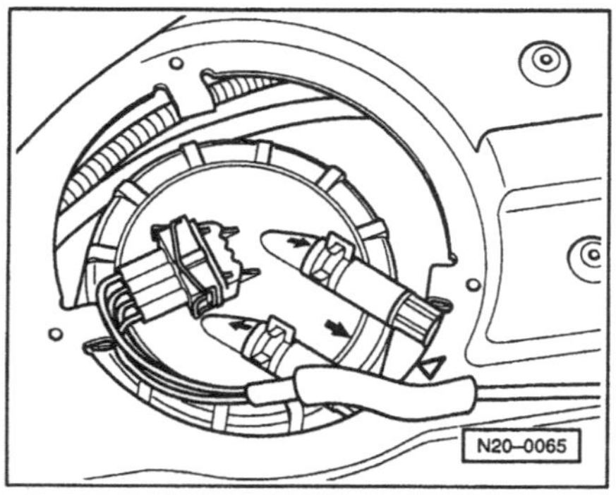

- ♦ *When inserting the fuel delivery unit ensure that the fuel gauge sender is not bent*
- ♦ *Coat flange seal with fuel when installing*
- ♦ *Ensure that fuel lines are correctly located and properly tightened*
- ♦ *Note installed position of fuel delivery unit flange: Marking on flange must align with marking on fuel tank*
- ♦ *Do not interchange the supply and return lines (return line is -blue-)*

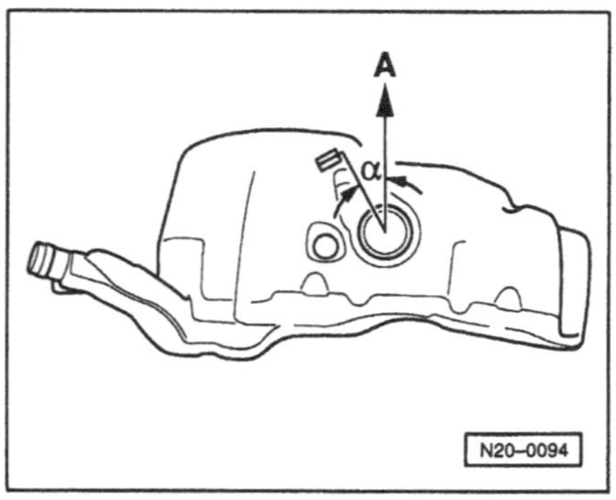

- ♦ *When the fuel delivery unit is correctly installed: Fuel gauge sender float points in direction of travel A:* α = 25 to 35°

Fuel tank, removing and installing

Special tools, testers and auxiliary items

- 3217 Collar wrench
- VAG 1383 A Engine/transmission jack

Removing

Observe safety precautions
⇒ page D 20-8

- Switch off ignition
- Disconnect battery ground strap

> ***CAUTION!***
> ***Obtain Anti-theft radio code before disconnecting battery ground strap.***

- Drain fuel tank and clean area around filler neck
- Remove retaining ring and splash shield from filler neck and unscrew mounting bolt
- Disconnect fuel tank mounting straps
  - support fuel tank using VAG 1383 A engine/transmission jack

- Lower jack just enough to allow pulling the supply lines, return lines and connector from the flange

> ***CAUTION!***
> ***The fuel system is under pressure! Before opening the system, place a rag around the connection and release the pressure by slowly loosening the connection.***

Note:

For vehicles with auxiliary heating, also disconnect the additional fuel lines mounted between the supply and return lines.

- Lower fuel tank

Installing

Install in reverse order of removal procedure but note the following:

- Route breather hoses free of kinks
- Ensure that fuel hoses are correctly located and tight
- Do not interchange the supply and return lines
  (return hose is -blue-)

Fuel pumps, checking

Special tools, testers and auxiliary items

- Fluke 83 Multimeter
- VAG 1348/3A Remote control with VAG 1348/3-2 Adaptor cable
- VAG 1466 Fuel analyzer
- VAG 1527B LED tester
- VW 1594 Adaptor kit
- 3217 Collar nut wrench
- VAG 1318 Pressure tester
- VAG 1318/1 Hose
- 1318/10 Adaptor
- 1318/11 Adaptor
- Measuring container
- Wiring diagram

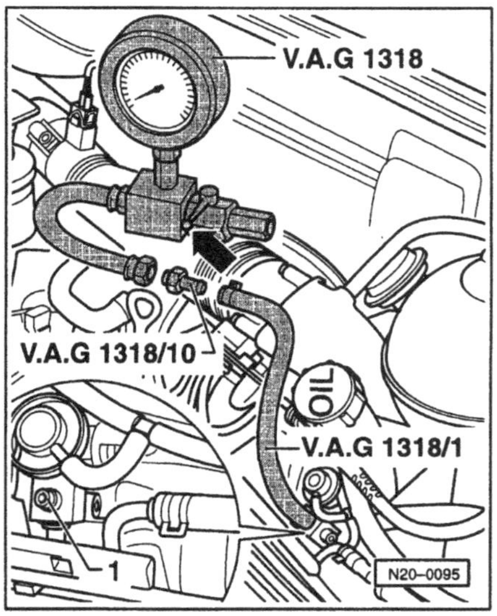

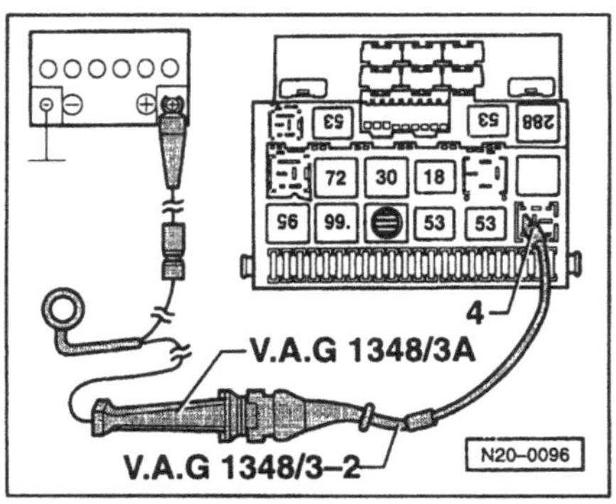

Checking conditions

- Battery voltage: 11.5 Volts minimum
- Fuse 18 OK

◄ – Remove sealing plug -1- on fuel pressure regulator bracket

– Connect VAG 1318 pressure gauge to test connection using VAG 1318/10 adapter and hose VAG 1318/1

- The pressure gauge lever must be closed (-arrow- at right angle to direction of flow)

> ***CAUTION!***
>
> ***The fuel system is under pressure! Before opening the system, place a rag around the connection and release the pressure by slowly loosening the connection.***

– Start engine and let idle

– Check fuel pressure

- Specification: approx. 2.5 bar (36 psi)

If fuel pressure does not build-up

– Switch off ignition

– Remove cover in front of fuse/relay panel

◄ – Remove fuel pump relay from fuse relay panel position 12

Notes:

- *If tools are required to pull relays or control modules out of the relay panel, first disconnect battery ground.*
- *Obtain radio Anti-theft code before disconnecting battery ground strap.*

– Connect remote control VAG 1348/3A between terminal 4 and battery positive (+) using adapter cable VAG 1348/3-2

– Operate remote control

If fuel pressure builds-up:

– Check activation of fuel pump relay

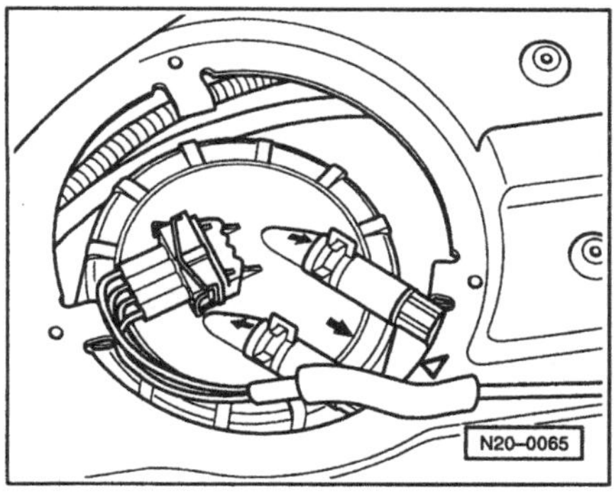

If fuel pressure is not built-up:

– Remove driver's seat
⇒ Repair Group 72

– Lift carpeting above the hand brake lever

– Remove access plate

– Disconnect 4-pin harness connector from fuel tank flange

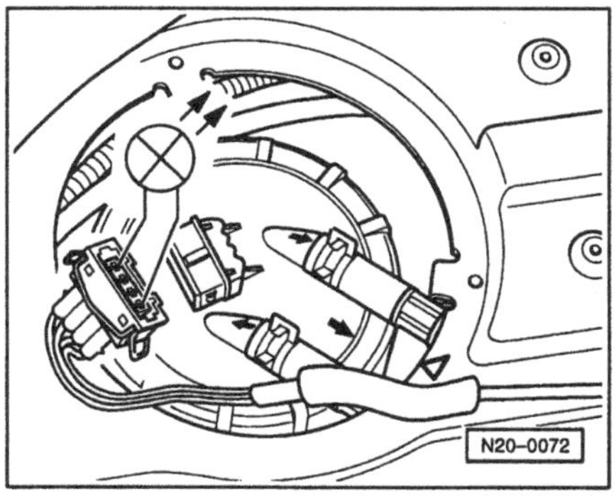

– Connect VAG 1527B LED tester to connector outer terminals using jumper wires from VW 1594 adaptor kit

– Operate remote control

- LED tester must light up

If LED does not light up:

– Locate and eliminate open circuit using wiring diagram

If LED lights up (voltage supply OK):

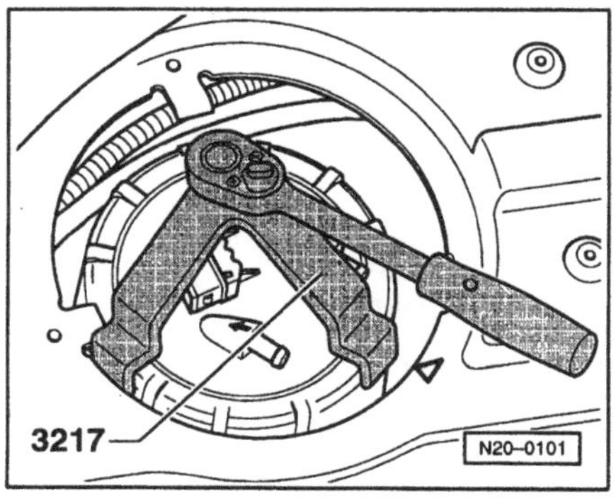

– Unscrew collar nut using 3217 tool

– Check if wire between flange and fuel pump is connected

If no open circuit can be found:

- Replace faulty fuel pump
⇒ page D 20-10

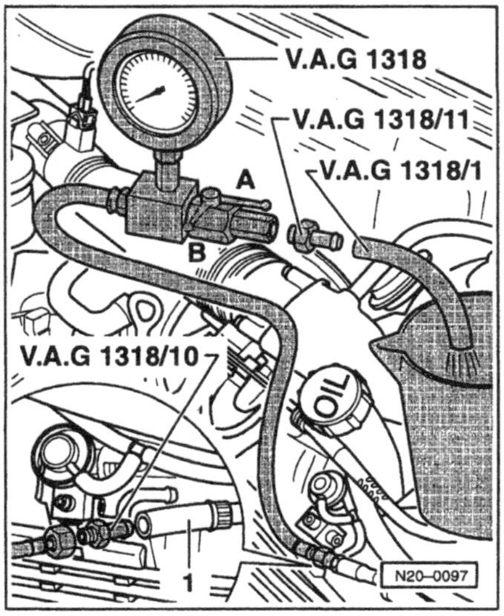

Delivery rate, checking

- Voltage supply OK
- VAG 1348/3A Remote control connected

– Remove filler cap from fuel tank filler neck

> ***CAUTION!***
>
> ***The fuel system is under pressure! Before opening the system, place a rag around the connection and release the pressure by slowly loosening the connection.***

– Disconnect fuel supply line -1- from fuel pipe

– Connect the VAG 1318 pressure gauge to fuel supply line -1- using 1318/10 adapter

– Push VAG 1318/1 hose onto adapter VAG 1318/11 on the pressure gauge and hold hose in a measuring container

– Open pressure gauge cut-off tap

♦ lever must point in direction of flow -A-

– Operate VAG 1348/3A remote control and slowly close lever until pressure gauge shows 3 bar (44 psi), once achieved, do not move the lever any further

– Empty measuring container

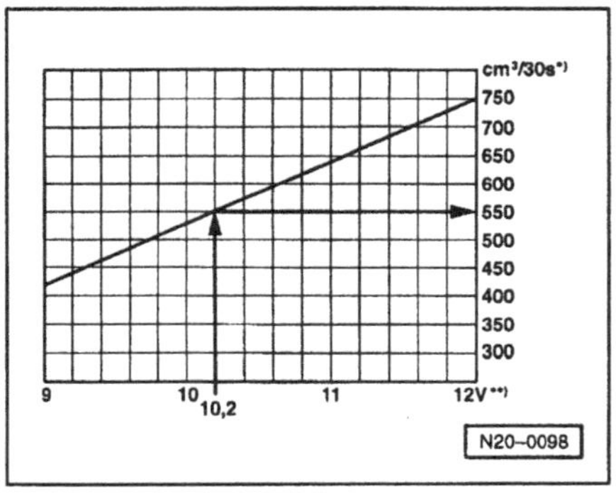

– Measure battery voltage using Fluke 83 multimeter

– Operate remote control for 30 seconds

– Compare the quantity of fuel delivered with specification.

*) Minimum delivery in cc's per 30 seconds

**) Voltage at fuel pump (running) with engine not running

(approx. 2 volts less than battery voltage)

Example:

For this example, 12.2 volts was measured at the battery. If voltage at the pump is approx. 2 volts less than battery voltage, this equates to a minimum delivery of 550 cc's in 30 seconds

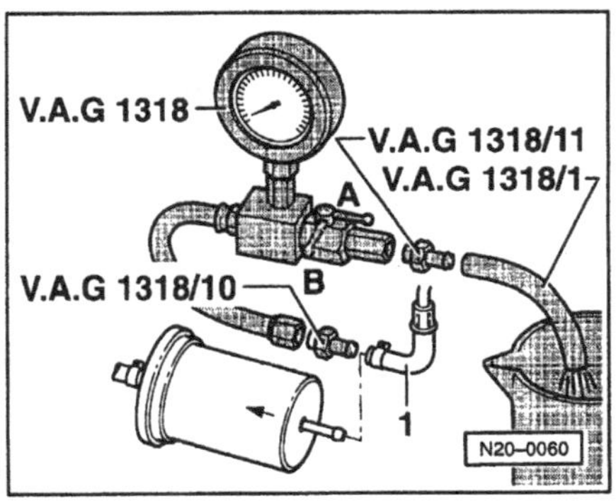

If the minimum delivery rate is not obtained:

– Check fuel lines for possible restrictions, kinks or blockages

– Disconnect supply line -1- from fuel filter inlet

– Connect VAG 1318 pressure gauge to hose using 1318/10 adaptor

– Repeat delivery rate check

If minimum delivery rate is now obtained:

– Replace fuel filter

If minimum delivery rate is still not obtained:

– Remove fuel delivery unit and check strainer for contaminants ⇒ page D 20-10

If no malfunctions detected up to this point, fuel pump is faulty

– Replace fuel delivery unit ⇒ page D 20-10

If minimum delivery rate has been attained but you still suspect an intermittent fuel supply system malfunction:

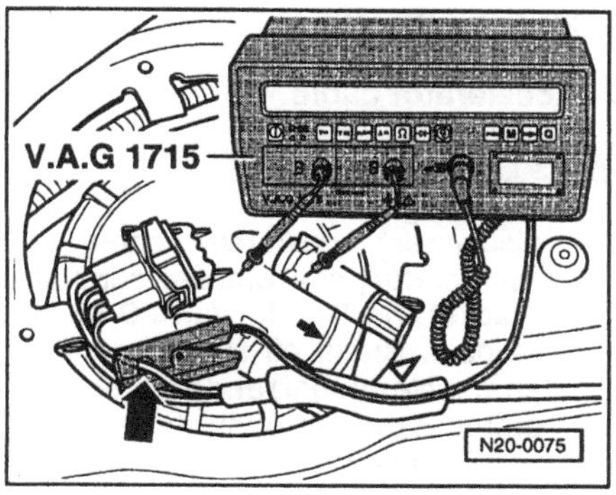

– Reconnect all disconnected fuel lines

– Remove driver's seat ⇒ Repair Group 72

– Lift carpet above the hand brake lever

– Remove access plate

◄ – Connect Fluke 83 multimeter to red/yellow harness wire with Fluke current measuring adaptor

– Start engine and let idle

– Measure fuel pump amperage draw

 ♦ Specification: 8 amps maximum

Note: *If fuel system malfunction is intermittent, perform check during a test drive, using a 2nd technician to read the measuring instruments.*

If amperage draw is exceeded, fuel pump is faulty

– Replace fuel delivery unit page ⇒ D 20-10

Fuel pump check valve, checking

♦ VAG 1348/3A Remote control connected

♦ VAG 1318 Pressure gauge connected to fuel supply line

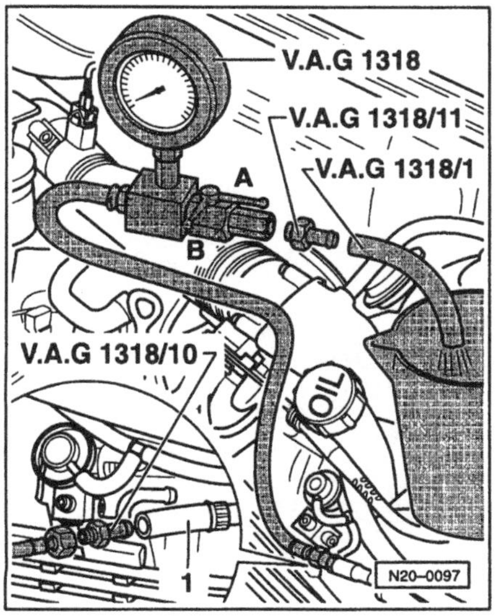

Note: *This setup checks the entire fuel supply line from the fuel delivery unit to the point at which the VAG 1318 pressure gauge is connected.*

◄ – Close pressure gauge tap (position -B-, lever at right angle to direction of flow)

– Operate remote control at short intervals until a pressure of approx. 3 bar (44 psi) has built-up

– If pressure builds up too high, lower excess by carefully opening the tap

> ***CAUTION!***
> ***Danger of fuel spray when opening pressure tap. Hold open end of pressure gauge over a suitable container to catch the overspray.***

– Observe pressure drop

 ♦ After 10 minutes pressure must not drop below 2.2 bar (32 psi)

– Check line connections for leaks and/or replace fuel delivery unit, if necessary ⇒ page D 20-10

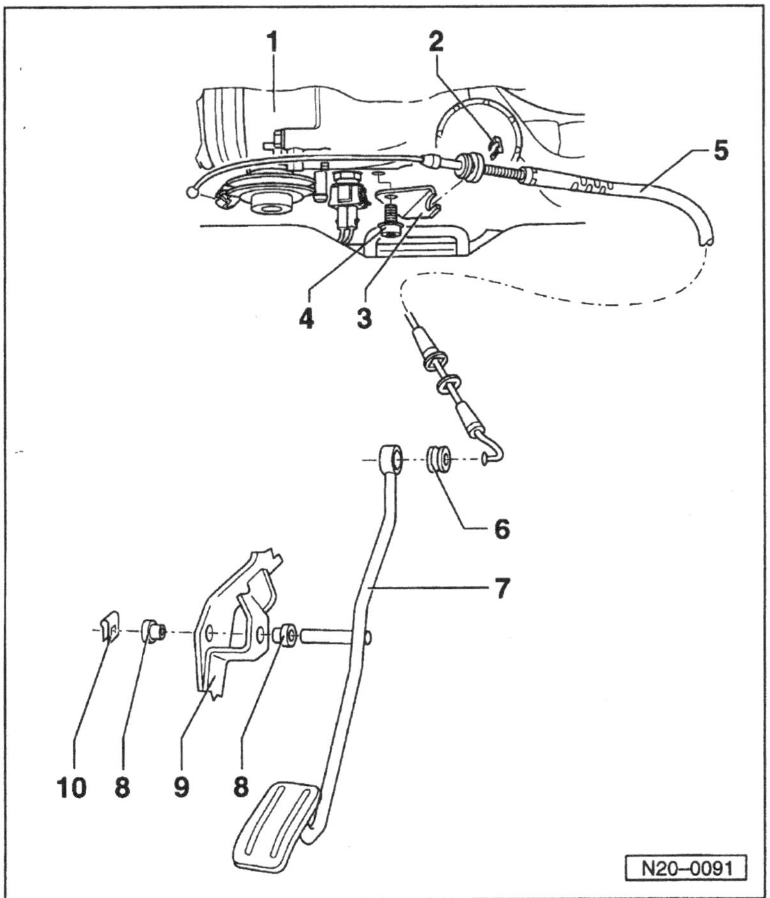

Accelerator mechanism, servicing

1 - **Throttle Valve Control Module J338**

2 - **Tab**

3 - **Support bracket**
- ♦ for accelerator cable

4 - **25 Nm (18 ft lb)**

5 - **Accelerator cable**
- ♦ adjusting:

⇒ page D 20-25

- ♦ removing:
  - – disconnect accelerator cable at accelerator pedal bracket, support bracket and Throttle Valve Control Module. Break off spreader clips (in vehicle interior) and pass accelerator cable through to engine compartment
- ♦ Do not reuse damaged accelerator cable, always replace

6 - **Rubber bushing**

7 - **Accelerator pedal**

8 - **Bushing**

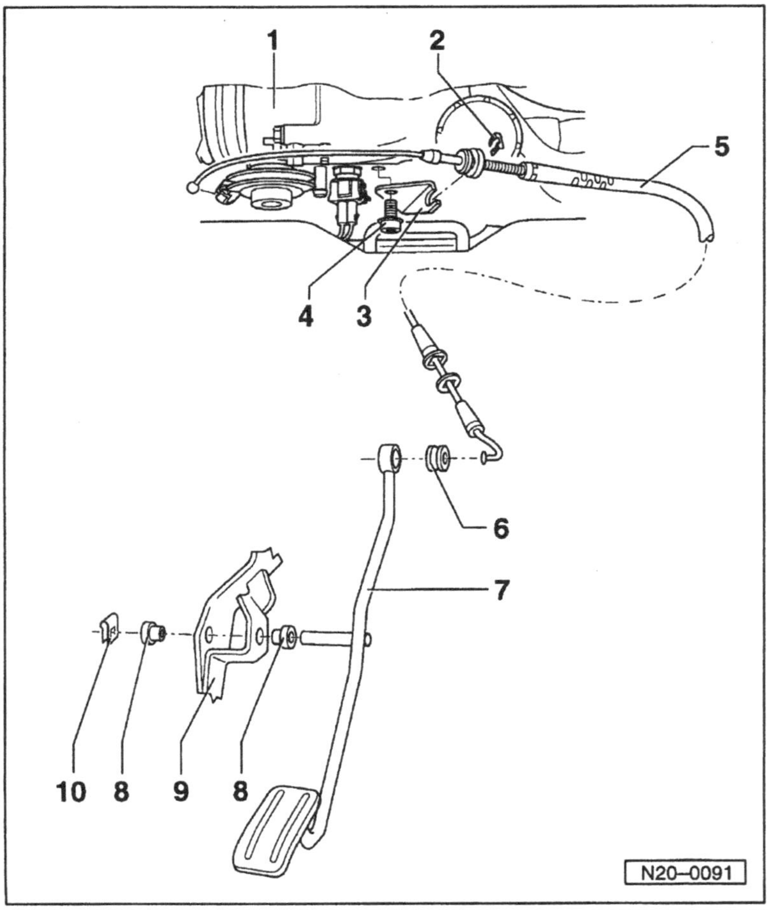

9 - **Accelerator pedal bracket**

10 - **Circlip**

Throttle cable, adjusting

Vehicles with manual transmission

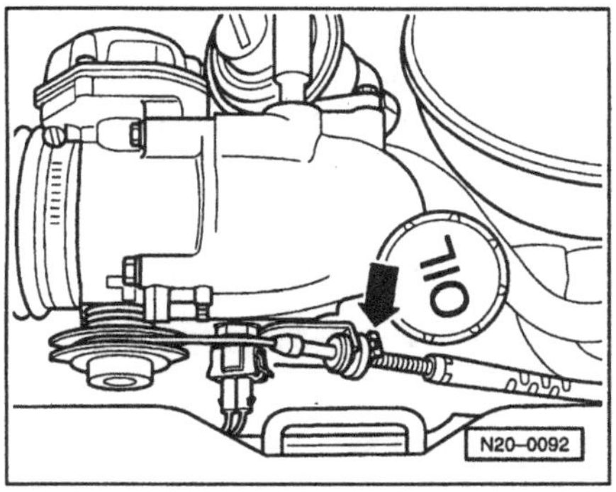

◄ – Adjust throttle cable by moving support bracket retainer -arrow- until the Wide Open Throttle position is obtained at the throttle body lever

Vehicles with automatic transmission

Special tools, testers and auxiliary items

- ♦ Fluke 83 Multimeter
- ♦ VW 1594 Adaptor kit
- ♦ 11 mm Spacer

Work sequence

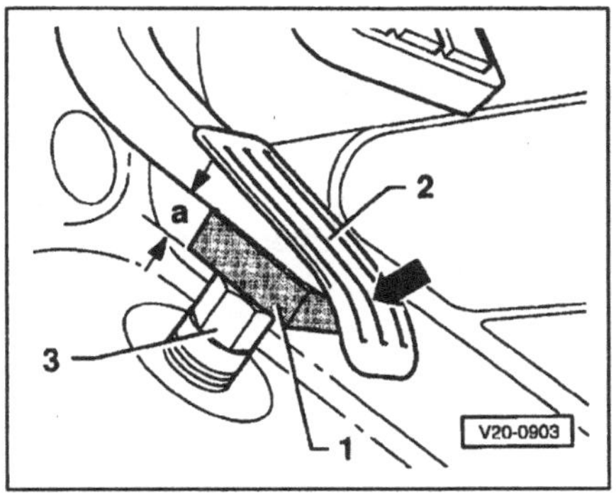

◄ – Clamp spacer -1- (a = 11 mm) between accelerator pedal -2- and stop -3- and hold accelerator pedal in this position

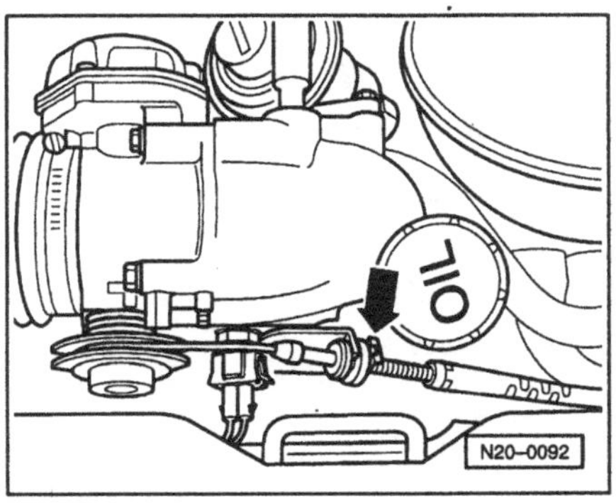

◄ – Fully open throttle body by pulling on outer cable and fix in this position using retainer -arrow-

– Release accelerator pedal

– Disconnect 2-pin harness connector from Kick Down switch F8 in engine compartment on bulkhead

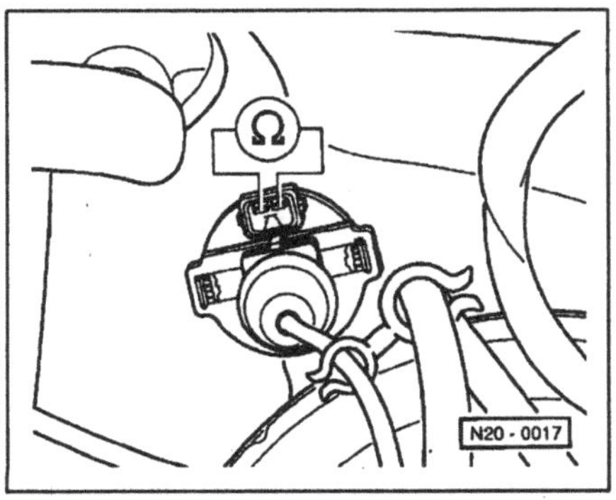

◄ – Connect multimeter to kick-down switch using jumper wires from VW 1594 adaptor kit

– Measure switch resistance

- ♦ Specification: ∞ Ω (open)

– Slowly move accelerator pedal in direction of Wide Open Throttle

Shortly after kick-down pressure point, resistance must drop to 0 Ω

- ♦ At this point, the pedal must be just off the stop

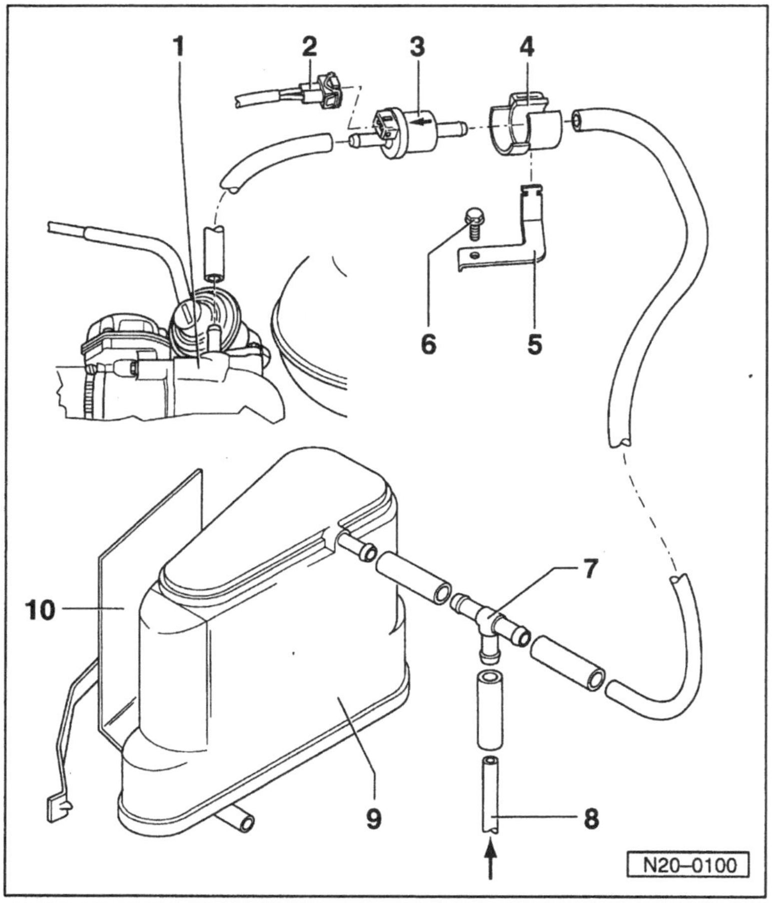

Evaporative Emissions system components, removing and installing

1 - Connection
- between intake manifold and Throttle Valve Control Module J338

2 - 2-pin harness connector
- green
- for EVAP canister purge regulator valve

3 - EVAP canister purge regulator valve N80
- when engine is warm, valve will be activated by ECM J220 (pulsed)
- installed position: arrow points in direction of flow
- checking:

⇒ Repair Group 01; Output Diagnostic Test mode

4 - Retaining ring
- for EVAP canister purge regulator valve

5 - Retainer
- for retaining ring

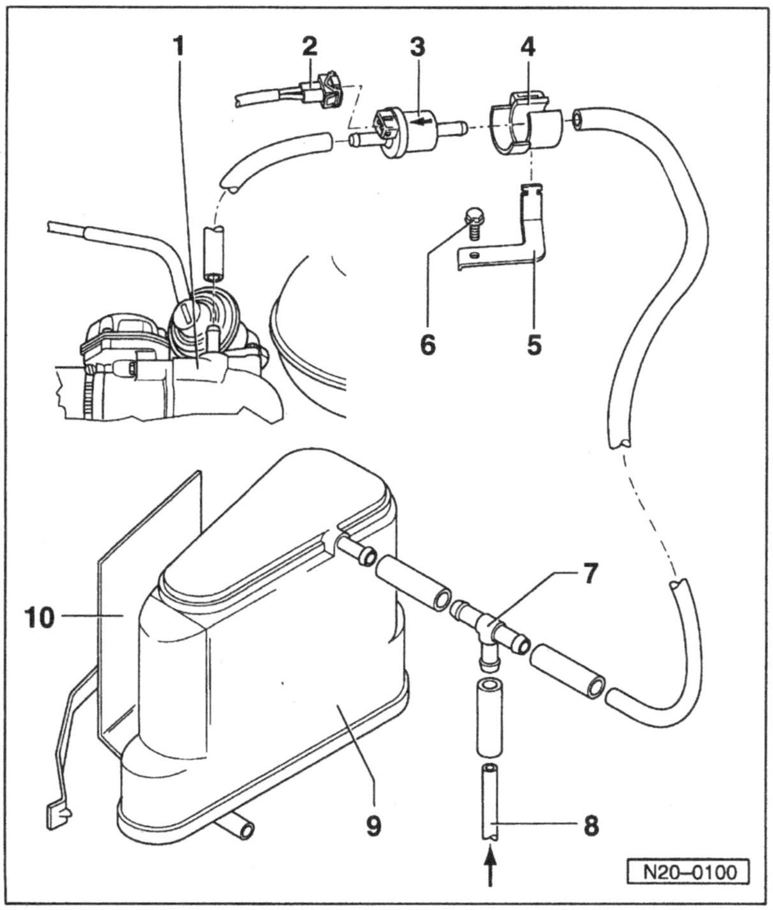

6 - 10 Nm (7 ft lb)

7 - Junction piece

8 - Vent line
- from fuel tank check valve

⇒ page D 20-4 (item 20)

9 - EVAP canister
- located in front left wheel housing
- remove left front wheel housing liner to obtain access

10 - Bracket
- for EVAP canister

Exhaust system components, removing and installing

Notes:

- *After performing work on the exhaust system, ensure that the system is not under tension and that there is sufficient clearance to the body. If necessary, loosen clamps and mufflers and align exhaust pipes such that there is sufficient clearance to the body over the full length of the exhaust and the supports are uniformly loaded.*
- *Replace self-locking nuts*

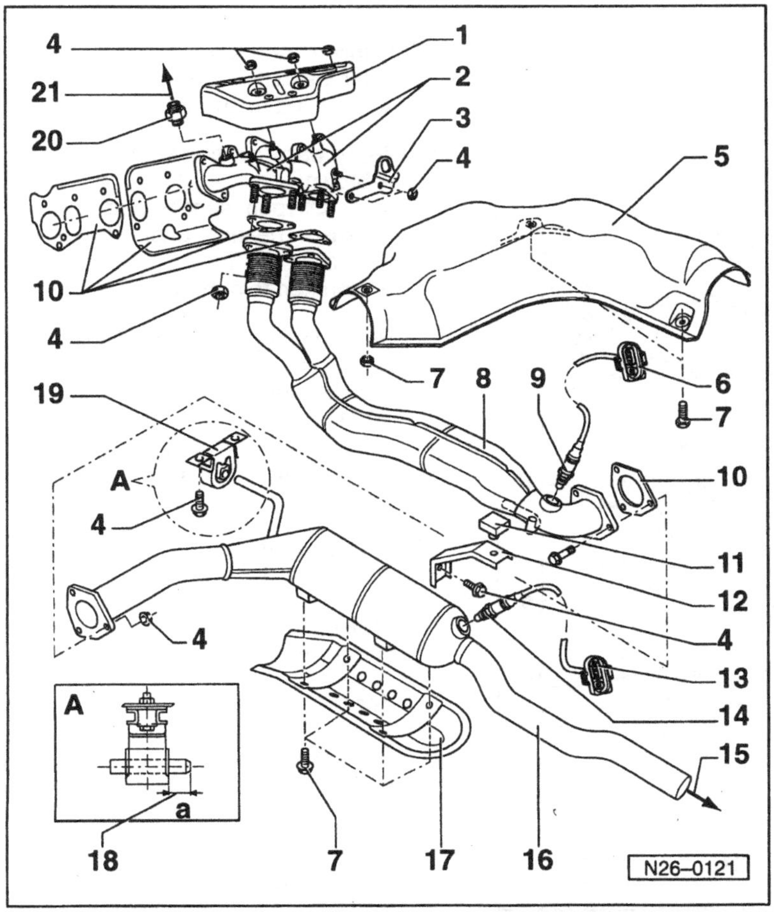

Exhaust system components, removing and installing

Note:

Align exhaust system longitudinally to maintain dimension -a-.

1 - Heat shield
- removing:
  - first remove pipe between EGR valve and exhaust manifold
- page D 26-10 (item 13)

2 - Exhaust manifold
- 2 piece

3 - Lifting eye

4 - M8 - 25 Nm (18 ft lb)
M10 - 40 Nm (30 ft lb)
- replace

5 - Heat shield
- for Three-Way catalyst

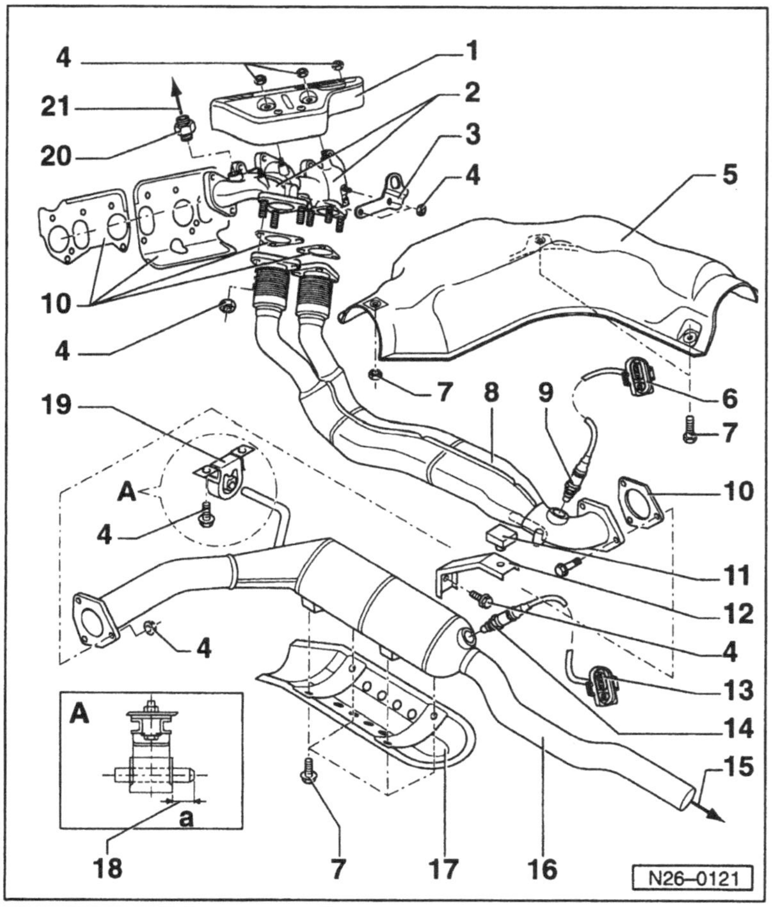

6 - 4-pin harness connector
- black
- mounted to sub-frame
- for Oxygen sensor and Oxygen sensor heating

⇒ Repair Group 24

7 - 10 Nm (7 ft lb)

8 - Front exhaust pipe

9 - Heated Oxygen sensor G39
- 50 Nm (37 ft lb)
- only grease threads using "G5"; do not allow "G5" to enter the sensor slots
- checking:

⇒ Repair Group 01

- Oxygen sensor and Oxygen sensor control, checking:

⇒ Repair Group 24

- Oxygen sensor heating, checking:

⇒ Repair Group 24

10 - Gasket
- replace

11 - Insulation rubber
- for front exhaust pipe (item 8)

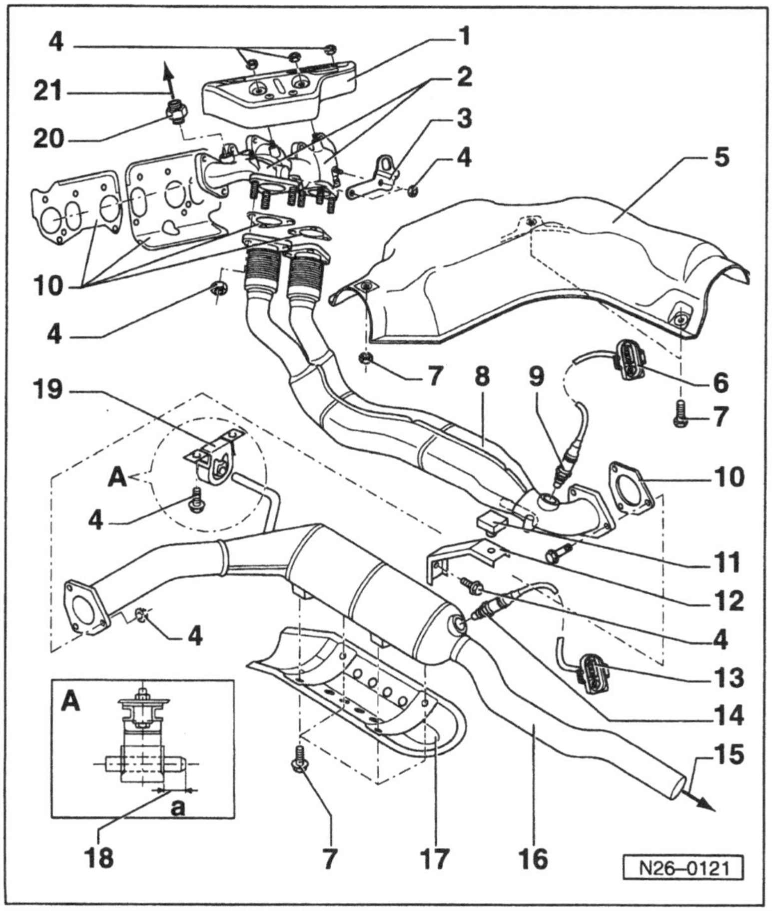

12 - Support bracket
- for insulation rubber
- mounted to sub-frame

13 - 4–pin harness connector
- brown
- for Oxygen sensor and Oxygen sensor heating after Three-Way catalyst
- mounted to sub-frame

14 - Heated Oxygen sensor 2 G108
- 50 Nm (37 ft lb)
- installation location: in Three-Way catalyst
- only grease threads using "G5"; do not allow "G5" to enter the sensor slots

15 - to front muffler

⇒ page D 26-7 (item 11)

16 - Three-Way Catalytic converter

17 - Heat shield

18 - Dimension -a-
- -a- = 10 mm minimum

19 - Mounting
- replace if damaged
- note installed position

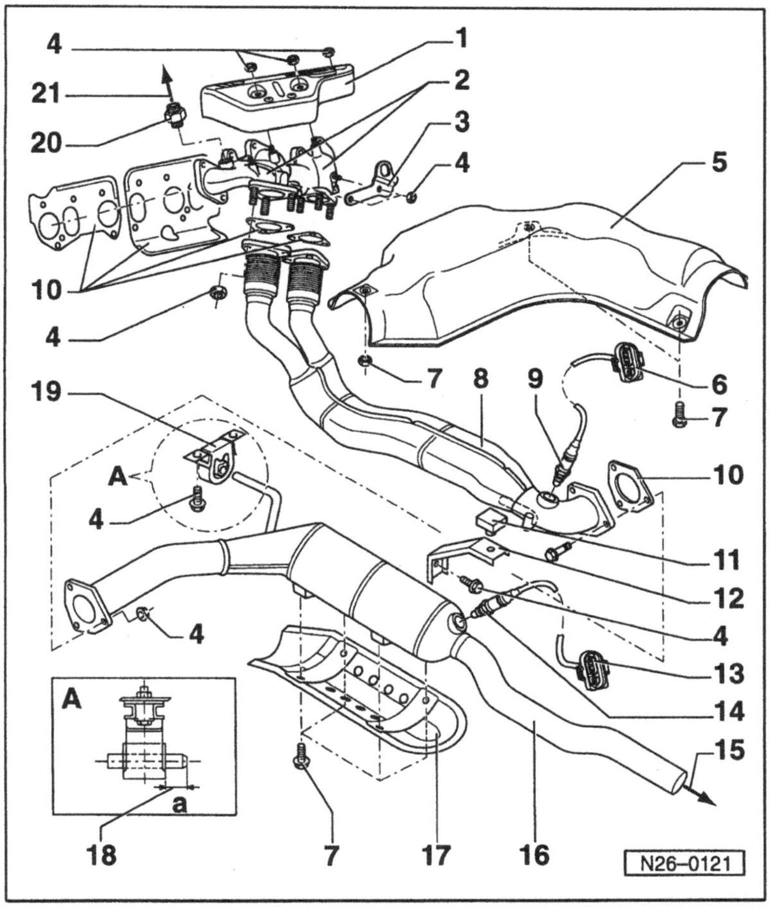

20 - **Connection**
- 35 Nm (26 ft lb)
- for pipe between EGR valve and exhaust manifold

21 - **to pipe**
- for exhaust gas outlet

⇒ page D 26-10 (item 13)

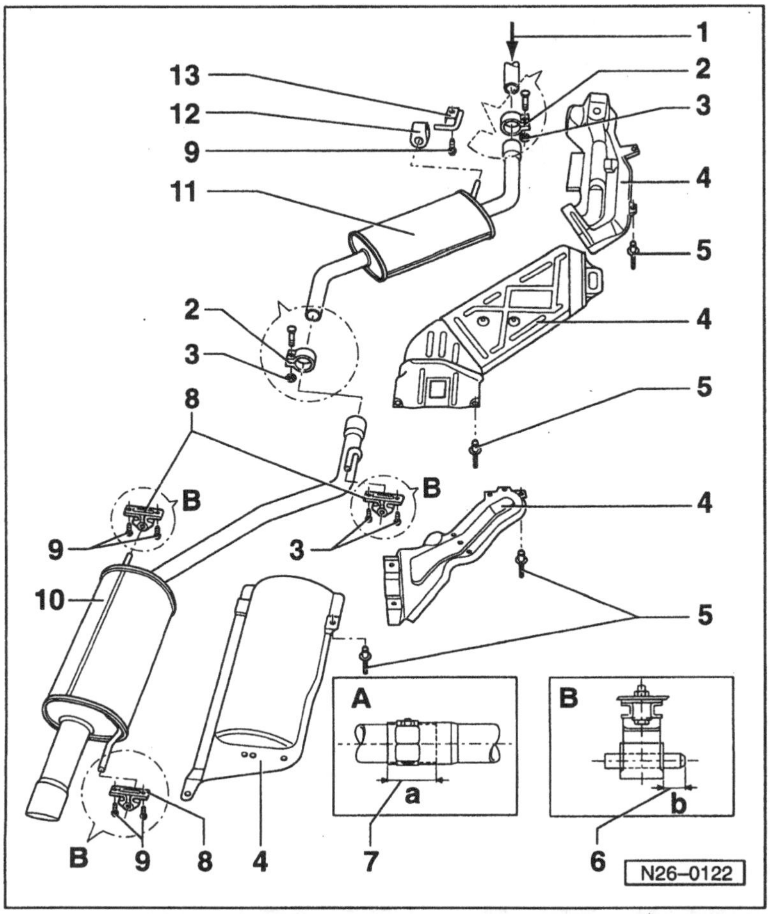

Muffler system and attachments, removing and installing

Note:

Align exhaust system longitudinally to maintain dimensions -a- and -b-.

1 - **from Three-Way catalyst**
⇒ page D 26-4 (item 16)

2 - **Clamp**

3 - **40 Nm (30 ft lb)**
- replace

4 - **Heat shield**

5 - **Pop rivet**

6 - **Dimension -b-**
- -b- =10 mm minimum

7 - **Dimension -a-**
- -a- = 50 ± 5 mm

8 - **Mounting**
- replace if damaged
- note installed position

9 - **25 Nm (18 ft lb)**

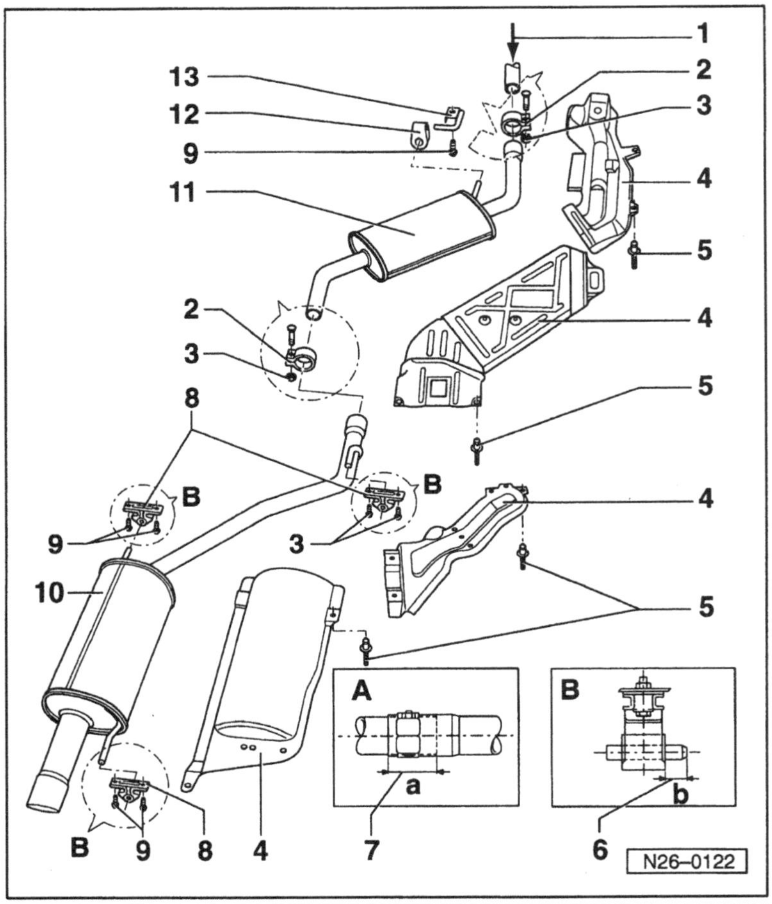

10 - **Rear muffler**

11 - **Front muffler**

12 - **Retaining ring**
- replace if damaged

13 - **Retainer**

Exhaust Gas Recirculation (EGR) system, overview

Notes:

- *Function/control of the EGR system is checked via Motronic On Board Diagnostic system.*
- *Components marked with an * are checked via On Board Diagnostic*

⇒ Repair Group 01
- *Components marked with ** are checked via Output Diagnostic Test Mode*

⇒ Repair Group 01
- *Always replace sealing rings and gaskets when assembling*
- *Vacuum lines and hose connections must be leak-tight*
- *Vacuum lines must not be blocked or kinked*

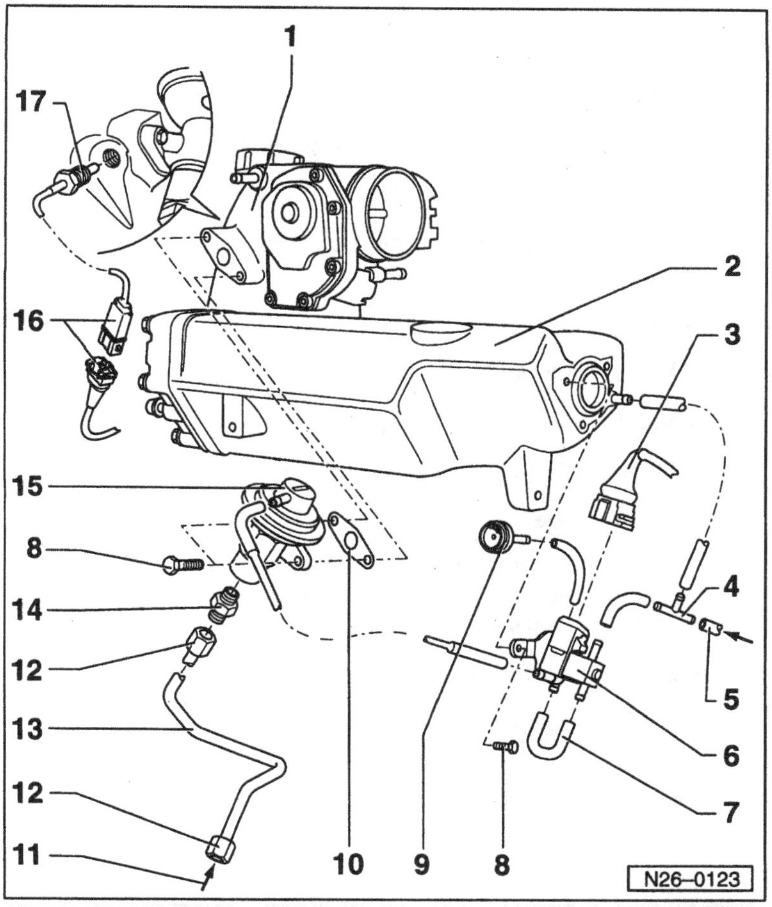

1 - Connection
- between intake manifold and Throttle Valve Control Module J338

2 - Intake manifold

3 - 2-pin harness connector
- brown
- for EGR valve N18

4 - Junction piece

5 - Vacuum line
- from Positive Crankcase Ventilation valve

⇒ Repair Group 24

6 - Exhaust Gas Recirculation valve N18*/**
- two-way valve
- checking:

⇒ Repair Group 01

7 - Connecting hose

8 - 10 Nm (7 ft lb)

9 - Air Cleaner
- can cause engine running problems if dirty

10 - Gasket
- replace

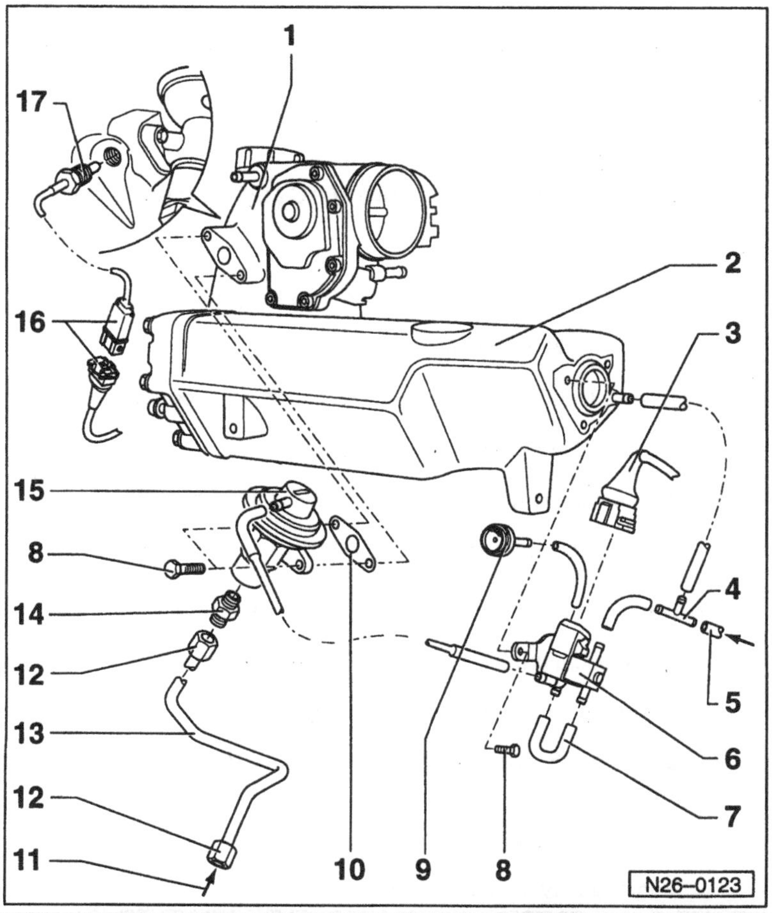

11 - from connection on exhaust manifold
- for exhaust gas inlet

⇒ page D 26-5, Item 20

12 - 30 Nm (22 ft lb)

13 - Pipe
- for exhaust gas intake

14 - Connection
- 35 Nm (26 ft lb)

15 - EGR valve
- checking

⇒ page D 26-11

16 - 2-pin harness connector
- black
- for exhaust gas recirculation temperature sensor G98

17 - EGR temperature sensor G98*
- 20 Nm (15 ft lb)

Exhaust Gas Recirculation (EGR) valve, checking

Special tools, testers and auxiliary items

- US 8012 Hand vacuum pump
- VAG 1551 Scan Tool or VAG 1552 Scan Tool with VAG 1551/3 adaptor cable

Checking conditions

- Vacuum lines and hose connections leak-tight
- Vacuum lines not blocked/kinked
- Engine oil temperature 50°C (122°F)minimum

Test sequence

– Connect VAG 1551 Scan Tool (VAG 1552) and select "address word 01" engine electronics with engine idling
⇒ Repair Group 01

Rapid data transfer	HELP
Select function XX	

◄ Display will appear as shown

– Press 0 and 8 buttons to select Function 08: "Read measuring value block." Press Q button to confirm input

Read measuring value block	HELP
Input display group number XX	

◄ Display will appear as shown

– Press 0 and 1 buttons to select "Display group number"

– Press Q button to confirm input

Read measuring value block 1			→
1	2	3	4

◄ Display will appear as shown (1 to 4 = display zones)

Only continue with check when

- engine coolant temp. is above 50 °C (122°F) (display zone 2)

– Press C button

– Press 0 and 2 buttons to select "Display group number"

– Press Q button to confirm input

Read measuring value block 2			→
1	2	3	4

◄ Display will appear as shown (1 to 4 = display zones)

– Read off figure shown in display zone 4

- Specification: EGRn. active (EGR system not active)

– Increase engine speed

– Read off figure displayed in display zone 4

- specification: EGR active (EGR system active)

– Disconnect vacuum hose from EGR valve

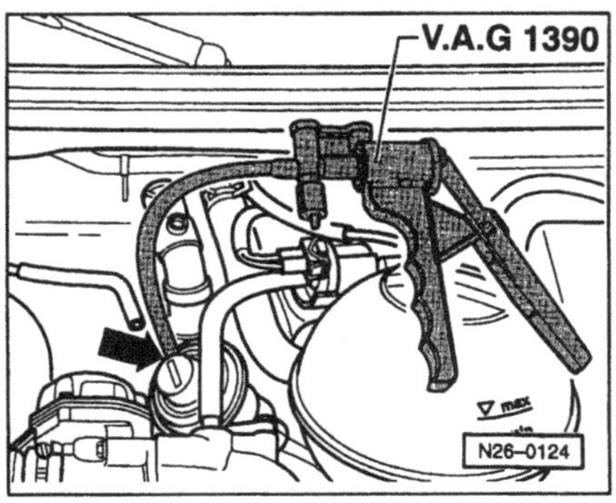

◄ – Connect US 8012 hand vacuum pump to valve -arrow- using piece of hose

– Operate hand vacuum pump

- idle quality must noticeably deteriorate

If NO:

- Press → button
- Press 0 and 6 buttons to select Function 06 “End output”
- Press Q button to confirm input
- Switch OFF ignition
- Check pipes and connections for blockage, clean if necessary, replace EGR valve if necessary
- Check EVAP canister purge regulator valve activation
⇒ Repair Group 01
- Check DTC memory
⇒ Repair Group 01

Secondary Air Injection system, function

The Secondary Air Injection system blows in air behind the exhaust valve for 65 seconds during the cold start (15 to 35°C [59 to 95°F]coolant temperature). This produces an oxygen–rich exhaust gas, causes afterburning, and reduces the catalyst heat-up time. Activation occurs via the Motronic ECM J220 via the Secondary Air Injection pump relay (J229) to Secondary Air Injection inlet valve (N112, change-over valve) and combi-valve. Additionally, after each engine start (up to max. 85 °C (185°F) engine temperature), the Secondary Air Injection system will (after a 20 second delay), switch in for 5 seconds during idle and is checked by On Board Diagnostic.

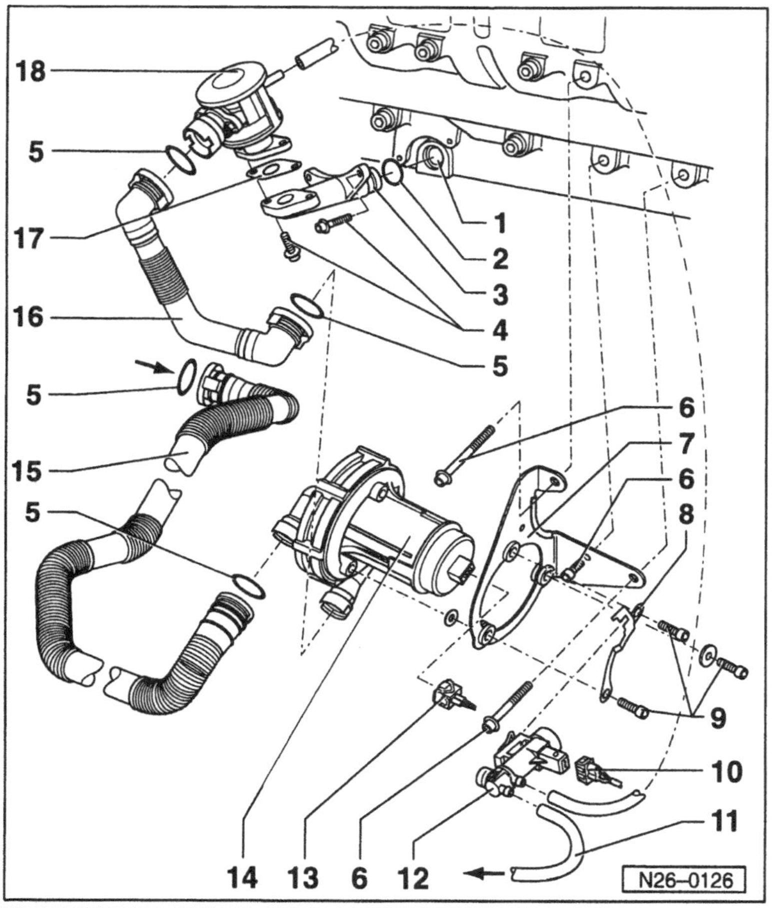

Secondary Air Injection system components, removing and installing

Notes:

- *Components marked with an * are checked by On Board Diagnostic:*

⇒ Repair Group 01

- *Components marked with ** are checked via Output Diagnostic Test Mode (DTM):*

⇒ Repair Group 01

- *Secondary Air Injection pump relay J299***

⇒ page D 26-18, Fig. 1

1 - Air port
- in cylinder head

2 - O-ring
- replace

3 - Connection

4 - 15 Nm (11 ft lb)

5 - O-ring
- replace if damaged

6 - 25 Nm (18 ft lb)

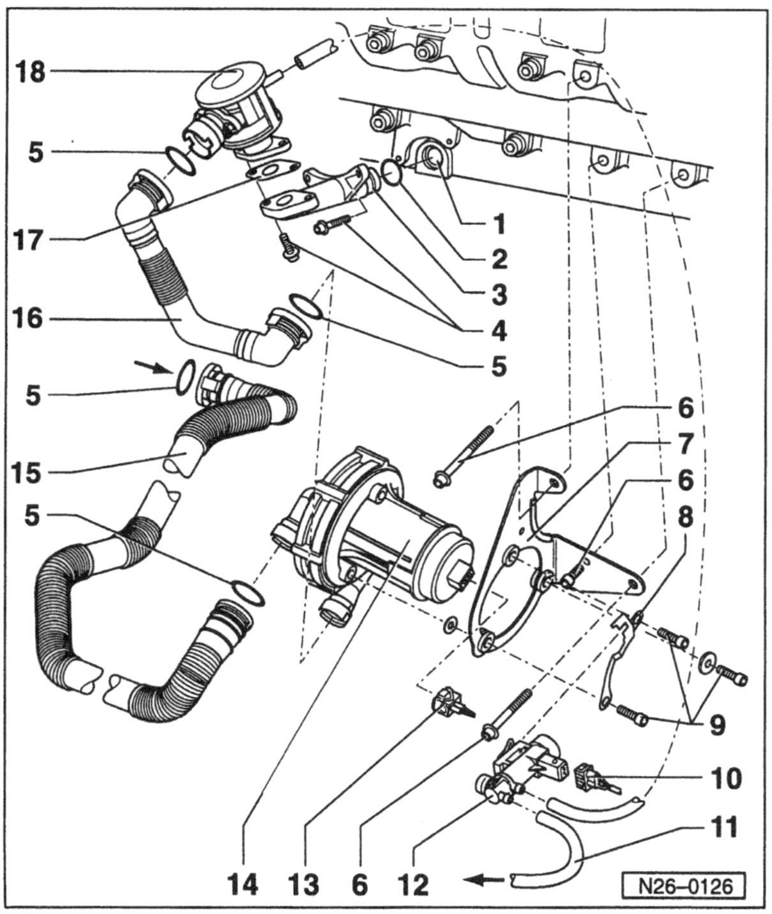

7 - Bracket
- for Secondary Air Injection pump motor
- mounted to intake manifold

8 - Retainer
- for Secondary Air Injection solenoid valve

9 - 10 Nm (7 ft lb)

10 - 2-pin harness connector
- black
- for Secondary Air Injection solenoid valve

11 - Vacuum pipe
- to junction piece between intake manifold and fuel pressure regulator

⇒ Repair Group 24

12 - Secondary Air Injection solenoid valve N112 */**

13 - 2-pin harness connector
- black
- for Secondary Air Injection pump motor

14 - Secondary Air Injection pump motor (V101)**

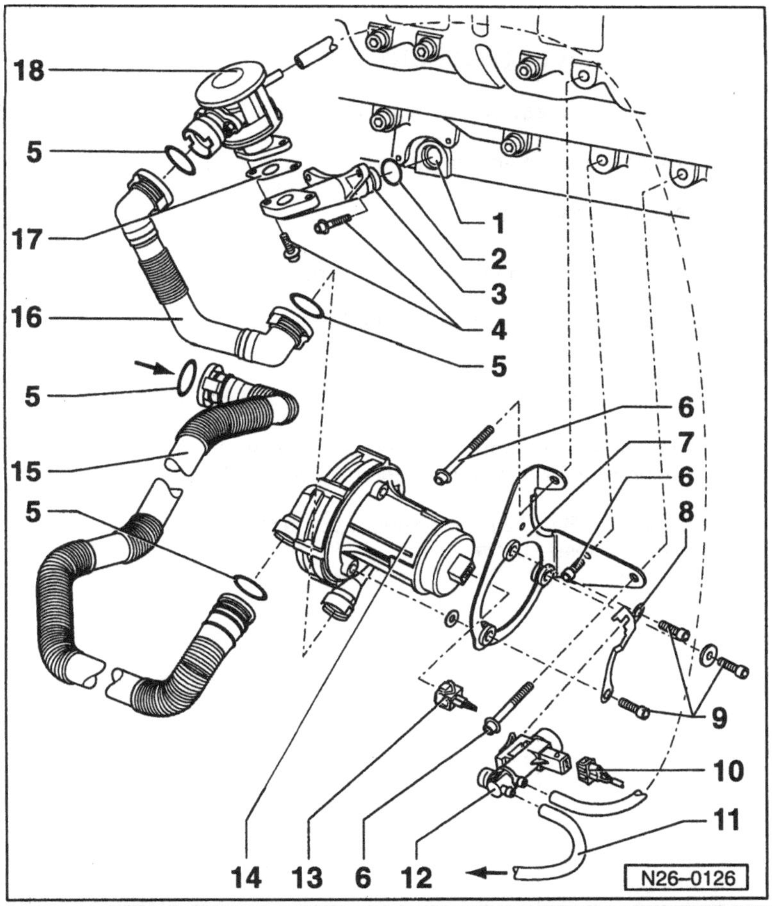

15 - **Intake hose**
- ensure that it is tightly seated
- from Air Cleaner upper section:

⇒ Repair Group 24

16 - **Pressure hose**
- ensure that it is tightly seated

17 - **Gasket**
- replace

18 - **Combi-valve**
- checking:

⇒ page D 26-19
- removing and installing:

⇒ page D 26-21

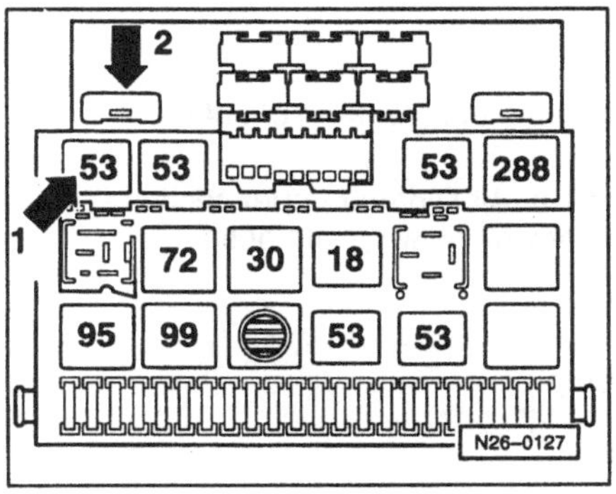

◄ **Fig. 1 Secondary Air Injection pump relay J299 (arrow 1)**

- with fuse S130 (arrow 2)

Note:

- *If tools are used to pull relays or control modules out of the fuse/ relay panel, first disconnect battery ground cable.*

CAUTION!
Obtain radio anti-theft code before disconnecting the battery ground cable.

Combi-valve, checking

Special tools, testers and auxiliary items

- US 8012 Hand vacuum pump

Checking conditions

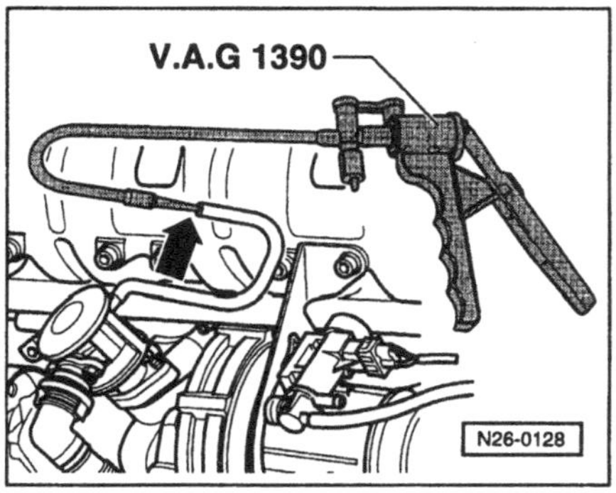

- Vacuum pipes and hose connections free of leaks
- Vacuum lines not blocked/kinked

– Remove insulation tray
⇒ Repair Group 50

– Disconnect vacuum hose from combi-valve from Secondary Air Injection solenoid valve N112

◄ – Connect US 8012 hand vacuum pump to combi-valve vacuum hose -arrow-

Note:
Do not use compressed air during the following check!

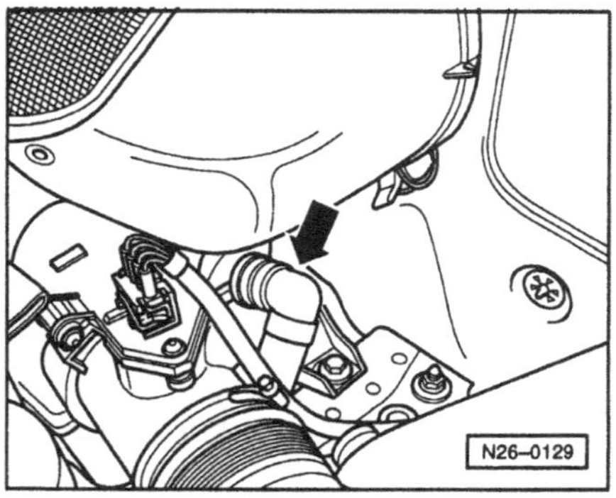

◄ – Detach hose to combi valve at Air Cleaner upper section -arrow- and pressurize slightly by blowing into hose

- combi-valve must be closed

– Operate hand vacuum pump

- combi-valve must open

If combi-valve does not open:

– Replace combi-valve
⇒ page D 26-21

Combi-valve, removing and installing

Removing

- Ensure that ignition is switched OFF
- Disconnect battery ground cable

> ***CAUTION!***
> ***Obtain radio anti-theft code before disconnecting the battery ground cable.***

- Remove sound dampener tray
⇒ Repair group 50

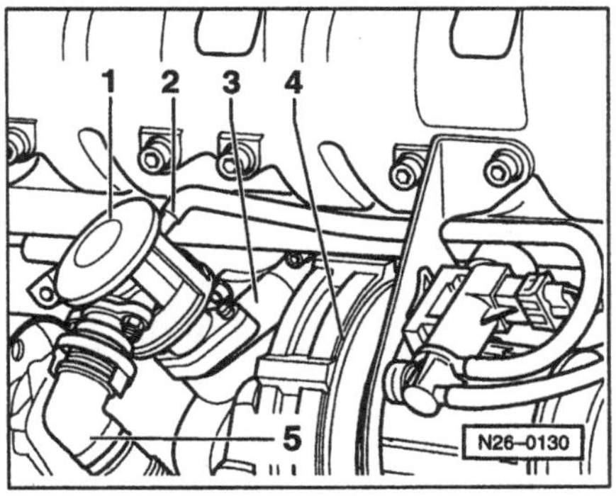

- ◄ Remove pressure hose -5- between combi-valve -1- and Secondary Air Injection pump -4-
- Disconnect vacuum hose -2- from combi-valve
- Unscrew combi-valve -1- from connection -3- and pull out

Installing

- Install in reverse order of removal procedure

2.4 Liter Diesel
Fuel Injection and Glow Plug
(Engine Code: AAB)

Section
E

WARNING!
Before proceeding with any work, please read the warnings and cautions immediately following this index. Also read any warning and caution that accompanies a procedure in the manual.

Please read these WARNINGS and CAUTIONS before proceeding with maintenance and repair work.

WARNING—

- Some repairs may be beyond your capability. If you lack the skills, tools and equipment, or a suitable workplace for any procedure described in this manual, we suggest you leave such repairs to an authorized Volkswagen dealer service department, or other qualified shop.

- Volkswagen is constantly improving its cars. Sometimes these changes, both in parts and specifications, are made applicable to earlier models. Therefore, before starting any major jobs or repairs to components on which passenger safety may depend, consult your authorized Volkswagen dealer about the Technical Bulletins that may have been issued since the editorial closing of this manual.

- Do not re-use any fasteners that are worn or deformed in normal use. Many fasteners are designed to be used only once and become unreliable and may fail when used a second time. This includes, but is not limited to, nuts, bolts, washers, self–locking nuts or bolts, circlips and cotter pins. Always replace these fasteners with new parts.

- Never work under a lifted car unless it is solidly supported on stands designed for the purpose. Do not support a car on cinder blocks, hollow tiles or other props that may crumble under continuous load. Never work under a vehicle that is supported solely by a jack. Never work under the car while the engine is running.

- If you are going to work under a car on the ground, make sure that the ground is level. Block the wheels to keep the car from rolling. Disconnect the battery negative terminal (ground strap) to prevent others from starting the vehicle while you are under it.

- Never run the engine unless the work area is well ventilated. Carbon monoxide (CO) kills.

- Do not attempt to work on your vehicle if you do not feel well. You increase the danger of injury to yourself and others if you are tired, upset or have taken medicine or any other substance that may impair you or keep you from being fully alert.

- Disconnect the battery negative (–) terminal (ground strap) whenever you work on the fuel system or the electrical system. Do not smoke or work near heaters or other fire hazards. Keep an approved fire extinguisher handy.

- Batteries produce explosive hydrogen gas. Keep sparks, lighted matches and open flame away from the top of the battery. If hydrogen gas escaping from the cap vents is ignited, it will ignite gas trapped in the cells and cause the battery to explode.

- Connect and disconnect battery cables, jumper cables or a battery charger only with the ignition switched off, to prevent sparks. Do not quick–charge the battery (for boost starting) for longer than one minute, and do not allow charging voltage to exceed 16.5 volts. Wait at least one minute before boosting the battery a second time.

- Illuminate your work area adequately but safely. Use a portable safety light for working inside or under the car. Make sure the bulb is enclosed by a wire cage. The hot filament of an accidentally broken bulb can ignite spilled fuel or oil.

- Tie long hair behind your head. Do not wear a necktie, a scarf, loose clothing, or a necklace when you work near machine tools or running engines. If your hair, clothing, or jewelry were to get caught in the machinery, severe injury could result.

- Finger rings, bracelets and other jewelry should be removed so that they cannot cause electrical shorts, get caught in running machinery, or be crushed by heavy parts.

- Catch draining fuel, oil, or brake fluid in suitable containers. Do not use food or beverage containers that might mislead someone into drinking from them. Store flammable fluids away from fire hazards. Wipe up spills at once, but do not store the oily rags, which can ignite and burn spontaneously.

- Always observe good workshop practices. Wear goggles when you operate machine tools or work with battery acid. Gloves or other protective clothing should be worn whenever the job requires working with harmful substances.

- The Air-Conditioning (A/C) system is filled with a chemical refrigerant, which is hazardous. The A/C system should be serviced only by trained technicians using approved refrigerant recovery/recycling equipment, trained in related safety precautions, and familiar with regulations governing the discharging and disposal of automotive chemical refrigerants.

- Do not expose any part of the A/C system to high temperatures such as an open flame. Excessive heat will increase system pressure and may cause the system to burst.

- Some aerosol tire inflators are highly flammable. Be extremely cautious when repairing a tire that may have been inflated using an aerosol tire inflator. Keep sparks, open flame or other sources of ignition away from the tire repair area. Inflate and deflate the tire at least four times before breaking the bead from the rim. Completely remove the tire from the rim before attempting any repair.

- Friction materials such as brake or clutch discs may contain asbestos fibers. Do not create dust by grinding, sanding, or by cleaning with compressed air. Avoid breathing asbestos fibers and asbestos dust. Breathing asbestos can cause serious diseases such as asbestosis or cancer, and may result in death.

- Greases, lubricants and other automotive chemicals contain toxic substances, many of which are absorbed directly through the skin. Read manufacturer's instructions and warnings carefully. Use hand and eye protection. Avoid direct skin contact.

- An airbag is operated by an explosive device. Handled improperly or without adequate safeguards, it can be accidently activated and cause serious personal injury. To prevent personal injury or airbag system failure, **only trained Volkswagen dealer service technicians** should test, disassemble or service the airbag system.

WARNINGS and CAUTIONS continued on next page ▶

Please read these WARNINGS and CAUTIONS before proceeding with maintenance and repair work.

WARNING (continued) —

- ALWAYS disconnect the airbag power supply before using a computer memory saver. Failure to disconnect the airbag power supply may result in accidental activation of the airbag.
- The airbag unit should not be removed, nor should any work be performed on the airbag system, without first reviewing the warnings and cautions that accompany the airbag system repair information in this manual.
- Never apply stickers or any other coverings on the steering wheel. Do not let chemical cleaners, oil or grease come into contact with the vinyl covering of the airbag unit.
- Never open or otherwise attempt to repair airbag system parts. Always use new parts. Never leave airbag parts or the partially disassembled airbag system unattended.
- Never use a test light or volt meter to conduct electrical tests on the airbag system. The airbag system must only be tested by trained Volkswagen Service technicians using special airbag tester equipment. The airbag system must only be tested while it is installed in the car.
- Do not expose an airbag unit to temperatures above 194°F (90°C) even for a brief period, while handling it during the repair process. Keep the unit clear of heat sources such as hot plates, soldering irons, heat lamps, welding equipment, or the like.
- Always replace airbag system components that have been mechanically damaged (bubbles, cracks, etc.).
- Always set down a removed airbag unit so that the horn pad is facing upward.
- When driving or riding in an airbag-equipped vehicle, never hold test equipment in your hands or lap while the vehicle is in motion. Objects between you and the airbag can increase the risk of injury in an accident.
- The storage, transportation and disposal of airbag units are subject to the laws for flammable solids.

CAUTION—

- If you lack the skills, tools and equipment, or a suitable workshop for any procedure described in this manual, we suggest you leave such repairs to an authorized Volkswagen dealer or other qualified shop. We especially urge you to consult an authorized Volkswagen dealer before beginning repairs on any car that may still be covered wholly or in part by any of the extensive warranties issued by Volkswagen of America, Inc.
- Volkswagen is constantly improving its cars and sometimes these changes, both in parts and specifications, are made applicable to earlier models. Therefore, part numbers listed in this manual are for reference only. Always check with your authorized Volkswagen dealer parts department for the latest information.
- Before starting a job, make certain that you have all the necessary tools and parts on hand. Read all the instructions thoroughly, do not attempt shortcuts. Use tools that are appropriate to the work and use only replacement parts meeting Volkswagen specifications. Makeshift tools, parts and procedures will not make good repairs.
- Use pneumatic and electric tools only to loosen threaded parts and fasteners. Never use these tools to tighten fasteners, especially on light alloy parts. Always use a torque wrench to tighten fasteners to the tightening torque specification listed.
- Be mindful of the environment and ecology. Before you drain the crankcase, find out the proper way to dispose of the oil. Do not pour oil onto the ground, down a drain, or into a stream, pond, or lake. Consult local ordinances that govern the disposal of wastes.
- When connecting cables or ground straps, all connections must be cleaned to bare metal. Be sure mounting bolts are tight.
- Do not replace fuse links with fuse links of other gauge or with standard wire. Always replace the entire length of the fuse link.
- Before doing any electrical welding on vehicles equipped with Anti-lock Brakes (ABS), disconnect the battery negative terminal (ground strap) and the ABS Control Module connector.
- On cars equipped with ABS, the ABS control unit cannot withstand temperatures from a paint–drying booth or a heat lamp in excess of 203°F (95°C) and should not be subjected to temperatures in excess of 185°F (85°C) for more than two hours.
- On cars equipped with anti-theft radios, make sure you know the correct radio activation code before disconnecting the battery or removing the radio. If the wrong code is entered when power is restored, the radio may lock up and be rendered inoperable, even if the correct code is then entered.
- When boost-charging the battery, first remove the fuses for the Engine Control Module (ECM), the Transmission Control Module (TCM), the ABS Control Module, and the On-Board computer. In cases where one or more of these components is not separately fused, disconnect the Control Module connector(s).
- Do not quick-charge the battery (for boost starting) for longer than one minute, and do not exceed 16.5 volts at the battery with the boosting cables attached. Wait at least one minute before boosting the battery a second time.

◀ **WARNINGS and CAUTIONS continued from previous page**

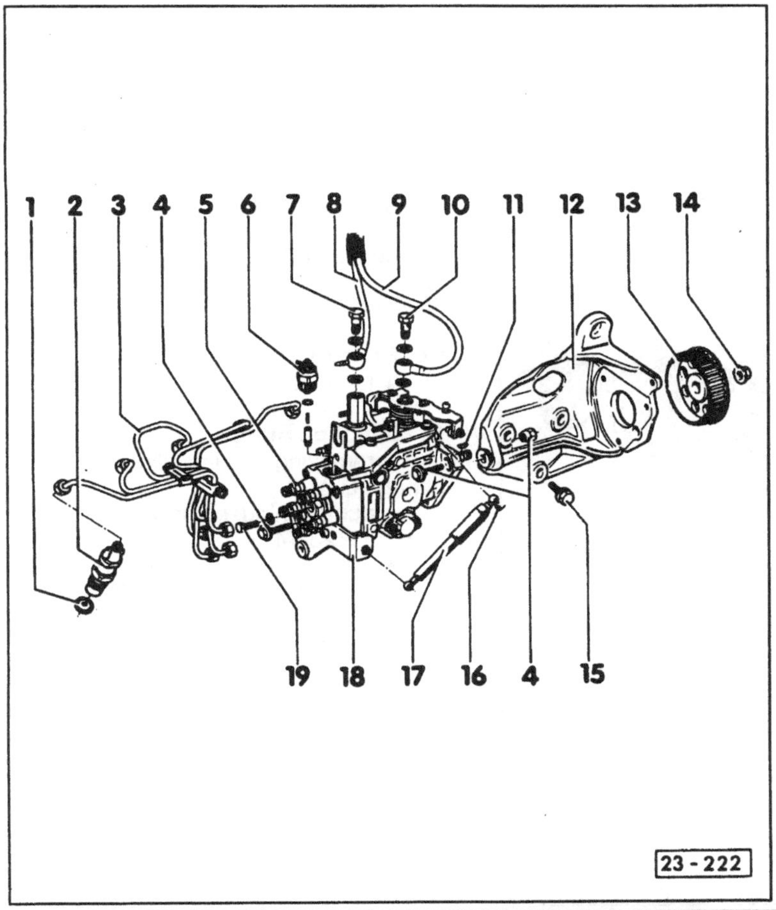

Fuel injection system, servicing

- Always replace all seals and gaskets
- Secure all fuel hoses with spring clips
- Rules for cleanliness:
⇒ page E 23-6
- Valve timing, checking:
⇒ page E 23-19
- Engine speed, adjusting
⇒ page E 23-23
- Fuel system leaks, checking
⇒ page E 23-7
- Fuel injection pump, servicing
⇒ page E 23-31

1 - Heat shield
- Replace
  - installed position
⇒ page E 23-27

2 - Fuel injector
- 70 Nm (52 ft lb)
- removing and installing:
⇒ page E 23-26
- servicing:
⇒ page E 23-28

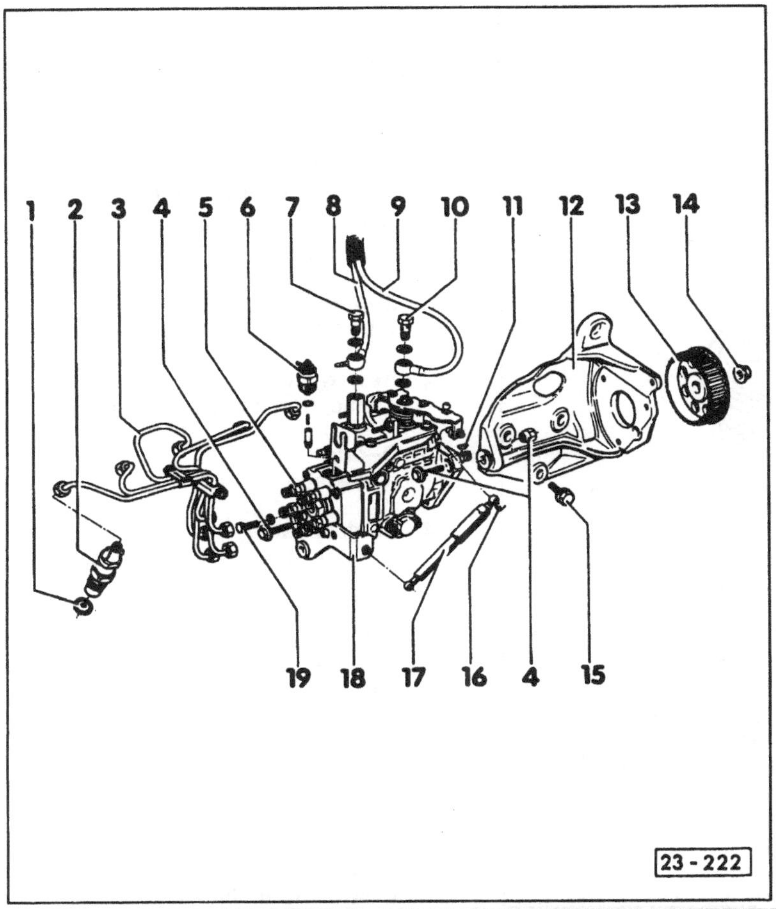

3 - Injector lines
- 25 Nm (18 ft lb)
- use 3035 counter-hold to remove
- always remove injector lines as a set
- do not alter shape or routing

4 - 25 Nm (18 ft lb)

5 - Connector
- removing, installing and sealing
⇒ page E 23-22

6 - Electro-magnetic stop control
- 40 Nm (30 ft lb)
- must click when ignition switched OFF and ON

7 - 25 Nm (18 ft lb)
- banjo bolt for return line
- marked "OUT"

8 - Fuel return line
- to fuel filter

9 - Fuel supply line
- from fuel filter

10 - 25 Nm (18 ft lb)

11 - Curved washer

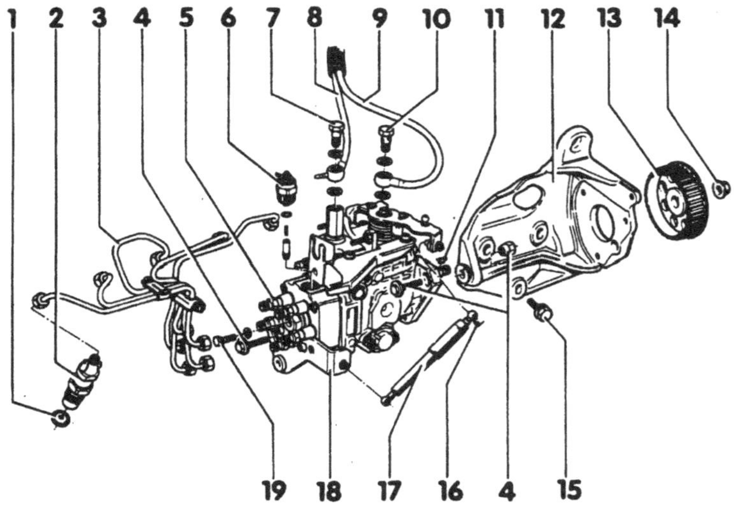

23 - 222

12 - Mounting bracket

13 - Injection pump gear sprocket
- removing:

⇒ page E 23-8

14 - 50 Nm (37 ft lb)

15 - 50 Nm (37 ft lb)

16 - Securing clip

17 - Shock absorber
- for load absorption

18 - Injection pump
- removing and installing:

⇒ page E 23-8

- pump timing, adjusting:

⇒ page E 23-14

- with the exception of the repairs described on page E 23-29, if a pump is faulty, it must be replaced. It is not possible to repair or service a pump in the workshop.

19 - 15 Nm (11 ft lb)
- if leaks occur, may be tightened to: 25 Nm (18 ft lb) max.

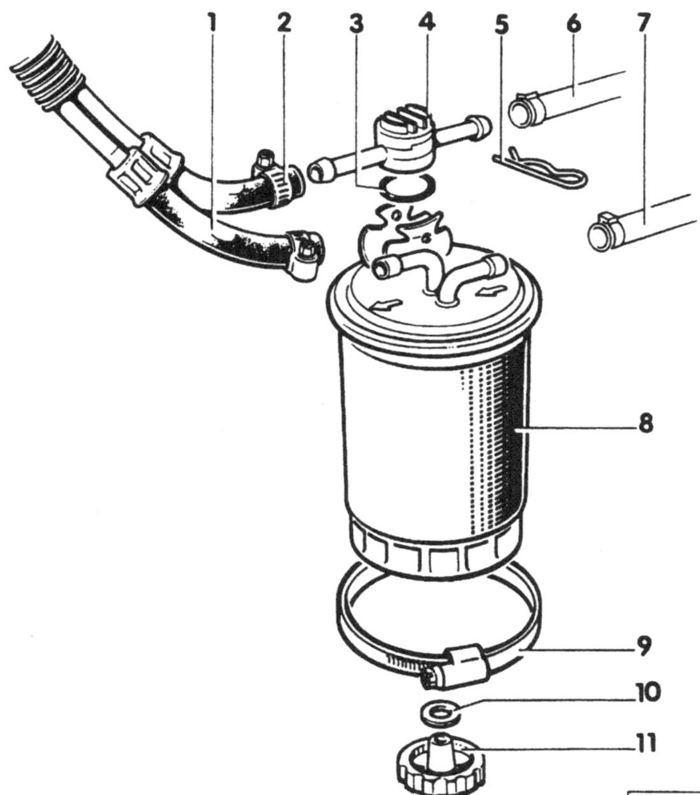

23 - 223

Fuel filter, removing and installing

- Always replace all seals and gaskets
- Secure all fuel hoses with spring clips
- Rules for cleanliness:

⇒ page E 23-6

1 - Supply line
- transparent, to injection pump

2 - Return line
- blue, from injection pump

3 - O–ring
– Replace

4 - Control valve
- installed position = direction of arrow to fuel tank
- below 15°C (59°F): Flow to filter open
- above 31°C (88°F): Flow to filter closed

5 - Retaining clip

6 - Return line
- blue, to fuel tank

7 - Supply line
- black, from fuel tank

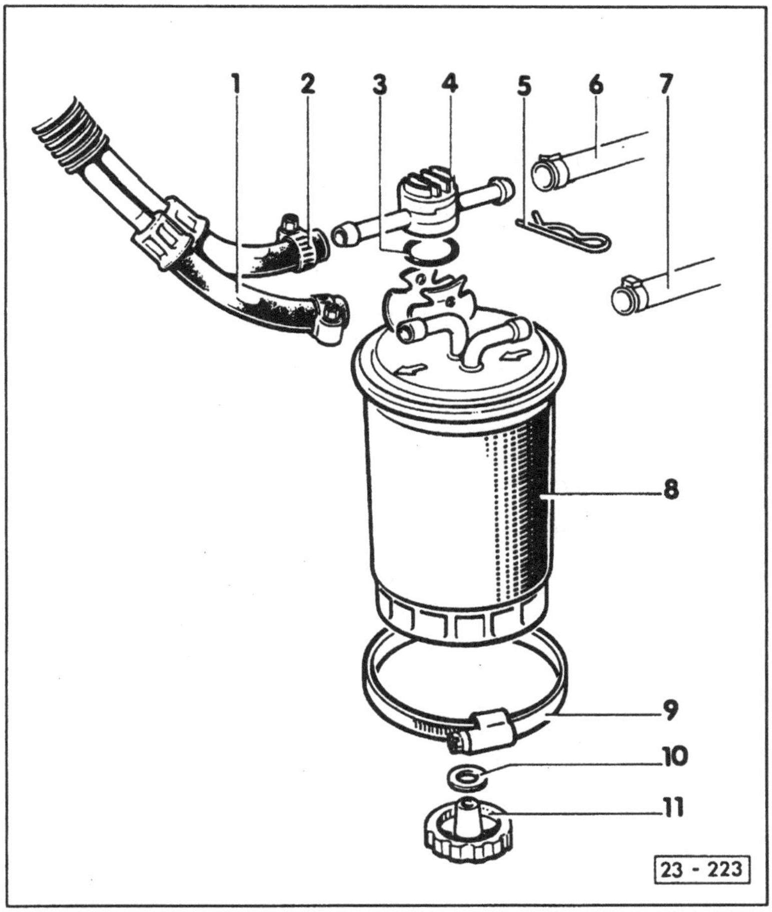

8 - **Fuel filter**
- ♦ direction of flow marked by arrows
- ♦ When replacing filter, release retaining clip -5- and remove control valve -4- with fuel lines connected

9 - **Mounting clamp**

10 - **Gasket**
- – Replace only if damaged

11 - **Drain plug**
- ♦ Loosen and allow approximately 100 cc's (6.1 cu. in.)of fluid to run out
- – To bleed: release retaining clip and remove control valve (with fuel lines connected)

Rules for cleanliness

When working on the fuel supply/injection system, pay careful attention to the following rules:

- Thoroughly clean all unions and adjacent areas before disconnecting
- Place parts that have been removed on a clean surface and cover them. Do not use fluffy cloths!
- Carefully cover opened components or seal them up if the repair can't be performed immediately
- Only install clean components
- Do not use parts that have been stored loose, in tool boxes etc.
- Only unpack replacement parts immediately prior to installation
- When the system is open:
  Do not use compressed air if it can be avoided.
  Do not move the vehicle unless absolutely necessary
- Ensure that Diesel fuel does NOT contact the coolant hoses! Immediately clean any hoses that have made contact with Diesel fuel. Always replace contaminated hoses.

Fuel system leakage, checking

– Run engine at idle and purge system of as much air as possible by opening throttle several times

– Detach fuel return line at injection pump

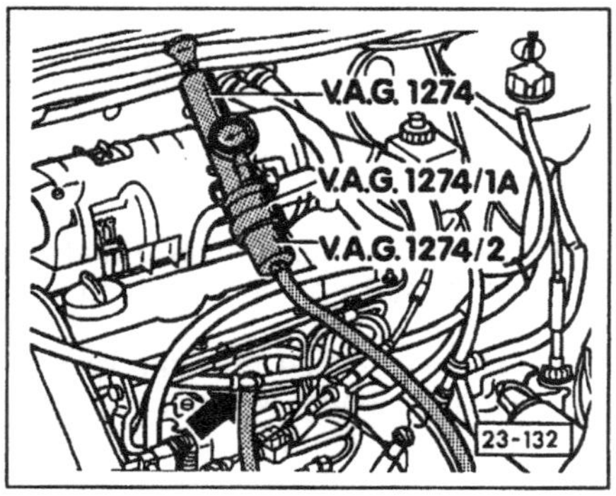

◄ – Attach adaptor line to injection pump in place of return line

– Crimp fuel supply line at fuel tank with hose clamp

– Build up pressure of 1.0 to 1.5 bar (15 to 22 psi) using hand pump

Note:

Air which could be in the system, and which becomes compressed, could make it necessary to pump up the system several times

If pressure continuously drops

– Locate and eliminate leak

Note:

By relocating the hose clamp, e.g., behind the fuel filter, the leak can be localized.

The return line can be pressurized by connecting the adaptor to the fuel pump supply line. The return and supply lines at the fuel tank as well as the supply line at the outlet of the fuel filter must then be disconnected.

Fuel injection pump, removing and installing

Removing

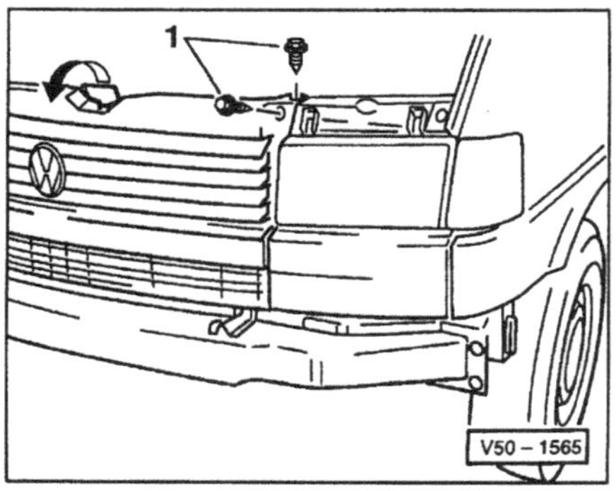

◄ – Remove sound dampening pan

– Unscrew mounting bolts -1- left and right

– Tilt radiator and lock carrier out and forward -arrow-

– Remove toothed belt guard from injection pump drive

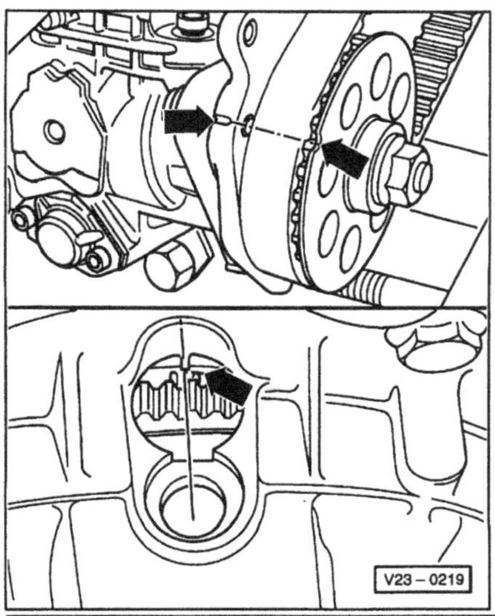

◄ – Turn crankshaft to cylinder number 1 TDC

- ♦ Marks on flywheel/clutch housing and injection pump wheel/ mounting bracket -arrows- must be aligned

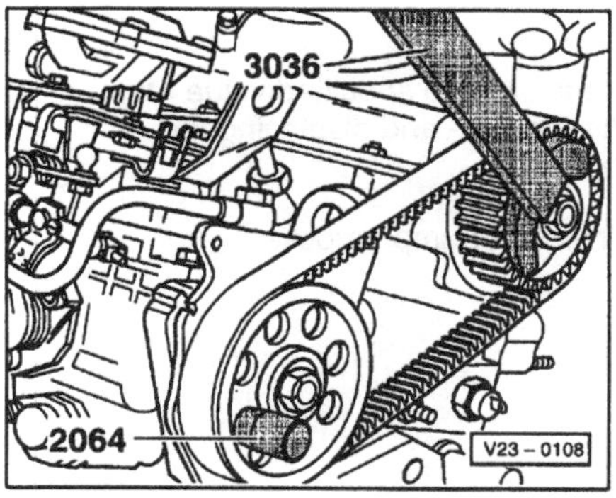

◄ – Lock injection pump sprocket with 2064 locking pin

– Hold injection pump sprocket with 3036 counter-hold tool

– Loosen mounting bolt, remove sprocket/toothed belt

– Loosen injection pump sprocket mounting nut approximately one turn and remove 2064 lock pin

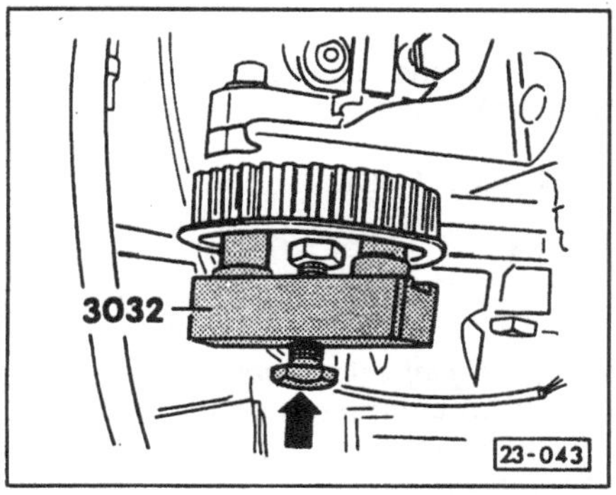

◄ – Pre-tension injection pump sprocket using puller

– Loosen injection pump sprocket from taper by tapping lightly on puller spindle -arrow-

– Unscrew mounting nut and remove injection pump sprocket

– Detach injection pipes, fuel supply line, fuel return line, shut-off line, throttle and Cold Start Accelerator cables

Note:

Use tubing wrench to loosen injection line.

– Unscrew injection pump mounting bolts from mounting bracket and remove pump

♦ to remove rear mounting bolt use 180 mm extension with 6 mm socket insert

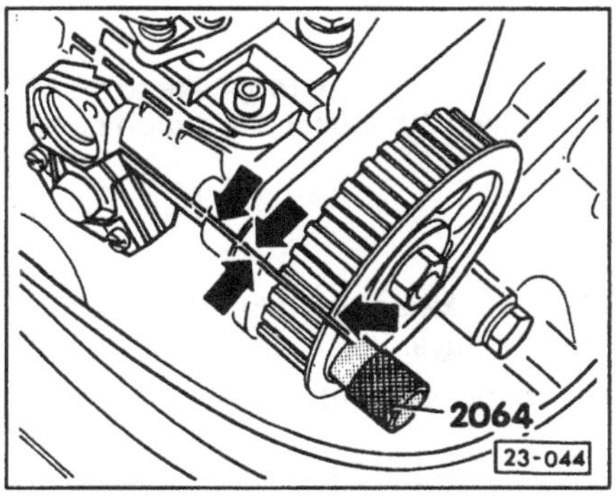

Installing

◄ – Install injection pump and make sure marks at injection pump flange and mounting bracket are in line -arrows-

– Install mounting bolts and tighten

♦ 25 Nm (18 ft lb)

– Place injection pump sprocket in position and turn until marks on sprocket and mounting bracket are in line -arrows-

– Lock injection pump sprocket with 2064 mandrel and tighten mounting nut

♦ 50 Nm (37 ft lb)

– Install toothed belt with injection pump drive sprocket

– Tighten injection pump mounting bolt, ensuring drive sprocket can still be turned by hand

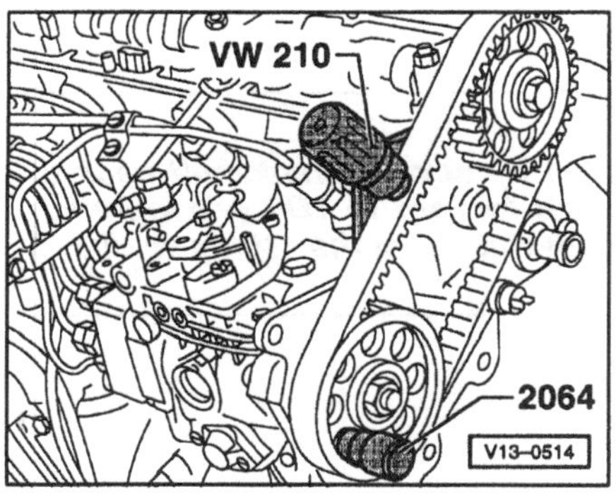

◄ – Check toothed belt tension

♦ specification: 12 to 13 scale value using VW 210

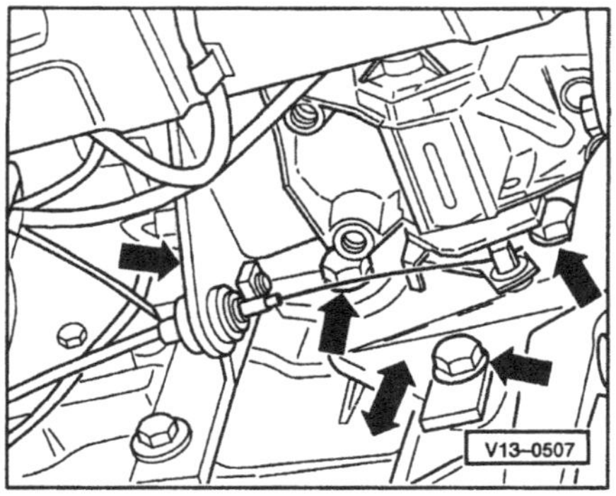

◄ – If necessary, tension toothed belt to specified value after loosening mounting bolts -arrows- and displacing the mounting bracket with pump

– Remove mandrel from injection pump sprocket

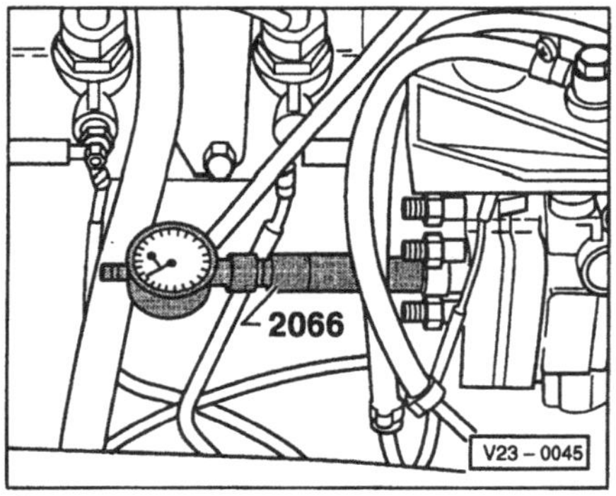

◄ – Screw in adaptor in place of plug, and install small dial gauge (0 to 3.0 mm range) with about 2.0 mm pretension

– Ensure that crankshaft is still at cyl 1 TDC

– Set start of injection as follows

Note:

To read the dial gauge when turning injection pump drive gear, lift vehicle and turn from below. When checking start of injection by turning crankshaft backward and forward, use a second technician to watch the marks on the flywheel/transmission.

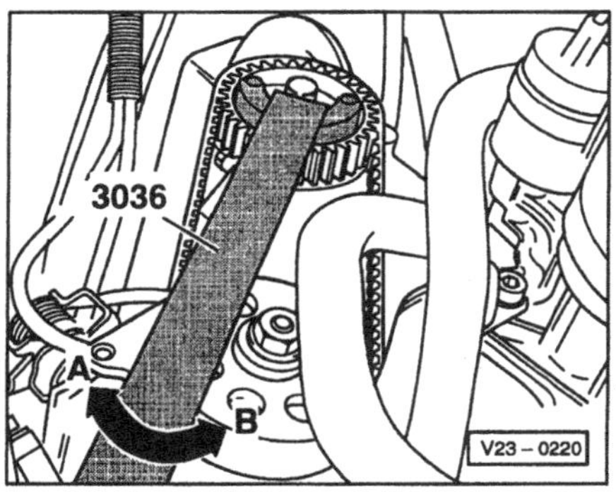

◄ – Turn injection pump sprocket anti-clockwise (opposite to normal direction) -arrow direction A- using 3036 until dial gauge needle stops moving

– Zero gauge

– Turn injection pump sprocket clockwise using 3036 tool -arrow- direction -B- until dial gauge displays:

♦ 1.00 + 0.02 mm stroke (start of injection)

– Hold injection pump sprocket in this position using 3036 tool

– Hand tighten fixing bolt to approximately

♦ 50 Nm (37 ft lb)

CAUTION!

Re-check start of injection by turning crankshaft back to zero on the dial gauge and forward to TDC (via vibration damper). This check will deviate from the set figure due to toothed belt slip.

– Start of injection must now be corrected again by a second adjustment, taking deviation into account, e.g.:

• First adjustment figure	=	1.00 *mm*
• Figure when checked	=	0.93 mm
• Deviation	=	–0.07 mm
• Second adjustment figure	=	1.07 mm

– After second adjustment tighten injection pump sprocket

♦ 100 Nm (74 ft lb)

– Connect fuel injection lines, fuel supply line, fuel return line, cut-off line and throttle cable

CAUTION!

Do not interchange the feed and return line banjo bolts. The inside diameter of the return line bolt is smaller and the hex is marked "OUT".

– Adjust idle and maximum engine speeds ⇒ page E 23-23

– Install toothed belt guard, radiator, lock carrier and engine cover

Fuel injection pump timing (static), checking and adjusting

Requirement

♦ Toothed belt tension OK

♦ Cold Start Accelerator knob NOT pulled out

– Remove sound–dampening pan

– Tilt radiator with lock carrier out and forward

– Remove toothed belt guard for injection pump drive

– Set engine to cylinder number 1 TDC

With engine removed

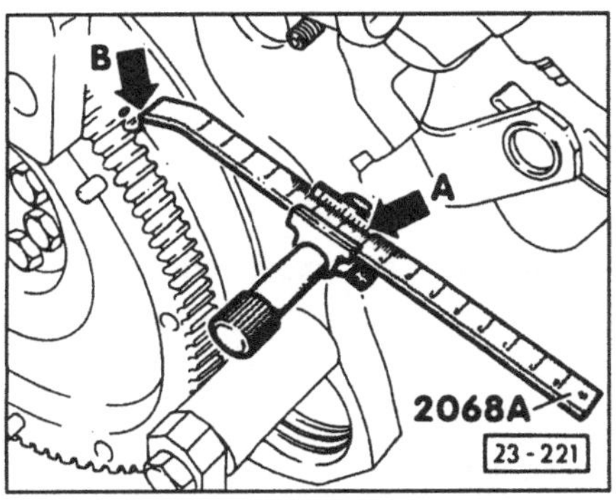

◄ – Set adjusting tool to 82 mm -arrow A-

♦ reference point is graduation on left of vernier scale

– Install adjusting tool as shown

– Turn crankshaft until TDC mark on flywheel and tip of adjusting tool -arrow B- and marks on injection pump gear and mounting bracket are aligned

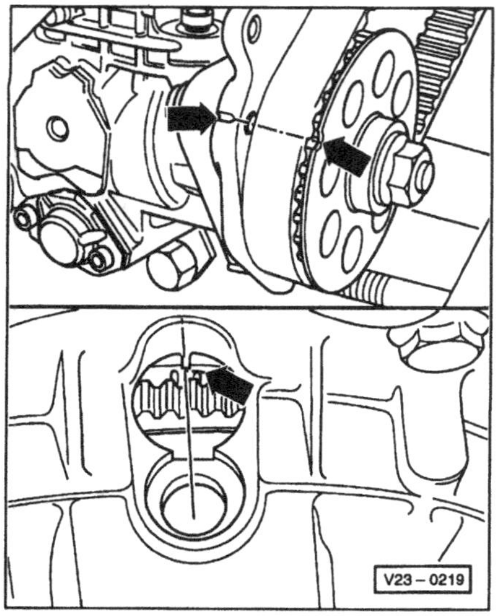

◄ **Engine installed**

– Turn crankshaft until TDC mark on flywheel, boss on bell housing and marks on injection pump gear and console align -arrows-

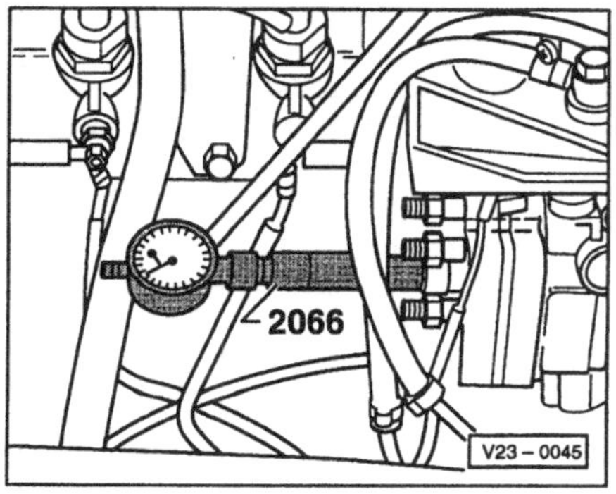

> ***CAUTION!***
>
> ***Always use a new washer for the plug, tightened to 25 Nm (18 ft lb).***

◄ – Screw in adaptor in place of plug, and install small dial gauge (0 to 3.0 mm range) with about 2.0 mm pre-tension

To read off dial gauge when turning injection pump drive gear, lift vehicle and turn from below. When checking start of injection by turning crankshaft backward and forward, a second person must watch the marks on the flywheel/transmission.

– Slowly turn crankshaft anti-clockwise (opposite to normal rotation), until dial gauge needle stops moving

– Zero gauge

– Turn crankshaft clockwise (normal rotation) until TDC mark on flywheel is aligned with reference mark

– Read off start of injection on dial gauge

Test figure:	0.93 ... 1.07 mm stroke
Setting figure:	1.00 + 0.02 mm stroke

Note:

If the value is within the specified tolerance, adjustment is not required.

– Adjust incorrect setting

Either

Turn injection pump after loosening mounting bolts from console and bracket

Or

Turn injection pump sprocket as follows:

Note:

To read off dial gauge when turning injection pump sprocket, lift vehicle and turn from below.

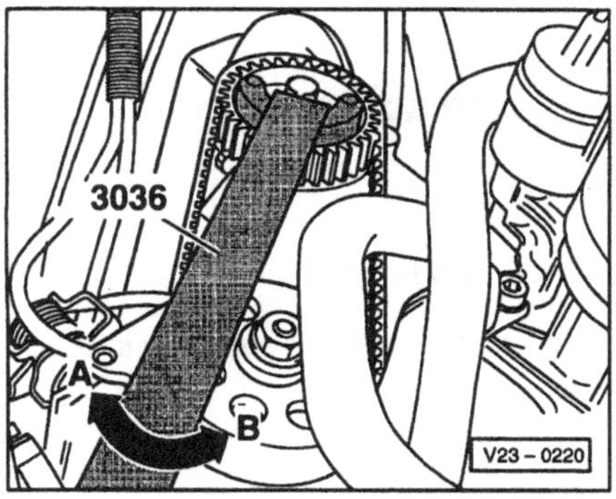

- Using 3036 counter-hold tool, hold injection pump sprocket and loosen approximately one turn
- Ensure that engine is still at TDC
- Using 3036 counter-hold tool, turn injection pump sprocket anti-clockwise (opposite to normal direction) -arrow- in direction -A- until dial gauge needle stops moving
- Zero gauge
- Using 3036 counter-hold tool, turn injection pump sprocket clockwise (normal rotation) -arrow- in direction -B- until gauge displays:
  - ♦ 1.00 ± 0.02 stroke (start of injection)
- Using 3036 counter-hold tool, hold injection pump sprocket in this position and tighten mounting bolt to approximately
  - ♦ 50 Nm (37 ft lb)

CAUTION!

Re-check start of injection by turning crankshaft back to zero on the dial gauge and forward to TDC (using vibration damper). This check will deviate from the set figure due to toothed belt slip.

- Start of injection must now be corrected by a second adjustment, taking the deviation into account

e.g.

• First adjustment figure	=	1.00 mm
• Figure when checked	=	0.93 mm
• Deviation	=	–0.07 mm
• Second adjustment figure	=	1.07 mm

- After second adjustment, tighten injection pump sprocket
  - ♦ 100 Nm (74 ft lb)
- Install toothed belt guard and radiator with lock carrier and sound dampening pan

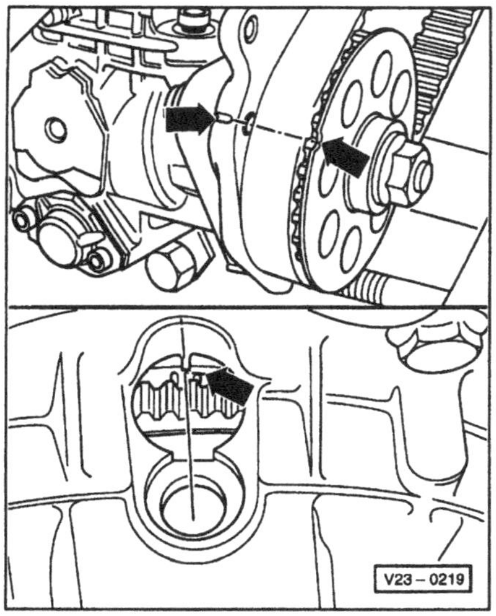

Valve timing, checking and adjusting

- Remove sound dampening pan
- Tilt radiator with lock carrier out and forward
- Remove cylinder head cover and toothed belt guard for injection pump drive
- Set crankshaft to cyl 1 TDC
  - ♦ Marks on flywheel/clutch housing and injection pump sprocket/ bracket must align -arrows-

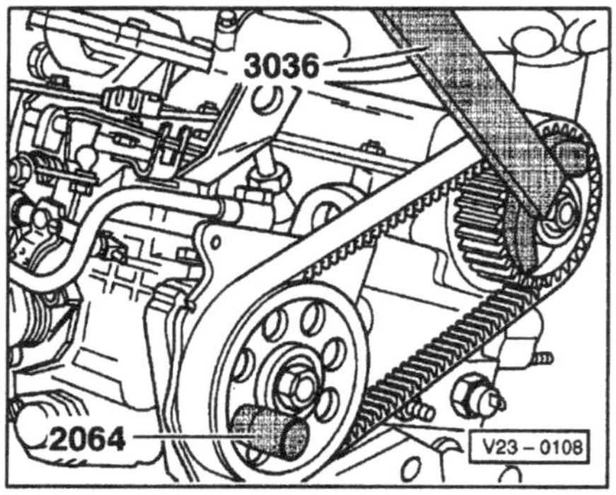

- Lock injection pump sprocket with 2064 mandrel
- Using 3036 counter-hold tool, hold injection pump sprocket and remove mounting bolt
- Remove sprocket together with toothed belt

- Ensure that TDC mark on flywheel is aligned with reference mark, adjust if necessary

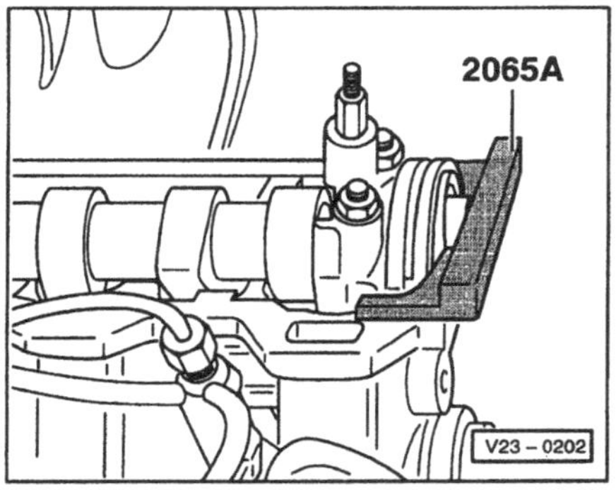

- Setting bar must fit in camshaft recess

If bar cannot be inserted,

- Adjust valve timing as follows:
- Turn crankshaft so setting bar can be inserted, then centralize bar as follows:
- Turn locked camshaft until one end of bar touches cylinder head
- Measure gap at other end of bar with feeler gauge
- Take half of this measurement and insert feeler gauge of this thickness between bar and head
- Turn camshaft so bar contacts feeler gauge
- Insert 2nd feeler gauge of same thickness between other end of bar and head
- Remove upper camshaft drive toothed belt guard and loosen camshaft sprocket mounting bolt approximately 1 turn
- Loosen camshaft sprocket on camshaft taper (by tapping with drift through hole in cover)

– Turn crankshaft until TDC mark on flywheel and boss on bell housing are aligned

– Tighten camshaft sprocket and remove setting bar

♦ 50 Nm (37 ft lb)

– Install injection pump drive sprocket with toothed belt

– Tighten drive sprocket mounting bolt until sprocket can just be turned by hand

– Adjust start of injection by turning injection pump sprocket ⇒ page E 23-14

Fuel injection pump connectors, correcting leaks

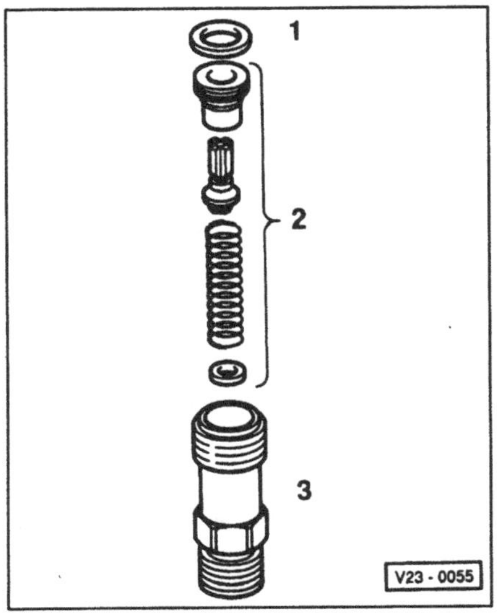

◄ 1 – Washer

2 – Pressure valve

3 – Connector

– Loosen injection line

– Tighten connector -3-

♦ 45 Nm (33 ft lb)

– Tighten injection line

♦ 25 Nm (18 ft lb)

If leak does not stop

– Install new connectors -3- and washers -1-

> ***CAUTION!***
> ***When installing new connectors, do not interchange the pressure valves.***

Idle and maximum speeds (no load), adjusting

Requirements

- ♦ Cold start accelerator cable must not be pulled out
- ♦ All electrical consumers switched OFF
- ♦ Engine oil temperature 60°C (140°F) minimum
- ♦ Measure engine speed using VAG 1367 ignition tester, using TDC sensor or VW 1324 adaptor

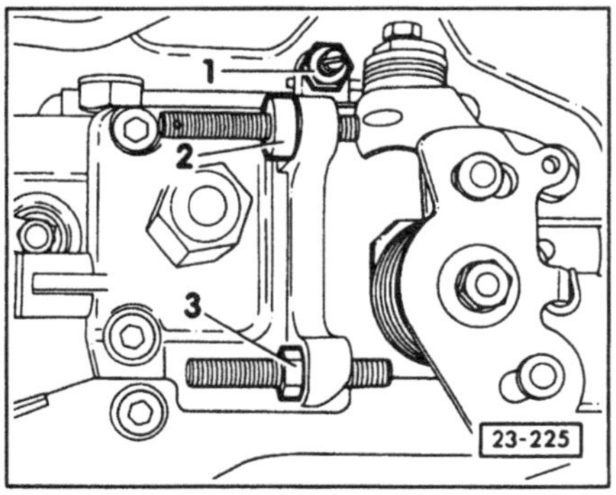

Idle speed

◄ 1 – Idle speed adjusting screw

2 – Residual volume adjusting screw

3 – Maximum speed adjusting screw

– Adjust idle speed using idle speed adjusting screw -1-

♦ specification: 850 ± 50 rpm

– Lock idle speed adjusting screw

Maximum speed (no load)

– Open throttle wide open and adjust maximum engine speed using maximum speed adjusting screw -3-

♦ specification: 4800 ± 100 rpm

– Lock maximum speed adjusting screw -3-

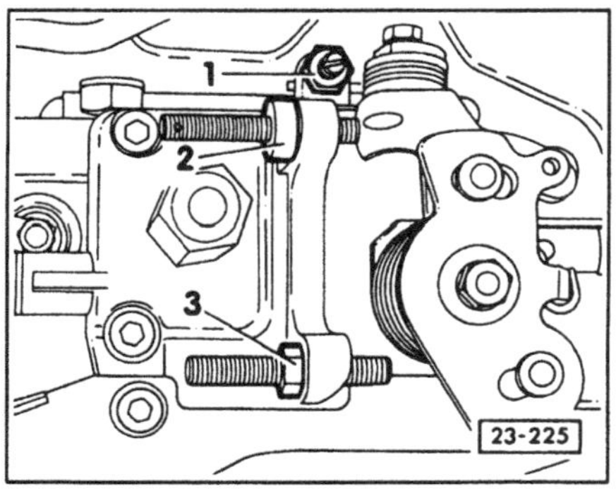

Residual volume adjusting screw

Notes:

◄ *The residual volume adjusting screw -2- is secured with an anti–tamper cap and must normally not be adjusted.*

The residual volume is set, using this screw, by the manufacturer on a test bench.

If the screw is turned, the following complaints may be heard:

Screw turned outwards (clearance at timing lever)

Residual volume is too small. This leads to performance complaints such as “flat spots” when starting off and/or accelerating from low engine speeds and/or experiencing jerking in all gears

If the above complaints are heard,

– Perform following basic setting on residual volume adjusting screw -2-:

– Remove anti-tamper cap

– Release adjusting screw -2- lock nut

Residual volume is too small

– Screw in adjusting screw until idle speed increases

♦ from point at which speed increase starts, turn adjusting screw back a half–turn

– Lock adjusting screw and secure with new anti–tamper cap

Residual volume too great (engine speed too high)

– Turn adjusting screw out until idle speed no longer decreases

– Turn adjusting screw in again until idle speed starts to increase

- ♦ from point at which engine speed starts to increase, turn adjusting screw back a half–turn

– Lock adjusting screw and secure using new anti–tamper cap

Fuel injectors, removing and installing

Note:
The first signs of injector trouble usually appear as follows:

- ♦ Misfiring
- ♦ Knocking in one more cylinders
- ♦ Engine overheating
- ♦ Loss of power
- ♦ Smoky black exhaust
- ♦ Increased fuel consumption
- ♦ Excessive blue smoke when starting from cold

Note:
Faulty injectors can be located by loosening the line union on each injector in turn with the engine running at fast idle. If the engine speed remains constant after loosening a line union, this denotes a faulty injector.

Removing

– Loosen injector lines using tubing wrench

– Remove injectors using 27 mm socket

> ***CAUTION!***
>
> ***Always remove fuel lines in a complete set. Do not alter the shape of fuel lines or attempt re-routing.***

Installing

> ***CAUTION!***
>
> ***Always install new heat shields between the cylinder head and fuel injectors.***

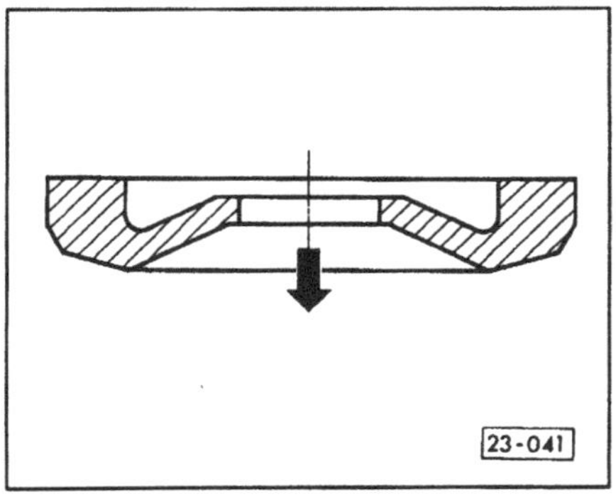

Installed position of heat shield

- ♦ -arrow- points towards cylinder
- ♦ tightening torque:

Injector lines = 25 Nm (18 ft lb)

Fuel injectors = 70 Nm (52 ft lb)

Fuel injectors, servicing

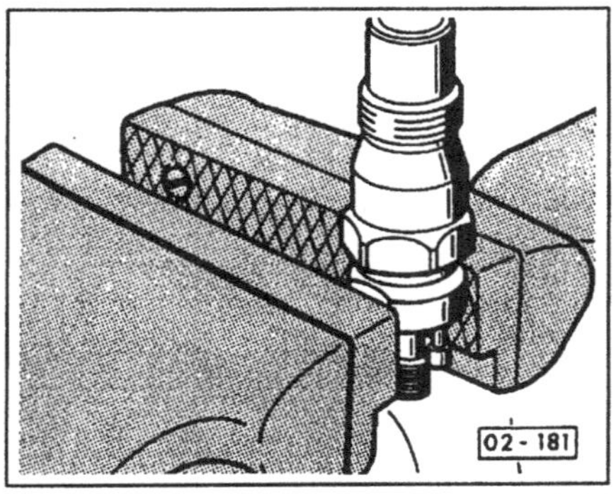

– Clamp upper part of injector in a vise and loosen hex-body

To prevent parts from falling out of the injector assembly

– Clamp lower section in a vise and then disassemble

Note:

When disassembling, keep all individual injector parts together and do not interchange any of them with parts from other injectors.

- ♦ Tightening torque for upper and lower sections
  70 Nm (52 ft lb)

Fuel Injector assembly

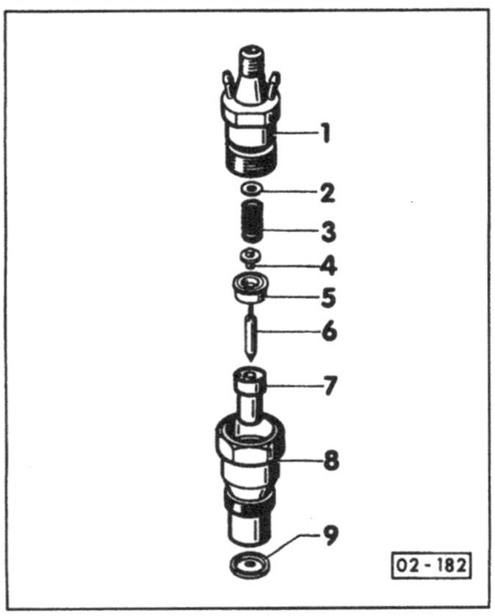

1 – Upper injector section

2 – Shim

3 – Spring

4 – Thrust pin

5 – Nozzle holder

6 – Needle

7 – Nozzle

8 – Lower injector section

9 – Heat shield

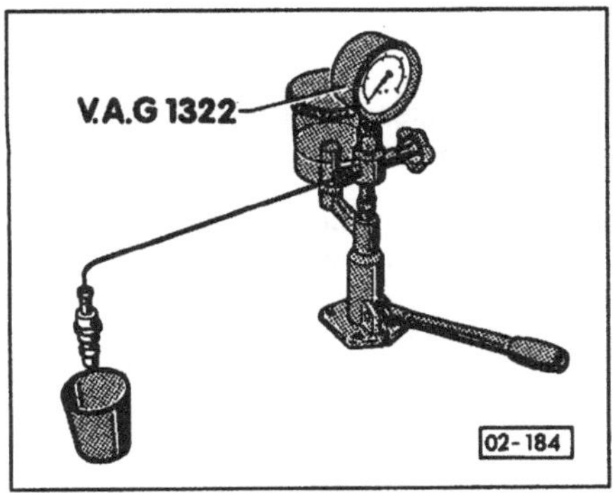

Fuel injectors, checking

◄ – Check injectors for: condition of needle tip, opening pressure, and possibility of leakage

> ***WARNING!***
> ***When testing injectors, take care not to expose the hands to the spray-stream because the fuel under high pressure will penetrate the skin which could result in serious injury.***

Fuel injector needle tip, visual check

– Inspect tip of fuel injector needle

If tip is broken off or bent

– Replace complete injector, or nozzle with new needle

Opening pressure, measuring using VAG 1322 test stand

– Open gauge valve

– Move tester lever down slowly and note pressure value at which injector just begins to spray

If measured opening pressure value is outside of specification

– Adjust by changing shims until opening pressure is within spec
  - ♦ specified pressures (bar)

New injector = 130 to 138 bar (1,885 to 2,001 psi)

Wear limit = 120 bar (1,740 psi)

Notes:

- ♦ *Thicker shim = increases opening pressure point*
- ♦ *Thinner shim = decreases opening pressure point*
- ♦ *Increasing shim thickness by 0.05 mm increases the pressure by about 5.0 bar (73 psi)*
- ♦ *Shims are available in thicknesses from 1.00 to 1.95 mm in 0.05 mm increments. Use the 3065 shim set box to store the shims.*
- ♦ *When servicing used injectors, set the opening pressure to the value for new injectors.*

Leakage test

– Open gauge valve

– Slowly press down on the pump lever until you can maintain a steady pressure of about 110 bar (1,595 psi) for 10 seconds

  - ♦ no fuel should leak from the nozzle tip

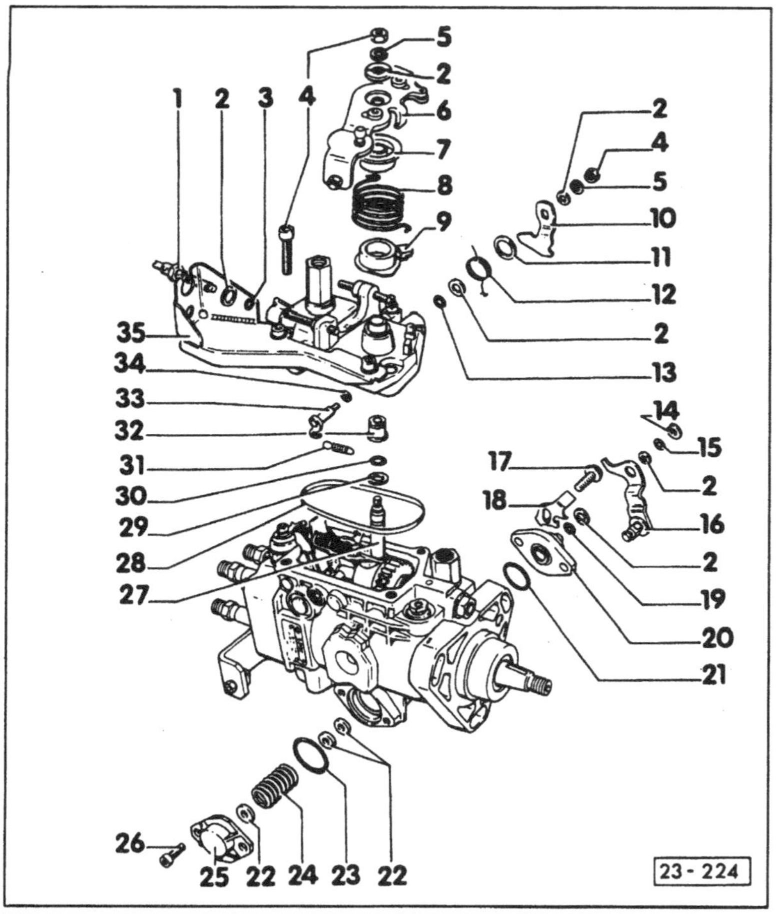

Fuel injection pump, servicing

♦ Observe Rules for cleanliness
⇒ page E 23-6

The following service operations can be performed on the injection pump:

♦ Throttle lever bushing -32-, throttle lever O-ring -30-, and gasket between pump cover and housing -28-, replacing:
⇒ page E 23-37

♦ Throttle return spring, replacing:
⇒ page E 23-35

♦ Volume adjustment screw O-ring -3-, replacing:
⇒ page E 23-40

♦ Idle speed shaft O-ring -13-, replacing:
⇒ page E 23-41

♦ Injection timing cover O-ring -23-, replacing:
⇒ page E 23-42

♦ CSA lever/cover O-ring for -19-/-21-, replacing:
⇒ page E 23-43

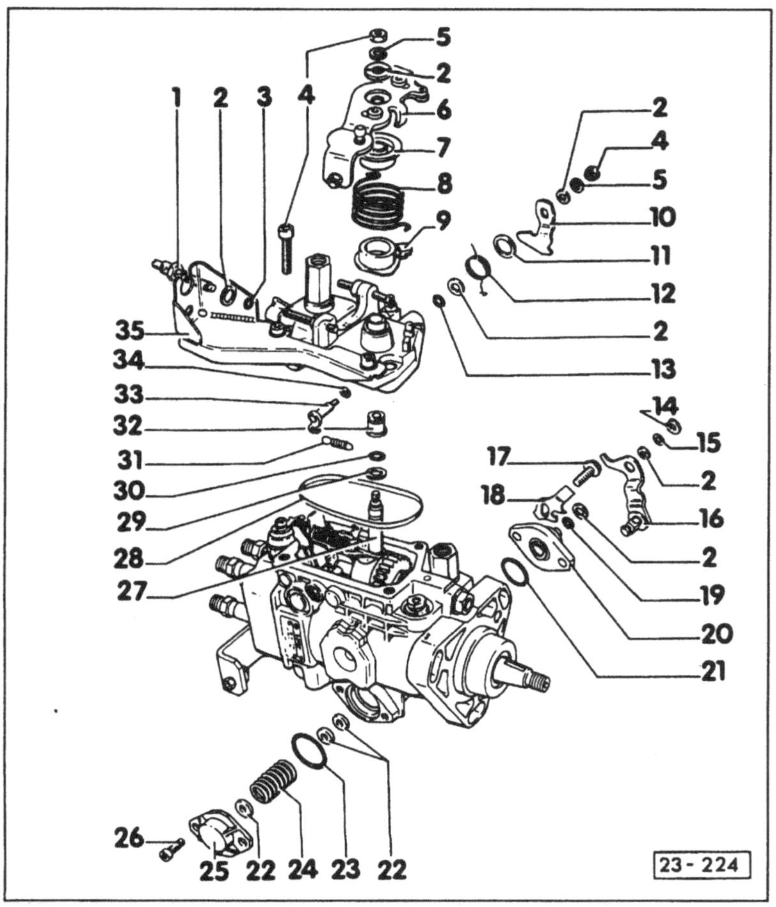

1 - Volume adjustment screw
– Mark installation position

2 - Washer

3 - O-ring
– Replace:
⇒ page E 23-40

4 - 10 Nm (7 ft lb)

5 - Spring washer

6 - Throttle lever
– Mark installation position:
⇒ page E 23-35

7 - Upper spring plate

8 - Return spring
♦ replacing:
⇒ page E 23-35

9 - Lower spring plate

10 - Idle speed adjustment lever

11 - Thrust washer

12 - Idle speed adjustment lever spring

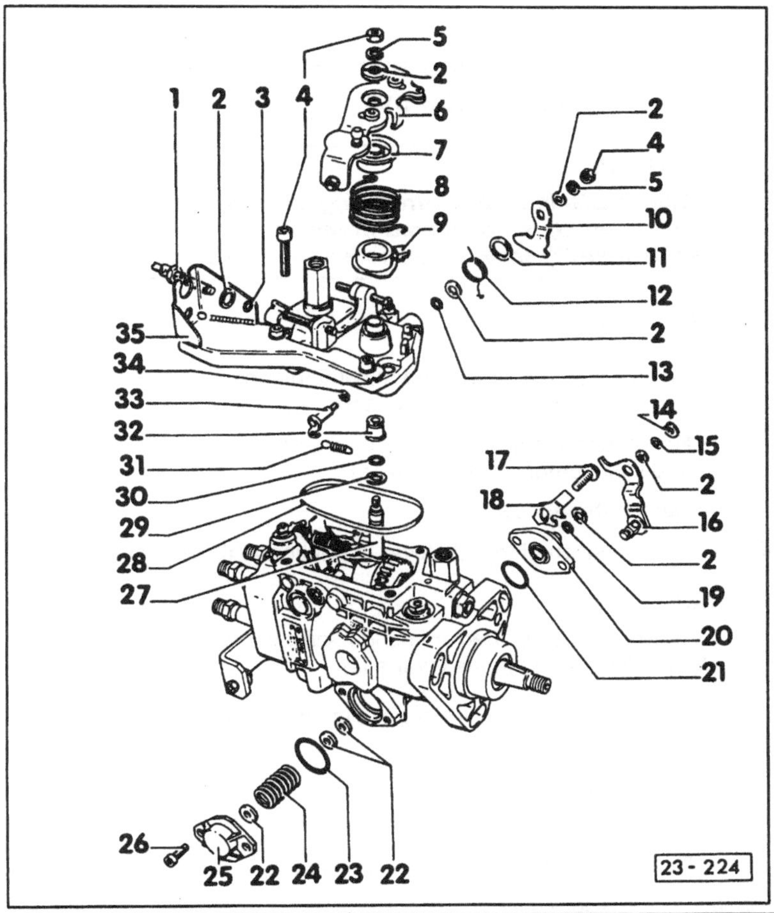

13 - O-ring
– Replace:
⇒ page E 23-37

14 - Circlip

15 - Spring washer

16 - Cold Start Accelerator (CSA) lever

17 - 10 Nm (7 ft lb)

18 - Stop plate
♦ for CSA lever (item 16)
♦ adjusting:
⇒ page E 23-43

19 - O-ring
– Replace:
⇒ page E 23-43

20 - CSA cover

21 - O–ring
– Replace:
⇒ page E 23-43

22 - Shim
♦ do not alter arrangement

23 - O–ring
– Replace:
⇒ page E 23-43

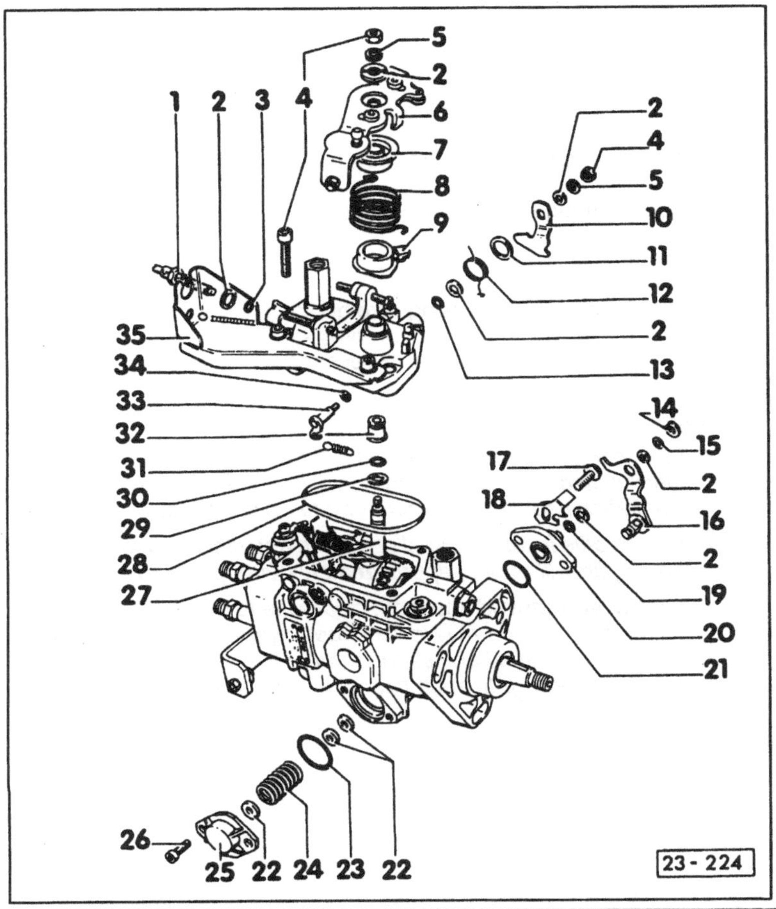

24 - Injection timing spring

25 - Injection timing cover

26 - 10 Nm (7 ft lb)

27 - Throttle lever shaft
– Push out with screwdriver handle

28 - Gasket
♦ *replacing:*
⇒ page E 23-37

29 - Thrust washer

30 - O–ring
– Replace

31 - Idle speed spring
– Detach when removing pump cover
♦ do not overstretch

32 - Bushing
♦ replacing:
⇒ page E 23-37

33 - Idle speed shaft

34 - Thrust washer

35 - Pump cover

Fuel injection pump throttle return spring, removing and installing

> ***CAUTION!***
>
> ***When replacing the return spring, ensure that the throttle lever (item 6) is not altered in relation to the throttle lever shaft (item 27) shown in exploded view 23-224, page E 23-31.***

Removing

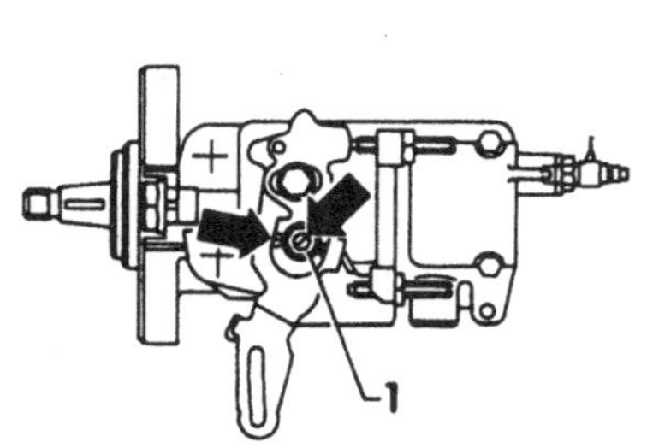

23-135

- Ensure that idle speed and maximum speed are within specifications, adjust if necessary
- Remove lock carrier mounting bolts and then tilt radiator and lock carrier out and forward
- Detach throttle cable
- ◄ Mark position of throttle lever in relation to throttle lever shaft

Note:

In some cases, etched markings -arrows- will be found on the throttle lever and throttle lever shaft.

- Disconnect shock absorber circlip and separate shock absorber from throttle lever
- Detach return spring
- Loosen mounting nut -4-
- Remove throttle lever and return spring

Installing

- Place new spring in position
- Place throttle lever in previously marked position
- Tighten mounting nut
  - ♦ 10 Nm (7 ft lb)
- Attach return spring (using wire hook)
- Check idle speed, adjust if necessary

Notes:

- ♦ *If the idle speed does not deviate more than 200 rpm from specification after fitting a new spring, the throttle lever installation position does not need to be changed.*
- ♦ *If the throttle lever is moved one tooth anti-clockwise to the shaft, the engine will race at approximately 4000 rpm at idle!*
- ♦ *If the lever is moved one tooth clockwise to the shaft, the engine will run at a considerably lower speed, approximately 500 rpm, or it will not start at all unless the throttle is opened and it will then stall during idling. In such cases, correct the throttle lever position.*

Throttle lever bushing in pump cover, pump cover gasket and "O" ring for throttle lever shaft, replacing

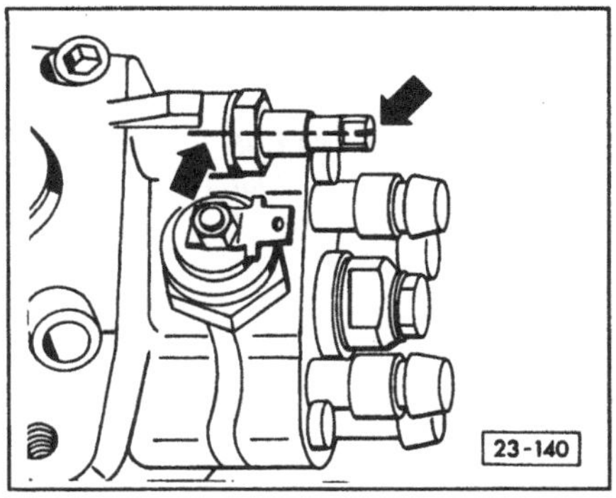

Note:

Item numbers (indicated without illustration in the following texts) refer to exploded view 23–224 ⇒ page E 23-31.

– Remove return spring and throttle lever:
⇒ page E 23-35

◄ – Mark position of volume adjustment screw in relation to the pump cover -arrows-

– Loosen locking nut, rotate against the locking sleeve and screw the volume adjustment screw out of pump cover

> ***CAUTION!***
>
> ***The slightest misadjustment of the volume adjustment screw can cause soot build–up and/or loss of engine power. For this reason, the same volume adjustment must be maintained after reassembling. Under no circumstance may the volume adjustment screw be screwed in past the starting position.***

– Remove injector lines

– Remove fuel return line

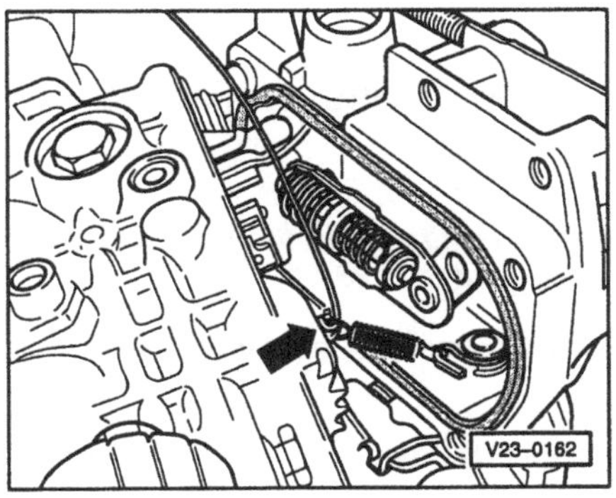

– Using an oil can, draw fuel out of the injection pump through the return line connection

– Remove cover bolts (4)

– Lift pump cover -35-, press throttle lever shaft -27- toward inside of cover (with screwdriver handle) when removing cover

◄ – Detach idle spring -31- (with self-made wire hook)

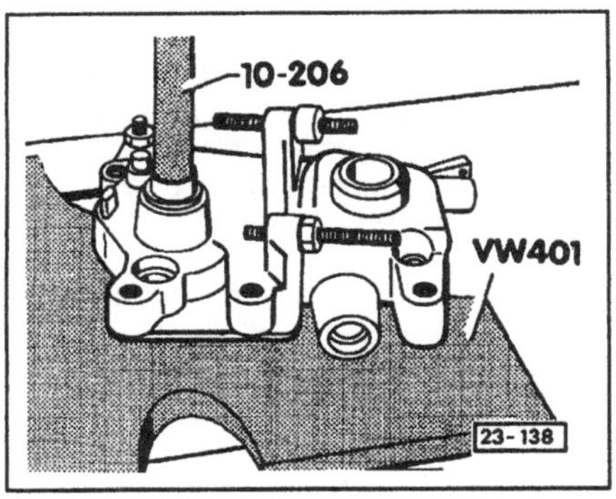

◄ – Remove pump cover and press out bushing -32- as shown

– Clean pump cover

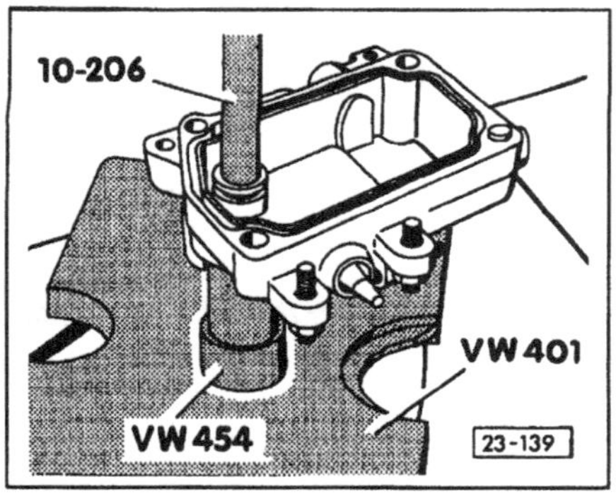

- Coat outside surface of new bushing with D6, and press into cover as shown, pressing in as far as collar
- Very carefully remove any surplus D6

Note:

Depending on pump version, various types of bushing are available. Select correct bushing by matching new bushing to the old.

- Install new throttle lever O-ring -30-
- Install new pump cover gasket -28-
  - ♦ the gasket is prevented from falling out during installation by small protrusions around the outside of the seal
- Coat throttle lever shaft and O-ring with diesel fuel and push into bushing, then place pump cover in position

> ***CAUTION!***
>
> ***Ensure that throttle lever thrust washer -29- is in position.***

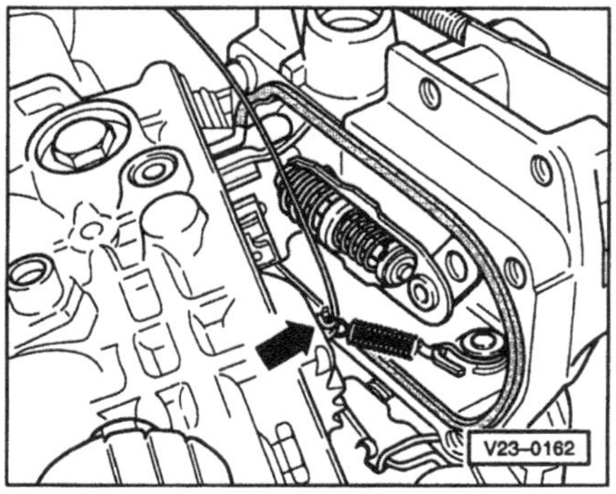

- Attach idle speed spring -31- with wire hook -arrow-
- Tighten pump cover
- Screw in volume adjustment screw -1- using new O-ring as shown
- Install return spring and throttle lever: ⇒ page E 23-35
- Run engine until warm and check idle and maximum speeds

Volume adjustment screw O-ring, replacing

Note:

Item numbers (indicated without illustration in the following texts) refer to exploded view 23–224 ⇒ page E 23-31.

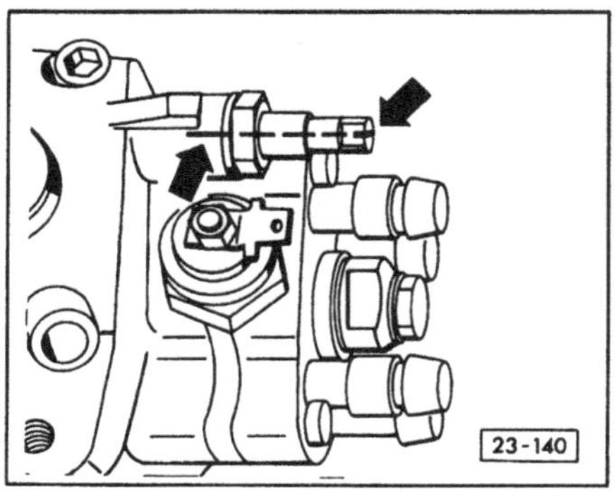

- Mark position of volume adjustment screw in relation to the pump cover -arrows-
- Loosen locking nut, rotate against the locking sleeve and screw the volume adjustment screw out of pump cover

> ***CAUTION!***
>
> ***The slightest misadjustment of the volume adjustment screw can cause soot build–up and/or loss of engine power. For this reason, the same volume adjustment must be maintained after reassembling. Under no circumstance may the volume adjustment screw be screwed in past the starting position.***

- Replace O-ring -3-
- Screw in volume adjustment screw as shown
- Run engine until warm and check idle and maximum speeds

Idle speed shaft O-ring, replacing

Note:

Item numbers (indicated without illustration in the following text) refer to exploded view 23–224 ⇒ page E 23-31.

– Remove pump cover (without replacing throttle lever bushing) ⇒ page E 23-37

– Remove idle speed lever nut -4- and lever -10-

– Push back idle speed shaft -33- and replace O-ring -13-

– Install pump cover ⇒ page E 23-37

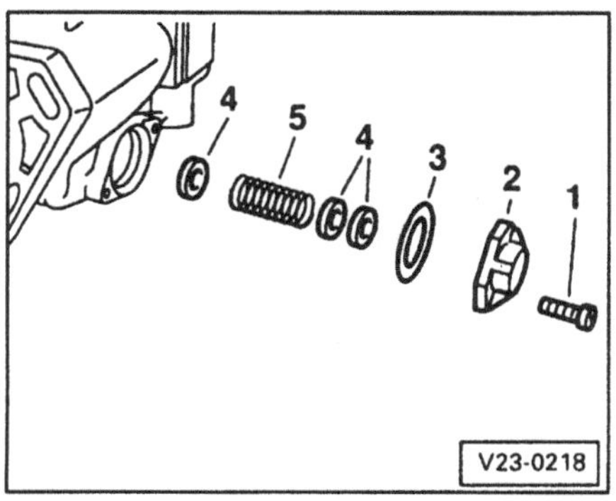

Injection timing cover O-ring, replacing

– Place clean cloth beneath injection pump

◄ – Remove cover screws -1-

– Remove and clean cover -2-

– Replace O-ring -3- and re-install cover with original shims -4-

CSA lever/cover O-ring, replacing

Note:

Item numbers (indicated without illustration in the following text) refer to exploded view 23–224 ⇒ page E 23-31.

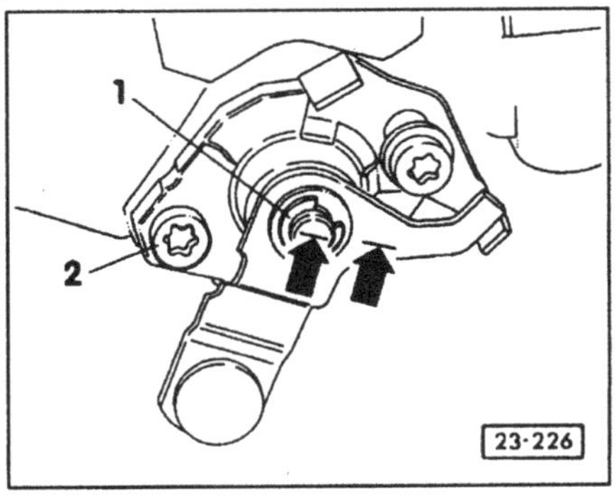

- Remove injection pump
- Mark position of CSA lever in relation to shaft -arrows-
- Remove circlip -1-
- Take off CSA lever
- Remove cover screws -2- and take off cover
- Replace O-rings -19-/-21- for cover/lever
- Install cover with stop plate
- Install CSA lever in previously marked position, secure and adjust as follows:

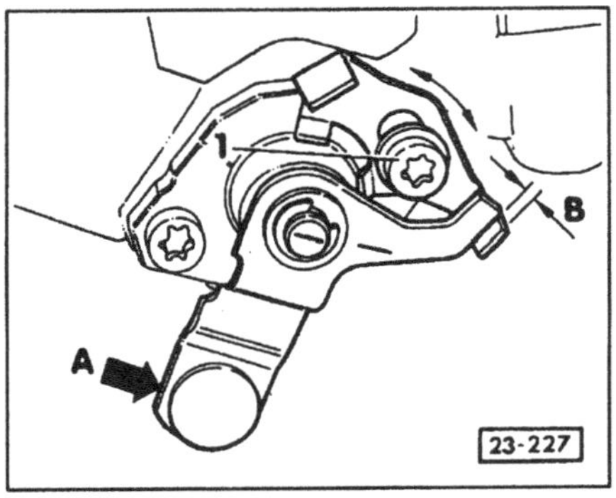

- Loosen stop plate mounting bolt -1- one half turn
- Move CSA lever by hand in adjustment direction -arrow A- until injection timer stroke (distinct resistance)
- With lever in this position, adjust stop plate gap to 1 mm -arrow B- and tighten mounting bolt
- Install injection pump

Glow plug system, checking

Requirements

- ♦ Engine cold
- ♦ Battery Voltage OK
- ♦ Voltage at glow plugs
  If no voltage, see wiring diagram

Amperage supply, checking using VAG 1315A

- Connect current supply to VAG 1315A tester
- Place glow plug wire in inductive pickup
- Press button for current measurement
- Glow, start engine and let idle
- During the extended glow period (approx. 120 seconds), record current draw with engine running
  - ♦ Current draw approx. 50 Amps: Glow plugs OK
  - ♦ Current draw below 50 A, check glow plugs

⇒ page E 28-2

Glow plugs, checking

Requirement

- ♦ battery voltage not less than 11.5 Volts

Note:

The current draw for the glow plug system with extended glow period (when engine is running during the extended glow period) is an approx. constant 10 Amp per glow plug. If system current is:

40 Amps = one glow plug is faulty

30 Amps = two glow plugs are faulty

20 Amps = three glow plugs are faulty

10 Amps = four glow plugs are faulty

0 Amps = all glow plugs are faulty

- Disconnect wiring and bus bar from glow plugs
- Connect VAG 1527 B LED tester between Battery plus and each of the glow plugs in turn
  - ♦ LED lights up: Glow plug is OK

LED does not light up:

- Replace faulty glow plug
  - ♦ tightening torque: 30 Nm (22 ft lb)

Notes:

- *To remove the cylinder 5 glow plug, disconnect the cylinder 5 injector line and injector.*
- *Do not exceed the 30 Nm (22 ft lb) tightening torque, otherwise the ring gap between the glow pin and thread will be squeezed together which could lead to premature glow plug failure.*
- *If no defects are found but engine is still hard to start, the glow plugs should be examined (injectors out) while glowing.*

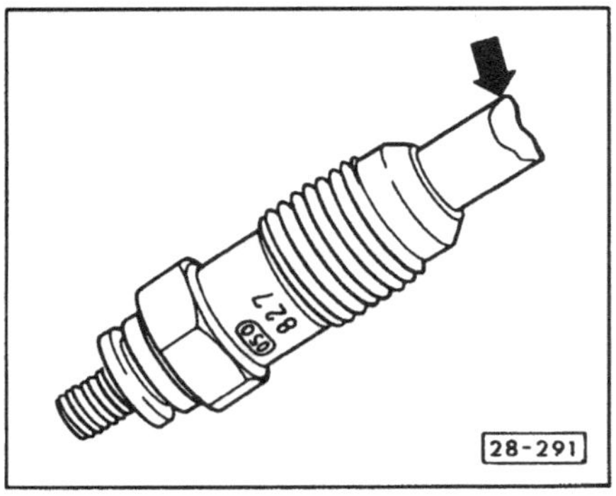

Glow plugs with burnt electrodes

Note:

- *Burnt glow plug electrodes are frequently caused by faulty injectors. Damage of this nature is not due to faults in or on the glow plugs.*
- *When damage of this nature is found -arrow-, it is not sufficient to merely replace the glow plug. The injector must also be tested for opening pressures and possible leakage.*

⇒ Repair Group 23

2.5 Liter 5–Cylinder, Fuel Injection and Ignition (Engine Codes: AAF, ACU)

Section F

WARNING!
Before proceeding with any work, please read the warnings and cautions immediately following this index. Also read any warning and caution that accompanies a procedure in the manual.

24 Multiport Fuel Injection (MFI) — Page

Vehicles built up to m.y. 1995

Vehicles built starting m.y. 1995

28 Ignition system

Page

Vehicles built up to m.y. 1995

Vehicles built starting m.y. 1995

Introduction

This Repair Manual booklet covers the EuroVan Fuel Injection & Ignition Repair Groups: 01, 24, and 28, for 5 cyl. Engine Codes: AAF and ACU.

Important!

The repair information for vehicles built **up to** m.y. 1995 has been kept seperate from the information applying to vehicles built **starting** m.y. 1995, use the Index to help you decide which material applies to your vehicle.

Please read these WARNINGS and CAUTIONS before proceeding with maintenance and repair work.

WARNING—

- Some repairs may be beyond your capability. If you lack the skills, tools and equipment, or a suitable workplace for any procedure described in this manual, we suggest you leave such repairs to an authorized Volkswagen dealer service department, or other qualified shop.

- Volkswagen is constantly improving its cars. Sometimes these changes, both in parts and specifications, are made applicable to earlier models. Therefore, before starting any major jobs or repairs to components on which passenger safety may depend, consult your authorized Volkswagen dealer about the Technical Bulletins that may have been issued since the editorial closing of this manual.

- Do not re-use any fasteners that are worn or deformed in normal use. Many fasteners are designed to be used only once and become unreliable and may fail when used a second time. This includes, but is not limited to, nuts, bolts, washers, self–locking nuts or bolts, circlips and cotter pins. Always replace these fasteners with new parts.

- Never work under a lifted car unless it is solidly supported on stands designed for the purpose. Do not support a car on cinder blocks, hollow tiles or other props that may crumble under continuous load. Never work under a vehicle that is supported solely by a jack. Never work under the car while the engine is running.

- If you are going to work under a car on the ground, make sure that the ground is level. Block the wheels to keep the car from rolling. Disconnect the battery negative terminal (ground strap) to prevent others from starting the vehicle while you are under it.

- Never run the engine unless the work area is well ventilated. Carbon monoxide (CO) kills.

- Do not attempt to work on your vehicle if you do not feel well. You increase the danger of injury to yourself and others if you are tired, upset or have taken medicine or any other substance that may impair you or keep you from being fully alert.

- Disconnect the battery negative (–) terminal (ground strap) whenever you work on the fuel system or the electrical system. Do not smoke or work near heaters or other fire hazards. Keep an approved fire extinguisher handy.

- Batteries produce explosive hydrogen gas. Keep sparks, lighted matches and open flame away from the top of the battery. If hydrogen gas escaping from the cap vents is ignited, it will ignite gas trapped in the cells and cause the battery to explode.

- Connect and disconnect battery cables, jumper cables or a battery charger only with the ignition switched off, to prevent sparks. Do not quick–charge the battery (for boost starting) for longer than one minute, and do not allow charging voltage to exceed 16.5 volts. Wait at least one minute before boosting the battery a second time.

- Illuminate your work area adequately but safely. Use a portable safety light for working inside or under the car. Make sure the bulb is enclosed by a wire cage. The hot filament of an accidentally broken bulb can ignite spilled fuel or oil.

- Tie long hair behind your head. Do not wear a necktie, a scarf, loose clothing, or a necklace when you work near machine tools or running engines. If your hair, clothing, or jewelry were to get caught in the machinery, severe injury could result.

- Finger rings, bracelets and other jewelry should be removed so that they cannot cause electrical shorts, get caught in running machinery, or be crushed by heavy parts.

- Catch draining fuel, oil, or brake fluid in suitable containers. Do not use food or beverage containers that might mislead someone into drinking from them. Store flammable fluids away from fire hazards. Wipe up spills at once, but do not store the oily rags, which can ignite and burn spontaneously.

- Always observe good workshop practices. Wear goggles when you operate machine tools or work with battery acid. Gloves or other protective clothing should be worn whenever the job requires working with harmful substances.

- The Air-Conditioning (A/C) system is filled with a chemical refrigerant, which is hazardous. The A/C system should be serviced only by trained technicians using approved refrigerant recovery/recycling equipment, trained in related safety precautions, and familiar with regulations governing the discharging and disposal of automotive chemical refrigerants.

- Do not expose any part of the A/C system to high temperatures such as an open flame. Excessive heat will increase system pressure and may cause the system to burst.

- Some aerosol tire inflators are highly flammable. Be extremely cautious when repairing a tire that may have been inflated using an aerosol tire inflator. Keep sparks, open flame or other sources of ignition away from the tire repair area. Inflate and deflate the tire at least four times before breaking the bead from the rim. Completely remove the tire from the rim before attempting any repair.

- Friction materials such as brake or clutch discs may contain asbestos fibers. Do not create dust by grinding, sanding, or by cleaning with compressed air. Avoid breathing asbestos fibers and asbestos dust. Breathing asbestos can cause serious diseases such as asbestosis or cancer, and may result in death.

- Greases, lubricants and other automotive chemicals contain toxic substances, many of which are absorbed directly through the skin. Read manufacturer's instructions and warnings carefully. Use hand and eye protection. Avoid direct skin contact.

- An airbag is operated by an explosive device. Handled improperly or without adequate safeguards, it can be accidently activated and cause serious personal injury. To prevent personal injury or airbag system failure, **only trained Volkswagen dealer service technicians** should test, disassemble or service the airbag system.

WARNINGS and CAUTIONS continued on next page ▶

Please read these WARNINGS and CAUTIONS before proceeding with maintenance and repair work.

WARNING (continued) —

- ALWAYS disconnect the airbag power supply before using a computer memory saver. Failure to disconnect the airbag power supply may result in accidental activation of the airbag.
- The airbag unit should not be removed, nor should any work be performed on the airbag system, without first reviewing the warnings and cautions that accompany the airbag system repair information in this manual.
- Never apply stickers or any other coverings on the steering wheel. Do not let chemical cleaners, oil or grease come into contact with the vinyl covering of the airbag unit.
- Never open or otherwise attempt to repair airbag system parts. Always use new parts. Never leave airbag parts or the partially disassembled airbag system unattended.
- Never use a test light or volt meter to conduct electrical tests on the airbag system. The airbag system must only be tested by trained Volkswagen Service technicians using special airbag tester equipment. The airbag system must only be tested while it is installed in the car.
- Do not expose an airbag unit to temperatures above 194°F (90°C) even for a brief period, while handling it during the repair process. Keep the unit clear of heat sources such as hot plates, soldering irons, heat lamps, welding equipment, or the like.
- Always replace airbag system components that have been mechanically damaged (bubbles, cracks, etc.).
- Always set down a removed airbag unit so that the horn pad is facing upward.
- When driving or riding in an airbag-equipped vehicle, never hold test equipment in your hands or lap while the vehicle is in motion. Objects between you and the airbag can increase the risk of injury in an accident.
- The storage, transportation and disposal of airbag units are subject to the laws for flammable solids.

CAUTION—

- If you lack the skills, tools and equipment, or a suitable workshop for any procedure described in this manual, we suggest you leave such repairs to an authorized Volkswagen dealer or other qualified shop. We especially urge you to consult an authorized Volkswagen dealer before beginning repairs on any car that may still be covered wholly or in part by any of the extensive warranties issued by Volkswagen of America, Inc.
- Volkswagen is constantly improving its cars and sometimes these changes, both in parts and specifications, are made applicable to earlier models. Therefore, part numbers listed in this manual are for reference only. Always check with your authorized Volkswagen dealer parts department for the latest information.
- Before starting a job, make certain that you have all the necessary tools and parts on hand. Read all the instructions thoroughly, do not attempt shortcuts. Use tools that are appropriate to the work and use only replacement parts meeting Volkswagen specifications. Makeshift tools, parts and procedures will not make good repairs.
- Use pneumatic and electric tools only to loosen threaded parts and fasteners. Never use these tools to tighten fasteners, especially on light alloy parts. Always use a torque wrench to tighten fasteners to the tightening torque specification listed.
- Be mindful of the environment and ecology. Before you drain the crankcase, find out the proper way to dispose of the oil. Do not pour oil onto the ground, down a drain, or into a stream, pond, or lake. Consult local ordinances that govern the disposal of wastes.
- When connecting cables or ground straps, all connections must be cleaned to bare metal. Be sure mounting bolts are tight.
- Do not replace fuse links with fuse links of other gauge or with standard wire. Always replace the entire length of the fuse link.
- Before doing any electrical welding on vehicles equipped with Anti-lock Brakes (ABS), disconnect the battery negative terminal (ground strap) and the ABS Control Module connector.
- On cars equipped with ABS, the ABS control unit cannot withstand temperatures from a paint–drying booth or a heat lamp in excess of 203°F (95°C) and should not be subjected to temperatures in excess of 185°F (85°C) for more than two hours.
- On cars equipped with anti-theft radios, make sure you know the correct radio activation code before disconnecting the battery or removing the radio. If the wrong code is entered when power is restored, the radio may lock up and be rendered inoperable, even if the correct code is then entered.
- When boost-charging the battery, first remove the fuses for the Engine Control Module (ECM), the Transmission Control Module (TCM), the ABS Control Module, and the On-Board computer. In cases where one or more of these components is not separately fused, disconnect the Control Module connector(s).
- Do not quick-charge the battery (for boost starting) for longer than one minute, and do not exceed 16.5 volts at the battery with the boosting cables attached. Wait at least one minute before boosting the battery a second time.

◀ **WARNINGS and CAUTIONS** continued from previous page

On Board Diagnostic, general information

Vehicles built up to m.y. 1995

- ♦ The Engine Control Module (ECM) J169 is equipped with Diagnostic Trouble Code (DTC) Memory
- ♦ If malfunctions occur in monitored sensors and/or components, they are stored in DTC Memory along with identifying data on the type of malfunction
- ♦ DTC display occurs after activation of the Scan Tool

⇒ page F 01-4

- ♦ DTC Memory must be erased after the malfunctions have been corrected or repaired

⇒ page F 01-8

- ♦ Malfunctions that affect Oxygen sensor control can only be read accurately after a test drive of at least 5 minutes

Malfunctions such as intermittent open circuits or loose terminals are stored and displayed as follows:

- ♦ If malfunctions occur for a maximum of 5 seconds, they are stored and considered to be "sporadic" and when displayed, they will show the letter code "SP".
- ♦ If malfunctions are present for more than 5 seconds, they are stored as DTC's and will be displayed like a permanent malfunction even though the malfunction is not occurring at the time of the reading

- ● California vehicles are equipped with a Malfunction Indicator (MIL) Lamp
- ● The MIL lamp in the instrument panel must light up when the ignition is turned ON and go out after the engine starts. As long as malfunctions occur in monitored sensors or components and the required DTC conditions are fulfilled, the MIL lamp will remain lit, even with the engine running

On Board Diagnostic system, technical data

Standard features
• Rapid data transfer
• Function 02: Diagnostic Trouble Code (DTC) Memory
• Function 03: Output Diagnostic Test Mode (DTM), (vehicles after 10/91)
• Function 04: Basic Setting (vehicles after 10/91)
• Function 08: Read measuring value block
• Function 09: Read individual measuring value, (vehicles after 10/91)
• Malfunction Indicator Lamp (MIL) in instrument panel (California ONLY)

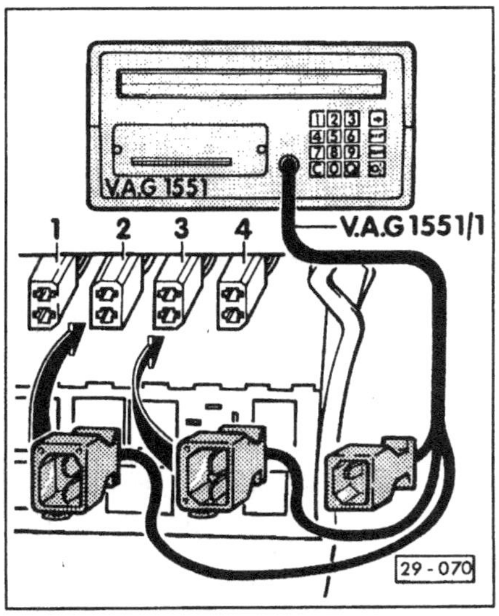

VAG 1551 Scan Tool, connecting and selecting Functions

Requirements

- ♦ battery voltage OK
- ♦ fuses 15, 18 and 21 OK
- ♦ engine and transmission ground connections OK:
  up to 7/92: engine and intake manifold
  after 7/92: transmission, battery and body near battery

– Fold down storage shelf in front of fuse/relay panel

– Connect VAG 1551 Scan Tool using VAG 1551/1 adaptor cable as follows:

◄ – First connect Scan Tool black connector to Data Link Connector

VAG On Board Diagnostic	HELP
1–Rapid data transfer	

◄ Displays will alternate as shown

VAG On Board Diagnostic	HELP
2–Diagnostic Trouble Code output	

◄ If display does not appear as shown:

– Do not connect Scan Tool white connector

– Check voltage supply to Scan Tool
⇒ page F 01-30

If display appears

- Connect white Scan Tool connector to white DLC in vehicle

  ♦ do not connect blue Scan Tool connector (not required)

Depending on which Scan Tool function is required:

- Switch ON ignition
  or
- Start engine

⇒ table, page F 01-7 to determine which Function to select

- Press Scan Tool HELP button (at any time) to obtain additional operating instructions

- Press → button to step through the program sequence

- Press 1 button to select "Rapid data transfer" operating mode

Rapid Data Transfer	HELP
Input address word XX	

◄ Display will appear as shown

- Press 0 and 1 buttons to select address word 01 "Engine electronics"

Rapid Data Transfer	Q
01–Engine electronics	

◄ Display will appear as shown

- Press Q button to enter input

Rapid Data Transfer	Q
Tester sends address word 01	

◄ Display will appear as shown

023906022E Digifant 1.2	1057→
Coding 000	WSC 00000

◄ Control module identification will be displayed on Scan Tool, e.g.:

Rapid Data Transfer	HELP
Control module does not respond!	

◄ If display appears as shown:

- Press HELP button to print a list of possible causes

After repairing possible causes:

- Press 0 and 1 buttons again to select address word 01 "Engine electronics"

- Press Q button to enter input

- Press → button

Rapid Data Transfer	HELP
Select function XX	

◄ Display will appear as shown

Note

If Function 02 "Read DTC Memory" is selected, turn ON printer using PRINT button (indicator lamp in the PRINT button lights up). With the printer switched ON, stored Trouble Codes and diagnostic information will automatically be displayed and printed out in sequence.

VAG 1551, selectable Functions

Function	Ignition ON	Engine idling
02 Check DTC memory	YES	NO
03 Output Diagnostic Test Mode •vehicles after 10/91	YES	NO
04 Basic setting •vehicles after 10/91 •only possible if coolant temperature is highter than 85°C. Until then, function is blocked • this function required for idle speed checking	NO	YES
05 Erase DTC Memory	YES	NO
06 End data transfer	YES	YES
08 Read measuring value block	YES	YES
09 Read individual measuring value block •vehicles after 10/91	YES	YES

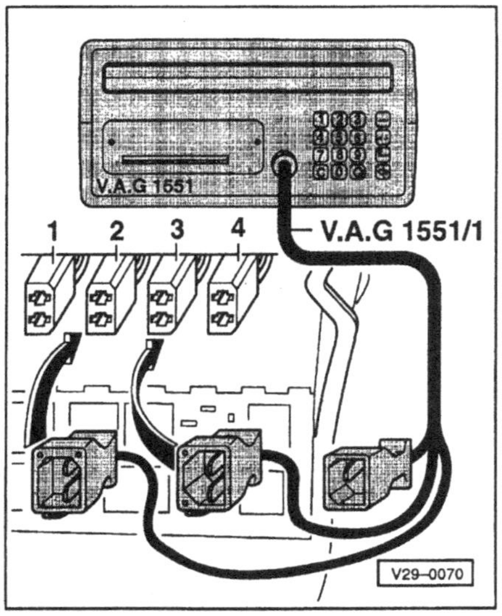

Functions 02 and 05: DTC Memory, checking and erasing

- Fold down storage shelf in front of relay panel
- Connect VAG 1551 Scan Tool using adaptor cable VAG 1551/1 as follows
- ◄ Connect Scan Tool black connector to Data Link Connector

VAG On Board Diagnostic	HELP
1–Rapid data transfer	

VAG On Board Diagnostic	HELP
2–Diagnostic trouble code output	

◄ Display will alternate as shown

◄ If display does not appear:

- Do not connect white Scan Tool connector
- Check voltage supply to Scan Tool ⇒ page F 01-30

If a display appears:

- Connect white Scan Tool connector to vehicle white DLC 3
  - ♦ do not connect blue Scan Tool connector (not required)
- Switch ON ignition
- Operate VAG 1551 Scan Tool while observing display
- Press 1 button to select "Rapid data transfer" operating mode
- Press PRINT button to switch ON printer
  - ♦ indicator light in PRINT button will light up
- Press 0 and 1 buttons to select address word 01 "Engine electronics"
- Press Q button to enter input
- Press → button
- Press 0 and 2 buttons to select function 02 "Check DTC Memory"
- Press Q button to enter input

"No faults recognized!"

◄ Display will show number of malfunctions (if any)

or

X Faults recognized!

If any displays other than these appear ⇒ page F 01-4

If NO malfunction is recognized:

- Press → button

Rapid data transfer	HELP→
Select function XX	

◄ Display will appear as shown

If one or more faults (malfunctions) are stored:

- Press 0 and 5 buttons to select function 05 "Erase DTC Memory"
- Press Q button to enter input

Rapid data transfer	→
DTC Memory is erased!	

◄ Display will appear as shown

> ***CAUTION!***
> ***If the ignition was switched OFF between checking and erasing DTC Memory; it will not be erased.***

- Press → button

Rapid data transfer	HELP
Select function XX	

◄ Display will appear as shown

- Press 0 and 6 buttons to select Function 06: "End data transfer"
- Press Q button to enter input

Rapid data transfer	Q
06–End output	

◄ Display will appear as shown

- Look up malfunctions in the Diagnostic Trouble Code Table, repair or replace as necessary
⇒ page F 01-12

Note:

The table lists the 5–digit trouble codes in sequence.

- Test drive vehicle for at least 5 minutes, ensuring that the following conditions are met:

♦ Engine Coolant Temperature must reach 85°C minimum

♦ Engine rpm must be raised to at least 3000 RPM

♦ Accelerator pedal must be pushed down briefly but completely, at least once

- Check DTC Memory again

Diagnostic Trouble Codes, table

Before replacing any components displayed by the Scan Tool:

- Check the wiring, terminal condition, harness connectors to the component and ground connections per the wiring diagram

● to check wiring: also see "Electrical Testing"
⇒ page F 01-31

Note:

DTC displays are only printed out if the Scan Tool is in the "Rapid data transfer" mode with the printer switched ON.

VAG 1551 Display	Possible Cause	Corrective Steps
65535 1111 No DTC recognized!	If there is a malfunction not recognized by On Board Diagnostic	– Continue troubleshooting, using wiring diagram
00518 2212 Throttle position sensor G69 Open circuit/short to ground	Wiring and/or G69 has short circuit to ground	– Check G69 wiring, starting page F 01-31, test steps 15, 34 and 35 and/or 31, 40 and 41
Open circuit/short to positive	Open circuit	
No DTC recognized, problem occurs sporadically	Open or short circuit in G69	– Check G69 wiring, starting page F 01-31 steps 15, 34 and 35 and/or 31, 40 and 41 – Check wiring and connectors for loose terminals, using wiring diagram – Check G69 ⇒ Repair Group 24
Implausible signal	G69 faulty	– Check G69, see page F 01-37
No signal	Open circuit	– Check G69 wiring, starting page F 01-31, steps 15, 34 and 35 and/or 31, 40 and 41
	G69 faulty	– Check G69 ⇒ Repair Group 24

VAG 1551 Display	Possible Cause	Corrective Steps
00519 2222 Manifold Absolute Pressure sensor G71	G71 in Digifant Engine Control Module faulty	– Check G71 ⇒ Repair Group 24
No signal	Vacuum line to Digifant Engine Control Module faulty or not connected	– Check vacuum line
00521 2242 CO Fuel Trim potentiometer G74	G74 faulty	– Check G 74 ⇒ Repair Group 24
Open circuit/short to positive	Open circuit	– Check G74 ⇒ page F 01-31, test step 13
No signal Short circuit to ground • for vehicles built after 7/92 • this code NOT for California	Wiring and/or G74 short circuit to ground	
00522 2312 Engine Coolant Temp sensor G62	G62 faulty	– Check G62 wiring ⇒ page F 01-31 steps 11 and/or 28
Open circuit/short to positive	Open circuit	
No DTC recognized, sporadic malfunction	Open circuit or short circuit G62	– Check G62 wiring ⇒ page F 01-31, steps 11 and/or 28 – Check wiring and connectors for loose terminals using wiring diagram ⇒ Repair Group 24

VAG 1551 Display	Possible Cause	Corrective Steps
00523 2322 Intake Air Temperature sensor G42	G42 faulty	– Check G42 wiring for short to ground
Short circuit to ground	Wiring shorted to ground	
Open circuit/short to positive	G42 faulty	– Check G42 wiring ⇒ page F 01-31 steps 12 and/or 29
	Open circuit	
No signal	G42 faulty	
	Open circuit	
No DTC recognized, sporadic malfunction	Open or short circuit in G42	– Check G42 wiring ⇒ page F 01-31 steps 12 and/or 29 – Check wiring and connectors for loose terminals using wiring diagram – Check G42 ⇒ Repair Group 24
00525 2342 Heated Oxygen sensor G39	G39 faulty	– Check G39 and Oxygen sensor control ⇒ Repair Group 24
No signal	Open circuit	– Check G 39 wiring ⇒ page F 01-31, steps 16 and/or 32
Short circuit to positive	G39 faulty	
	Wiring has short to positive	

VAG 1551 Display	Possible Cause	Corrective Steps
00537 2341 Oxygen sensor control	G39 faulty	– Check G39 and oxygen sensor control ⇒ Repair Group 24
Signal to positive	Wiring from G39 has short to positive	– Check intake system for leaks
	Control limit exceeded	
00545 2142 Signal from Transmission Control Module	Open circuit	– Check wiring and connectors for loose terminals using wiring diagram
No signal	Open circuit	
• this code applies to NON–California vehicles built after 10/91		

VAG 1551 Display	Possible Cause	Corrective Steps
00532 2234		
Supply voltage		
Signal too high	Battery voltage exceeds 15.5 Volts	– Check generator, using wiring diagrams. Repair or replace as necessary
Signal too low	Battery voltage below 6.1 Volts	– Check battery ⇒ Repair Group 27
• this code applies to NON–California vehicles built after 10/91		
01249 4411		
Injector cylinder 1	Open circuit and/or short to ground	– Check fuel injector wiring, ⇒ page F 01-31, test step 21
Faulty	Short to positive	– Check fuel injectors ⇒ Repair Group 24
• for California vehicles		
65535 1111		
Engine Control Module faulty	Faulty components in ECM J169	– Replace J169 ⇒ Repair Group 24

Function 03: Output Diagnostic Test Mode, checking

Vehicles built after 10/91

The following DTM components are activated via Output Diagnostic Test Mode (DTM) in the sequence given:

1 – Fuel pump relay J 17

2 – Idle Air Control valve N71

3 – EVAP canister purge regulator valve N80

– Fold down storage shelf in front of fuse/relay panel

– Connect VAG 1551 Scan Tool using adaptor cable VAG 1551/1 as follows:

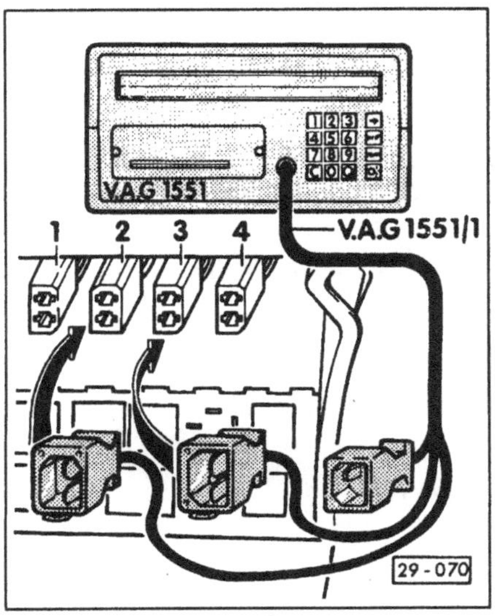

◄ – Connect black Scan Tool connector to black DLC 2 (Data Link Connector 2)

VAG On Board Diagnostic	HELP
1–Rapid data transfer	

VAG On Board Diagnostic	HELP
2–Blink code output	

◄ Display will alternate as shown

If display does NOT appear on Scan Tool:

- Do not connect Scan Tool white connector

- Check voltage supply to Scan Tool
⇒ page F 01-30

If display appears as shown:

- Connect white Scan Tool connector to vehicle white DLC 3

- Do not connect blue Scan Tool connector (not required)

- Switch ON ignition

- Operate VAG 1551 Scan Tool while observing display

- Press button 1 to select "Rapid data transfer" mode

- Press 0 and 1 buttons to select address word 01: "Engine electronics"

- Press Q button to enter input

- Press → button

- Press 0 and 3 buttons to select Function 03: "Output Diagnostic Test Mode"

Rapid data transfer	Q
03–Output Diagnostic Test Mode	

◄ Display will appear as shown

If a display other than these appears:
⇒ page F 01-4

- Trigger fuel pump relay J17

- Press Q button to enter input

Rapid data transfer	Q
03–Output Diagnostic Test Mode	

◄ Display will appear as shown

Note:

- *The fuel pump relay (fuse/relay panel location 12) must click until switched to the next output test by pressing the → button*
- *When triggering the fuel pump relay, the fuel pump must also run audibly*

If relay does NOT click:

- Perform electrical testing, steps 3 and/or 20
⇒ page F 01-31

- Trigger Idle Air Control valve N71

- Press → button

Output Diagnostic Test Mode	-
Fuel pump relay (J 17)	

◄ Display will appear as shown

Note:

The Idle Air Control valve must click until switched to the next Output test by pressing the → button.

If the Idle Air Control valve does not click:

- Disconnect harness connector -B- from Idle Air Control valve -A-

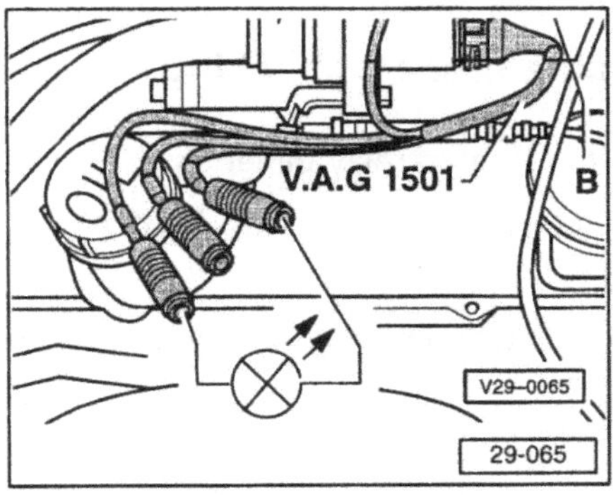

- Connect test adaptor VAG 1501 between valve and harness connector
- Connect US 1115 LED tester between terminals -1- and -3- test adaptor using jumper wires from VW 1594 adaptor kit

LED tester must blink

If LED blinks:

- Replace Idle Air Control valve

If NO:

- Perform electrical testing, steps 8 and/or 25 ⇒ page F 01-31
- Replace Digifant Engine Control Module, if necessary
- Trigger EVAP canister purge regulator valve N80
- Press → button

Output Diagnostic Test Mode
EVAP frequency vlave N 80

Display will appear as shown

Note:

The EVAP canister purge regulator valve must click until switched to the next Output test by pressing the button.

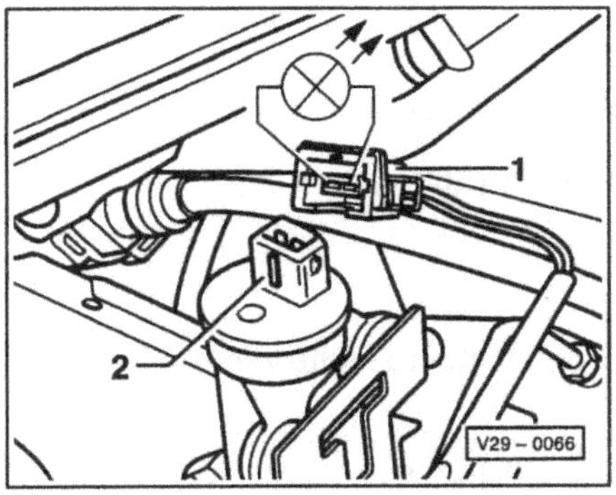

If the EVAP solenoid frequency valve does NOT click:

- Disconnect harness connector -1- from EVAP canister purge regulator valve -2-
- Connect VAG1527B LED tester between terminals of disconnected harness connector using jumper wires from VW 1594 adaptor kit
  - ♦ LED tester must blink

If LED blinks:

- Replace EVAP canister purge regulator valve

If LED does NOT blink:

- Perform electrical testing, step 5 and/or 22 ⇒ page F 01-31
- Replace ECM, if necessary

When Output Diagnostic Test checks have been completed:

- Press 0 and 6 buttons, select Function 06: "End data transfer"
- Press Q button to enter input
- Switch OFF ignition

Note:

If the ignition is not switched OFF before trying to start the engine, it will not turn over because the fuel injectors and ignition coil have not been activated.

Function 08:
"Read measuring value block", checking

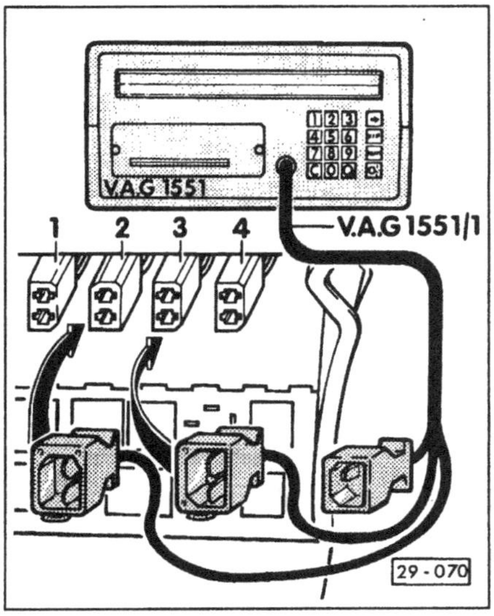

- Fold down storage shelf in front of relay panel
- Connect VAG 1551 Scan Tool using adaptor cable VAG 1551/1 as follows:
- ◄ Connect black Scan Tool connector to black vehicle Data Link Connector DLC2

VAG On Board Diagnostic	HELP
1–Rapid data transfer	

VAG On Board Diagnostic	HELP
2–Blink code output	

◄ Display will alternate as shown

If NO display appears on Scan Tool:

- Do not connect Scan Tool white connector
- Check voltage supply to Scan Tool
⇒ page F 01-30

If a display appears:

- Connect white Scan Tool connector to white vehicle Data Link Connector DLC 3
- Do not connect the blue Scan Tool connector (not required)

Depending on which Scan Tool function is required:

- Switch ON ignition
or
- Start engine

To determine which Function to select
⇒ table on page F 01-7

- Press Scan Tool HELP button (at any time) to obtain additional operating instructions
- Press → button to step through the program sequence
- Press 1 button to select "Rapid data transfer" operating mode

Rapid data transfer	HELP
Input address word XX	

◄ Display will appear as shown

- Press 0 and 1 buttons to select address word "Engine electronics"

Rapid data transfer	Q
01–Engine electronics	

◀ Display will appear as shown

– Press Q button to enter input

Read measurement block	HELP
Input display group number XX	

◀ Display will appear as shown

– Press → button

– Press 0 and 8 buttons to select
Function 08: "Read measuring value block"

– Press Q button to enter input

♦ Display will appear as shown

If any displays other than these appear:
⇒ page F 01-4

– Select desired display group number corresponding to display group overview

– Press Q button to enter display group number

♦ Example: Display Group 01

– Press 0 and 1 buttons to select display Group number 01

– Press Q button to enter input

Read measurement block 1			→
1	2	3	4

◀ Display group will appear as shown

Notes:

♦ *When function 08 "Read measurement block" is selected and display group numbers 01 to 05 are called up, the respective display group number is shown without the zero in the display*

♦ *When display group 00 is called up, the zeroes do not appear, only "Read measurement block" is shown on display*

♦ *Measurements are displayed in physical values*

Read measurement block 1									→
1	2	3	4	5	6	7	8	9	10

◀ ♦ *Measurements are shown in decimal form*

– Press -C- button before selecting any additional display groups

Display groups, overview

Vehicles built up to 9-91

Display group number	Parameters shown in display
00	Only used for individual testing, see Repair Group 24
01	1 = Engine Speed 2 = Manifold Absolute Pressure 3 = Engine Coolant Temperature 4 = Ignition timing point
02	1 = Engine Speed 2 = Intake Air Temperature 3 = for factory use only 4 = Fuel injection duration
03	1 = Engine Speed 2 = Engine Coolant Temperature 3 = for factory use only 4 = Fuel injection duration
04	1 = Engine Speed 2 = Manifold Absolute Pressure 3 = for factory use only 4 = Fuel injection duration
05	1 = Engine Speed 2 = Throttle Position Sensor 3 = for factory use only 4 = Fuel injection duration

Display groups, overview

Vehicles built after 10-91

Display group number	Parameters shown in display
00	Only used for individual testing, see Repair Group 24
01	1 = Engine Coolant Temperature 2 = Engine Speed 3 = Oxygen sensor signal voltage 4 = Ignition timing point
02	1 = Engine Coolant Temperature 2 = Engine Speed 3 = Throttle angle 4 = Engine load signal
03	1 = Engine Coolant Temperature 2 = Engine speed 3 = Intake Air Temperature 4 = Battery voltage
04	1 = Engine Coolant Temperature 2 = Engine Speed 3 = Ignition timing point 4 = Engine load signal
05	1 = Engine Coolant Temperature 2 = Engine Speed 3 = Throttle angle 4 = Battery voltage

For the following procedures:
⇒ Repair Group 24

- ♦ Heated Oxygen sensor and Oxygen sensor control, checking
- ♦ Acceleration/full throttle enrichment and deceleration fuel shut off, checking
- ♦ Throttle Position sensor, checking
- ♦ Engine Coolant Temperature sensor, checking
- ♦ Intake Air Temperature sensor, checking
- ♦ CO Fuel Trim potentiometer, checking
- ♦ Manifold Absolute Pressure sensor, checking

– Press → button to end "Read measuring block" Function

– Press 0 and 6 buttons to select Function 06: "End data transfer"

– Press -Q- button to enter input

Rapid data transfer	Q
06–End output	

◄ Display will appear as shown

VAG 1551 Scan Tool, voltage supply checking

Requirement

♦ Fuse 21 OK

– Switch Fluke 83 multimeter to 20 Volt scale

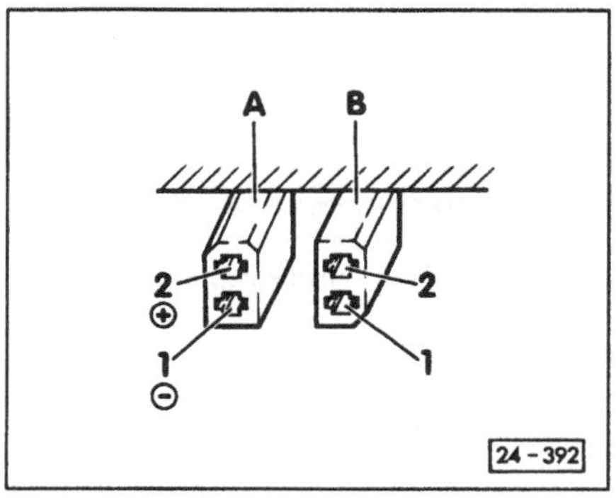

◄ – Measure voltage (and note polarity) at black Data Link Connector A in vehicle, using multimeter and jumper leads from VW 1594 adaptor kit

- ♦ terminal 1 = battery negative (–)
- ♦ terminal 2 = battery positive (+)

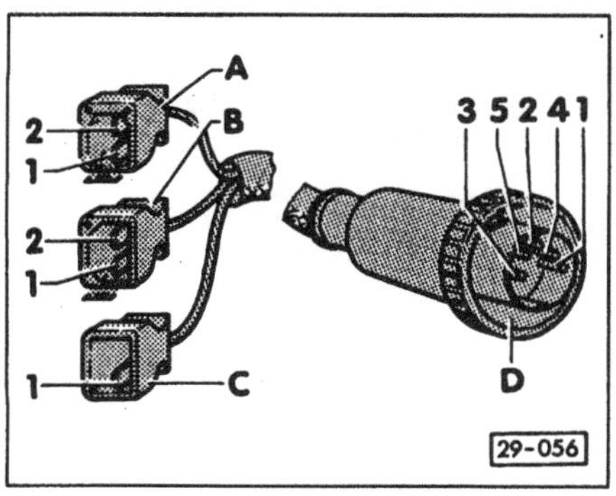

◄ – Check VAG 1551/1 Scan Tool adaptor cable for continuity

Data Link Connector terminal number			Scan Tool connector "D" terminal number
black	A	1 2	3 battery (–) 2 battery (+)
white	B	1 2	4 L wire 1 K wire
blue	C	1	5 lamp wire

Electrical wiring and components, testing

Using VAG 1598 Test Box and 1598/9 cable adaptor

> ***CAUTION!***
>
> ***ALWAYS switch the multimeter to the desired test range BEFORE connecting it to the circuit or component. Otherwise the Control Module, component or circuit could be damaged.***

- Use Fluke 83 multimeter (or equivalent) for all of the following electrical measurements
- Use the VAG1527B LED tester for the following tests
- Specified values are valid for ambient temperatures between 0 and + 40 °C
- If the measured values vary from the specified values, determine cause using wiring diagram
- If measured values vary only slightly from specified values, clean tester, test lead terminals and connectors
- Before replacing components, check the wiring and connectors especially when the specified values are less than 10 Ohms
- Repeat resistance measurements on components
- Use VAG 1598/9 adaptor wire and jumper wires from VW 1594 adaptor kit to connect testers to the VAG 1598 Test Box
- Vehicle connector terminal numbers match the VAG 1598 Test Box socket numbers

Requirements

- Battery voltage OK
- Fuses 15 and 18 OK
- Engine and transmission ground connections OK:
  up to 7/92: engine and intake manifold
  after 7/92: transmission, battery and body near battery
- Fuel pump and fuel pump relay OK

Vehicles with automatic transmission

Note:

If the Diagnostic Trouble Code (DTC) "No signal from automatic transmission" is stored in the Transmission Control Module (J 217) due to electrical testing, it must be erased after testing.
⇒ Repair Group 01 (Automatic transmission)

With ECM disconnected (49 states and Canada)

♦ California vehicles test table
⇒ page F 01-38

VAG 1698 Test Box, connecting

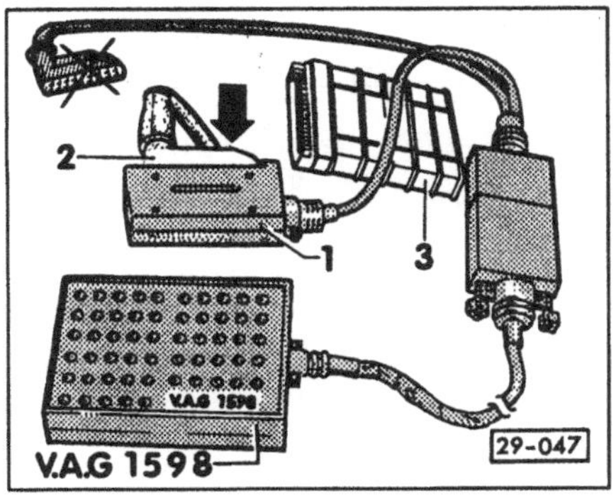

◄

– Switch OFF ignition

– Disconnect harness connector -2- from ECM -3-

♦ ECM -3- is installed in engine compartment on driver's side

– Connect VAG 1598 Test Box to wiring harness connector -2-

♦ Digifant Engine Control Module remains disconnected

Vehicles with automatic transmission

Note:

If the Diagnostic Trouble Code (DTC) "No signal from automatic transmission" is stored in the Transmission Control Module (J 217) due to electrical testing, it must be erased after testing. See Repair Group 01 (automatic transmission) for additional information.

– Switch Fluke 83 multimeter to 20 Volt range

Digifant system, electrical testing (49 states and Canada)

With ECM disconnected

49 States and Canada Vehicles				
Test step	**Test Box sockets**	**Item checked**	**• Test conditions – additional work**	**Specifications**
1	20 + 36 29 + 38	Voltage supply for ECM J169	– Switch ON ignition	Battery Voltage (approx.)
2	26 + 29	Wiring from starter terminal 50	– Operate starter,then switch OFF ignition	8 volts minimum
3	bridge 07 + 29	Wiring to fuel pump relay J17	• Ignition switched ON	Fuel pump must run audibly
4	2 + 20	Fuel injector wiring, N30, N31, N32, N33 and N83	• Ignition switched ON	Battery Voltage (approx)
5	04 + 29	EVAP canister purge regulator valve N 80	• Ignition switched ON – Remove fuse 18 – Bridge Test Box sockets 07 + 29 – Check injector resistance ⇒ Repair Group 24	Battery Voltage (approx)
6	20 + 27	Wiring to ignition coil N152	• Ignition switched ON	Battery Voltage app.
7	03 + 29	Cold start valve N17	• Ignition switched ON	Battery Voltage app.
8	25 + 29	IAC valve N71	• Ignition switched ON	Battery Voltage app.

Test step	Test Box sockets	Item checked	• Test conditions – additional work	Specifications
– Switch OFF ignition – Switch Fluke 83 multimeter to resistance range				
9[1]	37 + terminal with green wire	Wiring to A/C compressor	– Disconnect harness connector behind fuse/relay panel	1.5 Ohm maximum (continuity)

[1] Vehicles with A/C only

49 States and Canada Vehicles				
Test step	**Test Box sockets**	**Item checked**	**• Test conditions – additional work**	**Specifications**
10[1]	13 + terminal 1 11 + terminal 2 30 + terminal 3	Wiring to Camshaft Position sensor G40	– Disconnect Camshaft Position sensor harness connector	1.5 Ohm maximum (continuity)
11[2]	13 + 14	Engine Coolant Temperature sensor G62	See Repair Group 24	
12	13 + 15	Intake Air Temperature sensor G42 (inside of) CO Fuel Trim potentiometer G74 (Vehicles after 7/92)	—	Use chart from Repair Group 24 in step 11
13[4]	13 + 35	CO Fuel Trim potentiometer G74	—	0 to 2000 Ohms

[1] On Camshaft Position sensor harness connector.

[2] If a sensor malfunction is displayed via DTC but not detected by this test; it can be attributed to an intermittent open circuit in the temperature signal. In this case, also check the Engine Coolant Temperature sensor.
⇒ Repair Group 24

[3] Vehicles built up to 1/93

49 States and Canada Vehicles				
Test step	**Test Box sockets**	**Item checked**	**• Test conditions – additional work**	**Specifications**
14[1)]	13 + 35	Closed Throttle Position switch F60	– Throttle completely closed – Throttle wide open	1.5 Ohm maximum (continuity) Infinite Ohms (open)
15[2)]	01 + terminal 1 12 + terminal 2 13 + terminal 3	Throttle Position sensor wiring G69	– Disconnect harness connector from Throttle Position sensor G69	1.5 Ohm maximum (continuity)
16[3)]	20 + terminal 2 08 + terminal 3 08 + 20	Heated Oxygen sensor wiring G39	– Disconnect Heated Oxygen sensor G39 harness connector – Re–connect harness connector	1.5 Ohms maximum (continuity) Infinite Ohms (open)
17	32 + terminal 02	Gray/White wire on White Data Link Connector	—	1.5 Ohm maximum (continuity)

[1)] Vehicles built after 1/93

[2)] Throttle Position sensor harness connector.

[3)] Heated Oxygen sensor and Oxygen sensor heater harness connector.

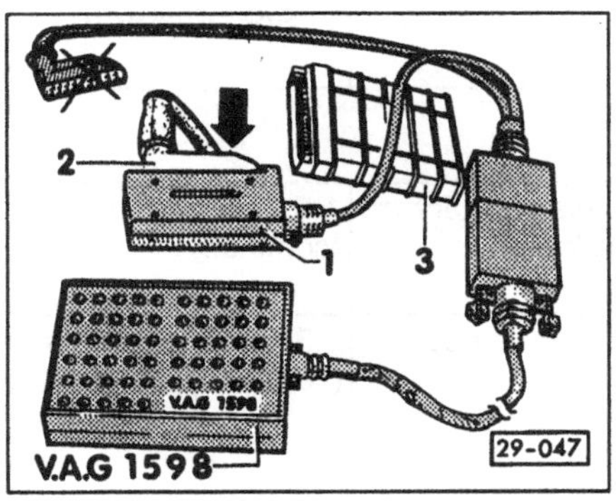

With ECM disconnected (California only)

VAG 1598 Test Box, connecting

♦ 49 States and Canada vehicles test table ⇒ page F 01-33

– Switch OFF ignition

◄ – Disconnect harness connector -2- from ECM 3

♦ ECM -3- is installed in the engine compartment on driver's side

– Connect VAG 1598 Test Box to wiring harness connector -2-

♦ Digifant Engine Control Module remains disconnected

Vehicles with automatic transmission

Note:

If the Diagnostic Trouble Code (DTC) "No signal from Automatic transmission" is stored in the Transmission Control Module (J 217) due to electrical testing, it must be erased after testing. *⇒ Repair Group 01 (Automatic transmission)*

– Switch Fluke 83 multimeter to 20 Volt range

Digifant system, electrical testing with ECM disconnected (California)

California Vehicles				
Test step	**Test Box sockets**	**Item checked**	• **Test conditions** – **additional work**	**Specifications**
18	01 + 07 19 + 35	Voltage supply for ECM J169	– Switch ON ignition	app. battery Voltage
19	25 + 35	Wiring from starter terminal 50	– Operate starter – Switch OFF ignition after this step is completed	8 Volts minimum
20	bridge 24 + 35	Wiring to fuel pump relay J17	• Ignition switched ON	Fuel pump must run audibly
21	EV11 + 20 EV21 + 21 EV31 + 03 EV41 + 02 EV51 + 22	Fuel injector wiring, N30, N31, N32, N33 and N83	• Ignition switched ON – Remove fuse 18 – Bridge terminals 24 + 35 – Check fuel injector resistance ⇒ Repair Group 24	battery Voltage
22	26 + 35	EVAP canister purge regulator valve N80	• Ignition switched ON	battery Voltage
23	01 + 06	Wiring to ignition coil N152	• Ignition switched ON	battery Voltage
24	05 + 35	Cold start injector N17	• Ignition switched ON	battery Voltage
25	23 + 35	Idle Air Control valve N71	• Ignition switched ON	battery Voltage

California Vehicles				
Test step	**Test Box sockets**	**Item checked**	• **Test conditions** – **additional work**	**Specifications**
– switch OFF ignition – switch Fluke 83 multimeter to resistance range				
26[1]	32 + terminal with green wire	Wiring to A/C compressor	– Disconnect harness connector behind fuse/relay panel	1.5 Ohms maximum (continuity)
27[2]	28 + terminal 01 37 + terminal 02 38 + terminal 3	Wiring to Camshaft position sensor (G 40)	– Disconnect harness connector at ignition distributor	1.5 Ohms maximum (continuity)

[1] Vehicles with A/C only.

[2] On Camshaft position sensor harness connector.

California Vehicles				
Test step	**Test Box sockets**	**Item checked**	**• Test conditions – additional work**	**Specifications**
28[1]	11 + 28	Engine Coolant Temperature sensor G62	See Repair Group 24	
29	28 + 30	Intake Air Temperature sensor G42	—	Use chart from Repair Group 24 in step 28
30	01 + 28	Closed Throttle Position switch F60	– Throttle completely closed	1.5 Ohms maximum (continuity)
			– Throttle wide open	Infinite Ohms (open)
31[2]	34 + terminal 01 33 + terminal 02 28 + terminal 03	Wiring to Throttle Position sensor G69	– Disconnect harness connector from Throttle Position sensor G69	1.5 Ohms maximum (continuity)

[1] If a malfunction in the sensor is displayed via DTC but not detected with this test, it can be attributed to an intermittent open circuit in the temperature signal path. In this case, also check the Engine Coolant Temperature sensor.

⇒ Repair Group 24

[2] Located on Throttle Position sensor harness connector.

California Vehicles				
Test step	**Test Box sockets**	**Item checked**	**• Test conditions – additional work**	**Specifications**
32[1]	01 + terminal 02 16 + terminal 03	Wiring to Heated Oxygen sensor G39	– Disconnect G39 harness connector	1.5 Ohms maximum (continuity)
	09 + 16 16 + 35		– Re–connect harness connector	Infinite Ohms (open)
33[2]	36 + terminal 02	Gray/White DLC wire	—	1.5 Ohms maximum (continuity)
	17 + terminal 01	Yellow/White DLC L–wire	—	1.5 Ohms maximum (continuity)

[1] On harness connector for Heated Oxygen sensor and Oxygen sensor heater.

[2] On the white DTC connector above the fuse/relay panel.

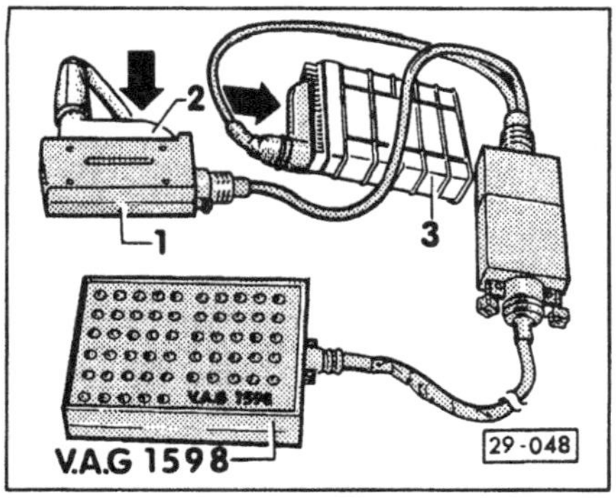

With ECM connected (49 states and Canada)

VAG 1598 Test Box, connecting

♦ For California vehicles test table
⇒ page F 01-38

– Read and observe ALL testing information
⇒ page F 01-31

– Switch OFF ignition

◄ – Connect VAG 1598 Test Box to ECM 3 and ECM harness connector 2 using adaptor cable 1

Vehicles with automatic transmission

Note:

If the Diagnostic Trouble Code (DTC) "No signal from Automatic transmission" is stored in the Transmission Control Module (J 217) due to electrical testing, it must be erased after testing.
⇒ Repair Group 01 (Automatic transmission)

– Switch Fluke 83 multimeter to 20 Volt range

Digifant system, electrical testing with ECM connected (49 states and Canada)

49 States and Canada Vehicles				
Test step	**Test Box sockets**	**Item checked**	**• Test conditions – additional work**	**Specifications**
34	01 + 12	Voltage supply for Throttle Position sensor G69	– Disconnect G69 harness connector	3.5 to 5.0 Volts
			– Switch ON ignition	4.5 to 5.0 Volts
35	12 + 13	Throttle Position sensor G69	• Ignition switched ON – Re–connect harness connector *Throttle setting:*	
			– Closed Throttle Position	0.3 to 1.7 Volts
			– Wide Open Throttle	3.0 to 5.0 Volts
36[1)]	31 + 30	Supply Voltage for Camshaft position sensor G40	• Ignition switched ON	10 Volts minimum
– Switch OFF ignition – Connect VAG 1527B LED tester (instead of multimeter) to Test Box using VW 1594/15 adaptor cable – Disconnect cold start valve harness connector – Disconnect main fuel injector harness connector at fuel rail				
37[1)]	11 + 13	Camshaft position sensor G40 signal	– Operate starter	LED tester must flicker
38[1)]	20 + 27	Ignition signal from ECM J169	– Operate starter	LED tester must flicker
39	10 + 13	RPM signal	– Operate starter	LED tester must flicker

[1)] Only perform if engine does not turn over.

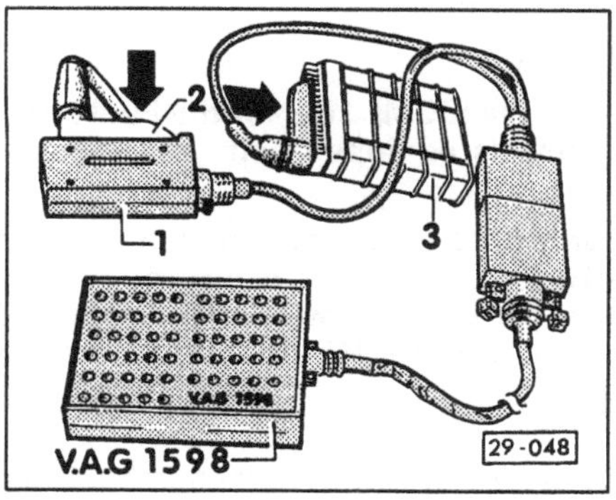

With ECM connected (California only)

VAG 1598 Test Box, connecting

♦ For 49 States and Canada vehicles test table
⇒ see page F 01-33

– Read and observe ALL of the testing information on
⇒ page F 01-31

– Switch OFF ignition

◄ – Connect VAG 1598 Test Box to ECM 3 and ECM harness connector 2 using adaptor cable 1

Vehicles with automatic transmission

Note:

If the Diagnostic Trouble Code (DTC) "No signal from automatic transmission" is stored in the Transmission Control Module (J 217) due to electrical testing, it must be erased after testing.
⇒ Repair Group 01 (automatic transmission)

– switch Fluke 83 multimeter to 20 Volt range

Digifant system, electrical testing with ECM connected (California)

California Vehicles				
Test step	**Test Box sockets**	**Item checked**	**• Test conditions – additional work**	**Specifications**
40	33 + 34	Voltage supply for Throttle Position sensor G69	– Disconnect G69 harness connector	3.5 to 5.0 Volts
	28 + 34		– Switch ON ignition	4.5 to 5.0 Volts
41	28 + 33	Throttle Position sensor G69	• Ignition switched ON – Re–connect harness connector *Throttle setting:*	
			– Closed Throttle Position	0.3 to 1.7 Volts
			– Wide Open Throttle	3.0 to 5.0 Volts
42[1)]	28 + 38	Supply Voltage for Camshaft position sensor G40	• Ignition switched ON	10 Volts minimum
– Switch OFF ignition – Connect VAG 1527B LED tester (instead of multimeter) to Test Box using VAG 1594/15 adaptor cable – Disconnect cold start valve harness connector – Disconnect main fuel injector harness connector at fuel rail				
43[1)]	28 + 37	Camshaft position sensor G40 signal	– Operate starter	LED tester must flicker
44[1)]	01 + 06	Ignition signal from Digifant ECM J169	– Operate starter	LED tester must flicker
45	18 + 28	RPM signal	– Operate starter	LED tester must flicker

[1)] Only perform if engine does not turn over.

On Board Diagnostic, general information

Vehicles built starting m.y. 1995

- The Engine Control Module (ECM) J169 for the Fuel Injection and Ignition system is equipped with a Diagnostic Trouble Code (DTC) memory.
- If malfunctions occur with sensors and/or components monitored by the On Board Diagnostic system, they will be stored in the DTC memory together with an indication of the type of malfunction. Check DTC memory to display stored malfunctions.

⇒ page F 01-52

- DTC memory must be erased once a malfunction has been eliminated.

⇒ page F 01-67

- Malfunctions relating to the Heated Oxygen sensor control system function can only be checked after a test drive of at least 10 minutes.
- Malfunctions due to a temporary open circuit in the wiring or a loose terminal, will also be stored. These malfunctions will be displayed as sporadic malfunctions "SP" and are erased automatically if they are not repeated after 40 engine starts.

Vehicles with Malfunction Indicator Lamp (MIL) ONLY:

- The instrument cluster MIL lamp must light up when the ignition is switched ON and go out when the engine starts. If malfunctions occur in sensors and/or components and monitoring conditions are satisfied, the MIL lamp will also light up (with engine running).

On Board Diagnostic system, technical data

System is equipped with:

- Diagnostic Trouble Code (DTC) memory: Permanent memory and Sporadic memory[1)]
- Rapid data transfer

Selectable Functions:

Function		Ignition switched ON	Engine idling
02	Check DTC memory	YES	YES
03	Output Diagnostic Test Mode (DTM)	YES	NO
04	Basic setting[1)]	NO	YES
05	Erase DTC memory	YES	YES
06	End data output	YES	YES
08	Read measuring value block	YES	YES

[1)] Will be erased after 40th engine start if malfunction has not recurred.

VAG 1551 Scan Tool, connecting

Test conditions

- ♦ Battery Voltage OK
- ♦ Fuse 21 OK
- ♦ Engine and transmission Ground connections OK (Engine Ground connection on cylinder head)

- Disconnect shelf in front of fuse/relay panel
- Connect VAG 1551 Scan Tool using VAG 1551/1 adaptor cable as follows:
- First connect the black plug for the VAG 1551 Scan Tool (Voltage supply) to black Data Link Connector -2-

VAG – On Board Diagnostic	HELP
1–Rapid data transfer*	
2–Blink code output*	

◄ – Display will appear as shown

* Appears alternately

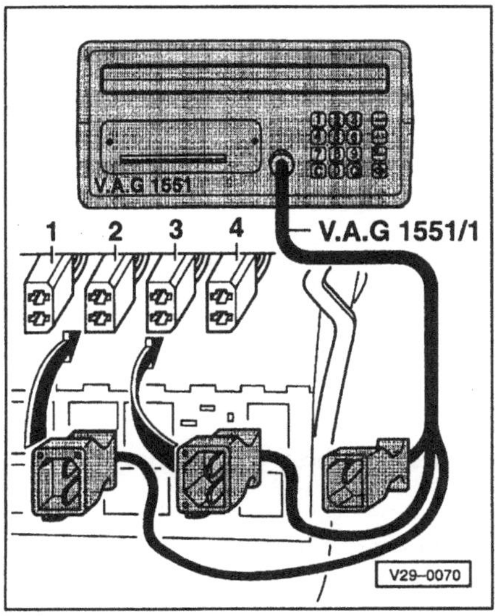

Note:

If the display remains blank, do not connect the white VAG 1551 plug! In this case check the Scan Tool Voltage supply. ⇒ F 01-81

◄ – Connect white plug to white Data Link Connector-3- (Blue plug is not used for this application)

Depending upon desired function

- Switch ON ignition

or

- Start engine
- Operate Scan Tool taking displayed information into account
- Press 1 button to select "Rapid data transfer"
- Press 0 and 1 buttons to select address word "Engine electronics"
- Press Q button to enter input

023 906 024 C Digifant 1.72	1640→

◄ VAG 1551 Scan Tool display will show ECM data:

- ♦ 023 906 024 C = ECM Part No. (for latest version ⇒ parts catalog)
- ♦ DIGIFANT 1.72 = System designation and version
- ♦ 1640 = Program level number

Control Module does not answer! HELP

◄ Display will appear as shown

- Print out list of Possible Causes by pressing HELP button

After eliminating Possible Causes

- Press 0 and 1 buttons to select address word "Engine electronics"
- Press Q button to enter input

Note:

Correct Engine Control Module and program level number details are only given with engine running.

- Press → button

Rapid data transfer	HELP
Select function XX	

◄ Display will appear as shown

- For additional steps, see repair procedures

Function 02: Diagnostic Trouble Code (DTC) memory, checking

- Connect VAG 1551 Scan Tool ⇒ page F 01-49
- Press 0 and 1 buttons to select address word "Engine electronics" with engine running
- Press Q button to enter input

If engine will not start:

- Operate starter for approx. 6 seconds, then leave ignition switched ON
- Press Print button to switch on printer
  - ♦ Print button LED lights up

Rapid data transfer	HELP
Select function XX	

◄ Display will appear as shown

- Press 0 and 2 buttons to select Function 02; "check DTC memory"
- Press Q button to enter input

X malfunctions recognized!

◄ The number of malfunctions stored or "No malfunction recognized!" will be shown on the display

Note:

If one or more malfunctions are stored, they will be displayed and printed out one after the other in sequence

Rapid data transfer	HELP
Select function XX	

◄ The display will then appear as shown

If no malfunctions are stored:

- Press → button
- Press 0 and 6 buttons to select Function 06: "End data output"
- Press Q button to enter input
- Locate and eliminate malfunctions printed out as per DTC table
⇒ page F 01-54
- Erase DTC memory
⇒ page F 01-67

Note:

If a malfunction is present which is not recognized by the On Board Diagnostic system, perform additional troubleshooting using the wiring diagram.

Diagnostic Trouble Code (DTC) table

Notes:

- *The DTC table is listed according to the 5 digit Diagnostic Trouble Code (DTC) code located in the upper left column of the chart*
- *Before replacing components indicated as being faulty, check the wiring and connectors to these components as well as the Ground connections using the wiring diagram. This is particularly relevant if malfunctions are output as "sporadic"*
- *For wiring check, also refer to the "Electrical checks" section*
⇒ page F 01-82

VAG 1551 Display	Possible Cause	Corrective Steps
No malfunction recognized!	If a malfunction is present: it is not recognized by On Board Diagnostic	Continue troubleshooting using wiring diagram
00515 2113 Camshaft Position sensor G40 Faulty	G40 faulty	– Check G40 ⇒ Repair Group 28, page F 28-35
	Incorrect trigger wheel	– Check wiring ⇒ page F 01-86, Test step 12
No malfunction type recognized/sporadic malfunction		

VAG 1551 Display	Possible Cause	Corrective Steps
00518 2212 Throttle Position sensor G69 Short to Ground	Wiring/G69 has short to Ground	– Check wiring together with G69 ⇒ page F 01-87, Test step 17
Open circuit/short to positive	Open circuit	
No signal	G69 faulty	
No malfunction type recognized/sporadic malfunction	For a brief period: Wiring open circuit, short circuit or open circuit in G69	– Check wiring together with G69 ⇒ page F 01-87, Test step 17 – Check wiring and connections for loose terminals using wiring diagram – Check G69 ⇒ Repair Group 24

VAG 1551 Display	Possible Cause	Corrective Steps
00519 2222 Manifold Absolute Pressure sensor G71	G71 in ECM faulty	– Check G71 ⇒ Repair Group 24, page F 24-105
No signal	Vacuum lines to ECM faulty or not connected	– Check vacuum lines
	Throttle Position sensor G69 faulty	– Trial replace G69
00522 2312 Engine Coolant Temperature sensor G62	G62 faulty, or connector is corroded causing incorrect working range	– Check wiring together with G62 ⇒ page F 01-86, Test step 13
Open circuit/short to positive	Wiring open circuit or short circuit to positive	
Impossible signal	Intermittent open circuit, short or open circuit in G62	– Check wiring together with G62 ⇒ page F 01-86, Test step 13
No malfunction type recognized/sporadic malfunction		– Check wiring and connections for loose terminals using wiring diagram – Check G62 ⇒ Repair Group 24, page F 24-101

VAG 1551 Display	Possible Cause	Corrective Steps
00523 2322 Intake Air Temperature sensor G42	G42 faulty	– Check wiring and G42 for short to Ground
Short to Ground	Wiring has short to Ground	
Open circuit/short to positive	G42 faulty	– Check wiring together with G42 ⇒ page F 01-86, Test step 14
	Wiring open circuit	
No signal	G42 faulty	
	Wiring open circuit	
00524 2142 Knock sensor 1 G61	Wiring open circuit/short circuit in sensor wiring	– Check wiring to G61 ⇒ page F 01-88, Test step 20
No signal	G61 faulty (knock sensor on right in direction of travel ⇒ F 01-92, Fig. 3)	– Replace G61 ⇒ Repair Group 28, page F 28-24, item 17
	No knock detection from Engine Control Module J169	– Replace J169 ⇒ Repair Group 24, page F 24-80, item 3

VAG 1551 Display	Possible Cause	Corrective Steps
00525 2342		
Heated Oxygen sensor G39	G39 faulty	– Check Heated Oxygen sensor and Oxygen sensor control ⇒ Repair Group 24, page F 24-92
No signal	Heated Oxygen sensor heater faulty	– Check Oxygen sensor heater Voltage supply ⇒ Repair Group 24
	Wiring open circuit	– Check wiring to G39 ⇒ page F 01-87, Test step -18-
Short circuit to positive	Short circuit to positive in wiring or G39	– Check wiring to G39 ⇒ page F 01-87, Test step -18-
	Wiring open circuit	– Check wiring and G39 for short to positive or Ground
Short circuit to Ground	Short circuit to Ground in wiring or G39	
	Fuel tank empty	– Fill tank/erase DTC memory ⇒ page F 01-67

VAG 1551 Display	Possible Cause	Corrective Steps
00532 2234		
Supply Voltage Signal too high	Battery Voltage above 15.5 Volts	– Check Generator ⇒ Wiring diagram
Signal too low	Battery Voltage less than 6.1 Volts	– Check battery – check Voltage supply for J169 ⇒ page F 01-84, Test step 1

VAG 1551 Display	Possible Cause	Corrective Steps
00537 2341		
Oxygen sensor control	Exhaust system leak between cylinder head and Three-way catalyst	– Check exhaust system: ⇒ Repair Group 26
Control limit exceeded	Misfiring	– Check ignition components ⇒ Repair Group 28, page F 28-22
	Intake Air system leaking	– Check intake air system for leaks (unmeasured air) ⇒ Repair Group 24, page F 24-116
	Injector(s) N30, N32, N32, N33, N83 faulty	– Check fuel injectors ⇒ Repair Group 24, page F 24-112
	Fuel pressure too low	– Check fuel pressure regulator ⇒ Repair Group 24, page F 24-106
	Fuel pressure too high	
	Oxygen sensor heater faulty	– Check Oxygen sensor heater Voltage supply and heater for continuity ⇒ Repair Group 24, page F 24-81 item 5
	EVAP canister purge regulator valve 1 N80 sticks (permanently open)	– Check N80 ⇒ page F 01-72, Output DTM

VAG 1551 Display	Possible Cause	Corrective Steps
Heated Oxygen sensor control continued		
Control limit not reached	Fuel pressure too high	– Check fuel pressure regulator ⇒ page F 24-106
	Injector(s) N30, N31, N32, N33, N83 faulty, leaking	– Check injector ⇒ page F 24-112
00540 2144		
Knock sensor 2 G66	Wiring open circuit/short circuit in sensor wiring	– Check wiring to G66 ⇒ page F 01-88, Test step 21
No signal	G66 faulty ⇒ page 01-46, Fig. 3 (left knock sensor)	– Replace G66 ⇒ page F 28-24, item 15
	No knock recognition from ECM J169	– Replace J169 ⇒ page F 24-80, item 3
00545 2314		
Engine/transmission electrical connection		
No signal	Wiring open circuit	– Check wiring and connections using wiring diagram

VAG 1551 Display	Possible Cause	Corrective Steps
00560 2411 Exhaust Gas Recirculation system	N18 EGR Vacuum Regulator Solenoid-valve faulty	– Check N18 ⇒ page F 01-74, Output DTM – Check wiring together with N18 ⇒ page F 01-89, Test steps 22, 23 – If necessary replace N18 ⇒ Repair Group 26
Signal to Ground	EGR temperature sensor G98 faulty	– Check wiring together with G98 ⇒ page F 01-89, Test step 24
	Wiring open circuit or short to Ground	– Locate malfunction using wiring diagram and repair as necessary
Signal to positive	Wire has short to positive	⇒ Wiring diagram
	EGR valve faulty	– Check EGR valve ⇒ Repair Group 26
	Vacuum lines faulty or not connected	– Check wiring: ⇒ Repair Group 26

VAG 1551 Display	Possible Cause	Corrective Steps
00703 Closed Throttle Position switch F60 Impossible signal	F60 faulty	– Check wiring together with F60 ⇒ page F 01-86, Test step 16 – Check Closed Throttle position switch F60 ⇒ Repair Group 24, page F 24-121
00740 Cyl 1 Crankshaft Position sensor G145	Wiring open circuit	– Check wiring to Camshaft Position sensor ⇒ page F 01-86, Test step 12
No signal	Incorrect Camshaft Position sensor rotor/ distributor	– Check Camshaft Position sensor ⇒ Repair Group 28, page F 28-35

VAG 1551 Display	Possible Cause	Corrective Steps
00758 Secondary Air Injection system faulty	Secondary Air Injection pump relay J299, Secondary Air Injection solenoid valve N112, Secondary Air Injection pump motor V101, faulty	– Perform Output Diagnostic Test Mode ⇒ page F 01-74 – Check wiring together with J299, N112 and V101 ⇒ page F 01-90, Test steps 25, 26
	Wiring open circuit or wire has short to positive	– Locate malfunction using wiring diagram and repair as necessary
	Vacuum lines or pressure hoses faulty or not connected	– Check lines and hoses: ⇒ Repair Group 26
	Secondary Air Injection pump faulty or not pumping, combi valve faulty or sticking, check–valve faulty or sticking	– Check Secondary Air Injection pump, combi-valve and check-valve: ⇒ Repair Group 26

VAG 1551 Display	Possible Cause	Corrective Steps
01087 Basic setting not performed	Basic setting not performed after replacing ECM	– Perform basic setting ⇒ Repair Group 24, page F 24-85
01249 to 01253 No. 1 Cyl. injector N30...	Wire or N30, N31, N32, N33, or N83 has short to positive	– Check N30, N31, N32, N33, or N83 ⇒ Repair Group 24, page F 24-112
Faulty	N30, N31, N32, N33, or N83 faulty	– Check wiring together with N30, N31, N32, N33, or N83 ⇒ page F 01-84, Test step 5/6
	Wiring open circuit/short to Ground	
65535 1111 Engine Control Module faulty	ECM internal components J169	– Replace J169 ⇒ Repair Group 24, page F 24-80, item 3

Function 05: Diagnostic Trouble Code (DTC) memory, erasing

Test conditions

♦ DTC's eliminated (if any)

– Perform a road test of at least 10 minutes duration; the following conditions must be met during the drive

♦ Engine coolant temperature must reach 80°C (176°F) minimum

♦ Accelerator pedal must be fully depressed (momentarily) until engine speed exceeds 4600 rpm

♦ Accelerate in 4th gear from approx. 50 km/h (30 mph) for approx. 4 seconds using half throttle

– Connect VAG 1551 Scan Tool
⇒ page F 01-49

– Press 0 and 1 buttons to select address word "Engine electronics" with engine running

– Press Q button to enter input

Rapid data transfer	HELP
Select function XX	

◄ Display will appear as shown

– Press 0 and 2 buttons to select Function 02: "Check DTC memory"

– Press Q button to enter input

Rapid data transfer	HELP
Select function XX	

◄ – Press → button until all malfunctions still stored have appeared and the display again reads as shown

– Press 0 and 5 buttons to select Function 05: "Erase DTC memory"

– Press Q button to enter input

Rapid data transfer	→
DTC memory is erased!	

◄ Display will appear as shown

– Press → button

Rapid data transfer	HELP
Select function XX	

◄ Display will appear as shown

– Press 0 and 6 buttons to select Function 06: "End data output"

– Press Q button to enter input

– Road test again and check DTC memory

♦ No malfunctions should be stored/displayed

Function 03: Output Diagnostic Test Mode (DTM)

The Output DTM activates the following components in the sequence shown

1. Fuel pump relay J17
2. Idle Air Control valve N71
3. EVAP canister purge regulator valve 1 N80
4. Secondary Air Injection pump relay J299[1)]
5. EGR vacuum regulator solenoid valve N18[1)]

Special tools, testers and auxiliary items

- ♦ VAG 1551 Scan Tool using VAG 1551/1 adaptor cable
- ♦ VW 1594 adaptor kit
- ♦ VAG 1527B LED Tester

[1)] Only for vehicles with a 6 pin fuel rail harness connector

Test sequence

– Connect VAG 1551 Scan Tool ⇒ page F 01-49

– With ignition switched ON press 0 and 1 buttons to select address word "Engine electronics"

– Press Q button to enter input

Rapid data transfer	HELP
Select function XX	

◄ Display will appear as shown

– Operate VAG 1551 Scan Tool taking displayed information into account

– Press 0 and 3 buttons to select Function 03: "Output Diagnostic Test Mode"

Rapid data transfer	Q
03 Output Diagnostic Test Mode (DTM)	

◄ Display will appear as shown

– Actuate fuel pump relay J17

– Press Q button to enter input

Output Diagnostic Test Mode (DTM)	→
Fuel pump relay J17	

◄ Display will appear as shown

Note:

The fuel pump relay (on the relay panel near the fuse box, relay position -12-) must click until switching to the next DTM component by pressing the → button.

During the activation of the fuel pump relay the fuel pump must be audibly heard running at intervals.

If the relay does not click:

– Check fuel pump relay using the wiring diagram

– Activate the Idle Air Control valve N71

– Press → button

Output Diagnostic Test Mode (DTM) →
Idle Air Control valve N71

◄ Display will appear as shown

Note:

The Idle Air Control valve must click, until switching to the next DTM component by pressing the → button.

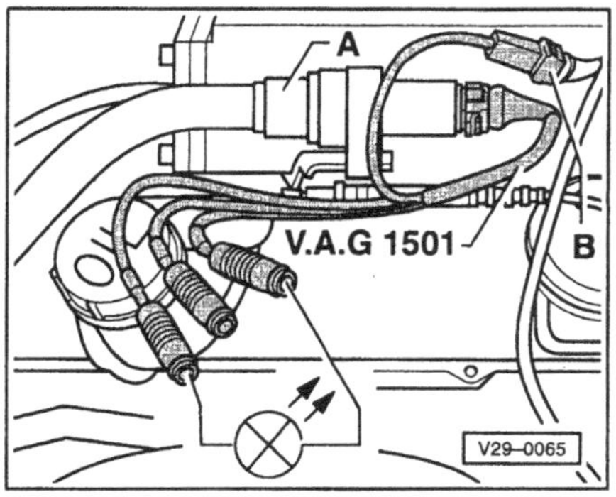

If Idle Air Control valve does not click

◄ – Disconnect harness connector -B- from Idle Air Control valve -A-, connect adaptor cable VAG 1501 between valve and connector

– Connect VAG 1527B LED tester between connectors -1- and -3- of adaptor cable using jumper wires from VW 1594 adaptor kit

♦ LED must flash

If LED flashes:

– Replace Idle Air Control valve

If LED does not flash:

– Perform electrical check, test step -10-, if necessary replace ECM
⇒ page F 01-85

Activate EVAP canister purge regulator valve 1 N80

– Press → button

Output Diagnostic Test Mode (DTM) →
EVAP canister purge regulator valve N80

◄ Display will appear as shown

Note:

The valve must click until switching to the next DTM component by pressing the → button

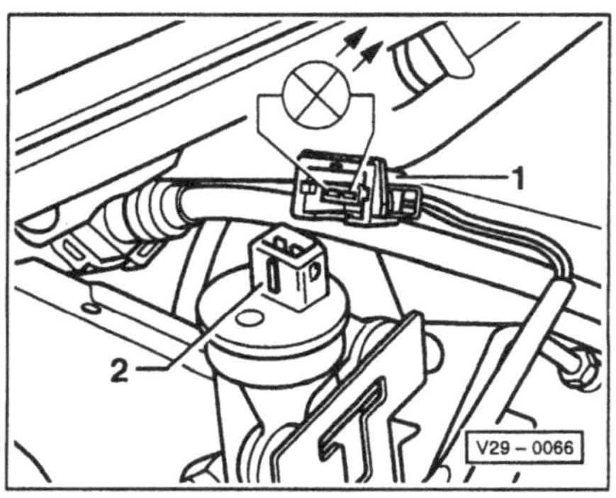

If valve does not click:

◄ – Disconnect harness connector-1- from Secondary Air Injection solenoid valve -2- and connect VAG 1527B LED tester to harness connector using jumper wires from VW 1594 adaptor kit

♦ LED must flash

If LED flashes:

– Replace Secondary Air Injection solenoid valve

If LED does not flash:

– Perform electrical check, test step -7-, replace ECM, if necessary
⇒ page F 01-85

– Activate Secondary Air Injection pump relay J299

– Press → button

Output Diagnostic Test Mode (DTM) →
Secondary Air Injection pump relay J299

◄ Display will appear as shown

The Secondary Air Injection pump relay J299 controls the Secondary Air Injection solenoid valve N112 and the Secondary Air Injection pump motor V101 in intervals, until the next DTM component is activated by pressing the → button

- ♦ The Secondary Air Injection solenoid valve N112 must be felt to switch

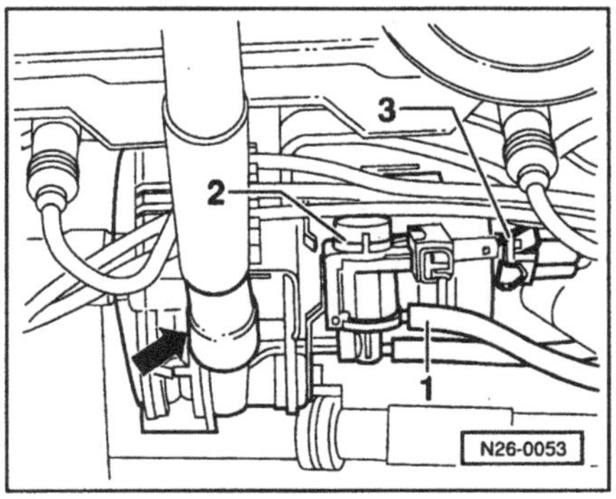

If the Secondary Air Injection pump motor does not run:

◄ – Disconnect (2-pin) harness connector -3- from Secondary Air Injection pump motor V101

– Connect VAG 1527B LED tester to the harness connector using jumper wires from the VW 1594 adaptor kit

- ♦ LED must light up

If LED lights up (Voltage supply OK):

– Replace the Secondary Air Injection pump motor V101

If the Secondary Air Injection solenoid valve does not switch:

– Disconnect the (2-pin) harness connector from the Secondary Air Injection solenoid valve N112

– Connect the VAG 1527B LED tester to the harness connector using jumper wires from the VW 1594 adaptor kit

- ♦ LED must light up

If LED lights up (Voltage supply OK):

– Replace Secondary Air Injection solenoid valve N112

If LED does not light up:

– Press → button until the Output DTM sequence completes

– Press 0 and 6 buttons to select
Function 06: "End data output"

– Press Q button to enter input

– Switch OFF ignition

– Perform electrical check, test steps 25 and 26 or (if necessary) locate short circuit using wiring diagram, correct as necessary
⇒ page F 01-90

If open circuit cannot be located:

– Replace Secondary Air Injection pump relay J299 or ECM J169 as necessary

– Activate EGR Vacuum Regulator solenoid valve N18

– Press → button

Output Diagnostic Test Mode (DTM) →
EGR Vacuum Regulator Solenoid valve N18

◄ Display will appear as shown

- ♦ EGR Vacuum Regulator solenoid valve N18 must click

If EGR valve does not click:

- Disconnect EGR valve harness connector and connect VAG 1527B LED tester to connector using jumper wires from VW 1594 adaptor kit

If LED flashes:

- Replace EGR Vacuum Regulator solenoid valve N18

If LED does not flash:

- Switch OFF ignition
- Reconnect harness connector to EGR valve
- Perform electrical check, test steps 22 and 23, replace ECM J169 if necessary
⇒ page F 01-89
- Press → button

Note:

After completion of Output Diagnostic Test Mode ; select Function 06: "End data output" and confirm with Q button. Then switch OFF the ignition.

If ignition is not switched OFF before attempting a start, the engine won't be able to start because the fuel injectors and ignition coil will not be activated.

- Switch OFF ignition

Function 08: Measuring value block, reading

The measured values in the Functions: "Reading measuring value block" and "Engine basic setting" are described during the individual component tests. The following table provides an overview.

Note:

To change to a different display group, press the -C- button.

Special tools, testers and auxiliary items

- VAG 1551 Scan Tool using adaptor cable VAG 1551/1

Measuring value block, display group overview

Display group 00 (decimal figures displayed)										
	Display zones									
	1	2	3	4	5	6	7	8	9	10
Display	Intake Air Temper-ature (°C)	Battery Voltage (Volts)	Engine Coolant Temper-ature (°C)	Air quantity (%)	Heated Oxygen sensor signal (Volts)	Heated Oxygen sensor control time counter	Heated Oxygen sensor status counter	Throttle Position sensor Voltage (Volts)	Fuel Injection period (ms)	Engine speed (rpm)
Spec[1)]	70 to 15	115 to 155	2 to 9	15 to 150	230 to 120	0	0 to 5[2)]	10 to 130	4 to 12	212 to 186
Corre-sponds to	12 to 65°C	10.8 to 14.4 Volts	80 to 110°C	5 to 60%	0.0 to 0.8 Volts	—	—	0.2 to 2.5 Volts	2 to 6 ms	775 to 1200 rpm

[1)] Specifications are valid for the Engine Control Module when in Function 04: "Basic setting".

[2)] The display will indicate high when there is no Heated Oxygen sensor signal (e.g. sensor cold). The display values can increase to 255 if for example the sensor heater or wiring is faulty. Check using Function 08 "Read measuring value block"

destination

	Display zones			
	1	2	3	4
Display group 01				
Display	xxxx rpm	xxx °C	x.x Volts	xxxxxxxx
Indicated	Engine speed	Engine Coolant Temperature	Heated Oxygen sensor Voltage	Adjustment conditions[2)]
Spec[1)]	775 to 1200	80 to 110	0.0 to 0.8	00000000
Display group 02				
Display	xxxx rpm	xx.xx ms	xx.xx Volts	xxx °C
Indicated	Engine speed	Fuel Injection period	Battery Voltage	Intake Air Temperature
Display group 03				
Display	xxxx rpm	xxx %	xx.xx ∠°	xxx %
Indicated	Engine speed	Engine load signal	Throttle valve angle (calculated value, dependent on Throttle Position sensor)	Idle Air Control valve opening

[1)] Specifications are valid when Engine Control Module is in Function 04: "Basic setting".

[2)] For relevance of numbers in 8 digit number block:
⇒ page F 01-80

	Display zones			
	1	2	3	4
Display group 04				
Display	xxxx rpm	xxx %	xxx	xxxxxxxx
Indicated	Engine speed	Engine load signal	Not relevant	Operating condition[1)]
Display group 05				
Display	xxxx rpm	xxx %	xxx	xxxxxxxx
Indicated	Engine speed	Duty cycle for: EVAP canister purge regulator valve	Not Relevant	Not relevant
Display group 06				
Display	xxx	xxx	xxx	xxx
Indicated	Learned mixture adaption value[2)]	Mixture adaption constant[2)]	Learned idle speed control value[2)]	Value stored in memory for Throttle Position sensor during "Basic setting"
Display group 07: Only for factory use.				

[1)] For relevance of values in 8 digit number block:
⇒ page F 01-80

[2)] Specification range not yet determined at time of printing

Relevance of figures in 8 digit number block

Relevance when displayed digit = 1									
X	X	X	X	X	X	X	X	Adjustment conditions (display group 01)	Operating condition (display group 04)
1								Not relevant	Overrun
	1							Signal from automatic transmission	Idling
		1						A/C compressor switched ON	Partially open throttle
			1					Closed Throttle Position switch open	Full load (Wide Open Throttle)
				1				Malfunction in Oxygen sensor control	Not relevant
					1			Throttle opened	Not relevant
						1		Engine speed over 2300 rpm	Not relevant
							1	Engine Coolant temperature below 80 °C	Not relevant

Additional measures
⇒ Repair procedures:

Notes:

- *Press → button to end "Read measuring value block"*
- *After terminating "Read measuring value block", select Function 06: "End data output" and confirm with Q.*

VAG 1551 Scan Tool Voltage supply, checking

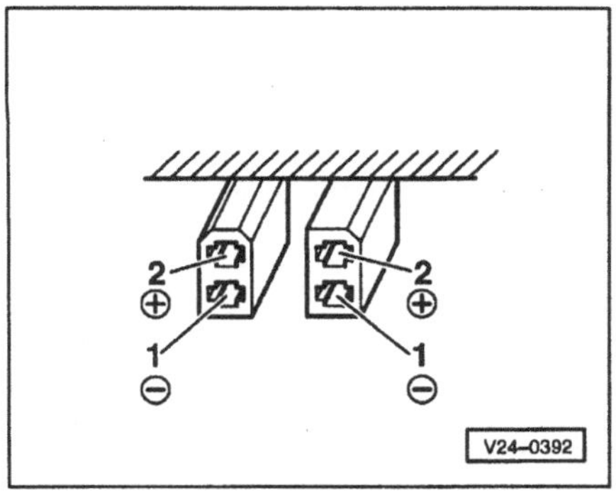

♦ Fuse 21 OK

– Check Voltage at black Data Link Connector -A- in vehicle (observe polarity when checking)

Terminal 1 = Battery negative (–)

Terminal 2 = Battery positive (+)

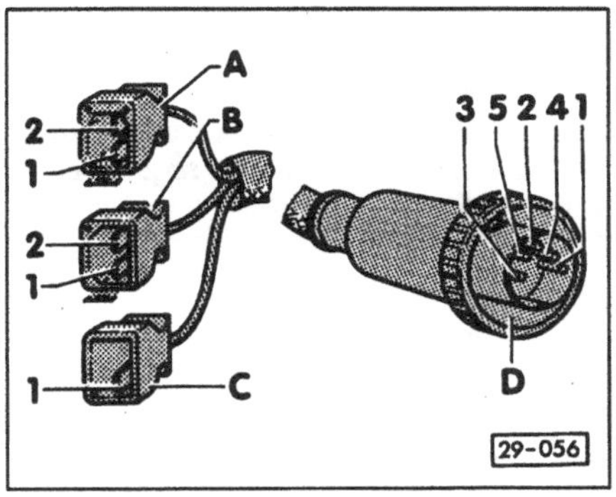

– Check VAG 1551/1 adaptor cable for continuity

Vehicle side		Scan Tool side	
Connector	Terminal	Connector D terminal	
Black -A-	1	3	Battery (–)
	2	2	Battery (+)
White -B-	1	4	L wire
	2	1	K wire
Blue -C-	1	5	Lamp wire

On Board Diagnostic system, electrical checks

Wiring/component checks using VAG 1598/18 Test Box

Special tools, testers and auxiliary items

♦ VAG 1598/18Test Box/adaptor cable

♦ VW 1594 Adaptor kit

♦ VAG 1527B LED tester

♦ Fluke 83 multimeter (or equivalent)

Notes:

♦ *The specifications given are valid within an ambient temperature range of 0 to + 40°C (32 to 104°F)*

♦ *If the measured values deviate from the specifications, determine the malfunction using the wiring diagram*

♦ *If the measured values only deviate slightly from the specifications, clean the sockets and plugs on the tester and measuring cables and repeat the check. Before replacing components, check the wiring and connections. in particular, for specifications less than 10 Ω, repeat the resistance measurement on the component*

♦ *To connect the various testers to the Test Box use jumper wires from the VW 1594 adaptor kit*

♦ *The vehicle wiring numbering and Test Box socket numbering are identical*

♦ *In addition to the checks described in the table, also check the wiring for short to ground (–) or battery positive (+) whenever necessary*

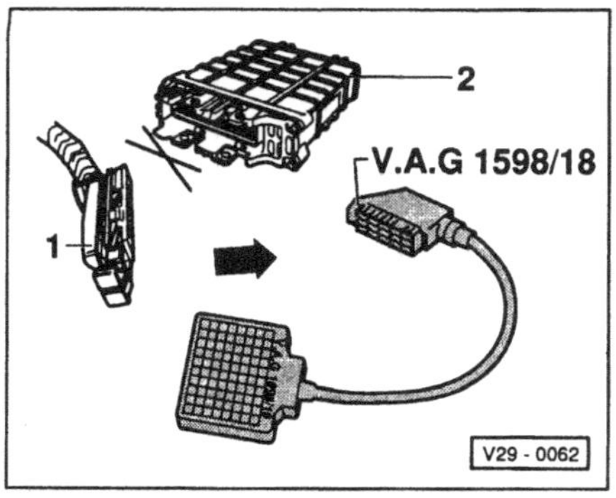

Test conditions

- Battery Voltage OK
- Fuses 15, 18 and 21 OK
- Ground connections on engine and transmission OK Engine: near knock sensor 1 Transmission: battery and body, near battery
- Fuel pump and fuel pump relay OK

– Switch OFF ignition

– Disconnect ECM harness connector -2- from ECM -3-

– Connect Test Box to ECM harness connector

– Perform electrical checks using table ⇒ page F 01-84

> ***CAUTION!***
>
> ***Switch the multimeter to the respective measuring range before connecting test cables. Observe test conditions and carry out any additional steps listed in the table to prevent damage to sensitive electronic components.***

Note:

After completing the electrical checks for vehicles with automatic transmission: Diagnostic Trouble Code "Engine / transmission electrical connection: open circuit" caused by the electrical check and stored in the Transmission Control Module must be erased.

⇒ Repair Group 01 (Automatic transmission 096)

Test table

– Measuring range: Switch multimeter to 20 Volt setting				
Test step	**Item checked**	**Test conditions / Additional steps**	**Test Box sockets**	**Specifications[1)]**
1	Voltage supply for Digifant ECM J169 via working relay	– Switch ON ignition	01 + 08 23 + 42	app. battery Voltage
2	—	—	—	—
3	Wire from starter terminal 50	– Operate starter	32 + 42	min. 8 Volts
4	Wire to fuel pump relay J17	Ignition switched ON	Bridge 31 + 42	Fuel pump must run audibly
5[3)]	Wire to the fuel injectors N30, N31, N32, N33 and N83[2)]	Ignition switched ON – Remove fuse 18 – Bridge Test Box sockets 31 + 42	01 + 02	app. battery Voltage
6[4)]	Wire to the fuel injectors N30, N31, N32, N33 and N83[2)]	Ignition switched ON – Remove fuse 18 – Bridge Test Box sockets 31 + 42	EV1 01 + 02 EV2 01 + 46 EV3 01 + 47 EV4 01 + 48 EV5 01 + 49	app. battery Voltage

1) Observe notes ⇒ page F 01-82

2) Fuel injector resistance, checking ⇒ Repair Group 24

3) Vehicles with 2 pin fuel rail connector

4) Vehicles with 6 pin fuel rail connector

this is a component to make a live reference to

– Measuring range: Switch multimeter to 20 Volt range				
Test step	**Item checked**	**Test conditions / Additional steps**	**Test Box sockets**	**Specifications[1)]**
7	EVAP canister purge regulator valve 1 N80	• Ignition switched ON	33 + 42	app. battery Voltage
8	Malfunction Indicator Lamp	• Ignition switched ON	Bridge 5 + 55	MIL must light up
9	Wiring to ignition coil N152	• Ignition switched ON	01 + 07	app. battery Voltage
10	Idle Air Control valve N71	• Ignition switched ON	30 + 42	app. battery Voltage
11	Wiring to A/C	• Ignition switched ON – Switch ON heater blower – Switch A/C to max. output	01 + 39	app. battery Voltage

[1)] Observe notes ⇒ page F 01-82

destination

– Ignition switched OFF – Measuring range: Switch multimeter to resistance setting –Ω–				
Test step	**Item checked**	**Test conditions / Additional steps**	**Test Box sockets**	**Specifications[1)]**
12	Wiring to Camshaft Position sensor G40	– Disconnect G40 at distributor – Bridge connector terminals 1 + 3	35 + 45	max. 1.5 Ω
		– Bridge connector terminals 1 + 3	35 + 44	max. 1.5 Ω
13[2)]	Engine Coolant Temperature sensor G62	—	12 + 35	Fig. 1 ⇒ page F 01-91
14	Intake Air Temperature sensor G42	—	35 + 37	Fig. 1 ⇒ page F 01-91
15[3)]	Wire to A/C compressor	– Separate single connector behind the relay panel	39 + terminal connector	max. 1.5 Ω

[1)] Observe notes ⇒ page F 01-82

[2)] If the On Board Diagnostic system indicates a sensor malfunction which is not established by this test, it could be caused by a temporary interruption in the temperature signal. In this case, additionally check the Engine Coolant Temperature sensor ⇒ Repair Group 24.

destination

Test step	Item checked	Test conditions / Additional steps	Test Box sockets	Specifications[1]
• Ignition switched OFF • Measuring range: Resistance range				
16	Closed Throttle Position switch F60	• Throttle closed	18 + 35	max. 10 Ω
		– Throttle opened		∞ Ω
17	Wiring to Throttle Position switch G69	– Disconnect 3 pin connector from Throttle Position sensor G69 – Bridge connector terminals 1 + 3	35 + 41	max. 1.5 Ω
		– Bridge connector terminals 1 + 2	35 + 40	
18	Wiring to Heated Oxygen sensor G39	– Disconnect G39 connector – Bridge connector terminals 2 + 3	17 + 20	max. 1.5 Ω
		– Reconnect G39 connector	17 + 20 17 + 42	∞ Ω
19	Wiring to white Data Link Connector	—	43 + terminal 2	max. 1.5 Ω
		—	28 + terminal 1[2]	

[1] Observe notes ⇒ page F 01-82

[2] Vehicles with 6 pin fuel rail connector

Test step	Item checked	Test conditions / Additional steps	Test Box sockets	Specifications[1]
• Ignition switched OFF • Measuring range: Resistance range				
20	Wiring to knock sensor 1 G61[2]	—	09 + 34 09 + 36 34 + 36	∞ Ω
		– Disconnect G61 connector (brown) – Bridge connector terminals 1 + 2	34 + 36	max. 1.5 Ω
		– Bridge connector terminals 1 + 3	09 + 36	max. 1.5 Ω
21	Wiring to knock sensor 2 G66[2]	—	10 + 24 10 + 25 24 + 25	∞ Ω
		– Disconnect G66 connector (black) – Bridge connect terminals 1 + 2	10 + 25	max. 1.5 Ω
		– Bridge connector terminals 1 + 3	10 + 24	max. 1.5 Ω

[1] Observe notes ⇒ page F 01-82

[2] Location ⇒ page F 01-92, Fig. 3

• Ignition switched OFF • Measuring range: Resistance range				
Test step	**Item checked**	**Test conditions / Additional steps**	**Test Box sockets**	**Specifications[1]**
22	EGR Vacuum Regulator solenoid valve N18	• Ignition switched ON	Briefly bridge 42 + 67	Valve must audibly click
23	Wiring to N18	• Ignition switched OFF	38 + 67	27 ... 31 Ω
		– Disconnect N18 harness connector		∞ Ω
		– Bridge connector terminals 1 + 2		max. 1.5 Ω
24	Wiring for EGR Temperature sensor G98	—	35 + 52	Fig. 2 ⇒ page F 01-91
		– Disconnect sensor harness connector		∞ Ω
		– Bridge connector terminals 1 + 2		max. 1.5 Ω

[1] Observe notes ⇒ page F 01-82

this is a component to create a reference to

• Ignition switched OFF • Measuring range: Resistance range				
Test step	**Item checked**	**Test conditions / Additional steps**	**Test Box sockets**	**Specifications[1]**
25	Secondary Air Injection pump relay J299	– Disconnect V101 harness connector	Briefly bridge 29 + 42	Relay must audibly click
	Secondary Air Injection solenoid valve N112			Relay switching must be felt
26	Secondary Air Injection pump motor V101	– Reconnect V101 harness connector	Bridge 29 + 42	Relay must audibly click and Secondary Air Injection pump motor must run

[1] Observe notes ⇒ page F 01-82

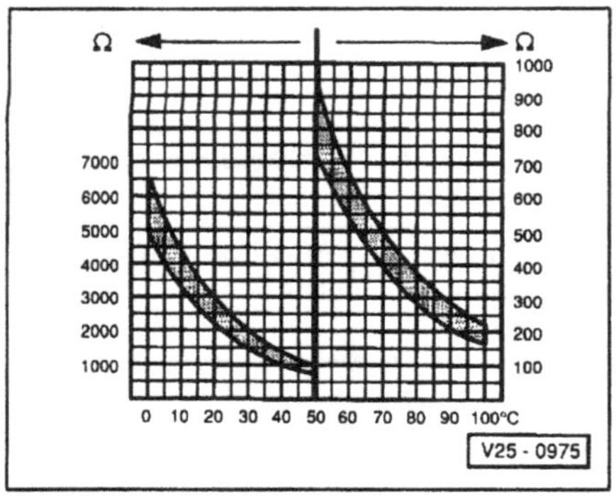

Fig. 1 Resistance chart for:

- G62 Engine Coolant Temperature sensor
- G42 Intake Air Temperature sensor

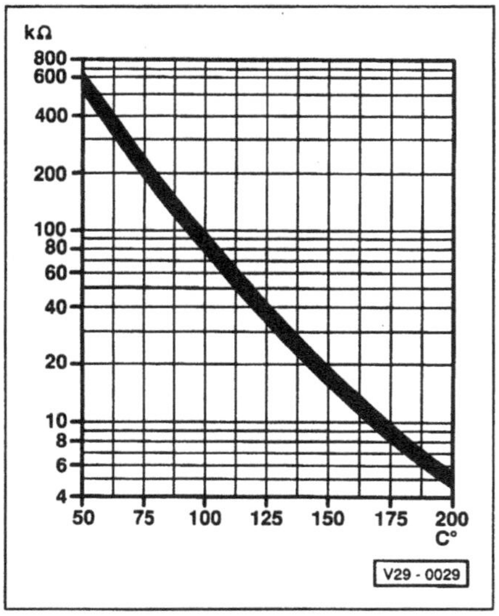

Fig. 2 Resistance chart for:

- G98 EGR Temperature sensor

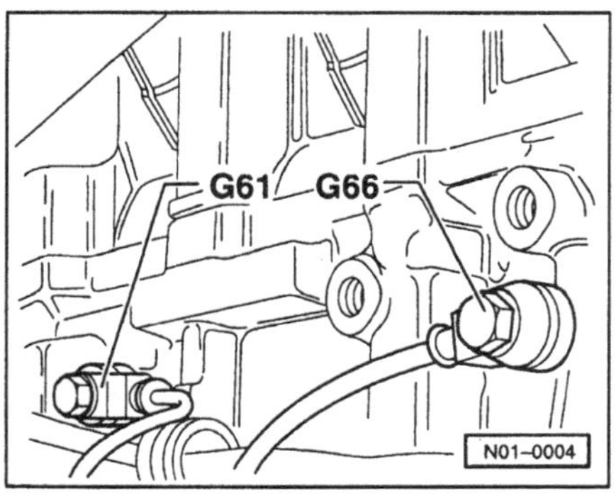

Fig. 3 Knock sensors G61 and G66

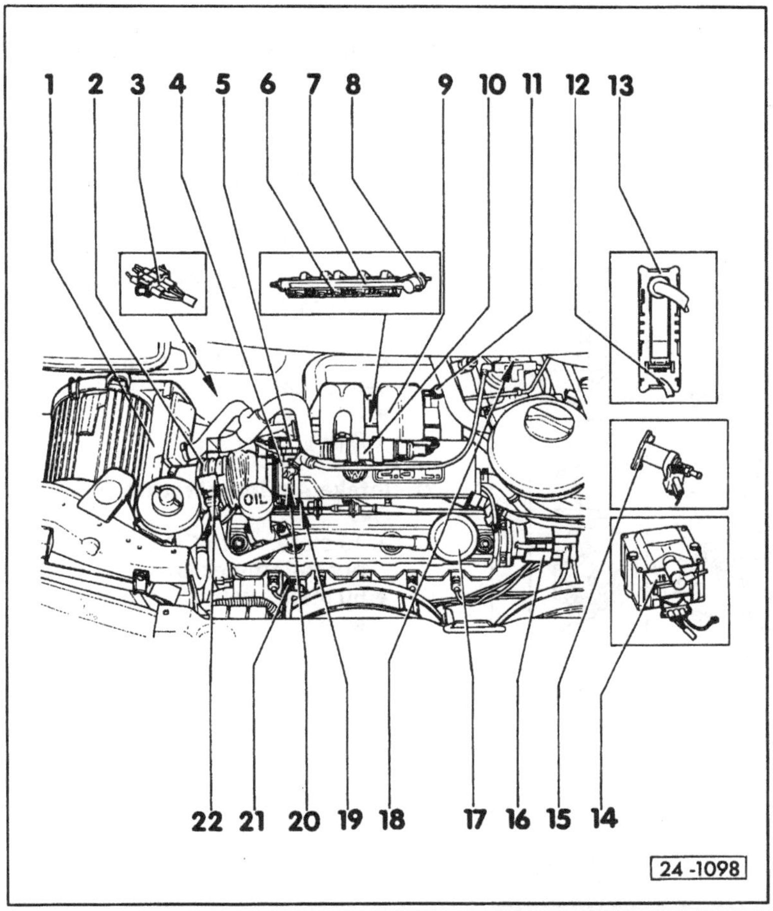

Digifant Fuel Injection System, component layout

Vehicles built up to m.y. 1995

Note:

This Repair section is for fuel injection only. For ignition system components:

⇒ Repair Group 28

1 - **Air Cleaner**
- ♦ with flap for intake air preheating

2 - **Intake hose**

3 - **3-pin harness connector**
- ♦ for Heated Oxygen Sensor

4 - **Throttle body**

5 - **Throttle Position sensor G69**

6 - **Fuel injectors N30, N31, N32, N33, N83**

7 - **Fuel rail**

8 - **Fuel pressure regulator**

9 - **Intake manifold**

10 - **Intake Air Control valve N71**

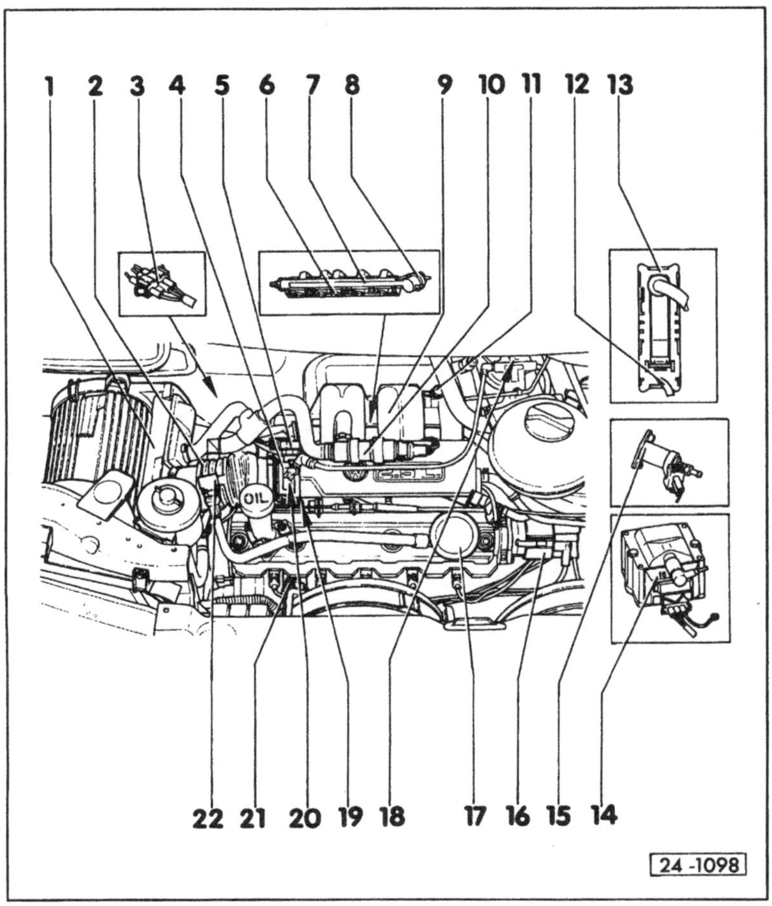

11 - **CO tap tube**

12 - **Vacuum hose**
- ♦ to intake manifold and/or check valve between intake manifold and brake booster

⇒ page F 24-7
- ♦ for Manifold Absolute Pressure sensor G71 in ECM J169

13 - **Digifant Engine Control Module J169**
- ♦ location: on left side of engine compartment (in driving direction)
- ♦ contains MAP sensor G71

14 - **Ignition coil N152**
- ♦ with power output stage
- ♦ location: under battery cover on left side (in driving direction)

15 - **Cold start injector**

16 - **Ignition distributor**
- ♦ with Camshaft Position sensor

⇒ Repair Group 28

17 - **Positive Crankcase Ventilation valve**

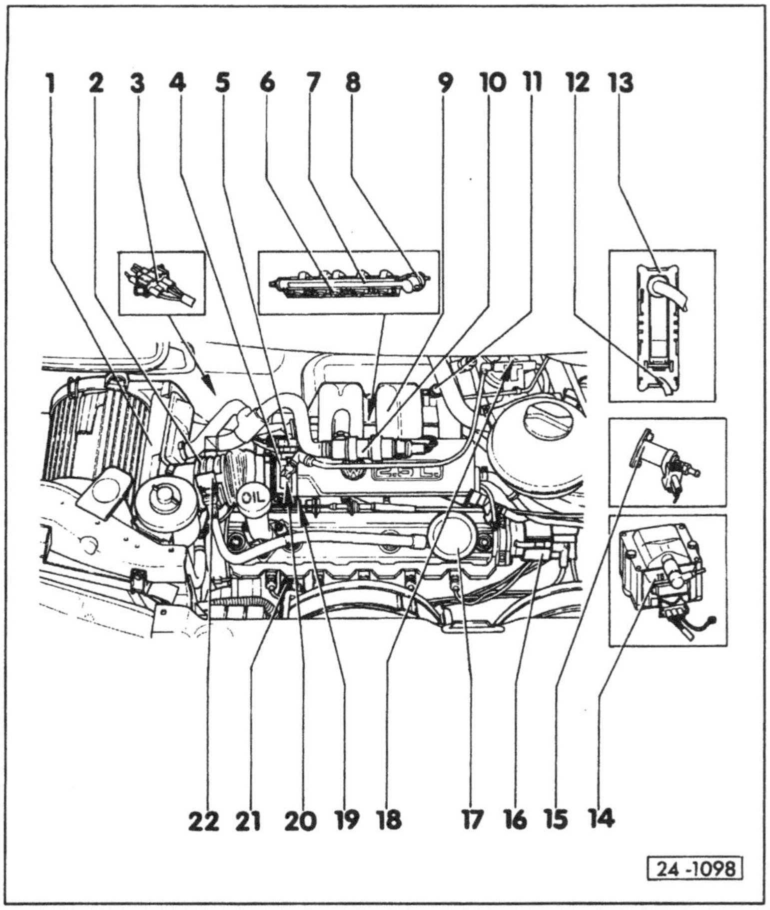

18 - EVAP canister purge regulator valve N 80
- EVAP system

⇒ Repair Group 20

19 - Closed Throttle Position switch F60
- mounted on throttle body

20 - Idle speed adjusting screw
- not for California

21 - Engine Coolant Temperature sensor G62
- blue
- 2-pin

22 - Intake Air Temperature sensor G42
- 49 state: with CO fuel trim potentiometer G74
- 50 state: with CO adjusting screw

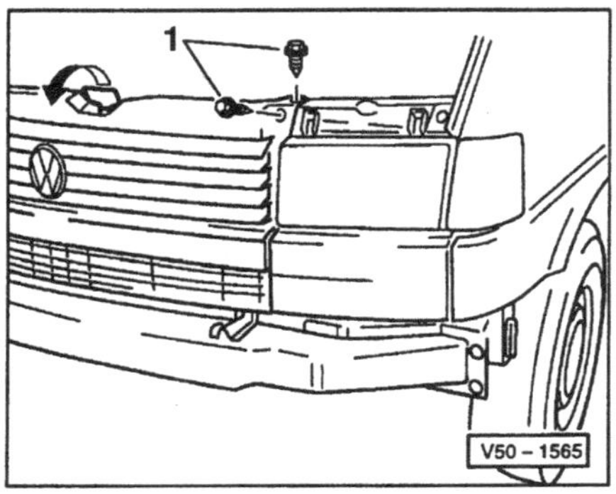

Upper radiator support, removing

◄
- Remove left and right mounting bolts -1-
- Tilt radiator and upper radiator support toward front (arrow)

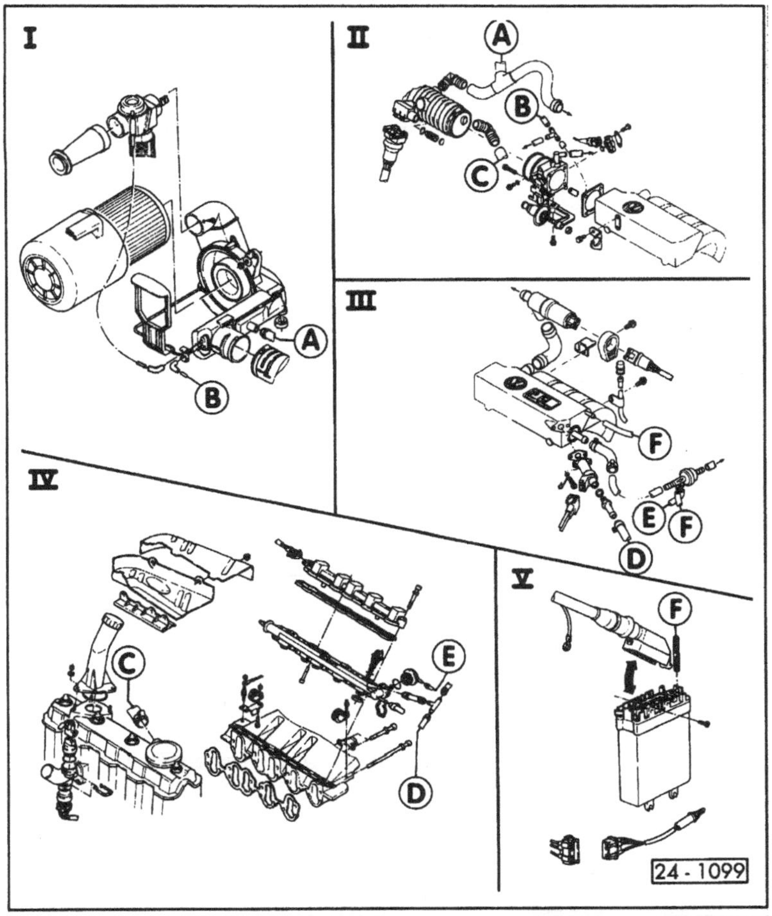

Fuel injection system, repairing

For Ignition system repairs
⇒ Repair Group 28

- The Engine Control Module for the fuel injection and ignition system is equipped with a Diagnostic Trouble Code (DTC) Memory. Before starting repairs or troubleshooting, activate DTC Memory and check the vacuum connections for leaks
- It is possible to exceed system limits while checking/adjusting. The control module will store these excursions as Diagnostic Trouble Codes; therefore, after completing all checking and adjusting, the DTC Memory must be erased
⇒ Repair Group 01
- Components tagged with an asterisk * are checked via On Board Diagnostic
- Components tagged by two asterisks ** are checked via Output Diagnostic Test Mode (DTM)
⇒ Repair Group 01
- Hose clamps are secured with screwed and locking clamps

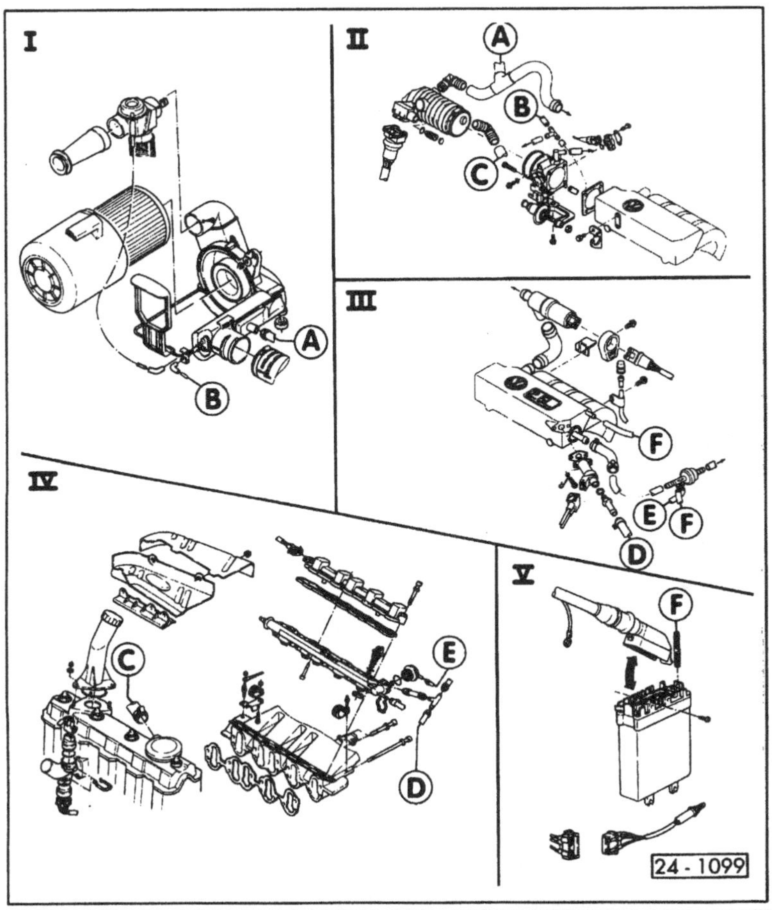

- Replace removed clamps with screw type clamps
- 10.5 Volts minimum is required for satisfactory operation of the electrical components
- Do NOT use sealants containing silicone. Silicone particles ingested by the intake air system could damage the Oxygen Sensor
- Observe all Safety precautions
⇒ page F 24-19
- Observe the Rules of Cleanliness
⇒ page F 24-20
- Technical data
⇒ page F 24-21
- Idle speed checking
⇒ page F 24-22
- For additional information regarding the On Board Diagnostic and electrical testing of the Digifant system
⇒ Repair Group 01

I – page F 24-7
II – page F 24-9
III– page F 24-12
IV– page F 24-14
V – page F 24-17

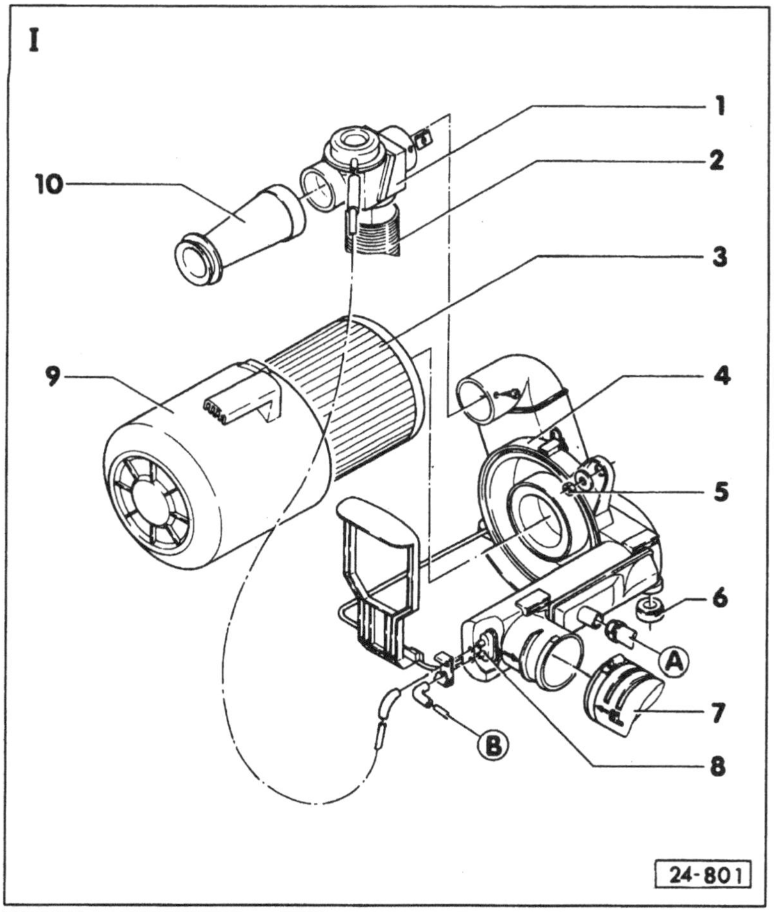

I – Intake air components, layout

A (this page) to A page F 24-9

B (this page) to B page F 24-9

1 - Intake air hose
- w/flap for intake air preheating
- checking

⇒ page F 24-61

2 - Hose from stove heater
- to hot air capture plate on exhaust manifold

⇒ page F 24-14 (item 4)

3 - Air Cleaner insert

4 - Air Cleaner housing

5 - 20 Nm (15 ft lb)

6 - Rubber washer

7 - Intake hose
- note installed position

8 - Temperature sensor/regulator
- for intake air preheating
- brass connector or connector with notch on top
- intake air preheating, checking

⇒ page F 24-61

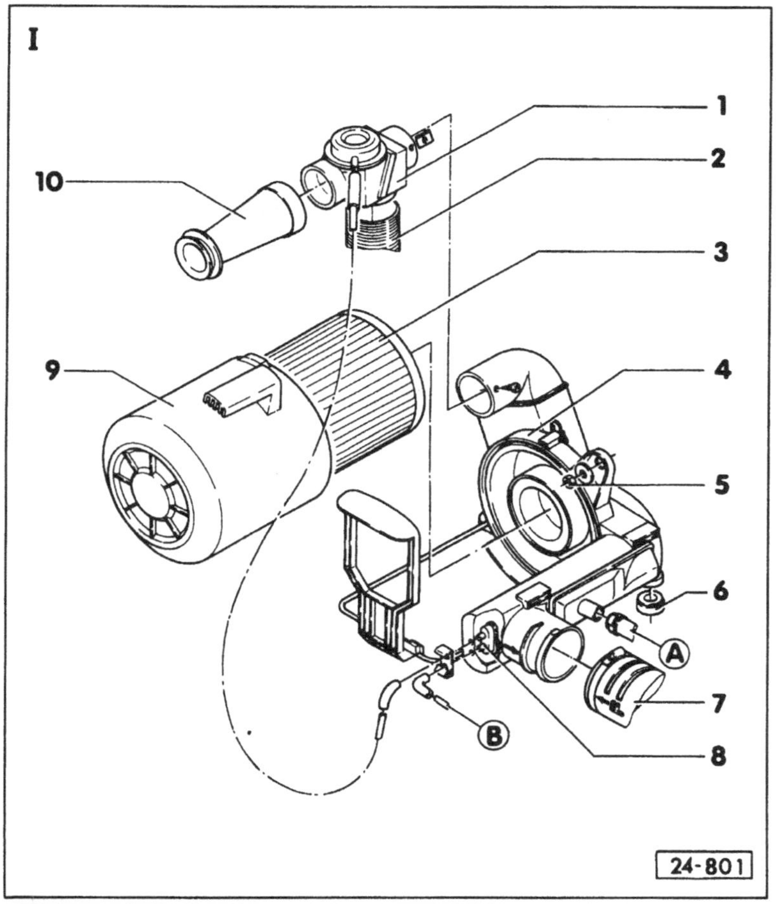

9 - Air Cleaner housing

10 - Snorkel
- note installed position

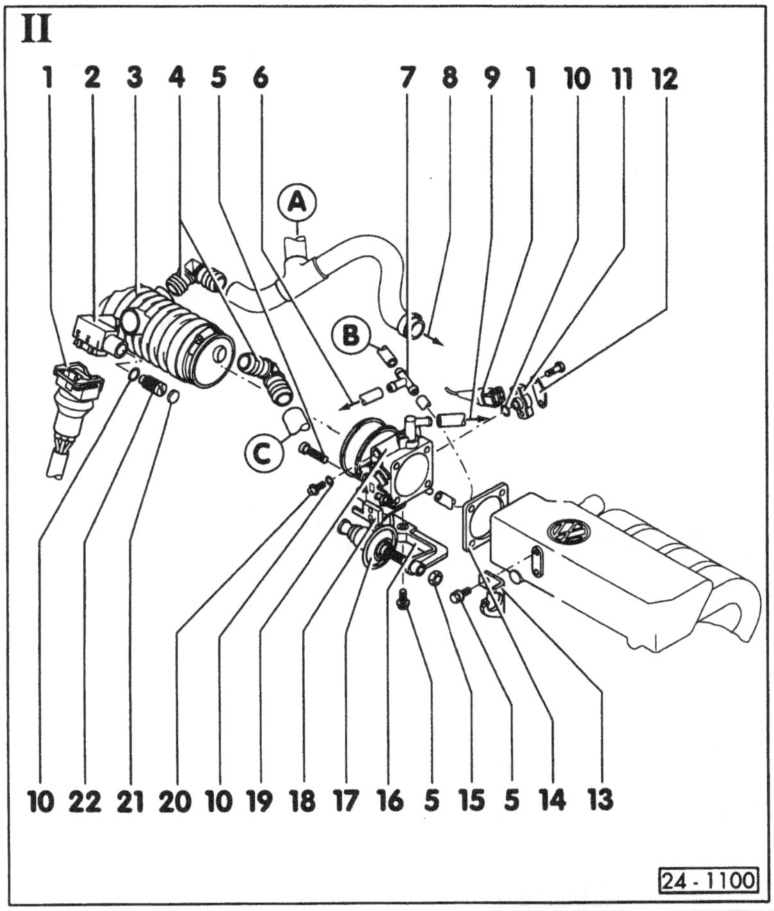

II – Throttle assembly, component layout

A (this page) to: page F 24-7

B (this page) to: page F 24-7

C (this page) to: page F 24-14

1 - Connector

2 - Intake Air Temperature sensor G42
- 49 state: with CO fuel trim potentiometer G74
- 50 state: with CO adjusting screw
- G42, checking

⇒ page F 24-42
- G74, checking

⇒ page F 24-43

3 - Intake air boot
- note installed position

4 - Angle connector

5 - M6 = 10 Nm (7 ft lb)
- M8 = 20 Nm (15 ft lb)

6 - to passenger compartment

7 - Tee connector

8 - to Idle Air Control valve N71**

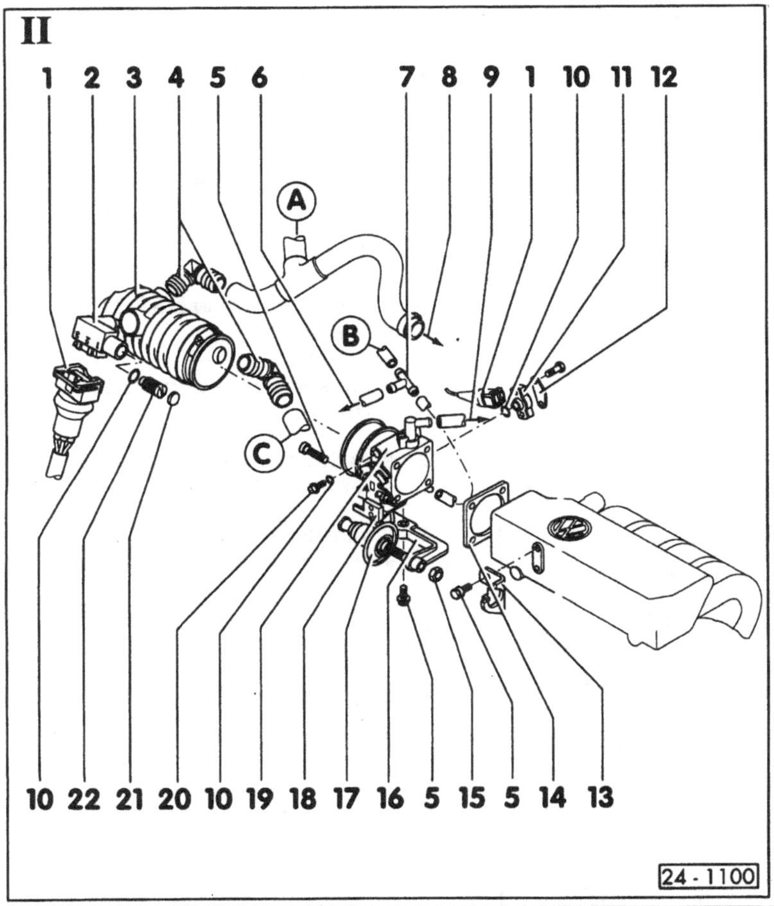

9 - EVAP canister purge regulator valve N80**

10 - O-ring
- replace if damaged

11 - Throttle Position sensor G69*
- 3-pin connector
- additional 4-pin connector for vehicles with automatic trans. routed to TCM J217
- checking

⇒ page F 24-37
- if replaced, perform idle check

⇒ page F 24-23

12 - Shield

13 - Bracket
- throttle cable, adjusting

⇒ Repair Group 20

14 - Gasket
- replace

15 - 20 Nm (15 ft lb)

16 - Bracket
- for dashpot

17 - Dashpot
- for manual transmission only
- checking/adjusting

⇒ page F 24-34

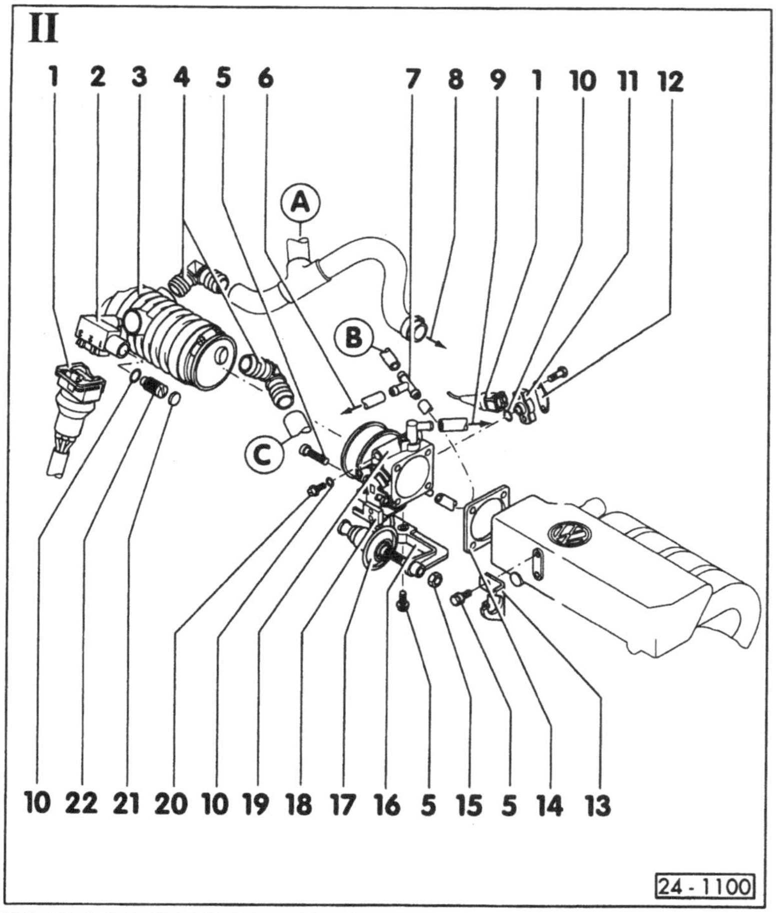

18 - Closed Throttle Position switch F60
- checking/adjusting

⇒ page F 24-43

19 - Throttle body
- basic throttle adjustment

⇒ page F 24-63

20 - Idle speed adjusting screw
- idle speed checking

⇒ page F 24-22

21 - Tamper-proof cap
- must be removed before CO adjustment can be performed

22 - CO adjusting screw
- idle speed checking

⇒ page F 24-22

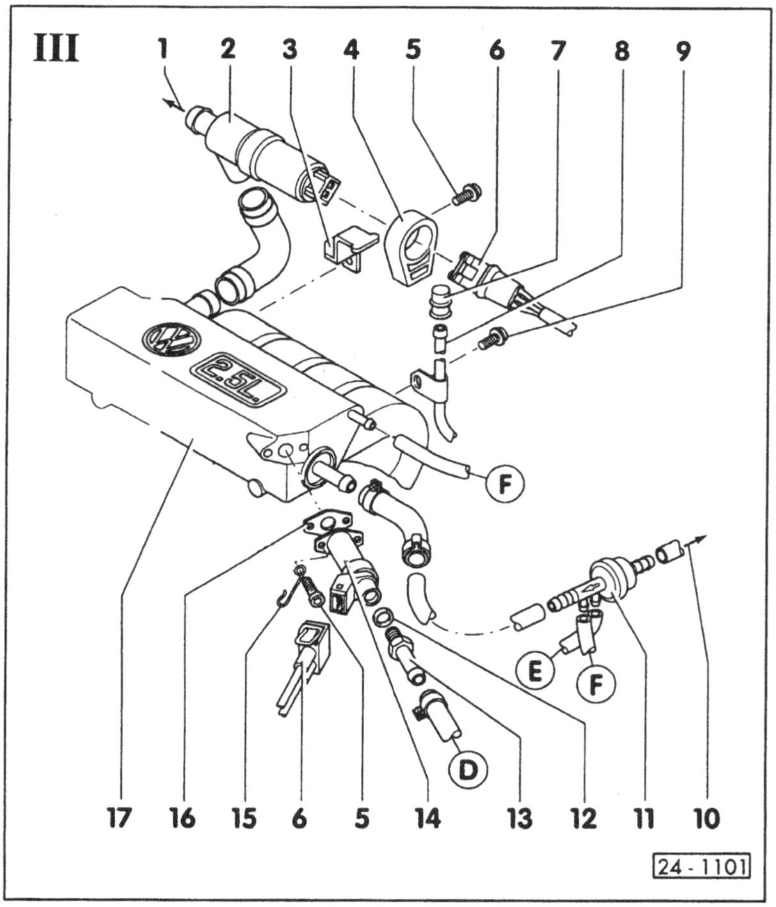

III – Fuel injection system, auxiliary components

D (this page) to: page F 24-14
E (this page) to: page F 24-14
F (this page) to: page F 24-17

1 - to intake air boot

2 - Idle Air Control valve N71**
- checking

⇒ page F 24-28

- resistance checking: 2 to 10 Ohms

3 - Attachment bracket
- for IAC valve**

4 - Mounting rubber
- absorbs shock and vibration
- for IAC valve**

5 - 10 Nm (7 ft lb)

6 - Harness connector to IAC valve

7 - Cap for CO tap tube
- ensure tight fit without leakage

8 - CO tap tube

9 - 15 Nm (11 ft lb)

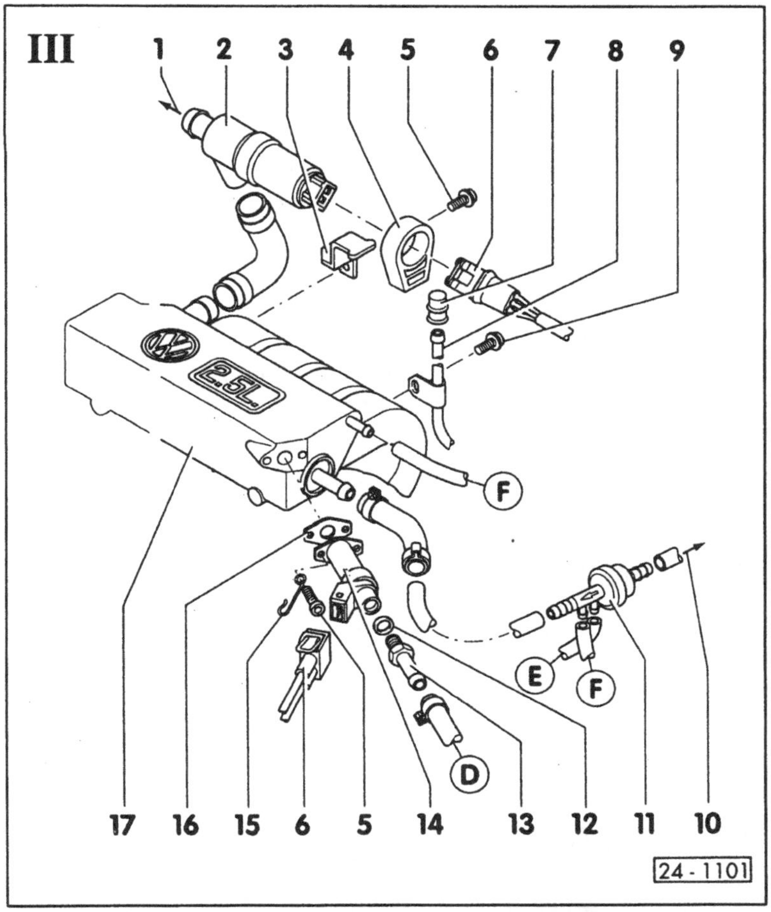

10 - to brake booster

11 - Check valve
- note flow orientation
- with vacuum connection to (F) ECM*

12 - Gasket
- replace

13 - 20 Nm (15 ft lb)

14 - Cold start injector
- checking

⇒ page F 24-50

15 - Guide wire
- for throttle cable

16 - Gasket
- replace

17 - Intake manifold
- with vacuum port connection (F) routed to ECM via check valve 11

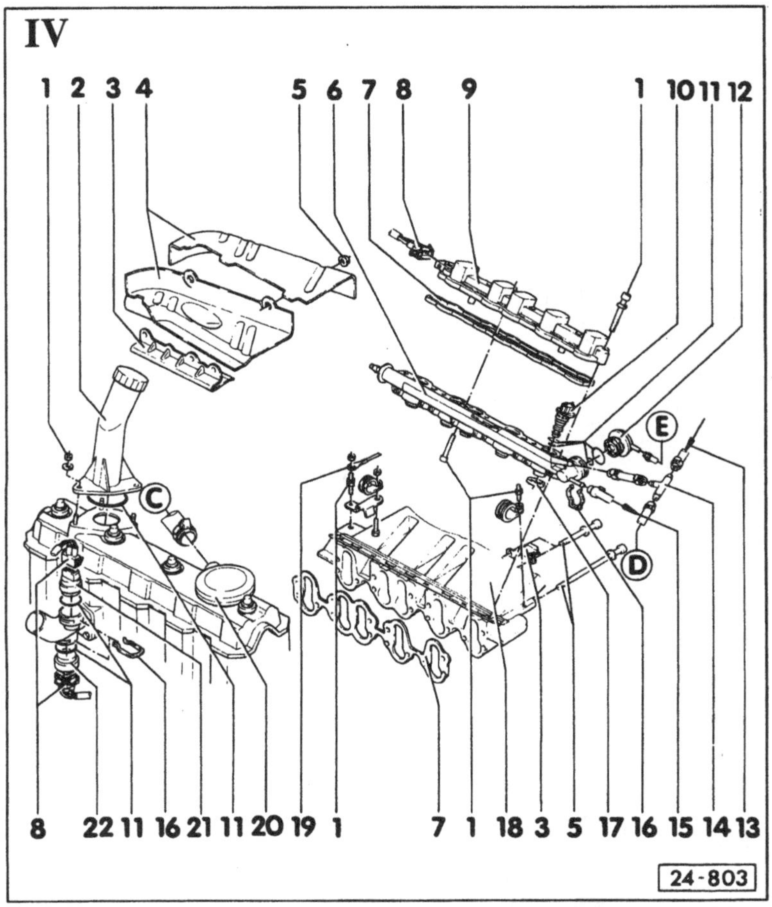

IV – Fuel Injection components, layout

C (this page) to: page F 24-9

D (this page) to: page F 24-12

E (this page) to: page F 24-12

1 - 10 Nm (7 ft lb)

2 - Oil filler pipe

3 - Bracket
- for hot air stove

4 - Hot air stove

5 - 25 Nm (18 ft lb)

6 - Fuel rail, lower section
- removing and installing

⇒ page F 24-52

7 - Gasket
- replace if damaged

8 - Harness connector for injectors
- 2-pin (49 state)
- 6-pin (California)

9 - Fuel rail, upper section
- removing/installing

⇒ page F 24-52

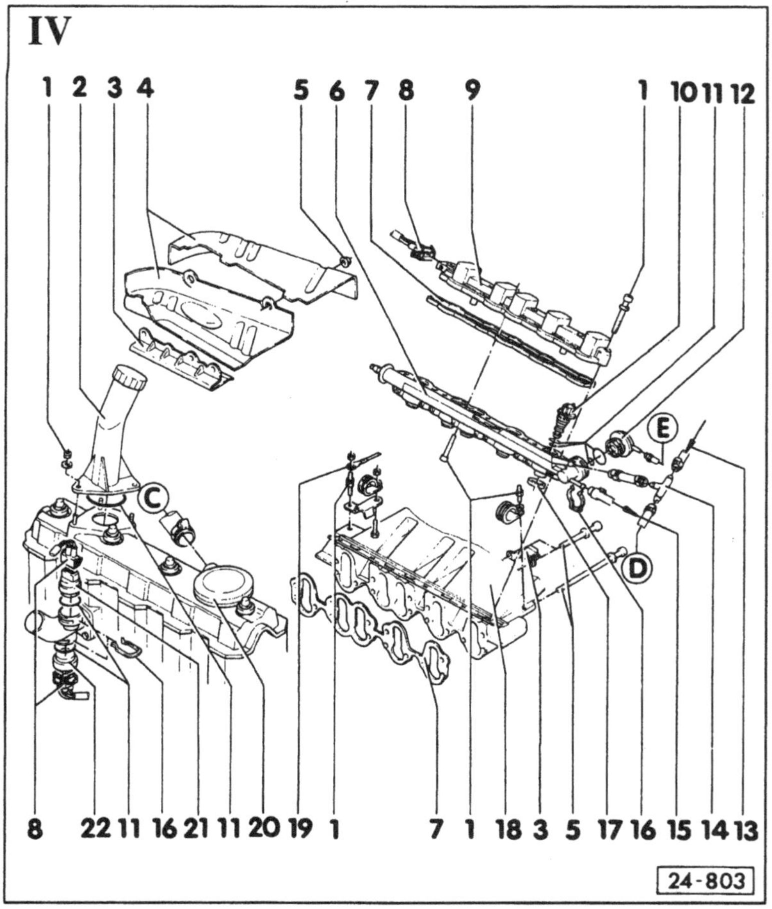

10 - Fuel injectors N30, N31, N32, N33, N83
- removing/installing

⇒ page F 24-52
- checking

⇒ page F 24-55
- California vehicles: check via On Board Diagnostic

11 - O-ring
- replace if damaged

12 - Fuel pressure regulator
- checking

⇒ page F 24-47

13 - Fuel supply line
- black

14 - Tee connector

15 - Fuel return line
- blue

16 - Retaining clip

17 - O-ring seal
- replace if damaged

18 - Intake manifold

19 - Ground connection

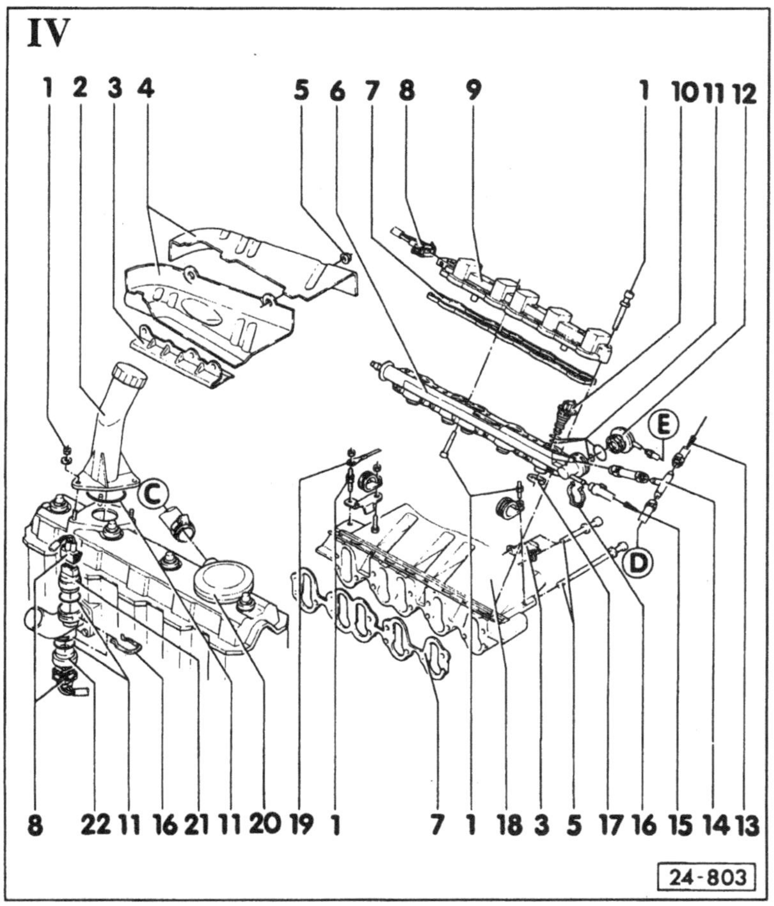

20 - Positive Crankcase Ventilation valve

21 - Engine Coolant Temperature sensor G62*
- blue
- 2-pin
- relieve cooling system pressure before removing
- checking

⇒ page F 24-40
- resistance checking

⇒ Repair Group 01

22 - Overheat fuse F51 and Engine Coolant Temperature sensor G2
- yellow
- 4-pin
- overheat fuse checking

⇒ Repair Group 19

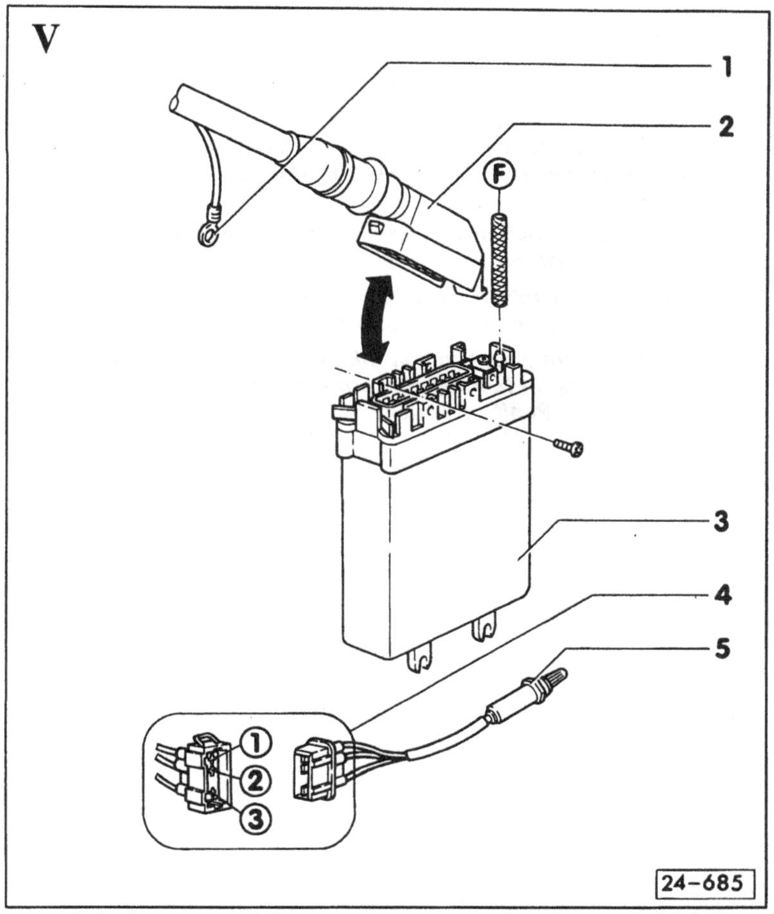

Digifant Engine Control Module, component layout

F (this page) to: page F 24-10

1 - Ground connection
- connected to chassis

2 - Engine Control Module harness connector
- switch OFF ignition BEFORE disconnecting or connecting!
- 38-pin

3 - Engine Control Module J169*
- for fuel injection system, Oxygen Sensor control, rpm governor, ignition system and OBD
- with Manifold Absolute Pressure sensor G71*, checking

⇒ page F 24-45

- if replaced, perform idle check

⇒ page F 24-22

- location: left engine compartment

4 - Harness connector
- 3-pin
- for Heated Oxygen Sensor G39* and for sensor heater
- mounted on right sub-assembly

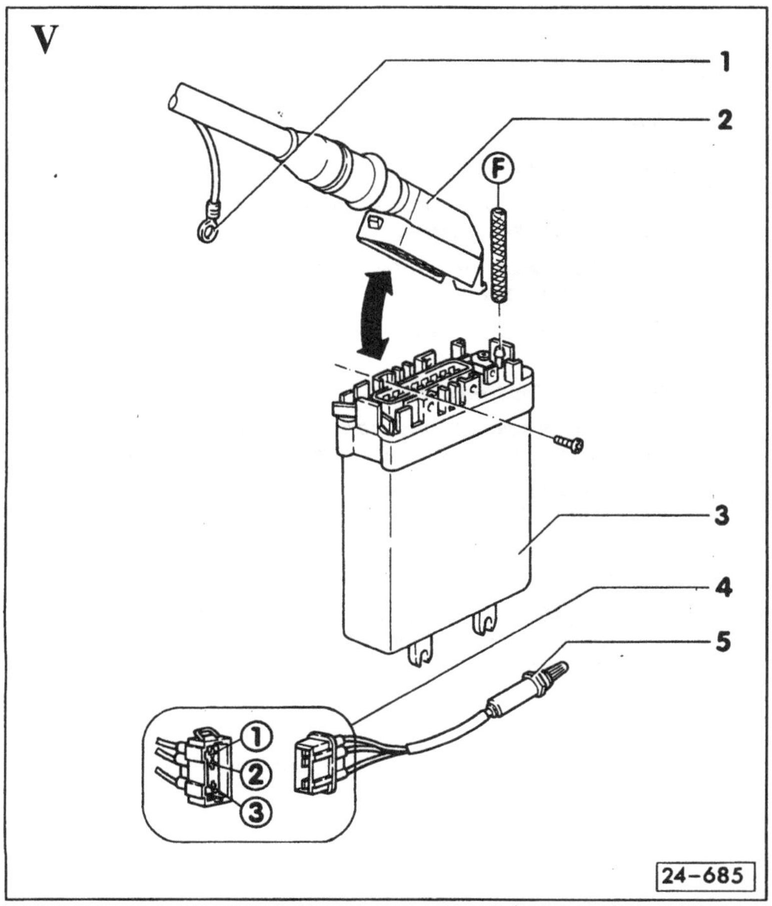

5 - Heated Oxygen sensor G39*
- 50 Nm (37 ft lb)
- Location: in front exhaust pipe
- lubricate threads with G5, but do not allow G5 to enter slotted area of probe
- voltage supply for probe heating via fuel pump relay J17
- voltage supply between terminals 1 (red/black) and 2 (brown) with engine running: approximately battery voltage
- check Oxygen sensor heater wires (white) for continuity

Safety precautions

> ***CAUTION!***
>
> ***Observe the following precautions to avoid personal injury as well as possible damage to the fuel injection system components:***
>
> - ***DO NOT touch or disconnect ignition wires while the engine is running and/or while cranking***
> - ***always switch OFF the ignition BEFORE disconnecting or connecting wiring or test measurements***
> - ***if the engine requires cranking without starting such as compression testing; disconnect harness connector from Camshaft Position sensor (on ignition distributor)***

Rules of Cleanliness

> ***CAUTION!***
>
> ***Rules of Cleanliness***
>
> ***Observe the following rules when working on the fuel supply/injection systems.***
>
> - ***carefully clean all connecting points and surrounding areas before opening***
> - ***store removed parts on a clean surface and keep them covered***
> - ***ONLY use lint free cloths***
> - ***carefully cover opened components or lines, or close them up if repair will not be performed right away***
> - ***ONLY use clean new parts: replacement parts should only be removed from their packages at the time of installation***
> - ***DO NOT use any parts that have been removed from their packaging or kept loose in tool boxes etc.***
> - ***if fuel system is opened up, avoid working with compressed air whenever possible; DO NOT move the vehicle***

Technical data

Vehicles built after 10/91

CAUTION	
Idle speed and CO content are NOT adjustable, they can ONLY be checked!	
Engine code	**AAF**
Idle speed	800 ± 25 RPM
CO content	0.3 to 1.2 volume%
Engine Control Module rpm cut–off	5500 RPM

Idle speed and CO content, checking

> ***CAUTION!***
>
> ***Idle speed and CO content are NOT adjustable, they can ONLY be checked.***

Requirements

- Engine Coolant Temperature 80°C (176°F) minimum
- All electrical consumers switched OFF (do not take measurements while radiator fan is running)
- A/C switched OFF
- Throttle cable adjustment OK
⇒ Repair Group 20
- Closed Throttle Position (CTP) switch OK
- DTC Memory cleared and any malfunctions corrected
⇒ Repair Group 01
- Ignition timing OK
⇒ Repair Group 28
- Idle Speed Control OK: with ignition ON, Idle Air Control valve must vibrate and hum
- Exhaust system must be leak-tight

Function 04: Engine basic setting, checking

Requirement

- ♦ Engine cold

Note:

Some engines have a production Crankshaft Position sensor installed. The VAG 1367 ignition tester can be connected to these engines, even when hot, without removing the distributor cap using adaptor cable VAG 1367/9.

- Remove splash shield from distributor cap

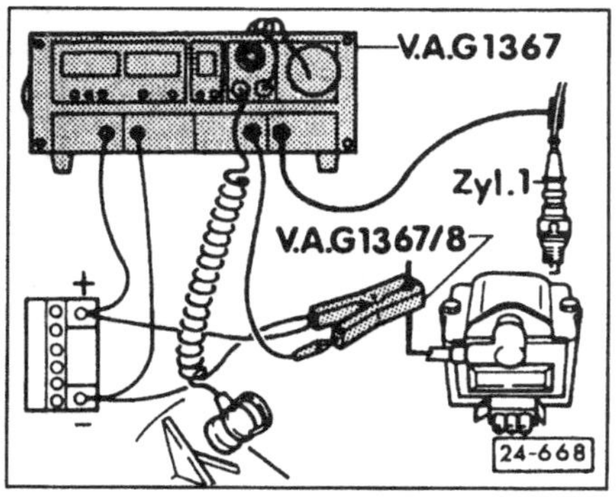

◄ – Connect VAG 1367 ignition tester using VAG 1367/8 inductive pickup

- Connect CO tester using VAG 1363/3 adaptor on CO tap tube

> ***CAUTION!***
>
> ***Ensure that the adaptor hose is tightly connected to the CO tap tube (with no leaks) to prevent measuring errors.***

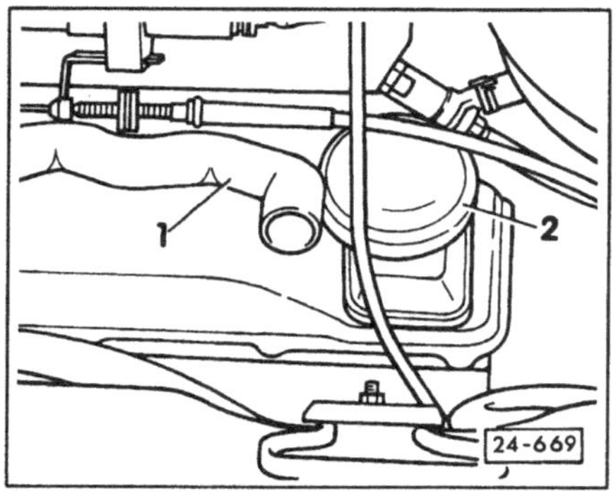

◄ – Disconnect crankcase breather hose -1- from the Positive Crankcase Ventilation valve -2- and then position the disconnected hose such that only fresh air is drawn in

- Connect VAG 1551 Scan Tool

⇒ Repair Group 01 for additional information

- Start engine and let warm up
  - ♦ engine oil temperature 80°C (176°F) minimum
- Allow to idle
  - ♦ do not allow idle speed to exceed 1500 RPM

Note:

If the engine stalls or shuts off, it can run with an increased idle speed for up to 4 minutes after re-starting. In this case wait until the engine speed drops before starting measurements.

- Operate VAG 1551 Scan Tool with respect to the displays shown
- Press 1 button to obtain Rapid Data Transfer
- Press 0 and 1 buttons to select 01 "Engine Electronics"
- Press Q button to enter input
- Press → button
- Press 0 and 4 buttons to select Function 04 "basic setting"

- ♦ When Function 04 is selected, idle speed is coordinated with the engine via the ECM
- ♦ If Throttle Position sensor is removed, installed or replaced on vehicles with automatic transmission, the TCM must be returned to the basic setting using the VAG 1551 Scan Tool ⇒ Repair Group 01

- Press Q button to enter input

Initiate basic setting	HELP
Input display group number	

◄ Display will appear as shown

- Press 0 button twice to select indicator group number
- Press Q button to enter input

System in basic setting
1 2 3 4 5 6 7 8 9 10

◄ Display will appear as shown

or

Function unknown/or can not be conducted at this time

◄ If the display appears as shown:

- Check the following possibilities:

♦ Minimum coolant temperature of 85°C (185°F) not yet attained

♦ Idle speed exceeds 1500 RPM

♦ Function 04 "Basic setting" using the VAG 1551 Scan Tool is not possible

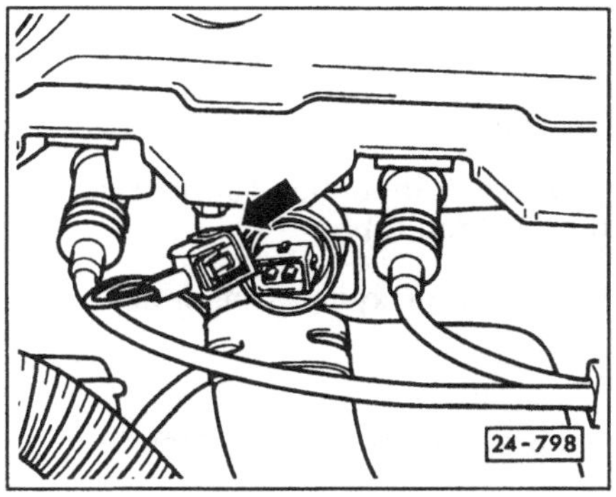

If YES:

◄ - Disconnect blue Engine Coolant Temperature sensor harness connector (arrow) with throttle in closed position

Note

If the engine shuts off before restarting, re-connect the ECT harness connector; otherwise, the ECM will default to the limp home mode, making accurate measurements impossible.

Vehicles up to 7/92

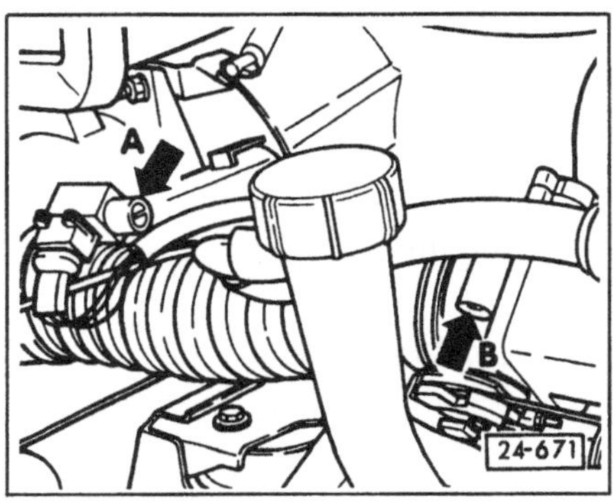

◄ - Check idle speed and CO content and adjust if necessary, by turning adjusting screws

A = CO adjusting screw

B = Idle speed adjusting screw

♦ Idle speed: 800 ± 25 RPM

♦ CO content: 0.7 ± 0.2 vol.%

- Replace tamper-proof cap after adjustment
- Push → button to end basic setting or re-connect Engine Coolant Temperature sensor harness connector

♦ Radiator cooling fan must not be running during this step

Vehicles after 7/92

- Check idle speed and CO content

♦ Idle speed: 775 to 825 RPM

♦ CO content: 0.3 to 1.2 vol. %

- Push → button to end basic setting or re-connect ECT sensor

♦ Radiator cooling fan must not be running during this step

- Activate and erase DTC Memory
⇒ Repair Group 01

  ♦ this will erase stored DTC caused by disconnecting ECT sensor G62

- Press 0 and 6 buttons to select Funct. 06: "end data transfer"
- Press Q button to enter input
- Let engine cool and remove distributor cap
- Remove VAG 1367 TDC sensor
- Re-install distributor cap

If specified values NOT obtained:

- Check intake air system for leaks
- Check exhaust system between cylinder head and three-way catalyst for leaks, including CO tap tube
- Check Heated Oxygen Sensor and Oxygen sensor control
- Test drive vehicle
- Activate DTC Memory, ensure that memory is clear
- Repeat idle speed check

Idle Air Control valve, checking

- Check the IAC valve using Output Diagnostic Test Mode
⇒ Repair Group 01 for additional information

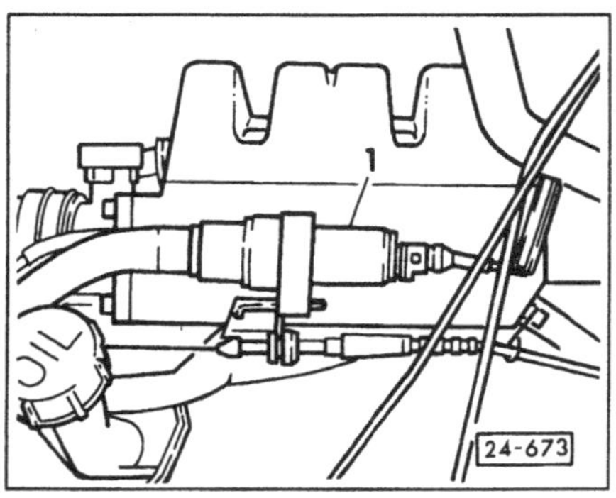

Function, checking

◄ - Switch ON ignition

  ♦ IAC valve 1 must vibrate and hum

If YES:

- Check IAC valve control

If NO:

- Switch OFF ignition
- Disconnect Idle Air Control valve harness connector from IAC valve -1-
- Switch Fluke 83 multimeter to resistance range
- Connect multimeter to IAC valve using jumper wires from VW 1594 adaptor kit
- Measure IAC valve resistance

  ♦ must be 2 to 10 Ohms

If NO:

– Replace IAC valve

If YES:

– Perform electrical checks, steps 8 and/or 25
⇒ Repair Group 01

Control, checking

Requirements

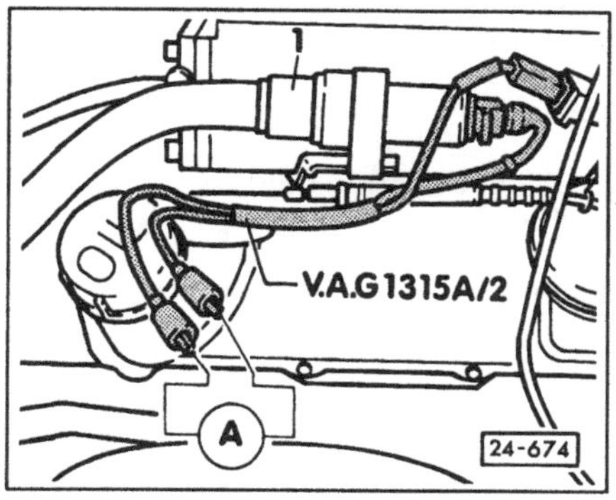

♦ Engine coolant temperature 80°C (176°F) minimum

♦ Idle speed check OK
⇒ page F 24-22

♦ Intake air system must be leak-tight

– Switch Fluke 83 multimeter to Amperage range

◄ – Disconnect Idle Air Control valve harness connector and insert adaptor cable VAG 1315A/2 between IAC valve and connector

– Connect multimeter to adaptor cable VAG 1315A/2 using jumper wires from VW 1594 adaptor kit

– Start engine and let idle

– Measure control current at idle speed (775 to 825 RPM),

♦ must be approximately 500 to 600 mA

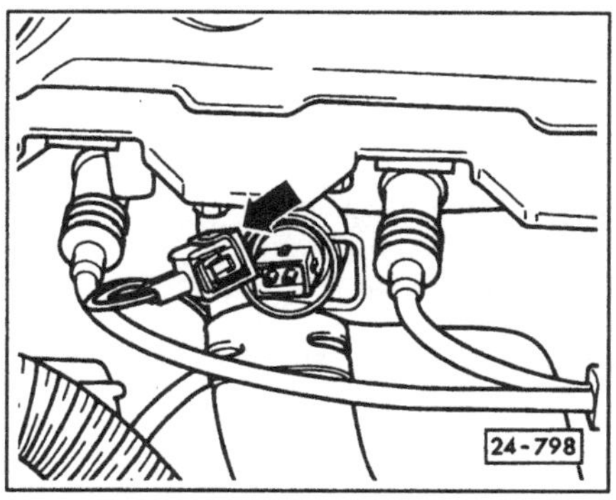

◄ – Disconnect harness connector from blue ECT sensor (arrow) with throttle closed

♦ must be approximately 500 to 600 mA

Note:

If engine shuts off before re-starting, re-connect the ECT harness connector; otherwise, the ECM will default to the limp home mode, making accurate measurements impossible.

If amperage values NOT obtained:

– Replace ECM J169

Note:

Control current for the Idle Air Control valve is dependent on engine load. The following loads can affect the control current and boost the amperage range to between 400 and 1000 mA:

♦ Engine cold

♦ A/C ON

♦ Electrical consumers switched ON

♦ Power steering turned to full lock position

♦ Ignition timing NOT OK

Heated Oxygen sensor and oxygen sensor control, checking

Requirements

- ♦ Idle speed check OK
- ♦ Exhaust system must be leak tight between three-way catalyst and cylinder head

– Connect VAG 1551 Scan Tool
⇒ Repair Group 01 for additional information

– Start engine and let idle

– Press 0 and 8 buttons to select Function 08: "Read measuring value block"

Read measurement block 1			
1	2	3	4

Display will appear as shown

Vehicles up to 9-91

Note:

In display group 00, only "Read measurement block" is shown on the display. Measurements are displayed in decimal form.

Only continue with check IF:

System in basic setting									
1	2	3	4	5	6	7	8	9	10

Displayed value in channel 3 is less than 10

- ♦ = coolant temperature greater than 85 °C (185 °F)

Vehicles after 7/92

Only continue with test IF:

- ♦ coolant temperature exceeds 85°C (185 °F) in channel 1

– Let engine idle for two minutes longer

– Connect CO tester to CO tap tube using adaptor VAG 1363/3

– Measure CO content

- ♦ 0.7 ± 0.2 vol.% (vehicles up to 7/92)
- ♦ 0.3 to 1.2 vol.% (vehicles after 7/92)

Read measurement block 1			
1	2	3	4

– Read oxygen sensor voltage in channel 3

- ♦ 0.0 to 0.75 Volts (fluctuation)

Vehicles up to 9-91

– Observe oxygen sensor signal in channel 5

System in basic setting									
1	2	3	4	5	6	7	8	9	10

Must be fluctuating by more than 14

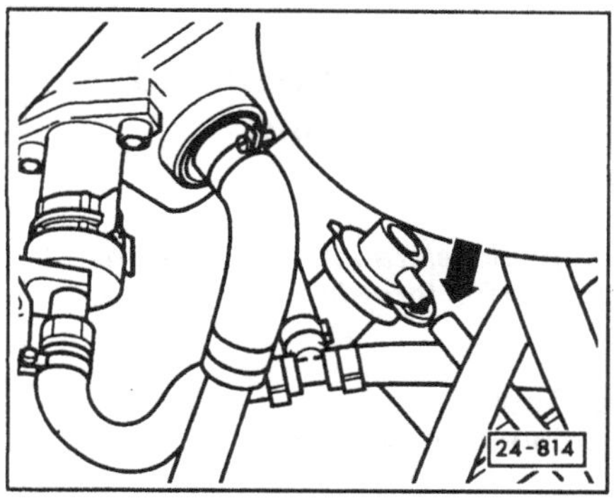

- Disconnect vacuum hose from fuel pressure regulator (arrow)
  - ♦ value must increase then drop back to original value
- Press → button
- Press 0 and 6 buttons to select Function 06: "end data transfer"
- Press Q button to enter input

If specified values NOT obtained:

- Check voltage supply for oxygen sensor heating
- Check oxygen sensor heating
⇒ page F 24-31
- Perform electrical checks, steps 16 and/or 32
⇒ Repair Group 01
- Replace Heated Oxygen Sensor G39

Dashpot, checking and adjusting

Manual transmission vehicles only

Requirement

♦ Basic throttle setting OK, checking:
⇒ page F 24-63

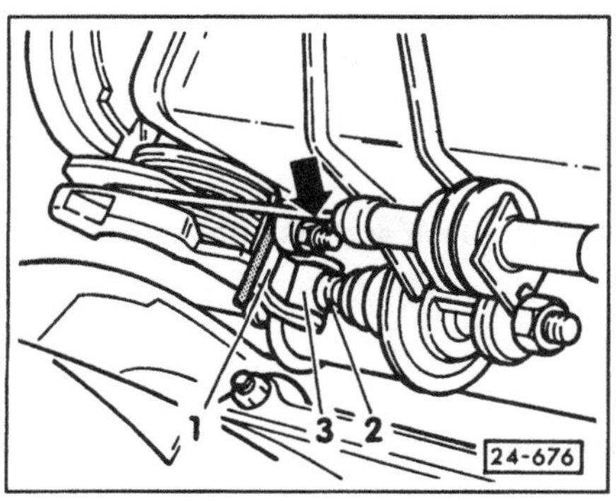

Checking

- Open throttle then close until piston -2- contacts roller -3-
- When condition satisfied, check dimension between limiter screw (arrow) and throttle -1- using feeler gage or drill
  - ♦ 1.5 to 2.5 mm

Adjusting

- Pinch 2 mm drill between limiting screw (arrow) and throttle -1-
- Adjust dashpot so piston -2- contacts roller -3-

Acceleration/full throttle enrichment and deceleration fuel shut–off, checking

Note:

The following test checks the deceleration fuel shut-off. If this test is OK, the acceleration and full throttle enrichment are also OK.

– Connect VAG 1551 Scan Tool
⇒ Repair Group 01 for additional information

– Start engine and let idle

– Press 0 and 8 buttons to select Function 08:
"Read measuring value block"

Read measurement block 1			
1	2	3	4

◄ Display will appear as shown

– Continue checking if:

♦ Engine coolant temperature exceeds 85°C (185 °F) (as shown in display channel 1)

Note:

Vehicles built up to 9-91, use Display channel 3.

– Let engine continue to idle 2 minutes longer

– Record value displayed in channel 4

– Raise engine speed to 3000 rpm minimum (vehicles up to 9/91 use channel 1) (vehicles after 9-91 use channel 2) by pressing accelerator pedal, then releasing

♦ displayed value in channel 4 (injection time) must increase, drop back to 0 ms and then match the recorded value

– Press → button

– Press 0 and 6 buttons to select Function 06:
"end data transfer"

– Press Q button to enter input

If displayed value does NOT increase and also does not return to 0 ms:

– Perform idle speed check
⇒ page F 24-22

– Check Throttle Position sensor
⇒ page F 24-37

– Perform electrical checks
⇒ Repair Group 01

Throttle position sensor, checking

- Vehicles with automatic transmissions have two potentiometers combined in one housing on the throttle body with two wires leading out of the potentiometer housing
- The 4-pin connector wiring goes to the Transmission Control Module J217
- Check the Automatic Transmission potentiometer by checking DTC Memory, see Repair Group 01
- The 3-pin connector wiring goes to the ECM J169

Note:

This connector is also used for automatic transmission vehicles.

- After removing, installing or replacing the TP sensor, check idle speed

⇒ page F 24-22

The ECM obtains the following information from the TP sensor:

With throttle in closed position:

- Switches OFF fuel supply during deceleration fuel shut off
- Idle speed control
- Ignition timing at idle

With throttle partially opened:

- injection quantity for acceleration enrichment

With throttle completely open:

- injection quantity for full throttle enrichment

Function 08, "Read measurement block"

- Switch ON ignition
- Connect VAG 1551 Scan Tool and select function 08
⇒ Repair Group 01 for additional information

```
Read measurement block 1
1          2          3          4
```

◄ Display will appear as shown

- Slowly open throttle until wide open, while opening:

- vehicles up to 9-91 observe angle display in channel 2
- vehicles after 10-91 observe angle display in channel 3
- numerical display value must increase uniformly over the entire opening range

Throttle position	Vehicles up to 9-91	Vehicles after 10-91
Closed	5 to 30 >°	0 >°
Wide open	100 >° minimum	80 >° minimum

- Press → button
- Press 0 and 6 buttons to select Function 06: "end data transfer"
- Press Q button to enter input

If displayed value does NOT increase uniformly:

- Perform electrical checks, steps 15, 34 and 35 and / or 31, 40 and 41

⇒ Repair Group 01

- Replace Throttle Position sensor G69, if necessary

Engine Coolant Temperature sensor, checking

Requirement

- ♦ Engine cold
- Connect VAG 1551 Scan Tool, see Repair Group 01 for additional information
- Start engine and let idle
- Select function 08: "Read measuring value block"

Read measurement block 1			
1	2	3	4

◄ Display will appear as shown

- Observe coolant temperature value in Scan Tool display
- ♦ Vehicles after 10-91 use display field 1
- ♦ Vehicles up to 9-91 use display field 3
- ♦ Temperature value must increase uniformly without interruption

Note:

If performance malfunctions occur during certain temperature ranges and the temperature value does not increase uniformly, the temperature signal is intermittent and the sensor should be replaced.

- Press → button
- Press 0 and 6 buttons to select Function 06: "end data transfer"
- Press Q button to enter input

If temperature value does NOT change:

- Perform electrical checks, steps 11 and/or 28
⇒ Repair Group 01

- Replace ECT sensor G62, if necessary
⇒ First relieve cooling system pressure

Intake Air Temperature sensor, checking

- Connect VAG 1551 Scan Tool
⇒ Repair Group 01 for additional information
- Switch ON ignition
- Press 0 and 8 buttons to select Function 08: "Read measuring value block"

Read measurement block 1			
1	2	3	4

◄ Display will appear as shown

- Remove IAT sensor G42 but do not disconnect from connector
- Note IAT value displayed via Scan Tool in channel 3

♦ vehicles up to 9/91 use channel 2
♦ vehicles after 10/91 use channel 3

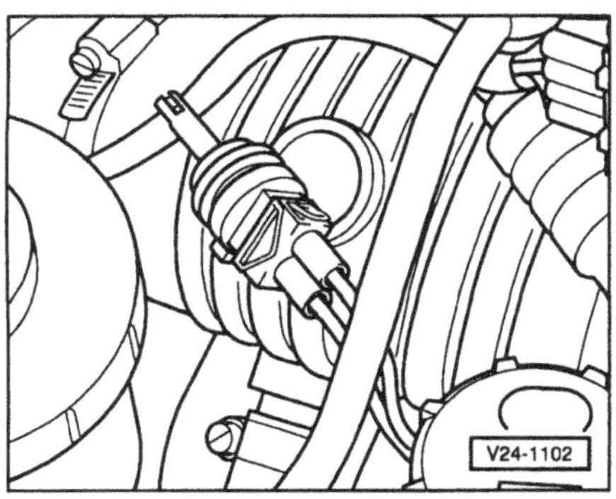

◄ - Spray IAT sensor with commercial cooling spray and observe temperature value on Scan Tool

♦ Temperature value must drop

- Press → button
- Press 0 and 6 buttons to select Function 06: "end data transfer"
- Press Q button to enter input

If temperature value does NOT change:

- perform electrical checks, step 12 and/or 29
⇒ Repair Group 01

- if necessary replace IAT sensor G42

CO fuel trim potentiometer, checking

Requirement

- ♦ Idle speed check OK

Vehicles up to 9/91

- Press 0 and 8 buttons to select Function 08: "Read measuring value block" in display group 00

System in basic setting									
1	2	3	4	5	6	7	8	9	10

◄ Display will appear as shown

- Read displayed value in channel 2

  ♦ Display must be 40 to 140

Note:

The displayed value depends on the CO adjustment performed during the idle check.

If specified values NOT obtained:

- Perform electrical checks, step 13 ⇒ Repair Group 01

- Replace ECM J169, if necessary

Vehicles after 10/91

- Connect VAG 1551 Scan Tool ⇒ Repair Group 01 for additional information

- Switch ON ignition

- Press 0 and 9 buttons to select Function 09: "read individual measurement" in channel 04

  ♦ Display must be 40 to 140

Read individual measurement
Channel 4 measurement XXX

◄ Display will appear as shown

Note:

The displayed value depends on the CO adjustment performed during the idle check.

Manifold Absolute Pressure sensor, checking

– Connect VAG 1551 Scan Tool
⇒ Repair Group 01 for additional information

– Start engine and let idle

– Select Function 08: "Read measurement block"

Read measurement block 1			
1	2	3	4

◄ Display will appear as shown

Note:

Only continue testing if coolant temperature exceeds 85°C (185°F).

– Read display value

- ♦ Vehicles up to 9/91 use channel 2
- ♦ Vehicles after 10/91 use channel 4
- ♦ Display must be 20 to 40% and fluctuating

If a constant value of approximately 90% is displayed:

– Check vacuum hose to ECM J169

– Replace ECM J169, if necessary

– Press → button

– Press 0 and 6 buttons to select Function 06:
"end data transfer"

– Press Q button to enter input

Closed Throttle Position switch, checking and adjusting

Function, testing

– Perform electrical checks, step 14 and/or 30
⇒ Repair Group 01

Adjusting

Requirements

♦ Basic throttle setting OK
⇒ page F 24-63

♦ CTP switch mounting screws loosened

♦ Throttle stop lever touching the limiting screw

– Slightly loosen mounting screws -1-

– Tightly press throttle lever -2- and CTP switch -3- together (arrow)

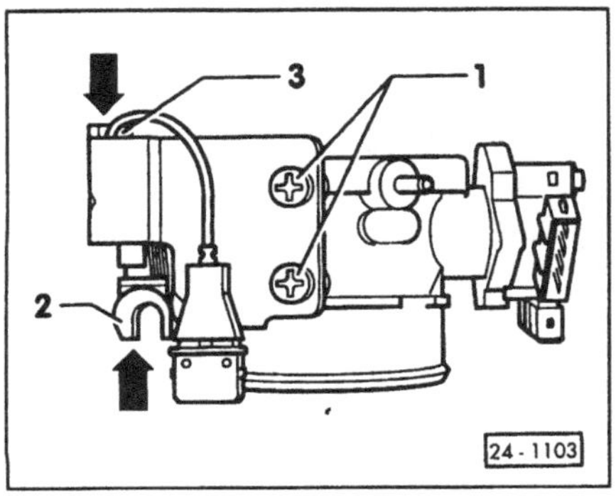

◄ – Tighten mounting screws -1-

– Open throttle

- ♦ CTP switch must audibly switch (click)

Fuel pressure regulator and residual pressure, checking

Note:

Fuel pressure is controlled by the fuel pressure regulator relative to intake manifold pressure.

> ***WARNING!***
>
> ***Fire hazard! DO NOT smoke or have anything in area that can ignite fuel.***
>
> ***Place rags around connections when loosening fittings to prevent fuel from spraying.***

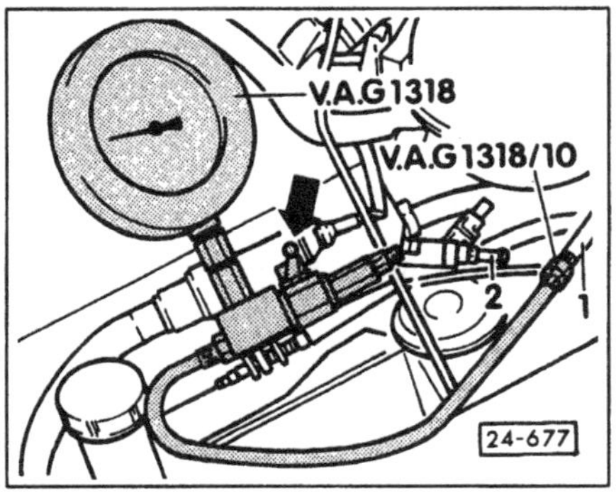

Requirement

- Fuel pump delivery quantity OK ⇒ Repair Group 20

Disconnect fuel line -1- from connection -2- on cold start injector

– Connect pressure gauge VAG 1318 to fuel line -1- using adaptor VAG 1318/10

> ***CAUTION!***
>
> ***VAG 1318 pressure tester shutoff must be closed, i.e. lever perpendicular to direction of flow (arrow).***

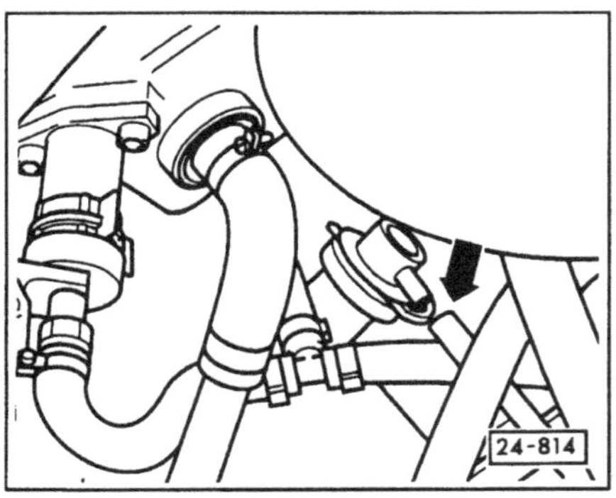

– Start engine and let idle

– Observe fuel pressure

- must be approximately 2.5 bar (36 psi)

– Disconnect vacuum hose from fuel pressure regulator (arrow)

- fuel pressure must increase to approximately 3.0 bar (44 psi)

– Switch OFF ignition

– Check residual pressure and for leakage by interpreting pressure drop on VAG 1318 gauge

- after 10 minutes, 2 bar (29 psi)(minimum) must still be present

If the residual pressure drops below 2 bar (29 psi):

– Start engine and let idle

– After pressure increases; switch OFF ignition and simultaneously clamp the fuel return line together at the fuel rail

– Watch for a pressure drop on VAG 1318 gauge

If pressure does NOT drop:

– Replace fuel pressure regulator

If pressure drops:

- Check fuel pump check valve
⇒ Repair Group 20
- Check hose connections and O–rings on fuel rail
- Check fuel injectors for leakage
- Check VAG 1318 pressure tester for leakage

> ***CAUTION!***
> ***Before disconnecting the VAG 1318, reduce fuel pressure by opening the fuel shutoff valve. Provide a container in front of the tester opening to catch any fuel that might spill out.***

Cold start injector, checking

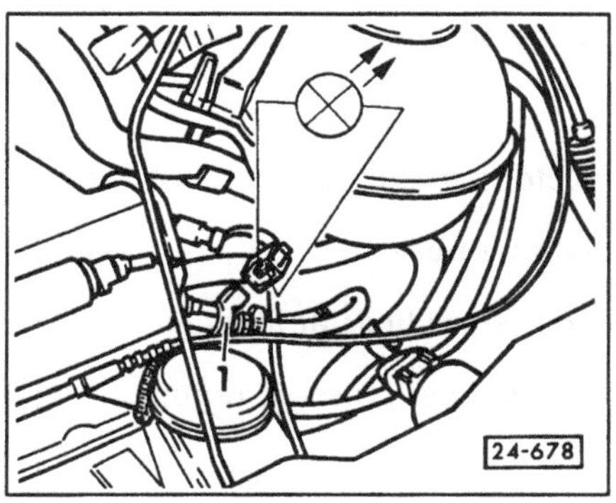

Voltage supply, checking

- Disconnect main fuel injector harness connector at fuel rail

◄ Disconnect cold start injector harness connector -1-

- Connect VAG 1527B LED tester to harness connector using jumper wires from VW 1594 adaptor kit

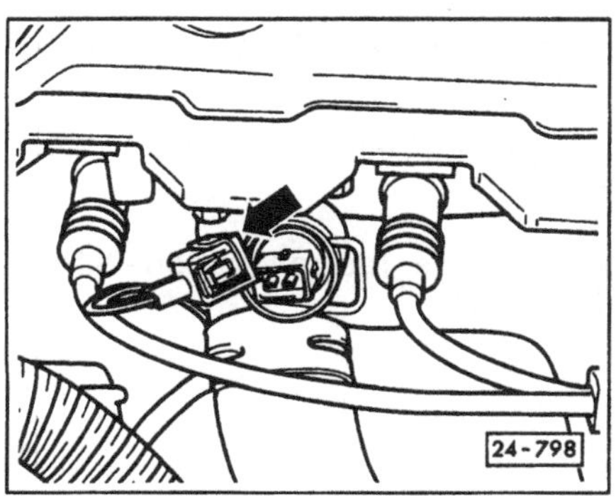

◄ - Disconnect blue ECT sensor harness connector (arrow)

- Operate starter
  - ♦ LED tester must light up for approximately 14 seconds

If LED does NOT light up:

- Perform electrical checks, steps 7 and/or 24
⇒ Repair Group 01
- Replace ECM J169, if necessary

Cold start injector, checking

Requirements

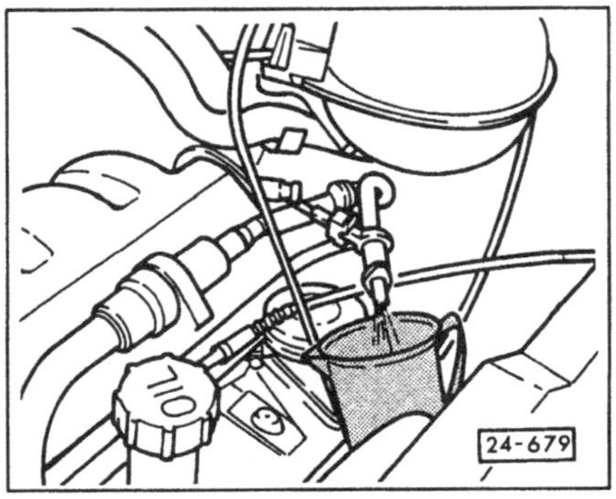

- ♦ Voltage supply OK
- ♦ Cold start injector harness connector connected
- ♦ Blue ECT sensor disconnected
- ♦ Main fuel injector harness connector disconnected (at fuel rail)

◄ – Remove cold start injector and hold in measuring container

– Operate starter

- ♦ cold start injector must spray in a uniform stream for approximately 1 to 4 seconds

– Dry off cold start injector nozzle

– Observe injector tip (nozzle)

- ♦ no drips or dampness may occur within one minute

If YES:

– Replace cold start injector N17

Fuel injectors, removing and installing

– Remove Air Cleaner housing and Air Cleaner element

– Remove intake hose

– Disconnect main fuel injector harness connector at fuel rail

– Disconnect crankcase breather hose

– Disconnect fuel supply and return lines at fuel rail

– Disconnect vacuum hose from fuel pressure regulator

– Remove fuel rail mounting screws

Note

To remove the socket head bolts, use an 1/8–in. drive ratchet and the SW5 3249 attachment.

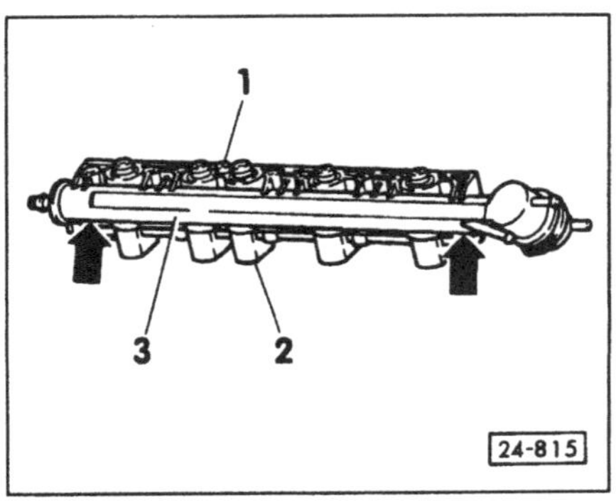

– Remove fuel rail assembly with fuel injectors on right side of vehicle toward the front

◄ – Remove screw -1- and pry off upper fuel rail section -2- from lower fuel rail section -3- (arrows)

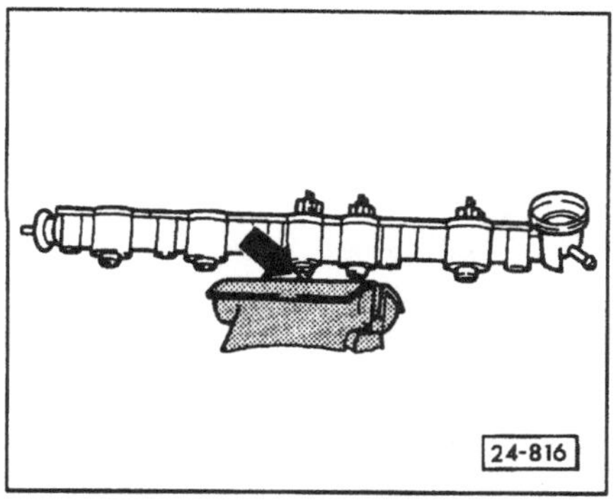

◄ – Press out injectors using M6 socket head bolt (arrow)

♦ place threaded side in vise

Installing

– Replace all damaged sealing rings, O-rings and gaskets

– Place gasket on upper section of fuel rail

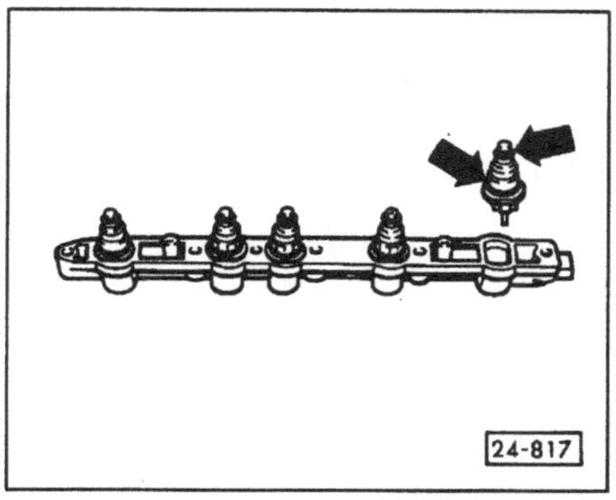

◄ – Lubricate fuel injector O-rings (arrows) with a light film of oil

– Insert fuel injectors into the upper fuel rail section

– Press upper fuel rail section (complete with fuel injectors) into the lower fuel rail section

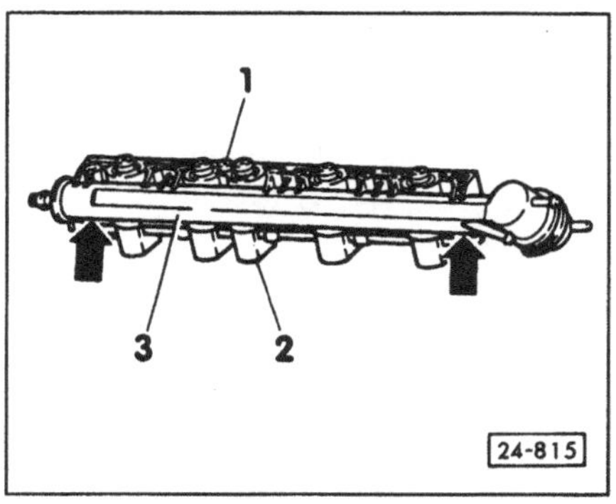

◄ – Tighten screw -1-

♦ 10 Nm (7 ft lb)

– Place fuel rail on intake manifold and tighten mounting screws

♦ 10 Nm (7 ft lb)

– Re-connect vacuum hose to fuel pressure regulator

– Re-connect fuel supply and return hoses

– Re-connect main fuel injector harness connector at fuel rail

– Re-connect Positive Crankcase Ventilation hose and attach to oil filler pipe

♦ ensure sufficient clearance between throttle body

– Install suction hose (note installation position)

– Install Air Cleaner insert and housing

Fuel Injectors, checking

Voltage supply, checking

Requirement

♦ Camshaft Position sensor OK, checking
⇒ Repair Group 28

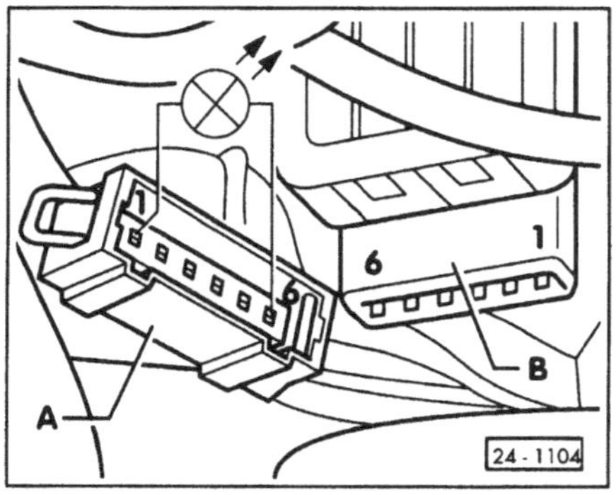

– Disconnect cold start injector harness connector

– Disconnect main fuel injector harness connector -A- from connector

– Connect VAG 1527B LED tester to connector terminal -6- using jumper wires from VW 1594 adaptor kit

  ♦ connect to terminals -1- and -2- for vehicles with a 2-pin connector

– Operate starter

  ♦ LED tester must flicker

– Repeat checks using terminals -2- and -6-, -3- and -6-, -4- and -6-, and -5- and -6-

  ♦ skip this step if vehicle has a 2-pin connector

If LED lights up continuously:

– Replace ground wire between battery and transmission

– Replace ECM J169

If LED flickers but does NOT light up:

– Perform electrical checks, step 4 and/or 21
⇒ Repair Group 01

– Replace ECM J169, if necessary

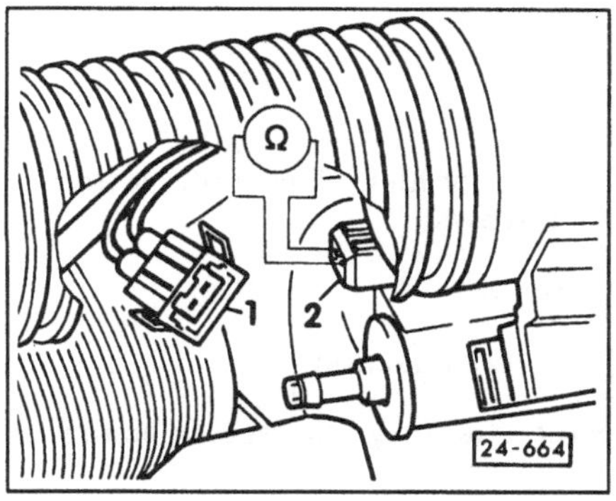

Resistance, checking

Vehicles with 2-pin connector

◄ – Switch Fluke 83 multimeter to resistance range

– Connect multimeter to connector -2- using jumper wires from VW 1594 adaptor kit

- ♦ must be 3.0 to 4.0 Ohms (indicating that all 5 injectors are OK)
- ♦ resistance for a single injector=15 to 20 Ohms

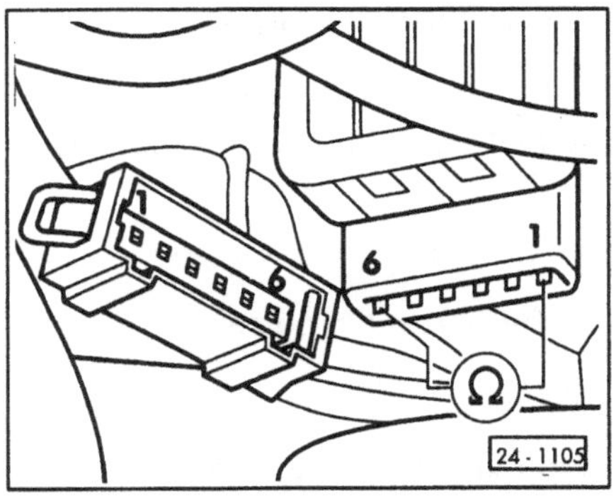

Vehicles with 6-pin connector

◄ – Switch Fluke 83 multimeter to resistance range

– Connect multimeter to connector -2- using jumper wires from VW 1594 adaptor kit

– Check resistance of individual injectors by measuring the following combinations:

Injector number	Terminal numbers
1	1 + 6
2	2 + 6
3	3 + 6
4	4 + 6
5	5 + 6

♦ resistance must be 12 to 18 Ohms

If specified values are NOT obtained:

– Remove fuel rail complete with injectors ⇒ page F 24-52

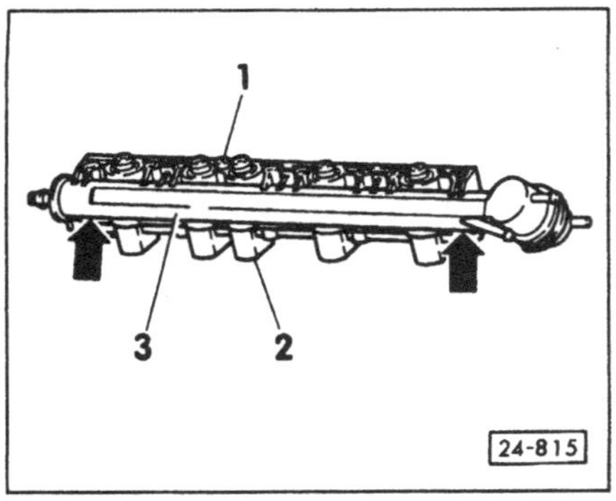

Vehicles with 2-pin connector

◄ – Remove screw -1- and pry upper fuel rail section -2- from lower fuel rail section -3- (arrows)

Vehicles with 2-pin connector

– Unclip cover from fuel rail upper section

– Repeat individual injector checking, replace injectors as needed

Fuel injector spray pattern, checking and leak testing

– Disconnect cold start injector harness connector

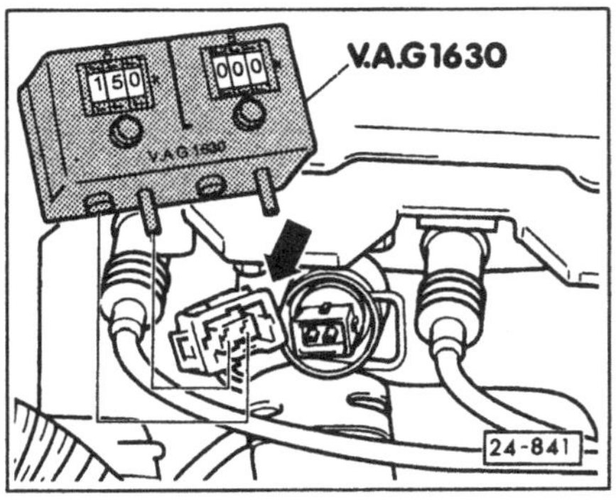

– Remove fuel rail complete with injectors ⇒ page F 24-52

◄ – Disconnect blue ECT sensor harness connector (arrow)

– Set VAG 1630 variable resistance box to 15000 Ohms and connect across blue ECT sensor harness connector using jumper wires from VW 1594 adaptor kit

– Connect fuel supply and return lines to fuel rail (arrow), using hose extensions as necessary

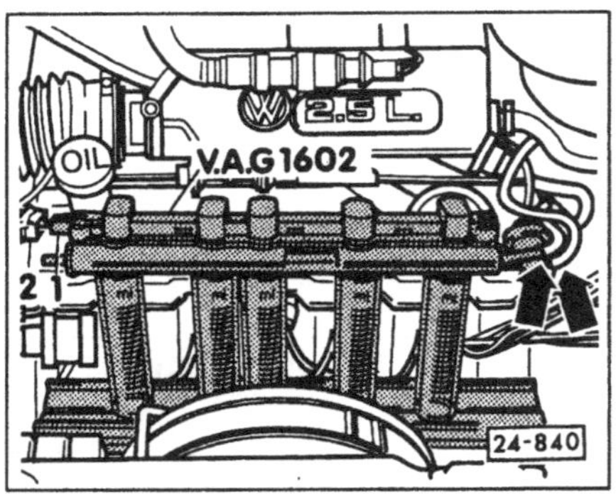

◄ – Insert fuel injectors into VAG 1602 fuel analyzer

– Extend connector -2- using jumper wires from VW 1594 adaptor kit and connect to fuel distributor harness connector -1-

– Operate starter for a few seconds

♦ Injectors must spray uniformly and in pulses

– Disconnect connection -2-

– Switch ON ignition for approximately 6 seconds

– Check injectors for leakage

♦ no more than 2 drops per minute per injector is acceptable

Note

Ensure that the O-rings are not damaged during fuel injector installation.

Intake air preheating, checking

Control flap, checking

Requirement

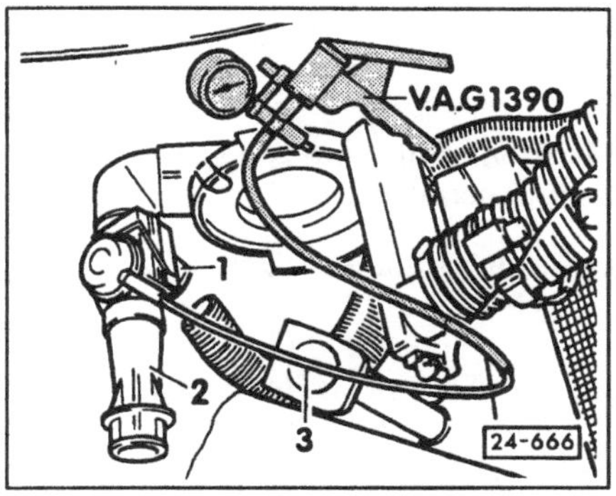

- ♦ Control flap vacuum element must be leak tight
- – Disconnect vacuum hose from temperature regulator vacuum element
- – Remove Air Cleaner housing and Air Cleaner element
- – Disconnect hose from stove hot air pipe
- – Check control flap position in air intake pipe by using a mirror or by touching
  - ♦ Control flap must close over hot air pipe -1-
- – Connect hand vacuum pump US 8026 to vacuum hose -3-
- – Operate pump and check for control flap ease of movement
- – Check for vacuum element function
  - ♦ Control flap must close off cold air pipe -2-

Temperature regulator, checking

- – Connect vacuum line -3- on temperature regulator (brass connector tube and/or with notch)
- – Start engine and let idle
- – Check position of control flap after 20 seconds (maximum)

Temperature of temperature controller	Position of control flap
below 20°C (68 °F)	cold air pipe 2 closed
above 30°C (86 °F)	hot air pipe 1 closed
between 20 and 30°C	between cold and hot air pipes

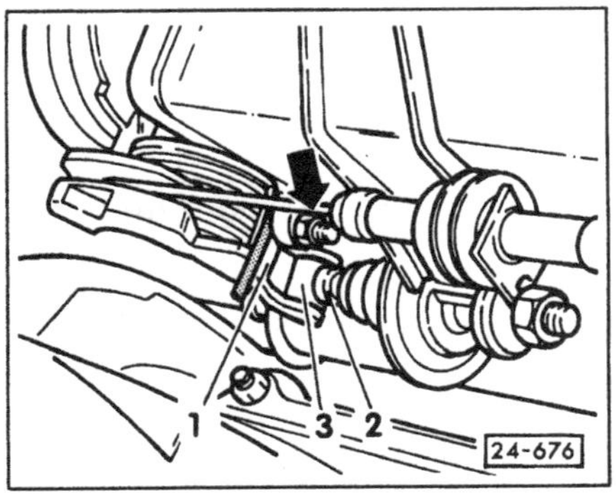

Throttle, basic setting

Note:

The limiting screw is adjusted at the factory and must not be changed. If the screw is accidentally turned, perform the basic throttle adjustment as follows.

◄ – Turn out limiting screw (arrow) until there is a gap between stop lever -1- and the limiting screw (arrow)

– Turn in the limiting screw until it touches lever -1-

Note

To determine the exact stop point of the limiter screw, place a thin piece of paper or cellophane between the limiting screw and lever -1-. By continuously tugging on the paper while turning the limiting screw the stop point will become obvious.

– After determining stop point, turn limiting screw in 1/2 turn further

– Check dashpot, adjust if necessary
⇒ page F 24-34

– Check throttle position sensor
⇒ page F 24-37

– Check idle speed
⇒ page F 24-22

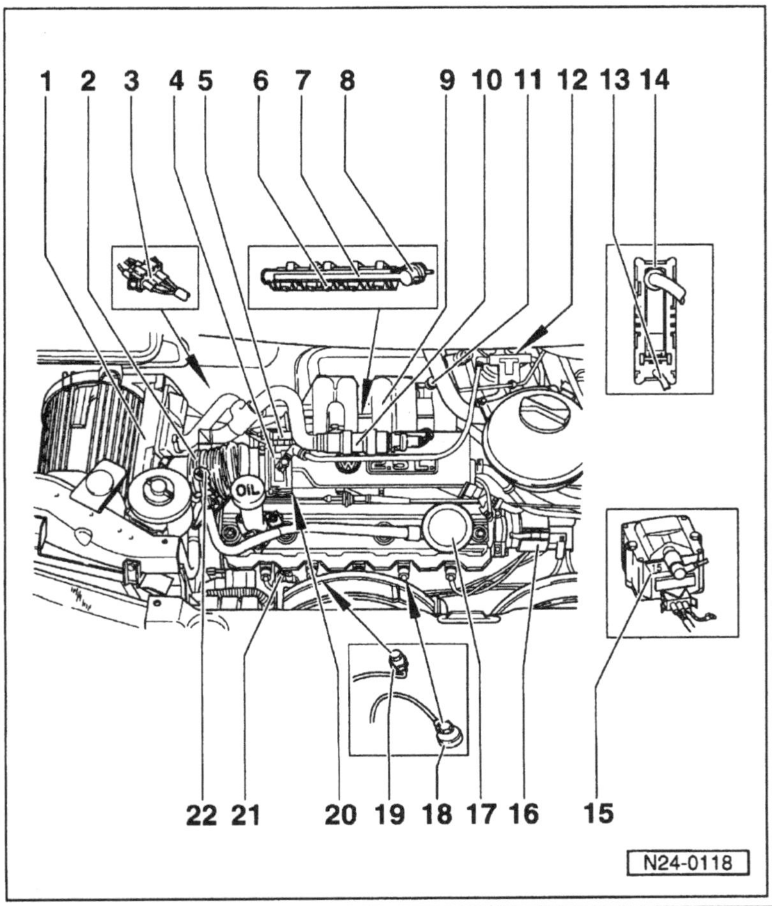

Digifant Fuel Injection system, component layout

Vehicles built starting m.y. 1995

Notes:

- *This section Fuel injection ONLY. For ignition system components:*
⇒ Repair Group 28
- *to Tilt lock carrier forward*
⇒ Fig. 1 page F 24-67

1 - Air Cleaner
- with regulating flap for intake air preheating

2 - Intake hose

3 - 3-pin connector
- for Heated Oxygen sensor G39 and Oxygen sensor heater

4 - Throttle body

5 - Throttle Position sensor G69

6 - Fuel injectors N30, N31, N32, N33, N83

7 - Fuel rail

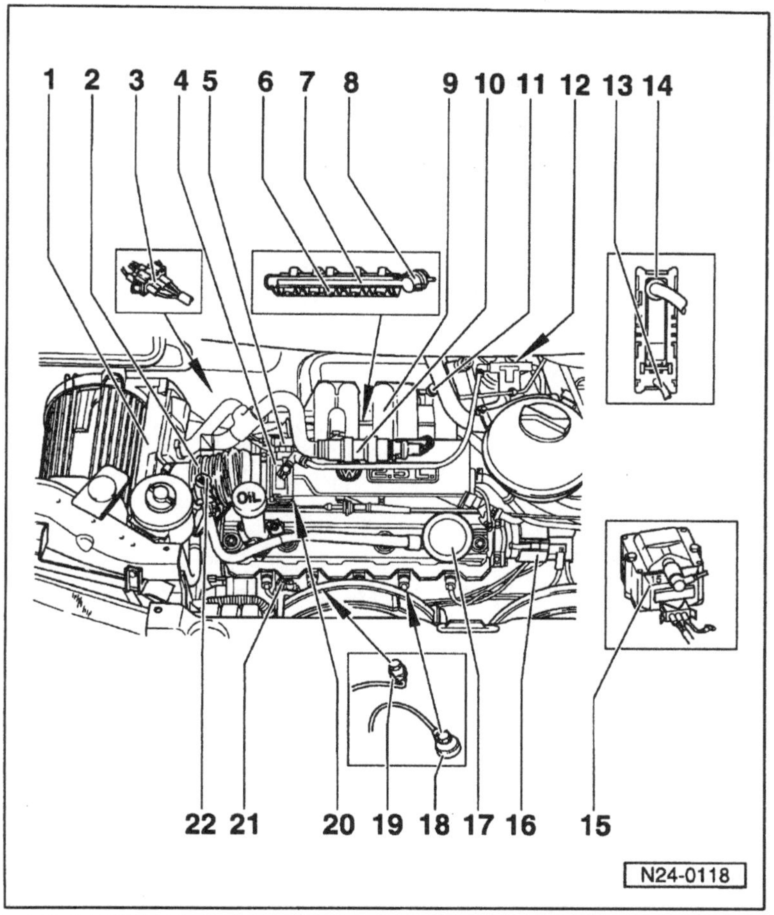

8 - Fuel pressure regulator

9 - Intake manifold

10 - Idle Air Control valve N71

11 - CO sampling tube

12 - EVAP canister purge regulator valve N80
- ♦ EVAP system

⇒ Repair Group 20

13 - Vacuum line connection to the ECM
- ♦ to T piece between intake manifold and fuel pressure regulator

⇒ page F 24-14, item D
- ♦ Manifold Absolute Pressure sensor G71 in J169 ECM

14 - Digifant Engine Control Module (ECM) J169
- ♦ location: in engine compartment on left
- ♦ with Manifold Absolute Pressure sensor G71

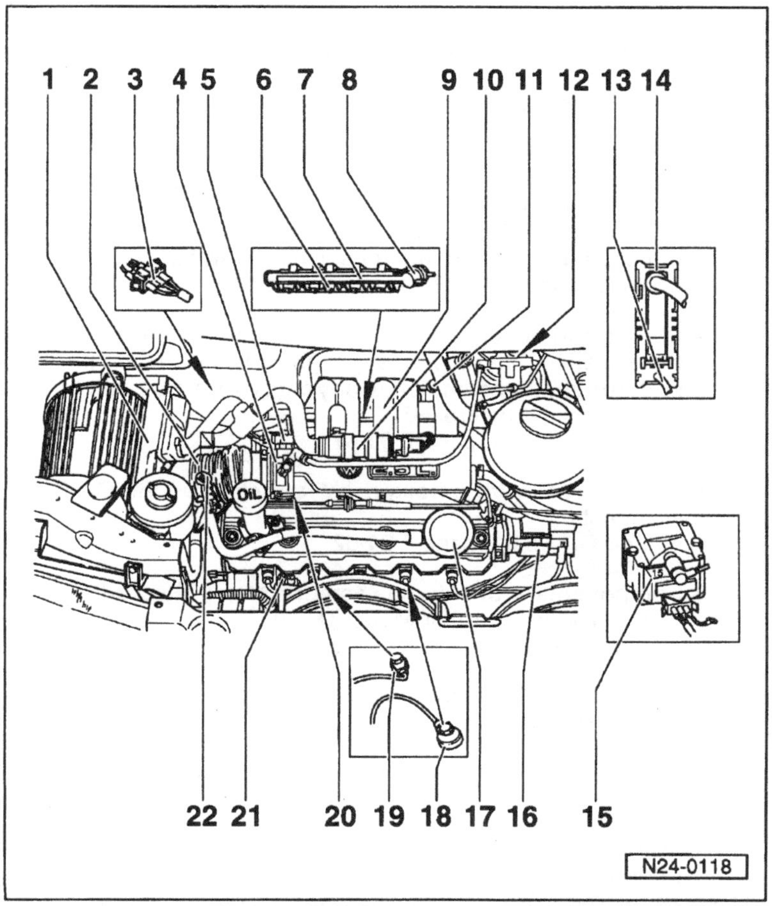

15 - Ignition coil N152

⇒ page F 28-23, item 1
- ♦ with ignition coil power output stage N152
- ♦ location: under battery cover on left in direction of travel

16 - Distributor
- ♦ with Camshaft Position sensor G40

⇒ page F 28-25

17 - Positive Crankcase Ventilation valve for crankcase breather

18 - Knock sensor 2 G66

⇒ page F 28-24, item 15

19 - Knock sensor 1 G61

⇒ page F 28-24, item 17

20 - Closed Throttle Position switch F60
- ♦ on Throttle body

21 - Engine Coolant Temperature sensor G62
- ♦ blue, 2-pin
- ♦ for Digifant fuel injection and ignition system

22 - Intake Air Temperature sensor G42

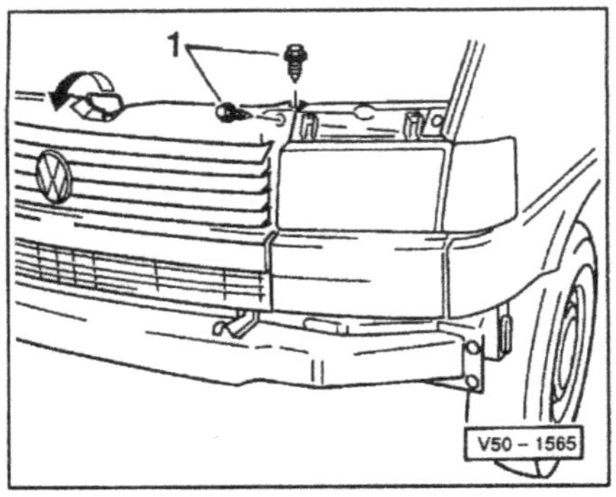

Fig. 1 Tilting lock carrier forward

– Remove mounting screws -1- on left and right

– Tilt radiator and lock carrier forward -arrow-

Fuel Injection system, servicing

Servicing Ignition system
⇒ Repair Group 28

♦ The Engine Control Module (ECM) for the fuel injection and ignition system is equipped with a Diagnostic Trouble Code (DTC) memory. Before carrying out repairs and troubleshooting, the DTC memory must be checked and all vacuum connections checked for leakage (outside air)

♦ Checks and adjustments can cause system control limits to be exceeded. These will be recognized as a DTC by the ECM and stored. After completing any checks or adjustments, DTC memory must be erased
⇒ Repair Group 01, page F 01-67

♦ Components with an asterisk * are checked via On Board Diagnostic
⇒ Repair Group 01, page F 01-52

♦ Components with a double asterisk ** are checked via Output Diagnostic Test Mode (DTM)
⇒ Repair Group 01, page F 01-69

♦ Hose connections are secured with screw-type or spring-type hose clips

♦ Always replace spring-type hose clips with screw-type hose clips

♦ Proper electrical component operation requires 10.5 Volts minimum

- Do not use sealants or products containing silicone! Particles of silicone drawn into the engine are NOT consumed during combustion and will damage the Heated Oxygen sensor

Safety precautions
⇒ page F 24-83

Rules for cleanliness
⇒ page F 24-84

Technical data
⇒ page F 24-82

Basic settings
⇒ page F 24-85

Intake system leak-checking (outside air)
⇒ page F 24-116

On Board Diagnostic and electrical check of the Digifant Fuel Injection and Ignition system
⇒ Repair Group 01, page F 01-82

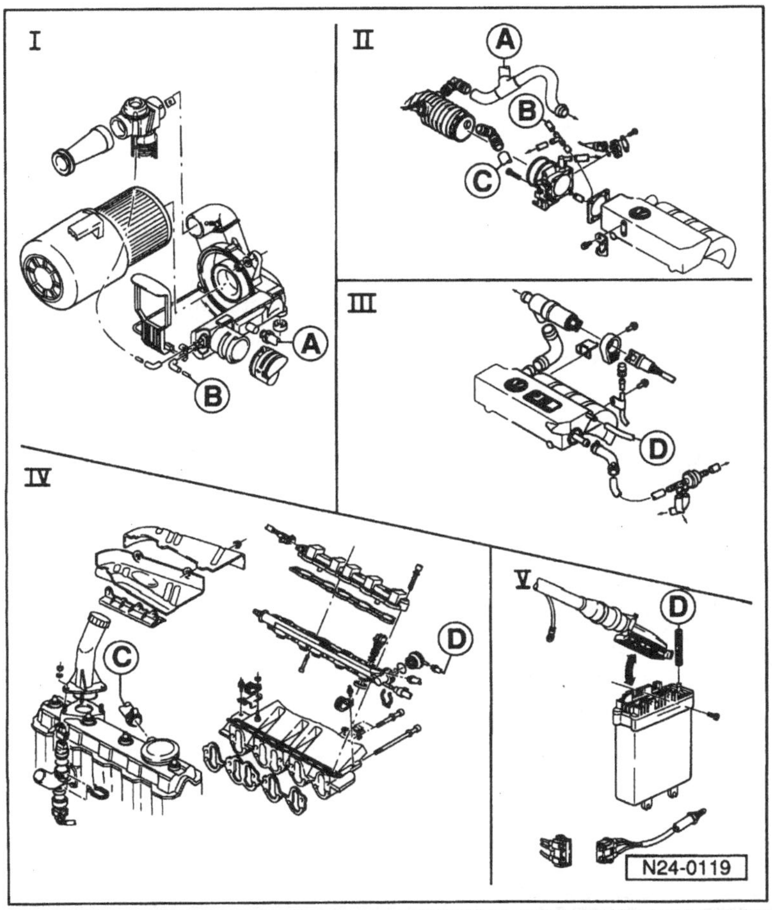

I ⇒ page F 24-71

II ⇒ page F 24-73

III ⇒ page F 24-75

IV ⇒ page F 24-77

V ⇒ page F 24-80

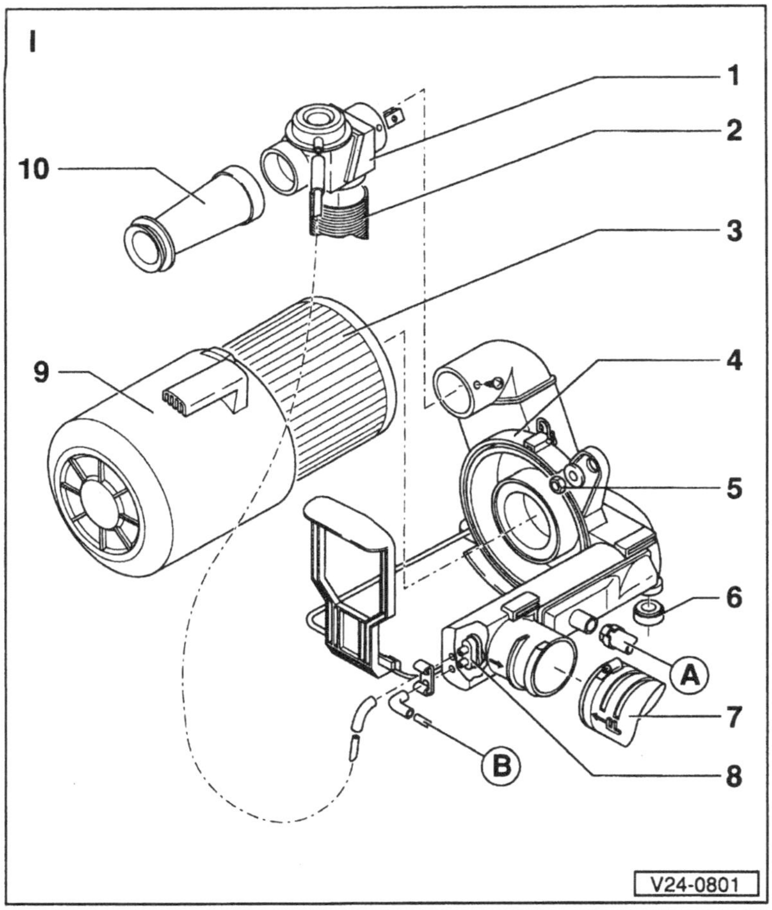

Part I

A ⇒ (goes to) page F 24-73

B ⇒ (goes to) page F 24-73

1 - Inlet Air pre-heater housing
- ♦ with regulating flap for intake air preheating, checking

⇒ page F 24-118
- – Note that there are two screws securing the pre-heater to the Air Cleaner housing elbow (only one is shown in the illustration)

2 - Hose
- ♦ from warm air collector plate on exhaust manifold

⇒ page F 24-77 (item 4)

3 - Air Cleaner element

4 - Air Cleaner housing

5 - 20 Nm (15 ft lb)

6 - Rubber washer

7 - Intake air hose
- ♦ note installed position

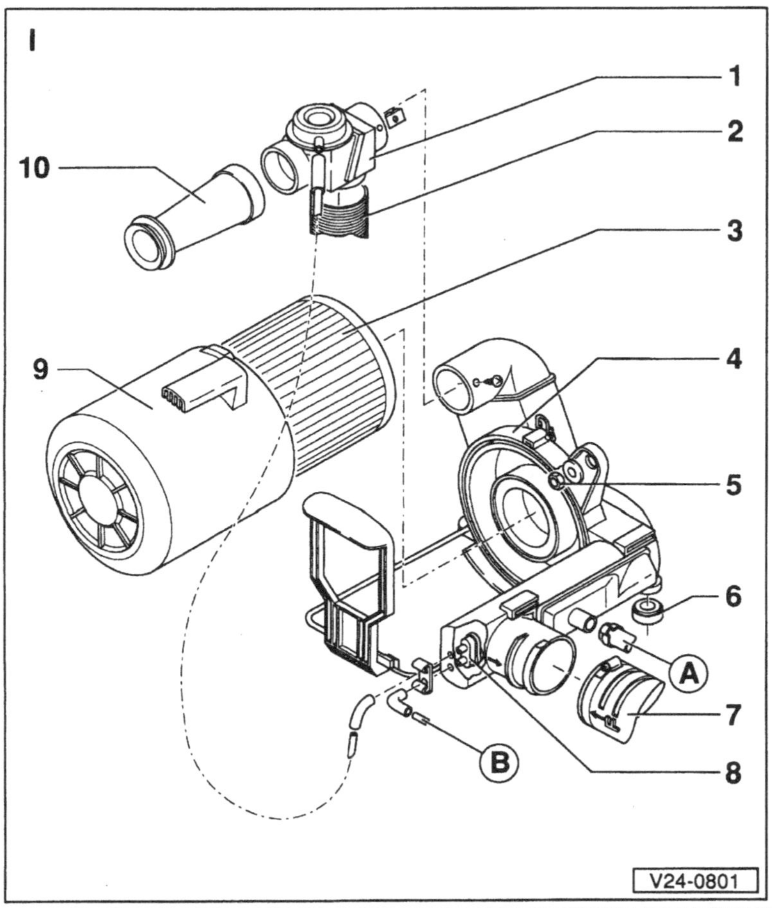

8 - Temperature regulator
- ♦ for intake air preheating
- ♦ metal connecting port (or notch) toward flap
- ♦ Checking intake air preheating

⇒ page F 24-118

9 - Air Cleaner element housing

10 - Inlet air snorkel
- – Note installed position

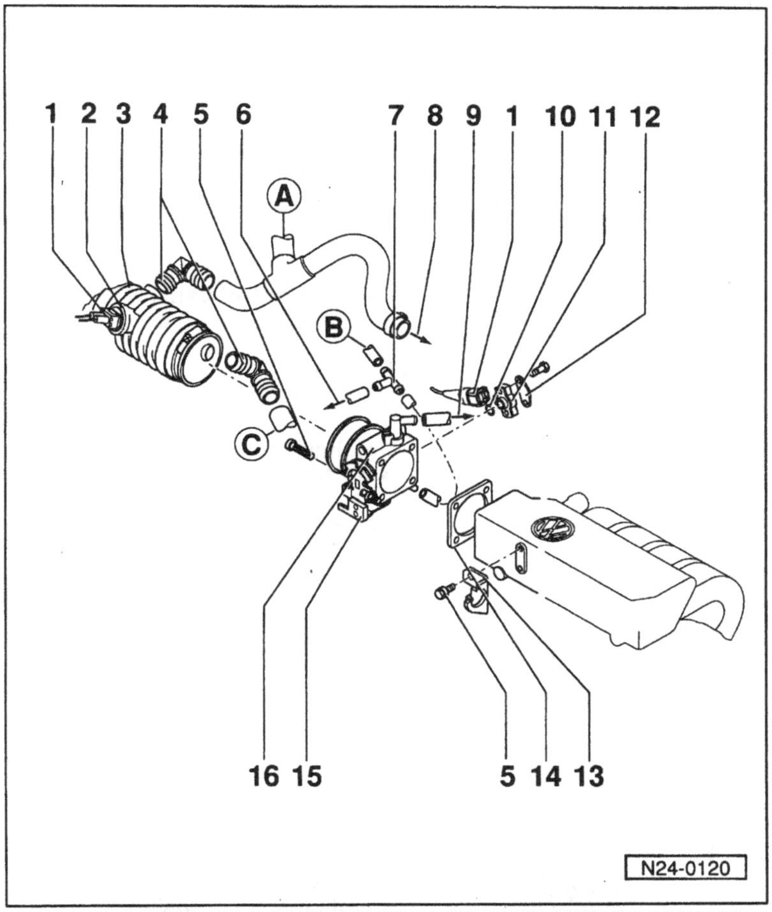

Part II

A ⇒ (goes to) page F 24-71

B ⇒ (goes to) page F 24-71

C ⇒ (goes to) page F 24-77

1 - Not Applicable to US Vehicles

2 - Not Applicable to US Vehicles

3 - Intake hose
- Note installed position

4 - Elbow

5 - M6 = 10 Nm (7 lt lb)
M8 = 20 Nm (15 ft lb)

6 - to vehicle interior

7 - T-piece

8 - to Idle Air Control valve (N71)**

9 - to EVAP canister purge regulator valve N80 **
♦ EVAP system
⇒ Repair Group 20

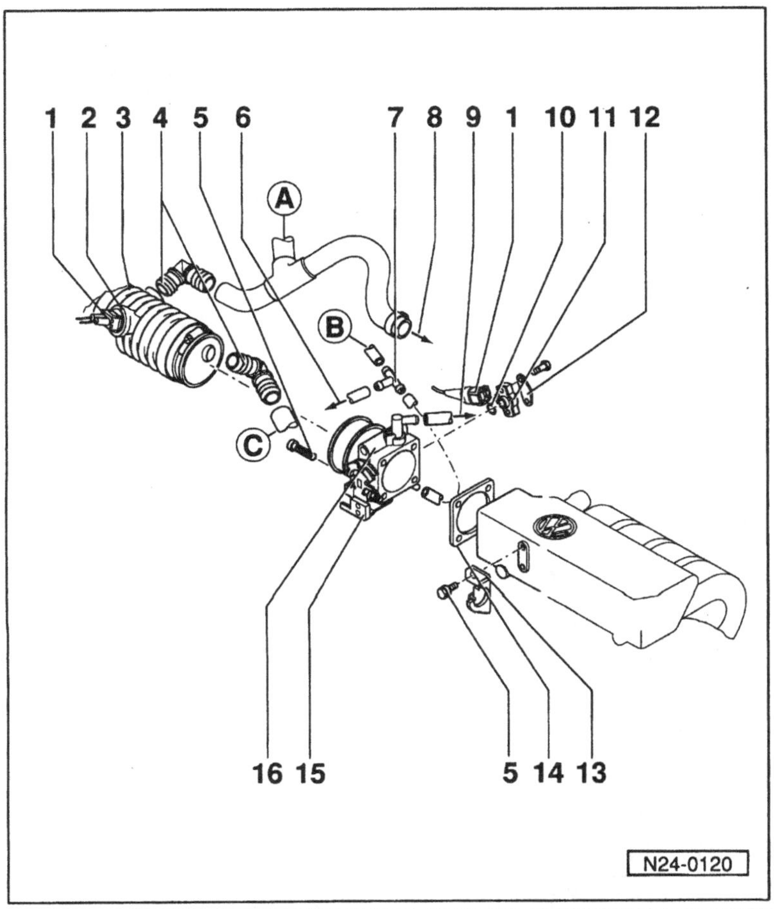

10 - O-ring
- Replace if damaged

11 - Throttle Position sensor G69*
♦ Checking:
⇒ page F 24-98

12 - Mounting plate

13 - Support bracket
♦ for accelerator cable
♦ accelerator cable, adjusting
⇒ Repair Group 20
♦ removing and installing parts of the fuel supply system, adjusting accelerator cable

14 - Gasket
♦ replace

15 - Closed Throttle Position switch F60
♦ checking and adjusting
⇒ page F 24-121

16 - Throttle Body

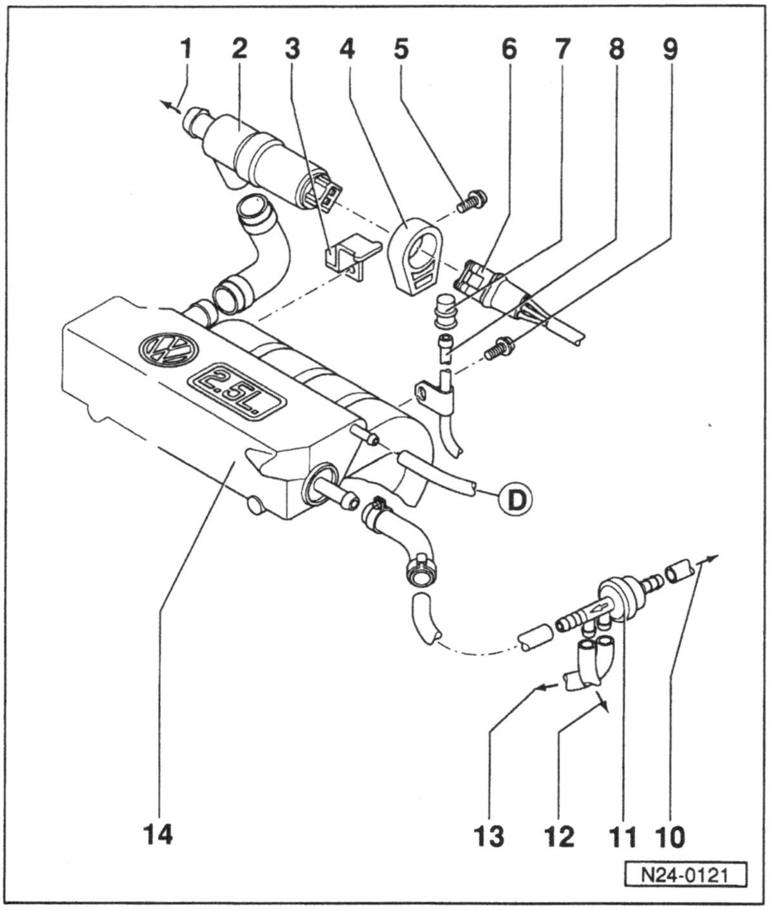

Part III

D ⇒ (goes to) page F 24-77 or F 24-80

- to fuel pressure regulator and ECM

1 - To Intake Air hose

2 - Idle Air Control valve N71**

- resistance: 2 - 10 Ω

3 - Bracket

- for Idle Air Control valve

4 - Retaining ring

- for Idle Air Control valve

5 - 10 Nm (7 ft lb)

6 - Harness connector

7 - Cap for CO sampling tube

– Ensure tight, leak-free installation

8 - CO sampling tube

9 - 15 Nm (11 ft lb)

10 - To brake servo

11 - Check valve

– Note installed position

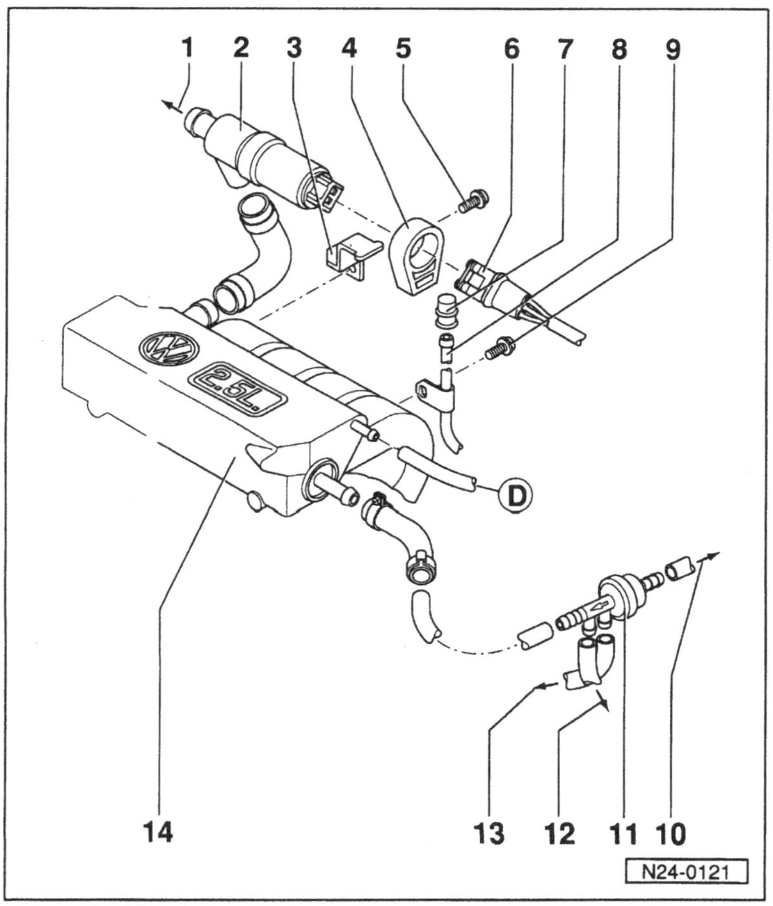

12 - Vacuum connection for EGR and Secondary Air Injection system

13 - to vehicle interior

14 - Intake manifold

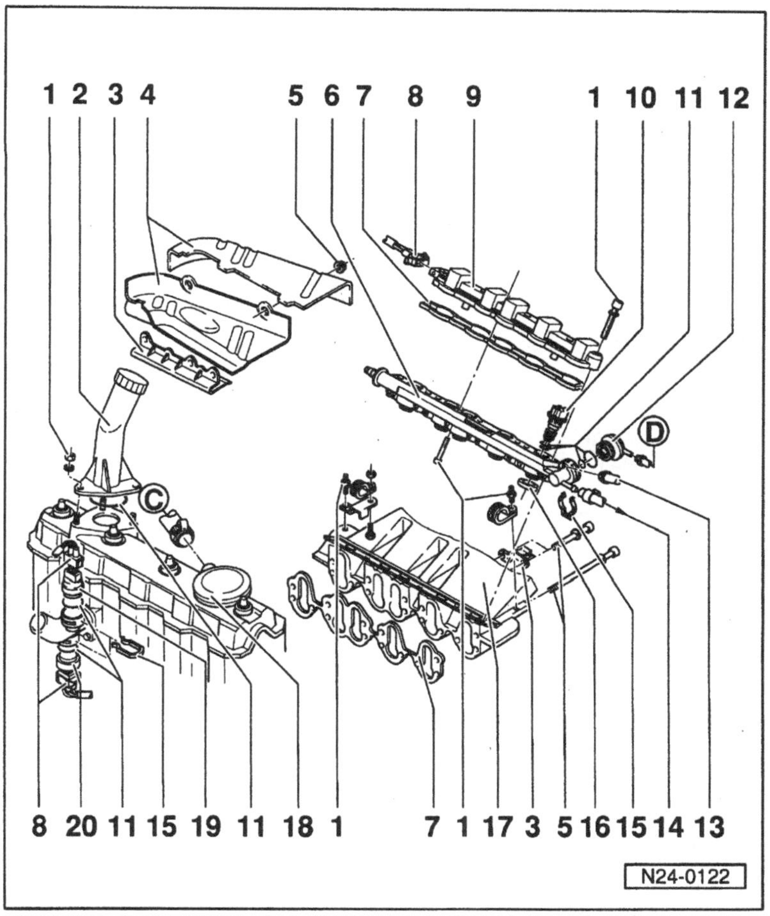

Part IV

C ⇒ (goes to) page F 24-73

D ⇒ (goes to) pages F 24-75 or F 24-80

1 - 10 Nm (7 ft lb)

2 - Oil filler pipe

3 - Bracket
- ♦ for warm air collector plate

4 - Warm air collector plate

5 - 25 Nm (18 ft lb)

6 - Fuel rail lower section
- ♦ removing and installing ⇒ page F 24-109

7 - Gasket
- – Replace if damaged

8 - 2-pin harness connector
- ♦ 6-pin, for vehicles with EGR and Secondary Air Injection system

9 - Fuel rail upper section
- ♦ with wiring guide
- ♦ removing and installing ⇒ page F 24-109

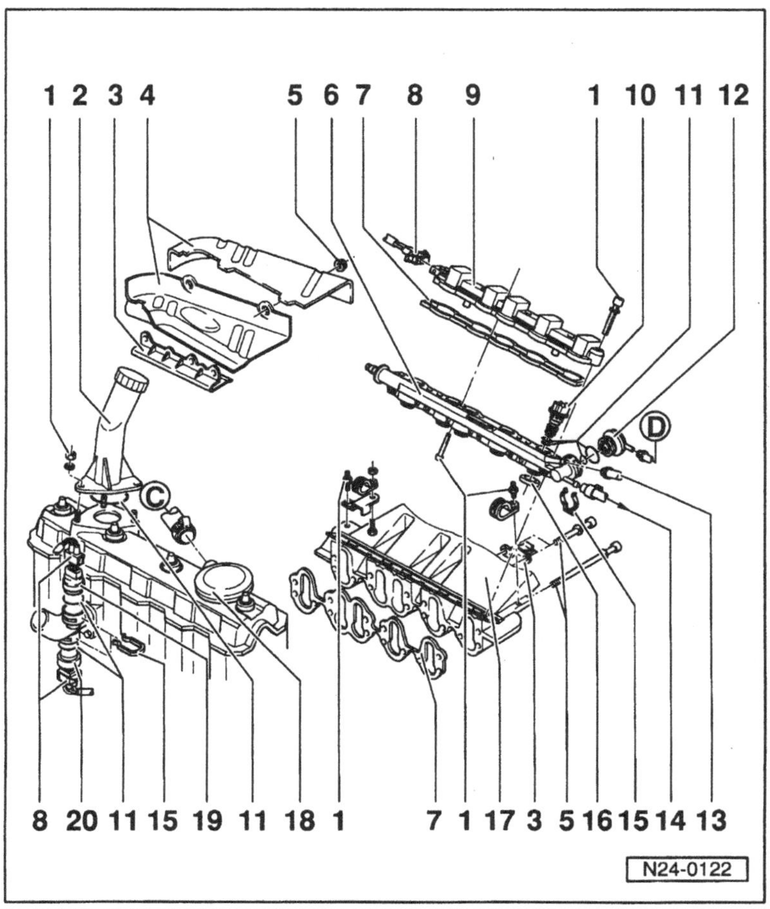

10 - Fuel injectors: N30, N31, N32, N33, N83
- ♦ resistance 15 to 20 Ω
- ♦ removing and installing ⇒ page F 24-109
- ♦ checking ⇒ page F 24-112

11 - O-ring
- – Replace if damaged

12 - Fuel pressure regulator
- ♦ fuel pressure regulator and residual pressure, checking ⇒ page F 24-106

13 - Fuel supply line
- ♦ black with white arrow
- ♦ from fuel pump assembly in fuel tank

14 - Fuel return line
- ♦ blue
- ♦ to fuel tank

15 - Retaining clip

16 - Seal
- – Replace if damaged

17 - Intake manifold

18 - Postive Crankcase ventilation valve for crankcase breather

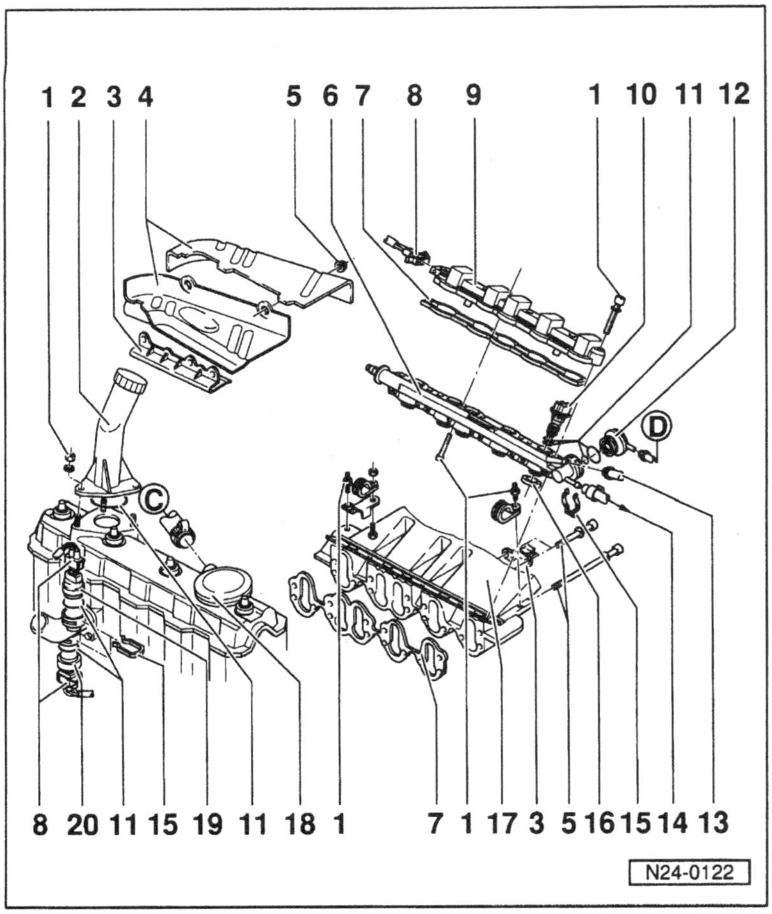

19 - Engine Coolant Temperature sensor G62*
- ♦ blue, 2-pin
- – Before removing, release pressure from cooling system, if necessary
- ♦ checking

⇒ page F 24-101
- ♦ resistance graph

⇒ Repair Group 01, page F 01-91

20 - Coolant CF51 with Engine Coolant Temperature sensor G2
- ♦ yellow, 4-pin

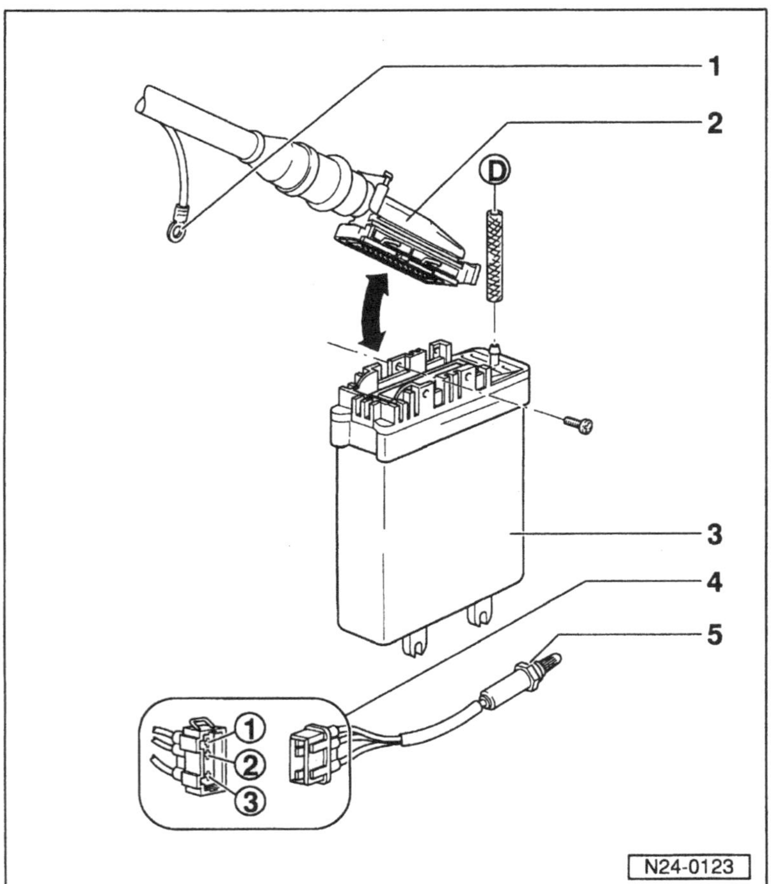

Part V

D ⇒ (goes to) page F 24-75 or F 24-77

1 - Chassis Ground connection
- ♦ attached to the body

2 - Engine Control Module harness connector

3 - Digifant Engine Control Module J169*
- ♦ for Fuel injection system, Oxygen sensor control, Knock control, Engine speed governor, On Board Diagnostic and Ignition
- ♦ with Manifold Absolute Pressure sensor G71*
- ♦ checking:

⇒ page F 24-105
- – Perform Engine Basic setting when replacing

⇒ page F 24-85

4 - 3–pin harness connector

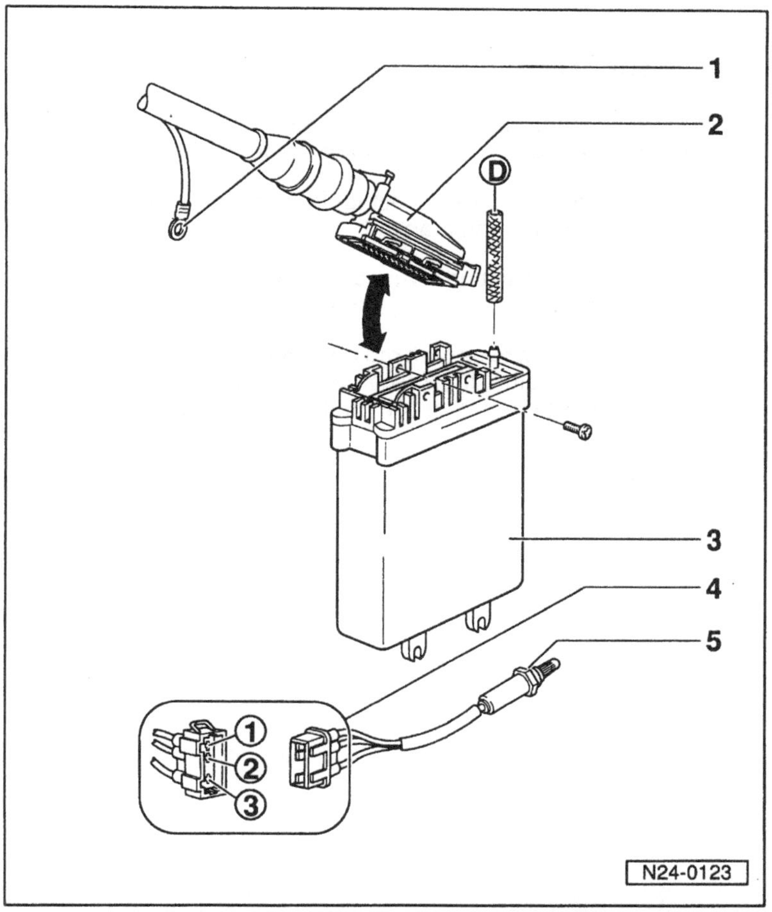

5 - Heated Oxygen sensor G39*

- ♦ 50 Nm (37 ft lb)
- ♦ location: in front exhaust pipe
- – Only grease threads with "G5"; do NOT allow "G5" to get into the slots on the sensor body
- ♦ Oxygen sensor heater Voltage supply via fuel pump relay J17**
- – Check Voltage supply between terminals -1- (red/ white) and -2- (brown), (with engine running): Specification: approx. battery Voltage
- – Check sensor heater for continuity on Heated Oxygen sensor connector (white wire)

Technical data

Engine code		ACU
Idle Speed checks [1]		
Idle speed	rpm	775 to 825 [2]
CO content	Vol. %	0.3 to 1.2 [2]
Digifant Engine Control Module (ECM) [3]		
RPM upper limit (cut-off point)	rpm	5500

[1] Observe test conditions
⇒ page F 24-90

[2] NOT adjustable

[3] If replaced, perform basic settings
⇒ page F 24-85

Safety precautions

To prevent injuries to persons and/or damage to the fuel injection and ignition system, observe the following points:

- Do not touch or disconnect ignition wiring when the engine is running or being cranked
- The ignition must be switched OFF before connecting or disconnecting injection or ignition system wiring or test leads
- If the engine is to be cranked but not started, e.g. when checking compression, first disconnect the Camshaft Position sensor harness connector (on ignition distributor housing)

Rules for cleanliness

When working on the fuel supply/injection system, carefully observe the following rules:

- Thoroughly clean all connections and the adjacent areas before disconnecting
- Place parts that have been removed on a clean surface and cover. Do not use fluffy cloths!
- Carefully cover opened components or seal, if the repair cannot be carried out immediately
- Only install clean components:

  Only unpack replacement parts just before installing

  Do not use parts that have been stored loose (e.g. in tool boxes etc.)
- When the system is open:

  Do not work with compressed air if it can be avoided

  Do not move the vehicle unless absolutely necessary

Function 04, "Engine basic settings"

Special tools, testers and auxiliary items

- ♦ VAG 1551 Scan Tool using adaptor cable VAG 1551/1
- ♦ VAG 1363A CO tester (or EPA approved equivalent)
- ♦ VAG 1363/3 adaptor
- ♦ VAG 1367 Engine Tester with VAG 1367/8 inductive pickup

Test conditions

- ♦ Engine oil temperature 80°C (176°F) minimum
- ♦ All electrical consumers switched OFF (engine radiator coolant fan must not run during the check/adjustments)
- ♦ A/C switched OFF
- ♦ Accelerator cable adjustment OK
⇒ Repair Group 20, Accelerator cable, adjusting
- ♦ Closed Throttle Position switch closed
- ♦ VAG 1551 Scan Tool connected
- ♦ No DTC's stored in DTC memory
⇒ Repair Group 01, page F 01-52

- ♦ Ignition timing OK
⇒ Repair Group 28, page F 28-31
- ♦ Idle Speed control OK (With ignition ON, Idle Air Control valve must vibrate and buzz)
- ♦ Exhaust system must be free of leaks

Test sequence

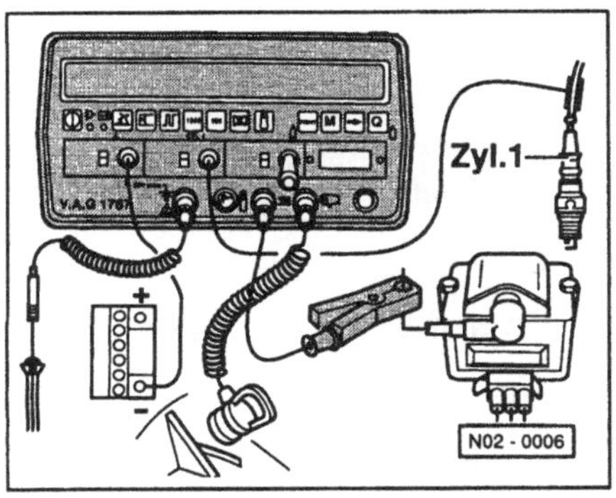

- ♦ Engine cold

Note:

Some vehicles have a TDC sensor installed as standard equipment. For these vehicles, the Engine Tester can be connected without disassembling the distributor cap (even with the engine at operating temperature) by using adaptor cable VAG 1367/9.

- Remove distributor cap from ignition distributor
- ◄ Connect VAG 1367 Engine Tester using inductive pickup VAG 1367/8
- Re-install ignition distributor cap

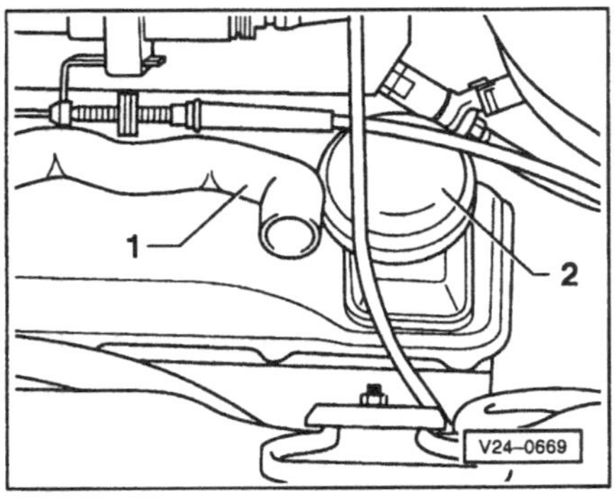

- Connect CO tester to CO sampling tube using VAG 1363/3 adaptor

Note:

To prevent incorrect readings, the adaptor must securely seal onto the CO sampling tube (free of leaks).

◄ - Pull crankcase breather hose -1- off pressure regulating valve -2- and position so that only fresh air can be drawn in

- Start engine and let idle (engine rpm must not exceed 1500 rpm)

Note:

If the engine stalls after restarting, it can run for up to 4 minutes at an increased rpm. In this case, do not continue until the rpm has again dropped below 1500 rpm.

- Operate Scan Tool taking displayed information into account
- Press 1 button to select "Rapid data transfer"
- Press 0 and 1 buttons to select address word 01 "Engine electronics"
- Press Q button to enter input
- Press → button
- Press 0 and 4 buttons to select Function 04: "Basic setting"
- Press Q button to enter input

Notes:

- *In the basic setting, the Digifant Engine Control Module is matched to the engine during idle*
- *If the Throttle Position sensor is removed, installed or replaced from a vehicle with an automatic transmission; the Transmission Control Module must be brought into the basic setting using the VAG 1551 Scan Tool*
- *Automatic transmission 098*

⇒ Repair Group 01 (Automatic transmission 098)

Basic setting	HELP
Input display group number XX	

◄ Display will appear as shown:

- Press 0 and 1 buttons to select "Display group number"
- Press Q button to enter input

Basic setting 1			→
1	2	3	4

◄ Display will appear as shown: (1 to 4 = Display channels)

Do not continue with check until:

- Engine temperature exceeds 85 °C (185 F) (display channel 2)
- All adjusting conditions are fulfilled (display channel 4)

⇒ Repair Group 01, page F 01-78

- Specification: 00000000

- Check idle speed and CO content
  - Idle speed: 775 to 875 rpm
  - CO content: 0.3 to 1.2 Vol.%

- Press → button
- Press 0 and 6 buttons to select Function 06: "End data output"
- Press Q button to enter input
- Allow engine to cool and remove distributor cap
- Remove TDC sensor
- Re-install distributor cap

If the specifications are not obtained:

- Check intake air system for leaks
⇒ page F 24-116
- Check exhaust system between cylinder head and Three-Way Catalyst for leaks (including the CO sampling tube and its cap)
- Check Heated Oxygen sensor and Oxygen sensor control
- Take vehicle for road test, repeat DTC memory check and then perform Function 04 "Engine basic setting" again

Idle speed control, checking

Functional check

To functionally test system, perform Output Diagnostic Test Mode (DTM)
⇒ Repair Group 01, page F 01-69

Checking regulation

- Check with Scan Tool VAG 1551 using Function 08, "Read measuring value block", with engine idling

Special tools, testers and auxiliary items

♦ VAG 1551 Scan Tool using adaptor cable VAG 1551/1

Test conditions

♦ No DTC's stored in DTC memory
⇒ page F 01-52, check DTC memory

♦ Scan Tool VAG 1551 connected and Function 08 "Read measuring value block" selected (Display group number 03)
⇒ page F 01-76

Read measuring value block 3			→
1	2	3	4

◄ Display will appear as shown: (1 to 4 = Display channels)

Note:

If something different is indicated on the display:
⇒ Scan Tool operating instructions

Test sequence

– Do not continue with check until engine temperature exceeds 85 °C (185 °F)

– Note value displayed in display channel 4

♦ Specification: 0 to 35 %

If specification not attained:

– Check valve resistance ⇒ page F 24-75 (item 2) or if necessary, Replace Digifant ECM J169

– Press → button

– Press 0 and 6 buttons to select Function 06, "End data output"

– Press Q button to enter input

Note:

The control current for idle speed control is dependent upon the engine load at idle. The following load conditions can cause the opening values to fluctuate between 0 and 35%:

♦ *Engine cold*

♦ *A/C switched ON*

♦ *Electrical consumers switched ON*

♦ *Power steering: wheels not in straight-ahead position*

♦ *Ignition timing not correct*

Heated Oxygen sensor, checking

– Check using Scan Tool VAG 1551 in Function 08, "Read measuring value block", with engine idling

Special tools, testers and auxiliary items

♦ Scan Tool VAG 1551 using adaptor cable VAG 1551/1

Test conditions

♦ Idle speed OK

♦ Exhaust system between three-way catalyst and cylinder head free of leaks

♦ Scan Tool VAG 1551 connected and Function 08, "Read measuring value block" selected (display group number 01) ⇒ page F 01-76

Read measuring value block 1			→
1	2	3	4

◄ Display will appear as shown: (1 to 4 = Display channels)

If something different is displayed: ⇒ Scan Tool operating instructions

Only continue testing if:

♦ Engine Coolant Temperature exceeds 85 °C (185 °F) ⇒ display channel 2

♦ Allow engine to idle for an additional 2 minutes

Read measuring value block 1 →
1 2 3 4

Test sequence

– Note Heated Oxygen sensor voltage (display channel 3)

♦ Specification: 0.0 to 0.8 Volts (fluctuating)

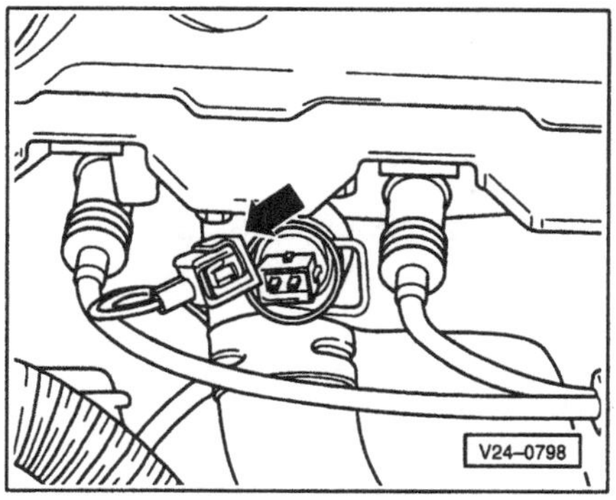

Vehicles with 2-pin fuel rail harness connector

– With throttle closed, disconnect (2-pin) Engine Coolant Temperature sensor -arrow-

♦ The Heated Oxygen sensor voltage in display channel 3 must rise and then drop back to the original figures

– Re-connect Heated Oxygen sensor harness connector

♦ Voltage (in display channel 3) must drop and then return to the original value

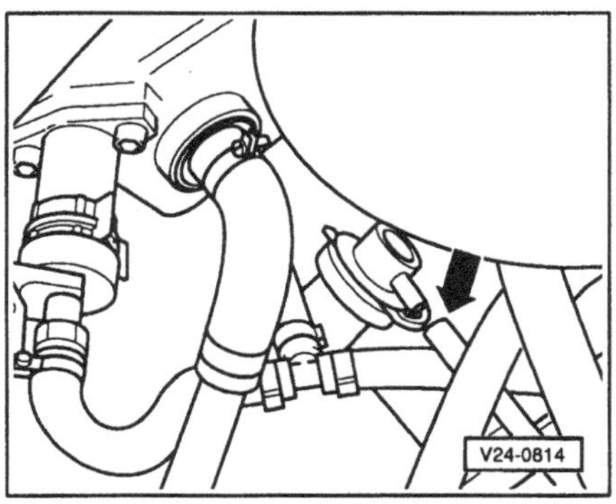

Vehicles with 6-pin fuel rail connector

– Pull vacuum hose off fuel pressure regulator and immediately plug off

♦ Displayed value must rise and then return to the original display value

All vehicles

– Press → button

– Press 0 and 6 buttons to select Function 06, "End data output"

– Press Q button to enter input

If specifications are not obtained:

– Check Heated Oxygen sensor heater Voltage supply and Heated Oxygen sensor heater for continuity
⇒ page F 24-92

– Perform electrical check test step 18
⇒ Repair Group 01, page F 01-87

– Replace Heated Oxygen sensor G39

– Check and erase DTC memory, if necessary, eliminate any malfunctions
⇒ Repair Group 01, page F 01-52

Engine operation, checking

– Check using Scan Tool VAG 1551 in Function 08, "Read measuring value block", with engine idling

Note:

This check establishes whether Digifant ECM J169 recognizes the engine operating conditions.

Special tools, testers and auxiliary items

♦ Scan Tool VAG 1551 using adaptor cable VAG 1551/1

Test conditions

♦ Scan Tool VAG 1551 connected and Function 08, "Read measuring value block" selected (Display group number 04)
⇒ Repair Group 01, page F 01-76

```
Read measuring value block 4        →
   1        2        3        4
```

◄ Display will appear as shown: (1 to 4 = Display channels)

Note:

If something different is displayed:
⇒ Scan Tool operating instructions

Checking sequence

Wide Open throttle

```
Read measuring value block 4        →
   ...rpm   ...%   ...km/h  00010000
```

◄ – Open throttle to wide open position while observing the value in the 4th position from the left in display channel 4

♦ Specification: 1

Partially open throttle

```
Read measuring value block 4        →
   ...rpm   ...%   ...km/h  00100000
```

◄ – Smoothly open the throttle while observing the display value in the 3rd position from the left in display channel 4

♦ Specification: 1

Closed throttle

```
Read measuring value block 4        →
   ...rpm   ...%   ...km/h  01000000
```

◄ – Observe the display value in the 2nd position from the left in display channel 4

♦ Specification: 1

Overrun:

– Raise engine speed above 3000 rpm

– Observe 1st position from left in display channel 4

```
Read measuring value block 4        →
   ...rpm   ...%   ...km/h  10000000
```

◄ – Close throttle abruptly

♦ Specification: above 1200 rpm = 1

Note:

- *Idle speed will be recognized below 1200 rpm*
- *Acceleration enrichment is also checked during the overrun cut-off check*

– Press → button

– Press 0 and 6 buttons to select Function 06, "End output"

– Press Q button to enter input

If specifications not obtained:

– Check and erase DTC memory, eliminate malfunctions if necessary
⇒ Repair Group 01, page F 01-52

– Check accelerator mechanism for ease of operation

– Check Throttle Position sensor
⇒ page F 24-98

Throttle Position sensor, checking

Note:

If Throttle Position sensor G69 has been removed, re-installed or replaced, then the Transmission Control Module J217 and the Throttle Position sensor must be matched to one another.
⇒ page F 24-88

Special tools, testers and auxiliary items

- Scan Tool VAG 1551 using adaptor cable VAG 1551/1
- Fluke 83 multimeter
- VW 1594 adaptor kit

Test sequence

Voltage supply, checking

– Disconnect 3-pin Throttle Position sensor harness connector

– Connect multimeter between outer terminals of harness connector, using jumper wires from the VW 1594 adaptor kit

– Switch ON ignition

- Specification: Approximately 5 Volts

If specification not obtained:

- Switch OFF ignition

- Perform electrical check, test step 17
⇒ Repair Group 01, page F 01-87, or if necessary, Replace ECM J169

Functional check

Check using VAG 1551 Scan Tool in Function 08, "Read measuring value block", with ignition switched ON

Test conditions

- ♦ VAG 1551 Scan Tool connected and Function 08, "Read measuring value block" selected (Display group number 03)
⇒ Repair Group 01, page F 01-76

Read measuring value block 3			→
1	2	3	4

◄ Display will appear as shown (1 to 4 = Display channels)

Note:

If something different is displayed:
⇒ Scan Tool operating instructions

- Check throttle angle on idle speed stop, (display channel 3)

  - ♦ Specification: 0 to 5 ∠°

- Slowly open throttle to wide open position and observe the angle displayed in display channel 3

  - ♦ displayed value must increase uniformly over complete range

- Check throttle angle at the wide open position stop (Display channel 3)

  - ♦ Specification: 80 to 90 ∠°

- Press → button

- Press 0 and 6 buttons to select Function 06, "End data transfer"

- Press Q button to enter input

If specifications are not obtained or do not increase uniformly:

- Perform electrical check, test step 17
⇒ Repair Group 01, page F 01-87

- Replace Throttle Position sensor G69, if necessary
⇒ page F 24-74, item 11

Engine Coolant Temperature sensor, checking

Functional check

– Check using VAG 1551 Scan Tool in Function 08, "Read measuring value block", with engine at idle

Special tools, testers and auxiliary items

♦ Scan Tool VAG 1551 using adaptor cable VAG 1551/1

Test conditions

♦ Engine cold

♦ Scan Tool VAG 1551 connected and Function 08, "Read measuring value block" selected (Display group number 01)
⇒ Repair Group 01, page F 01-76

Read measuring value block 1			→
1	2	3	4

◄ Display will appear as shown (1 to 4 = Display channels)

Note:

If something different is displayed:
⇒ Scan Tool operating instructions

Test sequence

– Observe Engine Coolant Temperature value in display channel 2

♦ value must increase uniformly without interruption

Notes:

♦ *If engine runs irregularly in certain temperature ranges and the displayed temperature does not increase uniformly; temperature signal is intermittent requiring sensor replacement*

♦ *If the Scan Tool display jumps by 2 to 5 °C, this is caused by the ECM, not by a malfunctioning sensor*

♦ *Interruption will be displayed as – 40 °C*

– Press → button

– Press 0 and 6 buttons to select Function 06, "End data output"

– Press Q button to enter input

If ECT value does not change:

– Perform electrical check, test step 13
⇒ Repair Group 01, page F 01-86

– Replace ECT sensor G62, after first releasing cooling system pressure
⇒ page F 24-79, item 19

Intake Air Temperature sensor, checking

Note:

This procedure NOT applicable to US vehicles!

Functional check

– Check with Scan Tool VAG 1551 in Function 08, "Read measuring value block", check with ignition switched ON

Special tools, testers and auxiliary items

♦ VAG 1551 Scan Tool using adaptor cable VAG 1551/1

♦ Freeze spray (commercially available)

Test conditions

● VAG 1551 Scan Tool connected and Function 08, "Read measuring value block" selected (Display group number 02)
⇒ Repair Group 01, page F 01-76

Read measuring value block 2			→
1	2	3	4

◄ Display will appear as shown: (1 to 4 = Display channels)

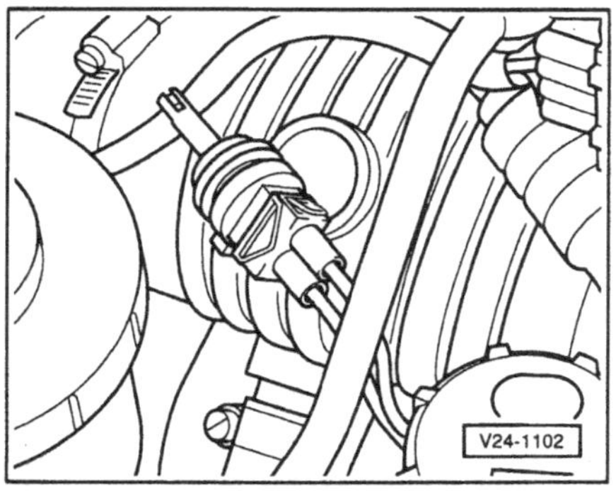

Test sequence

◄ – Remove Intake Air Temperature sensor (harness connector remains connected)

– Read Intake Air Temperature in display channel 4

♦ Specification: approximately ambient temperature

– Spray sensor with commercially available freeze spray

♦ Temperature value must decrease uniformly without interruption

Note:

Interruption will be shown as: – 40 °C.

– Press → button

– Press 0 and 6 buttons to select Function 06, "End data output"

– Press Q button to enter input

If temperature value does not change:

– Perform G42 electrical check, test step 14
⇒ Repair Group 01, page F 01-86

Manifold Absolute Pressure sensor, checking

Special tools, testers and auxiliary items

- ♦ VAG 1551 Scan Tool using adaptor cable VAG 1551/1

Functional check

– Check with engine idling, using Scan Tool in Function 08, "Read measuring value block", select Display Group 04

Test conditions

- ♦ VAG 1551 Scan Tool connected and Function 08, "Read measuring value block" selected (display group number 03)

⇒ Repair Group 01, page F 01-76

Read measuring value block 3			→
1	2	3	4

◄ Display will appear as shown, 1 to 4 = Display channels

Test sequence

– Do not continue with check until Engine Coolant Temp. is above 85 °C (185 °F), observe value in display channel 2

- ♦ Specification: 20 to 40% (fluctuating)

If specification not obtained:

– Check vacuum line to ECM J169, if necessary replace ECM

– Press → button

– Press 0 and 6 buttons to select Function 06, "End data output"

– Press Q button to enter input

Fuel pressure regulator and residual pressure, checking

Note:

The fuel pressure regulator controls fuel pressure relative to Manifold Absolute Pressure.

Special tools, testers and auxiliary items

- ♦ VAG 1318 Pressure tester
- ♦ 1318/10 adaptor
- ♦ 1318/11 adaptor
- ♦ 1318/16 adaptor

Test conditions

- ♦ Fuel pump delivery rate OK, checking

⇒ Repair Group 20

Note:

To prevent fuel spray when loosening connections, wrap a cloth around the connection.

Test sequence

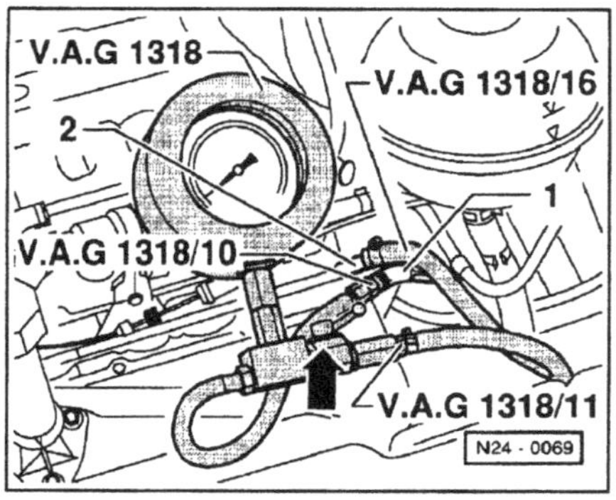

- Pull fuel line -1- off connection on fuel rail -2- and connect to VAG 1318 Pressure Tester, using adaptor 1318/10
- Connect pressure gauge VAG 1318, using adaptor 1318/11 and 1318/16 to fuel rail -2-
- Open pressure gauge shut-off
  - ♦ Handle in direction of flow -arrow-
- Start engine and let idle
  - ♦ Specification: Approximately 2.5 bar (36 psi) minimum

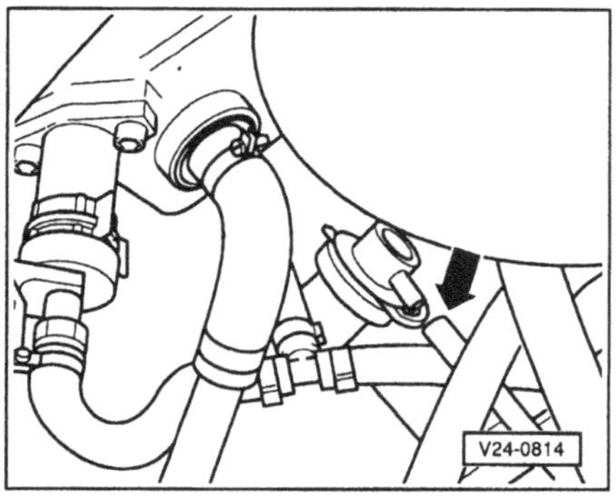

- Pull vacuum hose off fuel pressure regulator -arrow-
  - ♦ fuel pressure must rise to approximately 3.0 bar (44 psi) minimum
- Switch OFF ignition
- Check for leaks and evaluate residual pressure by watching pressure drop on gauge
  - ♦ After 10 minutes residual pressure must be 2 bar (29 psi) minimum

If residual pressure drops below 2 bar (29 psi):

- Start engine and let idle

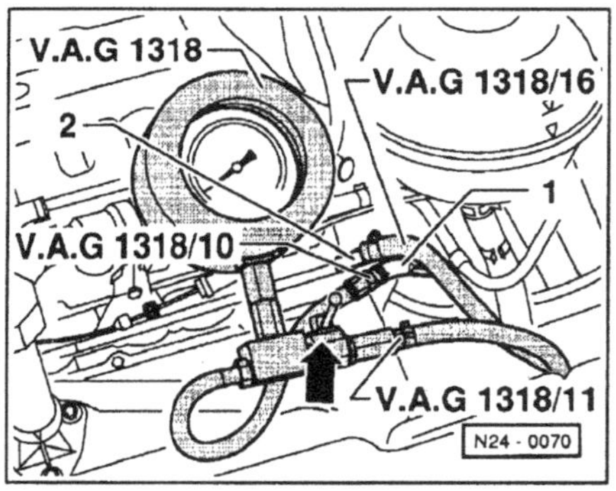

- After the pressure has built up, switch OFF ignition while simultaneously closing pressure gauge shut-off (handle perpendicular to direction of flow -arrow-)
- Observe pressure drop on gauge

If pressure drops again:

- Check fuel pump check valve
⇒ Repair Group 20

If pressure does not drop:

- Open pressure gauge shut-off (handle parallel to direction of flow -arrow-)
- Start engine and let idle

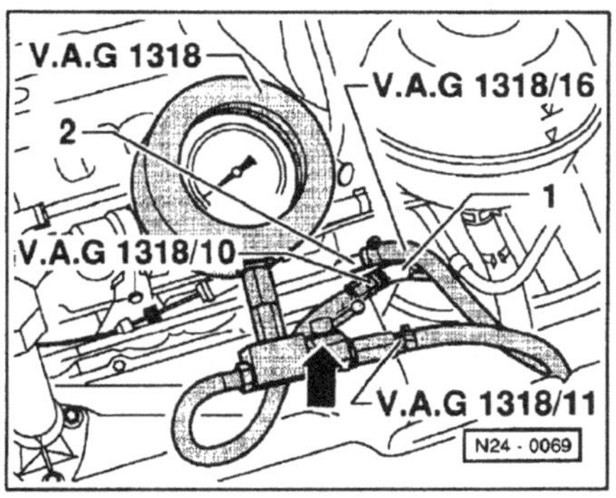

- After pressure has built up, switch OFF ignition while simultaneously clamping off blue fuel return line (-arrow-) on fuel rail

If pressure does not drop:

- Replace fuel pressure regulator

If pressure drops again:

- Check line connections, O-rings on fuel rail and fuel injectors for leaks
- Check VAG 1318 pressure tester for leaks

Fuel injectors, removing and installing

Special tools, testers and auxiliary items

- ♦ 3249 socket

Removing

- Remove Air Cleaner housing complete with filter element
- Remove intake air hose
- Disconnect main fuel injector harness connector from fuel rail
- Remove Positive Crankcase Ventilation breather hose
- Disconnect fuel supply and return lines from fuel distributor
- Disconnect vacuum hose from fuel pressure regulator
- Remove fuel rail attachment screws

Note:

The ratchet and key 3249 5 mm A/F ("1/8" drive) are particularly suitable for removing the socket head screws.

- Pull out fuel rail assembly (in direction of travel) complete with fuel injectors

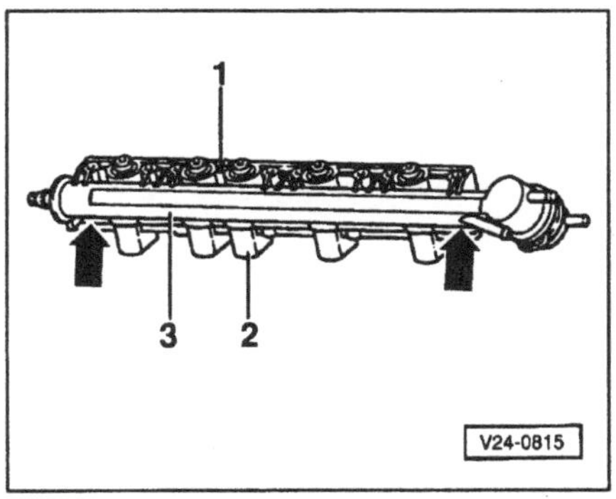

◄ – Remove screw -1- and pry upper section of fuel rail -2- fuel rail -3- at point indicated by -arrows-

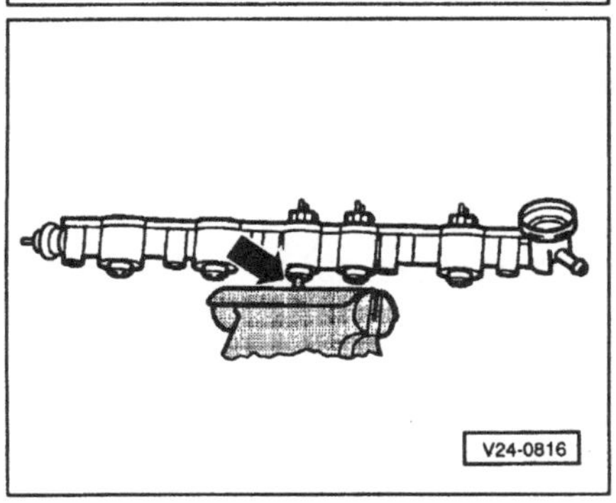

◄ – Clamp M6 socket head screw with threaded end in vise and force out fuel injector

Installing

Note:

Replace damaged fuel injector seals/gaskets and O-rings.

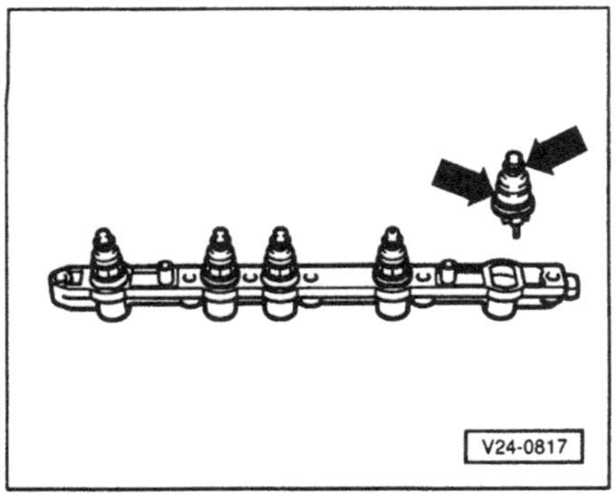

– Place gasket on fuel rail upper section

◄ – Insert fuel injectors into fuel rail upper section and moisten O-rings -arrows- with oil

– Press fuel rail upper section (complete with injectors) into the fuel rail

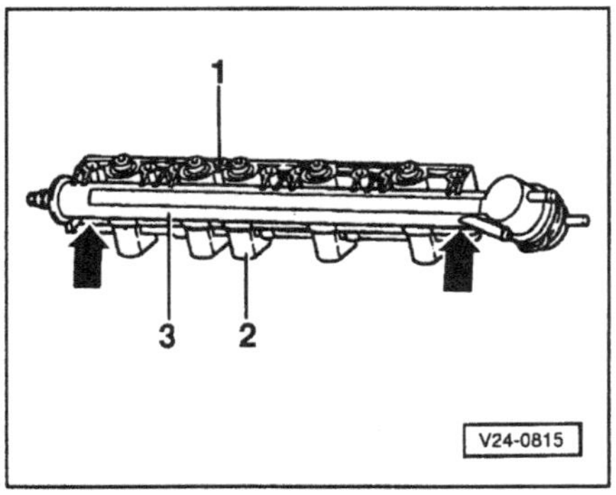

◄ – Tighten screw -1- to 10 Nm (7 ft lb)

– Place fuel rail on intake manifold and tighten attachment screws to 10 Nm (7 ft lb)

– Connect vacuum hose to fuel pressure regulator

– Connect fuel supply and return lines and fuel injector harness connector

– Install Positive Crankcase Ventilation breather hose and secure to oil filler pipe (ensure sufficient clearance to Throttle body)

– Install intake air hose (note position)

– Install Air Cleaner housing and filter element

Fuel injectors, checking

Special tools, testers and auxiliary items

♦ VW 1594 adaptor kit

♦ VAG 1527B LED tester

♦ VAG 1630 Digital potentiometer

♦ VAG 1602 Fuel Analyzer

Test conditions

♦ Camshaft Position sensor OK, checking ⇒ Repair Group 28, page F 28-35

Voltage supply and resistance, checking

– Check Voltage supply for all injectors

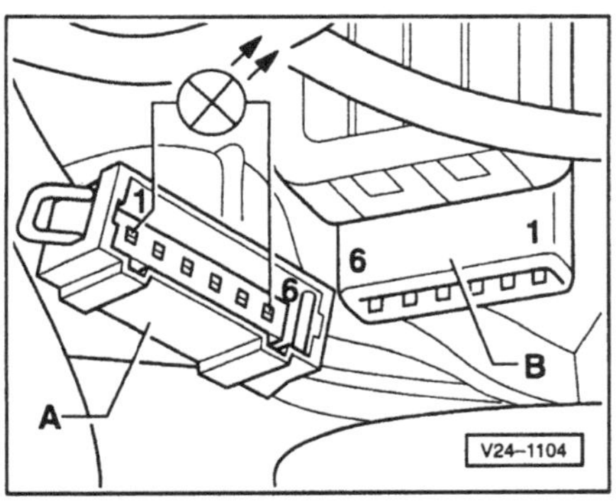

◄ – Disconnect harness connector -A- from main harness connector -B- and connect VAG 1527B LED tester between terminals 1 and 6 (vehicles with 2 pin connector between terminals 1 and 2) using jumper wires from VW 1594 adaptor kit

– Operate starter

♦ LED must flicker

– Repeat checks on terminals 2 and 6, 3 and 6, 4 and 6, and 5+6 (do not perform this check if it has the 2 pin connector)

If the LED is continuously lit:

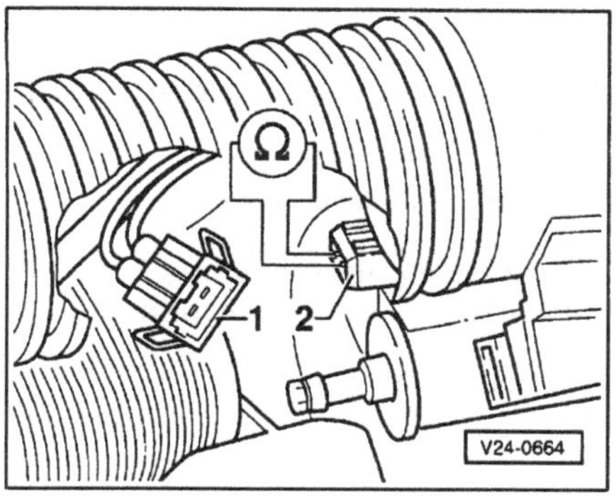

- Replace ground strap between battery and transmission
- Replace Engine Control Module J169

If LED does NOT light up or flicker:

- Perform electrical check, test steps 5 and 6 ⇒ Repair Group 01, page F 01-84, if necessary, replace ECM J169

Resistance checking

Vehicles with 2 pin fuel rail harness connector

◄ – Check resistance at connection -2- for all injectors, using multimeter and jumper wires from VW 1594 adaptor kit

- ♦ Specification: 3.0 to 4.0 Ω (= all 5 injectors OK)

Note:

Single injector OK = 15 to 20 Ω

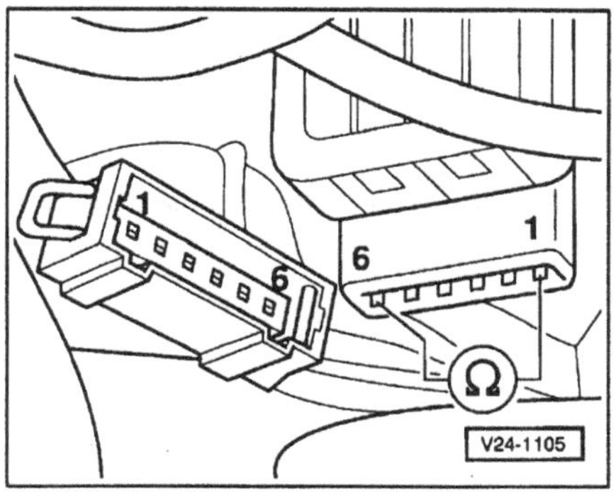

Vehicles with 6 pin fuel rail harness connector

◄ – Check fuel injector resistances individually, using multimeter on the main fuel rail harness connector

Fuel Injector Number:	1	2	3	4	5
Terminals:	1 + 6	2 + 6	3 + 6	4 + 6	5 + 6

Specification: 15 to 20 Ω

If the specification is not obtained:

- Remove fuel rail complete with injectors ⇒ page F 24-109

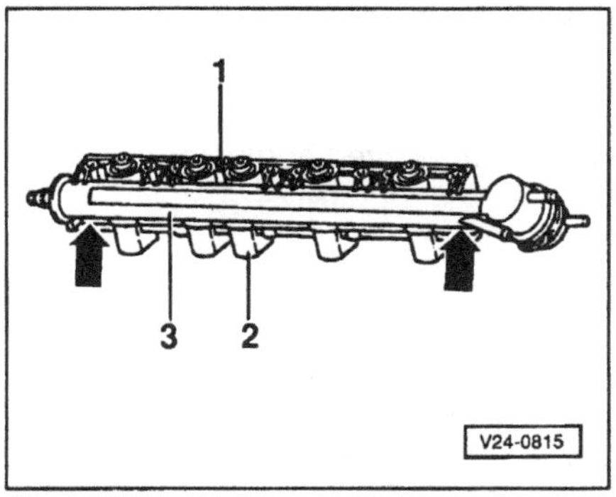

Vehicles with 2 pin fuel manifold connector

◄ – Remove bolt -1- and pry fuel rail upper section -2- from fuel rail section -3- as indicated by arrows

Vehicles with 6 pin fuel rail connector

- Unclip cover from fuel rail upper section
- Perform individual fuel injector checks, replace injector(s) as necessary

Spray pattern and leak–testing, checking

- Remove fuel rail complete with injectors ⇒ page F 24-109

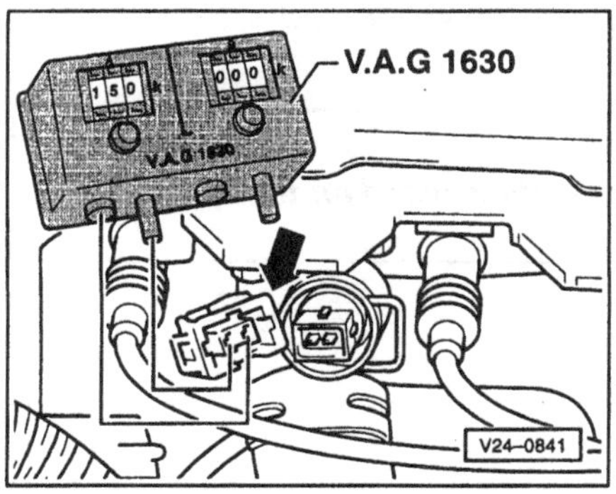

◄ – Disconnect Engine Coolant Temperature sensor -arrow-

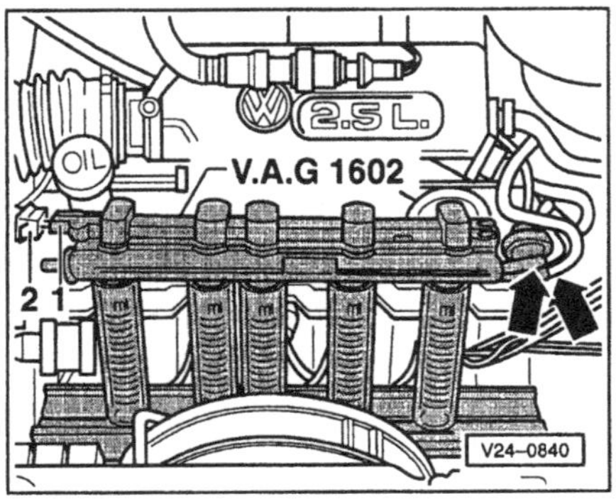

- Set VAG 1630 digital potentiometer (side A) to 15k and connect to disconnected harness connector using jumper wires from the VW 1594 adaptor kit
- Connect supply and return lines to fuel rail -arrows-, using extension hoses if necessary
- ◄ Place injectors in the VAG 1602 Fuel Analyzer
- Extend harness connector –2– using jumper wires from VW 1594 adaptor kit and connect to fuel rail connection -1-
- Disconnect ignition coil harness connector
- Operate starter
  - ♦ The fuel injectors must spray uniformly
- Switch OFF ignition and check injectors for leaks
  - ♦ No more than 2 drops per minute may leak from each injector

Note:

When installing the fuel injectors ensure that the O-rings are not damaged.

Intake air system, leak–testing (for outside air)

Special tools, testers and auxiliary items

- ♦ G 001 800 A1 Engine leak detector spray
- ♦ VAG 1363A CO tester (or EPA approved equivalent)
- ♦ VAG 1363/3 adaptor
- ♦ VAG 1367 Engine tester using VAG 1367/8 inductive pick-up

Notes:

- ♦ *If there is a leak, the vacuum in the intake system will cause the leak detector spray to be drawn in with the outside air. The leak detector spray reduces the fuel/air mixture ignitability, leading to reduced engine speed and a significant increase in CO content.*

CAUTION!

Always observe the precautions listed on the spray container.

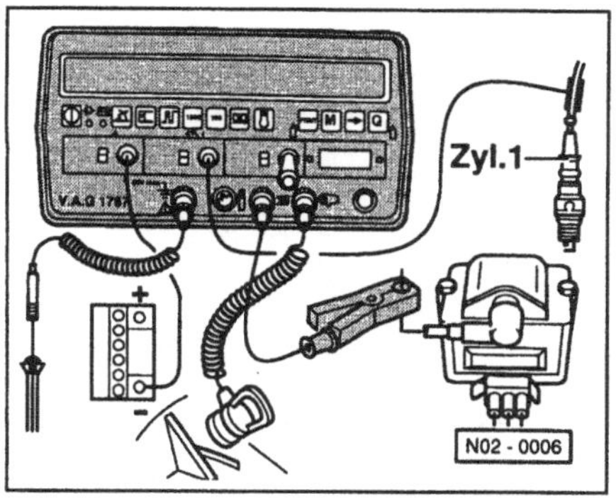

Test sequence

- Connect VAG 1367 Engine tester, using VAG 1367/8 inductive pick-up
- Connect CO tester to CO sampling tube, using VAG 1363/3 adaptor
- Start engine and let idle
- Systematically spray the intake system components, using engine leak detector spray

> ***CAUTION!***
> ***Always observe the precautions listed on the spray container.***

If engine rpm drops and the CO content changes:

- Check for leaks in those areas of the intake system that have been sprayed and eliminate any leak(s) as necessary

Intake air preheating, checking

Special tools, testers and auxiliary items

- ♦ US 8026 hand vacuum pump

Test conditions

- ♦ Regulating flap vacuum unit not leaking

Regulating flap, checking

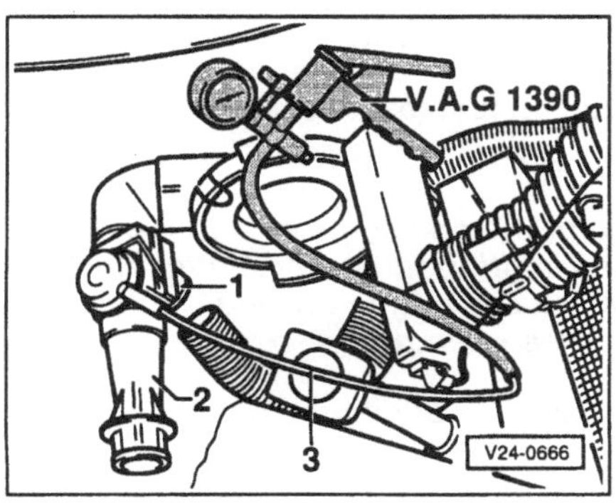

- Disconnect vacuum line from the temperature regulator flap vacuum unit
- Remove Air Cleaner with filter element
- Pull hose off warm air collector plate on warm air intake
- Check position of regulating flap in intake air housing, using a mirror or by feel
  - ♦ Regulating flap must close off warm air intake path -1-
- Connect vacuum line -3- to US 8026 vacuum pump
- Operate hand pump and check freedom of movement of regulating flap and function of vacuum unit
  - ♦ Regulating flap must close off cold air intake path -2-

Temperature regulator, checking

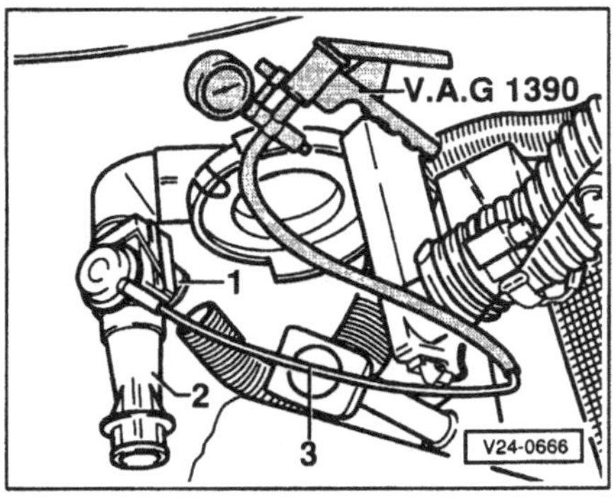

– Connect vacuum line -3- to Intake Air Temperature regulator (brass connecting port or with notch)

– Start engine and let idle

– Check position of regulating flap after 20 seconds max

Temperature of temperature regulator	Regulating flap position
below 20°C (68°F)	Cold air inlet path -2- closed
above 30°C (86°F)	Warm air inlet path -1- closed
Between 20 and 30°C (68 and 86°F)	Between cold and warm air inlet paths

Basic throttle adjustment

Note:

The limiting screw is set at the factory and must not be adjusted. However; if the screw is turned inadvertently, set it again as follows.

Test sequence

– Turn limiting screw -arrow- out until a gap exists between stop lever -1- and limiting screw -arrow-

– Turn limiting screw in, until it just touches lever -1-

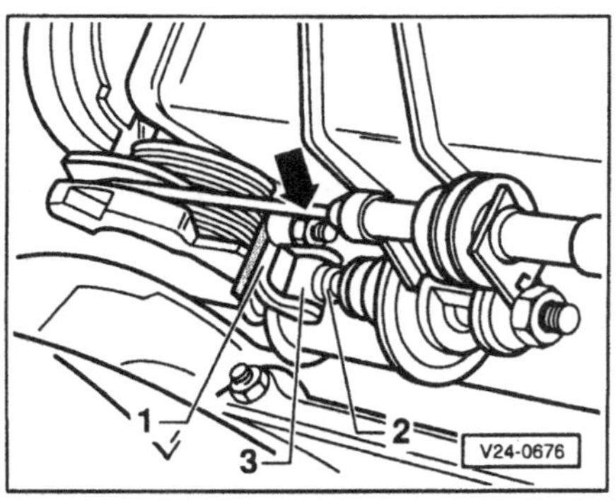

Note:

To determine the exact point of contact, place a thin piece of paper between lever -1- and limiting screw. By continually tugging on the paper, and at the same time turning the limiting screw, the exact point of contact can be determined.

– From this point, turn screw in an additional half turn

– Check Throttle Position sensor
⇒ page F 24-98

– Perform basic settings
⇒ page F 24-85

Closed Throttle Position switch, checking and adjusting

Test conditions

- ♦ Throttle basic setting OK
⇒ page F 24-120
- ♦ Closed Throttle Position switch mounting screws loosened
- ♦ Throttle body stop lever in contact with limiting screw

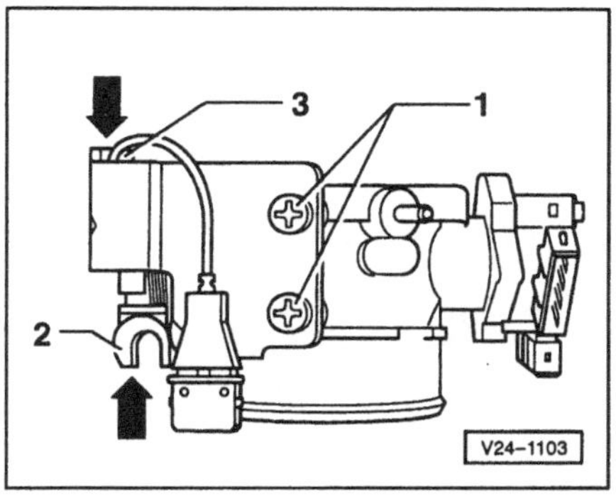

Function, checking

- Perform electrical check, test step 16
⇒ Repair Group 01, page F 01-87

Closed Throttle Position switch, adjusting

◄

- Lightly tighten mounting screws -1-
- Press throttle lever -2- and switch -3- tightly together -arrows-
- Tighten mounting screws -1-
- Open throttle
  - ♦ Closed Throttle Position switch must be heard to click

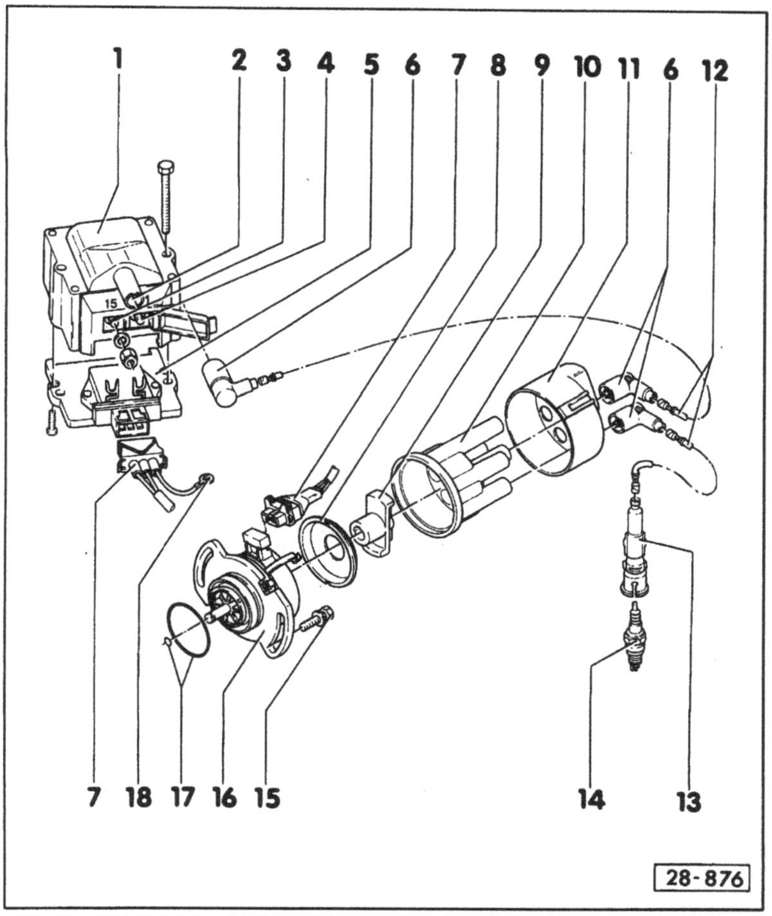

Digifant Ignition system, component layout

Vehicles built up to m.y. 1995

- Only Ignition system information covered in this Repair Group. For Fuel injection system information:

⇒ Repair Group 24

- The Fuel injection/Ignition Engine Control Module is equipped with On Board Diagnostic Functions
- Components identified with an asterisk * are checked via On Board Diagnostic
- Before repairs and troubleshooting, check DTC Memory, repair as needed and then erase DTC Memory

⇒ Repair Group 01

- Always observe Safety Precautions

⇒ page F 28-8

- Checking, adjusting, tune-up and spark plug data

⇒ page F 28-7

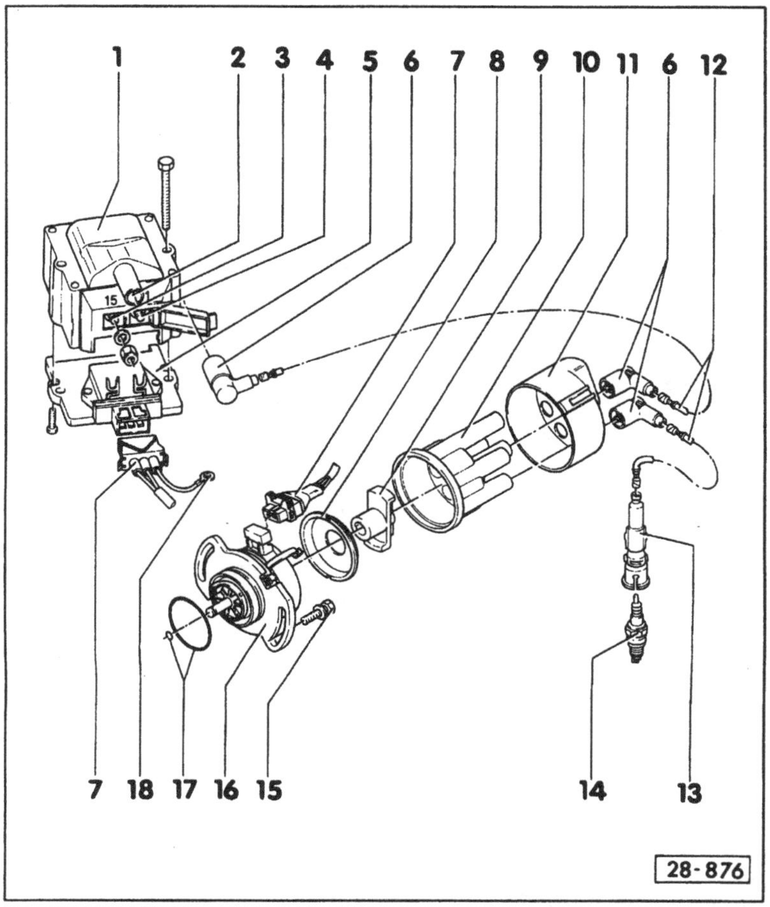

1 - Ignition coil
- checking

⇒ page F 28-19

- location: in driving direction left, under battery cover

2 - Terminal 4

3 - Terminal 15

4 - Terminal 1

5 - Ignition coil power output stage N157
- checking

⇒ page F 28-20

6 - Distributor cap connector for spark plug wire(s)
- RF suppression
- resistance check: 600 to 1400 Ohms

7 - Camshaft Position sensor harness connector

8 - Dust cap

9 - Ignition rotor
- identification "R1"
- resistance check: 600 to 1400 Ohms

10 - Distributor cap
- Check for cracks and leaks
- Check for contact wear
- Clean before installing
- Check carbon brush for wear and clearance

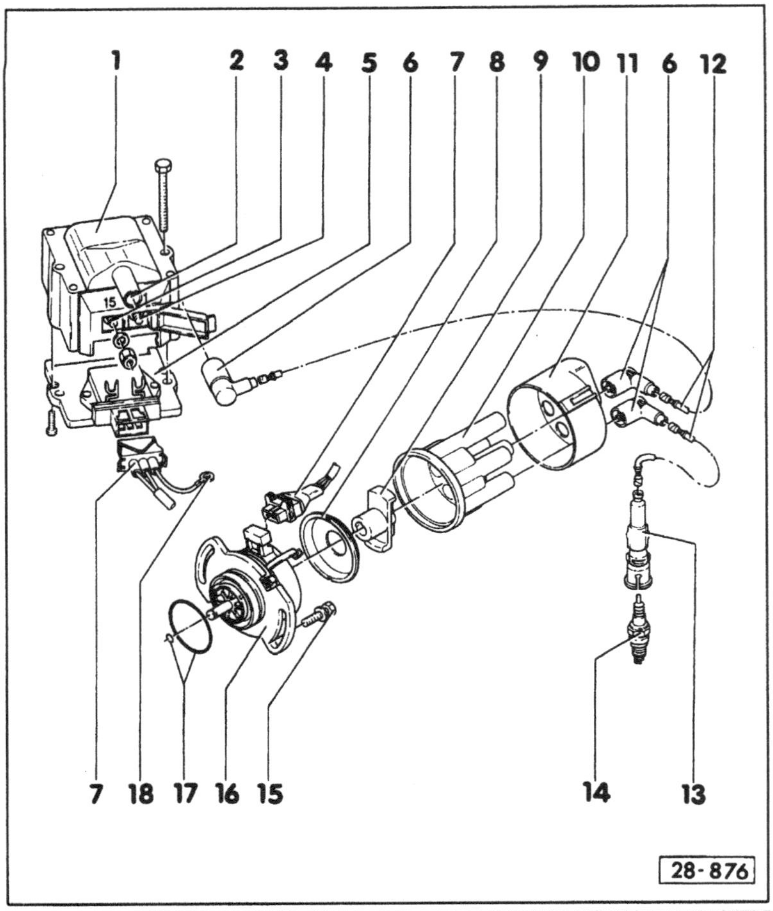

11 - RF shield for distributor cap

12 - Ignition wire
- Check for continuity

13 - Spark plug connector
- ♦ shielded
- ♦ resistance check: 4000 to 6000 Ohms

14 - Spark plug
- ♦ specifications and data

⇒ page F 28-7

15 - 10 Nm (7 ft lb)

16 - Ignition distributor housing
- ♦ w/Camshaft Position sensor G40*
- ♦ disassembling and assembling

⇒ page F 28-6
- ♦ installing:

⇒ page F 28-9
- ♦ checking ignition timing point and adjusting:

⇒ page F 28-11
- ♦ Cam Position sensor, checking:

⇒ page F 28-17

17 - O-ring
- Replace if damaged

18 - Ground strap
- ♦ fastened to housing

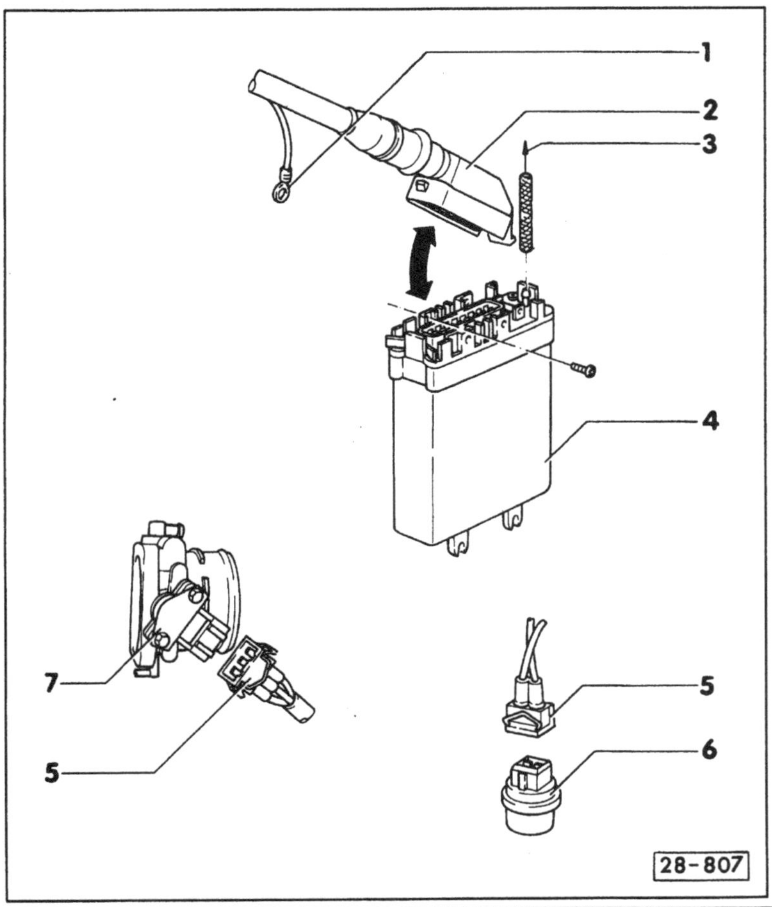

Engine Control Module (ECM), component layout

1 - Ground connection
- ♦ fastened to body

2 - 38-pin ECM harness connector
- Switch OFF ignition before disconnecting or connecting

3 - Vacuum line
- ♦ to intake hose of return valve between intake hose and brake booster

⇒ Repair Group 24
- ♦ for Manifold Absolute Pressure sensor G71* inside of ECM J169*

4 - Digifant Engine Control Module J169*
- ♦ for Fuel injection system, Oxygen sensor control, rpm limit, ignition and On Board Diagnostic
- ♦ location: left engine compartment
- ♦ with MAP sensor G71*, checking

⇒ Repair Group 24, page F 24-45
- If replaced, check idle speed

⇒ Repair Group 24, page F 24-23

5 - Engine Coolant Temperature sensor harness connector

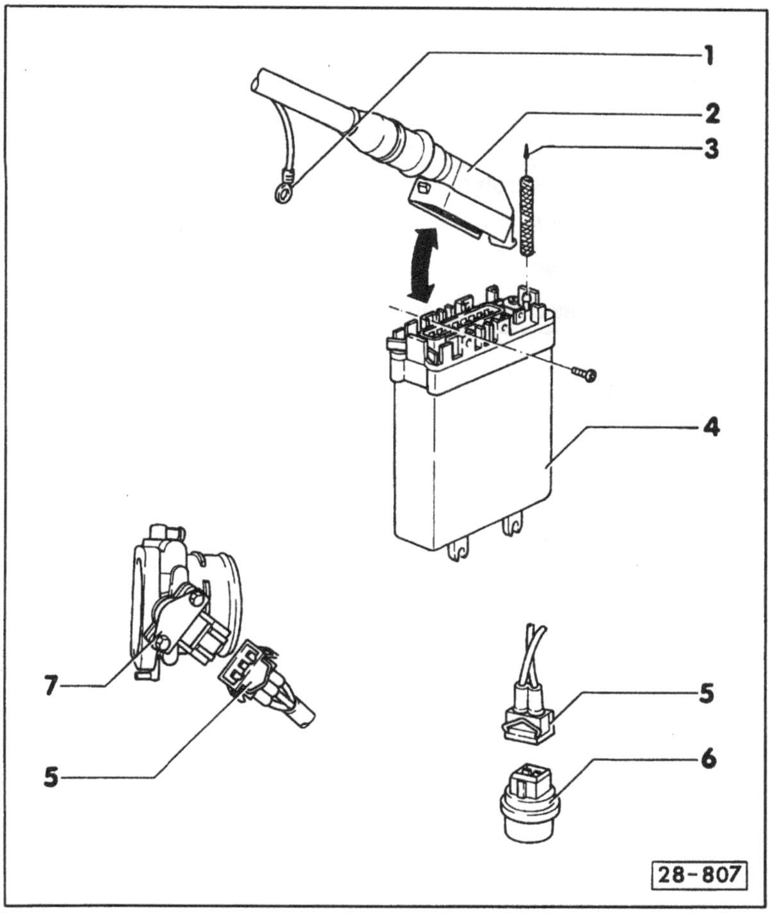

6 - Engine Coolant Temperature sensor G62*
- ♦ blue
- ♦ 2-pin
- – Reduce cooling system pressure before removing
- ♦ checking

⇒ Repair Group 24, page F 24-40
- ♦ resistance values

⇒ Repair Group 01, page F 01-91

7 - Throttle Position sensor G69*
- ♦ 3-point connection for manual transmission vehicles
- ♦ 4-point connector for automatic transmission vehicles (signal goes to Transmission Control Module J217)
- ♦ checking:

⇒ Repair Group 24, page F 24-37
- – Before replacing, perform idle check

⇒ Repair Group 24, page F 24-22

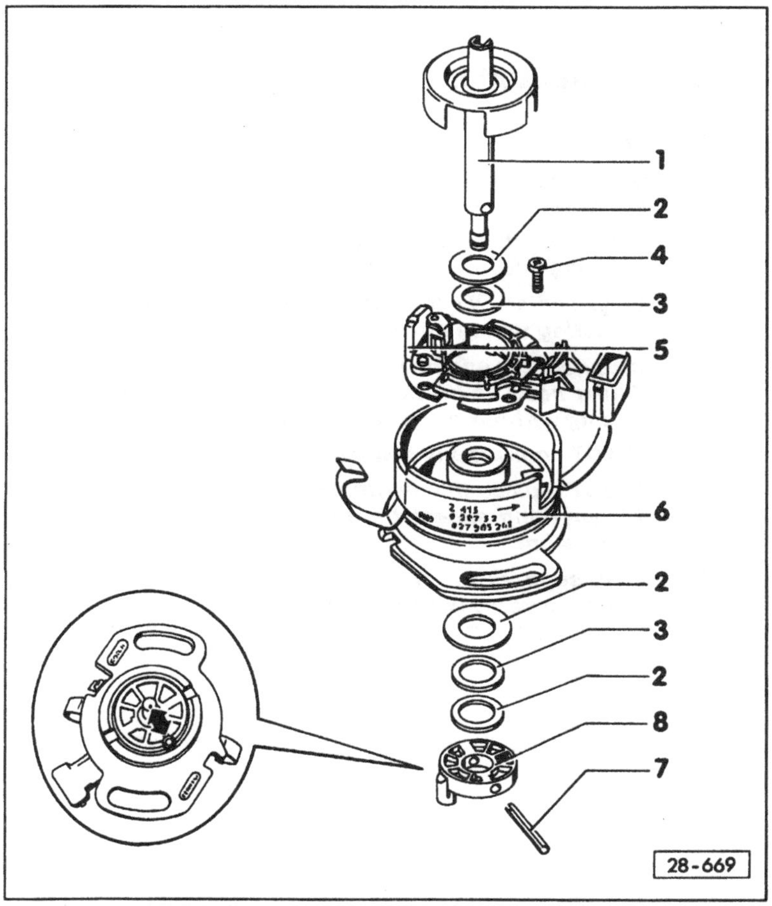

Ignition distributor, disassembly and assembly

Note:

During assembly, be sure that the clutch (item 8) on pin (item 7) moves easily, and distributor shaft play for item 1 is not reduced.

1 - Ignition distributor shaft
- ♦ with trigger wheel
- – Pull out of housing after removing pin (item 7)

2 - Washers

3 - Plastic spacer

4 - 3 Nm (27 inch lb)

5 - Camshaft Position sensor G40
- ♦ checking:

⇒ page F 28-17
- – Ensure that it is securely installed in distributor housing (item 6)

6 - Ignition distributor housing

7 - Pin

8 - Coupling
- – Before removing; position drive pin toward distributor shaft (item 1)

Tune-up, spark plugs and adjusting data

Engine Code	AAF
Ignition timing point:	
Checking value	4 to 8° BTDC
Adjusting value	6 ± 1° BTDC
These values checked / adjusted at	2000 to 2500/RPM
Firing order	1-2-4-5-3
Spark plugs	
Champion 101 000 026 AA	N9 BMC
Electrode gap	0.7 to 0.9 mm
Tightening torque	25 Nm (18 ft lb)

Safety precautions

CAUTION!

Observe the following precautions to avoid personal injury as well as possible damage to the ignition system.

- ***DO NOT touch or remove ignition wires while the engine is running and/or while cranking.***
- ***always switch OFF the ignition BEFORE disconnecting or connecting wiring or test measurements.***
- ***disconnect the engine speed sender (on lower left side of cylinder head on bracket) whenever the engine requires cranking without starting, such as checking compression.***
- ***DO NOT connect any condensers to terminal 1 (–).***
- ***DO NOT replace the distributor rotor (identification: R1) with anything except the production part, even for RF suppression.***
- ***for RF suppression only use 1000 Ohm resistance and spark plug wires with 5000 Ohms.***

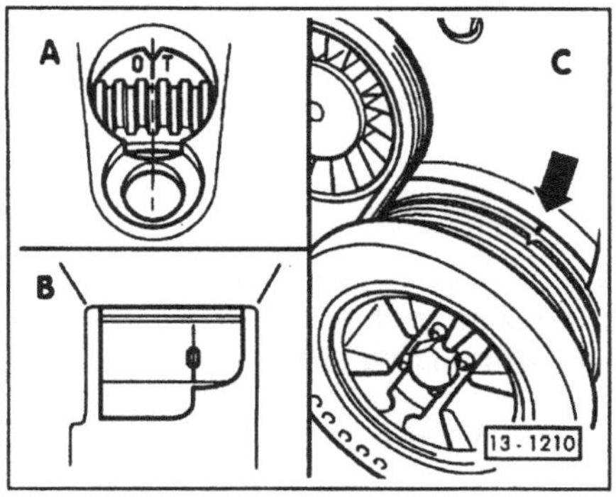

Ignition distributor, installing

Engine installed

- Position flywheel at TDC as shown in views -A- and -B-

Engine removed

- Align marking on vibration damper -C- with marking on lower toothed belt guard (arrow)

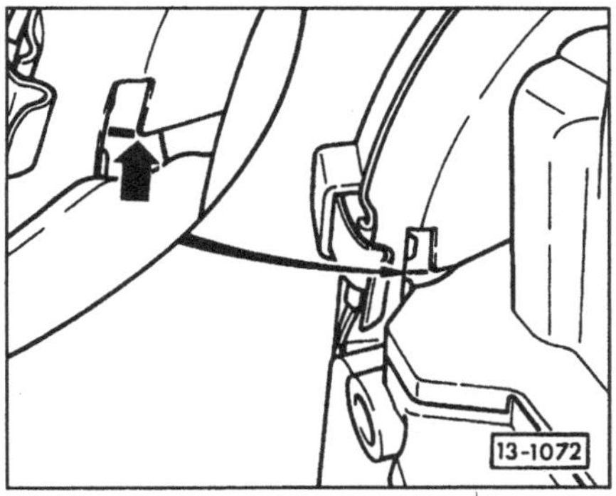

- Align mark on camshaft sprocket with marking on rear toothed belt guard (arrow)

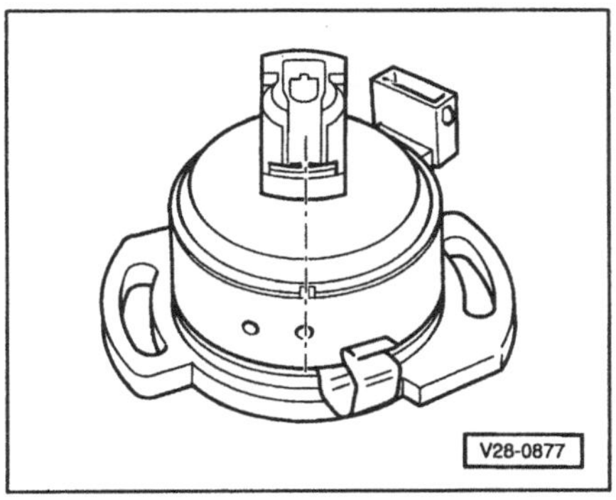

- Turn rotor until it points to cylinder #1 mark on distributor housing
- Insert distributor into engine (watch out for nearby components and obstructions)
- Clean distributor cap and inspect for cracks, tracking, etc., before installing; replace if necessary
- Start engine and let idle
- Check ignition timing, adjust if necessary

Ignition timing point, checking and adjusting

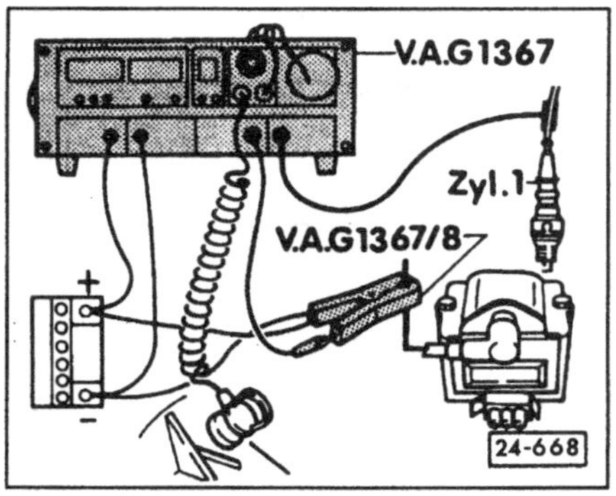

Requirement

♦ Engine cold

Note

Some vehicles require a TDC sensor along with adaptor VAG 1367/9. Connect the ignition tester to these vehicles with engine warm and without removing the distributor cap.

– Remove splash shield from distributor

◄ – Connect VAG 1367 engine tester, using VAG 1367/8 inductive pickup

– Connect VAG 1551 Scan Tool
⇒ Repair Group 01, page F 01-4

– Start engine and let idle until warm

♦ engine oil 80°C (176°F) minimum

♦ below 1500 rpm

Note

If the engine stalls or shuts off, it can run at increased idle speed for up to 4 minutes after re-starting. In this case, wait until engine speed drops before measuring the timing.

– Operate VAG 1551 with respect to the displays shown

– Press 1 to obtain Rapid data transfer

– Press 0 and 1 buttons to select address word 01, "Engine electronics"

– Press Q button to enter input

– Press → button

– Press 0 and 4 buttons to select Function 04, "Engine basic setting"

– Press Q button to enter input

Note

When Function 04 is selected, the idle speed is coordinated with the engine via the ECM.

Introduction of basic setting	HELP
Indicator group number input	

◄ Display will appear as shown

– Press the 0 button twice to select the indicator group number

– Press Q button to enter input

System in basic adjustment
1 2 3 4 5 6 7 8 9 10

Display will appear as shown

or

Function unknown/or can not be conducted at this time

If the display appears as shown:

- Check the following possibilities:

  ♦ Coolant temperature of 85°C (185°F) minimum not yet obtained

  ♦ Idle speed exceeds 1500 rpm

  ♦ Function 04,"Basic setting" using VAG 1551 Scan Tool is not possible

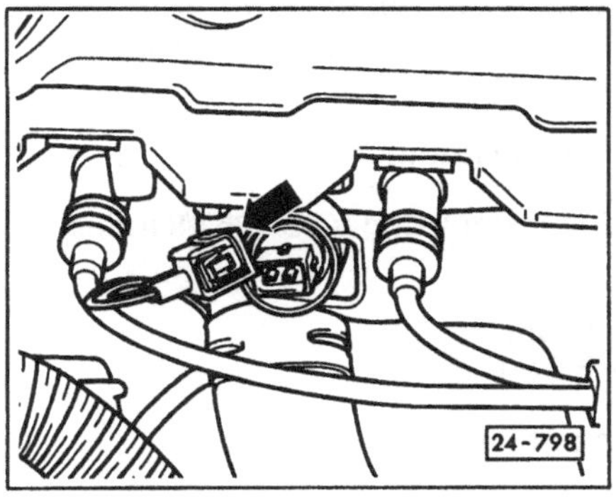

If YES:

- Disconnect blue Engine Coolant Temperature sensor harness connector (with throttle removed) -arrow-

Note:

If the engine shuts off; before restarting, re-connect the ECT harness connector; otherwise, the Digifant Engine Control Module will default to an emergency program making a test/adjustment impossible.

- Check ignition timing point

  ♦ Between 2000 and 2500 RPM

  ♦ Ignition timing must be between 4 and 8° BTDC and fluctuating

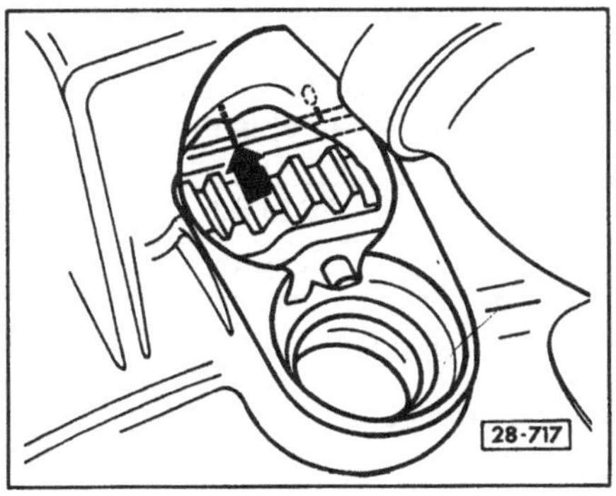

Ignition timing, checking with strobe light

Ignition timing mark flashes

- Adjust ignition timing point by turning the distributor

- Press → button to end Function 04, "Basic setting"

  ♦ Radiator cooling fan must not be running during measurement

- Check and erase Diagnostic Trouble Code memory
⇒ Repair Group 01

  ♦ this will erase the stored DTC caused by disconnecting ECT sensor G62

- Correct idle adjustment, if necessary, via Function 04, "Engine basic setting"
⇒ Repair Group 24, page F 24-23

- Press 0 and 6 buttons to select Function 06, "End data transfer"

- Press Q button to enter input

- Allow engine to cool

- Remove splash shield from distributor cap

- Remove VAG 1367 TDC sender from bell housing

Ignition timing advance (map), checking/adjusting

Requirements

- ♦ Ignition timing point adjustment OK
- ♦ DTC memory clear
- ♦ Engine cold

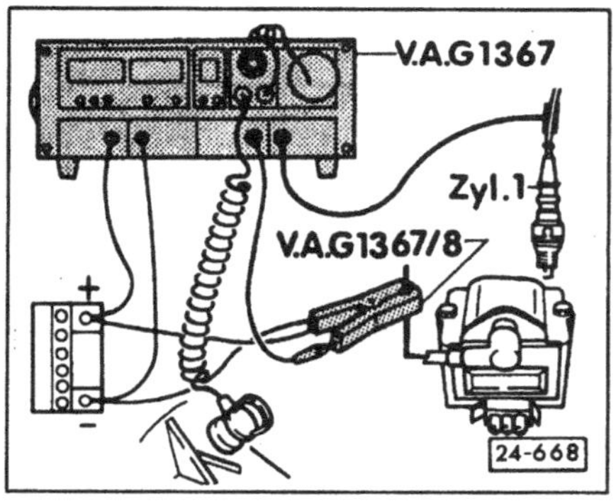

Note

Some vehicles require TDC sensor and adaptor VAG 1367/9. The ignition tester can be connected to these vehicles with the engine warm and without removing the distributor cap.

– Remove splash shield from distributor cap

◄ – Connect VAG 1367 engine tester using VAG 1367/8 inductive pickup

– Connect VAG 1551 Scan Tool
⇒ Repair Group 01, page F 01-4

– Start engine and let run until warm

  ♦ Engine oil 80°C (176°F) minimum

– Raise engine speed from idle to 2200 rpm

49 States: 26 to 36° BTDC
California 15 to 38° BTDC

◄ – Slowly raise engine speed to slightly exceed 2200 RPM until the ignition timing point (adjustment value) is displayed

49 States	26 to 36° BTDC
California	15 to 38° BTDC

If ignition timing point does not change

– Perform electrical check, Test step 10 or 27
⇒ Repair Group 01, page F 01-31

Note:

Use the VAG 1598 Test Box to perform these checks. If Test Box is not available, check Camshaft Position sensor.
⇒ page F 28-17

Camshaft Position sensor, checking

Voltage supply, checking

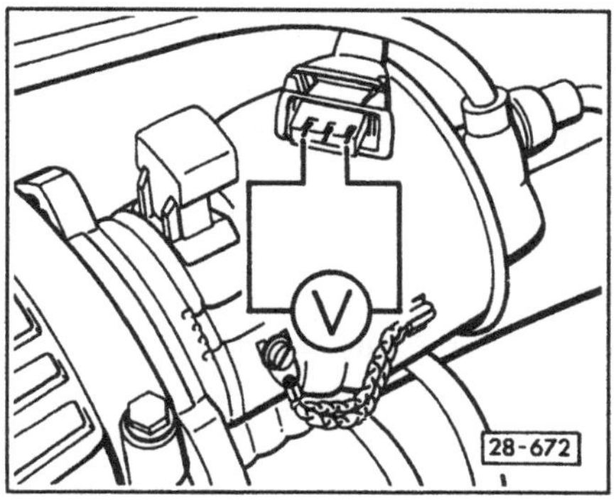

- Disconnect Camshaft Position sensor harness connector at ignition distributor
- ◄ Switch Fluke 83 multimeter to 20 Volt range
- Connect multimeter to outer terminals of connector, using jumper wires from VW 1594 adaptor kit
- Switch ON ignition
  - ♦ must be 10 Volts minimum

If NO:

- Replace Engine Control Module J169
- Switch OFF ignition

Function, checking

- Disconnect cold start valve harness connector
- Disconnect fuel injector harness connector at fuel rail
- Slide up the rubber boot on the Camshaft Position sensor harness connector (at ignition distributor)
- Re-connect Camshaft Position sensor connector

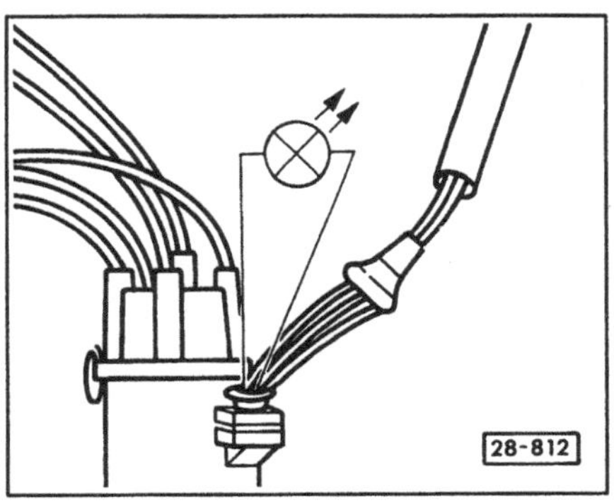

- ◄ Connect VAG 1527B LED tester to center terminal and brown / white outer wire of Camshaft Position sensor connector (while connected), using jumper wires from the VW 1594 adaptor kit
- Operate starter
  - ♦ LED tester must flicker

If NO:

- Replace Camshaft Position sensor

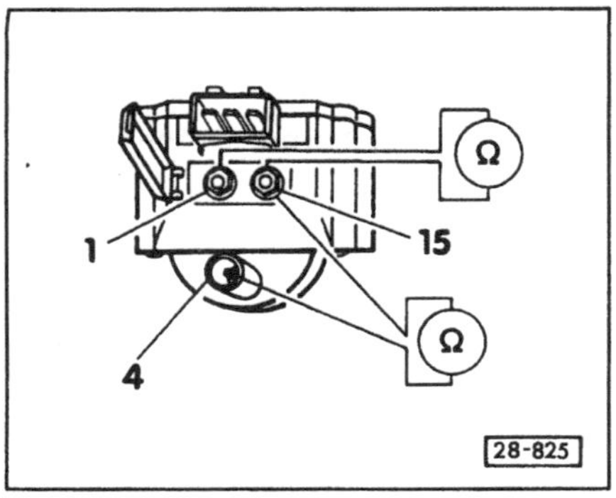

Ignition coil, checking

– Disconnect ignition wire and harness connector from ignition coil

– Switch Fluke 83 multimeter to resistance range

◄ – Connect multimeter between ignition coil terminals -1- and -15-, using jumper wires from VW 1594 adaptor kit

– Measure primary resistance

♦ must be 0.5 to 0.7 Ohms

– Connect multimeter between terminals -4- and -15-

– Measure secondary resistance

♦ must be 3000 to 4000 Ohms

If NO:

– Replace ignition coil N152 and power output stage N157

– Repeat test

Power output stage, checking

Requirements

♦ Electrical check, Test steps 6 or 23 OK
⇒ Repair Group 01, page F 01-31

♦ Ignition coil OK

Voltage supply, checking

– Remove 3-pin connector from ignition coil

– Switch Fluke 83 multimeter to 20 Volt range

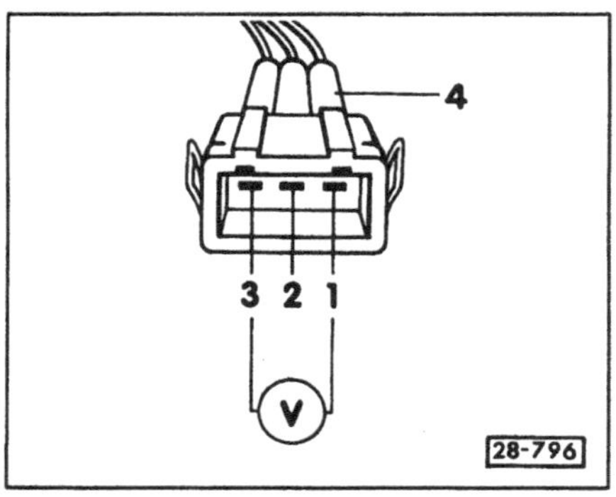

◄ – Connect multimeter between terminals -1- and -3- of connector, using jumper wires from VW 1594 adaptor kit

– Switch ON ignition

♦ must be approximately battery voltage

– Switch OFF ignition

Triggering, checking

– Disconnect cold start valve harness connector

– Disconnect fuel injector harness connector at fuel rail

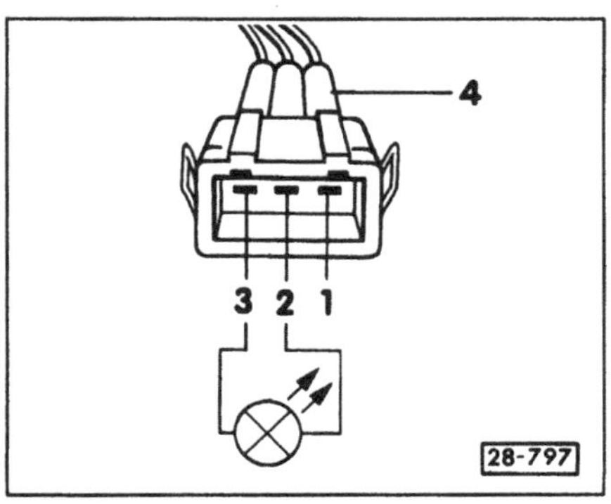

◄ – Connect VAG 1527B LED tester between terminals -2- and -3- of connector -4-, using adaptor VW 1594/15 from adaptor kit VW 1594

- Operate starter and check ignition signal from ECM
  - ♦ LED tester must flicker

If NO:

- Check Camshaft Position sensor
⇒ page F 28-17

If Camshaft Position sensor OK:

- Replace ECM J169
- Connect 3-pin harness connector and ignition wire to ignition coil

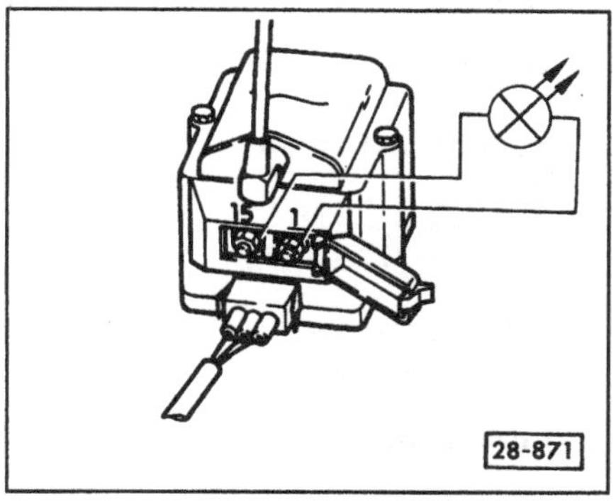

◄ - Connect VAG 1527B LED tester between terminals -1- and -15- of ignition coil, using jumper wires from VW 1594

> ***WARNING!***
>
> ***Electrical shock hazard. DO NOT touch the ignition coil terminals or test connections during following check.***

- Switch ON ignition
  - ♦ LED tester must light up for 1 to 2 seconds
- Operate starter
  - ♦ LED tester must flicker

If NO:

- Replace ignition coil power output stage

Digifant Ignition system, component overview

Vehicles starting m.y. 1995

Notes:

- ♦ *Only information specific to the ignition system is covered in this Repair Group. For Fuel injection system information,*
⇒ Repair Group 24
- ♦ *The Fuel Injection and Ignition system Engine Control Module is equipped with On Board Diagnostic capability.*
- ♦ *Components marked with an asterisk * are checked via the On Board Diagnostic system.*
- ♦ *Before performing repairs and/or troubleshooting, check the Diagnostic Trouble Code *(DTC) memory.*
⇒ Repair Group 01, page F 01-52

Safety precautions
⇒ page F 28-27

Checking and adjustment data, spark plugs
⇒ page F 28-28

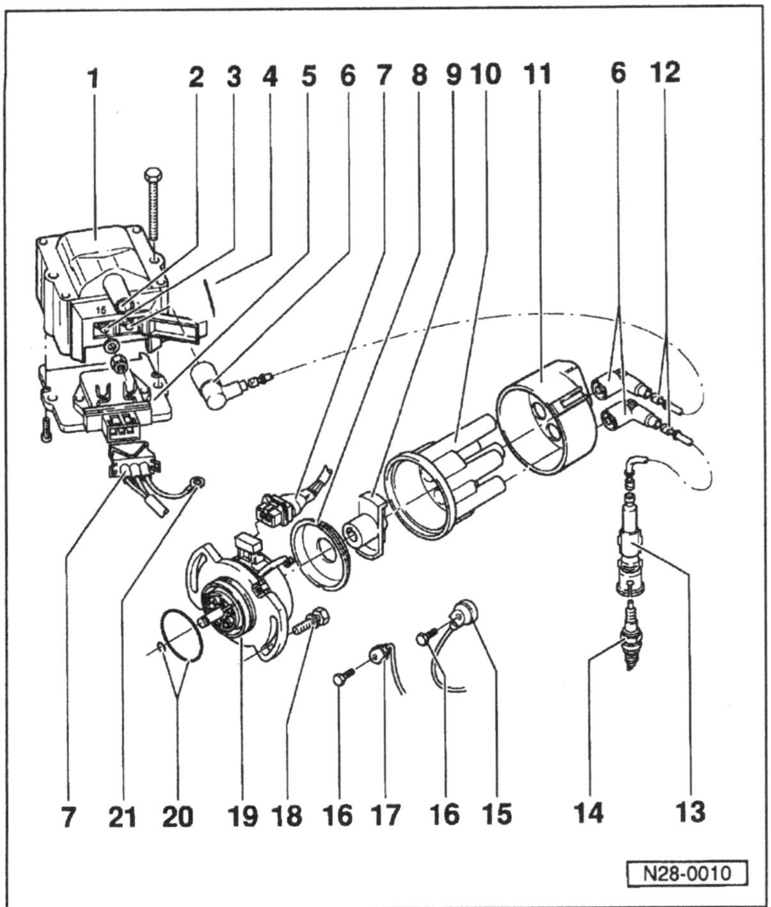

1 - Ignition coil N152
- checking:

⇒ page F 28-36

2 - Terminal 4

3 - Terminal 15

4 - Terminal 1

5 - Ignition coil power output stage N157
- checking:

⇒ page F 28-37

6 - RFI Suppressor
- 0.6 to 1.4 kΩ

7 - Connector

8 - Dust cap

9 - Rotor
- marking: R1
- 0.6 to 1.4 kΩ

10 - Distributor cap
- check for cracks and signs of arcing (carbon tracks)
- check electrode wear
- clean before fitting
- check carbon brush for wear and freedom of movement

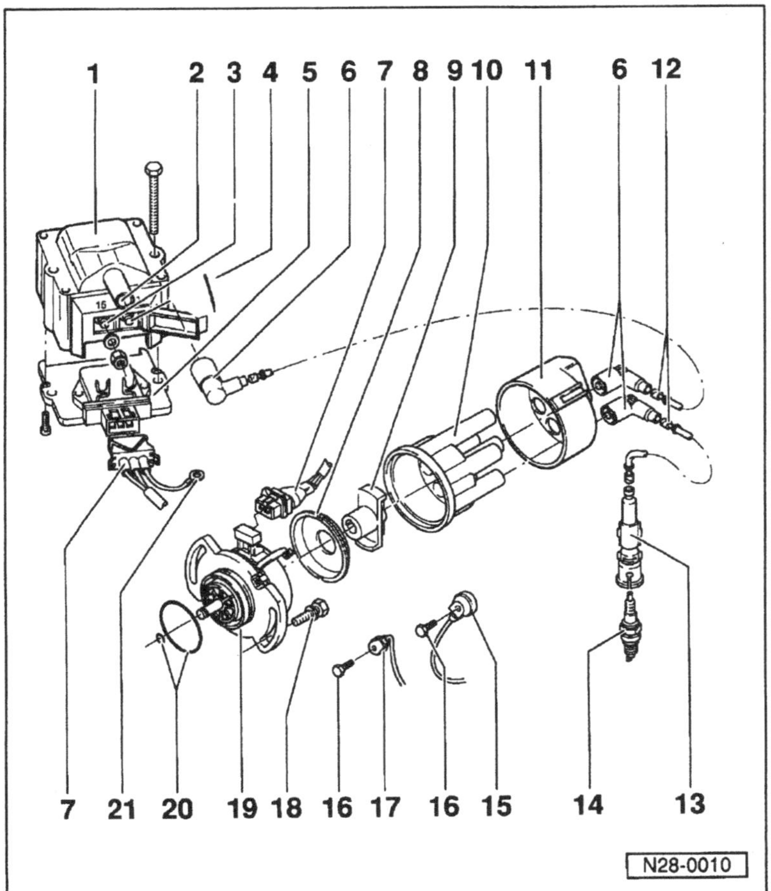

11 - RFI shield

12 - High tension cable
- check for continuity

13 - Spark plug connector
- 4000 to 6000 Ω

14 - Spark plug
- 30 Nm (22 ft lb)
- type and electrode gap

⇒ page F 28-28

15 - Knock sensor 2 G66**
- on left in direction of travel
- on engine block

16 - 20 Nm (15 ft lb)
- tightening torque influences the function of the knock sensor

17 - Knock sensor 1 G61*
- on right in direction of travel
- on engine block

18 - 10 Nm (7 ft lb)

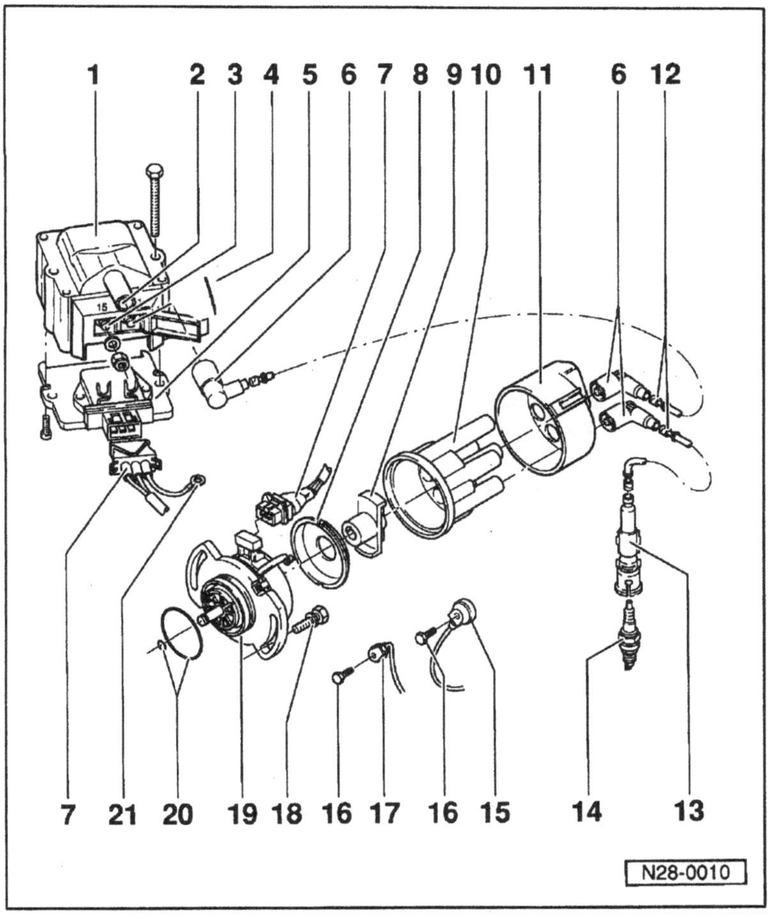

19 - Ignition Distributor with Camshaft Position sensor G40
- installing:

⇒ page F 28-29
- ignition timing, checking and adjusting:

⇒ page F 28-31
- Camshaft Position sensor. checking:

⇒ page F 28-35

20 - O-ring
- replace if damaged

21 - Ground strap

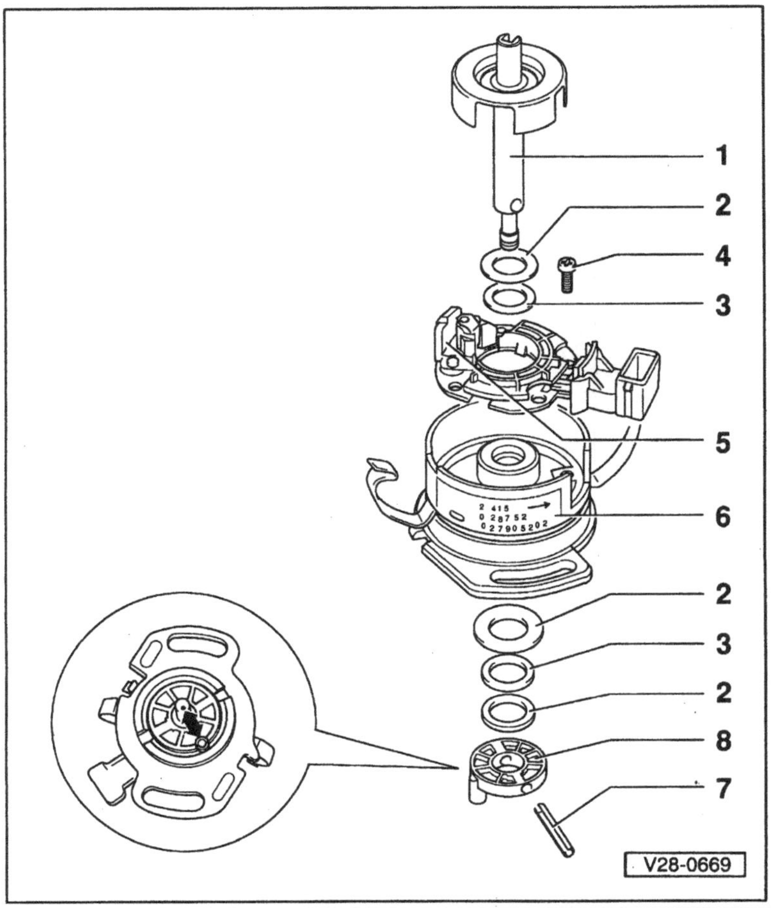

Ignition distributor, disassembling and assembling

Note:

When assembling, ensure that coupling (item 8) can be moved slightly on the pin (item 7) and distributor shaft (item 1) play is not restricted.

1 - Distributor shaft
- with Camshaft Position sensor trigger wheel
- pull out after removing spring pin (item 7)

2 - Shim(s)

3 - Plastic washer

4 - 3 Nm (127 in. lb)

5 - Camshaft Position sensor G40
- checking:

⇒ page F 28-35

6 - Distributor housing

7 - Spring pin

8 - Coupling
- before removing, mark position of drive dog to shaft (item 1)

Safety precautions

To prevent injuries to persons and/or damage to the fuel injection and ignition system components, observe the following points:

- Do not touch or disconnect ignition wires when the engine is running or cranking at starter speed.
- The ignition must be switched off when disconnecting or connecting injection and ignition system component wiring as well as test instrument cables.
- If the engine requires cranking at starter speeds but without starting, e.g. when checking compression: Disconnect the harness connector from the Engine Speed sensor (below bracket on left side of cylinder head).
- Do not connect a capacitor (of any description) to the ignition coil terminal 1 (–).
- Do not replace the 1000Ω (identification: R1) distributor rotor with a different type even for Radio Frequency Interference (RFI) suppression.
- For RFI suppression purposes only, high tension leads must have a resistance of 1000 Ω and spark plug connectors must have a resistance of 5000 Ω.

Test data, spark plugs

Engine code	ACU	
Ignition timing[1]		
Checking value	3 to 8° before TDC	
Adjusting value	6 ± 1° before TDC	
Engine speed	2000 to 2500 rpm	
Ignition timing at 2200 rpm[4]	23 to 33° BTDC	
Firing order	1–2–4–5–3	
Spark plugs	Manufacturers designation:	gap:
101 000 026 AA[3]	N9 BMC[3]	0.6 mm max.[2]
101 000 005 AE	W 8 DTC	0.7 to 0.9 mm
101 000 001 AE	14-8 DTU	0.7 to 0.9 mm
101 000 007 AB	N 7 BYC	0.7 to 0.9 mm
Tightening torque	25 Nm (18 ft lb)	

[1] Checking and adjusting ⇒ page F 28-31

[2] Gap between the ground electrode and center electrode

[3] Especially recommended for short journeys

[4] Ignition timing point, checking ⇒ page F 28-34

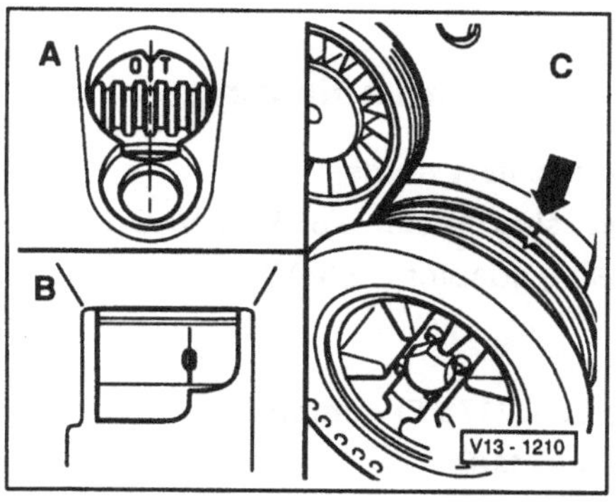

Ignition distributor, installing

Engine installed

◄ – Set flywheel -A- or drive plate -B- to TDC for cylinder #1

Engine removed

– Align marking on vibration damper -C- with marking on lower toothed belt guard -arrow-

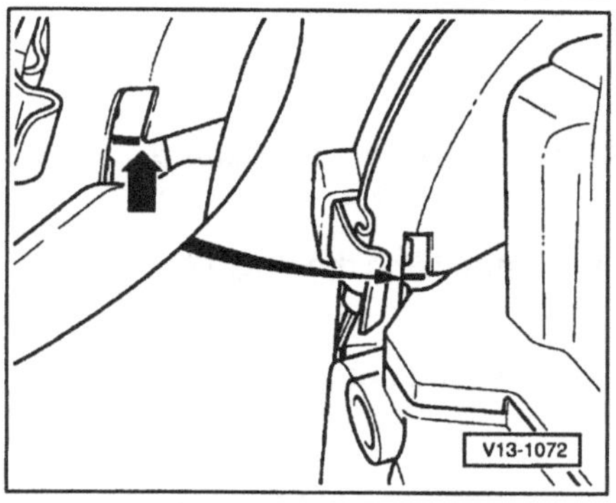

◄ – Align marks on camshaft sprocket with mark on rear toothed belt guard -arrow-

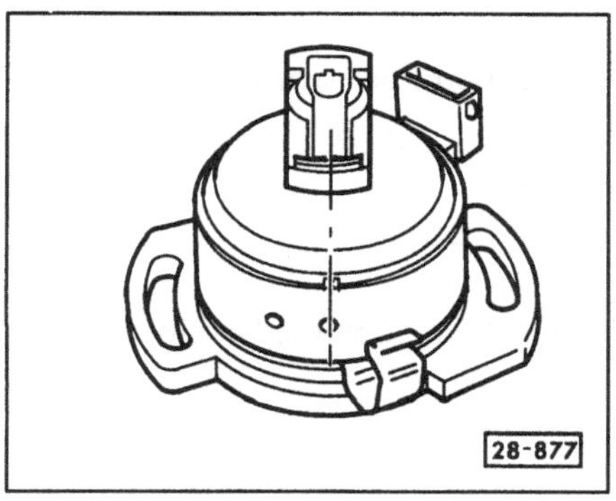

◄ – Position distributor rotor to point to cylinder #1 mark on housing

– Install ignition distributor

– Before installing, clean distributor cap and check for cracks and signs of tracking, replace if necessary

– Check and adjust ignition timing

Ignition timing, checking and adjusting

Special tools, testers and auxiliary items

- ♦ VAG 1367 Engine Tester, using inductive pick–up VAG 1 367/8
- ♦ VAG 1551 Scan Tool, using adaptor cable VAG 1551/1

Test conditions

- ♦ Engine oil temperature 80°C (176°F) minimum
- ♦ VAG 1551 Scan Tool connected

Test sequence

Note:

On some vehicles a TDC sensor is fitted as standard. Use adapter cable VAG 1367/9 to connect to a TDC sensor.

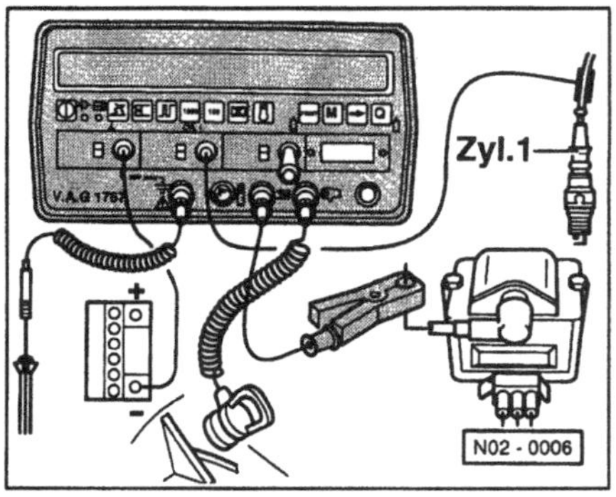

◄ – Connect VAG 1367 Engine Tester using the VAG 1367/8 inductive pickup

– Start engine and let idle (idle speed not to exceed 1500 rpm)

Note:

If the engine stalls, after restarting it can automatically run for up to 4 minutes at an increased speed. In which case do not continue until the speed drops off.

– Operate Scan Tool, taking the displayed information into account

– Press 1 button to select "Rapid data transfer"

– Press 0 and 1 buttons to select address word 01, "Engine electronics"

– Press Q button to enter input

– Press → button

– Press 0 and 4 buttons to select Function 04, "Basic setting"

– Press Q button to enter input

Note:

The Digifant Engine Control Module will be matched to the engine at idle speed, in the basic setting.

```
Basic setting                          HELP
Input display group number XX
```

◄ Display will appear as shown

– Press 0 and 1 buttons to select "Display group number"

– Press Q button to enter input

```
Basic setting 1                          →
   1        2        3        4
```

◄ Display will appear as shown, (1 to 4 = Display zones)

Do not continue with check until:

- ♦ Engine temperature exceeds 85°C (185°F) (display zone 2)
- ♦ All setting conditions have been fulfilled
  Specification: 00000000 (display zone 4)

⇒ page F 01-78

– Check ignition timing between 2000 and 2500 rpm

- ♦ Checking value: 3 to 8° before TDC (fluctuating)

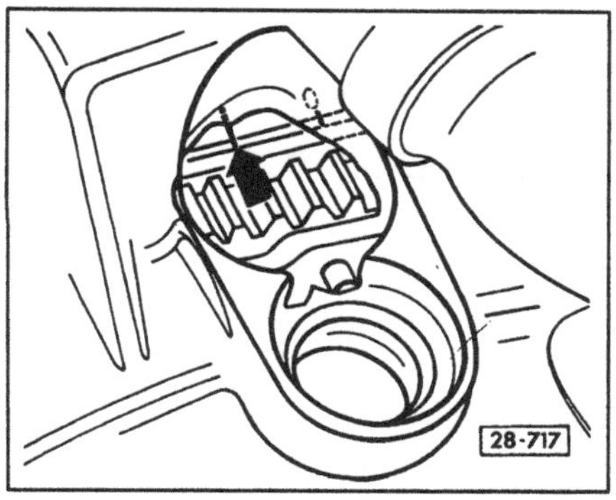

Using a stroboscope:

◄ – Point strobe at ignition timing mark

– If necessary, adjust ignition timing by turning the distributor

♦ Adjusting value: 6 ± 1° before TDC

– Allow engine to idle for at least 1 minute

– Press → button

– Press 0 and 6 buttons to select Function 06, "End data output"

– Press Q button to enter input

Ignition timing point, checking

Special tools, testers and auxiliary items

♦ VAG 1367 Engine Tester and inductive pick–up VAG 1367/8

Test conditions

♦ Ignition timing OK

♦ No malfunctions stored in DTC memory

♦ Engine oil temperature at least 80°C (176°F) minimum

Test sequence

Note:

On some vehicles a TDC sensor is installed as standard. Use adaptor cable VAG 1367/9 to connect the TDC sensor.

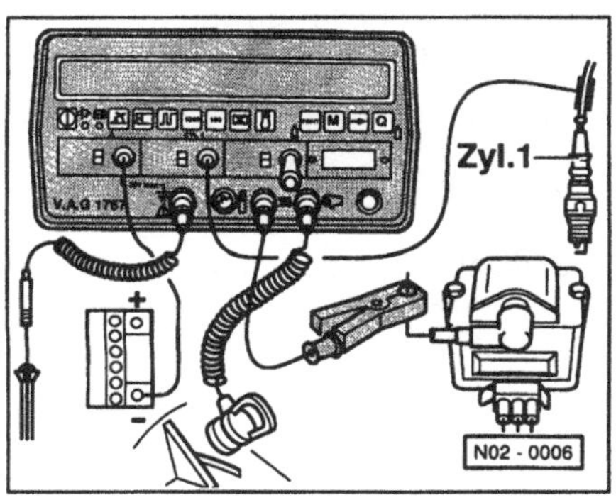

◄ – Connect VAG 1367 Engine Tester using VAG 1367/8 inductive pickup

– Start engine and let idle

– Set Engine Tester to 2200 rpm

– Slowly raise engine speed to slightly above 2200 rpm until ignition timing (advance angle) is displayed
♦ specification: 23 to 33° before TDC

If timing does not advance:

– Perform electrical checks, if necessary, replace ECM J169 ⇒ page F 01-82

Camshaft Position sensor, checking

Special tools, testers and auxiliary items

- Fluke 83 multimeter
- VW 1594 adaptor kit
- VAG 1527B LED tester
- Adaptor cable VAG 1315A/4

Test conditions

- DTC code "Camshaft Position sensor G40" recognized by On Board Diagnostic

Test sequence

– Perform electrical check, test step 12
⇒ Repair Group 01 page F 01-86

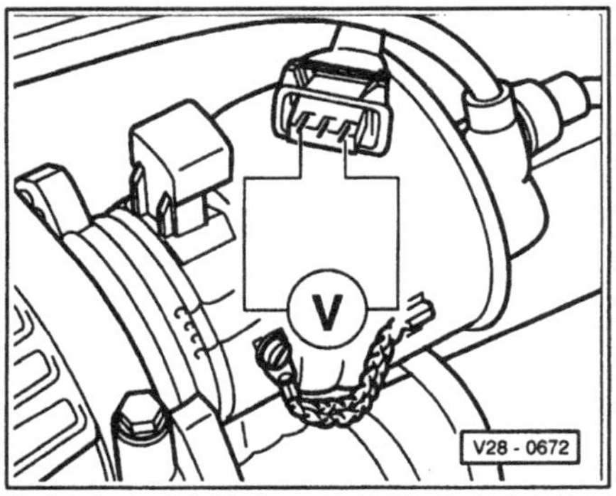

Voltage supply, checking

◄ – Disconnect 3-pin harness connector from Camshaft Position sensor G40

– Connect multimeter between terminals 1 and 3 of harness connector using VW 1594 adaptor leads

– Switch ON ignition

- Specification: At least 10 Volts

– Switch OFF ignition

If specifications are obtained:

– Replace Camshaft Position sensor
⇒ page F 28-26, item 5

Ignition coil, checking

Special tools, testers and auxiliary items

- Fluke 83 multimeter

Test sequence

– Disconnect coil wire from ignition coil and harness connector from power output stage

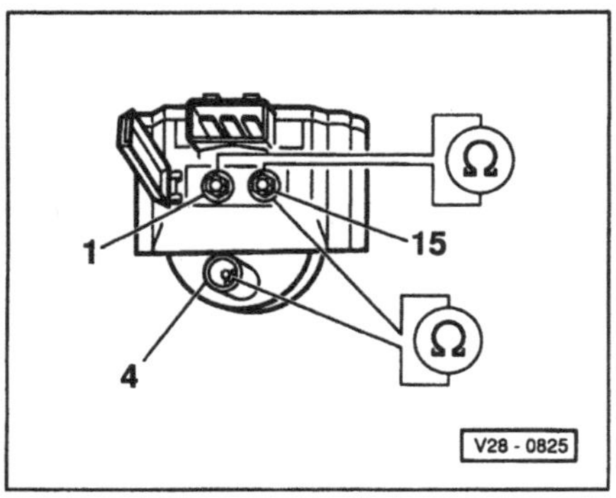

◄ – Check primary resistance by connecting multimeter between ignition coil terminals -1- and -15-

- Specification: 0.5 to 0.7 Ω

– Check secondary resistance by connecting multimeter between ignition coil terminals and 15

- Specification: 3000 to 4000 Ω

If specifications not obtained:

– Remove ignition coil and disconnect power output stage N157
⇒ page F 28-23, item 5

– Repeat check

Ignition coil power output stage, checking

Special tools, testers and auxiliary items

- ♦ Fluke 83 multimeter
- ♦ VW 1594 adaptor kit
- ♦ VAG 1527B LED tester

Test conditions

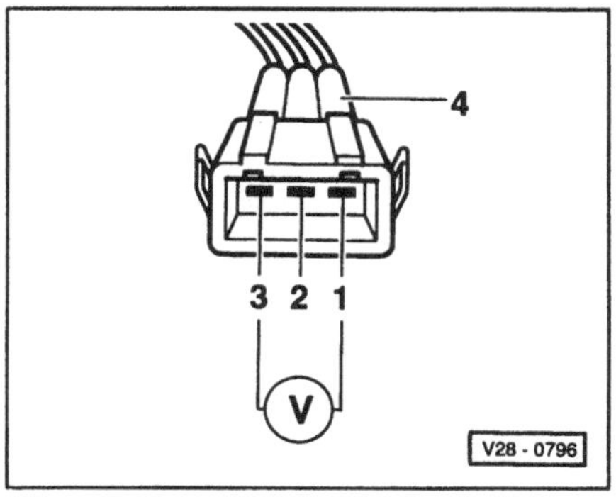

- ♦ Camshaft Position sensor OK
- ♦ Electrical check, test step 9 OK, checking ⇒ Repair Group 01, page F 01-85
- ♦ Ignition coil OK

Voltage supply, checking

- Disconnect ignition coil 3-pin harness connector
- ◄ Connect multimeter between terminals -1- and -3- of the harness connector using jumper leads from the VW 1594 adaptor kit
- Switch ON ignition
  - ♦ Specification: Approximately battery Voltage
- Switch OFF ignition

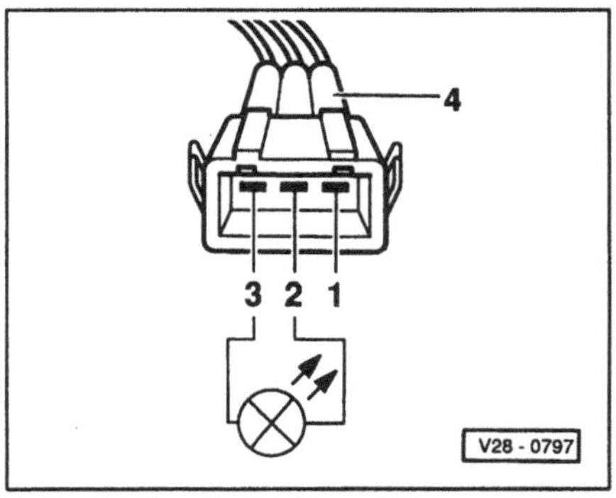

Activation, checking

- Remove fuse 18
- ◄ Connect VAG 1527B LED tester between terminals -2- and -3- of ignition coil harness connector, using jumper wires and adaptor VW 1594/15 from VW 1594 adaptor kit
- Operate starter and observe ignition signal from ECM
  - ♦ LED must flicker

If the LED does NOT flicker:

- Replace Digifant ECM J169
- Reconnect ignition coil harness connector and coil wire

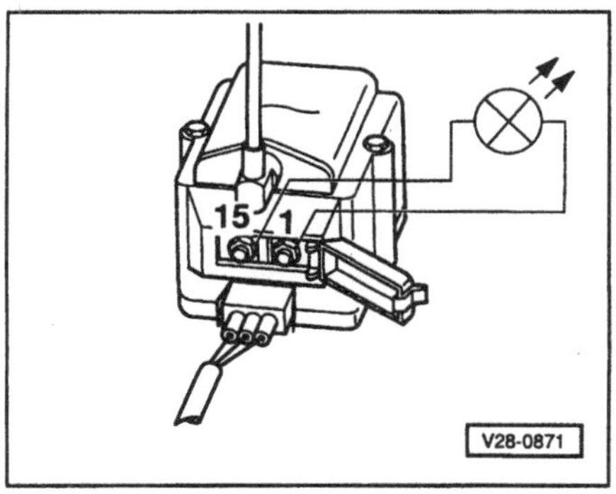

- ◄ Connect LED tester between terminals -1- and -15- of ignition coil, using jumper wires from VW 1594 adaptor kit

> ***CAUTION!***
> ***During the following check, do not touch the ignition coil terminals or test cables!***

- Switch ON ignition
  - ♦ LED must light up for 1 to 2 seconds
- Operate starter
  - ♦ LED must flicker
- Replace ignition coil power output stage, if necessary

2.8 Liter VR6, OBD II Fuel Injection and Ignition (Engine Code: AES)

Section G

WARNING!
Before proceeding with any work, please read the warnings and cautions immediately following this index. Also read any warning and caution that accompanies a procedure in the manual.

Please read these WARNINGS and CAUTIONS before proceeding with maintenance and repair work.

WARNING—

- Some repairs may be beyond your capability. If you lack the skills, tools and equipment, or a suitable workplace for any procedure described in this manual, we suggest you leave such repairs to an authorized Volkswagen dealer service department, or other qualified shop.

- Volkswagen is constantly improving its cars. Sometimes these changes, both in parts and specifications, are made applicable to earlier models. Therefore, before starting any major jobs or repairs to components on which passenger safety may depend, consult your authorized Volkswagen dealer about the Technical Bulletins that may have been issued since the editorial closing of this manual.

- Do not re-use any fasteners that are worn or deformed in normal use. Many fasteners are designed to be used only once and become unreliable and may fail when used a second time. This includes, but is not limited to, nuts, bolts, washers, self–locking nuts or bolts, circlips and cotter pins. Always replace these fasteners with new parts.

- Never work under a lifted car unless it is solidly supported on stands designed for the purpose. Do not support a car on cinder blocks, hollow tiles or other props that may crumble under continuous load. Never work under a vehicle that is supported solely by a jack. Never work under the car while the engine is running.

- If you are going to work under a car on the ground, make sure that the ground is level. Block the wheels to keep the car from rolling. Disconnect the battery negative terminal (ground strap) to prevent others from starting the vehicle while you are under it.

- Never run the engine unless the work area is well ventilated. Carbon monoxide (CO) kills.

- Do not attempt to work on your vehicle if you do not feel well. You increase the danger of injury to yourself and others if you are tired, upset or have taken medicine or any other substance that may impair you or keep you from being fully alert.

- Disconnect the battery negative (–) terminal (ground strap) whenever you work on the fuel system or the electrical system. Do not smoke or work near heaters or other fire hazards. Keep an approved fire extinguisher handy.

- Batteries produce explosive hydrogen gas. Keep sparks, lighted matches and open flame away from the top of the battery. If hydrogen gas escaping from the cap vents is ignited, it will ignite gas trapped in the cells and cause the battery to explode.

- Connect and disconnect battery cables, jumper cables or a battery charger only with the ignition switched off, to prevent sparks. Do not quick–charge the battery (for boost starting) for longer than one minute, and do not allow charging voltage to exceed 16.5 volts. Wait at least one minute before boosting the battery a second time.

- Illuminate your work area adequately but safely. Use a portable safety light for working inside or under the car. Make sure the bulb is enclosed by a wire cage. The hot filament of an accidentally broken bulb can ignite spilled fuel or oil.

- Tie long hair behind your head. Do not wear a necktie, a scarf, loose clothing, or a necklace when you work near machine tools or running engines. If your hair, clothing, or jewelry were to get caught in the machinery, severe injury could result.

- Finger rings, bracelets and other jewelry should be removed so that they cannot cause electrical shorts, get caught in running machinery, or be crushed by heavy parts.

- Catch draining fuel, oil, or brake fluid in suitable containers. Do not use food or beverage containers that might mislead someone into drinking from them. Store flammable fluids away from fire hazards. Wipe up spills at once, but do not store the oily rags, which can ignite and burn spontaneously.

- Always observe good workshop practices. Wear goggles when you operate machine tools or work with battery acid. Gloves or other protective clothing should be worn whenever the job requires working with harmful substances.

- The Air-Conditioning (A/C) system is filled with a chemical refrigerant, which is hazardous. The A/C system should be serviced only by trained technicians using approved refrigerant recovery/recycling equipment, trained in related safety precautions, and familiar with regulations governing the discharging and disposal of automotive chemical refrigerants.

- Do not expose any part of the A/C system to high temperatures such as an open flame. Excessive heat will increase system pressure and may cause the system to burst.

- Some aerosol tire inflators are highly flammable. Be extremely cautious when repairing a tire that may have been inflated using an aerosol tire inflator. Keep sparks, open flame or other sources of ignition away from the tire repair area. Inflate and deflate the tire at least four times before breaking the bead from the rim. Completely remove the tire from the rim before attempting any repair.

- Friction materials such as brake or clutch discs may contain asbestos fibers. Do not create dust by grinding, sanding, or by cleaning with compressed air. Avoid breathing asbestos fibers and asbestos dust. Breathing asbestos can cause serious diseases such as asbestosis or cancer, and may result in death.

- Greases, lubricants and other automotive chemicals contain toxic substances, many of which are absorbed directly through the skin. Read manufacturer's instructions and warnings carefully. Use hand and eye protection. Avoid direct skin contact.

- An airbag is operated by an explosive device. Handled improperly or without adequate safeguards, it can be accidently activated and cause serious personal injury. To prevent personal injury or airbag system failure, **only trained Volkswagen dealer service technicians** should test, disassemble or service the airbag system.

WARNINGS and CAUTIONS continued on next page ▶

Please read these WARNINGS and CAUTIONS before proceeding with maintenance and repair work.

WARNING (continued) —

- ALWAYS disconnect the airbag power supply before using a computer memory saver. Failure to disconnect the airbag power supply may result in accidental activation of the airbag.
- The airbag unit should not be removed, nor should any work be performed on the airbag system, without first reviewing the warnings and cautions that accompany the airbag system repair information in this manual.
- Never apply stickers or any other coverings on the steering wheel. Do not let chemical cleaners, oil or grease come into contact with the vinyl covering of the airbag unit.
- Never open or otherwise attempt to repair airbag system parts. Always use new parts. Never leave airbag parts or the partially disassembled airbag system unattended.
- Never use a test light or volt meter to conduct electrical tests on the airbag system. The airbag system must only be tested by trained Volkswagen Service technicians using special airbag tester equipment. The airbag system must only be tested while it is installed in the car.
- Do not expose an airbag unit to temperatures above 194°F (90°C) even for a brief period, while handling it during the repair process. Keep the unit clear of heat sources such as hot plates, soldering irons, heat lamps, welding equipment, or the like.
- Always replace airbag system components that have been mechanically damaged (bubbles, cracks, etc.).
- Always set down a removed airbag unit so that the horn pad is facing upward.
- When driving or riding in an airbag-equipped vehicle, never hold test equipment in your hands or lap while the vehicle is in motion. Objects between you and the airbag can increase the risk of injury in an accident.
- The storage, transportation and disposal of airbag units are subject to the laws for flammable solids.

CAUTION—

- If you lack the skills, tools and equipment, or a suitable workshop for any procedure described in this manual, we suggest you leave such repairs to an authorized Volkswagen dealer or other qualified shop. We especially urge you to consult an authorized Volkswagen dealer before beginning repairs on any car that may still be covered wholly or in part by any of the extensive warranties issued by Volkswagen of America, Inc.
- Volkswagen is constantly improving its cars and sometimes these changes, both in parts and specifications, are made applicable to earlier models. Therefore, part numbers listed in this manual are for reference only. Always check with your authorized Volkswagen dealer parts department for the latest information.
- Before starting a job, make certain that you have all the necessary tools and parts on hand. Read all the instructions thoroughly, do not attempt shortcuts. Use tools that are appropriate to the work and use only replacement parts meeting Volkswagen specifications. Makeshift tools, parts and procedures will not make good repairs.
- Use pneumatic and electric tools only to loosen threaded parts and fasteners. Never use these tools to tighten fasteners, especially on light alloy parts. Always use a torque wrench to tighten fasteners to the tightening torque specification listed.
- Be mindful of the environment and ecology. Before you drain the crankcase, find out the proper way to dispose of the oil. Do not pour oil onto the ground, down a drain, or into a stream, pond, or lake. Consult local ordinances that govern the disposal of wastes.
- When connecting cables or ground straps, all connections must be cleaned to bare metal. Be sure mounting bolts are tight.
- Do not replace fuse links with fuse links of other gauge or with standard wire. Always replace the entire length of the fuse link.
- Before doing any electrical welding on vehicles equipped with Anti-lock Brakes (ABS), disconnect the battery negative terminal (ground strap) and the ABS Control Module connector.
- On cars equipped with ABS, the ABS control unit cannot withstand temperatures from a paint–drying booth or a heat lamp in excess of 203°F (95°C) and should not be subjected to temperatures in excess of 185°F (85°C) for more than two hours.
- On cars equipped with anti-theft radios, make sure you know the correct radio activation code before disconnecting the battery or removing the radio. If the wrong code is entered when power is restored, the radio may lock up and be rendered inoperable, even if the correct code is then entered.
- When boost-charging the battery, first remove the fuses for the Engine Control Module (ECM), the Transmission Control Module (TCM), the ABS Control Module, and the On-Board computer. In cases where one or more of these components is not separately fused, disconnect the Control Module connector(s).
- Do not quick-charge the battery (for boost starting) for longer than one minute, and do not exceed 16.5 volts at the battery with the boosting cables attached. Wait at least one minute before boosting the battery a second time.

◀ **WARNINGS and CAUTIONS continued from previous page**

On Board Diagnostic System

On Board Diagnostic system, function

The J220 Engine Control Module (ECM) for the Fuel injection and Ignition systems is equipped with a Diagnostic Trouble Code (DTC) memory.

If malfunctions occur in monitored sensors and components, the malfunction will be stored in the DTC memory together with a text message describing the type of malfunction.

Malfunctions which only occur sporadically will have the additional description: "sporadic malfunction" shown on the print out. This type of malfunction is identified in the displays by /SP. The cause of /SP malfunctions for example, could be a loose terminal or intermittent open circuit. If the /SP malfunction does not occur again within 40 engine starts, it will be erased from DTC memory.

Stored malfunctions (DTC's) can be displayed once DTC memory has been checked.
⇒ page G 01-12

DTC memory must be erased once malfunctions have been eliminated.
⇒ page G 01-31

The Readiness code must be created again each time DTC memory is erased or when the Engine Control Module (ECM) voltage supply is interrupted.
⇒ page G 01-35

Malfunction Indicator Lamp (MIL), significance

If malfunctions are recognized by the Engine Control Module (ECM), they will switch on the Malfunction Indicator Lamp (MIL).

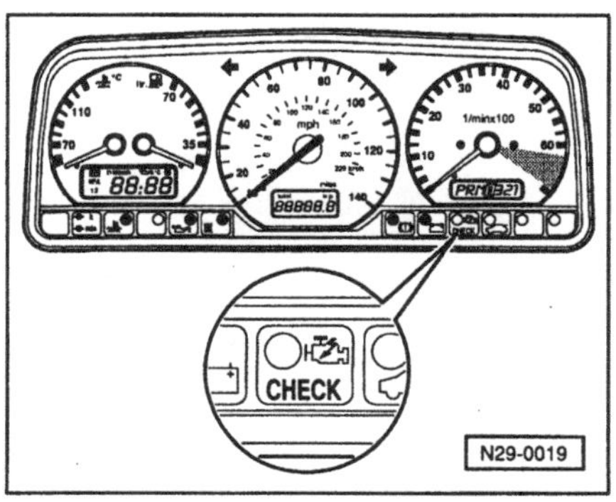

◄ Location of MIL lamp

Note:

The MIL lamp can switch on in the "Blinking" or "Permanently ON" mode. In either case, DTC memory must be checked.
⇒ page G 01-12

- *Blinking: There is a malfunction which can cause damage to the Three-Way catalyst if driven in this condition. In this case, do not drive the vehicle under full load or wide open acceleration!*
- *Permanently ON: There is a malfunction present which will increase exhaust emission levels. Check the Engine and/or Transmission Control Modules.*
- *If the MIL lamp does not light up, even though there is an engine running problem, or if a customer complains, after the MIL lamp has been functionally checked; DTC memory must be checked, because malfunctions which do not immediately switch the MIL lamp ON can still be stored!*

MIL lamp, functional check

– Switch ON ignition

♦ MIL lamp must light-up

If NO:

– Check MIL lamp wiring as follows:

Cause: Malfunction Indicator Lamp (K83) is not activated or does not light-up for open circuit	Remedy: – Switch OFF ignition – Connect VAG 1598/18 Test Box – Bridge Test Box sockets 1 and 5 – Switch ON ignition MIL lamp must light-up If MIL lamp does not light-up: – Switch OFF ignition – Check MIL lamp LED If LED is OK: – Locate/eliminate open circuit between ECM and MIL lamp via wiring diagram
	If no malfunction can be detected in wiring to MIL lamp:
Malfunction cause	**Control Module J220 faulty, replace.** **Erase DTC memory and create Readiness code.**

If MIL lamp lights-up (ignition switched ON) continue as follows:

– Start engine and let idle

♦ MIL lamp must go out after a few seconds

If MIL lamp does not go out:

– Check DTC memory
⇒ page G 01-12

If no DTC's are stored:

Cause: Malfunction Indicator Lamp (K83) is permanently activated by short to ground	Remedy: – Switch OFF ignition – Connect VAG 1598/18 Test Box – Measure resistance between Test Box socket 5 and ground: Specification: ∞ Ω If specification not obtained: Short to ground in signal wire between ECM J220 and MIL lamp – Locate and eliminate malfunction using wiring diagram
	If the specification ∞ Ω is obtained and no short to ground can be found:
Malfunction cause	**Engine Control Module J220 faulty, replace** **Erase DTC memory and create Readiness code**

On Board Diagnostic System, technical data

Control Module features

- Data transfer between Control Module and VAG 1551 / VAG 1552 Scan Tools is processed in the "Rapid data transfer" mode
- DTC memory is equipped with a non-volatile memory

Control Module identification

VAG 1551 Scan Tool, connecting and ECM selecting
⇒ page G 01-7

Control Module Functions

- *The ECM is equipped with a variety of Functions.*
- *Some Functions require the ignition ONLY to be switched ON, other Functions require the engine to be running.*
- *The table on the following page details which requirements apply to the individual Functions.*

Function	Requirement	
	Engine not running, ignition switched ON	Engine idling
02 Check DTC memory	Yes	Yes
03 Output Diagnostic Test Mode	Yes	No
04 Basic Setting	Yes[1)]	Yes[2)3)]
05 Erase DTC Memory	Yes	Yes
06 End Output	Yes	Yes
07 Code Control Module	Yes	No
08 Read Measuring Value Block	Yes	Yes

1) Must be performed if the ECM, engine or Throttle Valve Control Module has been replaced

2) Only possible when engine coolant temperature exceeds 80°C (176°F).
Function is blocked when temperatures are lower than 80°C (176°F).

3) Must be performed during idle speed check

VAG 1551 Scan Tool, connecting

Address Word 01 "engine electronics", selecting

Special tools, testers and auxiliary items

- VAG 1551 Scan Tool with adaptor cable VAG 1551/3

Note:

VAG 1552 Scan Tool can be functionally used instead of VAG 1551 Scan Tool, however; VAG 1552 has no print capability.

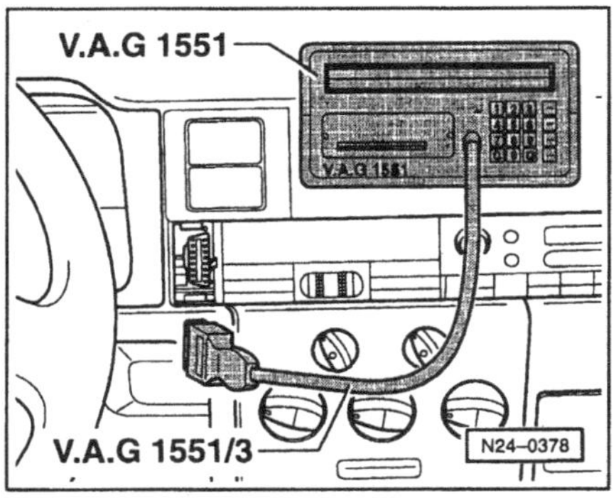

Requirements

- Fuses 15, 18, 19 and 21 OK
- Battery voltage 11 Volts minimum
- Engine/transmission ground connections OK
⇒ page G 24-4 (item 9)

Work sequence

◄ – Slide Data Link Connector (DLC) cover to expose DLC (on right side of steering column next to instrument cluster)

– Connect VAG 1551 Scan Tool using VAG 1551/3 adaptor cable

After Scan Tool has been connected and depending upon which Function is required:
⇒ page G 01-5

– Switch ON ignition or start engine (depending upon which Function is required)

If the display does not appear as shown in the work sequence:
⇒ Scan Tool operating instructions

If the display, "malfunction in data transfer" appears:

– Disconnect Scan Tool from DLC and then re-connect, repeat work step

VAG - On Board Diagnostic	HELP
1 - Rapid data transfer*	
2 - Blink code output*	

◄ Appears on display:

* Text lines 1 and 2 of display appear alternately

– Operate Scan Tool taking into account any displayed info.

– Press 1 button to select "Rapid data transfer" mode

– Press 0 and 1 buttons to select Address Word 01 "Engine electronics"

– Press Q button to enter input

021 906 259B MOTRONIC M5.9 AT V0 1→	
Coding 00001	WSC xxxxx

◄ VAG 1551 Scan Tool display shows Control Module identifying information, for example:

- 021 906 259B = Control Module Part Number

> ***CAUTION***
> ***Part numbers are for reference only. Always consult with the Parts department for the latest information.***

- MOTRONIC M5.9 = Fuel injection and Ignition system
- Coding 00001 = Coding variants
- WSC = Workshop code

Coding variants:

Coding	For following combinations:
00000	VR6 with manual transmission
00001	VR6 with automatic transmission

Note:

Accurate Control Module coding and identifying information is only possible when the engine is idling.

The ignition must be switched OFF once before Control Module Coding is entered into the ECM and made viewable via the Scan Tool display. Incorrect coding can lead to:

- *Engine running malfunctions*
- *Increased fuel consumption*
- *Increased emission levels*
- *Stored DTC's that did not actually occur*
- *Reduced transmission life*

If coding differs from vehicle version

– Check Control Module Coding
⇒ page G 01-10

– Press → button

Rapid data transfer Select Function XX	HELP

◄ Display will appear as shown

– For additional steps see repair procedures

Function 07, Control Module - coding

If correct vehicle coding is not displayed, or if the Control Module has been replaced; code Control Module as follows:

Special tools, testers and auxiliary items

- VAG 1551/VAG 1552 Scan Tool using VAG 1551/3 adaptor cable

Work sequence

– Connect VAG 1551/VAG 1552 Scan Tool

– With ignition switched ON, press 0 and 1 buttons to select Address word 01, "Engine Electronics"
⇒ page G 01-7

Rapid data transfer Select Function XX	HELP

◄ Display will appear as shown

– Press 1 button twice to select Function 11, "Login procedure"

– Press Q button to enter selection

Login procedure Input code number XXXXX	HELP

◄ Display will appear as shown

– Press buttons 0, 1, 2, 8 and 3 to select Login code 01283

– Press Q button to enter selection

Rapid data transfer Select Function XX	HELP

◄ Display will appear as shown

– Press 0 and 7 buttons to select Function 07, "Code Control Module"

– Press Q button to enter selection

Code Control Module	HELP
Input code number XXXXX	(0-32000)

◄ Display will appear as shown

– Enter appropriate code number for vehicle

– Press Q button to enter selection

Coding	For following combinations:
00000	VR6 with manual transmission
00001	VR6 with automatic transmission

021906259B MOTRONIC M5.9 AT V0 1 →	
Coding 00001	WSC XXXXX

◄ Display example shows Control Module identification

– Press → button

Rapid data transfer	HELP
Select Function XX	

◄ Display will appear as shown

– Press 0 and 6 buttons to select Function 06, "End output"

– Press Q button to enter selection

Function 02, DTC memory - checking

Special tools, testers and auxiliary items

- VAG 1551/VAG 1552 Scan Tool using VAG 1551/3 adaptor cable

Work sequence

– Connect Scan Tool

– With engine idling, press 0 and 1 buttons to select Address Word 01, "Engine Electronics"
⇒ page G 01-7

If engine will not start:

– *Operate starter for approx. 6 seconds and then leave ignition switched ON*

– Press Scan Tool PRINT button to switch ON printer

- warning lamp in PRINT button must light up

Rapid data transfer	HELP
Select Function XX	

◄ Display will appear as shown

– Press 0 and 2 buttons to select Function 02, "Check DTC memory"

– Press Q button to enter selection

X malfunctions recognized!

◄ The number of malfunctions stored or "No malfunction recognised!" will be shown on the display

If display shows anything different
⇒ Scan Tool operating instructions

If one or more DTC's are stored

- ♦ Stored DTC's will be displayed and printed out one after the other

Rapid data transfer	HELP
Select Function XX	

◄ The display will then appear

If no malfunction is stored:

- *Press → button*
- Press 0 and 6 buttons to select Function 06, "End output"
- Press Q button to enter selection
- Locate and eliminate malfunctions printed out per Diagnostic Trouble Code (DTC) table
⇒ page G 01-14

Erasing DTC memory
⇒ page G 01-31

Diagnostic Trouble Code (DTC), table

Notes:

- ♦ *The DTC codes are identified by using SAE or VAG codes.*
- ♦ *The "MIL" column gives the switch-on conditions for the MIL lamp.*
- ♦ *DTC codes which have the MIL switch-on condition shown as "5 secs." will be stored 5 seconds after detection.*
- ♦ *DTC codes which have the MIL switch-on condition shown as "Driving cycles": will initially be recognized from the engine start via the respective diagnostic Function until the engine is switched off.*
- ♦ *2 driving cycles are necessary for MIL switch-on conditions.*
- ♦ *Perform repairs on malfunctions with the "5 secs." MIL switch-on condition first, then repair malfunctions with the "2 driving cycles" switch-on condition next.*

After repairing a malfunction:

- Erase DTC memory
⇒ *page G 01-31*

- Create new Readiness code
⇒ *page G 01-35*

DTC code SAE	DTC code VAG	Diagnostic Trouble Code (DTC) Text	MIL	Corrective Steps
P0102	16486	Mass or Volume Air Flow Circuit Low Input	2 driving cycles	Check Mass Air Flow sensor ⇒ page G 24-66
P0103	16487	Mass or Volume Air Flow Circuit High Input		
P0112	16496	Intake Air Temperature Circuit Low Input	2 driving cycles	Check Intake Air Temp. sensor ⇒ page G 24-99
P0113	16497	Intake Air Temperature Circuit High Input		
P0116	16500	Engine Coolant Temperature Circuit Range/Performance		
P0117	16501	Engine Coolant Temperature Circuit Low Input	2 driving cycles	Check Engine Coolant Temperature sensor ⇒ page G 24-93
P0118	16502	Engine Coolant Temperature Circuit High Input		
P0120	16504	Throttle Position Sensor A Circuit Malfunction		Check Throttle Valve Control Module ⇒ page G 24-72
P0121	16505	Throttle Position Sensor A Circuit Range/Performance	2 driving cycles	Check Mass Air Flow sensor ⇒ page G 24-66
P0122	16506	Throttle Position Sensor A Circuit Low Input		

DTC code SAE	DTC code VAG	Diagnostic Trouble Code (DTC) Text	MIL	Corrective Steps
P0125	16509	Insufficient Coolant Temperature for Closed Loop Fuel Control	2 driving cycles	Check Engine Coolant Temperature sensor ⇒ page G 24-93 Check coolant thermostat ⇒ Repair Group 19
P0131	16515	02 Sensor Circuit (B1–S1) Low Voltage	2 driving cycles	Check Oxygen sensor and Oxygen control (before catalytic converter) ⇒ page G 24-28
P0132	16516	02 Sensor Circuit (B1–S1) High Voltage		Check Oxygen sensor aging and Oxygen sensor (before catalytic converter) ⇒ page G 24-60
P0133	16517	02 Sensor Circuit (B1–S1) Slow Response	2 driving cycles	
P0134	16518	02 Sensor Circuit (B1–S1) No Activity Detected		
P0135	16519	02 Sensor Heater Circuit (B1–S1) Malfunction	2 driving cycles	Check Oxygen sensor heating (before catalytic converter) ⇒ page G 24-38

DTC code SAE	VAG	Diagnostic Trouble Code (DTC) Text	MIL	Corrective Steps
P0137	16521	02 Sensor Circuit (B1–S2) Low Voltage	2 driving cycles	Check Oxygen sensor and Oxygen control (after catalytic convert-er) ⇒ page G 24-46
P0138	16522	02 Sensor Circuit (B1–S2) High Voltage		
P0140	16524	02 Sensor Circuit (B1–S2) No Activity Detected		
P0141	16525	02 Sensor Heater Circuit (B1–S2) Malfunction	2 driving cycles	Check Oxygen sensor heating (after catalytic converter) ⇒ page G 24-53

DTC code SAE	VAG	Diagnostic Trouble Code (DTC) Text	MIL	Corrective Steps
P0171	16555	(B1) System too Lean	2 driving cycles	Check Secondary Air Injection system ⇒ Repair Group 26
				Check intake air system for leaks ⇒ page G 24-128
				Check Oxygen sensor and Oxygen control (before catalytic con-verter) ⇒ page G 24-28
				Check Mass Air Flow sensor ⇒ page G 24-66
				Check fuel pump ⇒ Repair Group 20
				Check Fuel injectors ⇒ page G 24-121

DTC code SAE	VAG	Diagnostic Trouble Code (DTC) Text	MIL	Corrective Steps
P0172	16556	(B1) System too Rich	2 driving cycles	Check Oxygen sensor and Oxygen control (before catalytic converter) ⇒ page G 24-28
				Check fuel pressure regulator ⇒ page G 24-125
				Check exhaust system for leaks ⇒ Repair Group 26
P0300	16684	Random Misfire Detected	2 driving cycles / Blink	Check ignition system components ⇒ page G 28-2
				Check misfiring detection ⇒ page G 28-13
				Check ignition coil ⇒ page G 28-19
				Check Engine Speed sensor ⇒ page G 24-104
				Change type of fuel

DTC code SAE	VAG	Diagnostic Trouble Code (DTC) Text	MIL	Corrective Steps
P0301	16685	Cyl. 1 Misfire Detected	2 driving cycles / blink	Check Fuel injectors ⇒ page G 24-121
P0302	16686	Cyl. 2 Misfire Detected		Check ignition coil ⇒ page G 28-19
P0303	16687	Cyl. 3 Misfire Detected		
P0304	16688	Cyl. 4 Misfire Detected		Check misfiring detection ⇒ page G 28-13
P0305	16689	Cyl. 5 Misfire Detected		
P0306	16690	Cyl. 6 Misfire Detected		
—	16711	Knock Sensor 1 Circuit Low Input	5 secs.	Check knock sensor and knock control ⇒ page G 28-24
—	16716	Knock Sensor 2 Circuit Low Input	5 secs.	Check knock sensor and knock control ⇒ page G 28-24

DTC code SAE	VAG	Diagnostic Trouble Code (DTC) Text	MIL	Corrective Steps
P0341	16725	Camshaft Position Sensor Circuit Range/Performance	2 driving cycles	Check Camshaft Position sensor ⇒ page G 28-8
P0400	16784	Exhaust Gas Recirculation Flow Malfunction	2 driving cycles	Check EGR system ⇒ Repair Group 26
P0411	16795	Secondary Air Injection System Incorrect Flow Detected	2 driving cycles	Check Secondary Air Injection system ⇒ Repair Group 26
P0422	16806	Main Catalyst (B1) Efficiency Below Threshold	2 driving cycles	Check Oxygen sensor and Oxygen control (before catalytic converter) ⇒ page G 24-28

DTC code SAE	VAG	Diagnostic Trouble Code (DTC) Text	MIL	Corrective Steps
P0440	16824	EVAP Emissions Control System malfunction	2 driving cycles	Check EVAP canister purge regulator valve 1 ⇒ page G 01-77 ("Output Diagnostic Test Mode")
P0501	16885	Vehicle Speed sensor Range/Performance	2 driving cycles	Check vehicle speed signal ⇒ page G 24-106
P0506	16890	Idle Control System RPM Lower than Expected	2 driving cycles	Check fuel pressure regulator and residual pressure ⇒ page G 24-125 Check ignition timing ⇒ page G 28-11 Check speed signal ⇒ page G 24-106
P0507	16891	Idle Control System RPM Higher than Expected	2 driving cycles	Check battery voltage, Perform idle speed check ⇒ page G 24-25
P0510	16894	Closed Throttle Position switch malfunction	2 driving cycles	Check Throttle Valve Control Module ⇒ page G 24-72
P0605	16989	Control Module (internal malfunction)	2 trips	Change Control Module ⇒ page G 24-4 (item 12)

DTC code SAE	VAG	Diagnostic Trouble Code (DTC) Text	MIL	Corrective Steps
P1127	17535	Long Term Fuel Trim (B1) System too Rich	2 driving cycles	Check Mass Air Flow sensor ⇒ page G 24-66
				Check Oxygen sensor and Oxygen control (before catalytic converter) ⇒ page G 24-28
				Check Oxygen sensor and Oxygen control (after catalytic converter) ⇒ page G 24-46
				Check fuel pump ⇒ Repair Group 20
				Check Secondary Air Injection system ⇒ Repair Group 26
				Check Fuel injectors ⇒ page G 24-121

DTC code SAE	VAG	Diagnostic Trouble Code (DTC) Text	MIL	Corrective Steps
P1128	17536	Long Term Fuel Trim (B1) System too Lean	2 driving cycles	Check Oxygen sensor and Oxygen control (before catalytic converter) ⇒ page G 24-28
				Check Oxygen sensor and Oxygen control (after catalytic converter) ⇒ page G 24-46
				Check fuel pump ⇒ Repair Group 20
				Check Fuel injectors ⇒ page G 24-121
P1213	17621	Cyl. 1 Fuel Injector Circuit Short to B+	5 secs.	Check Fuel injectors ⇒ page G 24-121
P1214	17622	Cyl. 2 Fuel Injector Circuit Short to B+	5 secs.	
P1215	17623	Cyl. 3 Fuel Injector Circuit Short to B+	5 secs.	
P1216	17624	Cyl. 4 Fuel Injector Circuit Short to B+	5 secs.	
P1217	17625	Cyl. 5 Fuel Injector Circuit Short to B+	5 secs.	
P1218	17626	Cyl. 6 Fuel Injector Circuit Short to B+	5 secs.	

DTC code SAE	DTC code VAG	Diagnostic Trouble Code (DTC) Text	MIL	Corrective Steps
P1225	17633	Injector Circuit Cyl.1 Short to Ground	5 secs.	Check Fuel injectors ⇒ page G 24-121
P1226	17634	Injector Circuit Cyl.2 Short to Ground	5 secs.	
P1227	17635	Injector Circuit Cyl.3 Short to Ground	5 secs.	
P1228	17636	Injector Circuit Cyl.4 Short to Ground	5 secs.	
P1229	17637	Injector Circuit Cyl.5 Short to Ground	5 secs.	
P1230	17638	Injector Circuit Cyl.6 Short to Ground	5 secs.	
P1237	17645	Injector Circuit Cyl.1 Open Circuit	5 secs.	
P1238	17646	Injector Circuit Cyl.2 Open Circuit	5 secs.	
P1239	17647	Injector Circuit Cyl.3 Open Circuit	5 secs.	
P1240	17648	Injector Circuit Cyl.4 Open Circuit	5 secs.	
P1241	17649	Injector Circuit Cyl.5 Open Circuit	5 secs.	
P1242	17650	Injector Circuit Cyl.6 Open Circuit	5 secs.	

DTC code SAE	DTC code VAG	Diagnostic Trouble Code (DTC) Text	MIL	Corrective Steps
P1340	17748	Camshaft/Crankshaft Position sensor, Signals Out of Sequence	5 secs.	Check Engine Speed sensor ⇒ page G 24-104
P1401	17809	EGR Valve Power Stage Short to Ground	5 secs.	Check EGR valve, "Output Diagnostic Test Mode" ⇒ page G 01-77
P1402	17810	EGR Valve Circuit Short to B+	5 secs.	Check EGR valve ⇒ Repair Group 26
P1407	17815	EGR Temperature Sensor Signal too Low	2 driving cycles	Check EGR temperature sensor ⇒ Repair Group 26
P1408	17816	EGR Temperature Sensor Signal too High		

DTC code SAE	DTC code VAG	Diagnostic Trouble Code (DTC) Text	MIL	Corrective Steps
P1410	17818	Tank Ventilation Valve Short to B+	5 secs.	Check EVAP canister purge regulator valve ⇒ page G 01-77 ("Output Diagnostic Test Mode")
P1420	17828	Secondary Air Injection System Control Module Electrical Malfunction	5 secs.	Check Secondary Air Injection system ⇒ Repair Group 26
P1421	17829	Secondary Air Injection system control valve circuit short to Ground	5 secs.	
P1422	17830	Secondary Air Injection system control valve circuit,short to B+	5 secs.	
P1425	17833	Tank Ventilation Valve Short to Ground	5 secs.	
P1426	17834	Tank Ventilation Valve Open Circuit	5 secs.	Check EVAP canister purge regulator valve ⇒ page G 01-77 ("Output Diagnostic Test Mode")
P1440	17848	EGR Valve Power Stage Open	5 secs.	Check EGR valve ⇒ Repair Group 26

DTC code SAE	DTC code VAG	Diagnostic Trouble Code (DTC) Text	MIL	Corrective Steps
P1450	17858	Secondary Air Injection System Circuit Short to B+	5 secs.	
P1451	17859	Secondary Air Injection System Short to Ground	5 secs.	Check Secondary Air Injection pump relay J299 ⇒ wiring diagrams, Electrical troubleshooting and Component locations binder
P1452	17860	Secondary Air Injection System Open Circuit	5 secs.	
P1500	17908	Fuel pump relay Circuit Electrical Malfunction	5 secs.	Check fuel pump relay ⇒ wiring diagrams, Electrical troubleshooting and Component locations binder
P1502	17910	Fuel pump relay Circuit Short to B+	5 secs.	Check fuel pump ⇒ Repair Group 20

DTC code SAE	VAG	Diagnostic Trouble Code (DTC) Text	MIL	Corrective Steps
P1543	17951	Throttle Position Signal too Low	5 secs.	Check Throttle Valve Control Module ⇒ page G 24-72
P1544	17952	Throttle Actuation Signal too High	5 secs.	
P1580	17988	Throttle Actuator (B1) Malfunction	2 driving cycles	
P1582	17990	Idle Adaption at Limit	2 driving cycles	Check Throttle Valve Control Module ⇒ page G 24-72
				Check Intake air system for leaks ⇒ page G 24-128
				Check exhaust system for leaks ⇒ Repair Group 26
				Check fuel pressure regulator ⇒ page G 24-125

DTC code SAE	VAG	Diagnostic Trouble Code (DTC) Text	MIL	Corrective Steps
P1611	18019	MIL Call-up Circuit/Transmission Control Module Short to Ground	2 driving cycles	Check wiring between TCM and ECM ⇒ wiring diagrams, Electrical troubleshooting and Component locations binder
P1613	18021	MIL Call-up Open Circuit/Short to B+		Check MIL lamp LED ⇒ wiring diagrams, Electrical troubleshooting and Component locations binder, also check for heavy contact wear in ignition starter switch D, replace if necessary

Function 05, DTC memory - erasing

Special tools, testers and auxiliary items

♦ VAG 1551/VAG 1552 Scan Tool using VAG 1551/3 adaptor cable

Requirement

♦ All malfunction(s) eliminated

Note:

If DTC memory is erased, the Readiness code must be created again ⇒ page G 01-35.

Work sequence

– Perform road test of at least 10 minutes duration, during which the following requirements are fulfilled:

  ♦ Engine coolant temperature must reach 80°C (176°F) minimum

  ♦ Wide Open Throttle executed at least once while engine speed is above 4600 rpm

  ♦ Accelerate for approximately 4 seconds in 4th gear from approximately 50 km/h (30 mph), using Partially Open Throttle

– With engine idling, connect VAG 1551/VAG 1552 Scan Tool and select Address Word 01, "Engine Electronics" ⇒ page G 01-7


```
Rapid data transfer          HELP
Select Function XX
```

◄ Display will appear as shown

– Press 0 and 2 buttons to select Function 02, "Check DTC memory"

– Press Q button to confirm entry

```
Rapid data transfer          HELP
Select Function XX
```

◄ – Press → button until all stored DTC's have appeared and the display appears as shown

– Press 0 and 5 buttons to select Function 05, "Erase DTC memory"

– Press Q button to confirm entry

```
Rapid data transfer             →
DTC memory is erased!
```

◄ Display will appear as shown

– Press → button

```
Rapid data transfer          HELP
Select Function XX
```

◄ Display will appear as shown

– Press 0 and 6 buttons to select Function 06, "End output"

– Press Q button to confirm entry

– Perform another road test and Check DTC memory again

  ♦ No malfunctions should be displayed

Note:

If the same malfunction is stored in DTC memory after the road-test, check Control Module coding ⇒ page G 01-10.

Function 15, Readiness code - reading

Special tools, testers and auxiliary items

- ♦ VAG 1551/VAG 1552 Scan Tool using adaptor cable VAG 1551/3

Work sequence

– Connect Scan Tool

– With ignition switched ON, press 0 and 1 buttons to select Address Word 01, “Engine Electronics”
⇒ page G 01-7

```
Rapid data transfer                HELP
Select Function XX
```

◄ Display will appear as shown

– Press buttons 1 and 5 to select Function 15, “Readiness code”

– Press Q button to confirm entry

```
Readiness code
00000000 – Test complete
```

◄ Display must appear as shown when all diagnostic Functions have been completed

– Press → button

– Press 0 and 6 buttons to select Function 06, “End output”

– Press Q button to confirm entry

```
Readiness code
11101011 – Test not complete
```

◄ Display will appear as shown (for example) if one or more of the diagnostic checks has not been completed

– Press → button

Note:

If DTC memory was erased, Readiness code must be created again.

– Readiness code, creating:
⇒ page G 01-35

– Readiness code, reading:
⇒ page G 01-33

Relevance of 8 digit Readiness code number

Readiness code is created when ALL 8 cells are filled with zeroes.								
x	x	x	x	x	x	x	x	Diagnostic Function
							0	Three-Way Catalytic Converter
						0		Three-Way Catalytic Converter Heating
					0			Fuel Tank Ventilation System
				0				Secondary Air Injection System
			0					A/C
		0						Oxygen Sensor
	0							Oxygen Sensor Heating
0								Exhaust Gas Recirculation (EGR) System

Readiness code, creating

Note:

(05.96 ➤) When creating the Readiness code, each diagnostic Function will be individually recognised and displayed in an 8 digit number block allowing the viewer to immediately see which (if any) Function did not reach completion.

Special tools, testers and auxiliary items

- VAG 1551/VAG 1552 Scan Tool using adaptor cable VAG 1551/3

Notes:

- *During test sequence, engine must not be switched OFF!*
- *If specifications are obtained before the time limit expires, the test sequence can be advanced to the next step.*

Test sequence

Work step 1:

– Switch ON ignition

– Connect Scan Tool

– With ignition switched ON, press 0 and 1 buttons to select Address Word 01, “Engine Electronics”
⇒ page G 01-7

Relevance of 8–digit number block in display zone 4

Relevance if display 1								
1	2	3	4	5	6	7	8	Diagnostic conditions
							1	Malfunction stored in DTC memory
						1		ERROR-Bit = malfunction detected during diagnostic
					1			CYCLE Bit = Diagnostic completed
				1				ACTIVE Bit = Diagnostic currently active
			x					Function Bit [1)]
		x						Function Bit [1)]
	x							Function Bit [1)]
x								Function Bit [1)]

[1)] The relevance of the Function Bit varies depending upon the work step.

Notes:

- *There must not be any malfunctions stored in DTC memory and no malfunctions should be detected during this diagnostic.*
- *If the CYCLE bit has a 1, the diagnostic is completed and the test sequence can be implemented.*
- *The specifications for the function bits must only be satisfied during the diagnostic phase (ACTIVE bit = 1).*
- *An x in the diagnostic status box means the displayed value can be either a 0 or a 1.*

Work step 2:

```
Rapid data transfer                    HELP
Select Function XX
```

Display will appear as shown

- Press 0 and 2 buttons to select Function 02, "Check DTC memory" and confirm entry with Q button
- Press Q button to enter selection

```
X malfunctions recognised!
```

Display will show number of malfunctions stored or "No malfunction recognised!"

- Locate and eliminate malfunctions printed out as per Diagnostic Trouble Code (DTC) table

⇒ page G 01-14

- Press → button

Work step 3:

```
Rapid data transfer                    HELP
Select Function XX
```

Display will appear as shown

- Press 0 and 5 buttons to select Function 05, "Erase DTC memory"
- Press Q button to enter selection

```
Rapid data transfer                       →
DTC memory is erased!
```

Display will appear as shown

- Press → button

Work step 4:

- Start engine and let idle

Work step 5:

```
Rapid data transfer                    HELP
Select Function XX
```

Display will appear as shown

- Press 0 and 8 buttons to select Function 08, "Read measuring value block"
- Press Q button to enter selection

```
Read measured value block              HELP
Input display group number XXX
```

Display will appear as shown

- Press 1, 0 and 3 buttons to select "Display group number 103"
- Press Q button to enter selection

```
Read measured value block   103           →
    1          2          3               4
```

Display will appear as shown (1 to 4 = Display zones)

- Increase engine speed between 3000 and 3500 rpm and check specifications after 60 seconds

	Display zones			
	1	2	3	4
Display group 103				
Display	xx.xx ms	xxx.x°C	xxx.x°C	xxxx xxxx
Indicated	Engine load	Engine Coolant tempera-ture	Exhaust gas temperature	Diagnostic conditions
Specific.	---	At least 40°C	Approx. 360°C	xx1x xx00
Working range	1.4 to 2.4 ms	-46.5 to 141.0°C	0.0 to 999.9°C	x = Not relevant

Relevance of 8 digit number block in display zone 4								
1	2	3	4	5	6	7	8	Specifications of diagnostic conditions
		1						Oxygen control active
						0		Diagnostic reveals: NO malfunctions
							0	DTC memory: NO stored DTC's

– Press → button

Work step 6:

Diagnostic: Secondary Air Injection system

Test conditions

♦ Vehicle stationary, engine idling

```
Rapid data transfer                HELP
Select Function XX
```

◄ Display will appear as shown

– Press 0 and 4 buttons to select Function 04, "Basic setting"

– Press Q button to enter selection

```
Initiate basic setting             HELP
Input display group number XXX
```

◄ Display will appear as shown

– Press 1, 6 and 0 buttons to select "Display group number 160"

– Press Q button to enter selection

```
Basic setting 160                     →
     1        2        3              4
```

◄ Display will appear as shown (1 to 4 = Display zones)

– Start engine and let idle

– Check specifications after 20 seconds

	Display zones			
	1	2	3	4
Display group160				
Display	xxx.x°C	xx.x %	xx.x %	xxxx xxxx
Indicated	Engine Coolant temperature	Secondary Air Injection valve open	Secondary Air Injection pump running	Diagnostic conditions
Specs	At least 60°C	0.7%	25%	xx11 x100
		Secondary Air Injection valve causes deviations in Oxygen control	Secondary Air Injection valve causes deviations in Oxygen control	x = Not relevant
Working range	-46.5 to 141.0°C			

Relevance of 8 digit number block in display zone 4								
1	2	3	4	5	6	7	8	Specifications of diagnostic conditions
		1						Engine idling
			1					Vehicle stationary
					1			CYCLE bit = Diagnostic is active
						0		Diagnostic is malfunction free
							0	DTC memory is malfunction free

– Press C button

Work step 7:

```
Initiate basic setting              HELP
Input display group number XXX
```

◄ Display will appear as shown

– Press 1, 0 and 3 buttons to select “Display group number 103”

– Press Q button to enter input

```
Basic setting 103                      →
     1          2          3           4
```

◄ Display will appear as shown (1 to 4 = Display zones)

– Increase engine speed between 2200 and 3300 rpm and check specifications after 120 seconds

	Display zones 1	2	3	4
Display group 103				
Display	xx.xx ms	xxx.x°C	xxx.x°C	xxxx xxxx
Indicated	Engine load	Engine Coolant temperature	Exhaust gas temperature	Diagnostic conditions
Specs		At least 60°C	At least 360°C	xx1x xx00
	---		---	x = Not relevant
Working range	1.4 to 2.4 ms	-46.5 to 141.0°C	0.0 to 999.9°C	

Relevance of 8 digit number block in display zone 4								
1	2	3	4	5	6	7	8	Specifications of diagnostic conditions
		1						Oxygen control active
						0		Diagnostic is malfunction free
							0	DTC memory is malfunction free

– Press C button

Work step 8:

Diagnostic: Oxygen sensor aging (regulating frequency extended)

Initiate basic setting HELP
Input display group number XXX

◄ Display will appear as shown

– Press 1, 3 and 1 buttons to select "Display group number 131"

– Press Q button to enter input

Basic setting 131 →
1 2 3 4

◄ Display will appear as shown (1 to 4 = Display zones)

– Allow engine to idle for at least 30 seconds and then check the specifications

Note:

The 30 second idle period also applies to the EGR diagnostic.

	Display zones			
	1	2	3	4
Display group 131				
Display	xxxx rpm	x.xxx Volts	xxxx ms	xxxx xxxx
Indicated	Engine speed	Voltage of probe after Three-Way catalyst	Sensor aging	Diagnostic conditions
Specs	650 to 750 rpm	0.01 to 1.00 Volts fluctuating	–1200 to 1200 ms	xx11 x100
	---		Sensor aging: TV displacement by Oxygen control after catalyst	x = Not relevant
Working range	650 to 5500 rpm	0.01 to 1.00 Volts	–1200 to 1200 ms	

Relevance of 8 digit number block in display zone 4								
1	2	3	4	5	6	7	8	Specifications of diagnostic conditions
		1						Oxygen control (after catalytic converter) active
			1					Oxygen control (before catalytic converter) active
					1			CYCLE bit = Diagnostic active
						0		Diagnostic is malfunction free
							0	DTC memory is malfunction free

– Press C button

Work step 9:

Diagnostic: Oxygen control adaption in partial load range

```
Initiate basic setting          HELP
Input display group number XX
```

◄ Display will appear as shown

– Press 1, 2 and 5 buttons to select "Display group number 125"

– Press Q button to enter input

```
Basic setting  125                 →
    1        2        3        4
```

◄ Display will appear as shown (1 to 4 = Display zones)

Note:

Avoid over-revving before performing this step because the catalyst will store the extra Oxygen. As a result, the diagnostic will be blocked for at least 10 seconds.

– Perform road-test during which the following requirements are fulfilled

- ♦ Engage transmission range 2 (automatic) or 2nd gear (manual)
- ♦ Engine speed must be kept between 2500 and 4000 rpm

– Check specifications during road-test

- ♦ 2nd technician necessary

– Continue road-test until specifications are obtained

	Display zones			
	1	2	3	4
Display group 125				
Display	xxxx rpm	x.x%	x.x%	xxxx xxxx
Indicated	Engine speed	Oxygen sensor adaption under partial load	Oxygen sensor adaption at idle	Diagnostic conditions
Specs	2500 to 3500 rpm	–10 to 10%	–12.4 to 12.4%	01x1 x100
	Depending upon driving conditions			x = Not relevant
Working range	650 to 5500 rpm	–25 to 25%	–12.4 to 12.4%	

Relevance of 8 digit number block in display zone 4								
1	2	3	4	5	6	7	8	Specifications of diagnostic conditions
0								Reduced correction range active
	1							Partial load adaption active
			1					Oxygen control (before catalytic conv.) active
					1			CYCLE bit = Diagnostic is active
						0		Diagnostic is malfunction free
							0	DTC memory is malfunction free

– Press C button

– Continue with road-test for next test step (10)

Work step 10:

Diagnostic: EGR under partial load

Initiate basic setting HELP
Input display group number XX

◄ Display will appear as shown

– Press 1, 5 and 5 buttons to select "Display group number 155"

– Press Q button to enter input

Basic setting 155 →
1 2 3 4

◄ Display will appear as shown (1 to 4 = Display zones)

– Perform road-test during which the following requirements are fulfilled

♦ Engage transmission range 2 (automatic) or 2nd gear (manual)

♦ Engine speed must be kept between 2000 and 3500 rpm

– Check specifications during road-test

♦ 2nd technician necessary

♦ Road-test must be held constant for at least 20 seconds, until specifications are obtained

	Display zones			
	1	2	3	4
Display group 155				
Display	xxxx rpm	xx.x°C	xx.x°C	xxxx xxxx
Indicated	Engine speed	EGR temperature at idle	Temperature difference between idle and partial load	Diagnostic conditions
Specs	2000 to 3500 rpm	50°C minimum	approx. 50°C	1111 x100
	Depending upon driving conditions	30 seconds minimum		x = Not relevant
Working range	650 to 5500 rpm		No diagnostic at constant 50°C	

Relevance of 8 digit number block in display zone 4								
1	2	3	4	5	6	7	8	Specifications of diagnostic conditions
1								Engine temperature in permitted range
	1							Intake air temperature in permitted range
		1						Will only be recognised during road-test
			1					Altitude factor in permitted range
					1			CYCLE bit = Diagnostic is active
						0		Diagnostic is malfunction free
							0	DTC memory is malfunction free

– Press C button

Work step 11:

Diagnostic: Oxygen sensor adaption, Closed Throttle Position

Test conditions

- Coolant temperature 60°C (140°F) minimum
⇒ Display group 001, display zone 2

- Intake manifold temperature 80°C (176°F) maximum
⇒ Display group 003, display zone 4

Basic setting 125			→
1	2	3	4

◄ Display will appear as shown (1 to 4 = Display zones)

– Run engine at idle and check specifications after 40 seconds

	Display zones			
	1	2	3	4
Display group 125				
Display	xxxx rpm	x.x%	x.x%	xxxx xxxx
Indicated	Engine speed	Oxygen sensor adaption under partial load	Oxygen sensor adaption during idle	Diagnostic conditions
Specs	650 to 750 rpm	–23 to 23%	–12.4 to 12.4%	01x1 x100
				x = Not relevant
Working range	650 to 5500 rpm	–23 to 23%	–12.4 to 12.4%	

Relevance of 8 digit number block in display zone 4								
1	2	3	4	5	6	7	8	Specifications of diagnostic conditions
0								Reduced correction range active
	1							Partial load adaption active
			1					Oxygen control (before catalytic conv.) active
					1			CYCLE bit = Diagnostic is active
						0		Diagnostic is malfunction free
							0	DTC memory is malfunction free

– Press C button

Work step 12:

Diagnostic: Oxygen sensor aging, extended regulating frequency

Test conditions

- ♦ Vehicle stationary

Initiate basic setting	HELP
Input display group number XX	

◄ Display will appear as shown

– Press 1, 3 and 0 buttons to select "Display group number 130"

– Press Q button to enter selection

Basic setting 130			→
1	2	3	4

◄ Display will appear as shown (1 to 4 = Display zones)

– Increase engine speed between 2500 and 3500 rpm for 20 seconds and check specifications

	Display zones			
	1	2	3	4
Display group 130				
Display	xxxx rpm	xx s	x	xxxx xxxx
Indicated	Engine speed	Seconds	Period counter	Diagnostic conditions
Specs	2500 to 3500 rpm	0 to 2 seconds	10	1111 x100
		Period duration of Oxygen control (before catalytic converter)	Oxygen sensor periods recognized	
Working range	650 to 5500 rpm	0 to 3 seconds		

Relevance of 8 digit number block in display zone 4								
1	2	3	4	5	6	7	8	Specifications of diagnostic conditions
1								Oxygen control (before catalytic conv.) active
	1							Speed/load range OK
		1						Catalyst has its minimum temperature
			1					Sensor heating diagnostic (before cat. conv.)
					1			CYCLE bit = Diagnostic active
						0		Diagnostic is malfunction free
							0	DTC memory is malfunction free

– Press C button

Work step 13:

Diagnostic: Three-Way catalytic converter

Initiate basic setting HELP
Input display group number XX

◄ Display will appear as shown

– Press 1, 3 and 6 buttons to select "Display group number 136"

– Press Q button to enter selection

Basic setting 136 →
1 2 3 4

◄ Display will appear as shown (1 to 4 = Display zones)

– Increase engine speed between 2500 and 3500 rpm and check specifications after 120 seconds

	Display zones			
	1	2	3	4
Display group 136				
Display	xxxx rpm	xxx.x°C	x.xx	xxxx xxxx
Indicated	Engine speed	Exhaust gas temperature	Amplitude ratio	Diagnostic conditions
Specs	2500 to 3500 rpm	At least 360°C	max. 0.15	1111x100
				x = Not relevant
Working range	650 to 5500 rpm	0.0 to 999.9°C		

Relevance of 8 digit number block in display zone 4								
1	2	3	4	5	6	7	8	Specifications of diagnostic conditions
1								Oxygen control (before cat) active
	1							Catalyst has reached minimum temperature
		1						Load range OK
			1					Oxygen sensor (after cat) operationally ready
					1			CYCLE bit = Diagnostic active
						0		Diagnostic is malfunction free
							0	DTC memory is malfunction free

– Press C button

Work step 14:

Diagnostic: Fuel tank venting system

Test conditions

♦ Vehicle stationary

♦ All electrical consumers switched OFF (radiator fan must not run during the check)

♦ A/C switched OFF

Note:

The engine must not be loaded during this diagnostic because it will interrupt the diagnostic and will not re-start again until the engine is revved-up.

Initiate basic setting	HELP
Input display group number XX	

◄ Display will appear as shown

– Press 1, 5 and 0 buttons to select "Display group number 150"

– Press Q button to enter selection

Basic setting 150			→
1	2	3	4

◄ Display will appear as shown (1 to 4 = Display zones)

– Run engine for 30 seconds at idle and check specifications

	Display zones			
	1	2	3	4
Display group 150				
Display	xx%	x.x%	x.xx g/s	xxxx xxxx
Indicated	Opening degrees	Oxygen control	Idle speed control	Diagnostic conditions
Specs	0%	–7 to –23 or 7 to 23	max. 0.39 g/s	11xx xx00
	Fuel tank vent valve minimum opening	Oxygen control deviations during diagnostic	Oxygen control deviations during diagnostic	x = Not relevant
Working range	0 to 100%	–25 to 25		

Relevance of 8 digit number block in display zone 4								
1	2	3	4	5	6	7	8	Specifications of diagnostic conditions
1								Oxygen control (before catalytic converter) active
	1							Idle (Closed Throttle Position)
		1						Temp. when starting: warmer than –5°C
			0					Altitude: up to 2600 meters (1.6 miles) above sea level maximum
					1			CYCLE bit = Diagnostic active
						0		Diagnostic is malfunction free
							0	DTC memory is malfunction free

– Press → button

Work step 15:

– Display Readiness code
⇒ page G 01-33

If Readiness code still not OK:

– Perform work steps 16 to 23

Rapid data transfer HELP Select Function XX

Initiate basic setting HELP Input display group number XX

Basic setting 180 → 1 2 3 4

Work step 16:

Diagnostic: Vehicle Speed Sensor

◄ Display will appear as shown

– Press buttons 0 and 4 for the "Introduction of basic setting" function and confirm entry with Q button

◄ Display will appear as shown

– Press 1, 8 and 0 buttons to select "Display group number 180"

– Press Q button to enter selection

◄ Display will appear as shown (1 to 4 = Display zones)

– Perform road-test during which the following requirements are fulfilled

♦ Transmission with range 2 or 3 selected

♦ Check specifications during road-test (2nd technician necessary)

– Hold engine speed above 3500 rpm for 5 seconds

then

– Release accelerator pedal for 3 seconds

♦ After 3 seconds,driving speed must still be 20 km/h (12 mph) minimum and have been in overrun for 2 seconds minimum

	Display zones			
	1	2	3	4
Display group 180				
Display	xxxx rpm	xxx.x°C	km/h	xxxx xxxx
Indicated	Engine speed	Engine Coolant temperature	Vehicle speed	Diagnostic conditions
Specs	5 to 10 seconds, 3500 rpm minimum	80°C minimum	25 to 50 km/h	x111x100
				x = Not relevant
Working range	650 to 5500 rpm	-46.5 to 141.0°C		

Relevance of 8 digit number block in display zone 4								
1	2	3	4	5	6	7	8	Specifications of diagnostic conditions
	1							Engine speed for this check is OK
		1						Engine Coolant Temperature OK
			1					Overrun cut-off is active
					1			CYCLE bit = Diagnostic is active
						0		Diagnostic is malfunction free
							0	DTC memory is malfunction free

– Press C button

Work step 17:

Diagnostic: Knock Sensor 1

Test conditions

- Vehicle stationary

Initiate basic setting	HELP
Input display group number XX	

◄ Display will appear as shown

– Press 1, 4 and 5 buttons to select "Display group number 145"

– Press Q button to enter selection

Basic setting 145			→
1	2	3	4

◄ Display will appear as shown (1 to 4 = Display zones)

– Increase engine speed to 3200 rpm minimum

– Check specifications after 15 seconds

	Display zones			
	1	2	3	4
Display group 145				
Display	xxxx rpm	x	x	xxxx xxxx
Indicated	Engine speed	Knock sensor 1	Open circuit counter	Diagnostic conditions
Specs	3200 rpm, minimum	7 maximum	0	xxxx 1100
		Amplification factor of knock sensor signal	Open circuit diagnosed in wiring	x = Not relevant
Working range	650 to 5500 rpm			

Relevance of 8 digit number block in display zone 4								
1	2	3	4	5	6	7	8	Specifications of diagnostic conditions
				1				Knock sensor diagnostic is active
					1			CYCLE bit = Diagnostic is active
						0		Diagnostic is malfunction free
							0	DTC memory is malfunction free

– Press 3 button (VAG 1551) or ↑ button (VAG 1552)

Work step 18:

Diagnostic: Knock Sensor 2

Test conditions

♦ Vehicle stationary

– Press 1, 4 and 6 buttons to select "Display group number 146"

– Press Q button to enter selection

Basic setting 146			→
1	2	3	4

◄ Display will appear as shown (1 to 4 = Display zones)

– Increase engine speed to 3200 rpm minimum

– Check specifications after 15 seconds

	Display zones			
	1	2	3	4
Display group 146				
Display	xxxx rpm	x	x	xxxx xxxx
Indicated	Engine speed	Knock Sensor 2	Open circuit counter	Diagnostic conditions
Working range	650 to 5500 rpm			
Specs	3200 rpm minimum	7 maximum	0	xxxx 1100
		Amplification factor of knock sensor signal	Open circuit diagnosed	x = Not relevant

Relevance of 8 digit number block in display zone 4								
1	2	3	4	5	6	7	8	Specifications of diagnostic conditions
				1				Knock sensor diagnostic is active
					1			CYCLE bit = Diagnostic is active
						0		Diagnostic is malfunction free
							0	DTC memory is malfunction free

– Press C button

Work step 19:

Diagnostic: Oxygen sensor (before catalytic converter)

Initiate basic setting HELP Input display group number XXX

◄ Display will appear as shown

- Press 1, 1 and 5 buttons to select "Display group number 115"
- Press Q button to enter selection

Basic setting 115 → 1 2 3 4

◄ Display will appear as shown (1 to 4 = Display zones)

- Increase engine speed between 2200 and 2800 rpm and check specifications

	Display zones			
	1	2	3	4
Display group 115				
Display	xxx.x°C	xxx.x°C	x.xx Volts	xxxx xxxx
Indicated	Engine Coolant temperature	Exhaust gas temperature	Oxygen sensor Voltage (before catalytic conv.)	Diagnostic conditions
Specs	60°C minimum	Approx. 360°C	Fluctuating	1011 x100
		---	---	x = Not relevant
Working range	-46.5 to 141.0°C	0.0 to 999.9°C	0 to 1.0 Volt	

Relevance of 8 digit number block in display zone 4								
1	2	3	4	5	6	7	8	Specifications of diagnostic conditions
1								Oxygen sensor (before catalytic converter) is switched ON
	0							Oxygen sensor is operationally warm
		1						Oxygen sensor (before catalytic converter) operationally OK
			1					Oxygen control (before catalyst) is active
					1			CYCLE bit = Diagnostic is active
						0		Diagnostic is malfunction free
							0	DTC memory is malfunction free

- Press 3 button (VAG 1551) or ↑ button (VAG 1552)

Work step 20:

Diagnostic: Oxygen Sensor (after catalytic converter)

– Press 1, 1 and 6 buttons to select "Display group number 116"

– Press Q button to enter selection

Basic setting 116			→
1	2	3	4

◄ Display will appear as shown (1 to 4 = Display zones)

– Increase engine speed between 2200 and 2800 rpm for 15 seconds and check specifications

	Display zones			
	1	2	3	4
Display group 116				
Display	xxxx ms	xxx.x°C	x.xx V	xxxx xxxx
Indicated	Oxygen sensor (after catalytic converter) switching time delay	Exhaust gas temperature	Oxygen sensor Voltage (after catalytic converter)	Diagnostic conditions
Specs	0 to 1200 ms	At least 360°C	At least 0.6 Volts	1011 xx1 00
			Measured in overrun	x = Not relevant
Working range		0.0 to 999.9°C	0 to 1.0 Volt	

Relevance of 8 digit number block in display zone 4								
1	2	3	4	5	6	7	8	Specifications of diagnostic conditions
1								Sensor heating (after catalytic converter) is switched ON
	0							Oxygen sensor is operationally warm
		1						Oxygen sensor (after catalytic converter) is operationally ready
			1					Oxygen control (before cat. conv.) is active
						0		Diagnostic is malfunction free
							0	DTC memory is malfunction free

– Press C button

Work step 21:

Diagnostic: Oxygen Sensor heating (before and after catalytic converter)

Initiate basic setting	HELP
Input display group number XXX	

◄ Display will appear as shown

- Press 1, 2 and 0 buttons to select "Display group number 120"
- Press Q button to enter selection

Basic setting 120			→
1	2	3	4

◄ Display will appear as shown (1 to 4 = Display zones)

- Increase engine speed between 2200 and 2800 rpm and check specifications

	Display zones			
	1	2	3	4
Display group 120				
Display	xxx.x°C	xxx s	xx.x Ω	xxxx xxxx
Indicated	Exhaust gas temperature	Seconds	Resistance	Diagnostic conditions
Specs	At least 360°C	120 seconds	4.5 to 15.6 Ω	1111 x100
		Time between sensor heating switch-on and start of diagnostic	Oxygen sensor (before catalytic converter) heater resistance	x = Not relevant
Working range	0.0 to 999.9°C	0.0 to 500 seconds	0.0 to 65.0 Ω	

Relevance of 8 digit number block in display zone 4								
1	2	3	4	5	6	7	8	Specifications of diagnostic conditions
1								Sensor heating (before catalytic converter), switch-on
	1							Sensor (before catalytic converter), vaporisation point exceeded
		1						Sensor (before catalytic converter), operationally ready
			1					Sensor heating (before catalytic converter), operationally ready
					1			CYCLE bit = Diagnostic is active
						0		Diagnostic is malfunction free
							0	DTC memory is malfunction free

- Press 3 button (VAG 1551) or ↑ button (VAG 1552)

Diagnostic: Oxygen Sensor heating (before and after catalytic converter)

- Press 1, 2 and 1 buttons to select "Display group number 121"
- Press Q button to enter selection

Basic setting 121			→
1	2	3	4

◄ Display will appear as shown (1 to 4 = Display zones)

- Increase engine speed between 2200 and 2800 rpm and check specifications

	Display zones			
	1	2	3	4
Display group 121				
Display	xxx.x°C	xxx s	xx.x Ω	xxxx xxxx
Indicated	Exhaust gas temperature	Seconds	Resistance	Diagnostic conditions
Specs	At least 360°C	120 s	4.5 to 15.6 Ω	1111 x100
		Time between Oxygen sensor heating switch-on and start of diagnostic	Oxygen sensor (before catalytic converter) heater resistance	x = Not relevant
Working range	0.0 to 999.9°C	0.0 to 500 seconds	0.0 to 65.0 Ω	

Relevance of 8 digit number block in display zone 4								
1	2	3	4	5	6	7	8	Specifications of diagnostic conditions
1								Sensor heating (after catalytic converter), switch-on
	1							Sensor (after catalytic converter), vaporisation point exceeded
		1						Sensor (after catalytic converter), operationally ready
			1					Sensor heating (after catalytic converter), operationally ready
					1			CYCLE bit = Diagnostic active

Relevance of 8 digit number block in display zone 4								
						0		Diagnostic is malfunction free
							0	DTC memory is malfunction free

– Press C button

Work step 22:

Diagnostic: Throttle Valve Control Module

Note:

There are no specifications for this diagnostic. The values shown in the display zones are typical for this diagnostic. If other values are shown it does NOT indicate a system malfunction. The diagnostic functions run in the background during the check.

Initiate basic setting	HELP
Input display group number XXX	

◄ Display will appear as shown

– Press 1, 4 and 0 buttons to select "Display group number 140"

– Press Q button to enter selection

Basic setting 140			→
1	2	3	4

◄ Display will appear as shown (1 to 4 = Display zones)

– Run engine at idle

	Display zones			
	1	2	3	4
Display group 140				
Display	x.xx ms	xx%	x.x Volts	xxxx xxxx
Indicated	Engine load	Idle Air Control Valve position	Throttle Position sensor voltage	Diagnostic conditions
Specs	1.4 to 2.4 ms	65 to 85%	3.0 to 4.0 Volts	—

– Run engine at idle

– Press 3 button (VAG 1551) or ↑ button (VAG 1552)

Basic setting 141			→
1	2	3	4

◄ Display will appear as shown (1 to 4 = Display zones)

– Run engine at idle

	Display zones			
	1	2	3	4
Display group 141				
Display		xxx%		xxxx xxxx
Indicated	Throttle valve actuator	Throttle valve actuator	Throttle valve actuator	Diagnostic conditions
Specs	65 to 85%	65 to 85%	90 to 170	
	Actual position of throttle valve actuator	Throttle valve actuator specification	Throttle valve actuator integrator	

– Press 3 button (VAG 1551) or ↑ button (VAG 1552)

Basic setting 142			→
1	2	3	4

◄ Display will appear as shown (1 to 4 = Display zones)

– Run engine at idle

	Display zones			
	1	2	3	4
Display group 142				
Display	xx.x%	xx.x%	xx.x%	xxxx xxxx
Specs	65 to 85%	80 to 90%	20 to 30%	
	Throttle valve actuator emergency running cross section	Throttle valve actuator minimum stop	Throttle valve actuator maximum stop	

– Press → button

Work step 23:

– Read Readiness code
⇒ page G 01-33

– Press 0 and 6 buttons to select Function 06, “End output”

– Press Q button to enter selection

Function 03, “Output Diagnostic Test Mode”

The “Output Diagnostic Test Mode” (DTM) actuates the following components in the sequence shown:

1. Fuel Injector, Cyl. 1   N30
2. Fuel Injector, Cyl. 2   N31
3. Fuel Injector, Cyl. 3   N32
4. Fuel Injector, Cyl. 4   N33
5. Fuel Injector, Cyl. 5   N83
6. Fuel Injector, Cyl. 6   N84
7. EVAP canister purge regulator valve   N80
8. EGR vacuum regulator solenoid valve   N18
9. Secondary Air Injection solenoid valve   N112
10. Secondary Air Injection pump relay   J299

Special tools, testers and auxiliary items

- ♦ VAG 1551 Scan Tool with VAG 1551/3 adaptor cable
- ♦ VAG 1598/18 Test Box
- ♦ VW 1594 Adapter kit
- ♦ VAG 1527B LED Tester

Test conditions

- ● Fuses 15, 18 and S130 OK
- ● Throttle Position switch OK
⇒ checking, page G 24-72

Notes:

- ♦ *To activate the fuel injectors, the Throttle Position switch (in the Throttle Valve Control Module) must also be operated*
- ♦ *The “Output Diagnostic Test Mode” will activate each injector 5 times via the ECM*

Work sequence

– Connect VAG 1551/VAG 1552 Scan Tool

– With ignition switched ON, press 0 and 1 buttons to select Address word 01, “Engine Electronics”
⇒ page G 01-7

```
Rapid data transfer                    HELP
Select Function XX
```

◄ Display will appear as shown

– Operate Scan Tool taking displayed information into account

– Press 0 and 3 buttons to select Function 03 “Output Diagnostic Test Mode”

```
Rapid data transfer                       Q
03 “Output Diagnostic Test Mode”
```

◄ Display will appear as shown

"Output Diagnostic Test Mode" →
Injector cylinder 1 -N30

Cylinder 1 injector N30. activating

– Press Q button to enter selection

◄ Display will appear as shown

– Open throttle to Wide Open position and then close completely

- ♦ Cylinder 1 injector must click several times

Cylinders 2 through 6 Fuel injectors, individual activation

– Press → button

– Open throttle to Wide Open position and then close completely

- ♦ Cylinder 2 injector must click several times

To skip over an individual injector

– Press → button

If one or more injectors do NOT click:

– Proceed with "Output Diagnostic Test Mode" until completed

– Switch OFF ignition

– Check Fuel injector activation (resistance and amperage supply) ⇒ page G 24-121

"Output Diagnostic Test Mode" →
EVAP canister purge regulator valve -N80

EVAP canister purge regulator valve N80, activating

– Press → button

◄ Display will appear as shown

- ♦ EVAP canister purge regulator valve (mounted behind coolant expansion tank) must click until the next DTM component is selected by pressing → button

– Disconnect EVAP canister at EVAP canister purge regulator valve

– Attach piece of scrap hose to disconnected valve port

– Blow into hose (in direction of Throttle Valve Control Module) during "Output Diagnostic Test Mode"

- ♦ Valve must open and close

If valve does not open and close:

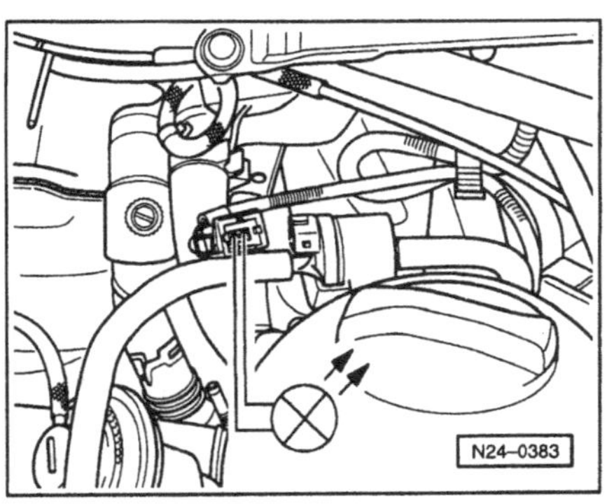

◄ – Disconnect 2-pin harness connector from N80 valve and connect VAG 1527B LED tester to disconnected connector using jumper wires from VW 1594 adaptor kit

- ♦ LED must flash

If LED flashes:

– Proceed with "Output Diagnostic Test Mode" until completed

– Switch OFF ignition

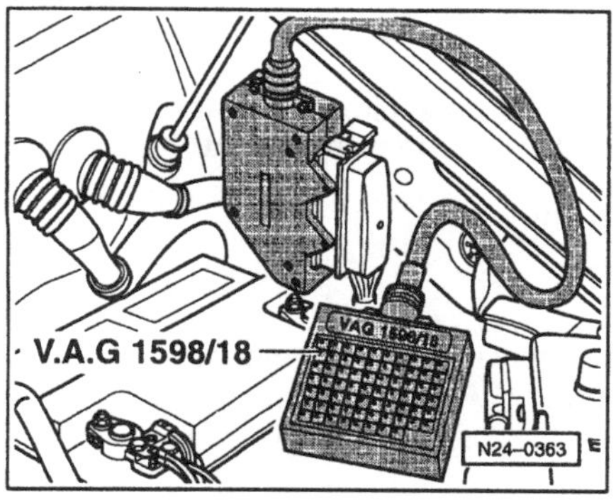

- Replace EVAP canister purge regulator valve N80
⇒ Repair Group 20

If LED does not flash:

- Switch OFF ignition
- Connect VAG 1598/18 Test Box to ECM harness connector

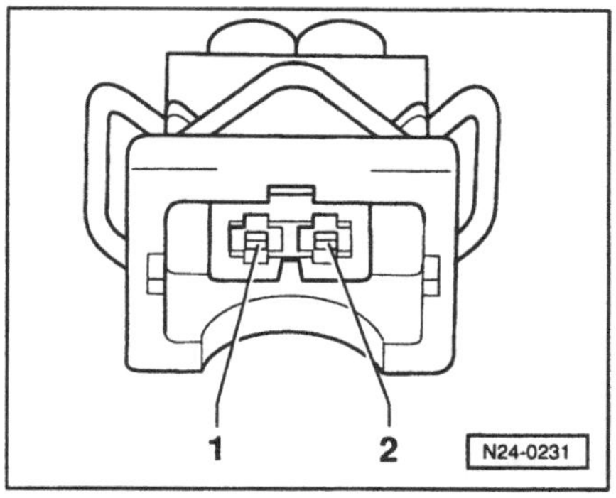

- Using wiring diagram, check for open circuit between Test Box socket 31 and terminal 1 of 2-pin harness connector
  - ♦ resistance: 1.5 Ω maximum

If wiring OK:

- Check N80 voltage supply using wiring diagram, replace ECM J220 if necessary
⇒ page G 24-7 (item 3)

EGR vacuum regulator solenoid valve N18, activating

- Press → button

"Output Diagnostic Test Mode" →
EGR vacuum regulator solenoid valve -N18

Display will appear as shown

- ♦ EGR valve must click until next DTM component is selected by pressing → button

If EGR valve does not click:

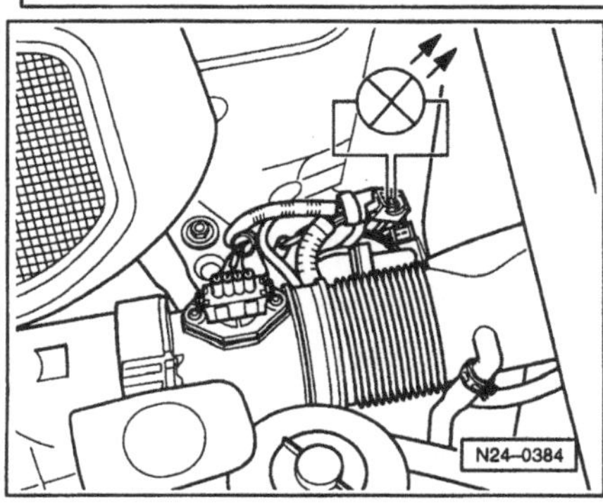

- Disconnect 2-pin harness connector from N18 valve and connect VAG 1527B LED tester to disconnected connector using jumper wires from VW 1594 adaptor kit
  - ♦ LED must flash

If LED flashes:

- Replace EGR vacuum regulator solenoid valve
⇒ Repair Group 26

If LED does not flash:

- Switch OFF ignition
- Connect VAG 1598/18 Test Box to ECM harness connector

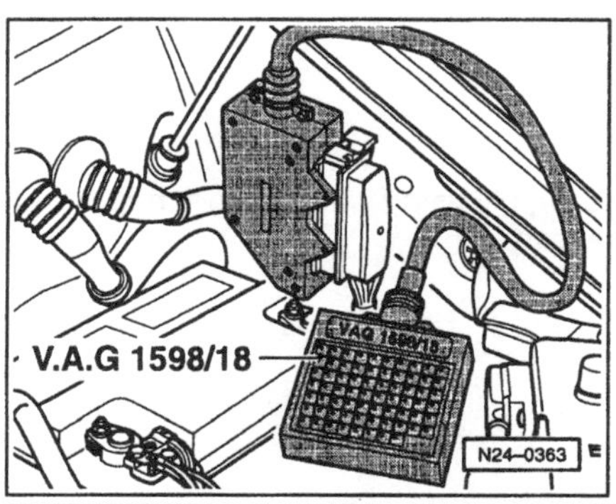

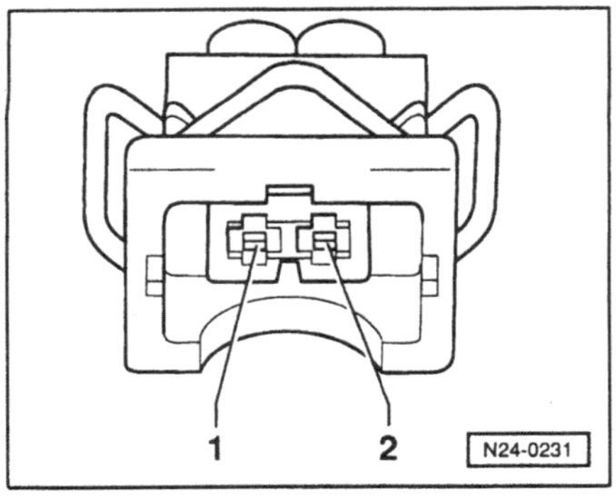

- Using wiring diagram, check for open circuit between Test Box socket 30 and terminal 2 of 2-pin harness connector
  - ♦ resistance: 1.5 Ω maximum

If wiring OK:

- Check valve N18 voltage supply using wiring diagram, replace ECM J220 if necessary
⇒ page G 24-7 (item 3)

Secondary Air Injection solenoid valve N112, activating

- Press → button

"Output Diagnostic Test Mode"	→
Secondary Air Injection solenoid valve N112	

Display will appear as shown

- ♦ Secondary Air Injection solenoid valve must click until next DTM component is activated by pressing → button

If valve does not click:

- Disconnect 2-pin harness connector from N112 valve and connect VAG 1527B LED tester to disconnected connector using jumper wires from VW 1594 adaptor kit
  - ♦ LED must blink

- Replace Secondary Air Injection solenoid valve N112
⇒ Repair Group 26

If LED does NOT blink:

- Switch OFF ignition
- Connect VAG 1598/18 Test Box to ECM harness connector

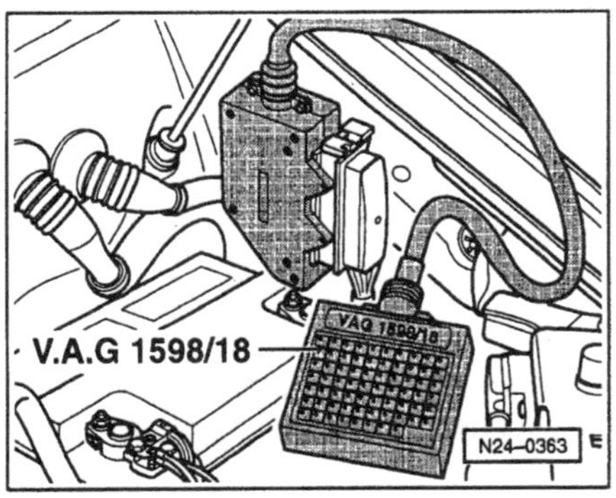

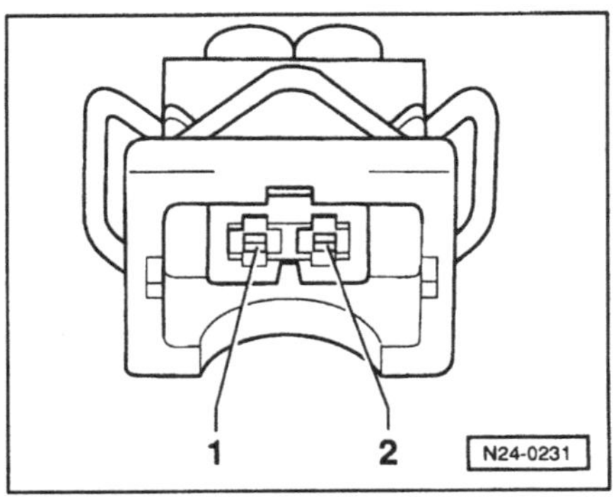

- Using wiring diagram, check for open circuit between Test Box socket 50 and terminal 1 of 2-pin harness connector
  - ♦ resistance: 1.5 Ω maximum

If wiring OK:

- Check N112 valve voltage supply using wiring diagram, replace J220 ECM if necessary
⇒ page G 24-7 (item 3)

Secondary Air Injection pump relay J299, activating

– Press → button

"Output Diagnostic Test Mode" →
Secondary Air Injection pump relay -J299

◄ Display will appear as shown

- ♦ The Secondary Air Injection pump relay J299 activates the Secondary Air Injection pump motor V101 which runs at intervals until the "Output Diagnostic Test Mode" is terminated by pressing the → button

If motor does NOT run at intervals:

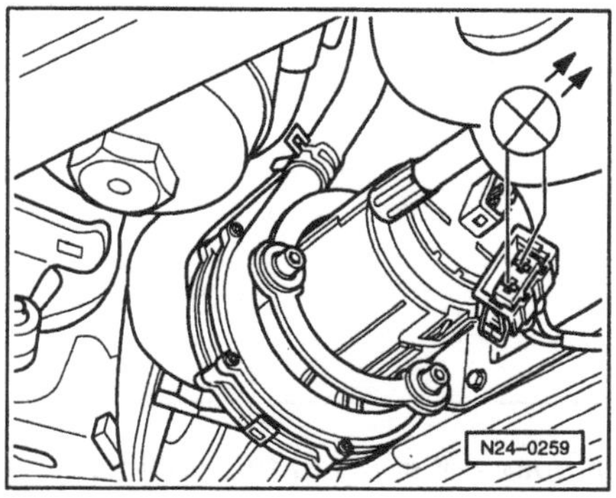

◄ – Disconnect 2-pin harness connector from V101 motor and connect VAG 1527B LED tester to disconnected connector using jumper wires from VW 1594 adaptor kit

- ♦ LED must blink

– Replace Secondary Air Injection pump motor V101
⇒ Repair Group 26

If LED does NOT blink:

– Check fuse S130
⇒ wiring diagram

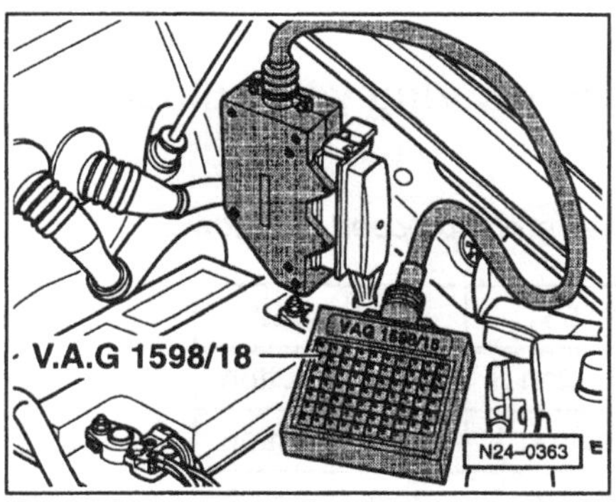

If fuse is OK:

– Switch OFF ignition

◄ – Connect VAG 1598/18 Test Box to ECM harness connector

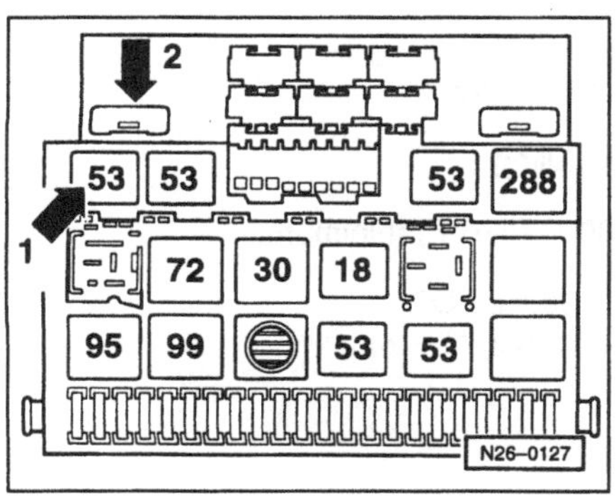

◄ – Remove Secondary Air Injection pump relay (arrow 1) from fuse/relay panel

Note:

- ♦ *If tools are required to remove relays or Control Modules from the fuse/relay panel, first disconnect the battery ground cable.*

> ***CAUTION!***
> ***Obtain the radio anti-theft code before disconnecting the battery ground cable!***

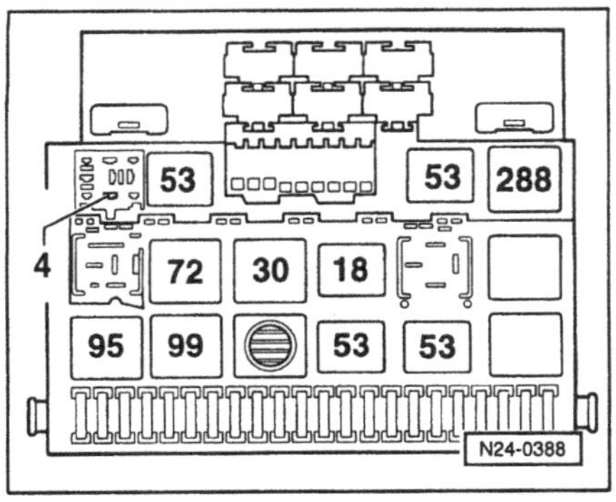

- Using wiring diagram, check for open circuit between Test Box socket 49 and terminal 4 of fuse/relay panel
  - ♦ resistance: 1.5 Ω maximum

If wiring OK:

- Check relay voltage supply using wiring diagram, replace relay if necessary replace Secondary Air Injection pump relay J299 if necessary

If relay OK:

- Replace ECM J220
⇒ page G 24-7 (item 3)

- Press → button

"Output Diagnostic Test Mode"	→
EVAP Canister Purge solenoid valve	N115

Display will appear as shown

> ***CAUTION!***
> ***Disregard this display! It does not apply to this vehicle.***

- Press → button

Rapid data transfer	HELP
Select Function XX	

Display will appear as shown

When you have completed "Output Diagnostic Test Mode" checks:

- Press 0 and 6 buttons to select Function 06 "End output"
- Press Q button to enter selection

Function 08, "Read measuring value block"

Note:
To change to another display group proceed as follows:

Display group	VAG 1551	VAG 1552
Higher	Press button 3	Press ↑ button
Lower	Press button 1	Press ↓ button
Skip	Press button C	Press button C

Test conditions

- ECM in Function 04 "Basic setting"
- Vehicle stationary, engine idling
- Engine oil temperature 80°C (176°F) minimum
- All electrical consumers switched OFF
  (radiator fan must not run during check)
- A/C switched OFF

Display group, overview

Display group 000 (decimal displayed value)		
• Engine idling, Control Module in "Basic setting" Function		
Display zones	**Specification**	**Corresponds to**
10 Partial load adaption value for Oxygen control (before catalytic converter)	118 to 138	–7 to 7%
9 Idle adaption value for Oxygen control (before catalytic converter)	241 to 255 or 0 to 14	–10 to 10%
8 Oxygen control	96 to 160	–5 to 5%
7 Idle air mass adaption value	112 to 144	–5 to 5 kg/h
6 Idle speed control (idle air mass)	112 to 144	–5 to 5 kg/h
5 Throttle angle	0 to 23	0 to 10 ∠°
4 Battery voltage	176 to 212	12.0 to 14.0 Volts
3 Engine speed	65 to 80	650 to 800 rpm
2 Engine load	28 to 58	1.4 to 2.4 ms
1 Engine coolant temperature	170 to 204	80 to 108°C

If one of the specifications not obtained:
⇒ page G 01-90, evaluating display group 000

For additional steps, see repair procedures

To terminate "Read measuring value block"

– Press → button

After terminating "Read measuring value block"

– Press 0 and 6 buttons to select Function 06, "End output"

– Press Q button to enter selection

Evaluating display group 000

Display zone: 1	Possible Malfunction cause	Corrective Steps
More than 204	♦ Engine Coolant Temperature sensor	– Check sensor ⇒ page G 24-93
Less than 170	♦ Engine Coolant Temperature sensor ♦ Thermostat faulty (open)	– Check sensor ⇒ page G 24-93 – Check thermostat ⇒ Repair Group 19
Display zone: 2	**Possible Malfunction cause**	**Corrective Steps**
More than 58	♦ Electrical consumer(s) switched ON ♦ Oxygen control at limit	– Switch OFF consumer(s) – Check Oxygen sensor and Oxygen control (before catalytic converter) ⇒ page G 24-28 – Check Oxygen sensor (before catalytic converter) for aging ⇒ page G 24-60
Less than 28	♦ Unmeasured air ♦ Fuel pressure regulator faulty or disconnected hose	– Check intake air system for leaks ⇒ page G 24-128 – Check fuel pressure regulator ⇒ page G 24-125

Display zone: 3	Possible Malfunction cause	Corrective Steps
Less than 65	♦ Transmission "Drive" range selected ♦ Throttle Valve Control Module faulty	– Selector lever in P or N position – Check Throttle Valve Control Module ⇒ page G 24-72
More than 80	♦ Throttle Position switch closed ♦ Throttle Valve Control Module faulty ♦ Unmeasured air	– Check Throttle Valve Control Module ⇒ page G 24-72 – Check intake air system for leaks ⇒ page G 24-128
Display zone: 4	Possible Malfunction cause	Corrective Steps
Less than 176	♦ Generator faulty ♦ Battery discharged/faulty	– Check Control Module voltage supply ⇒ page G 24-110 – Check generator, ⇒ Repair Group 27 – Check battery, ⇒ Repair Group 27
More than 212	♦ Voltage regulator faulty	– Check voltage regulator ⇒ Repair Group 27
Display zone: 5	Possible Malfunction cause	Corrective Steps
Less than 0	♦ Not possible	---
More than 23	♦ Throttle Valve Control Module "Basic setting" not performed ♦ Throttle Valve Control Module faulty ♦ Throttle cable out of adjustment	– Perform "Basic setting" ⇒ page G 24-90 – Check Throttle Valve Control Module ⇒ page G 24-72 – Adjust throttle cable ⇒ Repair Group 20

Display zone: 6 + 7	Possible Malfunction cause	Corrective Steps
Less than 112	♦ Unmeasured air after throttle body	– Check intake air system for leaks ⇒ page G 24-128
More than 144	♦ Increased engine load	– Switch OFF consumer
Display zone: 8	Possible Malfunction cause	Corrective Steps
Less than 96	♦ Mixture too rich, Oxygen control weakening mixture ♦ Oxygen control at limit ♦ Large fuel dump from EVAP canister ♦ Fuel pressure regulator faulty/hose fallen off	– Check Oxy. sensor/Oxy. control (before catalytic converter) ⇒ page G 24-28 – Check fuel pressure regulator ⇒ page G 24-125
More than 160	♦ Mixture too lean, Oxygen control enrichening mixture ♦ Unmeasured air ♦ Fuel injector(s) faulty ♦ Oxygen control at limit	– Check Oxy. sensor/Oxy. control (before cat. conv.) ⇒ page G 24-28 – Check intake air system for leaks ⇒ page G 24-128 – Check Fuel injectors ⇒ page G 24-121
128	♦ Shortage of fuel ♦ Oxygen control blocked	– Check fuel quantity in tank – Check Oxy. sensor/Oxy. control (before cat. conv.) ⇒ page G 24-28
Display zone: 9	Possible Malfunction cause	
Less than 241 or more than 14	♦ ⇒ page G 24-32, evaluating display group 25	
Display zone: 10	Possible Malfunction cause	
Less than 118 or more than 138	♦ ⇒ page G 24-32, evaluating display group 25	

Fuel injection system, servicing

For Ignition system servicing
⇒ Repair Group 28

Notes:

- *Engine compartment fuel lines must be secured with spring clips. The use of clamp or screw-type clips is not permitted.*
- *The Engine Control Module (ECM) for the Fuel injection and Ignition system is equipped with a Diagnostic Trouble Code (DTC) memory. Before performing repairs, adjustments or troubleshooting, the DTC memory must be checked and the vacuum connections checked for leakage (outside air).*
- *Components tagged with an * are checked via On Board Diagnostic.*

⇒ Repair Group 01, page G 01-12

- *Components tagged ** are checked via Output Diagnostic Test Mode (DTM).*

⇒ Repair Group 01, page G 01-77

- *Trouble-free electrical component operation requires 11.5 Volts (minimum).*
- *Do not use sealants containing silicone. Particles of silicone drawn into the engine, are not consumed during combustion and could damage the Oxygen sensor resulting in higher exhaust emission levels.*
- *Do not use terminal sprays or similar materials in the area of the Oxygen sensor connector. Oxygen sensors require reference air to function correctly which they receive via the cable. If terminal spray enters the sensor via the cable, it can lead to possible damage or driveability complaints.*

- *As a result of performing certain checks, the ECM can trigger and and store a DTC. Therefore after completing all checks and repairs, DTC memory must be checked for any possible DTC's and if necessary, erased.*

⇒ Repair Group 01, page G 01-12

Safety precautions
⇒ page G 24-22

Rules of cleanliness
⇒ page G 24-23

Technical data
⇒ page G 24-24

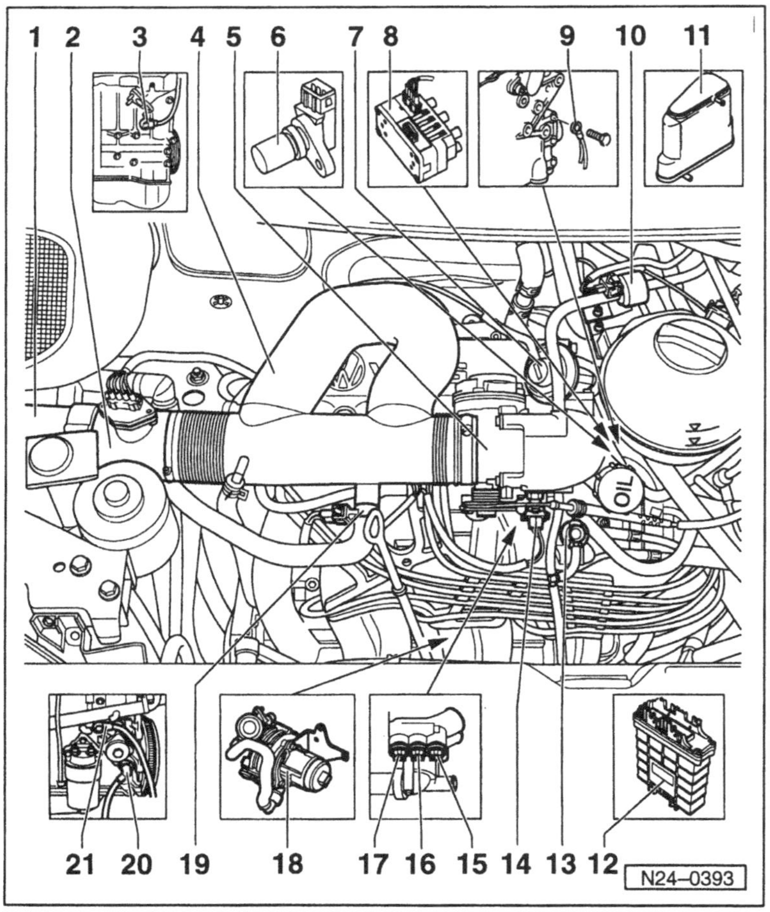

Motronic Fuel injection system

Component locations, overview

1 - Air Cleaner

2 - Mass Air Flow sensor G70

3 - Knock sensor 1 G61

⇒ Repair Group 28, page G 28-4 (item 13)

4 - Intake hose

- with heater element connection N79 for Positive Crankcase Ventilation system

5 - Throttle Valve Control Module J338

- heated by coolant

6 - Camshaft Position sensor G40

⇒ Repair Group 28, page G 28-2 (item 1)

7 - EGR valve

⇒ Repair Group 26

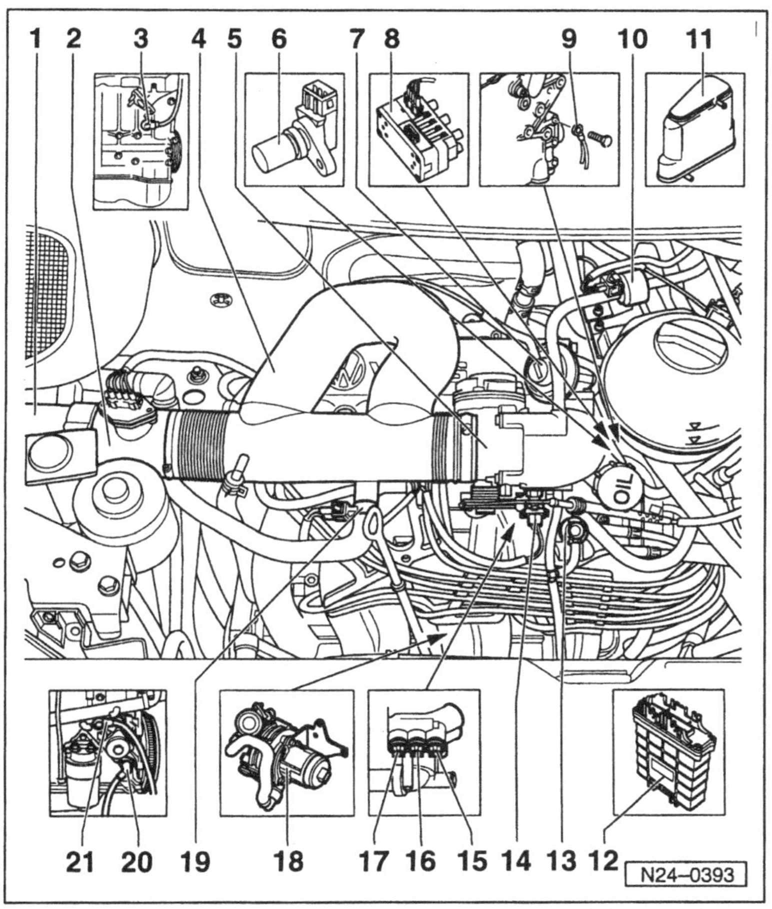

8 - Ignition coil N152

- With ignition cable identification, do not interchange

⇒ Repair Group 28, page G 28-2 (item 7)

9 - Ground connection

10 - EVAP canister purge regulator valve N80

- part of EVAP system

⇒ Repair Group 20

11 - EVAP canister

- location: front left wheel housing
- part of EVAP system

⇒ Repair Group 20

12 - Engine Control Module (ECM) J220

- location: engine compartment, left of battery

13 - Fuel pressure regulator

14 - Intake Air Temperature sensor G72

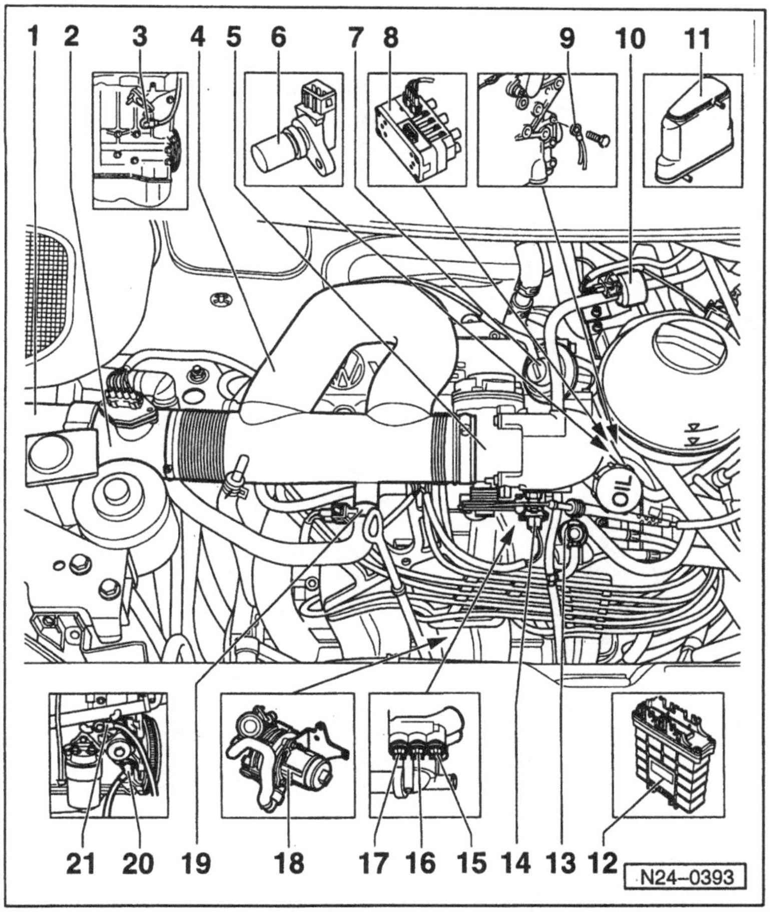

15 - **A/C Cut-out Thermal Switch F163 and 3rd Speed Coolant Fan Control Thermal Switch F165**
- ♦ brown, 4-pin
- ♦ for vehicles with A/C

⇒ Repair Group 87
- ♦ vehicles without A/C are plugged off

16 - **Engine Coolant Temperature sensor G62**
- ♦ blue, 2-pin
- ♦ for Motronic system

17 - **After-run Coolant Fan Control Thermal Switch F87 for Engine Coolant Temperature sensor G2**
- ♦ yellow, 4-pin

18 - **Secondary Air Injection Pump Motor V101**
- ♦ for EGR system

⇒ Repair Group 26

19 - **Positive Crankcase Ventilation Heating Element N79**
- ♦ for Positive Crankcase Ventilation system

20 - **Engine Speed sensor G28**

21 - **Knock sensor 2 G66**

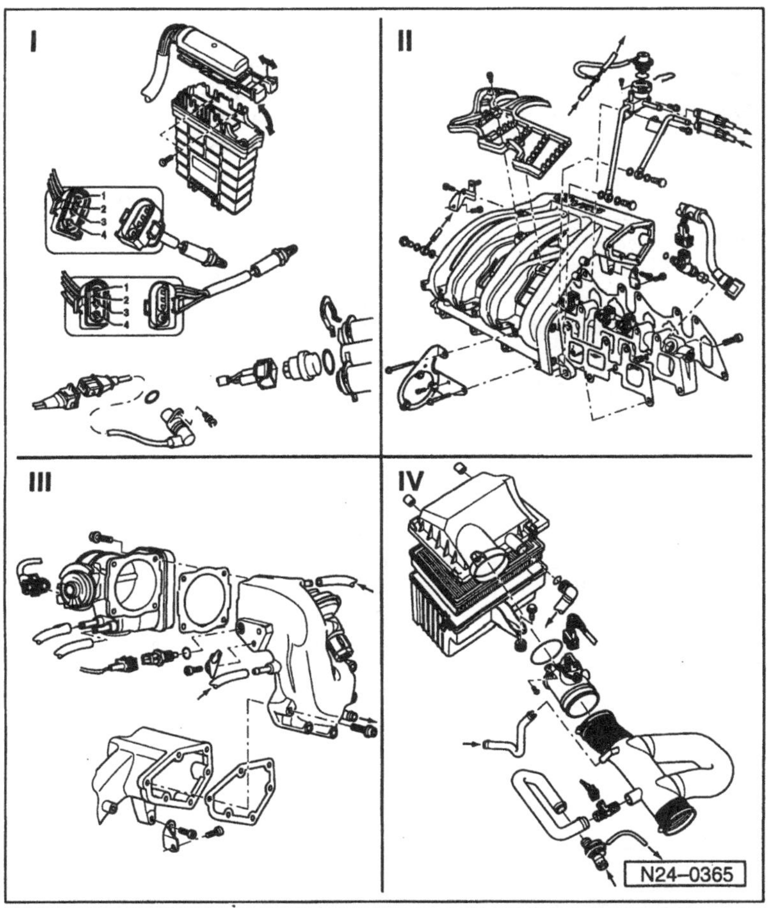

Fuel injection system, section overview

I - **Engine Control Module, Oxygen sensor, Engine Coolant Temperature sensor and Engine Speed sensor, removing and installing**

⇒ page G 24-7

II - **Intake Manifold assembly, disassembling and assembling**

⇒ page G 24-11

III - **Throttle Valve Control Module, removing and installing**

⇒ page G 24-15

IV - **Air Cleaner, Mass Air Flow sensor and Positive Crankcase Ventilation heating element, removing and installing**

⇒ page G 24-18

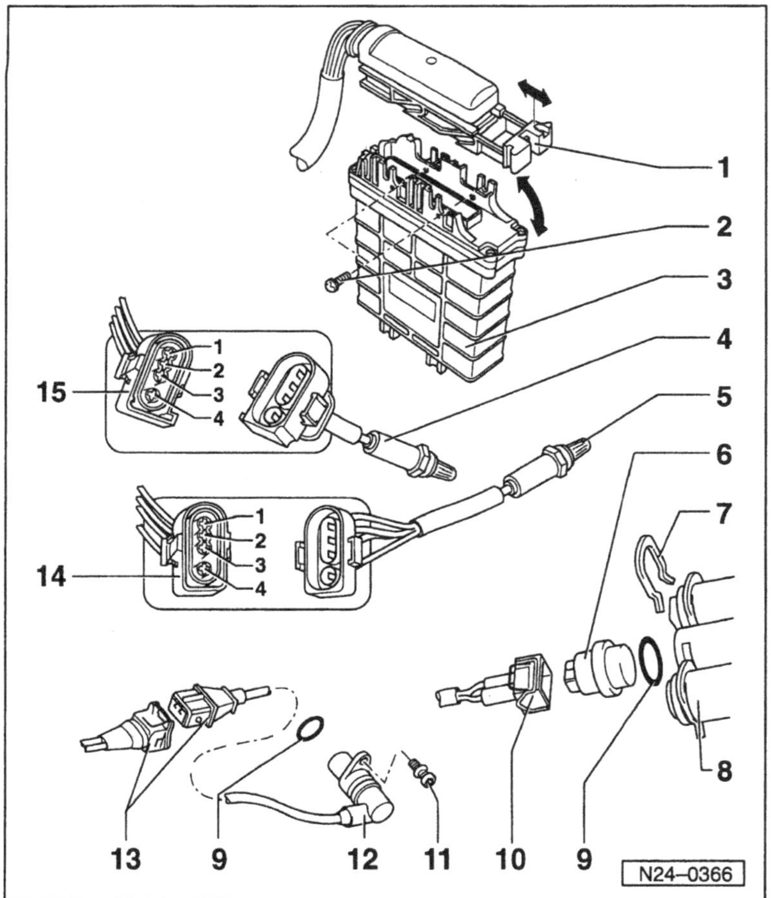

I - Engine Control Module, Oxygen sensor, Engine Coolant Temperature sensor and Engine Speed sensor, removing and installing

1 - ECM harness connector
- only disconnect or connect with ignition switched OFF
- unlatch to disconnect

2 - ECM mounting screws

3 - Engine Control Module J220*
- location: engine compartment, left of battery
- for Fuel injection and Ignition system, Throttle Valve Control Module, Oxygen control, knock control, EVAP canister purge regulator valve, speed governing via injectors or fuel pump relay and On Board Diagnostic
- if replaced, perform Basic setting

⇒ page G 24-90
- Voltage supply, checking

⇒ page G 24-110
- Control Module, coding

⇒ Repair Group 01, page G 01-10

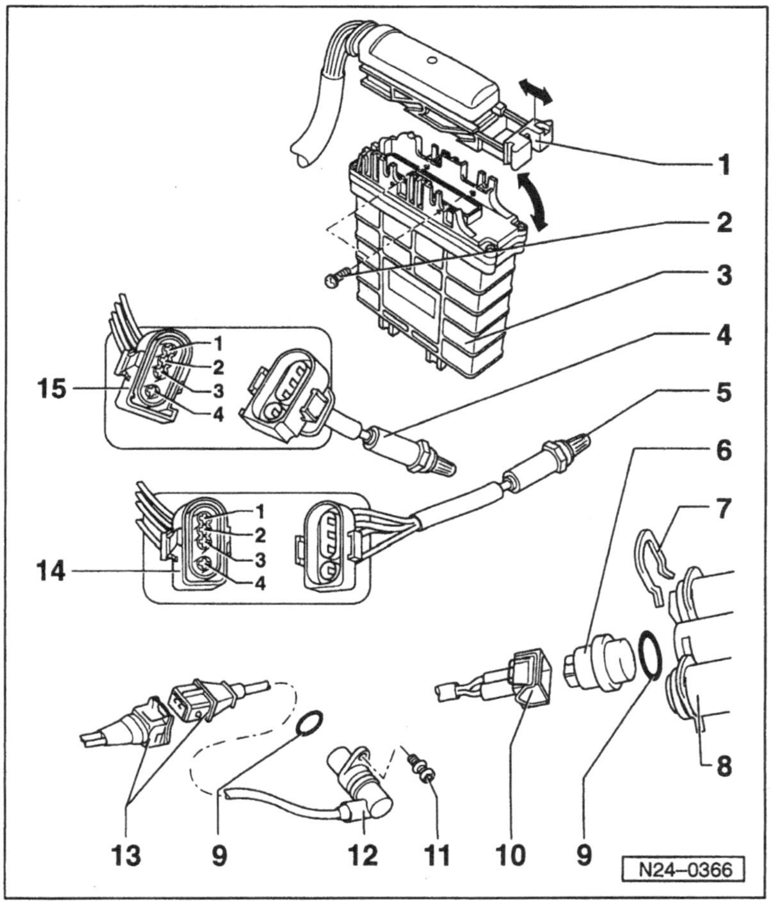

4 - Oxygen sensor (after catalytic converter) G108*
- 50 Nm (37 ft lb)
- location: in catalyst
- grease threads with G5; do NOT allow G5 to enter slots
- Oxygen sensor and Oxygen control, checking

⇒ page G 24-46
- sensor heating Voltage supply via fuel pump relay J17
- Oxygen sensor heater, checking

⇒ page G 24-53

5 - Heated Oxygen sensor (before catalytic converter) G39*
- 50 Nm (37 ft lb)
- location: in catalyst
- grease threads with G5; do NOT allow G5 to enter sensor slots
- Oxygen sensor and Oxygen control, checking

⇒ page G 24-28
- sensor heating Voltage supply via fuel pump relay J17
- Oxygen sensor heater, checking

⇒ page G 24-38

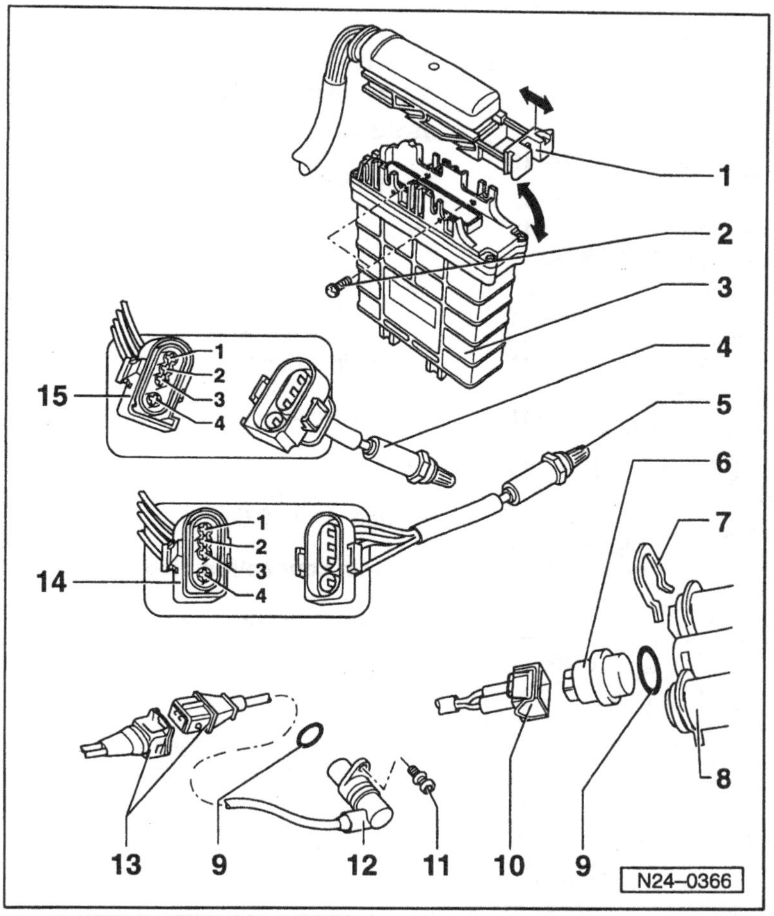

6 - Engine Coolant Temperature sensor G62*
- blue, 2-pin
- checking, ⇒ page G 24-93
- release cooling system pressure before removing (if necessary)

7 - Retaining clip
- ensure it is securely seated

8 - Thermostat housing

9 - O-ring
- replace if damaged

10 - Connector

11 - 10 Nm (7 ft lb)

12 - Engine Speed sensor G28
- location: cylinder block by intake

13 - 3-pin harness connector
- white
- for Engine Speed sensor

14 - 4-pin harness connector
- black
- mounted to sub-frame
- for Oxygen sensor and Oxygen sensor heating (before catalytic converter)

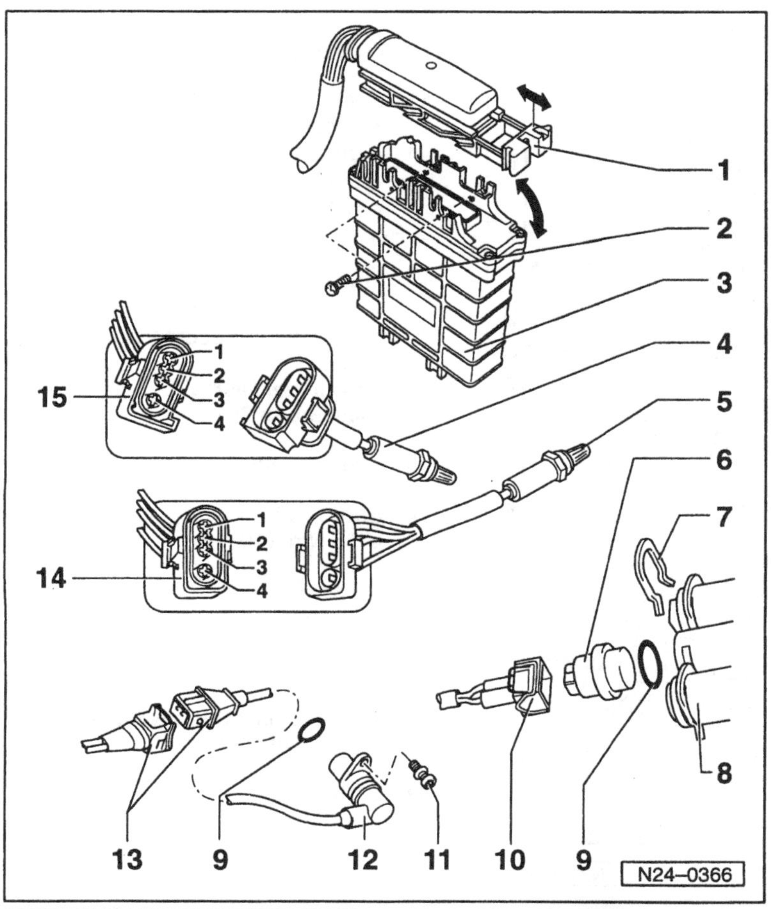

15 - 4-pin harness connector
- brown
- for Oxygen sensor and Oxygen sensor heater (after catalytic converter)

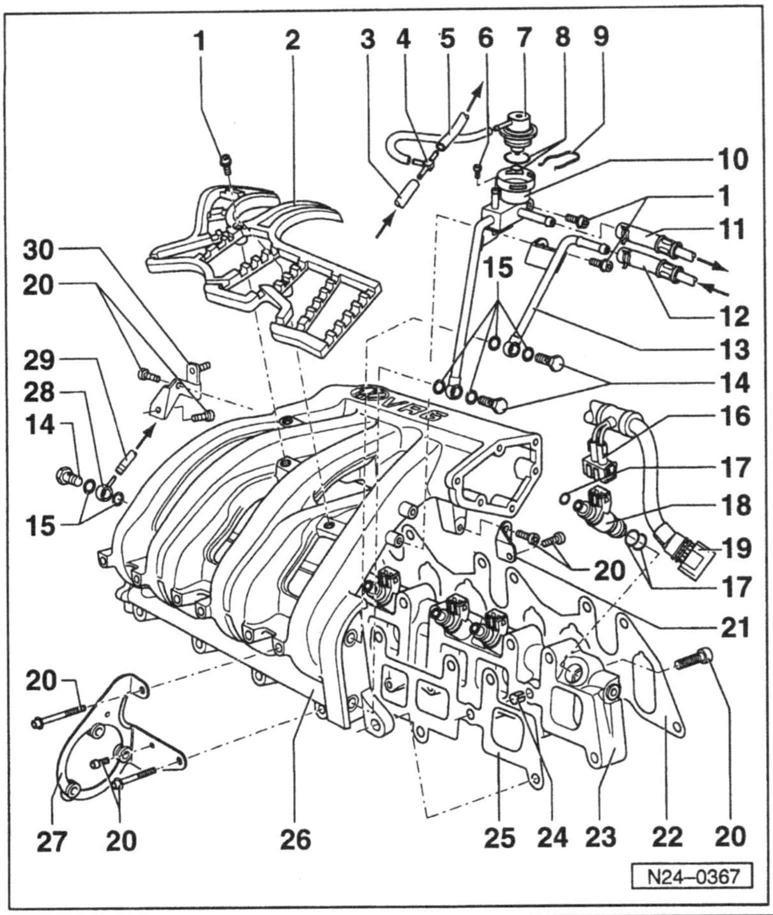

II - Intake manifold assembly, disassembling and assembling

1 - 10 Nm (7 ft lb)

2 - High tension cable guide

3 - Vacuum hose
- ♦ from Secondary Air Injection solenoid valve

⇒ Repair Group 26

4 - Tee piece

5 - Vacuum hose
- ♦ to connection

⇒ page G 24-16 (item 11)

6 - Test connection plug

7 - Fuel pressure regulator
- ♦ checking:

⇒ page G 24-125

8 - O-ring
- ♦ replace if damaged
- ♦ oil lightly before installing

9 - Retaining clip
- ♦ ensure it is seated securely

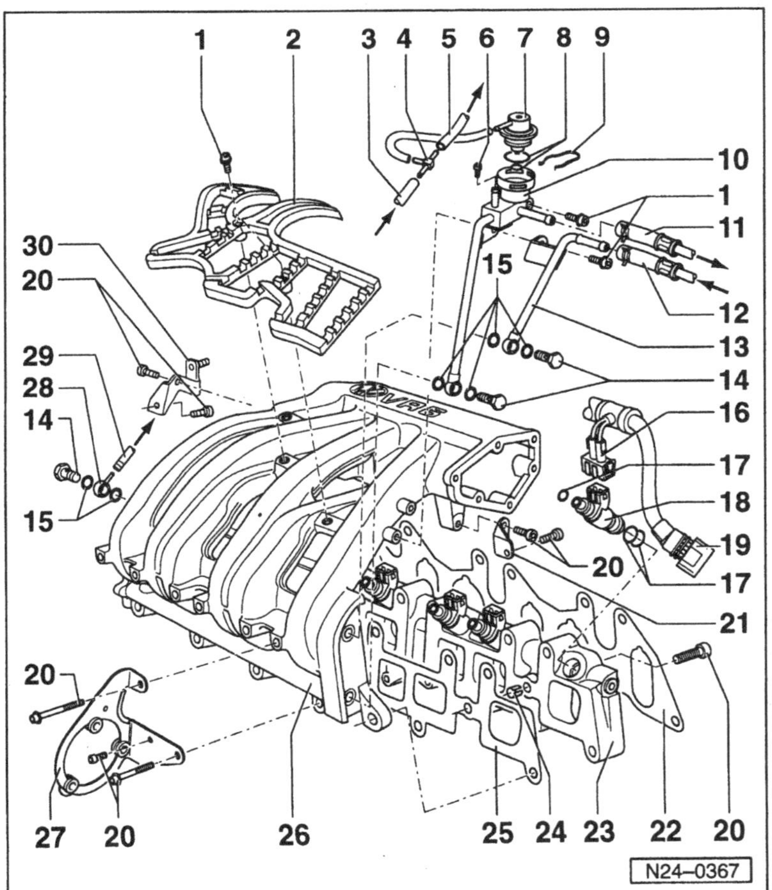

10 - Fuel pressure regulator bracket

11 - Fuel return line
- ♦ secure with spring clips
- ♦ ensure it is securely seated
- ♦ blue
- ♦ to fuel delivery unit in fuel tank

⇒ Repair Group 20

12 - Fuel supply line
- ♦ secure with spring-type clips
- ♦ ensure it is securely seated
- ♦ black
- ♦ from fuel filter:

⇒ Repair Group 20

13 - Fuel supply line

14 - Banjo bolt
- ♦ 15 Nm (10 ft lb)

15 - Oil seal
- ♦ replace

16 - 2-pin harness connector
- ♦ black
- ♦ for fuel injectors: N30, N31, N32, N33, N83, N84

17 - O-ring
- ♦ replace
- ♦ oil lightly before installing

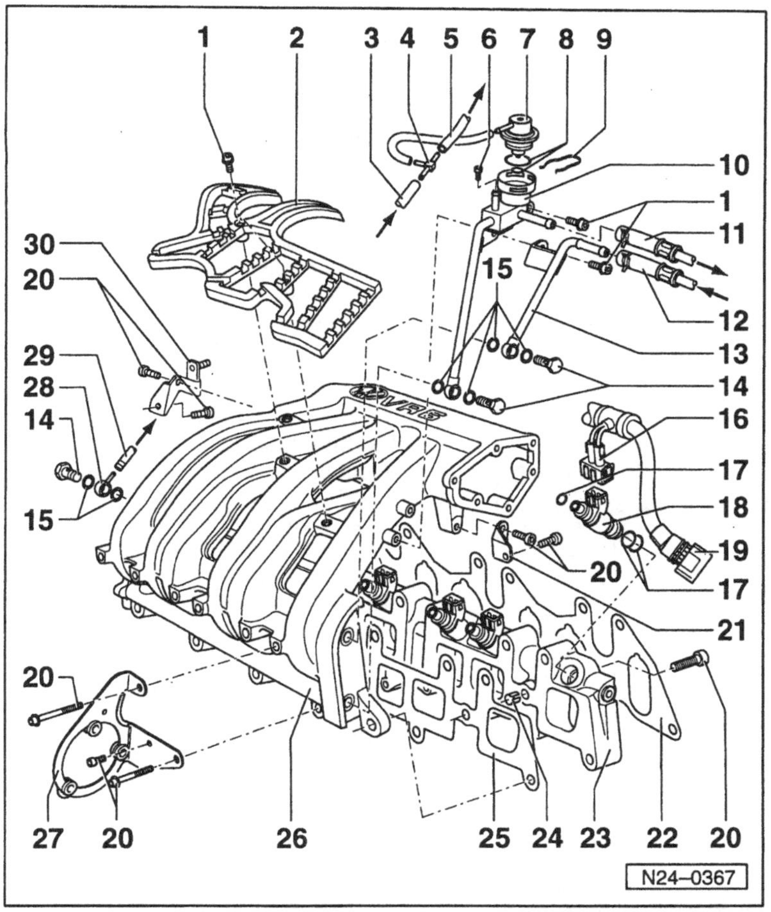

18 - Fuel Injectors N30, N31, N32, N33, N83, N84 */**
- removing and installing:

⇒ page G 24-119
- remove from lower intake manifold using 3047A tool
- checking:

⇒ page G 24-121

19 - Harness connector
- for fuel injectors: N30, N31, N32, N33, N83, N84

20 - 25 Nm (18 ft lb)

21 - Left rear support
- between intake manifold and cylinder head

22 - Lower intake manifold gasket
- replace
- note installed position

23 - Lower intake manifold
- removing and installing:

⇒ page G 24-119

24 - Dowel sleeve
- ensure it is securely seated

25 - Intake manifold gasket
- replace
- note installed position

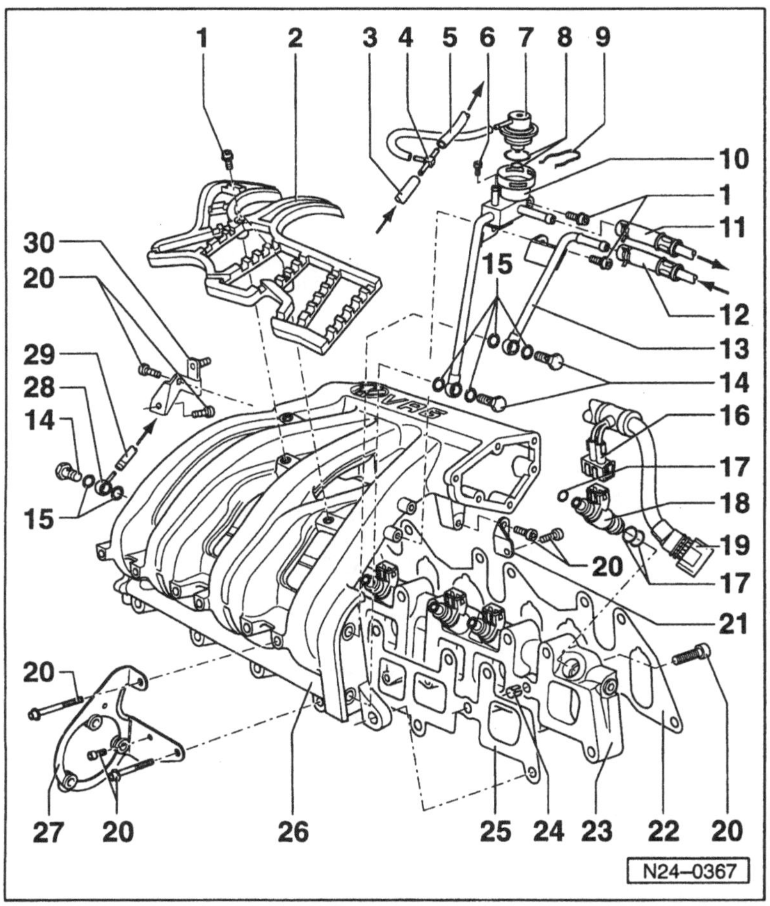

26 - Intake manifold
- removing and installing:

⇒ Repair Group 15

27 - Retainer
- for Secondary Air Injection pump motor:

⇒ Repair Group 26

28 - Hose connection
- mounted to lower intake manifold

29 - Connecting hose
- to intake hose

⇒ page G 24-18 (item 8)

30 - Right rear support
- between intake manifold and cylinder head

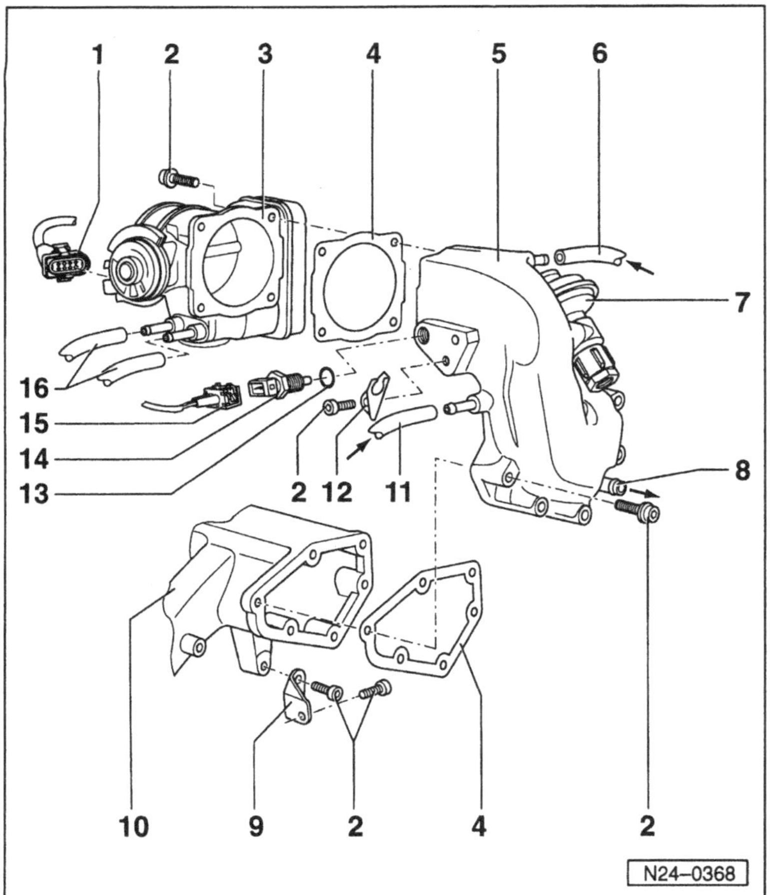

III -Throttle Valve Control Module, removing and installing

1 - 8-pin harness connector
- ♦ black
- ♦ for Throttle Valve Control Module J338
- ♦ only disconnect/connect with ignition Switched OFF

2 - 25 Nm (18 ft lb)

3 - Throttle Valve Control Module J338
- ♦ components: Throttle Position Actuator V60, Throttle Position sensor G88, Throttle Position sensor G69 and Closed Throttle Position switch F60
- ♦ heated by engine coolant
- ♦ checking:

⇒ page G 24-72
- ♦ if Throttle Valve Control Module is replaced, perform "Basic setting"

⇒ page G 24-90

4 - Gasket
- ♦ replace

5 - Connection

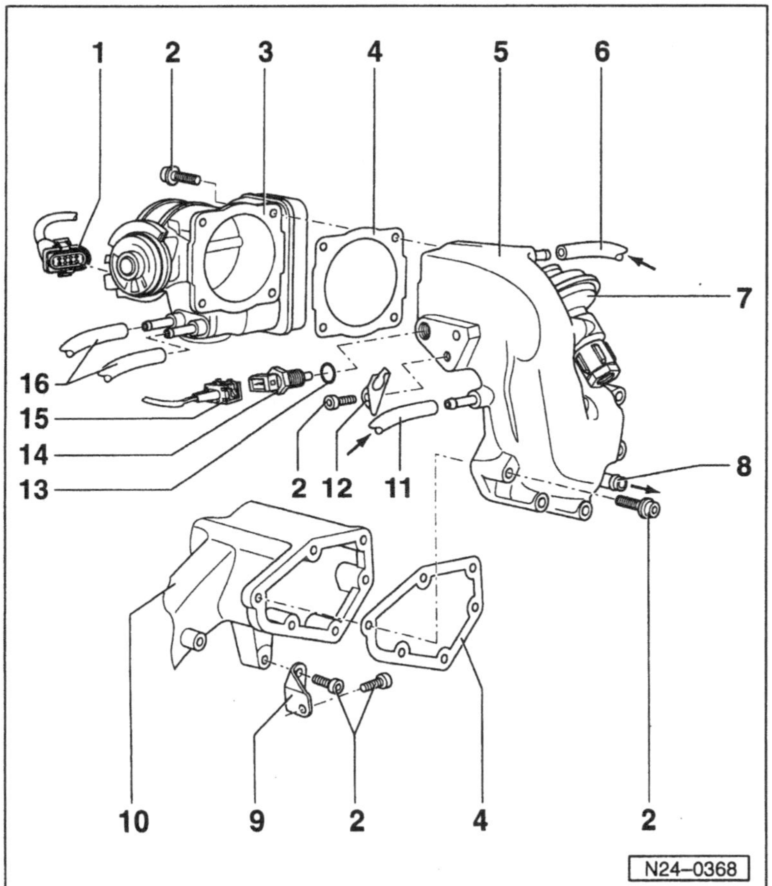

6 - Breather hose
- ♦ hose must not contact adjacent components!
- ♦ from EVAP canister purge regulator valve N80
- ♦ part of EVAP system

⇒ Repair Group 20

7 - Exhaust Gas Recirculation valve
- ♦ removing and installing:

⇒ Repair Group 26

8 - to Brake-servo vacuum line

9 - Left rear support
- ♦ between intake manifold and cylinder head

10 - Intake manifold
- ♦ disassembling and assembling:

⇒ page G 24-11
- ♦ removing and installing:

⇒ Repair Group 15

11 - Vacuum hose
- ♦ from junction piece for Fuel Pressure regulator / Secondary Air Injection solenoid valve

⇒ page G 24-11 (item 4)

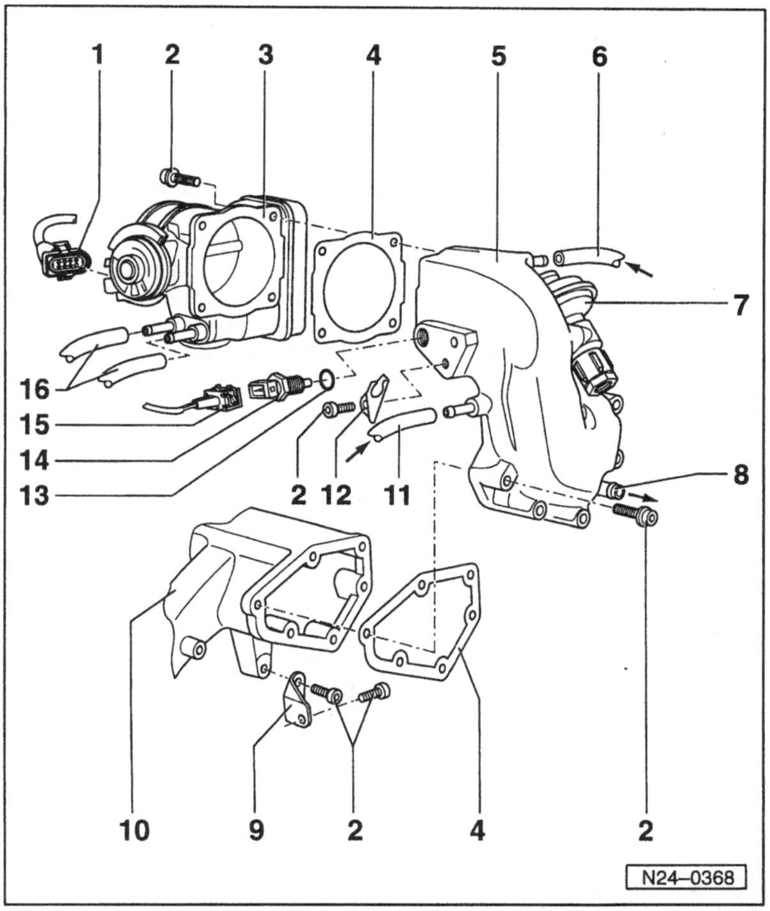

12 - Support bracket
- for accelerator cable
- accelerator cable, adjusting

⇒ Repair Group 20

13 - Oil seal
- replace

14 - Intake Air Temperature sensor G72*
- 15 Nm (10 ft lb)
- checking:

⇒ page G 24-99
- resistance values

⇒ Fig. 1, page G 24-21

15 - 2-pin harness connector
- black
- for Intake Air Temperature sensor

16 - Coolant hose

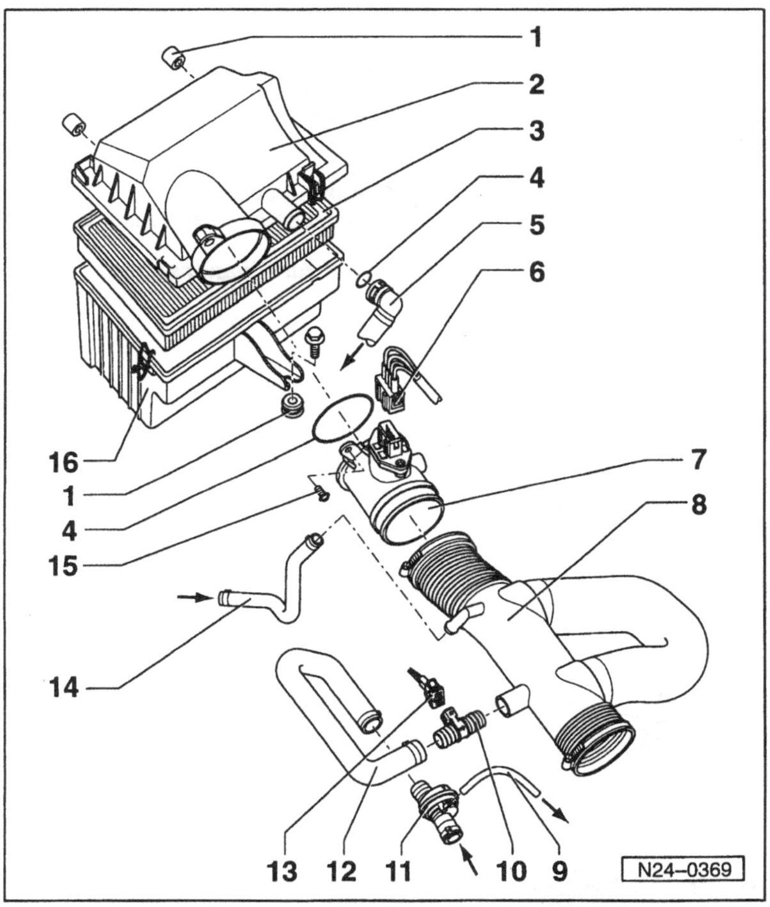

IV - Air Cleaner, Mass Air Flow sensor and Positive Crankcase Ventilation heater element, removing and installing

1 - Rubber mounting

2 - Air Cleaner upper section

3 - Filter element

4 - O-ring
- replace if damaged

5 - Intake hose
- ensure it is seated tightly
- to Secondary Air Injection Pump Motor V101:

⇒ Repair Group 26

6 - 4-pin harness connector
- black
- for Mass Air Flow sensor G70

7 - Mass Air Flow sensor G70*
- checking:

⇒ page G 24-66

8 - Intake hose
- ensure it is tightly seated

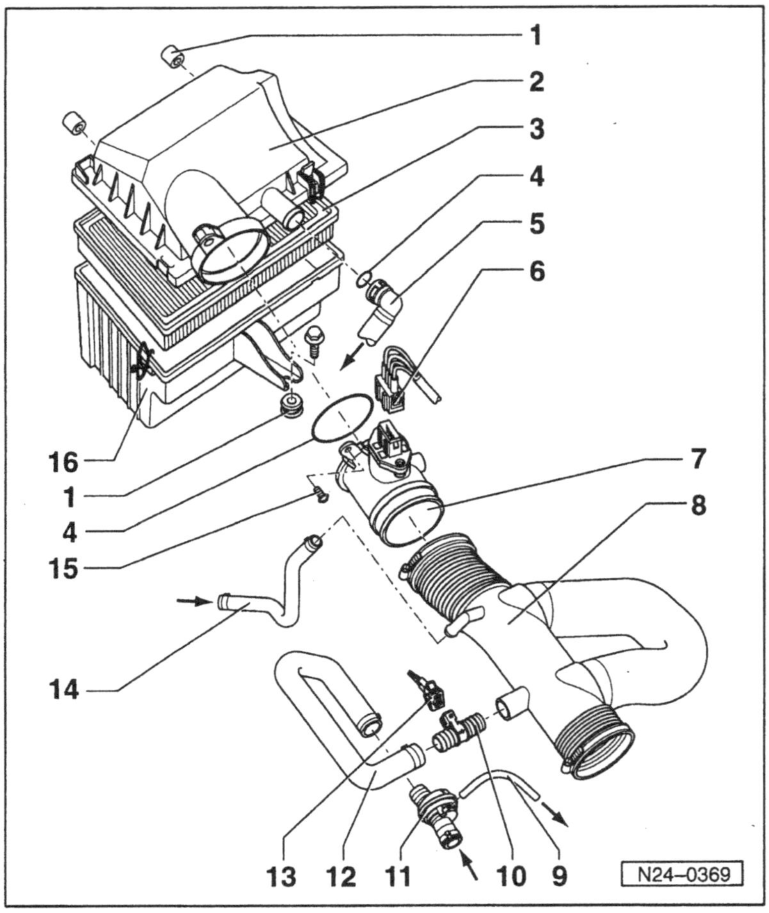

9 - Vacuum hose

- to junction piece for EGR valve /intake manifold

⇒ Repair Group 26

10 - Positive Crankcase Ventilation Heater Element N79

- for PCV valve
- arrow on heater element points toward intake hose
- resistance specification at ambient temperature (approximately 25°C or 77°F): 7 to 12 Ω

11 - Positive Crankcase Vent valve

- arrow on crankcase breather valve points to intake hose
- from cylinder head

12 - Connecting hose

13 - 2-pin harness connector

- black
- for heater element N79
- check heater element Voltage supply between terminals 1 and 2, with ignition switched ON: 11.5 Volts minimum

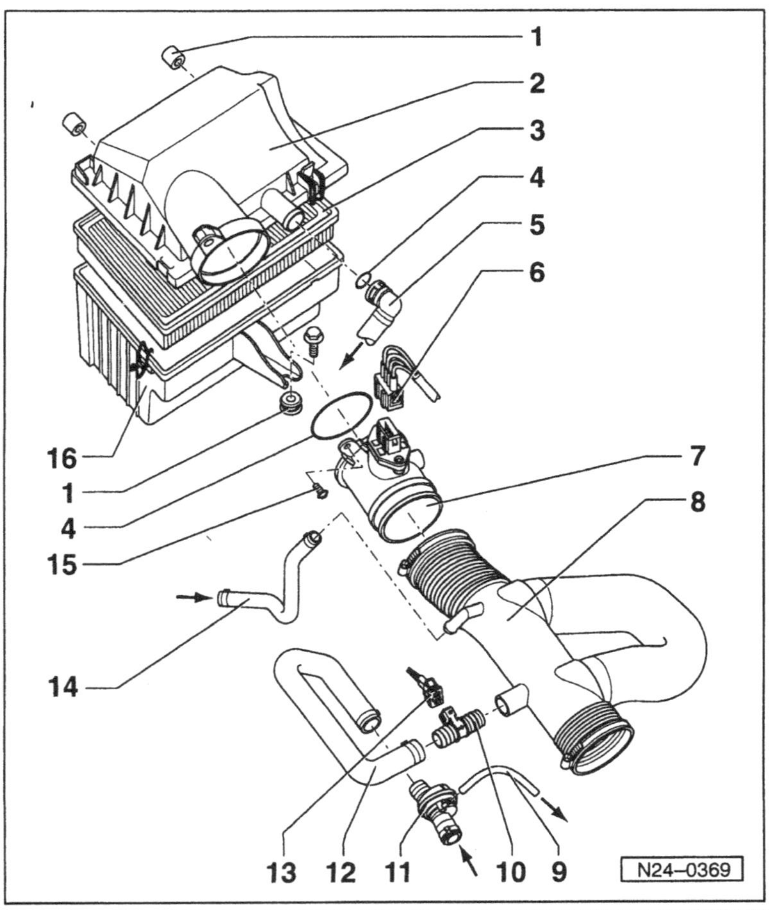

14 - Connecting hose

- from connection on lower intake manifold

⇒ page G 24-14 (item 28)

15 - Mounting screws

- for Mass Air Flow sensor G70

16 - Lower Air Cleaner section

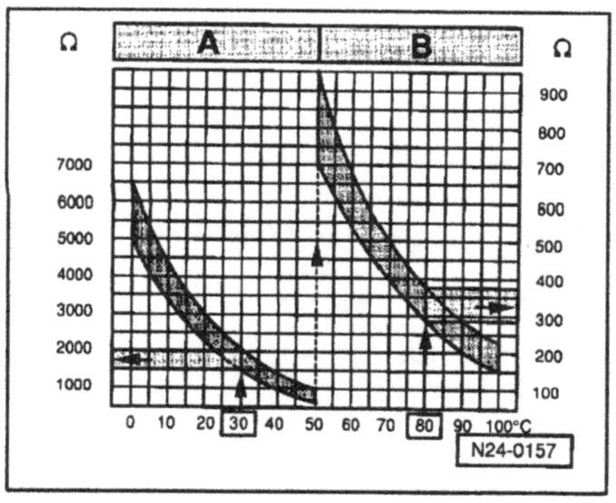

Fig. 1 Sensor resistance graph

- Diagram applies to both Engine Coolant Temperature sensor G62 and Intake Air Temperature sensor G72
- Scale -A- shows resistance values for temperature range 0 to 50°C, scale -B- shows values for temp range 50 to 100°C.

Examples:

- 30°C corresponds to a resistance between 1500 and 2000 Ω
- 80°C corresponds to a resistance between 275 and 375 Ω

Safety precautions

CAUTION!

The fuel system is under pressure! Before opening the system, place a rag around the connection and release the pressure by slowly loosening the connection.

To prevent injuries to persons and/or damage to the fuel injection and ignition system, observe the following:

- Do not touch or disconnect ignition wiring when engine is running or being turned at starter speed.
- Switch OFF ignition before connecting or disconnecting fuel injection or ignition system wiring or test cables.
- If engine requires cranking without starting, e.g., compression checking; disconnect 5-pin harness connector -arrow- from ignition coil.

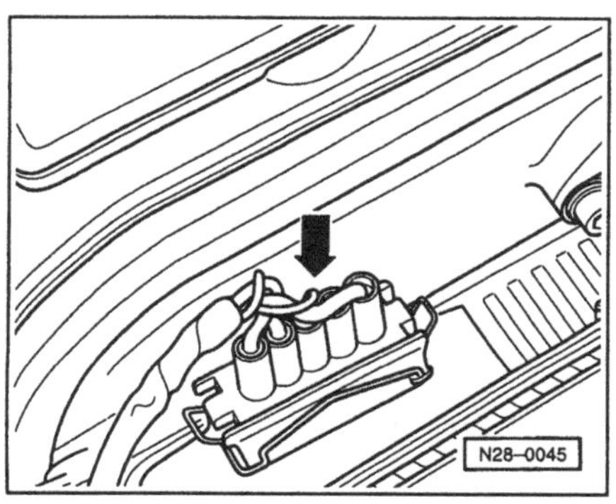

Rules of cleanliness

> ***CAUTION!***
> ***When working on the fuel system, carefully observe the following "Rules of cleanliness".***

- Thoroughly clean the fuel system line and hose connections as well as the surrounding area before disconnecting fuel connections.
- Place removed components on a clean surface and cover them up with plastic sheeting or paper. Don't use fluffy rags or materials that could leave lint!
- If the repair can't be carried out immediately,.carefully cover up any opened components or protectively seal them off.

Only install clean components:

- Only unpack replacement parts at the moment of installing
- Do not use parts that have been stored loose or without their protective packaging (e.g. in tool boxes, etc.)

When the fuel system is open:

- Do not work with compressed air if it can be avoided
- Do not move the vehicle if it can be avoided

Technical data

Engine code letters		**AES**
Idle speed check		
Idle speed[1]		650 to 750[3]
Engine Control Module[2]		
Part number		⇒ Parts dept. for latest info
Engine speed cut-off	rpm	5400 to 5800

[1] Not adjustable

[2] If replaced, perform Basic setting ⇒ page G 24-90

[3] If battery Voltage drops below 10.5 Volts, the idle speed will be automatically raised to 900 rpm

Idle speed, checking

- *Idle speed, ignition timing and CO content are NOT adjustable*
- *Idle speed is controlled by the Throttle Valve Control Module*
- *CO content is held within specification by Oxygen control. Malfunctions in Oxygen control are monitored by On Board Diagnostic, any malfunctions will be stored in DTC memory.*

Special tools, testers and auxiliary items

- VAG 1551/VAG 1552 Scan Tool with VAG 1551/3 adaptor cable

Requirements

- No malfunctions stored in DTC memory
⇒ page G 01-12

- Engine oil temperature 80°C (176°F) minimum

- All electrical consumers switched OFF
(radiator fan must not run during check)

- Throttle cable adjustment OK
⇒ Checking: Repair Group 20

- A/C switched OFF

- Exhaust system must be leak tight

Test sequence

– Connect VAG 1551 (VAG 1552) Scan Tool
⇒ Repair Group 01, page G 01-7

– With engine idling, press 0 and 1 buttons to select Address Word 01, "Engine Electronics"

Rapid data transfer	HELP
Select function XX	

◄ Display will appear as shown

– Press 0 and 4 buttons to select Function 04, "Basic setting"

– Press Q button to enter selection

Read measuring value block	HELP
Input display group number XX	

◄ Display will appear as shown

– Press 0 button twice to select "Display group number 1"

– Press Q button to enter selection

Basic setting 1			→
1	2	3	4

◄ Display will appear as shown (1 to 4 = Display zones)

Note:

The EVAP Canister Purge Regulator Valve N80 is closed when Function 04 is selected.

Do not continue with check until Engine Coolant Temperature exceeds 80°C (176°F)
⇒ Display zone 2, page G 24-27

– Briefly rev engine, then let idle for approximately 2 minutes

– Check specifications
⇒ Display zones 1 to 4, page G 24-27

	Display zones			
	1	2	3	4
Display group 1: Idle Speed, checking				
Display	xxxx rpm	xxx.x°C	xx.x%	xx.x ∠°
Indicated	Engine speed	Engine Coolant temperature	Oxygen control	Ignition angle
Working range	650 to 6000 rpm	---	–25.0 to 25.0%	0.0 to 40.0 ∠°
Spec	650 to 750 rpm	80.0 to 105.0°C	Must fluctuate by at least 2% range –5.0 to 5.0%	2.0 to 15.0 ∠°
	If specification not obtained: ⇒ page G 24-72, check Throttle Valve Control Module	---	If specification not obtained: ⇒ page G 24-28, check Oxygen sensor and control (before catalytic converter)	If specification not obtained: ⇒ page G 28-11, ignition timing, checking

– Press → button

– Press 0 and 6 buttons to select Function 06, "End output"

– Press Q button to enter selection

– Perform road test and repeat check

– Read Readiness code
⇒ page G 01-33

If DTC memory was erased, create Readiness code again
⇒ page G 01-35

Oxygen sensor and Oxygen control (before catalytic converter), checking

Special tools, testers and auxiliary items

- ♦ VAG 1551/1552 Scan Tool using VAG 1551/3 adaptor cable
- ♦ VAG 1598/18 Test Box
- ♦ Fluke 83 multimeter (or equivalent)
- ♦ VW 1594 Adaptor set
- ♦ Wiring diagram

Requirement

- ♦ Engine Coolant Temperature 80 °C (176°F) minimum

Functional check

– Connect VAG 1551 (VAG 1552) Scan Tool
⇒ Repair Group 01, page 01-7

– With engine idling, press 0 and 1 buttons to select Address Word 01, "Engine Electronics"

Rapid data transfer	HELP
Select function XX	

◄ Display will appear as shown

– Press 0 and 8 buttons to select Function 08, "Read measuring value block"

– Press Q button to enter selection

```
Read measuring value block        HELP
Input display group number XXX
```

◄ Display will appear as shown

– Press buttons 0, 2 and 5 for "Display group number 25"

– Press Q button to enter selection

```
Read measuring value block  25     →
   1          2          3         4
```

◄ Display will appear as shown (1 to 4 = Display zones)

– Check Oxygen control specifications (before catalytic converter) ⇒ Display zones 1 to 3

	Display zones			
	1	2	3	4
Display group 25: Oxygen control (before catalytic converter)				
Display	xx.x%	xx.x%	xx.x%	xxxxxxxx
Indicated	Oxygen control	Partial load adaption value	Idle speed adaption value	Oxygen control status (before catalytic conv.)
Working range	–25.0 to 25.0%	–16.4 to 16.4%	–16.4 to 16.4%	---
Spec	Value must fluctuate at least 2% within range –5.0 to 5.0%	–5.0 to 5.0% can fluctuate slightly	–5.0 to 5.0% (can fluctuate slightly)	Relevance ⇒ page G 24-34
	If specification not obtained ⇒ page G 24-30, continuation	If specification not obtained ⇒ page G 24-32		---

Continuation

If specification in Display zone 1 not obtained, or value does not fluctuate at least 2 %:

– Perform road-test to reduce possible build-up on Oxygen sensor and repeat check

If specification in Display zone 1 not obtained even after road test, or value does not fluctuate at least 2 %:

– Check Oxygen sensor heating ⇒ page G 24-38

If value displayed in Display zone 1 remains constant:

– Press C button

– Press 1, 1 and 5 buttons to select "Display group number 115"

– Press Q button to enter selection

```
Read measuring value block  115    →
   1          2          3         4
```

◄ Display will appear as shown (1 to 4 = Display zones)

– Note Oxygen sensor Voltage in Display zone 3 ⇒ page G 24-31

	Display zones			
	1	2	3	4
Display group 115: Oxygen sensor (before catalytic converter)				
Display	xxx.x°C	xxx.x°C	x.xxx Volts	xxxxxxxx
Indicated	Engine Coolant temperature	Exhaust Gas temperature (calculated)	Oxygen sensor Voltage (before cat)	Oxygen control status (before cat)
Working range	–46.5 to 141.0°C	0.0 to 999.9°C	0.000 to 1.000 Volts	---
Spec	80.0 to 105.0°C	140.0°C minimum	Voltage must fluctuate at least 0.3 Volts at least 30 times per minute in range 0.000 to 1.000 Volts	Relevance ⇒ page G 24-34
	---	---	If spec not obtained ⇒ page G 24-33	---

– Press → button

– Press 0 and 6 buttons to select Function 06, "End output"

– Press Q button to enter selection

– Switch OFF ignition

Evaluating display group 25

Display group: 25 Display zone: 2 + 3	Possible cause	Corrective Steps
Adaption figures in range: –5 to –16.4%	♦ Crankcase dilution: When the partial load adaption value (Display zone 2) is normal	– Oil change or a fast drive on an open road
	♦ Fuel pressure too high	– Check fuel pressure regulator ⇒ page G 24-125
	♦ Injector leaking	– Check fuel injectors ⇒ page G 24-121
	♦ Oxygen sensor heating	– Check Oxygen sensor heating ⇒ page G 24-38
Adaption figures in range: 5 to 16.4%	♦ Unmeasured air in air intake system or exhaust manifold/front pipe: When the partial load adaption value (Display zone 2) is normal	– Check intake air system for leaks (unmeasured air) ⇒ page G 24-128 – Check exhaust system ⇒ Repair Group 26
	♦ Fuel pressure too low	– Check fuel pressure regulator ⇒ page G 24-125
	♦ Check Oxygen sensor heating	– Check Oxygen sensor heating ⇒ page G 24-38
	♦ Injector not opening or only partly opening	– Check injectors ⇒ page G 24-121

Continued

Display group: 25 Display zone: 2 + 3	Possible cause	Corrective Steps
Adaption figures: constant 0.0%	◆ Oxygen control adaption not active	– Check whether Oxygen control adaption is active ⇒ page G 24-34 If Oxygen control adaption is not active: – Check Mass Air Flow sensor ⇒ page G 24-66

Evaluating display group 115

Display group: 115 Display zone: 3	Possible cause	Corrective Steps
Approx. 0.435 Volts	◆ Open circuit in wire 4 between Oxygen sensor and ECM	– Check basic Voltage ⇒ page G 24-35
Approx. 0.440 Volts	◆ Open circuit in wire 3 between Oxygen sensor and ECM	
Approx. 1.085 Volts	◆ Short to positive in wire 4 between Oxygen sensor and ECM	– Check Oxygen sensor wiring ⇒ page G 24-36
Approx. 0.000 Volts	◆ Short to Ground in wire 4 between Oxygen sensor and ECM	

Relevance of figures in 8 digit number block

Relevance when display = 1									
x	x	x	x	x	x	x	x	Oxygen control status (display group 25)	Oxygen control status (display group 115)
							1	Oxygen sensor (before catalytic converter) ready	Malfunction in DTC memory
						1		Oxygen sensor (after catalytic converter) ready	Malfunction detected during diagnostic
					1			Oxygen control (before catalytic converter) active	Diagnostic completed during drive
				1				Oxygen control adaption active	Diagnostic currently active
			1					Not relevant	Oxygen control (before catalytic converter) active
		1						Oxygen sensor Voltage initial sign	Oxygen sensor (before catalytic converter) ready
	1							Not relevant	Both Oxygen sensors cold
1								1 = Oxygen control regulating frequency rich 0 = Oxygen control regulating frequency lean	Sensor heating (before catalytic converter) ON

Basic Voltage, checking

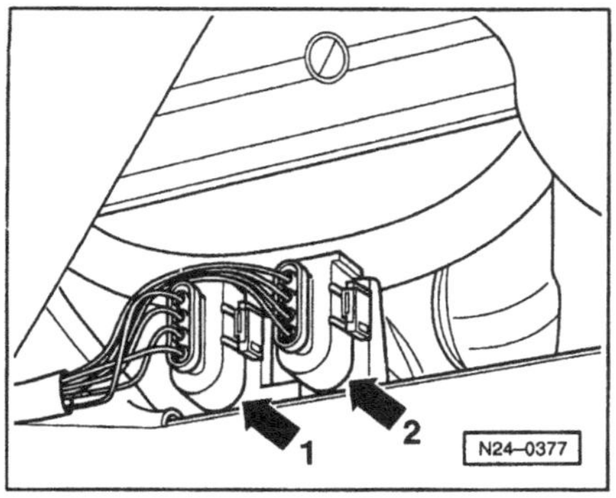

- Disconnect (black) 4-pin harness connector to Oxygen sensor -1- (before catalytic converter) G39

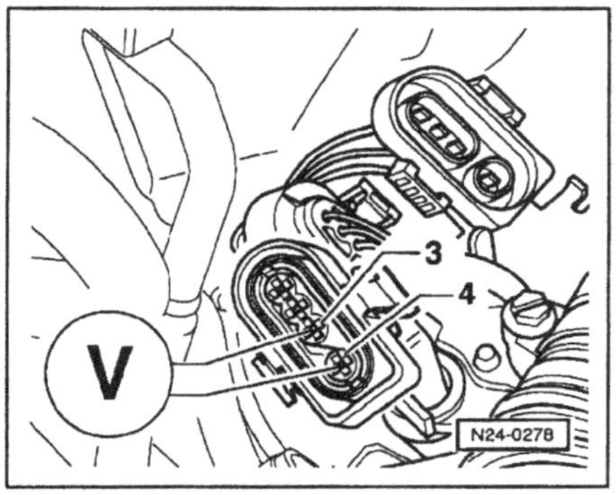

- Connect multimeter between terminals 3 + 4 using jumper wires from VW 1594 adaptor kit
- Start engine and measure basic Voltage
  - ♦ specification: 0.40 to 0.50 Volts
- Switch OFF ignition

If specification not obtained:

- Check Oxygen sensor wiring
⇒ page G 24-36

If specification obtained:

- Replace Oxygen sensor (before catalytic converter) G39

Oxygen sensor wiring, checking

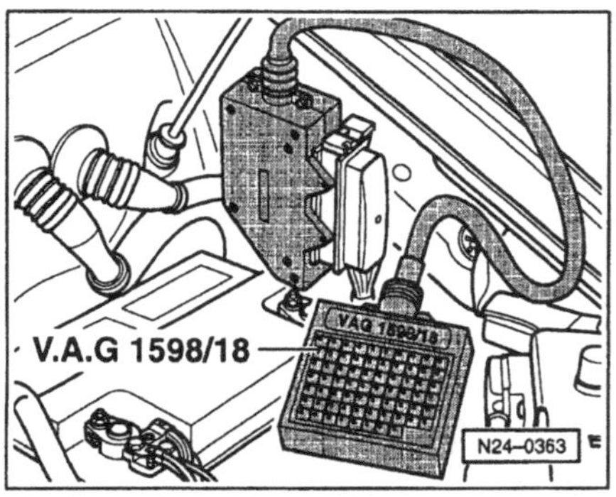

- Connect VAG 1598/18 Test Box to ECM harness connector

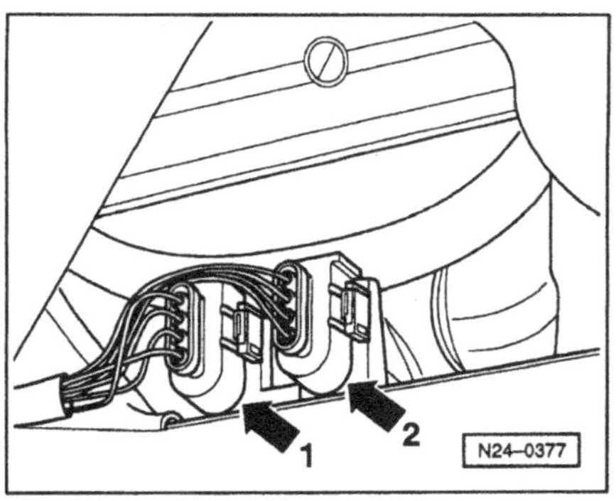

- Disconnect (black) 4-pin harness connector to Oxygen sensor -1- (before catalytic converter) G39

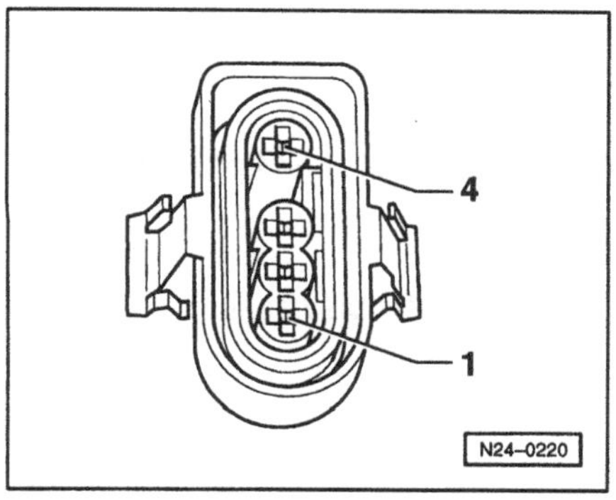

– Check wiring between Test Box and 4-pin ECM connector for open circuit using Wiring diagram, connect as follows:

– terminal 3 + socket 42

– terminal 4 + socket 20

♦ wire resistance: 1.5 Ω

– Check wires at 4-pin connector for shorting to one another

– terminal 4 + socket 42

♦ specification: ∞ Ω

– Check shielding for short to sensor wiring using Wiring diagram, connect as follows:

– terminal 4 + socket 56

– terminal 3 + socket 56

♦ specification: ∞ Ω

If wiring OK:

– Replace ECM J220

– Perform Basic setting ⇒ page G 24-90

– Read-out Readiness code ⇒ page G 01-33

If DTC memory was erased, create new Readiness code ⇒ page G 01-35

Oxygen sensor (before Catalytic Converter) heating, checking

Special tools, testers and auxiliary items

♦ VAG 1551/VAG 1552 Scan Tool using VAG 1551/3 adaptor cable

♦ VAG 1598/18 Test Box

♦ Fluke 83 multimeter (or equivalent)

♦ VW 1594 Adaptor kit

♦ Wiring diagram

Requirement

♦ Fuse 18 OK

Test sequence

– Connect VAG 1551 (VAG 1552) Scan Tool
⇒ Repair Group 01, page G 01-7

– With engine idling, press 0 and 1 buttons to select Address Word 01, "Engine Electronics"

Rapid data transfer	HELP
Select function XX	

Display will appear as shown

– Press 0 and 8 buttons to select Function 08 "Read measuring value block"

– Press Q button to enter selection

Read measuring value block HELP Input display group number XXX

◄ Display will appear as shown

– Press 1, 2 and 0 buttons to select "Display group number 120"

– Press Q button to enter selection

Read measuring value block 120 → 1 2 3 4

◄ Display will appear as shown (1 to 4 = Display zones)

– Check the resistance value for Oxygen sensor heating (before catalytic converter) (Display zone 3, page G 24-40)

	Display zones			
	1	2	3	4
Display group 120: Oxygen sensor heating (before catalytic converter)				
Display	xxx.x°C	xxx.xx seconds	xx.x Ω	xxxxxxxx
Indicated	Exhaust Gas temperature	Time until start of diagnosis after heating ON	Oxygen sensor heating resistance (before cata- lytic converter)	Oxygen control status (before catalic converter)
Working range	0.0 to 999.9°C	0.00 to 500.00 s	0.0 to 65.0 Ω	Relevance ⇒ page G 24-41
Spec	---	100.00 to 200.00 s	5.9 to 24.2 Ω	
	---	---	If specification not ob- tained: ⇒ page G 24-42: "continued"	---

– Press → button

– Press 0 and 6 buttons to select Function 06, "End output"

– Press Q button to enter selection

– Switch OFF ignition

Relevance of figures in 8 digit number block

								Relevance if display = 1
x	x	x	x	x	x	x	x	Oxygen control status (display group 120)
							1	Malfunction in DTC memory
						1		Malfunction detected during diagnostic
					1			Diagnostic completed during drive
				1				Diagnostic currently active
			1					Sensor heating (before cat. converter) ready
		1						Oxygen sensor (before cat. converter) ready
	1							Vapor point (before cat. converter) exceeded
1								1 = sensor heater (before catalytic converter) ON, alternating 0 and 1 = sensor heating is cycling

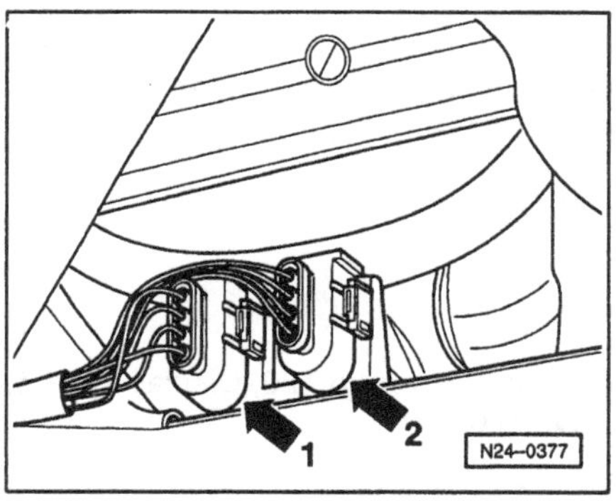

Continuation

- Disconnect (black) 4-pin connector to Oxygen sensor -1- (before catalytic converter) G39

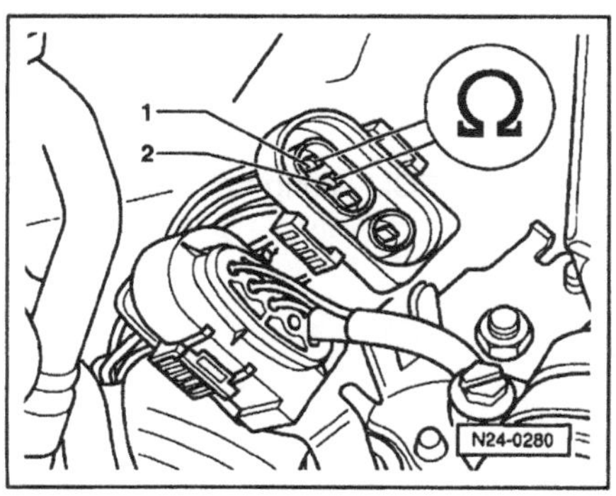

- Connect multimeter with aux. cables from VW 1594 to measure resistance at terminals 1 + 2 on connector to Oxygen sensor
- Measure resistance value
  - ♦ specification: 0.0 to 24.2 Ω

If specification not obtained:

- Replace Oxygen sensor (before catalytic converter) G39

If specification obtained:

- Switch multimeter to 20 Volt DC range

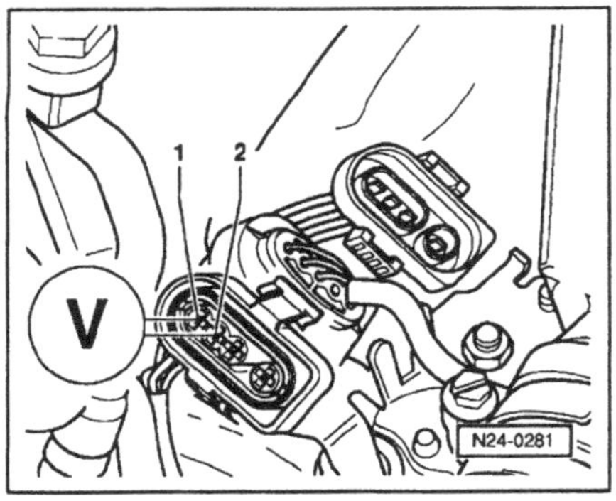

◄ – Connect multimeter between terminals 1 + 2 of ECM connector using jumper wires from VW 1594 adaptor kit

– Measure Voltage supply when display group 120, Display zone 4, 1st position from left = 1

♦ specification: 11.0 to 14.5 Volts

Measure Voltage supply when display group 120, Display zone 4, 1st position from left = alternating 0 and 1

♦ specification: between 0.0 and 12.0 Volts and alternating

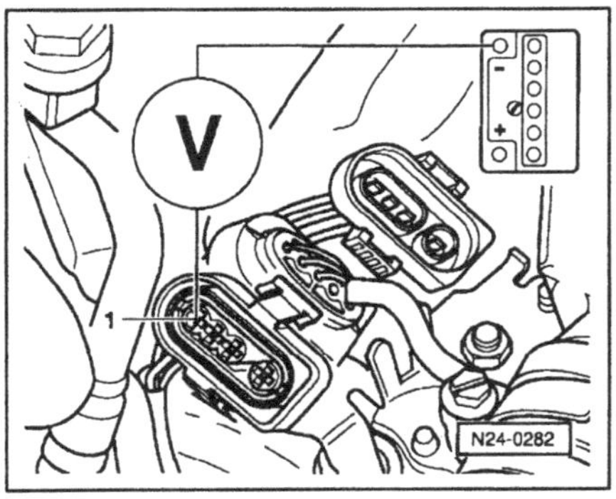

If no Voltage present:

◄ – Connect multimeter between terminal 1 of ECM connector + Ground using jumper wires from VW 1594 adaptor kit

♦ specification: 11.0 to 14.5 Volts

If again no Voltage present:

– Check wiring between terminal 1 and fuse/relay panel using wiring diagram

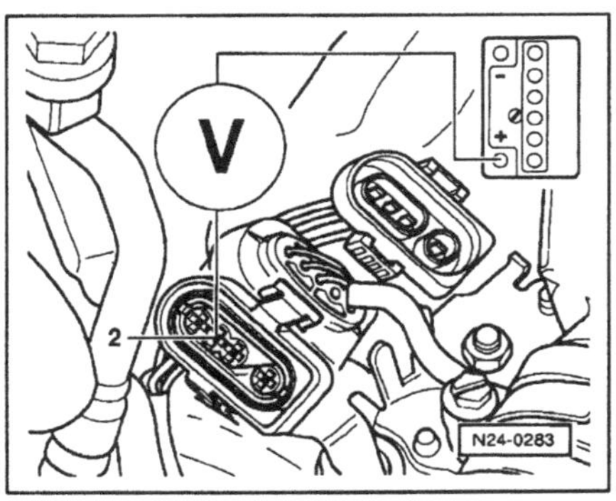

If Voltage present:

◄ – Connect multimeter between terminals 2 and B+ of ECM connector using jumper wires from VW 1594 adaptor kit

– Measure Voltage supply when display group 120, Display zone 4, 1st position from left = 1

♦ specification: 11.0 to 14.5 Volts

Measure Voltage supply when display group 120, Display zone 4, 1st position from left = alternating 0 and 1

♦ specification: between 0.0 and 12.0 Volts and alternating

– Switch OFF ignition

If Voltage not present:

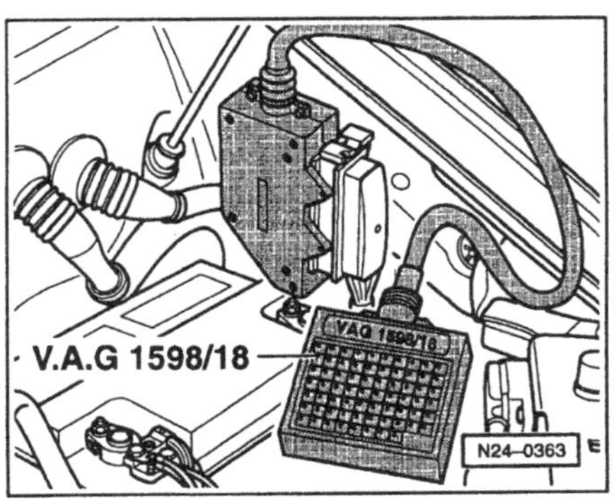

◄ – Connect VAG 1598/18 Test Box to ECM wiring harness

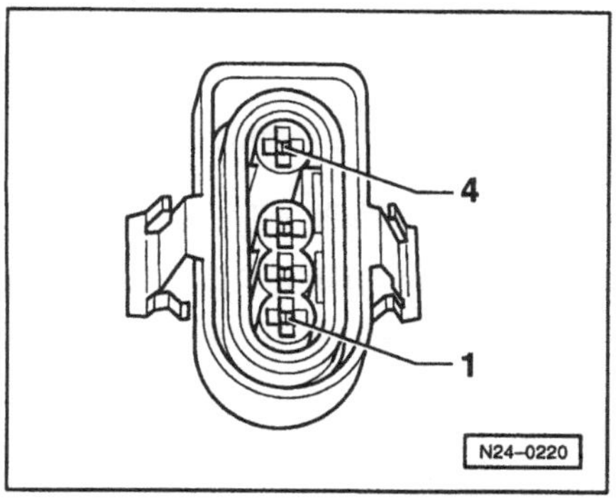

- Check for open circuit between Test Box and 4-pin harness connector using wiring diagram, connecting as follows:
  - terminal 2 + socket 12
  - ♦ wire resistance: 1.5 Ω maximum

If wiring OK:

- Replace Engine Control Module J220
- Perform Basic setting ⇒ page G 24-90
- Create Readiness code again ⇒ page G 01-35

If DTC memory has been erased:

- Read-out Readiness code ⇒ page G 01-33

Oxygen sensor and Oxygen control (after catalytic converter), checking

Special tools, testers and auxiliary items

- ♦ VAG 1551/1552 Scan Tool using VAG 1551/3 adaptor cable
- ♦ VAG 1598/18 Test Box
- ♦ Fluke 83 multimeter (or equivalent)
- ♦ VW 1594 Adaptor kit
- ♦ Wiring diagram

Requirement

- ♦ Engine Coolant Temperature 80°C (176°F) minimum

Functional check

- Connect VAG 1551 (VAG 1552) Scan Tool ⇒ Repair Group 01, page G 01-7
- With engine idling, press 0 and 1 buttons to select Address Word 01, “Engine Electronics”

Rapid data transfer	HELP
Select function XX	

Display will appear as shown

- Press 0 and 8 buttons to select Function 08, “Read measuring value block”
- Press Q button to enter selection

Read measuring value block HELP Input display group number XXX

◄ Display will appear as shown

– Press 1, 1 and 6 buttons to select "Display group number 116"

Read measuring value block 116 → 1 2 3 4

◄ Display will appear as shown (1 to 4 = Display zones)

– Note Oxygen sensor Voltage (Display zone 3)

	Display zones			
	1	2	3	4
Display group 116: Oxygen sensor (after catalytic converter)				
Display	xxx ms	xxx.x°C	x.xxx Volts	xxxxxxxx
Indicated	Regulating frequency	Exhaust Gas Temp (calculated)	Oxygen sensor Voltage (after catalytic converter)	Oxygen control status (after catalytic converter)
Working range	---	0.0 to 999.9°C	0.000 to 1.000 Volts	---
Specifi-cat	---	140.0°C minimum	0.000 to 1.000 Volts (can fluctuate slightly)	Relevance ⇒ page G 24-48
	---	---	If spec not obtained: ⇒ page G 24-48, continuation	---

Continuation

– Perform road-test to remove possible build-up on Oxygen sensor and repeat check

If spec in Display zone 3 not obtained even after road-test:

– Check Oxygen sensor heating ⇒ page G 24-53

– Raise engine speed above 3000 rpm

If figure in Display zone 3 remains constant ⇒ page G 24-48

Evaluating display group 116

Display group: 116 Display zone: 3	Possible cause	Corrective Steps
Approx. 0.435 Volts	♦ Open circuit in wire 4 between Oxygen sensor and ECM	– Check Basic Voltage ⇒ page G 24-49
Approx. 0.440 Volts	♦ Open circuit in wire 3 between Oxygen sensor and ECM	
Approx. 1.085 Volts	♦ Short to positive in wire 4 between Oxygen sensor and ECM	– Check Oxygen sensor wiring ⇒ page G 24-50
Approx. 0.000 Volts	♦ Short to ground in wire 4 between Oxygen sensor and ECM	

Relevance of figures in 8 digit number block

Relevance if display = 1								
x	x	x	x	x	x	x	x	Oxygen control status (display group 116)
							1	Malfunction in DTC memory
						1		Malfunction detected during diagnostic
					1			Diagnostic complete during drive
				1				Diagnostic currently active
			1					Oxygen control (before catalytic conv.) active
		1						Oxygen sensor (after catalytic conv.) ready
	1							Both Oxygen sensors cold
1								Sensor heating (after catalytic converter) ON

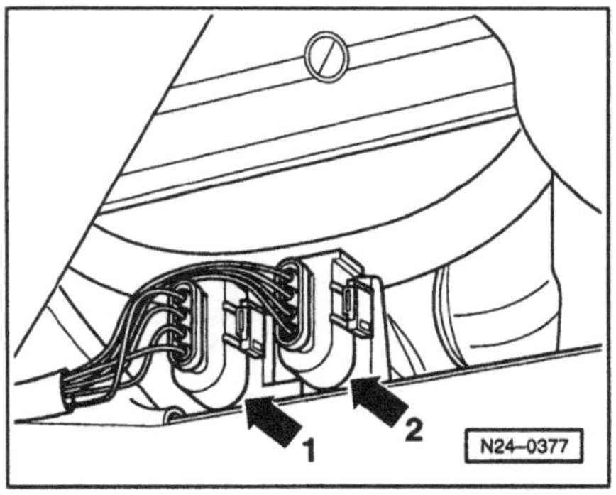

Basic Voltage, checking

◄ – Disconnect (brown) 4-pin connector to Oxygen sensor -2- (after catalytic converter) G108

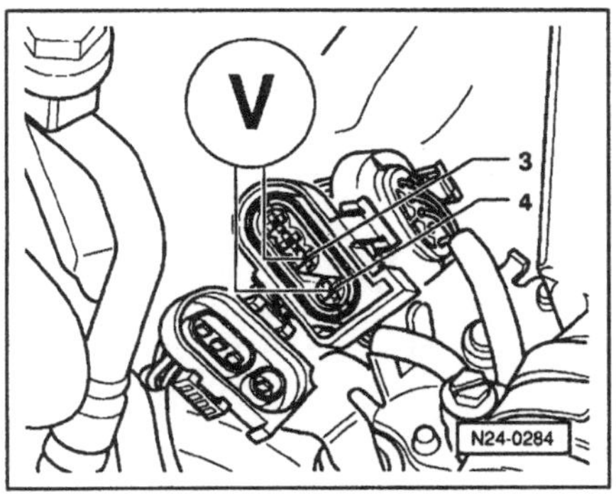

– Switch Fluke 83 multimeter to 2.0 Volt range

◄ – Connect multimeter between terminals 3 + 4 of ECM connector using jumper wires from VW 1594 adaptor kit

– Start engine and measure Basic Voltage
⇒ specification: 0.40 to 0.50 Volts

– Switch OFF ignition

If specification not obtained:

– Check Oxygen sensor wiring
⇒ page G 24-50

If specification obtained:

– Replace G108 Oxygen sensor (after catalytic converter)

Oxygen sensor wiring, checking

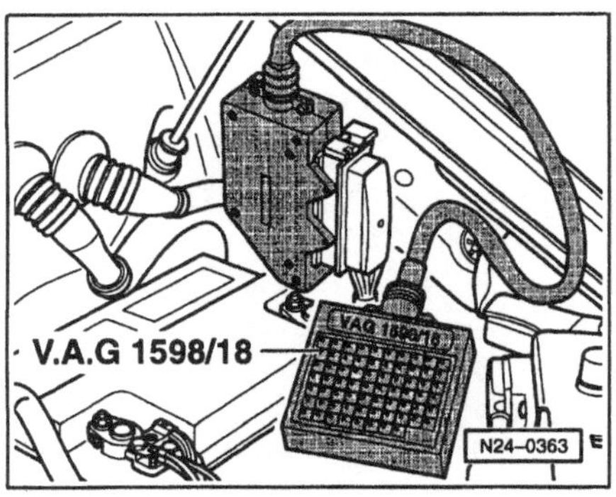

◄ – Connect VAG 1598/18 Test Box to ECM wiring harness

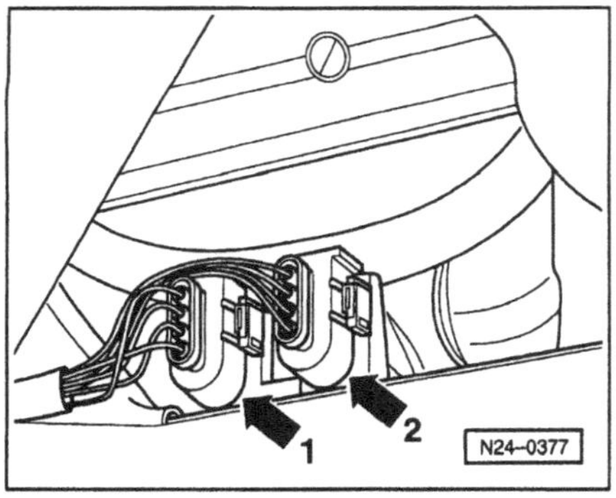

◄ – Disconnect (brown) 4-pin connector to Oxygen sensor -2- (after catalytic converter) G108

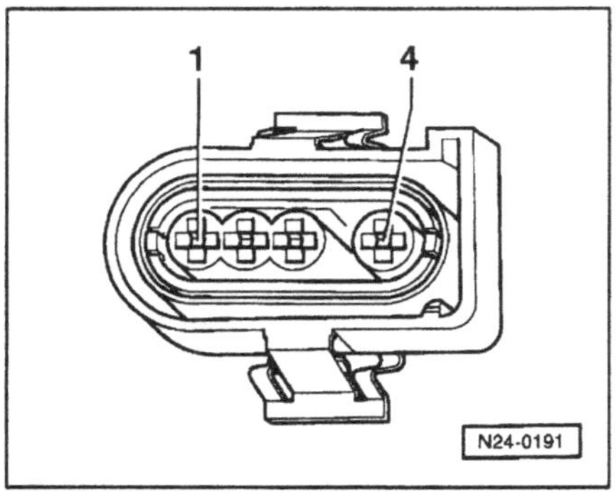

◄ – Check for open circuit between Test Box and 4-pin ECM connector using wiring diagram, connecting as follows:

- terminal 3 + socket 58
- terminal 4 + socket 13

♦ wire resistance: 1.5 Ω maximum

– Check wires to 4-pin connector for shorting to one another

- terminal 4 + socket 58

♦ specification: ∞Ω

– Check shielding for short to sensor wiring

- terminal 4 + socket 56
- terminal 3 + socket 56

♦ specification: ∞Ω

If wiring OK:

– Replace Engine Control Module J220

– Perform Basic setting
⇒ page G 24-90

– Read-out Readiness code
⇒ page G 01-33

If DTC memory was erased:

– Create Readiness code
⇒ page G 01-35

Oxygen sensor heating (after catalytic converter), checking

Special tools, testers and auxiliary items

- VAG 1551/1552 Scan Tool using VAG 1551/3 adaptor cable
- VAG 1598/18 Test Box
- Fluke 83 multimeter (or equivalent)
- VW 1594 Adaptor kit
- Wiring diagram

Requirement

- Fuse 18 OK

Test sequence

– Connect VAG 1551 (VAG 1552) Scan Tool ⇒ Repair Group 01, page 01-7

– With engine idling, press 0 and 1 buttons to select Address Word 01, "Engine Electronics"

Rapid data transfer	HELP
Select function XX	

◄ Display will appear as shown

– Press 0 and 8 buttons to select Function 08, "Read measuring value block"

– Press Q button to enter selection

Read measuring value block	HELP
Input display group number XXX	

◄ Display will appear as shown

– Press 1, 2 and 1 buttons to select "Display group number 121"

– Press Q button to enter selection

Read measuring value block 121			→
1	2	3	4

◄ Display will appear as shown (1 to 4 = Display zones)

– Check resistance value for Oxygen sensor heater (after catalytic converter) (Display zone 3, page G 24-55)

	Display zones			
	1	2	3	4
Display group 121: Oxygen sensor heating (after cat)				
Display	xxx.x°C	xxx.xx seconds	x.x Ω	xxxxxxxx
Indicated	Catalyst temperature	Time from heater ON to start of diagnostic	Oxygen sensor heating resistance (after cat)	Oxygen control status (after cat)
Working range	0.0 to 999.9°C	Approx. 150.00 s	0.0 to 65.0 Ω	Relevance ⇒ page G 24-55
Spec	---	---	5.9 to 24.2 Ω	
	---	---	If specification is not obtained: ⇒ page G 24-56, continuation	---

- Press → button
- Press 0 and 6 buttons to select Function 06, "End output"
- Press Q button to enter selection
- Switch OFF ignition

Relevance of figures in 8 digit number block

Relevance when display = 1								
x	x	x	x	x	x	x	x	Oxygen control status (display group 121)
							1	Malfunction in DTC memory
						1		Malfunction detected during diagnostic
					1			Diagnostic completed during drive
				1				Diagnostic currently active
			1					Sensor heating (after catalytic conv.) ready
		1						Oxygen sensor (after catalytic conv.) ready
	1							Vapor point (after catalytic conv.) exceeded
1								1 = sensor heating (after catalytic conv.) on alternating 0 and 1 = sensor heater is cycling

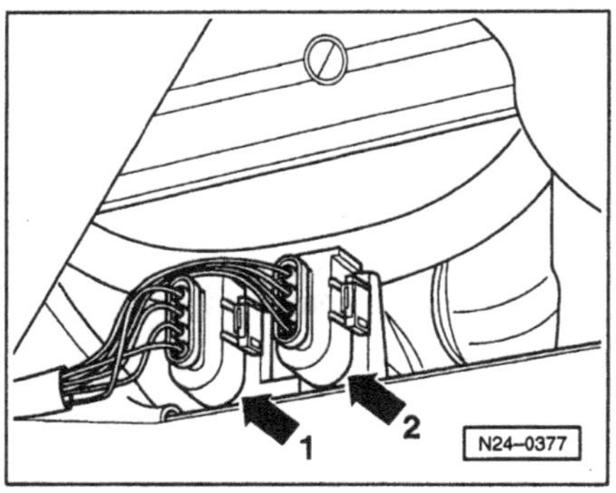

Continuation

- Disconnect (brown) 4-pin connector to Oxygen sensor -2- (after catalytic converter) G108

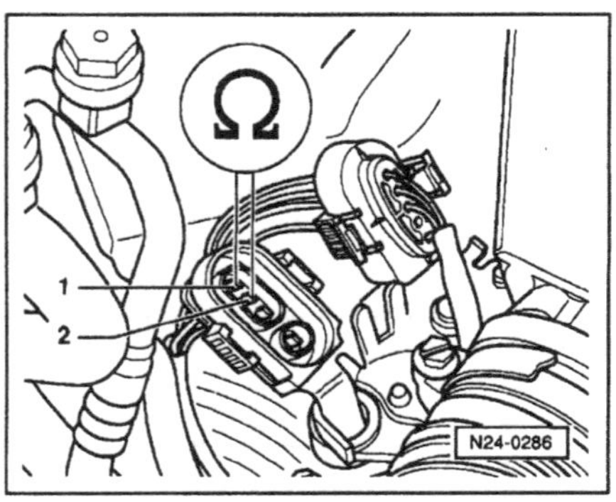

- Switch Fluke 83 multimeter to resistance range
- Connect multimeter to terminals 1 + 2 on Oxygen sensor connector, using jumper wires from VW 1594 adaptor kit
- Measure resistance

⇒ specification: 0.00 to 24.2 Ω

If specification not obtained:

- Replace G108 Oxygen sensor (after catalytic converter)

If specification obtained:

- Switch multimeter to 20 Volt DC range

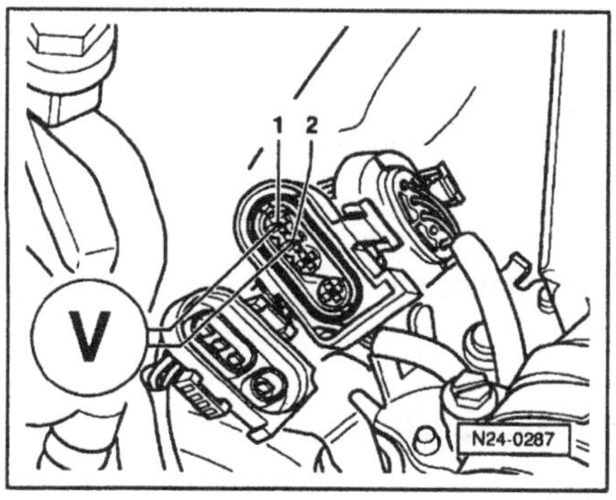

◄ – Connect multimeter between terminals 1 + 2 of ECM connector using jumper wires from VW 1594 kit

– Measure Voltage supply when display group 121, Display zone 4, 1st position from left = 1

♦ specification: 11.0 to 14.5 Volts

Measure Voltage supply when display group 121, Display zone 4, 1st position from left = alternating 0 and 1

♦ specification: between 0.0 and 12.0 Volts and alternating

If no Voltage present:

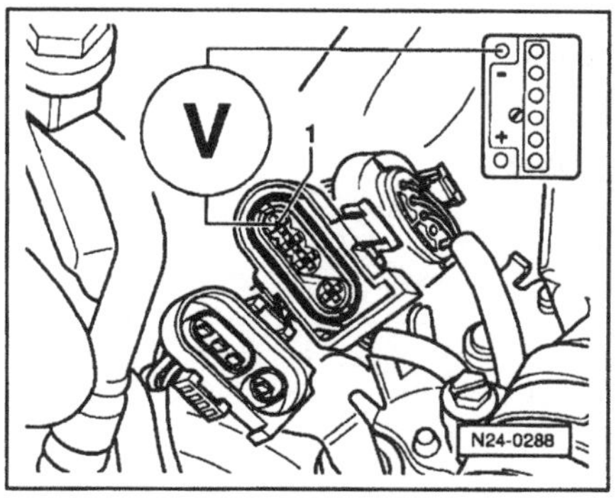

◄ – Connect multimeter between terminal 1 of ECM connector and Ground using jumper wires from VW 1594 adaptor kit
⇒ specification: 11.0 to 14.5 Volts

If no Voltage present, again:

– Check wiring between terminal 1 and fuse/relay panel using wiring diagram

If Voltage present:

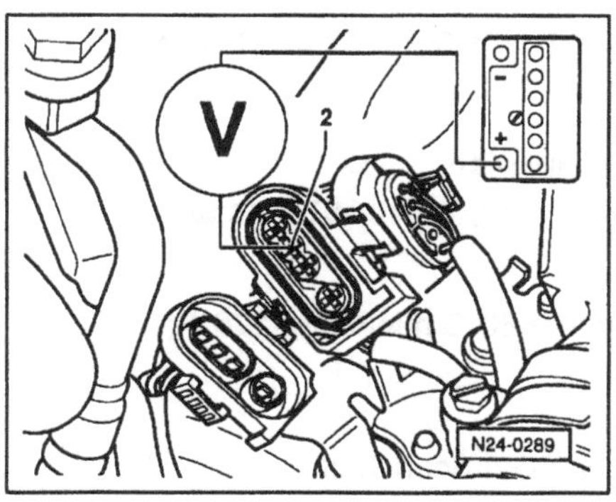

◄ – Connect multimeter between ECM connector terminals 2 and B+ using jumper wires from VW 1594 adaptor kit

– Measure Voltage supply when display group 121, Display zone 4, 1st position from left = 1

♦ specification: 11.0 to 14.5 Volts

– Measure Voltage supply when display group 121, Display zone 4, 1st position from left = alternating 0 and 1

♦ specification: between 0.0 and 12.0 Volts and alternating

– Switch OFF ignition

If specification not obtained:

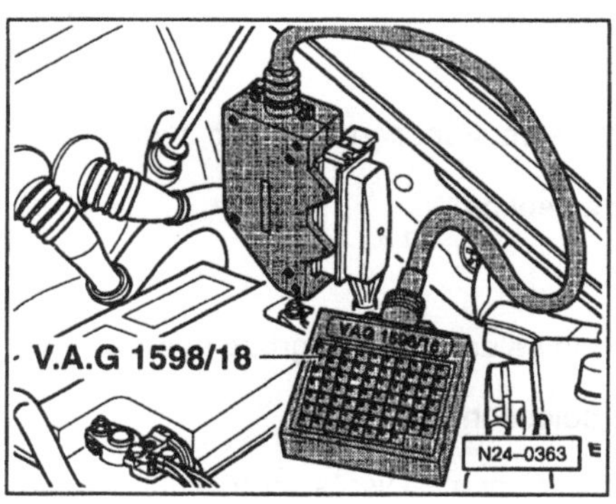

◄ – Connect VAG 1598/18 Test Box to ECM wiring harness

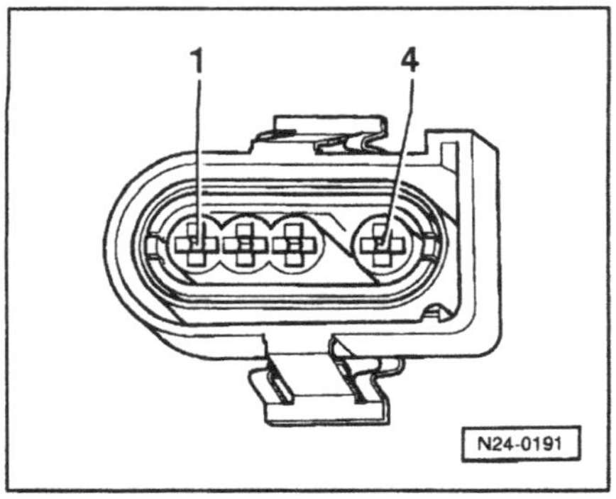

- Check for open circuit between Test Box and 4-pin harness connector using Wiring diagram, connecting as follows:
  - terminal 2 + socket 66
  - ♦ wire resistance: 1.5 Ω maximum

If wiring OK:

- Replace Engine Control Module J220
- Perform Basic setting
⇒ page G 24-90
- Create Readiness code again
⇒ page G 01-35

If DTC memory has been erased:

- Read-out Readiness code
⇒ page G 01-33

Oxygen sensor (before catalytic converter) aging, checking

Special tools, testers and auxiliary items

♦ VAG 1551/1552 Scan Tool using VAG 1551/3 adaptor cable

Requirement

♦ Engine Coolant Temperature 80°C minimum (176°F)

Functional check

- Connect VAG 1551 (VAG 1552) Scan Tool
⇒ Repair Group 01, page G 01-7
- With engine idling, press 0 and 1 buttons to select Address Word 01, "Engine Electronics"

Rapid data transfer	HELP
Select function XX	

Display will appear as shown

- Press 0 and 4 buttons to select Function 0, "Basic setting"
- Press Q button to enter selection

Introduce Basic setting	HELP
Input display group number XX	

Display will appear as shown

- Press 1, 3 and 0 buttons to select "Display group number 130"
- Press Q button to enter selection

Basic setting 130			→
1	2	3	4

Display will appear as shown (1 to 4 = Display zones)

- Rev engine between 2200 and 2800 rpm, check specs for Oxygen sensor aging (before catalytic conv.) ⇒ Display zones 1 to 4

Note:

- *To ensure exhaust gas temperature is within specification during test, maintain test rpm for at least 1 minute.*
- *Observe Oxygen control status in Display zone 4.*

	Display zones			
	1	2	3	4
Display group 130: Oxygen sensor aging (monitoring signal frequency of Oxygen sensor)				
Display	xxxx rpm	xx.xx seconds	xxx	xxxxxxxx
Indicated	Engine speed	Oxygen sensor (before catalytic converter) signal frequency	Valid Oxygen sensor signal frequency (counted)	Oxygen control status
Working range	650 to 6000 rpm	0.00 to 5.00 seconds	0 to 4	---
Spec	2200 to 2800 rpm	0.00 to 2.80 seconds	4	1111x100
	---	If specification not obtained: ⇒ page G 24-62, continuation		Relevance ⇒ page G 24-63

– Press C button

– Press 1, 3 and 1 buttons to select "Display group number 131"

– Press Q button to enter selection

Basic setting 131			→
1	2	3	4

◄ Display will appear as shown (1 to 4 = Display zones)

– Run engine at idle and check specifications

	Display zones			
	1	2	3	4
Display group 131: Oxygen sensor aging (Oxygen control signal frequency extended)				
Display	xxxx rpm	xx.xxx Volts	xxx ms	xxxxxxxx
Indicated	Engine speed	Oxygen sensor Voltage (after catalytic conv.)	Signal frequency (extended)	Oxygen control status
Working range	650 to 6000 rpm	0.000 to 1.000 Volts	---	---
Spec	2200 to 2800 rpm	0.500 to 0.700 Volts (can fluctuate slightly)	–600 to 600 ms	1111x100
	---	If specification not obtained: ⇒ page G 24-62, continuation		Relevance ⇒ page G 24-63

Continuation

If specification is not obtained:

– Drive vehicle to free up any Oxygen sensor build-up, repeat test

If specification still not obtained:

– Replace Oxygen sensor (before catalytic converter) G39

– Read-out Readiness code
⇒ page G 01-33

If DTC memory has been erased:

– Create Readiness code
⇒ page G 01-35

Relevance of figures in 8 digit number block

Relevance when display = 1									
x	x	x	x	x	x	x	x	Oxygen control status (display group 130)	Oxygen control status (display group 131)
							1	Malfunction in DTC memory	Malfunction in DTC memory
						1		Malfunctions detected during diagnostic	Malfunctions recognized during diagnostic
					1			Diagnostic completed during drive	Diagnostic completed during drive
				1				Diagnostic currently active	Diagnostic currently active
			1					Diagnostic for sensor heating (before catalytic converter) ready	Oxygen control (before catalytic converter) active
		1						Catalyst temperature within specified range	Oxygen control (after catalytic conv.) active
	1							Engine speed and load within specified range	Engine speed and load within specified range
1								Oxygen control (before catalytic conv.) active	Catalyst temperature within specified range

Engine operation, checking

Note:

This check will verify if the Engine Control Module recognizes the engine operating conditions.

Special tools, testers and auxiliary items

♦ VAG 1551/1552 Scan Tool using VAG 1551/3 adaptor cable

Requirement

♦ Engine oil temperature 80 °C (176 °F) minimum

Test sequence

– Connect VAG 1551 (VAG 1552) Scan Tool
⇒ Repair Group 01, page G 01-7

– With engine idling, press 0 and 1 buttons to select Address Word 01, "Engine Electronics"

Rapid data transfer	HELP
Select function XX	

◄ Display will appear as shown

– Press 0 and 8 buttons to select Function 08, "Read measuring value block"

– Press Q button to enter selection

Read measuring value block	HELP
Input display group number XXX	

◄ Display will appear as shown

– Press 0, 0 and 5 buttons to select "Display group number 5"

- Press Q button to enter selection

Read measuring value block 5			→
1	2	3	4

◄ Display will appear as shown (1 to 4 = Display zones)

- Check whether ECM recognizes operating mode (Display zone 4)

	Display zones			
	1	2	3	4
Display group 5: General engine data				
Display	xxx rpm	xx.xx ms	xxx km/h	Idle
Indicated	Engine speed	Engine load	Vehicle speed	Operating mode
Working range	650 to 6000 rpm	0.00 to 25.00 ms	---	---
Specifi-cat	650 to 750 rpm	---	0 km/h	Idle = closed throttle Partial load = slightly open throttle. Enrich. = Rev above 3000 rpm, then over-run (close throttle valve abruptly) Full load = only possible when driving

If specifications not obtained

- Check accelerator mechanism for ease of operation

- Check Throttle Valve Control Module ⇒ page G 24-72

Mass Air Flow sensor, checking

Special tools, testers and auxiliary items

- ♦ VAG 1551/1552 Scan Tool using VAG 1551/3 adaptor cable
- ♦ VAG 1598/18 Test Box
- ♦ Fluke 83 multimeter (or equivalent)
- ♦ VW 1594 Adaptor kit
- ♦ Wiring diagram

Requirements

- ♦ All electrical consumers Switched OFF (radiator fan must not run during the check)
- ♦ Air Conditioner Switched OFF

Test sequence

- Connect VAG 1551 (VAG 1552) Scan Tool ⇒ Repair Group 01, page G 01-7

- With engine idling, press 0 and 1 buttons to select Address Word 01, "Engine Electronics"

Rapid data transfer	HELP
Select function XX	

◄ Display will appear as shown

- Press 0 and 8 buttons to select Fuction 08, "Read measuring value block"

– Press Q button to enter selection

Read measuring value block HELP
Input display group number XXX

Display will appear as shown

– Press 0, 1 and 5 buttons to select “Display group number 15”

– Press Q button to enter selection

Read measuring value block 15 →
1 2 3 4

Display will appear as shown (1 to 4 = Display zones)

– Check load registration specification 1
(Display zones 2 and 3)

	Display zones			
	1	2	3	4
Display group 15: Load registration 1				
Display	xxx rpm	xx.xx ms	xx%	xx.x g/s
Indicated	Engine speed	Engine load	Engine load	Air mass
Working range	650 to 6000 rpm	0.00 to 25.00 ms	0 to 40%	---
Specifi- cat	650 to 750 rpm	1.00 to 3.00 ms	10 to 30%	3.0 to 4.0 g/s
	---	If specification not obtained: Check Voltage supply and wiring ⇒ page G 24-70		---

– Press C button

– Press buttons 0, 1 and 6 for “Display group number 16”

– Press Q button to enter selection

Read measuring value block 16 →
1 2 3 4

Display will appear as shown (1 to 4 = Display zones)

– Check load specification 2 (Display zone 3)

	Display zones			
	1	2	3	4
Display group 16: Load registration 2				
Display	xxx rpm	xx.xx ms	xx.xx ms	xx.xx ms

Evaluating display group16

Display group: 16 Display zone: 3	Possible cause	Corrective Steps
0.00 ms	♦ Wiring, open circuit in wire 3 or 4 between Mass Air Flow sensor and ECM	– Check Voltage supply ⇒ page G 24-69 – Check wiring ⇒ page G 24-70
Smallest value: 5.30 ms	♦ Wiring, open circuit in wire 1 or 2 between Mass Air Flow sensor and ECM	

Specifi-cat	650 to 750 rpm	1.00 to 3.00 ms	1.00 to 3.00 ms	1.00 to 3.00 ms
	---	---	If specification not obtained: ⇒ evaluating display group 16	---
Indicated	Engine speed	Engine load	Engine load	Engine load substitute value from throttle valve angle
Working range	650 to 6000 rpm	0.00 to 25.00 ms	0 to 25.00 ms	0.00 to 25.00 ms

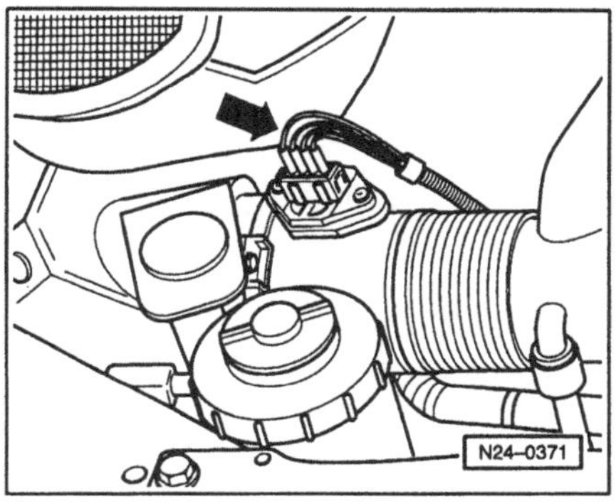

Voltage supply, checking

◄ – Disconnect 4-pin Mass Air Flow sensor harness connector-ar-row-

– Switch Fluke 83 multimeter to 20 Volt DC range

– Connect multimeter between harness connector terminals 1 + 3 using jumper wires from VW 1594 adaptor kit
⇒ specification: 9.0 to 14.5 Volts

If NO Voltage present:

– Switch OFF ignition

– Check wiring using wiring diagram

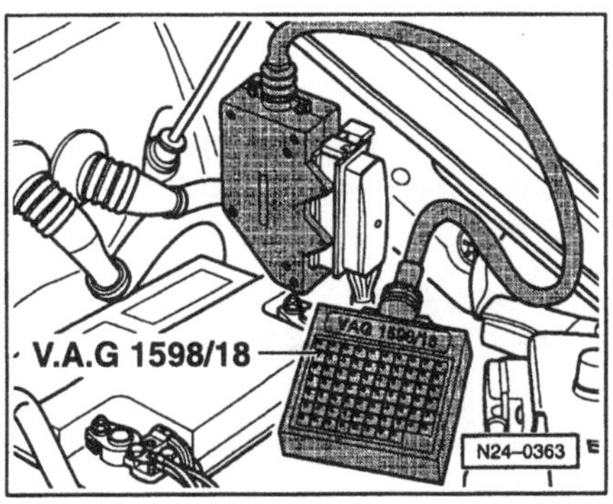

Wiring, checking

– Switch OFF ignition

◄ – Connect VAG 1598/18 Test Box to ECM wiring harness

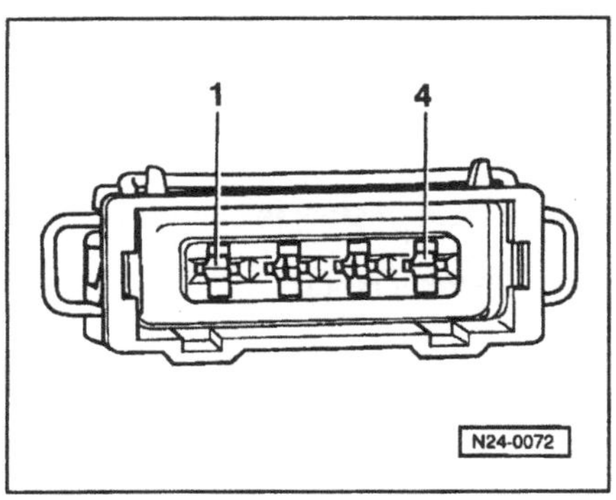

◄ – Check for open circuit between Test Box and 4-pin harness connector using wiring diagram, connecting as follows:
  – terminal 2 + socket 16
  – terminal 4 + socket 17
  ♦ wire resistance: 1.5 Ω maximum

– Check 4-pin connector wires for shorting to one another
  – terminal 4 + socket 16
  ♦ specification: ∞ Ω

– Switch Fluke 83 multimeter to 20 Volt DC range

– Check 4-pin harness connector wiring for short to B+ using wiring diagram, connecting as follows:
  – terminal 2 + vehicle Ground
  – terminal 4 + vehicle Ground
  ♦ specification: 0 Volts

If wiring OK:

– Replace Mass Air Flow sensor G70

– Read-out Readiness code
⇒ page G 01-33

If DTC memory has been erased:

– Create Readiness code
⇒ page G 01-35

Throttle Valve Control Module, checking

Note:

You must perform Function 04 "Basic setting" if the Throttle Valve Control Module J338 is removed, installed or replaced.
⇒ page G 24-90.

Special tools, testers and auxiliary items

♦ VAG 1551/1552 Scan Tool using VAG 1551/3 adaptor cable

♦ VAG 1598/18 Test Box

♦ Fluke 83 multimeter (or equivalent)

♦ VW 1594 Adaptor kit

♦ Wiring diagram

Voltage supply, checking

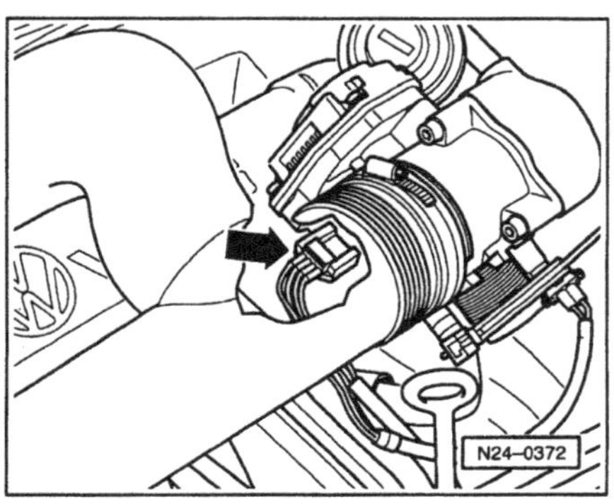

◄ – Disconnect 8-pin Throttle Valve Control Module connector

– Switch Fluke 83 multimeter to 20 Volts range

– Connect multimeter between harness connector terminals 3 + 7 using jumper wires from VW 1594 adaptor kit

– Switch ON ignition
⇒ specification: 9.0 to 14.5 Volts

– Connect multimeter between harness connector terminals 4 + 7
⇒ specification: 4.0 to 6.0 Volts

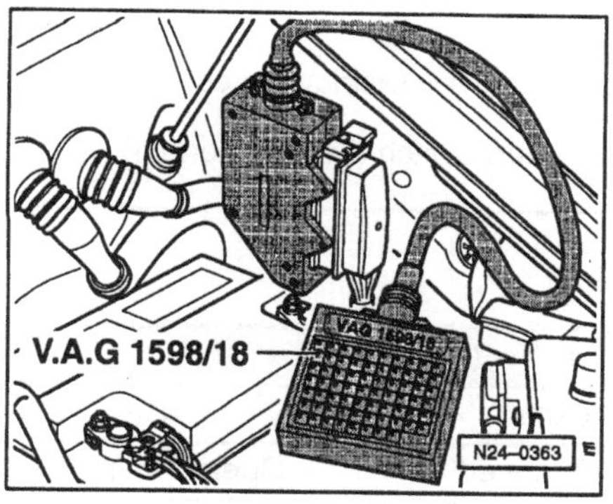

– Switch OFF ignition

If specifications not obtained:

◄ – Connect VAG 1598/18 Test Box to ECM wiring harness

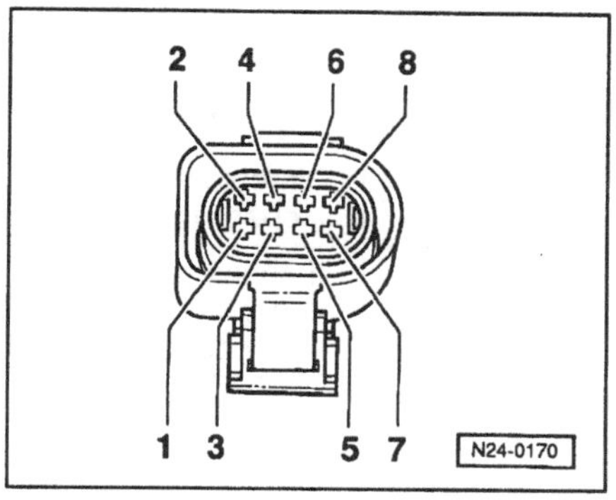

◄ – Check for open circuit between Test Box and 8-pin harness connector, using wiring diagram

– terminal 3 + socket 10

– terminal 4 + socket 41

– terminal 7 + socket 33

♦ wire resistance: Max. 1.5 Ω

– Check wiring at 8-pin connector for short to one another

– terminal 7 + socket 10

– terminal 7 + socket 41

– terminal 4 + socket 33

♦ specification: ∞ Ω

– Reconnect Throttle Valve Control Module

If wiring OK:

– Replace Engine Control Module J220

– Read-out Readiness code
⇒ page G 01-33

If DTC memory has been erased:

– Create Readiness code
⇒ page G 01-35

Closed Throttle Position switch, checking

– Connect VAG 1551 (VAG 1552) Scan Tool
⇒ Repair Group 01, page G 01-7

– With engine idling, press 0 and 1 buttons to select Address Word 01, "Engine Electronics"

Rapid data transfer Select function XX	HELP

◄ Display will appear as shown

– Press 0 and 8 buttons to select Function 08, "Read measuring value block"

– Press Q button to enter selection

Read measuring value block Input display group number XXX	HELP

◄ Display will appear as shown

– Press 0, 0 and 5 buttons to select "Display group number 5"

– Press Q button to enter selection

Read measuring value block 5			→
1	2	3	4

◄ Display will appear as shown (1 to 4 = Display zones)

– Check Closed Throttle Position Switch (Display zone 4)

	Display zones			
	1	2	3	4
Display group 5: General engine data				
Display	xxx rpm	xx.xx ms	xxx km/h	Text
Indicated	Engine speed	Engine load	Vehicle speed	Operating modes
Working range	650 to 6000 rpm	0.00 to 25.00 ms	---	---
Specification	650 to 1100 rpm	1.00 to 3.00 ms	0 km/h	Throttle valve closed = Idling Throttle valve slightly open = partial load
	---	---	---	If specification not obtained: ⇒ page G 24-76, continuation

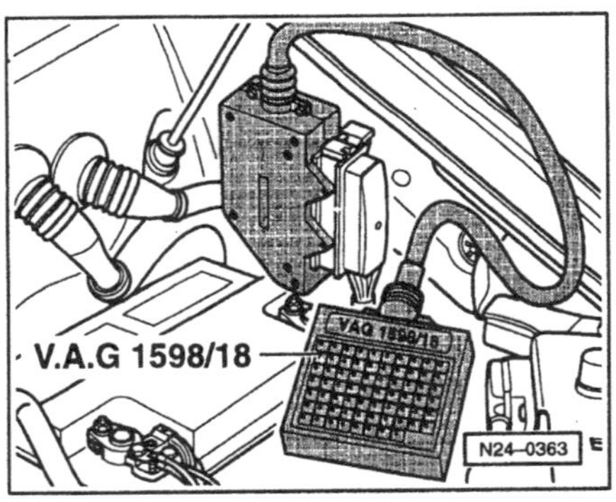

Continuation

– Switch OFF ignition

◄ – Connect VAG 1598/18 Test Box to ECM wiring harness

– Switch Fluke 83 multimeter to resistance range

– With closed throttle, connect multimeter between Test Box sockets 10 + 33

♦ specification: 5.0 Ω maximum

– Slowly open throttle valve

♦ specification: ∞Ω

If specification not obtained:

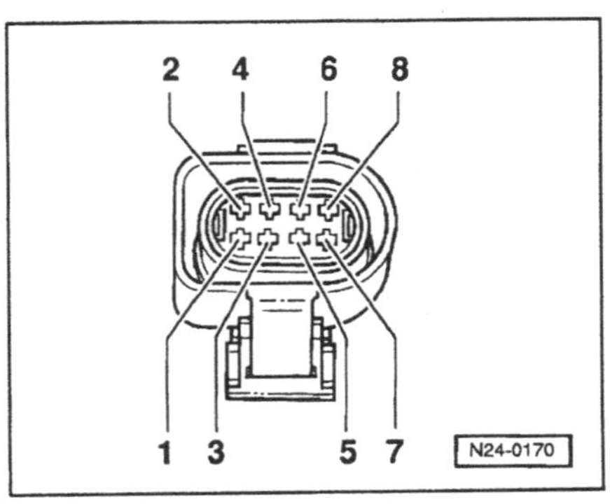

– Disconnect 8-pin Throttle Valve Control Module harness connector

◄ – Check for open circuit between Test Box and 8-pin harness connector using wiring diagram

– terminal 3 + socket 10

– terminal 7 + socket 33

♦ wire resistance:1.5 Ω maximum

- Check wiring at 8-pin connector for shorting to one another
  - terminal 7 + socket 10
  - ♦ specification: ∞ Ω
- Re-connect harness connector

If wiring OK:

- Replace Throttle Valve Control Module
- Perform Basic setting
⇒ page G 24-90
- Read-out Readiness code
⇒ page G 01-33

If DTC memory has been erased:

- Create Readiness code
⇒ page G 01-35

Throttle valve actuator, checking

Requirement

♦ Coolant temperature 80 °C (176 F°) minimum

Test sequence

- Connect VAG 1551 (VAG 1552) Scan Tool
⇒ Repair Group 01, page G 01-7
- With engine idling, press 0 and 1 buttons to select Address Word 01, "Engine Electronics"

Rapid data transfer	HELP
Select function XX	

◄ Display will appear as shown

- Press 0 and 8 buttons to select Function, "Read measuring value block"
- Press Q button to enter selection

Read measuring value block	HELP
Input display group number XXX	

◄ Display will appear as shown

- Press buttons 0, 3 and 7 for "Display group number 37"
- Press Q button to enter selection

Read measuring value block 37			→
1	2	3	4

◄ Display will appear as shown (1 to 4 = Display zones)

- Check idle speed control specs (Display zones 1 to 4)

	Display zones			
	1	2	3	4
Display group 37: Idling control				
Display	xxx rpm	xxx rpm	xx.x%	xx.x g/s
Indicated	Engine speed	Engine speed specification	Idle speed control	Air mass
Working range	650 to 6000 rpm	---	–16.0 to 16.0%	0.0 to 20.0 g/s
specification	650 to 750 rpm[1]	700 rpm	–4.0 to 4.0%	2.5 to 4.5 g/s
	If specification not obtained: ⇒ page G 24-83, continuation		If spec not obtained: ⇒ page G 24-81, evaluating display group 37	If spec not obtained: ⇒ page G 24-83

– Press C button

– Press 0, 3 and 6 buttons to select "Display group number 36"

– Press Q button to enter selection

Read measuring value block 36			→
1	2	3	4

◄ Display will appear as shown (1 to 4 = Display zones)

– Check idle speed control specs (Display zones 2 + 3)

	Display zones			
	1	2	3	4
Display group 36: Idling control				
Display	xx.x ∠°	x.xx g/s	x.xx g/s	---
Indicated	Throttle valve angle	Air mass adaption value during idle	Air mass adaption value with transmission range selected	---
Working range	0.0 to 90.0 ∠°	–1.70 to 1.70 g/s	–1.70 to 1.70 g/s	---
Specification	3.0 to 7.0 ∠°	–0.50 to 0.50 g/s	–0.40 to 0.40 g/s[1]	---
	---	If specification not obtained: ⇒ page G 24-82, evaluating display group 36		---

[1] Vehicles with manual transmission: "0" is always displayed.

Evaluating display group 37

Display group: 37 Display zone: 3	Possible cause	Corrective Steps
Idle control range: 4.0 to 16.0%	♦ Load increased (electrical consumers switched ON)	– Switch OFF electrical consumers
–4.0 to –16.0%	♦ Unmeasured air behind throttle valve (also note display group 36, Display zones 2 + 3)	– Check intake air system for leaks (unmeasured air) ⇒ page G 24-128 – Check exhaust system ⇒ Repair Group 26

Evaluating display group 36

Display group: 36 Display zone: 2	Possible cause	Corrective Steps
Air mass adaption value: 0.50 to 1.70%	♦ Load increased (electrical consumers switched ON)	– Switch OFF electrical consumers
–0.50 to –1.70%	♦ Unmeasured air behind throttle valve	– Check intake air system for leaks (unmeasured air) ⇒ page G 24-128 – Check exhaust system for leaks ⇒ Repair Group 26
Display zone: 3	**Possible cause**	**Corrective Steps**
Air mass adaption value: 0.40 to 1.70%	♦ Load increased (electrical consumers switched ON)	– Switch OFF electrical consumers
–0.40 to –1.70%	♦ Unmeasured air behind throttle valve	– Check intake air system for leaks (unmeasured air) ⇒ page G 24-128 – Check exhaust system for leaks ⇒ Repair Group 26

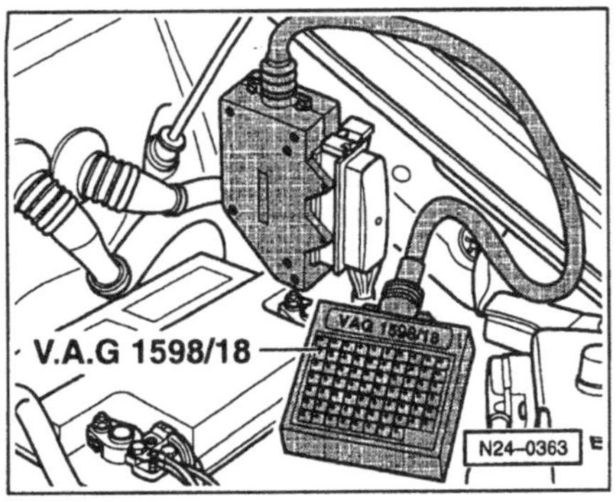

Continuation

- Switch OFF ignition
- Connect VAG 1598/18 Test Box to ECM wiring harness
- Switch ON ignition
- Switch Fluke 83 multimeter to resistance range
- With throttle valve closed, connect multimeter between Test Box sockets 27 + 53 using jumper wires from VW 1594 adaptor kit
  - ♦ specification: 3 to 200 Ω

If specification not obtained:

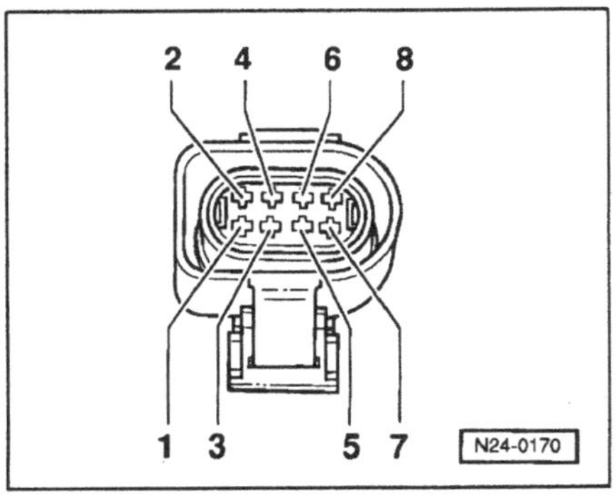

- Disconnect 8-pin Throttle Valve Control Module connector
- Check wiring for open circuit between Test Box and 8-pin connector using wiring diagram
  - terminal 1 + socket 27
  - terminal 2 + socket 53
  - terminal 7 + socket 33
  - terminal 8 + socket 62
  - ♦ wire resistance: 1.5 Ω maximum

- Check wiring at 8-pin harness connector for shorting to one another using wiring diagram
  - terminal 1 + socket 53
  - terminal 1 + socket 62
  - terminal 1 + socket 33
  - terminal 2 + socket 33
  - terminal 2 + socket 62
  - terminal 7 + socket 62
  - ♦ specification: ∞ Ω

If wiring OK:

- Replace Throttle Valve Control Module
- Perform Basic setting
⇒ page G 24-90
- Read-out Readiness code
⇒ page G 01-33

If DTC memory has been erased:

- Create Readiness code
⇒ page G 01-35

Throttle Valve Position sensor, checking

– Connect VAG 1551 (VAG 1552) Scan Tool
⇒ Repair Group 01, page G 01-7

– With engine idling, press 0 and 1 buttons to select Address Word 01, "Engine Electronics"

Rapid data transfer	HELP
Select function XX	

◄ Display will appear as shown

– Press 0 and 8 buttons to select Function 08, "Read measuring value block"

– Press Q button to enter selection

Read measuring value block	HELP
Input display group number XXX	

◄ Display will appear as shown

– Press 0, 0 and 3 buttons to select "Display group number 3"

– Press Q button to enter selection

Read measuring value block 3			→
1	2	3	4

◄ Display will appear as shown (1 to 4 = Display zones)

– Check Throttle Valve Position sensor specification (Display zone 3, page G 24-86)

	Display zones			
	1	2	3	4
Display group 3: Load registration 1				
Display	xxx rpm	xx.x g/s	xxx ∠°	xx.x°C
Indicated	Engine speed	Air mass	Throttle valve angle	Intake Air Temperature
Working range	650 to 6000 rpm	---	0 to 90 ∠°	–46.5 to 141.0°C
Specification	0 rpm	---	3 to 7 ∠°	Ambient temperature, approximately
	---	---	If spec not obtained: ⇒ page G 24-87, evaluating display group 3	---

– Slowly open throttle while observing throttle angle in Display zone 3

♦ displayed value must increase uniformly over complete range

– Press → button

– Press 0 and 6 buttons to select Function 06 "End output"

– Press Q button to enter selection

– Switch OFF ignition

Note:

The displayed value is dependent upon the Throttle Position sensor tolerances and does not correspond to the actual throttle opening angle. The maximum permissible displayed value is 90.0 ∠°.

If value does not increase uniformly:

– Replace Throttle Valve Control Module

– Perform Basic setting
⇒ page G 24-90

– Read-out Readiness code
⇒ page G 01-33

If DTC memory has been erased:

– Create Readiness code
⇒ page G 01-35

Evaluating display group 3

Display group: 3 Display zone: 3	Possible cause	Corrective Steps
0.0 ∠°	♦ Wiring open circuit	– Check wiring ⇒ page G 24-88
99.0 ∠°	♦ Short to Ground	

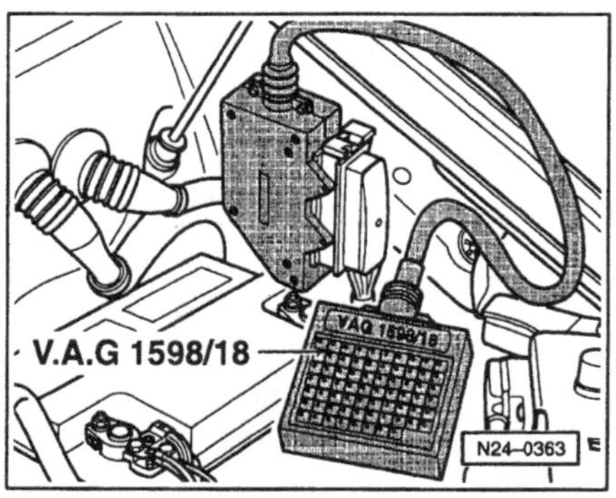

Wiring, checking

– Connect VAG 1598/18 Test Box to ECM wiring harness

– Switch Fluke 83 multimeter to resistance range

– Check wiring for short to Ground by connecting multimeter between Test Box sockets 01 + 40 using jumper wires from VW 1594 adaptor kit

♦ specification: ∞ Ω

– Switch multimeter to 20 Volt DC range

– Switch ON ignition

– Check wiring for short to positive, record Voltage value if necessary

– Switch OFF ignition

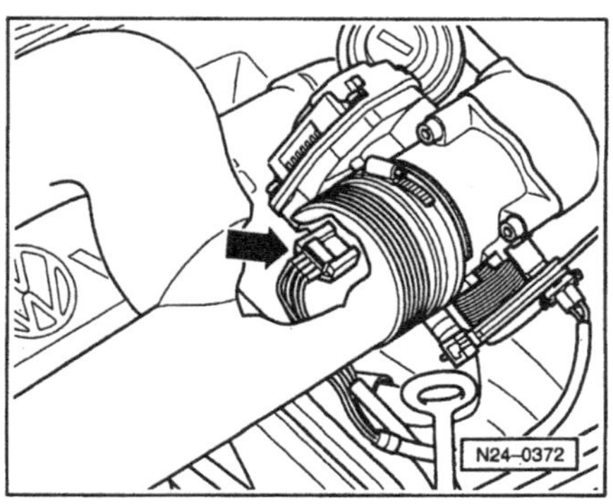

– Disconnect 8-pin Throttle Valve Control Module connector

Continuation (If Voltage present)

If approximately 5 Volts measured:
– Switch multimeter to resistance range

– Check wires for shorting to one another as follows

– Connect multimeter between Test Box sockets 40 + 41 using jumper wires from VW 1594 adaptor kit
⇒ specification: ∞ Ω

If Voltage was approximately equal to battery Voltage:
– Check wire for short to battery positive at 8-pin harness connector terminal 5 using wiring diagram

Continuation (NO Voltage present)

– Check wiring for open circuit between Test Box and 8-pin connector using wiring diagram
  – terminal 5 + socket 40
  ♦ wire resistance: 1.5 Ω maximum

If wiring OK:
– Replace Throttle Valve Control Module J338

– Perform Basic setting ⇒ page G 24-90

– Read-out Readiness code
⇒ page G 01-33

If DTC memory has been erased:
– Create Readiness code
⇒ page G 01-35

Function 04: Basic setting, performing

Notes:

♦ *Only perform Function 04 "Basic setting" if the Throttle Valve Control Module, Engine Control Module or engine was replaced.*

♦ *Function 04 "Basic setting" (with ignition switched ON) matches the Engine Control Module to the Throttle Valve Control Module.*

♦ *If the Basic setting is interrupted by the Control Module, it is possible that the Throttle body is not positioned on the mechanical stop due to dirt or contamination build-up such as carbon or an incorrectly adjusted accelerator cable. If this is the case, the malfunction "Basic setting not performed" will be stored in DTC memory. The next time the ignition is switched ON, Basic setting will automatically be performed again.*

Special tools, testers and auxiliary items

♦ VAG 1551/1552 Scan Tool using VAG 1551/3 adaptor cable

Requirement

♦ No malfunctions stored in DTC memory
⇒ page G 01-12, interrogating DTC memory

Test sequence

- Connect VAG 1551 (VAG 1552) Scan Tool
  ⇒ Repair Group 01, page G 01-7
- With ignition switched ON but engine not running, press 0 and 1 buttons to select Address Word 01, "Engine Electronics"

Rapid data transfer	HELP
Select function XX	

◄ Display will appear as shown

- Press 0 and 4 buttons to select Function 04, "Basic setting"
- Press Q button to enter selection

Initiate Basic setting	HELP
Input display group number XX	

◄ Display will appear as shown

- Press 0, 9 and 8 buttons to select "Display group number 98"
- Press Q button to enter selection

System in Basic setting 98			→
1	2	3	4

◄ Display will appear as shown (1 to 4 = Display zones)

Note:

After confirming Display group number 98, the Throttle Valve Actuator will move to the min., max. and then start positions. The Control Module stores the appropriate throttle valve angle in permanent memory. The throttle valve will then remain in the start position.

- Check specifications (Display zones 1 to 4, page G 24-92)

	Display zones			
	1	2	3	4
Display group 98: Basic setting Throttle Valve Control Module				
Display	x.xxx Volts	x.xxx Volts	Text	Text
Indicated	Throttle Position sensor Voltage	Throttle Position Actuator Voltage	Operating mode	Basic setting status
Working range	0.000 to 5.000 Volts	0.000 to 5.000 Volts	---	---
specifi-cation	---	---	Idle	ADP. (adaption) runs
	4.000 to 5.000 Volts	3.000 to 4.000 Volts	Idle	ADP. OK. (ADP. ERROR appears if: Basic setting is not successful)
	If specification is not obtained ⇒ page G 24-72, check Throttle Valve Control Module			

- Terminate Basic setting (after 30 seconds minimum) by pressing → button
- Press 0 and 6 buttons to select Function 06, "End output"
- Press Q button to enter selection

Engine Coolant Temperature sensor, checking

Special tools, testers and auxiliary items

- VAG 1551/1552 Scan Tool using VAG 1551/3 adaptor cable
- VAG 1598/18 Test Box
- Fluke 83 multimeter (or equivalent)
- VW 1594 Adaptor kit
- Wiring diagram

Note:

If an engine reaches operating temperature while stationary, or takes too long to reach operating temperature due to unfavorable conditions, it can lead to DTC P0116 or P0125 being stored in DTC memory. If so, erase DTC memory and bring the engine to operating temperature during a test drive.

Requirement

- Engine cold

Test sequence

– Connect VAG 1551 (VAG 1552) Scan Tool
⇒ Repair Group 01, page G 01-7

– With ignition switched ON but engine not running, press 0 and 1 buttons to select Address Word 01, “Engine Electronics”

Rapid data transfer	HELP
Select function XX	

◄ Display will appear as shown

– Press 0 and 8 buttons to select Function 08, “Read measuring value block”

– Press Q button to enter selection

Read measuring value block	HELP
Input display group number XXX	

◄ Display will appear as shown

– Press 0, 0 and 1 buttons to select “Display group number 1”

– Press Q button to enter selection

Read measuring value block 1			→
1	2	3	4

◄ Display will appear as shown (1 to 4 = Display zones)

– Check specification for Engine Coolant Temperature sensor (Display zone 2, page G 24-95)

	Display zones			
	1	2	3	4
Display group 1: Idle Speed Check				
Display	xxxx rpm	xxx.x°C	xx.x%	xx.x ∠°
Indicated	Engine speed	Engine Coolant temperature	Oxygen control	Ignition angle
Working range	650 to 6000 rpm	-46.5 to 141.0°C	–25.0 to 25.0%	0.0 to 50.0 ∠°
Specification	0 rpm	Ambient temperature[1] approximately	The value must fluctuate at least 3 % in range: –5.0 to 5.0%	2.0 to 15.0 ∠°
	---	If spec not obtained: ⇒ page G 24-96, evaluating display group 1	---	---

[1] If the displayed temperature deviates greatly from the ambient temperature of the sensor, check sensor wiring for resistance transfer / open circuit.

Continuation:

– Start engine and let idle

♦ temperature value must increase uniformly

If specification not obtained:

– Replace Engine Coolant Temperature sensor G62

– Press → button

– Press 0 and 6 buttons to select Function 06, "End output"

– Press Q button to enter selection

– Switch OFF ignition

Note:

♦ *The Scan Tool display increments in 1.5°C steps.*

If engine runs irregularly during certain temperature ranges and displayed temperature value does not increase smoothly:

– Replace Engine Coolant Temperature sensor G62

Evaluating display group 1

Display group: 1 Display zone: 2	Possible cause	Corrective Steps
Approx. –46.6°C	♦ Wiring open circuit or short to positive	– Check wiring ⇒ page G 24-95
Approx. 141.0°C	♦ Short to Ground	

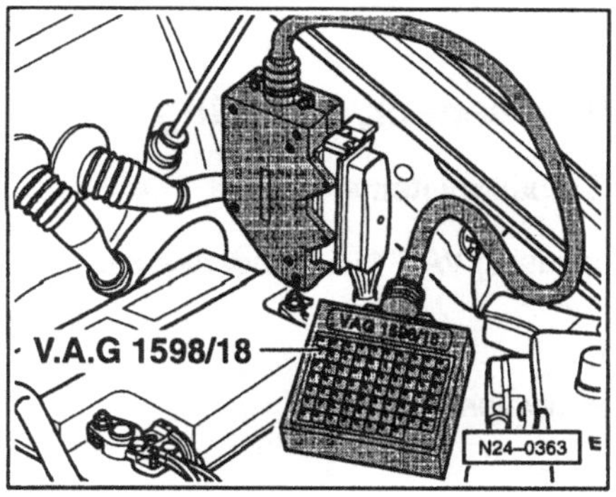

Wiring, checking

◄ – Connect VAG 1598/18 Test Box to ECM wiring harness

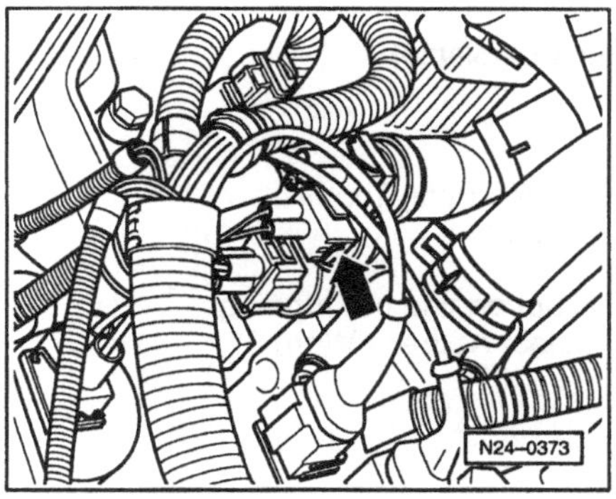

◄ – Disconnect 2-pin Engine Coolant Temperature sensor G62

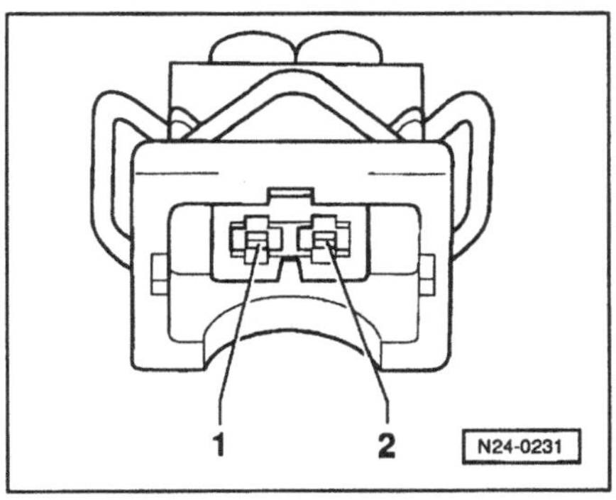

◄ – Check wiring for open circuit between Test Box and 2-pin connector using wiring diagram, connect as follows
  – terminal 1 + socket 14
  – terminal 2 + socket 33
  ♦ wire resistance: 1.5 Ω maximum

– Check wire for short between Control Module connector and 2-pin connector terminal 2 AND wire terminal 1 and Ground, using wiring diagram
  – terminal 2 + socket 14
  ♦ specification: ∞ Ω

– Additionally check both wires for short to battery positive
  ♦ specification: ∞ Ω

If wiring OK:

– Measure resistance at Engine Coolant Temperature sensor G62 terminals 1 + 2
  ♦ specification: ⇒ page G 24-21, Fig. 1

If specification not obtained:

– Replace Engine Coolant Temperature sensor G62

– Read-out Readiness code
⇒ Repair Group 01, page G 01-33

If DTC memory has been erased: Create Readiness code
⇒ Repair Group 01, page G 01-35

Intake Air Temperature sensor, checking

Special tools, testers and auxiliary items

- VAG 1551/1552 Scan Tool using VAG 1551/3 adaptor cable
- VAG 1598/18 Test Box
- Fluke 83 multimeter (or equivalent)
- VW 1594 Adaptor kit
- Wiring diagram
- Freeze-spray (commercially available)

Test sequence

– Connect VAG 1551 (VAG 1552) Scan Tool
⇒ Repair Group 01, page G 01-7

– With ignition Switched ON but engine not running, press 0 and 1 buttons to select Address Word 01, "Engine Electronics"

Rapid data transfer	HELP
Select function XX	

◄ Display will appear as shown

– Press 0 and 8 buttons to select Function 08, "Read measuring value block"

– Press Q button to enter selection

Read measuring value block	HELP
Input display group number XXX	

◄ Display will appear as shown

– Press 0, 0 and 3 buttons to select "Display group number 3"

– Press Q button to enter selection

Read measuring value block 3			→
1	2	3	4

◄ Display will appear as shown (1 to 4 = Display zones)

– Check specification for Intake Air Temperature sensor (Display zone 4)

	Display zones			
	1	2	3	4
Display group 3: Load registration 1				
Display	xxx rpm	xx.x g/s	xxx ∠°	xx.x°C
Indicated	Engine speed	Air mass	Throttle valve angle	Intake Air Temperature
Working range	650 to 6000 rpm	0.0 to 25.0 g/s	0 to 90 ∠°	-46.5 to 141.0°C
Specifi-cat	0 rpm	---	3 to 7 ∠°	Ambient temperature[1] approx.
	---	---	---	Continuation: ⇒ page G 24-101, evaluating display group 3

[1] If the displayed temperature deviates greatly from the ambient temperature of the sensor, check sensor wiring for resistance transfer / open circuit.

Evaluating display group 3

Display group: 3 Display zone: 4	Possible cause	Corrective Steps
–46.5°C	♦ Wiring open circuit or short to positive	– Check wiring, ⇒ page G 24-101
141.0°C	♦ Short to Ground	
Ambient temperature (approx.)	♦ Signal intermittently interrupted	– Check sensor ⇒ page G 24-103

Wiring, checking

– Switch OFF ignition

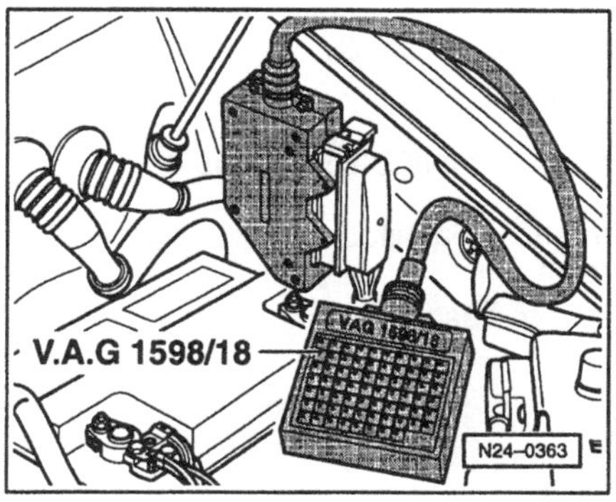

– Connect VAG 1598/18 Test Box to ECM wiring harness

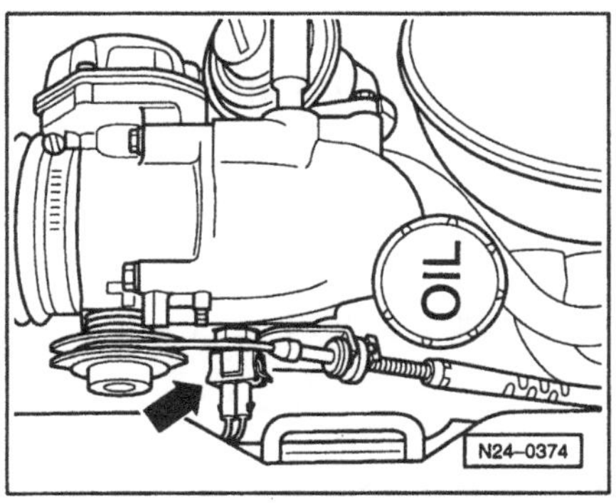

– Disconnect 2-pin connector for Intake Air Temperature sensor G72 -arrow-

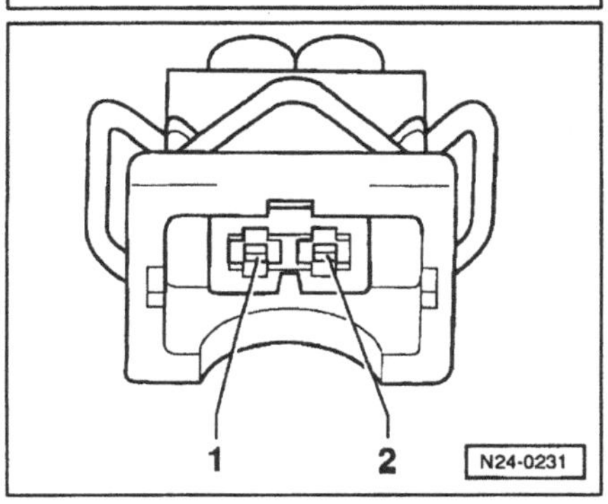

– Check wiring for open circuit between Test Box and 2-pin connector, using wiring diagram

– terminal 1 + socket 36

– terminal 2 + socket 33

♦ wire resistance: Max. 1.5 Ω

– Check wiring between ECM connector and 2-pin connector terminal 2 for short to wire terminal 1 and to vehicle Ground, using wiring diagram

– terminal 2 + socket 36

♦ specification: ∞ Ω

– Check both wires for possible shorting to Battery positive

♦ specification: ∞ Ω

If wiring OK:

– Switch Fluke 83 multimeter to resistance range

– Measure resistance between terminals 1+2 of Intake Air Temperature sensor G72
⇒ page G 24-21, Fig. 1

If specification not obtained:

– Replace Intake Air Temperature sensor G72

Continuation of check when display = ambient temperature

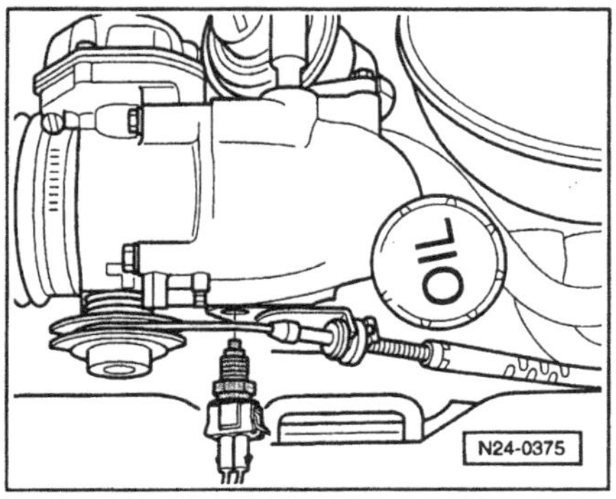

◄ – Remove Intake Air Temperature sensor G72
  ♦ connector remains connected

– Read Intake Air Temperature value in Display zone 4

– Spray sensor with (commercially available) freeze-spray while observing temperature value
  ♦ temperature value must decrease

If value does not decrease:

– Replace Intake Air Temperature sensor G72

– Read-out Readiness code
⇒ Repair Group 01, page G 01-33

If DTC memory has been erased:
– Create Readiness code
⇒ Repair Group 01, page G 01-35

Engine Speed (rpm) sensor, checking

Special tools, testers and auxiliary items

♦ VAG 1598/18 Test Box

♦ Fluke 83 multimeter (or equivalent)

♦ VW 1594 Adaptor kit

♦ Wiring diagram

Test sequence

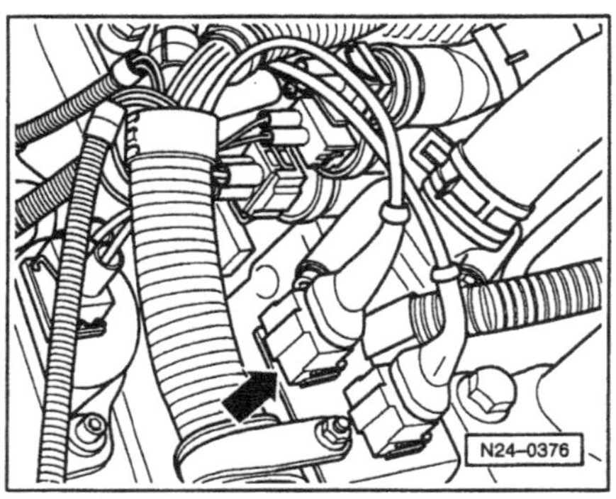

◄ – Disconnect (white) 3-pin Engine Speed sensor connector -arrow-

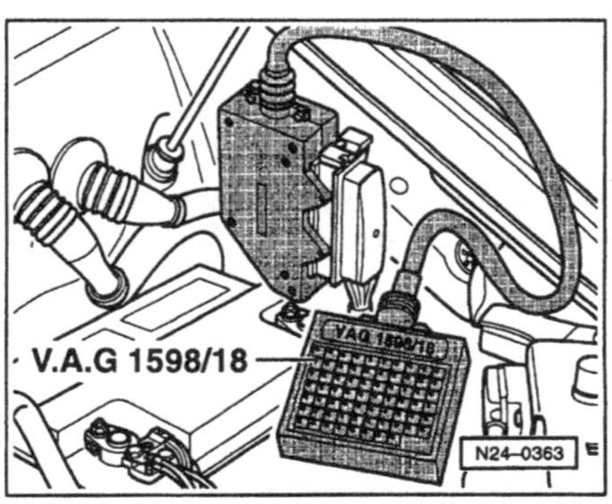

◄ – Connect VAG 1598/18 Test Box to ECM wiring harness

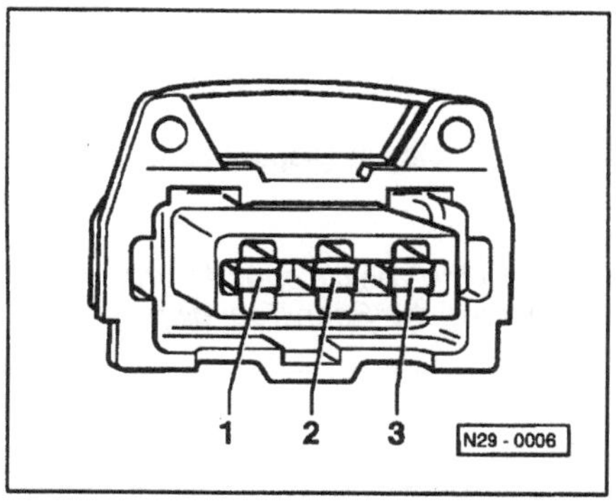

- Check for open circuit between Test Box and 3-pin harness connector using wiring diagram, connect as follows
  - terminal 1 + socket 67
  - terminal 2 + socket 68
  - terminal 3 + socket 56
  - ♦ wire resistance: 1.5 Ω maximum
- Check wires for possible shorting to one another
  - terminal 2 + socket 56
  - terminal 1 + socket 56
  - terminal 1 + socket 68
  - ♦ specification: ∞ Ω

If wiring OK:

- Replace Engine Speed sensor G28
⇒ Repair Group 01, page G 01-33

If DTC memory has been erased:
- Create Readiness code
⇒ Repair Group 01, page G 01-35

Vehicle Speed sensor (speed signal), checking

Special tools, testers and auxiliary items
- ♦ VAG 1551/1552 Scan Tool using VAG 1551/3 adaptor cable
- ♦ Fluke 83 multimeter (or equivalent)
- ♦ VW 1594 Adaptor kit
- ♦ Wiring diagram

Requirement
- ♦ Speedometer OK
⇒ checking, Repair Group 90

Test sequence

- Connect VAG 1551 (VAG 1552) Scan Tool
⇒ Repair Group 01, page G 01-7
- With engine idling, press 0 and 1 buttons to select Address Word 01, "Engine Electronics"

Rapid data transfer	HELP
Select function XX	

Display will appear as shown

- Press 0 and 8 buttons to select Function 08, "Read measuring value block"
- Press Q button to enter selection

Read measuring value block	HELP
Input display group number XXX	

Display will appear as shown

- Press 0, 0 and 5 buttons to select "Display group number 5"

Read measuring value block 5			→
1	2	3	4

◄ Display will appear as shown (1 to 4 = Display zones)

– Perform road-test and observe display in Display zone 3

Note:

You must drive the vehicle to check the vehicle speed signal. A second person is required to safely read the Scan Tool displays.

	Display zones			
	1	2	3	4
Display group 5: General engine data				
Display	xxx rpm	xx.xx ms	xxx km/h	Idle
Indicated	Engine speed	Engine load	Driving speed	Operating modes
Working range	650 to 6000 rpm	0.00 to 25.00 ms	---	---
Spec	---	---	Approx. driving speed	---
	---	---	If no driving speed displayed: ⇒ page G 24-108, continued	

– Press → button

– Press 0 and 6 buttons to select Function 06, “End output”

– Press Q button to enter selection

– Switch OFF ignition

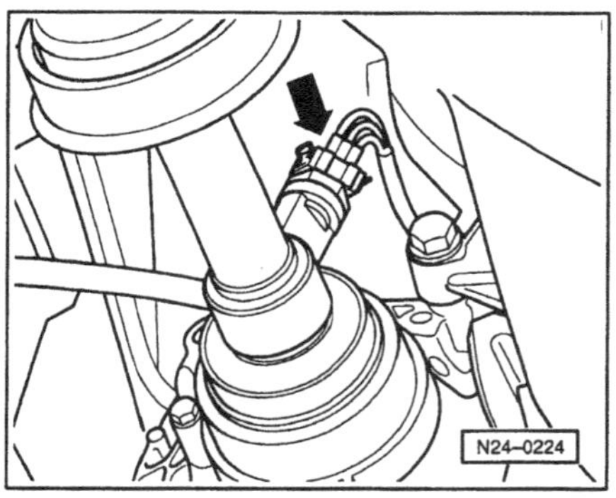

Continuation

If no driving speed indicated in Display zone 3

◄ – Disconnect 3-pin harness connector from Speedometer Vehicle Speed sensor -arrow-

– Switch ON ignition

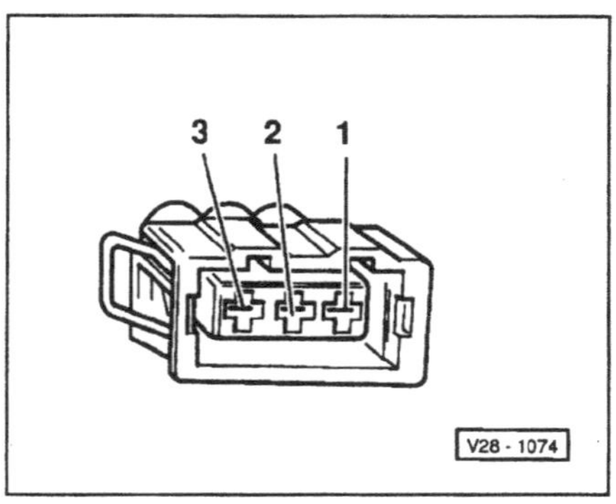

– Switch Fluke 83 multimeter to 20 Volt DC range

◄ – Connect multimeter between terminals 1+3 of harness connector using jumper wires from VW 1594 adaptor kit

- ♦ specification: 9 to 14.5 Volts

– Switch OFF ignition

– Reconnect Vehicle Speed sensor harness connector

If no Voltage present:

– Check wiring, using wiring diagram

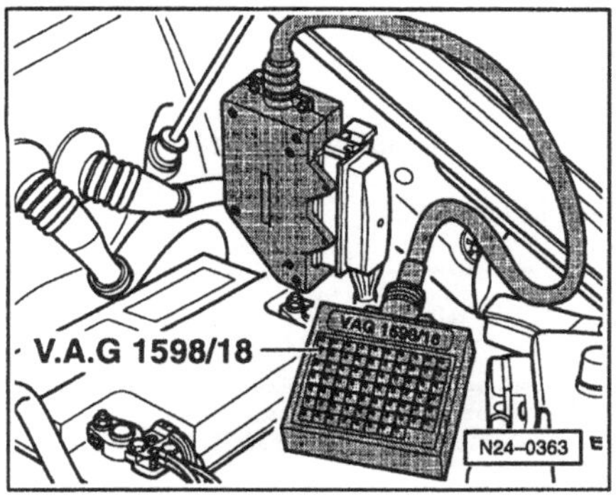

If Voltage between 9 and 14.5 Volts:

- Connect VAG 1598/18 Test Box to ECM wiring harness
- Switch multimeter to resistance range
- Check wiring for open circuit between central electric and Test Box socket 65 using wiring diagram
  - ♦ wire resistance: 1.5 Ω maximum
- Connect multimeter between sockets 56 + 65 using jumper wires from VW 1594 adaptor kit
- Switch ON ignition
- Raise left front wheel or push vehicle to excite sensor
  - ♦ Voltage must fluctuate between 0 and 4 Volts minimum

If wiring OK and Voltage present between terminals 1 + 3:

- Replace speedometer Vehicle Speed sensor G22
- Read-out Readiness code
⇒ Repair Group 01, page G 01-33

If DTC memory has been erased:
- Create Readiness code
⇒ Repair Group 01, page G 01-35

Engine Control Module (ECM) Voltage supply, checking

Special tools, testers and auxiliary items

- ♦ VAG 1551/1552 Scan Tool using VAG 1551/3 adaptor cable
- ♦ VAG 1598/18 Test Box
- ♦ Fluke 83 multimeter (or equivalent)
- ♦ VW 1594 Adaptor kit
- ♦ Wiring diagram

Test sequence

- Connect VAG 1551 (VAG 1552) Scan Tool
⇒ Repair Group 01, page G 01-7
- With ignition Switched ON but engine not running, press 0 and 1 buttons to select Address Word 01, "Engine Electronics"

Rapid data transfer Select function XX	HELP

Display will appear as shown

- Press 0 and 8 buttons to select Function 08, "Read measuring value block"
- Press Q button to enter selection

Read measuring value block Input display group number XXX	HELP

Display will appear as shown

– Press 0, 0 and 2 buttons to select "Display group number 2"

– Press Q button to enter selection

Read measuring value block 2			→
1	2	3	4

◄ Display will appear as shown (1 to 4 = Display zones)

– Check battery Voltage (Display zone 3)

	Display zones			
	1	2	3	4
Display group 2: General engine data				
Display	xxxx rpm	xx.xx ms	xx:xxx Volts	x.xx
Indicated	Engine speed	Injection period	Battery Voltage	Oxygen control adaption value for tank venting
Working range	650 to 6000 rpm	0.00 to 25.00 ms	0.000 to 16.500 Volts	0.1 to 1.0
Specifi-cation	0 rpm	---	12.000 to 14.500 Volts	---
	---	---	If spec not obtained: ⇒ page G 24-112 evaluating Display group 2	---

– Press → button

– Press 0 and 6 buttons to select Function 06, "End output"

– Press Q button to enter selection

Evaluating display group 2

Display group: 2 Display zone: 3	Possible cause	Corrective Steps
If no display appears on VAG 1551	♦ Fuse 15 faulty	– Replace fuse
	♦ Wiring open circuit	– Check Voltage supply terminal 15: ⇒ page G 24-113 – Check Voltage supply terminal 30: ⇒ page G 24-113
If displayed value fluctuates between 12.0 and 14.5 Volts	♦ Loose terminal	
0.0 to 12.0 Volts	♦ Battery discharged/faulty ♦ Voltage regulator faulty	– Check battery – Check Generator – Check Voltage regulator
14.5 to 16.5 Volts	♦ Generator faulty ♦ Voltage regulator faulty	– Check Generator – Check Voltage regulator

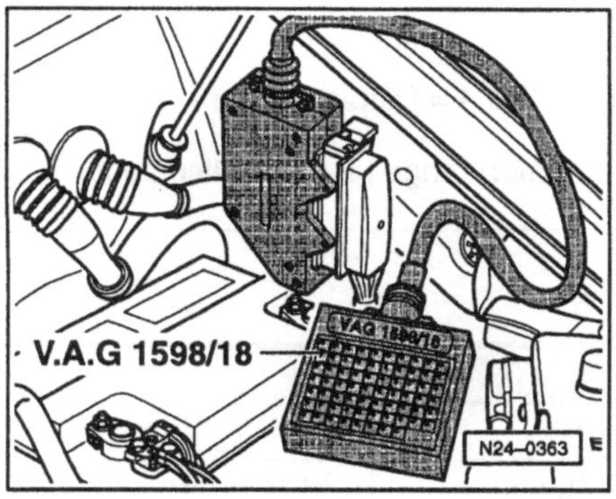

Voltage supply terminal 30, checking

– Switch OFF ignition

– Connect VAG 1598/18 Test Box to ECM wiring harness

– Switch Fluke 83 multimeter to 20 Volt DC range

– Connect multimeter between Test Box sockets 1 + 54 using jumper wires from VW 1594 adaptor kit

♦ specification: 12 to 14.5 Volts

If specification not obtained:

– Check wiring using wiring diagram

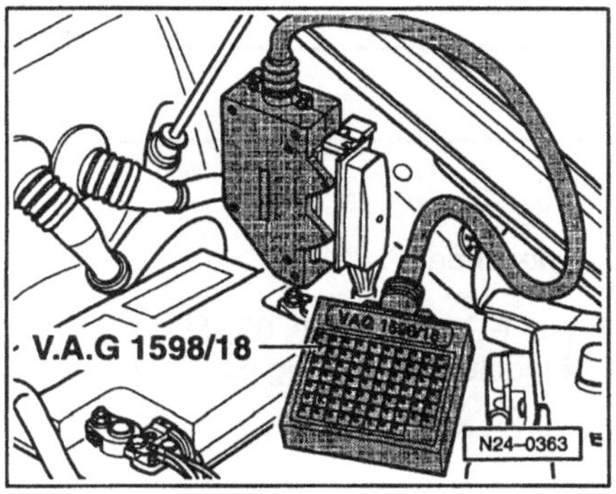

Voltage supply terminal 15, checking

– Switch OFF ignition

– Connect VAG 1598/18 Test Box to ECM wiring harness

– Switch ON ignition

– Connect multimeter between Test Box sockets 1 + 23 using jumper wires from VW 1594 adaptor kit

♦ specification: 12 to 14.5 Volts

If specification not obtained:

– Check wiring using wiring diagram

Automatic transmission (range signal), checking

Special tools, testers and auxiliary items

♦ VAG 1551/1552 Scan Tool using VAG 1551/3 adaptor cable

♦ VAG 1598/18 Test Box

♦ Fluke 83 multimeter (or equivalent)

♦ VW 1594 Adaptor kit

♦ Wiring diagram

Test sequence

– Connect VAG 1551 (VAG 1552) Scan Tool
⇒ Repair Group 01, page G 01-7

– With engine idling, press 0 and 1 buttons to select Address Word 01, "Engine Electronics"

Rapid data transfer	HELP
Select function XX	

Display will appear as shown

– Press 0 and 8 buttons to select Function 08, "Read measuring value block"

– Press Q button to enter selection

Read measuring value block	HELP
Input display group number XXX	

Display will appear as shown

– Press 0, 0 and 8 buttons to select "Display group number 8"

– Press Q button to enter selection

Read measuring value block 8			→
1	2	3	4

◄ Display will appear as shown (1 to 4 = Display zones)

– Observe automatic transmission range signal in Display zone 2

	Display zones			
	1	2	3	4
Display group 8: Signals to engine Control Module				
Display	xxxx rpm	Text	Text	Text
Indicated	Engine speed	Transmission range status	A/C status	A/C compressor status
Working range	650 to 6000 rpm	---	---	---
specification	650 to 750 rpm	P and N: NEUTRAL 1, 2, 3 and D: ON	---	---
	---	If spec not obtained: ⇒ page G 24-115	---	---

Continuation

If display does not appear as described

– Check wiring between engine ECM terminals 07, 11, 18 and 21 and Transmission Control Module using wiring diagram

A/C compressor (ON/OFF signal), checking

Special tools, testers and auxiliary items

- ♦ VAG 1551/1552 Scan Tool using VAG 1551/3 adaptor cable
- ♦ VAG 1598/18 Test Box
- ♦ Fluke 83 multimeter (or equivalent)
- ♦ VW 1594 Adaptor kit
- ♦ Wiring diagram

Requirements

- ♦ A/C Functions OK
- ♦ A/C switched OFF
- ♦ Vehicle interior temperature: 15°C (59°F) minimum
- ♦ No malfunctions (DTC's) stored in DTC memory ⇒ page G 01-12, checking DTC memory

Test sequence

– Connect VAG 1551 (VAG 1552) Scan Tool ⇒ Repair Group 01, page G 01-7

– With engine idling, press 0 and 1 buttons to select Address Word 01, "Engine Electronics"

Rapid data transfer	HELP
Select function XX	

◄ Display will appear as shown

– Press 0 and 8 buttons to select Function 08, "Read measuring value block"

– Press Q button to enter selection

Read measuring value block HELP Input display group number XXX

◄ Display will appear as shown

– Press 0, 0 and 8 buttons to select "Display group number 8"

– Press Q button to enter selection

Read measuring value block 8 → 1 2 3 4

◄ Display will appear as shown (1 to 4 = Display zones)

– Switch on A/C (lowest temp and highest blower speed)

– Check A/C specifications (Display zones 3 and 4)

	Display zones			
	1	2	3	4
Display group 8: Signals to Engine Control Module (ECM)				
Display	xxxx rpm	Text	Text	Text
Indicated	Engine speed	Transmission Range Selection	A/C status	A/C compressor status
Working range	650 to 6000 rpm	---	---	---
Specification	650 to 750 rpm[1)]	Neutral	A/C ON: A/C–HIGH A/C OFF: A/C–LOW	Compressor on = compr. ON Compressor off = compr. OFF
	---	---	If spec not obtained: ⇒ page G 24-118, continuation	

Note:

The A/C compressor will be switched OFF (Compr. OFF) when the ECM recognizes full load with A/C switched ON (A/C-HIGH).

Continuation

If display does not appear as described:

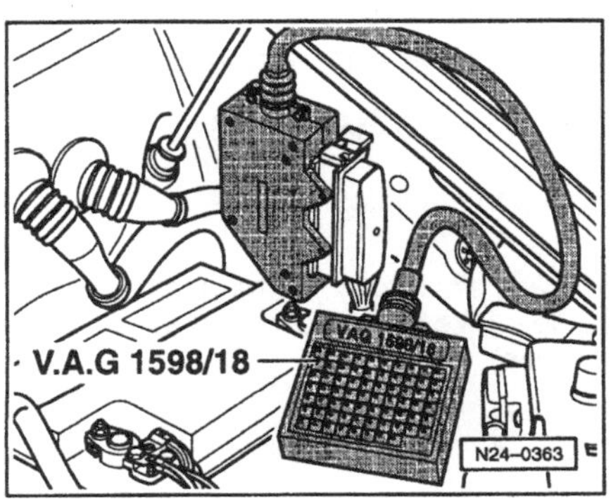

◄ – Connect VAG 1598/18 Test Box to ECM wiring harness

– Check wiring (for A/C open circuit) between Test Box sockets 37 and 39 respectively, using wiring diagram

- ♦ wire resistance: 1.5 Ω maximum

If specification not obtained:

– Check wiring using wiring diagram

Fuel injectors, removing and installing

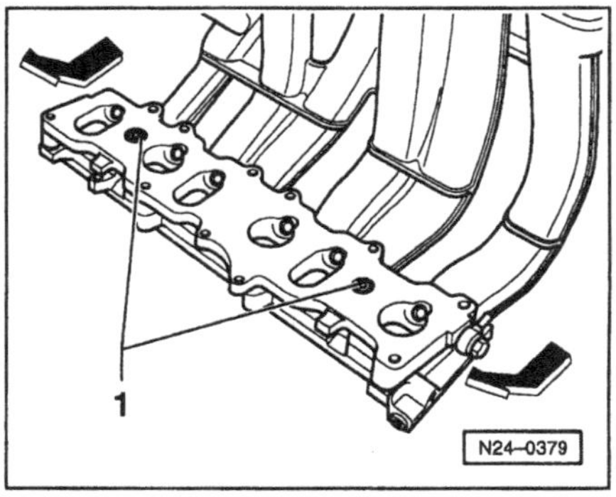

Special tools, testers and auxiliary items

- ♦ 3047A Extractor tool

Removing

– Remove intake manifold complete with lower intake manifold and Throttle Valve Control Module
⇒ Repair Group 15

– Disconnect all of the fuel injector harness connectors

◄ – Remove mounting bolts -1- from lower intake manifold

Note:

Before loosening, thoroughly clean the area of the intake manifold, lower intake manifold and fuel injectors.

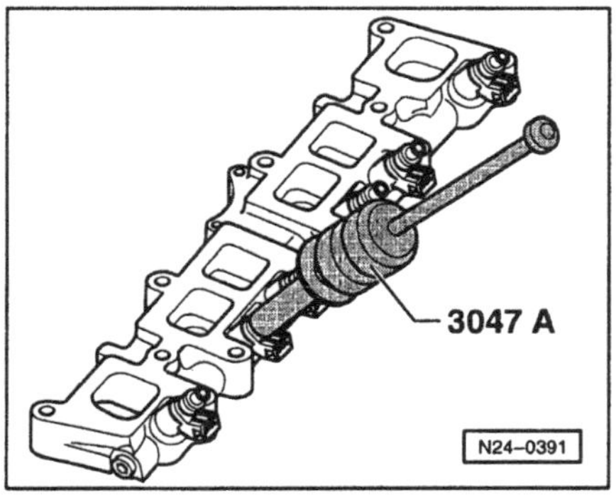

– Remove lower intake manifold (toward arrows) from intake manifold

Note:

Do not for any reason pry the lower intake manifold away from the intake manifold.

– Carefully pull injectors out of int. manifold/lower int. manifold

◄ ***Note:*** *Remove tight-fitting injectors from lower intake manifold using 3047 A extractor tool*

Installing

Notes:

- ♦ *Replace fuel injector O-rings. When installing injectors ensure that O-rings are not damaged*
- ♦ *Lightly coat O-rings with oil before installing*
- ♦ *Replace gasket between int. manifold and lower int. manifold*

– First install injectors in intake manifold (note installed position)

– Re-attach harness connectors to fuel injectors

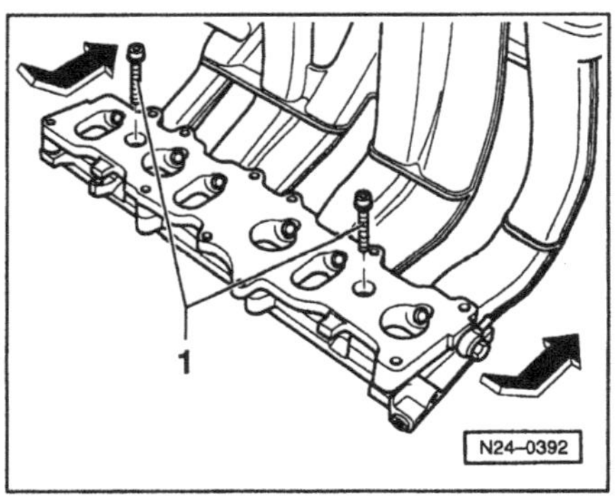

◄ – Install the intake manifold lower part onto intake manifold in direction of arrows (when installing intake manifold lower part observe fitting position of dowel sleeves)

– Insert mounting bolts -1- and tighten bolts

- ♦ tightening torque: 25 Nm (18 ft lb)

– Install the intake manifold with intake manifold lower part and Throttle Valve Control Module (when installing note position of dowel sleeves in cylinder head):
⇒ Repair Group 15

Fuel injectors, checking

Checking activation

Special tools, testers and auxiliary items

- ♦ VAG 1598/18 Test Box
- ♦ Fluke 83 multimeter (or equivalent)
- ♦ VAG 1527B LED tester
- ♦ VW 1594 Adaptor kit
- ♦ Wiring diagram

Requirements

- ♦ Engine speed sensor OK
⇒ checking, page G 24-104
- ♦ Fuel pump relay OK

Test sequence

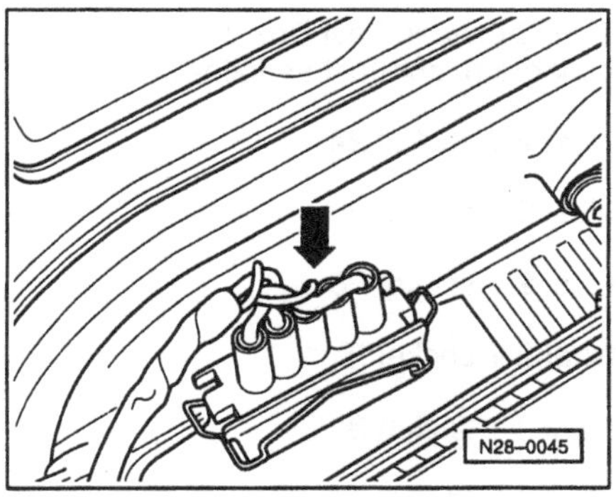

◄ – Disconnect 5-pin harness connector from ignition coil

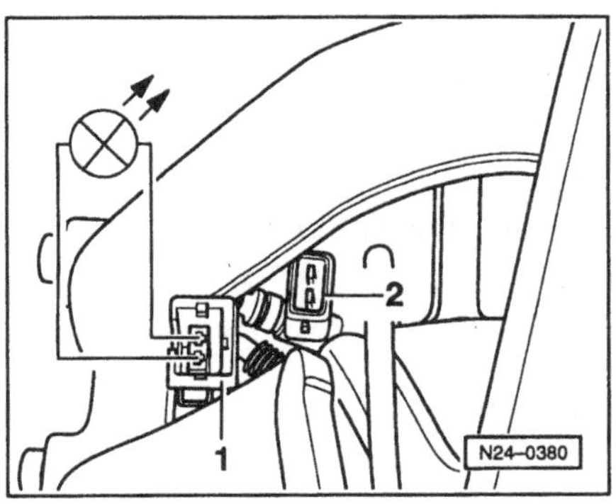

◄ – Disconnect connector -1- from connection -2- on all injectors

– Connect VAG 1527 B LED tester between Cyl. 1 injector connector terminals, using jumper wires from VW 1594 adaptor kit

– Operate starter and check Voltage supply to cylinder 1 injector

- ♦ LED must flicker

– Repeat injector check for Cyls. 2 to 6

– Switch OFF ignition

If LED does not flicker for any cylinder:

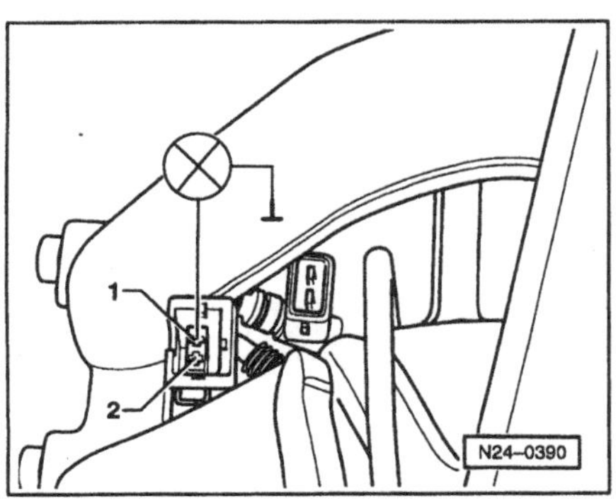

◄ – Connect LED tester between terminal 1 and Ground for cylinder 1 connector

– Operate starter

- ♦ LED must light up

If LED does not light up:

– Switch OFF ignition

– Check for open circuit between 2-pin connector terminal 1 and fuel pump relay J17 using wiring diagram

- ♦ wire resistance: max. 1.5 Ω

If LED flickers for one or more cylinders:

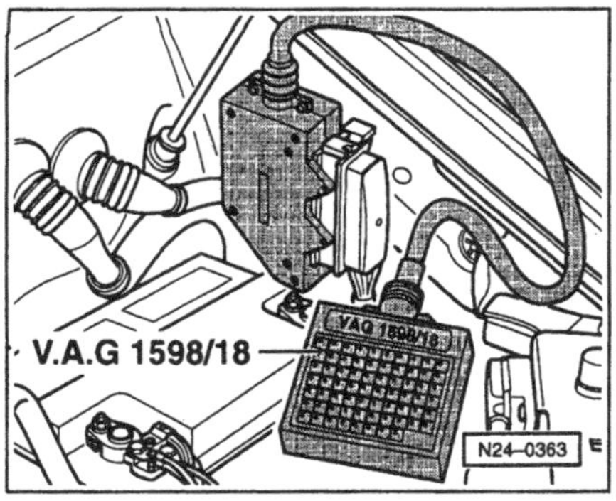

– Connect VAG 1598/18 Test Box to ECM wiring harness

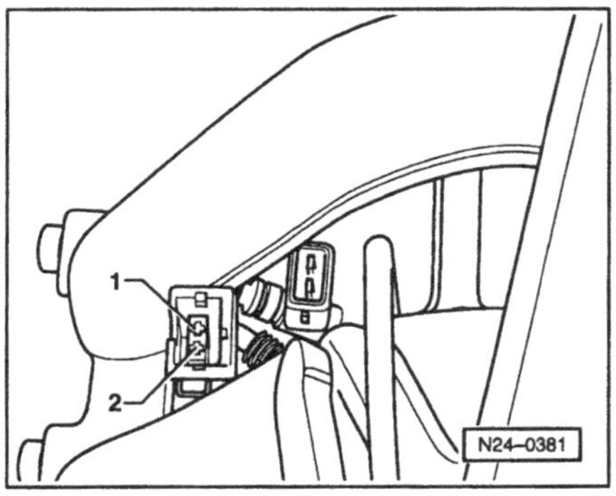

– Check wiring for open circuit between Test Box and injector connectors; using wiring diagram, connect as follows:

– Cyl. 1 connector, terminal 2 + socket 24

– Cyl. 2 connector, terminal 2 + socket 25

– Cyl. 3 connector, terminal 2 + socket 26

– Cyl. 4 connector, terminal 2 + socket 2

– Cyl. 5 connector, terminal 2 + socket 3

– Cyl. 6 connector, terminal 2 + socket 4

♦ wire resistance: 1.5 Ω maximum

– Check wires for shorting to one another

♦ specification: ∞ Ω

– Check for open circuit between terminal 1 of fuel injector connector

♦ wire resistance: 1.5 Ω maximum

– Check wires for shorting to one another

♦ specification: ∞ Ω

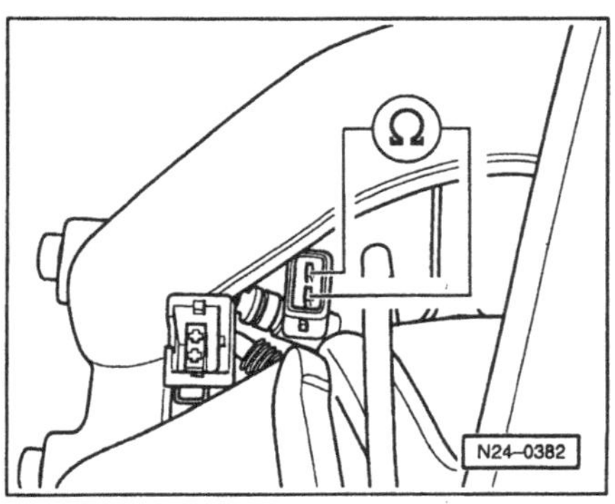

Fuel injector resistance, checking

– Measure fuel injector resistance between injector terminals

♦ specification: 15.0 to 21.5 Ω

If specification not obtained:

– Replace faulty fuel injector
⇒ page G 24-119

Fuel pressure regulator and residual pressure, checking

The fuel pressure regulator controls fuel pressure *relative to* Manifold Absolute Pressure.

Special tools, testers and auxiliary items

- VAG 1318 Pressure tester
- 1318/10 Adaptor
- VAG 1318/1 Hose

Requirement

- Fuel pump delivery rate OK
⇒ checking, Repair Group 20

Test sequence

> ***CAUTION!***
>
> ***Fuel system is pressurized! Wrap a cloth around the connection before loosening hose connections or opening a test connection. Carefully release pressure by pulling off the hose or by removing the plug.***

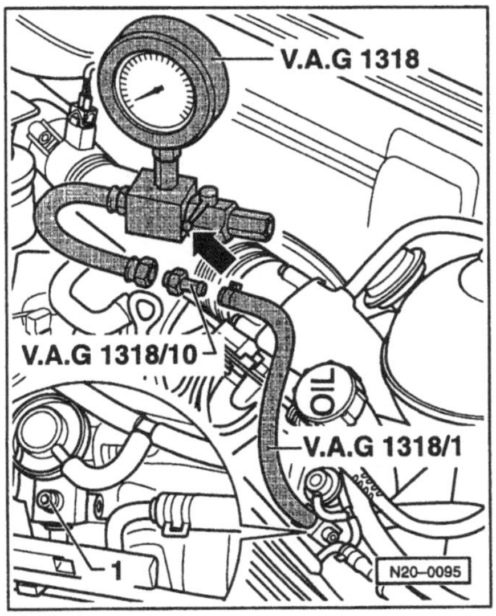

◄ – Remove plug -1- on fuel pressure regulator bracket

– Connect VAG 1318 pressure gauge to measuring connection using VAG 1318/10 adaptor with VAG 1318/1 hose

– Close pressure gauge shut-off

- lever must be perpindicular to flow -arrow-

– Start engine and let idle

– Measure fuel pressure

- specification: approximately 2.5 bar (36 psi)

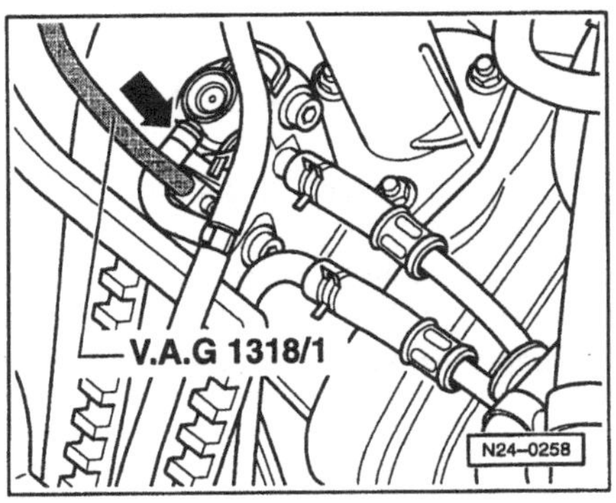

◄ – Pull vacuum hose off fuel pressure regulator -arrow-

- fuel pressure must increase to approximately 3.0 bar (44 psi)

– Switch OFF ignition

– Check for leaks and at same time measure residual pressure by watching pressure drop on gauge

- after 10 minutes residual pressure must be 2 bar (29 psi) minimum

If pressure drops below 2 bar (29 psi):

– Start engine and let idle

– After pressure has built-up, switch OFF ignition

– Immediately thereafter, clamp fuel return line (blue markings) positioned on fuel pressure regulator bracket

– Observe pressure drop on gauge

If pressure does not drop:

– Replace fuel pressure regulator

If pressure drops:

– Check fuel pump check valve
⇒ Repair Group 20

– Check fuel line connections and O-rings on lower intake manifold and fuel injectors for leaks

– Check pressure gauge for leaks

Note:

Before removing the pressure gauge, release any residual fuel pressure by opening the shut–off. Hold a container over the connection while doing this.

Intake air system, leak-checking (for outside air)

Special tools, testers and auxiliary items

- ♦ VAG 1551/1552 Scan Tool using VAG 1551/3 adaptor cable
- ♦ G 001 800 A1 Leak detector spray

Notes:

- ♦ *If there is a leak, manifold vacuum will draw the detector spray along with outside air into the source of the leak.*
- ♦ *Leak detector spray reduces mixture ignitability, leading to a drop in engine speed and a significant rise in CO content.*
- ♦ *Always observe safety precautions listed on the container.*

Test sequence

– Connect VAG 1551 (VAG 1552) Scan Tool
⇒ Repair Group 01, page G 01-7

– With engine idling, press 0 and 1 buttons to select Address Word 01, "Engine electronics"

Rapid data transfer	HELP
Select function XX	

◄ Display will appear as shown

– Press 0, 8 buttons, select Funct 08 "Read measuring value block"

– Press Q button to enter selection

Read measuring value block	HELP
Input display group number XXX	

◄ Display will appear as shown

– Press 0, 0 and 1 buttons to select "Display group number 1"

– Press Q button to enter selection

Read measuring value block 1			→
1	2	3	4

◄ Display will appear as shown (1 to 4 = Display zones)

– Note Oxygen control in Display zone 3

	Display zones			
	1	2	3	4
Display group 1: Idling test				
Display	xxxx rpm	xxx.x°C	xx.x%	xx.x ∠°
Indicated	Engine speed	Engine temperature	Oxygen control	Ignition angle
Working range	650 to 6000 rpm	---	–25.0 to 25.0%	0.0 to 40.0 ∠°
Spec	650 to 750 rpm	---	Value must fluctuate at least 2% in range –5.0 to 5.0%	2.0 to 15.0 ∠°

– Systematically spray intake system components with leak detector spray

If engine speed drops or Oxygen control value changes

– Press 0 and 6 buttons to select Function 06, “End output”

– Press Q button to enter selection

– Check suspected leak-sprayed area of intake system for leaks and eliminate as necessary

Motronic Ignition system, servicing

Notes:

- *Only components specifically relating to the ignition system are contained in this Repair Group. For fuel injection and ignition system shared components:*

⇒ Repair Group 24

- *The fuel injection and ignition system Control Module (ECM) is equipped with an On Board Diagnostic system*
- *Components marked with an * are automatically checked via the "On Board Diagnostic" system*
- *Check DTC memory before starting repairs and troubleshooting,*

⇒ Repair Group 01, page G 01-12

- *During some checks it is possible that the check itself can trigger the Control Module to recognize and store a malfunction. Therefore, after completing all checks and repairs; DTC memory must be checked and, if necessary, erased.*

⇒ Repair Group 01, page G 01-12

Safety precautions
⇒ Repair Group 24, page G 24-22

Technical data, spark plugs
⇒ page G 28-7

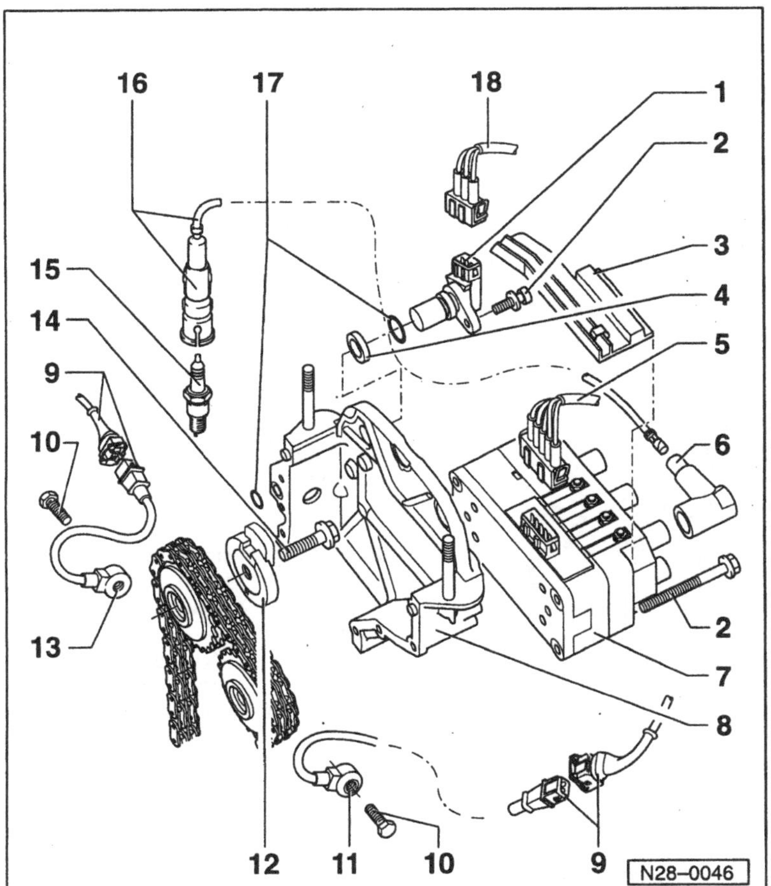

Ignition system, component overview

*Motronic Engine Control Module J220 * with connector*
⇒ Repair Group 24, page 24-7

1 - Camshaft Position sensor G40*
- checking

⇒ page G 28-8

- note spacer ring (item 4)
- to remove, unclip ignition coil cable duct (item 3)

2 - 10 Nm (7 ft lb)

3 - Cable duct
- for ignition coil N152 (item 7)

4 - Spacer ring

5 - 5-pin harness connector
- for ignition coil N152

6 - Suppressor
- 600 to 1400 Ω

7 - Ignition coil N152
- with ignition cable identification, do not interchange
- checking

⇒ page G 28-19

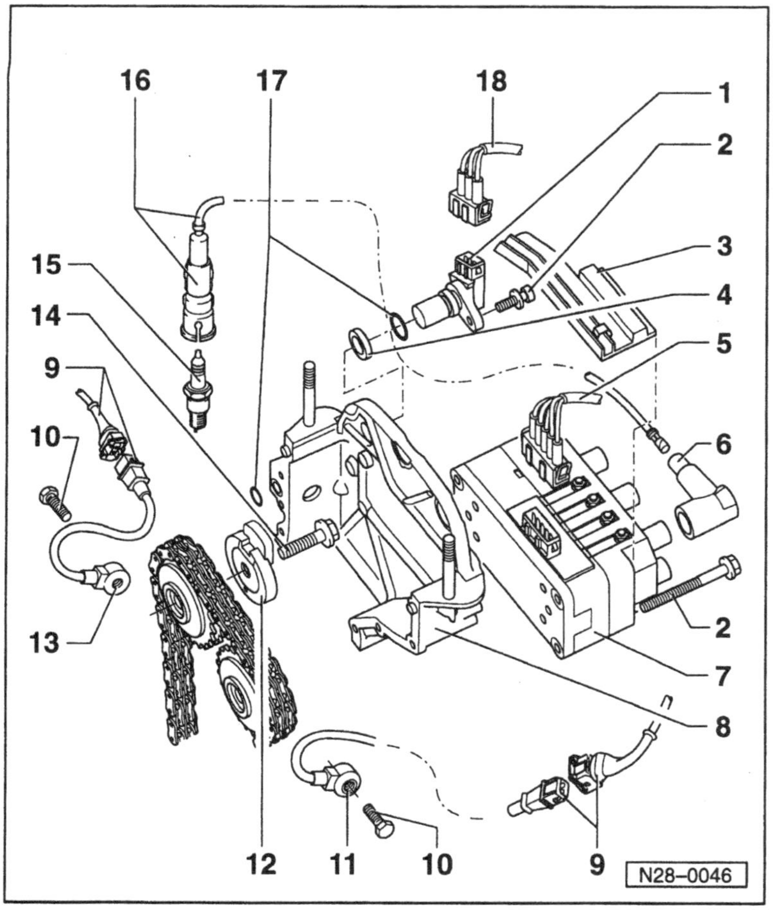

8 - Camshaft sprocket cover
- removing and installing

⇒ Repair Group 15

9 - 3-pin harness connector
- for knock sensor 1: white
- for knock sensor 2: black
- sensor and connector terminals are gold-plated

10 - 20 Nm (15 ft lb)
- tightening torque influences knock sensor function

11 - Knock sensor 2 G66*
- installation location: cylinder block, exhaust side
- knock sensor wiring, checking

⇒ page G 28-28

12 - Sensor wheel
- for Camshaft Position sensor G40
- contact surface of timing chain and sensor wheel must be dry when installing
- if sensor wheel has been removed, check timing after installation:

⇒ Repair Group 13

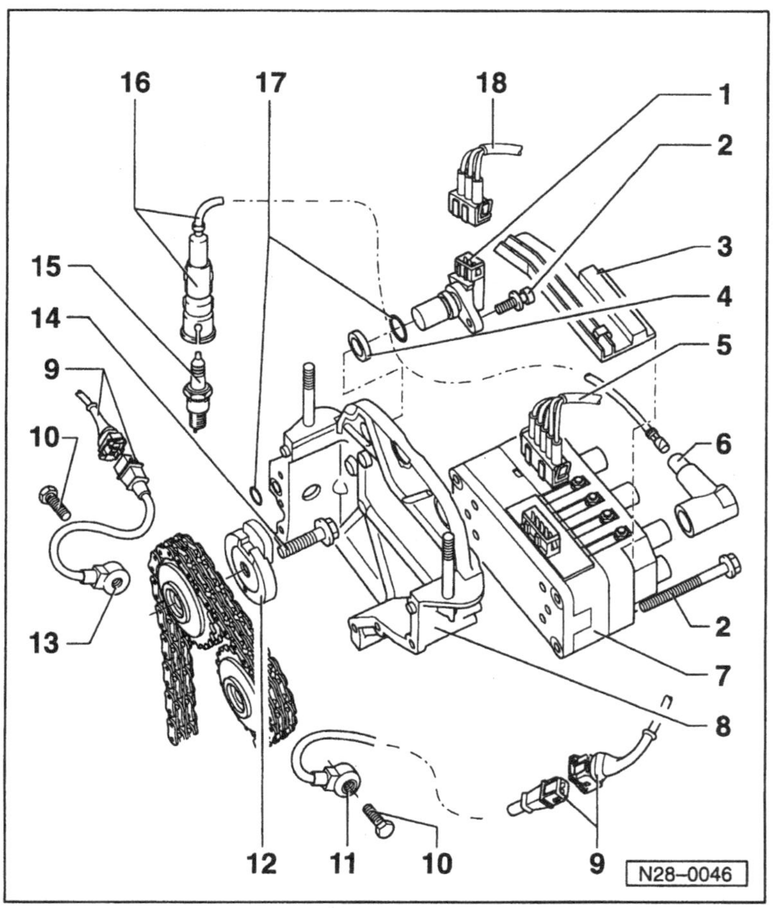

13 - Knock sensor 1 G61*
- installation location: cylinder block, exhaust side
- knock sensor wiring, checking

⇒ page G 28-28

14 - 100 Nm (75 ft lb)
- to remove and install: counter-hold with 24 mm open end wrench on camshaft
- oil bolt head terminal surface

15 - Spark plug
- 25 Nm (18 ft lb)
- remove and install using 3122B spark plug wrench
- technical data

⇒ page G 28-7

16 - Spark plug connector
- 4000 to 6000 Ω
- use tool 3277 A when pulling off or pressing on
- to pull off spark plug connector for cylinders 2, 4 and 6, remove radiator grille and fold lock carrier with radiator out forwards:

⇒ Repair Group 66

17 - O-ring
- replace

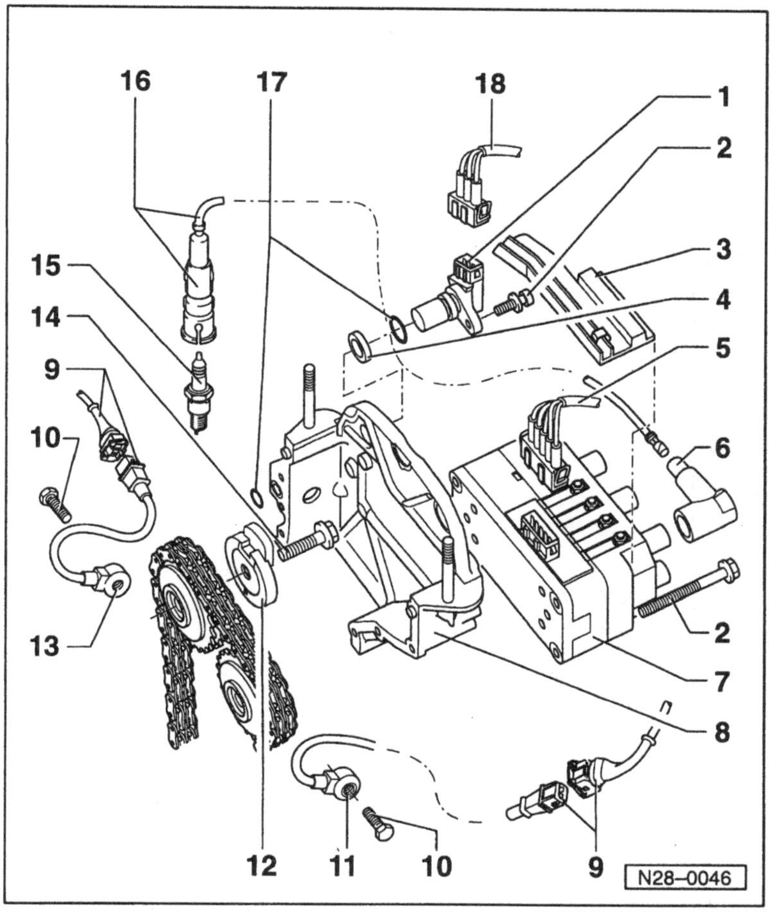

18 - **3-pin harness connector**
- black
- for Camshaft Position sensor G40

Safety precautions

To prevent injuries to persons and/or damage to the fuel injection and ignition system, note the following:

- Do not touch or disconnect ignition wiring when engine is running or being cranked
- Switch OFF ignition before connecting or disconnecting injection or ignition system wiring or tester cables

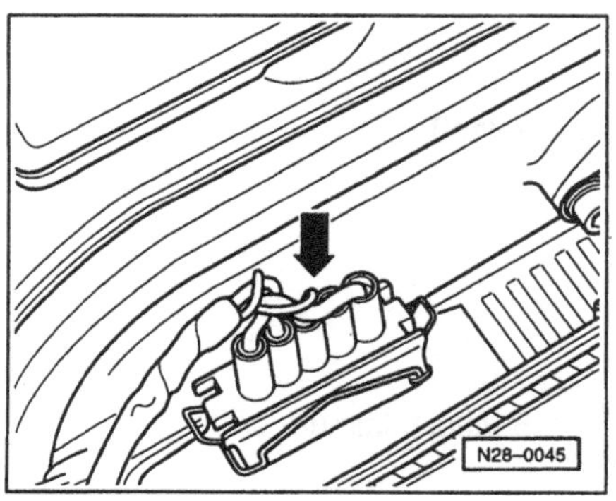

◄
- If engine requires cranking without starting, e.g. when checking compression, disconnect 5-pin harness connector from ignition coil -arrow-

Technical data, spark plugs

Engine code letters	AES
Ignition timing[1]	
Checking	⇒ page G 24-25 Idle speed checking
Firing order	1–5–3–6–2–4
Spark plugs[1)2)]	
VW/Audi	101 000 035 AH
OEM designation	BKR 5 EKUP
Electrode gap	0.7 mm[3]
Tightening torque	25 Nm (18 ft lb)

[1] Not adjustable

[2] Use tool 3277 A to remove and install spark plug connector on. Remove and install spark plugs with 3122 B spark plug wrench

[3] Gap between Ground electrode and center electrode insulation

Camshaft Position sensor, checking

Special tools, testers and auxiliary items

- VAG 1598/18 Test Box
- Fluke 83 multimeter (or equivalent)
- VW 1594 Adaptor kit
- Wiring diagram

Requirement

- Battery Positive Voltage: 11.5 Volts minimum

Test sequence

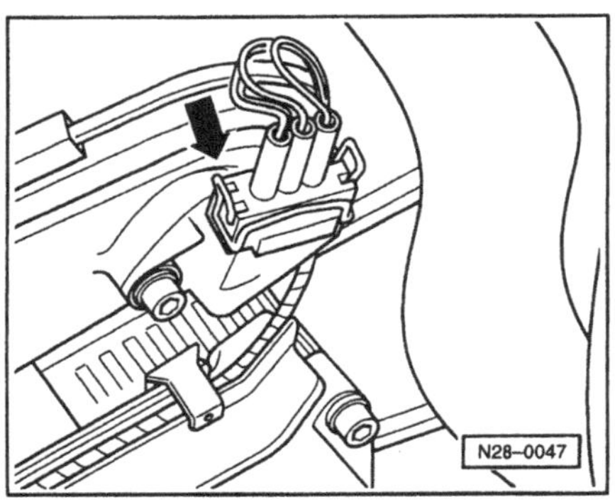

◄ – Disconnect 3-pin harness connector from Camshaft position sensor -arrow-

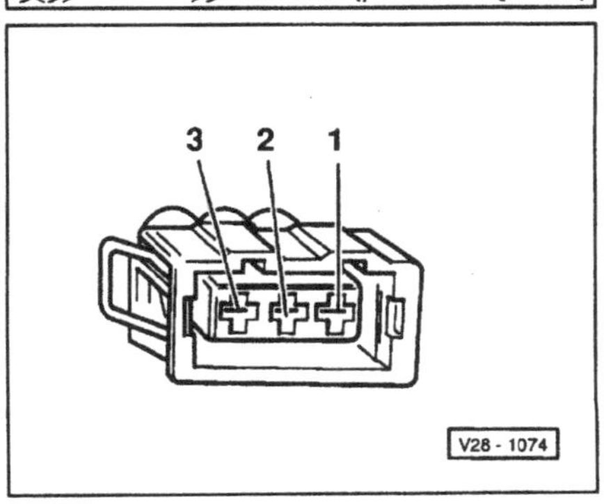

– Switch Fluke 83 multimeter to 20 Volt DC range

◄ – Connect multimeter between harness connector terminals 1 + 3 using jumper wires from VW 1594 adaptor kit

– Switch ON ignition

- specification: 11.5 Volts minimum

– Switch OFF ignition

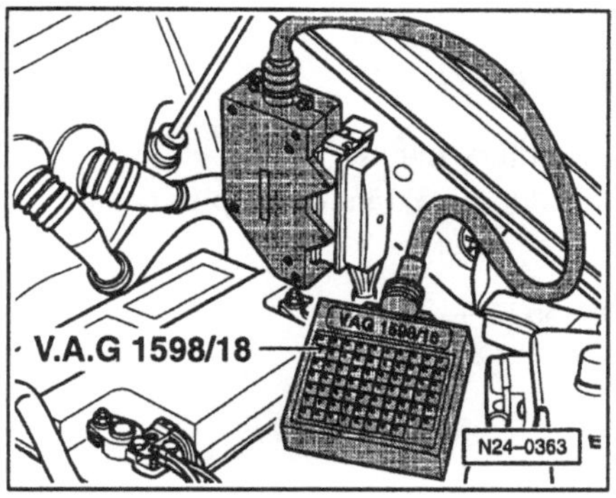

◄ – Connect Test Box VAG 1598/18 to ECM wiring harness

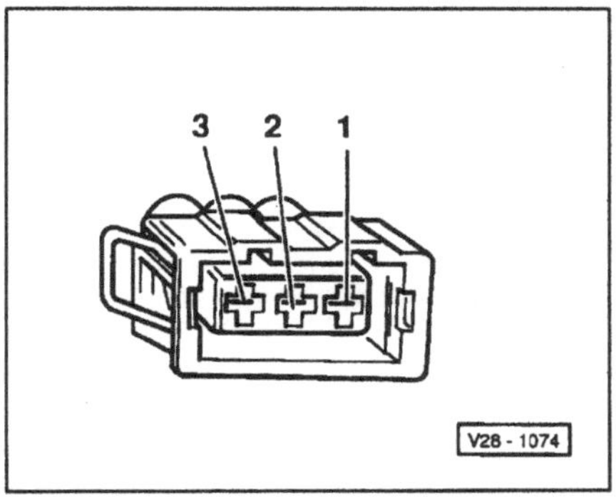

◄ – Check for open circuit between Test Box and 3-pin harness connector using wiring diagram, connecting as follows

- terminal 1 + socket 23
- terminal 2 + socket 44
- terminal 3 + socket 56
- ♦ Wire resistance: 1.5 Ω maximum

– Check wires for shorting to one another

- terminal 3 + socket 44
- terminal 3 + socket 23
- terminal 2 + socket 23
- ♦ specification: ∞ Ω

If wiring OK and voltage present between terminals 1 + 3:

– Replace Camshaft Position sensor G40
⇒ page G 28-2 (item 1)

If wiring OK and NO voltage between terminals 1 + 3:

– Replace Engine Control Module J220
⇒ page G 24-7 (item 3)

– Perform Basic setting
⇒ page G 24-90

– Read-out Readiness code
⇒ Repair Group 01, page G 01-33

If DTC memory has been erased:
– Create Readiness code
⇒ Repair Group 01, page G 01-35

Ignition timing, checking

Special tools, testers and auxiliary items

♦ VAG 1551/1552 Scan Tool using VAG 1551/3 adaptor cable

Requirements

♦ Electrical consumers switched OFF
(radiator fan must not run during checks)

♦ A/C switched OFF

Test sequence

– Connect VAG 1551 (VAG 1552) Scan Tool
⇒ Repair Group 01, page G 01-7

– With engine idling, press 0 and 1 buttons to select Address Word 01, "Engine electronics"

Rapid data transfer	HELP
Select function XX	

◄ Display will appear as shown

– Press 0 and 8 buttons to select Function 08, "Read measuring value block"

– Press Q button to enter selection

Read measuring value block	HELP
Input Display group number XXX	

◄ Display will appear as shown

– Press 0, 1 and 0 buttons to select "Display group number 10"

– Press Q button to enter selection

Read measuring value block 10			→
1	2	3	4

◄ Display will appear as shown (1 to 4 = Display zones)

– Check ignition specifications (Display zones 3 and 4)

	Display zones			
	1	2	3	4
Display group 10: Ignition 1				
Display	xxx rpm	xx.x ms	xx.x ∠°	xx.x ∠°
Indicated	Engine speed	Engine load	Ignition angle (map value)	Ignition angle
Working range	650 to 6000 rpm	0.0 to 25.0 ms	0.0 to 50.0 ∠° BTDC	0.0 to 40.0 ∠° BTDC
Spec	650 to 750 rpm	1.5 to 2.5 ms	11.0 to 13.0 ∠° BTDC	max. ± 2.0 ∠° deviation from display zone 3
	---	---	Test conditions: Intake Air Temperature 50°C max. If specification not obtained: ⇒ page G 24-72, Throttle Valve Control Mod. checking	

– Read-out Readiness code
⇒ Repair Group 01, page G 01-33

If DTC memory has been erased:

– Create Readiness code
⇒ Repair Group 01, page G 01-35

– Press → button

– Press 0 and 6 buttons to select Function 06, "End output"

– Press Q button to enter selection

Misfire recognition, checking

Special tools, testers and auxiliary items

♦ VAG 1551/1552 Scan Tool using VAG 1551/3 adaptor cable

Test sequence

– Connect VAG 1551 (VAG 1552) Scan Tool
⇒ Repair Group 01, page G 01-7

– With engine idling, press 0 and 1 buttons to select Address Word 01, "Engine electronics"

Rapid data transfer HELP
Select function XX

◄ Display will appear as shown

– Press 0 and 8 buttons to select Function 08, "Read measuring value block"

– Press Q button to enter selection

Read measuring value block HELP
Input Display group number XXX

◄ Display will appear as shown

– Press keys 1, 1 and 0 for "Display group number 110"

– Press Q button to enter selection

Read measuring value block 110 →
1 2 3 4

◄ Display will appear as shown (1 to 4 = Display zones)

– Check misfiring recognition spec (Display zones 2 to 4)

	Display zones			
	1	2	3	4
Display group 110: Misfire recognition 1				
Display	x.xx ms	xxx	xxx	xxxxxxxx
Indicated	Engine load	Misfire adversely affecting emissions level (total)	Misfire adversely affecting catalyst (total)	Misfire recognition status
Working range	0.00 to 25.00 ms	---	---	---
Spec	1.00 to 3.00 ms	0	0	00000000
	---	If specification not obtained: ⇒ page G 28-15, evaluating Display group 110		

– Read-out Readiness code
⇒ Repair Group 01, page G 01-33

If DTC memory has been erased:
– Create Readiness code
⇒ Repair Group 01, page G 01-35

– Press → button

– Press 0 and 6 buttons to select Function 06, "End output"

– Press Q button to enter selection

Evaluating Display group 110

Display group: 110 Display zone: 2 + 3	Possible cause	Corrective steps
More than 25	♦ Ignition coil malfunction ♦ Ignition cable malfunction ♦ Spark plug malfunction	– Check ignition coil ⇒ page G 28-19 – Check ignition system components ⇒ page G 28-2
	♦ Fuel injector malfunction ♦ Fuel shortage	– Check injectors ⇒ page G 24-121 – Check quantity of fuel in tank

Ignition timing control, checking

Special tools, testers and auxiliary items

- ♦ VAG 1551/1552 Scan Tool using VAG 1551/3 adaptor cable

Test conditions

- ♦ Electrical consumers switched OFF (radiator fan must not run during check)
- ♦ A/C switched OFF
- ♦ Engine oil temperature 80°C (176°F) minimum

Test sequence

– Connect VAG 1551 (VAG 1552) Scan Tool
⇒ Repair Group 01, page G 01-7

– With engine idling, press 0 and 1 buttons to select Address Word 01, "Engine electronics"

```
Rapid data transfer                HELP
Select function XX
```

◄ Display will appear as shown

– Press 0 and 8 buttons to select Function 08, "Read measuring value block"

– Press Q button to enter selection

```
Read measuring value block         HELP
Input Display group number XXX
```

◄ Display will appear as shown

– Press 0, 1 and 0 buttons to select "Display group number 10"

– Press Q button to enter selection

Read measuring value block 10			→
1	2	3	4

◄ Display will appear as shown (1 to 4 = Display zones)

– Check ignition timing control specifications (Display zones 1 to 4)

	Display zones			
	1	2	3	4
Display group 10: Ignition 1				
Display	xxx rpm	xx.x ms	xx.x ∠°	xx.x ∠°
Indicated	Engine speed	Engine load	Ignition angle (mapped value)	Ignition angle
Working range	650 to 6000 rpm	0.0 to 25.0 ms	0.0 to 40.0 ∠° BTDC	0.0 to 40.0 ∠° BTDC
Spec	650 to 750 rpm	1.9 to 2.1 ms	11.0 to 13.0 ∠° BTDC	max. ± 2.0 ∠° display zone 3 deviation
	2480 to 2520 rpm	1.7 to 1.9 ms	23.0 to 25.0 ∠° BTDC	Max. ± 2.0 ∠° display zone 3 deviation
	---	---	Test condition: Intake air temperature 50 °C max. If spec not obtained: ⇒ page G 28-18, continuation	

Continuation

– Operating modes, checking
⇒ page G 24-64

– Throttle Valve Control Module, checking
⇒ page G 24-72

– Knock sensor and knock control, checking
⇒ page G 28-24

If specification still not obtained:

– Replace Engine Control Module J220
⇒ page G 24-7 (item 3)

– Perform Basic setting
⇒ page G 24-90

– Read-out Readiness code
⇒ Repair Group 01, page G 01-33

If DTC memory has been erased:
– Create Readiness code
⇒ Repair Group 01, page G 01-35

Ignition coil, checking

Special tools, testers and auxiliary items

- VAG 1598/18 Test Box
- Fluke 83 multimeter (or equivalent)
- VAG 1527B LED Tester
- VW 1594 adaptor kit
- Wiring diagram

Requirements

- Battery Positive Voltage: 11.5 Volts minimum
- Engine Speed sensor OK
⇒ checking, page G 24-104
- Camshaft Position sensor OK
⇒ checking, page G 28-8

Test sequence

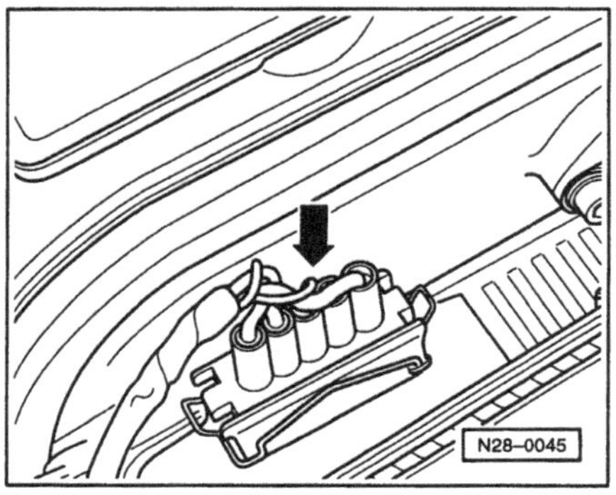

– Disconnect 5-pin harness connector from ignition coil

Voltage supply, checking

– Switch Fluke 83 multimeter to 20 Volt DC range

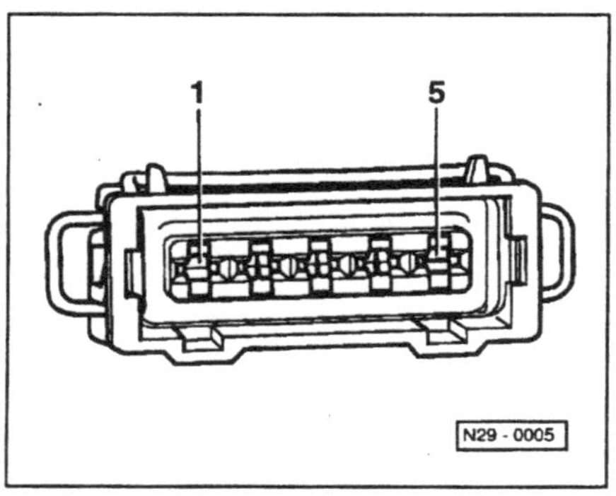

– Connect multimeter between terminals 1+5 of disconnected harness connector using jumper wires from VW 1594 adaptor kit

– Switch ON ignition and measure supply voltage

- must be 11.5 Volts minimum

– Switch OFF ignition

If no voltage present:

– Check for open circuit between 5-pin harness connector terminal 1 and Ground using wiring diagram

- wire resistance: 1.5 Ω maximum

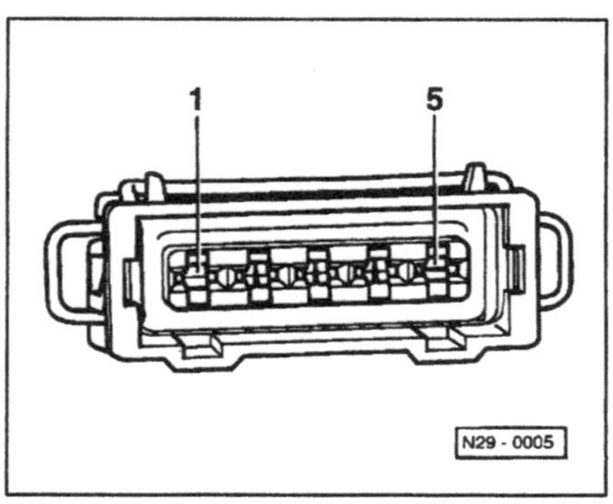

– Check for open circuit between 5-pin harness connector terminal 5 and fuse/relay panel using wiring diagram

- wire resistance: 1.5 Ω maximum

Activation, checking

> ***CAUTION!***
>
> ***Do not touch the ignition coil terminals or test cable attachments during the following test.***

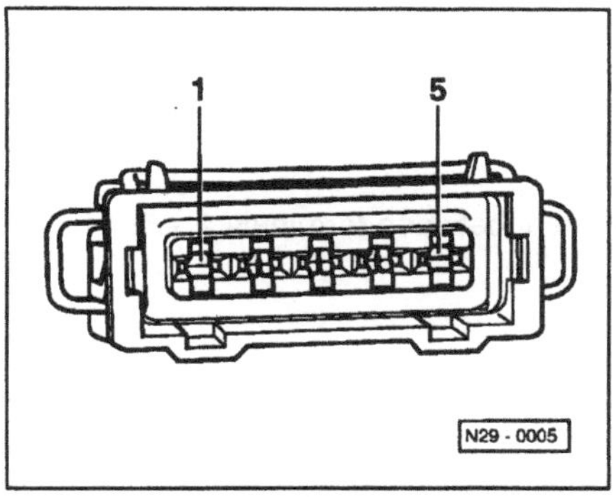

– Remove fuse 18 from fuse/panel

◄ – Using jumper wires from VW 1594 adaptor kit, connect VAG 1527B LED tester to disconnected connector:
  – terminals 5 + 2 (ignition output 1)
  – terminals 5 + 3 (ignition output 3)
  – terminals 5 + 4 (ignition output 2)

– Operate starter and check ignition signal from ECM J220
  ♦ LED must flicker

– Switch OFF ignition

If LED does not flicker:
– Replace ECM J220
⇒ page G 24-7 (item 3)

– Perform Basic setting:
⇒ page G 24-90

– Read-out Readiness code
⇒ Repair Group 01, page G 01-33

If DTC memory has been erased:
– Create Readiness code
⇒ Repair Group 01, page G 01-35

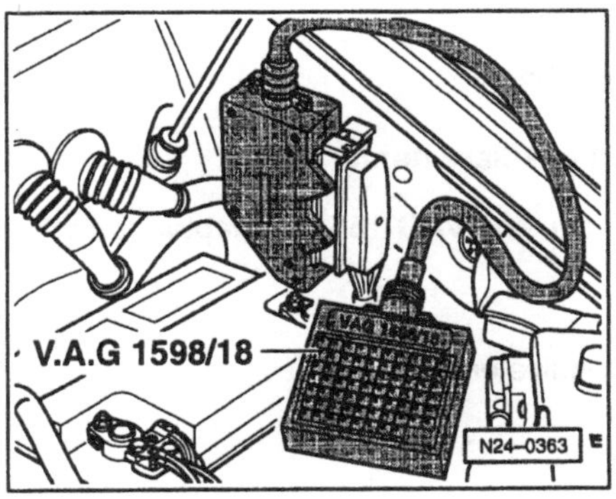

If LED flickers:

◄ – Connect Test Box VAG 1598/18 to ECM wiring harness

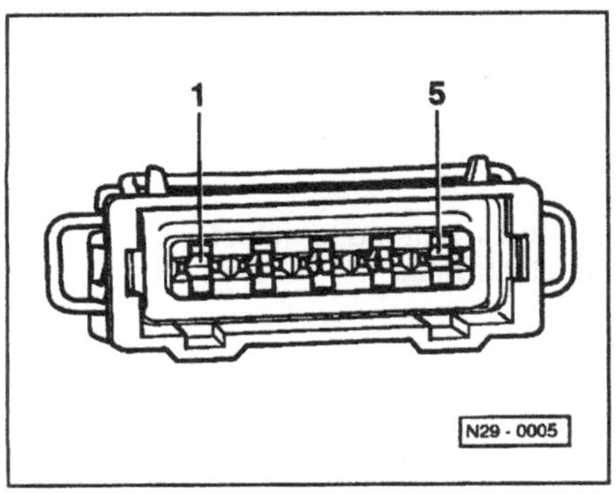

◄ – Check for open circuit between Test Box and 5-pin harness connector, using wiring diagram, connecting as follows:

  – terminal 2 + socket 8

  – terminal 3 + socket 60

  – terminal 4 + socket 52

  ♦ Wire resistance: 1.5 Ω maximum

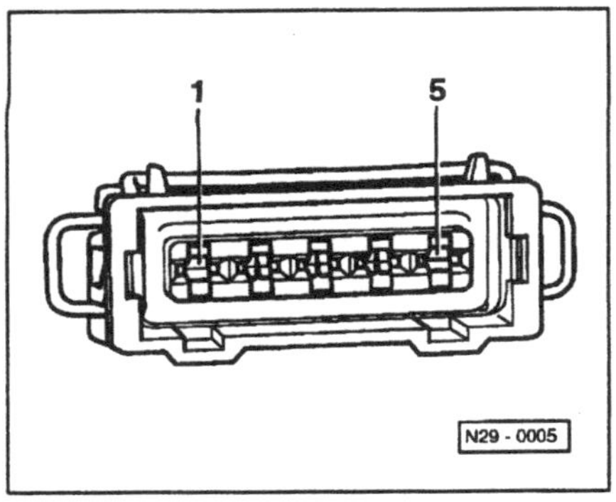

- Check wires for shorting to one another as follows:
  - terminal 2 + socket 60
  - terminal 2 + socket 52
  - terminal 3 + socket 52
  - ♦ specification: ∞ Ω

If wiring OK and voltage present between terminals 1 + 5:

- Replace ignition coil N152
⇒ page G 28-2 (item 7)

Secondary winding, checking

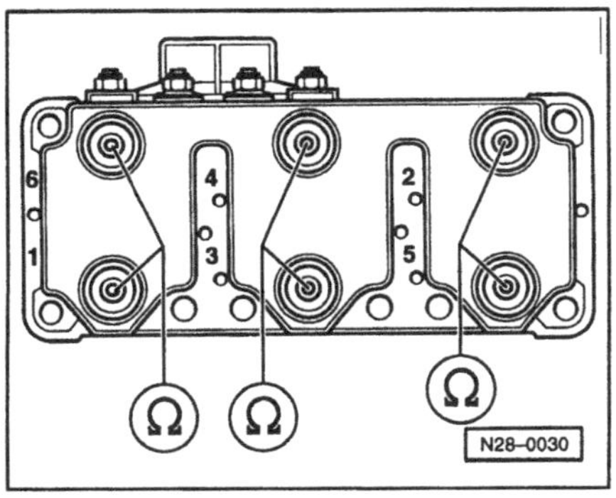

- Check secondary winding at terminal 4 between:
  - Cyl. 1 and Cyl. 6
  - Cyl. 3 and Cyl. 4
  - Cyl. 2 and Cyl. 5
  - ♦ specification: 3600 to 4400 Ω

If specifications not obtained:

- Replace ignition coil N152
⇒ page G 28-2 (item 7)

Knock control, checking

Special tools, testers and auxiliary items

- ♦ VAG 1551/1552 Scan Tool using VAG 1551/3 adaptor cable
- ♦ VAG 1598/18 Test Box
- ♦ Fluke 83 multimeter (or equivalent)
- ♦ VW 1594 Adaptor kit
- ♦ Wiring diagram

Test sequence

- Connect VAG 1551 (VAG 1552) Scan Tool
⇒ Repair Group 01, page G 01-7
- With engine idling, press 0 and 1 buttons to select Address Word 01, "Engine electronics"

Rapid data transfer	HELP
Select function XX	

Display will appear as shown

- Press 0 and 8 buttons to select Function 08, "Read measuring value block"
- Press Q button to enter selection

Read measuring value block HELP Input Display group number XXX

◄ Display will appear as shown

- Press 0, 4 and 5 buttons to select "Display group number 45" (Cylinders 1 to 4), or
- Press 0, 4 and 6 buttons to select "Display group number 46" (Cylinders 5 and 6)
- Press Q button to enter selection

Read measuring value block 45 → 1 2 3 4

◄ Display will appear as shown (1 to 4 = Display zones)

Note:

Check must be carried out during road-test because knock control is only active when engine load exceeds 3 ms.

- Perform road test and observe knock control specifications on display (2nd person required). During road test, engine Engine Coolant Temperature must exceed 80°C (176°F)

When temperature is reached, the following operating conditions must be performed several times:

- ♦ Closed throttle
- ♦ Partially open throttle
- ♦ Wide open throttle
- ♦ Overrun
- ♦ At Wide open throttle, engine rpm must exceed 3500

	Display zones			
	1	2	3	4
Display group 45: Knock control				
Display	xx.xx° ATDC	xx.xx° ATDC	xx.xx° ATDC	xx.xx° ATDC
Indicated	Ignition angle correction Cylinder 1	Ignition angle correction Cylinder 2	Ignition angle correction Cylinder 3	Ignition angle correction Cylinder 4
Working range	0.0 to 15.0° ATDC	0.0 to 15.0° ATDC	0.0 to 15.0° ATDC	0.0 to 15.0° ATDC
Spec	0.0 to 12.0° ATDC	0.0 to 12.0° ATDC	0.0 to 12.0° ATDC	0.0 to 12.0° ATDC
	If specification not obtained: ⇒ page G 28-27, evaluating Display group 45 and 46			

- Read-out Readiness code
⇒ Repair Group 01, page G 01-33

If DTC memory has been erased:
- Create Readiness code
⇒ Repair Group 01, page G 01-35

- Press → button
- Press 0 and 6 button to select Function 06, "End output"
- Press Q button to enter selection

Evaluating Display group 45 and 46

Display group: 45 Display zones: 1 to 4 Display group: 46 Display zones: 1 & 2	Possible cause	Corrective Steps
All cylinders more than 12° ATDC	♦ Knock sensor malfunction	– Continued ⇒ page G 28-28
	♦ Connector corroded	
	♦ Knock sensor not correctly tightened	– Loosen knock sensor and tighten to: 20 Nm (15 ft lb)
	♦ Engine auxiliary components loose	– Secure auxiliary components
	♦ Poor fuel quality	– Change type of fuel
One cylinder deviation greater than others	♦ Connector corroded	– Continued ⇒ page G 28-28
	♦ Engine damage	– Check compression pressure ⇒ Repair Group 13
	♦ Engine auxiliary components loose	– Secure auxiliary components

Knock sensor, checking

Special tools, testers and auxiliary items

- ♦ VAG 1598/18 Test Box
- ♦ Fluke 83 multimeter (or equivalent)
- ♦ VW 1594 Adaptor kit
- ♦ Wiring diagram

Test sequence

- Remove insulation tray ⇒ Repair Group 50

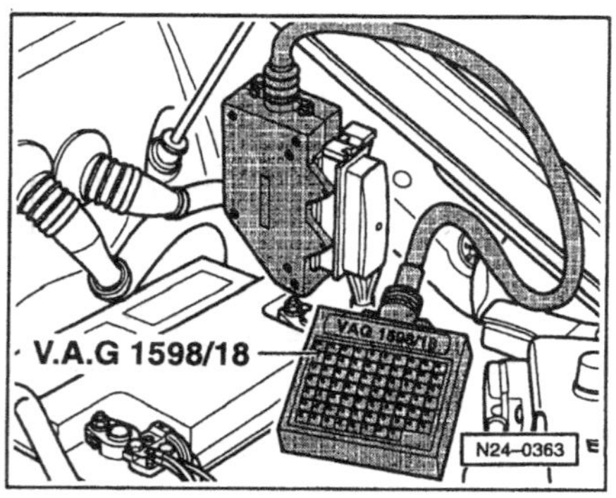

◄ – Connect VAG 1598/18 Test Box ECM wiring harness

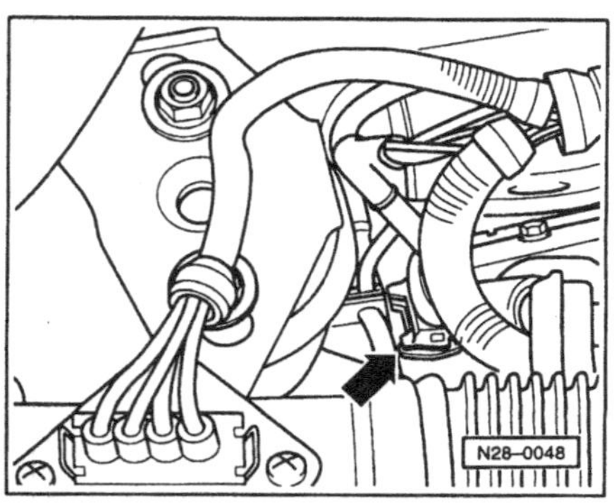

Knock sensor 1 G61

◄ – Disconnect white 3-pin harness connector to knock sensor 1 -arrow-

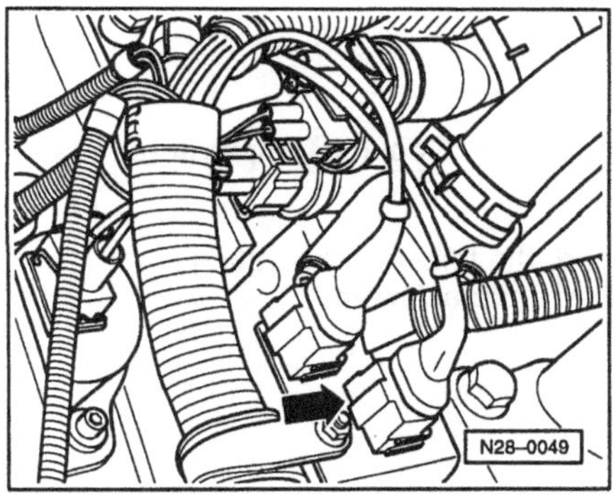

Knock sensor 2 G66

- Disconnect black 3-pin harness connector to knock sensor 2 -arrow-

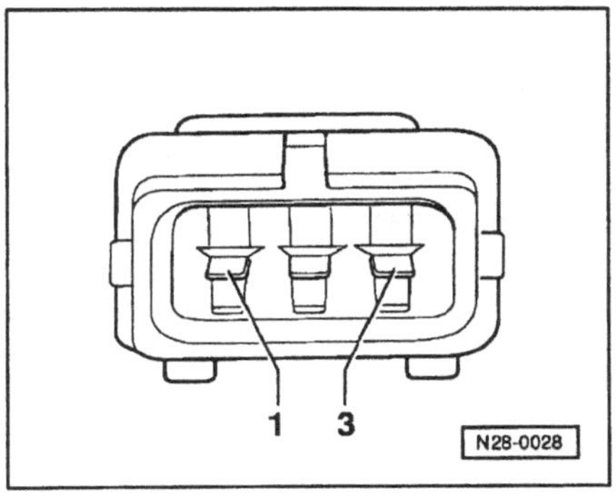

- Switch multimeter to resistance range
- Measure resistance between knock sensor terminals, connecting as follows:
  - between terminals 1 + 2
  - between terminals 1 + 3
  - between terminals 2 + 3
  - ♦ specification ∞ Ω

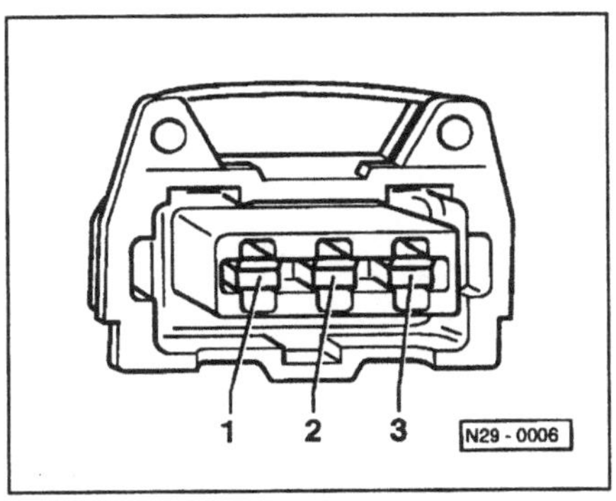

- Check for open circuit between Test Box and 3-pin harness connector using wiring diagram, connecting as follows:

	G61:	G66:
– terminal 1 + socket	34	57
– terminal 2 + socket	33	33
– terminal 3 + socket	56	56

♦ wire resistance: 1.5 Ω maximum

- Check wires for shorting to one another

	G61:	G66:
– terminal 2 + socket	34	57
– terminal 3 + socket	33	33
– terminal 3 + socket	34	57

♦ specification: ∞ Ω

If wiring OK:

- Loosen appropriate knock sensor and re-torque
  - ♦ 20 Nm (15 ft lb)
- Perform road test

– Perform road test

- ♦ during road test, engine Engine Coolant Temperature must exceed 80 °C (176°F)

When temperature is reached, the following operating conditions must be performed several times:

- ♦ Closed throttle
- ♦ Partially open throttle
- ♦ Wide open throttle
- ♦ Overrun
- ♦ At Wide open throttle, engine rpm must exceed 3500

– Check DTC memory for any stored DTC's

If DTC still present (malfunction stored again in DTC memory):

– Replace appropriate knock sensor, G61 and/or G66
⇒ page G 28-3

– Read-out Readiness code
⇒ Repair Group 01, page G 01-33

If DTC memory has been erased:
– Create Readiness code
⇒ Repair Group 01, page G 01-35